child development

A CULTURAL APPROACH

JEFFREY JENSEN ARNETT

Clark University

ASHLEY E. MAYNARD

University of Hawai'i at Mānoa

PEARSON

Boston   Columbus   Indianapolis   New York   San Francisco   Upper Saddle River
Amsterdam   Cape Town   Dubai   London   Madrid   Milan   Munich   Paris   Montréal   Toronto
Delhi   Mexico City   São Paulo   Sydney   Hong Kong   Seoul   Singapore   Taipei   Tokyo

Editorial Director: *Craig Campanella*
Editor in Chief: *Jessica Mosher*
Executive Editor: *Stephen Frail*
Senior Development Editors: *Julie Swasey, Deb Hartwell*
Development Editor: *Deb Hartwell*
Director of Marketing: *Brandy Dawson*
Marketing Manager: *Nicole Kunzmann*
Managing Editor: *Denise Forlow*
Project Manager: *Sherry Lewis*
Sr. Manufacturing and Operations Manager for Arts
   and Sciences: *Mary Fischer*
Senior Operations Specialist: *Diane Peirano*
Art Director: *Leslie Osher*

Text Design: *John Christiana*
Cover Design: *Wanda Espana/Wee Design Group*
Cover Art: *Danel Roldan*
Digital Media Director: *Brian Hyland*
Senior Digital Media Editor: *Peter Sabatini*
Digital Media Project Manager: *Caitlin Smith*
Full-Service Project Management: *Mary Tindle,*
   S4Carlisle Publishing Services
Composition: *S4Carlisle Publishing Services*
Printer/Binder: *R.R. Donnelley, Willard*
Cover Printer: *Lehigh Phoenix*
Text Font: *Sabon LT Std 10/13*

Credits and acknowledgments borrowed from other sources and reproduced, with permission, in this textbook appear on appropriate page within text.

Library of Congress Cataloging-in-Publication Data

Arnett, Jeffrey Jensen.
   Child development: a cultural approach / Jeffrey Jensen Arnett, Ashley Maynard.—1st ed.
      p. cm.
   ISBN-13: 978-0-205-84107-3
   ISBN-10: 0-205-84107-4
   1. Child development. 2. Child development—Cross-cultural studies. 3. Child psychology.   I. Maynard, Ashley, 1972-   II. Title.
   HQ767.9.A75 2013
   305.231—dc23

                                                                      2012027311

10 9 8 7 6 5 4 3 2 1

Student Editions
Hard Cover version   ISBN 10: 0-205-84107-4
                              ISBN 13: 978-0-205-84107-3
Paperback version   ISBN 10: 0-205-93889-2
                              ISBN 13: 978-0-205-93889-6
Books a' la Carte   ISBN 10: 0-205-93202-9
                              ISBN 13: 978-0-205-93202-3

*To my mom, who loved it all,
from start to finish.*
Jeffrey Jensen Arnett

To my teachers, who taught me how to learn.
Ashley E. Maynard

Contents

9 Emerging Adulthood 410

Infographic Maps

Preface

Welcome to *Child Development: A Cultural Approach*. Why a new textbook on child development? After all, there are already many textbooks available. For us, the most important motivation in writing this book was that we wanted to provide students with a portrayal of development that would cover the whole amazing range of human cultural diversity. As professors who have taught human development courses for years and were familiar with the available textbooks, we were struck by how narrow all of them seemed to be. They focused on human development in the United States as if it were the typical pattern for people everywhere, with only the occasional mention of people in other parts of the world. If you knew nothing about human development except what you read in a standard textbook, you would conclude that 95% of the human population must reside in the United States. Yet the United States is actually less than 5% of the world's population, and there is an immense range of patterns of human development in cultures around the globe, with most of those patterns strikingly different than the mainstream American model. And, even within the United States, cultural diversity is much greater than what is found in the typical textbook.

So, in writing this textbook, we decided to take a cultural approach. We set out to portray child development as it takes place across all the different varieties of cultural patterns that people have devised in response to their local conditions and the creative inspiration of their imaginations. Our goal was to teach students to *think culturally,* so that when they apply child development to the work they do or to their own lives, they understand that there is, always and everywhere, a cultural basis to development. The cultural approach also includes learning how to critique research for the extent to which it does or does not take the cultural basis of development into account. We provide this kind of critique at numerous points throughout the book, with the intent that students will learn how to do it themselves by the time they reach the end. *Thinking Culturally* questions appear in the margins of each chapter to promote students' abilities to think in this way.

We know from our experience as teachers that students find it fascinating to learn about the different forms that child development takes in various cultures, but there are also practical benefits to the cultural approach. It is more important than ever for students to have knowledge of the wider world because of the increasingly globalized economy and because so many problems, such as terrorism and climate change, cross borders. Whether they travel the globe or remain in their home towns, in a culturally diverse and globalized world, students will benefit from being able to apply the cultural approach and think culturally about development, whether in social interactions with friends and neighbors, or in their careers, as they may have patients or students or co-workers who come from different cultures.

The Chinese have an expression that loosely translates as "the frog in the well knows not of the great ocean," and it is often used as a cautionary reminder to look beyond our own experience and not to assume that what is true for ourselves is true for everyone else as well. We think all of us are like that frog, in a way (which is, in case you were wondering, why a frog is featured on the cover of this book). We've grown up in a certain cultural context. We've learned to think about life in a certain way. We've learned to think about development in a certain way. And most of us don't realize how broad and diverse our world really is. Our hope is that this book will help more students lift themselves out of the well and appreciate the wonderful diversity of child development.

The cultural approach makes this textbook much different from other child development textbooks, but there are other features that make this textbook distinct. This is the only major textbook to include a separate chapter on toddlerhood, the second and third years of life. Jeff had always been puzzled by the way other textbooks gloss over toddlerhood, usually including the second year of life as part of "infancy" and the third year of life as part of "early childhood." Yet any parent knows that years 2 and 3 are a lot different from what comes before or after, and Jeff remembered this well from his own experience as a father of twins. Infants cannot walk or talk, and once toddlers learn to do both in years 2 and 3, their experience of life—and their parents' experiences—change utterly. Toddlers are also different from older children, in that their ability for emotional self-regulation and their awareness of what is and is not acceptable behavior in their culture is much more limited.

This textbook is also set apart among major textbooks in that it includes an entire chapter on the stage of emerging adulthood. Emerging adulthood, roughly ages 18–25, is a new life stage that has arisen in developed countries over the past 50 years, as people have entered later into the commitments that structure adult life in most cultures: marriage, parenthood, and stable work. Jeff originally proposed the theory of emerging adulthood in 2000, and it has now become widely used in the social sciences. We think it is a fascinating and dynamic time of life, and we know students enjoy learning about it, as many of them are in that life stage or about to enter it.

This textbook is somewhat shorter than most other texts on child development. There is one chapter devoted to each phase of life, for a total of nine chapters. Each chapter is divided into three major sections, which correspond to the physical, the cognitive, and the emotional and social domains of development. This is an introductory textbook, and the goal is not to teach students everything there is to know about every aspect of child development, but to provide them with a foundation of knowledge on child development that hopefully will inspire them to learn more, in other courses and throughout life.

Applying the Cultural Approach

Cultural Videos

Extensive Cultural Coverage is woven into the narrative and on vivid display in images.

MyDevelopmentLab Cross-Cultural Videos, filmed in the United States, Mexico, and Botswana, and guided by series editor Ashley Maynard (University of Hawai'i at Mānoa) with important contributions from Bianca Dahl (Brown University), show how culture impacts development. Video guides, authored by Carol Miller of Anne Arundel Community College, at the end of every chapter section provide discussion questions to connect the videos with chapter content. Videos are available in multiple formats: on an instructor's DVD, tied to quizzes in MyDevelopmentLab, and linked to QR codes in the book to enable students to access the videos directly from their smart phones. Answers to discussion questions are available in the Instructor's Manual.

Cultural themes of infant social life

List the main features of infants' social worlds across cultures.

LEARNING OBJECTIVE 4.21

Although cultures vary in their customs of infant care, as they vary in most aspects of human development, there are several themes that occur frequently across cultures. If we combine what scholars have learned from observing infants in a variety of different cultures today, along with what other scholars have learned from studying human evolutionary history and the history of human societies, a common picture of the social world of the infant emerges (DeLoache & Gottlieb, 2000; Leakey, 1994; LeVine, 1977; LeVine et al., 1994; Richman et al., 2010; Small, 2005), characterized by the following features:

1. *Infants are with their mothers almost constantly for the early months of life.* Nearly all cultures have a period (usually 1–6 months) following birth when mother and infant do little but rest and recover from the birth together. After this rest period is over, the infant is typically strapped to the mother's back with a cloth as she goes back to her daily duties.
2. *After about 6 months, most daily infant care is done by older girls rather than the mother.* Once infants reach about 6 months old their care is delegated to older girls (usually 6 to 10 years old) so that the mother can devote her energy and attention to her work. Most often the girl is an older sister, but it could be any of a range of other people such as an older brother, cousin, grandmother, aunt, or a girl hired from outside the family. However, at night the infant sleeps with the mother.
3. *Infants are among many other people in the course of a day.* In addition to the mother and the caregiver who takes over at about age 6 months, infants are around many other people in the course of a day, such as siblings, aunts, cousins, grandparents, and neighbors.
4. *Infants are held or carried almost constantly.* In many traditional cultures, infants rarely touch the ground during their early months of life. This practice comes out of the belief that infants are highly vulnerable and must be shielded from dangers. Holding them close is a way of protecting them, and also a way of keeping them comforted, quiet, and manageable.
5. *Fathers are usually remote or absent during the first year.* As we saw in Chapter 3, in most cultures only women are allowed to observe and assist at birth, and this exclusion of men often continues during the first year. Fathers are rarely involved in the direct care of infants, partly because mothers breast-feed their infants frequently but also because

THINKING CULTURALLY

Of the five features of the infant's social world described here, how many are similar to and how many are different from the culture you are from? What do you think explains the differences?

Infants in many cultures are surrounded by adults all day, but cultures vary in how much the adults interact with infants. Here, two mothers and their babies with other family members and friends in the Samburu culture of Kenya.

Section 2 VIDEO GUIDE Theory of Mind Across Cultures (Length: 6:44)

This video contains several demonstrations of children from various countries performing tests of theory of mind.

1. How does acquiring a theory of mind impact a child's social interactions?

2. According to this video, does acquiring a theory of mind occur at the same age across cultures?

3. Can you think of any interactions that may help or hinder a child in developing a theory of mind?

▶ Watch the Video Theory of Mind Across Cultures in MyDevelopmentLab

Applying Your Knowledge and Thinking Culturally Questions

Applying Your Knowledge questions ask students to apply the chapter's content and cultural approach to real-life situations as well as to a wide range of future careers.

Thinking Culturally questions encourage students to think critically about the influence of culture on human development. Sample answers are provided in the Instructor's Manual.

DETERMINANTS OF ATTACHMENT QUAL

two-thirds of toddlers had secure one-third either insecure–avoidant other studies of American and Eur (NICHD Early Child Care Researc 2008). Disorganized–disoriented a

But what determines the qual early research, Ainsworth and her ing the same mother–child pairs i Situation (Ainsworth, 1977). The for four hours, from when the chil

When considering the mother behavior as observed in the Strang attachment was based mainly on *sensitive* means to be good at judg ample, sensitive mothers could tell others seemed to stop feeding whil ing them after they seemed full. To the children when they need it. Fo or talk soothingly when their chil cry for awhile before going to their

According to attachment theo and responsive behavior over the *ing model* of what to expect abo of need (Bowlby, 1969, 1980; Bre attachments have developed an int can rely upon to provide help and unsure that the mother will come working model of her as someone One reason the Strange Situation is that it is only by toddlerhood th developed an internal working m et al., 1978; Bowlby, 1969).

ATTACHMENT QUALITY AND LATER DEV

working model of the primary ca applied to other relationships. C

APPLYING YOUR KNOWLEDGE
... as a Nurse

Six-year-old Rosy from Mexico injured herself playing soccer. Her parents take this as evidence that girls should not play soccer, because it is too dangerous and they did not play soccer in the rural village they came from. What might you say to Rosy's parents?

codes to prev
potential dang
vocate safety r
It currently ha
and is expandi

Despite th
countries, dise
veloping coun
and disease (
much lower in
the leading ca
them die from

nt behavior is especially f the toddler is distressed.

APPLYING YOUR KNOWLEDGE

What are the implications of attachment theory for the debate discussed in Chapter 4 over whether or not a crying baby should be comforted?

THINKING CULTURALLY

How might a culture's values of individualism or collectivism influence toilet-training practices?

toilet trained by 18 months old and only about 60% by their third birthday (Bar et al., 2009; Schum et al., 2001). We'll look at the history of toilet training in m depth in the **Historical Focus: The History of Toilet Training** feature below.

Today, most American pediatricians believe it is best to be patient with toddl progress toward toilet training, and to time it according to when the toddler se ready (American Academy of Pediatrics [AAP], 2009). Most toddlers show signs readiness sometime between 18 and 30 months of age. Some key signs are

- staying "dry" for an hour or two during the day;
- regular bowel movements, occurring at about the same time each day;
- increased anticipation of the event, expressed through looks or words;
- directly asking to use the toilet or to wear underwear instead of a diaper.

Although toilet training usually begins during the toddler years, it rarely happ overnight. Typically it is a process that continues over several weeks, months, or e years. The earlier toilet training begins, the longer it takes to complete it (Blum 2004). After children are generally able to control urination and defecation, they may

"Focus" Features

Cultural Focus features offer in-depth coverage of development in a non-U.S. culture. Each Cultural Focus feature also includes a locator map that situates the culture being discussed in its larger geographic context.

Historical Focus features examine a developmental topic in its historical context to show how our views toward different stages of development change over time.

Research Focus features offer a detailed description of a research study including its premises, methods, results, and limitations.

CULTURAL FOCUS   Easing Birth Among the Cuna Indians

In many parts of the world today, birth is a social and religious event. Women give birth in their own homes, in the company of their closest female relatives and friends; the birth is assisted by a midwife whom the woman knows well. In many places the woman is believed to be especially vulnerable during birth, not just physically, but spiritually. Consequently, many cultures have developed religious beliefs and methods in an attempt to ensure the safety of mother and child.

One example was described by the French anthropologist Claude Levi-Strauss, who did ethnographic research on the Cuna Indians of Panama (Levi-Strauss, 1967). Normally, Cuna women are attended during birth by a midwife and female relatives. However, if labor becomes difficult, the midwife often calls on spiritual assistance from a *shaman*, a religious leader believed to have special powers and knowledge of the spirit world (see Chapter 2). Shamans are common in traditional cultures

The shaman's own spirit joins the animal spirits inside the womb to wage combat against Muu.

Does any of this do any good to the woman suffering a difficult labor? Medically, obviously not, but be careful before you dismiss the effects of the shaman's song too easily. There is abundant evidence of the **placebo effect**, which means that sometimes if people believe something affects them, it does, just by virtue of the power of their belief. In the classic example, if people are given a sugar pill containing no medicine and told it is a pain reliever, many of them will report experiencing reduced pain (Balodis et al., 2011). It was not the sugar pill that reduced their pain but their belief that the pill would relieve their pain.

So the shaman's song may have a placebo effect on the Cuna woman giving birth, if it helps promote her labor then at least to lessen her pain. Furthermore, according to Levi-Strauss, the shaman's song and the spiritual world it invokes allow the woman to make sense of her pain. By connecting her labor pain to the symbolic worldview of her shaman who believes in the spiritual world and the impact of the symbolic environment on of the woman's being, psychologically to "the task at hand" (Bates & Turner, 2003,

HISTORICAL FOCUS   The History of Toilet Training

Approaches to toilet training have shifted substantially in Western societies over the past century. These shifts provide an instructive example of how changes in cultural beliefs about children can interact with changes in technology.

In the historical record of the past 200 to 300 years, the emphasis was on teaching children to use the toilet at the earliest age possible (Mechling, 2008). Methods were often coercive, including scolding or physical punishment in case of an "accident." One U.S. government manual even urged parents to enforce the regularity of bowel movements for *infants* by inserting a curved stick into the baby's rectum at precise times each day (U.S. Department of Labor, 1932).

These early, harsh approaches to toilet training reflected a cultural belief in the appropriateness of strong parental authority (Dewar, 2010). Toddlers were to be toilet trained as soon as possible so that parents would be relieved of the mess and work of changing and cleaning their diapers; the needs of the parents were the top priority, not the needs of the children (Mechling, 2008). However, technological reasons—more precisely, the lack of technologies—were also involved. Keep in mind that before the late 20th century all diapers

20th century typically had three, four, or more children, and by the time the youngest one was in diapers, parents would have been changing and washing diapers for a long, long time.

Methods of toilet training evolved in the late 20th century, supported by changes in parenting beliefs as well as developments in technology. Parents became less concerned with establishing authority over children and more concerned with children's psychological well-being (Alwin, 1988). Child-care authorities warned that harsh, early toilet training could be psychologically damaging and that parents should be patient and allow the timing of toilet training to be determined by the toddler's readiness, as shown by their interest in using the toilet (Spock, 1966). Two key technological changes of the 1950s also contributed to more tolerant and patient methods: the invention of the disposable diaper and the electric washer and dryer. It was easier for parents to be more tolerant of their toddler's individual pace of toilet training once the parents no longer had to wash diapers by hand and could instead wash them in the electric washer or use disposables.

Today in developed countries most parents use disposable diapers. In the United States, from 1950 to today, there has been a steady rise in the proportion of parents using disposable diapers

RESEARCH FOCUS   Early Child Care and Its Consequences

One of the most striking changes of the last half century in Western countries is that mothers of young children now generally work outside the home (see **Map 5.2** on page 220). For example, in 1960 only 17% of American mothers of children under a year old were employed, but by the year 2000 this proportion had risen to over 60% (Smith et al., 2001). Similar changes took place in other Western countries (Scheiwe & Willekins, 2009). Because this change has happened so quickly and so recently, and because mothers have never before been employed in such large numbers, there has been a great deal of concern expressed about the potential consequence of this change for young children's development. Consequently, a great deal of research has been undertaken to explore this issue.

Beginning in the 1990s, the largest and most comprehensive study of early child care and its consequences was conducted in the United States, sponsored by the National Institute of Child Health and Human Development (NICHD). The "NICHD Study of Early Child Care" began in 1991 with over 1,300 young children (from infancy through early childhood) at 10 sites around the United States. The children and their families were followed longitudinally for 7 years (NICHD Early Child Care Research Network, 1997). The sample was diverse in socioeco-

Toddlers in high-quality child-care centers are as likely as children in home care to have secure attachments.

There were many notable and illuminating findings in the study. About three-fourths of the children in the study began nonmaternal child care by the age of 4 months. During infancy and toddlerhood most of this care was provided by relatives, but enrollment in child-care centers increased during toddlerhood, and beyond age 2 most children receiving nonmaternal care were in centers. Infants and toddlers averaged 33 hours a week in nonmaternal care. African American infants and toddlers experienced the highest number of hours per week of nonmaternal care and White infants and toddlers the lowest, with Latinos in between.

The most important variables related to children's development were hours per week in care and quality of care. Quality of care was assessed in three ways: (1) the caregivers' education, training in child care, and child-care experience; (2) the ratio of children to caregivers and the number of children per group; and (3) the interactions between caregivers and children (based on observations of mothers and nonmaternal caregivers). Notably, children from the highest and lowest SES backgrounds received the highest quality care and the children from near-poor backgrounds received the lowest, because the parents of the poorest children qualified for subsidies for high-quality care, whereas the parents of

Infographic Maps

Infographic Maps in every chapter provide a quick and effective way for students to visualize cultural, socioeconomic, and geopolitical variations in development.

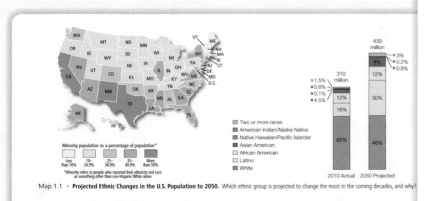

Map 1.1 • **Projected Ethnic Changes in the U.S. Population to 2050.** Which ethnic group is projected to change the most in the coming decades, and why?

Map 3.2 • **Neonatal and Maternal Mortality Worldwide.** How do neonatal and maternal mortality rates compare? What factors might explain why mortality rates are higher in developing countries than in developed countries?

Teaching and Learning Aids

Motor development

Describe the advances in motor development that take place during toddlerhood.   LEARNING OBJECTIVE 5.4

Toddlerhood is a time of dramatic advances in motor development. There are few physical advances more life changing than going from barely standing to walking, running, climbing, and jumping—and all this progress in gross motor development takes place during the toddler years. With regard to fine motor development, toddlers go from being able to place a small object inside a large object to holding a cup and building a tower of blocks.

GROSS MOTOR DEVELOPMENT: FROM TODDLING TO RUNNING, JUMPING, AND CLIMBING Next time you see a child about a year old trying to walk, observe closely. When children first begin to walk they spread their feet apart and take small, stiff-legged steps, shifting their weight from one leg to the other. In short, they toddle! This is, in fact, where the word *toddler* comes from, in reference to their tentative, unsteady, wide-stance steps.

On average, children begin to walk without support at about 11 months old, just as they are about to enter toddlerhood; but there is a wide range of normal variation around this average, from about 9 to 17 months (Adolph & Berger, 2006; Bayley, 2005). Children who walk at 9 months are no more likely than children who walk at 17 months to become Olympic athletes some day, they simply have different biological time lines for learning to walk.

By 15 months most toddlers can stand (briefly) on one leg and have begun to climb, although once they have climbed onto something, they are much less skilled at climbing down. For example, most can climb up stairs at this age but not (safely) down. By 18 months most can run, although at first they run with the same stiff-legged, wide-stance posture as they use for walking. By 24 months they can kick a ball or throw a small object, and their running has become more flexible and fluid. At this age they can now go down the stairs that they earlier learned to climb up, and more: They can squat for minutes at a time, stand on tiptoes, and jump up and down. Small wonder toddlers

At 12–18 months many toddlers can barely walk, but by their third year they can run and jump.

Learning Objectives

Learning objectives for each chapter are listed at the start of each chapter section as well as within the chapter alongside every section heading. Based on Bloom's taxonomy, these numbered objectives help students better organize and understand the material. The end-of-chapter summary is organized around these same objectives, as are all of the supplements and assessment material.

What Have You Learned? Questions

Review questions appear after each section to help students assess their comprehension of the material and their understanding of the influence that culture has on development. Sample answers are provided in the Instructor's Manual, making these questions ideally suited for classroom discussion or homework assignments.

WHAT HAVE YOU LEARNED?

1. What are some common themes of infant social life in non-Western cultures, and how do typical practices in Western cultures differ?
2. Why are infants in traditional cultures held or carried almost constantly?
3. According to Erikson's theory, how does the development of trust or mistrust in infancy affect later development?
4. What two qualities did Bowlby identify as important for the primary caregiver to have?

MyDevelopmentLab Icons

MyDevelopmentLab icons throughout the text provide numerous opportunities for students to learn the way they want to learn, including videos, simulations, and by providing additional information on particular topics.

- 👁 **Watch** (dozens of videos, including the new Cross-Cultural videos)
- ((**Listen** (streaming audio of the chapter)
- ✳ **Explore** (step-by-step tutorials on important concepts)
- ⊙→ **Simulate** (online simulations)
- ✓ **Study** and **Review** (online Study Plan, Chapter Quizzes, and Quick Reviews)
- 📖 **Read** (online readings feature additional information or more in-depth coverage of topics discussed in the text)

My Virtual Child Questions

To help students who are working with the My Virtual Child simulation to connect textbook concepts with the choices they are asked to make as they raise their virtual child, we have included thought questions related to My Virtual Child in the margin.

My Virtual Child

How do you think gender roles will change in your culture by the time your virtual child is your age?

Chapter Summary and Practice Test

End-of-Chapter Summary and Practice Tests, organized by learning objective, help students review and study, while MyDevelopmentLab provides additional resources online to help students achieve mastery of the material.

Summing Up

((•–[Listen to an audio file of your chapter in **MyDevelopmentLab**

SECTION 1   PHYSICAL DEVELOPMENT

5.1 Describe the typical changes in physical growth that take place in toddlerhood and explain the harmful effects of nutritional deficiencies on growth.

Toddlers' physical growth continues at a pace that is slightly reduced from infancy but is nevertheless faster than at any later time of life. Toddlers in developing countries often suffer protein and micronutrient deficiencies that impede their physical and cognitive development.

5.2 Describe the changes in brain development that take place during toddlerhood, and identify the two most common methods of measuring brain activity.

The brain's synaptic density peaks at the end of toddlerhood, followed by many years of synaptic pruning. The two most common methods of measuring brain activity are the EEG and the fMRI.

5.3 Describe the changes in sleeping patterns and sleeping arrangements that take place during toddlerhood.

Toddlers' episodes of night waking increase from 18 to

5.4 Describe the advances in motor development that take place during toddlerhood.

In their gross motor development, toddlers learn to walk, run, climb, and kick a ball. Toddlers in traditional cultures are often restricted in their movements to protect them from danger—especially cooking fires. Advances in fine motor development include holding a cup and building a tower of blocks. In their third year, toddlers may be able to brush their teeth, with some assistance.

5.5 Compare and contrast the process and timing of toilet training in developed countries and traditional cultures.

Children vary widely in the timing of learning toilet training, but most are toilet trained by the end of toddlerhood. In traditional cultures, toddlers usually learn controlled elimination through observing and imitating older children.

5.6 Distinguish the weaning process early in infancy from weaning later in toddlerhood.

nd or third year
traditional cul-
ending the tod-
e or coating the
stance.

Practice Test

✓•–[Study and Review in **MyDevelopmentLab**

1. _____ is a condition specific to toddlerhood in which protein deficiencies lead to varied symptoms such as swollen bellies, hair loss, and lack of energy.
   a. Kwashiorkor   c. Marasmus
   b. SIDS   d. Dysentery

2. What most characterizes early brain development in toddlerhood is
   a. the formation of the cerebral cortex.
   b. the steep increase in the density of synaptic connections among neurons.
   c. activity in the amygdala.
   d. the production of new brain cells.

3. During toddlerhood,
   a. sleeping alone is rare in traditional cultures.
   b. children sleep more than they did in infancy (because they are so much more active).
   c. naps are no longer needed.
   d. children sleep consistently throughout the night.

4. Toddlers
   a. who do not walk by 1 year are likely to have a gross motor problem.
   b. in traditional cultures are equal to toddlers from Western cultures in the development of their gross motor skills.
   c. can usually run before they can stand briefly on one leg.
   d. show the same pace of gross motor development as fine motor development.

5. In the West,
   a. most children show signs of readiness for toilet training by their first birthday.
   b. views about toilet training have stayed the same over the last several decades.
   c. children are toilet trained in a nearly identical way as their counterparts in traditional cultures.
   d. a sign of being ready to begin toilet training is when the child can stay "dry" for an hour or two during the day.

MyDevelopmentLab™

MyDevelopmentLab combines proven learning applications with powerful assessment to engage students, assess their learning, and help them succeed.

- **An individualized study plan for each student,** based on performance on chapter pretests, helps students focus on the specific topics where they need the most support. The personalized study plan arranges content from less-complex thinking, like remembering and understanding—to more-complex critical thinking skills—like applying and analyzing, and is based on Bloom's taxonomy. Every level of the study plan provides a formative assessment quiz.

- **My Virtual Child.** My Virtual Child is an interactive simulation that allows students to play the role of a parent and raise their own virtual child. By making decisions about specific scenarios, students can raise their child from birth to age 18 and learn firsthand how their own decisions and other parenting actions affect their child over time.

- **Media assignments** for each chapter—including videos with assignable questions—feed directly into the gradebook, enabling instructors to track student progress automatically.

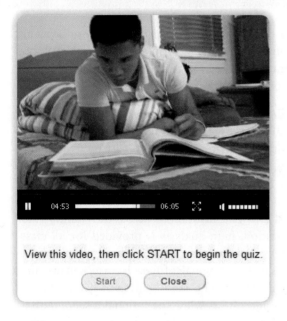

- **The Pearson eText** lets students access their textbook anytime and anywhere, and any way they want, including listening online.

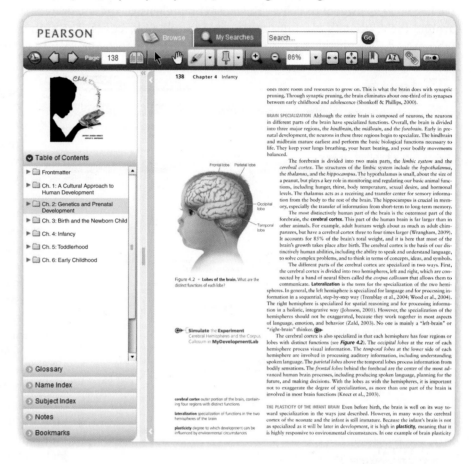

- **The MyDevelopmentLab Question Library** provides over 2,400 test items in the form of PreTests, Posttests, and Chapter Exams. These questions are parallel forms of questions found in the instructor test bank, ensuring that students using MyDevelopmentLab for review and practice will find their tests to be of similar tone and difficulty, while protecting the integrity of the instructor test bank.

With assessment tied to every video, application, and chapter, students get immediate feedback, and instructors can see what their students know with just a few clicks. Instructors can also personalize MyDevelopmentLab to meet the needs of their students.

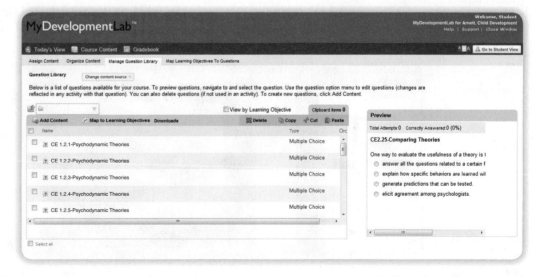

Teaching and Learning Package

A textbook is but one component of a comprehensive learning package. The author team that prepared the teaching and learning package had as its goal to deliver the most comprehensive and integrated package on the market. All supplements were developed around the textbook's carefully constructed learning objectives. The authors are grateful to reviewers and focus group members who provided invaluable feedback and suggestions for improving various elements of the program.

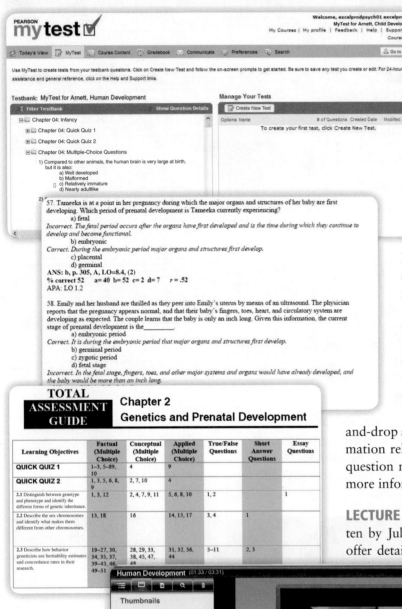

TEST BANK Written by Nicole Martin (Kennesaw State University), with David Hurford (Pittsburgh State University), Yuthika Kim (Oklahoma City Community College), and Julie McIntyre (Russell Sage College), the Test Bank contains over 3,000 questions, many of which were class-tested in multiple classes at both two-year and four-year institutions across the country prior to publication. Item analysis is provided for all class-tested items. All conceptual and applied multiple-choice questions include rationales for each correct answer and the key distracter. The item analysis helps instructors create balanced tests while the rationales serve both as an added guarantee of quality and as a time-saver when students challenge the keyed answer for a specific item. Each chapter of the test bank includes a two-page Total Assessment Guide, an easy-to-reference grid that organizes all test items by learning objective and question type.

The test bank comes with **Pearson MyTest,** a powerful test generation program that helps instructors easily create and print quizzes and exams. Questions and tests can be authored online, allowing instructors ultimate flexibility and the ability to efficiently manage assessments wherever and whenever they want. Instructors can easily access existing questions and then edit, create, and store, using simple drag-and-drop and Word-like controls. Data on each question provide information relevant to difficulty level and page number. In addition, each question maps to the text's major section and learning objective. For more information visit **www.PearsonMyTest.com.**

LECTURE POWERPOINT SLIDES WITH EMBEDDED VIDEOS Written by Julie McIntyre (Russell Sage College), the Lecture PowerPoints offer detailed outlines of key points for each chapter supported by selected visuals from the textbook, and include the videos featured in the in-text Video Guides. Standard Lecture PowerPoints without embedded videos are also available. A separate *Art and Figure* version of these presentations contains all art from the textbook for which Pearson has been granted electronic permissions. Clicker PowerPoints are also available for instructors who use personal response systems.

INSTRUCTOR'S MANUAL Written and compiled by Peggy Skinner (South Plains College) with Dorothy Marsil (Kennesaw State University), the Instructor's Manual includes a career-based supplement with discussion launchers focused on teaching, nursing, social work, and counseling. Each chapter offers integrated teaching outlines, lists of the key terms for each chapter for quick reference, and includes an extensive bank of lecture launchers, handouts, and activities, and suggestions for integrating third-party videos and web resources. Answers to the in-text features Applying Your Knowledge, Thinking Culturally, and What Have You Learned? are provided, as well as answers to each chapter's Video Guide. Detailed critical thinking problems with accompanying rubrics were written by Diana Joy of the Community College of Denver. A set of questions for using My Virtual Child with the cultural approach, written by Guyla Davis of Ouachita Baptist University, is also included. The electronic format features click-and-view hotlinks that allow instructors to quickly review or print any resource from a particular chapter. This tool saves prep work and helps you maximize your classroom time.

CLASSPREP Finding, sorting, organizing and presenting your instructor resources is faster and easier than ever before with ClassPrep. This fully searchable database contains hundreds and hundreds of our best teacher resources, including lecture launchers and discussion topics, in-class and out-of-class activities and assignments, handouts, video clips, photos, illustrations, charts, graphs and animations. Instructors can browse by topic, search by keyword, and filter results by asset type (photo, document, video, animation). Instructors can sort the resources into their own filing system, tag, rate and comment on individual resources, and even download most of the resources. ClassPrep also offers instructors the option to upload their own resources and present directly from ClassPrep. ClassPrep is available for instructors through MyDevelopmentLab. Please contact your Pearson representative for access.

ACCESSING ALL RESOURCES For a list of all student resources available with *Child Development: A Cultural Approach*, First Edition, go to **www.mypearsonstore.com**, enter the text ISBN (0-205-84107-4) and check out the "Everything That Goes with It" section under the book cover.

For access to all instructor supplements for *Child Development: A Cultural Approach*, First Edition go to **www.pearsonhighered.com/irc** and follow the directions to register (or log in if you already have a Pearson user name and password). Once you have registered and your status as an instructor is verified, you will be e-mailed a log-in name and password. Use your log-in name and password to access the catalog.

You can request hard copies of the supplements through your Pearson sales representative. If you do not know your sales representative, go to **www.pearsonhighered .com/replocator** and follow the directions. For technical support for any of your Pearson products, you and your students can contact **http://247.pearsoned.com**.

Acknowledgments

Writing a new child development textbook is an enormous enterprise, and this one has involved many talented and dedicated people. We are indebted to everyone who has contributed at each step of our writing of this book. We are especially grateful to Stephen Frail, who has shown careful dedication and abundant enthusiasm for the study of culture and development and who has made this book and the related projects possible. Julie Swasey pored over drafts and provided gentle and insightful editing, the way a weaver finishes a beautiful tapestry, making sure every thread is in place. Deb Hartwell assisted with figures and final polishing of the manuscript submission. The video series that we designed for this book came to life under the energetic guidance of Katie Toulmin, Nick Kaufman, Howard Stern, and the NKP Media crew. In filming the videos, Charles Castilla had just the right touch with the camera to make them personal and dignified. Bianca Dahl provided expert assistance in Botswana. Many thanks to Nicole Kunzmann, Senior Marketing Manager, who showed excellent skill in the marketing of the text and organized class testing, surveys, and focus groups that provided valuable feedback at every stage of the book's development. Thanks to Sherry Lewis and Denise Forlow for seeing the production of the book and ancillaries through to the finish. Alison Rodal, Market Development Manager, organized market testing and provided feedback that helped shape the project. Crystal McCarthy oversaw the development of the carefully integrated instructor and student support package. Peter Sabatini created the MyDevelopmentLab site. Carly Bergey and Ben Ferrini found the photos that exemplify the diversity of cultures discussed in the book. Wanda Espana designed the layout of the book. Thanks also go to J.C. Morgan at Precision Graphics and Maria Piper for their work on the art. Kevin Lear created the maps. And Anna Waluk and Estelle Simpson helped with permissions. Finally, we would like to thank the hundreds of reviewers who reviewed chapters, sections, and other materials in the course of the development of the book. We benefited greatly from their suggestions and corrections, and now instructors and students reading the book will benefit, too.

—Jeff Arnett & Ashley Maynard

I would also like to thank Jeff Arnett for inviting me to be a partner in this valuable and meaningful project.

—Ashley Maynard

The Development of Child Development: A Cultural Approach

The textbook you hold in your hands is the product of the most extensive development effort this market has ever witnessed. *Child Development: A Cultural Approach* reflects the countless hours and extraordinary efforts of a team of authors, editors, and reviewers that shared a vision for not only a unique human development textbook, but also the most comprehensive and integrated supplements program on the market. Over 200 manuscript reviewers provided invaluable feedback for making text as accessible and relevant to students as possible. Each chapter was also reviewed by a panel of subject matter experts to ensure accuracy and currency. Dozens of focus group participants helped guide every aspect of the program, from content coverage to the art style and design to the configuration of the supplements. In fact, some of those focus group participants were so invested in the project that they became members of the supplements author team themselves. Dozens of students compared the manuscript to their current textbooks and provided suggestions for improving the prose and design. We thank everyone who participated in ways great and small, and hope that you are as pleased with the finished product as we are!

INSTRUCTORS

Arkansas
Oscar Gomez, *Central Baptist College*

Arizona
Rosanne Dlugosz, *Scottsdale Community College*

California
Laurel Anderson, *Palomar College*
Jennifer Briffa, *Merritt College*
Dianna Chiabotti, *Napa Valley College*
Diana Deutsch, *Pierce College*
Dani Hodge, *California State University, San Bernadino*
Lynnel Kiely, *City Colleges of Chicago*
Denise Kennedy, *University of La Verne*
Jean Moylan, *California State University, Sacramento*
Deborah Muscari, *Gavilan College*
Wendy Orcajo, *Mt. San Jacinto College*
Jo Anne Pandey, *California State University, Northridge*
Melissa Paoloni, *Sacramento City College*
Nicole Porter, *Modesto Junior College*
Valerie Singleton, *California State University, Chico*
April Taylor, *California State University, Northridge*
Hsing-chen Tung, *San Diego State University*
Emily Scott-Lowe, *Pepperdine University*
Leonor Vazquez, *California State University, Los Angeles*
Anthony Verive, *College of the Desert*
Curtis Visca, *Saddleback College*
Gina Wilson, *MiraCosta College*
Juliana Fuqua, *Cal Poly Pomona*
Wendy Sanders, *College of the Desert*
Jamie Shepherd, *Saddleback College*

Colorado
Diana Joy, *Community College of Denver*
Jun Wang, *Colorado State University*

Delaware
Allison Cassidy, *Delaware Technical Community College*

Florida
Kathi Barrett, *Lake-Sumter Community College*
Norma Caltagirone, *Hillsborough Community College*
Carol Connor, *Florida State University*
Colleen Fawcett, *Palm Beach State College*
Christine Hughes, *University of Miami*
Madhavi Menon, *Nova Southeastern University*

Georgia
Valerie Misch, *Central Georgia Technical College*
Annette Wilson, *Armstrong Atlantic State University*

Iowa
Kari Terzino, *Des Moines Area Community College*

Illinois
Elbert Bolsen, *Columbia College*
Kelly Champion, *Northern Illinois University*
R.B. Church, *Northeastern Illinois University*
Carrie Dale, *Eastern Illinois University*

Ericka Hamilton, *Moraine Valley Community College*
Michael Meyerhoff, *Columbia College*
Elizabeth Rellinger Zettler, *Illinois College*

Kansas
Hira Nair, *Kansas City Kansas Community College*
Ruth Wallace, *Butler Community College*

Kentucky
April Grace, *Kentucky Community and Technical College System*

Maine
Alison Terry, *University of Maine, Farmington*

Massachusetts
Alfred Baptista, *Massasoit Community College*
Kyla McKay-Dewald, *Bristol Community College*
Martha Pott, *Tufts University*
Margaret Vaughan, *University of Massachusetts Boston*
Marcia Weinstein, *Salem State University*
Phyllis Wentworth, *Bristol Community College*

Maryland
Delaine Welch, *Frederick Community College*
Marlene Welch, *Carroll Community College*
Patricia Westerman, *Bowie State University*

Michigan
Laura C. Froyen, *Michigan State University*

Minnesota
David Schieffer, *Minnesota West Community & Technical College*
Hope Doerner, *Minneapolis Community and Technical College*

Missouri
Amy Kausler, *Jefferson College*
Michael Meehan, *Maryville University*
Bill Walkup, *Southwest Baptist University*

Mississippi
Lisa Thomas, *Mississippi College*

North Carolina
Margaret Annunziata, *Davidson County Community College*
Sharon Carter, *Davidson County Community College*
Sherry Forrest, *Craven Community College*
Karen Tinsley, *Guilford College*

Nebraska
Elizabeth Brewer, *Metropolitan Community College*
Kim Glackin, *Metropolitan Community College*
Susan Nordstrom, *Wayne State College*
Brigette Ryalls, *University of Nebraska at Omaha*

New Jersey
Miriam Linver, *Montclair State University*
Wallace Smith, *Union County College*
Sara Goldstein, *Montclair State University*

New Mexico
Kourtney Vaillancourt, *New Mexico State University*

New York
Melissa Ghera, *St. John Fisher College*
Melody Goldman, *Brooklyn College*

Sabrina Ismailer, *Hunter College*
Joseph Lao, *Hunter College*
Randolph Manning, *Suffolk County Community College*
Leigh McCallen, *The Graduate Center, CUNY*
Kristie Morris, *Rockland Community College*
Monida R. Sylvia, *Le Moyne College*

North Carolina
Karen Tinsley, *Guilford College*

Ohio
Michelle Abraham, *Miami University, Hamilton*
Karen Corcoran, *Ohio University*
Lisa Green, *Baldwin Wallace College*
Jamie Harmount, *Ohio University, Chillicothe Campus*

Oklahoma
Melinda Burgess, *Southwestern Oklahoma State University*
Stephen Burgess, *Southwestern Oklahoma State University*

Oregon
Tara Vargas, *Lewis & Clark College*

Pennsylvania
Heather Bachman, *University of Pittsburgh*
Nick Dominello, *Holy Family University*
Jaelyn Farris, *Penn State, Harrisburg*
Jason Baker, *Millersville University*

Rhode Island
Allison Butler, *Bryant University*

South Carolina
Bill Fisk, *Clemson University*

South Dakota
Jennifer Kampmann, *South Dakota State University*
Rebecca Martin, *South Dakota State University*

Tennessee
Steve Bradshaw, *Richmont Graduate University*
Lee Ann Jolley, *Tennessee Tech University*

Texas
Hsin-hui Lin, *University of Houston-Victoria*
Jeffrey Liew, *Texas A&M University*
Catherine Perz, *University of Houston-Victoria*
Elizabeth Rhoades, *University of Houston-Victoria*
Gaye Shook-Hughes, *Austin Community College*
Tyler Smith, *Baylor University*
Mario Tovar, *South Texas College*
Angela Williamson, *Tarrant County College*
Gaye Hughes, *Austin Community College*

Virginia
Tresia Samani, *Rappahannock Community College*

Washington, D.C.
Deborah Harris-O'Brien, *Trinity Washington University*

Wisconsin
Stacie Christian, *University of Wisconsin-Green Bay*
Ingrid Tiegel, *Carthage College*
Francesca Lopez, *Marquette University*

About the Authors

Jeffrey Jensen Arnett is a Research Professor in the Department of Psychology at Clark University in Worcester, Massachusetts. He received his Ph.D. in developmental psychology in 1986 from the University of Virginia, and did three years of postdoctoral work at the University of Chicago. From 1992 to 1998 he was Associate Professor in the Department of Human Development and Family Studies at the University of Missouri where he taught a 300-student life-span development course every semester. From 1998 to 2005 he was a Visiting Associate Professor in the Department of Human Development at the University of Maryland. In the fall of 2005 he was a Fulbright Scholar at the University of Copenhagen in Denmark.

His primary scholarly interest for the past 10 years has been in emerging adulthood. He coined the term, and has conducted research on emerging adults concerning a wide variety of topics, involving several different ethnic groups in American society. He is the editor of the *Journal of Adolescent Research,* and is on the editorial board of four other journals. He has published many theoretical and research papers on emerging adulthood in peer-reviewed journals, as well as the books *Human Development: A Cultural Approach* (2012, 1st edition, Pearson), *Adolescence and Emerging Adulthood: A Cultural Approach* (2013, 5th edition, Pearson), and *Emerging Adulthood: The Winding Road from the Late Teens Through the Twenties* (2004, Oxford University Press).

He lives in Worcester, Massachusetts, with his wife Lene Jensen and their twins, Miles and Paris. For more information on Dr. Arnett and his research, see **www.jeffreyarnett.com**.

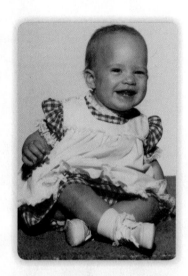

Ashley E. Maynard is Professor and Chair of the Department of Psychology at the University of Hawai'i at Mānoa, where she has been on the faculty since 2001. She received her Ph.D. in Psychology in 1999 from the University of California, Los Angeles and did two years of postdoctoral study in Anthropology and Cultural Psychology in the Department of Neuropsychiatry and Biobehavioral Sciences at UCLA.

Her primary research interest since 1995 has been the impact of cultural change at the macro level, such as economic and sociodemographic shifts, on socialization and cognition in childhood. She also studies the development of teaching in childhood and sibling interactions. She works with her students in Mexico, Costa Rica, Switzerland, and Hawai'i. She has won national awards for her research, including the James McKeen Cattell Award from the New York Academy of Sciences and the APA Division 7 (Developmental Psychology) Dissertation Award. She has published many articles on culture and human development in peer-reviewed journals, and in a volume she edited with Mary Martini *Learning in Cultural Context: Family, Peers, and School* (2005, Springer).

She lives, teaches, and writes in Honolulu, Hawai'i. For more information on Dr. Maynard and her research, please see **www.ashleymaynard.com**.

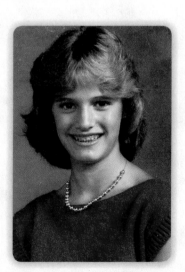

1

A Cultural Approach to Child Development

The Chinese have an expression for the limited way all of us learn to see the world: *jing di zhi wa,* meaning "frog in the bottom of a well." The expression comes from a fable about a frog that has lived its entire life in a small well. Swimming around in the water, the frog assumes that its tiny world is all there is. The frog believes that its perception is complete, but it has no idea how vast the world really is. It is only when a passing turtle tells the frog of the great ocean to the east that the frog realizes there is much more to the world than it had known.

All of us are like that frog. We grow up as members of a culture and learn, through direct and indirect teaching, to see the world from the perspective that becomes most familiar to us. Because the people around us usually share that perspective, we seldom have cause to question it. Like the frog, we rarely suspect how big and diverse our human species really is.

The goal of this book is to lift you out of the well, by taking a cultural approach to understanding **human development**, the ways people grow and change across the life span. This means that the emphasis of the book is on how persons develop as members of a culture. **Culture** is the dynamic pattern of a group's customs, practices, values, beliefs, art, and technology, handed down through language. In other words, a culture is a group's common way of life, passed on from one generation to the next. From the day we are born, all of us experience our lives as members of a culture (sometimes more than one), and this profoundly influences how we develop, how we behave, how we see the world, and how we experience life.

Biology is important, too, of course, and at various points we will discuss the interaction between biological and cultural or social influences.

> *“From the day we are born, all of us experience our lives as members of a culture.”*

However, human beings everywhere have essentially the same biological constitution, yet their paths through the life span are remarkably different depending on the culture in which their development takes place.

The tendency in most social science research, especially in psychology, has been to ignore or strip away culture in pursuit of universal principles of development (Jensen, 2011; Rozin, 2006). Research has focused mostly on studying human development in the American White middle class, because most researchers were American and they assumed that the processes of development they observed in the United States were universal (Arnett, 2008). But this is changing, and in recent years there has been increasing attention in psychology and other social science fields to the cultural context of human development (Shweder, 2011; Shweder et al., 2006). By now, researchers have presented descriptions of human development in places all over the world, and researchers studying American society have increased their attention to cultures within the United States that are outside of the White middle class.

Central to this book is the view that an emphasis on cultural context is essential to understanding human development. What it is like to grow up in the American middle class is different in many ways from growing up in Egypt, or Thailand, or Brazil—and also different from growing up in certain American minority cultures, such as urban African American culture or the culture of recent Mexican American immigrants. Throughout this book, we'll explore human development from the perspectives of many different cultures around the world. We'll also learn to analyze and critique research based on whether it does or does not take culture into account. By the time you finish this book, you should be able to *think culturally.*

Why is it important for you to understand human development using the cultural approach? Hopefully you will find it fascinating to learn about the marvelous diversity in the ways of life that children experience in different cultures. In addition, the cultural approach has many practical applications. Increasingly the world is approaching the *global village* that the social philosopher Marshall McLuhan (1960) forecast over half a century ago. In recent decades there has been an acceleration in the process of **globalization**, which refers to the increasing connections between different parts of the world in trade, travel, migration, and communication (Arnett, 2002b; Giddens, 2000; Ridley, 2010). Consequently, wherever you live in the world, in the course of your personal and professional life you are likely to have many contacts with people of other cultures. Those of you going into the nursing profession may one day have patients who have a cultural background in various parts of Asia or South America. Those of you pursuing careers in education will likely teach students whose families emigrated from countries in Africa or Europe. Your coworkers, your neighbors, possibly even your friends and family members may include people from a variety of different cultural backgrounds. Through the Internet you may have contact with people all over the world, via e-mail, Facebook and other social media, YouTube, and new technologies to come. Thus, understanding the cultural approach to human development is likely to be useful in all aspects of life, helping you to communicate with and understand the perspectives of others in a diverse, globalized world.

Not least, the cultural approach to human development will help you understand more deeply your own life and your place in the world. Think for a moment, of which culture or cultures are you a member? How has your cultural membership shaped your development and your view of the world? I am an American, and I have lived in the United States all my life. I am also White (or European American), ethnically, and a man; I am middle class and an urban resident. I am married to a Dane, and our family has spent a lot of time in Denmark. Those cultural contexts have shaped how I have learned to understand the world, as your cultural contexts have shaped your own understanding.

In the course of this book I will be your fellow frog, your guide and companion as we rise together out of the well to gaze at the broad, diverse, remarkable cultural panorama of the human journey. The book will introduce you to many variations in human development and cultural practices you did not know about before, which may lead you to see your own development and your own cultural practices in a new light. Whether you think babies should sleep with their parents, whether you think toddlers breast-feeding until age 3 is normal or abnormal, whether you think adolescents "naturally" draw closer to or further away from their parents, you are about to meet cultures with assumptions very different from your own. This will enrich your awareness of the variety of human experiences and may allow you to draw from a wider range of options of how you wish to live.

In this chapter we set the stage for the rest of the book. The first section provides a broad summary of human life today around the world and examines how culture developed out of our evolutionary history. The second section introduces the major theoretical conceptions of human development that contribute to developmental research. Finally, the third section provides an overview of child development as a scientific field, highlighting the methods and designs used in child development research.

human development way people grow and change across the life span; includes people's biological, cognitive, psychological, and social functioning

culture total pattern of a group's customs, beliefs, art, and technology

globalization increasing connections between different parts of the world in trade, travel, migration, and communication

APPLYING YOUR KNOWLEDGE
In the profession you are in or will one day be in, what is one way the cultural approach to human development might be applied to your work?

5

LEARNING OBJECTIVES

1.1 Distinguish between the demographic profiles of developed countries and developing countries in terms of population, income, and education.

1.2 Define the term *socioeconomic status* (SES) and explain why SES, gender, and ethnicity are important aspects of human development within countries.

1.3 Trace the evolutionary origins of the human species and summarize the features of the first human cultures.

1.4 Apply information about human evolution to how human development takes place today.

Humanity Today: A Demographic Profile

Because the goal of this book is to provide you with an understanding of how human development takes place in cultures all around the world, let's begin with a demographic profile of the world's human population in the early 21st century. Perhaps the most striking demographic feature of the human population today is the sheer size of it. For most of history the total human population was under 10 million (McFalls, 2007). Women typically had from four to eight children, but most of the children died in infancy or childhood and never reached reproductive age. The human population began to increase notably around 10,000 years ago, with the development of agriculture and domestication of animals (Diamond, 1992).

Population growth in the millennia that followed was very slow, and it was not until about 400 years ago that the world population reached 500 million persons. Since that time, and especially in the past century, population growth has accelerated at an astonishing rate (see **Figure 1.1**) (McFalls, 2007). It took just 150 years for the human population to double from 500 million to 1 billion, passing that threshold around the year 1800. Then came the medical advances of the 20th century, and the elimination or sharp reduction of deadly diseases like smallpox, typhus, diphtheria, and cholera. Subsequently, the human population reached 2 billion by 1930, then tripled to 6 billion by 1999. The 7 billion threshold was surpassed just 12 years later, in early 2011.

How high will the human population go? This is difficult to say, but most projections indicate it will rise to 9 billion by about 2050 and thereafter stabilize and perhaps slightly decline. This forecast is based on the worldwide decline in birthrates that has taken place in recent years. The **total fertility rate (TFR)** (number of births per woman) worldwide is currently 2.8, which is substantially higher than the rate of 2.1 that is the *replacement rate* of a stable population. However, the TFR has been declining sharply for over a decade and will decline to 2.1 by 2050 if current trends continue (Ridley, 2010).

total fertility rate (TFR) in a population, the number of births per woman

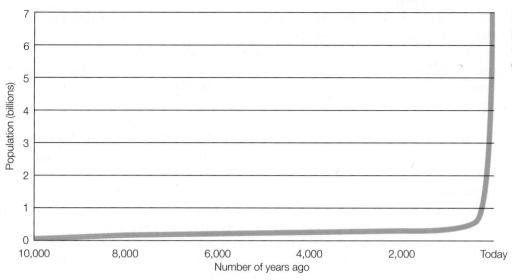

Figure 1.1 • **World population growth, past 10,000 years.** What happened in recent human history to cause population to rise so dramatically? **Source:** *Arnett, Human Development 1e.*

Variations across countries

Distinguish between the demographic profiles of developed countries and developing countries in terms of population, income, and education.

LEARNING OBJECTIVE 1.1

The population increase from now to 2050 will not take place equally around the world. On the contrary, there is a stark "global demographic divide" between the wealthy, economically developed countries that make up less than 20% of the world's population, and the economically developing countries that contain the majority of the world's population (Kent & Haub, 2005). Nearly all the population growth in the decades to come will take place in the economically developing countries. In contrast, nearly all wealthy countries are expected to decline in population during this period and beyond, because they have current fertility rates that are well below replacement rate.

For the purposes of this text, we'll use the term **developed countries** to refer to the most affluent countries in the world. Classifications of developed countries vary, but usually this designation includes the United States, Canada, Japan, South Korea, Australia, New Zealand, Chile, and nearly all the countries of Europe (Organization for Economic Cooperation and Development [OECD], 2010). For our discussion, developed countries will be contrasted with **developing countries**, which have less wealth than the developed countries but are experiencing rapid economic growth as they join the globalized economy. A brief profile of the developing country of India is presented in the **Cultural Focus: Incredible India!** feature on page 10. 📖

The current population of developed countries is 1.2 billion, about 18% of the total world population, and the population of developing countries is about 5.8 billion, about 82% of the world's population. Among developed countries, the United States is one of the few likely to gain rather than lose population in the next few decades. Currently there are about 310 million persons in the United States, but by 2050 there will be 439 million (Kotkin, 2010). Nearly all the other developed countries are expected to decline in population between now and 2050 (OECD, 2010). The decline will be steepest in Japan, which is projected to drop from a current population of 120 million to just 90 million by 2050, due to a low fertility rate and virtually no immigration.

There are two reasons why the United States is following a different demographic path than most other developed countries. First, the United States has a total fertility rate of 2.0, which is slightly below the replacement rate of

developed countries world's most economically developed and affluent countries, with the highest median levels of income and education

developing countries countries that have lower levels of income and education than developed countries but are experiencing rapid economic growth

Read the **Document** Developed Countries (OECD Classification) in **MyDevelopmentLab**

Nearly all the world population growth from now to 2050 will take place in developing countries. Here, a busy street in Delhi, India.

THINKING CULTURALLY

What are some potential political and social consequences of populations rising in developing countries and falling in developed countries in the coming decades?

THINKING CULTURALLY

What kinds of public policy changes might be necessary in the United States between now and 2050 to adapt to nearly 100 million more immigrants and a rise in the proportion of Latinos to 30%?

My Virtual Child

When thinking about how you will raise your virtual child, what are some ways that you will create a balance between individualism and collectivism?

individualistic cultural values such as independence and self-expression

collectivistic cultural values such as obedience and group harmony

2.1 but still higher than the TFR in most other developed countries (Population Reference Bureau, 2010). Second, and more importantly, the United States allows more legal immigration than most other developed countries do, and there are tens of millions of undocumented immigrants as well. The increase in population in the United States between now and 2050 will result entirely from immigration (Martin & Midgley, 2010). Both legal and undocumented immigrants to the United States come mainly from Mexico and Latin America, although many also come from Asia and other parts of the world. Consequently, as *Map 1.1* shows, by 2050 the proportion of the U.S. population that is Latino is projected to rise from 16% to 30% (Martin & Midgley). Canada, the United Kingdom, and Australia also have relatively open immigration policies, so they, too, may avoid the population decline that is projected for most developed countries (DeParle, 2010).

The demographic contrast of developed countries compared to the rest of the world is stark not only with respect to population but also in other key areas, such as income and education (see *Map 1.2*). With respect to income, about 40% of the world's population lives on less than two dollars per day, and 80% of the world's population lives on a family income of less than $6,000 per year (Kent & Haub, 2005; United Nations Development Programme [UNDP], 2006). At one extreme are the developed countries, where 9 of 10 persons are in the top 20% of the global income distribution, and at the other extreme is southern Africa, where half of the population is in the bottom 20% of global income. Africa's economic growth has been strong for the past decade, but it remains the poorest region in the world (McKinsey Global Institute, 2010).

A similar contrast between rich and poor countries exists regarding education. Your experience as a college student is a rare and privileged status in most of the world. In developed countries, virtually all children obtain primary and secondary education, and about 50% go on to tertiary education (college or other postsecondary training). However, in developing countries about 20% of children do not complete primary school and only about half are enrolled in secondary school (UNDP, 2006). College and other postsecondary education are only for the wealthy elite.

There are also some broad cultural differences between developed and developing countries, even though each category is very diverse. One important difference is that the cultures of Western developed countries tend to be based on **individualistic** values such as independence and self-expression (Greenfield, 2005). In contrast, developing countries tend to prize **collectivistic** values such as obedience and group harmony (Sullivan & Cottone, 2010). These are not mutually exclusive categories and

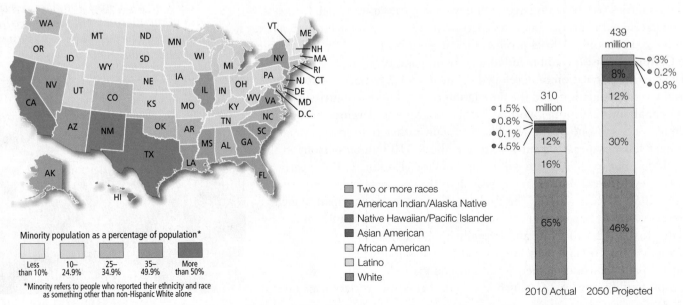

Minority population as a percentage of population*

| Less than 10% | 10–24.9% | 25–34.9% | 35–49.9% | More than 50% |

*Minority refers to people who reported their ethnicity and race as something other than non-Hispanic White alone

- Two or more races
- American Indian/Alaska Native
- Native Hawaiian/Pacific Islander
- Asian American
- African American
- Latino
- White

310 million
- 1.5%
- 0.8%
- 0.1%
- 4.5%
- 12%
- 16%
- 65%

439 million
- 3%
- 0.2%
- 0.8%
- 8%
- 12%
- 30%
- 46%

2010 Actual   2050 Projected

Map 1.1 • **Projected Ethnic Changes in the U.S. Population to 2050.** Which ethnic group is projected to change the most in the coming decades, and why?

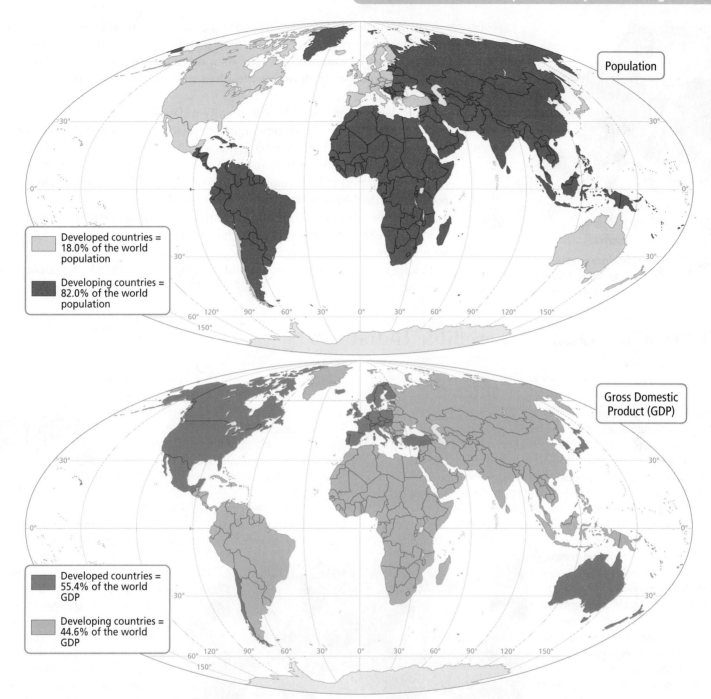

Map 1.2 • **Worldwide Variations in Population and Income Levels.** Developed countries represent only 18% of the world population yet they are much wealthier than developing countries. At what point in its economic development should a developing country be reclassified as a developed country?

each country has some balance between individualistic and collectivistic values. Furthermore, most countries contain a variety of cultures, some of which may be relatively individualistic whereas others are relatively collectivistic. Nevertheless, the overall distinction between individualism and collectivism is useful for describing broad differences between human groups. ◉

Within developing countries there is often a sharp divide between rural and urban areas, with people in urban areas having higher incomes and receiving more education and better medical care. Often, the lives of middle-class persons in urban areas of developing countries resemble the lives of people in developed countries in many ways, yet they are much different than people in rural areas of their own countries (UNDP, 2006). In this book, the term **traditional cultures** will be used to refer to

◉——[**Watch** the **Video** Differences Between Collectivistic and Individualistic Cultures in **MyDevelopmentLab**

traditional culture in developing countries, a rural culture that adheres more closely to cultural traditions than people in urban areas do

By age 10, many children in developing countries are no longer in school. Here, a child in Cameroon helps his mother make flour.

people in the rural areas of developing countries, who tend to adhere more closely to the historical traditions of their culture than people in urban areas do. Traditional cultures tend to be more collectivistic than other cultures are, in part because in rural areas close ties with others are often an economic necessity (Sullivan & Cottone, 2010).

This demographic profile of humanity today demonstrates that if you wish to understand human development, it is crucial to understand the lives of people in developing countries who make up the majority of the world's population. Most research on human development is on the 18% of the world's population that lives in developed countries—especially the 5% of the world's population that lives in the United States—because research requires money and developed countries can afford more of it than developing countries can (Arnett, 2008). However, it is clear that it would be inadequate to focus only on people in developed countries in a text on culture and child development. In this text, you will learn about child development as people experience it all over the world.

CULTURAL FOCUS   Incredible India!

One of the most fascinating and diverse places in the world, for anyone interested in human development, is India. The current population of India is 1.2 billion, making it the second most populous country in the world (after China), and by 2050 it will have more people than any other country, 1.5 billion (UNDP, 2011). Indians speak over 400 different languages, and there are over 200 distinct ethnic groups. Most Indians are Hindu (80%), but India also has millions of Muslims, Christians, Sikhs, Buddhists, and followers of other religions.

Although India is fabulously diverse, there are cultural traits across groups that are characteristically Indian (Kakar & Kakar, 2007). Family closeness is highly valued in India, and most households are multigenerational (Chaudhary & Sharma, 2012). Traditionally, women entered their husband's family household upon marriage, and the couples' children then grew up around the paternal grandparents and many aunts, uncles, and cousins. This system is still followed by most Indians, although in urban areas some middle-class couples choose to have their own household. Most marriages are arranged by parents and other respected family members (Chaudhary & Sharma, 2012). Traditionally, bride and groom did not meet until their wedding day, but now in most cases they meet each other briefly before marriage, in the presence of other family members.

One unique feature of Indian society is the **caste system**, which is an inherited social hierarchy. Indians believe in reincarnation, and this includes the belief that people are born into a caste position in the social hierarchy that reflects their moral and spiritual conduct in their previous life. People in high ranked castes tend to have the

most economic resources and the best access to education and health care, whereas people in the lowest castes tend to have little in the way of money or other resources. Attempts have been made to abolish the caste system in the past century, but it persists as a strong influence in Indian life (Kakar & Kakar, 2007).

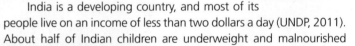

India is a developing country, and most of its people live on an income of less than two dollars a day (UNDP, 2011). About half of Indian children are underweight and malnourished (World Bank, 2011). Fewer than half of Indian adolescents complete secondary school. Only about half of adult women are literate, and about three-fourths of adult men. About two-thirds of India's population lives in rural villages, although there is a massive migration occurring from rural to urban areas, led mostly by young people.

Like many developing countries, India is rapidly changing. Its economy has been booming for the past two decades, lifting hundreds of millions of Indians out of poverty (UNDP, 2011). India is now a world leader in manufacturing, telecommunications, and services. If the economy continues to grow at its present pace India will lead the world in economic production by 2050 (Price Waterhouse Coopers, 2011). Life is changing rapidly for Indians, and children born today are likely to experience much different economic and cultural contexts than their parents or grandparents have known. India will be a country to watch in the decades to come, and we will learn about many aspects of human development in India in the course of this text.

Variations within countries

> Define the term *socioeconomic status* (SES) and explain why SES, gender, and ethnicity are important aspects of human development within countries.

The contrast between developed countries and developing countries will be used often in this text, as a general way of drawing a contrast between human development in relatively rich and relatively poor countries. However, it should be noted that there is substantial variation within each of these categories. All developed countries are relatively wealthy, but human development in Japan is quite different from human development in France or Canada. All developing countries are less wealthy than developed countries, but human development in China is quite different than human development in Brazil or Nigeria. At various points we will explore variations in human development within the broad categories of developed countries and developing countries.

Not only is there important variation in human development within each category of "developed" and "developing" countries, but there is additional variation within each country. Most countries today have a **majority culture** that sets most of the norms and standards and holds most of the positions of political, economic, intellectual, and media power. In addition, there may be many minority cultures defined by ethnicity, religion, language, or other characteristics.

Variations in human development also occur due to differences within countries in the settings and circumstances of individual lives. The settings and circumstances that contribute to variations in pathways of human development are called **contexts**. Contexts include environmental settings such as family, school, community, media, and culture, all of which will be discussed in this book. Three other important aspects of variation that will be highlighted are socioeconomic status, gender, and ethnicity.

SOCIOECONOMIC STATUS (SES) The term **socioeconomic status (SES)** is often used to refer to a person's *social class*, which includes educational level, income level, and occupational status. For children and adolescents, because they have not yet reached the social-class level they will have as adults, SES is usually used in reference to their parents' levels of education, income, and occupation. In most countries, SES is highly important in shaping human development. It influences everything from the risk of infant mortality to the quality and duration of children's education to the kind of work parents do and the kind of schools that children attend. Differences in SES are especially sharp in developing countries. In a country such as India or Saudi Arabia or Mexico, growing up as a member of the upper-class SES elite is very different from growing up as a member of the relatively poor majority, in terms of access to resources such as health care and education. However, even in developed countries there are important SES differences in access to resources throughout the course of human development. For example, in the United States infant mortality is higher among low-SES families than among high-SES families, in part because low-SES mothers are less likely to receive prenatal care (Daniels et al., 2006).

GENDER Gender is a key factor in development throughout the life span, in every culture (Carroll & Wolpe, 2005; Chinas, 1992). The expectations cultures have for males and females are different from the time they are born (Hatfield & Rapson, 2005). However, the degree of the differences varies greatly among cultures. In most developed countries today, the differences are relatively blurred: Men and women hold many of the same jobs, wear many of the same clothes (e.g., jeans, T-shirts), and enjoy many of the same entertainments. If you have grown up in a developed country, you may be surprised to learn

caste system in Hindu culture of India, an inherited social hierarchy, determined by birth

majority culture within a country, the cultural group that sets most of the norms and standards and holds most of the positions of political, economic, intellectual, and media power

contexts settings and circumstances that contribute to variations in pathways of human development, including SES, gender, and ethnicity, as well as family, school, community, media, and culture

socioeconomic status (SES) person's social class, including educational level, income level, and occupational status

My Virtual Child

Will your virtual child be part of the majority culture or the minority culture?

My Virtual Child

To which socioeconomic status will your virtual child belong? What are some ways that SES will impact your virtual child from the start of life?

APPLYING YOUR KNOWLEDGE
... as a Nurse

You are treating a child from a middle-class family from Mexico City. The parents speak English, and they are comfortable in the hospital setting in the United States. Do you think this family has more in common with those from the urban setting where you work, or are they more like people from rural areas?

THINKING CULTURALLY

What are some of the gender-specific expectations that exist in your culture (e.g., in the family, the school, the workplace, and the media)?

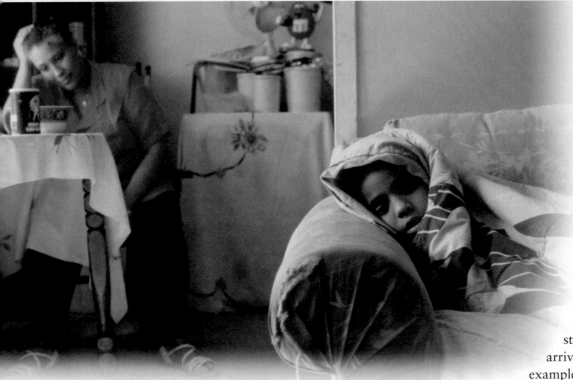

Within each country, SES is an influential context of human development. Here, a low-SES family in the United States.

My Virtual Child

What is your virtual child's ethnicity? How will ethnicity play a role in the development of your virtual child?

in the chapters to come how deep gender differences go in many other cultures. Nevertheless, gender-specific expectations exist in developed countries, too, as we will see.

ETHNICITY Finally, **ethnicity** is a crucial part of human development. Ethnicity may include a variety of components, such as cultural origin, cultural traditions, religion, and language. Race is different from ethnicity; race is simply the set of a person's physical traits that form the social categories designated as White, Black, Asian, and the like. Minority ethnic groups may arise as a consequence of immigration. There are also countries in which ethnic groups have a long-standing presence and may even have arrived before the majority culture. For example, Aboriginal peoples lived in Australia for many generations before the first European settlers arrived. Many African countries were constructed by European colonial powers in the 19th century and consist of people of a variety of ethnicities, each of whom has lived in their region for many generations. Often, ethnic minorities within countries have distinct cultural patterns that are different from those of the majority culture. For example, in the Canadian majority culture, premarital sex is common, but in the large Asian Canadian minority group, female virginity at marriage is still highly valued (Sears, 2012). In many developed countries, most of the ethnic minority groups have values that are less individualistic and more collectivistic than in the majority culture (Greenfield, 2005).

WHAT HAVE YOU LEARNED?

1. What factors have contributed to the massive growth of the human population in recent centuries?
2. Why are the populations of the United States and Canada expected to increase between now and 2050?
3. How do developed countries and developing countries differ with respect to population, income, and education?
4. How do SES, gender, and ethnicity contribute to variations in human development within countries?

The Origins of Human Diversity

Using a cultural approach to human development, we will see that humans are fabulously diverse in how they live. But how did this diversity arise? Humans are one species, so how did so many different ways of life develop from one biological origin? Before we turn our attention to the development of individuals, it is important to understand the

ethnicity group identity that may include components such as cultural origin, cultural traditions, race, religion, and language

development of the human species. Let's take a brief tour now of human evolutionary history, as a foundation for understanding the birth of culture and the historical context of individual human development today. For students who hold religious beliefs that may lead them to object to evolutionary theory, I understand that you may find this part of the text challenging, but it is nevertheless important to know about the theory of evolution and the evidence supporting it, as this is the view of human origins accepted by virtually all scientists. 📖

> 📖 **Read** the **Document** A More Extensive Account of Human Evolution in **MyDevelopmentLab**

Evolution and the birth of culture

Trace the evolutionary origins of the human species and summarize the features of the first human cultures.

LEARNING OBJECTIVE **1.3**

Evidence for the existence of humans like us goes back about 200,000 years. Physically, our species, *Homo sapiens*, has not changed much since then. However, the most dramatic changes in the ways that humans interact with their environments around the world are related to the advent of culture. Humans act in the world, and cultures change, moving the human species forward.

natural selection evolutionary process in which the offspring best adapted to their environment survive to produce offspring of their own

hominid evolutionary line that led to modern humans

hunter–gatherer social and economic system in which economic life is based on hunting (mostly by males) and gathering edible plants (mostly by females)

HUMAN ORIGINS To understand human origins it is important to know a few basic principles of the theory of evolution, first proposed by Charles Darwin in his 1859 book *The Origin of Species*. At the heart of the theory of evolution is the proposition that species change through the process of **natural selection**. In natural selection, the young of any species are born with variations on a wide range of characteristics. Some may be relatively large and others relatively small, some relatively fast and others relatively slow, and so on. Among the young, those who will be most likely to survive until they can reproduce will be the ones whose variations are best adapted to their environment. 👁

> 👁 **Watch** the **Video** Mechanisms of Evolution in **MyDevelopmentLab**

When did human evolution begin? According to biologists, the evolutionary line that eventually led to humans, known as the **hominid** line, split from other primates about six million years ago. The most important difference between early hominids and other primates was the development of *bipedal locomotion,* or walking on two legs. Evolutionary biologists have suggested that bipedal locomotion may have been a useful adaptation because it freed the hands for other things, such as carrying food, using a tool, or wielding a weapon against predators or prey (or other hominids) (Ember et al., 2011).

The Upper Paleolithic period beginning 40,000 years ago marked the birth of culture, including music. Here, a flute made by humans at the beginning of the Upper Paleolithic.

About three and half million years ago the hominid line split into two, with one line eventually dying out and the other a line of *Homo* species leading to modern humans (Shreeve, 2010). The most striking and important change during this period was the size of early *Homo*'s brain, which became over twice as large as the brain of early hominids. Simultaneously, the female *Homo*'s pelvis became wider to allow the birth of bigger-brained babies. Evolutionary biologists believe that the larger brains of early *Homo* babies meant that babies were born less mature than they were for earlier hominids, resulting in a longer period of infant dependency. This long period of infant dependency may have made it difficult for early *Homo* mothers to travel for long distances to accompany the males on hunting or scavenging expeditions (Wrangham, 2009). So, a **hunter–gatherer** way of life developed, in which females remained in a relatively stable home base, caring for children and perhaps gathering edible plants in the local area, while males went out to hunt or scavenge.

As the *Homo* species continued to evolve, it developed the ability to make tools and control fire. The earliest tools were apparently made by striking one stone against another to create a sharp edge. There is evidence that early *Homo*'s diet included

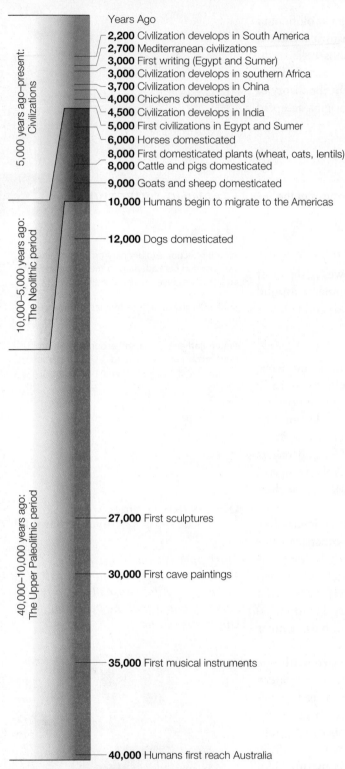

Years Ago

2,200 Civilization develops in South America
2,700 Mediterranean civilizations
3,000 First writing (Egypt and Sumer)
3,000 Civilization develops in southern Africa
3,700 Civilization develops in China
4,000 Chickens domesticated
4,500 Civilization develops in India
5,000 First civilizations in Egypt and Sumer
6,000 Horses domesticated
8,000 First domesticated plants (wheat, oats, lentils)
8,000 Cattle and pigs domesticated
9,000 Goats and sheep domesticated
10,000 Humans begin to migrate to the Americas

12,000 Dogs domesticated

27,000 First sculptures

30,000 First cave paintings

35,000 First musical instruments

40,000 Humans first reach Australia

5,000 years ago–present: Civilizations

10,000–5,000 years ago: The Neolithic period

40,000–10,000 years ago: The Upper Paleolithic period

Figure 1.2 • **Time line of human history from Upper Paleolithic period to the present.**

Homo sapiens species of modern humans

civilization form of human social life, beginning about 5,000 years ago, that includes cities, writing, occupational specialization, and states

state centralized political system that is an essential feature of a civilization

animals such as antelopes, wild pigs, giraffes, and even elephants. Controlling fire enabled our early ancestors to cook food, and because cooked food is used much more efficiently by the body than raw food, this led to another burst in brain size (Wrangham, 2009). Another evolutionary change during this period was that the size of the teeth and jaws diminished, because cooked food was easier to eat than raw food.

By 200,000 years ago the early hominid species had evolved into our species, **Homo sapiens** (Shreeve, 2011). *Homo sapiens* was different from earlier *Homo* species, with thinner and lighter bones—perhaps evolved for better running and hunting—smaller teeth and jaws, and most importantly, a brain about 30% larger than the brain of the *Homo* species that had just preceded us.

THE ORIGIN OF CULTURES AND CIVILIZATIONS Physically, *Homo sapiens* has changed little from 200,000 years ago to the present. However, a dramatic change in the development of the human species took place during the Upper Paleolithic period from 40,000 to about 10,000 years ago (Ember et al., 2011; Johnson, 2005). For the first time, art appeared: musical instruments; paintings on cave walls; small ivory beads attached to clothes; and human and animal figures carved from ivory or sculpted from clay. Several other important changes mark this period (see **Figure 1.2**), including the development of the first human burials, trade between human groups, the rapid development of tools, and the construction of the first boats.

The next period of dramatic change, from 10,000 years ago to about 5,000 years ago, is known as the Neolithic period (Johnson, 2005). During this time, humans broadened their food sources by cultivating plants and domesticating animals. The key contributor to this advance was climate change. The Upper Paleolithic was the time of the last Ice Age, when average global temperatures were about 10°C (50°F) below today's temperatures. As the climate became warmer and wetter, new plants evolved that were good human food sources, and humans began to try to produce more of the ones they liked best. Domestication of animals developed as a food source. Along with agriculture and animal care came new tools: mortars and pestles for processing plants into food, and the spindle and loom for weaving cotton and wool into clothing. Larger, sturdier dwellings were built (and furniture such as beds and tables) because people stayed in settled communities longer to tend their plants and animals.

The final major historical change that provides the basis for how we live today began around 5,000 years ago with the development of **civilization** (Ridley, 2010). The characteristics that mark civilization include cities, writing, specialization into different kinds of work, differences among people in wealth and status, and a centralized political system known as a **state**. The first civilizations developed around the same time in Egypt and Sumer (part of what is now Iraq). Because people in these civilizations kept written records and produced many goods, we have a good idea of how they lived. We know they had laws and sewer systems, and that their social classes included priests, soldiers, craftsmen, government workers, and slaves. We know they built monuments to their leaders, such as the pyramids that still stand in Egypt. They produced a vast range of goods including jewelry, sculpture, sailboats, wheeled wagons, and swords. Later civilizations developed in India (around 4,500 years ago), China (around 3,700 years ago), southern Africa (around 3,000 years ago), the Mediterranean area (Greece and Rome, around 2,700 years ago), and South America (around 2,200 years ago).

Why did civilizations and states arise? As agricultural production became more efficient, especially after the development of irrigation, not everyone in a cultural group had to work on food production. This allowed some members of the group to be concentrated in cities, away from food-production areas, where they could specialize as merchants, artists, musicians, bureaucrats, and religious and political leaders. Furthermore, as the use of irrigation expanded there was a need for a state to build and oversee the system, and as trade expanded there was a need for a state to build infrastructure such as roadways. Trade also connected people in larger cultural groups that could be united into a common state (Ridley, 2010).

THINKING CULTURALLY

What are some similarities and differences between life in the earliest civilizations and life today?

Human evolution and human development today

Apply information about human evolution to how human development takes place today.

LEARNING OBJECTIVE 1.4

What does this history of our development as a species tell us about human development today? First, it is important to recognize that how we develop today is based partly on our evolutionary history. We still share many characteristics with our hominid relatives and ancestors, such as a large brain compared to our body size, a relatively long period of childhood dependence on adults before reaching maturity, and cooperative living in social groups. Researchers working in the field of **evolutionary psychology** claim that many other characteristics of human development are influenced by our evolutionary history, such as aggressiveness and mate selection (Crawford & Krebs, 2008). We will examine their claims in the course of the book. ◉

A second important fact to note about our evolutionary history is that biologically we have changed little since the origin of *Homo sapiens* about 200,000 years ago, yet how we live has changed in astonishing ways (Ridley, 2010). Once we developed the large brain that is the most distinctive characteristic of our species, we became capable of altering our environments, so that it was no longer natural selection alone that would determine how we would live, but the cultures we created. As far as we can tell from the fossil record, all early hominids lived in the same way (Shreeve, 2010). Even different groups of early *Homo sapiens* seem to have lived more or less alike before the Upper Paleolithic period, as hunters and gatherers in small groups. Although we are a species that originated in the grasslands and forests of Africa, now we live in every environment on earth, from mountains to deserts, from tropical jungles to the Arctic. Although we are a species that evolved to live in small groups of a few dozen persons, now most of us live in cities with millions of other people. Although human females are capable of giving birth to at least eight children in the course of their reproductive lives, and probably did so through most of history, now most women have one, two, or three children—or perhaps none at all.

Today there are hundreds of different cultures around the world, all part of the human community but each with its distinct way of life. There are wide cultural variations in how we live, such as how we care for infants, what we expect from children, and how we respond to the changes of puberty. As members of the species *Homo sapiens* we all share a similar biology, but cultures shape the raw material of biology into widely different paths through the life span.

It is also culture that makes us unique as a species. Other animals have evolved in ways that are adaptive for a particular set of environmental conditions. They can learn in the course of their lifetimes, certainly, but the scope of their learning is limited. When

evolutionary psychology branch of psychology that examines how patterns of human functioning and behavior have resulted from adaptations to evolutionary conditions

◉─ **Watch** the **Video** Evolution and Sex: Michael Bailey in **MyDevelopmentLab**

APPLYING YOUR KNOWLEDGE
. . . as a Researcher

You are conducting a research study on the evolutionary bases of human development. One of your friends asks you, "Why is the topic of evolution important in developmental psychology?"

THINKING CULTURALLY

What evidence do you see today of human evolution continuing to occur? How do cultural practices alter the process of natural selection?

■□─┤**Read** the **Document** Do
Chimps Have Cultures? in
MyDevelopmentLab

◉─┤**Watch** the **Video** Culture Wars:
Evolution in **MyDevelopmentLab**

their environment changes, if their species is to survive it will do so not by learning new skills required by a new environment but through a process of natural selection that will enable those best suited *genetically* to the new environmental conditions to survive long enough to reproduce, while the others do not. ▭

In contrast, once humans developed the large brain we have now, it enabled us to survive in any environment by inventing and learning new skills and methods of survival, and then passing them along to others as part of a cultural way of life. We can survive and thrive even in conditions that are vastly different from our environment of evolutionary adaptation, because our capacity for cultural learning is so large and, compared to other animals, there is relatively little about us that is fixed by instinct. ◉

WHAT HAVE YOU LEARNED?

1. What are some of the major differences between early hominids and the *Homo* species?
2. When did the Upper Paleolithic period occur and what were the main features of human cultural change during that time?
3. How did climate change contribute to the human cultural advances of the Neolithic period?
4. What are the distinctive features of civilization? Which were the earliest civilizations and when did they begin?
5. How does the birth of culture make the human species different from other animals?

Section 1 VIDEO GUIDE Mechanisms of Evolution (Length: 3:30)

This video gives examples and descriptions of the evolutionary concepts of natural selection, genetic drift, and gene flow.

1. Describe an example of a chance event that could impact either the Green or Brown Beetle population.

2. Define gene flow and list an example of it either using the beetle population from the video or another type of insect or animal.

3. If a drought was causing the Brown Beetle population to grow due to natural selection, what should then occur if the weather balanced out again causing a more lush and less dry environment? Describe your answer in detail.

◉─┤**Watch** the **Video** Mechanisms of Evolution
in **MyDevelopmentLab**

SECTION 2 THEORIES OF HUMAN DEVELOPMENT

LEARNING OBJECTIVES

1.5 Summarize Freud's psychosexual theory and Erikson's psychosocial theory of human development and describe the main limitations of each.

1.6 Summarize the behaviorist theories of Watson, Skinner, and Bandura.

1.7 Summarize the constructivist theories of Piaget and Vygotsky.

1.8 Define the five systems of Bronfenbrenner's ecological theory and explain how it differs from stage theories.

Classic Theories

Conceptions of human development have been around for thousands of years (see the **Historical Focus: Ancient Conceptions of Human Development** feature on page 18). The scientific study of human development has been around for a relatively short time, only about 120 years. During that time there have been three major ways of conceptualizing human development: the psychodynamic approach, the behaviorist approach, and the constructivist approach.

Psychodynamic theories

Summarize Freud's psychosexual theory and Erikson's psychosocial theory of human development and describe the main limitations of each.

LEARNING OBJECTIVE 1.5

Psychodynamic approaches to human behavior examine the underlying psychological forces of human behavior, in particular the relationship between conscious and unconscious motivations. Development occurs through mastery of particular developmental challenges, and the growing person moves from one stage to the next.

FREUD'S PSYCHOSEXUAL THEORY The earliest scientific theory of human development was devised by Sigmund Freud (1856–1939), who was a physician in Vienna, Austria, in the late 19th century (Breger, 2000). Working with persons suffering from various mental health problems, Freud concluded that a consistent theme across patients was that they seemed to have experienced some kind of traumatic event in childhood. The trauma then became buried in their unconscious minds, or *repressed*, and continued thereafter to shape their personality and their mental functioning even though they could no longer remember it.

In an effort to address their problems, Freud developed the first method of psychotherapy, which he called *psychoanalysis*. The purpose of psychoanalysis was to bring patients' repressed memories from the unconscious into consciousness, by having them discuss their dreams and their childhood experiences while guided by the psychoanalyst. According to Freud, just making the repressed memories conscious would be enough to heal the patient.

HISTORICAL FOCUS   Ancient Conceptions of Human Development

Although human development is young as an area of the social sciences, people have been thinking for a long time about how we change with age throughout life. In this feature we examine two ancient ways of conceptualizing human development. As you read these conceptions, observe that they were written by and for men only. The absence of women from these conceptions of human development reflects the fact that in most cultures throughout history, men have held most of the power and have often kept women excluded from areas such as religious leadership and philosophy that inspired life-stage conceptions.

Probably the oldest known conception of the life course is in the *Dharmashastras,* the sacred law books of the Hindu religion, first written about 3,000 years ago (Kakar, 1998; Rose, 2004). In this conception there are four stages of a man's life, each lasting about 25 years in an ideal life span of 100 years.

Apprentice, ages 0–25

Householder, ages 26–50

Forest dweller, ages 51–74

Renunciant, ages 75–100

The apprentice stage comprises childhood and adolescence. This is the stage in which a boy depends on his parents, as he grows up and learns the skills necessary for adult life. In the householder stage, the young man has married and is in charge of his own household. This is a time of many responsibilities, ranging from providing for a family to taking care of elderly parents to engaging in productive work.

The third stage, forest dweller, begins when a man's first grandson is born. The ideal in this stage is for a man to withdraw from the world and literally live in the forest, devoting himself to prayer and religious study, and cultivating patience and compassion. Few Hindus ever actually withdraw to the forest, but even those who remain within society are supposed to begin to withdraw from worldly attachments. This means an end to sexual life, a decline in work responsibilities, and the beginning of a transfer of household responsibilities to the sons of the family.

The final stage of life is that of renunciant who goes even further than the forest dweller in rejecting worldly attachments. The purpose of life in this stage is simply to prepare for the end of this life and entry into the next (Hindus believe in reincarnation). Keep in mind, of course, that this stage *begins* at age 75, an age that few people reached thousands of years ago when the *Dharmashastras* were written and that even now marks the beginning of a rather short stage of life for most people who reach it.

In the life course according to the Jewish holy book the Talmud, 13 is the age of moral responsibility.

Another ancient conception of the life course comes from the Jewish holy book the Talmud, written about 1,500 years ago (Levinson, 1978). Like the Hindu *Dharmashastras,* the life course described in the Talmud goes up to age 100, but in smaller segments.

Age 5 is the age for beginning to read Scripture.

Age 10 is for beginning to learn the religious laws of the Jewish people.

Age 13 is the age of moral responsibility, when a boy has his Bar Mitzvah signifying that he is responsible for keeping the religious commandments, rather than his parents being responsible for him.

Age 15 is for first being able to discuss the Talmud.

Age 18 is for the wedding canopy.

Age 20 is for seeking an occupation.

Age 30 is for attaining full strength.

Age 40 is for understanding.

Age 50 is for giving counsel.

Age 60 is for becoming an elder and attaining wisdom.

Age 70 is for white hair.

Age 80 is for reaching a new, special strength of old age.

Age 90 is for being bent under the weight of the years.

Age 100 is for being as if already dead and passed away from the world.

Although these conceptions of human development were written in widely different places and times, they share certain similarities. They are ideal conceptions, a view of how we develop if all goes well: Preparation for life is made in youth, skills and expertise are gained in adulthood, and wisdom and peace are the fruits of old age. Furthermore, they view youth as a time of immaturity, adulthood as a time of great responsibilities and peak productivity, and the final stages of life as a preparation for death. These conceptions are also ideals in the sense that they assume that a person will live to old age, which is not something that most people could realistically expect until very recently.

One important difference among these ancient conceptions of human development is that they have very different ways of dividing up the life span, from just four stages in the *Dharmashastras* to 14 in the Talmud. This is a useful reminder that for humans the life span is not really divided into clear and definite biologically based stages, the way an insect has stages of larva, juvenile, and adult. Instead, conceptions of human development are only partly biological—infants everywhere cannot walk or talk, adolescents everywhere experience puberty—and are also culturally and socially based.

Freud's experiences as a psychoanalyst were the basis of his **psychosexual theory**. He believed that sexual desire was the driving force behind human development. Sexual desire arises from a part of the mind Freud called the *id*, and operates on the basis of the *pleasure principle*, meaning that it constantly seeks immediate and unrestrained satisfaction. However, from early in childhood, adults in the environment teach the child to develop a conscience, or *superego*, that restricts the satisfaction of desires and makes the child feel guilty for disobeying. At the same time as the superego develops, an *ego* also develops that serves as a mediator between id and superego. The ego operates on the *reality principle*, allowing the child to seek satisfaction within the constraints imposed by the superego. ✳

Although sexual desire is the driving force behind human development throughout life in Freud's theory, the locus of the sexual drive shifts around the body during the course of early development (see **Table 1.1**). Infancy is the *oral stage*, when sexual sensations are concentrated in the mouth. Infants derive pleasure from sucking, chewing, and biting. The next stage, beginning at about a year and a half, is the *anal stage*, when sexual sensations are concentrated in the anus. Toddlers derive their greatest pleasure from the act of elimination and are fascinated by feces. The *phallic stage*, from about age 3 to 6, is the most important stage of all in Freud's theory. In this stage sexual sensations become located in the genitals, but the child's sexual desires are focused particularly on the other-sex parent. Freud proposed that all children experience an *Oedipus complex* in which they desire to displace their same-sex parent and enjoy sexual access to the other-sex parent, as Oedipus did in the famous Greek myth.

According to Freud, the Oedipus complex is resolved when the child, fearing that the same-sex parent will punish his or her incestuous desires, gives up those desires and instead identifies with the same-sex parent, seeking to become more similar to that parent. In Freud's theory this leads to the fourth stage of psychosexual development, the *latency stage*, lasting from about age 6 until puberty. During this period the child represses sexual desires and focuses the energy from those desires on learning social and intellectual skills.

The fifth and last stage in Freud's theory is the *genital stage*, from puberty onward. The sexual drive reemerges, but this time in a way approved by the superego, directed toward persons outside the family. ✳

For Freud, everything important in development happens before adulthood. In fact, Freud viewed the personality as completed by age 6, in the first three stages of development. In each of those stages, either too much or too little gratification of desire could result in a *fixation* that would shape future development. For example, a child who had been overly frustrated in the oral stage, such as being weaned too early, would develop an adult personality that might include smoking cigarettes, nibbling fingernails, and a tendency to make "biting" remarks. A child who had been toilet trained too early or too severely might

psychosexual theory Freud's theory proposing that sexual desire is the driving force behind human development

✳ **Explore** the **Concept** The Id, Ego, and Superego in **MyDevelopmentLab**

✳ **Explore** the **Concept** Freud's Five Psychosexual Stages of Personality Development in **MyDevelopmentLab**

TABLE 1.1 Freud's Psychosexual Stages		
Age Period	**Psychosexual Stage**	**Main Features**
Infancy	Oral	Sexual sensations centered on the mouth; pleasure derived from sucking, chewing, biting
Toddlerhood	Anal	Sexual sensations centered on the anus; high interest in feces; pleasure derived from elimination
Early childhood	Phallic	Sexual sensations move to genitals; sexual desire for other-sex parent and fear of same-sex parent
Middle childhood	Latency	Sexual desires repressed; focus on developing social and cognitive skills
Adolescence	Genital	Reemergence of sexual desire, now directed outside the family

psychosocial theory Erikson's theory that human development is driven by the need to become integrated into the social and cultural environment

have an adult personality obsessed with cleanliness, detail, and order. A child who had, in the phallic stage, received attention from the other-sex parent that was sexually stimulating might have difficulty in adulthood forming a normal sexual relationship. The only way to remove these fixations, according to Freud, was through psychoanalysis.

From our perspective today, it easy to see plenty of gaping holes in Freud's theory (Breger, 2000). Sexuality is certainly an important part of human development, but human behavior is complex and cannot be reduced to a single motive. (Freud himself later added aggression as a drive alongside sexuality.) Also, although his theory emphasizes the crucial importance of the first six years of life, Freud never studied children. His view of childhood was based on the retrospective accounts of patients who came to him for psychoanalysis, mainly upper-class women in Vienna. (Yet, ironically, his psychosexual theory emphasized boys' development and virtually ignored girls.) Nevertheless, Freud's psychosexual theory was the dominant view of human development throughout the first half of the 20th century (Robins et al., 1999). Today, few people who study human development adhere to psychoanalysts (Grunbaum, 2006).

ERIKSON'S PSYCHOSOCIAL THEORY Even though Freud's theory was dominant in psychology for over a half century, from the beginning many people objected to what they regarded as an excessive emphasis on the sexual drive as the basis for all development. Among the skeptics was Erik Erikson (1902–1994). Although he was trained as a psychoanalyst in Freud's circle in Vienna, he doubted the validity of Freud's psychosexual theory. Instead, Erikson proposed a theory of development with two crucial differences from Freud's theory. First, it was a **psychosocial theory**, in which the driving force behind development was not sexuality but the need to become integrated into the social and cultural environment. Second, Erikson viewed development as continuing throughout the life span, not as determined solely by the early years as in Freud's theory.

Erikson (1950) proposed a sequence of eight stages of development (see **Table 1.2**). Each stage is characterized by a distinctive developmental challenge or "crisis" that the person must resolve. A successful resolution of the crisis prepares the person well for the next stage of development. However, a person who has difficulty with the crisis in one stage enters the next stage at high risk for being unsuccessful at that crisis as well. The stages build on each other, for better and for worse. We'll review all eight stages in this chapter and explore the first five stages, which take place between infancy and adolescence, over the course of this text.

In the first stage of life, during infancy, the developmental challenge is *trust versus mistrust*. If the infant is loved and cared for, a sense of basic trust develops that the

Erik Erikson was the first to propose a life span theory of human development.

Simulate the **Experiment** Closer Look Simulation: Development in **MyDevelopmentLab**

TABLE 1.2	Erikson's Eight Stages of Psychosocial Development	
Age Period	**Psychosocial Stage**	**Main Developmental Challenge**
Infancy	Trust vs. mistrust	Establish bond with trusted caregiver
Toddlerhood	Autonomy vs. shame and doubt	Develop a healthy sense of self as distinct from others
Early childhood	Initiative vs. guilt	Initiate activities in a purposeful way
Middle childhood	Industry vs. inferiority	Begin to learn knowledge and skills of culture
Adolescence	Identity vs. identity confusion	Develop a secure and coherent identity
Early adulthood	Intimacy vs. isolation	Establish a committed, long-term love relationship
Middle adulthood	Generativity vs. stagnation	Care for others and contribute to well-being of the young
Late adulthood	Ego integrity vs. despair	Evaluate lifetime, accept it as it is

world is a good place and need not be feared. If not well-loved in infancy, the child learns to mistrust others and to doubt that life will be rewarding.

In the second stage, during toddlerhood, the developmental challenge is *autonomy versus shame and doubt*. During this stage, the child develops a sense of self distinct from others. If the child is allowed some scope for making choices, a healthy sense of autonomy develops, but if there is excessive restraint or punishment, the child experiences shame and doubt.

In the third stage, during early childhood, the developmental challenge is *initiative versus guilt*. In this stage, the child becomes capable of planning activities in a purposeful way. With encouragement of this new ability a sense of initiative develops, but if the child is discouraged and treated harshly then guilt is experienced.

The fourth stage, during middle to late childhood, is *industry versus inferiority*. In this stage, children move out more into the world and begin to learn the knowledge and skills required by their culture. If a child is encouraged and taught well, a sense of industry develops that includes enthusiasm for learning and confidence in mastering the skills required. However, a child who is unsuccessful at learning what is demanded is likely to experience inferiority. ✳

The fifth stage is adolescence, with the challenge of *identity versus identity confusion*. Adolescents must develop an awareness of who they are, what their capacities are, and what their place is within their culture. For those who are unable to achieve this, identity confusion results.

The sixth stage, *intimacy versus isolation,* takes place in early adulthood. In this stage, the challenge for young adults is to risk their newly formed identity by entering a committed intimate relationship, usually marriage. Those who are unable or unwilling to make themselves vulnerable end up isolated, without an intimate relationship.

The seventh stage, in middle adulthood, involves the challenge of *generativity versus stagnation*. The generative person in middle adulthood is focused on how to contribute to the well-being of the next generation, through providing for and caring for others. Persons who focus instead on their own needs at midlife end up in a state of stagnation.

Finally, in the eighth stage, late adulthood, the challenge is *ego integrity versus despair*. This is a stage of looking back and reflecting on how one's life has been experienced. The person who accepts what life has provided, good and bad parts alike, and concludes that it was a life well spent can be considered to have ego integrity. In contrast, the person who is filled with regrets and resentments at this stage of life experiences despair. ✳

Erikson's psychosocial theory has endured better than Freud's psychosexual theory. Today, nearly all researchers who study human development would agree that development is lifelong, with important changes taking place at every phase of the life span (Baltes et al., 2006; Lerner, 2006). Similarly, nearly all researchers on human development today would agree with Erikson's emphasis on the social and cultural basis of development. However, not all of Erikson's proposed life stages have been accepted as valid or valuable. It is mainly his ideas about identity in adolescence and generativity in midlife that have inspired substantial interest and attention among researchers (Clark, 2010).

✳ **Explore** the **Concept** Erikson's First Four Stages of Psychosocial Development in **MyDevelopmentLab**

APPLYING YOUR KNOWLEDGE
. . . as a Day-Care Provider
You work at a day care where there are children ages 2 through 5. How might Erikson's theory explain the differences between the oldest and youngest children?

✳ **Explore** the **Concept** Erikson's Last Four Stages of Psychosocial Development in **MyDevelopmentLab**

APPLYING YOUR KNOWLEDGE
Based on your own experiences, which psychosexual theory of human development do you consider more valid, Erikson's or Freud's?

Behaviorism and learning theories

Summarize the behaviorist theories of Watson, Skinner, and Bandura.

LEARNING OBJECTIVE 1.6

Psychodynamic theories focus on the unconscious and on internal psychological conflicts that become the person's destiny. In response to Freud's psychoanalytic approach, those interested in a more scientific approach to psychology and to child development developed the theory of **behaviorism**. John Watson, an early behaviorist, argued that psychologists should observe and measure actual behavior, not hidden urges or thoughts

behaviorism theory that all thought and behavior can be explained in terms of learning mechanisms

conditioning the process by which a particular stimulus becomes linked to a particular response

about one's impulses. Behaviorists are also called *learning theorists* because they believe that anything can be learned, and that behavior can be shaped by the responses of others. Watson wrote:

> Give me a dozen healthy infants, well-formed, and my own specified world to bring them up in and I'll guarantee to take any one at random and train him to become any type of specialist I might select—doctor, lawyer, artist, merchant-chief and, yes, even beggar-man and thief, regardless of his talents, penchants, tendencies, abilities, vocations, and race of his ancestors. I am going beyond my facts and I admit it, but so have the advocates of the contrary and they have been doing it for many thousands of years. (Watson, 1930, p. 82)

Watson recommended that parents shake hands with their children in the morning, to socialize proper behavior (Watson, 1928). Although Watson was not able to turn children into any kind of person he wanted, the principles of learning theory continued in popularity, and indeed are still used in research and intervention today.

PAVLOV AND SKINNER: LAWS OF CONDITIONING Other psychologists were inspired to search for laws of behavior, based on the premise that everything humans do is learned through patterns of stimuli from the environment and the response. These psychologists, the early behaviorists, conducted experiments with animals and children and described laws of learning known as **conditioning**. Conditioning is a set of processes by which particular stimuli and responses become linked. Two types of conditioning form the basis of learning: classical conditioning and operant conditioning.

Classical conditioning is the process by which a neutral stimulus becomes associated with a meaningful stimulus, resulting in a conditioned response to the neutral stimulus. Perhaps the most famous example of classical conditioning comes from Ivan Pavlov's research with dogs. Pavlov was a Russian scientist who conducted research in the early 1900s on the digestion of animals. Like all dogs, Pavlov's dogs salivated (unconditioned response) at the presentation of food (meaningful, unconditioned stimulus). However, Pavlov soon noticed that the dogs also salivated when he rang a bell (neutral stimulus) at the presentation of food. Eventually, the dogs salivated at the ringing of the bell alone. Thus, the ringing of the bell had become associated with food, and the dogs produced the conditioned response of salivation to a previously neutral stimulus.

B. F. Skinner, the most influential American behaviorist, developed behaviorism into the middle and late 20th century through the study of operant conditioning. In *operant conditioning*, voluntary behavior can be modified through the use of reinforcement. Reinforcement is a consequence of a behavior that makes it more likely for the behavior to reoccur. For example, if you give a child a desirable reward, such as praise, it makes the child more likely to repeat the praised behavior. Skinner used the famous "Skinner box" to conduct learning experiments with rats and pigeons, showing how reinforcers could be used to shape behavior. Animal behavior could be shaped by providing rewards for only the desired behavior. For example, if the experimenter wanted the animal to turn in a certain direction, a reward, like a piece of food, would be given only when the animal turned in that direction.

The findings from behaviorism have practical applications for teachers and parents, who shape the behavior of children on a daily basis. Praise is a popular reinforcer in American culture, as are grades, stickers, or lively stamps in bright colors on outstanding work. What's interesting about reinforcing the behavior of children is that we have to adapt the reinforcer to the situation. We change the words of praise to correspond with the act being lauded. We give grades appropriate for the quality of the work. Not only do we adapt the reinforcers based on specific behaviors, but the motivations of children vary from those of animals, so we have to adapt to find reinforcers that are meaningful to children and the specific situations they are in. Principles of operant conditioning are used to encourage useful behaviors and to eliminate undesirable behaviors.

My Virtual Child

How might you use conditioning on your virtual child? Would parents across different cultures use conditioning in that same way?

APPLYING YOUR KNOWLEDGE
. . . as a Teacher

As a teacher, how might you need to vary rewards or other reinforcements in class?

SOCIAL LEARNING THEORY Early behaviorists believed that all behavior stems from learned responses, through the experiences of classical and operant conditioning. Later learning theorists such as Albert Bandura tested the idea that humans also learn from observing others, without directly experiencing any reinforcement or conditioning, forming the basis of **social learning theory**. Many animals and humans are social creatures who learn by watching others. More experienced individuals provide models of behavior that can be imitated, such as a father shaving his beard in front of his son or a mother playing tennis in front of her children. What is interesting is that not all behaviors are imitated—a model is more likely to be imitated when the observer is unsure about how to behave and when the model is someone the observer looks up to, who is similar to the observer, or whom the observer relies upon for guidance or nurturing (Bandura, 1977).

Social learning can also help explain how we learn negative behaviors, such as aggression. For example, in one classic experiment by Albert Bandura and his colleagues (1961), children in one group were shown a film that involved aggressive behavior by an adult, and children in the other group were shown a film that did not portray aggressive behavior. In a play session that followed, children in the group who had been shown the aggressive film behaved more aggressively toward an inflated doll ("Bobo") than children in the other group.

Learning theories, including social learning theory, are still used in many approaches to developmental research and these theories also have practical applications. Children and adults do learn through both classical and operant conditioning, and we do rely on each other to serve as models for behaviors we are striving to learn or to emulate (for better or worse). Learning theories are limited, however, in that they cannot account for many complex aspects of development, such as language development.

Good grades are usually positive reinforcers for high performance in school.

social learning theory focus on learning by observing social models without any direct reinforcement

Constructivist theories

| Summarize the constructivist theories of Piaget and Vygotsky. | **LEARNING OBJECTIVE** 1.7 |

Constructivist theories posit that knowledge is not a copy of reality, but rather that children and other people actively construct reality in the mind as they interact with objects and others in the world. Piaget and Vygotsky were constructivists who were contemporaries from different cultures.

PIAGET'S COGNITIVE CONSTRUCTIVIST THEORY Unquestionably, the most influential theory of cognitive development from infancy through adolescence is the one developed by the Swiss psychologist Jean Piaget (pee-ah-JAY), who lived from 1896 to 1980. Piaget's observations convinced him that children of different ages think differently, and that changes in cognitive development proceed in distinct stages (Piaget, 1954). Each stage involves a different way of thinking about the world. The idea of cognitive stages means that each person's cognitive abilities are organized into coherent **mental structures**; a person who thinks within a particular stage in one aspect of life should think within that stage in all other aspects of life as well, because all thinking is part of the same mental structure (Keating, 1990). Because Piaget focused on how cognition changes as the child interacts with the environment, his approach (and the approach of those who have followed in his tradition) is known as the **cognitive constructivist theory.** ✳

There are four stages of Piaget's theory (see **Table 1.3**): the sensorimotor stage (ages 0–2), the preoperational stage (ages 2–7), the concrete operations stage (ages 7–11) and the formal operations stage (ages 11–15 and up). We'll cover each theory in more detail throughout the course of this text.

According to Piaget, the driving force behind development from one stage to the next is **maturation**, a biologically driven program of developmental change that unfolds in interaction with the world (Inhelder & Piaget, 1958; Piaget, 2002). Each of

My Virtual Child

How is the environment that your virtual child interacts with different than the environment of a child from another culture? What impact do you think this will have on development?

✳—[**Explore** the **Concept** Piaget's Stages of Cognitive Development in **MyDevelopmentLab**

mental structures in Piaget's theory of cognitive development, the cognitive systems that organize thinking into coherent patterns so that all thinking takes place on the same level of cognitive functioning

cognitive constructivist theory Piaget's theory that the development of knowledge is driven by the child's interaction with objects in the world

maturation concept that an innate, biologically based program is the driving force behind development

TABLE 1.3 Stages of Cognitive Development in Piaget's Theory		
Ages	**Stage**	**Characteristics**
0–2	Sensorimotor	Capable of coordinating the activities of the senses with motor activities
3–6	Preoperational	Capable of symbolic representation, such as in language, but with limited ability to use mental operations
7–11	Concrete operations	Capable of using mental operations, but only in concrete, immediate experience; difficulty thinking hypothetically
12–15 and up	Formal operations	Capable of thinking logically and abstractly; capable of formulating hypotheses and testing them systematically; thinking is more complex; and can think about thinking (metacognition)

APPLYING YOUR KNOWLEDGE

Can you think of an example of something a 4-year-old could learn easily but a 1-year-old could not learn even with special teaching?

us has within our genotype a prescription for cognitive development that prepares us for certain changes at certain ages. A reasonably normal environment is necessary for cognitive development to occur, but the effect of the environment is limited. You cannot teach a 1-year-old something that only a 4-year-old can learn, no matter how sophisticated your teaching techniques are. By the time the 1-year-old reaches age 4, the biological processes of maturation will make it easy to understand the world as a typical child of 4 understands it, and no special teaching will be required.

Along with maturation, Piaget emphasized that cognitive development is driven by the child's efforts to understand and influence the surrounding environment (Demetriou & Raftopoulos, 2004; Piaget, 2002). Children actively construct their understanding of the world, rather than being merely the passive recipients of environmental influences. Piaget's view was in sharp contrast to the behaviorists (the leading theorists prior to Piaget), who viewed the environment as acting on the child through rewards and punishments rather than seeing the child as an active agent.

Piaget proposed that the child's construction of reality takes place through the use of **schemes**, which are cognitive structures for processing, organizing, and interpreting information. For infants, schemes are based on sensory and motor processes such as sucking and grasping, but after infancy, schemes become symbolic and representational, as words, ideas, and concepts. For example, all nouns are schemes—*tree, chair, dog*—because thinking of these words evokes a cognitive structure that allows you to process, organize, and interpret information.

The two processes involved in the use of schemes are assimilation and accommodation. **Assimilation** occurs when *new information is absorbed to fit an existing scheme*, sometimes being altered to fit the scheme. In contrast, **accommodation** entails *changing the scheme to adapt to the new information, which may involve developing a new scheme*. For example, if an infant has a scheme for "doggie," new examples of dogs the infant sees are assimilated into the scheme. But, if an infant sees a pony and says "doggie" (thinking that the animal has ears, four legs, and a tail), the parent may correct him by saying, "That's a horse," and the infant accommodates with a new scheme, for "horse." Assimilation and accommodation usually take place together in varying degrees; they are "two sides of the same cognitive coin" (Flavell et al., 2002, p. 5). For example, an infant who has been breast-feeding may use mostly assimilation and a slight degree of accommodation when learning to suck from the nipple on a bottle, but if sucking on a ball or a parent's finger the infant would be able to use assimilation less and need to use accommodation more.

People of other ages, too, use both assimilation and accommodation whenever they are processing cognitive information. One example is right in front of you. In the course of reading this text, you will read things that sound familiar to you from your own experience, so that you can easily assimilate them to what you already know. Other information, especially the information from cultures other than your own, will be contrary to the schemes you have developed from living in your culture and will require you to use accommodation in order to expand your knowledge and understanding of human development.

My Virtual Child

What knowledge will your virtual child need to acquire in order to develop skills important to his/her culture?

schemes cognitive structures for processing, organizing, and interpreting information

assimilation cognitive process of altering new information to fit an existing scheme

accommodation cognitive process of changing a scheme to adapt to new information

Even today, over 70 years after he first proposed it, Piaget's theory of cognitive development remains influential. Like all good theories, it has inspired a wealth of research (by Piaget and many others) to test its assertions and implications. And, like even the best theories, it has been modified and altered on the basis of research (Morra et al., 2008). We'll explore and evaluate each stage of his theory throughout the text.

VYGOTSKY'S SOCIAL CONSTRUCTIVIST THEORY In recent years a cultural approach to cognition has gained increased attention from scholars of human development. This approach is founded on the ideas of the Russian psychologist Lev Vygotsky (1896–1934). Vygotsky died of tuberculosis when he was just 37, and it took decades before his ideas about cognitive development were translated and recognized by scholars outside Russia. It is only in recent decades that his work has been widely influential among Western scholars, but his influence is increasing as interest in understanding the cultural basis of development continues to grow (Gardiner, 2001; Maynard & Martini, 2005; Segall et al., 1999).

Vygotsky's **social constructivist theory** is often referred to as a sociocultural theory, because in his view cognitive development is always both a social and a cultural process (John-Steiner & Mahn, 2003). It is social, because children learn through interactions with others and require assistance from others in order to learn what they need to know. It is cultural, because what children need to know is determined by the culture they live in. Vygotsky recognized that there are distinct cultural differences in the knowledge children must acquire—from agricultural skills in rural Asia, to caring for cattle in eastern Africa, to the verbal and scientific reasoning skills taught in Western schools. This is very different from Piaget's theory described earlier, which emphasizes the child's interactions with the physical environment and views cognitive development as essentially the same across cultures. However, Vygotsky's theory is also considered a constructivist theory, in that he posited that the child takes in information from the environment in order to build knowledge in the mind, but that the knowledge is actively constructed in a social process with others. Vygotsky emphasized the social contexts of development to a great extent.

Two of Vygotsky's most influential ideas are the zone of proximal development and scaffolding, both involving social interaction. The **zone of proximal development** is the difference between skills or tasks that children can accomplish alone and those they are capable of performing if guided by an adult or a more competent peer. According to Vygotsky, children learn best if the instruction they are provided is within the zone of proximal development, so that they need assistance at first but gradually become capable of performing the task on their own. For example, children learning a musical instrument may be lost or overwhelmed if learning entirely on their own, but can make progress if guided by someone who already knows how to play the instrument. 👁

Another key idea in Vygotsky's theory is **scaffolding**, which is the degree of assistance provided to children in the zone of proximal development. According to Vygotsky, scaffolding should gradually decrease as children become more competent at a task. When children begin learning a task, they require substantial instruction and involvement from an adult or more capable peer; but as they gain knowledge and skill, the teacher should gradually scale back the amount of direct instruction provided. For example, when infants and toddlers first learn language, parents' statements to them are usually very simple, but they become more complex as children's language mastery grows (Capone & McGregor, 2005). Scaffolding can occur at any age, whenever there is someone who is learning a skill or gaining knowledge from someone else. 👁

Scaffolding and the zone of proximal development underscore the social nature of learning in Vygotsky's theory. In his view, learning always takes place via a social process, through the interactions between someone who possesses knowledge and someone who is in the process of obtaining knowledge. The ideas of the zone of proximal development and scaffolding have been applied to toddlerhood and older children's learning as well, and will be explored further in later chapters.

social constructivist theory Vygotsky's theory that child development is driven by the child's interaction with more experienced others in social contexts

zone of proximal development difference between skills or tasks that children can accomplish alone and those they are capable of performing if guided by an adult or a more competent peer

scaffolding degree of assistance provided to the learner in the zone of proximal development, gradually decreasing as the learner's skills develop

👁—**Watch** the **Video** Zone of Proximal Development in **MyDevelopmentLab**

👁—**Watch** the **Video** Scaffolding in **MyDevelopmentLab**

In Vygotsky's theory, children's cognitive development is always both social and cultural. Here, a father in the Middle Eastern country of Oman shows his son how to weave a basket.

WHAT HAVE YOU LEARNED?

1. According to Freud's theory, what functions do the id, ego, and superego serve?
2. How is Erikson's theory similar to and different from Freud's?
3. How is classical conditioning different from operant conditioning?
4. How do people continue to use assimilation and accommodation as they develop?
5. How does Vygotsky's theory incorporate culture and social context in ways that go beyond Piaget?

Recent Theories

Recent theories of child development emphasize contexts, such as culture, more than in past theories. Bronfenbrenner's theory takes into account the surrounding contexts that affect the child, from the child's direct contacts to the cultural and economic forces that shape the way the child grows up. This book will take a stage approach to the study of child development and will place special emphasis on the cultural context.

Bronfenbrenner's ecological theory

1.8   **LEARNING OBJECTIVE**   Define the five systems of Bronfenbrenner's ecological theory and explain how it differs from stage theories.

An important recent theory of human development is Urie Bronfenbrenner's **ecological theory** (Bronfenbrenner, 1980, 2000, 2005; Bronfenbrenner & Morris, 1998). Unlike the theories proposed by Freud and Erikson, Bronfenbrenner's is not a stage theory of human development. Instead, his theory focuses on the multiple influences that shape human development in the social environment.

Bronfenbrenner presented his theory as a reaction to what he viewed as an over-emphasis in developmental psychology on the immediate environment, especially the mother–child relationship. The immediate environment is important, Bronfenbrenner acknowledged, but much more than this is involved in children's development. Bronfenbrenner's theory was intended to draw attention to the broader cultural environment that people experience as they develop, and to the ways the different levels of a person's

ecological theory Bronfenbrenner's theory that human development is shaped by five interrelated systems in the social environment

environment interact. In later writings (Bronfenbrenner, 2000, 2005; Bronfenbrenner & Morris, 1998), Bronfenbrenner added a biological dimension to his framework and it is now sometimes called a *bio-ecological theory*, but the distinctive contribution of the theory remains its portrayal of the cultural environment.

According to Bronfenbrenner, there are five key levels or *systems* that play a part in human development (see *Figure 1.3*):

1. The *microsystem* is Bronfenbrenner's term for the immediate environment, the settings where people experience their daily lives. Microsystems in most cultures include relationships with each parent, with siblings, and perhaps with extended family; with peers and friends; with teachers; and with other adults (such as coaches, religious leaders, and employers). Bronfenbrenner emphasizes that the child is an *active* agent in the microsystems. For example, children are affected by their parents, but children's behavior affects their parents as well; children are affected by their friends, but they also make choices about whom to have as friends. The microsystem is where most research in developmental psychology has focused. Today, however, most developmental psychologists use the term *context* rather than microsystem to refer to immediate environmental settings and relationships.

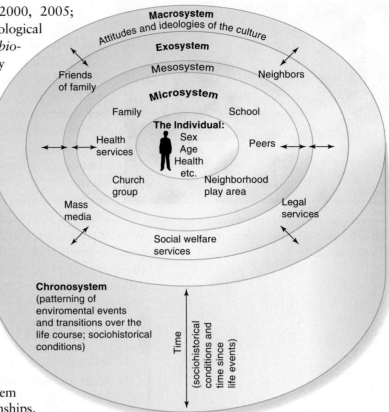

2. The *mesosystem* is the network of interconnections between the various microsystems. For example, a child who is experiencing abusive treatment from parents may become difficult to handle in relationships with teachers; or, if a parent's employer demands longer hours in the workplace, the parent's relationship with the child may be affected.

3. The *exosystem* refers to the societal institutions that have indirect but potentially important influences on development. In Bronfenbrenner's theory, these institutions include schools, religious institutions, and media. For example, in Asian countries such as South Korea, competition to get into college is intense and depends chiefly on adolescents' performance on a national exam at the end of high school; consequently, the high school years are a period of extreme academic stress.

4. The *macrosystem* is the broad system of cultural beliefs and values, and the economic and governmental systems that are built on those beliefs and values. For example, in countries such as Iran and Saudi Arabia, cultural beliefs and values are based in the religion of Islam, and the economic and governmental systems of those countries are also based on the teachings of Islam. In contrast, in most developed countries, beliefs in the value of individual freedom are reflected in a capitalist economic system and in governmental systems of representative democracy.

5. Finally, the *chronosystem* refers to changes that occur in developmental circumstances over time, both with respect to individual development and to historical changes. For example, with respect to individual development, losing your job is a much different experience at 15 than it would be at 45; with respect to historical changes, the occupational opportunities open to young women in many countries today are much broader than they were for young women half a century ago.

Figure 1.3 • **The systems in Bronfenbrenner's ecological theory.** How does this theory of human development differ from Freud's and Erikson's?

There are many characteristics of Bronfenbrenner's ecological theory that make it important and useful for the cultural approach that will be taken in this text. Many developmental theories make no mention of culture, but culture is an important component of Bronfenbrenner's theory. He recognizes that the cultural beliefs and values of the macrosystem are the basis for many of the other conditions of children's development. Furthermore, his theory recognizes the importance of historical contexts as influences on development, as we will see in this text. Also, Bronfenbrenner emphasized that children and adolescents are active participants in their development, not merely the passive recipients of external influences, and that will be stressed throughout this text as well.

APPLYING YOUR KNOWLEDGE

Why is a parent's employer-provided health insurance a mesosystem influence that policy makers should care about?

My Virtual Child

Describe the systems that will influence your virtual child's development.

In countries such as Iran, the macrosystem is based on Islam, which influences all aspects of life.

The structure of this textbook combines elements of Erikson's and Bronfenbrenner's approaches. Today there is a widespread consensus among researchers and theorists that human development is lifelong and that important changes take place throughout the life span, as Erikson proposed (Baltes et al., 2006). There is also a consensus in favor of Bronfenbrenner's view that it is not just the immediate family environment that is important in human development but multiple contexts interacting in multiple ways (Lerner, 2006).

This text takes a stage approach to the study of human development. Stages are a useful way of conceptualizing development because they draw our attention to the distinctive features of each age period, which helps us understand how people change over time (Arnett & Tanner, 2009). However, it should be kept in mind that for the most part, there are no sharp breaks between the stages. For example, toddlerhood is different from early childhood in many important ways, but the typical 34-month-old is not sharply different than the typical 37-month-old; nothing magical or dramatic occurs at 36 months to mark the end of one stage and the beginning of the next. To put it another way, scholars of human development generally regard development as *continuous* rather than *discontinuous* (Baltes et al., 2006).

WHAT HAVE YOU LEARNED?

1. Is Bronfenbrenner's theory more compatible with Freud's, Erikson's, or neither?
2. What role does culture play in Bronfenbrenner's ecological theory?
3. What are the microsystem environments that influence your development today? The mesosystem interactions?
4. What are the strengths and limitations of stage theories?

Section 2 VIDEO GUIDE Erik Erikson (Length: 1:56)

In this video the psychologist Erik Erikson is interviewed on his psychosocial theory of human development, including the stage of intimacy vs. isolation.

1. Describe the types of relationships that Erikson connects to the stage of intimacy vs. isolation.

2. Discuss Erikson's views on how the stage of intimacy vs. isolation relates to marriage.

3. Erikson discusses his thoughts on why some marriages among younger or less mature individuals might not be successful. Do you agree or disagree with these thoughts? Why?

⊙—[**Watch** the **Video** Erik Erikson in **MyDevelopmentLab**

LEARNING OBJECTIVES

1.9 Recall the five steps of the scientific method and the meanings and functions of hypotheses, sampling, and procedure in scientific research.

1.10 Describe some ethical standards for human development research.

1.11 Summarize the main methods used in research on human development.

1.12 Describe the major types of research designs used in human development research.

The Scientific Study of Human Development

The field of human development is based on scientific research, and to understand the research presented in this book it is important for you to know the essential elements of how the scientific process works. Here we look at this process and how it is applied to the study of child development.

The five steps of the scientific method

> Recall the five steps of the scientific method and the meanings and functions of hypotheses, sampling, and procedure in scientific research.

In its classic form, the **scientific method** involves five basic steps: (1) identifying a question to be investigated, (2) forming a hypothesis, (3) choosing a research method and a research design, (4) collecting data to test the hypothesis, and (5) drawing conclusions that lead to new questions and new hypotheses. *Figure 1.4* summarizes these steps.

STEP 1: IDENTIFY A QUESTION OF SCIENTIFIC INTEREST Every scientific study begins with an idea (Machado & Silva, 2007). A researcher wants to find an answer to a question that can be addressed using scientific methods. For example, in research on child development the question might be "How do infants who breast-feed differ in their physical and social development from infants who bottle-feed?" or "How does gender segregation in play groups in early childhood affect gender role development?" or "Why do adolescents in some cultures engage in risky behaviors while in other cultures they do not?" The question of interest may be generated by a theory or previous research, or it may be something the researcher has noticed from personal observation or experience.

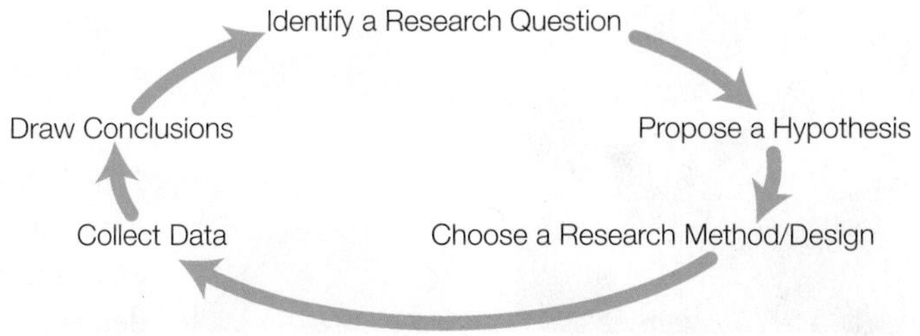

STEP 2: FORM A HYPOTHESIS In seeking to answer the question generated in Step 1, the researcher proposes one or more hypotheses. A **hypothesis** is the researcher's idea about one possible answer to the question of interest. For example, a researcher may be interested in the question "What is the effect of reading to toddlers on their performance in kindergarten?" and propose the hypothesis "Reading to toddlers will lead to increases in cognitive performance in

scientific method process of scientific investigation, involving a series of steps from identifying a research question through forming a hypothesis, selecting research methods and designs, collecting and analyzing data, and drawing conclusions

hypothesis in the scientific process, a researcher's idea about one possible answer to the question proposed for investigation

Figure 1.4 • **The steps of the scientific method**

Identify a Research Question

Propose a Hypothesis

Choose a Research Method/Design

Collect Data

Draw Conclusions

research method in the scientific process, the approach to investigating the hypothesis

research design plan for when and how to collect the data for a study

sample subset of a population for which data are collected in a scientific study

population in research, the entire category of people represented by a sample

procedure the way a study is conducted and the data are collected

kindergarten because children who are read to will be better equipped to learn how to read in school, compared to those who are not read to." The researcher would then design a study to test that hypothesis. The hypotheses of a study are crucial, because they influence the sampling, research methods, research design, data analysis, and interpretation that follow.

STEP 3: CHOOSE A RESEARCH METHOD AND A RESEARCH DESIGN Once the hypothesis is proposed, the investigator must choose a research method and a research design (Salkind, 2009). The **research method** is the approach to investigating the hypothesis. For example, in human development research two common research methods are questionnaires and interviews. The **research design** is the plan for when and how to collect the data for the study, for example the decision of whether to collect data at one time point or at more than one point. More detail on research methods and designs will be presented shortly.

STEP 4: COLLECT DATA TO TEST THE HYPOTHESIS After forming a hypothesis and choosing a research method and design, researchers who study human development seek to obtain a **sample**, which is a group of people who participate in a research study. The sample should represent the **population**, which is the entire category of people the sample represents. Suppose, for example, a researcher wants to study adolescents' attitudes toward contraception. Adolescents are the population, and the sample comprises the specific adolescents who participate in the study.

The goal in finding a sample is to seek out a sample that will be *representative* of the population of interest (Goodwin, 2009). To continue the example of a study of adolescents' attitudes toward contraceptive use, the waiting room of a clinic offering contraceptive services would probably not be a good place to look for a sample, because the adolescents coming to such a clinic would be quite likely to have more favorable attitudes toward contraception than adolescents in general; otherwise, why would they be in a place that offers contraceptive services? If the population of interest is adolescents in general, it would be better to sample them through schools or through a telephone survey that selects households randomly from the community.

APPLYING YOUR KNOWLEDGE

Think of a research question that interests you and a hypothesis based on the question. How would you find a representative sample for your study?

On the other hand, if a researcher is particularly interested in attitudes toward contraception among the population of adolescents who are already using or planning to use contraception, then a clinic offering contraceptive services would be a good place to find a sample. It depends on the population the researcher wishes to study and on the questions the researcher wishes to address. Again, the sample should be *representative* of the population of interest. If it is, then the findings from the sample will be *generalizable* to the population. In other words, the findings from the sample will make it possible to draw conclusions about not just the sample itself, but the larger population of people that the sample is intended to represent.

The **procedure** of the study is the way the study is conducted and the data are collected. One aspect of the procedure is the circumstances of the data collection. Researchers try to collect data in a way that will not be biased. For example, they must be careful not to phrase questions in an interview or questionnaire in a way that seems to lead people toward a desired response. They must also assure participants that their responses will be confidential, especially if the study concerns a sensitive topic such as sexual behavior or drug use.

If a sample of adolescents is obtained from a birth control clinic, what population does it represent?

STEP 5: DRAW CONCLUSIONS AND FORM NEW QUESTIONS AND HYPOTHESES Once the data for a study have been collected, statistical analyses are usually conducted to examine relationships between different parts of the data. Often, the analyses are determined by the hypotheses that generated the study. For example, a researcher

studying relationships with parents in middle childhood may hypothesize, based on a theory or on past research, that children in this stage are closer to their mothers than to their fathers. The scientist will then test that hypothesis with a statistical analysis comparing the quality of children's relationships with mothers and with fathers.

Once the data are analyzed they must be interpreted. When scientists write up the results of their research for publication in a scientific journal, they interpret the results of the study in light of relevant theories and previous research. After researchers write an article describing the methods used, the results of the statistical analyses, and the interpretation of the results, they typically submit the manuscript for the article to a professional journal. The editor of the journal then sends the manuscript out for review by other researchers. In other words, the manuscript is **peer-reviewed** for its scientific accuracy and credibility and for the importance of its contribution to the field. The editor typically relies on the reviews by the researchers' peers in deciding whether or not to accept the manuscript for publication. If the editor determines that the manuscript has passed the peer-review process successfully, the article is published in the journal. In addition to research articles, most journals publish occasional theoretical articles and review articles that integrate the findings from numerous other studies. Researchers studying human development also publish the results of their investigations in books, and often these books go through the peer-review process.

The results of research often lead to the development or modification of theories. A good **theory** is a framework that presents a set of interconnected ideas in an original way and inspires further research. Theories and research are intrinsically connected: A theory generates hypotheses that can be tested in research, and research leads to modifications of the theory, which generate further hypotheses and further research. There is no separate chapter on theories in this book, because theories and research are intrinsically connected and should be presented together. Theories are presented in every chapter in relation to the research they have generated and the questions they have raised for future research.

peer-review in scientific research, the system of having other scientists review a manuscript to judge its merits and worthiness for publication

theory framework that presents a set of interconnected ideas in an original way and inspires further research

APPLYING YOUR KNOWLEDGE

Find an article pertaining to human development in a newspaper or magazine and evaluate whether it meets the standards of scientific research.

Ethics in human development research

| Describe some ethical standards for human development research. | LEARNING OBJECTIVE | 1.10 |

Imagine that you were a child development researcher who was interested in language development, and you hypothesized that the number of words spoken to a toddler would influence the size of the toddler's vocabulary a year later. So, you designed a study in which families with toddlers were randomly assigned to two groups: In one group, parents were trained to speak frequently to their toddlers, whereas in the other group the parents were given no instructions. Is this research design ethical?

Imagine that you were a child development researcher interested in the question of what makes teenagers argue with their parents. So, you proposed a study in which you invited mothers and their adolescent children to come into a laboratory situation, where they were provided with a list of possible secrets that teenagers might keep from their parents, and asked to pick one of them to discuss, while being filmed by the researchers. Is this research design ethical?

Imagine that you were a child development researcher who was working to develop a drug to promote memory enhancement in children. In experiments with rats the drug had been shown to enhance memory, in that after receiving the drug, the rats had increased success in running mazes they had run before. However, the rats receiving the drug also died earlier than the rats in the control group. Would it be ethical to conduct a study on children in which one group received the drug and another group did not?

APPLYING YOUR KNOWLEDGE

Of the three hypothetical studies described here, which do you think would be likely to receive IRB approval and which not?

informed consent standard procedure in social scientific studies that entails informing potential participants of what their participation would involve, including any possible risks, and giving them the opportunity to agree to participate or not

◉▶ Simulate the Experiment
Ethics of Psychological Research
in **MyDevelopmentLab**

**APPLYING YOUR KNOWLEDGE
. . . as a Nurse**

There is a new medical study being conducted on your ward. A child you are treating is eligible and would like to participate, but her parents haven't given their consent. Can the child still participate?

These are the kinds of ethical issues that arise in the course of research on child development. To prevent ethical violations, most institutions that sponsor research, such as universities and research institutes, require proposals for research to be approved by an *institutional review board (IRB)*. IRBs usually comprise people who have research experience themselves and therefore can judge whether the research being proposed follows reasonable ethical guidelines. In addition to IRBs, professional organizations such as the Society for Research on Child Development (SRCD) often have a set of ethical guidelines for researchers. ◉▶

The requirements of IRBs and the ethical guidelines of professional organizations usually include the following components (Fisher, 2003; Rosnow & Rosenthal, 2005):

1. *Protection from physical and psychological harm.* The most important consideration in human development research is that the persons participating in the research will not be harmed by it.
2. *Informed consent prior to participation.* One standard ethical requirement of human development research is **informed consent**. Participants in any scientific study are supposed to be presented with a *consent form* before they participate (Salkind, 2009). Consent forms typically include information about who is conducting the study, what the purposes of the study are, what participation in the study involves, what risks (if any) are involved in participating, and what the person can expect to receive in return for participation. Consent forms also usually include a statement indicating that participation in the study is voluntary, and that persons may withdraw from participation in the study at any time. The use of consent forms is not always possible (for example, in telephone surveys), but whenever possible they are included in the procedure for researchers studying human development. For persons under age 18, the consent of one of their parents is also usually required as part of a study's procedures.
3. *Confidentiality.* Researchers are ethically required to take steps to ensure that all information provided by participants in human development research is confidential, meaning that it will not be shared with anyone outside the immediate research group and any results from the research will not identify any of the participants by name.
4. *Deception and debriefing.* Sometimes human development research involves deception. For example, a study might involve having children play a game but fix the game to ensure that they will lose, because the objective of the study is to examine how children respond to losing a game. IRBs require researchers to show that the deception in the proposed study will cause no harm. Also, ethical guidelines require that participants in a study that involves deception must be *debriefed*, which means that following their participation they must be told the true purpose of the study and the reason for the deception.

WHAT HAVE YOU LEARNED?

1. Why is it important to use a representative sample in research?
2. What is the function of peer review?
3. How are theories and research connected?
4. Define the term *informed consent* and explain why it is important.

✳ Explore the Concept Diversity
in Psychological Inquiry in
MyDevelopmentLab

Methods and Designs in Research

Although all investigators of human development follow the scientific method in some form, there are many different ways of investigating research questions. Studies vary in the methods used and in their research designs. ✳

Research methods

> Summarize the main methods used in research on human development.

Researchers study human development in a variety of academic disciplines, including psychology, sociology, anthropology, education, social work, family studies, and medicine. They use various methods in their investigations, each of which has both strengths and limitations (see **Table 1.4**). We'll examine each of the major research methods next, then consider an issue that is important across methods, the question of reliability and validity. 👁

👁—⌐**Watch** the **Video** Research
Methods in **MyDevelopmentLab**

QUESTIONNAIRES The most commonly used method in social science research is the questionnaire (Salkind, 2009). Usually, questionnaires have a *closed-question* format, which means that participants are provided with specific responses to choose from (Shaughnessy et al., 2011). Sometimes the questions have an *open-ended question* format, which means that participants are allowed to state their response following the question. One advantage of closed questions is that they make it possible to collect and analyze responses from a large number of people in a relatively short time. Everyone responds to the same questions with the same response options. For this reason, closed questions have often been used in large-scale surveys. Questionnaires often produce **quantitative** data, which can be counted and analyzed with statistics.

Although questionnaires are a dominant method in the study of human development, the use of questionnaires has certain limitations (Arnett, 2005a). When a closed-question format is used, the range of possible responses is already specified, and the participant must choose from the responses provided. The researcher tries to cover the responses that seem most plausible and most likely, but it is impossible in a few brief response options to do justice to the depth and diversity of human experience. For example, if a questionnaire contains an item such as "How close are you to your siblings? A. very close; B. somewhat close; C. not very close; D. not at all close," it is probably true that children who choose "very close" really are closer to their siblings than children who choose "not at all close." But this alone does not begin to capture the complexity of the sibling relationship.

INTERVIEWS Interviews are intended to provide the kind of individuality and complexity that questionnaires usually lack. An interview allows a researcher to hear people describe their lives in their own words, with all the uniqueness and richness that such descriptions make possible. Interviews also enable a researcher to know the whole person and see how the various parts of the person's life are intertwined. For example,

quantitative data that is collected in numerical form

TABLE 1.4 Research Methods: Advantages and Limitations

Methods	Advantages	Limitations
Questionnaire	Large sample, quick data collection	Preset responses, no depth
Interview	Individuality and complexity	Time and effort of coding
Observations	Actual behavior, not self-report	Observation may affect behavior
Ethnographic research	Entire span of daily life	Researcher must live among participants; possible bias
Case studies	Rich, detailed data	Difficult to generalize results
Biological measurements	Precise data	Expensive; relation to behavior may not be clear
Experiment	Control, identification of cause and effect	May not reflect real life
Natural experiment	Illuminate gene–environment relations	Unusual circumstances; rare

an interview on an adolescent's family relationships might reveal how the adolescent's relationship with her mother is affected by her relationship with her father, and how the whole family has been affected by certain events—perhaps a family member's loss of a job, psychological problems, medical problems, or substance abuse.

Interviews provide qualitative data, which can be interesting and informative. **Qualitative** data are nonnumerical and include not only interview data, but also data from other nonnumerical methods such as descriptive observations, video recordings, or photographs. (Note that interviews, observations, and video recordings can be coded, and the codes can be quantified for later statistical analysis.) However, like questionnaires, interviews have limitations (Shaughnessy et al., 2011). Because interviews do not typically provide a range of specific responses the way questionnaires do, interview responses have to be coded according to some plan of classification. For example, if you asked emerging adults the interview question "What do you think makes a person an adult?" you might get a fascinating range of responses. However, to make sense of the data and present them in a scientific format, at some point you would have to code the responses into categories—legal markers, biological markers, character qualities, and so on. Only in this way would you be able to say something about the pattern of responses in your sample. Coding interview data takes time, effort, and money. This is one of the reasons far more studies are conducted using questionnaires than interviews.

OBSERVATIONS Another way researchers learn about human development is through *observations*. Studies using this method involve observing people and recording their behavior either on video or through written records. In some studies the observations take place in the natural environment. For example, a study of aggressive behavior in children might involve observations on a school playground. In other studies the observations take place in a laboratory setting. For example, many laboratory studies of attachments between toddlers and their parents have been conducted in which the parent leaves the room briefly and the toddler's behavior is observed while the parent is absent and when the parent returns. Whether in the natural environment or the laboratory, after the observations are completed the data are coded and analyzed.

Observational methods have an advantage over questionnaires and interviews in that they involve actual behavior rather than self-reports of behavior. However, the disadvantage of observations is that the people being observed may be aware of the observer and this awareness may make their behavior different than it would be under normal conditions. For example, parents being observed in a laboratory setting with their children may be nicer to them than they would be at home.

ETHNOGRAPHIC RESEARCH Researchers have also learned about human development through **ethnographic research** (Jessor et al., 1996). In this method researchers spend a considerable amount of time with the people they wish to study, often by actually living among them. Information gained in ethnographic research typically comes from researchers' observations, experiences, and informal conversations with the people they are studying. Ethnographic research is commonly used by anthropologists, usually in studying non-Western cultures. Anthropologists usually report the results of their research in an *ethnography,* which is a book that presents an anthropologist's observations of what life is like in a particular culture. Ethnographic research is also used by some social scientists today to study a particular aspect of their own culture (e.g., Douglass, 2005).

The main advantage of the ethnographic method is that it allows the researcher to learn how people behave in their daily lives. Other methods capture only a slice or summary of people's lives, but the ethnographic method provides insights into the whole span of daily experience. The main disadvantage of the ethnographic method is that it requires a great deal of time, commitment, and sacrifice by the researcher. It means that researchers must give up their own lives for a period of time, from a few weeks to years, in order

Observations allow researchers to assess behavior directly rather than through self-report. Here, the attachment between toddler and parent is assessed.

qualitative data that is collected in nonnumerical form

ethnographic research research method that involves spending extensive time among the people being studied

to live among the people whose lives they wish to understand. Also, an ethnographic researcher is likely to form relationships with the people being studied, which may bias the interpretation of the results.

CASE STUDIES The case study method entails the detailed examination of the life of one person or a small number of persons. The advantage of a case study is in the detail and richness that is possible when only one or a few persons are being described. The disadvantage of the case study is that it is especially difficult to generalize the results to larger groups of people on the basis of only one or a few people's experiences.

Some of the most influential studies in the history of human development research were case studies. For example, Jean Piaget initially based his ideas about infants' cognitive development on his detailed observations of his own three children (Piaget, 1936/1952). Also, Charles Darwin recorded an extensive case study of the early years of his son Doddy, as we'll see in more detail in the **Research Focus: Darwin's Diary** feature on page 36. Today the case study method is sometimes used in mental health research to describe a case that is unusual or that portrays the characteristics of a mental health issue in an especially vivid way. It is also used in combination with other methods, as a way of providing a sense of the whole of a person's life (Arnett, 2004).

Ethnographic research entails living among the people in the culture of interest. Here, the renowned anthropologist Margaret Mead talks to a mother in the Manus culture of Papua New Guinea.

BIOLOGICAL MEASUREMENTS Biological changes are a central part of human development, so research includes measurements of biological functioning. This includes research on hormonal functioning, brain functioning, and the genetic basis of development. Some of this research involves measuring biological characteristics, such as hormone levels, and relating the results to data using other methods, such as questionnaires on aggressive behavior. Research on brain functioning often involves measuring brain activity during different kinds of behavior, like listening to music or solving a math problem. Research on genetics increasingly involves directly examining the chemical structure of genes.

Biological methods have the advantage of providing precise measurements of many aspects of human functioning. They allow researchers to gain knowledge into how biological aspects of development are related to cognitive, social, and emotional functioning. However, biological methods tend to rely on expensive equipment. Also, although biological measurements can be precise, their relation to other aspects of functioning is often far from exact. For example, if levels of a certain hormone are positively associated with aggressive behavior, it may be that the hormone causes the aggressive behavior, or it could be that aggressive behavior causes levels of the hormone to rise. Methods in brain research yield data from monitoring the brain's electrical activity or recording images of the brain while it is engaged in various activities, but those data can be difficult to interpret (Gergen, 2011).

EXPERIMENTAL RESEARCH An approach used in many kinds of scientific research is the **experimental research method**. In the simplest form of this design, participants in the study are randomly assigned to either the *experimental group,* which receives a treatment of some kind, or the *control group,* which receives no treatment (Goodwin, 2009). Because participants were randomly assigned to either the experimental group or the control group, it can be reasonably assumed that the two groups did not differ prior to the experiment. A true experiment is the only way to establish cause. Many studies are quasi-experimental or observational, and cause cannot be inferred; these are considered correlational studies.

In an experiment there are independent variables and dependent variables. The **independent variable** is the variable that is different for the experimental group than for the control group. The **dependent variable** is the outcome that is measured to calculate the results of the experiment. For example, in the classic "Bobo" doll experiment by Albert Bandura and his colleagues (1961), children in the experimental group were shown a film

experimental research method research method that entails comparing an *experimental group* that receives a treatment of some kind to a *control group* that receives no treatment

independent variable in an experiment, the variable that is different for the experimental group than for the control group

dependent variable in an experiment, the outcome that is measured to calculate the results of the experiment by comparing the experimental group to the control group

RESEARCH FOCUS   Darwin's Diary

Charles Darwin is best known for his book *The Origin of Species* (1859), which laid out his theory of evolution and dramatically changed how humans view themselves in relation to nature. However, 20 years before he published *The Origin of Species,* Darwin embarked on a different project. He decided to keep a diary record of the development of his first child, Doddy. Already Darwin was intensely interested in how and why animal species differ from one another. By keeping a careful record of Doddy's development, Darwin hoped to find evidence toward answering questions such as "What is innate and what is learned?"; "What skills emerge in the first years of a child's life, and at what ages?"; and "How are human children different from other young primates?" In his diary, Darwin recorded observations and insights concerning Doddy's cognitive, language, social, and moral development (Keegan & Gruber, 1985).

In observing Doddy's cognitive development, Darwin noted that it was at about 4 months of age that Doddy first became able to coordinate simple actions:

Darwin kept a diary of his son Doddy's development.

> Took my finger to his mouth & as usual could not get it back in, on account of his own hand being in the way; then he slipped his own back & so got my finger in.—This was not chance & therefore a kind of reasoning. (p. 12)

About two weeks later, at 4½ months of age, Doddy showed further evidence of being able to coordinate his actions: tracking an object with his eyes and reaching for it.

> May 9th a watch held close to face: he extended his hand to it—Had made feeble trials for two or three days before. (p. 16)

As we will see in Chapter 4, beginning to coordinate actions in this way was later recognized by psychological researchers as an important marker of early cognitive development. Doddy's first word was "ouchy," at 11 months, but at this age he used it to refer to a wide range of objects. At 12 months, Doddy began to use the word "mum" to refer specifically to food, and Darwin noted the importance of the tone of voice Doddy used, as well as the similarity to communication in birds:

> He ceased crying for food, but instead cries "mum"—his word for food & to this word he gives the most strongly marked [questioning] sound at the end . . . which one ordinarily gives

to "what?" . . . [It may be] analogous to cry for food of nesting birds. (p. 28)

With regard to social development, Darwin observed, as later researchers would, that Doddy's first smiles were the expression of internal states rather than being intended as communication. "When little under five weeks old, smiled but certainly not from pleasure" (p. 3). Over the course of the next months Darwin recorded how smiling changed from an expression of internal feelings to a social act directed toward others. Darwin also noted Doddy's aggressive behavior. On one occasion when Doddy was 13 months old, he became angry when his nurse tried to take a piece of cake away from him: "He tried to slap her face, went scarlet, screamed & shook his head" (p. 29). Because Doddy had never been physically punished, Darwin concluded that this act of aggression must have been instinctive rather than learned.

Darwin viewed moral development as evident in Doddy from about 1 year old, and linked it to the ability to understand what others were seeking to communicate. This incident occurred when Doddy was about 13 months old:

> I repeated several times in a reproaching voice, "Doddy won't give poor Papa a kiss—naughty Doddy." He unquestionably was made slightly uncomfortable by this . . . [His discomfort] showed something like first shades of moral sense. (p. 28)

About a year later, at just over 2 years old, Doddy showed further moral development, in his pride at his kindness to his younger sister:

> Doddy was generous enough to give Anny the last mouthful of gingerbread & today he again put his last crumb on the sofa for Anny to run to then cried in rather a vain-glorious tone "oh kind Doddy." (p. 36)

The diary method has been used by curious investigators of human development both before and after Darwin (Jaeger, 1985). Today, the diary method continues to be used, but usually in a way that combines the diaries of a variety of different people rather than relying on one account.

that involved aggressive behavior by an adult, and children in the control group were shown a film that did not portray aggressive behavior. The independent variable was the content of the film each group was shown. In a play session that followed, children in the treatment group were more aggressive toward an inflated doll ("Bobo") than children in the control group. The dependent variable was the children's aggressiveness. ⊙➤

Another area of human development research for which the experimental research method is commonly used is for **interventions**. Interventions are programs intended to change the attitudes or behavior of the participants. For example, a variety of programs have been developed to prevent adolescents from starting to smoke cigarettes, by promoting critical thinking about cigarette advertising or by attempting to change attitudes associating smoking with peer acceptance (e.g., Horn et al., 2005). The adolescents participating in such a study are randomly assigned to either the experimental group receiving the intervention or the control group that does not receive the intervention. After the intervention, the two groups are assessed for their attitudes and behavior regarding smoking. If the intervention worked, the attitudes and/or behavior of the experimental group should be less favorable toward smoking than those of the control group.

The advantage of the experimental method is that it allows the researcher a high degree of control over participants' behavior. Rather than monitoring behavior that occurs naturally, the researcher attempts to change the normal patterns of behavior by assigning some persons to an experimental group and some to a control group. This allows for a clearer and more definite measure of the effect of the experimental manipulation than is possible in normal life. However, the disadvantage of the experimental method is the flip side of the advantage: Because participants' behavior has been altered through experimental manipulation, it is difficult to say if the results would apply in normal life.

⊙➤ **Simulate** the **Experiment** Distinguishing Independent and Dependent Variables in **MyDevelopmentLab**

Intervention programs are one type of experimental research. Here, adolescents participate in an anti-drug use program.

NATURAL EXPERIMENTS A **natural experiment** is a situation that exists naturally—in other words, the researcher does not control it—but that provides interesting scientific information to the perceptive observer (Goodwin, 2009). One natural experiment used frequently in human development research is adoption. Unlike in most families, children in adoptive families are raised by adults with whom they have no genetic relationship. Because one set of parents provides the child's genes and a different set of parents provides the environment, it is possible to examine the relative contributions of genes and environment to the child's development. Similarities between adoptive parents and adopted children are likely to be due to the environment provided by the parents, because the parents and children are biologically unrelated. Similarities between adopted children and their biological parents are likely to be due to genetics, because the environment the children grew up in was not provided by the biological parents.

Twin studies make use of another type of natural experiment. Identical or *monozygotic (MZ) twins* have exactly the same genes, whereas fraternal or *dizygotic (DZ) twins* have about half their genes in common, the same as other siblings. By comparing the degree of similarity in MZ compared to DZ twins, we gain information about the extent to which a characteristic is genetically based. If MZ twins are more similar on a characteristic than DZ twins are, this may be due to genetics, since MZ twins are more genetically similar. Of special interest are studies of MZ twins adopted into different families. The results of this extraordinary natural experiment are striking and informative, as we shall see in the chapters to come.

Natural experiments provide the advantage of allowing for exceptional insights into the relation between genes and the environment. However, they have disadvantages as well. Families who adopt children are not selected randomly but volunteer and go through an extensive screening process, which makes adoption studies difficult

intervention program intended to change the attitudes or behavior of the participants

natural experiment situation that exists naturally but provides interesting scientific information

reliability in scientific research, the consistency of measurements across different occasions

validity in scientific research, the extent to which a research method measures what it claims to measure

to generalize to biological families. Also, natural experiments such as MZ twins being adopted into different families are extremely rare, and consequently such studies can only provide answers to a limited range of questions.

RELIABILITY AND VALIDITY In scientific research it is important that research methods have *reliability* and *validity*. **Reliability** refers to the consistency of measurements (Salkind, 2009). There are a variety of types of reliability, but in general, a method has high reliability if it obtains similar results on different occasions. For example, if a questionnaire asked girls in their senior year of high school to recall when their first menstrual period occurred, the questionnaire would be considered reliable if most of the girls answered the same on one occasion as they did when asked the question again six months later. Or, if children were interviewed about the quality of their friendships with their classmates, the measure would be reliable if the children's answers were the same in response to two different interviewers (Goodwin, 2009).

Validity refers to the truthfulness of a method (Shaughnessy et al., 2011). A method is valid if it *measures what it claims to measure*. For example, IQ tests are purported to measure intellectual abilities, but as we shall see in Chapter 7, this claim is controversial. Critics claim that IQ tests are not valid (i.e., that they do not measure what they claim to measure). Notice that a measure is not necessarily valid even if it is reliable. It is widely agreed that IQ tests are reliable—people generally score about the same on one occasion as they do on another—but the validity of the tests is disputed. In general, validity is more difficult to establish than reliability. We will examine questions of reliability and validity throughout the text.

Research designs

1.12 **LEARNING OBJECTIVE** Describe the major types of research designs used in human development research.

cross-sectional research research design that involves collecting data from people of a variety of ages on a single occasion

In addition to choosing a research method, researchers must also choose a design for their study. Common research designs in the study of human development include cross-sectional and longitudinal designs (see *Table 1.5*).

CROSS-SECTIONAL RESEARCH The most common type of research design in the study of human development is **cross-sectional research**. In cross-sectional research, data are collected on a single occasion (Goodwin, 2009). Then, the researcher examines potential relations between variables in the data, based on the hypotheses of the study. For example, researchers interested in promoting health among adolescents may ask a sample of teenagers to fill out a questionnaire reporting their physical health and how much they exercise, based on the hypothesis that exercising promotes better physical health. They then analyze the data to see if the amount of exercise is related to physical health (see *Figure 1.5* for a hypothetical illustration of this relationship). ✳

✳─[**Explore** the **Concept** Cross-Sectional and Longitudinal Research Designs in **MyDevelopmentLab**

Cross-sectional research has both strengths and weaknesses. The main strength is that these studies can be completed quickly and inexpensively. Data collection is done on one occasion, and the study is finished. These features explain why cross-sectional research is so widely used among researchers.

However, there are weaknesses as well in the cross-sectional research design. Most importantly, cross-sectional research yields a *correlation* between variables, and correlations

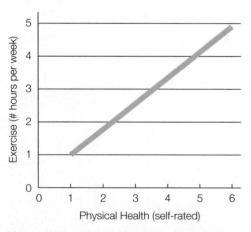

Figure 1.5 • **Physical health and exercise are correlated—but which causes which?**

TABLE 1.5 Research Designs: Advantages and Limitations		
Method	**Advantages**	**Limitations**
Cross-sectional	Quick and inexpensive	Correlations difficult to interpret
Longitudinal	Monitors change over time	Time, expense, attrition

can be difficult to interpret. A **correlation** is a statistical relationship between two variables, such that knowing one of the variables makes it possible to predict the other. A *positive correlation* means that when one variable increases or decreases, the other variable changes in the same direction; a *negative correlation* means that when one variable increases the other decreases. In the example just provided, the researcher may find a positive correlation between exercising and physical health. But does this mean that exercising causes better physical health, or that people with better physical health are more inclined to exercise? Based on cross-sectional research alone, there is no way to tell. ✳

It is a basic statistical principle of scientific research that *correlation does not imply causation,* meaning that when two variables are correlated it is not possible to tell whether one variable caused the other. Nevertheless, this principle is frequently overlooked in research on human development. For example, there are hundreds of studies showing a correlation between parenting behaviors and children's functioning. Frequently this correlation has been interpreted as causation—parenting behaviors cause children to function in certain ways—but in fact the correlation alone does not show this (Pinker, 2002). It could be that children's characteristics cause parents to behave in certain ways, or it could be that the behavior of both parents and children is due to a third variable, such as SES or cultural context. We will explore this issue and other *correlation versus causation* questions in later chapters.

LONGITUDINAL RESEARCH The limitations of cross-sectional research have led some researchers to use a **longitudinal research** design, in which the same persons are followed over time and data are collected on two or more occasions. The length of longitudinal research designs varies widely, from a few weeks or months to years or even decades. Most longitudinal studies take place over a relatively short period, a year or less, but some studies have followed their samples over an entire lifetime, from infancy to old age (e.g., Friedman & Martin, 2011).

The great advantage of the longitudinal research design is that it allows researchers on human development to examine the question that is at the heart of the study of human development: "How do people change over time?" In addition, the longitudinal research design allows researchers to gain more insight into the question of correlation versus causation. For example, suppose a cross-sectional study of children shows a marked difference in average body size reached by age 18: People born in earlier birth *cohorts,* or historical periods, tend to be smaller on average than people born in later birth cohorts. Does this mean that simply being born later caused an increase in body size? From a cross-sectional study, there is no way to tell; it could be that the culture has changed over the years, and that the older children grew up in a setting where they had fewer calories than the younger children did. This kind of explanation for age differences is called a **cohort effect;** people of different ages vary because they grew up in different *cohorts* or historical periods. You would need to find out what kinds of changes occurred, and

✳ Explore the **Concept** Correlations Do Not Show Causation in **MyDevelopmentLab**

APPLYING YOUR KNOWLEDGE

From your daily life, think of an example of how you or people you know may have mistaken correlation for causation. How would you design a study to show whether or not causation is truly involved?

correlation statistical relationship between two variables such that knowing one of the variables makes it possible to predict the other

longitudinal research research design in which the same persons are followed over time and data are collected on two or more occasions

cohort effect in scientific research, an explanation of group differences among people of different ages based on the fact that they grew up in different *cohorts* or historical periods

Longitudinal studies follow the same persons over time. Here, an American girl in toddlerhood, early childhood, middle childhood, and adolescence.

when they occurred, in order to link those changes to body size. There are a number of variables other than access to calories that may be at play, including the kinds of calories the younger children had access to, whether the children were doing physical work, and whether there was an epidemic of childhood disease in the older group.

Longitudinal research designs have disadvantages as well. Most importantly, they take a great deal more time, money, and patience than a cross-sectional research design does. Researchers do not learn the outcome to the investigation of their hypothesis until weeks, months, or years later. Over time, it is inevitable that some people will drop out of a longitudinal study, for one reason or another—a process called *attrition*. Consequently, the sample the researcher has at Time 1 is likely to be different than the sample that remains at Time 2, 3, or 4, which limits the conclusions that can be drawn. In most studies, dropout is highest among people from low-SES groups, which means that the longer a longitudinal study goes on, the less likely it is to represent the SES range of the entire population.

Throughout this text, studies using a wide variety of research methods and research designs will be presented. For now, the methods and designs just described will provide you with an introduction to the approaches used most often.

> ### APPLYING YOUR KNOWLEDGE
>
> *Choose a topic on child development that you would be interested in studying. Which methodological approach would you use, and why?*

WHAT HAVE YOU LEARNED?

1. What are some advantages and disadvantages of using ethnographic methods of research?
2. What are reliability and validity and why are they important in scientific research?
3. What is a correlation and why does it not necessarily show causation?
4. Give an example of a study with a cross-sectional research design and one using a longitudinal research design.

Section 3 VIDEO GUIDE Robert Guthrie: Before Informed Consent (Length: 2:59)

In this video you will see a discussion of the controversial experiment that was conducted on veterans at a VA hospital in Tuskegee, Alabama. The ethics of the research being conducted are explored and various examples of unethical and questionable practices are discussed.

1. List at least two aspects of the experiment that would be considered unethical according to today's standards and explain why.

2. Do you feel that race is an important factor in the discussion of this experiment? Why or why not?

3. Imagine that you are a researcher who has been instructed to conduct an experiment similar to the one discussed in this clip. What protocols would you include to ensure that your study is ethical and that none of your subjects is harmed?

Watch the **Video** Robert Guthrie: Before Informed Consent in **MyDevelopmentLab**

Summing Up

SECTION 1   HUMAN DEVELOPMENT TODAY AND ITS ORIGINS

1.1 Distinguish between the demographic profiles of developed countries and developing countries in terms of population, income, and education.

Developed countries have been the focus of most research on human development, but they hold only about 18% of the world's population. The majority of the world's population (82%) lives in developing countries, and as the total population rises from 7 billion now to 9 billion in 2050, nearly all the increase will take place in developing countries. Most people in developing countries are poor and live in rural areas, but these countries are experiencing rapid economic development and a massive migration to urban areas.

1.2 Define the term *socioeconomic status* (SES) and explain why SES, gender, and ethnicity are important aspects of human development within countries.

SES includes educational level, income level, and occupational status. It influences access to resources such as education and health care. Gender shapes expectations and opportunities in most cultures throughout life. Ethnicity often includes a distinct cultural identity.

1.3 Trace the evolutionary origins of the human species and summarize the features of the first human cultures.

Humans arose from earlier hominids and developed distinctive characteristics such as large brains, long infancy, tool use, and control of fire. Our species, *Homo sapiens,* first appeared about 200,000 years ago.

The Upper Paleolithic period (40,000–10,000 years ago) is the first time human cultures became distinct from one another in their art and tools. During the Neolithic period (10,000–5,000 years ago), humans first domesticated plants and animals. The first civilizations around 5,000 years ago marked the origin of writing, specialized work, and a centralized state.

1.4 Apply information about human evolution to how human development takes place today.

Humans are one species, but since the birth of culture, human groups have developed remarkably diverse ways of life. Our exceptionally large brain has allowed us to create cultural practices that enable us to live in a wide range of environments.

KEY TERMS

human development *p. 4*	individualistic *p. 8*	socioeconomic status (SES) *p. 11*	civilization *p. 14*
culture *p. 4*	collectivistic *p. 8*	ethnicity *p. 12*	state *p. 14*
globalization *p. 5*	traditional cultures *p. 9*	natural selection *p. 13*	evolutionary psychology *p. 15*
total fertility rate (TFR) *p. 6*	caste system *p. 10*	hominid *p. 13*	
developed countries *p. 7*	majority culture *p. 11*	hunter–gatherer *p. 13*	
developing countries *p. 7*	contexts *p. 11*	*Homo sapiens* *p. 14*	

SECTION 2   THEORIES OF HUMAN DEVELOPMENT

1.5 Summarize Freud's psychosexual theory and Erikson's psychosocial theory of human development and describe the main limitations of each.

Freud's psychosexual theory of development emphasized the sexual drive as the primary motivator of human behavior. He proposed five stages of psychosexual development, but believed that the early stages were crucial and that most of later development was determined by age 6. Erikson proposed a psychosocial theory of development that emphasized social and cultural influences and proposed that important changes take place throughout the life span. In his theory of eight stages throughout the life span, each stage is characterized by a distinctive "crisis" with two possible resolutions, one healthy and one unhealthy. Erikson's theory may not be applicable across cultures.

1.6 Summarize the behaviorist theories of Watson, Skinner, and Bandura.

Behaviorist theories emphasize observable behavior and the mechanisms of learning. Humans and other animals learn through conditioning, including classical and operant conditioning. In classical conditioning stimuli are associated with responses, and in operant conditioning reinforcers cause behaviors to recur. Social learning theory emphasizes the use of models for behavior and the ways that learning can occur through observation of others, without direct reinforcement.

1.7 Summarize the constructivist theories of Piaget and Vygotsky.

Piaget and Vygotsky both emphasized that knowledge is not a copy of reality, but rather knowledge and

behaviors are constructed by the mind as the child or person interacts with the environment. Piaget emphasized the role of the child's interaction with and action on objects in the development of qualitatively different stages in cognitive development. Vygotsky emphasized social contexts as sources of information for the child to build knowledge in the mind.

1.8 Define the five systems of Bronfenbrenner's ecological theory and explain how it differs from stage theories.

Bronfenbrenner's ecological theory emphasizes the different systems that interact in a person's development, including microsystems, the mesosystem, the exosystem, the macrosystem, and the chronosystem. It is not a stage theory and instead emphasizes the multiple influences that shape human development in the social environment.

KEY TERMS

psychosexual theory *p. 19*

psychosocial theory *p. 20*

behaviorism *p. 21*

conditioning *p. 22*

social learning theory *p. 23*

mental structures *p. 23*

cognitive constructivist theory *p. 23*

maturation *p. 23*

schemes *p. 24*

assimilation *p. 24*

accommodation *p. 24*

social constructivist theory *p. 25*

zone of proximal development *p. 25*

scaffolding *p. 25*

ecological theory *p. 26*

SECTION 3 HOW WE STUDY HUMAN DEVELOPMENT

1.9 Recall the five steps of the scientific method and the meanings and functions of hypotheses, sampling, and procedure in scientific research.

The scientific method entails five main steps: (1) identifying a research question, (2) forming a hypothesis, (3) choosing a research method and a research design, (4) collecting data, and (5) drawing conclusions that lead to new questions and new hypotheses.

1.10 Describe some ethical standards for human development research.

Research on human development is required to follow ethical guidelines, which are laid out by professional organizations and enforced by IRBs. The main guidelines include protecting participants from physical or psychological harm, informed consent prior to

participation, confidentiality, and debriefing after participation if deception was used.

1.11 Summarize the main methods used in research on human development.

A variety of specific methods for data collection are used in the study of human development, ranging from questionnaires and interviews to ethnographic research to experiments. Each method has both strengths and weaknesses. Two important qualities in research methods are reliability (consistency of measurement) and validity (the accuracy of measurement in reflecting real life).

1.12 Describe the major types of research designs used in human development research.

Common research designs include cross-sectional and longitudinal. Each design has both strengths and weaknesses.

KEY TERMS

scientific method *p. 29*

hypothesis *p. 29*

research method *p. 30*

research design *p. 30*

sample *p. 30*

population *p. 30*

procedure *p. 30*

peer-reviewed *p. 31*

theory *p. 31*

informed consent *p. 32*

quantitative *p. 33*

qualitative *p. 34*

ethnographic research *p. 34*

experimental research method *p. 35*

independent variable *p. 35*

dependent variable *p. 35*

intervention *p. 37*

natural experiment *p. 37*

reliability *p. 38*

validity *p. 38*

cross-sectional research *p. 38*

correlation *p. 39*

longitudinal research *p. 39*

cohort effect *p. 39*

Practice Test

✓● Study and Review in MyDevelopmentLab

1. The United States
   a. is the developed country that will experience the steepest decline in population between now and 2050.
   b. is one of the few developed countries that will experience an increase in population, due largely to immigration.
   c. is expected to have approximately the same proportion of Latinos by 2050, but far fewer African Americans.
   d. has a total fertility rate that is lower than most developed countries due to the availability of birth control.

2. If a researcher wanted to measure the socioeconomic status (SES) of her adult participants, she would need to ask them about all of the following **EXCEPT** their
   a. educational level.
   b. number of children.
   c. income level.
   d. occupational status.

3. Which of the following occurred during the Neolithic period?
   a. The climate got much colder.
   b. Humans began to bury their dead for the first time.
   c. The domestication of animals developed.
   d. People lived an unsettled life and often slept in temporary housing.

4. Which of the following best represents the impact of evolution on human development?
   a. Biologically, humans have changed drastically since the origin of *Homo sapiens*.
   b. Our development of bipedal locomotion is the most distinctive characteristic of our species.
   c. Cultures shape the raw material of biology into widely different paths throughout the life span.
   d. Instincts reduce humans' capacity for cultural learning more than they reduce animals' capacity for cultural learning.

5. According to Freud
   a. attachment security is the driving force behind human development throughout life.
   b. everything important in development happened before adulthood.
   c. a small percentage of children experience an Oedipus complex that leads them to want to have sexual access to their opposite-sex parents.
   d. the root of mental health problems in his patients was that they seemed to have experienced some type of traumatic event during puberty.

6. A child learns to pull a tab in order to make a bell stop ringing. Pulling the tab is evidence of
   a. social learning.
   b. classical conditioning.
   c. operant conditioning.
   d. Pavlovian conditioning.

7. According to Piaget, if a child has a scheme for "Daddy" and calls all men "Daddy," the child is using
   a. assimilation.
   b. accommodation.
   c. maturation.
   d. concrete operations.

8. The American belief in the value of individual freedom as demonstrated in its capitalist economic system and its governmental system of representative democracy reflects which system of Bronfenbrenner's theory?
   a. exosystem
   b. chronosystem
   c. microsystem
   d. macrosystem

9. _____ generates hypotheses that can be tested in research.
   a. An unbiased sample
   b. A theory
   c. The research design
   d. The research method

10. In the famous case of Henrietta Lacks, an African American woman's cancer cells were removed from her cervix without her knowledge by a surgeon right before her death in 1951. Researchers wanted to study these HeLa cells to learn about the genes that cause cancer and those that suppress it. The ethical requirement of _____ would protect against this happening today.
    a. informed consent
    b. deception
    c. confidentiality
    d. generalizability of the findings

11. Which of the following is true regarding research methods?
    a. Qualitative data is considered unscientific among most researchers in the field of psychology.
    b. The strength of the case study approach is the ability to generalize the findings.
    c. The ethnographic method allows the researcher to learn how people behave in their daily lives.
    d. The most commonly used method in social science research is the open-ended interview.

12. Which of the following is a problem with cross-sectional research?
    a. Participants tend to drop out of the study.
    b. It tends to be more expensive to conduct than longitudinal research.
    c. It tends to be more time-consuming than longitudinal research.
    d. It yields a correlation, which may be difficult to interpret.

2 Genetics and Prenatal Development

In a small village in rural Turkey, 22-year-old Aysun is pregnant with her first child. She has been married for five years, and she had begun to despair that she would never become pregnant. Aysun felt she was doing all she could to make it happen, even eating everything her mother had told her would help her conceive a son, such as fried foods, spicy foods, and red foods such as beef and tomato sauce. Her mother-in-law occasionally muttered that her barren state was a punishment from Allah, for Aysun failing to be sufficiently obedient to her husband, Hasan. Aysun herself suspected that someone had cast the evil eye on her, but she could not think who it might be.

In any case, now that she is pregnant, all that can be forgotten. Hasan is proud of her, Aysun's family is delighted, and even her mother-in-law has warmed up to her a bit. Now in her fourth month of pregnancy, Aysun has begun to receive occasional visits from the village midwife, who has provided advice on how to have a successful pregnancy. In particular, she has advised avoiding strong smells, menstruating women, and cold drafts, all of which are believed to bring about miscarriage and deformities. To her relief, Aysun has begun to feel the baby moving, indicating that the soul has entered it, and every time she feels it she thanks Allah and prays that her baby will be safe and healthy (based on Delaney, 2000).

In the city of Oslo, Norway, 32-year-old Vera is pregnant with her first child. She is not married, but she has been living with her partner Jens for 5 years, and both of them feel they are now ready to become parents. They have finished their education and established their careers and they have had a few years together to enjoy being a couple. Now it seems natural to them to enter the next phase of their lives by becoming parents. At the clinic during their most recent prenatal checkup, Vera and Jens were enthralled as they watched the 5-month-old fetus in the ultrasound image, moving around and opening and closing its mouth. They know their lives are about to change dramatically, and that there will be sacrifices. Vera has already had a taste of the sacrifices in store, by giving up alcohol and cigarettes during her pregnancy. But both of them yearn for something beyond themselves to be devoted to, and both believe that parenthood will be joyful and fulfilling, even amidst its challenges (based on Ravn, 2005).

Two women, both mothers-to-be, both experiencing pregnancy with a combination of joy, hope, and fear. Yet in some ways they are experiencing pregnancy in markedly different ways, due to their cultural context. For Aysun, as for most women in rural areas of developing countries, there is little in the way of technology or medical care to provide her with information about how to promote the healthy development of her fetus. Instead, she relies on folk beliefs, the midwife's years of experience, and social support from her family. For Vera, as for most women in developed countries, medical care and technological aids are available throughout pregnancy. Yet she and her husband face formidable challenges in altering their lives to make room for the demands of raising a small child while continuing to pursue their careers.

> " *Pregnancy is experienced in many different ways around the world, but everywhere it is a momentous event.* "

Pregnancy is experienced in many different ways around the world, but everywhere it is a momentous event. In this chapter we examine the process of prenatal development, from its genetic beginnings until the final months of pregnancy. The first section of the chapter covers the basics of genetics and how a new human life begins. In the next section we examine prenatal development and prenatal care for both mother and baby to enhance the likelihood that all will go well. Sometimes problems arise in the course of pregnancy or in becoming pregnant in the first place, so the final section of the chapter addresses prenatal complications and infertility.

LEARNING OBJECTIVES

2.1 Distinguish between genotype and phenotype and identify the different forms of genetic inheritance.

2.2 Describe the sex chromosomes and identify what makes them different from other chromosomes.

2.3 Describe how behavior geneticists use heritability estimates and concordance rates in their research.

2.4 Describe how the concept of epigenesis frames gene–environment interactions, and connect epigenesis to the concept of reaction range.

2.5 Explain how the theory of genotype → environment effects casts new light on the old nature–nurture debate.

2.6 Outline the process of meiosis in the formation of reproductive cells and specify how the process differs for males and females.

2.7 Describe the process of fertilization and conception.

Genetic Basics

In all organisms, humans included, individual development has a genetic beginning. To understand the role of genetics in human development, it is important to have a basic foundation of knowledge about genes and how they function. (((

((•⎡**Listen** to the **Podcast** Genetics in **MyDevelopmentLab**

Genotype and phenotype

Distinguish between genotype and phenotype and identify the different forms of genetic inheritance.

LEARNING OBJECTIVE 2.1

⁕⎡**Explore** the **Concept** Building Blocks of Genetics in **MyDevelopmentLab**

Nearly all cells in the human body contain 46 **chromosomes** in 23 pairs, with 1 chromosome in each pair inherited from the mother and the other inherited from the father (see **Figure 2.1**). The chromosomes are composed of complex molecules known as **DNA (deoxyribonucleic acid)** (see **Figure 2.2**). The DNA in the chromosomes is organized into segments called **genes,** which are the basic units of hereditary information. Genes contain paired sequences of chemicals called *nucleotides,* and these sequences comprise instructions for the functioning and replication of the cells. There are about 23,000 genes in our 46 chromosomes, the total human **genome**, with all together about 3 billion nucleotide pairs (International Human Genome Sequencing Consortium, 2004; Lander et al., 2001). ⁕

Not all 23,000 genes are expressed in the course of development. The totality of an individual's genes is the **genotype**, and the person's actual characteristics are called the **phenotype**. In part, the difference between genotype and phenotype is a consequence of the person's environment. For example, if you were born with a genotype that included exceptional musical ability, this talent might never be developed if your environment

chromosomes sausage-shaped structures in the nucleus of cells, containing genes, which are paired, except in reproductive cells

DNA (deoxyribonucleic acid) long strand of cell material that stores and transfers genetic information in all life forms

gene segment of DNA containing coded instructions for the growth and functioning of the organism

genome entire store of an organism's hereditary information

genotype organism's unique genetic inheritance

phenotype organism's actual characteristics, derived from its genotype

47

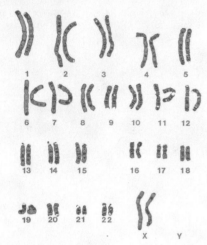

Figure 2.1 • **The human genome.** The 46 chromosomes in the human genome are organized into 23 pairs.

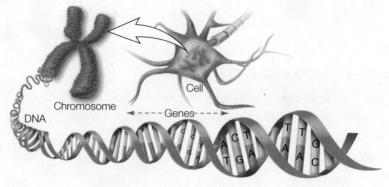

Figure 2.2 • **The chemical structure of DNA.** DNA is composed of nucleotide pairs.

provided no access to musical instruments or musical instruction. Consequently, the musical ability present in your genotype would not be apparent in your phenotype.

Another aspect of genetic functioning that influences the relation between genotype and phenotype is **dominant–recessive inheritance** (Jones, 2006). On every pair of chromosomes there are two forms of each gene, one on the chromosome inherited from the mother and one on the chromosome inherited from the father. Each form of the gene is called an **allele**. On many of these pairs of alleles, dominant–recessive inheritance occurs. This means that only one of the two genes—the *dominant gene*—influences the phenotype, whereas the *recessive gene* does not, even though it is part of the genotype. For example, if you inherited a gene for curly hair from one parent and straight hair from the other, you would have curly hair, because curly hair is dominant and straight hair is recessive. Recessive genes are expressed in the phenotype only when they are paired with another recessive gene. A clear pattern of dominant–recessive inheritance is evident only for traits determined by a single gene, which is not true of most traits, as we will see shortly. Some other examples of dominant and recessive characteristics are shown in **Table 2.1**. ✳

The table shows clear-cut examples of dominant and recessive genes, but sometimes there is **incomplete dominance**, in which the phenotype is influenced primarily, but not exclusively, by the dominant gene. One example of incomplete dominance involves the sickle-cell trait that is common among black Africans and their descendants such as African Americans (see **Figure 2.3**). Most blood cells are shaped like a disk, but when a person inherits two recessive genes for the sickle-cell trait the blood cells become hook-shaped, like the blade of a sickle. This results in a condition called *sickle-cell anemia*, in which the sickle-shaped blood cells clog up the blood vessels and cause pain, susceptibility to disease, and early death. About 1 in 500 Africans (and African Americans) have this disorder, and it also occurs (less commonly) in people whose ancestors came from India or the Mediterranean region (Quinn et al., 2004).

However, if a person inherits only one recessive gene for the sickle-cell trait, along with a normal dominant gene, the dominance is incomplete, and a portion—but not

✳ ⌐**Explore** the **Concept**
Dominant and Recessive Traits
in **MyDevelopmentLab**

**APPLYING YOUR KNOWLEDGE
. . . as a Teacher**

You have a set of identical (MZ) twins in your third-grade classroom. They seem to have different personalities. One of them excels at playing music and the other does not, taking an interest instead in sports. How do you explain this difference?

dominant–recessive inheritance pattern of inheritance in which a pair of chromosomes contains one dominant and one recessive gene, but only the dominant gene is expressed in the phenotype

allele on a pair of chromosomes, each of two forms of a gene

incomplete dominance form of dominant–recessive inheritance in which the phenotype is influenced primarily by the dominant gene but also to some extent by the recessive gene

TABLE 2.1 Traits With Single-Gene Dominant–Recessive Inheritance

Dominant	Recessive
Curly hair	Straight hair
Dark hair	Blonde hair
Facial dimples	No dimples
Normal hearing	Deafness (some forms)
Normal vision	Nearsighted vision
Freckles	No freckles
Unattached ear lobe	Attached ear lobe
Can roll tongue in U-shape	Cannot roll tongue

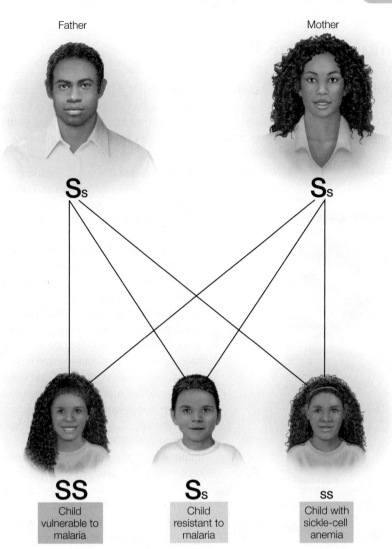

Father

Mother

S_s

S_s

SS
Child
vulnerable to
malaria

S_s
Child
resistant to
malaria

ss
Child with
sickle-cell
anemia

Figure 2.3 • **Incomplete dominance in sickle-cell inheritance.** Two recessive genes for the sickle-cell trait results in sickle-cell anemia, but having one dominant and one recessive gene provides protection against malaria.

all—of the person's blood cells will be sickle shaped. This portion is not large enough to cause sickle-cell anemia, but it is large enough to make the person resistant to malaria, a blood disease that is spread by mosquitoes. Malaria is often fatal, and even when it is not, it can cause brain damage and other enduring health problems. It occurs worldwide in developing countries but is especially common in Africa, killing over a million people a year. In many central African countries over 50% of children are affected (Finkel, 2007a).

This explains why the sickle-cell trait evolved especially among Africans. With two recessive genes for the sickle-cell trait a person will have sickle-cell anemia, but a person who has one recessive gene for the sickle-cell trait and one normal dominant gene will have enhanced resistance to malaria. Because the effects of contracting malaria are so severe, in evolutionary terms it is an advantage genetically to have the sickle-cell trait to protect against malaria, even if it also raises the risk of sickle-cell anemia.

Most characteristics in human development are not determined solely by a single pair of genes. Despite what you may have heard about the supposed existence of a "gay gene" or "religion gene" or "crime gene," no such genes have been found, nor are they likely to be, as we'll see in the **Research Focus: The Human Genome Project** feature. Although single gene pairs sometimes play a crucial role in development, as in the case of sickle-cell anemia, more commonly the influence of genes is a consequence of **polygenic inheritance**, the interaction of multiple genes rather than just one (Lewis, 2005). This is true for physical characteristics such as height, weight, and skin color, as well as for characteristics such as intelligence, personality, and susceptibility to various diseases (Hoh & Ott, 2003; Karlsson, 2006; Rucker & McGuffin, 2010).

polygenic inheritance expression of phenotypic characteristics due to the interaction of multiple genes

RESEARCH FOCUS   The Human Genome Project

Since the structure of DNA was first discovered in 1953 by James Crick and James Watson, research on genetics has boomed. It has especially grown in recent years as more advanced technological instruments have allowed researchers to examine the characteristics of individual genes.

One of the most exciting scientific projects on genetics has been the Human Genome Project. Beginning in 1990, this project engaged a team of scientists in the goal of describing the chemical features of every single gene in the human genome. This goal was reached in 2000, and a map of the human genome has now been published (Gottlieb, 2004; International Human Genome Sequencing Consortium, 2004; Moore, 2001; Pinker, 2004; "Special report on the human genome," 2010; Weaver, 2005). It contains many surprising and important findings:

1. There are only about 23,000 protein coding genes in the human genome, far fewer than the 100,000 genes scientists had expected to find. For comparison, worms have about 19,000 genes, and fruit flies about 13,000.

2. The 23,000 protein-coding genes are only 3% of the human genome. The other 97%, which does not code for proteins, is sometimes dismissed as "junk," but this is just another way of saying we do not yet know what function it serves.

3. Many genes can make multiple proteins, not just one protein as scientists had believed.

4. An especially important type of gene called a **regulator gene** directs the activities of other genes. For example, precisely the same gene that produces legs in humans also produces the four legs of a dog and the many legs of a caterpillar, and it is

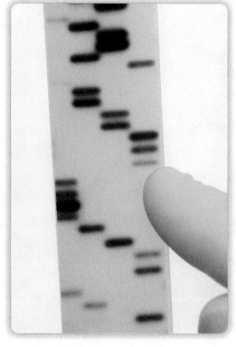

a regulator gene that tells it what type of legs to make. Consequently, there are far more similarities among the genes of different species than had previously been known, with the differences among related species often being mainly due to the activities of regulator genes.

5. Most human characteristics are polygenic, meaning that they are due to the collaboration of multiple genes rather than a single gene. Genes respond to the activities of other genes and alter their activities accordingly.

The remarkable accomplishments of the Human Genome Project raised hopes that genetic therapies will soon be available for the many human disorders that have a genetic origin. **Gene therapy** would replace genes causing a disorder with genes that did not cause the disorder. Already techniques of gene therapy have been developed in scientific research on animals, and studies have begun to include human participants. So far, however, these techniques have shown mixed results. For example, in one study gene therapy successfully relieved symptoms for some patients with a severe disorder of the immune system, whereas other patients experienced serious side effects (Ralph et al., 2004).

The prospects for gene therapy are complicated by the fact that most human characteristics are polygenic, involving multiple genes. Consequently, gene therapy that alters the activity of one gene might have unintended and unwelcome consequences on other aspects of the person's functioning. Nevertheless, the use of gene therapy is certain to grow in the years to come, not only for disorders but for some aspects of normal functioning.

The sex chromosomes

2.2   **LEARNING OBJECTIVE**   Describe the sex chromosomes and identify what makes them different from other chromosomes.

regulator gene gene that directs the activities of other genes

gene therapy method of treating genetic disorders that involves replacing the affected genes with genes that do not have the disorder

sex chromosomes chromosomes that determine whether an organism is male (XY) or female (XX)

Of the 23 pairs of chromosomes, one pair is different from the rest. These are the **sex chromosomes**, which determine whether the person will be male or female (Jones, 2006). In the female this pair is called XX; in the male, XY. The Y chromosome is notably smaller than other chromosomes and contains only one-third the genetic material. All eggs in the mother contain an X chromosome but sperm may carry either an X or a Y chromosome. So, it is the father's sperm that determines what the sex of the child will be. Ironically, many cultures mistakenly believe that the woman is responsible for the child's sex, and blame her if she fails to have sons (LeVine et al., 1994).

Many cultures also have beliefs about how to predict the baby's sex (DeLoache & Gottlieb, 2000). According to ancient Mayan beliefs, sex can be predicted from the mother's age and the month of conception; if both are even or odd, it's a girl, but if one is odd and one even, it's a boy. In Chinese tradition there is a similar calculation, also based on mother's age and the month of conception. In the West today many people believe that if the mother is "carrying high"—the fetus feels high in the uterus—a girl is on the way, but if the mother is "carrying low" it's a boy. Another belief is that if the mother craves sweet foods, the baby will be a girl, but if she craves sour or salty foods she will soon have a boy. And in some countries it is believed that if the mother-to-be's right breast is larger than the left she will have a boy, but if the left breast is larger she will have a girl. None of these beliefs has the slightest scientific basis, but they demonstrate how important gender is to a child's future in most cultures, even before birth.

The sex of the developing organism also has biological consequences for prenatal development. Having only one X chromosome makes males more vulnerable than females to a variety of recessive disorders that are linked to the X chromosome (Narayanan et al., 2006). The reason for this is that if a female has one X chromosome that contains the recessive gene for a disorder, the disorder will not show up in her phenotype because the dominant gene on her other X chromosome will prevent it from being expressed. She will be a carrier of the disorder to the next generation but will not have the disorder herself. In contrast, if a male receives one X chromosome containing the recessive gene for a disorder, he will definitely have the disorder because he has no other X chromosome that may contain a dominant gene to block its expression. His Y chromosome cannot serve this function. An example of this pattern of **X-linked inheritance** is shown in **Figure 2.4** for hemophilia, a disorder in which the blood does not clot properly and the

My Virtual Child

What are some beliefs that your culture holds about how to predict a baby's sex?

APPLYING YOUR KNOWLEDGE ... as a Nurse

You meet a couple who has three sons, and they want to conceive a daughter. The mother says it is the man's sperm that determine the sex of the embryo. What could you say to help this couple?

X-linked inheritance pattern of inheritance in which a recessive characteristic is expressed because it is carried on the male's X chromosome

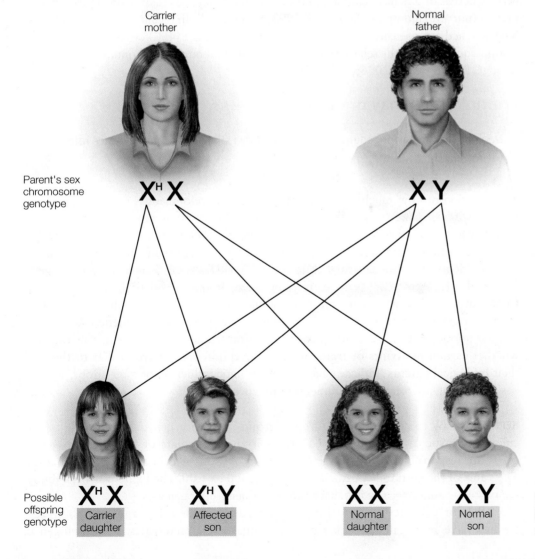

Figure 2.4 • **X-Linked inheritance in hemophilia.** Why are males more vulnerable to recessive disorders carried on the X chromosome?

person may bleed to death from even a minor injury. Because of X-linked inheritance, males are at greater risk for a wide variety of genetically based problems, including learning disabilities and mental retardation (James et al., 2006; Snow, 2010).

WHAT HAVE YOU LEARNED?

1. How is phenotype influenced by the environment?
2. Why did the sickle-cell trait develop among Africans?
3. What determines the sex of a child?
4. What is X-linked inheritance, and what genetic risks are associated with it?

Genes and Environment in Human Development

There is no doubt that genes have some influence on human development, but how much? Scholars have long debated the relative importance of genes and the environment in human development. In this **nature–nurture debate**, some scholars have claimed that development can be explained by genes (nature) and that environment matters little, whereas others have claimed that development depends mainly on environmental factors (nurture) (compare Baumrind, 1993; Scarr, 1993). In recent years, most scholars have reached a consensus that both genes and environment play key roles in human development, although the relative strength of nature and nurture continues to be debated (Dodge, 2007; Lerner, 2006; Pinker, 2004).

Principles of behavior genetics

2.3 | **LEARNING OBJECTIVE** | Describe how behavior geneticists use heritability estimates and concordance rates in their research.

The question of how much genes influence human development is at the heart of the field of **behavior genetics** (Gottesman, 2004; Plomin, 2009). Researchers who work in behavior genetics estimate the influence of genes on development by comparing people who share different amounts of their genes, mainly through twin studies and adoption studies. Identical or **monozygotic (MZ) twins** have 100% of their genes in common. Fraternal or **dizygotic (DZ) twins** and siblings have 40–60% of their genes in common. Consequently, when MZ twins are more similar than DZ twins or siblings, this indicates that genetics play a strong role. Adoptive children have no genetic resemblance to their adoptive families. Consequently, adoption studies allow a researcher to study whether certain behaviors or traits of adoptive children are more similar to those of their biological parents (indicating a stronger genetic influence) or their adoptive families (indicating a stronger environmental influence).

HERITABILITY By comparing these different groups, behavior geneticists are able to calculate a statistic called **heritability**. Heritability is an estimate of the extent to which genes are responsible for the differences among persons within a specific population. The value of the heritability estimate ranges from 0 to 1.00. The higher the heritability, the more the characteristic is believed to be influenced by genetics.

Behavior genetics has flourished in the past two decades, and heritability estimates have been calculated for a wide range of characteristics. For intelligence,

nature–nurture debate debate among scholars as to whether human development is influenced mainly by genes (nature) or environment (nurture)

behavior genetics field in the study of human development that aims to identify the extent to which genes influence behavior, primarily by comparing persons who share different amounts of their genes

monozygotic (MZ) twins twins who have exactly the same genotype; also called identical twins

dizygotic (DZ) twins twins that result when two ova are released by a female instead of one, and both are fertilized by sperm; also called fraternal twins

heritability statistical estimate of the extent to which genes are responsible for the differences among persons within a specific population, with values ranging from 0 to 1.00

heritability estimates for children and adolescents have been found to be about 0.50, meaning that about half the variation in their IQ scores has been attributed to genetic influences (Turkheimer et al., 2009). With regard to personality characteristics, heritability estimates range from 0.40 to 0.50 for a wide array of characteristics such as sociability, activity level, and even religiosity (Bouchard & McGue, 2003).

Heritability estimates have been criticized for giving a misleading impression of the influence of genetics on development (Collins et al., 2000; Rutter, 2012). According to the critics, to state that a trait is heritable implies that we know with precision how much genes contribute to its development, but this is not so. Heritability estimates are simply estimates based on comparisons of persons with different amounts of genetic material in common, not direct measures of the activity of genes. Heritability estimates are a measure not just of genetic influence but of *how much the environment allows the genes to be expressed*. In other words, heritability estimates measure phenotype rather than genotype.

This can be seen in the studies finding that heritability of intelligence increases from childhood to adulthood (McGue & Christensen, 2002). Obviously genes do not change during this time, but the environment changes to allow greater expression of genetic potentials. Other studies find that heritability of intelligence is higher in middle-class families than in poor families (McCartney & Berry, 2009; Turkheimer et al., 2009). This is not because middle-class families have different kinds of genes than poor families do, but because the greater economic resources of middle-class families make it more likely that children's genotypic potential for intelligence will be expressed in their phenotype. ((•

CONCORDANCE RATES Another statistic of genetic influence used in behavior genetics is **concordance rate**. This is a percentage that indicates the degree of similarity in phenotype among pairs of family members. Concordance rates range from 0% to 100%. The higher the concordance rate, the more similar the two persons are.

In many studies, comparisons of concordance rates are made between MZ and DZ twins. When concordance rates are higher among MZ than DZ twins, this indicates that the basis for the disorder is partly genetic. For example, concordance rates for schizophrenia, a severe mental disorder involving hallucinations and disordered patterns of thinking and behavior, are 50% for MZ twins and 18% for DZ twins (Gottesman, 1994). This means that when one MZ twin has schizophrenia, 50% of the time the other twin has schizophrenia as well. For DZ twins, when one twin has schizophrenia, the other twin has the disorder only 18% of the time. Adoption studies also sometimes use this statistic, comparing concordance rates between parents and adopted children, parents and biological children, and adoptive or biological siblings.

Gene–environment interactions: Epigenesis and reaction ranges

| Describe how the concept of epigenesis frames gene–environment interactions, and connect epigenesis to the concept of reaction range. | **LEARNING OBJECTIVE** 2.4 |

Studies of heritability show not only that genes influence development but also that the environment influences how genes are expressed. A related idea is **epigenesis**, which means that development results from the bidirectional interactions between genotype and environment (Gottlieb, 2004; Gottlieb & Lickliter, 2007). According to epigenetic theory, genetic activity responds constantly to environmental influences. Development is influenced by genes but not purely determined by them (Caspi & Moffitt, 2006). ◉

MZ twins have the same genotype.

My Virtual Child

Can you think of a trait other than intelligence that has a higher or lower heritability for your virtual child when compared to a child of a different culture?

((•—[**Listen** to the **Podcast** Heritability and Onset of Schizophrenia Disorder in **MyDevelopmentLab**

concordance rate degree of similarity in phenotype among pairs of family members, expressed as a percentage

epigenesis in development, the continuous bidirectional interactions between genes and environment

◉—[**Watch** the **Video** Special Topics: Epigenetics—A Revolutionary Science in **MyDevelopmentLab**

Genes establish a reaction range for height, and environment determines where a person's height falls within that range. Here, sisters of the Hamer tribe in Ethiopia, a tribe known for being exceptionally tall.

Here is an example of epigenesis. Girls normally begin menstruating around age 11–16, toward the lower end of this range under healthy conditions and toward the higher end when nutrition is insufficient or the girl is suffering from medical problems (Neberich et al., 2010). Clearly it is part of the human-female genotype for menstruation to be initiated somewhere in this age range, with the timing influenced by environmental conditions. Furthermore, when girls' environmental conditions change, their menstrual patterns may also change. Girls who experience severe weight loss often stop menstruating (Roberto et al., 2008). If their nutritional intake improves, they begin menstruating again. This demonstrates a continuous interaction between genotype and environment, with menstruation being "turned on" genetically as part of puberty but "turned off" if environmental conditions are dire, then turned on again once the nutritional environment improves.

As this example illustrates, often when genes influence human development it is by establishing boundaries for environmental influences rather than specifying a precise characteristic. In other words, genes establish a **reaction range** of potential expression, and environment determines where a person's phenotype will fall within that range (McCartney & Berry, 2009). To take another example, height is known to be influenced by genes. You can probably tell this just by looking at your own height in relation to other members of your family. However, the genes for height simply establish the reaction range's upper and lower boundaries, and where a person's actual height ends up—the phenotype—is determined by environmental influences such as nutrition and disease.

Evidence for this is clear from the pattern of changes in height in societies around the world over the past century. In most Western countries, average height rose steadily in the first half of the 20th century as nutrition and health care improved (Freedman et al., 2006). The genes of their populations could not have changed in just a generation or two; instead, the improving environment allowed them to reach a higher point in their genetic reaction range for height. In other countries, such as China and South Korea, improvements in nutrition and health care came later, in the second half of the 20th century, so increases in height in those countries have taken place only recently (Wang et al., 2010). However, people are unlikely ever to grow to be 10 or 20 feet tall. In recent decades in Western countries there has been little change in average height, indicating that the populations of these countries have reached the upper boundary of their reaction range for height.

The theory of genotype → environment effects

2.5 **LEARNING OBJECTIVE** | Explain how the theory of genotype → environment effects casts new light on the old nature–nurture debate.

reaction range range of possible developmental paths established by genes; environment determines where development takes place within that range

theory of genotype → environment effects theory proposing that genes influence the kind of environment we experience

passive genotype → environment effects in the theory of genotype → environment effects, the type that results from the fact that in a biological family, parents provide both genes and environment to their children

One influential theory of behavior genetics is the **theory of genotype → environment effects** proposed by Sandra Scarr and Kathleen McCartney (Plomin, 2009; Scarr, 1993; Scarr & McCartney, 1983). According to this theory, both genotype and environment make essential contributions to human development. However, the relative strengths of genetics and the environment are difficult to unravel because our genes actually influence the kind of environment we experience. That is the reason for the arrow in the term *genotype → environment effects*. Based on our genotypes, we *create our own environments,* to a considerable extent.

THE THREE FORMS OF GENOTYPE → ENVIRONMENT EFFECTS These genotype → environment effects take three forms: passive, evocative, and active. **Passive genotype → environment effects** occur in biological families because *parents provide both genes and environment for their children.* This may seem obvious, but it has profound implications for how we think about development. Take this father–daughter example. Dad has been good at drawing things ever since he was a boy, and now he makes a living as a graphic artist. One of the first birthday presents he gives to his little girl is a set of crayons and colored pencils for drawing. She seems to like it, and he provides her with increasingly sophisticated materials as she grows up. He also teaches her a number of drawing skills as she seems ready to learn them. By the time she reaches adolescence, she's quite a proficient artist herself, and draws a lot of the art for school clubs and social events. She goes to college and majors in architecture, then goes on to become an architect. It is easy to see how she became so good at drawing, given an environment that stimulated her drawing abilities so much—right?

Not so fast. It is true that Dad provided her with a stimulating environment, but he also provided her with half her genes. If there are any genes that contribute to drawing ability—such as genes that contribute to spatial reasoning and fine motor coordination—she may well have received those from Dad, too. The point is that in a biological family, it is very difficult to separate genetic influences from environmental influences because *parents provide both,* and they are likely to provide an environment that reinforces the tendencies they have provided to their children through their genes.

So, you should be skeptical when you read studies that claim that parents' behavior is the cause of the characteristics of their biological children. Remember from Chapter 1: Correlation is not necessarily causation! Just because there is a *correlation* between the behavior of parents and the characteristics of their children does not mean the parents' behavior *caused* the children to have those characteristics. Maybe causation was involved, but in biological families it is difficult to tell. The correlation could be due to the similarity in genes between the biological parents and their children rather than to the environment the biological parents provided. One good way to unravel this tangle is through adoption studies. These studies avoid the problem of passive genotype → environment effects because one set of parents provided the children's genes but a different set of parents provided the environment. We'll look at an extraordinary case of adoption in the **Cultural Focus: Oskar and Jack: A Story of Genes, Environments, and Cultures** feature on page 56.

Evocative genotype → environment effects occur when a person's inherited characteristics evoke responses from others in their environment. If you had a son who started reading at age 3 and seemed to love it, you might buy him more books. If you had a daughter who could sink 20-foot jump shots at age 12, you might arrange to send her to basketball camp. Did you ever babysit or work in a setting where there were many children? If so, you probably found that children differ in how sociable, cooperative, and obedient they are. In turn, you may have found that you responded differently to them, depending on their characteristics. It was probably easier for you to be warm and supportive toward children who were cheerful and cooperative, and you may have found yourself becoming frustrated and raising your voice toward children who were disobedient and disruptive. This is what is meant by evocative genotype → environment effects—with the crucial addition of the assumption that characteristics such as reading ability, athletic ability, and sociability are at least partly based in genetics.

Active genotype → environment effects occur when people seek out environments that correspond to their genotypic characteristics, a process called *niche-picking.* The child who is faster than her peers may be motivated to try out for a sports team; the adolescent with an ear for music may ask for piano lessons; the emerging adult for whom reading has always been slow and difficult may prefer to begin working full-time after high school rather than going to college or university. The idea here is that people are often drawn to environments that match their inherited abilities.

GENOTYPE → ENVIRONMENT EFFECTS OVER TIME   The three types of genotype → environment effects operate throughout childhood, adolescence, and adulthood, but their relative balance changes over time (Scarr, 1993). In childhood, passive genotype → environment

When parents and children are similar, is the similarity due to genetics or environment?

APPLYING YOUR KNOWLEDGE
. . . as a Researcher

You are volunteering in a rural village outside of Nairobi, Kenya. You notice a group of children younger than 10 who are noticeably taller than their own siblings who are 14. How might you explain this difference?

APPLYING YOUR KNOWLEDGE

Think of one of your abilities and describe how the various types of genotype → environment effects may have been involved in your development of that ability.

evocative genotype → environment effects in the theory of genotype → environment effects, the type that results occur when a person's inherited characteristics evoke responses from others in the environment

active genotype → environment effects in the theory of genotype → environment effects, the type that results when people seek out environments that correspond to their genotypic characteristics

CULTURAL FOCUS Oskar and Jack: A Story of Genes, Environments, and Cultures

As this chapter describes, understanding the interplay between genes and environments is one of the most important, complex, and fascinating issues in the study of human development. One approach that has been helpful in unraveling these interactions is research on twins, especially twins separated early in life and raised in different environments. The Minnesota Study of Twins Reared Apart, led by Thomas J. Bouchard, Jr., of the University of Minnesota, has been studying separated twins since 1979, and the results have been groundbreaking and sometimes astounding (Segal et al., 1999; Segal, 2005).

Among the most remarkable cases in the Minnesota study is the story of identical twins Oskar and Jack (Segal, 2005). They were born in Trinidad in 1933, but within six months their parents split up. Oskar left for Germany with his Catholic mother, while Jack remained in Trinidad in the care of his Jewish father. Thus, unlike most separated twins, who at least remain within the same culture and country, Oskar and Jack grew up with the same genotype but with different cultures, different countries, and different religions. Furthermore, Oskar migrated with his mother to Germany in 1933, the year the Nazis rose to power. And Jack was raised as a Jew, at a time when Jews were targeted for extermination by the Nazis.

In some ways, the twins' childhood family environments were similar—as in similarly miserable. Oskar's mother soon moved to Italy and left him in Germany in the care of his grandmother, who was stern and harsh. Jack's father alternated between ignoring him and beating him. Both boys felt like outsiders, Oskar as half-Jewish in a country where that background was becoming increasingly dangerous, and Jack as a White boy in a mostly Black country, and as half-German at a time when Germans were becoming increasingly feared and hated. Despite these similarities, their cultures were about as different as could be. Oskar was an enthusiastic member of the Hitler Youth, and he learned to despise Jews and to keep his own half-Jewish background hidden. Jack was raised as a Jew and at 16 was sent by his father to Israel to join the navy, where he met and married an American Jew. At age 21 he and his wife moved to the United States.

What were the results of this extraordinary natural experiment in the two men's adult development? The extensive data collected by the Minnesota team, which included a week of tests and interviews with the men as well as interviews with their family members and others close to them, indicated that they had highly similar adult personalities. Both were described by themselves and others as short-tempered, demanding, and absent minded. Their wives commented that they walked, moved, and even tripped in exactly the same way. In addition, they shared a remarkable range of unusual, quirky personal habits. Both read books from back to front, sneezed loudly in elevators, liked to wear rubber bands on their wrists, and wrapped tape around pens and pencils to get a better grip.

What does the case study of Oskar and Jack tell us about genetics, environment, and culture?

However, their cultural identities and worldviews were as far apart as one might imagine, given the vastly different cultures they grew up in. Oskar repented his membership in the Hitler Youth as an adult, and lamented the Holocaust that had taken millions of Jewish lives under the Nazis—but he considered himself very German, and he and Jack disagreed vehemently over the responsibility and justification for bombings and other acts of war conducted during World War II. Neither twin participated much in religious observances as an adult, but Jack had a strongly Jewish identity and argued bitterly with Oskar over relations between Israel and the Palestinians. Thus, despite all their similarities in personality, because of their different cultural environments they ultimately had very different identities—starkly separate understandings of who they are and how they fit into the world around them. As Oskar told Jack when they met again in adulthood, "If we had been switched, I would have been the Jew and you would have been the Nazi."

effects are especially pronounced, and active genotype → environment effects are relatively weak. This is because the younger a child is, the more parents control the daily environment the child experiences and the less autonomy the child has to seek out environmental influences outside the family.

However, the balance changes as children move through adolescence and into adulthood (Plomin, 2009). Parental control diminishes, so passive genotype → environment effects also diminish. Autonomy increases, so active genotype → environment effects also increase. In adulthood, passive genotype → environment effects fade entirely (except in cultures where persons continue to live with their parents even in adulthood), and active genotype → environment effects move to the forefront. Evocative genotype → environment effects remain relatively stable from childhood through adulthood.

The theory of genotype → environment effects has been the source of vigorous debate (Pinker, 2004). Many scholars question the theory's claim that characteristics such as sociability, reading ability, and athletic ability are substantially inherited (Baumrind, 1993; Lerner, 2006), citing evidence that these complex traits are reinforced by the child's interactions with the environment and by what is available. Further, the idea that the influence of the environment is limited by the ways genes shape it seems like it doesn't tell the whole story. For example, there are many examples of children around the world developing in typical patterns of physical, cognitive, and social development in spite of harsh or limiting environmental conditions. However, even given the controversy and debate, it is currently an influential theory, and you should be familiar with it as part of your understanding of human development.

APPLYING YOUR KNOWLEDGE

Some critics of the theory of genotype → environment effects have argued that it is a pessimistic theory because it holds that the influence of the environment is limited by the ways genes shape the environment. Do you agree with this critique? Are there conditions in which it might be a good thing for the influence of the environment to be limited?

WHAT HAVE YOU LEARNED?

1. How do adoption studies and twin studies help unravel the relation between genetics and environment?

2. How does the concept of *reaction range* include both genetic and environmental influences?

3. What are the three types of genotype → environment effects?

4. How do the three types of genotype → environment effects change throughout the life span?

Genes and Individual Development

When does individual human development begin? The answer may surprise you. The process of forming a new human being actually begins long before sperm and egg are joined. Sperm and eggs themselves go through a process of development. In this section we look at the genetic basis of prenatal development, beginning with sperm and egg formation.

Sperm and egg formation

Outline the process of meiosis in the formation of reproductive cells and specify how the process differs for males and females.

LEARNING OBJECTIVE 2.6

The only cells in the human body that do not contain 46 chromosomes are the reproductive cells or **gametes**: the sperm in the male and the egg or **ovum** (plural, *ova*) in the female. Gametes form in the testes of the male and the ovaries of the female through a process called **meiosis** (see *Figure 2.5*). Meiosis is a variation of **mitosis**, the normal

gametes cells, distinctive to each sex, that are involved in reproduction (egg cells in the ovaries of the female and sperm in the testes of the male)

ovum mature egg that develops in ovaries, about every 28 days in human females

meiosis process by which gametes are generated, through separation and duplication of chromosome pairs, ending in four new gametes from the original cell, each with half the number of chromosomes of the original cell

mitosis process of cell replication in which the chromosomes duplicate themselves and the cell divides into two cells, each with the same number of chromosomes as the original cell

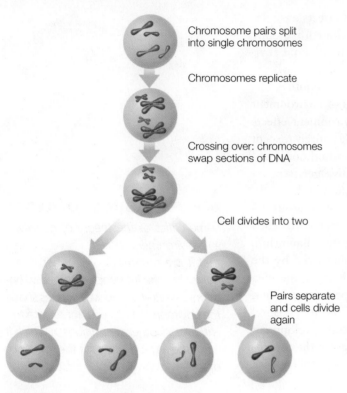

Chromosome pairs split into single chromosomes

Chromosomes replicate

Crossing over: chromosomes swap sections of DNA

Cell divides into two

Pairs separate and cells divide again

Figure 2.5 • **The creation of gametes through meiosis.** How does meiosis differ from mitosis?

process of cell replication in which the chromosomes duplicate themselves and the cell divides to become two cells, each containing the same number of chromosomes as the original cell (Pankow, 2008). In meiosis, cells that begin with 23 pairs of chromosomes first split into 46 single chromosomes, then replicate themselves and split into two cells, each with 23 pairs of chromosomes like the original cell. So far the process is just like mitosis. But then the pairs separate into single chromosomes and split again, this time into gametes that have 23 unpaired chromosomes instead of the original 46. So, at the end of the process of meiosis, from the original cell in the testes or ovaries, four new cells have been created, each with 23 chromosomes.

There are some important sex differences in the process of meiosis (Jones, 2006). In males meiosis is completed before sperm are released, but in females the final stage of meiosis takes place only when and if the ovum is fertilized by a sperm (more on this shortly). Also, in males the outcome of meiosis is four viable sperm, whereas in females meiosis produces only one viable ovum along with three *polar bodies* that are not functional.

Did you ever think about why you are different from your brothers or sisters, even though both of you have 23 chromosomes each from Mom and Dad? I know I am constantly amazed at how different my twins are. Here's the explanation for sibling diversity. Something fascinating and remarkable happens at the outset of the process of meiosis. After the chromosomes first split and replicate, but before the cell divides, pieces of genetic material are exchanged between the alleles in each pair, a process called **crossing over** (refer again to Figure 2.5). Crossing over mixes the combinations of genes in the chromosomes, so that genetic material that originated from the mother and father is rearranged in a virtually infinite number of ways (Pankow, 2008). Your parents could have had dozens, hundreds, even millions of children together, and none of them would be exactly like you genetically (unless you have an identical twin).

Here is another interesting fact about the production of gametes. Upon reaching puberty, males begin producing millions of sperm each day. There are 100 to 300 million sperm in the typical male ejaculation (Johnson, 2008). In contrast, females have already produced all the ova they will ever have *while they are still in their own mothers' womb*. Because crossing over begins when ova are created, this means that the development of a unique genotype for each individual begins before the individual's mother is born!

Females are born with about 1 million ova, but this number diminishes to about 40,000 by the time they reach puberty, and about 400 of these will mature during a woman's child-bearing years (Johnson, 2008; Moore & Persaud, 2003). Most women run out of viable ova some time in their forties, but men produce sperm throughout their adult lives (although the quantity and quality of the sperm may decline with age) (Finn, 2001).

THINKING CULTURALLY

In your culture, what are the beliefs about the best age for a woman to conceive a child? For a man?

Conception

2.7 **LEARNING OBJECTIVE** Describe the process of fertilization and conception.

crossing over at the outset of meiosis, the exchange of genetic material between paired chromosomes

When sexual intercourse takes place between a man and a woman, many millions of sperm from the man begin making their way through the woman's reproductive organs—first into the vagina, then through the cervix, through the uterus, and up the fallopian tubes toward the ovaries. Hundreds of millions of sperm may seem like more than enough, but keep in mind that sperm are composed of a single cell, not much more than 23 chromosomes and a tail, so they are not exactly skilled at navigation. The

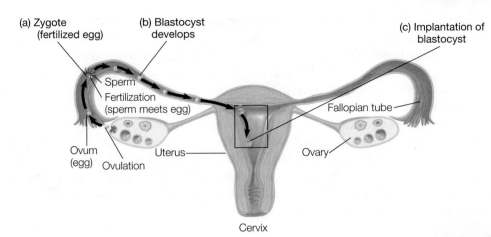

(a) Zygote (fertilized egg)

(b) Blastocyst develops

(c) Implantation of blastocyst

Sperm

Fertilization (sperm meets egg)

Fallopian tube

Ovum (egg)

Ovulation

Uterus

Ovary

Cervix

Figure 2.6 • **The ovulation process.** The two ovaries alternate ovulation in each monthly cycle.

distance from the vagina to the ovaries is vast for such a small object as a sperm. Furthermore, the woman's body responds to sperm as a foreign substance and begins killing them off immediately. Usually only a few hundred sperm make it up the fallopian tubes to where fertilization can take place (Jones, 2006).

Within the woman, there are two ovaries that release an ovum in alternating months. During the early part of the woman's cycle the ovum is maturing into a **follicle**. The follicle consists of the ovum plus other cells that surround it and provide nutrients. About 14 days into a woman's cycle, the mature follicle bursts and *ovulation* takes place as the ovum is released into the fallopian tube (see *Figure 2.6*). The ovum is 2,000 times larger than a sperm because it contains so much cytoplasm, the fluid that will be the main source of nutrients in the early days after conception (Johnson, 2008). The cytoplasm will provide nutrients for the first two weeks of growth if the ovum is fertilized, until it reaches the uterus and begins drawing nutrients from the mother. ✳

It is only during the first 24 hours after the ovum enters the fallopian tube that fertilization can occur. It takes sperm from a few hours to a whole day to travel up the fallopian tubes, so fertilization is most likely to take place if intercourse occurs on the day of ovulation or the two previous days (Wilcox et al., 1995). Sperm can live up to five days after entering the woman's body, but most do not last more than two days (Johnson, 2008).

When sperm reach the ovum they begin to penetrate the surface of the cell, aided by a chemical on the tip of the sperm that dissolves the ovum's membrane. Once the sperm penetrates the ovum's membrane, the head of the sperm detaches from the tail and continues toward the nucleus of the cell while the tail remains outside. The moment a sperm breaks through, a chemical change takes place in the membrane of the ovum that prevents any other sperm from getting in.

When the sperm head reaches the nucleus of the ovum, the final phase of meiosis is triggered in the ovum (Johnson, 2008). Fertilization takes place as the 23 chromosomes from the ovum pair up with the 23 chromosomes from the sperm and a new cell, the **zygote**, is formed from the two gametes. The zygote's 46 paired chromosomes constitute the new organism's unique genotype, set once and for all at the moment of conception. ◉

Although this is how conception usually takes place, there are occasional variations. One of the most common variations is that two ova are released by the woman instead of one, and both are fertilized by sperm, resulting in DZ twins (recall that DZ stands for *dizygotic*—two zygotes). This takes place overall about once in every 60 births, although there are substantial ethnic variations, ranging from 1 in every 25 births in Nigeria to 1 in every 700 births in Japan (Gall, 1996). In general, Asians have the lowest rates of DZ twins and Africans the highest (Mange & Mange, 1998).

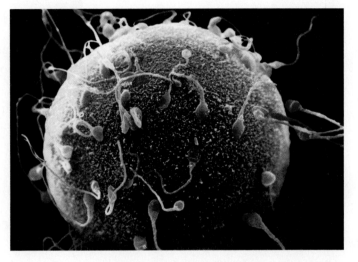

Fertilization can take place only in the first 24 hours after the ovum enters the fallopian tube.

✳ **Explore** the **Concept** Female Reproductive Organs in **MyDevelopmentLab**

◉ **Watch** the **Video** Period of the Zygote in **MyDevelopmentLab**

follicle during the female reproductive cycle, the ovum plus other cells that surround the ovum and provide nutrients

zygote following fertilization, the new cell formed from the union of sperm and ovum

In addition to ethnic background, some of the factors that increase the likelihood of DZ twins are a family history of twins, age (older women are more likely to release two eggs at once), and nutrition (women with healthy diets are more likely to have DZ twins) (Bortolus et al., 1999). Today, another common cause of DZ twins is infertility treatments, which we will discuss in more detail later in the chapter.

Twins can also result when a zygote that has just begun the process of cell division splits into two separate clusters of cells, creating MZ twins (recall that MZ stands for *monozygotic*—one zygote). MZ twins are less common than DZ twins, occurring about 1 in every 285 births (Zach et al., 2001). In contrast to DZ twins, MZ twins are not more common in some ethnic groups than others. They take place at the same frequency all around the world. Also unlike DZ twins, MZ twins do not run in families and are not predicted by age or nutrition.

My Virtual Child

Based on your ethnic background and other factors, are you at a high or low risk for having twins?

WHAT HAVE YOU LEARNED?

1. Can you provide a brief description of crossing over?
2. How does gamete production differ in males and females?
3. What factors determine whether conception will occur?
4. What are the two types of twins and how do they differ in causes and frequencies?

Section 1 VIDEO GUIDE A Preference for Sons (Length: 4:07)

In this video, individuals from various countries are interviewed regarding gender preferences and even forms of gender selection.

1. What are your thoughts on gender-selective abortion in other countries? Did your viewing of this clip impact your thoughts?

2. Describe your reaction to IVH gender selection that occurs in some of the countries discussed in this clip.

3. What are some of the reasons provided by individuals in this clip why boys are preferred over girls in the countries of Taiwan, India, and South Korea?

▶ **Watch** the **Video** A Preference for Sons
in **MyDevelopmentLab**

LEARNING OBJECTIVES

2.8 Describe the structures that form during the germinal period, and identify when implantation takes place.

2.9 Outline the major milestones of the embryonic period and identify when they take place.

2.10 Describe the major milestones of the fetal period and identify when viability occurs.

2.11 Recall some approaches to prenatal care in traditional cultures.

2.12 Summarize scientifically based information on prenatal care.

2.13 Identify the major teratogens in developing countries and developed countries.

Prenatal Development

When sperm and ovum unite to become a zygote, a remarkable process is set in motion. If all goes well, about nine months later a fully formed human being will be born. Now we look closely at this process, from conception to birth (summarized in *Table 2.2*). ✳

✳ **Explore** the **Concept** Life Stages and Approximate Ages in Human Development: Prenatal in **MyDevelopmentLab**

The germinal period (first 2 weeks)

Describe the structures that form during the germinal period, and identify when implantation takes place.

LEARNING OBJECTIVE 2.8

The first two weeks after fertilization are called the **germinal period** (Jones, 2006). This is the period when the zygote travels down the fallopian tubes to the uterus and implants in the uterine wall. As it travels, it begins cell division and differentiation. The

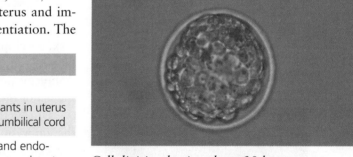

Cell division begins about 30 hours after conception.

TABLE 2.2 Milestones of Prenatal Development

Trimester	Period	Weeks	Milestones
First	Germinal	1–2	Zygote divides and forms blastocyst, which implants in uterus and begins forming the amnion, placenta, and umbilical cord
	Embryonic	3–4	Three layers form: the ectoderm, mesoderm, and endoderm; neural tube develops and produces neurons; heart begins beating; ribs, muscles, and digestive tract form
		5–8	Arms and legs develop, then fingers and toes; placenta and umbilical cord function; digestive system develops; liver produces blood cells; embryo responds to touch
	Fetal	9–12	Genitals form and release sex hormones; fingernails, toenails, and taste buds develop; heartbeat audible with stethoscope
Second		13–24	Mother feels movement; fetus kicks, turns, hiccups, sucks thumb, breathes amniotic fluid; responds to sounds, especially music and familiar voices; vernix and lanugo develop on skin
Third		25–38	Lungs develop fully; over two-thirds of birth weight is gained; brain development accelerates; sleep–wake cycles resemble newborn's

germinal period first 2 weeks after conception

blastocyst ball of about 100 cells formed by about one week following conception

trophoblast in the blastocyst, the outer layer of cells, which will go on to form structures that provide protection and nourishment to the embryo

embryonic disk in the blastocyst, the inner layer of cells, which will go on to form the embryo

amnion fluid-filled membrane that surrounds and protects the developing organism in the womb

placenta in the womb, gatekeeper between mother and fetus, protecting the fetus from bacteria and wastes in the mother's blood, and producing hormones that maintain the blood in the uterine lining and cause the mother's breasts to produce milk

umbilical cord structure connecting the fetus to the placenta

embryonic period weeks 3–8 of prenatal development

gestation in prenatal development, elapsed time since conception

ectoderm in the embryonic period, the outer layer of cells, which will eventually become the skin, hair, nails, sensory organs, and nervous system (brain and spinal cord)

mesoderm in the embryonic period, the middle of the three cell layers, which will become the muscles, bones, reproductive system, and circulatory system

endoderm in the embryonic period, the inner layer of cells, which will become the digestive system and the respiratory system

neural tube in the embryonic period, the part of the ectoderm that will become the spinal cord and brain

neuron cell of the nervous system

first cell division does not occur until 30 hours after conception, but after that, cell division takes place at a faster rate. By one week following conception there is a ball of about 100 cells known as a **blastocyst**. The blastocyst is divided into two layers. The outer layer of cells, called the **trophoblast**, will form the structures that provide protection and nourishment. The inner layer of cells, the **embryonic disk**, will become the embryo of the new organism.

During the second week after conception, *implantation* occurs as the blastocyst becomes firmly embedded into the lining of the uterus. Since the ovum was released from the ovary, the follicle from which it was released has been generating hormones that have caused the uterus to build up a bloody lining in preparation for receiving the blastocyst. Now the blastocyst is nourished by this blood.

The trophoblast begins to differentiate into several structures during this second week. Part of it forms a membrane, the **amnion**, which surrounds the developing organism and fills with fluid, helping to keep a steady temperature for the organism and protect it against the friction of the mother's movements (Johnson, 2008). In between the uterine wall and the embryonic disk a round structure, the **placenta**, begins to develop. The placenta will allow nutrients to pass from the mother to the developing organism and permit wastes to be removed. It also acts as a gatekeeper, protecting the developing organism from bacteria and wastes in the mother's blood, and it produces hormones that maintain the blood in the uterine lining and cause the mother's breasts to produce milk. An **umbilical cord** also begins to develop, connecting the fetus to the placenta.

Implantation is the outcome of the germinal period if all goes well. However, it is estimated that over half of blastocysts never implant successfully, usually due to chromosomal problems that have caused cell division to slow down or stop (Johnson, 2008). If implantation fails, the blastocyst will be eliminated from the woman's body along with the bloody uterine lining during her next menstrual period.

The embryonic period (weeks 3–8)

2.9 **LEARNING OBJECTIVE** Outline the major milestones of the embryonic period and identify when they take place.

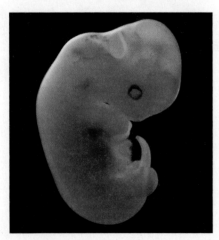

👁 Watch the Video The Embryonic Period: A Critical Period of Human Development in **MyDevelopmentLab**

In the fourth week of embryonic development, the heart has begun to beat and major organ systems are forming.

During the germinal period the trophoblast differentiated faster than the embryonic disk, developing the structures to protect and nurture the organism during pregnancy. Now, differentiation occurs rapidly in the embryonic disk. Over the 6 weeks of the **embryonic period**, 3–8 weeks' **gestation** (the time elapsed since conception), nearly all the major organ systems are formed (Fleming, 2006). 👁

During the first week of the embryonic period—the third week after conception—the embryonic disk forms three layers. The outer layer, the **ectoderm**, will become the skin, hair, nails, sensory organs, and nervous system. The middle layer, the **mesoderm**, will become the muscles, bones, reproductive system, and circulatory system. The inner layer, the **endoderm**, will become the digestive system and the respiratory system.

The nervous system develops first and fastest (Johnson, 2008). By the end of week 3, part of the ectoderm forms the **neural tube**, which will eventually become the spinal cord and brain. Once formed, the neural tube begins producing **neurons** (cells of the nervous system) in immense quantities, over 250,000 per minute. In the fourth week the shape of the head becomes apparent, and the eyes, nose, mouth, and ears begin to form. The heart begins to beat during this week, and the ribs, muscles, and digestive tract appear. By the end of the fourth week the embryo is only one-quarter inch long but already remarkably differentiated. Nevertheless, even an expert embryologist would have trouble at this point judging whether the embryo was to become a fish, a bird, or a mammal.

During weeks 5–8, growth continues its rapid pace. Buds that will become the arms and legs appear in week 5, developing webbed fingers and toes that lose their webbing by week 8. The placenta and the umbilical cord become fully functional (Jones, 2006). The digestive system develops, and the liver begins producing blood cells. The heart develops separate chambers. The top of the neural tube continues to develop into the brain, but the bottom of it looks like a tail in week 5, gradually shrinking to look more like a spinal cord by week 8.

By the end of the eighth week, the embryo is just one inch (2½ centimeters) long and ¹⁄₃₀ of an ounce (1 g) in weight. Yet all the main body parts have formed, and all of the main organs except the sex organs. Furthermore, the tiny embryo responds to touch, especially around its mouth, and it can move (Moore & Persaud, 2003). Now the embryo looks distinctly human (Johnson, 2008).

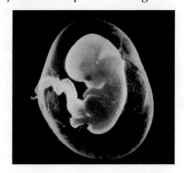

By the end of the eighth week, the embryo is just 1 inch long but all the major organs have formed except the sex organs.

The fetal period (week 9–birth)

Describe the major milestones of the fetal period and identify when viability occurs.

LEARNING OBJECTIVE 2.10

During the **fetal period**, lasting from 9 weeks after conception until birth, the organs continue to develop, and there is tremendous growth in sheer size, from ¹⁄₃₀ of an ounce in weight and 1 inch long at the beginning of the fetal period to an average (in developed countries) of 7½ pounds (3.4 kg) and 20 inches (51 cm) by birth. 👁

By the end of the third month the genitals have formed. After forming, the genitals release hormones that influence the rest of prenatal development, including brain organization, body size, and activity level, with boys becoming on average somewhat larger and more active (Cameron, 2001; DiPietro et al., 2004). Also during the third month, fingernails, toenails, and taste buds begin to develop. The heart has developed enough so that the heartbeat can now be heard through a stethoscope.

After 3 months, the typical fetus weighs about 3 ounces and is 3 inches long. A good way to remember this is as "three times three"—3 months, 3 ounces, 3 inches. Or, you can think of it as 100 days, 100 grams, 100 millimeters. Prenatal development is divided into three 3-month periods called **trimesters**, and the end of the third month marks the end of the first trimester.

During the second trimester, the fetus becomes active and begins to respond to its environment (Henrichs et al., 2010). By the end of the fourth month the fetus's movements can be felt by the mother. Gradually over the course of the second trimester the activity of the fetus becomes more diverse. By the end of the second trimester it breathes amniotic fluid in and out; it kicks, turns, and hiccups; it even sucks its thumb. It also responds to sounds, including voices and music, showing a preference (indicated by increased heart rate) for familiar voices, especially the voice of the mother. A slimy white substance called *vernix* covers the skin, to protect it from chapping due to the amniotic fluid, and downy hair called *lanugo* helps the vernix stick to the skin. By birth the fetus usually sheds its lanugo, although sometimes babies are born with lanugo still on, then shed it in the early weeks of life.

By the end of the second trimester, 6 months after conception, the typical fetus is about 14 inches long (36 cm) and weighs about 2 pounds (0.9 kg). Although it seems well-developed in many aspects of its behavior, it is still questionable in its *viability*, meaning its ability to survive outside of the womb. Babies born before 22 weeks rarely survive, even with the most advanced technological assistance. Even at 26 weeks, near the end of the second trimester, the survival rate is only 50%, and the survivors often have disabilities—14% have severe mental disabilities and 12% have cerebral palsy, which entails extensive physical and neurological disabilities (Lorenz et al., 1998). And this survival rate is only for babies that happen to be born in developed countries or in a wealthy family in a developing country. In most of the world, babies born before the end of the second trimester have no access to advanced medical care and will not survive (OECD, 2009).

👁 **Watch** the **Video** Fetal Development in **MyDevelopmentLab**

By the end of the second trimester, the fetus hiccups, sucks its thumb, and responds to voices and music.

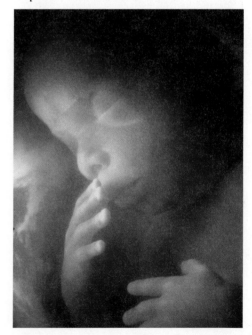

fetal period in prenatal development, the period from week 9 until birth

trimester one of the three 3-month periods of prenatal development

The main obstacle to viability at the beginning of the third trimester is the immaturity of the lungs. The lungs are the last major organ to become viable, and even a baby born in the seventh or early eighth month may need a respirator to breathe properly. Weight gain is also important. During the last trimester the typical fetus gains over 5 pounds, and this additional weight helps it sustain life. Babies born weighing less than 5.5 pounds are at risk for a wide range of problems, as we will see in detail in Chapter 3.

The brain is even less mature than the lungs in the third trimester, but its immaturity does not represent an obstacle to viability. As described in Chapter 1, in humans, early brain immaturity was an adaptation that occurred in the course of our evolutionary development to enable us to have an exceptionally large brain yet still fit through the birth canal. More than any other animal, humans are born with immature brains, which is why human babies are vulnerable and need parental care longer than other animals do. Nevertheless, more brain development occurs in the last 2 months of prenatal development than in any previous months. Neurons are created in vast numbers, up to 500,000 per minute, and the connections between them become increasingly elaborate (Capone & Kaufmann, 2008). 👁

By the third trimester, brain development has progressed to the point where, at 28 weeks, the sleep–wake cycles of the fetus are similar to those of a newborn infant. The fetus becomes increasingly aware of the external environment, especially in its ability to hear and remember sounds (James, 2010). In one study, mothers were asked to read Dr. Seuss's *The Cat in the Hat* to their fetuses every day during the last 6 weeks of pregnancy (DeCasper & Spence, 1986). After birth, the babies showed a preference for a recording of their mother reading *The Cat in the Hat*, by sucking on a plastic nipple in order to turn it on. They sucked harder to hear *The Cat in the Hat* than they did for recordings of their mothers reading similar rhyming stories they had not heard before. Fetuses respond to their internal environment as well. When the mother is highly stressed, the fetus's heart beats faster and its body movements increase (DiPietro et al., 2002). 👁

WHAT HAVE YOU LEARNED?

1. What is the function of the placenta?
2. How often does implantation fail, and why?
3. What three layers are formed from the embryonic disk, and what will each become?
4. What is the major obstacle to viability in the last trimester? How does the threshold for viability differ between developed countries and developing countries?
5. To what extent are fetuses aware of the external environment?

Prenatal Care

Because prenatal development carries risks for both mother and fetus, all cultures have developed customs and practices to try to promote a healthy outcome. First we look at some of the practices of prenatal care in traditional cultures, then we look at the scientific approach to prenatal care that has developed recently.

Prenatal care in traditional cultures

2.11 **LEARNING OBJECTIVE** Recall some approaches to prenatal care in traditional cultures.

All cultures have a store of advice about what a woman should and should not do during pregnancy (DeLoache & Gottlieb, 2000). What kind of guidelines or advice have you heard? You might ask your mother, your grandmother, and other mothers you know what advice they followed and where they obtained it.

Sometimes pregnancy advice seems practical and sensible. The practical advice reflects the collected wisdom that women pass down to each other over generations, based on their own experiences. Other times the advice may seem odd, especially to someone outside the given culture. Customs that seem peculiar to an outsider may arise because pregnancy is often perilous to both mother and fetus. Cultures sometimes develop their prenatal customs out of the desire to ensure that pregnancy will proceed successfully, but without the scientific knowledge that would make such control possible.

Here are a few examples. Among the Beng people of the West African nation of Ivory Coast, a variety of precautions are advocated for pregnant women (Gottlieb, 2000). As her belly swells, the pregnant woman is advised to rub it with oil made from a local tree, so that her skin will not become uncomfortably tight—a good piece of practical advice. She is also advised to avoid drinking palm wine during the early months of pregnancy; again, practical advice drawn from the experience of women who drank alcohol during pregnancy, with unfortunate results. On the other hand, she is also advised to avoid eating meat from the bushbuck antelope while pregnant, and warned that if she does her baby may emerge from the womb striped like the antelope. Her husband must stop hunting while she is pregnant, because it is believed that if he unwittingly killed a pregnant animal, his wife and her baby would also die. The mother-to-be must also be on her best behavior while pregnant. If she steals something while pregnant, it is believed that her child will develop the long arm of a thief; if she casts a curse on an enemy, it is believed that her baby will become a witch.

Thousands of miles away, on the Indonesian island of Bali, people have a similar mix of beliefs about foods to avoid and the danger of witches (Diener, 2000). Various foods are classified as "hot" or "cold," not because of their temperature but because of how they are believed to affect bodily functioning. "Hot" foods are to be avoided during pregnancy, including eggplant, mango, and octopus. Also, a pregnant mother should not accept food from someone who is spiritually impure, such as a menstruating woman or someone who has recently had a death in the family. Witches are believed to be especially attracted to the blood of a pregnant woman and her unborn child, so pregnant women are advised to obtain a magic charm and wear it on their belt or hang it on the gate of their yard, for protection.

The Warlpiri, an Aboriginal culture of Australia, have beliefs about foods and animal spirits that a pregnant woman must avoid (Pierroutsakos, 2000). No animals with spiked body parts should be eaten—such as anteaters, possums, or lizards—because those spikes can appear in the fetus and make pregnancy and birth dangerous to the mother. "Strong" foods should also be avoided, such as emu, rabbit, and bandicoot (a rodent). Where the Warlpiri live, different areas are believed to be associated with different animals, and a pregnant woman must take special care concerning the animal associated with the area where her baby was conceived. (The Warlpiri are nomadic, and move from place to place frequently.) So, for example, if she conceived her child in the land of the wild dogs, it is believed that she and everyone she knows must avoid harming or killing a wild dog while she is pregnant, or she will suffer a miscarriage.

One helpful method of prenatal care common in many traditional cultures is massage (Field, 2004; Jordan, 1994). The prenatal massage is usually performed by a **midwife** (a person who assists women in pregnancy and childbirth) in the course of her visits to the pregnant woman. Typically, the woman lies on the floor on a blanket, and the midwife kneels or sits on a stool beside her. Then the midwife spreads an oil on the woman's abdomen and begins the massage with light circular movements. While the massage is taking place, the midwife asks the woman various questions about how the pregnancy is going. As part of the massage, the midwife probes to determine the fetus's position in the uterus. If the fetus is turned in an unfavorable position, so that it would be likely to come out feet first rather than head first, the midwife will attempt an *inversion* to turn the fetus's head toward the vaginal opening. This is sometimes painful, but as we will see in Chapter 3, a head-first birth is much safer than a feet-first birth, for both baby and mother.

midwife person who assists in pregnant women's prenatal care and the birth process

My Virtual Child

Does your culture hold any prenatal customs?

THINKING CULTURALLY

How are magical thoughts about pregnancy, particularly foods and activities to avoid during pregnancy, related to dangerous conditions that many people of the world find themselves in?

Prenatal massage has benefits for mother and fetus. Here, a midwife and a pregnant woman in Guatemala.

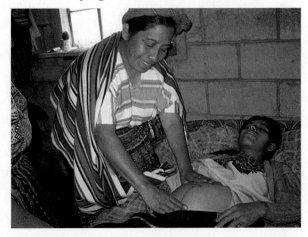

After massaging the abdomen, the midwife massages the woman's back. Carrying a baby is a great strain on a woman's back, especially in the last trimester, so the back massage is helpful for relieving the mother's discomfort.

Prenatal massage has a long history in many cultures (Jordan, 1994). In recent years, it has also begun to be used by midwives, nurses, and physicians in developed countries. By now, a substantial amount of research has accumulated to support the benefits of massage for mother and fetus. Benefits to the mother include lower likelihood of back pain, less swelling of the joints, and better sleep (Field, 2004). Babies whose mothers received prenatal massage score higher on scales of their physical and social functioning in the early weeks of life (Field et al., 2006).

Scientifically based prenatal care

2.12	LEARNING OBJECTIVE	Summarize scientifically based information on prenatal care.

Some of the examples of prenatal customs just provided may strike you as strange, but they are understandable as a human attempt to control events that are highly important but also mysterious. Until recently, and even in developed cultures, people had little idea, scientifically, how to promote the well-being of a pregnant woman and her fetus, so they devised customs based on what little knowledge they possessed from experience. In developed countries, including the United States, there are varying beliefs about pregnancy and prenatal care based on cultural factors such as ethnicity and religious differences. The customs that people follow can be seen as their theories—sometimes accurate and sometimes not—about how prenatal development takes place and how it can be made safer.

Scientific guidelines for prenatal care focus mostly on four key areas: medical evaluations, diet, exercise, and avoidance of potentially harmful influences called *teratogens* (see *Table 2.3*) (World Health Organization [WHO], 2009). In most cultures today, pregnant women receive assistance from others in promoting and maintaining their health during pregnancy. In developing countries, women typically receive support from their mothers, mothers-in-law, other family members, and friends (DeLoache & Gottlieb, 2000). Men are usually excluded from anything involving pregnancy and

---

TABLE 2.3 Essentials of Prenatal Care

Before Pregnancy

- Have a medical examination to ensure there are no diseases that may affect prenatal development. If not fully vaccinated, obtain vaccinations for diseases, such as rubella, that can damage prenatal development. (Vaccinations may be unsafe during pregnancy.)
- Avoid tobacco, alcohol, and other drugs, which may make it more difficult to become pregnant and are damaging to prenatal development.

During Pregnancy

- *Diet.* Maintain a balanced diet, including protein, grains, fruits, and vegetables. Avoid excessive fats and sugars and obtain sufficient iron and iodine. Gain 25–35 pounds in total; avoid dieting as well as excessive weight gain.
- *Exercise.* Engage in mild to moderate exercise regularly, including aerobic exercise, to stimulate circulatory system and muscles, as well as Kegel exercises to strengthen vaginal muscles. Avoid strenuous exercise and high-risk sports, such as long-distance running, contact sports, downhill skiing, waterskiing, and horseback riding.
- *Teratogens.* Avoid tobacco, alcohol, and other drugs. Avoid exposure to X-rays, hazardous chemicals, and infectious diseases.
- *Get regular prenatal checkups.* Regular medical visits are recommended during the entire pregnancy, beginning between week 8 and week 12. Ideally, women will see a doctor every four weeks after week 12, until week 28, when weekly visits are recommended for the duration of the pregnancy.

birth. In developed countries, pregnant women often receive help and support from the father-to-be, as well as from mothers, mothers-in-law, other family members, friends, and health care providers. In both developing and developed countries, this supportive network can help the pregnant woman monitor her health and the health of her unborn child throughout the course of the pregnancy.

PRENATAL HEALTH EVALUATIONS One key conclusion of research on prenatal care is that pregnant women should receive regular evaluations from a skilled health care worker, beginning as soon as possible after conception, to monitor the health of mother and fetus and ensure that the pregnancy is proceeding well. Most women in developed countries have access to physicians, nurses, or certified midwives who can provide good prenatal care. However, some poor women may not have access to such care, especially in the United States. The percentage of women in the United States who begin prenatal care in their first trimester varies greatly based on ethnicity and SES, as shown in **Map 2.1**.

Pregnant women in developing countries are much less likely than those in developed countries to receive prenatal care from a skilled health care worker. The World Health Organization's *Making Pregnancy Safer* program has focused on working with governments to set up programs that provide pregnant women with such care (WHO, 2009). Currently 99% of maternal and infant deaths occur in developing countries—only 1% occur in developed countries—and the WHO program is focused on the 70 countries with the highest death rates, mostly in Africa and South Asia.

DIET As recently as the middle of the 20th century, women in developed countries were being advised by their doctors to limit their weight gain during pregnancy to no more than 15 pounds (Olson, 2008). By now, scientific studies have shown that women should typically gain 25–35 pounds during pregnancy, and women who gain less than 20 pounds are at risk for having babies who are preterm and low birth weight (Ehrenberg et al., 2003). Pregnant women should eat somewhat more than they did prior to pregnancy, but only by about 300 calories a day. Women should also drink more fluids during pregnancy than they normally do, as the fetus needs fluids for healthy development and a pregnant woman's body also requires more.

In many ways, a healthy pregnancy diet resembles a healthy diet any other time: a good balance of protein, grains, fruits, and vegetables, and avoidance of foods with excessive sugar or fat content. However, there are some nutrients that are of special importance during pregnancy, most notably iron and iodine. Iron-rich foods such as

Simulate the **Experiment**
Teratogens and Their Effects
in **MyDevelopmentLab**

My Virtual Child

How will your or your partner's virtual pregnancy differ from pregnancies in different cultures?

THINKING CULTURALLY

Are there any beliefs in your culture about what a woman should eat or should avoid eating before or during pregnancy? Do the same beliefs apply to men during any point of the conception and gestation continuum?

Map 2.1 • **Ethnic Variations in Prenatal Care Within the United States.** How does prenatal care differ for White women compared with other ethnic groups? What economic factors might account for these variations?

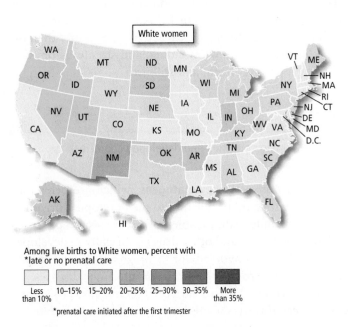

Among live births to White women, percent with
*late or no prenatal care

| Less than 10% | 10–15% | 15–20% | 20–25% | 25–30% | 30–35% | More than 35% |

*prenatal care initiated after the first trimester

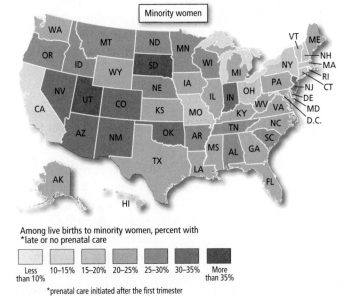

Among live births to minority women, percent with
*late or no prenatal care

| Less than 10% | 10–15% | 15–20% | 20–25% | 25–30% | 30–35% | More than 35% |

*prenatal care initiated after the first trimester

Moderate exercise is part of good prenatal care.

APPLYING YOUR KNOWLEDGE
...as a Nurse

One of your pregnant patients tells you that in her culture women are advised to move around as little as possible during pregnancy. What would you tell her?

beef, duck, potatoes (including skin), spinach, and dried fruits are important for building the blood supply of mother and fetus. The WHO estimates that nearly one-half of women worldwide are deficient in iron, placing them at risk for having preterm and low-birth-weight babies (WHO, 2009). Even with a healthy diet including iron-rich foods, health authorities recommend an iron supplement from the 12th week of pregnancy onward.

Iodine is also crucial, because low iodine intake during pregnancy increases the risks of miscarriage, stillbirth, and abnormalities in fetal brain development. In developed countries salt has been iodized since the 1920s, so women receive adequate iodine as part of a normal diet. However, in developing countries most women do not use iodized salt and consequently they often experience iodine deficiencies. The WHO and other major health organizations have made a strong push recently to make iodine supplements available in developing countries, as will be explained in more detail in Chapter 3.

EXERCISE Like advice on diet, advice on exercising during pregnancy has changed as a scientific body of knowledge has developed. Until a few decades ago, it was widely believed in developed countries that pregnancy was a kind of disability or illness, and a pregnant woman was viewed as too fragile and weak to take a walk or carry a bag of groceries, much less exercise (Murkoff & Mazel, 2008). However, it is now clear that mild to moderate exercise enhances the health of the pregnant woman and her fetus (although any planned exercise program should be cleared with a skilled health care professional before proceeding).

Aerobic exercise such as walking, jogging, or swimming, stimulates the circulatory and muscular systems of a woman's body (McArdle et al., 2009). It increases her ability to process oxygen, a benefit for both her and the fetus, and increases muscle tone and strength (thus lowering the likelihood of backache and constipation). Also highly useful are *Kegel exercises,* which involve tensing the muscles of the vagina and anus as tightly as possible for 8–10 seconds before gradually relaxing them (Murkoff & Mazel, 2008). These exercises strengthen the vagina muscles to prepare it for the delivery of the fetus. Certain kinds of strenuous exercise and high-risk sports should be avoided during pregnancy, including downhill skiing, waterskiing, horseback riding, any contact sports, and jogging more than two miles.

Aerobic exercises during pregnancy are especially advisable for women whose daily lives do not require much physical activity, including most women in developed countries (Stotland et al., 2010). For most women in developing countries, and for some women in developed countries, their work in factories or fields requires a great deal of daily exertion, and the risks of too much strenuous physical activity are greater than the risks of too little exercise. Heavy lifting, continuous standing, and strenuous physical exertion raise the risks of miscarriage, preterm birth, and stillbirth.

Teratogens

2.13 **LEARNING OBJECTIVE** | Identify the major teratogens in developing countries and developed countries.

An essential part of good prenatal care is avoiding **teratogens**, which are behaviors, environments, and bodily conditions that could be harmful to the developing organism (Haffner, 2007). Common teratogens include malnutrition and disease (especially in developing countries) as well as alcohol, tobacco, and other drugs (especially in developed countries). Certain kinds of work are also best avoided during pregnancy if they involve exposure to teratogens such as X-rays, hazardous chemicals, or infectious diseases.

Both the embryo and the fetus are vulnerable to a variety of teratogens. The embryonic period, especially, is a *critical period* for prenatal development, meaning that it is

teratogen behavior, environment, or bodily condition that can have damaging influence on prenatal development

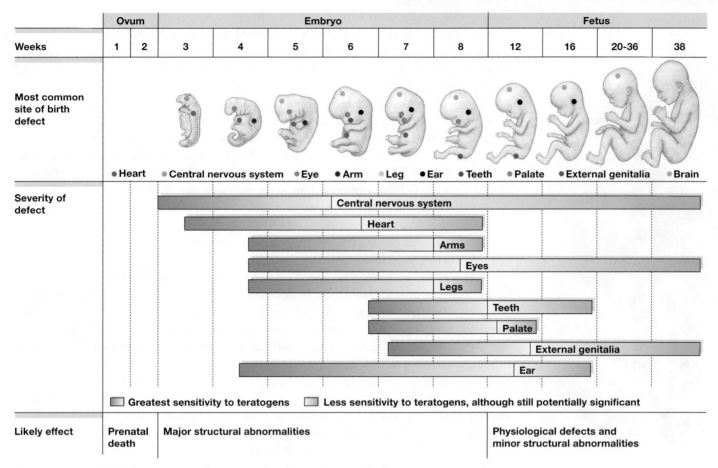

Figure 2.7 • **Timing of teratogens.** Vulnerability to teratogens is greatest in the embryonic period. **Source:** Moore, 1974.

a period when teratogens can have an especially profound and enduring effect on later development, as **Figure 2.7** illustrates. This is because the embryonic period is when all the major organ systems are forming at a rapid rate. However, some teratogens can do damage during the fetal period.

MALNUTRITION Probably the most common teratogen worldwide is malnutrition (Kalter, 2010). Medical experts recommend that pregnant women gain 25–35 pounds, and that they eat a healthy, balanced diet of proteins, grains, fruit, and vegetables (Martin et al., 2002). However, if you recall from Chapter 1 that 40% of the world's population lives on less than two dollars a day, you can imagine that most mothers who are part of that 40% receive a prenatal diet that falls far short of the ideal.

Furthermore, about half the world's population is rural, and the diet of people in rural areas often varies substantially depending on the time of year. They may eat fairly well during summer and fall when their crops provide food, but less well during winter and spring when fresh food is unavailable. Consequently, prenatal health may depend greatly on when the child was conceived.

Dramatic evidence of this effect has been shown in recent decades in China (Berry et al., 1999). In the 1980s China had the highest incidence in the world of two serious prenatal disorders, *anencephaly*, in which parts of the brain are missing or malformed, and *spina bifida*, which is an extreme distortion in the shape of the spinal column. It was discovered that in both of these disorders the main cause is a deficiency of folic acid, a nutrient found especially in fruits and vegetables. Furthermore, researchers observed that the traditional marriage period in China is January and February, and most couples try to conceive a child as soon after marriage as possible. Consequently, the early months of pregnancy typically take place in winter and

Malnutrition is a common teratogen in developing countries. Here, a pregnant woman in rural Zambia.

APPLYING YOUR KNOWLEDGE
. . . as a Nurse

How would you intervene in a community that has never had children vaccinated and doesn't believe in vaccines?

AIDS (acquired immune deficiency syndrome) sexually transmitted infection caused by HIV, resulting in damage to the immune system

early spring, when rural women are least likely to have fruits and vegetables as part of their diet. After this pattern was discovered, the Chinese government established a nationwide program to provide mothers with supplements of folic acid, and since that time the incidence of anencephaly and spina bifida has been sharply reduced (De Wals et al., 2007).

Many other countries have also taken steps to reduce folic-acid deficiencies in pregnant mothers. After research established that folic acid was the key to preventing anencephaly and spina bifida, governments in many countries passed laws requiring folic acid to be added to grain products such as cereals, bread, pasta, flour, and rice. Almost immediately, the incidence of both disorders fell sharply (Honein et al., 2001). Medical authorities now recommend that women begin taking folic acid supplements and eating plenty of fruits and vegetables even when they are trying to become pregnant, because the damage from lack of folic acid can take place in the early weeks of pregnancy, before the woman knows for sure that she is pregnant (de Villarreal et al., 2006).

It is not only in developing countries or rural areas that nutritional deficiencies can be problematic during pregnancy. In developed countries healthy food may be widely available, but that does mean that all mothers eat a healthy, balanced diet. They may have deficiencies of protein and other nutrients, especially if they live in poverty. In the United States, the federal government administers the WIC program, for women, infants, and children. WIC is designed to help low-income mothers make sure that they and their children are getting adequate nutrition. In some developed countries, particularly in the United States, mothers may be obese, which makes them more likely to develop diabetes during pregnancy and to require a cesarean delivery. Maternal obesity also makes it more likely that babies will be born with a range of problems including spina bifida, heart defects, and cleft palate (Doheny, 2009).

Prenatal nutrition influences risks for serious prenatal problems as well as the risk of premature delivery and low birth weight (Ilich & Brownbill, 2010). Furthermore, malnutrition during pregnancy can have effects that appear many years later. For example, in the country of Gambia in western Africa, research has shown that children born during the "hungry season" (the time span between harvests when food is most scarce) are at greater risk of dying from illness and disease in their twenties (Moore et al., 1997). In Finland, prenatal malnutrition has been shown to be a risk factor for the development of schizophrenia in emerging adulthood (Wahlbeck et al., 2001).

INFECTIOUS DISEASES Infectious diseases are far more prevalent in developing countries than in developed countries (WHO, 2009). Many of these diseases influence prenatal development. One of the most prevalent and serious is *rubella* (also known as *German measles*). The embryonic period is a critical period for exposure to rubella. Over half of infants whose mothers contracted the illness during this period have severe problems including blindness, deafness, mental retardation, and abnormalities of the heart, genitals, or intestinal system (Eberhart-Phillips et al., 1993). During the fetal period effects of rubella are less severe, but can include low birth weight, hearing problems, and skeletal defects (Brown & Susser, 2002). Since the late 1960s a vaccine given to children has made rubella rare in developed countries—girls retain the immunity into adulthood, when they become pregnant—but it remains widespread in developing countries where children are less likely to receive the vaccine (Plotkin et al., 1999; WHO, 2009).

Another common infectious disease of prenatal development is **AIDS (acquired immune deficiency syndrome)**, a sexually transmitted infection (STI) caused by the human immunodeficiency virus (HIV), which damages the immune system. HIV/AIDS can be transmitted from mother to child during prenatal development through the blood, during birth, or through breast milk. HIV/AIDS damages brain development prenatally, and infants with HIV are unlikely to survive to adulthood unless they receive an expensive "cocktail" of medications rarely available in the developing countries where AIDS is most common (Susser, 2011). In developing countries mother–child transmission of HIV/AIDS has been dramatically reduced in recent years through three strategies: (1) effective medicines given to mothers prior to birth and to infants; (2) cesarean sections for AIDS-infected mothers; and (3) the use of infant formula in place of breast-feeding (Blair et al., 2004; Sullivan, 2003). However, 95% of all HIV infections take place in Africa, and few African mothers or infants have access to the three strategies that are effective against HIV/AIDS (WHO, 2010b).

Other STIs that can affect the fetus include herpes, gonorrhea, and syphilis. Herpes is a virus and cannot be treated with antibiotics. In order to avoid the risk of the fetus contracting herpes during delivery, the fetus of a mother with herpes will likely be delivered via Cesarean section. Gonorrhea and syphilis can be treated with antibiotics, and if treated early, should not affect the developing fetus.

ALCOHOL In developed countries, the teratogen that causes the most widespread damage to prenatal development is alcohol (Sokol et al., 2003). Although it used to be believed that moderate alcohol use would cause no harm during pregnancy, recent research has shown that the only safe amount of alcohol for a pregnant woman is *none at all*. Even one or two drinks a few days a week puts the developing child at risk for lower height, weight, and head size at birth, and for lower intelligence and higher aggressiveness during childhood (Willford et al., 2006). 👁

When mothers drink heavily during pregnancy, their infants are at risk for **fetal alcohol spectrum disorder (FASD)**, which includes facial deformities, heart problems, misshapen limbs, and a variety of cognitive problems such as mental retardation and attention and memory deficits (Mattson et al., 2010). Infants born with FASD face a lifetime of trouble, and the more alcohol their mothers drank during pregnancy, the worse their problems are likely to be (Barr & Streissguth, 2001). In childhood and adolescence, their cognitive deficits make it difficult for them to succeed academically or socially in school (Korkman, et al., 2003). In adolescence, FASD raises the risk of delinquency, alcohol and drug abuse, and depression and other mental health problems (Baer et al., 2003; Mattson et al., 2010). Rates of FASD are especially alarming, as high as 10%, in some Native American and Canadian First Nations communities where alcoholism is prevalent (Caetano et al., 2006; Tough et al., 2007). 👁

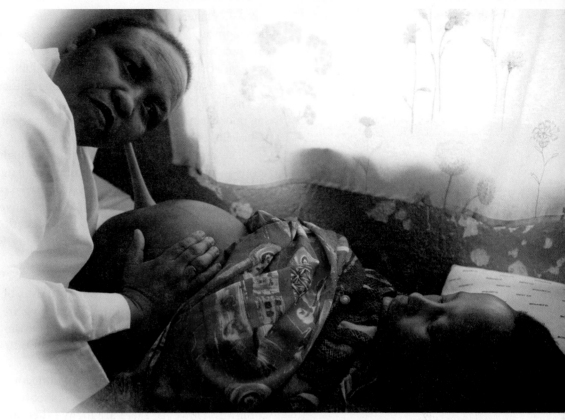

Pregnant women in developing countries who have AIDS rarely receive adequate medical treatment. Here, a woman at a clinic for HIV/AIDS patients in Lesotho.

fetal alcohol spectrum disorder (FASD) set of problems that occur as a consequence of high maternal alcohol use during pregnancy, including facial deformities, heart problems, misshapen limbs, and a variety of cognitive problems

👁─⌐**Watch** the **Video** Fetal Alcohol Damage in **MyDevelopmentLab**

👁─⌐**Watch** the **Video** Fetal Alcohol Syndrome: Sidney in **MyDevelopmentLab**

Heavy alcohol use in pregnancy causes fetal alcohol spectrum disorder (FASD), which includes a variety of severe developmental problems.

secondhand smoke smoke from a cigarette inhaled by those near the smoker

TOBACCO Maternal cigarette smoking has a wide range of negative effects on prenatal development. Women who smoke during pregnancy are at higher risk for miscarriage and premature birth, and smoking is the leading cause of low birth weight in developed countries (Espy et al., 2011). Maternal smoking raises the risks of health problems in infants, such as impaired heart functioning, difficulty breathing, and even death (Jaakkola & Gissler, 2004). Prenatal exposure to smoking predicts problems in childhood, including poorer language skills, problems with attention and memory, and behavior problems (Cornelius et al., 2011; Sawnani et al., 2004).

The problems appear to continue through adolescence. In one study, boys whose mothers had smoked heavily during pregnancy were four times more likely to have conduct disorders by adolescence, compared to boys whose mothers had not smoked, and girls were five times more likely to have substance abuse problems (Weissman et al., 1999). With smoking as with alcohol use, the more the mother uses the substance during pregnancy, the more likely the baby will be born with serious and enduring problems.

Fathers' smoking is also a peril to prenatal development. The **secondhand smoke** from fathers' smoking leads to higher risks of low birth weight and childhood cancer (Rückinger et al., 2010). Rates of smoking are generally higher in developed countries than in developing countries, but they are rising rapidly in developing countries around the world as their economies grow (WHO, 2012).

OTHER TERATOGENS Malnutrition and infectious diseases are the most common teratogens in developing countries, with alcohol and tobacco most common in developed countries. However, there are many other potential teratogens. Maternal use of drugs such as cocaine, heroin, and marijuana causes physical, cognitive, and behavioral problems in infants (Messinger & Lester, 2008; National Institute on Drug Abuse, 2001). Certain prescription drugs can also cause harm. For example, Accutane, a drug used to treat severe acne, can cause devastating damage to major organs such as the brain and heart during embryonic development (Honein et al., 2001). Even nonprescription drugs such as cold medicines can be damaging to prenatal development, so women who are pregnant or seeking to become pregnant should always check with their doctors about any medications they may be taking (Morgan et al., 2010). Other potential teratogens include environmental pollution, radiation, excessive caffeine, and severe maternal stress. Interestingly, socioeconomic status has also been considered a teratogen because poor women may be more likely to be exposed to these and other harmful substances. Poor women may be more likely to come into contact with environmental hazards or work in dangerous conditions than their wealthier counterparts.

Essentially, the close biological connection between mother and embryo or fetus means that whatever she is experiencing—for good or for ill—may also be experienced by the baby growing within her. Experiences that damage the health of the mother carry a strong risk of damaging the health of the baby as well. The rapid rate of growth of the embryo and fetus makes them especially vulnerable.

Even experiences that may be harmless or healthy for the mother can be dangerous to the baby. For example, moderate alcohol use of one to two drinks a day is actually healthy for adults, but unhealthy for prenatal development. The placenta does provide some protection to the embryo or fetus, preventing some teratogens from entering and causing damage. However, the protection it provides is limited, and many teratogens manage to cross the placental barrier.

My Virtual Child

What teratogens will you or your partner likely be exposed to during pregnancy? Would this hold true in a different culture?

APPLYING YOUR KNOWLEDGE

How might you help lower-income women deal with risk factors in pregnancy, such as stress or insufficient nutrition?

WHAT HAVE YOU LEARNED?

1. What are some prenatal care practices in traditional cultures that contribute to the health of mother and fetus and some that do not?

2. What are some benefits of prenatal massage to both mother and fetus?

3. Why is regular prenatal care from a skilled health care worker important during pregnancy, and how does access to this care vary around the world?

4. Why are nutrients such as iodine and iron of special importance during pregnancy?

5. Which two infectious diseases are common teratogens in developing countries, and what are their effects on prenatal development?

6. How much alcohol is safe for a mother to consume during pregnancy? What are the features of fetal alcohol spectrum disorder?

Section 2 VIDEO GUIDE Pregnancy and Prenatal Care Across Cultures (Length: 8:14)

In this video expectant mothers from various countries are interviewed regarding their pregnancy experiences. There is also an interview with a Mayan midwife regarding her role in prenatal care.

1. Do you think the American expectant mother's experience is typical of most expectant mothers in the United States? Why or why not?

2. Compare and contrast the American expectant mother's experience with the Mayan expectant mother's experience.

3. Describe the role of the midwife interviewed here. What are some advantages of seeing a doctor vs. a midwife as listed by the mothers in this clip?

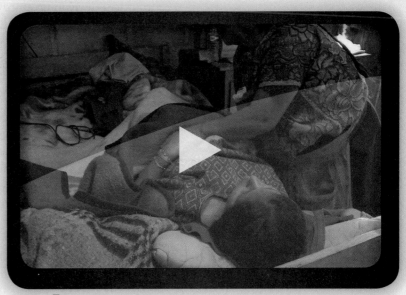

Watch the **Video** Pregnancy and Prenatal Care Across Cultures in **MyDevelopmentLab**

LEARNING OBJECTIVES

2.14 Explain how chromosomal disorders occur.

2.15 Describe the three main techniques of prenatal diagnosis, and explain who is likely to seek genetic counseling and for what purposes.

2.16 List the major causes of infertility for both men and women.

2.17 Describe the current treatments for infertility.

2.18 Compare rates of infertility worldwide, and contrast the views of infertility in developed and developing countries.

Risks in the Prenatal Period

Most pregnancies proceed without major problems and end with the birth of a healthy infant. However, many things can go wrong in the course of prenatal development. Chromosomal disorders affect less than one percent of children born, but the effects can range from quite serious to unnoticeable. Women who are pregnant or who think they may become pregnant may consider diagnostic testing of themselves, their partners, and their developing embryos.

Chromosomal disorders

| 2.14 | LEARNING OBJECTIVE | Explain how chromosomal disorders occur. |

In the course of the formation of the gametes during meiosis, sometimes errors take place and the chromosomes fail to divide properly. Consequently, instead of ending up with 46 chromosomes in each cell, the person has 45 or 47 (or even, in rare cases, 48 or 49), and problems occur. It is estimated that as many as half of all conceptions involve too many or too few chromosomes, but most of the zygotes that result either never begin to develop or are spontaneously aborted early in the pregnancy (Borgaonkar, 1997; Johnson, 2008). In 1 out of 200 live births, the child has a chromosomal disorder. There are two main types of chromosomal disorders: (1) those that involve the sex chromosomes and (2) those that take place on the 21st pair of chromosomes, resulting in a condition known as Down syndrome.

SEX CHROMOSOME DISORDERS The sex chromosomes are especially likely to be involved in chromosomal disorders. A person may have an extra X chromosome (resulting in XXX or XXY), or an extra Y chromosome (XYY), or may have only an X and no second sex chromosome. About 1 in every 500 infants has some type of sex chromosome disorder.

The XXY condition is known as Klinefelter's syndrome, but not all males who have an extra X chromosome exhibit the symptoms of the syndrome. Those with Klinefelter's syndrome may have weak muscles, low sperm count, and delayed language development. The X0 condition is known as Turner syndrome. These females tend to be short in stature, with no menstrual cycle and resulting sterility. In the case of XYY males, there is usually accelerated physical growth, with normal levels of testosterone. Some of these males have learning delays.

Generally, there are two common consequences of sex chromosome disorders (Batzer & Rovitsky, 2009). One is that the person has some type of cognitive deficit, such as mental retardation (ranging from mild to severe), a learning disorder, or speech impairments. The other kind of problem is that the person has some abnormality in the development of the reproductive system at puberty, such as underdeveloped testes and penis in boys or no ovulation in girls. One of the functions of the sex chromosomes is to direct the production of the sex hormones, and having too few or too many sex chromosomes disrupts this process. However, treatment with hormone supplements is often effective in correcting the problem.

DOWN SYNDROME When there is an extra chromosome on the 21st pair, the condition is known as **Down syndrome** or *trisomy-21*. Persons with Down syndrome have distinct physical features, including a short, stocky build, an unusually flat face, a large tongue, and an extra fold of skin on the eyelids. They also have cognitive deficits, including mental retardation and speech problems (Pennington et al., 2003). Many also have problems in their physical development, such as hearing impairments and heart defects.

Their social development varies widely. Some children with Down syndrome smile less readily than other persons and have difficulty making eye contact, but others are exceptionally happy and loving. Supportive and encouraging parents help children with Down syndrome develop more favorably (Sigman, 1999). Intervention programs in infancy and preschool have been shown to enhance their social, emotional, and motor skills (Carr, 2002). In adulthood, with adequate support many are able to hold a job that is highly structured and involves simple tasks.

However, people with Down syndrome age faster than other people (Berney, 2009). Their total brain volume begins to decrease as early as their twenties. Various physical ailments that may develop for other people in late adulthood begin to afflict people with Down syndrome in their thirties and forties, including leukemia, cancer, Alzheimer's disease, and heart disease (Hassold & Patterson, 1999). As a result, their life expectancy is considerably lower than in the general population. However, with medical treatment most are able to live into at least their fifties or sixties (Roizen & Patterson, 2003).

PARENTAL AGE AND CHROMOSOMAL DISORDERS Children with chromosomal problems are almost always born to parents who have no disorder (Batzer & Ravitsky, 2009). Chromosomal problems occur not because the parents have an inherited problem that they pass on to their children, but usually because of the age of the parents, especially the mother. For example, the risk of Down syndrome rises with maternal age, from 1 in 1,900 births at age 20 to 1 in 30 births at age 45 (Meyers et al., 1997). The risk of chromosomal disorders is low for mothers in their twenties and rises only slightly in the thirties, but rises steeply after age 40 (see *Figure 2.8*) (Heffner, 2004).

Recall that a woman's gamete production takes place while she is still in the womb of her own mother. The older she gets, the longer the eggs have been in her ovaries. When conception takes place and the last part of meiosis is completed in the ovum, the older the woman, the greater the likelihood that the chromosomes will not separate properly because they have been suspended in that final stage of meiosis for so long. The father's sperm is the cause of the chromosomal disorder in 5–10% of cases, but it is unclear if the risk increases with the father's age (Crow, 2003; Fisch et al., 2003; Muller et al., 2000).

Down syndrome genetic disorder due to carrying an extra chromosome on the 21st pair

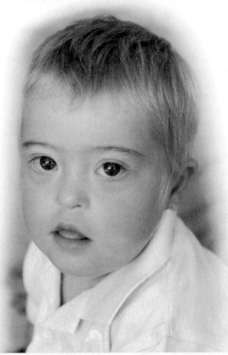

Persons with Down syndrome typically face a wide range of physical and cognitive problems.

—⟦**Watch** the **Video** Down Syndrome in **MyDevelopmentLab**

My Virtual Child

What prenatal diagnosing techniques are available in your culture? Does your or your partner's background increase the likelihood of using these techniques?

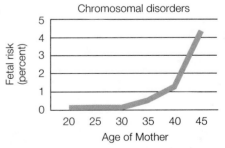

Figure 2.8 • **Chromosomal disorders and maternal age.** Why does the risk rise so steeply after age 40?

Prenatal diagnosis

LEARNING OBJECTIVE   Describe the three main techniques of prenatal diagnosis, and explain who is likely to seek genetic counseling and for what purposes.

ultrasound machine that uses sound waves to produce images of the fetus during pregnancy

amniocentesis prenatal procedure in which a needle is used to withdraw amniotic fluid containing fetal cells from the placenta, allowing possible prenatal problems to be detected

chorionic villus sampling (CVS) prenatal technique for diagnosing genetic problems, involving taking a sample of cells at 5–10 weeks gestation by inserting a tube into the uterus

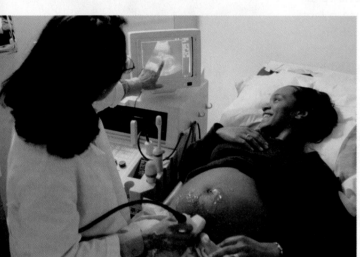

Ultrasound allows medical professionals and parents to monitor prenatal development.

Watch the **Video** Prenatal Ultrasound in **MyDevelopmentLab**

Watch the **Video** Chorionic Villus Testing in **MyDevelopmentLab**

Various technologies are used to monitor the course of prenatal development. Even before pregnancy, some couples who are at risk for potential problems seek prenatal genetic counseling in order to inform themselves about the nature and degree of the risks they face.

TECHNIQUES OF PRENATAL MONITORING In developed countries, a variety of techniques are available to monitor the growth and health of the fetus and detect prenatal problems. Common methods include ultrasound, amniocentesis, and chorionic villus sampling (CVS).

Ultrasound. In **ultrasound**, high-frequency sound waves are directed toward the uterus, and as they bounce off the fetus they are converted by computer into an image that can be viewed on a screen. Ultrasound technology has improved in recent years and the image is usually distinct enough to make it possible to measure the fetus's size and shape and to monitor its activities. Studies have also found that viewing ultrasound images helps promote a feeling of parental involvement and attachment even before birth (Righetti et al., 2005). I remember well the thrill of seeing my twins on the ultrasound monitor and marveling as they grew from two clumps of cells to full-grown fetuses.

Ultrasound is sometimes used to screen for Down syndrome, which can be detected 13 weeks into prenatal development (Reddy & Mennui, 2006). It is also used for pregnancies that involve multiple fetuses, because these are high-risk pregnancies in which it is common for some of the fetuses to be developing less favorably than others. However, today ultrasound is used for most normal pregnancies in developed countries, not just for those that are high risk (Merz, 2006). It is cheap, easy, and safe, and it allows doctors to monitor fetal growth and gives parents the enjoyment of seeing the fetus as it is developing in the womb. It also allows parents to learn the sex of the child before birth, if they wish. However, ultrasound is also sometimes used to abort female fetuses in cultures where males are more highly valued. Both India and China today have millions more males than females due to selective abortions of female fetuses over recent decades (Abrejo et al., 2009).

Amniocentesis. In **amniocentesis**, a long hollow needle is inserted into the pregnant woman's abdomen and, using the ultrasound image for guidance, a sample of the amniotic fluid is withdrawn from the placenta surrounding the fetus. This fluid contains fetal cells sloughed off in the course of prenatal development, and the cells can be examined for information on the fetus's genotype. Amniocentesis is conducted 15–20 weeks into pregnancy. It is used only for women who are at risk for prenatal problems due to family history or age (35 or older) because it carries a small risk of triggering miscarriage. It can detect 40 different defects in fetal development with 100% accuracy (Brambati & Tului, 2005).

Chorionic villus sampling (CVS). Like amniocentesis, **chorionic villus sampling (CVS)** entails sampling and analyzing cells early in development to detect possible genetic problems. CVS takes place at 5–10 weeks into the pregnancy; the sample is obtained from the cells that are beginning to form the umbilical cord. Guided by ultrasound, a tube is inserted through the vagina and into the uterus to obtain the cell sample. CVS entails a slight but genuine risk of miscarriage or damage to the fetus, so it is used only when there is a family history of genetic abnormalities or the woman is age 35 or over (Brambati & Tului, 2005). It is 99% accurate in diagnosing genetic problems.

GENETIC COUNSELING Even before pregnancy, couples whose family history places them at risk for having children with genetic disorders may seek *genetic counseling,* which involves analyzing the family history and genotypes of prospective parents to identify possible risks (Coughlin, 2009). Those with risks that merit genetic counseling include persons who have an inherited genetic condition or a close relative who has one; couples with a history of miscarriages or infertility; and older couples (women over 35 and men over 40) (Fransen et al., 2006). The decision to obtain genetic counseling may be difficult, because the results may require the couple to make the choice between trying to become pregnant and risking that the child will have a genetic disorder, or deciding not to pursue pregnancy. However, the knowledge obtained from genetic counseling enables people to make an informed decision.

In the first step of genetic counseling, the counselor takes a comprehensive family history from each prospective parent, seeking to identify patterns that may indicate problematic recessive or X-linked genes. Then each partner provides a blood, skin, or urine sample that can be used to analyze their chromosomes to identify possible problems, such as the presence of an extra sex chromosome. With the information obtained from genetic counseling, the couple can then decide whether or not they wish to attempt pregnancy (Coughlin, 2009).

> **APPLYING YOUR KNOWLEDGE**
>
> *What ethical issues might be raised by prenatal diagnosis techniques and genetic counseling?*

WHAT HAVE YOU LEARNED?

1. What are the major features and consequences of Down syndrome?
2. How is the relation of age to chromosomal disorders different for women and men?
3. Why is an ultrasound done at the same time as an amniocentesis?
4. What are the risks and limitations of the three main techniques of prenatal diagnosis?

Infertility and Reproductive Technology

Most women of reproductive age (roughly age 15–40) who have sexual intercourse on a regular basis will become pregnant within a year or two. However, for some couples becoming pregnant is more problematic. **Infertility** is defined as the inability to attain pregnancy after at least a year of regular sexual intercourse without contraception. Rates of infertility in the United States have been remarkably consistent over the past century at about 10–15% of couples (Johnson, 2008; Marsh & Ronner, 1996).

infertility inability to attain pregnancy after at least a year of regular sexual intercourse

Causes of infertility

List the major causes of infertility for both men and women.

LEARNING OBJECTIVE **2.16**

About half the time the source of infertility is in the male reproductive system and about half the time in the female reproductive system (Jones, 2006). Among men, there are three main sources of infertility (Jequier, 2011): (1) too few sperm may be produced; (2) the quality of the sperm may be poor, due to disease or defects in the sperm manufacturing process in the testicles; or (3) the sperm may be low in *motility* (movement) and therefore unable to make it all the way up the fallopian tubes. These problems may be genetic or they may be caused by behavior such as drug abuse, alcohol abuse, or cigarette smoking. Or, they may be due simply to age—it takes three times longer for men over 40 to impregnate a partner than it does for men

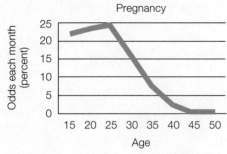

Figure 2.9 • **Fertility and maternal age.**
Why does fertility decline after the mid-twenties?

under 25, because the quantity and quality of sperm production decreases with age (Kidd et al., 2001).

Among women, infertility is most often caused by problems in ovulation (National Women's Health Information Center, 2011). Inability to ovulate can be caused by disease, or it can be due to drug abuse, alcohol abuse, or cigarette smoking, or to being extremely underweight or overweight. However, age is the most common cause of inability to ovulate (Maheshwari et al., 2008). As you learned early in the chapter, females are born with all the eggs they will ever have in their ovaries, and the quality of those eggs deteriorates gradually after puberty. Fertility decreases for women throughout their twenties and thirties but especially drops after age 40, when they become more likely to have menstrual cycles with no ovulation at all (see **Figure 2.9**).

Infertility treatments

2.17   LEARNING OBJECTIVE   Describe the current treatments for infertility.

We now know that men and women contribute equally to infertility. However, this knowledge is very recent, coming only in about the past 50 years. For most of human history in most cultures, infertility has been regarded almost exclusively as a female problem, and women suffering from it were described not as infertile but as "barren" (Marsh & Ronner, 1996). In the West, for over 2,000 years, from about the fourth century B.C.E. to the 1800s, the reigning explanation for infertility was based on a theory that both women and men must produce a seed in order for conception to occur, and that the seed was released through orgasm. This theory is discussed in detail in the **Historical Focus: How Are Babies Made?** feature on page 80. Because men generally reach orgasm a whole lot easier than women do, the main advice given to infertile couples was for the husband to give more attention to bringing sexual pleasure to his wife. As one advice writer stated in 1708, "The womb must be in a state of delight" or sex would be fruitless (Marsh & Ronner, 1996, p. 15). This theory was wrong, but at least it did no harm. Other treatments for infertility were not just ineffective but damaging to women's health, including surgery on the woman's reproductive anatomy and bloodletting (which is pretty much what it sounds like: making a cut in a blood vessel in the arm and letting blood run out until the alleged imbalance was restored).

During the course of the 20th century, treatments for infertility became more scientifically based and technologically advanced. Today there are a variety of approaches to treating infertility. These methods are used by infertile couples as well as by gay and lesbian couples and by single women. A variety of related methods for overcoming infertility are grouped under the term **assisted reproductive technologies (ART)**, including artificial insemination, fertility drugs, and in vitro fertilization (IVF). ART methods are used in response to a wide variety of infertility problems in either the male or female reproductive system, or both (Hansen et al., 2005). Most infertility treatments are quite costly, and lower SES groups may not have the same access to treatments as those in higher SES groups.

ARTIFICIAL INSEMINATION The oldest effective treatment for infertility is **artificial insemination**, which involves injecting the man's sperm directly into the woman's uterus, timed to coincide with her ovulation (Schoolcraft, 2010). It was first developed in the 19th century when physicians believed the primary cause of infertility was a too-tight cervix (the opening between the vagina and the uterus). Today, artificial insemination most often occurs as *donor insemination,* in which a man other than the woman's husband or partner provides the sperm. Most often this approach is due to problems in the husband or partner's sperm production, but increasingly this procedure is chosen

 Read the **Document** Historical Approaches to Infertility in **MyDevelopmentLab**

assisted reproductive technologies (ART) methods for overcoming infertility that include artificial insemination, fertility drugs, and IVF

artificial insemination procedure of injecting sperm directly into the uterus

by lesbian couples or single women who wish to have a child. Artificial insemination is the simplest and most effective reproductive technology, with a success rate of over 70% per trial (Wright et al., 2004).

FERTILITY DRUGS If the primary problem is that the woman cannot ovulate properly, the most common approach is to stimulate ovulation through fertility drugs. The drugs mimic the activity of the hormones that normally provoke ovulation. Usually fertility drugs stimulate both the quality and the quantity of follicles in each cycle. Over half of the women who take the drugs become pregnant within six cycles (Schoolcraft, 2010).

Fertility drugs work for many women, but they also carry serious risks, including blood clots, kidney damage, and damage to the ovaries (Lauersen & Bouchez, 2000). The purpose of the drugs is to stimulate the development of follicles in the ovaries, but often more than one follicle develops, resulting in the release of two, three, or more ova. Consequently, use of fertility drugs produces high rates of multiple births, about 10–25% depending on the drug (Schoolcraft, 2010). Usually this means twins, but there is also the possibility of triplets or more. You may have seen magazine stories or television shows about multiple births of six, seven, or eight infants and how adorable they are, but the consequences of multiple births are often tragic. The more babies conceived at once, the higher the risk for miscarriages, premature birth, and serious developmental difficulties.

IN VITRO FERTILIZATION (IVF) If fertility drugs are unsuccessful in achieving pregnancy, the next step in the ART method is **in vitro fertilization (IVF)**. In IVF, after fertility drugs are used to stimulate the growth of numerous follicles in the woman's ovaries, the ripe ova are then removed and combined with the man's sperm so that fertilization will take place. After a few days it is possible to tell which of the zygotes have developed and which have not, so the most promising two or three are placed into the woman's uterus in the hope that one will continue to develop. In vitro fertilization success rates have steadily improved in recent years, and are currently about 35% per attempt for women under age 35 (American Pregnancy Association, 2011). However, the success rate declines sharply with age and is less than 10% in women 40 or older.

When the first IVF baby was born in 1978 there were concerns that babies conceived in this way might be abnormal in some way. However, by now many of these babies have grown to adulthood without any problems. Today IVF is the basis of thousands of pregnancies per year, almost entirely in developed countries because of the technology and expense it requires.

Multiple births often receive extensive media attention, but the consequences of such births are often tragic, with higher risks of miscarriages, premature birth, and serious developmental difficulties.

APPLYING YOUR KNOWLEDGE

Because fertility drugs frequently result in multiple births, should there be legal restrictions on how they can be used?

My Virtual Child

Is your virtual child most likely a product of infertility treatment? Why or why not?

in vitro fertilization (IVF) form of infertility treatment that involves using drugs to stimulate the growth of multiple follicles in the ovaries, removing the follicles and combining them with sperm, then transferring the most promising zygotes to the uterus

HISTORICAL FOCUS   How Are Babies Made?

You probably knew long before you took this class the basics of how a human life begins: the sperm from a man, ejaculated during sexual intercourse, unites with the egg from a woman, released once every 28 days or so in the course of her menstrual cycle. However, it may surprise you to learn that this knowledge is very recent, less than 200 years old (Marsh & Ronner, 1996).

In the West, the dominant theory of conception for over two millennia was the *semence theory*: Both men and women emit "seed" during intercourse, and pregnancy takes place when the seeds meet and unite. This is not as close to modern knowledge as you might think at first glance. In this theory, both men and women were required to have an orgasm during intercourse in order for their seeds to be released. People knew, of course, that women menstruated, but they had no idea that menstruation was connected to the release of an egg by the woman. They believed that women released their eggs during orgasm, just as men release their own "seed."

The semence theory was first proposed by Hippocrates, the influential Greek physician who is widely credited with founding the medical profession around 400 B.C.E. This view remained dominant for over 2,000 years. Then in 1667 a Dutch scientist, Renier de Graaf, was the first to describe the contents in the ovaries of a mammal. De Graaf concluded that the ova of the female rabbit he examined were the sole source of new rabbits, and that the

The animalcule

same principle applied to all other mammals, including human beings. In his view, the sperm were "mere manure for the ovum," that is, they stimulated the ovum to grow and develop but did not contribute any material. This became known as the *ovist theory* of prenatal development.

However, in 1677 Anton van Leeuwenhoek, the Dutch scientist who invented the microscope, used his new device to examine sperm. The microscope seemed to Leeuwenhoek and others to show that the head of the sperm contained a tiny **animalcule,** essentially a microscopic human being (see illustration). He reached a conclusion at the opposite extreme of de Graaf's: That sperm were the sole origin of life, and the women's womb merely provided a place for the animalcule to grow gradually from microscopic size to a human baby.

Neither the ovists nor the animalculists disputed that orgasm of both man and woman was necessary in order for development to begin. For the next 200 years, both popular and medical opinion continued to hold that mutual orgasm was required to initiate the process. During those 200 years the debate between ovists and animalculists continued to rage. It was only toward the end of the 19th century that scientists learned enough about ovulation and menstruation to realize that female orgasm had nothing to do with ovulation, and that neither the ovists nor the animalculists were right about conception and prenatal development.

Infertility worldwide

2.18   **LEARNING OBJECTIVE**   Compare rates of infertility worldwide, and contrast the views of infertility in developed and developing countries.

Although worldwide the average infertility rate is about 10–15%, there is variation among countries. Especially notable is what population experts call the **infertility belt** across Central Africa (including countries such as Cameroon, the Sudan, and the Republic of the Congo), where rates of infertility are as high as 30% (refer to *Map 2.2*). Total fertility rates in Africa are substantially higher than anywhere else in the world, but they would be even higher if not for the high rates of infertility in some African countries. The reasons for high rates of infertility across the infertility belt are not well understood, but possible explanations include malnutrition and high rates of sexually transmitted infections (STIs) (World Health Organization, 2004).

Across cultures, most people wish to have children and infertility is experienced as a source of frustration and distress (van Balen & Inhorn, 2002). However, there are definite cultural differences in how seriously infertility is viewed and how it is framed socially. In the individualistic West, infertile couples often experience a sense of sadness and loss. In one Swedish study, couples seeking infertility treatments often felt frustration over missing out on a major focus of life, and they experienced a negative effect on their sexual relationship (Hjelmstedt et al., 1999). They felt that they were unable to live up to social and personal expectations for having a child. Other studies have found that infertility often creates strains in the marital relationship; but in the long

animalcule microscopic human being

infertility belt geographical area in central Africa with infertility rates as high as 30%, apparently due to high rates of malnutrition and STIs

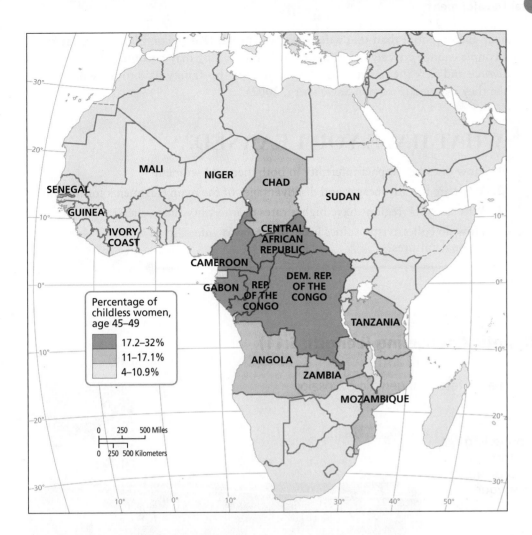

Map 2.2 • **The "Infertility Belt."** In certain countries in Central Africa, infertility rates are as high as 30%. The reasons for this are unclear although malnutrition and high rates of STIs are probable factors.

run, about half of couples report that the experience of infertility made their relationship closer and stronger (Schmidt et al., 2005).

Outside the West, cultures tend to be more collectivistic, and the social consequences of infertility are even more profound. Infertility is often deeply stigmatized. This is especially true for women, who are usually blamed for the problem and for whom motherhood is essential to their identity and their place within the social world (Inhorn & van Balen, 2002; Sembuya, 2010). In many cultures, infertility means much more than that the couple will miss out on the joys of raising a child. It may mean that there will be no one to continue the family tradition of remembering and worshipping the ancestors, a responsibility that often falls on the oldest son, especially in Asian and African cultures. It may also mean that the status of the wife is lowered in relation to her husband, her in-laws, and the community, because infertility is viewed more as her failure than his. Even if she has a daughter, she may still be seen as inadequate if she fails to produce a son. This is ironic because, as we discussed earlier in the chapter, biologically it is the father and not the mother who determines the sex of the child.

Few people in developing countries have access to reproductive technologies like fertility drugs and IVF. Women may try herbal remedies provided by a midwife. Others may seek supernatural remedies. For example, in Ghana women often consult a shaman (religious leader believed to have special powers), who focuses on trying to appease the wrath of the gods believed to be inflicting infertility on the woman as a punishment (Leonard, 2002).

If infertility persists, it is viewed in many cultures as grounds for the husband to divorce his wife or take another wife. For example, in Vietnam it is generally accepted that if a man's wife is infertile he will attempt to have a child with another "wife," even though having more than one wife is actually illegal (Pashigian, 2002). In Cameroon, if a couple cannot conceive a child, the husband's family may encourage him to obtain a divorce and seek the return of the "bride-wealth" his family paid to the wife's family when they married (Feldman-Salvelsberg, 2002).

WHAT HAVE YOU LEARNED?

1. How does age impact infertility in both men and women?
2. What are the advantages and disadvantages of the main treatments for infertility?
3. Why do some regions have higher rates of infertility than others?
4. How do collectivistic values influence the way infertility is viewed in some traditional cultures?

Section 3 VIDEO GUIDE   Genetic Counseling (Length: 5:11)

In this video an interview is conducted with a professional genetic counselor.

1. What are your thoughts on genetic counseling after viewing this clip? Did you have any thoughts or opinions on genetic counseling prior to viewing the clip? If so, did viewing this clip change your opinion?

2. Would you/Did you seek genetic counseling during your pregnancy? Why or why not? Would you recommend it to others?

3. The professional interviewed in this clip lists several reasons why individuals might consider genetic counseling. List and describe at least three of these reasons.

◉—⌐ **Watch** the **Video** Genetic Counseling
in **MyDevelopmentLab**

Summing Up

((•—[**Listen** to an audio file of your chapter in **MyDevelopmentLab**

SECTION 1   GENETIC INFLUENCES ON DEVELOPMENT

2.1 Distinguish between genotype and phenotype and identify the different forms of genetic inheritance.

There are 46 chromosomes in the human genome, organized into 23 pairs. The totality of an individual's genes is the genotype, and the person's actual characteristics are called the phenotype. Genotype and phenotype may be different, due to dominant–recessive inheritance, incomplete dominance, and environmental influences. Most human characteristics are polygenic, meaning that they are influenced by multiple genes rather than just one.

2.2 Describe the sex chromosomes and identify what makes them different from other chromosomes.

The sex chromosomes determine whether the person will be male or female. In the female this pair is called XX; in the male, XY. Having only one X chromosome makes males more vulnerable than females to a variety of recessive disorders that are linked to the X chromosome.

2.3 Describe how behavior geneticists use heritability estimates and concordance rates in their research.

Heritability estimates indicate the degree to which a characteristic is believed to be influenced by genes within a specific population. Concordance rates indicate the degree of similarity between people with different amounts of their genes in common, for example MZ and DZ twins.

2.4 Describe how the concept of epigenesis frames gene–environment interactions, and connect epigenesis to the concept of reaction range.

Epigenesis is the concept that development results from bidirectional interactions between genotype and environment. The concept of reaction range also involves gene-environment interactions, because it means that genes set a range for development and environment determines where development falls within that range.

2.5 Explain how the theory of genotype → environment effects casts new light on the old nature–nurture debate.

Rather than viewing nature and nurture as separate forces, this theory proposes that genes influence environments through three types of genotype → environment effects: passive (parents provide both genes and environment to their children); evocative (children evoke responses from those who care for them); and active (children seek out an environment that corresponds to their genotype). The three types of effects operate throughout the life span and their relative balance changes with time.

2.6 Outline the process of meiosis in the formation of reproductive cells and specify how the process differs for males and females.

In meiosis, cells that begin with 23 pairs of chromosomes split and replicate repeatedly until they form four gametes, each with 23 individual chromosomes. In males the outcome of meiosis is four viable sperm, but in females meiosis produces only one viable ovum. Also, males produce millions of sperm daily beginning in puberty, whereas females produce all the eggs they will ever have while still in their mother's womb.

2.7 Describe the process of fertilization and conception.

About 14 days into a woman's cycle an ovum is released into the fallopian tube. For the next 24 hours, fertilization can occur in which the 23 chromosomes from the ovum pair-up with the 23 chromosomes from the sperm and a new cell, the zygote, is formed from the two gametes. The zygote's 46 paired chromosomes constitute the new organism's unique genotype, set once and for all at the moment of conception.

KEY TERMS

chromosomes *p. 47*	polygenic inheritance *p. 49*	heritability *p. 52*	active genotype → environment effects *p. 55*
DNA (deoxyribonucleic acid) *p. 47*	regulator gene *p. 50*	concordance rate *p. 53*	
gene *p. 47*	gene therapy *p. 50*	epigenesis *p. 53*	gametes *p. 57*
genome *p. 47*	sex chromosomes *p. 50*	reaction range *p. 54*	ovum *p. 57*
genotype *p. 47*	X-linked inheritance *p. 51*	theory of genotype → environment effects *p. 54*	meiosis *p. 57*
phenotype *p. 47*	nature–nurture debate *p. 52*		mitosis *p. 57*
dominant–recessive inheritance *p. 48*	behavior genetics *p. 52*	passive genotype → environment effects *p. 54*	crossing over *p. 58*
	monozygotic (MZ) twins *p. 52*		follicle *p. 59*
allele *p. 48*	dizygotic (DZ) twins *p. 52*	evocative genotype → environment effects *p. 55*	zygote *p. 59*
incomplete dominance *p. 48*			

SECTION 2 PRENATAL DEVELOPMENT AND PRENATAL CARE

2.8 Describe the structures that form during the germinal period, and identify when implantation takes place.

During the germinal period a ball of cells called the blastocyst forms and implants in the lining of the uterus. The blastocyst has two layers, the embryonic disk that will become the embryo of the new organism and the trophoblast that will form the supporting structures of the amnion, placenta, and umbilical cord.

2.9 Outline the major milestones of the embryonic period and identify when they take place.

During the embryonic period (3–8 weeks after conception) all the major organ systems are initially formed, except the sex organs. Rapid development of organs during this period makes it a critical period for the effects of teratogens.

2.10 Describe the major milestones of the fetal period and identify when viability occurs.

During the fetal period (week 9–birth) organ systems continue to develop and there is immense growth in size. Viability is rare before the third trimester because of the immaturity of the lungs. By 28 weeks the fetus has sleep–wake cycles similar to a newborn baby's and can remember and respond to sound, taste, and the mother's movements.

2.11 Recall some approaches to prenatal care in traditional cultures.

In traditional cultures prenatal care often includes massage as well as folk knowledge that may or may not have practical consequences. For instance, many cultures advise pregnant women to avoid certain types of food.

2.12 Summarize scientifically based information on prenatal care.

Essential elements of prenatal care include regular evaluations by a health care professional and guidelines concerning diet, exercise, and avoiding teratogens. Pregnant women are advised to gain 25–35 pounds in the course of pregnancy, and light to moderate exercise is encouraged.

2.13 Identify the major teratogens in developing countries and developed countries.

The major teratogens are malnutrition and infectious diseases in developing countries and alcohol and tobacco in developed countries. The embryonic period is a critical period for prenatal development since all the major organ systems are forming at a rapid rate. However, some teratogens can do damage during the fetal period as well.

KEY TERMS

germinal period *p. 61*	umbilical cord *p. 62*	neural tube *p. 62*	AIDS (acquired immune deficiency syndrome) *p. 70*
blastocyst *p. 62*	embryonic period *p. 62*	neuron *p. 62*	
trophoblast *p. 62*	gestation *p. 62*	fetal period *p. 63*	fetal alcohol spectrum disorder (FASD) *p. 71*
embryonic disk *p. 62*	ectoderm *p. 62*	trimester *p. 63*	
amnion *p. 62*	mesoderm *p. 62*	midwife *p. 65*	secondhand smoke *p. 72*
placenta *p. 62*	endoderm *p. 62*	teratogen *p. 68*	

SECTION 3 PREGNANCY PROBLEMS

2.14 Explain how chromosomal disorders occur.

Chromosomal disorders occur when the chromosomes fail to divide properly during meiosis. These disorders may involve the sex chromosomes or may take place on the 21st pair of chromosomes, resulting in a condition known as Down syndrome. Risks of chromosomal disorders rise with parental age.

2.15 Describe the three main techniques of prenatal diagnosis, and explain who is likely to seek genetic counseling and for what purposes.

Prenatal diagnosis may include ultrasound, amniocentesis, and chorionic villus sampling (CVS). Couples who may be at high risk for genetic disorders sometimes seek genetic counseling prior to attempting pregnancy.

2.16 List the major causes of infertility for both men and women.

Male infertility may be caused by too few sperm, poor quality of sperm, or low motility of sperm. Female infertility is most often caused by problems in ovulation. Infertility in both men and women is often due to age, but it can also be genetic or caused by behavior such as drug abuse, alcohol abuse, or cigarette smoking.

2.17 Describe the current treatments for infertility.

Treatments for infertility are termed *assisted reproductive technologies* (ART) and include artificial insemination, fertility drugs, and IVF.

2.18 Compare rates of infertility worldwide, and contrast views of infertility in developed and developing countries.

Although worldwide the average infertility rate is about 10–15%, there is variation among countries. Rates of infertility are as high as 30% in the "infertility belt" of central Africa, possibly due to high rates of malnutrition and STIs.

KEY TERMS

Down syndrome *p. 75*
ultrasound *p. 76*
amniocentesis *p. 76*

chorionic villus sampling (CVS) *p. 76*
infertility *p. 77*

assisted reproductive technologies (ART) *p. 78*
artificial insemination *p. 78*

in vitro fertilization (IVF) *p. 80*
animalcule *p. 80*
infertility belt *p. 80*

Practice Test

✓●─ Study and Review in **MyDevelopmentLab**

1. Keisha has inherited one recessive gene for the sickle-cell trait along with one normal dominant gene. As a result of this _____, she is resistant to malaria and does not have sickle-cell anemia.
   a. dominant–recessive inheritance
   b. incomplete dominance
   c. polygenic inheritance
   d. reaction range

2. Who has the greatest risk of developing hemophilia, which is an X-linked recessive disorder?
   a. a female who has one X chromosome that contains the gene for this disorder
   b. a male who has one X chromosome that contains the gene for this disorder
   c. males and females with one X chromosome that contains the gene for the disorder will have equal risk
   d. only Native Americans, due to their unique genetic makeup

3. Which of the following questions would a behavioral geneticist be most likely to ask?
   a. "Why are children in the same family so different from one another?"
   b. "Are preterm babies more likely to have learning difficulties during the school years?"
   c. "How can prenatal tests be used to detect Down syndrome?"
   d. "What effects does alcohol have on the developing organism?"

4. Why has there has been little change in the average height in Western countries over the last few decades?
   a. The population has become overweight or obese, which negatively affects height.
   b. People in Western countries have been exposed to more diseases.
   c. People have reached the upper boundary of their reaction range for height.
   d. Evolutionary influences are causing all populations to decrease in height.

5. John is short for his age and is very coordinated. Although exposed to a variety of activities, none has particularly interested him. His father, who used to wrestle when he was younger, signs John up for wrestling thinking this could be the perfect sport. He convinces John to give it a try and John goes on to become a champion wrestler. This is an example of
   a. passive genotype → environment effects.
   b. evocative genotype → environment effects.
   c. active genotype → environment effects.
   d. heritability.

6. As a result of the process of crossing over
   a. the risk of Down syndrome is increased.
   b. boys are more likely to be born with a learning disability.
   c. women are at increased risk for infertility.
   d. each child born to a set of parents is genetically unique (with the exception of identical twins).

7. S. J. is most likely to have DZ twins if
   a. she has Asian biological parents.
   b. she is in her late teens.
   c. she is concerned about gaining too much weight and severely restricts her calorie intake.
   d. her mother had DZ twins.

8. If a woman learns that her infertility problem is due to a problem with the _____ successfully implanting, something went wrong during the germinal period.
   a. zygote   c. fetus
   b. blastocyst   d. trophoblast

9. During the embryonic period
   a. the blastocyst forms.
   b. the zygote is created.
   c. the zygote attaches to the uterine wall.
   d. the nervous system develops.

10. Saad, a baby born 6 weeks prematurely, is more at risk of not surviving than Nona, a baby who is full term because Saad's _____ is/are still immature.
    a. small intestines
    b. heart
    c. lungs
    d. spleen

11. In traditional cultures, prenatal massage
    a. is usually done only when there is reason to believe that the fetus is not developing properly.
    b. is usually considered dangerous.
    c. has beneficial effects for both mother and fetus.
    d. is almost exclusively performed by the pregnant mother herself in complete isolation.

12. K. M. is an American woman of healthy weight who went to the doctor for her second prenatal checkup. What would be LEAST LIKELY recommended by her physician?
    a. to increase her fluid intake
    b. to avoid exercise as much as possible, especially aerobic activities
    c. to increase her caloric intake
    d. to be sure she is getting enough iron and folic acid in her diet

13. K. L.'s baby was born blind, deaf, and with mental retardation. It is most likely that during her pregnancy she
   a. contracted AIDS.
   b. had rubella.
   c. had a severe nutritional deficiency.
   d. ate foods that were too high in folic acid.

14. A child who has an X0 chromosomal makeup (where 0 denotes a missing chromosome where there is supposed to be a 23rd pair) will most likely:
   a. be a male with Down syndrome.
   b. be a female who will later experience problems in the development of the reproductive system.
   c. be a typical female who will not experience cognitive or physical problems.
   d. not survive past the age of 3.

15. Carissa has a family history of Down syndrome and is in her 5th week of pregnancy. She decides that she would like to find out as early as possible whether her unborn child has Down syndrome or any other genetic abnormality. What test is she most likely to get?
   a. fetal monitoring
   b. ultrasound
   c. amniocentesis
   d. chorionic villus sampling

16. Sam would be LEAST LIKELY to be infertile if
   a. his sperm have been found to be low in motility.
   b. he is under the age of 25.
   c. he smokes marijuana and binge drinks.
   d. his sperm count has been found to be low.

17. Fertility drugs
   a. lead to pregnancy in virtually all women if they take them long enough.
   b. decrease a woman's chances of having DZ twins.
   c. are also known in the medical community as in vitro fertilization.
   d. carry risks such as blood clots and kidney damage.

18. A married woman from a non-Western, collectivistic culture has been unable to have a child for over three years. Which of the following is most likely?
   a. She will have a higher status relative to her husband.
   b. She will get a lot of social support from her mother- and father-in-law.
   c. She will try IVF.
   d. She will be blamed for this "problem."

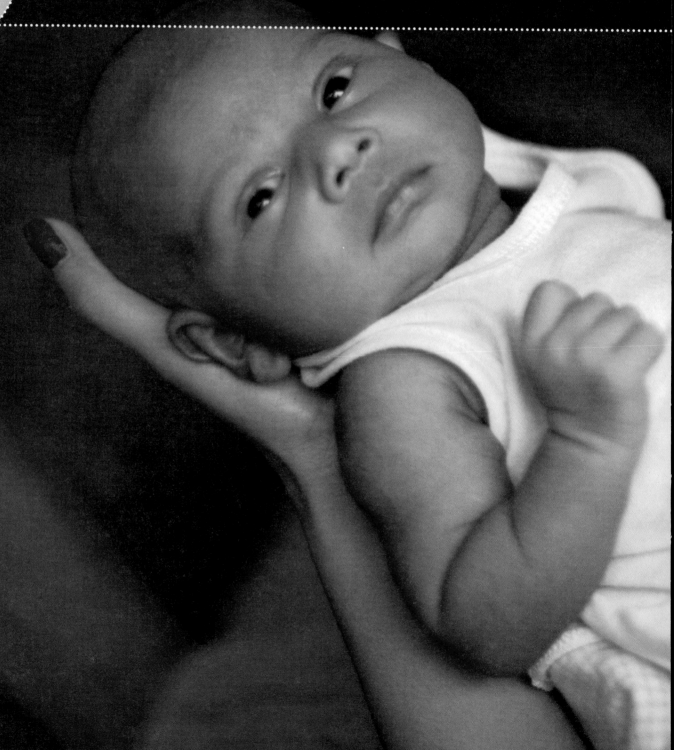

3 Birth and the Newborn Child

It is Dawn in Yucatan, Mexico, and in a small village a man makes his way quickly toward the hut of Doña Juana, the village midwife. The man's wife has been pregnant for nearly nine months, and now it seems her time has come. He awakens Doña Juana, who gathers her birth equipment and follows him to his hut.

When they arrive they greet the mother-to-be, lying comfortably on a hammock, and the women who will help during the birth process: her own mother, her aunt, and her sister. Doña Juana inquires and learns that for several hours the contractions have been weak and far apart but persistent, and now they seem to be growing stronger and closer together. Nevertheless, it appears that the birth is still some hours off, and Doña Juana and the other women settle in and begin to share tales of their own birth experiences and other births they have witnessed. Dona Juana explains the birth process to the expectant mother, demonstrating different birthing positions as she speaks. The other women— all mothers themselves—join in, demonstrating their own favorite birth positions.

The Yucatec Maya, like people in many cultures, believe that the time surrounding birth is a time of great vulnerability to evil spirits. As the birth approaches, the midwife directs the helpers to keep all doors and windows shut and stuff all cracks in the hut with rags, to keep the evil spirits out.

Some births are easy and some are difficult, and this one is going to be on the difficult side. Labor now continues for several hours, with the contractions growing steadily more frequent and intense. With each contraction, the expectant mother throws her arms back around the neck of her own mother and lifts herself up on the hammock almost to a sitting position, making use of gravity to position the baby for exiting through the birth canal. When the contraction subsides, the woman reclines again to rest as the midwife and the other birth helpers massage her abdomen, back, and legs.

By now it is nearly midday, and the midwife is becoming concerned. She fears that at this rate the woman will be too exhausted to push adequately once the time comes. Cracking a raw egg into a cup, she gives it to the woman to swallow. Immediately the woman vomits, and this brings on an especially strong contraction.

Now the contractions are reaching a new level of intensity, and the midwife instructs the woman to push as hard as she can with each one. During the contractions the other women urge the mother-to-be on with a rhythmic chorus of words: "Come on, bring it down, let's go!" In between contractions the expectant mother complains of the pain, and the other women scold her gently. "Don't be lazy! Just push like you're supposed to, and everything will be fine."

On the third contraction that follows the baby at last emerges, to exclamations of joy and relief. It's a girl! Doña Juana quickly suctions the mucus from the baby's nose and mouth so she can breathe, then lays her on the mother's abdomen. The mother smiles wearily and looks down at her new daughter. A few minutes later the placenta is delivered, and the midwife hands it carefully to a helper who will bury it later in a special ritual. Now the midwife cuts the umbilical cord and cauterizes the stump with the flame of a candle. While the helpers clean up, the mother breast-feeds her baby for the first time. (Adapted from Jordan, 1993.)

Across cultures, the birth of a new human being is usually regarded as a joyful event, worthy of celebration (DeLoache & Gottlieb, 2000). At the same time, it is often a physically challenging and potentially perilous process, for both mother and child, especially when modern medical assistance is not available. In this chapter we will look at the birth process, followed by cultural variations in birth beliefs, then at the history of birth in the West and birth variations today around the world. We will then move on to care of the newborn, before ending with the characteristics of the newborn child.

> *Across cultures, the birth of a new human being is usually regarded as a joyful event.*

LEARNING OBJECTIVES

3.1 Describe the three stages of the birth process.

3.2 Name two common types of birth complications and explain how they can be overcome by cesarean delivery.

3.3 Compare and contrast cultural variations in birth beliefs.

3.4 Explain the role of the midwife and compare and contrast cultural practices and medical methods for easing the birth process.

3.5 Summarize the history of birth in the West from the 15th century to today and compare various childbirth methods used today.

3.6 Describe the differences in maternal and neonatal mortality both within and between developed countries and developing countries.

The Birth Process

Toward the end of pregnancy, hormonal changes take place that trigger the beginning of the birth process. Most importantly, the hormone **oxytocin** is released from the woman's pituitary gland. When the amount of oxytocin in the expectant mother's blood reaches a certain threshold level, her uterus begins to contract on a frequent and regular basis, and the birth process begins.

oxytocin hormone released by pituitary gland that causes labor to begin

Stages of the birth process

Describe the three stages of the birth process.

LEARNING OBJECTIVE 3.1

The birth process is generally divided into three stages: labor, delivery of the baby, and delivery of the placenta and umbilical cord, as shown in **Figure 3.1** (Mayo Clinic Staff, 2011). There is immense variability among women in the length and difficulty of this process, depending mostly on the size of the woman and the size of the baby, but in general women's first births are longer and more difficult.

Stage 1: Labor

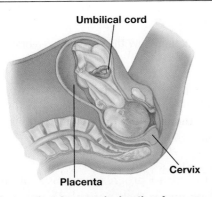

Contractions increase in duration, frequency, and intensity, causing the cervix to dilate.

Stage 2: Delivery

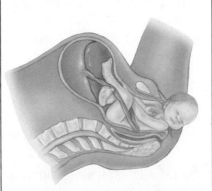

The mother pushes, and the baby crowns and then exits the birth canal and enters the world.

Stage 3: Expelling of Placenta & Umbilical Cord

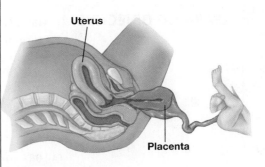

Contractions continue as the placenta and umbilical cord are expelled.

Figure 3.1 • **The three stages of the birth process.** Which stage is longest and most difficult?

91

labor first stage of the birth process, in which the cervix dilates and the muscles of the uterus contract to push the fetus into the vagina toward the cervix

delivery second stage of the birth process, during which the fetus is pushed out of the cervix and through the birth canal

The first stage of the birth process, **labor**, is the longest and most taxing stage, averaging about 12 hours for first births and 6 hours for subsequent births (Lyon, 2007). During labor, contractions of the muscles in the uterus cause the woman's cervix to dilate (open) in preparation for the baby's exit. By the end of labor, the cervix has opened to about 10 centimeters. Labor is painful because the contractions of the muscles of the uterus must occur with increasing intensity, frequency, and duration in order to dilate the cervix and move the fetus down the neck of the uterus and through the vagina. The contractions of the uterus are painful in the same way (and for the same reasons) a cramp is painful—pain results when muscles contract intensely for an extended period.

The second stage of the birth process, **delivery**, usually takes a half hour to an hour, but again there is wide variation (Murkoff & Mazel, 2008). Now the mother's efforts to push will help move the fetus through the cervix and out of the uterus. Contractions continue to help, too, but for most women the contractions are now less frequent, although they remain 60–90 seconds long. Usually the woman feels a tremendous urge to push during her contractions.

At last *crowning* occurs, meaning that the baby's head appears at the outer opening of the vagina. At this point, if she is giving birth in a hospital she may be given an *episiotomy*, which is an incision to make the vaginal opening larger. The purpose of the episiotomy is to make the mother's vagina less likely to tear as the fetus's head comes out, and to shorten this part of the birth process by 15 to 30 minutes. However, critics of episiotomies say they are often unnecessary, and in response to such criticism the rate of episiotomies in the United States declined from about 90% in 1970 to just 20% in 2000 (Cassidy, 2006). Episiotomies are quite common in other parts of the world, such as in Latin America, where they are considered routine (Althabe et al., 2005).

Now the baby has arrived, but the birth process is not yet over. In this third and final stage, contractions continue as the placenta and umbilical cord are expelled from the uterus (Lyons, 2007). This process usually happens within a few minutes, at most a half hour. The contractions are mild and last about a minute each. Although the expulsion of the placenta and umbilical cord is usually brief, care must be taken that the entire placenta comes out. If it does not, the uterus will be unable to contract properly and the mother will continue to bleed, perhaps even to the point of threatening her life. Beginning to breast-feed the newborn triggers contractions that help expel the placenta, and when advanced medical care is available the mother may be given an injection of synthetic oxytocin for the same purpose.

If the mother has had an episiotomy or her vagina has torn during delivery, she will be stitched up at this time. At this point, too, the umbilical cord must be cut and tied. There are many interesting cultural beliefs surrounding the cutting of the umbilical cord and the disposal of the placenta, as we will see later in the chapter.

Birth complications

3.2   LEARNING OBJECTIVE   Name two common types of birth complications and explain how they can be overcome by cesarean delivery.

We have just examined the birth process as it occurs if all goes well, but of course there are many times when all does not go well. Two of the most common birth complications are *failure to progress* and the *breech presentation* of the fetus.

FAILURE TO PROGRESS AND BREECH PRESENTATION   "Failure to progress" means that the woman has begun the birth process but it is taking longer than normal. The woman may stimulate progress by walking around, taking a nap, or having an enema. She may also be given herbal medicines or synthetic oxytocin (most often Pitocin) to stimulate her contractions.

Breech presentation is when the fetus is turned around so that the feet or buttocks are positioned to come first out of the birth canal, rather than the head. About 4% of fetuses present in the breech position (Martin et al., 2005). Breech births are dangerous to the baby because coming out feet- or buttocks-first can cause the umbilical cord to be constricted during delivery, potentially leading to insufficient oxygen and brain damage within minutes. Consequently, attempts are usually made to avoid a breech presentation. Midwives have long used their skills to massage the expectant mother's abdomen and turn the fetus from breech presentation to head-first (as described in Chapter 2), but it must be done with extreme care to avoid tearing the placenta from the uterine wall. Today physicians in hospitals also seek to turn breech fetuses at about the 37th week of pregnancy. Doctors often use drugs to relax the muscles of the uterus as they attempt to turn the fetus with the massage (Hofmeyr, 2002).

CESAREAN DELIVERY If failure to progress takes place during delivery, or if a fetus in breech position cannot be turned successfully, or if other problems arise in the birth process, the woman may be given a **cesarean delivery**, or **C-section**. The C-section involves cutting open the mother's abdomen and retrieving the baby directly from the uterus. The C-section has been around for a long time—according to legend it is named for the Roman emperor Julius Caesar, who supposedly was born by this method about 2,000 years ago—but until recent decades mothers nearly always died from it, even as the baby was saved. Today, with the standardization of sterile procedures and the use of antibiotics, it is very safe, although it takes women longer to heal from a cesarean than from a vaginal birth (Connolly & Sullivan, 2004). C-sections are generally safe for infants as well, and if the mother has a sexually transmitted infection, such as HIV or genital herpes, it is safer than a vaginal birth because it protects the infant from the risk of contracting the disease during the birth process. There can be complications from C-sections, such as infection, a longer hospital stay, and the inability of the mother to breast-feed if she must take antibiotics. As *Map 3.1* shows, rates of C-sections vary widely among countries and do not seem to be related to world region or level of economic development (Organisation for Economic Co-operation and Development [OECD], 2009; World Health Organization [WHO], 2010a).

breech presentation positioning of the fetus so that feet or buttocks, rather than the head, are positioned to come first out of the birth canal

cesarean delivery, or **C-section** type of birth in which mother's abdomen is cut open and fetus is retrieved directly from the uterus

APPLYING YOUR KNOWLEDGE
. . . as a Nurse

One of your patients is a pregnant woman who is HIV positive and is nervous about having a C-section delivery. What might you say to reassure her of its benefits?

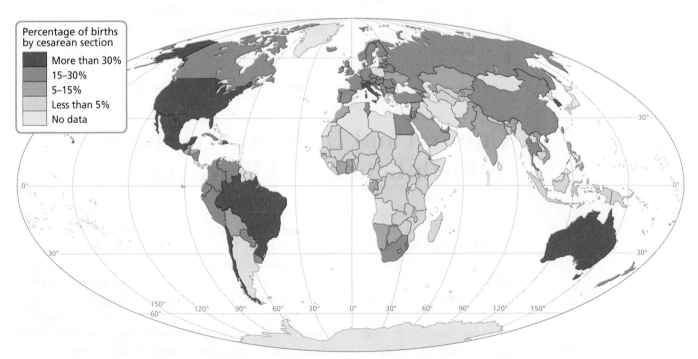

Percentage of births by cesarean section

More than 30%
15–30%
5–15%
Less than 5%
No data

Map 3.1 • **Cesarean Section Rates, Selected Countries.** Which countries have the highest rates of cesarean sections? What determines whether a country has high or low rates?

Critics of high C-section rates claim that they are performed far more than is necessary, and that they are often performed not so much to protect the mother and baby as to fatten the wallets of doctors (C-sections are a type of surgery and thus cost far more than a vaginal birth) or to make the timing of the birth predictable and convenient for the mother. However, C-section rates are not substantially higher in countries that rely mostly on private medical insurance and where doctors get paid more for doing more C-sections (like the United States), than in countries like China, Italy, and Canada that have a national health care system that does not pay doctors per C-section (WHO, 2010a). More likely, high rates of C-sections result from extreme caution by doctors seeking to avoid disaster during births.

Some of the countries that have the lowest rates of C-sections also have very low rates of birth complications, which seems to indicate that many C-sections performed in other countries are unnecessary (WHO, 2010a). Specifically, the countries that have the lowest rates of birth problems as well as the lowest rates of C-sections are the countries of northern Europe, where doctors and mothers alike share a cultural belief that birth should be natural and that technical intervention should take place only when absolutely necessary (Ravn, 2005). However, rates of C-sections are also low in countries like India and in most of Africa, where many people lack access to hospital facilities that could provide C-sections when necessary (WHO, 2010a).

For women who have had a C-section, there is a possibility of having a vaginal birth with the next baby, known as a VBAC (*vaginal birth after cesarean section*) (Shorten, 2010). As part of a more general movement in developed countries toward natural, less technological birth experiences, rates of VBAC rose in the 1980s and 1990s, and by the late 1990s about one-fourth of American women who had their first baby by C-section had a VBAC with their next baby (Roberts et al., 2007). A National Institutes of Health (NIH) panel reviewed the evidence related to the safety of VBACs in 2010 and declared that a VBAC is safe for nearly all women.

WHAT HAVE YOU LEARNED?

1. What role does oxytocin play in the birth process?
2. Why is it important that the entire placenta be expelled?
3. What are the potential dangers involved with a breech birth?
4. Which countries have the highest C-section rates and which the lowest? What explains the differences?

Cultural and Historical Variations in Birth Beliefs and Practices

Around nine months after conception, if survival has been sustained through the amazing, dramatic, and sometimes hazardous events of the germinal, embryonic, and fetal periods, a child is born. Even for the child who has made it this far, the hazards are far from over. Birth inspires especially intense beliefs in every culture because it is often difficult and sometimes fatal, to mother or child or both. The difficulties and dangers of birth are unique to the human species (Cassidy, 2006). Polar bear mothers, who weigh an average of 500 pounds, give birth to cubs whose heads are smaller than the heads of newborn humans. Even gorillas, one of our closest primate relatives, have babies who average only 2% of their mother's weight at birth, compared to 6% for humans.

Recall from Chapter 1 that over the course of human evolutionary history, the size of the brain more than tripled. Yet the rest of the female body did not grow three times larger, nor did the female pelvis triple in size. Consequently, birth became more problematic among humans than among any other animal, as it became increasingly difficult for the large-brained, big-headed fetus to make it through the birth canal out into the world.

Humans responded to this danger by developing cultural beliefs and practices intended to explain why labor is difficult and to alleviate the pain and enhance the safety of mother and child. Some of these beliefs and practices were surely helpful; others were indisputably harmful. Some of the most harmful beliefs and practices were developed not in traditional cultures but in the West, through the interventions of the medical profession from the 18th to the mid-20th century. It is only in the past 50 years that scientifically-based medical knowledge has led to methods that are genuinely helpful to mothers and babies in the birthing process.

Variations in birth beliefs

> Compare and contrast cultural variations in birth beliefs.

LEARNING OBJECTIVE 3.3

Cultural beliefs about birth are sometimes designed to protect mother and baby, and sometimes designed to isolate them and protect others. The placenta is one aspect of the birth process that is often the focus of distinct beliefs.

BELIEFS AND RITUALS SURROUNDING BIRTH As noted at the outset of the chapter, across cultures a successful birth is marked with a joyful celebration (Newton & Newton, 2003). For example, among the Ila people of Zimbabwe, women attending the birth will shower praise upon the woman having the baby. After the birth, her husband comes in to congratulate her, and other male relations also enter the hut to clasp her hand and provide her with gifts.

However, there are also cultural practices that frame birth and its aftermath with some degree of fear and wariness. Perhaps because birth is often dangerous, many traditional cultures have developed beliefs that it puts a woman in a state of being spiritually unclean (Newton & Newton, 2003). In some cultures, birth must take place away from where most people reside, so that others will not be contaminated by it. For example, among the Arapesh of New Guinea, birth is allowed to take place only at the outskirts of the village, in a place reserved for other contaminating activities such as excretion and menstruation.

Many cultures have beliefs that the mother remains unclean long after the birth and must be kept away from others, for her own sake as well as theirs (Newton & Newton, 2003). In traditional Vietnam (but not today), the mother was to avoid going out for at least 30 days after birth, in order not to contaminate the rest of the village or endanger herself or her infant; even her husband could not enter her room but could only speak to her from outside the door. Some cultures have rituals for women to purify themselves after birth, and not just non-Western cultures. In the Bible, the twelfth chapter of the book of Leviticus is devoted to ritual purification of women after childbirth, and until recent decades the Catholic church had a special ritual for new mothers to purify themselves.

Why would such beliefs develop? A frequent motivation for the development of cultural beliefs appears to be the desire for control. As the great early 20th-century anthropologist Bronislaw Malinowski observed, "the function of [magical beliefs] is to ritualize optimism, to enhance [our] victory in the faith of hope over fear . . . [people] resort to magic only where chance and circumstances are not fully controlled" (Jones & Kay, 2003, p. 103). Birth is often fraught with pain and peril. Humans, faced with this unpleasant prospect, develop beliefs they hope will enable them to avoid, or at least minimize, the pain and peril. It is a comfort to believe that if certain rituals are

THINKING CULTURALLY

In your own culture, in what ways (if any) is birth viewed as potentially contaminating? In what ways is it celebrated?

performed, the mother, the baby, and everyone else will make it through the process unscathed.

MEANINGS OF THE PLACENTA The placenta is a component of the birth process that has often carried its own special cultural beliefs. Perhaps because delivery of the placenta is potentially dangerous, many cultures have developed beliefs that the placenta itself is potentially dangerous and must be disposed of properly so that no unpleasant consequences will result (Jones & Kay, 2003). Failure to do so is believed to carry consequences as minor as pimples on the baby or as major as the baby's death.

In some cultures the methods for disposing of the placenta are clear and simple: burial, burning, throwing it in a river, or keeping it in a special place reserved for placentas. For example, among the Navajo, a Native American culture, the custom was to bury the placenta in a sacred place to underscore the baby's bonds to the ancestral land (Selander, 2011). In other cultures, the traditions surrounding the placenta are more elaborate and involve beliefs that the placenta has a spirit or soul of its own. In these cultures, the placenta is not simply thrown away but given a proper burial similar to that given to a person. For example, in several parts of the world, including Ghana, Malaysia, and Indonesia, the placenta is treated as the baby's semihuman sibling (Cassidy, 2006). Following delivery, the midwife washes the placenta and buries it as she would a stillborn infant. In some cultures the burial includes prayers to the placenta requesting it to not harm the newborn child or the mother.

In developed countries the placenta is recognized as having special value as a source of hormones and nutrients. Hospitals give their placentas to researchers, or to cosmetic manufacturers who use them to make products such as hair conditioner (Jones & Kay, 2003). Some people in Western countries even advocate consuming part of the placenta, on top of "placenta pizza" or blended into a "placenta cocktail" (Weekley, 2007)!

The (rare) practice of consuming part of the placenta is inspired by the fact that many other mammalian mothers, from mice to monkeys, eat the placenta. The placenta is full of nutrients that can provide a boost to an exhausted new mother about to begin nursing. It also contains the hormone oxytocin, which helps prevent postpartum hemorrhage. Few human cultures have been found to have a custom of eating the placenta, although in some parts of the Philippines midwives add placental blood to a porridge intended to strengthen the new mother (Cassidy, 2006). Also, in traditional Chinese medicine, dried placenta is sometimes used to stimulate maternal milk production (Tierra & Tierra, 1998).

Variations in birth practices

| 3.4 | **LEARNING OBJECTIVE** | Explain the role of the midwife and compare and contrast cultural practices and medical methods for easing the birth process. |

Around the world, the majority of women give birth at home, with the help of midwives. In the past, most birthing women in Western cultures were assisted by midwives, but this practice shifted toward doctors and hospitals in the past two centuries. There are both natural and medical ways of easing the birth process and ensuring the health and well-being of the mother and baby.

WHO HELPS? Although there is great cultural variation in beliefs about birth, there is relatively little variation among traditional cultures in who assists with the birth. Almost always, the main assistants are older women (Bel & Bel, 2007). In one early study of birth practices in 60 traditional cultures, elderly women assisted in 58 of them (Ford, 1945). Women are often attended by older female relatives, such as their mothers or aunts, or by midwives. Midwives tend to be older women who have had children themselves but are now beyond childbearing age. They have direct experience with childbirth but no longer have young children to care for, so that they are available and able when called to duty.

There are a variety of ways a woman may become a midwife (Cosminsky, 2003). In some cultures, such as in Guatemala and the Ojibwa tribe of Native Americans, she receives what she believes to be a supernatural calling in a dream or vision. In other cultures, the position of midwife is inherited from mother to daughter. Still other cultures allow women to volunteer to be midwives. Regardless of how she comes to the position, typically the woman who is to be a midwife spends several years in apprenticeship to a more experienced midwife before taking the lead in assisting with a birth. Through apprenticeship she learns basic principles of hygiene, methods to ease the birth, and practices for prenatal and postnatal care.

Midwives are usually the main birth assistants in rural areas of developing countries. Here, a midwife attends to a pregnant woman in her Cambodian village home.

Cultures have varied widely in how they regard midwives. Most often, the midwife has a highly respected status in her culture, and is held in high regard for her knowledge and skills. However, in some cultures midwives have been regarded with contempt or fear. In India, for example, midwives come from the *castes* (social status groups; see Chapter 1) that have the lowest status (Cosminsky, 2003). Birth is believed to be unclean and polluting, so only the lowest castes are deemed fit to be involved in it. In the West, midwives administered most births until the 15th through the 17th centuries when they were frequently persecuted (Ehrenreich, 2010). However, in recent decades, midwifery has become more prevalent and accepted in Western countries, as we will see in more detail later in the chapter. Though most babies in the United States today are delivered by medical doctors, an increasing number of hospitals allow for the involvement of a midwife to assist women in labor.

In developed countries today, the woman may have her spouse or partner present, whereas he would usually be excluded from the birth in developing countries (DeLoache & Gottlieb, 2000). She may have her mother present, or her mother-in-law, and one or more sisters. There may also be a midwife, especially in developing countries, and health personnel, especially in developed countries. These caregivers may assist the woman with the comfort strategies described below. Rarely in traditional cultures, men have been found to be the main birth attendants, such as in some parts of Mexico and the Philippines. More typically, not only are men not the main attendants at birth but they are forbidden from being present (Newton & Newton, 2003). However, sometimes fathers assist by holding up the mother as she leans, stands, or squats to deliver the baby (Jordan, 1993).

EASING THE BIRTH Traditional cultures have devised many ways of attempting to ease the birth process. For starters, in most traditional cultures, children are much more aware of the processes of pregnancy and of labor and delivery. They are usually present when their mothers are visited by midwives for prenatal consultations, and they grow up believing that childbirth is part of a natural process of life. Strategies for helping mothers through labor begin long before birth. As noted in Chapter 2, often the role of midwife includes prenatal visits, every few weeks beginning in about the fourth month of pregnancy. When visiting the prospective mother, the midwife typically gives her an abdominal massage. This is believed to make the birth easier, and it also allows the midwife to determine the position of the fetus. If the fetus is in the breech position, she turns it.

In addition to massaging the pregnant woman's abdomen, the midwife often gives the mother herbal tea, intended to prevent miscarriage and promote healthy development of the fetus. She also gives the mother advice on diet and exercise. In many cultures in Asia and South America, foods are classified as "hot" or "cold" (a cultural definition, not on the basis of whether they are actually hot or cold; refer back to Chapter 2), and the mother is forbidden from eating "hot" foods (Cosminsky, 2003). These food classifications have no scientific basis, but they may help to reassure the expectant mother and enhance her confidence going into the birth process.

When the woman begins to go into labor, the midwife is called, and the expectant mother's female relatives gather around her. Sometimes the midwife gives the mother-to-be medicine intended to ease the pain of labor and birth. Many cultures have used herbal medicines, but in the Ukraine, traditionally the first act of the midwife upon arriving at the home of a woman in labor was to give her a generous glass of whiskey (Newton & Newton, 2003). Expectant mothers may be fed special foods to strengthen them for the labor to come. In some cultures women are urged to lie quietly between contractions, in others they are encouraged to walk around or even to exercise.

During the early part of labor, the midwife may use the intervals between contractions to explain to the expectant mother what is to come—how the contractions will come more and more frequently, how the woman will eventually have to push the baby out, and what the woman's position should be during the birth (Bel & Bel, 2007). Sometimes the other women present add to the midwife's advice, describing or even demonstrating their own positioning when giving birth. As labor continues, often the midwife and other women present with the mother will urge her on during contractions with "birth talk," calling out encouragement and instructions, and sometimes even scolding her if she screams too loud or complains too much (Bergström et al., 2009, 2010).

The longer the labor, the more exhausted the mother and the greater the potential danger to mother and child. Consequently, cultures have created a wide variety of practices intended to speed it up, as we'll see in the **Cultural Focus: Easing Birth Among the Cuna Indians** feature. The most widespread approach, appearing in cultures in all parts of the world, is to use some kind of imagery or metaphor associated with opening up or expulsion (Bates & Turner, 2003). For example, in the Philippines a key (for "opening" the cervix) and a comb (for "untangling" the umbilical cord) are placed under the laboring woman's pillow. In parts of Southeast Asia, people assisting the laboring woman unlock all doors, windows, and cupboards, and forbid others from uttering words such as "stuck" or "fastened." In other cultures, ropes are unknotted, bottles are uncorked, or animals are let out of their pens. Several cultures use the imagery of the flower, placing flowers in the room with the woman in the hope that as the buds of the flower open, so will her cervix. These methods have no direct effect on the birth, of course, but they may give the birth mother emotional and social support.

Emotional and social support help ease the birth for women in developed countries as well (da Motta et al., 2006). Here are some strategies recommended by health professionals to ease the woman's discomfort (Mayo Clinic Staff, 2011):

- Rock in a rocking chair.
- Roll on a birthing ball.
- Breathe in a steady rhythm, fast or slow, depending on what is most comfortable.
- Take a warm shower or bath.
- Place a cool, damp cloth on the forehead.

APPLYING YOUR KNOWLEDGE
. . . as a Nurse

You have a patient who wants to include a midwife in the birthing room. The hospital where you work allows this. Why might a midwife be helpful to the mother?

- Take a walk, stopping to breathe through contractions.
- Have a massage between contractions.

Medical interventions are also common in developed countries. Women in labor often receive an **epidural**, which involves the injection of an anesthetic drug into the spinal fluid to help them manage the pain while remaining alert (Vallejo et al., 2007). If administered in the correct dosage, an epidural allows enough feeling to remain so that the woman can push when the time comes, but sometimes synthetic oxytocin has to be administered because the epidural causes contractions to become sluggish. Rates of receiving epidurals for women having a vaginal birth vary widely in developed countries, for example 76% in the United States, 52% in Sweden, 45% in Canada, and 24% in New Zealand (Lane, 2009). The reasons for these variations are not clear.

An important part of the strategy for easing the birth in many cultures is the physical position of the mother. In nearly all cultures some kind of upright position is used, most commonly kneeling or sitting, followed in prevalence by squatting or standing

epidural during birth process, injection of an anesthetic drug into the spinal fluid to help the mother manage the pain while also remaining alert

placebo effect psychological phenomenon in which people believe something affects them and it does, just by virtue of the power of their belief

My Virtual Child

Will your culture influence how you or your partner attempt to ease the process of birth?

CULTURAL FOCUS   Easing Birth Among the Cuna Indians

In many parts of the world today, birth is a social and religious event. Women give birth in their own homes, in the company of their closest female relatives and friends; the birth is assisted by a midwife whom the woman knows well. In many places the woman is believed to be especially vulnerable during birth, not just physically, but spiritually. Consequently, many cultures have developed religious beliefs and methods in an attempt to ensure the safety of mother and child.

One example was described by the French anthropologist Claude Levi-Strauss, who did ethnographic research on the Cuna Indians of Panama (Levi-Strauss, 1967). Normally, Cuna women are attended during birth by a midwife and female relatives. However, if labor becomes difficult, the midwife often calls on spiritual assistance from a *shaman*, a religious leader believed to have special powers and knowledge of the spirit world (see Chapter 2). Shamans are common in traditional cultures around the world.

Among the Cuna Indians, difficult births are believed to be caused by the spirit of the womb, Muu, who may, for no apparent reason, decide to hold on to the fetus and prevent it from coming out. The shaman's job is to invoke magic that will release the fetus from Muu's grip. He sits down next to the woman giving birth and begins by singing a long and detailed song describing why he has been summoned to help her and how he and his fellow spirits plan to launch an attack on Muu. Then, as the song continues, he calls upon the spirits of other animals for assistance, such as woodboring insects to cut through Muu's fingers and burrowing insects to help push the fetus along the birth canal.

The shaman's own spirit joins the animal spirits inside the womb to wage combat against Muu.

Does any of this do any good to the woman suffering a difficult labor? Medically, obviously not, but be careful before you dismiss the effects of the shaman's song too easily. There is abundant evidence of the **placebo effect**, which means that sometimes if people believe something affects them, it does, just by virtue of the power of their belief. In the classic example, if people are given a sugar pill containing no medicine and told it is a pain reliever, many of them will report experiencing reduced pain (Balodis et al., 2011). It was not the sugar pill that reduced their pain but their belief that the pill would reduce their pain.

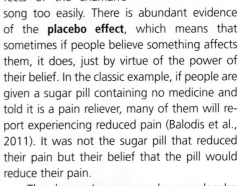

The shaman's song may have a placebo effect on the Cuna woman giving birth, if not to promote her labor then at least to ease her pain. Furthermore, according to Levi-Strauss, the shaman's song and the spiritual world it invokes allow the woman to make sense of her pain. By connecting her labor pain to the symbolic worldview of her culture, she gives it meaning and order. For a woman who believes in the spiritual world the shaman describes, "The impact of the symbolic environment is to concentrate the whole of the woman's being, psychologically and physiologically, upon the task at hand" (Bates & Turner, 2003, pp. 93–94).

(Newton & Newton, 2003). Often a woman will lean back on a hammock or bed between contractions, but take a more upright position as birth becomes imminent. Lying flat was the most prevalent delivery position in developed countries during the 20th century, but it is rarely used in traditional cultures, as it makes delivery more difficult by failing to make use of gravity. In developed countries today, many hospitals use a semisitting, half-reclining position (Murkoff & Mazel, 2008).

After birth, typically the baby is laid on the mother's abdomen until the placenta and umbilical cord are expelled from her uterus. Although there is often great joy and relief at the birth of the baby, the attention of the birth attendants and the mother is immediately directed toward delivering the placenta. A variety of strategies are used to promote the process, such as massage, medication, rituals involving opening or expelling, or attempts to make the woman sneeze or vomit (Cosminsky, 2003). Most common across cultures is the use of herbal medicines, administered as a tea or a douche (a liquid substance placed into the vagina). In developed countries, synthetic oxytocin may be used to promote contractions that will expel the placenta.

After the placenta is expelled, the umbilical cord is cut. Usually the cord is tied with thread, string, or plant fiber. In traditional cultures, some of the customs involved in cutting or treating the cord are unwittingly hazardous to the baby (Cosminsky, 2003). Tools used to cut the cord include bamboo, shell, broken glass, sickles, and razors, and they may not be clean, resulting in transmission of disease to the baby. Methods for treating the cut cord include, in one part of northern India, ash from burned cow dung mixed with dirt, which is now known to increase sharply the baby's risk of tetanus.

Variations on birth in the West

3.5   **LEARNING OBJECTIVE**   Summarize the history of birth in the West from the 15th century to today and compare various childbirth methods used today.

Given the perils of birth throughout human history one might assume that once modern scientific medicine developed, mothers and babies were safer than in the superstitious past. However, this is not quite how the story goes. On the contrary, making birth "medical" made the dangers for mothers and babies worse, not better, for *over a century*. Here we'll look first at the struggle between midwives and doctors for priority in assisting the birth. Then we'll look at the problems involved in medical approaches to birth in the 20th century, and the more favorable trends of recent decades.

HISTORICAL VARIATIONS In the West, as in other cultures, most births throughout most of history were administered by midwives (Ehrenreich, 2010). The role of midwife was widely valued and respected. Most did their work for little or no pay, although families would often present them with a gift after the birth.

This began to change in the 15th century, as a witch-hunting fervor swept over Europe. Midwives became widely suspected of being witches, and many of them were put to death (Cassidy, 2006). After the witch-hunting fervor passed, midwifery revived, but to keep out any remaining witches midwives were required to have licenses, issued by the Catholic church.

In the early 18th century a new challenge arose to the status of midwives. Medical schools were established throughout Europe, and many of the new doctors considered delivering babies to be the domain of physicians. Gradually in the course of the 18th and 19th centuries, as doctors became more numerous, they took over a steadily higher proportion of births, at first with unfortunate results for mothers as we'll see in the **Historical Focus: The Tragic History of Doctor-Assisted Births in the**

HISTORICAL FOCUS The Tragic History of Doctor-Assisted Births in the 19th Century

In the course of the 19th century, it became increasingly common for doctors in the West to be called upon to assist in births. The medical profession was gaining in prestige, and the care and assistance of expectant mothers became a distinct field within medicine called **obstetrics**. Increasingly, mothers felt they would be safer if attended by a physician. Unfortunately, medical training at the time often included virtually nothing about assisting a birth. All the doctors-to-be were men, and in many medical schools it was considered improper for a man to see a woman's genitals under any circumstances. Consequently, medical students learned about assisting a birth only from reading books and attending lectures, which sometimes included a demonstration with a mannequin playing the role of Mom and a rag doll to play the baby (Cassidy, 2006).

This may sound humorously idiotic, but the consequences of doctors' ignorance were anything but amusing for mothers and babies. For many physicians, the first birth they assisted after medical school was also the first birth they ever witnessed; for years they learned by trial and error, at the mothers' and babies' expense. Many of the doctors used forceps, a set of "iron hands" intended to help ease the baby's head out of the vagina. Forceps were first invented in the 16th century, but came into widespread use in the 18th and 19th centuries. By the end of the 19th century, half of all American births involved the use of forceps (Ehrenreich, 2010). Forceps were sometimes useful in the hands of an experienced, well-trained doctor—and still are, in rare cases—but doctors of the time were rarely experienced or well trained. Consequently, the use of forceps frequently resulted in damage to the baby or the mother. In the course of the 20th century, as the damage done by forceps was increasingly recognized, their use diminished. By the

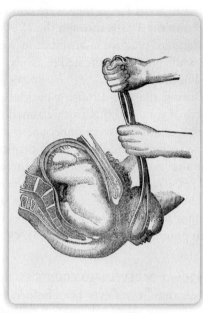

Nineteenth-century illustration of use of forceps.

early 21st century they were used in only 4% of American births (Cassidy, 2006).

Even worse than the pervasive and unnecessary use of forceps in doctor-assisted births in the 19th century was the spread of disease. At the time, it was not known that disease is transmitted by bacteria and viruses, so no one understood that it was necessary for doctors to wash their hands before examining a patient to avoid spreading infection. Consequently, hospitals became disease factories, and as more and more mothers gave birth in hospitals—hoping they would be safer there than at home—more and more of them became afflicted with diseases spread by doctors. And as medical schools in the United States and Europe began providing students with more direct involvement in births, the students, too, became carriers of disease.

Doctors and medical students would go from doing an autopsy on a cadaver to examining the vagina of a woman in labor, unwittingly spreading disease along the way. Vast numbers of women died following childbirth from what was called *childbed fever* or *puerperal sepsis*. Records show that in many European and American hospitals in the 19th century about 1 in 20 mothers died from childbed fever, and during occasional epidemics the rates were much higher (Nuland, 2003). Records from one Boston hospital in 1883 showed that 75% of mothers giving birth suffered from childbed fever, and 20% died from it (Cassidy, 2006). Few people realized that doctors were contaminating the mothers, and doctors were reluctant to accept the evidence once it began to emerge (Nuland, 2003). For centuries childbed fever had been attributed to causes such as bad air, self-poisoning by the mother's vaginal fluids, or the mother's milk gone astray in her body; doctors, who saw themselves as bringing enlightened science to the birth process, were not eager to accept that they were actually making it worse.

19th Century feature. Even in the early 20th century, midwives still assisted at about 50% of births, but by 1930 this proportion had dwindled to 15%, and by 1973 to just 1% (Cassidy, 2006).

In obstetrics, as in other branches of medicine, a more scientific basis of knowledge, care, and treatment developed during the 20th century. However, progress was slow. In the early decades of the 20th century medical training remained inadequate. A 1912 survey of 120 medical schools found that the majority of professors of obstetrics admitted that they were inadequately trained to teach their subject (Cassidy, 2006). Although hand washing became standard among doctors by the early 20th century, inadequate washing still caused many deaths. It was not until the 1940s that it became standard for obstetricians to wash their hands and also wear rubber gloves in examining women.

obstetrics field of medicine that focuses on prenatal care and birth

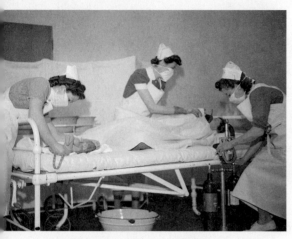

In the mid-20th century birth in developed countries often took place in a condition of "Twilight Sleep," in which the mother was heavily medicated. Shown here is a 1946 photo of a new mother under sedation after giving birth in a London hospital.

👁—⌐**Watch** the **Video** Drug-Free Deliveries in **MyDevelopmentLab**

natural childbirth approach to childbirth that avoids medical technologies and interventions

electronic fetal monitoring (EFM) method that tracks the fetus's heartbeat, either externally through the mother's abdomen or directly by running a wire through the cervix and placing a sensor on the fetus's scalp

In natural childbirth, husbands or partners often assist with breathing techniques designed to manage the pain.

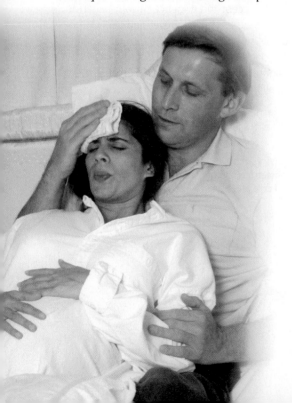

The development of antibiotics at this time cured the cases of fever from infection that did occur (Carter & Carter, 2005).

In some ways, obstetrical care of women grew still worse in the early 20th century. Doctors increasingly used drugs to relieve mothers' pain during birth. In the early 20th century a new drug method was developed that resulted in a condition that became known as *Twilight Sleep* (Cassidy, 2008). After being injected with narcotics (mainly morphine), a woman giving birth in Twilight Sleep became less inhibited, which helped her relax during her contractions and promoted dilation of her cervix, making the use of forceps less likely. Women still felt pain, but afterward they remembered none of it, so as far as they were concerned, the birth had been painless and problem free. From the 1930s through the 1960s use of Twilight Sleep and other drug methods was standard practice in hospitals in Western countries, and women nearly always gave birth while heavily medicated (Cassidy, 2006). If you live in a Western country, ask your grandmother about it.

During the late 1960s, a backlash began to develop against the medicalization of birth (Lyon, 2009). Critics claimed that medical procedures such as forceps, episiotomies, and drugs were unnecessary and had been created by the medical profession mainly to make childbirth more profitable. These critics advocated **natural childbirth** as an alternative. Although this term was first proposed in the 1930s, it was only in the 1960s and the decades that followed that a variety of drug-and-technology-free approaches to birth became popular, as part of more general trends toward greater rights for women, a greater push for consumer rights, and a growing interest in natural health practices (Thompson, 2005). 👁

BIRTH TODAY IN DEVELOPED COUNTRIES In developed countries today, the birth process is better than it has ever been before, for both mothers and babies, and parents have many choices about where they will give birth, who assists or is present with them, and how natural the delivery will be. The natural childbirth movement has had many positive effects on how birth is assisted in mainstream medicine. Although most births in developed countries still take place in a hospital, birth has become less like an operation performed by a physician and more of a collaboration between doctors, nurses (often including nurse-midwives), and mothers. Ninety-nine percent of births in the United States occur in hospitals. Most out-of-hospital births occur in women's homes, while some occur at birthing centers, and medical clinics (MacDorman et al., 2010).

Several technological developments have made the birth process less painful and safer for both mother and baby. Epidurals are a great improvement over being knocked out by Twilight Sleep and similar drug methods. The "vacuum," a cup attached to the head of the fetus and linked to an extracting machine that uses vacuum power to pull firmly but steadily, serves the same function as forceps but with less likelihood of damage to either mother or baby (WHO, 2011b). **Electronic fetal monitoring (EFM)** is another common technology used in births in developed countries. EFM tracks the fetus's heartbeat, either externally through the mother's abdomen or directly by running a wire through the cervix and placing a sensor on the fetus's scalp. In the United States, about 85% of births include EFM (Martin et al., 2005). Changes in the fetal heart rate may indicate distress and call for intervention (Sachs et al., 1999). However, heart rate changes are not easy to interpret and do not necessarily indicate distress, so use of EFM may increase the rate of unnecessary C-sections (Thacker & Stroup, 2003).

Natural childbirth methods vary in their details, but all reject medical technologies and interventions as unhelpful to the birth process or even harmful. The premise is that a substantial amount of the pain women experience in childbirth is based on the anxiety created by fear of the medical setting and lack of understanding of the birth process. Consequently, natural childbirth typically entails a nonmedical setting for birth, usually the woman's home, and includes classes in which the parents-to-be learn about the birth process. The remainder of the pain experienced in childbirth can be managed by learning relaxation and breathing techniques. Another important component of natural childbirth approaches is for the expectant mother to have the physical and emotional support of her husband or partner or others who could assist with the relaxation and breathing techniques.

No differences have been found in maternal and neonatal health outcomes between natural childbirth and medical methods (Bergström et al., 2009). However, most participants in natural childbirth methods report that it lowered their anxiety about the birth and made them feel that they were more knowledgeable about and more in control of the birth process (Westfall & Benoit, 2004). Natural childbirth methods remain popular today, especially in northern Europe. In most countries where women have the option of medical methods to lower the pain of birth most of them choose these methods, but in northern Europe the majority of women choose to make the birth experience as natural as possible, in a home rather than a hospital (Ravn, 2005).

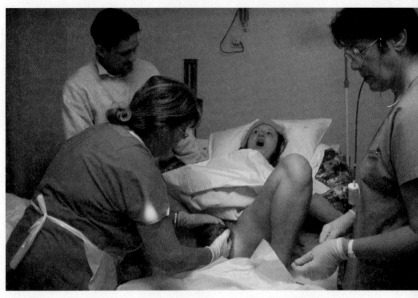

In developed countries, the husband or other family members often assist with strategies to ease the birth process. Here, an American man assists as his wife gives birth.

In recent decades midwifery has seen a revival, and currently about 10% of births in the United States are assisted by midwives (MacDorman et al., 2010). In the United States, Native Americans are the ethnic group most likely to be assisted by midwives, with Caucasians and Asian Americans being the least likely (Parker, 1994). Many midwives now receive formal training and are certified and licensed as nurse-midwives, recognizing their special training in nursing and midwifery, rather than simply learning their skills from an older midwife as in the past. In Europe, midwives are much more common than in the United States, especially in northern Europe. In Norway, for example, 96% of births are assisted by midwives (Cosminsky, 2003).

Fathers are now involved, too. Prior to the 1960s they were totally excluded from the birth, but by the late 1970s the majority of fathers were present when their wives gave birth (Simkin, 2007). In general, the father's presence seems to benefit the mother during birth (Kainz et al., 2010). When fathers are present, mothers experience slightly shorter labor and express greater satisfaction with the birth experience (Hodnett et al., 2007). For fathers, being present at the birth evokes intense feelings of wonder and love for the mother and child (Erlandsson & Lindgren, 2009). However, some fathers also experience intense fears for their health and well-being (Eriksson et al., 2007).

My Virtual Child

How does your culture influence how you or your partner will decide to give birth to your virtual child? Who will be present at the delivery?

My Virtual Child

Is your virtual child at a higher risk for infant mortality?

Cultural variations in neonatal and maternal mortality

Describe the differences in maternal and neonatal mortality both within and between developed countries and developing countries.

LEARNING OBJECTIVE **3.6**

Outside developed countries, few pregnant women have access to any modern medical technologies. As you can see from **Map 3.2,** rates of infant and maternal mortality are vastly higher in developing countries than in developed countries. In the over 80% of the world's population that lives outside developed countries, birth remains fraught with pain and peril. However, there are some hopeful signs. Maternal mortality has decreased substantially in developing countries over the past 30 years, due to improvements in nutrition and access to health care (Hogan et al., 2010; Rajaratnam et al., 2003).

APPLYING YOUR KNOWLEDGE

If you were pregnant or the partner of a pregnant woman, how "natural" would you want the childbirth to be, and why? Where would you want the baby to be delivered? Who would you like to be present?

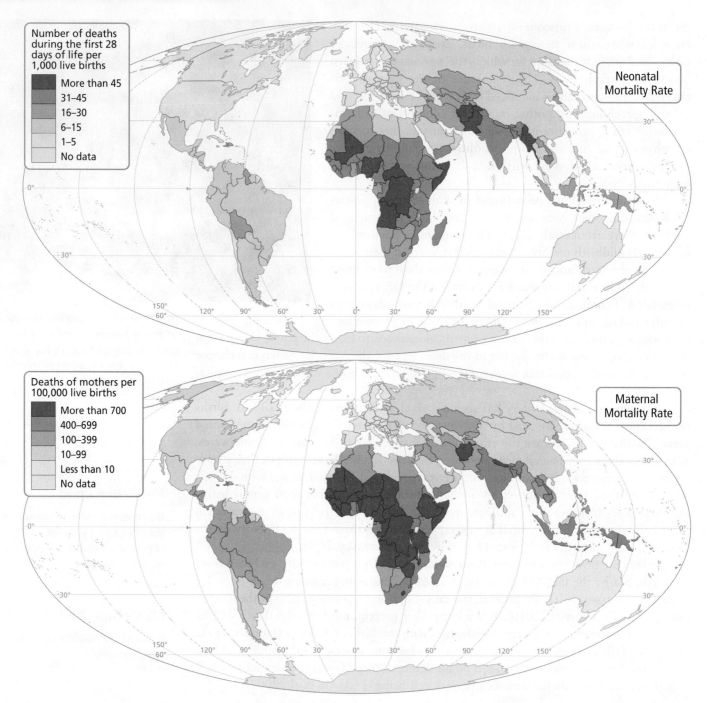

Map 3.2 • **Neonatal and Maternal Mortality Worldwide.** How do neonatal and maternal mortality rates compare? What factors might explain why mortality rates are higher in developing countries than in developed countries?

There is also substantial variation in neonatal and maternal mortality within developed countries, especially within the United States (UNDP, 2011). Neonatal mortality is over twice as high for African Americans as for Whites, due primarily to greater poverty and lower access to high-quality medical care among African Americans (Centers for Disease Control and Prevention [CDC], 2010a). However, neonatal mortality has dropped steeply in the United States since 1980, by over half among Whites and by nearly half among African Americans (U.S. Bureau of the Census, 2010). Current rates among Latinos and Asian Americans are similar to those for Whites (CDC, 2010a). For maternal mortality, the trends are in the opposite direction. Maternal mortality is over three times as high among African Americans as among Whites and has been rising steadily in both groups since 1980, for reasons that are not clear (U.S. Bureau of the Census, 2010).

WHAT HAVE YOU LEARNED?

1. Provide two examples of cultural beliefs regarding birth.
2. What are some cultural beliefs and practices concerning the disposal of the placenta?
3. Who is typically present at birth, across cultures, and who is not?
4. What position do mothers typically take when giving birth, and why?
5. What was Twilight Sleep, and what birthing methods developed as a counter-reaction to the medicalized approach to birth?
6. What are the factors influencing maternal and neonatal mortality today within both developed countries and developing countries?

Section 1 VIDEO GUIDE Labor (Length: 10:35)

This video gives an overview of labor and delivery. It contains a video simulation of the process as well as actual footage of labor and delivery from a real birth.

1. While the video narrator tells us that the actual trigger for labor is still a mystery, he provides a few possibilities. Explain those possibilities.

2. List at least three of the signals a woman may experience to let her know she is about to begin labor.

3. Describe in detail the three stages of labor.

◉─〔Watch the **Video** Labor in **MyDevelopmentLab**

LEARNING OBJECTIVES

3.7 Identify the features of the two major scales most often used to assess neonatal health.

3.8 Identify the neonatal classifications for low birth weight and describe the consequences and major treatments.

3.9 Describe neonates' patterns of waking and sleeping, including how and why these patterns differ across cultures.

3.10 Describe the neonatal reflexes, including those that have a functional purpose and those that do not.

3.11 Describe the neonate's sensory abilities with respect to touch, taste and smell, hearing, and sight.

The Neonate's Health

fontanels soft spots on the skull between loosely joined pieces of the skull that shift during birth process to assist passage through the birth canal

neonate newborn baby, up to 4 weeks old

neonatal jaundice yellowish pallor common in the first few days of life due to immaturity of the liver

At birth, babies are covered with vernix, which protects their skin.

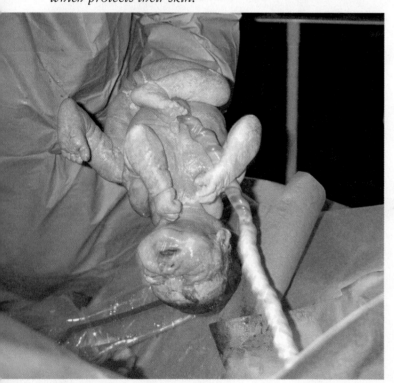

And so out comes baby at last, after nine months or so inside the womb. If you were expecting cuddly and cute from the beginning, you may be in for a surprise. The baby may be covered with fine, fuzzy hair called lanugo. This hair will be shed after a few days, fortunately. The skin may also be coated all over with an oily, cheesy substance called vernix, which protected the skin from chapping while in the womb. When my twins were born I was amazed to see that they were covered with this white substance, which I had never known about until that moment.

The head may be a bit misshapen as a consequence of being squeezed through the birth canal. One evolutionary solution to the problem of getting large-brained human fetuses out of the womb is that the skull of the infant's head is not yet fused into one bone. Instead, it is composed of several loosely joined pieces that can move around as necessary during the birth process. In between the pieces are two soft spots called **fontanels**, one on top and one toward the back of the head. It will take about 18 months before the pieces of the skull are firmly joined and the fontanels have disappeared.

It was only 9 months ago that sperm and ovum united to make a single cell, but by birth the newborn baby has 10 trillion cells! The typical newborn child, or **neonate**, is about 50 centimeters (20 in.) long and weighs about 3.4 kilograms (7.5 lb). Neonates tend to lose about 10% of their weight in their first few days, because they lose fluids and do not eat much (Verma et al., 2009). By the fifth day they start to regain this weight, and by the end of the second week most are back up to their birth weight.

About half of all neonates have a yellowish look to their skin and eyeballs in the first few days of life. This condition, known as **neonatal jaundice**, is due to the immaturity of the liver (Madlon-Kay, 2002). In most cases, neonatal jaundice disappears after a few days as the liver begins to function normally, but if it lasts more than a few days it should be treated, or it can result in brain damage (American Academy of Pediatrics [AAP] Committee on Quality Improvement, 2011). The most effective treatment is a simple one, *phototherapy,* which involves exposing the neonate to colored light; blue works best (AAP, 2011).

Measuring neonatal health

> Identify the features of the two major scales most often used to assess neonatal health.

In the transition from the fetal environment to the outside world, the first few minutes are crucial. Especially important is for neonates to begin to breathe on their own, after months of obtaining their oxygen through their mothers' umbilical cord. Most neonates begin to breathe as soon as they are exposed to air, even before the umbilical cord is cut. However, if they do not, the consequences can become severe very quickly. Deprivation of oxygen, a condition known as **anoxia**, results in swift and massive death of brain cells. If a neonate suffers anoxia for even a few minutes, the result can be permanent cognitive deficits, including mental retardation (Hopkins-Golightly et al., 2003).

Because the transition from the fetal environment is crucial and occasionally problematic, methods have been developed for assessing neonatal health. In Western countries, two of the most widely used methods are the Apgar scale and the Brazelton Neonatal Behavioral Assessment Scale (NBAS).

THE APGAR SCALE The **Apgar scale** is named after its creator, the pediatrician Virginia Apgar (1953). The letters *APGAR* also correspond to the five subtests that comprise the scale: **A**ppearance (color), **P**ulse (heart rate), **G**rimace (reflex irritability), **A**ctivity (muscle tone), and **R**espiration (breathing). The neonate is rated on each of these five subscales, receiving a score of 0, 1, or 2 (see *Table 3.1*), with the overall score ranging from 0 to 10. Neonates are rated twice, first about a minute after birth and then after 5 minutes, because sometimes a neonate's condition can change quickly during this time, for better or worse.

A score of 7 to 10 means the neonate is in good to excellent condition. Scores in this range are received by over 98% of American babies (Martin et al., 2005). If the score is from 4 to 6, anoxia is likely and the neonate is in need of assistance to begin breathing. If the score is 3 or below, the neonate is in life-threatening danger and immediate medical assistance is required. In addition to their usefulness immediately after birth, Apgar scores indicate the neonate's risk of death in the first month of life, which can alert physicians that careful monitoring is necessary (Casey et al., 2001).

THE BRAZELTON SCALE Another widely used scale of neonatal functioning is the **Brazelton Neonatal Behavioral Assessment Scale (NBAS)**. The NBAS rates neonates on 27 items assessing *reflexes* (such as blinking); *physical states* (such as irritability and excitability),

TABLE 3.1 The Apgar Scale

Total Score: 7–10 = Good to excellent condition; 4–6 = Requires assistance to breathe; 3 or below = Life-threatening danger

Score	0	1	2
Appearance (Body color)	Blue and pale	Body pink, but extremities blue	Entire body pink
Pulse (Heart rate)	Absent	Slow—less than 100 beats per minute	Fast—100–140 beats per minute
Grimace (Reflex irritability)	No response	Grimace	Coughing, sneezing, and crying
Activity (Muscle tone)	Limp and flaccid	Weak, inactive, but some flexion of extremities	Strong, active motion
Respiration (Breathing)	No breathing for more than 1 minute	Irregular and slow	Good breathing with normal crying

Source: *A Proposal for the New Method of Evaluation of the Newborn Infant* in ANESTHESIA AND ANALGESIA, Volume no. 32.

anoxia deprivation of oxygen during birth process and soon after that can result in serious neurological damage within minutes

Apgar scale neonatal assessment scale with five subtests: Appearance (color), Pulse (heart rate), Grimace (reflex irritability), Activity (muscle tone), and Respiration (breathing)

Brazelton Neonatal Behavioral Assessment Scale (NBAS) 27-item scale of neonatal functioning with overall ratings "worrisome," "normal," and "superior"

responses to social stimulation, and *central nervous system instability* (indicated by symptoms such as tremors). Based on these 27 items, the neonate receives an overall rating of "worrisome," "normal," or "superior" (Nugent & Brazelton, 2000; Nugent et al., 2009).

In contrast to the Apgar scale, which is administered immediately after birth, the NBAS is usually performed about a day after birth but can be given any time in the first two months. The NBAS most effectively predicts future development if it is given a day after birth and then about a week later. Neonates who are rated normal or superior at both points or who show a "recovery curve" from worrisome to normal or superior have good prospects for development over the next several years, whereas neonates who are worrisome at both points or go down from normal or superior to worrisome are at risk for early developmental problems (Ohgi et al., 2003).

For at-risk neonates as well as others, the NBAS can help inform parents about the abilities and characteristics of their infants. In one study of Brazilian mothers, those who took part in an NBAS-guided discussion of their infants a few days after birth were more likely to smile, vocalize, and establish eye contact with their infants a month later, compared to mothers in a control group who received only general health care information (Wendland-Carro et al., 1999). In an American study of full-term and preterm neonates, parents in both groups who participated in an NBAS program interacted more confidently with their babies than parents who did not take part in the program (Eiden & Reifman, 1996).

The NBAS has also been used in research to examine differences among neonates across cultures and how those differences interact with parenting practices (Nugent et al., 2009). For example, studies comparing Asian and White American neonates on the NBAS have found the Asian neonates tend to be calmer and less irritable (Muret-Wagstaff & Moore, 1989). This difference may be partly biological, but it also appears to be related to parenting differences. Asian mothers tended to respond quickly to neonates' distress and attempt to soothe them, whereas White mothers were more likely to let the neonates fuss for a while before tending to them. In another study, in Zambia, many of the infants were born with low birth weights and were rated worrisome on the NBAS a day after birth (Brazelton et al., 1976). However, a week later most of the worrisome neonates had become normal or superior on the NBAS. The researchers attributed this change to the Zambian mothers' custom of carrying the infant close to their bodies during most of the day, providing soothing comfort as well as sensory stimulation.

My Virtual Child

How do you think your virtual child will score on the NBAS? What cultural explanations can you think of to help explain the score?

Low birth weight

3.8 **LEARNING OBJECTIVE** Identify the neonatal classifications for low birth weight and describe the consequences and major treatments.

The weight of a baby at birth is one of the most important indicators of its prospects for survival and healthy development. Neonates are considered to have **low birth weight** if they are born weighing less than 2,500 grams (about 5.5 pounds). Some neonates with low birth weights are **preterm**, meaning that they were born 3 or more weeks earlier than the optimal 40 weeks after conception. Other low-birth-weight neonates are **small for date**, meaning that they weigh less than 90% of other neonates who were born at the same *gestational age* (number of weeks since conception). Small-for-date neonates are especially at risk, with an infant death rate four times higher than that of preterm infants (Regev et al., 2003).

Rates of low-birth-weight neonates vary widely among world regions (UNICEF, 2004a). As **Map 3.3** shows, the overall rate worldwide is 14%. Asia and Africa have the highest rates, and Europe the lowest. The current rates in the United States (8%) and Canada (6%) are lower than in developing regions of the world but higher than in Europe. Within the United States, rates of low birth weight are about twice as high among African Americans as among other ethnic groups, for reasons that may include

low birth weight term for neonates weighing less than 2,500 grams (5.5 lb)

preterm babies born at 37 weeks gestation or less

small for date term applied to neonates who weigh less than 90% of other neonates who were born at the same gestational age

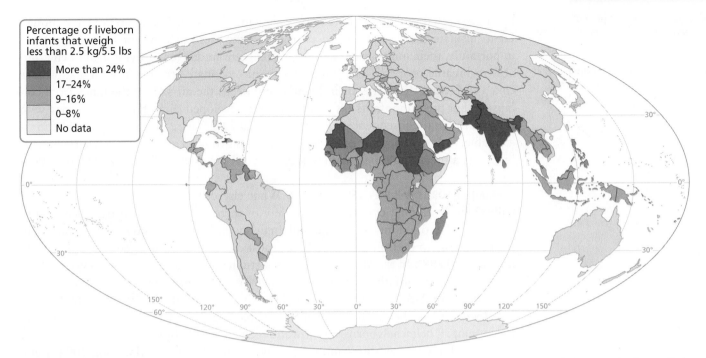

Percentage of liveborn
infants that weigh
less than 2.5 kg/5.5 lbs

- More than 24%
- 17–24%
- 9–16%
- 0–8%
- No data

lower likelihood of good prenatal care and higher levels of stress (Casey Foundation, 2010; Giscombé & Lobel, 2005).

The causes of low birth weight also vary widely among world regions. In developing countries, the main cause is that mothers are frequently malnourished, in poor health, and receive little or no prenatal care. In developed countries, the primary cause of low birth weight is the mother's cigarette smoking (Rückinger, Beyerlein, et al., 2010). Other contributors to low birth weight are multiple births (the more babies in the womb at once, the lower the birth weights), use of alcohol or other drugs during pregnancy, and young or old maternal age (under 17 or over 40) (Gavin et al., 2011).

CONSEQUENCES OF LOW BIRTH WEIGHT Low-birth-weight babies are at high risk of death in their first year of life. Even in developed countries with advanced medical care, low birth weight is the second most common cause of death in infancy, next to genetic birth defects (Martin et al., 2005). **Very-low-birth-weight** neonates, who weigh less than 1,500 grams (about 3.3 lb) at birth, and **extremely-low-birth-weight** neonates, who weigh less than 1,000 grams (about 2.2 lb) at birth, are at especially high risk for early death (Tamaru et al., 2011). Usually these neonates are born many weeks before full term. Even in the United States, which has the most advanced medical technology in the world, the chance of surviving through the first year is only 50% for a baby born before 25 weeks gestation (National Institute of Child Health and Human Development [NICHD], 2004). In developing countries, where low birth weight is most common, deaths due to low birth weight contribute to higher overall rates of infant mortality, which we will discuss in more detail later in the chapter.

Why are low-birth-weight neonates at such high risk for death? If they were small for date at birth, it was likely due to factors that interfered with their prenatal development, such as poor maternal nutrition, maternal illness or disease, or exposure to teratogens such as nicotine or alcohol (see Chapter 2). Consequently, they were already less healthy than other neonates when they were born, compounding their risk.

For preterm neonates, their physical systems are inadequately developed at birth. Their immune systems are immature, leaving them vulnerable to infection (Stoll et al., 2004). Their central nervous systems are immature, making it difficult for them to perform basic

Map 3.3 • Rates of Low Birth Weight Around the World. Why are rates so high in developing countries?

very low birth weight term for neonates who weigh less than 1,500 grams (3.3 lb) at birth

extremely low birth weight term for neonates who weigh less than 1,000 grams (about 2.2 lb) at birth

My Virtual Child

Does your environment put your virtual child at risk for being low birth weight?

Babies born with low birth weights are at risk for multiple problems. Unlike this neonate in Uganda, most low-birth-weight neonates in developing countries do not have access to advanced medical care.

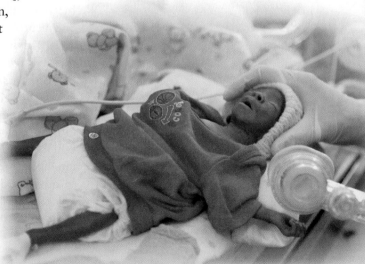

surfactant substance in lungs that promotes breathing and keeps the air sacs in the lungs from collapsing

kangaroo care recommended care for preterm and low-birth-weight neonates, in which mothers or fathers are advised to place the baby skin-to-skin on their chests for 2–3 hours a day for the early weeks of life

functions such as sucking to obtain nourishment. Their little bodies do not have enough fat to insulate them, so they are at risk of dying from insufficient body heat. Most importantly, their lungs are immature, so they are in danger of dying from being unable to breathe properly. The lungs of a mature neonate are coated with a substance called **surfactant** that helps them breathe and keeps the air sacs in the lungs from collapsing, but preterm infants often have not yet developed surfactant, a deficiency with potentially fatal consequences (Porath et al., 2011). Where advanced medical care is available, mainly in developed countries, preterm neonates are often given surfactant at birth (via a breathing tube), making their survival much more likely (Mugford, 2006).

TREATMENT FOR LOW-BIRTH-WEIGHT BABIES What else can be done for low-birth-weight babies? In developing countries, where few of them receive medical treatment, traditional methods of infant care are helpful. In many traditional cultures, young infants are strapped close to their mother's body for most of the time as she goes about her daily life (Small, 1998). In the West, this has been studied as a method called **kangaroo care**, in which mothers or fathers are advised to place their preterm newborns skin-to-skin on their chests for 2–3 hours a day during the early weeks of life (Warnock et al., 2010).

Research has shown that kangaroo care has highly beneficial effects on neonatal functioning. It helps newborns stabilize and regulate bodily functions such as heart rate, breathing, body temperature, and sleep–wake cycles (Ferber & Makhoul, 2004; Reid, 2004). Preterm infants treated with kangaroo care are more likely to survive their first year, and they have longer periods of sleep, cry less, and gain weight faster than other preterm infants (Charpak et al., 2005; Kostandy et al., 2008). Mothers benefit as well. Kangaroo care gives them more confidence in caring for their tiny, vulnerable infant, which leads to more success in breast-feeding (Feldman et al., 2003; Ferber & Makhoul, 2004). The effects of kangaroo care on low-birth-weight babies are so well established that now it is used in over three-fourths of neonatal intensive care units in the United States (Engler et al., 2002). An Italian study found that kangaroo care was practiced in two-thirds of the neonatal intensive care units (de Vonderweid & Leonessa, 2009).

The other traditional method of infant care that is helpful for low-birth-weight babies is *infant massage*. This is a widespread custom in Asia, India, and Africa, not just for vulnerable babies but for all of them (McClure, 2000). In the West, infant massage developed because low-birth-weight babies are often placed in an *isolette,* a covered, sterile chamber that provides oxygen and a controlled temperature. The isolette protects neonates from infection but also cuts them off from sensory and social stimulation. Infant massage, pioneered in the West by Tiffany Field and her colleagues (Field, 1998; Field et al., 2010), was intended to relieve the neonate's isolation.

Research has now established the effectiveness of massage in promoting the healthy development of low-birth-weight babies. Preterm neonates who receive three 15-minute massages a day in their first days of life gain weight faster than other preterm babies, and they are more active and alert (Field, 2001; Field et al., 2010). The massages work by triggering the release of hormones that promote weight gain, muscle development, and neurological development (Dieter, et al., 2003; Ferber et al., 2002; Field et al., 2010). In the United States, currently 38% of hospitals practice massage in their neonatal intensive care units (Field et al., 2010).

Kangaroo care has many benefits for low-birth-weight babies.

Although kangaroo care and massage can be helpful, low-birth-weight babies are at risk for a variety of problems throughout childhood, adolescence, and adulthood. In childhood, low birth weight predicts physical problems such as asthma and cognitive problems that include language delays and poor school performance (Davis, 2003; Marlow et al., 2005). In adolescence, low birth weight predicts relatively low intelligence-test scores and greater likelihood of repeating a grade (Martin et al., 2008). In adulthood, low birth weight predicts brain abnormalities, attention deficits, and low educational attainment (Fearon et al., 2004; Hofman et al., 2004; Strang-Karlsson et al., 2008).

The lower the birth weight, the worse the problems. Most neonates who weigh 1,500 to 2,500 grams at birth (3.3 to 5.5 lb) are likely to show no major impairments after a few years as long as they receive adequate nutrition and medical care, but neonates weighing less than 1,500 grams, the very low-birth-weight and extremely low-birth-weight babies, are likely to have enduring problems in multiple respects (Davis, 2003; Saigal et al., 2003; Taylor et al., 2000). With an unusually healthy and enriched environment, some of the negative consequences of low birth weight can be avoided, even for very low-birth-weight babies (Doyle et al., 2004; Martin et al., 2008). However, in developed countries as well as in developing countries, low-birth-weight babies are most likely to be born to parents who have the fewest resources (UNICEF, 2004a; WHO, 2011a).

WHAT HAVE YOU LEARNED?

1. Why do neonates have fontanels?
2. What does *APGAR* stand for, and what constitutes a "good" or "excellent" score on the scale?
3. How has the NBAS been used to inform parents and in neonatal research?
4. What distinguishes a small-for-date infant from a preterm infant?
5. What physical systems of preterm babies are inadequately developed at birth? What are some health implications of this?
6. What are the long-term consequences for low birth weight?

Physical Functioning of the Neonate

Physical functioning in the first few weeks of life is different in some important ways when compared to the rest of life. Neonates sleep more and have a wider range of reflexes than the rest of us do. Their senses are mostly well developed at birth, although hearing and especially sight take some weeks to mature.

Neonatal sleeping patterns

Describe neonates' patterns of waking and sleeping, including how and why these patterns differ across cultures.

LEARNING OBJECTIVE 3.9

As discussed in Chapter 2, even in the womb there are cycles of waking and sleeping, beginning at about 28 weeks gestation. Once born, most neonates spend more time asleep than awake. The average for neonates is 16 to 17 hours of sleep a day, although there is great variation, from about 10 hours to about 21 (Peirano et al., 2003).

Neonates not only sleep much of the time, but the pattern and quality of their sleep is different than it will be later in infancy and beyond. Rather than sleeping 16–17 hours straight, they sleep for a few hours, wake up for a while, sleep a few more hours, and wake up again. Their sleep–wake patterns are governed by when they get hungry, not whether it is light or dark outside (Davis et al., 2004). Of course, neonates' sleep–wake patterns do not fit very well with how most adults prefer to sleep, so parents are often sleep-deprived in the early weeks of their children's lives (Burnham et al., 2002). By about 4 months of age most infants have begun to sleep for longer periods, usually about six hours in a row at night, and their total sleep has declined to about 14 hours a day.

Another way that neonates' sleep is distinctive is that they spend an especially high proportion of their sleep in **rapid eye movement (REM) sleep**, so called because during

rapid eye movement (REM) sleep phase of the sleep cycle in which a person's eyes move back and forth rapidly under the eyelids; persons in REM sleep experience other physiological changes as well

Most neonates sleep 16–17 hours a day.

 **Simulate** the **Experiment** Stages
of Sleep in **MyDevelopmentLab**

Explore the **Concept** Virtual
Brain: Sleep and Dreaming
in **MyDevelopmentLab**

this kind of sleep a person's eyes move back and forth rapidly under the eyelids. A person in REM sleep experiences other physiological changes as well, such as irregular heart rate and breathing and (in males) an erection. Adults spend about 20% of their sleep time in REM sleep, but neonates are in REM sleep about one-half the time they are sleeping (Burnham et al., 2002). Furthermore, adults do not enter REM until about an hour after falling asleep, but neonates enter it almost immediately. By about 3 months of age, time spent in REM sleep has fallen to 40%, and infants no longer begin their sleep cycle with it.

In adults, REM sleep is the time when dreams take place. Are neonates dreaming during their extensive REM sleep periods? It is difficult to say, of course—they're not telling—but researchers in this area have generally concluded that the answer is no. Neonate's brain-wave patterns during REM sleep are different from the patterns of adults. For adults, REM brain waves look similar to waking brain waves, but for infants the REM brain waves are different than during either waking or non-REM sleep (Arditi-Babchuck et al., 2009). Researchers believe that for neonates, REM sleep stimulates brain development (McNamara & Sullivan, 2000). This seems to be supported by research showing that the percentage of REM sleep is even greater in fetuses than in neonates, and greater in preterm than in full-term neonates (Arditi-Babchuck et al., 2009; de Weerd & van den Bossche, 2003).

In addition to neonates' distinctive sleep patterns, they have a variety of other states of arousal that change frequently. When they are not sleeping, they may be alert but they may also be drowsy, dazed, fussing, or in a sleep–wake transition.

So far this description of neonates' sleep–wake patterns has been based on research in Western countries, but infant care is an area for which there is wide cultural variation that may influence sleep–wake patterns. In many traditional cultures, neonates and young infants are in physical contact with their mothers almost constantly, and this has important effects on the babies' states of arousal and sleep–wake patterns. For example, among the Kipsigis of Kenya, mothers strap their babies to their backs in the early months of life as they go about their daily work and social activities (Anders & Taylor, 1994; Super & Harkness, 2009). Swaddled cozily on Mom's back, the babies spend more time napping and dozing during the day than a baby in a developed country would. At night, Kipsigis babies are not placed in a separate room but sleep right alongside their mothers, so they are able to feed whenever they wish. Consequently, for the first year of life they rarely sleep more than three hours straight, day or night. In contrast, by 8 months of age American babies typically sleep about eight hours at night without waking.

Neonatal reflexes

<table>
<tr><td>**3.10**</td><td>**LEARNING OBJECTIVE**</td><td>Describe the neonatal reflexes, including those that have a functional purpose and those that do not.</td></tr>
</table>

reflex automatic response to certain kinds
of stimulation

 Watch the **Video** Reflexes
in **MyDevelopmentLab**

 Watch the **Video** Development
of the Grasp Reflex
in **MyDevelopmentLab**

Looking at a newborn baby, you might think that it will be many months before it can do much other than just lie there. Actually, though, neonates have a remarkable range of **reflexes**, which are automatic responses to certain kinds of stimulation. A total of 27 reflexes are present at birth or shortly after (Futagi et al., 2009). Some examples are shown in *Table 3.2*.

Some reflexes have clear survival value. Sucking and swallowing reflexes allow the neonate to obtain nourishment from the mother's breast. The **rooting reflex** helps neonates find the breast, because it causes them to turn their heads and open their mouths when touched on the cheek or the side of the mouth. The grasping reflex helps neonates hang on when something is placed in their palms. The **Moro reflex** serves a similar function, causing neonates to arch their backs, fling out their arms, and then bring their arms quickly together in an embrace, in response to a sensation of falling backward or a loud sound. Reflexes for coughing, gagging, sneezing, blinking, and shivering regulate neonates' sensory systems and help them avoid things in the environment that may be unhealthy.

TABLE 3.2 Neonatal Reflexes

Reflex	Stimulation	Response	Disappears by . . .
Stepping	Hold baby under arms with feet touching floor	Makes stepping motions	2 months
Moro	Dip downward suddenly, or loud sound	Arch back, extend arms and legs outward, bring arms together swiftly	3 months
Babkin	Press and stroke both palms	Mouth opens, eyes close, head tilts forward	3 months
Sucking	Object or substance in mouth	Sucking	4 months
Rooting	Touch on cheek or mouth	Turn toward touch	4 months
Grasping	Object placed in palm	Hold tightly	4 months
Swimming	Baby is immersed in water	Holds breath, swims with arms and legs	4 months
Tonic neck	Baby laid on back	Head turns to side, legs and arms take "fencing position" with arms and legs extended on side head is turned, flexed on the other side	5 months
Babinski	Stroke sole of foot	Foot twists in, toes fan out	8 months

rooting reflex reflex that causes the neonate to turn its head and open its mouth when it is touched on the cheek or the side of the mouth; helps the neonate find the breast

Moro reflex reflex in response to a sensation of falling backward or to a loud sound, in which the neonate arches its back, flings out its arms, and then brings its arms quickly together in an embrace

Some reflexes are precursors of voluntary movements that will develop later. The stepping reflex can be observed about a month after birth, by holding an infant under the arms at a height that allows its feet to just touch the floor. Expression of the stepping reflex disappears after about two months, but will reappear as voluntary movement later in the first year when the infant starts walking. The swimming reflex is one of the most surprising and remarkable. At about 1 month old, an infant placed face down in water will automatically hold its breath and begin making coordinated swimming movements. After 4 months this reflex has disappeared, and will become voluntary swimming movements only many years later.

Other reflexes appear to have no apparent purpose, other than their obvious entertainment value. With the *Babkin reflex,* a neonate whose palms are firmly stroked will open its mouth, close its eyes, and tilt its head forward. With the *Babinski reflex,* when the sole of the neonate's foot is stroked, it will respond by twisting its foot inward as it fans out its toes (Singerman & Lee, 2008).

Most neonatal reflexes fade away after a few months, as they are replaced by voluntary behavior. However, in the early weeks of life, reflexes serve as important indicators of normal development and healthy functioning (Schott & Rossor, 2003). Both the Apgar and the NBAS include items on reflex responses as an indirect measure of the neonate's neurological development.

The Moro reflex is present at birth, but disappears by 3 months of age.

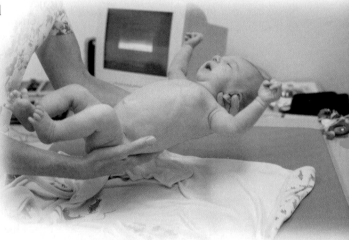

Neonatal senses

Describe the neonate's sensory abilities with respect to touch, taste and smell, hearing, and sight.

LEARNING OBJECTIVE 3.11

The neonate's senses vary widely in how well developed they are at birth. Touch and taste are well developed, even in the womb, but sight does not mature until several months after birth. Let's look at each of the neonate's senses, from the most to the least developed.

Explore the **Concept** Virtual Brain: Mechanisms of Perception in **MyDevelopmentLab**

TOUCH Touch is the earliest sense to develop. Even as early as 2 months gestation, the rooting reflex is present. By 7 months gestation, 2 months before a full-term birth, all the fetus's body parts respond to touch (Tyano et al., 2010). Most neonatal reflexes involve responses to touch.

Given that touch develops so early and is so advanced at birth, it is surprising that until recent decades, most physicians believed that neonates could not experience pain (Noia et al., 2008). In fact, surgery on neonates was usually performed without anesthetics. Physicians believed that even if neonates felt pain, they felt it only briefly, and they believed that the pain was less important than the danger of giving anesthetic medication to such a young child. This belief may have developed because neonates who experience pain (for example, boys who are circumcised) often either recover quickly and behave normally shortly afterward, or fall into a deep sleep immediately afterward, as a protective mechanism. Also, in response to some types of pain, such a being pricked on the heel, neonates take longer to respond (by several seconds) than they will a few months later (Tyano et al., 2010).

In recent years, research has established clearly that neonates feel pain. Their physiological reactions to pain are much like the reactions of people at other ages: their heart rates and blood pressure increase, their palms sweat, their muscles tense, and their pupils dilate (Warnock & Sandrin, 2004; Williams et al., 2009). They even have a specific kind of high-pitched, intense cry that indicates pain (Simons et al., 2003). Evidence also indicates that neonates who experience intense pain release stress hormones that interfere with sleep and feeding and heighten their sensitivity to later pain (Mitchell & Boss, 2002). For these reasons, physicians' organizations now recommend pain relief for neonates undergoing painful medical procedures (Noia et al., 2008). To minimize the dangers of anesthetics, nonmedical methods such as drinking sugar water can be used, or local rather than general anesthesia (Holsti & Grunau, 2010).

TASTE AND SMELL Like touch, taste is well developed even in the womb. The amniotic fluid that the fetus floats in has the flavor of whatever the mother has recently eaten, and neonates show a preference for the smells that were distinctive in the mother's diet in the days before birth (Schaal et al., 2000). In one study, when women drank carrot juice during pregnancy, their neonates were more likely to prefer the smell of carrots (Menella, 2000). Neonates exposed to the smell of their mother's amniotic fluid and another woman's amniotic fluid orient their attention to their mother's fluid (Marlier et al., 1998). In fact, neonates find the smell of their mother's amniotic fluid soothing, and cry less when it is present (Varendi et al., 1998).

Neonates and infants prefer sweet tastes to sour ones.

In addition to showing an early preference for whatever is familiar from the womb, neonates have a variety of innate responses to tastes and smells. Like most children and adults, neonates prefer sweet tastes and smells over bitter or sour ones (Booth et al., 2010). If they smell or taste something bitter or sour, their noses crinkle up, their foreheads wrinkle, and their mouths show a displeased expression (Bartoshuk & Beauchamp, 1994).

Preference for sweet tastes is present before birth. When an artificial sweetener is added to amniotic fluid, fetuses' swallowing becomes more frequent (Booth et al., 2010). After birth, preference for sweet tastes is demonstrated with a facial expression that looks like pleasure, and with a desire to consume more. As just noted, tasting something sweet can have a calming effect on neonates who are in pain. Preference for sweet tastes may be adaptive, because breast milk is slightly sweet (Porges & Lispitt, 1993). Enjoying the sweet taste of breast milk may make neonates more likely to nurse successfully.

In addition to their innate preferences, neonates quickly begin to discriminate smells after birth. At 2 days after birth, breast-feeding neonates show no difference in response between their mother's breast smell and the breast smell of another lactating mother, but by 4 days they orient more toward their mother's smell (Porter & Reiser, 2005).

HEARING Hearing is another sense that is quite well developed before birth. As noted in Chapter 2, fetuses become familiar with their mother's voice and other sounds. After birth, they recognize distinctive sounds they heard in the womb.

Neonates have an innate sensitivity to human speech that is apparent from birth (Vouloumanos & Werker, 2004). Studies on this topic typically assess neonates' preferences by how vigorously they suck on a plastic nipple; the more frequently they suck, the stronger their preference for or attention to the sound. Using this method, studies have found that neonates prefer their mother's voice to other women's voices, and their mother's language to foreign languages (Vouloumanos et al., 2010). However, they show no preference for their father's voice over other male voices (Kisilevsky et al., 2003). This may be partly because they heard his voice less while in the womb, and partly because neonates generally prefer high-pitched voices over low-pitched voices.

Neonates can distinguish small changes in speech sounds. In one study, neonates were given a special nipple that would produce a sound of a person saying "ba" every time they sucked on it (Aldridge et al., 2001). They sucked with enthusiasm for a minute or so, then their sucking pace slowed as they got used to the sound and perhaps bored with it. But when the sound changed to "ga," their sucking pace picked up, showing that they recognized the subtle change in the sound and responded to the novelty of it. Changes in neonate's sucking patterns show they also recognize the difference between two-syllable and three-syllable words, and between changes in emphasis such as when ma-*ma* changes to *ma*-ma(Sansavini et al., 1997).

In addition to their language sensitivity, neonates show a very early sensitivity to music (Levitin, 2007). At only a few days old, they respond when a series of musical notes changes from ascending to descending order (Trehub, 2001). After a few months, infants respond to a change in one note of a six-note melody, and to changes in musical keys (Trehub et al., 1985). One study even found that neonates preferred classical music over rock music (Spence & DeCasper, 1987).

Like language awareness, musical awareness begins prenatally. Neonates prefer songs their mother's sang to them during pregnancy to songs their mother sang to them for the first time after birth (Kisilevsky et al., 2003). Neonate's musical responses may simply reflect their familiarity with sounds they heard before birth, but it could also indicate an innate human responsiveness to music (Levitin, 2007). Music is frequently a part of human cultural rituals, and innate responsiveness to music may have served to enhance cohesiveness within human cultural groups.

Although neonates hear quite well in many respects, there are also some limitations to their hearing abilities that will improve over the first two years of life (Tharpe & Ashmead, 2001). One reason for these limitations is that it takes awhile after birth for the amniotic fluid to drain out of their ears. Another reason is that their hearing system is not physiologically mature until they are about two years old.

Neonates are unable to hear some very soft sounds that adults can hear (Watkin, 2011). Overall, their hearing is better for high-pitched sounds than for midrange or low-pitched sounds (Aslin et al., 1998; Werner & Marean, 1996). They also have difficulty with **sound localization**, that is, with telling where a sound is coming from (Litovsky & Ashmead, 1997). In fact, their abilities for sound localization actually become worse for the first two months of life, but then improve rapidly and reach adult levels by 1 year old (Watkin, 2011).

SIGHT Sight is the least developed of the neonate's senses (Atkinson, 2000). Several key structures of the eye are still immature at birth, specifically, (1) the muscles of the *lens,* which adjust the eyes' focus depending on the distance from the object; (2) the cells of the *retina,* the membrane in the back of the eye that collects visual information and converts it into a form that can be sent to the brain; (3) *cones,* which identify colors, and (4) the *optic nerve,* which transmits visual information from the retina to the brain. ✳

At birth, neonates' vision is estimated to range from 20/200 to 20/600, which means that the clarity and accuracy of their perception of an object 20 feet away is comparable to a person with normal 20/20 vision looking at the same object from 200 to 600 feet away (Cavallini et al., 2002). Their visual acuity is best at a distance of 8–14 inches. Vision improves steadily as their eyes mature, and reaches 20/20 sometime

APPLYING YOUR KNOWLEDGE
. . . as a Researcher

Why is it adaptive for neonates to be able to distinguish sounds such as "ba" and "ga" and stress patterns such as ma-*ma and* ma-ma?

✳─ Explore the Concept Light and the Optic Nerve in **MyDevelopmentLab**

sound localization perceptual ability for telling where a sound is coming from

APPLYING YOUR KNOWLEDGE ... *as a Parent*

Given what you have learned here about neonate's sight preferences, how would you design a mobile for your newborn's room?

Explore the **Concept** Virtual Brain: The Visual System in **MyDevelopmentLab**

in the second half of the first year. Their capacity for *binocular vision*, combining information from both eyes for perceiving depth and motion, is also limited at birth but matures quickly, by about 3–4 months old (Atkinson, 2000). Color vision matures at about the same pace. Neonates can distinguish between red and white but not between white and other colors, probably because the cones are immature (Kellman & Arterberry, 2006). By 4 months old, infants are similar to adults in their perception of colors (Alexander & Hines, 2002; Dobson, 2000).

Just as with taste and hearing, neonates show innate visual preferences (Colombo & Mitchell, 2009). ("Preference" is measured by how long they look at one visual stimulus compared to another. The longer they look, the more they are presumed to prefer the stimulus.) Even shortly after birth they prefer patterns to random designs, curved over straight lines, three-dimensional rather than two-dimensional objects, and colored over gray patterns. Above all, they prefer human faces over any other pattern (Pascalis & Kelly, 2009). This indicates that they are born with cells that are specialized to detect and prefer certain kinds of visual patterns (Csibra et al., 2000).

WHAT HAVE YOU LEARNED?

1. How are neonates' sleep patterns distinct from those of adults?
2. What function does the rooting reflex serve?
3. When do neonatal reflexes disappear?
4. Which senses are most developed at birth? Which least?
5. What does research indicate concerning neonates' experience of pain?
6. Which visual pattern do neonates prefer the most?

Section 2 VIDEO GUIDE Premature Births and the NICU (Length: 5:11)

This video contains an overview of information about premature births and the Neonatal Intensive Care Unit.

1. What are some of the advances in care that technology has provided to the NICU?

2. In this video, the speaker discusses several reasons why babies might end up in the NICU. List some of the causes that were mentioned and highlight those that can be controlled by the mother as well as those that cannot be controlled by the mother.

3. What are some of the complications (both long and short term) that premature babies might encounter?

Watch the **Video** Premature Births and the NICU in **MyDevelopmentLab**

LEARNING OBJECTIVES

3.12 Describe the cultural customs surrounding breast-feeding across cultures and history.

3.13 Identify the advantages of breast-feeding and where those advantages are largest.

3.14 Describe neonates' types of crying and how crying patterns and soothing methods vary across cultures.

3.15 Describe the extent to which human mothers "bond" with their neonates and the extent to which this claim has been exaggerated.

3.16 Describe the reasons for postpartum depression and its consequences for children.

Nutrition: Is Breast Best?

One of the most heavily researched topics regarding neonates is the question of how they should be fed. Specifically, attention has focused on whether breast-feeding should be recommended for all children, and if so, for how long. Here we examine the evolutionary and historical basis of breast-feeding, the evidence for its benefits, and the efforts to promote breast-feeding in developing countries.

Evolutionary and historical perspectives on breast-feeding

Describe the cultural customs surrounding breast-feeding across cultures and history.   **LEARNING OBJECTIVE** **3.12**

Both mother and baby are biologically prepared for breast-feeding. In the mother, the preparation begins well before birth. Early in pregnancy the **mammary glands** in her breasts expand greatly in size as milk-producing cells multiply and mature. By 4 months gestation the breasts are ready to produce milk. At birth, the mother's **let-down reflex** in her breasts causes milk to be released to the tip of her nipples whenever she hears the sound of her infant's cry, sees its open mouth, or even thinks about breast-feeding (Walshaw, 2010).

Infants are ready for breast-feeding as soon as they are born. The sucking and rooting reflexes are at their strongest 30 minutes after birth (Bryder, 2009). As noted earlier in this chapter, within a few days neonates recognize their mother's smell and the sound of her voice, which helps orient them for feeding.

Our closest primate relatives, chimpanzees, breast-feed for about four years. In the human past, archeological and historical evidence indicate that in most cultures infants were fed breast milk as their primary or sole food for two–three years, followed by two–three more years of occasional nursing. There are also indications that breast-feeding in the human past took place at frequent intervals. Among the Kung San of Central Africa, a modern hunter–gatherer culture, infants feed about every 13 minutes, on average, during their first year of life (Sellen, 2001). In traditional, nonindustrial cultures it is typical for infants to be bound to or close to their mothers almost constantly, day and night, allowing for frequent feeding. This has led anthropologists to conclude that this was probably the pattern for 99% of human history (Small, 1998).

Such frequent feeding is, of course, very demanding on the mother, and many cultures have developed ways of easing this responsibility. One common way has been substituting mothers' milk with milk from other species, especially cows or goats, two

mammary glands in females, the glands that produce milk to nourish babies

let-down reflex in females, a reflex that causes milk to be released to the tip of the nipples in response to the sound of her infant's cry, seeing its open mouth, or even thinking about breast-feeding

wet nursing cultural practice, common in human history, of hiring a lactating woman other than the mother to feed the infant

Wet nursing has a long history in Europe. Here, a wet nurse and baby in France in 1895.

species that are domesticated in many cultures and so readily available. Another way is **wet nursing**, which means hiring a lactating woman other than the mother to feed the infant. Wet nursing is a widespread custom as old as recorded human history. European records indicate that by the 1700s in some countries a majority of women employed a wet nurse to breast-feed their babies (Fildes, 1995).

In the late 1800s, manufactured substitutes such as condensed milk and evaporated milk began to be developed and marketed in the West by large corporations such as Borden and Nestlé (Bryder, 2009). The corporations claimed that these milk substitutes were not only more convenient than breast milk but also cleaner and safer. Doctors were persuaded—thanks in part to generous payments from the corporations—and they in turn persuaded new mothers to use the milk substitutes. By the 1940s only 20–30% of babies in the United States were breast-fed, and the percentage stayed in this range until the 1970s (Small, 1998). By then, scientific evidence was accumulating that breast milk was far better than any substitute, and health organizations such as UNICEF and the World Health Organization (WHO) began to wage worldwide campaigns to promote breast-feeding.

In recent years, rates of breast-feeding have risen to over 70% in the United States and Canada due to government-sponsored campaigns touting the health benefits, and breast-feeding has become nearly universal in northern Europe (Greve, 2003; Ryan et al., 2006). In developed countries, the higher the mother's age, educational level, and socioeconomic status, the more likely she is to breast-feed her infant (Schulze & Carlisle, 2010). Within the United States, rates of breast-feeding are higher among Latinos (80%) and Whites (79%) than among African Americans (65%), but rates have risen across all ethnic groups in recent years (CDC, 2008). It should be noted that these rates are for *any duration* of breast-feeding; across ethnic groups, less than half the neonates who breast-feed initially are still breast-feeding at age 6 months. Worldwide only about half of all infants are breast-fed even for a short time (UNICEF, 2011).

Benefits of breast-feeding

3.13 **LEARNING OBJECTIVE** | Identify the advantages of breast-feeding and where those advantages are largest.

My Virtual Child

In what ways does your culture support breast-feeding?

What benefits of breast-feeding have been demonstrated by scientific research in recent decades? The list is a long one, and includes:

Disease protection. Breast milk contains antibodies and other substances that strengthen the baby's immune system, and breast-feeding has been found to reduce the risk of a wide range of illnesses and diseases, such as diphtheria, pneumonia, ear infections, asthma, and diarrhea, among many others (AAP, 2005a; Godfrey & Meyers, 2009).

Cognitive development. Breast-fed infants tend to score higher than bottle-fed infants on measures of cognitive functioning, perhaps because the nutrients in breast milk promote early brain development (Kramer et al., 2008). This finding holds up even after controlling for many other factors such as parents' intelligence and education (Feldman & Eidelman, 2003). The benefits are mainly for infants who are preterm or low birth weight and consequently are at risk for cognitive difficulties (Ip et al., 2007; Schulze & Carlisle, 2010).

Reduced obesity. Breast-feeding for at least six months reduces the likelihood of obesity in childhood (AAP, 2005a; Shields et al., 2010). This is especially important in developed countries, where rates of obesity have risen dramatically in recent decades.

Better health in childhood and adulthood. In addition to protection from illnesses and disease early in life, breast-feeding promotes long-term health in a variety of ways, such as promoting bone density, enhancing vision, and improving cardiovascular functioning (Gibson et al., 2000; Owen et al., 2002). ◉

◉ **Watch** the **Video** Breastfeeding in **MyDevelopmentLab**

Mothers also benefit from breast-feeding (Godfrey & Meyers, 2009). In the days following birth, breast-feeding triggers the release of the hormone oxytocin, which reduces bleeding in the uterus and causes the uterus to return to its original size. Nursing the neonate also helps mothers return to their prepregnancy weight, because it burns 500–1,000 calories per day. Nursing has long-term effects as well on mothers' health, strengthening their bones, and reducing their risk of ovarian and breast cancer even many years later (Ip et al., 2007). Furthermore, breast-feeding acts as a natural form of birth control because it suppresses ovulation, making it less likely that a woman will conceive another child quickly once she resumes sexual contact with her husband (Bellamy, 2005). Though breast-feeding may suppress ovulation, it does not eliminate the chance that a woman will ovulate, and should not be considered a reliable form of contraception in women who do not wish to become pregnant.

How long should mothers breast-feed their infants? The World Health Organization (WHO) recommends breast-feeding for two years, with solid foods introduced to supplement breast milk at 6 months of age. As just noted, few women today breast-feed for the recommended time. However, even breast-feeding for only a few days after birth provides important benefits for infants. The first milk the mother produces is **colostrum**, a thick, yellowish liquid that is extremely rich in protein and antibodies that strengthen the neonate's immune system (Napier & Meister, 2000). Colostrum is especially important for neonates to receive, but it lasts only a few days. Perhaps because of its odd appearance, colostrum is erroneously believed in many cultures to be bad for babies. For example, in India many mothers avoid giving colostrum to their babies, substituting it with a mix of butter and honey they believe is healthier (Small, 1998).

Even in developed countries, where good health care is widely available, breast-feeding provides advantages for infants and mothers. However, in developed countries the advantages of breast-feeding are relatively small, as we will see in the **Research Focus: How Much Does Breast-Feeding Matter?** feature on page 120. In contrast, breast-feeding is crucial in developing countries, where risks of many diseases are higher and infants may not receive the vaccinations that are routine in developed countries. In developed countries, breast-feeding helps infants avoid illnesses such as gastrointestinal infections, but in developing countries breast-feeding can be literally a matter of life and death. UNICEF estimates that 1.5 million babies die each year in developing countries because they are bottle-fed rather than breast-fed (UNICEF, 2011). This is not only due to losing the advantages of breast-feeding but to making infant formula with unsafe water, as we will soon see in more detail.

If breast-feeding is so important to infants' health, why don't more mothers nurse in the early months of their children's lives? Some women have difficulty with breast-feeding, either because their infant cannot latch on properly (often a problem with low-birth-weight babies) or because they produce insufficient breast milk (Bryder, 2009). However, there are a number of practical obstacles as well. In developed countries, many mothers are employed outside the home, which makes breast-feeding more difficult (but not impossible; some use a breast pump to make milk available in their absence). Breast-feeding also makes it more difficult for fathers to take part in feeding (except via the pumped breast milk) and more challenging for fathers and mothers to share the care of the baby more or less equally, as many couples in developed countries would prefer (Genesoni & Tallandini, 2009; Wolf, 2007). One of my most cherished memories of early fatherhood is of the nights in their first few months of life when I would get up to do the 3 A.M. feeding and it would be just me and the twins, the whole world silent and sleeping around us. When fathers are able to feed the neonate it also helps mothers recover from the physical strain of giving birth (Simkin, 2007).

In developing countries, sometimes mothers have infectious diseases such as HIV/AIDS, tuberculosis, or West Nile virus that could be transmitted through breast milk, so they are advised not to breast-feed (CDC, 2002). However, only a small percentage of women have such diseases. A much larger contributor to low rates of breast-feeding

The benefits of breast-feeding are especially important in developing countries, where risks to early development are higher. Here, a mother nurses her baby in the Southeast Asian country of Laos.

My Virtual Child

If you chose to breast-feed your virtual child, how long will that child be breast-fed? How has your culture influenced that decision?

APPLYING YOUR KNOWLEDGE

What public policies might help women who choose to breast-feed?

colostrum thick, yellowish, milky liquid produced by mammalian mothers during the first days following birth, extremely rich in protein and antibodies that strengthen the baby's immune system

Numerous studies have found benefits of breast-feeding for children and mothers alike across a wide range of areas. In developing countries, breast-feeding is crucial to infant health, because these populations receive little in the way of vaccines and other medical care to protect them from widespread diseases. But what about in developed countries? How much difference does breast-feeding make to the long-term development of children?

There are so many studies of breast-feeding in developed countries that it is sometimes difficult to make sense of them all and come to a general conclusion about their results and implications. One way of boiling down a large number of studies into a comprehensible summary is a statistical method called a **meta-analysis**, which combines the results from many studies to estimate the overall conclusion to be drawn from the research.

In the most comprehensive meta-analysis of breast-feeding studies yet conducted, Stanley Ip and colleagues (2007) screened over 9,000 studies and selected nearly 500 that met their criteria for valid research methods and design. The conclusions of their meta-analysis generally support the conclusions stated in this chapter, that breast-feeding is associated with a wide variety of benefits for infants and mothers.

However, the authors of the meta-analysis also warned that readers "should not infer causality based on these findings" (Ip et al., 2007, p. v). Why not? Because most studies of breast-feeding benefits find a correlation between breast-feeding and benefits, and as we saw in Chapter 1, correlation does not mean causation. One reason to be skeptical of causation claims in studies of breast-feeding is that breast-feeding status is based on *self-selection,* meaning that women choose to breast-feed (or not), and those who choose to breast-feed tend to be different in many ways than women who do not. Most notably, the authors observed, women who breast-feed generally have more education and higher IQs. Consequently, the differences between the two groups that are attributed to breast-feeding may actually be due to their differences in education and IQ.

To get around this problem, studies sometimes *control for* education when comparing breast-feeding and non-breast-feeding groups. This means that the educational differences between the two groups are taken into account statistically. Although controlling for education is helpful in assessing more accurately the consequences of breast-feeding, it does not entirely resolve the issue. The problem is that breast-feeding and education are **confounded**, which means that they are entwined in people's lives in a way that is not easy to disentangle through statistical strategies. Education tends to be connected to a lot of other aspects of mothers' lives, such as attention to prenatal care, access to health care resources, likelihood of having a stable partner, likelihood of smoking, and household income, among others. Controlling for education in statistical analyses does not make all those other differences disappear.

So what can be done to find out accurately how much difference breast-feeding makes in babies' and mothers' outcomes? Ethical standards (see Chapter 1) probably would prohibit assigning new mothers into breast-feeding and non-breast-feeding groups, given what appear to be the benefits of breast-feeding. However, one study that approximated this design was conducted by Canadian researcher Michael Kramer and his colleagues in Belarus in Eastern Europe. The researchers gained the cooperation of 31 maternity hospitals and clinics and the study involved over 17,000 women who—note carefully—stated their intention to breast-feed. Kramer and colleagues randomly assigned the women into two groups, with one group receiving an intervention designed to promote and support breast-feeding by providing women with advice, information, and instruction, whereas the women in the control group received no intervention.

The women and their babies were then followed up by Kramer and colleagues for the next 7 years (so far). Over the course of the first year, women in the intervention group were more likely to exclusively breast-feed when their babies were 3 months old (46% vs. 11%) and more likely to be breast-feeding at any level at 12 months (19% vs. 11%), although by then breast-feeding rates were low in both groups (Kramer et al., 2008). Babies in the intervention group were less likely to have gastrointestinal infections during their first year (Kramer et al., 2008). However, at age 6, there were no differences between children in the two groups in asthma or allergy problems (Kramer et al., 2008), nor in the likelihood of obesity (Kramer et al., 2009). Perhaps the most striking finding was that, at age 6, the children in the intervention group were significantly higher in IQ, by 6 points (Kramer et al., 2008). This is especially notable because most studies on the cognitive effects of breast-feeding find that no effects remain after controlling for education and other confounding variables, unless the children were born preterm or low birth weight (Schulze & Carlisle, 2010). The result found by Kramer and colleagues seems to indicate a small but clear positive effect of breast-feeding on children's cognitive development.

However, this study, impressive as it is, is hardly the last word on this complex topic. Remember, all the mothers in the study had indicated their intention to breast-feed; all were self-selected, in other words. So, the results do not apply to mothers who do not intend to breast-feed, or to their children. Also, how important is it that the study was conducted in Belarus? Belarus is not easily classified as either a developed country or a developing country. It is part of Europe, but it is a relatively poor European country (United Nations Development Programme [UNDP], 2011), and its median levels of income, education, and health care access are nowhere near that of Western European countries. Would the same benefits from a breast-feeding intervention be found in a more developed country than Belarus? Like most studies, the research by Kramer and colleagues opens up new questions to be investigated.

is that many mothers in developing countries have been deceived, by the marketing campaigns of corporations selling infant formula, into believing the formula is actually better for infants than breast milk is.

This is false. Infant formula today is better than the condensed or evaporated milk of a century ago, because it is fortified with many of the components that make breast milk healthy, but even the best infant formula today is not as good for infants as breast milk is. Worse yet, infant formula is typically mixed with water, and in many developing countries the available water is not purified and may contain disease. Consequently, not only do infants fed with formula miss out on the health benefits of breast milk, but they are imperiled by the diseases that may be contained in the water mixed with the powdered formula.

In response to this situation, the WHO and UNICEF initiated a worldwide effort beginning in the early 1990s to promote breast-feeding (UNICEF, 2011; WHO, 2000b). These organizations have attempted to educate women about the advantages of breast-feeding for them and their infants. They have also worked with hospitals to implement programs to get breast-feeding off to a good start in the first days of the neonate's life. In this "Baby-Friendly Hospital Initiative," hospital personnel educate mothers about breast-feeding prior to the birth, help them with the first feeding shortly after birth, show them how to maintain lactation (milk flow), and organize them into breast-feeding support groups (Merewood et al., 2005; Merten et al., 2005).

The WHO/UNICEF initiative has been successful, with rates of breast-feeding increasing wherever it has been implemented (UNICEF, 2011). However, because most births in developing countries today take place in homes, most mothers are unlikely to come into contact with the Baby-Friendly Hospital Initiative. With only half of infants worldwide breast-fed for even a short time, clearly there remains much room for improvement.

meta-analysis statistical technique that combines the results from many studies into one summary statistic to evaluate the overall outcome of research in an area

confounded problem in statistical analyses when variables are entwined in people's lives in a way that is not easy to disentangle

THINKING CULTURALLY

Given that marketing infant formula in developing countries persuades many women to bottle-feed rather than breast-feed, in the mistaken belief that drinking formula will be better for their babies, should developing countries make it illegal to sell infant formula?

WHAT HAVE YOU LEARNED?

1. What cultural pattern of breast-feeding do anthropologists believe has prevailed for most of human history?
2. In what parts of the world is breast-feeding most and least prevalent today?
3. What are the advantages of breast-feeding, and why are they important?
4. What is colostrum and what role does it have in breast-feeding?
5. Is infant formula an adequate substitute for breast milk? Why or why not? Where and where not?

Social and Emotional Aspects of Neonatal Care

There are few events that change the life of an adult more than having a baby! My wife and I had our twins relatively late—I was 42 and she was 33—and by then we had been together as a couple for over 10 years. We were used to late and long dinners, and to lazy weekends waking up late, reading for hours, and taking long walks. All that went out the window when the twins were born. In the early weeks it seemed like all we did all day long—and half the night—was feed them, change them, dress them, walk them, and adore them.

Neonates need not only protection and nutrition, they need social and emotional care as well. Here we look at neonates' crying patterns and the soothing methods that cultures have developed, and at the first social contacts between neonates and others, sometimes called "bonding." In closing the chapter we examine the postpartum depression sometimes experienced by new mothers.

Crying and soothing

3.14 **LEARNING OBJECTIVE** Describe neonates' types of crying and how crying patterns and soothing methods vary across cultures.

Because human newborns are so immature and dependent in the early months of life, they need some way of signaling their needs to those who care for them, and their most frequent and effective signal is crying. Adults tend to find the crying of an infant hard to bear, so they have developed many creative ways of soothing them.

CRYING Three distinct kinds of crying signals have been identified (Wood & Gustafson, 2001):

Fussing. This is a kind of warm-up cry, when babies are mildly distressed. If no response comes soon, it develops into full-blown crying. It is fairly soft in volume, an unsteady whimper punctuated by pauses and long intakes of breath.
Anger cry. A cry that expels a large volume of air through the vocal cords.
Pain cry. Sudden onset, with no fussing to herald it. Baby takes a large intake of breath and holds it, then lets loose.

Most parents can tell the difference between an anger cry and a pain cry by the time the infant is about a month old (Zeskind et al., 1992). However, there are lots of other reasons an infant may cry, without a distinctive cry to go with them: hungry, lonely, wet or soiled diaper, tired, uncomfortable, too warm, too cold, or any other kind of frustration. Crying that falls into this general category is usually referred to as a *basic cry* or *frustration cry* (Wood & Gustafson, 2001).

Across a variety of cultures with different infant-care practices, daily crying duration follows what is known as the "crying curve" (Barr, 2009): stable for the first three weeks of life, rising steadily and reaching a peak by the end of the second month, then declining. *Figure 3.2* shows the pattern for American infants. Sometimes crying has a clear source, but there is a lot of crying in the early months for no particular reason. This is important for parents to remember, because distress in neonates often triggers distress in those around them (Out et al., 2010). *Table 3.3* presents a way to remember the normal features of crying in the first three months of life.

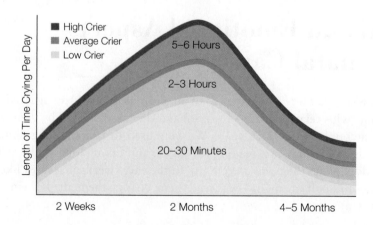

Figure 3.2 • **Daily crying duration in the early months.** In their first months of life, infants often cry for no apparent reason.

swaddling practice of infant care that involves wrapping an infant tightly in cloths or blankets

TABLE 3.3 Period of PURPLE Crying in the Early Months

A crying baby is difficult for others to bear, especially when the crying is frequent and does not appear to take place for an evident reason. Here is a way to remind parents and others of the normal features of crying in the early months of life.

P	Peak pattern	Crying peaks around age 2 months and then declines
U	Unpredictable	Crying in the early months often comes and goes unpredictably, for no apparent reason
R	Resistant to soothing	Crying may continue despite parents' best soothing efforts
P	Pain-like face	Crying babies may look like they are in pain even though they are not
L	Long lasting	Babies cry for longer in the early months, sometimes 30–40 minutes or more
E	Evening crying	Babies usually cry most in the afternoon and evening

The word **Period** means that the crying has a beginning and an end.

SOOTHING AND RESPONDING TO CRIES Although daily crying *duration* is consistent across cultures, there is wide variation in the *frequency* and *intensity* of crying in infancy. Crying episodes are longer and more intense in cultures where infants are left on their own a lot and have relatively little time when they are being carried around. Four out of 5 American infants have daily crying episodes in the early months of life of at least 15 minutes that do not have any apparent cause (Eisenberg, et al., 2008). In contrast, infants in cultures where babies are held or carried around much of the day rarely have prolonged episodes of crying. For example, in a study comparing infants in South Korea and the United States, the American infants cried for much longer periods, and this appeared to be explained by differences in parenting (Small, 1998). Korean infants spent much less of their time alone than American infants did, Korean mothers carried their infants twice as long per day as the American mothers did, and Korean mothers responded immediately to their infants' cries whereas American mothers often let the infant cry it out.

The relation between parenting and infant crying has also been demonstrated experimentally. In one study, researchers divided American mothers and their newborns into two equal groups (Hunziker & Barr, 1986). The mothers in Group A were asked to carry their babies for at least three hours a day, and mothers in Group B were not given any special instructions. Infants' mothers in both groups kept diaries of when and how long their babies cried. When the infants were 8 weeks old, the frequency of crying was the same in both groups, but the duration of crying was only about half as long in Group A, the babies who were held more often, as it was in Group B.

In traditional cultures babies are typically held for most of the day, either by their mothers or by another adult woman or an older sibling, usually a sister. When neonates in traditional cultures cry, two common responses are breast-feeding and swaddling (DeLoache & Gottlieb, 2000). Crying often signals hunger, so offering the breast soothes the baby, but even if babies are not hungry they can find consolation in suckling, in the same way that babies in developed countries are soothed by a pacifier.

In **swaddling**, babies are wrapped tightly in cloths so that their arms and legs cannot move. Often the baby is laid on a cradle board and the cloths are wrapped around the board as well as around the baby. Swaddling is an ancient practice, with evidence of it going back 6,000 years (DeMeo, 2006).

THINKING CULTURALLY

How does the framework of individualism and collectivism from Chapter 1 help to explain the Korean practice of carrying their infants much of the time and responding immediately to their cries and the American practice of leaving infants on their own much of the time and sometimes letting them "cry it out"?

APPLYING YOUR KNOWLEDGE
. . . as a Day-Care Provider

You have children of different ages in your day care. Is it healthy for young children of different ages to interact with each other? What might be the benefits for younger and older children?

Crying spells are longer and more intense in cultures where neonates are left alone for a substantial part of the day.

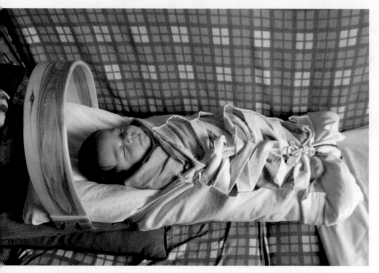

Swaddling babies to reduce crying spells is a long tradition in many cultures. Here, a Navajo baby in Arizona is swaddled to a traditional cradleboard.

Swaddling has long been widely used in many cultures, from China to Turkey to South America, in the belief that neonates find it soothing and that it helps them sleep and ensures that their limbs grow properly (van Sleuwen et al., 2007). It fell out of favor in Western cultures in the 17th century, when it became regarded as cruel and unnatural. However, swaddling has recently become more common in the West as studies have indicated that it reduces crying and does not inhibit motor development (Thach, 2009).

What else can parents and other caregivers do to soothe a crying neonate? First, of course, any apparent needs should be addressed, in case the baby is hungry, cold, tired, uncomfortable, injured, or needs a diaper change. For crying that has no apparent source, parents have devised a wide range of methods, such as (Eisenberg et al., 2008):

- Lifting baby up and holding to the shoulder
- Soothing repetitive movements such as rocking gently back and forth or riding in a car or carriage
- Soothing sounds such as singing, a fan or vacuum cleaner, or recordings of nature sounds like waves breaking on a beach
- A warm-water bath
- A pacifier or a finger to suck on
- Distraction, with some new sight or sound

The common theme of these methods appears to be offering a new source of sensory stimulation, especially something gently repetitive. When my twins were neonates we usually tried to soothe them by holding them to the shoulder or singing to them, but if those methods did not work their crying was almost always soothed by the gentle movements of the battery-operated infant seat we called their "wiggly chair." Parents with a crying neonate will often go to great lengths to make the crying stop, so there are many such items on the market today that promise to help parents achieve this goal.

There is also the option of not responding to crying, until the infant stops. For decades, developmental psychologists have debated whether ignoring crying is a good or bad idea. Some argue that ignoring it is a good idea (unless of course the infant has a clear need for food or other care), because parents who respond will reinforce the infant's crying and thus make crying more likely the next time the infant wants attention (Crncek et al., 2010; Gewirtz, 1977; Van IJzendoorn & Hubbard, 2000). Others argue that ignoring it is a bad idea, because infants whose cries are ignored will cry even more in order to get the attention they need (Bell & Ainsworth, 1972; Lohaus et al., 2004). Different studies have reported different findings, so all that can be concluded at this point is that responses to crying do not appear to be strongly related to infants' development (Alvarez, 2004; Hiscock & Jordan, 2004; Lewis & Ramsay, 1999).

About 1 in 10 Western babies have crying patterns of extreme duration, a condition known as **colic**. Babies are considered to be colicky if they fit the "rule of threes" (Barr, 2009): the crying goes on for more than 3 hours a day over more than 3 days at a time for more than 3 weeks. Colic usually begins in the second or third week of life and reaches its peak at 6 weeks, thereafter declining until it disappears at about 3 months of age (Barr & Gunnar, 2000; St. James-Roberts et al., 2003).

The causes of colic are unknown, but it exists primarily in Western cultures, where infants receive relatively little carrying time (Richman et al., 2010). Remedies for colic are also unknown. Babies with colic are inconsolable. None of the soothing methods described above work with them. Fortunately, there appear to be no long-term effects of colic, in babies' physical, emotional, or social development (Barr, 2009; Eisenberg et al., 2008). However, this may be of little comfort to parents who must endure the persistent crying of an inconsolable infant for many weeks. Colic is a risk factor for parents' maltreatment of their babies (Zeskind & Lester, 2001), so it is important for parents to seek help and support if they feel themselves reaching the breaking point.

APPLYING YOUR KNOWLEDGE
. . . as a Researcher

Considering that colic places neonates at risk for parental maltreatment, how would you design a program to prevent such maltreatment?

colic infant crying pattern in which the crying goes on for more than 3 hours a day over more than 3 days at a time for more than 3 weeks

Bonding: Myth and truth

Describe the extent to which human mothers "bond" with their neonates and the extent to which this claim has been exaggerated.

LEARNING OBJECTIVE   **3.15**

In some species, especially among birds such as geese, the first minutes after birth are a critical period for relations between mother and offspring. Geese form an instant and enduring bond to the first moving object they see, a phenomenon known as **imprinting**. Usually this first object is their mother, of course, and imprinting quickly to her promotes their survival because they will follow her everywhere she goes when they begin waddling around soon after birth. Konrad Lorenz (1957), who first identified the imprinting process, showed that geese would imprint to any moving object they saw soon after birth (including him—see the photo).

Some physicians, learning of this research, applied it to humans and asserted that in humans, too, the first few minutes and hours after birth are critical to mother–infant **bonding** (Klaus & Kennell, 1976). Without contact with the mother shortly after birth, these physicians claimed, the baby's future development is jeopardized. However, when systematic research was done to test this hypothesis, it turned out not to be true (Lamb, 1994; Redshaw, 1997; Weinberg, 2004). Humans are not birds, and they are not at risk for later emotional and social problems if they do not bond with a caregiver in the first minutes, hours, or days after birth.

Nevertheless, this is a rare example of a false idea having good effects. As described earlier in the chapter, in developing countries the birth process had become overly medical by the 1950s and 1960s. Although bonding claims were false, the possibility that they were true led hospitals all over the world to reexamine their policies of sedating the mother and separating mother and child immediately after birth (Lamb, 1994). Subsequently, during the 1970s and after, hospital policies changed so that mother, child, and even father could all be in close contact after the birth. This may not be necessary for the baby's successful later development, but there is no reason not to allow it, and it does alleviate parents' anxieties and promotes feelings of warmth and confidence in caring for their newborn child (Bergström et al., 2009).

imprinting instant and enduring bond to the first moving object seen after birth; common in birds

bonding concept that in humans the first few minutes and hours after birth are critical to mother–infant relationships

Goslings will imprint to the first moving object they see, which is usually—but not always—the mother goose. Here, the biologist Konrad Lorenz leads three goslings on a swim.

Postpartum depression

Describe the reasons for postpartum depression and its consequences for children.

LEARNING OBJECTIVE   **3.16**

Although the birth of a child is generally greeted with joy, some parents experience a difficult time emotionally in the early months of their baby's life. In one study of new mothers in 11 countries, **postpartum depression** was found at similar rates in all of them, about 10% (Oates et al., 2004). In Western countries this condition was often seen as an illness requiring possible intervention of health professionals, whereas in non-Western countries social support from family members was relied upon for making it through. Studies in the United States and the United Kingdom report that about 4% of fathers also experience postpartum depression in the months following the birth of their child (Dennis, 2004; Ramchandani et al., 2005).

postpartum depression in parents with a new baby, feelings of sadness and anxiety so intense as to interfere with the ability to carry out simple daily tasks

Across countries, about 10% of new mothers experience postpartum depression.

Low emotional states in mothers following birth may be due to rapid hormonal changes, as the high concentrations of estrogen and progesterone in the mother's body return to normal levels. However, postpartum depression is deeper and more enduring. Feelings of sadness and anxiety become so intense that they interfere with the ability to carry out simple daily tasks. Other symptoms include extreme changes in appetite and difficulty sleeping. Postpartum depression often peaks about four weeks after childbirth—long after the mother's hormones would have returned to normal levels—and in 25–50% of mothers who experience postpartum depression it lasts 6 months or longer (Beck, 2002; Clay & Seehusen, 2004).

Why do some women and not others develop postpartum depression? Women are more at risk for postpartum depression if they have had previous episodes of major depression or if they have close family members who have experienced major depression (Bloch et al., 2006). This suggests that for postpartum depression, as for other forms of depression, some people may have a genetic vulnerability to becoming depressed when they experience intense life stresses. Women are also more likely to experience postpartum depression if they lack social support from a husband or partner (Iles et al., 2011). Thus even if a mother has a genetic vulnerability to depression, it is unlikely to be expressed unless she also experiences a social and cultural context in which social support is lacking. For fathers, postpartum depression may result from the challenges of reconciling their personal and work-related needs with the demands of being a father (Genesoni & Tallandini, 2009; Ramchandani et al., 2005).

Mothers' and fathers' postpartum depression is related to children's developmental problems in infancy and beyond. Numerous studies of mothers with postpartum depression have found that their infants are more likely than other infants to be irritable, to have problems eating and sleeping, and to have difficulty forming attachments (Herrera et al., 2004; Martins & Griffin, 2000). In later development, the children are at risk for being withdrawn or displaying antisocial behavior (Nylen et al., 2006). Children of fathers with postpartum depression have been found to have similar risks for their development (Kane & Garber, 2004; Ramchandani et al., 2005).

Of course, all of these studies are subject to the research design problem we discussed in Chapter 2, of passive and evocative genotype → environment effects. That is, the children in these studies received not only their environment from their parents but also their genes, and it is difficult to tell whether the relation between their problems and their parents' depression is due to genetics or environment (the problem of passive genotype → environment effects). Also, the studies usually assume that the mother's depression affected the child, but it could also be that the mothers became depressed in part because their infant was especially irritable and difficult (evocative genotype → environment effects). However, observational studies of mothers with postpartum depression have found that they talk to and look at their infant less than other mothers, and that they also touch them less and smile less often at them (Righetti-Veltema et al., 2002). This suggests that the behavior of depressed mothers is different in ways that may affect infants, even if passive and evocative genotype → environment effects are also involved.

WHAT HAVE YOU LEARNED?

1. Describe the "crying curve." When does crying reach its peak in neonates?
2. What is the relation, if any, between parenting practices and infant crying?
3. How have claims that humans bond with their neonates influenced hospital policies in the United States?
4. What are the consequences of postpartum depression for children? Why do genotype → environment effects make it difficult to tell?

Section 3 VIDEO GUIDE Breast-feeding Practices Across Cultures (Length: 6:19)

In this video mothers, and expectant mothers, from various countries are interviewed about their views on breast-feeding.

1. Were you surprised to see that many of the women interviewed have similar reasons for breast-feeding (regardless of their culture)? What are some of the benefits of breast-feeding that they mentioned?

2. Although she was not asked the question about how she would comfort her child, how do you think the expectant mother from the United States would answer? Do you think that she would answer in a way similar to the mothers from the other countries? Would the American mother have additional options that the other mothers may not?

3. What are your thoughts on the lengths of time that the mothers planned to breast-feed and the reasons that they had for the lengths?

Watch the **Video** Breastfeeding Practices Across Cultures in **MyDevelopmentLab**

Summing Up

((•─ **Listen** to an audio file of your chapter in **MyDevelopmentLab**

SECTION 1   BIRTH AND ITS CULTURAL CONTEXT

3.1 Describe the three stages of the birth process.

The three stages of the birth process are labor, delivery, and expelling of the placenta and umbilical cord. During labor, the contractions of the muscles in the uterus cause the mother's cervix to dilate in preparation for the baby's exit. By the end of labor, the cervix has opened to about 10 centimeters. During delivery, the woman pushes the fetus through the cervix and out of the uterus. In the final stage of the birth process, contractions continue as the placenta and umbilical cord are expelled.

3.2 Name two common types of birth complications and explain how they can be overcome by cesarean delivery.

Two common birth complications are failure to progress, which occurs when the birth process is taking longer than normal, and the breech presentation of the fetus, which means the fetus is turned around so that the feet or buttocks are positioned to come first out of the birth canal. Both complications can be overcome through the use of a C-section, which today is generally safe for mothers and infants.

3.3 Compare and contrast cultural variations in birth beliefs.

Because birth is often dangerous, many traditional cultures—such as the Arapesh of New Guinea and the traditional Vietnamese—have developed beliefs that childbirth puts a woman in a state of being spiritually unclean. The placenta is often disposed of with care in traditional cultures because of beliefs that it is potentially dangerous or even semihuman.

3.4 Explain the role of the midwife and compare and contrast cultural practices and medical methods for easing the birth process.

In most cultures, women giving birth are attended by female relatives and an older woman ("midwife" or similar title) who has experience assisting in the birth process. The midwife eases birth pain through massage techniques, reassurance, and herbal medicines. In developed countries, an anesthetic drug called an epidural is often injected into a woman's spinal fluid to help manage the pain.

3.5 Summarize the history of birth in the West from the 15th century to today and compare various childbirth methods used today.

There have been attempts over the past several centuries to make birth safer for baby and mother alike. Some of those attempts were disastrous, such as the deadly infections spread to mothers unwittingly by 19th-century doctors. In the early 20th century the attempts were overzealous and overly medical, as birth was taken over by doctors and hospitals, with the maternal experience disregarded. In the past 50 years most of the West has moved toward a more reasonable middle ground, seeking to minimize medical intervention but making it available when necessary.

3.6 Describe the differences in maternal and neonatal mortality both within and between developed countries and developing countries.

In recent decades birth has become routinely safe and humane in developed countries, although there is considerable variation based on SES and ethnicity. Childbirth remains highly dangerous in developing countries where little medical intervention is available, although mortality rates are decreasing due to recent improvements in nutrition and access to health care.

KEY TERMS

oxytocin *p. 91*

labor *p. 92*

delivery *p. 92*

breech presentation *p. 93*

cesarean delivery or (C-section) *p. 93*

epidural *p. 99*

placebo effect *p. 99*

obstetrics *p. 101*

natural childbirth *p. 102*

electronic fetal monitoring (EFM) *p. 102*

SECTION 2   THE NEONATE

3.7 Identify the features of the two major scales most often used to assess neonatal health.

Two of the most widely used methods of assessing neonatal health are the Apgar scale and the Brazelton Neonatal Behavioral Assessment Scale (NBAS). The Apgar scale, which is administered immediately after birth, assesses infants on five subtests with a total rating of 1–10. The NBAS, which is administered any time from 1 day to 2 months after birth, relies on a 27-item scale and assigns infants an overall rating of "worrisome," "normal," or "superior."

3.8 Identify the neonatal classifications for low birth weight and describe the consequences and major treatments.

Low-birth-weight neonates weigh less than 5.5 pounds and very-low-birth-weight neonates weigh less than 3.3 pounds; extremely-low-birth-weight babies weight less than 2.2 pounds. Low birth weight is related to a variety of physical, cognitive, and behavioral problems, not just in infancy but throughout life. Close physical contact and infant massage can help ameliorate the problems.

3.9 Describe neonates' patterns of waking and sleeping, including how and why these patterns differ across cultures.

Neonates sleep an average of 16 to 17 hours a day (in segments of a few hours each), about 50% of it in REM sleep. By 4 months old the typical infant sleeps for 14 of every 24 hours, including about six hours straight at night, and the proportion of REM sleep declines to 40%. These patterns may vary across cultures due to differences in parenting practices such as how much time mothers spend holding their babies.

3.10 Describe the neonatal reflexes, including those that have a functional purpose and those that do not.

There are 27 reflexes present at birth or shortly after, including some related to early survival (such as sucking and rooting) and others that have no apparent function (such as the *Babkin* and *Babinski* reflexes).

3.11 Describe the neonate's sensory abilities with respect to touch, taste and smell, hearing, and sight.

Touch and taste develop prenatally to a large extent, and neonate's abilities are similar to adults'. Neonates also quickly begin to discriminate smells after birth, showing a preference for the smell of their mother's breast. Hearing is also quite mature at birth, although neonates hear high-pitched sounds better than other sounds and their ability to localize sound does not mature until about 1 year old. Sight is the least developed of the senses at birth, due to the physiological immaturity of the visual system at birth, but it reaches maturity by the end of the first year.

KEY TERMS

fontanels *p. 106*

neonate *p. 106*

neonatal jaundice *p. 106*

anoxia *p. 107*

Apgar scale *p. 107*

Brazelton Neonatal Behavioral Assessment Scale (NBAS) *p. 107*

low birth weight *p. 108*

preterm *p. 108*

small for date *p. 108*

very low birth weight *p. 109*

extremely low birth weight *p. 109*

surfactant *p. 110*

kangaroo care *p. 110*

rapid eye movement (REM) sleep *p. 111*

reflex *p. 112*

rooting reflex *p. 112*

Moro reflex *p. 112*

sound localization *p. 115*

SECTION 3 CARING FOR THE NEONATE

3.12 Describe the cultural customs surrounding breast-feeding across cultures and history.

In the human past, evidence indicates that in most cultures children were fed breast milk as their primary or sole food for two to three years. To ease the burden of frequent feedings, the custom of wet nursing (hiring a lactating woman other than the mother to feed the infant) is a widespread custom as old as recorded human history.

3.13 Identify the advantages of breast-feeding and where those advantages are largest.

Breast-feeding is beneficial to infants in many ways, including offering protection from disease in infancy and better health in childhood and adulthood, healthy cognitive development, and reduced obesity. For mothers, breast-feeding helps their bodies return to normal after pregnancy and serves as a natural contraceptive. The advantages are especially pronounced in developing countries. Nevertheless, worldwide only about half of all infants are breast-fed even for a short time.

3.14 Describe neonates' types of crying and how crying patterns and soothing methods vary across cultures.

Three distinct kinds of crying signals have been identified: fussing, anger, and pain. Crying frequency rises steadily beginning at 3 weeks of age and reaches a peak by the end of the second month, then declines. This pattern is similar across cultures, but duration and intensity of crying are lower in cultures where babies are held or carried throughout much of the day and night.

3.15 Describe the extent to which human mothers "bond" with their neonates and the extent to which this claim has been exaggerated.

Some physicians have claimed on the basis of animal studies that the first few minutes and hours after birth are critical to mother–infant "bonding." This has now been shown to be false, but the claims had the beneficial effect of changing hospital policies to allow more contact between mothers, fathers, and neonates.

3.16 Describe the reasons for postpartum depression and its consequences for children.

Many mothers experience mood fluctuations in the days following birth as their hormones return to normal levels, but some mothers experience an extended period of postpartum depression, as do some fathers. The basis of postpartum depression appears to be a combination of genetic vulnerability to depression and a social and cultural context that does not provide enough social support.

KEY TERMS

mammary glands *p. 117*

let-down reflex *p. 117*

wet nursing *p. 118*

colostrum *p. 119*

meta-analysis *p. 121*

confounded *p. 120*

swaddling *p. 123*

colic *p. 125*

imprinting *p. 125*

bonding *p. 125*

postpartum depression *p. 127*

Practice Test

✓•—[Study and Review in **MyDevelopmentLab**

1. Juanita's cervix is 10 centimeters dilated so she
   a. is just beginning the labor stage.
   b. requires an episiotomy.
   c. has completed labor and is ready to deliver the baby.
   d. requires a C-section.

2. C-sections
   a. are performed when the baby is in the breech position and attempts to turn the baby into a head first position have not been successful.
   b. require the same recovery time as a vaginal birth if they are performed correctly.
   c. have been proven safe only in the case where there is a failure to progress.
   d. are performed at equally small rates around the world because they are seen as a last resort.

3. In traditional cultures, birth is allowed to take place only in certain settings. The LEAST LIKELY explanation is
   a. so others will not be contaminated.
   b. to feel a sense of control over an often perilous situation.
   c. to find a place where medical help is available if complications arise.
   d. so that the mother or her infant will not be endangered.

4. Surita is a midwife in a traditional culture. She is most likely to
   a. have spent time as an apprentice to a more experienced midwife.
   b. be childless so she is able to devote more time to this work.
   c. be a young woman because she will be able to practice midwifery for longer than her older counterparts.
   d. exclude other relatives from being present to reduce possible contamination.

5. Which of the following is true about birthing practices?
   a. Recently, midwifery has seen a revival, and about 50% of births in the United States are assisted by midwives.
   b. In the early 1900s, the intervention of doctors often made the birth process less dangerous because they now had better expertise and medical equipment.
   c. In the 1960s, doctors began administering drugs such as ether and chloroform, which offered pain relief without any side effects.
   d. Twilight Sleep was a drug used in the early 20th century that promoted dilation of the cervix and resulted in mothers forgetting the events of birth.

6. In developing countries
   a. most pregnant women now have access to modern medical technologies.
   b. giving birth is relatively free of risks because of modernization and globalization.
   c. maternal mortality has decreased over the past 30 years.
   d. rates of infant mortality are lower than in developed countries because of more holistic and natural approaches to childbirth.

7. The five characteristics that are evaluated in the Apgar scale are
   a. the Babinski, Moro, stepping, swimming, and grasping reflexes.
   b. color, heart rate, reflex irritability, muscle tone, and breathing.
   c. reaction to cuddling, startling, intelligence, vocal response, and visual response.
   d. sucking reflex, responses to social stimulation, and disease symptoms.

8. Preterm babies are considered at risk because
   a. their immune systems are immature.
   b. they have too much surfactant in their lungs.
   c. their bodies generate too much heat.
   d. their gestational age is 40 weeks and that is still too early to perform basic functions such as sucking.

9. Compared to adults, neonates
   a. spend a lower proportion of their sleep in REM.
   b. enter REM sooner after falling asleep.
   c. spend less time sleeping.
   d. do not experience eye movements under the eyelids or brain-wave changes during REM sleep.

10. Which of the following reflexes has no apparent survival value?
    a. the rooting reflex   c. the Babinski reflex
    b. the Moro reflex   d. the grasping reflex

11. The earliest sense to develop is
    a. taste.   c. vision.
    b. touch.   d. hearing.

12. Breast-feeding
    a. is more common among women from low socioeconomic status groups.
    b. increased in popularity as formulas came on to the market because the formulas were very expensive and women worried about product safety.
    c. is something both mother and baby are biologically prepared to do.
    d. rates have stayed about the same in the United States since the 1940s.

13. Which of the following statements about breast-feeding is most accurate?
    a. Babies in developing countries are more at risk for health problems if their mothers do not breast-feed them than are babies in developed countries.
    b. Breast-feeding promotes better health in childhood, but does not have any influence on long-term health.
    c. Breast-fed babies are more likely than bottle-fed babies to become obese in childhood because they are used to eating on demand.
    d. The colostrum that mothers produce in the first weeks after birth can be dangerous to babies so doctors advise using formula until the mother begins producing milk.

14. American infants
    a. are less likely to experience colic than are babies in non-Western cultures.
    b. typically experience colic until they are about a year of age.
    c. show the same frequency, intensity, and duration of crying as babies from all over the world.
    d. have been found to cry more than babies from cultures where they are held or carried for much of the day.

15. Which of the following statements about bonding is most accurate?
    a. There is a critical period for mother–child relations in all species.
    b. Imprinting is another name for the stepping reflex.
    c. In humans, if there is no contact with the mother shortly after birth, the baby's future development is at risk.
    d. Konrad Lorenz showed that following the first moving object after birth has survival value.

16. Postpartum depression
    a. is less common among women who have had previous episodes of major depression because they tend to seek preventive treatment.
    b. is experienced by men as well as by women.
    c. has a genetic component and, therefore, has not been correlated with levels of social support.
    d. has been linked with developmental outcomes for babies, but only among male babies.

4 Infancy

133

Dawn breaks, and little Makori, age 6 months, wakes up in the arms of his mother. He has been sleeping next to her all night, as he does every night. Several times he woke up hungry and nuzzled around until he found her breast and suckled for awhile. Now he finds himself hungry again, and he whimpers softly. Drowsily, his mother draws him comfortably next to her and lets him feed.

Elsewhere in the household, others are stirring. Evan, age 10, Makori's oldest brother, is starting a cooking fire in the corner of the hut. Sister Marisera, age 7, has gone outside with Getonto, age 4, to fetch water from the well. Their father is not present. Like many men of this Gusii (goo-SEE) village, he has migrated to a larger city in Kenya to look for work, and comes home only rarely.

Makori's mother now rises and, with Makori on her hip, goes about preparing breakfast. When Marisera returns with the water, she takes over care of Makori so the mother can make a simple breakfast of warm cereal. Marisera will be responsible for caring for her younger siblings for most of the day.

After breakfast, their mother departs for the fields, where she will work all morning tending the family's crops. Evan leaves for school, and Marisera is left with the younger boys. The fields are only a short walk away, and Marisera will come by with the younger children at least once an hour so that Makori can feed on his mother's breast milk.

Otherwise, Makori spends most of his morning bound to his sister's back with a tightly wound cloth while Marisera goes about her morning tasks such as cleaning up after breakfast and feeding the family's three goats. Sometimes Makori dozes off for awhile, nuzzled against his sister's warm back.

At lunchtime Makori's mother comes back from the fields, and his brother from school, and the family has their meal together. Shortly after lunch Makori's aunt and grandmother come to visit. All afternoon the women talk together as they prepare food for the evening meal. Makori feeds frequently from his mother's breast and watches with interest as his older siblings play or go about their chores.

It is rare that anyone speaks directly to Makori—the Gusii believe there is no sense in talking to infants, who understand little and cannot reply—but he is always in the arms or on the lap of one of the women or his older siblings. In the course of the day, he never touches the ground. The Gusii believe that infants are especially vulnerable to disease and to witchcraft, and therefore require constant care and protection in order to survive their first year of life.

Evening falls, and dinner is prepared, enjoyed, and cleaned up afterward. As night comes on, Makori ends his day just as he began it, sleeping securely against the warm skin of his mother.

Does Makori's daily life sound quite a bit different than the lives of infants you have observed? It probably does, given that infants in developed countries have a daily pattern that differs from Makori's in many ways. Yet Makori's life is far more typical of the human experience in infancy, both historically and today, in most parts of the world.

In a sense, little Makori's daily life is similar to the life of infants everywhere. In all cultures, infants have limited mobility and do not yet use language (the word *infant* means literally "without speech"), although they have a variety of ways of communicating. In all cultures, infants cannot do much for themselves and rely heavily on others for care and protection. However, even in infancy cultural variations are vast. In some cultures infants are carried around for most of the day and breast-feed often, as in Makori's case, whereas in others, they lie by themselves for a substantial proportion of the day—and night. In this chapter we will explore both cultural similarities and variations in infants' development. Beginning in this chapter and throughout the rest of the book, the chapters will be divided into three major sections: physical development, cognitive development, and emotional and social development.

> *He is always in the arms or on the lap of one of the women or his older siblings.*

LEARNING OBJECTIVES

4.1 Explain the gains in height and weight, the two basic principles of physical growth, and the growth of teeth in this period.

4.2 Identify the different parts of the brain and describe how the brain changes in the first few years of life.

4.3 Describe how infant sleep changes in the course of the first year and evaluate the risk factors for SIDS, including the research evidence regarding cosleeping.

4.4 Describe how infants' nutritional needs change during the first year of life and identify the reasons and consequences for malnutrition in infancy.

4.5 List the major causes and preventive methods of infant mortality and describe some cultural approaches to protecting infants.

4.6 Describe the major changes during infancy in gross and fine motor development.

4.7 Describe when and how infants develop depth perception and intermodal perception.

Growth and Change in Infancy

We begin this section by examining physical growth (height and weight), the emergence of the first teeth, and infant brain development. Then we'll examine changes in sleeping patterns, the dangers of SIDS, and cultural variations in where infants sleep (and with whom).

Bodily growth

> Explain the gains in height and weight, the two basic principles of physical growth, and the growth of teeth in this period.

LEARNING OBJECTIVE 4.1

Bodily growth in infancy is remarkably rapid as babies increase in height and weight. This rapid growth follows two principles: from the head to the tail and from the core of the body outward. Teeth make their first appearance in the infancy period.

CHANGES IN HEIGHT AND WEIGHT Babies grow at a faster rate in their first year than at any later time of life (Adolph & Berger, 2005). Birth weight doubles by the time the infant is 5 months old, and triples by the end of the first year, to about 10 kilos (22 lb) on average. If this rate of growth continued for the next three years, the average 4-year-old would weigh 600 pounds! But the rate of weight gain decreases steeply after the first year.

Babies especially accumulate fat in the early months, which helps them maintain a constant body temperature. At 6 months, a well-nourished baby looks on the plump side, but by 1 year children lose much of their "baby fat," and the trend toward a lower ratio of fat to body weight continues until puberty (Fomon & Nelson, 2002).

Height also increases dramatically in the first year, from about 50 centimeters (20 in.) to about 75 centimeters (30 in.), at the rate of about 2 cm per month. Unlike weight, growth in height in the first year is uneven, occurring in spurts rather than steadily. Studies that have monitored height closely have found that infants may grow very little for several days or even weeks, then spurt a half inch in just a day or two

Most babies are plump and have large heads in proportion to their bodies.

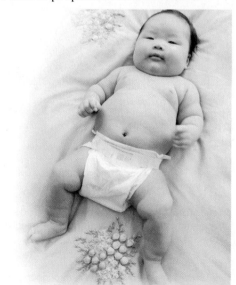

Figure 4.1 • **The cephalocaudal principle of body growth.** Growth begins with the head and then continues downward to the rest of the body.

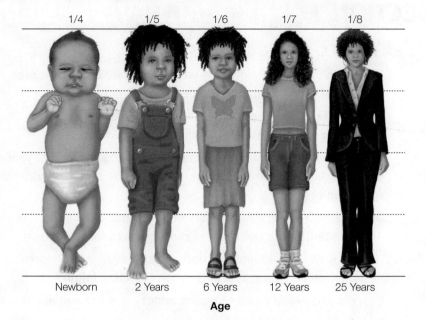

| 1/4 | 1/5 | 1/6 | 1/7 | 1/8 |

Newborn 2 Years 6 Years 12 Years 25 Years

Age

(Lampl et al., 2001). Girls tend to be shorter and lighter than boys, at birth and throughout childhood, until puberty when they briefly surpass boys in height (Geary, 2010).

Another way growth is uneven in infancy is that it tends to begin at the top, with the head, and then proceed downward to the rest of the body (Adolph & Berger, 2005). This is called the **cephalocaudal principle** (*cephalocaudal* is Latin for "head to tail"). So, for example, the head is one-quarter of the neonate's body length, but only one-eighth of an adult's (see *Figure 4.1*). In addition, growth proceeds from the middle of the body outward, which is the **proximodistal principle** (*proximodistal* is Latin for "near to far"). So, for example, the trunk and arms grow faster than the hands and fingers. Control of the body follows a similar pattern. For example, infants are able to hold up their heads before they can control their legs and feet, and they can control their hands as a whole before they can control individual fingers.

TEETH AND TEETHING Most babies have no visible teeth at birth, although their teeth have begun to grow beneath their gums. For most infants the first tooth appears between 5 and 9 months of age. As the first teeth break through the skin of the gums, or even in the weeks before, most babies experience discomfort and pain called **teething**. There is a vast range of variability in teething among infants, from constant pain to no discomfort at all. The first teeth and the molars tend to be especially painful.

There are several signs that a baby has begun teething, even if a tooth has not yet broken through (Trajanovska et al., 2010). Teething stimulates saliva production, so parents may notice there is more drooling, more coughing, and perhaps a rash around the mouth. Babies often seize the opportunity for something to bite when teething, including their own hands if nothing else is available, because the counterpressure of the bite relieves the pressure from under the gums. Watch your fingers! You may be surprised how strong a teething baby's bite can be.

Not many of us become more cheerful when in pain, at any age, so it is not surprising that teething babies also tend to become irritable. Some may be reluctant to breast- or bottle-feed, because the suction created from feeding adds to their discomfort (fortunately, most can also eat solid foods by the time they begin teething). And, of course, they become more likely to wake up at night with teething pain. Parents who celebrated when their child began "sleeping through the night" at about 4 months old may find that this was a temporary rather than permanent transition, as the baby now wakes up and cries for relief from teething (Sarrell et al., 2005).

Fortunately, there is a range of strategies to help relieve the infant's teething pain (Trajanovska et al., 2010). Something to bite or chew on, such as a cold wet washcloth

Teething is often uncomfortable and painful.

cephalocaudal principle principle of biological development that growth tends to begin at the top, with the head, and then proceeds downward to the rest of the body

proximodistal principle principle of biological development that growth proceeds from the middle of the body outward

teething period of discomfort and pain experienced by infants as their new teeth break through their gums

or a "teething ring," can provide the counterpressure on the gums that helps relieve the pain. Something cold to drink or eat can be soothing, and it is a good idea to supplement the fluids lost to drooling with extra fluids to drink. Finally, topical pain relievers rubbed on the gums can also be effective.

Brain development

> Identify the different parts of the brain and describe how the brain changes in the first few years of life.

LEARNING OBJECTIVE 4.2

Recall from Chapter 3 that humans have relatively large brains at birth compared to other animals, thus making the birth process more painful and dangerous. But even though the human brain is relatively large at birth, it is also relatively immature, compared to the brains of other animals (Johnson, 2001). We come out when we do because if we waited any longer, our brains would be too big for us ever to make it through the birth canal. Consequently, much of the basic brain development that takes place prenatally for other animals takes place in the first year for humans. Note, for example, that other animals are mobile at birth or within a few days or weeks, but humans cannot even crawl for about six months and cannot walk until the end of their first year.

Here we will look first at basics of infant brain growth, then at the specialized functions of different parts of the brain. Then we'll explore the special sensitivity of brain development during infancy.

BRAIN GROWTH As you learned in Chapter 2, during the second trimester of prenatal development, neurons are produced at the astonishing rate of 250,000 per minute. The pace then slows considerably in the third trimester, as the focus of development shifts to other organs and to overall size. After birth, the brain resumes its explosive growth. The neonate's brain is about 25% the size of an adult's brain, but by age 2 it will reach 70%. ✳

There are about 100–200 billion brain cells, or *neurons*, in the average infant brain (Kostovic & Vasung, 2009). Neurons differ from other cells in the body in that they are not directly connected to each other. Instead, they are separated by tiny gaps called *synapses*. Neurons communicate across the synapses by releasing chemicals called **neurotransmitters**. The **axon** of the neuron releases neurotransmitters, and the **dendrites** receive them. ✳

The brain growth that occurs in the first two years of life does not involve production of more and more neurons. In fact, the number of neurons in the brain drops by age 2 to about one-half what it was at birth (de Haan & Johnson, 2003). There are two other ways that brain growth takes place during infancy. First, the dendritic connections between neurons multiply vastly, a process known as **overproduction** or **exuberance** (Kostovic & Vasung, 2009). At birth the neurons have few interconnections, but by age 2 each neuron is connected to hundreds or even thousands of other cells. The greatest density of connections appears in toddlerhood, as we'll see in Chapter 5. The second way the brain grows in infancy is through **myelination**, the process by which the axons become encased in a *myelin sheath*, an envelope of fatty material that increases the speed of communication between neurons (Gale et al., 2004). Myelination is especially active in the early years of life but continues at a slower rate until about age 30 (Taylor, 2006). ⏵

As neurons create vast networks of dendrites to connect to other neurons, a process begins that enhances the precision and efficiency of the connections. "Use it or lose it" is the principle that applies, as dendritic connections that are used become stronger and faster and those that are unused wither away, in a process called **synaptic pruning** (Kostovic & Vasung, 2009). If you were growing carrots in a backyard garden and you had planted thousands of seeds, how would you ensure that they would thrive? The best way would be to prune or pluck out the weaker shoots to allow the stronger

neurotransmitters chemical that enables neurons to communicate across synapses

axon part of the neuron that transmits electric impulses and releases neurotransmitters

dendrites part of the neuron that receives neurotransmitters

overproduction/exuberance burst in the production of dendritic connections between neurons

myelination process of the growth of the myelin sheath around the axon of a neuron

synaptic pruning process in brain development in which dendritic connections that are used become stronger and faster and those that are unused whither away

✳ **Explore** the **Concept** Virtual Brain in **MyDevelopmentLab**

✳ **Explore** the **Concept** of The Synapse in **MyDevelopmentLab**

 **Simulate** the **Experiment**
Neurotransmitters: Communication Between Neurons in **MyDevelopmentLab**

ones more room and resources to grow on. This is what the brain does with synaptic pruning. Through synaptic pruning, the brain eliminates about one-third of its synapses between early childhood and adolescence (Shonkoff & Phillips, 2000).

BRAIN SPECIALIZATION Although the entire brain is composed of neurons, the neurons in different parts of the brain have specialized functions. Overall, the brain is divided into three major regions, the *hindbrain*, the *midbrain*, and the *forebrain*. Early in pre-natal development, the neurons in these three regions begin to specialize. The hindbrain and midbrain mature earliest and perform the basic biological functions necessary to life. They keep your lungs breathing, your heart beating, and your bodily movements balanced.

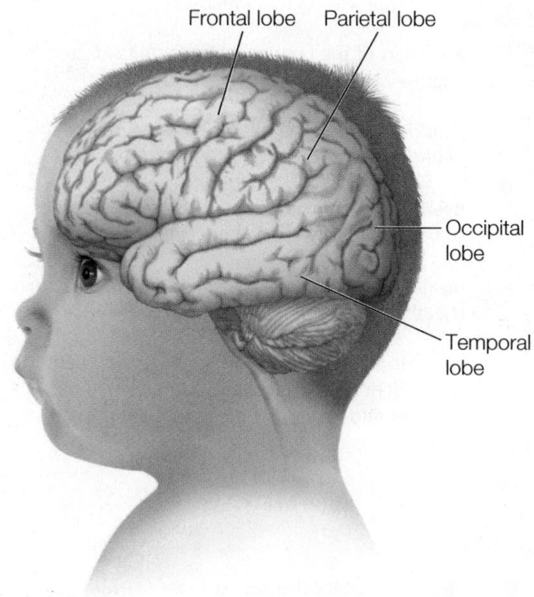

The forebrain is divided into two main parts, the *limbic system* and the *cerebral cortex*. The structures of the limbic system include the *hypothalamus*, the *thalamus*, and the *hippocampus*. The hypothalamus is small, about the size of a peanut, but plays a key role in monitoring and regulating our basic animal func-tions, including hunger, thirst, body temperature, sexual desire, and hormonal levels. The thalamus acts as a receiving and transfer center for sensory informa-tion from the body to the rest of the brain. The hippocampus is crucial in mem-ory, especially the transfer of information from short-term to long-term memory.

The most distinctively human part of the brain is the outermost part of the forebrain, the **cerebral cortex**. This part of the human brain is far larger than in other animals. For example, adult humans weigh about as much as adult chim-panzees, but have a cerebral cortex three to four times larger (Wrangham, 2009). It accounts for 85% of the brain's total weight, and it is here that most of the brain's growth takes place after birth. The cerebral cortex is the basis of our dis-tinctively human abilities, including the ability to speak and understand language, to solve complex problems, and to think in terms of concepts, ideas, and symbols.

The different parts of the cerebral cortex are specialized in two ways. First, the cerebral cortex is divided into two hemispheres, left and right, which are con-nected by a band of neural fibers called the *corpus callosum* that allows them to communicate. **Lateralization** is the term for the specialization of the two hemi-spheres. In general, the left hemisphere is specialized for language and for processing in-formation in a sequential, step-by-step way (Tremblay et al., 2004; Wood et al., 2004). The right hemisphere is specialized for spatial reasoning and for processing informa-tion in a holistic, integrative way (Johnson, 2001). However, the specialization of the hemispheres should not be exaggerated, because they work together in most aspects of language, emotion, and behavior (Zald, 2003). No one is mainly a "left-brain" or "right-brain" thinker. ◉▶

The cerebral cortex is also specialized in that each hemisphere has four regions or lobes with distinct functions (see **Figure 4.2**). The *occipital lobes* at the rear of each hemisphere process visual information. The *temporal lobes* at the lower side of each hemisphere are involved in processing auditory information, including understanding spoken language. The *parietal lobes* above the temporal lobes process information from bodily sensations. The *frontal lobes* behind the forehead are the center of the most ad-vanced human brain processes, including producing spoken language, planning for the future, and making decisions. With the lobes as with the hemispheres, it is important not to exaggerate the degree of specialization, as more than one part of the brain is involved in most brain functions (Knect et al., 2003).

THE PLASTICITY OF THE INFANT BRAIN Even before birth, the brain is well on its way to-ward specialization in the ways just described. However, in many ways the cerebral cortex of the neonate and the infant is still immature. Because the infant's brain is not as specialized as it will be later in development, it is high in **plasticity**, meaning that it is highly responsive to environmental circumstances. In one example of brain plasticity

Frontal lobe   Parietal lobe

Occipital lobe

Temporal lobe

Figure 4.2 • **Lobes of the brain.** What are the distinct functions of each lobe?

◉▶⎡**Simulate** the **Experiment**
Cerebral Hemispheres and the Corpus Callosum in **MyDevelopmentLab**

cerebral cortex outer portion of the brain, contain-ing four regions with distinct functions

lateralization specialization of functions in the two hemispheres of the brain

plasticicty degree to which development can be influenced by environmental circumstances

that is particularly relevant across cultures, infants can learn any language (or languages) that they hear regularly. Hearing infants are born with the ability to hear the sounds of any spoken language in the world, but exposure to sounds from a specific language, along with a decline in plasticity, means that infants stop being able to detect sounds from languages they are not hearing by about 10 months of age.

The high plasticity of the infant brain makes it adaptable but also vulnerable (Gale et al., 2004). On the plus side, if a part of the brain is damaged in infancy due to an accident or disease, other parts of the brain can often take over the functions of the damaged portion, whereas this is less possible later in development once greater specialization has taken place. On the minus side, environmental deprivation can have permanent effects if it takes place in infancy, whereas later its effects would not be as profound or long lasting.

Imagine that, starting tomorrow, for three years you lived in conditions of great deprivation, with little food, little interaction with others, and nothing interesting to do. At the end of it, you might be very hungry and not very happy, but it is likely your weight would soon return to normal and your intellectual skills and abilities would be unaffected in the long run. This is what has usually happened to prisoners of war who had been subject to such grim conditions (Moore, 2010).

If the same kind of deprivation had happened to you in the first three years of your life, the effects would have been much worse. We know this because of a horrible natural experiment that took place in Romania beginning in the 1960s. Government policies to increase the birth rate resulted in hundreds of thousands of children whose families could not afford to care for them. In the early 1990s, after Communist regimes fell in Eastern European countries, Western visitors to Romania were shocked at the conditions in the country's orphanages. Infants and young children in the orphanages had been given little in the way of nutrition and even less in love, attention, and cognitive stimulation. They were kept in large, dim, bare rooms, attended by a small number of indifferent caregivers. In response to widespread outrage, the orphanages were soon closed and the children were adopted into homes in other countries, mostly in Canada and Great Britain.

The children had all been deprived, but they were adopted at different ages. Over the course of the next several years, it was clear that age at adoption made a big difference in their cognitive development (O'Connor et al., 2000; Rutter et al., 2004). All the children recovered dramatically in physical size after a year or two in their new homes, but the degree of cognitive recovery depended strongly on age at adoption, with those adopted earlier faring better than those adopted later. As shown in *Figure 4.3*, by age 6 the Romanian children who had been adopted when less than 6 months old were no different in their rate of cognitive impairment than British children adopted at the same age (Beckett et al., 2006). However, Romanian children adopted at 6–24 months old had cognitive abilities significantly lower than the Romanian or British children adopted earlier, and Romanian children adopted at age 24–42 months had cognitive abilities that were lower still. This indicates that after about 6 months of age, the damage to the brain due to early deprivation often could not be entirely undone even by years of exposure to a more stimulating environment. Plasticity of the infant brain is high but diminishes steeply over the first few years of life.

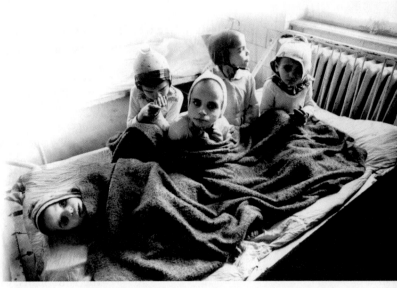

The cognitive recovery of adopted Romanian orphans depended greatly on the age at which they were adopted.

Figure 4.3 • **Romanian adoptees' cognitive abilities, by age of adoption.** The later the age of adoption, the lower their cognitive abilities.
Source: Based on data from: *Do the effects of early severe deprivation on cognition persist into early adolescence? Findings from the English and Romanian adoptees study.* Child Development, 77, 696–711.

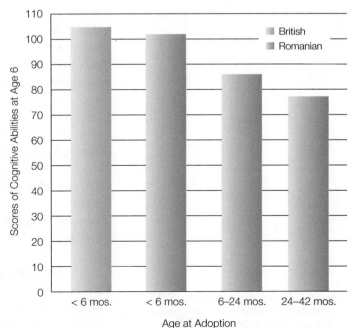

Sleep changes

4.3 **LEARNING OBJECTIVE** | Describe how infant sleep changes in the course of the first year and evaluate the risk factors for SIDS, including the research evidence regarding cosleeping.

As described in Chapter 3, neonates sleep for 16–17 hours a day in periods of a few hours, and are in REM sleep about half this time. By 3–4 months old, infants sleep for longer periods, up to 6–7 hours in a row at night, and REM sleep has declined to about 40%. By age 6 months, cultural practices influence how much infants sleep. American infants sleep about 14 hours a day at this age, including daytime naps (Murkoff et al., 2003). However, among the Kipsigis people of Kenya studied by Charles Super and Sara Harkness (1986), infants slept only about 12 hours a day at 6 months of age, perhaps because they spent much of the day strapped to their mothers or an older sibling, and so expended less energy than American infants do. Super and colleagues (1996) also studied infants in the Netherlands and compared their sleep patterns to American infants. The Dutch infants slept about 16 hours a day at 6 months, 2 hours more than the Americans, due to Dutch cultural beliefs emphasizing rest and early bedtimes for young children.

Two important issues of sleep in infancy are the risk of dying during sleep and the issue of whom infants should sleep with. For both issues, there are important cultural variations.

SUDDEN INFANT DEATH SYNDROME (SIDS) When infants are 2–4 months of age, they are at highest risk for **sudden infant death syndrome (SIDS)**. Infants who die of SIDS do not have any apparent illness or disorder, they simply fall asleep and never wake up. SIDS is the leading cause of death for infants 1–12 months of age in developed countries (Moon et al., 2007). Infants of Asian descent are less likely to die of SIDS than those of European or African descent, and African American and Native American infants are at especially high risk, with rates 4–6 times higher than White Americans (Pickett et al., 2005). The higher rates of SIDS among African Americans and Native Americans are part of a larger pattern than begins with poorer prenatal care and continues with greater vulnerability in the first year of life. ◉

◉─┤**Watch** the **Video** SIDS in **MyDevelopmentLab**

Although deaths from SIDS have no clear cause, there are several factors known to put infants at risk (Kinney & Thach, 2009; Moon et al., 2007), including stomach sleeping, low birth weight and low APGAR scores, and soft bedding. One theory is that babies' vulnerability to SIDS at 2–4 months old reflects the transition from reflex behavior to intentional behavior (Lipsitt, 2003). For their first two months of life, when infants' breathing is blocked, a reflex causes them to shake their heads, bring their hands to their face, and push away the cause of the obstruction. After two months of age, once the reflex disappears, most babies are able to do this as intentional, learned behavior, but some are unable to make the transition, perhaps due in part to respiratory and muscular vulnerabilities. When these infants experience breathing difficulties during sleep, instead of being able to shake off the difficulty, they die.

One thing that is certain is that sleeping on the back instead of the stomach makes an enormous difference in lowering the risk of SIDS. In 1994, in response to growing research evidence of the risks of stomach-sleeping, pediatricians in the United States launched a major "BACK to Sleep" campaign to inform parents and health professionals of the importance of putting infants to sleep on their backs. Over the next decade, the prevalence of stomach sleeping among American infants declined from 70% to 20% and SIDS deaths declined by nearly one-half (Kochanek et al., 2004; National Center for Health Statistics, 2005). In response to similar campaigns in other countries, SIDS declined by 90% in the United Kingdom and by over 50% in many other developed countries (see **Figure 4.4**) (National Sudden and Unexpected Infant/Child Death &

sudden infant death syndrome (SIDS) death within the first year of life due to unknown reasons, with no apparent illness or disorder

Pregnancy Loss Resource Center, 2010). In addition to placing infants to sleep on their backs, the American Academy of Pediatrics [AAP] (2000) recommends the following:

- Providing a firm sleep surface with no soft objects near the infant
- Avoiding smoking during pregnancy and near the infant because of secondhand smoke
- Avoiding overheating (lightly clothe the infant)
- Giving the baby a pacifier before sleep

COSLEEPING: WHO SLEEPS WITH WHOM? With whom should infants sleep? Should they sleep by themselves, in a crib or even a room of their own, or should they sleep alongside a parent or a sibling?

If you are a member of a Western culture, you may assume that it is better for infants to have their own crib and room within a few weeks after birth, so that they can learn to be independent and the parents can enjoy their marital intimacy without disruption (or without as much disruption, at least). Prominent pediatricians and health authorities in the United States and other Western countries warn against **cosleeping**, in which the infant sleeps in the same bed as the parents, arguing that it leads to excessive dependence by infants and can endanger the emotional health of infants or even lead to SIDS (AAP Task Force on Infant Positioning and SIDS, 2000). In a survey of American pediatricians, 88% recommended that babies sleep in a crib in a room of their own (Small, 1998).

However, this is one of many issues in this book where what is normal and seems healthy and "natural" in Western countries is actually extremely unusual worldwide. Outside of the West, nearly all cultures have some form of cosleeping during infancy (Small, 2005). Many of the parents in these cultures view the Western practice of nightly isolation of infants as "a form of child neglect or worse" (DeLoache & Gottlieb, 2000, pp. 16–17). They believe infants are highly vulnerable to injury, illness, and death, and that sleeping beside the mother is necessary to protect them. This arrangement also makes it easy for the infant to breast-feed when necessary during the night, without disturbing others and arousing the mother only slightly. Typically a child sleeps beside the mother until the next child is born, which is usually when the child is 2–4 years old.

In a study comparing sleeping arrangements among Guatemalan Maya and European Americans, all the Mayan mothers coslept with their infants until the next child was born, whereupon the child would cosleep with the father or in a bed alongside the mother and the new baby (Morelli et al., 1992). The mothers explained that cosleeping helped promote a close parent–child attachment, highly valued in their collectivistic culture. The Mayan mothers were appalled when they heard how American infants typically sleep alone, and regarded this practice as cold and cruel. In contrast, few of the American mothers coslept with their infants, explaining that they wanted the child to become independent and that cosleeping would foster a degree of dependency that would be emotionally unhealthy.

But it is not just in traditional cultures like the Guatemalan Maya that cosleeping is the norm. In Japan and South Korea, two of the most technologically advanced countries in the world, almost all infants cosleep with their mothers, and children continue to sleep with or near their mothers until puberty (Mindell et al., 2010). Like the Mayan mothers, Asian mothers justify their cosleeping practices on the basis of collectivistic values, explaining that this is one way for children to learn from a very early age that they are closely tied to others in bonds of interdependence and mutual obligation. Will cosleeping automatically foster interdependence instead of independence? No, it is not

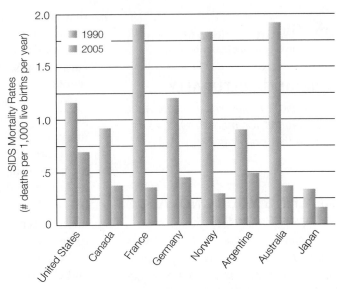

Figure 4.4 • **The impact of reduction campaigns on SIDS rates.** Why did rates of SIDS decline so much over this period?

In most cultures, mothers and infants cosleep.

My Virtual Child

Will you choose to cosleep with your infant? How is your choice reflective of your cultural values?

cosleeping cultural practice in which infants and sometimes older children sleep with one or both parents

⊙—⌐ **Watch** the **Video** Cosleeping
in **MyDevelopmentLab**

THINKING CULTURALLY

What might cosleeping indicate about expectations for marital relations in a culture that practices it?

**APPLYING YOUR KNOWLEDGE
. . . as a Parent**

You want to cosleep with your newborn daughter, but your spouse is afraid the child will not learn to become independent. What might you tell him or her in response?

custom complex distinctive cultural pattern of behavior that reflects underlying cultural beliefs

that simple. Sleeping arrangements are just one of many activities where infants are socialized to the norms of their culture. ⊙

Importing the cultural practice of cosleeping may not fit seamlessly with American cultural values or practices. American parents who choose to cosleep with their infants would be advised to emulate the sleeping conditions in cultures where cosleeping is the norm: a firm mattress (not a pillow top), light bedding, giving the infant a pacifier, and going to sleep sober (Germo et al., 2007). Intoxication can lead to less awareness of the infant next to you and can cause accidental smothering.

Cultural customs regarding infant sleeping arrangements are a good example of a **custom complex**, that is, a distinctive cultural pattern of behavior that is based on underlying cultural beliefs. Cosleeping tends to reflect collectivistic beliefs, that members of the culture are closely bound to one another (Small, 1998). In contrast, having infants sleep alone tends to reflect an individualistic belief that each person should learn to be self-sufficient and not rely on others any more than necessary.

Parents in an individualistic culture may fear that cosleeping will make infants and children too dependent. However, children who cosleep with their parents in infancy are actually more self-reliant (e.g, able to dress themselves) and more socially independent (e.g., can make friends by themselves) than other children are (Keller & Goldberg, 2004).

What about the danger of SIDS? Don't cultures where cosleeping is the norm have high rates of SIDS, if cosleeping is a risk factor for SIDS as most American pediatricians believe? On the contrary, SIDS is almost unknown in cultures where cosleeping is the norm. In the United States, however, where most parents do not cosleep, rates of SIDS are among the highest in the world.

There appear to be several reasons for this pattern (McKenna & McDade, 2005). First, most parents and infants in cosleeping cultures sleep on relatively hard surfaces such as a mat on the floor or a futon, thus avoiding the soft bedding that is sometimes implicated in SIDS. Second, infants who cosleep breast-feed more often and longer than infants who do not, and these frequent episodes of arousal in the course of the night make SIDS less likely. Third, cosleeping mothers tend to lay their infants on their backs to make the mother's breast more easily accessible for breast-feeding. Thus back-sleeping developed as a widespread cultural practice for practical reasons long before research showed that it lessened the risk of SIDS.

Some American cultures have a long tradition of infant cosleeping. It is a common practice among African Americans (Milan et al., 2007), and in the rural culture of the Appalachian Mountains, children typically sleep alongside their parents for the first two years of life (Abbott, 1992). In many developed countries, the prevalence of cosleeping in infancy has grown in recent years as research has shown that it causes no emotional harm and may even be protective against SIDS (Mindell et al., 2010; Willinger et al., 2003). Cosleeping infants may be at risk for SIDS if their parents are obese or consume alcohol or other drugs before sleeping, but otherwise cosleeping is more often a protective factor than a risk factor for SIDS (McKenna & McDade, 2005).

WHAT HAVE YOU LEARNED?

1. How do the cephalocaudal and proximodistal principles apply to infant growth?
2. How can parents tell when teething is occurring?
3. How "plastic" is the infant brain and how does plasticity change beyond infancy?
4. How and why do cultures vary in who sleeps with whom during infancy? Does cosleeping make SIDS more likely or less likely?

Infant Health

Infants' health depends a great deal on where they happened to be born, that is, on their cultural, economic, and social context. Here we look first at how nutritional needs change over the first year, then at the prevalence and effects of malnutrition. This will be followed by an examination of infant mortality rates and causes, immunizations, and cultural beliefs and practices to protect babies.

Nutritional needs

Describe how infants' nutritional needs change during the first year of life and identify the reasons and consequences for malnutrition in infancy.

LEARNING OBJECTIVE **4.4**

Infants need a lot of food, and they need it often. In fact, during the first year of life nutritional energy needs are greater than at any other time of life, per pound/kilo of body weight (Vlaardingerbroek et al., 2009). Infants also need more fat in their diets than at any later point in life, to fuel the growth of their bodies and (especially) their brains.

INTRODUCTION OF SOLID FOODS As noted in Chapter 3, the best way to obtain good high-fat nutrition during infancy is through breast milk. Whether they breast-feed or not, infants also start eating some solid foods during the first year of life. Cultures vary widely in when they introduce solid food to infants, ranging from those that introduce it after just a few weeks of life to those that wait until the second half of the first year. Age 4–5 months is common, in part because that is an age when infants can sit up with support and also the age when they often begin to show an interest in what others are eating (Small, 2005).

At 4–5 months old infants still have a gag reflex that causes them to spit out any solid item that enters their mouths. Consequently, at first more food usually ends up on them than in them! The ability to chew and swallow does not develop until the second half of the first year (Napier & Meister, 2000).

In the West, pediatricians generally recommend introducing solid food during the fifth or sixth month of life (Seach et al., 2010). Usually the first solid food is rice cereal mixed with breast milk or formula, made thin when first introduced and gradually thickened as the baby becomes used to eating it (National Center for Education in Maternal and Child Health, 2002). This is followed by pureed fruits and vegetables (at about 6 months), then, in cultures and families that consume meats, pureed meats (at 7–8 months).

In traditional cultures, too, the first foods to be introduced have been mashed, pureed, or prechewed. For example, among the Balinese in Indonesia, even in the first weeks of life mothers give their babies soft prechewed foods such as bananas to supplement breast milk (Diener, 2000). In the course of the first year, the range of foods provided to the baby widens, but the mother typically chews the food first.

MALNUTRITION IN INFANCY Because infants have such great nutritional needs, and because their brains and bodies are growing at a faster rate than at any later time of life, the effects of malnutrition in infancy are especially severe and enduring. Malnutrition is faced by families in poverty, all over the world, including in the United States. Infants are capable of thriving mainly on breast milk, along with a little solid food after the early months, so malnutrition in infancy is usually due to the mother being unable or unwilling to breast-feed. Often the problem is that the mother is so ill or malnourished herself that she is unable to produce an adequate supply of breast milk. Or, she may have a disease that can be communicated through breast milk, such as tuberculosis or HIV, and she has been advised not to breast-feed. She may also have been misled to believe that infant formula is better for her baby than breast milk (see Chapter 3), so she has stopped breast-feeding and instead gives her infant the formula substitute, which

My Virtual Child

How has your culture influenced the manner in which you've introduced solid foods to your virtual child?

Infants with marasmus waste away from lack of nourishment.

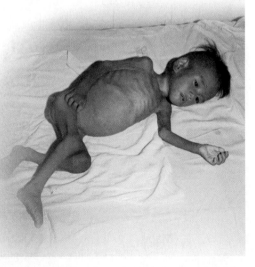

marasmus disease in which the body wastes away from lack of nutrients

may not be available in sufficient quantity. If the infant's mother has died—not uncommon in the areas of the world where infant malnutrition is most common—there may be no one else who can breast-feed the baby or otherwise provide adequate nutrition.

Malnourished infants are at risk for **marasmus,** a disease in which the body wastes away from lack of nutrients. The body stops growing, the muscles atrophy, the baby becomes increasingly lethargic, and eventually death results. Even among infants who survive, malnutrition impairs normal development for years to come (Galler et al., 2010; Nolan et al., 2002). However, studies in Guatemala and several other countries have found that nutritional supplements for infants in poor families have enduring beneficial effects on their physical, cognitive, and social development (Pollitt et al., 1996).

Infant mortality

4.5 **LEARNING OBJECTIVE** List the major causes and preventive methods of infant mortality and describe some cultural approaches to protecting infants.

The first year of life has always been a perilous period for the human species. Human females typically have a reproductive span of at least 20 years, from the late teens through the late thirties, and with regular sexual intercourse most would have at least 3–7 children during that span. Yet, as we saw in Chapter 1, until recently in human history there was little increase in the total human population. This means that many children died before reaching reproductive age, and based on current patterns it seems likely that many of them died in infancy. Even now, worldwide, the first year of life has the highest risk of death of any period in the entire life span (UNICEF, 2008).

CAUSES AND PREVENTION OF INFANT MORTALITY As noted in Chapter 3, most infant mortality is in fact neonatal mortality. That is, it takes place during the first month of life and is usually due to severe birth defects or low birth weight, or is an indirect consequence of the death of the mother during childbirth (UNICEF, 2008). As with neonatal mortality, rates of infant mortality vary vastly between developed countries and developing countries (see **Map 4.1**).

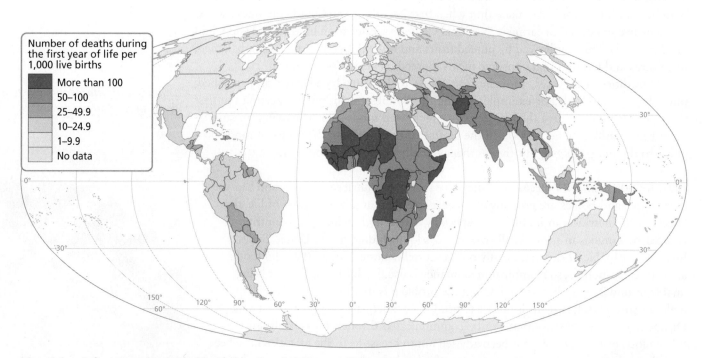

Number of deaths during the first year of life per 1,000 live births

- More than 100
- 50–100
- 25–49.9
- 10–24.9
- 1–9.9
- No data

Map 4.1 • **Infant Mortality Rates Worldwide.** How do infant mortality rates compare with neonatal mortality rates (as shown in Map 3.2 on page 104)? What are some potential causes of the high infant mortality rates in developing countries?

With regard to deaths beyond the first month but within the first year, in addition to deaths due to malnutrition, diseases are another major cause of infant mortality worldwide. Malaria, a blood disease spread by mosquitoes (see Chapter 2), is a major killer of infants, responsible for about 1 million infant deaths per year, mainly in Africa (Finkel, 2007a). Dysentery, an illness of the digestive system, is also one of the top sources of infant mortality, especially in tropical regions where dysentery bacteria thrive.

Overall, the number-one source of infant mortality beyond the first month but within the first year is diarrhea (UNICEF, 2008). Infants with diarrhea lose fluids and eventually die from dehydration if untreated. Diarrhea may be caused by a range of digestive illnesses, and is often a consequence of bottle-feeding in unsanitary conditions. In developing countries, infants who bottle-feed have a mortality rate five times higher than those who breastfeed (Bahl et al., 2005), and many of the deaths are due to diarrhea caused by mixing formula powder with unclean water.

Diarrhea can be cured easily through simple, inexpensive **oral rehydration therapy (ORT)**. ORT involves having infants with diarrhea drink a solution of salt and glucose mixed with (clean) water. Since 1980 the World Health Organization (WHO) has led an international effort to reduce infant deaths through providing ORT, and the effort has reduced the worldwide rate of infant deaths due to diarrhea from 4.5 million per year to less than 2 million (Boschi-Pinto et al., 2009). However, the reason the rate is still as high as 2 million per year is that even now, in the parts of the world where infant diarrhea is most common, this simple, inexpensive remedy is often unavailable.

Although millions of infants worldwide die yearly from lack of adequate nutrition and medical care, in the past half century many diseases that formerly killed infants and young children have been reduced or even eliminated due to vaccines that provide immunization (Centers for Disease Control and Prevention [CDC], 2006b). Smallpox has been eradicated, measles and polio have been eliminated in large regions of the world, and diphtheria, tetanus, and yellow fever have been greatly reduced in prevalence, all due to immunization programs.

Typically, children receive vaccinations for these diseases in the first or second year of life. However, there is a great deal of variability worldwide in how likely children are to be vaccinated. As of 2006, coverage was 66% of children in Africa, 69% in South Asia, and over 90% in Europe and the Americas (CDC, 2006b). In recent years, a major effort to provide immunization to all children has been made by the WHO, UNICEF, and private foundations, and the rate of immunization has been increasing, especially in Africa (UNICEF, 2008).

Although rumors have circulated that some vaccinations may actually cause harm to children, for example by triggering autism, scientific studies have found no basis for these claims (Rodier, 2009). Unfortunately, some parents have been deceived by these claims and consequently refused to have their children vaccinated, which, ironically—and sadly—exposes their children and other people's children to the genuine danger of contracting infectious diseases.

Vaccines have been so effective for several generations that some parents believe that their children will not be threatened by diseases the vaccines would protect against, causing some parents not to vaccinate their children. Some parents fear the side effects of vaccines, such as fever, rashes, or mild cases of the disease, and choose not to vaccinate. However, the U.S. Centers for Disease Control maintain that vaccines are safe, and that rates of infant vaccination have been increasing (CDC, 2011a).

CULTURAL BELIEFS AND PRACTICES TO PROTECT INFANTS Perhaps the most striking feature of the infant's social environment in traditional cultures is the parents' acute awareness of infants' vulnerability and their resulting motive to do whatever they can to make the infant's survival most likely. The cultural practices of secluding infants in their early weeks, cosleeping with them, and constantly carrying them developed out of long and painful human experience with high infant mortality.

oral rehydration therapy (ORT) treatment for infant diarrhea that involves drinking a solution of salt and glucose mixed with clean water

APPLYING YOUR KNOWLEDGE
. . . as a Researcher

In Hawaii, a "Baby Luau" is a big party held to mark a baby's first birthday. What might be a cultural–historical reason for this?

APPLYING YOUR KNOWLEDGE
. . . as a Day-Care Provider

How would you respond to parents who express reluctance to have their infant vaccinated, fearing it would be harmful instead of helpful?

Increased prevalence of vaccinations in infancy has greatly reduced infant mortality worldwide. Here, an infant receives a vaccination in Mozambique.

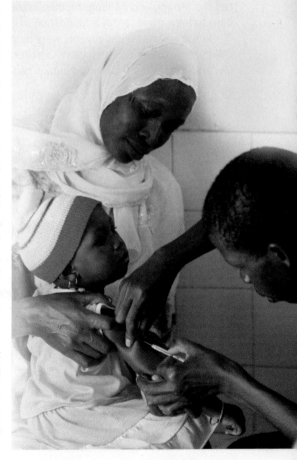

HISTORICAL FOCUS   Protecting Infants the Puritan Way

In the year 1630 about 1,000 people sailed from England to America, where they hoped to build a new society free from the corruptions they perceived as widespread in English society (Reese, 2000). In the new land they wished to "purify" the practice of the Christian religion by disposing of the hierarchy and elaborate ceremonies that went along with religious services in the Church of England, and for this reason they became known as "Puritans." A few months after leaving England they arrived in Massachusetts Bay, and they soon settled in small villages throughout the northeastern part of what eventually became the United States.

It was important to the Puritans to protect their children from the "common corruptions of this evil world," and they sought to do so from the beginning, naming their newborns after elements of their faith such as "Grace," "Redeemed," and "Mercy." Puritans believed that infants were born depraved and prone to sin, and that newborns should be baptized as soon as possible, no longer than eight days after birth. But they saw baptism as only the first step toward a child's redemption from sin. All through infancy, in the course of daily activities like feeding and bathing, mothers were counseled to quote the Bible to their infants to lay a foundation of godly thinking.

In some ways Puritan parents were more nurturing toward their children than other English parents were. Unlike many parents in the England they had left behind, Puritans generally did not send their children to a wet nurse and did not swaddle them. Breast-feeding was recommended for the first year, and at weaning parents often sent their child to a relative's home for a period, in an effort to make the transition easier for both mother and child.

Like children in many cultures, Puritan children were subject to a variety of illnesses, and like adults in many cultures, Puritan adults developed a wide range of treatments that were useless at best and sometimes harmful. For colic, the recommended treatment was to feed the infant a broth made from the boiled intestines and skin of a wolf. For the flu, the recommended treatment was to place a spider in a nut shell, wrap it with silk, and hang it around the infant's neck. For illnesses of all kinds, bloodletting (making a cut in the arm and letting a quantity of blood run out) was the standard treatment. It is probably not necessary to emphasize how unwise this was. Of course, the Puritans' intentions were good. They believed they were helping their children, not harming them.

Although from a modern perspective Puritans are often seen as overly strict and rigid in what they required of children as well as adults, they understood that infants were too immature to follow rules and limits. Parents were encouraged to be kind and indulgent with their infants, the better to win their trust and eventually win them to God's will. Restrictions and punishments would come soon enough, in the second year of life and beyond.

Many cultures resort to magic in an effort to protect their babies. Here, a baby from the Hamer Tribe of Ethiopia wears jewelry the mother has adorned her with to ward off disease.

Historically, parents had no immunizations or other medical care for their infants, but they often went to great lengths to try and protect their babies from death, as you will see in the **Historical Focus: Protecting Infants the Puritan Way** feature above. Although they knew nothing about the physiological causes of illness and had no effective medical remedies, they attempted to devise practices that would allow their infants to avoid harm. In medieval Europe, for example, where an estimated one of every three babies died before their first birthday, a popular belief was that teething was a common cause of death (Fontanel & d'Hartcourt, 1997). This is a case of the common human tendency, discussed in Chapter 1, to confuse correlation and causation. Teething often takes place about midway through the first year. When their infants began suffering symptoms such as fevers and diarrhea after teething began, the parents concluded that teething was the cause, having no idea that the real source of the symptoms was a disease such as malaria, typhus, or cholera. So, they addressed the illness by placing a charm or amulet around the child's neck, or by placing leeches on the baby's gums, sadly to no good effect.

Today, too, in cultures or in immigrant groups where medical remedies for infant illness are not trusted or are not readily available, parents often resort to magical practices intended to protect their babies from disease and death. Observations today in places with little access to medical care offer many poignant examples of the cultural practices that have developed to try to protect infants. For example, the people of Bali, in Indonesia, believe that infants should be treated like gods, since they have just arrived from the spirit world, where the gods dwell (Diener, 2000). Consequently, infants should be held constantly and should never touch the ground, out of respect for their godly status. If an infant dies, this is often interpreted as indicating that the infant was not shown the proper respect and so decided to return to the spirit world.

The Fulani people of West Africa believe that a sharp knife should always be kept near the baby to ward off the witches and evil spirits that may try to take its soul (Johnson, 2000). Compliments to the baby should be avoided at all costs, as this may only make the baby seem more valuable and beautiful and so all the more attractive to the evil spirits. Instead, the Fulani people believe parents should give the infant an unattractive nickname like "Cow Turd," so that the evil spirits will think the baby is not worth taking.

Finally, many cultural groups who immigrate to the United States continue to use folk remedies to avoid or treat illness. For example, some Guatemalan Maya and Somali parents ward against "Evil Eye" by tying a special string around the infant's wrist. Many Hmong and Vietnamese parents rub coins on children's skin to help expel illness. "Coining" involves first rubbing the skin with medicated oil and then rubbing the edge of a coin over the area to draw out the illness. This practice typically causes symmetrical abrasions with well-defined borders, and these skin blotches should not be automatically mistaken for abuse (Fontes & O'Neill-Arana, 2008).

gross motor development development of motor abilities including balance and posture as well as whole-body movements such as crawling

fine motor development development of motor abilities involving finely tuned movements of the hands such as grasping and manipulating objects

> **THINKING CULTURALLY**
>
> *What cultural practices to protect infants are you familiar with?*

WHAT HAVE YOU LEARNED?

1. What kinds of solid foods should infants eat; beginning when?
2. Can the consequences of malnutrition be reversed if later nutrition improves?
3. What is the major cause of infant mortality, and why is the rate so high if there is a simple remedy?
4. How do the rates of infant vaccination vary in different world regions and how have vaccinations influenced rates of infant mortality over the past century?
5. How is the correlation–causation error reflected in the ways some cultures have sought to protect infants from harm?

Baby on the Move: Motor and Sensory Development

One of the most striking features of human neonates is how little they are able to move around. Even if you hold neonates up, their heads flop to one side because their neck muscles are not yet strong enough to support their heads. But over the course of the first year they develop from immobile to highly mobile, a huge change not just in their lives but in the lives of those who care for them. Sensory development in the first year is more subtle, but advances take place, especially in the sense of sight. ◉

Watch the **Video** Motor Development in Infants and Toddlers in **MyDevelopmentLab**

Motor development

Describe the major changes during infancy in gross and fine motor development.

LEARNING OBJECTIVE 4.6

Over the first year of life remarkable advances take place in motor development. The changes occur in **gross motor development**, which includes balance and posture as well as whole-body movements such as crawling, and in **fine motor development**, which entails more finely tuned movements of the hands such as grasping and manipulating objects.

In many traditional cultures infants are strapped to their mothers' backs for most of the day. Here, a mother and infant in rural Vietnam.

👁️⊸[**Watch** the **Video** Gross Motor Skills in **MyDevelopmentLab**

APPLYING YOUR KNOWLEDGE
. . . as a Nurse

A mother is worried that her baby hasn't crawled yet and fears something is wrong. What can you tell her?

APPLYING YOUR KNOWLEDGE

How would the advances in gross motor development over the first year influence the infant's social relationships?

GROSS MOTOR DEVELOPMENT Ask a parent of an infant what's new, and it's quite likely you'll hear about some new milestone of gross motor development that has recently been achieved. "Emma can now sit up on her own without falling over!" or "Juan is suddenly crawling all over the house!" or "Maru took her first steps yesterday!" There are many achievements of gross motor development over the first year, including holding the head up without support, rolling over, sitting without support, crawling, standing, cruising (walking while holding on to something), and (for some) walking. Most children achieve these skills in this sequence, although sometimes the order of skills varies and sometimes children skip steps in the sequence. There is more variability in the timing of each milestone of gross motor development than in the sequence. As you can see in **Table 4.1**, for each milestone there is a normal range of variation of several months. Infants could reach the milestones anywhere within those ranges and still be developing normally. 👁️

How much of infants' gross motor development is *ontogenetic*—meaning that it takes place due to an inborn, genetically based, individual timetable—and how much of it is due to experience and learning? As with most aspects of development, both genetics and environment are involved. Certainly the highly consistent sequence of gross motor milestones suggests an ontogenetic timetable. There is also evidence for genetic group differences, with infants of African heritage reaching most motor milestones earlier than other infants (Kelly et al., 2006). However, most developmental psychologists view gross motor development in infancy as a combination of the genetic timetable, the maturation of the brain, support and assistance from adults for developing the skill, and the child's own efforts to practice the skill (Adolf & Berger, 2006; Thelen, 2001).

Looking at infant gross motor development across cultures provides a vivid picture of how genetics and environment interact. In many traditional cultures it is a common practice for infants to be strapped onto their mothers' backs for most of the day, as the mothers go about their daily business of tending crops, preparing food, and other kinds of work (Pretorius et al., 2002). In some cultures a common infant-care practice in the first few months of life is swaddling, which was discussed in Chapter 3. If infants are strapped to their mothers' backs or swaddled for most of the day, they receive little practice in developing gross motor skills. These restrictive practices are partly to free the mother to work, but cultures that swaddle infants also believe that swaddling protects the infant from sickness and other threats to health (DeLoache & Gottlieb, 2000). In rural regions of Turkey, infants are swaddled for the first few months and then carried around by their mother and other family members, as discussed in the **Cultural Focus: Infant Care in Rural Turkey** feature.

Even after they learn to crawl at about 6 months old and walk at about 1 year, infants in traditional cultures are restricted in their exercise of these new motor skills. If they are allowed to crawl around and explore they might wander into the cooking fire,

---

TABLE 4.1 Milestones of Gross Motor Development in Infancy

Milestone	Average Age	Age Range*
Holding head up unsupported	6 weeks	3 weeks–4 months
Rolling over	4½ months	2–7 months
Sitting without support	7 months	5–9 months
Crawling	7 months	5–11 months
Standing	11 months	5–12 months
Walking with support (cruising)	11½ months	7–12 months
Walking	12 months	9–17 months

*Age ranges provided are for 90% of American infants.
Source: Based on Bayley Scales of Infant and Toddler Development, Third Edition (Bayley-III).

or be trampled by livestock, or tumble off a cliff, or any number of other bad things, so it is viewed as best to keep them in someone's arms at all times. As we saw with the story of Makori that opened this chapter, infants from the Gusii culture of Kenya are held or carried the majority of their waking hours throughout the first year (see *Figure 4.5*) (LeVine et al., 1994, p. 160).

In contrast, some cultures actively promote infants' gross motor development. For example, the Kipsigis people of Kenya begin encouraging gross motor skills from early on (Super & Harkness, 2009). When only 2–3 months old, infants are placed in shallow holes, kept upright by rolled blankets, months before they would be able to sit on their own. At about the same age, parents start encouraging their infants to practice walking by holding them up and bouncing their feet on the ground. Similarly, in Jamaica

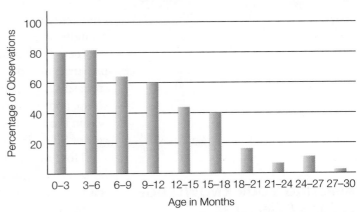

Figure 4.5 • **Holding of Gusii infants by age.** How does the percentage during the first year compare to infants in your culture? **Source:** Childcare and culture: Lessons from Africa, LeVine (1994).

CULTURAL FOCUS   Infant Care in Rural Turkey

Turkey is a Muslim country of about 70 million people located at the intersection of Asia and Europe. It has experienced rapid economic development in recent decades, but as in many developing countries, the changes are taking place mainly in urban areas and the lives of people in rural areas continue to follow the traditional ways (DeLoache & Gottlieb, 2000).

Rural villagers in Turkey make their livelihood mainly by farming. Most families have enough land to raise crops to provide for their own needs, with a little left over to sell at the market. Most also have sheep, goats, and perhaps a few cows, to provide dairy products and meat. Houses are made of mudbrick and usually have two large rooms used for all activities, from eating and sleeping to entertaining. Since the 1970s the villages have had electricity, and families typically have a washing machine, a television, and a few other electronic devices.

The Turks regard children as a great blessing and celebrate the birth of each child. They believe that it is essential to have children in order to have a happy life, and that children strengthen the parents' marriage. Infants and young children are typically treated with a great deal of love and indulgence.

Infants are breast-fed for at least the first 18 months of life. Turks believe that breast-feeding the infant gives the mother "milk rights," meaning that in return the grown child will be obligated to take care of her in her old age. Traditionally, if the mother was unable to produce sufficient milk, another woman in the village would become the infant's "milk mother." That woman's

children would become the infant's "milk siblings," and in adulthood they would be forbidden to marry just as biological siblings are. Today, however, women who cannot produce milk usually obtain bottles and formula rather than arranging for a milk mother.

Infants are swaddled most of the time during their first months of life. Turkish people believe that swaddling makes infants feel secure and helps them sleep soundly. They also believe that swaddling protects infants' health and well-being.

After swaddling has ended, infants are held almost constantly by their mothers and other family members and family friends. They are rarely allowed to crawl around once they become capable of doing so, because of the fear that they will find something dirty or dangerous and put it in their mouths. But there is almost always someone around who is happy to hold a baby, given the child-focused beliefs of rural Turkish culture.

Turkish villagers do not celebrate or even keep track of birthdays, but they often have a party when the infant's first tooth comes in. There is music and dancing, and a special food is prepared for the occasion, "tooth bulgur" made of bulgur wheat and chickpeas cooked into a soft paste. Turks believe this paste helps infants' teeth come in without pain. Wishful thinking, perhaps, but it also reflects the Turkish belief that babies should experience as little pain and as much joy and love as possible.

Turks value children highly and treat infants with abundant love and indulgence.

mothers massage and stretch their babies' arms and legs beginning in early infancy to promote strength and growth, and like the Kipsigis, beginning at 2–3 months of age they help them practice walking (Hopkins & Westra, 1990). In some Western countries, pediatricians now recommend "tummy time" for infants, that is, placing them on their stomachs for a short period each day to encourage them to learn to push up, roll over, sit up, and stand (Ianelli, 2007). Tummy time is viewed as more important now than it was in the past because infants are now supposed to sleep on their backs to reduce the risk of SIDS, and so spend less time on their stomachs.

How much does it matter, ultimately, if cultural practices hinder or promote infants' gross motor development? A little in the short run, perhaps, but not much in the long run. For the most part, infants in cultures where they are strapped to the mother's back or swaddled learn to crawl and walk at about the same age as infants in cultures that neither bind their infants nor make special efforts to support gross motor development (Adolph et al., 2010). One exception is the Ache people, a South American Indian culture (Kaplan & Dove, 1987). Ache mothers have extremely close contact with their infants, strapping, carrying, or holding them 93% of daylight time and 100% of the night hours. Consequently, Ache children do not typically begin walking until about age 2, a year later than the norm across cultures. However, this appears to be partly because Ache infants enjoy being carried around so much that they often refuse to walk even after they are able! In any case, there is no difference in gross motor development by age 6 between Ache children and children in less restrictive cultures.

Infants in cultures where gross motor development is actively stimulated may develop slightly earlier than in cultures where parents make no special efforts. In a study comparing Jamaican immigrant infants in England with native-born English mothers, the Jamaican immigrant infants walked slightly earlier, evidently because their mothers encouraged them to walk and practiced with them, but the two groups were no different in when crawling began (Hopkins & Westra, 1990). In some African cultures that actively stimulate gross motor development, infants walk a few weeks earlier than children in the West (Adolph et al., 2010). Here again, however, by age 6 there are no differences in gross motor development between children in the cultures that promote early motor achievement and cultures that do not. Thus it appears that cultural practices can slightly speed up or slow down the ontogenetic timetable for gross motor development in infancy, but the influence of the environment is relatively small and transient for this particular area of development.

FINE MOTOR DEVELOPMENT One of the evolutionary developments that makes humans anatomically distinctive among animals is the **opposable thumb**, that is, the position of our thumbs opposite our fingers. (Place your thumb now against your fingers and you will see what I mean.) The opposable thumb is the basis of fine motor development, the deft movements of our hands that enable us to make a tool, pick up a small object, or thread a needle. During the first year of life, the ability for fine motor movements makes remarkable progress.

The principal milestones of fine motor development in infancy are reaching and grasping. Oddly, infants are better at reaching during the first month of life than they are at 2 months of age (Spencer et al., 2000). Neonates will extend their arms awkwardly toward an interesting object, an action called *prereaching*, although it is more like a swipe or a swing than a well-coordinated reach. By 2 months, however, prereaching no longer takes place (Lee et al., 2008). Prereaching is a reflex that occurs in response to an object, and like many reflexes it disappears within the first months of life.

At about 3 months of age, reaching reappears, but in a more coordinated and accurate way than in the neonate. Reaching continues to develop over the course of the

APPLYING YOUR KNOWLEDGE
. . . as a Researcher

You are conducting research with Mayan Indians in Mexico. You notice that babies younger than 1 year are always held or carried on someone's back. They never get the chance to crawl. Yet they walk at about the same time as other infants you've seen at home (around their first birthday). How can you explain this?

THINKING CULTURALLY

In the United States, there seem to be a lot of books on getting your baby to sleep through the night. Why aren't there similar books on teaching children to walk sooner?

opposable thumb position of the thumb apart from the fingers, unique to humans, that makes possible fine motor movements

first year, becoming smoother, more direct, and more capable of adjusting to changes in the movement and position of the object (Berthier & Carrico, 2010).

Grasping is also a neonatal reflex, and this means it is not under intentional control (Schott & Rossor, 2003). Neonates will automatically grasp whatever is placed in their hands. Like reaching, grasping becomes smoother and more accurate during the first year, as infants learn to adjust the positions of their fingers and thumbs even before their hand reaches the object, and to adjust further once they grasp the object, in response to its size, shape, and weight (Daum et al., 2011). By the end of the first year, infants are able to grasp a spoon well enough to begin to feed themselves—although this does not guarantee the food will always end up in their mouths!

At the same time as infants' abilities for reaching and grasping are advancing, they are learning to coordinate the two. They use the combination to help them explore the environment around them. By 5 months of age, once they reach and grasp an object, they might hold it with one hand as they explore it with the other, or transfer it from one hand to the other (Keen, 2005).

Learning to coordinate reaching and grasping is the basis of further development of fine motor skills, and an essential part of human motor functioning. However, during infancy it can also be a dangerous ability to have. Beginning at about 4 to 5 months, what is the first thing infants do with an object after reaching and grasping it? They put it in their mouths, of course—whether it is edible or not. (How this tendency somehow survived natural selection is a good question.) At this age they can mainly grasp objects that pose no danger, because their grasping ability is not yet fine enough to enable them to grasp objects they could choke on. However, by 9–12 months of age infants learn the "pincer grasp" that allows them to hold a small object between their thumb and forefinger, such as a marble, a coin, or a crayon stub (Murkoff et al., 2003). This allows them to begin feeding themselves small pieces of food, but the tendency to taste even the untasteable remains at this age, so others have to be especially vigilant in monitoring what infants reach, grasp, and place in their mouths.

By 9–12 months infants are able to grasp small objects.

APPLYING YOUR KNOWLEDGE
. . . as a Parent

What are the implications of gross and fine motor development for safety precautions in your household?

Sensory development

Describe when and how infants develop depth perception and intermodal perception.

LEARNING OBJECTIVE **4.7**

As described in Chapter 3, the senses vary in how developed they are at birth. Taste and touch are nearly mature, hearing is well-developed in most respects, and sight is the least mature of the senses.

DEPTH PERCEPTION One important aspect of vision that develops during infancy is **depth perception,** the ability to discern the relative distance of objects in the environment (Kavšec, 2003). The key to depth perception is **binocular vision,** the ability to combine the images of each eye into one image. Because our two eyes are slightly apart on our faces, they have slightly different angles on the visual field before them, and combining these two angles into one image provides a perception of the depth or distance of the object. That is, it indicates the location of the object in relation to the observer and in relation to other objects in the visual field. Binocular vision begins to develop by about 3 months of age (Brown & Miracle, 2003; Slater et al., 2002).

Depth perception becomes especially important once babies become mobile. Prior to that time, their lack of depth perception is harmless, but once they begin to crawl and then walk they may run into things or fall off the edge of surfaces unless they can use depth perception to anticipate hazards.

My Virtual Child

What kind of hazards might your virtual child encounter as he or she explores the environment? Are these similar to hazards that could be found in other environments?

depth perception ability to discern the relative distance of objects in the environment

binocular vision ability to combine the images of the two eyes into one image

intermodal perception integration and coordination of information from the various senses

Simulate the **Experiment** The Visual Cliff in **MyDevelopmentLab**

Figure 4.6 • **The visual cliff experiment.** Infants' reluctance to cross the "visual cliff" shows their ability for depth perception.

This was first demonstrated in a classic experiment by Eleanor Gibson and James Walk (1960). Gibson's inspiration for the experiment was a recent trip to the Grand Canyon, where her fear that her young children would tumble over the edge inspired her to wonder when children develop an awareness of depth that allows them to avoid such mishaps. Back in the lab, she and Walk designed a clever experiment. They made a glass-covered table with a checkered pattern below the glass, but on one half of the table the checkered pattern was just below the surface whereas on the other half it was about two feet below, giving the appearance of a "visual cliff" in the middle of the table (see *Figure 4.6*).

The infants in the study (ages 6–14 months) were happy to crawl around on the "shallow" side of the cliff, but most would not cross over to the "deep" side, even when their mothers stood on the other side of it and beckoned them encouragingly. This showed that they had learned depth perception.

But *when* did they learn it? All the infants in the study could crawl or walk, otherwise they would not have had much chance of crossing the cliff even if they wanted to, but by that age they already had depth perception. A subsequent experiment added further information. The researchers used 2–3-month-old infants as the participants, and placed them first on the shallow side of the visual cliff and then on the deep side, while monitoring the babies' heart rates (Campos et al., 1970). Their heart rates decreased when they were placed on the deep side, indicating that they were interested but not afraid. This was taken to indicate that at 2–3 months of age, before they could crawl, infants had depth perception but their lack of experience with crawling meant that they did not experience fear of the visual cliff.

INTERMODAL PERCEPTION Studies of infants' sensory abilities typically try to isolate a single sense so that it can be studied without interference from the others, but of course this is not how the senses function in real life. Shake a rattle in front of 6-month-old baby and she sees it, hears it, reaches out and touches it, then tastes it, effortlessly coordinating all her senses at once.

The integration and coordination of sensory information is called **intermodal perception**. Even neonates possess a rudimentary form of this ability. When they hear a sound they look in the direction it came from, indicating coordination of auditory and visual responses (Morrongiello et al., 1994). Over the course of the first year intermodal perception develops further. One-month-old infants recognize objects they have put in their mouths but have not seen before, indicating integration of touch and sight (Schweinle & Wilcox, 2004). Four-month-old infants look longer at a video of a puppet jumping up and down in time with music than at the same puppet when the jumping does not match the music, suggesting that the correspondence of visual and auditory stimuli appeals to them (Spelke, 1979). By 8 months, infants can even match an unfamiliar person's face with the correct voice when the faces and voices vary on the basis of age and gender, indicating a developing ability to coordinate visual and auditory information (Patterson & Werker, 2002). Thus the early development of intermodal perception helps infants learn about their physical and social world (Banks, 2005).

WHAT HAVE YOU LEARNED?

1. How do cultural practices such as swaddling influence the timing of gross motor development?
2. What is the pincer grasp and at what age do infants master it?
3. How does the visual cliff experiment demonstrate when and how infants learn depth perception?
4. Give an example of intermodal perception in an 8-month-old infant.

Section 1 VIDEO GUIDE Infant Fine Motor Development Across Cultures (Length: 3:26)

This video displays several instances of babies from various countries at differing stages of fine motor development.

1. The narrator tells us that certain developmental milestones occur at very similar ages across cultures. Does this surprise you? Why or why not?

2. Can you think of any related skills that the pincer grasp might be a precursor for? What about skills related to grasping? In what ways would these primitive skills be so important across cultures?

3. Many first attempts of grasping by young babies are unsuccessful. Why do you think they continue to try and eventually succeed?

👁 ─[**Watch** the **Video** Infant Fine Motor Development Across Cultures in **MyDevelopmentLab**

LEARNING OBJECTIVES

4.8 Describe the first four sensorimotor substages.

4.9 Explain how object permanence develops over the course of the first year.

4.10 Summarize the major critiques of Piaget's sensorimotor theory.

4.11 Explain how attention and habituation change during infancy.

4.12 Explain how short-term and long-term memory expand during infancy.

4.13 Describe the major scales used in measuring infant development and explain how habituation assessments are used to predict later intelligence.

4.14 Evaluate the claim that educational media enhance infants' cognitive development.

4.15 Describe the course of language development over the first year of life.

4.16 Describe how cultures vary in their stimulation of language development.

---

sensorimotor stage in Piaget's theory, the first two years of cognitive development, which involves learning how to coordinate the activities of the senses with motor activities

schemes cognitive structures for processing, organizing, and interpreting information

assimilation cognitive process of altering new information to fit an existing scheme

accommodation cognitive process of changing a scheme to adapt to new information

Piaget's Sensorimotor Stage

The sensorimotor stage of Piaget's theory is characterized by the infant's developing maturation and use of the sensory systems (particularly vision, touch, and hearing), and the motor system (manipulating objects, self-locomotion). The infant learns about the world through sensorimotor activity, exploring and building schemas in the mind about how the world works.

The sensorimotor substages

4.8	**LEARNING OBJECTIVE**	Describe the first four sensorimotor substages.

Based on his own research and his collaborations with his colleague Barbel Inhelder, Piaget devised a theory of cognitive development to describe the stages that children's thinking passes through as they grow up (Inhelder & Piaget, 1958; Piaget, 1972) (see Chapter 1). The first two years of life Piaget termed the **sensorimotor stage**. Cognitive development in this stage involves learning how to coordinate the activities of the senses (such as watching an object as it moves across your field of vision) with motor activities (such as reaching out to grasp the object). During infancy, the two major cognitive achievements, according to Piaget, are the advance in sensorimotor development from reflex behavior to intentional action and the attainment of object permanence.

According to Piaget, the sensorimotor stage can be divided into six substages (Piaget, 1952, 1954). The first four substages take place during the first year of life and will be described here. The last two sensorimotor stages develop in the second year and will be covered in Chapter 5, on toddlerhood.

Substage 1: Simple reflexes (0–1 month). In this substage, cognitive activity is based mainly on the neonatal reflexes described in Chapter 3, such as sucking, rooting, and grasping. Reflexes are a type of **scheme,** because they are a way of processing and organizing information. However, unlike most schemes, for which there is a balance of **assimilation** and **accommodation,** reflex schemes are weighted

Watch the **Video**
Sensorimotor Development
in **MyDevelopmentLab**

Explore the **Concept** Infant's
Perceptual and Cognitive Milestones
in **MyDevelopmentLab**

heavily toward assimilation, because they do not adapt much in response to the environment.

Substage 2: First habits and primary circular reactions (1–4 months). In this substage, infants' activities in relation to the world become based less on reflexes and more on the infants' purposeful behavior. Specifically, infants in this substage learn to repeat bodily movements that occurred initially by chance. For example, infants often discover how tasty their hands and fingers can be in this substage. While moving their hands around randomly, one ends up in their mouth and they begin sucking on it. Finding this sensation pleasurable, they repeat the movement, now intentionally. The movement is *primary* because it focuses on the infant's own body, and *circular* because once it is discovered it is repeated intentionally.

Substage 3: Secondary circular reactions (4–8 months). Like primary circular reactions, secondary circular reactions entail the repetition of movements that originally occurred by chance. The difference is that primary circular reactions involve activity that is restricted to the infant's own body, whereas secondary circular reactions involve activity in relation to the external world. For example, Piaget recorded how his daughter Lucienne at this age accidentally kicked a mobile hanging over her crib. Delighted at the effect, she now repeated the behavior intentionally, over and over, each time squealing with laughter (Crain, 2000).

Substage 4: Coordination of secondary schemes (8–12 months). In this substage, for the first time the baby's actions begin not as accidents but as intentional, goal-directed behavior. Furthermore, rather than exercising one scheme at a time, the infant can now coordinate schemes. For example, at this age Piaget's son Laurent was able to move an object (Piaget's hand) out of the way in order to reach another object (a matchbox), thus coordinating three schemes: moving something aside, reaching, and grasping.

Object permanence

Explain how object permanence develops over the course of the first year.

LEARNING OBJECTIVE 4.9

Another important cognitive advance in infancy is the initial understanding of **object permanence**. This is the awareness that objects (including people) continue to exist even when we are not in direct sensory or motor contact with them. The achievement of object permanence indicates that infants are able to mentally represent objects. ◉

From his observations and simple experiments, Piaget concluded that infants have little understanding of object permanence, or mental representation, for much of the first year of life (Piaget, 1952). When infants under 4 months drop an object, they do not look to see where it went. Piaget interpreted this as indicating that, to the infants, the object ceased to exist once they could not see or touch it. From 4 to 8 months, infants who drop an object will look briefly to see where it has gone, but only briefly, which Piaget interpreted as indicating that they are unsure whether the object still exists. If infants at this age are shown an interesting object—Piaget liked to use his pocket watch—and then the object is placed under a blanket, they will not lift up the blanket to look for it.

It is only at 8–12 months that infants begin to show a developing awareness of object permanence. Now, when shown an interesting object that then disappears under a blanket, they will pick up the blanket to find it. However, their grasp of object permanence at this age is still rudimentary, as Piaget showed by making the task slightly more complicated. After an 8–12 month old successfully solved the object-under-the-blanket task several times, Piaget introduced a second blanket next to the first, showed the infant the object, and this time placed it under the second blanket. Infants at this age then looked for the object—but not under the second blanket, where they had just seen it hidden, but under the first blanket, where they had found it before!

◉—[**Watch** the **Video**
Object Permanence in
MyDevelopmentLab

object permanence awareness that objects (including people) continue to exist even when we are not in direct sensory or motor contact with them

At age 8–12 months infants still have an incomplete understanding of object permanence.

Piaget called this the *A-not-B error*. The infants were used to finding the object under blanket A, so they continued to look under blanket A, not blanket B, even after they had seen the object hidden under blanket B. To Piaget, this error indicated that the infants believed that their own action of looking under blanket A was what had caused the object to reappear. They did not understand that the object continued to exist irrespective of their actions, so they did not yet fully grasp object permanence.

Limited understanding of object permanence could explain why infants love the game "peek-a-boo," in which adults cover their face with their hands or an object (such as a cloth), then suddenly reveal it. One study found that this game was played by adults and infants across a diverse range of cultures, including Brazil, Greece, India, Iran, Indonesia, South Korea, and South Africa (Fernald & O'Neill, 1993). Infants everywhere delighted in the game, and across cultures there were developmental changes. In the early months, infants enjoyed the game but responded only when the other person's face reappeared. Beginning at about 5 months, babies would begin to smile and laugh even before the other person reappeared, indicating that they were anticipating the event. By 12 months old infants would initiate the game themselves, by holding a cloth up to the adult's face or putting it over their own. Perhaps infants everywhere love "peek-a-boo" because to them, given their limited understanding of object permanence, the other person's face seems to disappear when it is obscured, then suddenly, magically reappears. 👁

Watch the **Video** Hidden Elephant in **MyDevelopmentLab**

Evaluating Piaget's sensorimotor theory

4.10 | **LEARNING OBJECTIVE** | Summarize the major critiques of Piaget's sensorimotor theory.

You may have noticed that some of the examples discussed previously involved Piaget's children. Actually, Piaget initially based his theory of sensorimotor development on his careful observations and experiments with his own three children, Laurent, Lucienne, and Jacqueline. It is remarkable—and it is a testimony to Piaget's brilliance—that a theory based on just three children within the same Swiss family became the reigning theory of infant cognitive development.

Even today, over 70 years after he first proposed it, Piaget's theory of infant cognitive development remains influential. Like all good theories, it has inspired a wealth of research (by Piaget and many others) to test its assertions and implications. And, like even the best theories, it has been modified and altered on the basis of research (Morra et al., 2008).

In recent decades, methods of testing infants' cognitive abilities have become much more technologically advanced. Studies using these methods have generally concluded that Piaget's theory was correct in its overall description of infant cognitive development (Marcovitch et al., 2003). However, some critics argue that the theory may have underestimated infants' cognitive abilities, especially with regard to object permanence.

Infants' motor development occurs along with their cognitive development, so when they fail to look under a blanket for a hidden object, could it be they lack the motor coordination to search for the object rather than that they believe it is has disappeared? One line of research by Renee Baillargeon and colleagues has tested this hypothesis by using the "violation of expectations method." This method is based on the assumption that infants will look longer at an event that has violated their expectations, and if they look longer at an event violating the rule of object permanence this indicates some understanding of object permanence, without requiring any motor movements. For example, at age 5–6 months, infants will look longer when a toy they have seen hidden at one spot in a sandbox emerges from a different spot (Baillargeon, 2008; Newcombe & Huttenlocher, 2006). This seems to indicate an expectation that it should have emerged from the same spot, as a permanent object would. Even at 2–3 months infants look longer at events that are physically impossible (Wang et al., 2005), perhaps showing a more advanced understanding of objects than Piaget would have predicted.

Some critics of Piaget's sensorimotor theory argue that mistakes regarding object permanence may reflect memory development rather than a failure to understand the properties of objects. For example, with respect to the A-not-B error, the longer the delay between hiding the object under blanket B and the infant's attempts to find it, the higher the likelihood of making the error, suggesting that with a longer delay the infant may simply have forgotten where it was placed (Diamond, 1985).

Another criticism of Piaget's sensorimotor theory is cultural (Maynard, 2008). The theory was originally based on his own three Swiss children, and nearly all subsequent research has been on children in the West (Mistry & Saraswathi, 2003). However, one of the few non-Western studies, of infants in Ivory Coast, found that infants there developed through the sensorimotor stages earlier than Piaget had described (Dasen et al., 1978), perhaps because their parents encouraged them to develop motor skills.

Overall, however, Piaget's sensorimotor theory has held up well over many decades. Many parts of it have been supported by research, and so far no other comprehensive theory has come along to replace it. However, the information processing approach described next views infant cognitive development quite differently.

WHAT HAVE YOU LEARNED?

1. According to Piaget, how much of an effect does the environment have on our cognitive development?
2. How do secondary circular reactions differ from primary circular reactions?
3. What is the A-not-B error and how is it used to measure infants' understanding of object permanence?
4. What role does memory play in infants' mastery of object permanence?

Information Processing in Infancy

Piaget's theory and the research it inspired focuses on how thinking changes with age. To Piaget, we do not simply have a greater cognitive capacity as we age and develop, we actually think differently at each life stage.

The **information processing approach** to understanding cognitive development is quite different. Rather than viewing cognitive development as *discontinuous*, that is, as separated into distinct stages, the way Piaget did, the information processing approach views cognitive change as *continuous*, meaning gradual and steady. In this view, cognitive processes remain essentially the same over time (Halford, 2005). The focus is not on how **mental structures** and ways of thinking change with age but on the thinking processes that exist at all ages. Nevertheless, some studies of information processing compare people of various ages to show how thinking capacities change developmentally. ◉▸

The original model for the information processing approach was the computer (Hunt, 1989). Information processing researchers and theorists have tried to break down human thinking into separate parts in the same way the functions of a computer

information processing approach approach to understanding cognitive functioning that focuses on cognitive processes that exist at all ages, rather than on viewing cognitive developing in terms of discontinuous stages

mental structure in Piaget's theory of cognitive development, the cognitive systems that organize thinking into coherent patterns so that all thinking takes place on the same level of cognitive functioning

THINKING CULTURALLY

Among some cultures, such as the Maya of Mexico, parents view a child's development as proceeding along a set course and therefore offer little external stimulation. How does this contrast to the American ideal of providing a lot of cognitive stimulation?

APPLYING YOUR KNOWLEDGE

Are Piaget's approach and the information processing approach to cognitive development incompatible, or could they be combined?

◉▸ **Simulate** the **Experiment** The Information Processing Model in **MyDevelopmentLab**

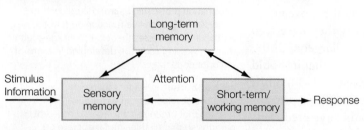

Figure 4.7 • **Information processing model.** The components of the model operate simultaneously.

are separated into capacities for *attention*, *processing*, and *memory*. In the case of object permanence, for example, someone taking the information processing approach would examine how infants draw their attention to the most relevant aspects of the problem, process the results of each trial, remember the results, and retrieve the results from previous trials to compare to the most recent trial.

Recent models of information processing have moved away from a simple computer analogy and recognize that the brain is more complex than any computer (Ashcraft, 2009). Rather than occurring in a step-by-step fashion as in a computer, in humans the different components of thinking operate simultaneously, as *Figure 4.7* illustrates. Nevertheless, the focus of information processing remains on the components of the thinking process, especially attention and memory. Let's look next at how attention and memory develop during infancy.

Attention

| 4.11 | LEARNING OBJECTIVE | Explain how attention and habituation change during infancy. |

Information processing begins with stimulus information that enters the senses, but much of what you see, hear, and touch is processed no further. For example, as you read this, there may be sounds in the environment, other sights in your visual field, and the feeling of your body in the seat where you are reading, but if you are focusing on what you are reading most of this information goes no further than sensory memory. The only information you proceed to process is the information on which you focus your attention.

In infants the study of attention has focused on **habituation**, which is the gradual decrease in attention to a stimulus after repeated presentations. For example, infants will look longer at a toy the first time it is presented than the fourth or fifth time. A complementary concept, **dishabituation**, is the revival of attention when a new stimulus is presented following several presentations of a previous stimulus. For example, if you show infants a picture of the same face several times in a row, then show a new face, they will generally dishabituate to the new face, that is, they will pay more attention to it than to the "old" face. Habituation and dishabituation can be studied by monitoring infants' looking behavior, but infants rarely lie still for long even if they are paying attention to something, so two other methods have been frequently used: heart rate (heart rate declines when a new stimulus is presented and gradually rises as habituation takes place) and sucking rate (infants suck on a pacifier more frequently when a new stimulus is presented and gradually decline in their sucking rate with habituation).

During the course of the first year of life, it takes less and less time for habituation to occur. When presented with a visual stimulus, neonates may take several minutes before they show signs of habituating (by changing their looking time, heart rate, or sucking rate). By 4–5 months old, habituation in a similar experiment takes only about 10 seconds, and by 7–8 months only a few seconds (Domsch et al., 2010; Kavšek & Bornstein, 2010). This appears to be because with age infants become more efficient at perceiving and processing a stimulus.

Even when they are a few months old, infants of the same age vary in their rates of habituation, and these individual differences tend to be stable over time. Some infants are more efficient than others at processing information; consequently, they habituate

habituation gradual decrease in attention to a stimulus aftere repeated presentations

dishabituation following habituation, the revival of attention when a new stimulus is presented more quickly. Infants who habituate relatively slowly appear to do so not because they are especially good at sustaining their attention but because they seem to get stuck on the stimulus and have difficulty disengaging from it. Speed of habituation positively predicts memory ability on other tasks in infancy, as well as later performance on intelligence tests (Courage et al., 2004; Rose et al., 2005).

In the second half of the first year, infants' patterns of attention become increasingly social. They direct their attention not just to whatever sensations are most stimulating but to what the people around them are attending to, engaging in *joint attention*. By the end of the first year they often notice what important people around them are paying attention to, and will look or point in the same direction. One experiment showed that 10-month-old infants were less likely to look or point in the direction an adult was faced if the adult's eyes were closed or blindfolded, indicating that the infants were aware of the adults' attentional patterns and matched their own to them (Brooks & Meltzoff, 2005).

Joint attention is the basis not just of infants' information processing development but of language and emotional communication (Van Hecke et al., 2007). This makes sense; one way infants and children learn new words is to observe what another person is doing or looking at when they use a word. Often this takes place during social interactions between infants and others, but it can also take place from infants observing where the attention of another person is directed. As we will see in more detail later in the chapter, not all cultures encourage social interactions with infants. A cultural analysis of this issue showed that in cultures where social interactions with adults are limited, infants and young children learn a great deal of their language by observing adults' language use and "listening in," that is, using joint attention to discern the meaning of words (Akhtar, 2005).

Joint attention develops by the end of the first year.

Memory

Explain how short-term and long-term memory expand during infancy.

LEARNING OBJECTIVE 4.12

Infants' memory abilities expand greatly during the first year of life, both for short-term and for long-term memory. One reflection of the development of short-term memory is their improvement in the object permanence task. As noted earlier, object permanence is a test of short-term memory as well as a test of knowledge of the properties of objects. Memory studies using object permanence tasks show that the number of locations infants can remember and search to look for a hidden object increases sharply in the second half of the first year (Morra et al., 2008).

Long-term memory also improves notably over the course of the first year. In one experiment, researchers tied a string to the foot of infants 2 to 6 months old and taught them to move a mobile hanging above their cribs by kicking their foot (Rovee-Collier, 1999). The 2-month-olds forgot the training within a week—they no longer kicked to make the mobile move when the string was tied to their legs—but the 6-month-olds remembered it for about three weeks, demonstrating their longer long-term memories.

Further experiments showed an interesting distinction between *recognition memory* and *recall memory* (Hildreth et al., 2003). After the mobile-kicking trick appeared to be lost from the infants' memories, the researchers gave the infants a hint by making the mobile move. The infants *recognized* this clue and began kicking again to make the mobile move, up to a month later, even though they had been unable to *recall* the memory before being prompted. The older the infant was, the more effective the prompting. From infancy onward, recognition memory comes easier to us than recall memory (Flavell et al., 2002).

WHAT HAVE YOU LEARNED?

1. What are the key features of the information processing approach and how does it differ from Piaget's approach?
2. What is the difference between habituation and dishabituation?
3. How is joint attention related to language development?
4. How does memory change during infancy, especially with regard to recognition and recall memory?

Assessing Infant Development

Given the many remarkable changes in development that happen over the course of the first year, researchers have long been interested in evaluating infants to see if they are developing normally. These assessments include cognitive development as well as other aspects of development. We'll also evaluate efforts to improve infants' cognitive development through media stimulation.

Approaches to assessing development

4.13 LEARNING OBJECTIVE

Describe the major scales used in measuring infant development and explain how habituation assessments are used to predict later intelligence.

There are a variety of methods used to measure infant development, including the scales approach of Gesell and Bayley. More recently, research on infants' cognitive development has focused on information processing, especially the processes of attention and memory.

THE SCALES OF GESELL AND BAYLEY One approach to assessing infant development was pioneered by Arnold Gesell (1934, 1946). Gesell constructed an assessment of infant development that included four subscales: motor skills (such as sitting), language use, adaptive behavior (such as exploring a new object), and personal–social behavior (such as using a spoon). Following the model of intelligence tests, which produce an *intelligence quotient (IQ)* as an overall measure of mental abilities, Gesell combined the results of his assessment into a **developmental quotient (DQ)** as an overall measure of infants' developmental progress. Just as for IQs, for DQs 100 is set as the **median** or middle score. Gesell recognized that what he had produced was different from an IQ test, but he hoped it would be similarly useful for assessing current abilities and predicting future development.

Gesell's scale for infants is no longer used, but his approach was continued by Nancy Bayley, who produced the **Bayley Scales of Infant Development,** now in their third edition, the Bayley-III (Bayley, 2005). The Bayley-III can assess development from age 3 months to age 3½ years. There are three main scales on the Bayley-III:

1. *Cognitive scale.* This scale measures mental abilities such as attention and exploration. For example, at 6 months it assesses whether the baby looks at pictures in a book; at 23–25 months it assesses whether a child can match similar pictures.
2. *Language scale.* This scale measures use and understanding of language. For example, at 17–19 months it assesses whether the child can identify objects in a picture, and at 38–42 months it assesses whether the child can name four colors.
3. *Motor scale.* This scale measures fine and gross motor abilities, such as sitting alone for 30 seconds at 6 months, or hopping twice on one foot at 38–42 months.

developmental quotient (DQ) in assessments of infant development, the overall score indicating developmental progress

median in a distribution of data, the score that is precisely in the middle, with half the distribution lying above and half below

Bayley Scales of Infant Development widely used assessment of infant development from age 3 months to 3½ years

As with Gesell's scales, the Bayley scales produce an overall DQ. However, one problem with the Bayley scales is that the reliability of the scales is low (see Chapter 1 for information on reliability). Consequently, especially at the youngest ages, an infant's score on one occasion may be quite different than the same infant's score a week or a month later (Bornstein et al., 1997). Infants' states of arousal and motivation vary greatly from one hour or even minute to the next, so an infant's DQ in the testing session may simply reflect the state that he or she was in at the moment rather than more enduring and stable mental abilities.

Neither Gesell's assessment nor the Bayley scales predict later IQ or school performance well. In fact, Bayley scores in infancy hardly predict later development at all (Hack et al., 2005). If you look closely at the previous examples, this should not be surprising, as the Bayley scales measure quite different kinds of abilities than the verbal and spatial abilities that later IQ tests measure and that schoolwork requires. (Let's face it, hopping on one foot is not likely to be predictive of any kind of school performance or any kind of work you are likely to do as an adult, unless you become a ballet dancer.) The only exception to this is at the lower extreme. An infant who scores very low on the Bayley scales may have serious developmental problems. Consequently, the Bayley scales are used mainly as a screening tool, to identify infants who have serious problems in need of immediate attention, rather than as predictors of later development for children within the normal range.

INFORMATION PROCESSING APPROACHES TO INFANT ASSESSMENT Efforts to predict later intelligence using information-processing approaches have shown greater promise. The focus of these approaches has been on habituation. As noted earlier, infants vary in how long it takes them to habituate to a new stimulus, such as a sight or a sound (Colombo, 2002). Some are "short-lookers" who habituate quickly, others are "long-lookers" who take more time and more presentations of the stimulus before they habituate. The shorter the habituation time, the more efficient the infant's information processing abilities. They look for a shorter length of time because it takes them less time to take in and process information about the stimulus.

Longitudinal studies have found that short-lookers in infancy tend to have higher IQ scores later in development than long-lookers do (Kavšek, 2004; Rose et al., 2005; Sigman et al., 2000). In one study, short-lookers in infancy had higher IQs and higher educational achievement when the researchers followed up with them 20 years later, as adults (Fagan et al., 2007). Habituation assessments in infancy have also been found to be useful for identifying infants who have developmental problems (Kavšek & Bornstein, 2008). Furthermore, habituation assessments tend to be more reliable than assessments of DQ, that is, they are more likely to be consistent when measured across more than one occasion (Kavšek, 2004). The most recent version of the Bayley scales now includes a measure of habituation (Bayley, 2005), which may improve reliability and predictive validity above previous versions of the scale.

Can media enhance cognitive development? The myth of "Baby Einstein"

| Evaluate the claim that educational media enhance infants' cognitive development. | **LEARNING OBJECTIVE** | **4.14** |

In addition to efforts to assess infants' cognitive development, efforts have also been made to enhance it. One effort of this kind that has become popular in some developed countries is educational media products for infants. ⊙

In the early 1990s a study was published claiming that listening to the music of Mozart enhanced cognitive functioning (Rauscher et al., 1993). The study was conducted with university students, not babies, and the "effect" lasted only 10 minutes,

⊙─ **Watch** the **Video** Baby TV in **MyDevelopmentLab**

Educational media products for infants have not been demonstrated to enhance cognitive development.

and subsequent studies failed to replicate even a 10-minute effect (Rauscher, 2003). Nevertheless, the study received worldwide attention and inspired the creation of a vast range of educational media products claiming to promote infants' cognitive development.

Do they work? The answer appears to be no. Many studies investigating this question have concluded that educational media products have no effect on infants' cognitive development. In fact, one study of 8- to 16-month-olds found that for every hour of "educational" DVDs viewed per day, the DVD viewers understood 8 to 16 *fewer* words than babies who watched no DVDs (Guernsey, 2007). The authors interpreted this surprising finding as due to the fact that the DVD viewers may have spent less time interacting with the people around them. That is, they were watching DVDs instead of interacting socially, and the DVD watching did not compensate for the deficit in social interaction. Similar results were found in another study (DeLoache et al., 2010). Fortunately, national studies have found that only 17% of babies in the United States watch educational media products for an hour or more per day, and the average is only about 13 minutes (Guernsey, 2007; Roberts & Foehr, 2004).

These findings suggest that Piaget was right that children's cognitive maturity has its own innate timetable and that it is fruitless (and perhaps even detrimental) to try to hurry it along. So what can you do to promote infants' healthy cognitive development? Talk to them, read to them, respond to them—and be patient. They will grow up soon enough.

WHAT HAVE YOU LEARNED?

1. What was Gesell's approach to measuring infant intelligence?
2. What are the features of the Bayley scale? How accurate are the scales in predicting later intelligence?
3. What is a new way of measuring infant intelligence and how successful is it?
4. Why should we be cautious about applying the "Mozart effect" to infants?

My Virtual Child

What languages will your virtual child be exposed to during infancy?

👁 ⌐ **Watch** the **Video** Language Development in **MyDevelopmentLab**

The Beginnings of Language

According to the traditional beliefs of the Beng people of Ivory Coast (in Africa), in the spirit world all people understand all languages (Gottlieb, 2000). Babies have just come from the spirit world when they are born, so they understand whatever is said in any language. However, during the first year, memory of all other languages fades and babies come to understand only the language they hear around them. Except for the part about the spirit world, this is actually a pretty accurate summary of how babies' language development takes place in the course of the first year of life, as we will learn next. (See ***Table 4.2*** for the milestones of infant language development.) 👁

First sounds and words

4.15 **LEARNING OBJECTIVE** | Describe the course of language development over the first year of life.

cooing prelanguage "oo-ing" and "ah-ing," and gurgling sounds babies make beginning at about 2 months old

Very early on, babies begin to make the sounds that will eventually develop into language (Waxman & Lidz, 2006). First is **cooing,** the "oo-ing" and "ah-ing" and gurgling sounds babies make beginning at about 2 months old. Often cooing takes place in

TABLE 4.2 Milestones of Infant Language Development

Age	Milestone
2 months	Cooing (preverbal and gurgling sounds)
4–10 months	Babbling (repetitive consonant–vowel combinations)
8–10 months	First gestures (such as "bye-bye")
10–12 months	Comprehension of words and simple sentences
12 months	First spoken word

Note: For each milestone there is a normal range, and babies who are somewhat later in reaching the milestones may nevertheless have normal language development.

interactions with others, but sometimes it takes place without interactions, as if babies are discovering their vocal apparatus and trying out the sounds it can make.

By about 4–6 months old, cooing develops into **babbling,** repetitive consonant-vowel combinations such as "ba-ba-ba" or "do-do-do-do." When my son Miles was 3–4 months old he repeated the sounds "ah-gee" so often that for a while we called him "Mr. Ah-Gee." Babbling appears to be universal among infants. In fact, babies the world over appear to babble with the same sounds initially, regardless of the language of their culture (Lee at al., 2010). Deaf infants exposed to sign language have a form of babbling, too, using their hands instead of sounds (van Beinum, 2008). However, after a couple of months, infants begin to babble in the sounds distinctive to their culture and cease to babble in sounds they have not heard used by the people around them. By the time infants are about 9 months old, untrained listeners can distinguish whether a recording of babbling is from an infant raised amidst French, Arabic, or Chinese (Oller et al., 1997). ◉

By around 8–10 months, infants begin to use gestures to communicate (Goldin-Meadow, 2009). They may lift their arms up to indicate they wish to be picked up, or point to an object they would like to have brought to them, or hold out an object to offer it to someone else, or wave bye-bye. Using gestures is a way of evoking behavior from others (for example, being picked up after lifting their arms in request), and also a way of evoking verbal responses from others (such as a spoken "bye-bye" in response to the infant's gestured bye-bye), at a time when infants still cannot produce words of their own.

Infants' first words usually are spoken a month or two before or after their first birthday. Typical first words include important people ("Mama," "Dada"), familiar animals ("dog"), moving objects ("car"), foods ("milk"), and greetings or farewells ("hi," "bye-bye") (Waxman & Lidz, 2006).

Most infants can speak only a few words, at most, by the end of their first year, but they understand many more words than they can speak. In fact, at all ages, language *comprehension* (the words we understand) exceeds language *production* (the words we use), but the difference is especially striking and notable during infancy. Even as early as 4 months old infants can recognize their own name (Mandel et al., 1995). By their first birthday, although infants can speak only a word or two, they understand about 50 words (Menyuk et al., 1995).

The foundations of language comprehension are evident very early in the abilities of infants to recognize changes in language sounds (Werker & Fennell, 2009). To test this ability, researchers play a spoken sound repeatedly for an infant (for example, "ba, ba, ba, ba"), then change it slightly ("pa, pa, pa pa"). If an infant looks in the direction of the sound when it changes, this is taken to indicate awareness of the change. Even when only a few weeks old, infants show this awareness (Saffran et al., 2006).

Furthermore, like babbling, discrimination of simple sounds appears to be universal at first, but becomes more specialized toward the end of the first year to the language of the infant's culture. In one study, American and Japanese infants were compared at 6 and 12 months (Iverson et al., 2003). At 6 months, the American and Japanese infants

◉ **Watch** the **Video** Speech Development in **MyDevelopmentLab**

babbling repetitive prelanguage consonant–vowel combinations such as "ba-ba-ba" or "do-do-do-do," made by infants universally beginning at about 6 months old

were equally responsive to the distinction between "ra" and "la," even though there are no "r" or "l" sounds in the Japanese language, so the Japanese infants would not have heard this distinction before. However, by 12 months old the American infants could still recognize the "r" versus "l" distinction but the Japanese infants could not, as their language skills were now more specialized to their own language. ◉

Infant-directed (ID) speech

<table>
<tr><td>**4.16**</td><td>**LEARNING OBJECTIVE**</td><td>Describe how cultures vary in their stimulation of language development.</td></tr>
</table>

◉⌐Watch the Video Stimulating Language Development in **MyDevelopmentLab**

infant-directed (ID) speech special form of speech that adults in many cultures direct toward infants, in which the pitch of the voice becomes higher than in normal speech, the intonation is exaggerated, and words and phrases are repeated

◉⌐Watch the Video Child-Directed Speech in **MyDevelopmentLab**

APPLYING YOUR KNOWLEDGE

How do the findings just presented on language development relate to Piaget's concept of maturation?

Suppose you were to say to an adult, "Would you like something to eat?" How would you say it? Now imagine saying the same thing to an infant. Would you change how you said it?

In many cultures, people speak in a special way to infants, called **infant-directed (ID) speech** (Bryant & Barrett, 2007). In ID speech, the pitch of the voice becomes higher than in normal speech, and the intonation is exaggerated. Grammar is simplified, and words and phrases are more likely to be repeated than in normal speech. Topics of ID speech often pertain to objects ("Look at the birdie! See the birdie?") or emotional communication ("What a good girl! You ate your applesauce!"). ◉

Why do people often use ID speech with infants? One reason is that the infants seem to like it. Even when ID speech is in a language they do not understand, infants show a preference for it by the time they are 4 months old, as indicated by paying greater attention to ID speech in an unfamiliar language than to non-ID speech in the same language (Singh et al., 2009).

And why do infants like ID speech? One theory is that infants prefer it because it is more emotionally charged than other speech (Trainor et al., 2000). Also, at a time when language is still new to them, ID speech helps infants unravel language's mysteries. The exaggeration and repetition of words gives infants cues to their meaning (Soderstrom, 2007). By exaggerating the sounds used in making words, ID speech provides infants with information about the building blocks of speech they will use in the language of their culture (Kuhl, 2004). The exaggerations of ID speech also separate speech into specific words and phrases more clearly than normal speech does (Thiessen et al., 2005).

ID speech is common in Western cultures (Bryant & Barrett, 2007). Japanese studies have also found that ID speech is common in Japan (Mazuka et al., 2008). Outside the developed countries, however, there is more variability. Some traditional cultures use ID speech, such as the Fulani of West Africa, who say single words and phrases to their infants from their very first days of life in an effort to stimulate their language development (Johnson, 2000). However, in other traditional cultures parents do not use ID speech and make no special effort to speak to infants. For example, among the Gusii of Kenya, parents speak to infants substantially less than American parents do (LeVine, 1994; Richman et al., 2010). Remember little Makori, the Gusii baby introduced at the beginning of the chapter? The Gusii, like people in many traditional cultures, carry their infants around almost constantly and have a great deal of physical contact with them, including cosleeping at night, but they do not view it as necessary or useful to speak to infants. Similarly, the Ifaluk people of Micronesia believe there is no point in speaking to infants because they cannot understand what you say (Le, 2000). Nevertheless, despite receiving no ID speech, children in these cultures learn their language fluently within a few years, just as children in cultures with ID speech do.

Does this mean you do not need to speak to your own infants, in your culture? Definitely not. In cultures such as the Gusii and the Ifaluk, parents may not speak directly to their infants very often, but infants are part of a language-rich environment all day long. Although no one spoke directly to

Adults in many cultures use infant-directed speech, with high pitch and exaggerated intonation.

Makori, he was surrounded by conversation from his mother, sister, and other relatives. Instead of spending the day with one parent and perhaps a sibling, as infants do in cultures where ID speech is common, infants in traditional cultures typically have many adults and children around them in the course of the day. Families are bigger, extended family members live either in the same household or nearby, and interactions with other community members are more common (Akhtar & Tomasello, 2000). Perhaps ID speech developed because, in the small nuclear families that are typical of Western countries today, without ID speech infants may have very little other language stimulation. The success of children in traditional cultures in learning their languages despite having no ID speech shows that listening to others' conversations in a language-rich environment is also an effective way of acquiring a language (Akhtar, 2005). 👁

By the end of their first year infants have laid an important foundation for language and can comprehend many words, but their language production is still very limited. The real explosion in language development comes in the second year, so in the next chapter we will examine the origins and growth of language in greater detail.

WHAT HAVE YOU LEARNED?

1. Which develops first in infants' language, comprehension or production? How do we know this?
2. At what age are infants able to distinguish between their native language and other languages?
3. What is ID speech and why do infants prefer it?
4. Why is ID speech more common in Western cultures? Are children in cultures without ID speech delayed in their language development? Why or why not?

My Virtual Child

Will you use infant-direct speech with your virtual child? Why or why not?

👁 **Watch** the **Video** Language Learning in **MyDevelopmentLab**

APPLYING YOUR KNOWLEDGE
. . . as a Day-Care Provider
How can you encourage language use among the children in your care?

Section 2 VIDEO GUIDE Object Permanence Across Cultures (Length: 3:56)

In this video we see demonstrations of children at various ages being tested to see if they grasp the concept of object permanence or not. The children from many different cultures show that this is a universal concept.

1. According to this video, object permanence is universal across cultures. Why would this be such an important concept for children to acquire?

2. What game is commonly played with babies that can be connected to object permanence and why?

3. Do you feel that object permanence can be related to the early development of trust? Why or why not?

👁 **Watch** the **Video** Object Permanence Across Cultures in **MyDevelopmentLab**

LEARNING OBJECTIVES

4.17 Define infant temperament and describe three ways of conceptualizing it.

4.18 Explain how the idea of goodness-of-fit pertains to temperament on both a family level and a cultural level.

4.19 Identify the primary emotions and describe how they develop during infancy.

4.20 Describe infants' emotional perceptions and how their emotions become increasingly social over the first year.

4.21 List the main features of infants' social worlds across cultures.

4.22 Compare and contrast the two major theories of infants' social development.

Temperament

Have you had any experience in caring for infants, perhaps as a babysitter, older sibling, or parent? If so, you have probably observed that they differ from early on in how they respond to you and to the environment. As a parent I have certainly observed this in my twins, who have had virtually the same environment all their lives and yet are very different in their emotional responses and expressions. Ask any parents of more than one child about this issue, and they will probably tell a similar tale (Ganiban et al., 2011).

In the study of human development, these kinds of differences in emotionality are viewed as indicators of **temperament**. Temperament includes qualities such as activity level, irritability, soothability, emotional reactivity, and sociability. You can think of temperament as the biologically based raw material of personality (Goldsmith, 2009; Rothbart et al., 2000). Researchers on temperament believe that all infants are born with certain tendencies toward behavior and personality development, and the environment then shapes those tendencies in the course of development. Let's look at three related ways of conceptualizing temperament, then at some of the challenges involved in measuring and studying it (see **Table 4.3** for a summary). 👁

👁⊶⎡**Watch** the **Video** Temperament at **MyDevelopmentLab**

Conceptualizing temperament: Three approaches

4.17 | **LEARNING OBJECTIVE** | Define infant temperament and describe three ways of conceptualizing it.

Temperament was originally proposed as a psychological concept by Alexander Thomas and Stella Chess, who in 1956 began the New York Longitudinal Study (NYLS). Thomas and Chess wanted to see how infants' innate tendencies would be shaped into personality in the course of development through childhood and adolescence. Using parents' reports, which we will discuss in detail in the **Research Focus: Measuring Temperament** feature on page 168, they assessed infant temperament by judging qualities such as activity level, adaptability, intensity of reactions, and quality of mood. On this basis the infants were classified into three categories: easy, difficult, and slow-to-warm-up.

temperament innate responses to the physical and social environment, including qualities of activity level, irritability, soothability, emotional reactivity, and sociability

TABLE 4.3 Three Conceptions of Infant Temperament

| Thomas and Chess | | Rothbart | | Buss and Plomin | |
Quality	Description	Quality	Description	Quality	Description
Activity level	Ratio of active time to inactive time	Activity level	Frequency and intensity of gross motor activity	Activity	Overall activity level
Attention span	Length of time devoted to an activity before moving on to the next	Attention span/ persistence	Duration of attention to a single activity	Attention span	Duration of attention to a single activity
Intensity of reaction	Emotional expressiveness, e.g., crying, laughing	Fearful distress	Fear/distress in response to novel or intense stimulation	Emotionality	Emotional reactivity
Rhythmicity	Regularity of physical functions such as feeding and sleeping	Irritable distress	Expression of distress when frustrated	Soothability	Responsiveness to attempts to soothe when distressed
Distractibility	Extent to which new stimulation stops current behavior, e.g., when crying	Positive affect	Frequency of expression of happiness and other positive emotions	Sociability	Degree of interest in others, positive or negative responses to social Interactions
Approach/ Withdrawal	Response to new object or person	Self-regulation	Ability to suppress an initial response to a situation and execute a more adaptive response		
Adaptability	Adjustment to changes in routines				
Threshold of responsiveness	Stimulation required to evoke a response				
Quality of mood	General level of happy versus unhappy mood				

1. *Easy* babies (40% of the sample) were those whose moods were generally positive. They adapted well to new situations and were generally moderate rather than extreme in their emotional reactions. 👁
2. *Difficult* babies (10%) did not adapt well to new situations, and their moods were intensely negative more frequently than other babies. 👁
3. *Slow-to-warm-up* babies (15%) were notably low in activity level, reacted negatively to new situations, and had fewer positive or negative emotional extremes than other babies. 👁

By following these babies into adulthood in their longitudinal study, Thomas and Chess were able to show that temperament in infancy predicted later development in some respects (Chess & Thomas, 1984; Ramos et al., 2005; Thomas et al., 1968). The difficult babies in their study were at high risk for problems in childhood, such as aggressive behavior, anxiety, and social withdrawal. Slow-to-warm-up babies rarely seemed to have problems in early childhood, but once they entered school they were sometimes fearful and had problems academically and with peers because of their relatively slow responsiveness.

Perhaps you noticed that the three categories in the classic Thomas and Chess study added up to only 65% of the infants they studied. The other 35% could not be classified as easy, difficult, or slow-to-warm-up. It is clearly a problem to exclude 35% of infants, so other temperament researchers have avoided categories, instead rating all infants on the basis of temperamental traits.

Mary Rothbart and her colleagues have kept some of the Thomas and Chess temperament qualities, such as activity level and attention span, but they added a dimension

👁—Watch the **Video** Temperament: Easy in **MyDevelopmentLab**

👁—Watch the **Video** Temperament: Difficult in **MyDevelopmentLab**

👁—Watch the **Video** Temperament: Inhibited in **MyDevelopmentLab**

RESEARCH FOCUS Measuring Temperament

Temperament is conceptualized as an innate, biologically based quality that is the basis of personality development. However, when Thomas and Chess began studying temperament, no biological measurements were available, so they used parents' reports of infants' behavior as the source of their temperament classifications. Even today, most studies of infant temperament are based on parents' reports (Rothbart & Bates, 2006).

There are some clear advantages to using parents' reports. After all, parents see their infants in many different situations on a daily basis over a long period of time. In contrast, a researcher who assesses temperament on the basis of the infants' performance on tasks administered in the laboratory sees the infant only on that one occasion. Because infants' states change so frequently, the researcher may assess infants as having a "difficult" temperament when in fact the infant is simply in a temporary state of distress—hungry, perhaps, or tired, or cold, or hot, or in need of a diaper change. Parental reports of infant temperament on questionnaires are also quick, inexpensive, and easy to administer.

However, parents are not always accurate appraisers of their infants' behavior. For example, mothers' prenatal beliefs about children's tendencies predict their later ratings of their infants' temperament (Kiang et al., 2004). Mothers who are depressed are more likely to rate their infants' temperament negatively, perhaps because they find even normal infant behavior more stressful than other mothers do (Clarke-Stewart et al., 2000). Mothers' and fathers' ratings of their infants' temperament show only low to moderate levels of agreement (Atella et al., 2003). Parents tend to rate their twins or other siblings as less similar in temperament than researchers do, and this has been interpreted as indicating that parents exaggerate the differences between their children (Saudino, 2003).

What are the options besides parents' reports? Thomas and Chess recommend that researchers observe infants' behavior in naturalistic settings (e.g., at home, at the park) on several occasions, to avoid the problem of observing on just one occasion

Temperament is difficult to assess in a research setting because infants' emotional states fluctuate so much.

when the infant may have been in an unusually bad or good mood. Of course, this takes considerably more time and money than a simple parental questionnaire, and even a series of observations may not be as valid as the experiences parents accumulate over months of caring for their infants. Another approach has been to have parents keep daily diaries of their infants' behavior (e.g., sleeping, fussing, crying). Reports using this method have been shown to correlate well with temperament ratings based on parental reports or performance on laboratory tasks (Atella et al., 2003; St. James-Roberts & Plewis, 1996).

Because temperament is regarded as biologically based, it makes sense to have biological assessments of it, especially now that the tools for such assessments are widely available (Joyce, 2010). One simple but effective biological measure of infant temperament is heart rate. Extremely shy children tend to have consistently high heart rates, beginning in infancy (Kagan, 2003). Also, their heart rates show a greater increase in response to new stimulation such as new toys, new smells, or new people; compared to other children (Kagan, 1998). In one longitudinal study, infants who were highly reactive to new stimulation at 4 months of age had higher heart rates before birth as well as at 2 weeks of age (Kagan, 1994).

Other biological assessments of temperament have been developed, including measures of brain activity. We will discuss those assessments in later chapters, as they have been made in toddlerhood and early childhood rather than in infancy. Although infant temperament can predict later development to some extent, predictions are more accurate when assessments of temperament are made after age 2 (Joyce, 2010; Kagan & Fox, 2006). Fussing, crying, and rapid changes in states are common in infancy across a wide range of infants. It is only after age 2 that children's moods and behavior settle into more stable patterns that predict later development. But can temperament still be assumed to be innate and biologically-based once the environment has been experienced for two years or more?

of *self-regulation*, the ability to manage negative emotions (Rothbart, 2004; Rothbart et al., 2011). Similarly, David Buss and Robert Plomin (1984) include activity level and intensity of emotional reactions (which they call "emotionality") in their model, but add *sociability*, which refers to positive or negative responses to social interactions. Both models have been moderately successful in predicting children's functioning from infant temperament (Buss, 1995; Rothbart & Bates, 2006).

Goodness-of-fit

Explain how the idea of goodness-of-fit pertains to temperament on both a family level and a cultural level.

LEARNING OBJECTIVE **4.18**

Across the three conceptualizations, the core of temperament seems to be in activity level, attention span, and a general tendency toward positive or negative emotions. All three approaches also view temperament as the raw material of personality, which is then shaped by the environment. Thomas and Chess (1977) proposed the concept of **goodness-of-fit**, meaning that children develop best if there is a good fit between the temperament of the child and environmental demands. In their view, difficult and slow-to-warm-up babies need parents who are aware of their temperaments and willing to be especially patient and nurturing.

Subsequent studies have provided support for the idea of goodness-of-fit, finding that babies with negative temperamental qualities were able to learn to control their emotional reactions better by age 3 if their parents were understanding and tolerant (Warren & Simmens, 2005). Other research has shown that babies who are low in emotional reactivity respond more favorably to face-to-face interaction with a parent than babies who are high in emotional reactivity (Jahromi et al., 2004). Conversely, parents who respond to an infant's difficult temperament with anger and frustration are likely to find that the infant becomes a child who is defiant and disobedient, leading to further conflict and frustration for both parents and children (Calkins, 2002).

There may also be something like a cultural goodness-of-fit, given that different cultures have different views of the value of personality traits such as activity level and emotional expressiveness. In general, Asian babies have been found to be less active and irritable than babies in the United States and Canada, and appear to learn self-regulation earlier and more easily (Chen et al., 2005; Ramsay & Lewis, 2001). This temperamental difference may be, in part, the basis for differences later in childhood, such as Asian children being more likely to be shy. However, in contrast to the North American view of shyness as a problem to be overcome, in Asian cultures, shyness is viewed more positively. The child—and the adult—who listens rather than speaks is respected and admired. Consequently, studies of Chinese children have shown that shyness is associated with academic success and being well liked by peers (Chen et al., 1995). Now that China is changing so rapidly, both culturally and economically, there is some evidence that shyness is becoming less valued and related to poor rather than favorable adjustment in childhood (Chen, 2011; Chen et al., 2005). We'll cover more on this in later chapters.

My Virtual Child

How will your culture influence your virtual child's temperament?

WHAT HAVE YOU LEARNED?

1. What do the main ways of conceptualizing and measuring temperament have in common?
2. What dimension did Mary Rothbart and her colleagues add to the Thomas and Chess model of temperament?
3. What does *sociability* refer to, as conceptualized by Buss and Plomin?
4. Give an example of how goodness-of-fit varies from one culture to the next.

Infants' Emotions

Expressing and understanding emotions goes deep into our biological nature. As Charles Darwin observed in 1872 in *The Expression of Emotions in Man and Animals*, the strong similarity between emotional expressions in humans and other mammals indicates that

goodness-of-fit theoretical principle that children develop best if there is a good fit between the temperament of the child and environmental demands

primary emotions most basic emotions, such as anger, fear, disgust, surprise, and happiness

secondary emotions emotions that require social learning and a sense of self, such as embarrassment, shame, and guilt; also called sociomoral emotions

human emotional expressions are part of a long evolutionary history. Tigers snarl, wolves growl, chimpanzees—and humans, too—bare their teeth and scream. Darwin also observed that emotional expressions were highly similar among humans in different cultures. Recent researchers have confirmed that people in various cultures can easily identify the emotions expressed in photographs of people from outside their culture (Ekman, 2003).

Primary emotions

| 4.19 | **LEARNING OBJECTIVE** | Identify the primary emotions and describe how they develop during infancy. |

Infants are born with a limited range of emotions that become differentiated into a wider range in the course of the early years of life. Studies of emotional development distinguish between two broad classes of emotion (Lewis, 2008). **Primary emotions** are the most basic emotions, the ones we share with animals, such as anger, fear, disgust, surprise, and happiness. Primary emotions are all evident within the first year of life. **Secondary emotions** are emotions that require social learning and a sense of self, such as embarrassment, shame, and guilt. Secondary emotions are also called *sociomoral emotions*, because infants are not born knowing what is embarrassing or shameful but have to learn this from their social environment and make an evaluation of a situation based on their sense of self. Secondary emotions develop mostly in the second year of life, so we will look at the development of primary emotions here and secondary emotions in Chapter 5. ◗→

Three primary emotions are evident in the early weeks of life: distress, interest, and pleasure (Lewis, 2002, 2008). Distress is evident in crying, of course, and we have seen in this chapter how infants' interest can be assessed from the first days of life by where they turn their attention. We have also seen, in Chapter 3, that neonates show a facial expression of pleasure when tasting a sweet substance. Gradually in the first months of life these three emotions become differentiated into other primary emotions: distress into anger, sadness, and fear; interest into surprise; and pleasure into happiness. Let's look at how each of these primary emotions develops over the first year. ◉

Anger is expressed early in the form of a distinctive anger cry, as described in Chapter 3, but as an emotional expression separate from crying, it shows development over the course of the first year (Dodge et al., 2006; Lewis, 2010). In one study of infants at 1, 4, and 7 months of age, the babies' responses were observed as their forearms were held down so that they could not move them for a few minutes, a condition none of them liked much (Oster et al., 1992). The 1-month-old infants showed clear distress, but raters (who did not know the hypotheses of the study) did not classify their distress responses as anger. The 4-month-old infants were also distressed, but about half of them showed their distress in facial expressions that could be clearly identified as anger. By 7 months, nearly all the infants showed a definite anger response. Another study also observed the clear expression of anger in 7-month-olds, in response to having an attractive object taken away (Sternberg et al., 1983). As infants become capable of intentional behavior in the second half of the first year, their expressions of anger often occur when their intentions are thwarted (Izard & Ackerman, 2000).

Sadness is rare in the first year of life, except for infants with depressed mothers. When mothers are depressed, by 2–3 months

◉→ **Simulate** the **Experiment** Facial Expressions of Emotion in **MyDevelopmentLab**

◉→ **Watch** the **Video** Basic Emotions in **MyDevelopmentLab**

Infants universally exhibit the primary emotions. Can you tell which primary emotion is represented in each photograph?

old infants, too, show facial expressions of sadness (Herrera et al., 2004). Could this be a case of passive genotype → environment interactions? Perhaps both infants and mothers have a genetic predisposition toward sadness in such families. This is something to consider, but in one study nondepressed mothers were instructed to look depressed in a 3-minute interaction with their infants (Cohn & Tronick, 1983). The infants responded with distress, suggesting that sad infants with depressed mothers are responding to their mothers' sadness rather than being genetically predisposed to sad emotional expressions.

Fear develops by 6 months of age (Gartstein et al., 2006). By then infants show facial expressions of fear, for example in response to a toy that moves toward them suddenly and unexpectedly (Buss & Goldsmith, 1998). Fear also becomes social at this age, as infants begin to show *stranger anxiety* in response to unfamiliar adults (Grossman et al., 2005). Stranger anxiety is a sign that the infant has begun to develop attachments to familiar persons, a topic we will discuss in detail in Chapter 5.

Surprise, indicated by an open mouth and raised eyebrows, is first evident about half way through the first year (Camras et al., 1996). It is most often elicited by something in the infant's perceptual world that violates expectations. For example, a toy such as a jack-in-the-box might elicit surprise, especially the first time the jack pops out.

Finally, the development of happiness is evident in changes in infants' smiles and laughter that take place during the early months. After a few weeks, infants begin to smile in response to certain kinds of sensory stimulation—after feeding, or while urinating, or while having their cheeks stroked (Murkoff et al., 2003). However, it is not until the second or third month of life that the first **social smile** appears, an expression of happiness in response to interacting with others (Fogel et al., 2006). The first laughs occur about a month after the first smiles (Nwokah et al., 1999). Beginning at this age both smiles and laughs can be elicited by social interactions or by sensory or perceptual events, such as tickling or kisses or games such as peek-a-boo (Fogel et al., 2006). By the end of the first year, infants have several different kinds of smiles that they show in response to different people and in different situations (Bolzani et al., 2002). ◉

Watch the **Video** Social and Personality Development in **MyDevelopmentLab**

Infants' emotional perceptions

Describe infants' emotional perceptions and how their emotions become increasingly social over the first year.

LEARNING OBJECTIVE 4.20

Infants not only communicate emotions from the first days of life, they also perceive others' emotions. At just a few days old, neonates who hear another neonate cry often begin crying themselves, a phenomenon called **emotional contagion** (Geangu et al., 2010). This response shows that they recognize and respond to the cry as a signal of distress (Gazzaniga, 2009). Furthermore, they are more likely to cry in response to the cry of a fellow neonate than in response to an older infant's cry, a chimpanzee's cry, or a recording of their own cry, showing that they are remarkably perceptive at discriminating among cries.

At first, infants are better at perceiving emotions by hearing than by seeing. Remember, their auditory system is more developed than their visual system in the early weeks of life. When shown faces in the early weeks, neonates tend to look mainly at the boundaries and edges rather than at the internal features such as mouth and eyes that are most likely to express emotion. By 2–3 months old, infants' eyesight has improved substantially and they have begun to be able to discriminate between happy, sad, and angry faces (Haan & Matheson, 2009; Hunnius et al., 2011). To test this, researchers often use a habituation method. In this method, infants are presented with the same photograph of the same facial expression repeatedly until they no longer show any interest in it, that is, they become habituated. Then they are shown the same face with

social smile expression of happiness in response to interacting with others, first appearing at age 2–3 months

emotional contagion in infants, crying in response to hearing another infant cry, evident beginning at just a few days old

social referencing term for process of becoming more adept at observing others' emotional responses to ambiguous and uncertain situations, and using that information to shape one's own emotional responses

a different facial expression, and if they look longer at the new facial expression this is taken to indicate that they have noticed the difference.

Another interesting way of showing that infants perceive emotions is to show no emotion at all. By age 2–3 months, when parents interacting with their infants are told by researchers to show no emotion for a time, the infants respond with distress (Adamson & Frick, 2003; Tronick, 2007). This method, known as the *still-face paradigm*, shows that infants quickly learn to expect certain emotional reactions from others, especially others who are familiar and important to them (Mesman et al., 2009).

More generally, infants' responses to the still-face paradigm demonstrate that from early on, emotions are experienced through relations with others rather than originating only within the individual (Tronick, 2007). In the early weeks of life infants have smiles that are stimulated by internal states and cries that may be due to being hungry, tired, or cold, but infants soon learn to discern others' emotions and adjust their own emotions in response. By the time they are just 2–3 months old, when infants vocalize or smile they expect the others they know and trust to respond in expected ways, as they have in the past, which is why the still-face paradigm disturbs infants so much.

Another indicator of the development of emotional perception during the first year is in infants' abilities to match auditory and visual emotion. In studies on this topic, infants in the laboratory are shown two photographs with markedly different emotions, such as happiness and sadness. Then a vocal recording is played, matching one of the facial emotions but not the other, and the infants' attention is monitored. By the time they are 7 months old, infants look more at the face that matches the emotion of the voice, showing that they expect the two to go together (Kahana-Kalman & Walker-Andrews, 2001; Soken & Pick, 1999).

Gradually over the first year, infants become more adept at observing others' emotional responses to ambiguous and uncertain situations and using that information to shape their own emotional responses. Known as **social referencing,** this is an important way that infants learn about the world around them. In studies testing social referencing abilities, typically a mother and infant in a laboratory situation are given an unfamiliar toy to play with, and the mother is instructed by the researchers to show positive or negative emotion in relation to the toy. Subsequently, the infant will generally play with the toy if the mother showed positive emotion toward it but avoid it if the mother's emotion was negative. This response appears by the time infants are about 9–10 months old (Mumme & Fernald, 2003).

My Virtual Child

Describe your virtual child's social environment. How has your culture influenced it?

WHAT HAVE YOU LEARNED?

1. How do secondary emotions differ from primary emotions?
2. At what age do infants develop stranger anxiety to unfamiliar adults?
3. What do infant responses to the still-face paradigm demonstrate about their emotions?
4. How do researchers test social referencing in an experimental setting?

The Social World of the Infant

The social world of the infant is a crucial part of understanding infant development, because it affects every aspect of development, from physical and motor development to cognitive, emotional, and, of course, social development. Humans are built for social interactions and social relationships from Day 1. We have seen many examples of this here and in Chapter 3. Human infants recognize the smell and voice of their mother from the first few days of life. When they cry it is often some kind of social interaction that soothes them. They learn about the world through joint attention and social referencing.

Humans' social environments grow gradually more complex in the course of development as they enter new contexts such as school, community, and workplace. During infancy, social experience and social development occurs within a relatively small circle, a group of persons who are part of the infant's daily environment, and usually there is one person who provides the most love and care—typically, but not always, the mother. Here, let's look first at the broad cultural pattern of the infant's social world, then at two theories of infant social development.

Cultural themes of infant social life

List the main features of infants' social worlds across cultures.

LEARNING OBJECTIVE **4.21**

Although cultures vary in their customs of infant care, as they vary in most aspects of human development, there are several themes that occur frequently across cultures. If we combine what scholars have learned from observing infants in a variety of different cultures today, along with what other scholars have learned from studying human evolutionary history and the history of human societies, a common picture of the social world of the infant emerges (DeLoache & Gottlieb, 2000; Leakey, 1994; LeVine, 1977; LeVine et al., 1994; Richman et al., 2010; Small, 2005), characterized by the following features:

1. *Infants are with their mothers almost constantly for the early months of life.* Nearly all cultures have a period (usually 1–6 months) following birth when mother and infant do little but rest and recover from the birth together. After this rest period is over, the infant is typically strapped to the mother's back with a cloth as she goes back to her daily duties.

2. *After about 6 months, most daily infant care is done by older girls rather than the mother.* Once infants reach about 6 months old their care is delegated to older girls (usually 6 to 10 years old) so that the mother can devote her energy and attention to her work. Most often the girl is an older sister, but it could be any of a range of other people such as an older brother, cousin, grandmother, aunt, or a girl hired from outside the family. However, at night the infant sleeps with the mother.

3. *Infants are among many other people in the course of a day.* In addition to the mother and the caregiver who takes over at about age 6 months, infants are around many other people in the course of a day, such as siblings, aunts, cousins, grandparents, and neighbors.

4. *Infants are held or carried almost constantly.* In many traditional cultures, infants rarely touch the ground during their early months of life. This practice comes out of the belief that infants are highly vulnerable and must be shielded from dangers. Holding them close is a way of protecting them, and also a way of keeping them comforted, quiet, and manageable.

5. *Fathers are usually remote or absent during the first year.* As we saw in Chapter 3, in most cultures only women are allowed to observe and assist at birth, and this exclusion of men often continues during the first year. Fathers are rarely involved in the direct care of infants, partly because mothers breast-feed their infants frequently but also because care of infants is typically believed to be part of a woman's role but not a man's.

These features are still the dominant worldwide pattern in developing countries (Richman et al., 2010; Small, 2005), but the pattern in developed countries has become quite different over the past two centuries, especially in Western countries. The typical social environment for infants

> **THINKING CULTURALLY**
>
> *Of the five features of the infant's social world described here, how many are similar to and how many are different from the culture you are from? What do you think explains the differences?*

Infants in many cultures are surrounded by adults all day, but cultures vary in how much the adults interact with infants. Here, two mothers and their babies with other family members and friends in the Samburu culture of Kenya.

trust versus mistrust in Erikson's psychosocial theory, the first stage of development, during infancy, in which the central crisis is the need to establish a stable attachment to a loving and nurturing caregiver

attachment theory Bowlby's theory of emotional and social development, focusing on the crucial importance of the infant's relationship with the primary caregiver

in developed countries is the "nuclear family" consisting of a mother, father (perhaps), and (perhaps) one sibling. Most infants in Western developed countries sleep in a separate room from the time they are born (Keller & Goldberg, 2004). Mother and infant are alone together for much of the time, and the infant may be left in a crib, stroller, or infant seat for a substantial proportion of the day (Baildum et al., 2000). Fathers in developed countries today are more involved than ever in infant care, although still not usually as much as mothers are (Hawkins et al., 2008; Lewis et al., 2009).

Nevertheless, like infants in developing countries, infants in developed countries nearly always grow up to be capable of functioning well socially in their culture. They develop friendships with peers, they find adults outside the family with whom they form relationships, such as teachers, and they grow to adulthood and form work relationships and intimate relationships with persons outside the family, with most eventually starting a new family of their own. Clearly infants can develop well socially in a variety of cultural contexts. What seems to be crucial to infants' social development across cultures is to have at least one social relationship with someone who is devoted to their care, as we will see next.

The foundation of social development: Two theories

4.22 **LEARNING OBJECTIVE** Compare and contrast the two major theories of infants' social development.

Both Erikson and Bowlby viewed the first attachment relationship as crucial to future emotional and social development.

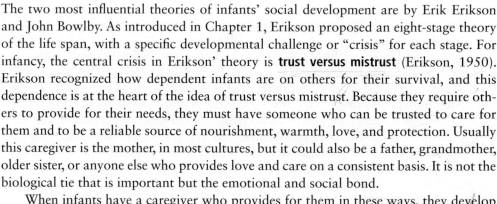

The two most influential theories of infants' social development are by Erik Erikson and John Bowlby. As introduced in Chapter 1, Erikson proposed an eight-stage theory of the life span, with a specific developmental challenge or "crisis" for each stage. For infancy, the central crisis in Erikson' theory is **trust versus mistrust** (Erikson, 1950). Erikson recognized how dependent infants are on others for their survival, and this dependence is at the heart of the idea of trust versus mistrust. Because they require others to provide for their needs, they must have someone who can be trusted to care for them and to be a reliable source of nourishment, warmth, love, and protection. Usually this caregiver is the mother, in most cultures, but it could also be a father, grandmother, older sister, or anyone else who provides love and care on a consistent basis. It is not the biological tie that is important but the emotional and social bond.

When infants have a caregiver who provides for them in these ways, they develop a basic trust in their social world. They come to believe that others will be trustworthy, and to believe that they themselves are worthy of love. However, if adequate love and care are lacking in the first year, infants may come to mistrust not only their first caregiver but others in their social world. They learn that they cannot count on the goodwill of others, and they may shrink from social relations in a world that seems harsh and unfriendly. This basic trust or mistrust lasts long beyond infancy. Remember, in Erikson's theory each stage builds on previous stages, for better or worse. Developing trust in infancy provides a strong foundation for all future social development, whereas developing mistrust is likely to be problematic not only in infancy but in future life stages.

A similar theory of infant social development was proposed a few years later by John Bowlby (1969/1982). Like Erikson's theory, Bowlby's **attachment theory** focused on the crucial importance of the infant's relationship with the primary caregiver. Like Erikson, Bowlby believed that the quality of this first important social relationship influenced emotional and social development not only in infancy but in later stages of development as well. Like Erikson, Bowlby viewed trust as the key issue in the infant's first attachment to another person. In Bowlby's terms, if the primary caregiver is *sensitive* and *responsive* in caring for the infant, the infant will learn that others, too, can be trusted in social relationships. However, if these qualities are lacking in the primary caregiver, the infant will come to expect—in infancy and in later development—that others, too, may not be reliable social partners. 👁

There are also important differences between the two theories. As we learned in Chapter 1, Erikson's psychosocial theory was a deliberate contrast to Freud's psychosexual theory. However, Bowlby's theory had quite different origins, in evolutionary theory and in research on mother–offspring relationships in animal species. Also, Bowlby's theory inspired methods for evaluating the infant–caregiver relationship that led to a research literature that now comprises thousands of studies (Cassidy & Shaver, 2008; Grossman et al., 2005). Most of this research has been on toddlers rather than infants, so we will save a detailed analysis of Bowlby's theory and the research it generated for the next chapter. 👁

👁 ⌐**Watch** the **Video** Parent–Child Attachments in **MyDevelopmentLab**

👁 ⌐**Watch** the **Video** Attachment in **MyDevelopmentLab**

WHAT HAVE YOU LEARNED?

1. What are some common themes of infant social life in non-Western cultures, and how do typical practices in Western cultures differ?

2. Why are infants in traditional cultures held or carried almost constantly?

3. According to Erikson's theory, how does the development of trust or mistrust in infancy affect later development?

4. What two qualities did Bowlby identify as important for the primary caregiver to have?

Section 3 VIDEO GUIDE Social Referencing (Length: 1:04)

This is a brief video of a demonstration of an adult and child interacting.

1. In this demonstration, the adult stops singing and begins to ignore the child. What was the purpose of this ceasing of the interaction?

2. We see the child smile at a person or object off camera, but then choosing to still interact with the adult on camera. Does this have any significance and why?

3. What do you feel is the objective of the demonstration in this video?

👁 ⌐**Watch** the **Video** Social Referencing in **MyDevelopmentLab**

Summing Up

((•⁣—[**Listen** to an audio file of your chapter in **MyDevelopmentLab**

SECTION 1 PHYSICAL DEVELOPMENT

4.1 Explain the gains in height and weight, the two basic principles of physical growth, and the growth of teeth in this period.

The physical developments of infancy include a tripling of weight and an inch-per-month growth in height. The cephalocaudal principle means that physical growth tends to begin at the top, with the head, and then proceeds downward to the rest of the body. The proximodistal principle means that growth proceeds from the middle of the body outward. For most infants the first tooth appears between 5 and 9 months of age. Teething pain can be soothed with something to bite or chew on or something cold to drink or eat, or by using medications.

4.2 Identify the different parts of the brain and describe how the brain changes in the first few years of life.

The brain is separated into two hemispheres connected by the corpus callosum, and each hemisphere has four lobes with distinct functions. Brain development in infancy is concentrated in the expansion of dendritic connections and myelination. Studies of infants and children exposed to extreme deprivation indicate that the brain is especially vulnerable in the first year of life.

4.3 Describe how infant sleep changes in the course of the first year and evaluate the risk factors for SIDS, including the research evidence regarding cosleeping.

Sleep needs for American infants decline during the first year. SIDS is most common at age 2–4 months. Sleeping on the back rather than the stomach greatly reduces the risk of SIDS. In cultures where infants sleep alongside their mothers on a firm surface the risk of SIDS is very low. Historically and worldwide today, mother–infant cosleeping is far more common than putting babies to sleep in a room of their own.

4.4 Describe how infants' nutritional needs change during the first year of life and identify the reasons and consequences for malnutrition in infancy.

The best way to obtain good high-fat nutrition during infancy is through breast milk. The timing of the introduction of solid food varies among cultures, from the first week of life to some time in the second half of the first year. Malnutrition in infancy is usually due mainly to the mother being unable or unwilling to breast-feed.

4.5 List the major causes and preventive methods of infant mortality and describe some cultural approaches to protecting infants.

Malnutrition is a common source of infant mortality, but the most common source is diarrhea. Diarrhea can be cured by oral rehydration therapy (ORT), though access to clean water makes this treatment unavailable in some parts of the world. The cultural practices of secluding infants in their early weeks, cosleeping with them, and constantly carrying them developed out of long and painful human experience with high infant mortality.

4.6 Describe the major changes during infancy in gross and fine motor development.

Achievements in gross motor development in infancy include rolling over, crawling, and standing. Cultural differences in restricting or encouraging gross motor development make a slight difference in the timing of gross motor achievements, but little difference in the long run. Reaching and grasping are two of the fine motor milestones of the first year.

4.7 Describe when and how infants develop depth perception and intermodal perception.

Increased adeptness at binocular vision around 3 months of age enables infants to develop depth perception during the first year. Infants also become better at intermodal perception or coordinating their senses.

KEY TERMS

cephalocaudal principle *p. 136*
proximodistal principle *p. 136*
teething *p. 136*
neurotransmitters *p. 137*
axon *p. 137*
dendrites *p. 137*

overproduction or exuberance *p. 137*
myelination *p. 137*
synaptic pruning *p. 137*
cerebral cortex *p. 138*
lateralization *p. 138*
plasticity *p. 138*

sudden infant death syndrome (SIDS) *p. 140*
cosleeping *p. 141*
custom complex *p. 142*
marasmus *p. 144*
oral rehydration therapy (ORT) *p. 145*

gross motor development *p. 147*
fine motor development *p. 147*
opposable thumb *p. 150*
depth perception *p. 151*
binocular vision *p. 151*
intermodal perception *p. 152*

SECTION 2 COGNITIVE DEVELOPMENT

4.8 Describe the first four sensorimotor substages.

Substage 1 is based on neonatal reflexes; 2 is based more on purposeful behavior; 3 entails the repetition of movements that first occurred by chance; and 4 is based on intentional, goal-directed behavior.

4.9 Explain how object permanence develops over the course of the first year.

Object permanence has begun to develop by the end of infancy, but it is not complete until the end of the second year.

4.10 Summarize the major critiques of Piaget's sensorimotor theory.

Some critics argue that the theory may have underestimated infants' cognitive abilities. Another criticism of Piaget is cultural, because nearly all research has been on children in the West.

4.11 Explain how attention and habituation change during infancy.

Infants pay more attention to a stimulus they have not seen before. Habituation develops more quickly during the course of the first year, and at any given age, quickness of habituation is positively related to later cognitive achievements. Increasingly during the first year, infants learn from joint attention with others.

4.12 Explain how short-term and long-term memory expand during infancy.

Both short-term and long-term memory improve notably over the course of the first year, though recognition memory comes easier than recall memory.

4.13 Describe the major scales used in measuring infant development and explain how habituation assessments are used to predict later intelligence.

The Bayley scales are widely used to measure infants' development, but scores on the Bayley do not predict later cognitive development. Efforts to predict later intelligence using information processing approaches have shown greater promise. These assessments measure habituation by distinguish between "short-lookers" and "long-lookers," with short-lookers higher in later intelligence.

4.14 Evaluate the claim that educational media enhance infants' cognitive development.

Many studies investigating this question have concluded that educational media products have no effect on infants' cognitive development and may even be detrimental.

4.15 Describe the course of language development over the first year of life.

When they first begin to babble at about 6 months, infants use a wide range of sounds, but within a few months they more often make the sounds from main language they hear around them. First words are usually spoken around the end of the first year; infants can already understand about 50 words by this time.

4.16 Describe how cultures vary in their stimulation of language development.

Many cultures use infant-directed (ID) speech to their babies, and babies appear to enjoy hearing it. However, even in cultures that do not use ID speech, children become adept users of language by the time they are a few years old.

KEY TERMS

sensorimotor stage *p. 154*

schemes *p. 154*

assimilation *p. 154*

accommodation *p. 154*

object permanence *p. 155*

information processing approach *p. 157*

mental structure *p. 157*

habituation *p. 158*

dishabituation *p. 158*

developmental quotient (DQ) *p. 160*

median *p. 160*

Bayley Scales of Infant Development *p. 160*

cooing *p. 162*

babbling *p. 163*

infant-directed (ID) speech *p. 164*

SECTION 3 EMOTIONAL AND SOCIAL DEVELOPMENT

4.17 Define infant temperament and describe three ways of conceptualizing it.

Temperament includes qualities such as activity level, attention span, and emotional reactivity. Thomas and Chess conceptualized temperament by classifying infants as easy, difficult, and slow-to-warm-up. Rothbart and colleagues added a dimension of *self-regulation*, the ability to manage negative emotions, and Buss and Plomin added *sociability*, which refers to positive or negative responses to social interactions.

4.18 Explain how the idea of goodness-of-fit pertains to temperament on both a family level and a cultural level.

Goodness-of-fit means that children develop best if there is a "good fit" between the temperament of the child and environmental demands. It varies culturally, given that different cultures have different views of the value of personality traits such as emotional expressiveness.

4.19 Identify the primary emotions and describe how they develop during infancy.

Primary emotions such as anger, fear, and happiness are evident within a few months after birth, although sadness tends to develop after infancy.

4.20 Describe infants' emotional perceptions and how their emotions become increasingly social over the first year.

Infants are socially aware of others' emotions from the first days of life, and respond with distress to the distress of others. Toward the end of the first year they draw emotional cues from how others respond to ambiguous situations.

4.21 List the main features of infants' social worlds across cultures.

Infants are typically cared for by their mothers (in early months) and then by older siblings. They are surrounded by other people and held or carried often. In Western developed countries infants have a smaller social world and more time alone, but they also learn to function socially.

4.22 Compare and contrast the two major theories of infants' social development.

The key to healthy social development, according to Erikson and Bowlby, is a strong, reliable attachment to a primary caregiver. Their theories differ in their origins and Bowlby's theory has inspired thousands of studies.

KEY TERMS

temperament *p. 166*
goodness-of-fit *p. 169*
primary emotions *p. 170*
secondary emotions *p. 170*
social smile *p. 171*
emotional contagion *p. 171*
social referencing *p. 172*
trust-versus-mistrust *p. 174*
attachment theory *p. 174*

Practice Test

✓●⌐Study and Review in MyDevelopmentLab

1. Siwen goes to the doctor and expresses concern that her infant's head is too big for his body. The doctor tells her that this is normal because of
   a. the fact that head size varies widely.
   b. the cephalocaudal principle.
   c. the proximodistal principle.
   d. the fact that after infancy, growth slows down considerably.

2. Tara and Paul adopted their baby daughter, Oksana, from a Romanian orphanage five years ago. She was physically and emotionally deprived until they adopted her at age 2½. It is most likely that Oksana
   a. stayed underweight for much of her life.
   b. had more cognitive impairment than she would have had if she had been adopted before 6 months of age.
   c. will have greater brain plasticity later in development because of her nurturing environment.
   d. will show no signs of cognitive impairment due to synaptic pruning.

3. SIDS is almost unknown in cultures where cosleeping is the norm because
   a. babies tend to sleep on hard mats.
   b. parents tend to put cloth on both sides of their babies so they remain on their sides.
   c. babies are less likely to be breast-fed and therefore, parents are less likely to roll over on them.
   d. babies are less likely to be aroused during the night in these quieter settings.

4. Marasmus is
   a. a disease common among malnourished women with HIV.
   b. most common during childhood and contracted through breast milk.
   c. an infant disease characterized by muscle atrophy and abnormal drowsiness.
   d. a deadly disease resulting from contaminated water being used to dilute formula.

5. If you were a pediatrician working in a developing country, you would likely use oral rehydration therapy to treat
   a. dysentery.
   b. diarrhea.
   c. small pox and malaria.
   d. yellow fever.

6. Mahori was strapped to his mother's back for the first year of his life. Which of the following statements is true?
   a. Mahori's parents gave him extra "tummy time" to develop his muscles.
   b. Mahori's motor development will be similar to an American child if they are compared during kindergarten.
   c. The sequence of his motor development will be different from that of babies in cultures where walking during infancy is actively encouraged.
   d. When it comes to Mahori's motor development, environment plays a stronger role than genetics.

7. The key to depth perception is
   a. the development of the pincer grasp.
   b. the development of intermodal perception.
   c. being able to walk.
   d. binocular vision, the ability to combine the images of each eye into one image.

8. Maha starts to begin rooting while being held by her mother's friend, who quickly passes Maha back to her mother to be breast-fed. Based on Piaget's sensorimotor substages, how old is Maha?
   a. 0–1 month
   b. 1–4 months
   c. 4–8 months
   d. 8–12 months

9. Object permanence is
   a. something infants are born with.
   b. knowing that an object appears in a place because the infant looked for it there.
   c. knowing that an object continues to exist even when it is out of sight.
   d. acquired by 3 months of age.

10. Critics of Piaget's sensorimotor theory argue that the likelihood of making the A-not-B error depends on
    a. the sex of the child.
    b. the time of day the child is tested.
    c. the delay between hiding and searching.
    d. the color of the object.

11. Speed of _____ is a good predictor of later memory and intelligence.
    a. habituation
    b. making the A-not-B error
    c. accommodation
    d. secondary circular reactions

12. John is able to name all of the state capitals without his teacher providing any hints. This is an example of
    a. recognition memory.
    b. joint attention.
    c. recall memory.
    d. habituation.

13. Scores on the Bayley Scales of Infant Development
    a. are useful as a screening tool because those who score very low may have developmental problems.
    b. are predictive of later IQ or school performance.
    c. are no longer used because they are considered out of date.
    d. are calculated for use with children ages 3 months to 9 years.

14. Compared to infants who do not watch educational programming, those who watch 2–3 hours per day
    a. learn to speak earlier.
    b. score higher on cognitive tests.
    c. show no verbal or cognitive advantage.
    d. develop better attention spans.

15. Babbling
    a. is found only in infants from the Western Hemisphere.
    b. occurs only if the infant can hear.
    c. develops before cooing.
    d. is universal.

16. Use of infant-directed speech
    a. is less common in cultures outside the West.
    b. leads to slower development of language than the style of language typically spoken with adults.
    c. involves speaking in a lower than normal tone and using less repetition than in normal speech.
    d. has been shown to be less interesting to babies than normal speech; a reason why many parents do not use this type of "baby talk."

17. Temperament
    a. has been measured using the same nine components across various studies.
    b. has been assessed using only cross-sectional methods.
    c. is considered to have a biological basis.
    d. has no bearing whatsoever on later development.

18. Which of the following best illustrates a good fit between caregiver and child?
    a. an irritable baby who is reared by parents who are rigid and intolerant
    b. a "difficult" infant whose parents respond with anger and frustration
    c. a slow-to-warm-up baby whose parents are understanding and tolerant
    d. a baby with a tendency toward negative emotions whose parents try to overcome this by encouraging face-to-face interactions with others

19. Of the emotions listed below, _____ is the emotion an infant would likely display later in development than the others.
    a. fear   c. disgust
    b. shame   d. anger

20. When mothers waiting on the "deep side" of the visual cliff express fearful emotions, none of their 12-month-old infants are willing to cross. This finding illustrates
    a. habituation.   c. the still-face paradigm.
    b. social referencing.   d. goodness-of-fit.

21. Which of the following is a common feature of infant social life in most cultures throughout history?
    a. Infants spend a lot of their day in the company of their fathers.
    b. Infants are cared for exclusively by their mothers until they become old enough to walk.
    c. Infants are often kept away from older adults so that they'll be less vulnerable to the spread of disease.
    d. Infants are surrounded by others and carried or held almost constantly.

22. Erikson and Bowlby both view _____ as the key issue in an infant's attachment to others.
    a. love   c. age
    b. trust   d. personality

5 Toddlerhood

Sometimes on a pleasant day I walk to a nearby park to have my lunch, and one day recently as I was eating at a picnic table, I observed two moms and their young children at the adjacent table. Each mom had an infant about 6 months old in a stroller, and the infants lay in their strollers peacefully, each of them examining a soft colorful toy the mom had given them. One mom also had a boy who appeared to be perhaps 3 or 4 years old. The boy wandered back and forth between the moms and the playground, climbing on the ladders and sliding down slides, returning to the picnic table occasionally for food or just to check in.

The other mom had a girl who appeared to be perhaps 2 years old, and it was this toddler who drew the most attention. Unlike the infants, who were not going anywhere without their moms' knowledge and consent, the toddler was moving around constantly, climbing on the picnic table, peering into the stroller at her little sister, chasing a squirrel, curiously picking up items off the ground. Unlike the older boy, the toddler could not be allowed to go off on her own because she had less of a sense of what was safe and what to avoid. At one point she climbed on the picnic table and stood precariously on one of the seats, then slipped and hurt her leg, crying until her mother came and soothed her. She did not speak much herself, unlike the older boy, but she was the subject of many statements from her mother and she seemed to understand whatever she was told: "Would you like some juice?" "Look at the squirrel!" "Don't pick that up, it's yucky." When the moms and their children finally left the park, the boy helped his mother push the stroller, while the other mom carried her toddler daughter on her hip as she pushed her other daughter along.

Development during toddlerhood, the second and third years of life, rivals development during infancy for events of drama and

> **❝By their third birthday, toddlers' social world has greatly expanded. ❞**

importance. On their first birthday most infants are barely able to walk without support; by their third birthday toddlers can run, jump, and climb stairs. On their first birthday infants speak only a handful of words; by their third birthday toddlers have achieved remarkable fluency in the language of their culture and are able to understand and speak about nearly any topic under the sun. On their first birthday infants have little in the way of emotional regulation, and show their anger and their exuberance with equal unrestraint; by their third birthday, toddlers have begun to grasp well the moral worldview of their culture, and they exhibit the sociomoral emotions of guilt, embarrassment, and shame. On their first birthday the social world of most infants is limited to parents, siblings, and perhaps some extended family members; but by their third birthday toddlers' social world has greatly expanded. Anthropologist Margaret Mead (1930/2001) described the change from infancy to toddlerhood as going from being a "lap child," in almost constant physical contact with the mother, to being a "knee child" who is attached to the mother but also spends a lot of time in a wider social circle—especially with siblings and older children as part of a mixed-age play group.

In this chapter we examine all of these changes in detail, beginning with the physical changes of toddlerhood, including physical growth, motor development, and the socialization of physical functions through toilet training and weaning. Then we focus on theories of cognitive development and look at language development, from the evolutionary basis of language to the burst of language use that begins at about 18 months of age, to the social and cultural context of language development. Finally, we look at socioemotional development in toddlerhood, including the development of the sociomoral emotions and emotional regulation, the birth of the self, gender development, attachments to mothers and others, and the toddler's widening social world.

LEARNING OBJECTIVES

5.1 Describe the typical changes in physical growth that take place in toddlerhood and explain the harmful effects of nutritional deficiencies on growth.

5.2 Describe the changes in brain development that take place during toddlerhood, and identify the two most common methods of measuring brain activity.

5.3 Describe the changes in sleeping patterns and sleeping arrangements that take place during toddlerhood.

5.4 Describe the advances in motor development that take place during toddlerhood.

5.5 Compare and contrast the process and timing of toilet training in developed countries and traditional cultures.

5.6 Distinguish the weaning process early in infancy from weaning later in toddlerhood.

Growth and Change in Years 2 and 3

During the second and third years of life, physical growth slows down from its blazing pace of the first year, but it remains more rapid than it will be at any later time of life. This is true for bodily growth as well as for brain development. Sleep patterns change substantially too, in years 2 and 3. Toddlerhood is also a time of dramatic advances in both gross and fine motor development.

Bodily growth

> Describe the typical changes in physical growth that take place in toddlerhood and explain the harmful effects of nutritional deficiencies on growth.

LEARNING OBJECTIVE 5.1

The growth of the body is swift and steady during the toddler years. *Figure 5.1* shows the changes in height and weight for American girls. Patterns of growth are similar in other developed countries (UNICEF, 2009). Throughout childhood the average boy is slightly taller and heavier than the average girl.

During toddlerhood, children lose the "baby fat" of infancy and become leaner as they become longer (Fomon & Nelson, 2002). They no longer need as much fat to keep their bodies at a constant temperature. Also, the head, which was one-fourth of the neonate's length, is one-fifth of the 2-year-old's height. The rest of the body will continue to grow faster than the head, and by adulthood the head will be one-eighth the size of the whole body.

Toddlers in developing countries often do not grow as rapidly as toddlers in developed countries. Typically, at birth and for the first 6 months of life, rates of growth are similar in developed countries and developing countries (LeVine et al., 1994), because during the early months infants in most cultures rely mainly on breast milk or infant formula and eat little solid food. However, starting around 6 months of age, when they begin eating solid food as a larger part of their diet, children in developing countries receive less protein and begin to lag in their growth. According to the World Health Organization (WHO, 2010c), about one-fourth of children worldwide have diets that are deficient in protein, nearly all of them in developing countries. By the time they

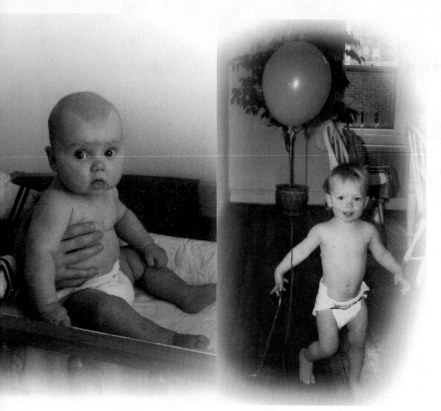

Toddlers lose a lot of their "baby fat" and often become leaner as they grow longer. This is my daughter Paris at 4 months and 18 months.

kwashiorkor protein deficiency in childhood, leading to symptoms such as lethargy, irritability, thinning hair, and swollen body, which may be fatal if not treated

micronutrients dietary ingredients essential to optimal physical growth, including iodine, iron, zinc, and vitamins A, B_{12}, C, and D

Toddlers who do not receive enough protein in their diets sometimes suffer from kwashiorkor, as does this boy in Uganda.

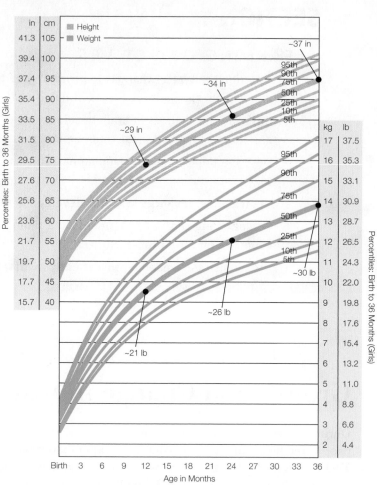

Figure 5.1 • **Growth chart for American girls from birth through age 3.** Growth slows from infancy to toddlerhood but remains rapid.

reach their first birthday, the height and weight of average children in developing countries are comparable to the bottom 5% of children in developed countries, and this pattern continues through childhood into adulthood.

Protein deficiency not only limits the growth of children in developing countries but it makes them vulnerable to disease and early death. One outcome specific to toddlerhood is **kwashiorkor,** in which protein deficiency leads to a range of symptoms such as lethargy, irritability, and thinning hair (Medline, 2008). Often the body swells with water, especially the belly. Toddlers with kwashiorkor may be getting enough food in the form of starches such as rice, bread, or potatoes, but not enough protein. Kwashiorkor lowers the effectiveness of the immune system, making toddlers more vulnerable to disease, and over time can lead to coma followed by death. Improved protein intake can relieve the symptoms of kwashiorkor, but earlier damage to physical and cognitive development is likely to be permanent.

In addition to protein, toddlers need a diet that contains **micronutrients** such as iron, zinc, and vitamins A, B_{12}, C, and D. Perhaps the most crucial micronutrient deficiency worldwide is iodine. About one-third of the world's population has a dietary deficiency of iodine, especially in Africa and South Asia (Zimmermann et al., 2008). In young children a lack of iodine inhibits cognitive development, resulting in an estimated IQ (intelligence quotient) deficiency of 10 to 15 points, a substantial margin. Fortunately, adding iodine to a diet is simple—through iodized salt—and cheap, costing only a few cents per person per year. Unfortunately, one-third of the world's children still lack this simple micronutrient. Some children in developed countries also lack sufficient micronutrients. One national study of toddlers in the United States found that iron deficiency prevalence rates were about 7% overall and were twice as high among Latino toddlers (12%) as among White or African American toddlers (both 6%) (Brotanek et al., 2007). Iron deficiency makes toddlers tired and irritable.

Brain development

Describe the changes in brain development that take place during toddlerhood, and identify the two most common methods of measuring brain activity.

LEARNING OBJECTIVE   **5.2**

The brain continues its rapid growth during the toddler years. As noted in Chapter 4, it is not the production of new brain cells that marks early brain development. In fact, the brain has only about one-half as many neurons at age 2 as it did at birth. What most distinguishes early brain development is the steep increase in **synaptic density,** the number of synaptic connections among neurons (Huttenlocher, 2003). These connections multiply immensely in the first three years, and toddlerhood is when peak production of new synapses is reached in the frontal lobes, the part of our brain that is the location of many of our most distinctively human cognitive qualities, such as reasoning, planning, and creativity. During toddlerhood new synapses in the frontal cortex are produced at the mind-boggling rate of 2 million per second, reaching a total by age 2 of more than 100 trillion (see *Figure 5.2*) (Johnson, 2001; Shonkoff & Phillips, 2000). The peak of synaptic density comes right at the end of toddlerhood, around the third birthday (Thompson & Nelson, 2001).

After the peak of synaptic density, a long process of synaptic pruning begins. In synaptic pruning, the connections between neurons become fewer but more efficient, with the synapses that are used becoming more developed, while unused synapses wither away (see Chapter 4). Synaptic pruning will remove about one-third of synapses in the frontal cortex from early childhood to adolescence, and after a new burst of synaptic density in early adolescence the process of synaptic pruning will continue at a slower rate through adolescence and into adulthood (Blakemore, 2003; Thompson et al., 2000).

Methods of assessing brain activity provide evidence of the rapid growth of the toddler brain. One widely used method, the **EEG (electroencephalogram),** measures the electrical activity of the cerebral cortex. Every time a synapse fires it emits a tiny burst of electricity, which allows researchers to measure the overall activity of the cerebral cortex as well as activation of specific parts of it. EEG research on toddlers has found a sharp increase in overall cortical activity from 18 to 24 months (Bell & Wolfe, 2007), reflecting important advances in cognitive and language development that we will examine later in this chapter. Another common method, **fMRI (functional magnetic resonance imaging),** requires a person to lie still inside a machine that uses a magnetic field to record changes

synaptic density density of synapses among neurons in the brain; peaks around age 3

EEG (electroencephalogram) device that measures the electrical activity of the cerebral cortex, allowing researchers to measure overall activity of the cerebral cortex as well as activation of specific parts of it

fMRI (functional magnetic resonance imaging) method of monitoring brain activity in which a person lies inside a machine that uses a magnetic field to record changes in blood flow and oxygen use in the brain in response to different kinds of stimulation

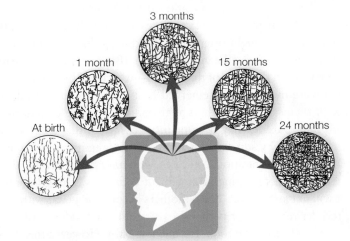

Figure 5.2 • **Changes in synaptic density from birth to age 2.** Synaptic connections increase throughout the first two years, with the greatest density occurring at the end of toddlerhood.

Figure 5.3 • **fMRI machine.** It is not until after toddlerhood that most children can lie still long enough to have an fMRI.

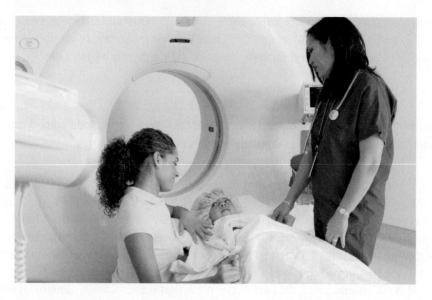

in blood flow and oxygen use in the brain in response to different kinds of stimulation, such as music (see **Figure 5.3**). Unlike the EEG, an fMRI can detect activity in any part of the brain, not just the cerebral cortex. The fMRI method is not often used with toddlers, perhaps because they are too wiggly and incapable of restraining their movements. However, one study solved this problem by assessing toddlers (age 21 months) and 3-year-olds as they slept, and found that toddlers showed greater frontal lobe activity in response to speech than the older children did, reflecting the brain's readiness for rapid language acquisition during the toddler period (Redcay et al., 2008).

Sleep and (more) teething

<table>
<tr><td>**5.3**</td><td>**LEARNING OBJECTIVE**</td><td>Describe the changes in sleeping patterns and sleeping arrangements that take place during toddlerhood.</td></tr>
</table>

Sleep declines from 16 to 18 hours a day in the neonate to about 15 hours a day by the first birthday, and further to about 12 to 13 hours by the second birthday. The toddler not only sleeps less than the infant but also has more of a night-sleeping, day-waking arousal schedule. This comes as a great relief to their parents! Most toddlers take only one nap during the day by the time they reach 18 months old, compared to the two or more naps a day typical of infants (Iglowstein et al., 2003).

However, this does not mean that toddlers consistently sleep through the night. In fact, one study of toddlers in Israel, England, and Australia found that episodes of waking in the night increased in frequency from 1½ to 2 years of age (Scher et al., 2004). There are two reasons why waking at night often increases during this time. First, there is a resurgence of teething between 13 and 19 months of age (Bong et al., 2008). This time it is the molars—the large teeth in the back of the mouth—which are bigger and more painful as they emerge than were the teeth that emerged in infancy. Second, toddlers develop a more definite sense of themselves and others as they approach age 2, and if they sleep in a bed separate from their parents they become more aware of this separation and more intentional about relieving it by summoning a parent or going into the parents' room.

What about the toddlers in traditional cultures, who have been sleeping alongside their mothers through infancy? This sleeping arrangement continues through the beginning of toddlerhood, but it will not last forever. When mothers become pregnant with another child, usually when the toddler reaches 2 or perhaps 3 years old, the toddler is ousted from that cozy spot beside her at night to make room for the new baby. However, this does not mean that toddlers now sleep alone. Instead, they now sleep alongside older siblings, or perhaps the father (Owens, 2004). Throughout life, sleeping alone is rare in traditional cultures.

APPLYING YOUR KNOWLEDGE
. . . as a Nurse

One of your patients is an American grandmother who is very critical of her Japanese daughter-in-law, who co-sleeps with her 2-year-old granddaughter. The grandmother asserts that this is unhealthy for the granddaughter. How do you respond?

Motor development

| Describe the advances in motor development that take place during toddlerhood. | **LEARNING OBJECTIVE** 5.4 |

Toddlerhood is a time of dramatic advances in motor development. There are few physical advances more life changing than going from barely standing to walking, running, climbing, and jumping—and all this progress in gross motor development takes place during the toddler years. With regard to fine motor development, toddlers go from being able to place a small object inside a large object to holding a cup and building a tower of blocks.

GROSS MOTOR DEVELOPMENT: FROM TODDLING TO RUNNING, JUMPING, AND CLIMBING Next time you see a child about a year old trying to walk, observe closely. When children first begin to walk they spread their feet apart and take small, stiff-legged steps, shifting their weight from one leg to the other. In short, they toddle! This is, in fact, where the word *toddler* comes from, in reference to their tentative, unsteady, wide-stance steps.

On average, children begin to walk without support at about 11 months old, just as they are about to enter toddlerhood; but there is a wide range of normal variation around this average, from about 9 to 17 months (Adolph & Berger, 2006; Bayley, 2005). Children who walk at 9 months are no more likely than children who walk at 17 months to become Olympic athletes some day, they simply have different biological time lines for learning to walk.

By 15 months most toddlers can stand (briefly) on one leg and have begun to climb, although once they have climbed onto something, they are much less skilled at climbing down. For example, most can climb up stairs at this age but not (safely) down. By 18 months most can run, although at first they run with the same stiff-legged, wide-stance posture as they use for walking. By 24 months they can kick a ball or throw a small object, and their running has become more flexible and fluid. At this age they can now go down the stairs that they earlier learned to climb up, and more: They can squat for minutes at a time, stand on tiptoes, and jump up and down. Small wonder toddlers move around so much, with so many new abilities to try out!

Through the third year, toddlers' gross motor skills continue to develop as they gain more flexibility and balance. They become better at using visual information to adjust their walking and running in response to changes in surfaces, so they become less likely to stumble and fall (Berger et al., 2005). **Table 5.1** summarizes the major milestones in gross motor development during toddlerhood.

The research just described is based on Western, mostly American toddlers. What about toddlers in traditional cultures? As you will recall from Chapter 4, infants in traditional cultures are held or carried most of the time to keep them safe and secure. Toddlers in traditional cultures are allowed slightly more mobility—it is much harder to keep a toddler still than it is an infant—but they continue to be held and carried for about half their waking hours (LeVine, 1977; LeVine et al., 1994). Nevertheless, they are equal to toddlers in developed countries in the development of their gross motor skills (Greenfield et al., 2003). In fact, toddlers in Africa (as well as African Americans) tend to reach gross motor milestones earlier than toddlers of European backgrounds (Kelly et al., 2006).

At 12–18 months many toddlers can barely walk, but by their third year they can run and jump.

TABLE 5.1 Milestones of Gross Motor Development in Toddlerhood

Age *(Months)*	Milestone
9–16	Stand alone
9–17	Walk without support
11–19	Stand on one leg
11–21	Climb onto chairs, beds, up stairs, etc.
13–17	Walk backward
14–22	Run
16–30	Walk on tiptoes
17–30	Jump in place
22–36	Walk up and down stairs

Note: The range shown is the age period at which 90% of toddlers achieve the milestone.

My Virtual Child

How will you baby-proof your home now that your virtual child is mobile? Are there any precautions that you will likely take that someone in a different environment may not need to consider, or vice versa?

APPLYING YOUR KNOWLEDGE
. . . as a Preschool Teacher

What are some ways you can ensure a safe learning environment in your preschool classroom?

Toddlers become capable of eating with a spoon and show a right- or left-hand preference for self-feeding.

The reason for restricting toddlers' movements is the same as for infants: to keep them safe and away from harm. Fire is especially a danger, as many traditional cultures have a cooking fire burning perpetually—during the day for cooking meals, during the night for warmth. Because toddlers are so active and so heedless of potential dangers, and because they trip and tumble a lot as they develop their walking and running skills, there is a danger that they will fall into a cooking fire unless their movements are restricted. For toddlers in traditional cultures, other common potential dangers are falling off a cliff, falling into a lake or river, or being trampled by livestock. Holding and carrying toddlers for much of their waking hours makes mishaps less likely.

For the same safety reasons, parents in developed countries "baby-proof" their homes once their children become mobile, removing sharp objects and other potential sources of harm (McKenzie, 2004). Parents of toddlers should also place gates at the top of stairs to prevent the child from falling, add locks to cabinets containing sharp objects and household chemicals, install outlet covers to prevent electrocution, and take other measures to protect against potential sources of harm or injury (Eisenberg & Eggum, 2008).

FINE MOTOR DEVELOPMENT: FROM SCRIBBLING TO BUILDING WITH BLOCKS Toddler gains in fine motor development are not as revolutionary as their gains in gross motor development, but they are certainly substantial. Already at 12 months they have come a long way in the course of infancy, and can hold an object in one hand while performing an action on it with the other; for example, they can hold a container with the right hand while placing rocks into it with the left hand (Kopp, 2003). At 12 months most have come to show a definite right- or left-hand preference for self-feeding, and over the next 6 months they try a variety of grips on their spoons until they find a grip they will use consistently (McCarty et al., 2001). During the first year of toddlerhood they also learn to hold a cup, scribble with a pencil or crayon, build a tower of three to four blocks, and turn the pages of a book (Kopp, 2003).

The second year of toddlerhood, from the second to the third birthday, is marked by fewer major advances and more by extending the advances of the previous year. The block tower rises to eight to 10 blocks, the scribbling becomes skillful enough to draw a semistraight line, and an attempt to copy a circle may result in something that actually looks somewhat like a circle (Chen et al., 2010). Toddlers in their third year of life can even begin to brush their teeth, with a little assistance. ***Table 5.2*** summarizes the major milestones in fine motor development during toddlerhood.

TABLE 5.2 Milestones of Fine Motor Development in Toddlerhood

Age (Months)	Milestone
7–15	Hold writing instrument (e.g., pencil, crayon)
8–16	Coordinate actions of both hands
10–19	Build tower of 2 blocks
10–21	Scribble vigorously
12–18	Feed self with spoon
15–23	Build tower of 3–4 blocks
20–28	Draw straight line on paper
24–32	Brush teeth
26–34	Build tower of 8–10 blocks
29–37	Copy circle

Note: The range shown is the age period at which 90% of toddlers achieve the milestone.

WHAT HAVE YOU LEARNED?

1. What are the most important nutritional deficiencies in toddlerhood, and how do they influence health?
2. How do synaptic density and synaptic pruning change during toddlerhood?
3. What are the two reasons why night-waking increases from 1½ to 2 years of age?
4. How do sleeping arrangements change in the course of toddlerhood in traditional cultures?
5. To what extent do cultures restrict toddlers' movements, and why?
6. What specific fine motor abilities do toddlers lack at their first birthday but develop by their third birthday?

Socializing Physical Functions: Toilet Training and Weaning

Eating and eliminating wastes are two physical functions that humans share with other animals, but for humans these functions become socialized from an early age. Here we look at how toddlers become toilet trained and weaned.

Toilet training

Compare and contrast the process and timing of toilet training in developed countries and traditional cultures.

LEARNING OBJECTIVE 5.5

The toddler years are when most children first learn to control their urination and defecation and become "toilet trained." Expectations for exactly when during the toddler years this should happen have changed substantially over the past half century in the United States (Blum et al., 2004). During the mid-20th century, pediatricians advocated early toilet training—the earlier the better—and in 1957 a study reported that 92% of American toddlers were toilet trained by the time they were 18 months old (Goode, 1999). Gradually, pediatricians and parents concluded there was little reason to require toilet training so early, and in more recent studies only about 25% of toddlers were

THINKING CULTURALLY

How might a culture's values of individualism or collectivism influence toilet-training practices?

toilet trained by 18 months old and only about 60% by their third birthday (Barone et al., 2009; Schum et al., 2001). We'll look at the history of toilet training in more depth in the **Historical Focus: The History of Toilet Training feature** below.

Today, most American pediatricians believe it is best to be patient with toddlers' progress toward toilet training, and to time it according to when the toddler seems ready (American Academy of Pediatrics [AAP], 2009). Most toddlers show signs of readiness sometime between 18 and 30 months of age. Some key signs are

- staying "dry" for an hour or two during the day;
- regular bowel movements, occurring at about the same time each day;
- increased anticipation of the event, expressed through looks or words;
- directly asking to use the toilet or to wear underwear instead of a diaper.

Although toilet training usually begins during the toddler years, it rarely happens overnight. Typically it is a process that continues over several weeks, months, or even years. The earlier toilet training begins, the longer it takes to complete it (Blum et al., 2004). After children are generally able to control urination and defecation, they may occasionally have an "accident" when they are especially tired, excited, or stressed (Murkoff

HISTORICAL FOCUS   The History of Toilet Training

Approaches to toilet training have shifted substantially in Western societies over the past century. These shifts provide an instructive example of how changes in cultural beliefs about children can interact with changes in technology.

In the historical record of the past 200 to 300 years, the emphasis was on teaching children to use the toilet at the earliest age possible (Mechling, 2008). Methods were often coercive, including scolding or physical punishment in case of an "accident." One U.S. government manual even urged parents to enforce the regularity of bowel movements for *infants* by inserting a curved stick into the baby's rectum at precise times each day (U.S. Department of Labor, 1932).

These early, harsh approaches to toilet training reflected a cultural belief in the appropriateness of strong parental authority (Dewar, 2010). Toddlers were to be toilet trained as soon as possible so that parents would be relieved of the mess and work of changing and cleaning their diapers; the needs of the parents were the top priority, not the needs of the children (Mechling, 2008). However, technological reasons—more precisely, the lack of technologies—were also involved. Keep in mind that before the late 20th century all diapers were cloth and had to be washed by hand. This certainly gave parents a strong incentive to toilet train their children early. Keep in mind, too, that families before the late

Approaches to toilet training have changed in recent decades with experts now recommending a "child-centered" approach.

20th century typically had three, four, or more children, and by the time the youngest one was in diapers, parents would have been changing and washing diapers for a long, long time.

Methods of toilet training evolved in the late 20th century, supported by changes in parenting beliefs as well as developments in technology. Parents became less concerned with establishing authority over children and more concerned with children's psychological well-being (Alwin, 1988). Child-care authorities warned that harsh, early toilet training could be psychologically damaging and that parents should be patient and allow the timing of toilet training to be determined by the toddler's readiness, as shown by their interest in using the toilet (Spock, 1966). Two key technological changes of the 1950s also contributed to more tolerant and patient methods: the invention of the disposable diaper and the electric washer and dryer. It was easier for parents to be more tolerant of their toddler's individual pace of toilet training once the parents no longer had to wash diapers by hand and could instead wash them in the electric washer or use disposables.

Today in developed countries most parents use disposable diapers. In the United States, from 1950 to today, there has been a steady rise in the proportion of parents using disposable diapers and a steady decline in the proportion of toddlers becoming toilet trained before 18 months old. A "child-centered" approach to toilet training is recommended by experts, part of a more general child-centered approach to parenting that places the needs of children above the needs of parents—a reversal of the historical pattern (Brazelton & Sparrow, 2004). Some experts now advocate "toilet learning" because "toilet training" carries the baggage of the harsh, bad old days (Eisenberg et al., 1994). Parents use books and videos to introduce the idea of toilet training to their children and gradually teach them how to use the toilet regularly, often beginning with a child-sized training toilet. Disposable diapers make the wait a lot easier for parents to bear!

et al., 2003). Even after children have ceased having accidents during the day, they may not have consistent control at night. For this reason, it is common for children to wear "training pants"—in between diapers and underwear—for a period after learning toilet training. Even at age 5, about one-fourth of children have an occasional accident, usually at night (Fritz & Rockney, 2004).

Toddlers in developed countries usually have this process guided and supervised by parents, but for toddlers in traditional cultures, older siblings and other older children are often the guides. *Toilet training* is probably not the right term to use to refer to this process in traditional cultures, because they rarely have toilets—so let's call it "controlled elimination." By age 2 or 3 most toddlers in traditional cultures spend the majority of their waking hours in groups with children of mixed ages, and they learn controlled elimination from watching and imitating other children (LeVine, 1994). Parents may be involved as well. For example, among the Ifaluk people on the Pacific Ocean islands of Micronesia, when toddlers reach about age 2 their parents encourage them to relieve themselves in the nearby lagoon, not in or near the house, and reprimand them if they fail to comply (Le, 2000).

My Virtual Child

How has your culture influenced the decisions you've made regarding toilet training your virtual child?

Weaning

| Distinguish the weaning process early in infancy from weaning later in toddlerhood. |

LEARNING OBJECTIVE 5.6

As mentioned in Chapter 3, cultures vary widely in whether and how long mothers breast-feed their children. However, based on what we know of human history and of practices today in traditional cultures, it is clear that breast-feeding for two to three years has been the most typical human custom (see **Map 5.1**) (Small, 1998). The World Health Organization recommends breast-feeding for the first two years.

If breast-feeding takes place for only a few weeks or months during infancy, the transition from breast to bottle usually takes place fairly smoothly, especially if the bottle is introduced gradually (Murkoff et al., 2003). Infants may protest at first the change from the familiar breast to the unfamiliar bottle, especially if the nipple of the bottle requires a substantial accommodation in sucking technique. But this usually

APPLYING YOUR KNOWLEDGE
. . . as a Researcher

Toddlers in many cultures are weaned around age 2. What is an evolutionary explanation for weaning around this age?

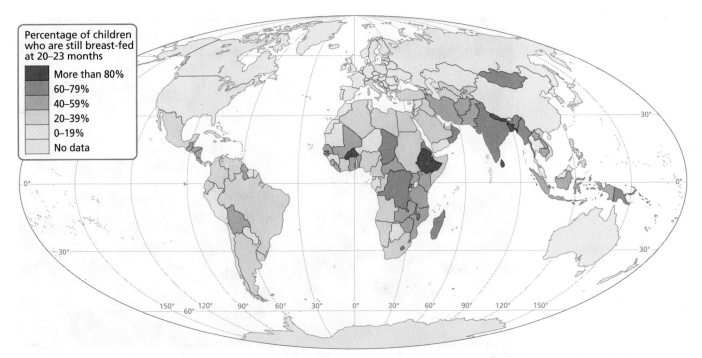

Percentage of children who are still breast-fed at 20–23 months

- More than 80%
- 60–79%
- 40–59%
- 20–39%
- 0–19%
- No data

Map 5.1 • **Cultural Variations in the Length of Breast-Feeding.** Which countries and regions have the highest rates of breast-feeding at 20–23 months, and which the lowest? What cultural and economic differences might explain these variations?

weaning cessation of breast-feeding

passes quickly: They get hungry, they want to eat, the bottle contains milk, so they drink from the bottle. However, the longer breast-feeding continues into toddlerhood, the more challenging **weaning** becomes when the mother decides the time has come for the child to stop drinking breast milk. As we will see in more detail later in the chapter, the toddler is much more socially aware than the infant, and much more capable of exercising intentional behavior. The toddler can also speak up, in a way the infant cannot, to make demands and protest prohibitions.

Consequently, most traditional cultures have customary practices for weaning toddlers from the breast. Often, the approach is gentle and gradual at first, but becomes harsher if the toddler resists. For example, in Bali (an island that is part of Indonesia) parents feed their babies some solid food from the first few days of life, and attempt gradual weaning beginning about age 2. However, if the gradual approach does not work, mothers coat their breasts with bitter-tasting herbs (Diener, 2000). Similarly, toddlers in rural villages in Turkey are weaned at about age 2, but if they persist in trying to breast-feed, the mother coats her breasts with tomato paste. The child usually cries and protests, but the method works without fail (Delaney, 2000).

Other cultures separate mother and toddler during weaning, so that the toddler will have no choice but to get used to life without breast-feeding. Among the Fulani people of West Africa, toddlers are sent to their grandmother's household during weaning. If the toddler complains about not breast-feeding, the grandmother may offer her own breast, but the toddler quickly loses interest upon discovering that there is no milk in it (Johnson, 2000).

There are variations in age of weaning across ethnic and socioeconomic groups in the United States (Hla et al., 2003). Women who work full-time tend to wean children earlier than those who work part-time. Child-led weaning has become an increasingly popular practice among middle-class parents in the United States. If the child is allowed to lead the weaning process, nursing continues until the child decides it is time to stop. This means that weaning may not occur until the child is 2½ to 7 years old, and one day he may say, "I don't want to nurse anymore," and that is the end of nursing. In mother–child pairs where nursing continues past age 2, it is typical for nursing to occur with decreasing frequency, usually once per day.

Toddlers in traditional cultures often breast-feed until they are about 2 years old. Here, a mother of the Yanomamo people of the Amazon rain forest nurses her toddler.

WHAT HAVE YOU LEARNED?

1. How have views on toilet training changed throughout history?
2. What are the signs that toddlers are ready to begin toilet training?
3. How does controlled elimination in traditional cultures differ from toilet training in developed countries?
4. Why is weaning more difficult in toddlerhood than in infancy?
5. What practices do traditional cultures use if toddlers resist weaning?

Section 1 VIDEO GUIDE Gross Motor Development Across Cultures (Length: 4:22)

In this video, we observe how gross motor skills such as crawling and walking proceed at different rates within and across cultures. We also interview Karen Adolph, a leading researcher of motor development.

1. Karen Adolph notes that in some cultures, toddlers do not crawl at all or learn to crawl only after they have mastered walking. What cultural factors might influence this?

2. Should parents be concerned if their child takes longer than other children to achieve a gross motor milestone, such as learning to walk? Why or why not?

3. According to Adolph's longitudinal research, at what point do infants and toddlers have a solid grasp of their gross motor abilities? What is the relevance of this for parents who are trying to baby-proof their house?

Watch the **Video** Gross Motor Development Across Cultures in **MyDevelopmentLab**

LEARNING OBJECTIVES

5.7 Outline the cognitive achievements of toddlerhood in Piaget's theory.

5.8 Explain Vygotsky's sociocultural theory of cognitive development and contrast it with Piaget's theory.

5.9 Summarize the evidence for the biological and evolutionary bases of language.

5.10 Describe the milestones in language development that take place during the toddler years.

5.11 Identify how parents' stimulation of toddlers' language varies across cultures and evaluate how these variations relate to language development.

Cognitive Development Theories

You have already been introduced to Piaget and Vygotsky and their theories of infant cognitive development (see Chapters 1 and 4). Here their theories continue into toddlerhood.

Cognitive development in toddlerhood: Piaget's theory

5.7 **LEARNING OBJECTIVE** | Outline the cognitive achievements of toddlerhood in Piaget's theory.

Piaget proposed that cognitive development during the first two years of life follows a sequence of six sensorimotor stages. As we saw in Chapter 4, during infancy the primary cognitive advance of the first four stages of sensorimotor development is from simple reflexes to intentional, coordinated behavior. Neonates have a wide range of reflexes and little intentional control over their behavior, but by the end of the first year infants have lost most of their reflexes and can perform intentional actions that combine schemes, such as moving one object aside in order to reach another. In the second year of life—during toddlerhood—the final two stages of sensorimotor development are completed.

SENSORIMOTOR STAGE 5: TERTIARY CIRCULAR REACTIONS Piaget called the fifth stage of sensorimotor development *tertiary circular reactions* (age 12–18 months). In this stage, toddlers intentionally try out different behaviors to see what the effects will be. In the previous stage, *secondary circular reactions*, the action first occurs by accident and then is intentionally repeated, but in tertiary circular reactions the action is intentional from the beginning. Like secondary circular reactions, tertiary circular reactions are circular because they are performed repeatedly.

For example, at 17 months my twins discovered how to flush the toilet, and one day they flushed and flushed and flushed until the flushing system broke and the water began overflowing. I discovered this as I sat downstairs reading the newspaper and suddenly observed water whooshing out of the vents in the ceiling! I ran upstairs and there they were, standing in three inches of water, giggling with glee, absolutely delighted. I don't recall thinking of Piaget at that moment, but I'll bet he would have been pleased. To Piaget, in this stage toddlers become like little scientists, experimenting on the objects around them in order to learn more about how the world works. My twins certainly learned that day about what happens when you flush a toilet repeatedly.

SENSORIMOTOR STAGE 6: MENTAL REPRESENTATIONS The final stage of sensorimotor development, from 18 to 24 months, is the stage of **mental representations**. Now, instead of trying out a range of actions as in tertiary circular reactions, toddlers first think about the possibilities and select the action most likely to achieve the desired outcome. Piaget gave the example of his daughter Lucienne, who sought to obtain a small chain from inside the matchbox where her father had placed it. First she turned the box upside down; then she tried to jam her finger into it, but neither of these methods worked. She paused for a moment, holding the matchbox and considering it intently. Then she opened and closed her mouth, and suddenly slid back the cover of the matchbox to reveal the chain (Crain, 2000). To Piaget, opening and closing her mouth showed that she was pondering potential solutions, then mimicking the solution that had occurred to her.

Mental representation is a crucial milestone in cognitive development, because it is the basis of the most important and most distinctly human cognitive abilities, including language. The words we use are mental representations of objects, people, actions, and ideas.

OBJECT PERMANENCE IN TODDLERHOOD Object permanence also develops further during toddlerhood. As described in Chapter 4, by their first birthday infants will look for an object that they observe being hidden behind or under another object. However, even at 12 months they still make the "A-not-B error." That is, if they find an object under blanket A, and then a second blanket B is added and they observe the object being hidden under blanket B, they nevertheless tend to look under blanket A, where they found the object the first time.

Toddlers learn to avoid the A-not-B error and search for the object where they last saw it hidden. However, even though the A-not-B error is less common in toddlerhood than in infancy, search errors happen occasionally on this task in toddlerhood and even into early childhood, up to ages 4 and 5 (Hood et al., 2003; Newcombe & Huttenlocher, 2006). But we can say with some confidence that toddlers have attained object permanence once they generally avoid the A-not-B error.

Object permanence is a major advance of cognitive development in toddlerhood, but it is not a distinctly human achievement. In fact, chimpanzees and human toddlers have equal success on object permanence tasks at age 2 (Call, 2001; Collier-Baker & Suddendorf, 2006). Understanding the permanence of the physical world is crucial to being able to function in that world, so it is not surprising that humans and nonhuman primates would share this fundamental ability (Brownell & Kopp, 2007).

DEFERRED IMITATION The ability for mental representation of actions also makes possible **deferred imitation,** which is the ability to repeat actions observed at an earlier time. Piaget's favorite example of deferred imitation involved his daughter Jacqueline, who witnessed another child exploding into an elaborate public tantrum and then repeated the tantrum herself at home the next day (Crain, 2000). Deferred imitation is a crucial ability for learning because it means that when we observe something important to know, we can repeat it later ourselves. Deferred imitation is a frequent part of toddlers' pretend play, as they observe the actions of other children or adults—making a meal, feeding a baby, digging a hole—and then imitate those actions later in their play (Lillard, 2007).

mental representations Piaget's final stage of sensorimotor development in which toddlers first think about the range of possibilities and then select the action most likely to achieve the desired outcome

deferred imitation ability to repeat actions observed at an earlier time

My Virtual Child

Your virtual child has shown symbolic thinking through advanced make-believe play with a dollhouse. How might a child from a different culture show symbolic thinking?

Toddlers' play is often based on deferred imitation. Here, a toddler in Peru offers a bottle to her doll.

Piaget proposed that deferred imitation begins at about 18 months, but subsequent research has shown that it develops much earlier than he had thought (Bauer, 2006). Deferred imitation of facial expressions has been reported as early as 6 weeks of age, when infants exposed to an unusual facial expression from an unfamiliar adult imitated it when the same adult appeared before them the next day (Meltzoff & Moore, 1994). At 6 months of age, infants can imitate a simple sequence of events a day later, such as taking off a puppet's glove and shaking it to ring a bell inside the glove (Barr & Hayne, 2003).

However, if there is a longer delay, toddlers are more proficient at deferred imitation than infants are. In a series of studies, children 9, 13, and 20 months old were shown two-step sequences of events such as placing a car on a track to make a light go on, then pushing a rod to make the car run down a ramp (Bauer et al., 2000; 2001; 2003). After a 1-month interval, shown the same materials, fewer than half of the 9-month-olds could imitate the steps they had seen previously, compared with about two-thirds of the 13-month-olds and nearly all the 20-month-olds. Other studies have shown that better deferred imitation among toddlers than among infants may be due principally to advances in the maturity of the brain. Specifically, the *hippocampus*, that part of the brain especially important in long-term memory encoding and recall, is still in a highly immature state of development during infancy but matures substantially during toddlerhood (Bauer et al., 2003; Liston & Kagan, 2002). ✳

CATEGORIZATION Piaget also believed that mental representation in toddlerhood is the basis of categorization. Once we are able to represent an image of a house mentally, for example, we can understand the category "house" and understand that different houses are all part of that category. A toddler can observe houses of different colors, styles, and sizes and still recognize that they all fall under the same general category of "house." These categories, in turn, become the basis for language, because each noun and verb represents a category (Waxman, 2003). The word *truck* represents the category "truck" containing every possible variety of truck; the word *run* represents the category "run" containing all varieties of running, and so on.

Here, too, recent experiments seem to indicate that Piaget underestimated children's early abilities. Infants and toddlers are able to do more than he had thought. Even infants as young as a few months old have been shown to have a rudimentary understanding of categories. This can be demonstrated by their patterns of looking at a series of images. As we have seen, infants tend to look longer at images that are new or unfamiliar, and their attention to images is often used in research to infer what they know and do not know. In one study, 3- and 4-month-old infants were shown photographs of cats (Quinn et al., 1993). After a series of cat photos, the infants were shown two new photos, one of a cat and one of a dog. They looked longer at the dog photo, indicating that they had been using a category for "cat," and looked longer at the dog photo because it did not fit.

However, research has generally confirmed Piaget's insight that categorization becomes more advanced during toddlerhood. For example, one study compared children who were 9, 12, and 18 months old (Gopnik et al., 1999). The children were given four different toy horses and four different pencils. At 9 months, they played with the objects but made no effort to separate them into categories. At 12 months, some of the children would place the objects into categories and some would not. By 18 months, nearly all the children would systematically and deliberately separate the objects into a "horse" category and a "pencil" category.

By the time they are 2 years old, toddlers can go beyond the appearance of objects to categorize them on the basis of their functions or qualities. In a study demonstrating this ability, 2-year-olds were shown a machine and a collection of blocks that appeared to be identical (Gopnik et al., 1999). Then they were shown that two of the blocks made the machine light up when placed on it, whereas others did not. The researcher

APPLYING YOUR KNOWLEDGE

Give an example of real-life learning by deferred imitation at age 2, 7, 14, and 25.

✳ **Explore** the **Concept** Encoding, Storage, and Retrieval in Memory in **MyDevelopmentLab**

picked up one of the blocks that had made the machine light up and said, "This is a blicket. Can you show me the other blicket?" The 2-year-olds were able to choose the other block that had made the machine light go on, even though it looked the same as the blocks that had not had that effect. Although *blicket* was a nonsense word the toddlers had not heard before, they were able to understand that the category "blicket" was defined by causing the machine to light up.

Vygotsky's cultural theory of cognitive development

Explain Vygotsky's sociocultural theory of cognitive development and contrast it with Piaget's theory.

LEARNING OBJECTIVE **5.8**

Although most studies of toddlers' cognitive development pay little attention to cultural context, in recent years a cultural approach to cognition has gained increased attention from scholars of human development. This approach is founded on the ideas of the Russian psychologist Lev Vygotsky (1896–1934). In Chapter 1, we examined two of Vygotsky's most influential ideas: the **zone of proximal development** and scaffolding. Here, we delve deeper into these ideas and explore the role of private speech and guided participation in children's development.

PRIVATE SPEECH AND THE USE OF LANGUAGE As they learn in the zone of proximal development and have conversations with those guiding them, children begin to speak to themselves in a self-guiding and self-directing way, first aloud and then internally. Vygotsky called this **private speech** (Winsler, 2009). As children become more competent in what they are learning, they internalize their private speech and gradually decrease its use. Toddlerhood and early childhood are crucial periods in Vygotsky's theory, because it is during these life stages that children are most likely to use private speech and make the transition from using it aloud to using it internally (Feigenbaum, 2002). Toddlers use private speech to work through new concepts and experiences as they explore the world. A toddler may comment on how a toy works, for example, "This goes there." As the child gets older, he may comment on social experiences as a reminder of rules, "I share my toys." Children may also give themselves encouragement, such as "You can do it" when approaching something new or scary.

Private speech continues throughout life. In fact, Vygotsky believed that private speech was necessary to all higher order cognitive functioning. In recent years, studies have shown that adolescents and adults use private speech when solving tasks of diverse kinds and diverse levels of difficulty (Medina et al., 2009). You may notice that you use private speech when trying to remember something or when studying for exams. Private speech can be helpful as you try to remember facts or when you try to work out what you think about a particular situation or problem. Parents and teachers can encourage private speech by modeling its use in classrooms.

Language is a centrally important developmental skill in Vygotsky's theory. He thought that we advance thinking through the social tool of language. For example, having a complex number system with the concept of zero allows for advanced scientific thinking. A language with the numbers "one," "two," and "many" will not lead to the development of calculus. Vygotsky thought that the child develops language through interacting with others. Language is first a social tool, which then becomes internalized. As the child's own language develops, her thinking advances, and she is able to understand the social and physical worlds with increasing sophistication. One way that language advances thinking is by building a scaffold for thought. As discussed in Chapter 1, a scaffold is a tool or social guidance that provides help to a learner so that she can accomplish something with help that very soon she will be able to accomplish on her own—the way a scaffold on the side of a building allows workers to work up

APPLYING YOUR KNOWLEDGE

Think of a recent time when you have used private speech. What was it about the task that evoked private speech on that occasion?

zone of proximal development difference between skills or tasks that children can accomplish alone and those they are capable of performing if guided by an adult or a more competent peer

private speech in Vygotsky's theory, self-guiding and self-directing comments children make to themselves as they learn in the zone of proximal development and have conversations with those guiding them; first spoken aloud, then internally

guided participation teaching interaction between two people (often an adult and a child) as they participate in a culturally valued activity

high safely. Through learning words, the child is able to learn concepts and build on them to develop knowledge.

GUIDED PARTICIPATION One scholar who has been important in extending Vygotsky's theory is Barbara Rogoff (1990, 1995, 1998, 2003). Her idea of **guided participation** refers to the interaction between two people (often an adult and a child) as they participate in a culturally valued activity. The guidance is "the direction offered by cultural and social values, as well as social partners" (Rogoff, 1995, p. 142) as learning takes place. As an example of guided participation, Rogoff (2003) describes a toddler and caregiver in Taiwan "playing school" together. As part of the game, the caregiver teaches the toddler to stand up and bow down to the teacher at the beginning and end of class, teaching not only the routine of the classroom but the cultural value of respect for teachers' authority. The teaching in guided participation may also be indirect. For example, from her research with the Mayan people of Guatemala, Rogoff (2003) describes how toddlers observe their mother making tortillas and attempt to imitate them. Mothers give them a small piece of dough and help their efforts along by rolling the dough into a ball and starting the flattening process but otherwise do not provide explicit teaching, allowing toddlers to learn through observing and then attempting to imitate their mother's actions.

Guided participation is used in formal and informal education settings, in school and in apprenticeship processes, though it is mostly thought of as the tacit or implicit learning that happens in informal settings. In formal educational settings, guided participation is used in cultural practices such as lining up, taking turns, greetings and goodbyes. For example, in the preschool, there is often "circle time," where children and their teachers gather in a circle and sing a "Good morning" song where each person is greeted with, "Good morning." Children do not automatically know these kinds of social rules that help society function; they have to be taught routines through social interaction in learning settings. Guided participation occurs in many settings where physical skills are being learned. Think of dance classes or golf lessons. A teacher helps the student learn the proper steps or the proper body position to do the activity. The task is demonstrated, and the teacher may guide the learner's body in the proper form until the learner can do it by himself. As adults, we continue to learn via guided participation in such activities as foreign language instruction, cooking, art, and dance.

My Virtual Child

In what activities will you engage in guided participation with your virtual child? Are these activities similar to those found in other cultures?

THINKING CULTURALLY

When celebrating holidays within your culture, what are some examples of guided participation you have seen?

In Vygotsky's theory, children's cognitive development is always both social and cultural. Here, a father in the Middle Eastern country of Oman shows his son how to weave a basket.

WHAT HAVE YOU LEARNED?

1. How does toddlers' understanding of object permanence develop beyond what infants know?

2. Describe the concepts of deferred imitation and categorization and explain how they develop during toddlerhood.

3. Describe the concept of private speech and explain how it reflects or leads to the development of ideas in the child's mind.

4. Describe the practice of guided participation and explain how this practice helps people learn.

5. How is Rogoff's idea of guided participation similar to Vygotsky's zone of proximal development?

Language Development

Of all the qualities that distinguish humans from other animals, language may be the most important. Other species of animals have their own ways of communicating, but language allows humans to communicate about a vastly broader range of topics. Using language, humans can communicate about not just what is observable in the present, the way other animals might communicate about food or predators in their immediate environment, but about an infinite range of things beyond the present moment. With language, too, we can communicate not just about things that exist but about things that might exist, things that we imagine. As linguist Derrick Bickerton remarks, "Only language could have broken through the prison of immediate experience in which every other creature is locked, releasing us into infinite freedoms of space and time" (Leakey, 1994, p. 119).

In Chapter 4 we looked at the beginnings of language in infancy. However, by the end of infancy most children can speak only a few words. It is during toddlerhood that language development has its most rapid and important advances. Toddlers go from speaking a few words at their first birthday to being fluent users of language by their third birthday. Let's examine the course of this remarkable achievement, looking first at the biological and evolutionary bases of language, then at specific language milestones of toddlerhood, and finally, at the cultural and social context of toddlers' language use.

The biological and evolutionary bases of language

Summarize the evidence for the biological and evolutionary bases of language.

LEARNING OBJECTIVE 5.9

You may have heard that some primates have learned how to use language. Attempts to teach language to apes have a long history in the social sciences, going back over a half century. In the earliest attempts, researchers treated baby chimpanzees as closely as possible to how a human infant would be treated, having the chimpanzees live in the researcher's household as part of the family and making daily efforts to teach the chimps how to speak. Years of these efforts yielded nothing but the single word "mama"—and a badly disordered household. It turned out that chimpanzees, like other nonhuman primates, lack the vocal apparatus that makes human speech possible.

In the 1960s, researchers hit on the clever idea of teaching apes sign language; these attempts were much more successful. One famous chimpanzee, Washoe, learned to use about 100 signs, mostly involving requests for food (Small, M., 2001). She

Chimpanzees can learn to use some sign language in a limited way, but they lack the infinite generativity of human language.

infinite generativity ability to take the word symbols of a language and combine them in a virtually infinite number of new ways

Broca's area portion of the left frontal lobe of the human brain that is specialized for language production

Wernicke's area portion of the left temporal lobe of the human brain that is specialized for language comprehension

Simulate the **Experiment**
Broca's Area and Wernicke's Area
in **MyDevelopmentLab**

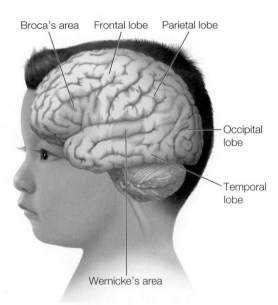

Broca's area   Frontal lobe   Parietal lobe

Occipital lobe

Temporal lobe

Wernicke's area

Figure 5.4 • **Illustration of the brain lobes showing location of Broca's area and Wernicke's area.**

even learned to lie and to make jokes. However, she never learned to make original combinations of signs (with one possible exception, when she saw a duck for the first time and signed "water bird"). Mostly, Washoe and other primates who have learned sign language simply mimic the signs they have been taught by their human teachers. They lack the most important and distinctive feature of human language, which is **infinite generativity,** the ability to take the word symbols of a language and combine them in a virtually infinite number of new ways.

A variety of human biological characteristics shows that we are a species uniquely built for language (Kenneally, 2007). First, humans have a unique vocal apparatus. We are able to make a much wider range of sounds than the other primates because, for us, the larynx is located lower in the throat, which creates a large sound chamber, the pharynx, above the vocal cords. We also have a relatively small and mobile tongue that can push the air coming past the larynx in various ways to make different sounds, and lips that are flexible enough to stop and start the passage of air.

Second, two areas in the left hemisphere of the human brain are specifically devoted to language functions (Nakano & Blumstein, 2004; Pizzamiglio et al., 2005). **Broca's area** in the left frontal lobe is specialized for language production, and **Wernicke's area** in the left temporal lobe is specialized for language comprehension (see *Figure 5.4*). If damage to one of these areas occurs in adulthood, the specialized language function of the area is also damaged; but if damage takes place in childhood, other areas of the brain can compensate—with compensation being greater the younger the brain injury takes place (Akshoomoff et al., 2002; Huttenlocher, 2002). In addition to Broca's and Wernicke's areas, many other regions of the brain contribute to language use (Dick et al., 2004). In fact, some linguists argue that the extraordinary size of the human brain in comparison to other species is due mainly to the evolution of language (Pinker, 2004).

Third, genes specifically devoted to language development have recently been identified (Gazzaniga, 2008; Pinker, 2004). Because Broca's and Wernicke's areas have long been known to be part of normal brain anatomy, the genetic basis of language was clear. However, identifying the specific genes for language strengthens our knowledge of how deeply language is embedded in human phylogenetic (species) development.

Undoubtedly the development of language gave humans a substantial evolutionary advantage over nonhuman primates (Small, M., 2001). Language would have made it easier to communicate about the location of food sources and about how to make tools, which would in turn enhance survival. Many evolutionary biologists believe that language also conferred an evolutionary advantage because of its social function. During the course of human evolution, the size of human groups gradually increased (Leakey, 1994), leading to an increased need for communication that would allow them to function effectively. Because language abilities improved the efficiency of group functioning, groups that excelled in language would have been more likely than other groups to survive and reproduce. Within groups, too, using language effectively would have given people an advantage in obtaining mates, food, and status, so natural selection would have favored language abilities in the course of human evolutionary history (Pinker, 2004).

Milestones of toddler language: From first words to fluency

Describe the milestones in language development that take place during the toddler years.

Toddlers' advances in language begin slowly but then rise sharply, so that in less than two years they go from speaking a few words to being highly adept language users. Especially notable is the amazing burst of language development that occurs at 18 to 24 months.

APPLYING YOUR KNOWLEDGE
How, specifically, would language have conferred an evolutionary advantage to early humans in obtaining mates, food, and status?

TWELVE MONTHS TO 18 MONTHS: SLOW EXPANSION For the first 6 months of toddlerhood, language develops at a steady but slow pace. From 12 to 18 months old, toddlers learn to speak one to three new words a week, reaching 10 words by 15 months old and 50 words by about 18 months old, on average, in American studies (Bloom, 1998). There is a wide range of variability around these averages. Toddlers may speak their 10th word anywhere from 13 to 19 months old, and their 50th word anywhere from 14 to 24 months old, and still be considered within the normal range (Newman, 2008). Just as the timing of taking first steps has no relation to later athletic ability, generally speaking, the timing of speaking the first, 10th, or 50th word has no relation to later verbal ability.

The first 50 words tend to be words that are part of toddler's daily routines (Waxman & Lidz, 2006), and include

- important people ("Mama," "Dada"),
- familiar animals ("dog," "kitty"),
- body parts ("hair," "tummy"),
- moving objects ("car," "truck"),
- foods ("milk," "cookie"),
- actions ("eat," "bath"),
- household items ("cup," "chair"),
- toys ("ball," "bear"),
- greetings or farewells ("hi," "bye-bye").

Toddlers first learn words they need to use in practical ways to communicate with the people around them, usually as part of shared activities (Newman, 2007). Often at this age they speak in partial words, for example, "bah" for bird, "meh" for milk, or "na-na" for "banana."

From 12 to 18 months most toddlers use one word at a time, but a single word can have varied meanings. Toddler's single words are called **holophrases,** meaning that for them a single word can be used to represent different forms of whole sentences (Flavell et al., 2002). For example, "cup" could mean "Fill my *cup* with juice," or "I dropped the *cup* on the floor," or "Hand me my *cup,* I can't reach it," or "Here, take this *cup,*" depending on when and how and to whom it is said.

Another way toddlers make the most of their limited vocabulary is to have a single word represent a variety of related objects. This is called **overextension** (Bloom, 2000). For example, when the son of two language researchers learned the name of the furry family dog, Nunu, he applied it not only to the original Nunu but to all dogs, as well as to other fuzzy objects such as slippers, and even to a salad with a large black olive that apparently reminded him of Nunu's nose (de Villiers & de Villiers, 1978).

Toddlers also exhibit **underextension,** applying a general word to a specific object (Woodward & Markman, 1998). When I was a child, my family had a cat named Kitty, who received that name because my brother was told that it was "the kitty," and began calling it Kitty, and the name stuck. He did not realize that *kitty* was the (slang) name for the larger category, "cats," but mistook it for the proper name of that particular cat.

holophrase single word that is used to represent a whole sentence

overextension use of a single word to represent a variety of related objects

underextension applying a general word to a specific object

Toddlers exhibit overextension when they use a single word (such as "raspberry") to represent a variety of related objects (such as strawberries and other red berries).

Underextension often occurs in this way, with a toddler first applying a new word to a specific object, then learning later to apply it to a category of objects.

Here, as at all ages, *production* (speaking) lags behind *comprehension* (understanding) in language development. Although toddlers do not reach the 50-word milestone in production until about 18 months old, they usually achieve 50-word comprehension by about 13 months old (Menyuk et al., 1995). During toddlerhood, comprehension is a better predictor of later verbal intelligence than production is (Reznick et al., 1997).

EIGHTEEN MONTHS TO 24 MONTHS: THE NAMING EXPLOSION   After learning to speak words at a slow rate for the first half of their second year, toddlers' word production suddenly takes off from 18 to 24 months. The pace of learning new words doubles, from one to three words per week to five or six words per week (Kopp, 2003). This is known as the *naming explosion* or *vocabulary spurt* (Bloom et al., 1985; Goldfield & Reznick, 1990). After just one time of being told what an object is called, toddlers this age will learn it and remember it, a process called **fast mapping** (Gopnik et al., 1999; Markman & Jaswal, 2004). Fast mapping is due not just to memory but to toddlers' ability to quickly infer the meaning of words based on how the word is used in a sentence and how it seems to be related to words they already know (Dixon et al., 2006). By their second birthday, toddlers have an average vocabulary of about 200 words (Dale & Goodman, 2004). This rapid pace of learning and remembering words will continue for years, but it is especially striking at 18 to 24 months because this is when it begins (Ganger & Brent, 2004). Girls' vocabulary increases faster than boys' vocabulary during this period, initiating a gender difference in verbal abilities that will persist throughout childhood (Lovas, 2011).

Two of the most notable words toddlers learn during this period are *gone* and *no*. Using "gone" reflects their growing awareness of object permanence, as it signifies that something has disappeared from view but still exists somewhere (Gopnik et al., 1999). Using "no" reflects their budding sense of self ("me," "my," and "mine" also begin to be used at this age). Saying "no" can be short for "You may want me to do to that, but I don't want to do it!" Of course, they also begin to hear "No!" more often around this age, as their mobility and curiosity leads them to behavior that the adults around them may regard as dangerous or destructive (Kopp, 2003). During this 18- to 24-month period they also learn to name one or two colors, at least six body parts, and emotional states like "tired" and "mad" (Eisenberg et al., 2006; Kopp, 2003).

Toward the end of the 18- to 24-month period, toddlers begin to combine spoken words for the first time. Their first word combinations are usually two words, in what is called **telegraphic speech** (Bloom, 1998; Brown, 1973). Telegraphic speech takes similar forms in a variety of languages, from English to German to Finnish to Samoan: "See doggie," "Big car," "My ball," "More cookie," or "Mommy gone" (Bochner & Jones, 2008; Slobin, 1972). Like a telegram in the old days, telegraphic speech strips away connecting words like *the* and *and*, getting right to the point with nouns, verbs, and modifiers.

An interesting feature of telegraphic speech is that it already shows an initial knowledge of syntax (word order). Toddlers say "See doggie," not "Doggie see"; they say "My ball," not "Ball my." Similar to the one-word holophrases used earlier, telegraphic speech implies more understanding of language than it states explicitly: "Big car" means "Look at the big car," "My ball" means 'This is my ball," and so on.

Verbal production is the most striking advance of the 18- to 24-month period, but comprehension also advances notably as toddlers become faster and more efficient in processing words. In one series of experiments, toddlers 15 to 24 months old were shown pictures of two objects at a time while a recorded voice said "Where's the _____?" and named one of the objects (Fernald et al., 2006). At 15 months, toddlers waited until the whole word had been spoken before looking at the object the

fast mapping learning and remembering a word for an object after just one time of being told what the object is called

telegraphic speech two-word phrases that strip away connecting words, such as *the* and *and*.

word referred to, but by 24 months they would shift their gaze even before the word had been completely spoken, for example looking at the shoe as soon as they heard the "sh" part spoken.

TWENTY-FOUR MONTHS TO 36 MONTHS: BECOMING ADEPT AT LANGUAGE During the third year, toddlers continue to expand their speaking vocabulary at the same rapid pace that began at 18 to 24 months. They learn to use prepositions such as *under*, *over*, and *through* (Eisenberg et al., 1994). They also use words that reflect a more complex understanding of categories. For example, they understand that a bear is not only a bear but also an animal (Kopp, 2003). ◉

They continue to exhibit overextension and underextension, but with diminishing frequency as their vocabulary expands. They continue to use telegraphic speech as well, but now in three- and four-word statements ("Ball under bed!") rather than two words. Increasingly during the third year they begin to speak in short, complete sentences. At this age my son Miles would point to the moon and protest, "It's too high!" as if he expected us to do something about it.

By the end of the third year most toddlers are remarkably skilled language users (Maratsos, 1998). They can communicate with others about a wide range of topics. They can speak about events that are happening in the present as well as about past and future events. Toddlers raised in homes where Chinese is spoken have learned that raising or lowering the pitch of a word changes its meaning. French toddlers have learned how to make nasal sounds and say "Voilà!" and !Kung San toddlers in Botswana have learned how to click their tongues against various parts of their mouths to make the words of their language (Small, M., 2001). Although their pronunciation of words is not as precise as it will become later, by the time they reach age 3 most toddlers can speak clearly enough to make themselves understood about nearly anything they wish.

Furthermore, without any explicit instruction, by the end of the third year toddlers have learned grammar—the rules of their language—no matter how complex those rules may seem to someone who does not speak it. Consider this example, from Turkish (Slobin, 1972). In Turkish, the rules of grammar, also called syntax, are different from English. In English, "The girl fed the dog" has quite a different meaning from "The dog fed the girl." The *subject* (girl) is supposed to go first, followed by the *verb* (fed) and then the *object* (dog). However, in Turkish the object is indicated not by the order of the words but by attaching the suffix *u*. So, "The girl fed the dog-u" means the same as "The dog-u fed the girl." Turkish toddlers use the *u* rule correctly by their third year, just as English-speaking children learn the correct use of English syntax by their third year (Aksu-Koç & Slobin, 1985).

The marvelous ability that young children have to learn the rules of their language is one more indication of the biological basis of language. A half century ago, many psychologists argued that language has no biological origin and children learn it solely through imitation and parental reinforcement. Parents encourage language use by smiling and nodding, reinforcing the child's verbal behavior. The behaviorist B. F. Skinner (refer back to Chapter 1) led the learning theory approach to language acquisition. He believed that children learned language through imitating speech that they heard, while adults reinforced the sounds that best approximated the language the child was learning. The linguist Noam Chomsky (1957, 1969) took a nativist perspective and protested that language is too complex to be learned in this way. Observing that all children learn the basic rules of grammar of their language at about the same age, 2 to 3 years old, Chomsky proposed that children are born with a **language acquisition device (LAD)** that enables them to perceive and grasp quickly the grammatical rules in the language around them. Today language researchers generally agree that language development is a biological potential that is then nurtured by social interaction, although there is still a lively debate about the nature of the biological foundation of language and the kinds of social stimulation needed to develop it (Hoff, 2009).

◉ **Watch** the **Video** EMT Program and Language Development in **MyDevelopmentLab**

language acquisition device (LAD) according to Chomsky, innate feature of the brain that enables children to perceive and grasp quickly the grammatical rules in the language around them

overregularization applying grammatical rules even to words that are the exception to the rule

Toddlers' language mastery is evident not only in how well they use the rules of their language but also in the mistakes they make. As they learn the grammar of their language, they make mistakes that reflect **overregularization**, which means applying grammatical rules even to words that are an exception to the rule.

Here are two examples from English that illustrate overregularization. First, the plural of most English nouns can be obtained by adding *s* to the singular form, but there are irregular exceptions, such as "mice" as the plural of "mouse," and "feet" as the plural of "foot." In the third year, toddlers sometimes make mistakes with these kinds of words, saying "mouses" instead of "mice" and "foots" instead of "feet." Second, the rule for the past tense of an English verb is to add *ed* to the end, but there are irregular exceptions, such as "went" as the past tense of "go" and "threw" as the past tense of "throw." In the third year toddlers sometimes make mistakes with these exceptions, saying "Mommy *goed* to the store" or "I *throwed* the ball." Overregularizations of this kind continue into middle childhood (Kidd & Lum, 2008).

APPLYING YOUR KNOWLEDGE

Give some examples of over regularization in addition to the ones provided here.

Learning language in a social and cultural context

5.11 **LEARNING OBJECTIVE** | Identify how parents' stimulation of toddlers' language varies across cultures and evaluate how these variations relate to language development.

Humans are biologically built for learning language, but not for learning any specific language. There are over 60,000 different human languages in the world (Small, M., 2001), but none of them come preinscribed on our brains. Whatever language we learn must come from our social and cultural environment.

This was first shown in a bizarre experiment conducted about 800 years ago. Frederick II, the Holy Roman Emperor (1194–1250), decided he wanted to find out what language infants would speak "naturally," if they were left to their own resources. He chose a group of neonates in an orphanage and instructed their caregivers never to speak in their presence. What language would the babies begin to speak spontaneously, on their own? Would it be Latin, the language of scholars at that time? Would it be German, Frederick's own language, or (God forbid) French, the language of his chief rivals?

The answer turned out to be, as you may have guessed, none of the above. Tragically, all of the infants died. This is a poignant illustration of how we are poised for language to be part of the human social environment, and of how humans need language to develop properly, not just in their language development but in their social development.

PARENTS' STIMULATION OF TODDLERS' LANGUAGE DEVELOPMENT What kind of social environment do toddlers need in order to develop their language skills? In American research, the focus has been on how parents foster language development in young children, and the subsequent language differences that result. For example, American girls are typically more talkative than American boys. This may be because mothers typically talk more to toddler girls than they do to boys. In addition to studies of gender differences, several studies have examined social-class differences in parents' language stimulation and how this is related to the pace of toddlers' language development (Hoff, 2004; Lee & Burkam, 2002). For example, one study videotaped parent–child interactions in the homes of low-, middle-, and high-income families on several occasions, beginning when the children were 7 to 9 months old and continuing until they were about 30 months old (Hart & Risley, 1999). There were striking differences in how many words were spoken to children of different income levels. Parents in high-income families talked the most to their children, averaging about 35 words a minute; parents in middle-income families talked to their children an average of about 20 words a minute; and parents of low-income families provided the least language stimulation, just 10 words per minute. By 30 months old there were substantial differences in the toddlers' vocabularies, averaging 766 words in the high-income families and just 357 words in the low-income families.

In another study, children and mothers were videotaped in laboratories, first when the children were 9 months old and then when they were 13 months old; each mother–child pair engaged in free play with toys provided by the experimenters (Tamis-LeMonda et al., 2001). The study focused on maternal responsiveness to the children's vocalizations and how this related to attaining language milestones when the children were reassessed later in toddlerhood, in their third year. Maternal responsiveness included affirmations ("Good job!" for speaking a word correctly), imitations (saying "cup" after the child said "ca" and pointed to a cup), and expansions (saying "Where did the ball go?" after the child said "ba?"). Maternal responsiveness was positively correlated with earlier timing of all four language milestones later in toddlerhood: first word, 50-word spoken vocabulary, first word combinations, and first use of past tense. That is, children whose mothers responded more often to their vocalizations tended to reach these milestones earlier than other children.

So, it seems there is solid evidence that the family language environment in infancy and toddlerhood influences children's language development at least through toddlerhood, right? Well, not so fast. These studies provide classic examples of the hazards of interpreting relations between parents' behavior and children's outcomes in biological families, due to passive genotype–environment effects (see Chapter 2). Can you see why? The studies do show that parents' language stimulation is related to toddlers' language achievements. However, the parents provided not only the language environment to the children in the study but their genotype as well. There is ample evidence from adoption and twin studies that verbal abilities are inherited to a substantial extent (Loehlin et al., 1997). Consequently, it is not clear how much the relation between parental behavior and children's development was due to parents' behavior and how much of it was due to genes—including the genes that influence verbal abilities. In studies of parents and children in biological families, genes and environment are *confounded*, which means they are closely related and difficult to separate.

This is not to say that family language environments do not matter in toddlers' language development. Of course they do. It is just that, in studies with this kind of confound between genetics and environment, it is impossible to tell how much. To identify more definitely how much the family language environment matters, it would be necessary to conduct these kinds of studies in adoptive families or twin families, but so far, in studies of toddler's language development, this has not been done. In early childhood and beyond, the influence of teacher's language use on children's language development provides more definite evidence of an environmental effect, because teachers and children have no genetic relationship (Huttenlocher et al., 2002).

CULTURAL VARIATIONS IN TODDLERS' LANGUAGE ENVIRONMENTS The other notable feature of most research on toddlers' language development, in addition to the passive genotype–environment issue just described, is its assumption that most toddler language use takes place in a parent–toddler dyad—just the two of them. This assumption may be true for the families being studied in

My Virtual Child

How will you stimulate your virtual child's language development? How will your activities differ from a parent in a different environment?

Toddlers in traditional cultures often experience a language-rich environment. Here, a Mongolian family shares a meal and conversation.

developed countries, but the social environment that most toddlers experience world-wide is much different from this, and consequently their language environment differs as well.

Once they learn to walk and begin to talk, toddlers in most cultures spend most of their days not with their parents but in mixed-age groups of other children, including an older girl, often an older sister, who is mainly responsible for caring for them. When toddlers are with their parents, usually many other people are around as well, such as siblings, extended-family members, and neighbors. This makes for a language-rich environment, because there is talking going on around them almost constantly, with so many people present. However, relatively little of this talk may be directed specifically at the toddler, because there are so many other people around and because others may not see it as necessary to speak directly to toddlers in order to stimulate their language development.

In fact, the others in a toddlers' social environment may even see it as bad parenting to speak often with toddlers. The Gusii people of Kenya believe that encouraging young children to speak is a mistake, because it makes it more likely that they will grow up to be selfish and disobedient (see Chapter 4) (LeVine et al., 1994). Their children learn the Gusii language as proficiently as American children learn English, but they learn it from being frequently in social groups where adults and older children are using language, not from having their language development stimulated directly in frequent daily inter-actions with their parents.

This is not an isolated example. Studies comparing children in different cultures have found that direct stimulation of toddlers' language development is a practice en-couraged in some cultures but discouraged in others. One study compared Japanese mothers and Canadian mothers in their interactions with their young children (Minami & McCabe, 1995). In Japanese culture, being talkative is considered im-polite and undesirable, especially for males, because the Japanese believe it is better to blend in harmoniously with the group than to call attention to yourself (Markus & Kitayama, 2003; Rothbaum et al., 2001). Consequently, the Japanese mothers in the study often discouraged their children from talking, especially their boys. In contrast, the Canadian mothers encouraged their children to talk more, by asking them questions and suggesting they provide more details. This approach was inter-preted by the researchers as being based on a belief system favoring individualism and self-expression.

As this study illustrates, in learning language children also learn a way of seeing the world and the values and beliefs of their culture. Another example of this can be found in Bambi Schieffelin's (1986, 1990) ethnography of the Kaluli people of New Guinea, a traditional culture where the people sustain life through hunting, fishing, and growing crops. In this culture, children spend most of their daily lives in a multiage extended-family group. Mothers rarely speak directly to infants, because they believe their babies would not understand. Instead, they sometimes speak on the infant's behalf, in a high-pitched voice (e.g., "Please feed me!").

Once infants grow to be toddlers and begin to talk, mothers and others direct speech at them. However, the emphasis is not on the toddlers expressing themselves and saying what they want and need, but on repeating what the other person has said. Mothers will say something on behalf of the toddler, such as "Give me the stick," then say the phrase "Say like that," encouraging the toddler to repeat what the mother has said just like she said it. Instead of the Western value of "Be yourself," which is promoted by asking toddlers questions about child-oriented topics, toddlers are be-ing taught the value predominant among the Kaluli and many other cultures: "Do as you're told." In this way, the acquisition of language is simultaneously the acquisition of cultural beliefs.

APPLYING YOUR KNOWLEDGE
. . . as a Day-Care Provider
You notice that some children in your classroom are very quiet while others are very talkative. What factors may contribute to these differences?

THINKING CULTURALLY
What are some of the ways that adults in your culture encourage—or discourage—toddlers' language use?

WHAT HAVE YOU LEARNED?

1. What biological characteristics do humans have that makes language possible?

2. How would the development of language have provided an evolutionary advantage?

3. What is the "naming explosion" and when does it occur?

4. What changes in language development take place during the third year, and what kinds of mistakes are 2- and 3-year-olds most likely to make?

5. What do American studies indicate about parental stimulation of toddlers' language development, and why are the results of these studies difficult to interpret?

6. How do Japanese and Canadian parents differ in the way they stimulate language in toddlers, and how are these variations related to cultural values?

Section 2 VIDEO GUIDE Language Development Across Cultures (Length: 7:40)

In this video, we talk to parents from different cultural backgrounds about how they communicate with their infants and toddlers and ask them what, if anything, they do to foster their child's language development.

1. Discuss the three factors mentioned in the clip that influence toddler language development. What are some additional factors that might also impact toddler language development?

2. Do you think that the U.S. mother interviewed here discussed a situation typical of most children across the United States? Why or why not?

3. Discuss your thoughts on the mother from Africa stating that she does not read to her baby because the baby is too young. What age do you think it is appropriate to begin reading to children and why?

Watch the Video Language Development Across Cultures in MyDevelopmentLab

LEARNING OBJECTIVES

5.12 Describe how emotional development advances during toddlerhood and identify the impact of culture on these changes.

5.13 Describe the changes in self-development that take place during toddlerhood.

5.14 Distinguish between *sex* and *gender* and summarize the evidence for the biological basis of gender development.

5.15 Describe the essential features of attachment theory and identify the four classifications of attachment.

5.16 Identify the key factors influencing the quality of toddlers' attachment to their mothers, and explain what effect attachment quality has on development.

5.17 Summarize the major critiques of attachment theory, including the cultural critique.

5.18 Compare and contrast the typical patterns of father involvement with infants and toddlers in traditional cultures and developed countries.

5.19 Describe relationships with siblings, peers, and friends during toddlerhood.

5.20 Identify the characteristics of autism spectrum disorders and recognize how they affect prospects for children as they grow to adulthood.

5.21 Identify the typical rates of television use in toddlerhood and explain some consequences of toddlers' TV watching.

My Virtual Child

What strategies might you use to help your virtual child regulate his or her emotions? How has your culture influenced your parenting in this area?

Emotional Development in Toddlerhood

Toddlerhood is the stage of life when we first learn how to regulate our emotions. As part of this process we learn emotions such as shame and guilt that reflect our responses to the expectations and requirements of others.

Toddlers' emotions

5.12 **LEARNING OBJECTIVE** | Describe how emotional development advances during toddlerhood and identify the impact of culture on these changes.

As toddlers become more self-aware, they learn that the people in their cultural environment regard some behaviors as good and others as bad, some as right and some as wrong, and they learn to feel negative emotions when they do something defined as bad or wrong. They also begin to learn how to regulate their emotions.

EMOTIONAL SELF-REGULATION From the early months of life, infants tend to show how they feel. Happy or sad, hungry or mad, they let you know. Gradually during the first year, infants develop the rudiments of emotional regulation. They learn to turn their attention away from unpleasant stimulation (Axia et al., 1999). The people around them soothe their distress with the kinds of strategies we discussed in Chapter 4, such as cuddling and rocking. In many cultures, frequent breast-feeding is used as an emotional regulator, to quiet babies whenever they begin to fuss (DeLoache & Gottlieb, 2000; LeVine et al., 1994).

During toddlerhood, emotional self-regulation advances in four ways (Kopp, 1989; Thompson & Goodvin, 2007).

1. First, toddlers develop *behaviors* that can help them regulate their emotions. For example, toddlers who are frightened may run to a trusted adult or older sibling, or cling to a comforting blanket or stuffed animal.

2. Second, toddlers use *language* to promote emotional self-regulation. As noted earlier in the chapter, from about 18 months old toddlers begin to use words to identify and talk about their emotions. Throughout toddlerhood and beyond, talking about feelings with others enhances children's understanding of their own and others' emotions, which in turn promotes their emotional self-regulation (Bugental & Grusec, 2006; Parke & Buriel, 2006).

3. Third, *external requirements* by others extend toddlers' capacities for emotional self-regulation. In toddlerhood, parents begin to convey and enforce rules that require emotional self-regulation: no hitting others no matter how angry you are, no jumping on the table no matter how happy you are, and so on (Calkins, 2002). Cultures vary in their requirements for emotional self-regulation, with collectivistic cultures such as China and Japan tending toward stiffer requirements than the more individualistic cultures of the West (Bornstein, 2006; Laible, 2004; Shweder et al., 2006).

4. Fourth and finally, emotional self-regulation in toddlerhood is promoted by the development of the *sociomoral emotions* (Thompson & Goodvin, 2007). Becoming capable of guilt, shame, and embarrassment motivates toddlers to avoid these unpleasant emotional states. Because they may be admonished by others for expressing primary emotions too strongly (e.g., yelling angrily in a grocery store) or in the wrong context (e.g., laughing loudly in a quiet restaurant), they learn emotional self-regulation as part of an effort to win approval from others and avoid their disapproval.

If emotional self-regulation increases from infancy to toddlerhood, why is it toddlerhood that is associated with tantrums—and why is age 2 popularly known in some cultures as the "terrible twos"? Perhaps it is that for toddlers, abilities for emotional self-regulation increase but so do expectations for emotional control. Consequently, when they have the brief but intense outburst of anger, crying, and distress that constitutes a tantrum it is more noticed than the more frequent outbursts of infants (Calkins, 2002). Perhaps it is also that toddlers have a more developed sense of self, including the ability to protest with a tantrum when they don't get their way (Grolnick et al., 2006). ◉

There must also be a cultural explanation involved. It is interesting to observe that in Western countries, such as the United States and the United Kingdom, it is widely accepted that toddlerhood tantrums are normal and even inevitable (Potegal & Davidson, 2003). One popular American advice book for parents of toddlers asserts that "Tantrums are a fact of toddler life, a behavior that's virtually universal . . . turning little cherubs into little monsters" (Murkoff et al., 2003, p. 336). Yet outside the West, toddler tantrums are rarely mentioned, and toddlerhood is not seen as an age of "terrible" behavior. In African and Asian cultures, by the time toddlerhood is reached, children have already learned that they are expected to control their emotions and their behavior, and they exercise the control required of them (Holodynski, 2009; Miller et al., 2010). It may be that tantrums and the allegedly terrible twos are not inevitable at all, but a consequence of Western cultural beliefs in the value of self-expression, which children have already learned well by toddlerhood.

LEARNING THE SOCIOMORAL EMOTIONS As described in Chapter 4, infants across cultures display a range of recognizable *primary emotions* from early in life, including anger, fear, and happiness. In toddlerhood new emotions appear, including guilt, shame, embarrassment, envy, and pride. These are known as *secondary emotions* because they develop later than the primary emotions and they are based on what toddlers experience in their social environment and how they evaluate themselves within that environment (Lewis, 2000). All toddlers

◉ **Watch** the **Video** Emotional Regulation in Early Childhood in **MyDevelopmentLab**

APPLYING YOUR KNOWLEDGE
. . . as a Teacher

You notice that some children in your preschool classroom don't show much emotion and are able to control their behavior better than other children. Might there be a cultural explanation for this variation?

Toddlers become capable of sociomoral emotions such as shame.

have a capacity for developing secondary emotions, as indicated by the fact these emotions appear across a wide range of cultures and are accompanied by characteristic body postures such as, for shame, lowering their eyes, bowing their heads, or covering their faces with their hands (Barrett & Nelson-Goens, 1997). However, what evokes the secondary emotions depends on what toddlers have been taught in their social and cultural environment.

The secondary emotions are called **sociomoral emotions** because they are evoked based on what the toddler has learned about culturally based standards of right and wrong (Mascolo & Fischer, 2007). When toddlers experience guilt, shame, or embarrassment, it is not just because they have made the cognitive comparison between what they have done and what others have expected of them. It is also because they have begun to learn to feel good when they conform to the expected standard and bad when they do not. Thus by age 2 most toddlers have begun to develop a conscience, an internalized set of moral standards that guides their behavior and emotions (Kochanska, 2002; Thompson, 2006).

Another important sociomoral emotion that first develops in toddlerhood is **empathy,** the ability to understand and respond helpfully to another person's distress. Even neonates have an early form of empathy, as indicated by crying when they hear the cry of another infant. Throughout the first year, infants respond to the distress of others with distress of their own. However, true empathy requires an understanding of the self as separate from others, so it develops along with self-awareness in toddlerhood (Gopnik et al., 1999). It is only in the second and especially the third year that toddlers have enough of a developed self to understand the distress of others and respond, not by becoming distressed themselves but by helping other persons relieve their distress (Nichols et al., 2009). In one study, toddlers responded to a researcher's feigned distress by offering a hug, a comforting remark, or a favorite stuffed animal or blanket (Hoffman, 2000). This demonstrates the beginning of **prosocial behavior,** which is behavior intended to help or benefit others (Svetlova et al., 2010).

Although the triggers of the sociomoral emotions are learned from the social environment, there are probably some that are universal. Children everywhere seem to be taught not to hurt the people around them and not to damage or destroy things (Rogoff, 2003). However, even in toddlerhood there are cultural differences in how the sociomoral emotions are shaped. Cultural differences are especially sharp regarding the emotions of pride and shame, that is, in how good a person should feel about individual accomplishments and how quickly, easily, and often shame should be evoked. In Western countries, especially in the United States, pride is often viewed positively (Bellah et al., 1985; Twenge, 2006). Children are praised and encouraged to feel good about themselves for accomplishments such as hitting a ball, dancing in a show, or learning something new. Everybody on the soccer team gets a trophy, win or lose. Shame, in contrast, is applied with hesitation, as parents and others worry that shame may harm the development of children's self-esteem.

In most non-Western cultures, however, pride is seen as a greater danger than shame. In Japanese and Chinese cultures, for example, children are taught from early on not to call attention to themselves and not to display pride in response to personal success (Akimoto & Sanbonmatsu, 1999). For example, in one study of mothers' and 2½ year-olds' conversations about misbehavior in China and the United States, American mothers tended to frame the misbehavior as an emotionally positive learning experience—"Now you know not to do that next time, don't you?"—in order to preserve their toddlers' self-esteem. In contrast, Chinese mothers cultivated shame in their toddlers by emphasizing the negative consequences and negative feelings that resulted from the misbehavior

sociomoral emotions emotions evoked based on learned culturally based standards of right and wrong; also called *secondary emotions*

empathy ability to understand and respond helpfully to another person's distress

prosocial behavior positive behavior toward others, including kindness, friendliness, and sharing

(Miller et al., 1997). To the Chinese mothers, teaching their toddlers shame was a way of teaching them to be considerate of others, and a way of preparing them to grow up in a collectivistic culture that emphasizes the value of consideration for others.

Learning the sociomoral emotions is an important part of becoming a member of a culture. To function in a culture it is necessary to know the rules and expectations for behavior and to avoid violating them; the sociomoral emotions are experienced as unpleasant, so children and adults alike generally conform to cultural expectations in order to avoid the sociomoral emotions. However, according to Erik Erikson's theory (1950), it is important for parents not to press the sociomoral emotions so hard as to thwart the toddler's budding sense of selfhood. In Erikson's life-span theory (see Chapter 1), toddlerhood is the stage of **autonomy versus shame and doubt.** Toddlers are just gaining a sense of themselves as individuals and learning that they can make choices and decisions and express them to others—which is why "No!" is a popular word during this life stage. When parents allow toddlers to exercise autonomy with reasonable limits, for example by allowing them to do something like spoon some food onto their plate when you could do it for them a lot quicker (and more neatly), toddlers gain a healthy confidence in their abilities to handle life's challenges. However, if parents are harsh and impatient with toddler's attempts to begin to do some things for themselves, toddlers may experience shame and doubt that will undermine their trust in themselves when they are faced with new tasks and new relationships.

autonomy versus shame and doubt in Erikson's lifespan theory, the main crisis of the toddlerhood stage, when toddlers gain a healthy confidence in their ability to make choices and express them to others *or* parents are harsh and impatient and toddlers experience shame and doubt that undermines their trust in themselves

self-recognition ability to recognize one's image in the mirror as one's self

self-reflection capacity to think about one's self as one would think about other persons and objects

The birth of the self

Describe the changes in self-development that take place during toddlerhood.

LEARNING OBJECTIVE 5.13

Even in the early weeks of life there is evidence that infants have the beginnings of a sense of self, a sense of being distinct from the external environment. Many of the topics introduced in Chapter 4 on infancy can be interpreted as reflecting the beginnings of self-awareness. Infants recognize the smell of their mother's breast and the sound of her voice after just a few days of life, indicating an awareness of a difference between their own smells and sounds and those of others. In the first month they display a stronger rooting reflex in response to another person touching their cheek than in response to their own hand performing the same movement (Rochat & Hespos, 1997). After a month or two they begin responding in interactions with others by smiling, moving, and vocalizing, thus showing an awareness of themselves and others as distinct social partners. By the middle of the first year they recognize and respond to their own name when it is spoken by others, indicating the beginning of a name-based identity. By the end of the first year, they search for hidden objects and examine objects and put them in their mouths, all behaviors showing an awareness of the distinction between themselves and the external world (Harter, 2006b; Thompson, 2006).

Although self-awareness begins to develop during infancy, it advances in important ways during toddlerhood. It is during the second and third years of life that children first demonstrate **self-recognition.** This was demonstrated in a classic experiment in which toddlers were secretly dabbed on the nose with a red spot, then placed in front of a mirror (Lewis & Brooks-Gunn, 1979). Upon seeing the child with the red nose in the mirror, 9- and 12-month-old infants would reach out to touch their reflection as if it were someone else, but by 18 months most toddlers rubbed their own nose, recognizing the image as themselves. ◉

About the same time self-recognition first appears (as indicated in the red-nose test) toddlers also begin to use personal pronouns for the first time ("*I,*" "*me,*" "*mine*"), and they begin to refer to themselves by their own names (Lewis & Ramsay, 2004; Pipp et al., 1987). These developments show that by the second half of their second year toddlers have the beginnings of **self-reflection,** the capacity to think about themselves as they

THINKING CULTURALLY

How does the birth of the self in toddlerhood help explain toddlers' responses to scoldings from parents?

◉—⌐**Watch** the **Video** Self Awareness Task in **MyDevelopmentLab**

gender identity awareness of one's self as male or female

sex biological status of being male or female

gender cultural categories of "male" and "female"

would think about other persons and objects. Self-reflection enables toddlers to develop the sociomoral emotions described earlier. As toddlers become more self-aware, they learn that the people in their cultural environment have expectations for how to behave and they learn to feel negative emotions when they do something defined as bad or wrong.

Gender identity and the biology of gender development

| 5.14 | **LEARNING OBJECTIVE** | Distinguish between *sex* and *gender* and summarize the evidence for the biological basis of gender development. |

❋ **Explore** the **Concept** Different Gender Stereotypes in **MyDevelopmentLab**

◉ **Watch** the **Video** Gender Versus Sex in **MyDevelopmentLab**

◉ **Watch** the **Video** Understanding Self and Others in **MyDevelopmentLab**

Gender socialization begins early in all cultures.

Another aspect of self-development that begins in toddlerhood is the formation of a **gender identity.** Between 18 and 30 months of age is when children first identify themselves and others as male or female (Martin et al., 2002). At age 2 they can also apply gender terms like *boy* and *girl*, *woman* and *man* to others (Campbell et al., 2004; Raag, 2003). ❋

Before proceeding further, let's clarify the difference between *sex* and *gender*. In general, social scientists use the term **sex** to refer to the biological status of being male or female. **Gender,** in contrast, refers to the cultural categories of "male" and "female" (Tobach, 2004). Use of the term *sex* implies that the characteristics of males and females have a biological basis. Use of the term *gender* implies that characteristics of males and females may be due to cultural and social beliefs, influences, and perceptions. For example, the fact that males are somewhat larger than females throughout life is a sex difference. However, the fact that girls in many cultures have longer hair than boys is a gender difference. The distinction between a sex difference and a gender difference is not always as clear as in these examples, as we will see in this and other chapters. The degree to which differences between males and females are biological or cultural is a subject of great importance and heated debate in the social sciences. ◉

Even before toddlerhood, in all cultures people communicate gender expectations to boys and girls by dressing them differently, talking to them differently, and playing with them differently (Hatfield & Rapson, 2006). In a classic experimental study (Sidorowicz & Lunney, 1980), adults were asked to play with a 10-month-old infant they did not know. All adults played with the same infant, but some were told it was a girl, some were told it was a boy, and some were given no information about its sex. There were three toys to play with: a rubber football, a doll, and a teething ring. When the adults thought the child was male, 50% of the men and 80% of the women played with the child using the football. When they thought the child was female, 89% of the men and 73% of the women used the doll in play.

In the early years, it is mainly parents who are the deliverers of cultural gender messages (Ruble et al., 2006; Whiting & Edwards, 1988). They give their children names, and usually the names are distinctively male or female. They dress boys differently from girls and provide them with different toys to play with (Bandura & Bussey, 2004). Toys are gender-specific custom complexes, representing distinctive cultural patterns of behavior that are based on underlying cultural beliefs (see Chapter 4). Toys for boys—such as guns, cars, and balls for playing sports—reflect the expectation that boys will be active, aggressive, and competitive. Toys for girls—such as dolls, jewelry, and playhouses—reflect the expectation that girls will be nurturing, cooperative, and attractive in appearance. Children readily learn cultural messages about gender roles in toddlerhood, and by early childhood they help enforce these roles with other children. However, gender development has a biological basis as well; *sex* and *gender* are intertwined. Let's look at the biological basis of gender development here, and then explore gender socialization in depth in Chapter 6. ◉

GENDER AND BIOLOGY The cultural and social basis of gender development is well-substantiated. However, there is also a biological basis to gender development. To put this in terms of the distinction between sex and gender just described, sex differences sometimes underlie gender differences—but not always, as we shall see. There are three elements to the biological basis of gender development: evolutionary, ethological, and hormonal.

In the evolutionary view, males and females develop differently because over the course of many millennia of human evolution, different characteristics promoted survival for the two sexes (Buss, 2004). For males, survival was promoted by aggressiveness, competitiveness, and dominance. The aggressiveness and competitiveness of boys in early childhood is an outcome of a long evolutionary history. For human females, in contrast, over the course of many millennia of evolution, survival was promoted by being nurturing, cooperative, and emotionally responsive to others. In this view, the cooperativeness and emotional responsiveness of girls in early childhood, and their interest in playing house and playing with dolls, is an outcome of a long evolutionary history (Buss, 2000).

Ethology, the study of animal behavior, also provides evidence of the biological basis of human gender differences. The gender differences that exist among humans are also true of our closest primate and mammalian relatives (Diamond, 1992; Pinker, 2004). Like human males, the males in those species closely related to us are also more aggressive, competitive, and dominant than females; and males who are highest in these qualities gain greater sexual access to females. Like human females, females in closely related species also are more nurturing and cooperative than males are, and they have primary responsibility for caring for young children. Like human children, the young of closely related species also play in same-sex groups. The similarity of sex-specific behavior across related species is strong evidence for a biological basis for human gender differences.

Hormonal evidence also supports the biological basis of human gender differences. Throughout life, beginning even prenatally, males and females differ in their hormonal balances, with males having more androgens and females more estrogens. In fact, males must receive a burst of androgens in their third month of prenatal development in order to develop into males. These hormonal differences influence human development and behavior. The strongest evidence for this is in studies of children who have hormonal abnormalities. Girls who were exposed to high levels of androgens in the womb are more likely than their peers to show male play behavior in early childhood, including playing with "male" toys like trucks and a preference for male playmates (Hines, 2004). Boys who were exposed to high levels of estrogens in the womb are more likely than their peers to show female play behavior in early childhood, including playing with "female" toys like dolls and a preference for female playmates (Knickmeyer & Baron-Cohen, 2006). In animal studies, too, females whose levels of prenatal androgen are increased experimentally show increased aggression and more active play than their animal peers, and less interest in caring for their offspring (Maccoby, 2002).

THE LIMITS OF BIOLOGY Taken together, the evidence from evolutionary theory, ethological research, and research on hormonal abnormalities makes a strong case for the biological basis of human gender differences. There is little doubt that gender differences are accentuated and reinforced by the socialization environment, in every culture. At the same time, there is little doubt that human males and females are biologically different and that these differences are evident in their development in toddlerhood and beyond, in all cultures.

However, there is good reason to be skeptical and wary of attributing all human gender differences mainly to biology. In the course of human history, especially in the last century, gender roles have changed dramatically, even though biologically we have not changed (Brumberg, 1997). It is only 100 years ago that women were excluded from higher education and from virtually all professions. It was widely believed, even among scientists—who were all male—that women were biologically incapable of strenuous intellectual work.

My Virtual Child

How will you communicate gender expectations to your virtual child? Will you communicate messages that are consistent with cultural expectations?

My Virtual Child

How do you think gender roles will change in your culture by the time your virtual child is your age?

APPLYING YOUR KNOWLEDGE

How is the case of children with hormonal abnormalities an example of a natural experiment, where there can be no random assignment to conditions but where the data may still be useful (see Chapter 1)? Are there any limitations to its validity as a natural experiment?

ethology study of animal behavior

Today in an era when women exceed men in university participation in most countries in the world and are close to or equal to men in their representation in medicine, law, business, and other fields, these beliefs seem preposterous. Yet just a century ago, the most knowledgeable people of the time were certain these beliefs were true. That fact should give us pause before we assert that the biological basis of children's gender differences today is indisputable. The changes in women's roles over the past century demonstrate the enormous influence that culture can have on the raw material of biology in human development. As cultures change, gender roles can change, even though the underlying biology of human development remains the same.

The other issue worth mentioning here is that when we speak of gender differences, we are comparing one-half of the human species to the other, over 3 billion persons to the other 3 billion-plus persons. There is a tendency among social scientists to describe gender differences by stating that "boys are X, whereas girls are Y" (including in the section you just read). However, these generalizations almost always overstate the differences between the two genders. Even where there are legitimate gender differences, in early childhood and beyond, there are also many exceptions. To put it another way, the variability within each gender is usually much greater than the differences between the two genders, for most characteristics. Consequently, we should be careful not to let our perceptions of gender differences prejudge our estimations of the qualities or abilities of individual boys or girls or men or women. ✳

✳ **Explore** the **Concept** Adults' Perceptions of Boys and Girls in **MyDevelopmentLab**

WHAT HAVE YOU LEARNED?

1. What are four ways that emotional regulation develops during toddlerhood?
2. Why is age 2 described as the "terrible twos" in some cultures but not in others?
3. Why are secondary emotions also called "sociomoral emotions"?
4. What is the red-nose test and how does it demonstrate self-recognition?
5. What is gender identity and when does it first develop?
6. Describe some ways that parents communicate gender-role socialization to infants and toddlers.

One Special Person: Attachment Theory and Research

From infancy to toddlerhood, the social world expands. However, crucial to social development remains the relationship with one special person, usually but not always the mother, who provides love and care reliably. In the field of human development the study of this relationship in infancy and toddlerhood has focused on attachment theory and research based on this theory.

Attachment theory

5.15 **LEARNING OBJECTIVE** | Describe the essential features of attachment theory and identify the four classifications of attachment.

Because the long dependency of children on adults is such a distinctive characteristic of our species, the question of how the attachments between human children and adults develop has long been of great interest to human development scholars. Attachment theory was first introduced in our discussion of infant social development (see Chapter 4). Here we examine the features of attachment theory in more detail, including ways of evaluating the quality of parent–child attachment and critiques of attachment theory.

BOWLBY'S THEORY Through most of the 20th century there was strong consensus that human infants become attached to their mothers because mothers provide them with food. Hunger is a distressing physical state, especially for babies, who are growing rapidly and need to be fed often. Mothers relieve this distressing state and provide the pleasure of feeding. Over time, infants come to associate the mother with the relief of distress and the experience of pleasure. This association becomes the basis for the love that infants feel for their mothers. This was the dominant view in psychology in the first half of the 20th century. However, around the middle of the 20th century, the British scholar John Bowlby (1969/1982) began to observe that many research findings that were appearing at the time were inconsistent with this consensus.

There were three findings that were especially notable to Bowlby. First, French psychiatrist René Spitz (1945) reported that infants raised in institutions suffered in their physical and emotional development, even if they were fed well. Spitz studied infants who entered an orphanage when they were 3 to 12 months old. Despite adequate physical care, the babies lost weight and seemed listless and passive, a condition Spitz called *anaclitic depression*. Spitz attributed the infants' condition to the fact that one nurse had to care for seven infants and spent little time with each except for feeding them and changing their diapers. (Anaclitic means "leaning upon," and Spitz chose this term because the infants had no one to lean upon.) The infants showed no sign of developing positive feelings toward the nurse, even though the nurse provided them with nourishment. Other studies of institutionalized infants reported similar results (Rutter, 1996). 👁

The second set of findings that called feeding into question as the basis of the infant–mother bond involved primates, specifically rhesus monkeys. In a classic study, Harry Harlow (1958) placed baby monkeys in a cage with two kinds of artificial "mothers." One of the mothers was made of wire mesh, the other of soft terry cloth. Harlow found that even when he placed the feeding bottle in the wire mother, the baby monkeys spent almost all their time on the cloth mother, going to the wire mother only to feed. Again, a simple link between feeding and emotional bonds seemed called into question.

The third set of findings noted by Bowlby proved the most important for his thinking. These findings came from the field of *ethology*, which, as we have noted, is the study of animal behavior. Ethologists reported that for some animals, the bond between newborns and their mothers was instantaneous and occurred immediately after birth. Konrad Lorenz (1965), a German ethologist, showed that newborn goslings would bond to the first moving object they saw after hatching and follow it closely, a phenomenon he called *imprinting* (see Chapter 3). To Lorenz and other ethologists, the foundation of the bond between the young of the species and their mothers was not nourishment but protection. Imprinting to the mother would cause the young to stay close to her and thereby be protected from harm.

Considering these three sets of findings, Bowlby concluded that the emotional tie between infants and their mothers was based on children's need for protection and care for many years. Thus as Bowlby described it, the *attachment* that develops between children and caring adults is an emotional bond that promotes the protection and survival of children during the years they are most vulnerable. The child's **primary attachment figure** is the person who is sought out when the child experiences some kind of distress or threat in the environment, such as hunger, pain, an unfamiliar person, or an unfamiliar setting. Usually the primary attachment figure is a parent, and is most often the mother because in nearly all cultures mothers are primarily the ones who are most involved in the care of infants. However, the primary attachment figure could also be the father, a grandparent, an older sister, or anyone else who is most involved in the

John Bowlby, originator of attachment theory. (Photo by Jürgen Schadeberg)

👁—[**Watch** the **Video** Institution Care/ Adoption and Foster Care: Nathan Fox in **MyDevelopmentLab**

Harlow's studies showed that attachments were not based on nourishment. As shown here, the monkeys preferred the cloth "mother" even though the wire "mother" provided nourishment.

primary attachment figure person who is sought out when a child experiences some kind of distress or threat in the environment

stranger anxiety fear in response to unfamiliar persons, usually evident in infants by age 6 months

secure base role of primary attachment figure, allows child to explore world while seeking comfort when threats arise

separation anxiety discomfort experienced by infants and young children when apart from attachment figures, especially when a stranger is present

Strange Situation laboratory assessment of attachment entailing a series of introductions, separations, and reunions involving the child, the mother, and an unfamiliar person

◉─[**Watch** the **Video** Stranger Anxiety in **MyDevelopmentLab**

APPLYING YOUR KNOWLEDGE
. . . as a Researcher

You are sent to a local Polynesian village to do the "red nose" test with some toddlers aged 12–20 months (refer back to p. 211). The instructions call for the mother to sit near the mirror. However, the toddlers seem to want an older sibling to sit nearby rather than their mothers. Is it ok to change the protocol to include the older sibling instead of the mother?

infant's care. Separation from the primary attachment figure is experienced by the child as especially threatening, and the loss of the primary attachment figure is a catastrophe for children's development (Bowlby, 1980).

Although infants can discriminate among the smells and voices of different people in their environment from early on, in their first months they can be held and cared for by a wide range of people, familiar as well as unfamiliar, without protesting. However, by about the middle of the first year of life, this begins to change. Gradually they become more selective, developing stronger preferences for familiar others who have cared for them, and **stranger anxiety** emerges in response to being approached, held, or even smiled at by people they do not recognize and trust. Stranger anxiety exists in a wide range of cultures beginning at about age 6 months and grows stronger in the months that follow (Super & Harkness, 1986), as *Table 5.3* illustrates. So, if an infant or toddler turns away, frowns, or bursts into tears in response to your friendly overtures, don't take it personally! ◉

There is an evolutionary basis for the development of stranger anxiety at about age 6 months (Bowlby, 1967). This is the age when infants first become mobile, and learning to crawl allows them to begin to explore the environment but also carries the risk that they may crawl themselves into big trouble. Learning to stay close to familiar persons and avoid unfamiliar persons helps infants stay near those who will protect them and keep them safe.

Although it promotes survival for children to stay close to caring adults, it also promotes survival for children to learn about the world around them. Consequently, under normal conditions young children use their primary attachment figure as a **secure base** from which to explore the surrounding environment (Bowlby, 1969/1982). If a threat appears in the environment, attachment behavior is activated and children seek direct physical contact with their attachment figure.

According to Bowlby, attachment develops gradually over the first two years of life, culminating in a *goal-corrected partnership* in which both persons use language to communicate about the child's needs and the primary attachment figure's responses. Over time, the child becomes steadily less dependent on the care and protection of the primary attachment figure. However, even into adulthood, the child may seek out the primary caregiver for comfort during times of crisis.

VARIETIES OF ATTACHMENT: THE STRANGE SITUATION Bowlby was a theorist, not a researcher, and he did not conduct studies to test his theory directly. Research on attachment was pioneered by Mary Ainsworth, a colleague of Bowlby (Ainsworth & Bell, 1969; Ainsworth et al., 1978). Ainsworth followed Bowlby's theory in viewing the child's attachment as being most evident in the response to separation from the primary attachment figure. She had observed that along with stranger anxiety, infants and toddlers experience **separation anxiety** when apart from attachment figures, especially if a stranger is present.

TABLE 5.3	Percentage of Children Who Cried Following Departure of Mother		
		Age and Percentage	
Age	African Bushman (*n*=25)	Antigua, Guatemala (*n*=36)	Israeli Kibbutz (*n*=122)
5 months	0		
9 months		50	30
11 months		85	
14 months	100		62
20 months		70	30
25 months	80	32	
35 months	30		

To evoke children's attachment behavior, Ainsworth devised a laboratory procedure she called the **Strange Situation** (Ainsworth et al., 1978). The Strange Situation is a series of introductions, separations, and reunions involving the child, the mother, and an unfamiliar person (see *Figure 5.5*). It was devised for toddlers, ages 12 to 24 months, because this is an age that is old enough so that attachment has developed to a point where it can be assessed.

In the Strange Situation the mother and toddler first come into the laboratory room and are left for a few minutes to become used to it. There are toys and the toddler may begin to play with them. A series of episodes follows in which a "stranger" enters the room, the mother leaves the room, the mother returns, the mother leaves again, and the mother returns again. When she returns the second time, the mother is supposed to pick the child up.

On the basis of toddlers' responses to the Strange Situation, four classifications of attachment were developed (Ainsworth et al., 1978; Ammaniti et al., 2005). The first three were proposed by Ainsworth, and the fourth was added by later researchers.

> **Secure attachment.** Toddlers in this category use the mother as a secure base from which to explore, in the first part of the Strange Situation when only the mother and toddler are present. Upon separation, securely attached toddlers usually cry or vocalize in protest. When the mother returns, they greet her happily by smiling and perhaps going to her to be hugged and held.
>
> **Insecure–avoidant attachment.** These toddlers show little or no interaction with the mother when she is present, and no response to the mother's departure or return. When these toddlers are picked up in the last episode of the Strange Situation, they may immediately seek to get down.
>
> **Insecure–resistant attachment.** Toddlers classified as insecure–resistant are less likely than others to explore the toys when the mother is present, and they show greater distress when she leaves the room. When she returns, they show ambivalence, running to greet the mother in seeming relief but then pushing her away when she attempts to comfort or pick them up.
>
> **Disorganized–disoriented attachment.** Toddlers in this category show extremely unusual behavior in response to the Strange Situation (Ammaniti et al., 2005; van IJzendoorn et al., 1999). They may seem dazed and detached when the mother leaves the room, but with outbursts of anger, and when the mother returns they may seem fearful. Some freeze their movements suddenly in odd postures. This kind of attachment is especially shown by toddlers who show other signs of serious problems, such as autism or Down syndrome. Their mothers are more likely to have used alcohol or drugs during pregnancy and are more likely to have had psychological problems.

Although attachment classification is based on behavior throughout the Strange Situation, Ainsworth viewed the toddler's reunion behavior as the best indicator of the quality of attachment (Ainsworth et al., 1978). Toddlers with secure attachments seemed delighted to see their mothers again after a separation and often sought physical contact with her, whereas toddlers with insecure attachments either responded little to her return (avoidant) or seemed both relieved and angry at her (resistant). ⦿➤

Figure 5.5 • **The Strange Situation.** The Strange Situation features a series of episodes in which (a) the mother leaves the room, (b) the toddler is alone with the stranger, and (c) the mother returns to the room and is reunited with the toddler.

secure attachment healthiest classification of parent–child attachment, in which the child uses the parent as a secure base from which to explore, protests when separated from parent, and is happy when the parent returns

insecure–avoidant attachment classification of parent–child attachment in which there is relatively little interaction between them and the child shows little response to the parent's absence and may resist being picked up when the parent returns

insecure–resistant attachment classification of parent–child attachment in which the child shows little exploratory behavior when the parent is present, great distress when the parent leaves the room, and ambivalence upon the parent's return

disorganized–disoriented attachment classification of parent–child attachment in which the child seems dazed and detached, with possible outbursts of anger, when the parent leaves the room, and exhibits fear upon parent's return

⦿➤ **Simulate** the **Experiment** Attachment Classifications in the Strange Situation in **MyDevelopmentLab**

Quality of attachment

Identify the key factors influencing the quality of toddlers' attachment to their mothers, and explain what effect attachment quality has on development.

LEARNING OBJECTIVE **5.16**

If toddlers differ in the quality of their attachments, what determines those differences? And what implications does attachment quality in toddlerhood have for later development?

Attachment behavior is especially activated if the toddler is distressed.

APPLYING YOUR KNOWLEDGE

What are the implications of attachment theory for the debate discussed in Chapter 4 over whether or not a crying baby should be comforted?

DETERMINANTS OF ATTACHMENT QUALITY Ainsworth's early research indicated that about two-thirds of toddlers had secure attachments to their mothers, with the remaining one-third either insecure–avoidant or insecure–resistant (Ainsworth et al., 1977). Many other studies of American and European children since then have found similar results (NICHD Early Child Care Research Network, 2006b; van IJzendoorn & Sagi-Schwartz, 2008). Disorganized–disoriented attachment is rare.

But what determines the quality of toddlers' attachments to their mothers? In her early research, Ainsworth and her colleagues observed families in their homes, including the same mother–child pairs they later observed in the laboratory in the Strange Situation (Ainsworth, 1977). The home observations were extensive: every three weeks for four hours, from when the children were 3 weeks old to just past their first birthday.

When considering the mother–child interactions in the home in relation to their behavior as observed in the Strange Situation, Ainsworth concluded that the quality of attachment was based mainly on how sensitive and responsive the mother was. To be *sensitive* means to be good at judging what the child needs at any given time. For example, sensitive mothers could tell when their children had had enough to eat, whereas others seemed to stop feeding while the children were still hungry or tried to keep feeding them after they seemed full. To be *responsive* means to be quick to assist or soothe the children when they need it. For example, responsive mothers would hug or pick up or talk soothingly when their children were distressed, whereas others would let them cry for awhile before going to their assistance.

According to attachment theory, based on the degree of their mothers' sensitive and responsive behavior over the first year of life, children develop an *internal working model* of what to expect about her availability and supportiveness during times of need (Bowlby, 1969, 1980; Bretherton & Mulholland, 1999). Children with secure attachments have developed an internal working model of the mother as someone they can rely upon to provide help and protection. Children with insecure attachments are unsure that the mother will come through when they need her. They have an internal working model of her as someone who is unpredictable and cannot always be trusted. One reason the Strange Situation is first assessed in toddlerhood rather than infancy is that it is only by toddlerhood that children are cognitively mature enough to have developed an internal working model of their primary attachment figure (Ainsworth et al., 1978; Bowlby, 1969).

ATTACHMENT QUALITY AND LATER DEVELOPMENT According to Bowlby (1969), the internal working model of the primary caregiver formed in infancy and toddlerhood is later applied to other relationships. Consequently, the attachment to the primary caregiver established in the first two years shapes expectations and interactions in relationships with others throughout life, from friends to teachers to romantic partners to one's own future children. Securely attached children are able to love and trust others because they could love and trust their primary caregiver in their early years. Insecurely attached children display hostility, indifference, or overdependence on others in later relationships, because they find it difficult to believe others will be worthy of their love and trust (Thompson, 1998).

This is a bold and intriguing claim. How well does it hold up in research? A number of longitudinal studies on attachment have by now followed samples from toddlerhood through adolescence or emerging adulthood, and they provide mixed support for the predictions of attachment theory. Some longitudinal studies show a relationship between attachment quality assessed in toddlerhood and later emotional and social development, but other studies do not (Egeland & Carlson, 2004). The current view is that attachment quality in infancy and toddlerhood establishes tendencies and expectations that may then be modified by later experiences in childhood, adolescence, and beyond (McCarthy & Maughan, 2010; Thompson, 2008). To put this in terms of the theory, the internal working model established early may be modified substantially by later experiences.

Only disorganized–disoriented attachment is highly predictive of later problems (Ammaniti et al., 2005; van IJzendoorn et al., 1999; Vondra & Barnett, 1999). Toddlers with this attachment classification exhibit high hostility and aggression in early and middle childhood, and are likely to have cognitive problems as well (Weinfield et al., 2004). In adolescence and beyond, toddlers who had been classified as disorganized–disoriented are at higher risk for behavior problems and psychopathology (van IJzendoorn et al., 1999). However, this type of attachment is believed to be due to underlying problems in neurological development, not to the behavior of the primary caregiver (Barnett et al., 1999; Macfie et al., 2001). Since Ainsworth's classic studies, researchers have also investigated toddlers' attachments to fathers and other nonmaternal caregivers. We examine one such study in the **Research Focus: Early Child Care and Its Consequences** feature. ◉

Watch the **Video** Lisa: Adjusting to Day Care: Part 1 in **MyDevelopmentLab**

RESEARCH FOCUS   Early Child Care and Its Consequences

One of the most striking changes of the last half century in Western countries is that mothers of young children now generally work outside the home (see **Map 5.2** on page 220). For example, in 1960 only 17% of American mothers of children under a year old were employed, but by the year 2000 this proportion had risen to over 60% (Smith et al., 2001). Similar changes took place in other Western countries (Scheiwe & Willekins, 2009). Because this change has happened so quickly and so recently, and because mothers have never before been employed in such large numbers, there has been a great deal of concern expressed about the potential consequence of this change for young children's development. Consequently, a great deal of research has been undertaken to explore this issue.

Beginning in the 1990s, the largest and most comprehensive study of early child care and its consequences was conducted in the United States, sponsored by the National Institute of Child Health and Human Development (NICHD). The "NICHD Study of Early Child Care" began in 1991 with over 1,300 young children (from infancy through early childhood) at 10 sites around the United States. The children and their families were followed longitudinally for 7 years (NICHD Early Child Care Research Network, 1997). The sample was diverse in socioeconomic (SES) background, ethnicity, and geographical region. Multiple methods were used to assess the children and their families, including observations, interviews, questionnaires, and standardized tests. Multiple aspects of the care children received were also assessed, including quantity, stability, quality, and type of care. A wide range of children's developmental domains were examined, including physical, social, emotional, cognitive, and language development.

Toddlers in high-quality child-care centers are as likely as children in home care to have secure attachments.

There were many notable and illuminating findings in the study. About three-fourths of the children in the study began nonmaternal child care by the age of 4 months. During infancy and toddlerhood most of this care was provided by relatives, but enrollment in child-care centers increased during toddlerhood, and beyond age 2 most children receiving nonmaternal care were in centers. Infants and toddlers averaged 33 hours a week in nonmaternal care. African American infants and toddlers experienced the highest number of hours per week of nonmaternal care and White infants and toddlers the lowest, with Latinos in between.

The most important variables related to children's development were hours per week in care and quality of care. Quality of care was assessed in three ways: (1) the caregivers' education, training in child care, and child-care experience; (2) the ratio of children to caregivers and the number of children per group; and (3) the interactions between caregivers and children (based on observations of mothers and nonmaternal caregivers). Notably, children from the highest and lowest SES backgrounds received the highest quality care and the children from near-poor backgrounds received the lowest, because the parents of the poorest children qualified for subsidies for high-quality care, whereas the parents of the near-poor children did not.

The results of the study regarding early childhood will be discussed in Chapter 6, but for infants and toddlers, the focus of the study was on how child-care arrangements might be related to attachment (NICHD Early Child Care Research Network, 1997, 2005). The observations measured how *sensitive* and *responsive* caregivers were with the children, the two most important determinants of

(continued)

attachment quality according to attachment theory. As measured by the Strange Situation, attachments to mothers were no different for toddlers receiving nonmaternal care than for toddlers receiving only maternal care. However, insecure attachments were more likely if the nonmaternal care was low in quality, for more than 10 hours per week, or if mothers were low in sensitivity. Maternal sensitivity was especially important. Toddlers whose mothers were relatively high in sensitivity were usually securely attached, even if the quality of nonmaternal care was below average and the number of hours in care was more than 10 per week; in contrast, toddlers whose mothers were relatively low in sensitivity were often insecurely attached even if they received high-quality nonmaternal child care.

This was an impressively ambitious and comprehensive study, but even this study has limitations. Most notably, the children were not randomly assigned into child-care groups. The choices about the care they received and how many hours per week they were in care were made by their parents, not the researchers. Consequently, the outcomes of the children's child-care experiences were interwoven with many other variables, such as parents' income, education, and ethnicity. In statistical analyses it is possible to "control for" these other variables in seeking to determine the consequences of child-care experiences, but not so much as to resemble the more definite results that random assignment into child-care groups would have provided. This is an example of how social scientists are rarely able to create an ideal experimental situation in their research, but must usually take human behavior as they find it and do their best to unravel the daunting complexity of real life.

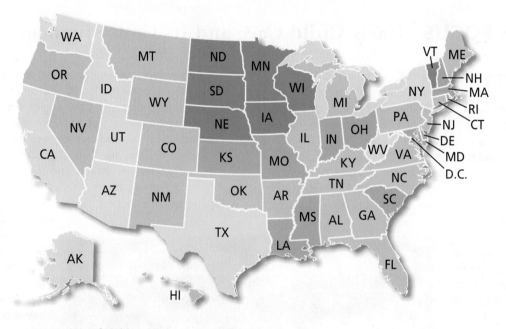

Percentage of children under 6 years old with both parents in the labor force

| 49.9–59.9% | 60–64.9% | 65–69.9% | More than 70% |

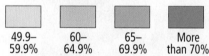

Map 5.2 • **American Children With Working Parents.** Many American children live in households in which both parents are working. Which states have the highest percentage of working parents? How will this influence the need for early child care in these states?

Critiques of attachment theory

5.17   LEARNING OBJECTIVE   Summarize the major critiques of attachment theory, including the cultural critique.

Attachment theory is undoubtedly one of the most influential theories of human development. It has generated hundreds of studies since Bowlby first articulated it over 40 years ago (Atkinson & Goldberg, 2004; Cassidy & Shaver, 2008; Sroufe et al., 2005). However, it has also generated critiques that have pointed to limitations of the theory.

THE CHILD EFFECT CRITIQUE The "child effect" is one of the most common critiques of attachment theory. It claims the theory overstates the mother's influence and understates the child's influence on quality of attachment, in two related ways. First, it fails to recognize that children are born with different temperaments (see Chapter 4) (Bakermans-Kranenburg et al., 2004). If, in the Strange Situation, a toddler is highly anxious when the mother leaves the room, then behaves aggressively by pushing her away when she returns, it could be due to a difficult temperament, not to the mother's failure to be sufficiently sensitive and responsive (Atkinson et al., 1999; van IJzendoorn et al., 2004).

Second, in attachment theory the direction of influence is one-way, from parents to children, but increasingly in recent decades researchers of human development have emphasized that parent–child relations are *reciprocal* or *bidirectional*. Parents influence their children, but children also influence their parents. For example, mothers of toddlers with a disorganized–disoriented attachment classification have been found to behave differently in the Strange Situation than other mothers. They may fail to respond when their toddlers become distressed, and may hold them at arm's length when picking them up, rather than comforting them by holding them close (Lyons-Ruth et al., 1999; van IJzendoorn et al., 1999). These mothers sometimes appear confused, frustrated, or impatient. This could be a failure to be sensitive and responsive, but it is also possible that the mothers are responding to the toddler's behavioral difficulties (Barnett et al., 1999). Most likely is that the mothers and disorganized–disoriented toddlers are influencing each other in a negative bidirectional cycle (Lyons-Ruth et al., 1999; Symons, 2001).

Jerome Kagan (2000), who has conducted decades of research on young children, proposes that it is highly unlikely that infants and toddlers are as vulnerable and impressionable to parental influence as the attachment theorists suppose. On the contrary, Kagan believes that infants and toddlers have evolved to be capable of developing well in response to a wide range of variations in parenting. Parents do not need to be ideally sensitive and responsive in order for their children to grow up to be capable of forming healthy attachments to others.

Although it is now widely acknowledged that child effects contribute to attachment quality, there is evidence from several sources indicating that attachment also depends on parental care. First, toddlers sometimes exhibit different attachments to fathers than to mothers (Shonkoff & Phillips, 2000). If attachment were due mainly to temperament or bidirectional effects, one would expect toddlers' attachments to be consistent across caregivers. Second, attachment quality has been found to be affected by family events such as parental divorce, job loss, or financial problems (Thompson & Raikes, 2003). Again, if attachment were due primarily to child characteristics, one would expect consistency regardless of external events. Finally, behavior genetics studies have found little genetic contribution to attachment (O'Connor & Croft, 2001). If temperament were a major contributor to attachment quality, one would expect attachment quality to be heritable, as temperament is, yet current evidence indicates it is not.

THE CULTURAL CRITIQUE As we have seen, cultures vary widely in the care they provide for infants and toddlers. Overall, in traditional cultures infants and mothers are in close contact throughout the first year of life, and in the second year toddlers spend most of their time being cared for by an older girl, often a sibling, and playing in mixed-age groups. In the West, infants are also cared for mainly by mothers, but they typically have their own bedroom from the beginning and are left on their own for a considerable amount of time, including at night. Autonomy and independence are encouraged from an early age.

To what extent are these differences reflected in attachment relationships? Remember, attachment is supposed to be a universal, species-wide phenomenon. According to Bowlby, it developed in the course of human evolution due to the extended vulnerability that all human infants, toddlers, and children share. Consequently, attachment should

Is early attachment the basis of all future love relationships?

be evident in similar ways across cultures. In the decades of research since Bowlby proposed his theory, researchers have concluded that children's attachments are "recognizably the same" across cultures (Cassidy & Shaver, 2008, p. xiii).

Some aspects of attachment may be universal. In all cultures, infants and toddlers develop attachments to the people around them who provide loving, protective care (van IJzendoorn & Sagi-Schwartz, 2008). There is evidence that parents in many cultures have a common view of what constitutes a securely attached child. One study involved mothers of toddlers in six cultures: China, Columbia, Germany, Israel, Japan, and the United States (Posada et al., 1995). Across cultures, mothers described an "ideally secure" child in similar ways, as relying on the mother in times of need but also being willing to explore the surrounding world—in short, using her as a secure base from which to explore, much as described in attachment theory. Other studies involving multiple cultures have found that secure attachment is the most common classification in all cultures studied so far (van IJzendoorn & Sagi, 2010).

However, cultural variations have also been found. One study compared Strange Situation results for toddlers in the United States, Japan, and several northern European countries (van IJzendoorn & Kroonenberg, 1988). In all countries, the majority of toddlers were found to be securely attached (see ***Figure 5.6***). However, the U.S. and northern European toddlers were more likely than Japanese toddlers to be classified as insecure–avoidant. In contrast, insecure–resistant attachment was especially common among the Japanese toddlers, compared to toddlers in the other countries. These differences were attributed to cultural differences in typical patterns of care. Specifically, a U.S. and northern European cultural emphasis on early independence was deemed to make insecure–avoidant attachment more likely, whereas in Japan mothers are rarely apart from their children and encourage a high degree of dependency in children. Consequently, their toddlers may have found the Strange Situation more stressful than the European or American toddlers did, making the insecure–resistant attachment classification more likely.

In traditional cultures, any kind of insecure attachment is probably rare. Infants are soothed immediately at the first sign of distress, often with breast-feeding. Toddlers are typically cared for by an older sister and also have frequent contact with the mother. However, as we have seen, weaning can be a major event in the lives of toddlers

Mothers and children in Japan often have very close relationships.

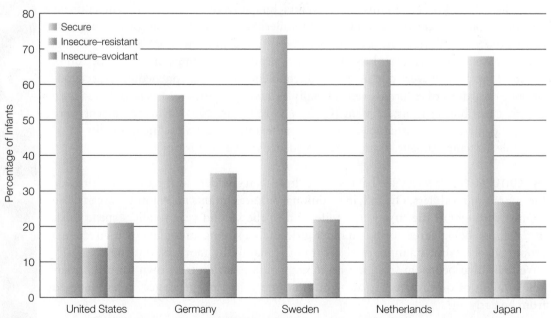

Figure 5.6 • **Cultural variations in the Strange Situation.** Across cultures, most toddlers exhibit secure attachment in response to the Strange Situation. In this study toddlers in Japan were more likely to be classified as insecure–resistant and less likely to be classified as insecure–avoidant than toddlers in other countries. **Source:** Based on van IJzendoorn & Kroonenberg, 1988.

in traditional cultures, and it may have an influence on the security of attachment. In one of Ainsworth's (1977) earliest studies, on mother–child attachments in Uganda, she observed that toddlers in Uganda often changed in attachment after weaning, suddenly showing a sharp increase in insecurity, including "a remarkable increase in their fear of strangers" (p. 143).

In general, the traditional, non-Western norm of maternal care emphasizes interdependence and collectivism to a greater extent than is found in attachment theory (Morelli & Rothbaum, 2007; Rothbaum et al., 2000; Rothbaum & Morelli, 2005). Attachment theorists emphasize that sensitive and responsive maternal care should provide love and care while also encouraging self-expression and independence, but this is not an ideal found in all or even most cultures. For example, Rothbaum and colleagues (2007) describe the Japanese concept of **amae** (*ah-ma-eh*), which is a very close, physical, indulgent relationship between the mother and her young child. This is the ideal in Japan, but to some attachment researchers it fits the description of the kind of mothering that promotes insecure–resistant attachment (George & Solomon, 1999). Also, attachment researchers describe how toddlers with secure attachments grow up to be children who are self-reliant, socially assertive, and have high self-esteem, but these traits are not viewed as virtues in all cultures (Rothbaum et al., 2000).

Overall, attachment theory has held up quite well in the decades since Bowlby first proposed it. However, at this point relatively few studies have been conducted outside Western cultures, so there is more to be learned about the forms attachments may take in different cultures (Morelli & Rothbaum, 2007).

WHAT HAVE YOU LEARNED?

1. What research findings led to Bowlby's development of attachment theory?
2. How does attachment develop in the first two years of life?
3. How did Mary Ainsworth research attachment theory?
4. What have studies on the consequences of early child care found? What are the limitations of such studies?
5. To what extent do longitudinal studies of attachment support Bowlby's theory?
6. Is attachment universal? What cultural variations have been found?

The Social World of the Toddler

In toddlerhood as in infancy, the social world includes ties to family, especially mothers and fathers. However, in toddlerhood relations with siblings, peers, and friends become more prominent. Toddlerhood is also when autistic spectrum disorders first appear for some children, a serious disruption in their social development. Media use continues to be important in toddlerhood, especially television.

The role of fathers

Compare and contrast the typical patterns of father involvement with infants and toddlers in traditional cultures and developed countries.

LEARNING OBJECTIVE 5.18

In nearly all cultures, mothers play a central role in the care of infants and toddlers. As we have seen, fathers in traditional cultures are often excluded entirely from the birth process; in the weeks after birth, the mother and neonate are usually together constantly,

---

APPLYING YOUR KNOWLEDGE
. . . as a Day-Care Provider

Katal is a Mayan toddler who has just relocated from Mexico with her parents. Her only other caregivers, her grandparents, stayed behind. You notice Katal is not easily soothed when her parents leave, and when they return, she rushes to them but then seems to shun their attempts to comfort her. Would you classify Katal as an insecure–resistant child?

APPLYING YOUR KNOWLEDGE

Given the long period of immaturity that the young of the human species have, is attachment necessarily universal? Would it be possible for a child to grow to maturity without forming attachments of some kind?

amae Japanese word for very close, physical, indulgent relationship between the mother and her young child

polygyny cultural tradition in which men have more than one wife

whereas the father may or may not be involved in early care. There are two reasons that mothers have historically been the primary caretakers of infants and toddlers. The first reason is biological. Because breast milk has usually been the main form of nourishment for human infants during the first half year, the mother tends to be the one who cares for the infant, more than anyone else. Consequently, by toddlerhood mothers are usually the primary attachment figure (Bowlby, 1969; Cassidy & Shaver, 2008).

The second reason has a cultural basis. In most cultures through nearly all of human history, male and female gender roles have been separate and distinct (Gilmore, 1990; Hatfield & Rapson, 1996). In their adult roles, women have been expected to run the household and care for children, whereas men have been expected to protect and provide for the family (Arnett, 1998). In their leisure time women relax with children and other women, and men relax with other men (Gilmore, 1990). Consequently, in most cultures, historically, fathers have been on the periphery of the emotional lives of children.

FATHERS IN TRADITIONAL CULTURES Although fathers are rarely involved in daily child care in traditional cultures, they are part of the child's social environment in other ways. For example, in China the father's traditional role is provider and disciplinarian (Ho, 1987). Care and nurturance is left to the mother. In Latin America, too, the tradition is that the father provides for the family and has unquestioned authority over his children, although in many Latin American cultures this role coexists with warm, affectionate relations with his children (Halgunseth et al., 2006). Many cultures in Africa have a tradition of **polygyny,** meaning that men often have more than one wife (Westoff, 2003). (*Polygamy* is a more general term referring to having two or more spouses, regardless of whether they are wives or husbands.) Households are composed of each wife and her children, with the father either living separately or rotating among them. Here, too, his role is that of provider and disciplinarian, and the children are not usually emotionally close to him (Nsamenang, 1992). Polygyny has become less common in recent decades.

Although the most common cultural pattern worldwide is that fathers serve as providers but are otherwise remote from the emotional lives of infants and toddlers, there are some notable exceptions. Fathers in the Warlpiri culture of aboriginal Australia have a close relationship with their toddlers, but forge a unique bond with their daughters, as we'll see in the **Cultural Focus: Toddlerhood in Aboriginal Australia** feature. Among the Manus people of New Guinea studied by Margaret Mead (1930/2001), during the first year of life the infant and mother are together almost constantly, and the father is involved only occasionally. However, once the child enters toddlerhood and begins to walk, the father takes over most child care. The toddler sleeps with the father, plays with him, rides on his back, and goes along on his daily fishing expeditions. Later in childhood, if the parents quarrel and separate, the children often choose to stay with the father, indicating that by then he has become the primary attachment figure.

A similar nurturing role for the father is found among the Aka people of central Africa, who lived until very recently by hunting and gathering, as all humans did until about 10,000 years ago (Hewlett, 2004). Aka fathers have been called "the most nurturing fathers yet observed" (Engle & Breaux, 1998, p. 5). They frequently hold their infants and toddlers, about five times as much as men in similar hunter–gatherer cultures (Hewlett, 2004). Mothers and fathers share infant and toddler care more or less equally, and both of them have nurturing, affectionate attachments to their children.

Fathers in modern developed countries do more child care than they did in the past, but still not as much as mothers do.

FATHERS IN DEVELOPED COUNTRIES The examples of the Manus and the Aka show the flexibility and potential variation of human cultural patterns of fatherhood. Here, as in so many aspects of development, humans have no single biologically driven species-wide pattern of behavior, but learn to behave in ways valued in their cultural traditions. Despite the exceptions, there is a clear norm across human cultures of fathers being relatively remote and removed from close care of infants and toddlers.

CULTURAL FOCUS Toddlerhood in Aboriginal Australia

Humans first arrived on the island continent of what is now known as Australia about 40,000 years ago. The first humans brought with them a hunter–gatherer way of life that still is the basis of life for many of their descendants, the Aboriginal Australians. Groups of a few families migrated according to the change of seasons and the availability of food and water, hunting animals such as kangaroos, emus, and lizards, and gathering fruits, seeds, and roots. However, immigrants from the United Kingdom began to arrive in the 18th century, and today, Aboriginal Australians comprise less than 2% of the total Australian population of about 15 million (Frydenberg & Lodge, 2007). The culture of Aboriginal Australians has been impacted in many ways by the majority culture, and many of them now live a Western lifestyle in the cities. Others still live the traditional nomadic way of life, and they will be the focus here, specifically the Warlpiri culture of Aboriginal Australians (Pierroutsakos, 2000).

The Warlpiri, like people in many traditional cultures you have read about in this book, believe babies should never be left alone and should rarely, if ever, be placed on the ground. Consequently, it is not until toddlerhood that the children practice much gross motor activity. Nevertheless, they begin to walk around their first birthday and are soon toddling about the camp. Mothers must spend a substantial portion of their day gathering the fruits, seeds, and roots that provide nourishment for their families. When out gathering, they usually will not take their toddler along, so they can focus on the work they are doing. However, in the camp there are always sisters, aunts, or grandmothers who can watch the toddler while the mother is at work. Co-wives also help; the Warlpiri are polygynous.

Warlpiri toddlers breast-feed at least through age 2; traditionally, they breast-fed until they were about 5 years old! Breast-feeding provides nourishment and also serves as a natural contraceptive, inhibiting ovulation so that children will not be too closely spaced. At night, Warlpiri toddlers sleep on the ground in the arms of their mothers by the family campfire.

Warlpiri parents are loving, gentle, and generous with their toddlers. Except when they are out gathering food, mothers are with their toddlers nearly all the time, often kissing them and speaking to them in "baby talk" (infant-directed speech, discussed in Chapter 4). Fathers also have close, affectionate relationships with their toddlers, especially doting on their daughters. Part of the father's role includes protecting his daughters from harm, not just in childhood but through adolescence and adulthood. Both mothers and fathers fear that illness and disease may strike their young children, and they use magical methods to ward off these perils, including singing, storytelling, and body painting.

Most Warlpiri children do not speak their first understandable words until about age 2, perhaps because their language includes few short words. During the first two years, parents often mimic their infants' and toddlers' vocalizations, as a kind of teasing but affectionate baby talk. Although they begin speaking words later than toddlers in most other cultures, Warlpiri toddlers nevertheless become proficient speakers of their native language by the age of 3.

Aboriginal cultures in Australia were nearly destroyed in the 20th century when the government adopted a policy of forced assimilation and relocation from their traditional lands into government settlements. However, in recent decades this policy was repealed and the Australian government has helped Aboriginal groups return to their ancestral lands. Although Aboriginal cultures have been changed through these experiences, and many of them have adopted the urban way of life of the Australian majority, it is remarkable that many others have been able to sustain something like their traditional way of life.

Warlpiri fathers often dote on their daughters.

In some ways, the role of fathers in developed countries today is in line with the pattern historically and in traditional societies. Across developed countries, fathers interact less with their infants and toddlers than mothers do, and provide less care such as bathing, feeding, dressing, and soothing (Chuang et al., 2004; Day & Lamb, 2004; Lamb & Lewis, 2005; Schwalb et al., 2004). In the United States, about one-third of toddlers live with single mothers; nonresident fathers are less involved in care of their toddlers than fathers who live in the household, although involvement is greater among nonresident fathers who are African American or Latino than among Whites (Cabrera & Garcia-Coll, 2004). When fathers do interact with their infants and toddlers, it tends to

👁—Watch the **Video**
Rough and Tumble Play in
MyDevelopmentLab

be in play rather than care, especially in physical, highly stimulating, rough-and-tumble play (Lamb, 2000; Paquette, 2004). Dad is the one throwing the kids in the air and catching them, or wrestling with them, but usually he has not been the one feeding them applesauce or changing their diapers. 👁

However, there is a definite trend toward greater father involvement, as gender roles have become more flexible and egalitarian in developed countries (Pleck & Masciadrelli, 2004). American fathers have been found to spend about 85% as much time as mothers do in caring for their young children, and Canadian fathers about 75% (Pleck & Masciadrelli, 2004; Sandberg & Hofferth, 2001; Zuzanek, 2000). Fathers are more likely to provide near-equal care for young children when the mother and father work similar numbers of hours outside the home, and when marital satisfaction is high (NICHD Early Child Care Network, 2000). Like the examples of the Manus and the Aka, the findings of recent changes in fathers' care for young children in developed countries show that parenting is to a large extent a learned rather than innate behavioral pattern that can change as a culture changes.

The wider social world: Siblings, peers, and friends

5.19 | **LEARNING OBJECTIVE** | Describe relationships with siblings, peers, and friends during toddlerhood.

THINKING CULTURALLY

What hypothesis could you propose about how sibling relationships in toddlerhood in developing countries might differ from sibling relationships in developed countries, and what would be the basis for your hypothesis?

In studies of social development in toddlerhood, the focus has been on relations with parents, especially attachments to mothers. However, among the many ways toddlerhood is distinct from infancy is that the toddler's social world broadens to include a wider range of people, including siblings, peers, and friends.

SIBLINGS: YOUNGER AND OLDER We have seen already how important sibling relationships are for toddlers in traditional cultures, where an older sibling, usually a sister, often takes over the main responsibility for child care from the mother. Toddlers in these cultures most certainly develop an attachment to the older siblings who care for them, but from the limited evidence available, it appears to be a secondary attachment rather than the primary attachment (Ainsworth, 1977; LeVine et al., 1994). That is, under most conditions toddlers are content to be under the care of older siblings, but in times of crisis they want the care and comfort of their mothers. 👁

👁—Watch the **Video** Sibling Rivalry in
MyDevelopmentLab

In developed countries, too, studies show that toddlers have attachments to siblings (Shumaker et al., 2011). One study used an adaptation of the Strange Situation to examine American toddlers' attachments to older siblings (Samuels, 1980). Two-year-old toddlers and their mothers were asked to come to the backyard of an unfamiliar home, sometimes with—and sometimes without—a 4-year-old sibling present. When no older sibling was present, the toddlers mostly responded to the mother's departure with distress and to her return with great relief, much as they do in the standard Strange Situation. However, when the older sibling was there along with the toddler, the toddler rarely showed distress when the mother left the backyard. The older sibling provided the emotional comfort and security of an attachment figure, making this outdoor Strange Situation less strange and intimidating.

APPLYING YOUR KNOWLEDGE
. . . as a Teacher

One of your Mexican students in your grade 3 classroom tells you that she spends her evening and weekends caring for her younger siblings, one of whom is in kindergarten and one of whom is a toddler. She helps their mother bathe them and she helps prepare meals, sometimes even preparing dinner on her own. What do you think about this?

A substantial amount of research on toddlers' relations with siblings has focused on how they respond to the birth of a younger sibling. Overall, their reaction tends to be negative. Often, following the birth of a younger sibling, toddlers' attachment to the mother changes from secure to insecure, as they feel threatened by all the attention given to the new baby (Teti et al., 1996). Some toddlers display problems such as increased aggressiveness toward others, or become increasingly whiny, demanding, and disobedient (Hughes & Dunn, 2007). They may regress in their development toward toilet training or self-feeding. Sometimes mothers become less patient and responsive with their toddlers, under the stress of caring for both a toddler and a new baby (Dunn & Kendrick, 1982).

What can parents do to ease the transition for toddlers? Studies indicate that if mothers pay special attention to the toddler before the new baby arrives and explain the feelings and needs of the baby after the birth, toddlers respond more positively to their new sibling (Howe et al., 2001; Hughes & Dunn, 2007; Teti et al., 1996). However, the reality is that across cultures, conflict is more common with siblings than in any other relationship throughout childhood and adolescence, as we will see in more detail in Chapter 6.

What if the toddler is the younger sibling rather than the older sibling? Here there is both an upside and a downside. The upside is that once younger siblings are no longer infants but toddlers, and develop the ability to talk, walk, and share in pretend play, older siblings show less resentment and become much more interested in playing with them (Hughes & Dunn, 2007). By their second year of life, toddlers often imitate their older siblings and look to them for cues on what to do and how to do it (Barr & Hayne, 2003).

The downside is that conflict rises as toddlers become increasingly capable of asserting their own interests and desires. In one study that followed toddlers and their older siblings from when the toddlers were 14 months old to when they were 24 months old, home observations showed that conflict increased steadily during this period and became more physical (Dunn & Munn, 1985). In another study, 15- to 23-month-old toddlers showed remarkably advanced abilities for annoying their older siblings (Dunn, 1988). For example, one toddler left a fight with an older sibling to go and destroy an object the older sibling cherished; another toddler ran to find a toy spider and pushed it in his older sibling's face, knowing the older sibling was afraid of spiders!

In sum, toddlers' relations with younger and older siblings are often characterized by ambivalence, a combination of positive and negative emotions. It is important to add that there is a great range of individual differences here. In other words, some toddlers get along a lot better with their siblings than others do, for reasons such as gender similarity or difference, spacing between siblings, and the mesh or clash of personalities (Hughes & Dunn, 2007).

Toddlers often react negatively to the birth of a younger sibling.

⊙─⎡**Watch** the **Video** Play in Early Childhood in **MyDevelopmentLab**

Toddlers in developed countries engage in advanced forms of play with their friends.

PEERS AND . . . FRIENDS? In most cultures, toddlerhood is a time of forming the first social relations outside the family. In traditional cultures, this usually means being part of a peer play group that may include siblings and cousins as well as other children. These play groups usually include children of a variety of ages, but toddlerhood is when children first come into the group after having been cared for during infancy mainly by the mother and an older girl. ⊙

In developed countries, too, peer relations expand in toddlerhood, often in the form of some kind of group care such as a child-care center (Rubin, Bukowski, et al., 2006). Research observing toddlers in these settings has found that their peer play interactions are more advanced than early studies had reported. One influential early study reported that toddlers engaged exclusively in *solitary play*, all by themselves, or *parallel play*, in which they would take part in the same activity but without acknowledging each other (Parten, 1932). However, more recent studies have found that toddlers engage in not only solitary and parallel play but in *simple social play*, where they talk to each other, smile, and give and receive toys, and even in *cooperative pretend play*, involving a shared fantasy such as pretending to be animals (Howes, 1996; Hughes & Dunn, 2007).

Furthermore, toddlers who know each other well tend to engage in more advanced forms of play than unacquainted toddlers. In one study of toddlers attending the same child-care center, even young toddlers (16–17 months old) engaged in simple social play (Howes, 1985). By 24 months, half of the toddlers engaged in cooperative pretend play, and this kind of play was observed in all the toddlers between 30 and 36 months old. This is a striking contrast to studies of social relations among unacquainted toddlers, which had found mainly solitary and parallel play, with cooperative pretend play not appearing until at least age 3 (Howes, 1996; Hughes & Dunn, 2007)

Clearly toddlers are capable of playing with each other in a variety of ways, but do they really form friendships? A substantial and growing body of research suggests they

Toddler friends smile and laugh more with each other than they do with nonfriends. Here, three boys in South Africa share a laugh.

do (Goldman & Buysse, 2007). Their friendships appear to have many of the same features of friendships at other ages, such as companionship, mutual affection, and emotional closeness (Rubin, Bukowski, et al., 2006). Even shortly after their first birthday, toddlers prefer some of their child-care or play-group peers over others and seek them out as companions when they are together (Shonkoff & Phillips, 2000). Like older children and even adults, toddlers choose each other as friends based partly on similarities, such as activity level and social skills (Rubin, Bukowski, et al., 2006). Toddlers who become friends develop favorite games they play when together (Howes, 1996). Toddler friends share emotions more frequently with each other than they do with nonfriends. They smile and laugh more, but also have more conflicts, although conflicts between toddler friends are milder and more quickly resolved than among nonfriends (Ross & Lollis, 1989). Friendships do change in quality with age, as we will see in the chapters to come, but even in toddlerhood many of the features of friendship are evident.

Autistic spectrum disorders: A disruption in social development

5.20 **LEARNING OBJECTIVE**

Identify the characteristics of autism spectrum disorders and recognize how they affect prospects for children as they grow to adulthood.

In 1938, a well-known child psychiatrist received a visit from parents concerned about their little boy, Donald (Donovan & Zucker, 2010). According to the parents, even as a baby Donald had displayed "no apparent affection" (p. 85) for his parents, and still did not. He never cried when separated from them or wished to be comforted by them. Nor did he seem interested in other adults or children, appearing to "live within himself" (p. 85) with no need for social relations. Furthermore, Donald's use of language was peculiar. He was often unresponsive to his parents' instructions and requests, and did not even react to his own name. Yet certain unusual words captivated him and he would repeat them over and over again: *trumpet vine, business, chrysanthemum*. He enjoyed repetition not only of words but of behaviors, such as spinning round objects.

This description became the basis of the initial diagnosis of what became known as **autism,** and the main features of the diagnosis are the same today as they were for Donald: (1) lack of interest in social relations, (2) abnormal language development, and (3) repetitive behavior. Many children with autism also prefer to have highly predictable routines and hate to have them disrupted. Some also have exceptional, isolated mental skills—Donald, for example, could multiply large numbers instantly in his head—but this is rare. The majority of children with autism are low in intelligence and exhibit some degree of intellectual disability (Lord, 2010). About 1 in 500 children is affected by autism.

Another 4 in 100 children have some but not all features of autism and are classified as having an **autism spectrum disorder (ASD),** also referred to as a *pervasive developmental disorder*. These rates are consistent across Asia, Europe, and North America, with some variation based on diagnostic criteria used (Centers for Disease Control and Prevention [CDC], 2011a). The origins of the disorders are unclear. ASDs are believed to have a genetic basis, as evidence of abnormal brain development is present in the unusually large brains of children who will later develop the disorders (Hadjikhani et al., 2004). Various environmental causes for the disorders have been proposed, from dietary contributors to toddlerhood vaccines, but none of them has been supported by research. Rates of autism and ASD have increased in recent decades in developed countries, but there is no consensus on the reasons for the increase (CDC, 2011a). It may be that disorders

👁—⌐**Watch** the **Video** Against Odds: Children with Autism in **MyDevelopmentLab**

autism developmental disorder marked by a lack of interest in social relations, abnormal language development, and repetitive behavior

autism spectrum disorder (ASD) a category of developmental disorders that includes autism, Asperger syndrome, and Pervasive Developmental Disorder Not Otherwise Specified

once diagnosed as schizophrenia or mental retardation are now diagnosed as autism or ASD due to increased awareness of the disorders (Donovan & Zucker, 2010). Physicians in many countries now routinely screen toddlers for the disorders, whereas they did not in the past (CDC, 2011a).

Usually the diagnosis of autism or ASD is made during toddlerhood, between 18 and 30 months of age (Filipek et al., 2000). However, studies analyzing home videos of infants later diagnosed with autism indicate that signs of the disorder are already present in infancy (Dawson et al., 1998; Werner et al., 2000). Even at 8 to 10 months old, infants with autism show little or no evidence of normal social behaviors. They do not engage in joint attention with parents, or point to objects to show to others, or look at others, or respond to their own name. During infancy some of this behavior could be attributed to differences in temperament, but the diagnosis of autism becomes more definite in toddlerhood with the failure to develop language skills during a period that is normally a time of dramatic advances. About half of children with autism never develop language skills well enough to communicate about even basic needs, and the half who do develop some language skills are nevertheless impaired in their ability to communicate with others (Hale & Tager-Flusberg, 2005). Their social deficits compound their language deficits: Their lack of interest in others and lack of ability to understand others' perspectives makes it difficult for them to engage in the normal exchange of conversation that other people perform without effort, even in toddlerhood.

Toddlers with autism have deficits in their social and language development. Here, a boy plays alone at a school for children with autism in Beijing, China.

What happens to children with autism when they grow up? There is a range of outcomes for children with autism or ASD. Eighty-five percent of children with autism continue to live with parents, siblings, or other relatives (Donvan & Zucker, 2010). Some live in government-sponsored group homes, and in rare cases they are able to function at a high enough level to live alone, as Donald (now in his 70s) does. In some ways autism becomes more problematic in adulthood than in childhood, because adults with autism often lack emotional regulation as children with autism do but are bigger and can cause more disruption. They also develop sexual desires, without the social knowledge of the appropriate expression of those desires. There is no cure for autism and few effective treatments, but with help, many children and adults with autism can learn some skills for daily living, such as wearing clean clothes, asking for directions (and then following them), and keeping track of money. Children with a mild form of autism such as Asperger's syndrome can live very productive lives, especially if they focus on topics that interest them and channel that interest into an appropriate professional direction. Early intervention with cognitive behavioral therapy or other effective treatments can help children with autism or ASD develop cognitive and social skills. Intervention should be geared toward the child's specific needs, so that each child learns the skills that help him or her progress.

Media use in toddlerhood

Identify the typical rates of television use in toddlerhood and explain some consequences of toddlers' TV watching.

LEARNING OBJECTIVE **5.21**

Media use among toddlers is more limited than it will be at later ages, when it will include everything from computers to cell phones to magazines. However, media use, especially television, is a typical part of daily life in most countries, even during toddlerhood. According to a national study in the United States, 58% of children under age 3

Television shows with prosocial themes can inspire prosocial behavior in toddlers.

watch TV every day, and 30% even have a TV in their bedroom (Rideout & Hamel, 2006). African American and Latino toddlers watch more TV than toddlers in other ethnic groups, initiating a pattern of ethnic differences that will continue throughout life (Anand & Krosnick, 2005).

Already in the second year of life, toddlers have begun to understand that the images on the TV screen are not real. In one study, 9-month-old infants and 14- and 19-month-old toddlers were shown a video in which a woman demonstrated how to play with a variety of toys for young children (Pierroutsakos & Troseth, 2003). The infants reached out to the screen and attempted to grasp, hit, or rub the toys, but the toddlers did not. However, other studies have shown that toddlers sometimes interact with televised images by talking to them, which suggests that for toddlers the television/reality boundary is not completely clear (Garrison & Christakis, 2005).

How does TV-watching influence toddlers? Surveys indicate that a majority of American parents fear that TV may harm their young children (Rideout et al., 2003; Woodward & Gridina, 2000). However, with television, as with other media we will examine in future chapters, the effects depend very much on the media content. In one American study, one group of 2-year-olds was shown the TV show *Barney and Friends*, featuring a large, purple, talking dinosaur who encourages behavior such as kindness and sharing. This group was then compared in free play to another group of 2-year-olds who had not seen the show (Singer & Singer, 1998). The toddlers in the *Barney* group showed more prosocial behavior, such as sharing, and less aggressiveness, along with a greater tendency to engage in symbolic play. In a national (American) study, 70% of parents of children under age 3 reported that their toddlers had imitated positive behavior they had seen on television, such as sharing or helping, whereas only 27% had imitated aggressive behavior such as hitting or kicking (Rideout & Hamel, 2006).

With regard to the effects of TV-watching on cognitive development, evidence is mixed, with some studies indicating that watching TV helps toddlers expand their vocabularies and others reporting that it may be detrimental to language development (Courage & Setliff, 2009). Again, content matters. One study had parents report toddlers' TV-viewing patterns every three months from age 6–30 months, then assessed the toddlers' language development at 30 months (Linebarger & Walker, 2005). Watching educationally oriented programs such as *Dora the Explorer* resulted in greater vocabularies and higher expressive language scores than watching other programs did. Other studies have found that TV can inspire imaginative play among toddlers (Weber, 2006). I remember this well from when my twins were toddlers, how they would watch a TV show or a video and then invent their own elaborate games pretending to be characters they had watched, such as the *Teletubbies* or *Peter Pan*. We even bought them Teletubbies dolls to facilitate the games.

Even if TV sometimes inspires prosocial or creative behavior, a persistent concern about television use from toddlerhood onward is the **displacement effect**; that is, the fact that time spent watching TV is time not spent doing other activities such as reading or playing with other children (Weber, 2006). In 2001, the American Academy of Pediatrics recommended that children under 2 years old should not watch television at all, and children 2 years and older should be limited to no more than 2 hours of TV a day (American Academy of Pediatrics Committee on Public Education, 2001). The basis for this recommendation was not that television content is damaging but that young children would benefit more from active learning through experiences such as

APPLYING YOUR KNOWLEDGE

How does the displacement effect change—if at all—from toddlerhood through adulthood?

displacement effect in media research, term for how media use occupies time that may have been spent on other activities

play and conversations with others (Kirkorian et al., 2008). It should be added that in many households the television is on nearly all the time, and consequently even toddlers are exposed to TV content that is a long way from Barney (Rideout & Hamel, 2006). Many children's shows still contain aggressive content, and children can learn aggressive behavior from these shows. Furthermore, children who watch a lot of TV consume the junk food that is advertised and they don't exercise as much as children who watch less TV or no TV at all. ◉

Watch the **Video** Limitations on TV Commercials for Children in **MyDevelopmentLab**

WHAT HAVE YOU LEARNED?

1. What are some exceptions to the typical pattern of father involvement with infants and toddlers in traditional cultures?

2. How is the typical pattern of father involvement with infants and toddlers in developed countries changing?

3. How do toddlers respond to the birth of a younger sibling? How do toddlers' relations with younger siblings differ from their relations with older siblings?

4. What kinds of play are typical between toddlers?

5. What are the main features, causes, and consequences of autism?

6. What are some of the consequences—both positive and negative—of toddlers' TV use?

Section 3 VIDEO GUIDE Separation Anxiety Across Cultures (Length: 6:10)

In this video, we explore the development of attachment among infants and toddlers by observing how children at different ages and from various cultures react to being approached by strangers and separated from their primary caregivers.

1. Describe an instance when you have witnessed a child experiencing separation or stranger anxiety.

2. The clip here shows examples of separation and stranger anxiety. Discuss the difference between pure separation anxiety and the impact that including a stranger can have on a child's reaction.

3. Which of Piaget's concepts is linked to separation anxiety? Explain this connection.

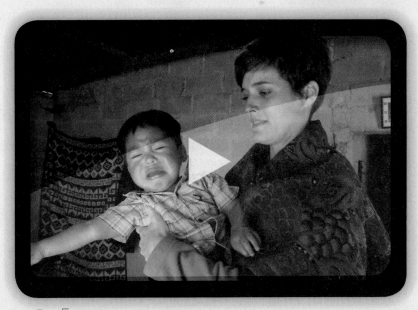

Watch the **Video** Separation Anxiety Across Cultures in **MyDevelopmentLab**

Summing Up

((•—[**Listen** to an audio file of your chapter in **MyDevelopmentLab**

SECTION 1 PHYSICAL DEVELOPMENT

5.1 Describe the typical changes in physical growth that take place in toddlerhood and explain the harmful effects of nutritional deficiencies on growth.

Toddlers' physical growth continues at a pace that is slightly reduced from infancy but is nevertheless faster than at any later time of life. Toddlers in developing countries often suffer protein and micronutrient deficiencies that impede their physical and cognitive development.

5.2 Describe the changes in brain development that take place during toddlerhood, and identify the two most common methods of measuring brain activity.

The brain's synaptic density peaks at the end of toddlerhood, followed by many years of synaptic pruning. The two most common methods of measuring brain activity are the EEG and the fMRI.

5.3 Describe the changes in sleeping patterns and sleeping arrangements that take place during toddlerhood.

Toddlers' episodes of night-waking increase from 18 to 24 months of age, in part due to teething of molars. In traditional cultures, toddlers sleep with their mothers until the next child is born, after which they sleep with other family members.

5.4 Describe the advances in motor development that take place during toddlerhood.

In their gross motor development, toddlers learn to walk, run, climb, and kick a ball. Toddlers in traditional cultures are often restricted in their movements to protect them from danger—especially cooking fires. Advances in fine motor development include holding a cup and building a tower of blocks. In their third year, toddlers may be able to brush their teeth, with some assistance.

5.5 Compare and contrast the process and timing of toilet training in developed countries and traditional cultures.

Children vary widely in the timing of learning toilet training, but most are toilet trained by the end of toddlerhood. In traditional cultures, toddlers usually learn controlled elimination through observing and imitating older children.

5.6 Distinguish the weaning process early in infancy from weaning later in toddlerhood.

When weaning takes place in the second or third year of life, toddlers often resist. Customs in traditional cultures for promoting weaning include sending the toddler to a relative's household for awhile or coating the mother's breast with an unpleasant substance.

KEY TERMS

kwashiorkor *p. 184*
micronutrients *p. 184*

synaptic density *p. 185*
EEG (electroencephalogram) *p. 185*

fMRI (functional magnetic resonance imaging) *p. 185*

weaning *p. 192*

SECTION 2 COGNITIVE DEVELOPMENT

5.7 Outline the cognitive achievements of toddlerhood in Piaget's theory.

According to Piaget, the ability for mental representations develops in the second half of the second year and is the basis for important aspects of later cognitive functioning, including problem solving and language. Object permanence also reaches near-completion during this period. Deferred imitation and categorization also require mental representation.

5.8 Explain Vygotsky's sociocultural theory of cognitive development and contrast it with Piaget's theory.

Unlike Piaget and most other cognitive theorists and researchers, Vygotsky emphasized the cultural basis of cognitive development in childhood. His concepts of private speech and the role of guided participation in learning help to explain how children gain cultural knowledge from adults.

5.9 Summarize the evidence for the biological and evolutionary bases of language.

Humans have areas in the brain specifically devoted to language functions. Language conferred an evolutionary advantage to humans because it helped humans build and use technology, coordinate action, and improve communication.

5.10 Describe the milestones in language development that take place during the toddler years.

At 18 months, most toddlers speak about 50 words, usually in holophrases. By 24 months, most speak about 200 words and combine some words in telegraphic speech. By their third birthdays, most can easily use the language of their culture in full sentences.

5.11 Identify how parents' stimulation of toddlers' language varies across cultures and evaluate how these variations relate to language development.

Cultures vary widely in how much they encourage toddlers' language development, from stimulating language use through direct interactions, to allowing toddlers to be present among conversing adults but otherwise not speaking to them much, to actually discouraging them from talking. Regardless of cultural practices, toddlers generally learn to use their language well by the time they reach age 3.

KEY TERMS

mental representations *p. 195*

deferred imitation *p. 195*

zone of proximal development *p. 197*

private speech *p. 197*

guided participation *p. 198*

infinite generativity *p. 200*

Broca's area *p. 200*

Wernicke's area *p. 200*

holophrases *p. 201*

overextension *p. 201*

underextension *p. 201*

fast mapping *p. 202*

telegraphic speech *p. 202*

language acquisition device (LAD) *p. 203*

overregularization *p. 204*

SECTION 3 EMOTIONAL AND SOCIAL DEVELOPMENT

5.12 Describe how emotional development advances during toddlerhood and identify the impact of culture on these changes.

Sociomoral emotions developing in toddlerhood include guilt, shame, embarrassment, envy, and pride. They are called sociomoral emotions because they indicate that toddlers have begun to learn the moral standards of their culture. Toddlers in Western cultures have occasional tantrums, perhaps because they have a more developed sense of intentionality than infants do and so are more likely to protest when thwarted. However, tantrums are rare outside the West where cultures place less emphasis on self-expression.

5.13 Describe the changes in self-development that take place during toddlerhood.

The birth of the self in toddlerhood is indicated in the development of self-recognition and self-reflection and the expression of sociomoral emotions. Gender identity also develops during this time, as children begin to identify themselves and others as male or female and to apply gender terms.

5.14 Distinguish between *sex* and *gender* and summarize the evidence for the biological basis of gender development.

Sex is the biological status of being male or female, whereas *gender* refers to the cultural categories of "male" and "female." The biological basis of gender is indicated in evolutionary theory, ethological studies, and hormonal studies. However, changes in male and female roles in recent times have shown that these roles can change dramatically over a relatively short time and therefore biological assumptions about gender should be viewed with skepticism.

5.15 Describe the essential features of attachment theory and identify the four classifications of attachment.

In formulating attachment theory, Bowlby emphasized the evolutionary need for a person who would provide protection and care during the vulnerable early years of life. Ainsworth developed the Strange Situation to assess attachment quality, and concluded that it showed three distinct types of attachment: secure, insecure–avoidant, and insecure–resistant. The young child forms an internal working model depending on the mother's sensitivity and responsiveness. Disorganized–disoriented is a fourth classification, added by later researchers.

5.16 Identify the key factors influencing the quality of toddlers' attachment to their mothers, and explain what effect attachment quality has on development.

The quality of attachment is based mainly on how sensitive and responsive a mother is toward her child. Attachment quality as assessed in toddlerhood does not consistently predict later outcomes, except for the unusual disorganized–disoriented attachment type.

5.17 Summarize the major critiques of attachment theory, including the cultural critique.

Attachment theory has been criticized for not acknowledging temperament sufficiently and for overlooking bidirectional effects. Toddlers in all cultures appear to become attached to those who care for them most, but there are important cultural variations in patterns and norms of attachment.

5.18 Compare and contrast the typical patterns of father involvement with infants and toddlers in traditional cultures and developed countries.

Fathers in traditional cultures usually serve as family providers but are remote from toddlers' emotional lives, although there are exceptions. Across cultures, fathers tend to provide less physical and emotional care than mothers, but this is changing as gender roles and work responsibilities change.

5.19 Describe relationships with siblings, peers, and friends during toddlerhood.

Across cultures, toddlers often react negatively to the birth of a younger sibling. When toddlers themselves are the younger siblings, their older siblings enjoy playing with them more than when they were infants, but conflict tends to rise as toddlers become more capable of asserting their own desires. With friends, toddler play takes a variety of forms, including solitary play, parallel play, simple social play, and cooperative pretend play. Toddlers' friendships often have qualities similar to friendships at older ages, including companionship, mutual affection, and emotional closeness.

5.20 Identify the characteristics of autism spectrum disorders and recognize how they affect prospects for children as they grow to adulthood.

Autism is a developmental disorder marked by a lack of interest in social relations, abnormal language development, and repetitive behavior. The social and language deficits of autism make social development problematic in childhood and beyond.

5.21 Identify the typical rates of television use in toddlerhood and explain some consequences of toddlers' TV watching.

Toddlers in many countries watch TV every day. Television watching in toddlerhood may promote prosocial behavior if the TV content is prosocial, but there are concerns about the displacement effect, especially for children under 2 years old. Parents should be cautioned that some TV content contains aggressive behavior, and that children who watch a lot of TV may develop unhealthy habits.

KEY TERMS

sociomoral emotions *p. 210*

empathy *p. 210*

prosocial behavior *p. 210*

autonomy versus shame and doubt *p. 211*

self-recognition *p. 211*

self-reflection *p. 211*

gender identity *p. 212*

sex *p. 212*

gender *p. 212*

ethology *p. 213*

primary attachment figure *p. 215*

stranger anxiety *p. 216*

secure base *p. 216*

separation anxiety *p. 216*

Strange Situation *p. 217*

secure attachment *p. 217*

insecure–avoidant attachment *p. 217*

insecure–resistant attachment *p. 217*

disorganized–disoriented attachment *p. 217*

amae *p. 223*

polygyny *p. 224*

autism *p. 228*

autism spectrum disorder (ASD) *p. 228*

displacement effect *p. 230*

Practice Test

✔—Study and Review in MyDevelopmentLab

1. _____ is a condition specific to toddlerhood in which protein deficiencies lead to varied symptoms such as swollen bellies, hair loss, and lack of energy.
   a. Kwashiorkor
   b. SIDS
   c. Marasmus
   d. Dysentery

2. What most characterizes early brain development in toddlerhood is
   a. the formation of the cerebral cortex.
   b. the steep increase in the density of synaptic connections among neurons.
   c. activity in the amygdala.
   d. the production of new brain cells.

3. During toddlerhood,
   a. sleeping alone is rare in traditional cultures.
   b. children sleep more than they did in infancy (because they are so much more active).
   c. naps are no longer needed.
   d. children sleep consistently throughout the night.

4. Toddlers
   a. who do not walk by 1 year are likely to have a gross motor problem.
   b. in traditional cultures are equal to toddlers from Western cultures in the development of their gross motor skills.
   c. can usually run before they can stand briefly on one leg.
   d. show the same pace of gross motor development as fine motor development.

5. In the West,
   a. most children show signs of readiness for toilet training by their first birthday.
   b. views about toilet training have stayed the same over the last several decades.
   c. children are toilet trained in a nearly identical way as their counterparts in traditional cultures.
   d. a sign of being ready to begin toilet training is when the child can stay "dry" for an hour or two during the day.

6. If you are a toddler from a traditional culture, you would likely
   a. have experienced some customary practice for being weaned.
   b. be abruptly weaned at age 1.
   c. be given formula instead of breast milk.
   d. still be breast-feeding at age 5.

7. When children generally avoid making the A-not-B error, they
   a. show the ability to categorize.
   b. have attained object permanence.
   c. understand scaffolding.
   d. use tertiary circular reactions.

8. According to Vygotsky, _____ is required for cognitive development.
   a. social interaction
   b. formal education
   c. strong parent–child attachment
   d. emotional self-regulation

9. When it comes to learning what we consider language, the most significant difference between apes and humans is
   a. the inability for apes to learn more than a few signs.
   b. the faster pace of humans' sign language.
   c. the inability of apes to generate word symbols in an infinite number of ways.
   d. the inability of apes to make requests.

10. Which is an example of overextension?
    a. A child saying, "He hitted me with a stick."
    b. A child saying, "The moon looks happy tonight."
    c. A child calling all men "Dada."
    d. A child saying "I no like peas."

11. Research has shown that
    a. direct stimulation of language development is discouraged in some cultures.
    b. genetics plays very little role in verbal ability.
    c. language development in American children is not linked to income level of parents.
    d. maternal responsiveness to American children's vocalizations has no impact on when children reach language milestones.

12. Which of the following is a sociomoral emotion?
    a. anger   c. fear
    b. pride   d. happiness

13. Researchers secretly dabbed a red spot on the nose of babies of different ages and then placed them in front of a mirror. They were testing
    a. gender identity.   c. stranger anxiety.
    b. sex roles.   d. self-recognition.

14. Gender identity
    a. develops much more quickly in females than males.
    b. refers to the ability of children to identify themselves as male and female.
    c. is demonstrated when a child prefers to be with the same-sex parent or grandparent.
    d. develops around age 5.

15. Secure attachment is characterized by
    a. a willingness to use the caregiver as a secure base to explore the environment.
    b. a tendency to be self-centered.
    c. acting both relieved and angry at their caregiver after seeing her again after separation.
    d. a dependency on the mother for approval of all activities.

16. Research has shown that a child with a(n) _____ attachment classification is most likely to have later problems such as hostility, psychopathology, and cognitive deficits.
    a. insecure–resistant   c. disorganized–disoriented
    b. insecure–avoidant   d. goal-corrected

17. Which of the following best describes attachment across cultures?
    a. Autonomy and independence are encouraged from an early age across cultures.
    b. In all cultures, infants and toddlers develop attachments to the people around them who provide loving, protective care.
    c. Insecure–resistant attachment is the most common classification in all cultures because many children find the Strange Situation to be very stressful.
    d. Children from the United States and Japan tend to be classified the same way in studies employing the Strange Situation paradigm.

18. In developed countries, fathers would most likely be observed in which of the following activity with their infants or toddlers?
    a. bathing them   c. soothing them
    b. feeding them   d. playing with them

19. During toddlerhood
    a. those who know each other well usually engage in solitary play rather than other forms of play.
    b. friendships seem to have many of the same features of friendships at other ages.
    c. there seems to be no preference for play partners; they play equally with whatever children are present.
    d. children are not yet capable of engaging in simply social play or cooperative pretend play.

20. Which behavior would be most characteristic of a child who has been diagnosed with autism?
    a. a preoccupation with talking to strangers
    b. a preoccupation with repetitive movements
    c. a preoccupation with looking at faces
    d. a preoccupation with pointing at objects until others look at them

21. Research on media has shown that
    a. in the United States it is virtually unheard of to have a TV in a young child's bedroom.
    b. children are only able to learn to model aggressive behaviors at this age because prosocial behaviors require more advanced cognitive development.
    c. the effects of television and other media depend on the content.
    d. the displacement effect is no longer considered a major problem because of all the media options available.

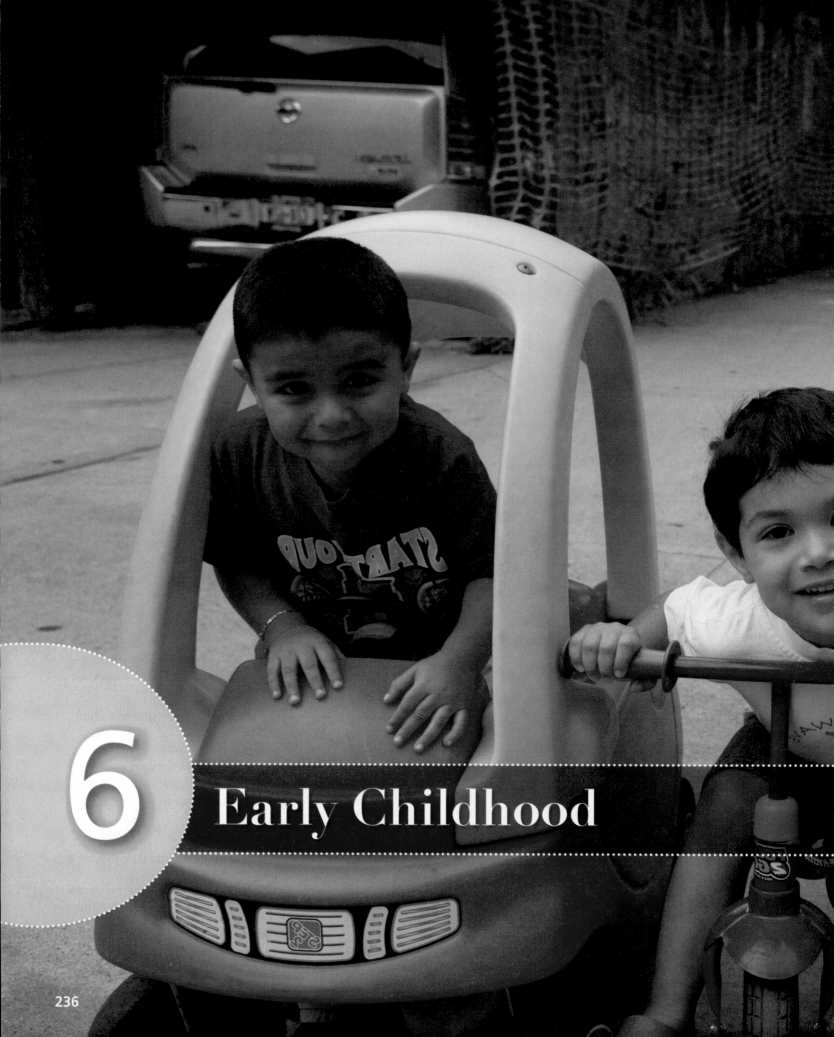

6 Early Childhood

237

It is midmorning in a day care center in Aalborg, Denmark, and Lars Olsen, age 4, is playing a game with his friend Pelle (pronounced *Pell-Uh*). "Look out!" he shouts to Pelle, holding up a toy airplane with a little pilot in it. "There's gonna be a crash!" Pelle, with no airplane of his own, has taken a plastic banana from the kitchen play area and straddled a small stuffed bear on it. "You can't catch me! I'm too fast!" he exclaims, and dashes away with Lars in pursuit. Lars catches up to him and hits his toy plane against Pelle's banana airplane, and the airplanes crash to the ground along with the laughing boys.

"Come, children!" calls the boys' preschool teacher, Birgitte. "It's story time." The children, familiar with this daily ritual, sit on the floor in a semi-circle in front of Birgitte as she begins to read the story of the day. Lars enjoys the story, and the "Letter Learning Time" that comes after it. He has learned most of his letters already, and looks forward to being able to read.

In the afternoon his mother picks him up on the way from her job at an accounting firm, and the two of them go home. Soon his father arrives home from work, too, and Lars watches television while his parents prepare dinner.

After dinner, Lars watches more TV as his parents clean up, then he and his father play a board game. Bedtime comes at 8 P.M. sharp. His mother puts him to bed, reading him a story before giving him a kiss and wishing him good night.

Meanwhile, an ocean away in a Mayan village in Guatemala, 5-year-old Maricela (Mari) helps her mother make the day's tortillas. Mari flattens a ball of dough into a tortilla as her mother cooks. When her brother Roberto toddles over to join them, Mari jumps up to hold him away from the fire. He is not yet 2 years old, and she is responsible for keeping him away from danger. She carries him outside, where they play a chasing game for a while. They notice their father coming home from the fields for the midday meal, and they run to greet him. Soon Mari's older brother and sister will be coming home from school to join them.

In the afternoon and evening, Mari continues to work alongside her mother and take care of her little brother. There is water to be fetched and firewood to be gathered, and Roberto must be watched constantly. Her aunt and her cousin Gina come by, and she and Gina play with their dolls, pretending that the dolls are taking tortillas into the village square to sell. Mari's older sister is currently the one who sells the tortillas in town, but Mari knows that within a few years this duty will fall to her.

In the evening the family gathers around the ever-smoldering fire, and Mari sits on her father's lap. Before long Mari is asleep, and the next morning she will have no memory of being passed from her father to her older sister, or of falling asleep by her sister's side next to the fire.

As we have seen in the previous two chapters, from birth onward children's development can be very different depending on their culture. In early childhood the cultural contexts of development expand in several important ways, as the stories of Lars and Mari show. Children begin to learn culturally specific skills, through participation in daily tasks with their parents and siblings in some cultures, as in Mari's case, or through participation in group care and preschool in other cultures, as for Lars. Their play comes to include pretend play, and the materials of their fantasy games are drawn from their cultural environment—airplanes for Lars, tortillas for Mari. They become increasingly aware of their culture's differential gender expectations for boys and girls. And they develop an awareness of their culture's values and moral order. By sleeping alone in his bedroom, Lars is learning the cultural value of individualism; by sleeping alongside others, Mari is learning that she is always intertwined with others in bonds of mutual support and obligation.

We will explore all of these areas in the course of this chapter. First, we examine the changes in physical and motor development that occur in early childhood.

> *. . . the materials of their fantasy games are drawn from their cultural environment . . .*

LEARNING OBJECTIVES

6.1 Describe the physical growth and change that takes place during early childhood.

6.2 Describe the changes in brain development that take place during early childhood and the aspects of brain development that explain "infantile" amnesia.

6.3 Identify the main nutritional deficiencies and the primary sources of injury, illness, and mortality during early childhood in developed and developing countries.

6.4 Describe changes in gross and fine motor abilities during early childhood, and explain how these changes may have a cultural basis.

6.5 Describe the development of handedness and identify the consequences and cultural views of left-handedness.

Growth From Age 3 to 6

The pace of bodily growth continues to decline in the period from toddlerhood to early childhood, as it did from infancy to toddlerhood. A variety of parts of the brain make crucial strides forward, although brain development still has a long way to go. Optimal growth in the body and the brain require adequate health and nutrition, which are lacking in much of the world during early childhood.

Bodily growth

> Describe the physical growth and change that takes place during early childhood. **LEARNING OBJECTIVE 6.1**

From age 3 to 6 the typical American child grows 2–3 inches per year and adds 5 to 7 pounds. The typical 3-year-old is about 35 inches tall and weighs about 30 pounds; the typical 6-year-old is about 45 inches tall and weighs about 45 pounds. Throughout this period, boys are slightly taller and heavier than girls, although the average differences are small. Both boys and girls gain more in weight than in height during early childhood, but most add more muscle than fat. From toddlerhood to early childhood, most children lose their remaining "baby fat" and their bodily proportions become similar to those of adults.

In developing countries, average heights and weights in early childhood are considerably lower, due to lower nutrition and higher likelihood of childhood diseases. For example, the average 6-year-old in Bangladesh is only as tall as the average 4-year-old in Sweden (Leathers & Foster, 2004).

Within developing countries, too, differences in socioeconomic status influence gains in height and weight in early childhood. As noted in earlier chapters, economic differences tend to be large in developing countries; most have a relatively small middle- and upper-class and a large population of low-income people. Wealthier people have more access to nutritional foods, so their children are taller and weigh more than poorer children of the same age (Ogden et al., 2002). Given roughly equal levels of nutrition and health care, individual differences in height and weight gains during childhood are due to genetics (Chambers et al., 2001).

By their third birthday, most children have a full set of 20 teeth (McGregor et al., 1968). These are their *primary* or "baby" teeth that will be replaced by 32 permanent

By age 5, about 40% of North American children have at least one cavity.

teeth in the course of childhood, beginning at about age 6. However, this replacement process takes place slowly, lasting until about age 14, so children use their baby teeth for up to 10 years and have to learn how to take care of them to prevent tooth decay.

In developed countries, children usually have their first visit to the dentist around age 3 (Bottenberg et al., 2008; Chi et al., 2011). Most children learn how to brush their teeth in early childhood, and in developed countries it is increasingly common for children's dental care to include fluoride rinses and sealants (plastic tooth coatings). Some countries and local areas also add fluoride to the water system, which greatly reduces children's rates of cavities. Nevertheless, about 40% of North American children have at least one dental cavity by age 5 (World Health Organization [WHO], 2008a), primarily due to inconsistent dental care and to diets that are heavy in sugars and starches that cause cavities. Children in developing countries are less likely to have diets loaded with sugars and starches, but they are also less likely to have fluoride in their water systems and less likely to have access to regular dental care that would provide fluoride rinses and sealants. Overall, children in most developing countries have more tooth decay in early and middle childhood than children in developed countries do (WHO, 2008b).

Brain development and "infantile" amnesia

6.2 | **LEARNING OBJECTIVE** | Describe the changes in brain development that take place during early childhood and the aspects of brain development that explain "infantile" amnesia.

The size of the brain continues to increase gradually during early childhood. At age 3 the brain is about 70% of its adult weight, and at age 6, about 90% (Bauer et al., 2009). In contrast, the average 6-year-old's body weight is less than 30% what it will be in adulthood, so the growth of the brain outpaces the rest of the body (Nihart, 1993).

The frontal lobes grow faster than the rest of the cerebral cortex during early childhood (Anderson & Jacobs, 2008; Blumenthal et al., 1999). Growth in the frontal lobes underlies the advances in emotional regulation, foresight, and organizing that take place during the preschool years (Diamond, 2004). Maturation of the frontal lobes and connections with other parts of the brain help preschool children regulate both positive and negative emotions (Rothbart et al., 2011). Because of these important changes, temper tantrums usually subside and children are better able to express and understand a range of emotions. Throughout the cerebral cortex, growth from age 3 to 15 takes place not gradually but in spurts within the different lobes, followed by periods of vigorous synaptic pruning (Thompson et al., 2000).

During early childhood the number of neurons continues the decline that began in toddlerhood via synaptic pruning. The increase in brain size and weight during early childhood is due to an increase in dendritic connections between neurons and to myelination (see Chapter 4 p. 141, if you need to refresh your memory about myelination). Four parts of the brain are especially notable for their myelination during early childhood (see *Figure 6.1*).

In the **corpus callosum**, the band of neural fibers connecting the right and left hemispheres of the cerebral cortex, myelination peaks during early childhood, although it continues at a slower pace through adolescence. The corpus callosum allows for coordination of activity between the two hemispheres, so increased myelination of this area of the brain enhances the speed of functioning throughout the cerebral cortex.

corpus callosum band of neural fibers connecting the two hemispheres of the brain

Substantial myelination also takes place in early childhood in the **cerebellum**, a structure at the base of the brain involved in balance and motor movements. Increased myelination enhances connections between the cerebellum and the cerebral cortex. This change underlies the child's increasing abilities to jump, run, climb, and throw a ball.

In the **reticular formation**, a part of the brain involved in attention, myelination is completed by age 5, which helps explain the increase in attention span that takes place in the course of early childhood. For example, by age 4 or 5 most children could easily sit through a 10–15 minute period in preschool while a story is read aloud, whereas most toddlers would be unable to sit still and pay attention for so long.

Similarly, myelination in the **hippocampus** is completed by age 5. The hippocampus is involved in the transfer of information from short-term to long-term memory, so the completion of myelination by age 5 may explain why *autobiographical memory* (memory for personal events and experiences) is limited prior to this age (Pathman et al., 2011). However, myelination in the hippocampus is gradual, and most adults can remember some autobiographical events that happened before age 5 (Howe et al., 2009). For example, in one study children who had been hospitalized for a medical emergency at ages 2–13 were interviewed 5 years later (Peterson & Whalen, 2001). Even the children who were only 2 years old at the time of the injury recalled the main features of their injury experience accurately 5 years later, although memory for details of the experience improved with age.

Other studies have found that many children and adults have autobiographical memories for events and experiences that happened as early as age 2, but remember little or nothing prior to this age (Courage & Cowan, 2009). The inability to remember anything prior to age 2 is known as **infantile amnesia**. One recent theory proposes that autobiographical memory before age 2 is limited because the awareness of self becomes stable at about 2 years of age and serves as a new organizer around which events can be encoded, stored, and retrieved in memory as personal, that is, as having happened "to me" (Howe et al., 2009). Another perspective proposes that encoding memories is promoted by language development, because language allows us to tell ourselves a narrative of events and experiences; consequently, most autobiographical memory is encoded only after language development accelerates at age 2 (Newcombe et al., 2007). ✳

Autobiographical memory may also be partly cultural. In a study comparing adults' autobiographical memories, White American adults remembered more events prior to age 5 than Chinese adults did, and their earliest memory was 6 months earlier on average (Wang, 2006). The interpretation proposed by the authors was that the greater individualism of British and American cultures promotes greater attention to individual experiences and consequently more and earlier autobiographical memories.

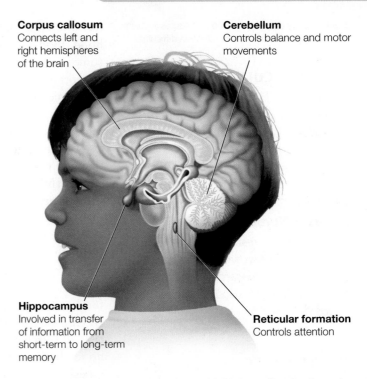

Corpus callosum
Connects left and right hemispheres of the brain

Cerebellum
Controls balance and motor movements

Hippocampus
Involved in transfer of information from short-term to long-term memory

Reticular formation
Controls attention

Figure 6.1 • **Four brain structures with high myelination in early childhood.** In which structures is myelination completed by age 5?

cerebellum structure at the base of the brain involved in balance and motor movements

reticular formation part of the lower brain, involved in attention

hippocampus stucture involved in transfer of information from short-term to long-term memory

infantile amnesia inability to remember anything that happened prior to age 2

✳ **Explore** the **Concept** Virtual Brain: Learning and Memory in **MyDevelopmentLab**

APPLYING YOUR KNOWLEDGE
What is your earliest memory? Is there any way for you to tell if it really happened or how accurate it is?

Health and safety in early childhood

Identify the main nutritional deficiencies and the primary sources of injury, illness, and mortality during early childhood in developed and developing countries.

LEARNING OBJECTIVE **6.3**

By early childhood, children are not as vulnerable to health threats as they were in infancy and toddlerhood (UNICEF, 2008). Nevertheless, there are many health and safety concerns associated with this period. Proper nutrition is essential to a child's healthy development, yet in developing countries the rates of malnutrition are alarmingly high. Children in developing countries remain vulnerable to some illnesses and diseases, and children worldwide are subject to high rates of injuries compared to other periods of the life course.

anemia dietary deficiency of iron that causes problems such as fatigue, irritability, and attention difficulties

Many children in developed countries have nutritional deficiencies despite an abundance of food. Here, a child in London eats a fast food meal that is high in fat and sugar.

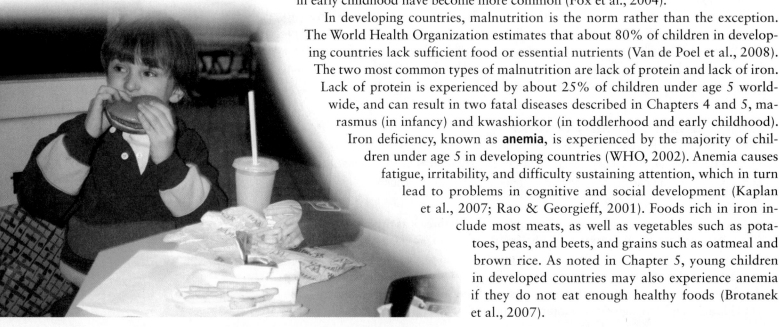

NUTRITION AND MALNUTRITION   As the rate of physical growth slows down in early childhood, food consumption diminishes as well. Children may have some meals, or even some whole days, where they eat little. This can be alarming to parents, but it is nothing to worry about as long as it does not happen over an extended period and is not accompanied by symptoms that may indicate illness or disease. Appetites vary a lot from day to day in early childhood, and the 5-year-old who barely touched dinner one night may eat nearly as much as Mom and Dad the next night (Hursti, 1999).

Children generally learn to like whatever foods the adults in their environment like and provide for them. In India kids eat rice with spicy sauces, in Japan kids eat sushi, while in Mexico kids eat chili peppers. Nevertheless, a myth persists among many North American parents that kids in early childhood will only eat a small range of foods high in fat and sugar content, such as hamburgers, hot dogs, fried chicken, and macaroni and cheese (Zehle et al., 2007). This false belief then becomes a self-fulfilling prophecy, as children who eat foods high in sugar and fat lose their taste for healthier foods (Black et al., 2002). The assumption that young children like only high-fat and sugar foods also leads parents to bribe their children to eat healthier foods—"If you eat three more bites of carrots, then you can have some pudding"—which leads the children to view healthy foods as a trial and unhealthy foods as a reward (Birch et al., 2003). These cultural practices contribute to high rates of childhood obesity in many developed countries, as we will see in more detail in Chapter 7. Obesity in American children under age 5 is a growing problem, particularly in Latino and Native American children. Recent data indicate that rates of obesity for White and African American children are similar, at 11.4% and 11.7% respectively. However, the rate of obesity for Latino preschool children is 16%, and the rate for Native American children is 19% (Centers for Disease Control and Prevention, 2010c). Being overweight at such a young age can lead to health problems later, such as diabetes, hypertension, and depression. 👁

Because young children in developed countries often eat too much of unhealthy foods and too little of healthy foods, many of them have specific nutritional deficiencies despite living in cultures where food is abundant. Calcium is the most common nutritional deficiency in the United States, with one-third of American 3-year-olds consuming less than the amount recommended by health authorities (Wagner & Greer, 2008). Calcium is especially important for the growth of bones and teeth, and is found in foods such beans, peas, broccoli, and dairy products such as milk and cheese. Over the past 30 years, as children have consumed less milk and more soft drinks, calcium deficiencies in early childhood have become more common (Fox et al., 2004).

In developing countries, malnutrition is the norm rather than the exception. The World Health Organization estimates that about 80% of children in developing countries lack sufficient food or essential nutrients (Van de Poel et al., 2008). The two most common types of malnutrition are lack of protein and lack of iron. Lack of protein is experienced by about 25% of children under age 5 worldwide, and can result in two fatal diseases described in Chapters 4 and 5, marasmus (in infancy) and kwashiorkor (in toddlerhood and early childhood). Iron deficiency, known as **anemia**, is experienced by the majority of children under age 5 in developing countries (WHO, 2002). Anemia causes fatigue, irritability, and difficulty sustaining attention, which in turn lead to problems in cognitive and social development (Kaplan et al., 2007; Rao & Georgieff, 2001). Foods rich in iron include most meats, as well as vegetables such as potatoes, peas, and beets, and grains such as oatmeal and brown rice. As noted in Chapter 5, young children in developed countries may also experience anemia if they do not eat enough healthy foods (Brotanek et al., 2007).

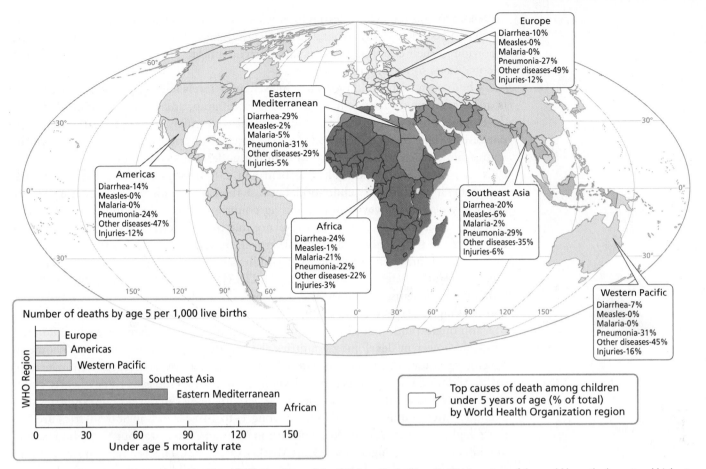

Europe
Diarrhea-10%
Measles-0%
Malaria-0%
Pneumonia-27%
Other diseases-49%
Injuries-12%

Eastern Mediterranean
Diarrhea-29%
Measles-2%
Malaria-5%
Pneumonia-31%
Other diseases-29%
Injuries-5%

Americas
Diarrhea-14%
Measles-0%
Malaria-0%
Pneumonia-24%
Other diseases-47%
Injuries-12%

Southeast Asia
Diarrhea-20%
Measles-6%
Malaria-2%
Pneumonia-29%
Other diseases-35%
Injuries-6%

Africa
Diarrhea-24%
Measles-1%
Malaria-21%
Pneumonia-22%
Other diseases-22%
Injuries-3%

Western Pacific
Diarrhea-7%
Measles-0%
Malaria-0%
Pneumonia-31%
Other diseases-45%
Injuries-16%

Number of deaths by age 5 per 1,000 live births

WHO Region
Europe
Americas
Western Pacific
Southeast Asia
Eastern Mediterranean
African

0   30   60   90   120   150
Under age 5 mortality rate

Top causes of death among children under 5 years of age (% of total) by World Health Organization region

Map 6.1 • **Worldwide Mortality Rates and Causes of Death in Children Under Age 5.** Which regions of the world have the lowest and highest rates of childhood deaths? How do the causes of death vary by region?

ILLNESS AND DISEASE In developing countries, the causes of death in early childhood are usually illnesses and diseases, especially pneumonia, malaria, and measles (UNICEF, 2008). Malnutrition is believed to be indirectly responsible for about half of early childhood deaths, because lack of sufficient food reduces the effectiveness of the body's immune system. **Map 6.1** highlights global mortality rates and major causes of death in children under age 5.

However, remarkable progress has been made in recent decades in reducing mortality in children under age 5. From 1960 to 2006, the number of deaths worldwide of children under age 5 declined from 20 million to under 10 million, even though the world's population more than doubled during that time (UNICEF, 2008). The decline is due to a variety of factors, especially improved food production in developing countries and increased prevalence of childhood vaccinations.

In developed countries, where most children receive vaccinations and have access to adequate food and medical care, minor illnesses are common in early childhood, with most children experiencing 7–10 per year (Kesson, 2007). Minor illnesses help build up the immune system, so that children typically experience them less frequently with age.

Deaths worldwide among children age 5 and under have declined by half in the past 50 years, largely due to increased childhood vaccinations. Here, a Red Cross volunteer in El Salvador gives an oral vaccination to a 6-year-old boy.

INJURIES Do you remember becoming injured at all in early childhood? If you do, you are in good company. Most young children—and their parents—can count on spending a portion of their childhood nursing an injury; a minor "boo-boo" if they're lucky, but in some cases something more serious.

Children in early childhood have high activity levels and their motor development is advanced enough for them to be able to run, jump, and climb, but their cognitive development is not yet advanced enough for them to anticipate situations that might be dangerous. This combination leads to high rates of injuries in early childhood. In the United States each year, one-third of children under 10 become injured badly enough to receive medical attention (Field & Behrman, 2003). Boys are more likely than girls to become injured in early childhood, because their play tends to be rougher and more physically active. However, in developing countries, most of the injuries and deaths that take place in early childhood occur not due to high activity levels but as a consequence of the prevalence of automobile travel. In developed countries, the most common cause of injury and death in early childhood is motor vehicle accidents (National Highway Traffic Safety Administration [NHTSA], 2011; Safe Kids Worldwide, 2002). Other common causes of injury and death in early childhood are drowning, falls, fire, and choking (Overpeck et al., 1999).

You might think that rates of injury and death due to accidents in early childhood would be lower in developing countries than in developed countries, since people in developing countries are less likely to own the cars that are the predominant source of early childhood injury and death in developed countries. However, rates of early childhood injury and death due to accidents are actually higher in developing countries. For example, rates of unintentional injury among 1- to 14-year-olds in South Africa are five times higher than in developed countries; in Vietnam, rates are four times higher, and in China three times higher (Safe Kids Worldwide, 2002). This is due to more stringent safety codes in developed countries, such as requiring child seats in cars, strict building codes to prevent fires, and lifeguards in public swimming areas where drowning is a potential danger. An organization called Safe Kids Worldwide (2009) is working to advocate safety measures for young children in both developed and developing countries. It currently has chapters in 16 countries, including China, Brazil, India, and Canada, and is expanding steadily.

Despite the high rates of accidental injury among young children in developing countries, disease is a far greater danger. Only 3% of deaths of children under 5 in developing countries are due to injuries, and virtually all the other 97% are due to illness and disease (UNICEF, 2008). In contrast, even though rates of accidental injuries are much lower in developed countries than in developing countries, accidental injuries are the leading cause of death for young children in developed countries because so few of them die from illness or disease.

My Virtual Child

What can you do to make your child's environment safe for play and exploration?

APPLYING YOUR KNOWLEDGE
. . . as a Nurse

Six-year-old Rosy from Mexico injured herself playing soccer. Her parents take this as evidence that girls should not play soccer, because it is too dangerous and they did not play soccer in the rural village they came from. What might you say to Rosy's parents?

WHAT HAVE YOU LEARNED?

1. What are the average differences in height and weight between children in developed and developing countries? What accounts for these differences?

2. What parts of the brain experience the most notable changes in early childhood?

3. What is the main nutritional deficiency among young children in the United States? How can this deficiency be explained in an environment where food is available in abundance?

4. How has mortality for children age 5 and under changed in the past century worldwide?

Motor Development

One thing for certain about motor activity in early childhood is that there is a lot of it. Children of this age are frequently on the move, enjoying and extending the development of their new motor abilities.

Gross and fine motor skills

Describe changes in gross and fine motor abilities during early childhood, and explain how these changes may have a cultural basis.

LEARNING OBJECTIVE 6.4

In many ways, gross motor development in early childhood extends abilities that first appeared in toddlerhood. Toddlers can hop a step or two with both feet, but from age 3 to 6 young children learn to make more hops in a row and to hop on one foot. Toddlers can jump, but from age 3 to 6 children learn to jump farther from a standing position and to make a running jump. Toddlers begin to climb stairs, but age 3 to 6 is when children learn to climb stairs without support, alternating their feet. Toddlers can throw a ball, but from age 3 to 6, children learn to throw a ball farther and more accurately, and they become better at catching a ball, too. They also increase their running speed and their ability to stop suddenly or change direction. Gender differences in gross motor development appear in early childhood, with boys generally becoming better at skills emphasizing strength or size, such as jumping and throwing a ball, and girls becoming better at body-coordination skills, such as balancing on one foot (Cratty, 1986; Lung et al., 2011). In the preschool period, girls tend to be better than boys at activities involving fine motor skills, such as writing, drawing, and turning the pages of a book (Lung et al., 2011).

Fine motor development in early childhood involves a similar extension of skills that arose in toddlerhood, along with some new skills. As toddlers they could already pick up a small object using two fingers, but now they learn to do it more quickly and precisely. They could already hold a crayon and scribble on a piece of paper, but in early childhood they learn to draw something that is recognizable to others, such as a person, animal, or building. By age 6 they can even draw shapes such as a circle or triangle, and their first letters and some short words, perhaps including their own name. New fine motor skills learned in early childhood include putting on and removing their clothes, using scissors, and using a knife to cut soft food (Cratty, 1986; Piek et al., 2008). Their growing fine motor abilities allow children to learn to do many things their parents had been doing for them, such as using utensils to feed themselves, putting on a coat or shoes, and brushing their teeth.

Of course, nearly all the research on this topic has been done in the West, and to some extent the gross and fine motor skills just described are culturally specific. How can using scissors be a milestone of motor development in a culture where people do not use scissors? In one interesting example of this, researchers asked 10- to 15-year-olds in a New Guinea tribe to draw a person (Martlew & Connolly, 1996). Because they had never tried to draw anything before—their tribe has no written language and no tools to write with or materials to write on—their drawings were very simple and unelaborated. But this does not mean their fine motor skills were less developed than those of much younger children in developed countries who are used to drawing from toddlerhood onward. It could be simply that the task was unfamiliar to them, and that there are fine motor skills specific to their own culture that they excel in. Recently, efforts have been made to develop assessments of gross and fine motor development that are culturally relevant, by basing the norms for motor milestones on local cultural patterns (Scherzer, 2009).

Gross motor skills advance from toddlerhood to early childhood.

Handedness

6.5   **LEARNING OBJECTIVE**   Describe the development of handedness and identify the consequences and cultural views of left-handedness.

handedness preference for using either the right or left hand in gross and fine motor activities

Once children begin drawing or writing in early childhood, they show a clear preference for using their right or left hand, but **handedness** appears long before early childhood. In fact, even prenatally, fetuses show a definite preference for sucking the thumb of their right or left hand, with 90% preferring the right thumb (Hepper et al., 2005). The same 90% proportion of right-handers continues into childhood and throughout adulthood in most cultures (Hinojosa et al., 2003).

If handedness appears so early, that must mean it is determined genetically, right? Actually, the evidence is mixed on this issue. Adopted children are more likely to resemble their biological parents than their adoptive parents in their handedness, suggesting a genetic origin (Carter-Salzman, 1980). On the other hand (pun intended), identical twins are more likely than ordinary siblings to *differ* in handedness, even though identical twins share 100% of their genotype and other siblings only about 50% (Derom et al., 1996). This appears to be due to the fact that twins usually lie in opposite ways within the uterus, whereas most singletons lie toward the left. Lying toward one side allows for greater movement and hence greater development of the hand on the other side, so most twins end up with one being right-handed and one being left-handed while most singletons end up right-handed.

Nevertheless, as usual, culture is also a big part of the picture. Historically, many cultures have viewed left-handedness as dangerous and evil and have suppressed its development in children (Schacter & Ransil, 1996). In Western languages, the word *sinister* is derived from a Latin word meaning "on the left," and many paintings in Western art depict the devil as left-handed. In many Asian and Middle Eastern cultures, only the left hand is supposed to be used for wiping up after defecation, and all other activities are supposed to be done mainly with the right hand. In Africa, even today, using the left hand is suppressed in many cultures from childhood onward, and the prevalence of left-handedness in some African countries is as low as 1%, far lower than the 10% figure in cultures where left-handedness is tolerated (Provins, 1997).

Why have so many cultures regarded being left-handed as evil or dangerous?

Why do so many cultures regard left-handedness with such fear and contempt? Perhaps negative cultural beliefs about left-handedness developed because people noticed that left-handedness was associated with a greater likelihood of various problems. Left-handed infants are more likely to be born prematurely or to experience an unusually difficult birth, and there is evidence that brain damage prenatally or during birth can contribute to left-handedness (Powls et al., 1996). In early and middle childhood, lefthanders are more likely to have problems learning to read and to have other verbal learning disabilities (Natsopoulos et al., 1998). This may have something to do with the fact that about one-fourth of left-handers process language in both hemispheres rather than primarily in the left hemisphere (Knecht et al., 2000). In adulthood, people who are left-handed have lower life expectancy and are more likely to die in motor vehicle accidents (Martin & Freitas, 2002), probably because they are more likely to swerve into oncoming traffic, at least in countries where drivers move forward on the right-hand side of the road.

However, this explanation is not entirely convincing because left-handedness is associated not only with greater likelihood of some types of problems but with excellence and even genius in certain fields. Left-handed children are more likely to show exceptional verbal and math abilities (Bower, 1985; Flannery & Leiderman, 1995). Left-handers are especially likely to have strong visual–spatial abilities, and consequently they are more likely than right-handers to become architects or artists (Holtzen, 2000). Some of the greatest artists in the Western tradition have been left-handed, including Leonardo da Vinci, Michaelangelo, and Pablo Picasso (Schacter & Ransil, 1996). It is worth keeping in mind that the majority of left-handers are in the normal range in their cognitive development, and show neither unusual problems nor unusual gifts. Hence the widespread cultural prejudice against left-handers remains mysterious.

APPLYING YOUR KNOWLEDGE
. . . as a Nurse

At their son Brahim's three-year checkup, his parents complain that he uses his left hand to eat and worry that he may develop left-handedness. They have tried to get him to use his right hand by restricting his left hand at mealtimes, but, when left to his own devices, he goes back to using his left hand. What can you tell them to help them not worry about this?

WHAT HAVE YOU LEARNED?

1. What kinds of changes in the ability to climb stairs occur in children between the ages of 3 and 6?

2. What gender differences in gross motor development appear in early childhood?

3. What new self-care skills accompany improvements in fine motor development in early childhood?

4. What are some genetic and environmental explanations for handedness?

Section 1 VIDEO GUIDE The Growing Child (Length: 1:13)

This video explains many aspects of physical development in the early childhood years, including concepts such as lateralization, automaticity, and rates of growth.

1. In this video, the narrator mentions skills that children are better able to complete due to automaticity. Explain automaticity and list at least three activities that children are better able to perform.

2. What are some benefits of children gaining hand preference?

3. The narrator of this video tells us that the rate of physical growth slows in the early childhood years. What impact would this have on the food and nutritional requirements of children in this age group?

Watch the **Video** The Growing Child
in **MyDevelopmentLab**

Theories of Cognitive Development

In the course of early childhood, children make many remarkable advances in their cognitive development. Several theories shed light on these developments, including Piaget's preoperational stage; "theory of mind," which examines how children think about the thoughts of others; and theories of cultural learning that emphasize the ways that young children gain the knowledge and skills of their culture. These theories complement each other to provide a comprehensive picture of cognitive development in early childhood.

Piaget's preoperational stage of cognitive development

| 6.6 | LEARNING OBJECTIVE | Explain the features of Piaget's preoperational stage of cognitive development. |

In Piaget's theory, early childhood is a crucial turning point in children's cognitive development because this is when thinking becomes *representational* (Piaget, 1952). During the first two years of life, the sensorimotor stage, thinking takes place primarily in association with sensorimotor activities such as reaching and grasping. Gradually toward the end of the sensorimotor period, in the second half of the second year, children begin to internalize the images of their sensorimotor activities, marking the beginning of representational thought.

However, it is during the latter part of toddlerhood and especially in early childhood that we become truly representational thinkers. Language requires the ability to represent the world symbolically, through words, and this is when language skills develop most dramatically. Once we can represent the world through language, we are freed from our momentary sensorimotor experience. With language we can represent not only the present but the past and the future, not only the world as we see it before us but the world as we previously experienced it and the world as it will be—the coming cold (or warm) season, a decline in the availability of food or water, and so on. We can even represent the world as it has never been, through mentally combining ideas—flying monkeys, talking trees, and people who have superhuman powers.

These are marvelous cognitive achievements, and yet early childhood fascinated Piaget not only for what children of this age are able to do cognitively but also for the kinds of mistakes they make. In fact, Piaget termed the age period from 2 to 7 the **preoperational stage**, emphasizing that children of this age were not yet able to perform mental *operations,* that is, cognitive procedures that follow certain logical rules. Piaget specified a number of areas of preoperational cognitive mistakes that are characteristic of early childhood, including conservation, egocentrism, animism, and classification. 👁

CONSERVATION According to Piaget, children in early childhood lack the ability to understand **conservation**, the principle that the amount of a physical substance remains the same even if its physical appearance changes. In his best known demonstration of this mistake, Piaget showed young children two identical glasses holding equal amounts of water and asked them if the two amounts of water were equal. The children typically answered "yes"—they were capable of understanding that much. Then Piaget poured the contents from one of the glasses into a taller, thinner glass, and asked the children again if the two amounts of water were equal. Now most of the children answered "no," failing to understand that the *amount* of water remained the same even though the *appearance* of the water changed. Piaget also demonstrated that children made this error with other substances besides water, as shown in *Figure 6.2.* 👁

👁—Watch the **Video** The Preoperational and Concrete Operational Stage in **MyDevelopmentLab**

preoperational stage cognitive stage from age 2 to 7 during which the child becomes capable of representing the world symbolically—for example, through the use of language—but is still very limited in ability to use mental operations

conservation mental ability to understand that the quantity of a substance or material remains the same even if its appearance changes

👁—Watch the **Video** Conservation Tasks in **MyDevelopmentLab**

Type of Conservation	Modality	Change in Physical Appearance	Average Age Conservation Is Grasped
Number	Number of elements in a collection	Rearranging or dislocating elements	6–7 years
Substance (mass)	Amount of a malleable substance (e.g., clay or liquid)	Altering shape	7–8 years
Length	Length of a line or object	Altering shape or configuration	7–8 years
Area	Amount of surface covered by a set of plane figures	Rearranging the figures	8–9 years
Weight	Weight of an object	Altering shape	9–10 years
Volume	Volume of an object (in terms of water displacement)	Altering shape	14–15 years

Figure 6.2 • **Various substances used in Piaget's conservation task.** What cognitive limitations in young children lead to mistakes in these tasks?

View 1   View 2

Figure 6.3 • **Piaget's three mountains task.** How does performance on this task indicate egocentrism?

⊙─[**Watch** the **Video** Egocentrism Task in **MyDevelopmentLab**

My Virtual Child

When your virtual child begins displaying animism, how will you respond?

centration Piaget's term for young children's thinking as being *centered* or focused on one noticeable aspect of a cognitive problem to the exclusion of other important aspects

reversibility ability to reverse an action mentally

egocentrism cognitive inability to distinguish between one's own perspective and another person's perspective

animism tendency to attribute human thoughts and feelings to inanimate objects and forces

classification ability to understand that objects can be part of more than one cognitive group, for example an object can be classified with red objects as well as with round objects

Piaget interpreted children's mistakes on conservation tasks as indicating two kinds of cognitive deficiencies. The first is **centration**, meaning that young children's thinking is *centered* or focused on one noticeable aspect of a cognitive problem to the exclusion of other important aspects. In the conservation of liquid task, they notice the change in height as the water is poured into the taller glass but neglect to observe the change in width that takes place simultaneously.

Second, young children lack **reversibility**, the ability to reverse an action mentally. When the water is poured from the original glass to the taller glass in the conservation task, anyone who can reverse that action mentally can see that the amount of water would be the same. Young children cannot perform the mental operation of reversibility, so they mistakenly believe the amount of water has changed.

EGOCENTRISM   Another cognitive limitation of the preoperational stage, in Piaget's view, is **egocentrism**, the inability to distinguish between your own perspective and another person's perspective. To demonstrate egocentrism, Piaget and his colleague Barbel Inhelder (1969) devised what they called the "three mountains task" (see **Figure 6.3**). In this task a child is shown a clay model of three different mountains of varying sizes, one with snow on top, one with a red cross, and one with a house. The child walks around the table to see what the mountain looks like from each side, then sits down while the experimenter moves a doll to different points around the table. At each of the doll's locations, the child is shown a series of photographs and asked which one indicates the doll's point of view. In the early years of the preoperational stage, children tend to pick the photo that matches their own perspective, not the doll's. ⊙

One aspect of egocentrism is **animism**, the tendency to attribute human thoughts and feelings to inanimate objects and forces. According to Piaget, when young children believe that the thunder is angry or the moon is following them, it reflects their animistic thinking. It also reflects their egocentrism, in that they are attributing the thoughts and feelings that they might have themselves to things that are inanimate.

Children's play with stuffed animals and dolls is a good example of animistic thinking. When they play with these toys, children frequently attribute human thoughts and feelings to them, often the thoughts and feelings they might have themselves. This is play, but it is a kind of play they take seriously. At age 5, my daughter Paris would sometimes "find" a stuffed puppy or kitten on our porch that she would treat as if it were a live animal that would now be her pet. If you humorously suggested that this might be an especially easy pet to care for, being stuffed—as I made the mistake of doing one day—she took great offense and insisted it was a real animal. To her, at that moment, it was.

CLASSIFICATION   Preoperational children also lack the capacity for **classification**, according to Piaget, meaning that they have difficulty understanding that objects can be simultaneously part of more than one "class" or group. He demonstrated this by showing children a drawing of four blue flowers and 12 yellow flowers and asking them, "Are there more yellow flowers, or are there more flowers?" In early childhood, children would typically answer "More yellow flowers," because they did not understand that yellow flowers could be part of the class "yellow flowers" and simultaneously part of the class "flowers."

Here, as with conservation, the cognitive limitations of centration and lack of reversibility are at the root of the error, in Piaget's view. Young children center on the fact that the yellow flowers are yellow, which leads them to overlook that the yellow flowers are also flowers. They also lack reversibility in that they cannot perform the mental operation of placing the yellow and blue flowers together into the "flowers" class and then moving them back into the "yellow flowers" and "blue flowers" classes, respectively.

PREOPERATIONAL SUBSTAGES: SYMBOLIC FUNCTION AND INTUITIVE THOUGHT Age 2 to 7 is a long period with many changes in a child's cognitive development. Although Piaget called this age span the preoperational stage, he also separated it into two substages. The **symbolic function substage** is the first substage, lasting from about age 2 to 4. This is when the child first becomes capable of representational thought and of using symbols to represent the world. As mentioned earlier, language is the most important indicator of the capacity to think in terms of symbols, because words are symbols. Play is another area where symbolic functions are evident early in the preoperational stage. Children of this age can use a stick to represent a magic wand, or dirt and water to represent chocolate pudding.

The second substage of the preoperational stage is the **intuitive thought substage**, lasting from age 4 to 7. During this period children become highly curious about the world, frequently asking "Why?" when others provide them with information. This shows that they have begun to think logically, because their questions indicate that they are wondering about how one event leads to another event. Through their questions they learn more about the nature of the world, and they expand their knowledge. However, they are unable to explain how they know what they know. This is why Piaget called this substage *intuitive*; children in this substage do not know why they know something, they just know it. For example, even if they happen to state the correct answer when faced with a conservation or classification problem, they have difficulty explaining why their answer is correct. Here, too, the preoperational child's cognitive functioning is framed by Piaget primarily in terms of what is yet to be learned.

EVALUATING PIAGET'S THEORY Piaget's theory of preoperational thought in early childhood has been challenged in the decades since he proposed it. The criticisms focus on two issues: claims that he underestimated children's cognitive capabilities, and claims that development is more continuous and less stagelike than he proposed.

Many studies over the past several decades have shown that children ages 2–7 are cognitively capable of more than Piaget recognized. With regard to conservation tasks, it has been shown that even 3-year-old children can give correct answers in conservation of number tasks, as long as only two or three items are used (Gelman, 1969; Vilette, 2002). By the time children learn to count to 10 or more, usually by age 4 or 5, they can use counting to solve conservation of number tasks involving larger numbers of items. By age 6—still in the preoperational stage, according to Piaget—they do not even need to count to solve the task, because they understand that the number of items remains the same if no items are added or removed (Klahr & MacWhinney, 1998).

In other ways, too, children ages 2–7 are less prone to cognitive errors than Piaget proposed. Regarding egocentrism, when the three mountains task is modified so that familiar objects are used instead of the three mountain model, children give less egocentric responses (Newcombe & Huttenlocher, 1992). Studies using other methods also show that 2- to 7-year-old children are less egocentric than Piaget thought. As described in Chapter 5, even toddlers show the beginnings of an ability to take others' perspectives, when they discern what they can do to annoy a sibling (Dunn, 1988). By age 4, children switch to shorter, simpler sentences when talking to toddlers or babies, showing a distinctly unegocentric ability to take the perspective of the younger children (Bryant & Barrett, 2007).

Regarding Piaget's stage claims, research has shown that the development of cognitive skills in childhood is less stagelike and more continuous than Piaget believed (Bibok et al., 2009). Remember, Piaget's stage theory asserts that movement from one stage to another represents a wholesale cognitive shift, a change not just in specific cognitive skills but in how children think. In this view, children ages 2–7 are incapable of performing mental operations, and then in the next stage they become able to do so. However, as we have just seen, research has generally shown that the ability to perform mental operations changes gradually over the course of childhood (Case, 1999).

How does animism reflect young children's egocentrism?

symbolic function substage first substage of the preoperational stage, lasting from about age 2 to age 4, when the child first becomes capable of representational thought and of using symbols to represent the world

intuitive thought substage second substage of the preoperational stage, lasting from age 4 to 7, during which children begin to understand how one event leads to another event but cannot say why they know what they know

Understanding thinking: The development of "theory of mind"

LEARNING OBJECTIVE   Explain what "theory of mind" is and the evidence for how it develops during early childhood.

Current research on cognitive development in early childhood has moved beyond Piaget's theories. One popular area of research in recent years is **theory of mind**, the ability to understand thinking processes in one's self and others. Having a theory of mind involves knowing that one has a mind, that other people have minds, and that minds do certain kinds of things. When you have an understanding of mind, you can be aware of mental states in which you think, dream, understand, believe, and even trick or deceive. ◉

Understanding how others think is a challenge even for adults, but the beginnings of theory of mind appear very early, in infancy. Through behavior such as joint attention and the use of prelanguage vocalizations, infants show that they understand that others have mental states such as intentionality (Tomasello & Rakoczy, 2003). By age 2, as they begin to use language more, children show increasing recognition that others have thoughts and emotions that can be contrasted with their own (e.g., "That man is mad!" or "I like applesauce. Brother no like applesauce."). At age 2, children begin to use words that refer to mental processes, such as "think," "remember," and "pretend" (Flavell et al., 2002). By age 3, children know it is possible for them and others to imagine something that is not physically present (such as an ice cream cone). They can respond to an imaginary event as if it has really happened, and they realize that others can do the same (Andrews et al., 2003). This understanding becomes the basis of pretend play for many years to come.

However, there are limits to 3-year-olds' theory of mind, and crucial changes take place in the course of early childhood. They are better than 2-year-olds at understanding that others have thoughts and feelings that are different than their own, but they find it difficult to take others' perspectives. Perspective-taking ability advances considerably from age 3 to 6 (Bigelow & Dugas, 2008), when children's understanding of their own and others' minds also increases dramatically. There are several factors related to these changes, including the maturation of the prefrontal cortex (Stone et al., 1998) and having siblings (Perner et al., 1994). Many early studies found that having older siblings was a benefit in developing theory of mind skills (Lewis et al., 1996) and more recent studies have found that there is a benefit for the older sibling as well (Peterson, 2000). If you have a sibling, you can understand why having siblings would help a child develop theory of mind. There is another child in the house with whom you have to negotiate, play, and generally get along with.

This change is vividly demonstrated in recent research involving *false-belief tasks*. In one experiment testing understanding of false beliefs, children are shown a doll named Maxi who places chocolate in a cabinet and then leaves the room (Amsterlaw & Wellman, 2006). Next another doll, his mother, enters the room and moves the chocolate to a different place. Children are then asked, where will Maxi look for the chocolate when he returns? Most 3-year-old children answer erroneously that Maxi will look for the chocolate in the new place, where his mother stored it. In contrast, by age 4 most children recognize that Maxi will believe falsely that the chocolate is in the cabinet where he left it. The proportion of children who understand this correctly rises even higher by age 5. ◉

In another well-known test of theory of mind, children are shown a box that appears to contain a kind of candy called "Smarties" and asked what they think is in the box (Gopnik & Astington, 1988). After they answer "candy" or "Smarties" they are shown that the box in fact contains pencils. Then they are asked what another person, who has not been shown the contents, will think is in the box. "Candy" or "Smarties"

◉—Watch the **Video** Theory of Mind in **MyDevelopmentLab**

APPLYING YOUR KNOWLEDGE
. . . as a Parent

When you complain of a headache, your 3-year-old daughter offers you her teddy bear for comfort. How can you explain this?

◉—Watch the **Video** False Belief Task in **MyDevelopmentLab**

theory of mind ability to understand thinking processes in one's self and others

is the correct answer, showing theory of mind; "pencils" is incorrect. Most children pass the test by the time they are 4 or 5 years old.

By age 6, nearly all children solve false-belief tasks easily. Notice the similarity to Piaget's description of the developmental course of egocentrism. Poor understanding of theory of mind can be seen as a kind of egocentrism, and with Piaget's egocentrism tasks as well as false-belief tasks, children make great advances in the course of early childhood.

Some theory of mind research has now been done in other cultures, enough to show that the development of theory of mind depends strongly on cultural context and language. For example, Chinese languages have several different forms of the word *belief,* some of which signify that the belief is false; the use of these forms of *belief* in false-belief tasks make it easy for Chinese children to solve them (Tardif et al., 2004). Also, not all languages have words to signify mental states. Among the Quechua people of Peru studied by Penelope Vinden (1996), their language has no terms for mental states. Perhaps for this reason, children there do poorly on false-belief tasks not just in early childhood but through middle childhood as well.

Cultural learning in early childhood

Identify the ways that cultural learning takes place in early childhood.

LEARNING OBJECTIVE 6.8

In Piaget's depiction of cognitive development, the young child is like a solitary little scientist gradually mastering the concepts of conservation and classification and overcoming the errors of egocentrism and animism. Vygotsky's sociocultural theory of learning takes a much different approach, viewing cognitive development as a social and cultural process (see Chapter 5). Children learn not through their individual interactions with the environment but through the social process of guided participation, as they interact with a more knowledgeable member of the culture (often an older sibling or parent) in the course of daily activities.

Early childhood is a period when this kind of cultural learning comes to the fore. More than in toddlerhood, young children have the capacity for learning culturally specific skills. The Mayan example that began this chapter provides one illustration. A 5-year-old can readily learn the skills involved in making tortillas, whereas a 2-year-old would not have the necessary learning abilities, motor skills, or impulse control (Rogoff, 2003). In many cultures, the end of early childhood, ages 5–6, is the time when children are first given important responsibilities in the family for food preparation, child care, and animal care (LeVine & New, 2008). During early childhood they acquire the cultural learning necessary for these duties, sometimes through direct instruction but more often through observing and participating in adults' activities.

It is not only in traditional cultures that cultural learning takes place via guided participation. For example, a child in an economically developed country might help his parents prepare a grocery shopping list, and in the course of this process learn culturally valued skills such as reading, using lists as tools for organization and planning, and calculating sums of money (Rogoff, 2003). Children in Western countries are also encouraged to speak up and hold conversations. For example, over dinner American parents often ask their young children a series of questions ("What songs did you sing at preschool? What did you have for a snack?"), thereby preparing them for the question-and-answer structure of formal schooling they

How is cultural learning taking place here?

will enter in middle childhood (Martini, 1996). This is in contrast to cultures from Asia to northern Canada in which silence is valued, especially in children, and children who talk frequently are viewed as immature and low in intelligence (Rogoff, 2003).

Two factors make cultural learning in developed countries different from cultural learning in traditional cultures. One is that children in developed countries are often apart from their families for a substantial part of the day, in a preschool or another group-care setting. Cultural learning takes place in the preschool setting, of course—recall the example of Lars that began this chapter—but it is mostly a more direct kind of instruction (e.g., learning letters) rather than the cultural learning that takes place through guided participation in daily activities within the family. Second, the activities of adults in a complex economy are less accessible to children's learning than the activities that children learn through guided participation in traditional cultures, such as child care, tending animals, and food preparation. Most jobs in a complex economy require advanced skills of reading, analyzing information, and using technology, so there is a limit to which children can learn these skills through guided participation, especially in early childhood.

WHAT HAVE YOU LEARNED?

1. According to Piaget, what two kinds of cognitive deficiencies are evident in children's mistakes on conservation tasks?
2. What are the two main issues raised by critics of Piaget's theory of preoperational thought?
3. What advances in theory of mind take place between the ages of 2 and 3?
4. What two factors make cultural learning in developed countries different from cultural learning in traditional cultures?

Early Childhood Education

Traditionally in many cultures, formal schooling has started at about age 7. This is the age at which children have been viewed as first capable of learning the skills of reading, writing, and math. However, because the need to learn how to use words and numbers is so strong in the modern information-based economy, in many countries school now begins earlier than ever. In developed countries about three-fourths of 3- to 5-year-old children are enrolled in group child care, preschool, or kindergarten (UNESCO, 2006, p. 20). In developing countries, the percentages are lower but rising. In the United States, about half of American states now fund some preschool programs for 4-year-old children, usually focusing on children from low-income families. ◉

Watch the **Video** Early Literacy Development in **MyDevelopmentLab**

The importance of preschool quality

| 6.9 | **LEARNING OBJECTIVE** | Identify the features that are most important in preschool quality. |

Watch the **Video** Choosing the Right School in **MyDevelopmentLab**

What are the cognitive and social effects of attending preschool? For the most part, attending preschool is beneficial for young children (Campbell et al., 2002). Cognitive benefits of attending preschool include higher verbal skills and stronger performance on measures of memory and listening comprehension (Clarke-Stewart & Allhusen, 2002). Children from low-income families especially benefit cognitively from preschool (Loeb et al., 2004; Vandell, 2004). They perform better on tests of school readiness than children of similar backgrounds who did not attend preschool. ◉

There are also social benefits to attending preschool. Children who attend preschool are generally more independent and socially confident than children who remain home (National Institute of Child Health and Human Development [NICHD] Early Child Care Research Network, 2006). However, there appear to be social costs as well. Children attending preschool have been observed to be less compliant, less respectful toward adults, and more aggressive than other children (Belsky et al., 2006). Furthermore, these negative social effects may endure long past preschool age. In one large national (U.S.) longitudinal study, children who attended preschool for more than 10 hours per week were more disruptive in class once they entered school, in follow-ups extending through sixth grade (NICHD Early Child Care Research Network, 2006).

Yet these findings concerning the overall positive or negative outcomes associated with preschool can be misleading. Preschool programs vary vastly in quality, and many studies have found that the quality of preschool child care is more important than simply the fact of whether children are in preschool or not (Clarke-Stewart & Allhusen, 2002; Maccoby & Lewis, 2003; NICHD Early Child Care Research Network, 2006).

What factors should parents consider when searching for a high-quality preschool experience for their children? There is a broad consensus among scholars of early childhood development that the most important features include the following (Lavzer & Goodson, 2006; National Association for the Education of Young Children [NAEYC], 2010; Vandell et al., 2005):

- *Education and training of teachers.* Unlike teachers at higher grade levels, preschool teachers often are not required to have education or credentials specific to early childhood education. Preschool teachers who have training in early childhood education provide a better social and cognitive environment.
- *Class size and child–teacher ratio.* Experts recommend no more than 20 children in a classroom, and a ratio of children to preschool teachers no higher than five to ten 3-year-olds per teacher or seven to ten 4-year-olds per teacher.
- *Age-appropriate materials and activities.* In early childhood, children learn more through active engagement with materials rather than through formal lessons or rote learning.
- *Teacher–child interactions.* Teachers should spend most of their time in interactions with the children rather than with each other. They should circulate among the children, asking questions, offering suggestions, and assisting them when necessary.

Notice that the criteria for high-quality preschools do not include intense academic instruction. Here again there is a broad consensus among early childhood scholars that preschool teaching should be based on *developmentally appropriate educational practice* (NAEYC, 2010). At the preschool age, this means that learning should involve exploring and discovering through relatively unstructured, hands-on experiences—learning about the physical world through playing in a water or sand area, for example, or learning new words through songs and nursery rhymes, as you will see in the **Research Focus: The Montessori Preschool Program** feature on page 256. In contrast, structured academic learning, with worksheets and memorization tasks, mostly in large groups, is discouraged as developmentally inappropriate for preschool children. Several studies have shown the benefits of developmentally appropriate educational practice for preschool children, both cognitively and socially (Hart et al., 1998; Huffman & Speer, 2000). Generally, a constructivist approach (see Chapter 1) that is *child-centered*, like Montessori programs, benefits children's learning because children are allowed to explore and discover—through play, touch, art, and individual interest—in a largely self-paced and self-structured way. *Teacher-directed* approaches stress academic learning and are almost always given at a set pace, where all children must follow along.

APPLYING YOUR KNOWLEDGE
. . . as a Preschool Teacher

The parent of one of your students questions why you spend so much time letting the children play with sand and sing songs rather than teaching them academic skills. How do you respond?

My Virtual Child

What type of preschool program would you choose for your virtual child? Why?

RESEARCH FOCUS   The Montessori Preschool Program

About a century ago, an Italian doctor named Maria Montessori developed a new approach to enhancing the cognitive development of young children. She had observed that children from poor families were often well behind their peers by the time they entered school, and she sought to find a way to assist them in preschool so that they would have a better chance of school success.

Montessori (1964) was focused on making her approach appropriate for the developmental stage of early childhood. She believed that young children should not be subjected to tests and grades. In her view, children have a natural desire to learn about the world that should be encouraged and enhanced. The program she developed emphasizes learning through self-directed exploration. Children are provided with a variety of different materials and activities, and they learn in a self-directed way as they choose from among the options. Teachers are present and sometimes facilitate small-group activities to enhance children's development of social skills, but the emphasis is on allowing children to learn through self-initiated discovery.

Children attending Montessori schools show cognitive and social advantages.

Montessori's design for preschool programs proved instantly popular, and remains popular today. There are thousands of Montessori preschool programs worldwide, but until recently they had not been evaluated systematically through research. Now studies by developmental psychologist Angeline Lillard (2008; Lillard & Else-Quest, 2006) have demonstrated the validity of Montessori's insights.

Lillard compared two groups of 3- to 6-year-old children. One group of children had attended a Montessori preschool, and the other group attended other types of preschools. All the children in the non-Montessori group had originally applied to Montessori schools but were not able to enter due to space limitations, with admission determined by a random lottery. This was a crucial aspect of the study design; do you see why? If the researchers had simply compared children in Montessori schools with children in non-Montessori schools, any differences would have been difficult to interpret, because there may have been many other differences between the families of children in the two types of schools (e.g., children in Montessori schools may have more-educated parents). Because the families of children in the non-Montessori schools had also applied to get their children into the Montessori schools, it can be assumed that the family backgrounds of the children in the two groups were similar.

The children who attended Montessori preschools were more advanced in both cognitive and social development than the children who attended the other preschools. Cognitively, the Montessori children scored higher on tests of reading and math skills than the other children. They also performed better on a card-sorting task that tested the ability to apply decision rules. Socially, in playground observations the Montessori children engaged more in cooperative play and less in rough, chaotic play such as wrestling. In sum, the Montessori approach appears to provide children with a setting that encourages self-initiated, active learning and thereby enhances cognitive and social development.

Cross-national variations

6.10   LEARNING OBJECTIVE   Describe the distinctive practices of Japanese preschools and how they reflect cultural values.

THINKING CULTURALLY

How does the Japanese practice of having children wear identical uniforms in preschool represent a custom complex? That is, what cultural beliefs underlie this cultural practice?

Although attending preschool has become a typical experience among children in developed countries, there is great variation in how countries structure preschool and what they wish young children to learn. In most countries, parents hope for social benefits from preschool, but there is variation between countries in the expectations of cognitive and academic benefits. In some countries, such as China and the United States, learning basic academic skills is one of the primary goals of having children attend preschool (Johnson et al., 2003; Tobin et al., 2009). In other countries, such as Japan and most of Europe, learning academic skills is a low priority in preschool (Hayashi et al., 2009). Rather, preschool is mainly a time for learning social skills such as how to function as a member of a group.

Japan is of particular interest in this area, because Japanese students have long been at or near the top of international comparisons in reading, math, and science from middle childhood through high school (National Center for Education Statistics [NCES], 2011). You might expect, then, that one reason for this success is that they begin academic instruction earlier than in other countries, but just the opposite turns out to be true. In one study of Japanese and American parents and preschool teachers, only 2% of the Japanese listed "to give children a good start academically" as one of the top three reasons for young children to attend preschool (Tobin et al., 2009). In contrast, over half the Americans named this as one of the top three reasons. There was a similarly sharp contrast in response to the item "to give children the experience of being a member of the group." Sixty percent of Japanese endorsed this reason for preschool, compared to just 20% of the Americans.

Preschools in Japan teach nothing about reading and numbers. Instead, the focus is on group play, so that children will learn the values of cooperation and sharing. Preschool children wear identical uniforms, with different colors to indicate their classroom membership. They each have the same equipment, which they keep in identical drawers. Through being introduced to these cultural practices in preschool, children also learn collectivistic Japanese values.

Japanese preschools emphasize group play and cooperation.

Preschool as a cognitive intervention

Describe early intervention programs and their outcomes.

LEARNING OBJECTIVE **6.11**

One type of preschool experience that focuses intensively on cognitive development is the **early intervention program**. These are programs directed at young children who are at risk for later school problems because they come from low-income families. The goal of early intervention programs is to give these children extra cognitive stimulation in early childhood so that they will have a better opportunity to succeed once they enter school.

By far the largest early intervention program in the United States is Project Head Start. The program began in 1965 and is still going strong, with about 1 million American children enrolled each year (Office of Head Start, 2010). The program provides one or two years of preschool, but it also includes other services. Children in the program receive free meals and health care. Parents receive health care as well as job-training services. Parents are also directly involved in the Head Start program, serving on councils that make policies for the centers and sometimes serving as teachers in the classroom. Canada has a similar program focusing on First Nations minority children who are often at risk for later school problems.

Do these programs work? The answer is not simple. The main goal of Head Start originally was to raise the intelligence of children from low-income backgrounds so that their academic performance would be enhanced once they entered school. Children in Head Start show a boost in IQ and academic achievement after their participation in the program, compared to children from similar backgrounds who did not take part, so in this respect, yes, the program worked. However, a consistent pattern in Head Start and many other early intervention programs is that the IQ and achievement gains fade within 2 or 3 years of entering elementary school (Barnett & Hustedt, 2005).

early intervention program program directed at young children who are at risk for later problems, intended to prevent problems from developing

This is not surprising in view of the fact that children in the program typically enter poorly funded, low-quality public schools after their Head Start experience, but nevertheless the fading of the initial gains was unexpected and fell short of the original goals of the program.

However, there have been some favorable results from the Head Start program, too (Brooks-Gunn, 2003; Resnick, 2010). Children who have participated in Head Start are less likely to be placed in special education or to repeat a grade. It should be kept in mind that Head Start is a program with a million children in tens of thousands of programs, and inevitably the programs vary in quality (Resnick, 2010; Zigler & Styfco, 2004). The more parents are involved in the program, the more their child demonstrates benefits in terms of academic and social skills (Marcon, 1999).

Head Start was designed to serve children ages 4–6 and give them a "head start" in school readiness, but in the 1990s a new program, Early Head Start, was initiated for low-income families and their children under the age of 3 (Raikes et al., 2010). The goal of this program was to see if greater effects on cognitive and social development could be obtained by beginning the intervention at an earlier age. Sometimes the program entails center care, sometimes home visits by skilled child care workers, and sometimes a mix of the two. Research on the effects of Early Head Start is now in progress, but so far the mixed programs (center care combined with home visits) appears to have the strongest positive effects on cognitive and social development (Robinson et al., 2009).

Some small-scale, intensive early intervention programs have shown a broader range of enduring effects. One of the best known is the High Scope Preschool Project, which entailed a full-day two-year preschool program for children from low-income families (Schweinhart et al., 2004). The High Scope children showed the familiar pattern of an initial gain in IQ and academic achievement followed by a decline, but they demonstrated many other benefits of the program, compared to a control group. In adolescence, the girls were less likely to become pregnant and the boys were less likely to be arrested, and both boys and girls were more likely to graduate from high school and attend college (see **Figure 6.4**). At age 27, the High Scope participants were more likely to be married and to own their home, less likely to have spent time in prison, and their monthly income was higher. At age 40, High Scope participants still displayed benefits of the program in a wide range of areas, including income and family stability. This program shows that an intensive, high-quality early intervention program can have profound and lasting benefits.

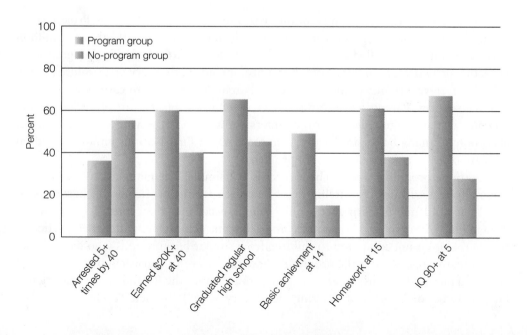

Figure 6.4 • **Major findings of the High Scope preschool study.** High Scope participants showed better academic performance, IQ scores, and earning potential and were less likely to be arrested later in life than other children.

WHAT HAVE YOU LEARNED?

1. What constitutes developmentally appropriate educational practice for preschool children?
2. How do Japanese preschools differ from American preschools?
3. What is the goal of early intervention programs?
4. How have results of small-scale early intervention programs such as the High Scope Preschool Project differed from those of programs such as Head Start?

Language Development

As we saw in Chapter 5, by age 3 children are remarkably adept at using language. Nevertheless, their language development from age 3 to 6 continues at a remarkable pace, in areas including vocabulary, grammar, and pragmatics.

Advances in vocabulary and grammar

Explain how advances in vocabulary and grammar occur in early childhood.

LEARNING OBJECTIVE   6.12

Perhaps the most amazing advance at this age is the growth in children's vocabulary. The average 3-year-old has a vocabulary of about 1,000 words; by age 6, the average vocabulary has increased to over 2,500 words (Bloom, 1998). This means they are adding words nearly every day (Clark, 1995). Interestingly, language development does not proceed at the same pace in all families around the world. Children in lower-SES families tend to lag behind children in the middle class in vocabulary development (Hart & Risley, 1995), and this can lead to lower performance in school. Children in lower-SES families are not exposed to as many different words, and they have smaller vocabularies and use simpler grammar than children in the middle class. However, even children in poorer families acquire new words regularly and build their vocabularies over the preschool period.

How does children's language progress so quickly? Clearly children's brains are built for learning language, as noted in the previous chapter, and early childhood is a **sensitive period** for language learning, when the capacity for learning new words is especially pronounced (Pinker, 1994). As we learned in Chapter 5, young children add new words to their vocabulary through a process known as *fast mapping* (Ganger & Brent, 2004; Swingley, 2010). This means that as young children learn new words they begin to form a mental map of interconnected sets of word categories. When they hear a word the first time they instantly connect it to one of these categories based on how the word is used in a sentence and how it seems to be related to words they already know, to help discern its meaning.

The kinds of words children fast-map earliest depend partly on the language. Children learning Eastern languages such as Chinese, Japanese, and Korean tend to learn more verbs than nouns at first, because sentences often emphasize verbs but only imply the nouns without speaking them (Kim et al., 2000). In contrast, children learning English and other Western languages fast-map nouns earlier than verbs, because nouns are prominent in these languages. In both Eastern and Western languages, modifiers (such as *large, narrow, pretty, low*) are added more slowly than nouns and verbs (Mintz, 2005).

As young children add new words to their vocabulary, they also continue to learn **grammar**, which is a language's distinctive system of rules. Some examples of rules

sensitive period in the course of development, a period when the capacity for learning in a specific area is especially pronounced

grammar a language's distinctive system of rules

This is a wug.

**Now there is another one.
There are two of them.
There are two _____.**

Figure 6.5 • **Berko's language study.** How do the results of this study show young children's grasp of grammar?

include single/plural forms; past, present, and future tense; word order; and use of articles (such as "a" and "the") and prepositions (such as "under" and "by"). Without any formal training, young children grasp the grammatical rules of their language with few errors simply by hearing and using the language in daily interactions. By age 4, it is estimated that children use correct grammar in 90% of their statements (Guasti, 2000; Pinker, 1994).

But how do we know they have really learned the rules of their language? Couldn't they simply be repeating what they hear older children and adults say? In a classic study investigating this question, Jean Berko (1958) had young children respond to questions involving nonsense words (see **Figure 6.5**). Although they had never heard the words before—Berko had made them up—the children were able to apply the grammar of English and use nouns in plural and possessive forms. As noted in Chapter 5 (p. 207), the readiness with which children learn grammar indicates that they possess what Chomsky (1965) called a language acquisition device, which is an innate capacity for grasping quickly a language's rules.

Pragmatics: Social and cultural rules of language

6.13	**LEARNING OBJECTIVE**	Describe how children learn pragmatics in early childhood, and identify to what extent these social rules are culturally based.

pragmatics social and cultural context of language that guides people as to what is appropriate to say and not to say in a given social situation

THINKING CULTURALLY

Can you think of examples of how pragmatics have changed in your culture compared to a century ago?

How might the language used in this kind of play demonstrate a grasp of pragmatics?

In order to use language effectively, children must learn not only vocabulary and grammar but the social rules or **pragmatics** for using language in interaction with others. Pragmatics guide us in knowing what to say—and what not to say—in a given social situation. For example, children learn to say "please" when asking for something and "thank you" when they receive something.

Even before they begin speaking, children begin learning pragmatics through gestures, for example when they wave "bye-bye" to someone when leaving. By the age of 2, they know the pragmatics of a basic conversation, including taking turns speaking (Pan & Snow, 1999). However, at this age they have not yet grasped the pragmatics of sustaining a conversation on one topic, and they tend to change topics rapidly as new things occur to them, without much awareness of the other person's perspective.

By age 4, children are more sensitive to the characteristics of their conversational partner and will adjust their speech accordingly. In one study using hand puppets, 4-year-olds used different kinds of speech when acting out different puppet roles (Anderson, 2000). When playing a socially dominant role such as teacher or doctor they used commands frequently, whereas when playing subordinate roles such as student or patient they spoke more politely.

The use of pragmatics represents not only social understanding but cultural knowledge. All cultures have their own rules for what kinds of speech can be used in what kinds of situations. For example, some cultures require children to address adults with respectful titles, such as "Mr." for adult men. Many cultures have words that are classified as "bad words" that are not supposed to be spoken, especially by children.

These are the kinds of pragmatics children learn in the course of early childhood, but while they are learning them there can be some embarrassing moments for parents along the way. One day when she was about 3 years old my daughter Paris and I were going through the checkout line in the grocery store, and she said to the clerk, apropos of nothing, "When

I grow to a mommy, I'm going to have a baby in my tummy!" On another occasion, at age 4 my son Miles was talking about how he planned to live to be 100 years old and asked me if I would still be around by then. "Probably not," I said. "You're only four years old, and I'm forty-six." "Ooohhh," he said with genuine concern in his voice, "then you don't have many years left!" Adults understand intuitively that young children lack a sense of pragmatics, so they tend to find such moments amusing rather than offensive. By middle childhood, most children learn when it is culturally appropriate to speak and when it is best to keep your thoughts to yourself.

My Virtual Child

What are some cultural rules that your virtual child will need to learn in order to communicate with others in your environment?

WHAT HAVE YOU LEARNED?

1. What changes to a child's vocabulary occur between the ages of 3 and 6?
2. How do children learning Eastern languages differ from children learning Western languages in the kinds of words that they fast-map earliest?
3. Give an example of a young child showing an early understanding of pragmatics.
4. How do pragmatics represent cultural knowledge?

Section 2 VIDEO GUIDE Theory of Mind Across Cultures (Length: 6:44)

This video contains several demonstrations of children from various countries performing tests of theory of mind.

1. How does acquiring a theory of mind impact a child's social interactions?

2. According to this video, does acquiring a theory of mind occur at the same age across cultures?

3. Can you think of any interactions that may help or hinder a child in developing a theory of mind?

⊙—Watch the Video Theory of Mind Across Cultures in MyDevelopmentLab

LEARNING OBJECTIVES

6.14 Identify advances in emotional understanding and self-regulation during early childhood.

6.15 Describe moral development in early childhood, including empathy, modeling, and morality as cultural learning.

6.16 Describe the roles that parents and peers play in gender socialization, and explain how gender schemas lead to self-socialization.

6.17 Describe the four types of parenting "styles" and the outcomes associated with each, and explain why those outcomes are complex.

6.18 Describe the major cultural variations in approaches to parenting.

6.19 Describe the main cultural variations in how parents discipline young children, and explain how cultural context influences children's responses to discipline.

6.20 Identify the most common features of sibling relationships worldwide, and describe how children with no siblings differ from other children.

6.21 Explain how the quality of friendships changes from toddlerhood to early childhood, and describe the role of play and aggression in young children's friendships.

6.22 Identify the rates and consequences of media use in early childhood.

Emotional Regulation and Gender Socialization

APPLYING YOUR KNOWLEDGE
. . . as a Preschool Teacher

A child in your class loves to answer questions and regularly blurts out answers. What might you do to help the child learn the appropriate behavior?

After the emotional volatility and intensity of the toddler years, children make great advances in emotional self-regulation in early childhood. Also notable in their emotional development during this time is increasing empathy and a greater grasp of the moral system of their culture, learned in part by modeling their behavior after the behavior of others who are important in their lives. With regard to gender development, early childhood is a life stage of great importance, with children gaining a fuller understanding of the gender roles and expectations of their culture and beginning to enforce those gender roles on others as well as on themselves.

Emotional regulation

6.14 LEARNING OBJECTIVE

Identify advances in emotional understanding and self-regulation during early childhood.

Early childhood is a time of great advances in emotional development, specifically in emotional understanding and self-regulation. With respect to emotional understanding, in the course of early childhood children become adept at understanding the sources of other people's expressed emotions (Eisenberg & Fabes, 2006). In studies that show children cards depicting expressed emotions, by age 5 children are usually accurate in explaining the emotions of the situation (e.g., "She's happy because she got a present," or "He's sad because his mom scolded him"). They are also adept at understanding how emotional states are the basis of subsequent actions, for example that an angry child is more likely to hit someone (Kagan & Hershkowitz, 2005).

Young children become more adept not only at understanding others' emotions but at controlling their own. In fact, **emotional self-regulation** is considered to be one of the major developmental tasks of early childhood (Grolnick et al., 2006). Developing emotional self-regulation is crucial to social relations, because maintaining harmonious social relations often requires us to restrain our immediate impulses—to wait in line, to let others go first in a game or a conversation, or to take fewer pieces of candy than we really want. Across cultures, early childhood is a time when expectations for emotional self-regulation increase (Whiting & Edwards, 1988). From age 2 to 6, extremes of emotional expression such as temper tantrums, crying, and physical aggression decrease (Alink et al., 2006; Carlson, 2003). In the brain, the development of the frontal cortex promotes this process, because this is the part of the brain most involved in emotional self-regulation (Bell & Wolfe, 2007).

Another key reason why emotional outbursts decline during early childhood is that children learn strategies for regulating their emotions (Grolnick et al., 2006). Experimental studies have identified the strategies that young children use when presented with an emotionally challenging situation, such as being given a disappointing prize after being led to expect a very attractive prize (Eisenberg & Fabes, 2007). Some of the most effective strategies are leaving the situation; talking to themselves; redirecting their attention to a different activity; and seeking comfort from an attachment figure. These strategies are part of what researchers call *effortful control,* when children focus their attention on managing their emotions (Cipriano & Stifter, 2010). Parents can help young children develop effortful control, by providing emotional and physical comfort when their children are upset, by suggesting possible strategies for managing emotions, and by modeling effortful control themselves (Katz & Windecker-Nelson, 2004).

Children vary in their success at achieving emotional self-regulation in early childhood, depending both on their temperament and on the socialization for self-regulation provided by parents and others. Children who have problems of **undercontrol** in early childhood have inadequately developed emotional self-regulation. These children are at risk for **externalizing problems**, such as aggression and conflict with others, in early childhood and beyond (Cole et al., 2003). However, developing **overcontrol**, an excessive degree of self-regulation of emotions, is also problematic. This can lead to **internalizing problems**, such as anxiety and depression, in early childhood and beyond (Grolnick et al., 2006). Throughout life, internalizing problems is more common among females and externalizing problems is more common among males (Frick & Kimonis, 2008; Ollendick et al., 2008).

Successful emotional regulation means developing a level of effortful control that is between the two extremes. As Erik Erikson (1950) noted in proposing that early childhood is the stage of **initiative vs. guilt** (see Chapter 1), children need to learn emotional control but without being so tightly regulated that they feel excess guilt and their ability to initiate activities is undermined. But different cultures have different views of what the optimal level of emotional control is (Chen et al., 2007). Behavior that looks like undercontrol in one culture could be valued as a healthy expression of vigor in another culture, at least for boys (LeVine & New, 2010). Behavior that looks like overcontrol in one culture could be valued as the virtue of reticence in another culture (Rogoff, 2003).

emotional self-regulation ability to exercise control over one's emotions

undercontrol trait of having inadequate emotional self-regulation

externalizing problems problems that involve others, such as aggression

overcontrol trait of having excessive emotional self-regulation

internalizing problems problems that entail turning distress inward, toward the self, such as depression and anxiety

initiative vs. guilt in Erikson's lifespan theory, the early childhood stage, in which the alternatives are learning to plan activities in a purposeful way, or being afflicted with excess guilt that undermines initiative

My Virtual Child

What are some strategies that you might use to help your virtual child learn to regulate his or her emotions in a culturally appropriate way?

Extreme expressions of emotion decrease in the course of early childhood as effortful control develops.

Moral development

6.15   **LEARNING OBJECTIVE**   Describe moral development in early childhood, including empathy, modeling, and morality as cultural learning.

Watch the Video Moral Development in **MyDevelopmentLab**

As described in Chapter 5, toddlerhood is when the sociomoral emotions first appear, such as guilt, shame, embarrassment, and pride. Even in toddlerhood, the sociomoral emotions are shaped by cultural standards. Toddlers feel guilt, shame, or embarrassment when they violate the expected standards for behavior indicated by those in their social environment, and pride when they comply.

One sociomoral emotion that is especially important to moral development in early childhood is empathy. As we have seen, toddlers and even infants show indications of empathy, but the capacity for empathy develops further in early childhood (Eisenberg & Valiente, 2004). Children become better at perspective-taking, and being able to understand how others think and feel makes them more empathic. Empathy promotes prosocial behavior such as being generous or helpful. It contributes to the moral understanding of principles such as avoiding harm and being fair, because through empathy children understand how their behavior would make another person feel. As empathy increases, prosocial behavior increases over the course of early childhood (Eisenberg et al., 2006).

In early childhood, moral development advances further as children gain a more detailed and complex understanding of the rules and expectations of their culture. Toddlers know when others approve or disapprove of something they have done, and usually respond with the appropriate sociomoral emotion. However, in early childhood there is greater awareness of the rule or expectation that evoked the approval or disapproval. Also, young children are more capable than toddlers of anticipating the potential consequences of their actions and avoiding behaviors that would be morally disapproved (Grolnick et al., 2006).

Young children do not inherently know the rules and expectations of their culture and must learn them, sometimes by unknowingly violating them and then observing the consequences in the responses of their parents and others. For example, one day when our twins were about 4 years old, they got into the laundry room in the basement and took cups of liquid detergent and spread it all over the basement furniture—sofa, table, loveseat, VCR, CD player—all of which were ruined! I don't think they had any intention or awareness of doing something wrong, although after we found out what they had done they knew from our response they should never do it again.

A good example of cultural learning of morality can be found in the research of Richard Shweder, who has compared children, adolescents, and adults in India and the United States (2009) (Shweder et al., 1990). Shweder has found that by about age 5, children already grasp the moral standards of their culture, and their views change little from childhood to adolescence to adulthood.

Shweder found that there are some similarities in moral views in early childhood in India and the United States, but also many differences. At age 5, children in both countries have learned that it is wrong to take others' property ("steal flowers from a neighbor's garden") or to inflict harm intentionally ("kick a dog sleeping on the side of the road"). However, young children also view many issues with a different moral perspective depending on whether they live in India or the United States. Young children in the United States view it as acceptable to eat beef, but young children in India view it as wrong. Young children in India view it as acceptable for more of a father's inheritance to go to his son than to his daughter, but young children in the United States view it as wrong. Young children in both cultures have the ability to understand their culture's moral rules, even though the moral rules they have learned by early childhood are quite different.

How do children learn moral rules so early in life? There are several ways. Sometimes moral rules are taught explicitly. The Ten Commandments of the Jewish and Christian religions are a good example of this. Parents often rely on religious institutions as sources of correct moral behavior. Churches and temples can be places where children learn the moral codes valued by their parents. Sometimes morality is taught through stories, in both formal settings, like Sunday school, and informal settings, like the family dinner table. Barbara Rogoff (2003) gives examples of storytelling as moral instruction in a variety of cultures, including Canadian First Nations people, Native Americans, and the Xhosa people of South Africa. Among the Xhosa (pronounced ZO-sa), it is usually the elders that tell the stories, but the stories have been told many times before, and even young children soon learn the stories and participate in the narrative.

What is it like for immigrant children to learn the rules and expectations of the cultural groups they are engaged in? For many immigrant children, the rules for proper behavior at home are different from the rules at school, and children must bridge the culture between home and school by adapting their behavior in the two settings (Rothstein-Fisch et al., 2010).

Young children also learn morality through custom complexes (see Chapter 4). Remember, the essence of the custom complex is that every customary practice of a culture contains not just the customary practice itself but cultural beliefs, often including moral beliefs. Shweder (Shweder et al., 1990) gives an example of this kind of moral learning in India. Like people in many cultures, Indians believe that a woman's menstrual blood has potentially dangerous powers. Consequently, a menstruating woman is not supposed to cook food or sleep in the same bed as her husband. By the end of early childhood, Indian children have learned not just that a menstruating woman does not cook food or sleep with her husband (the cultural practice) but that it would be *wrong* for her to do so (the moral belief).

A variation on the custom complex can be found in American research on *modeling*. Research extending over more than 30 years has shown that young children tend to model their behavior after the behavior of others they observe (Bandura, 1977; Bussey & Bandura, 2004). Most of this research has been experimental, involving situations where children observe other children or adults behaving aggressively or kindly, selfishly or generously; then children's own behavior in a similar experimental situation is observed. Children are especially likely to model their behavior after another person if the other person's behavior is rewarded. Also, they are more likely to model their behavior after adults who are warm and responsive or who are viewed as having authority or prestige. According to modeling theory, after observing multiple occasions of others' behavior being rewarded or punished, children conclude that the rewarded behavior is morally desirable and the punished behavior is forbidden (Bandura, 2002). So, by observing behavior (and its consequences) they learn their culture's principles of moral conduct. ◉

In addition to grasping early their culture's moral principles, young children begin to display the rudiments of moral reasoning. By the age of 3 or 4, children are capable of making moral judgments that involve considerations of justice and fairness (Helwig, 2008). By age 4 they understand the difference between telling the truth and lying, and they believe it is wrong to tell lies even when the liar is not caught (Bussey, 1992). However, their moral reasoning tends to be rigid at this age. They are more likely than older children to state that stealing and lying are always wrong, without

Moral lessons are often communicated through stories. Here, a village elder tells children stories in Tanzania.

THINKING CULTURALLY

Can you think of a childhood story or fairy tale told in your culture that communicates a moral lesson?

◉ **Watch** the **Video** Moral Development in **MyDevelopmentLab**

My Virtual Child

How will you teach morality to your virtual child? Do these teachings reflect your cultural background?

regard to the circumstances (Lourenco, 2003). Also, their moral judgments tend to be based more on fear of punishment than is the case for older children and adults (Gibbs, 2003). Their moral reasoning will become more complex with age, as we will see in later chapters.

Teaching moral rules is a large part of parenting young children. Sometimes the hardest part is keeping a straight face. My wife and I bought a nice leather chair for our living room when our twins turned 4 years old, thinking that by now they were old enough to know they should be gentle with a nice piece of furniture. Wrong! Within 2 weeks they had put several large scratches in it. When confronted, they confessed at first, but then retracted their confession and looked for an alibi. "We didn't do it, Daddy," claimed Paris, lawyer for the defense. "Well, then who did?" I demanded. She cast her eyes down, as if it were painful for her to reveal the true offender. "Santa Claus," she said.

Gender development

6.16   LEARNING OBJECTIVE

Describe the roles that parents and peers play in gender socialization, and explain how gender schemas lead to self-socialization.

In all cultures, gender is a fundamental organizing principle of social life. All cultures distinguish different roles and expectations for males and females, although the strictness of those roles and expectations varies widely. Of course, many other animals, including all our mammal relatives and certainly our primate cousins, have male–female differences in their typical patterns of behavior and development. What makes humans distinctive is that, unlike other animals, we require culture to tell us how males and females are supposed to behave.

GENDER IDENTITY AND GENDER SOCIALIZATION Early childhood is an especially important period with respect to gender development. Recall from Chapter 5 that even earlier, at age 2, children attain *gender identity*, that is, they understand themselves as being either male or female (Ruble et al., 2006). However, in early childhood, gender issues intensify. By age 3–4, children associate a variety of things with either males or females, including toys, games, clothes, household items, occupations, and even colors (Ruble et al., 2006).

Furthermore, they are often adamant and rigid in their perceptions of maleness and femaleness, denying, for example, that it would be possible for a boy to wear a ponytail and still remain a boy, or for a girl to play roughly and still remain a girl (Blakemore, 2003)! One reason for their insistence on strict gender roles at this age may be cognitive. It is not until age 6 or 7 that children attain **gender constancy**, the understanding that maleness and femaleness are biological and cannot change (Ruble et al., 2006). Earlier, children may be so insistent about maintaining **gender roles** because they believe that changing external features like clothes or hairstyles could result in a change in gender.

The similarity of children's gender roles and gender behavior across cultures is striking, and there is a biological basis to some gender differences, as we saw in Chapter 5. However, children in virtually all cultures are also subject to intense gender socialization.

GENDER SOCIALIZATION As we learned in Chapter 5, parents play an active role in delivering cultural gender messages to their children (Ruble et al., 2006; Whiting & Edwards, 1988). They may give their children distinctively male or female names, dress them in gender-specific colors and styles, and provide them with cars or dolls to play with (Bandura & Bussey, 2004).

APPLYING YOUR KNOWLEDGE
. . . as a Nurse

New grandmother Natalie wonders where newborn Nicole will receive male gender role socialization while being raised by her two mothers. What can you tell her?

gender constancy understanding that maleness and femaleness are biological and cannot change

gender roles cultural expectations for appearance and behavior specific to males or females

Parents' important role in gender socialization continues in early childhood. They continue to give their children the clothes and toys they believe are gender appropriate. They express approval when their children behave in gender-appropriate ways, and disapproval when their children violate gender expectations (Gelman et al., 2004; Leaper & Smith, 2004). In conversations, parents sometimes communicate gender expectations directly (e.g., "Don't cry, you're not a little girl, are you?"). They also communicate indirectly, by approving or not contradicting their children's gender statements (e.g., "Only boys can be doctors, Mommy"). Parents also provide models, through their own behavior, language, and appearance, of how males and females are supposed to be different in their culture (Bandura & Bussey, 2004).

Fathers become especially important to gender socialization in early childhood and beyond. They are more insistent about conformity to gender roles than mothers are, especially for boys (David et al., 2004; Wood et al., 2002). They may not want their daughters to play rough and tumble games, but they are adamant that their boys not be "sissies" or "wimps." As we will see in later chapters, males' greater fear of violations of gender roles is something that continues throughout life in many cultures.

Peers also become a major source of gender socialization in early childhood. Once children learn gender roles and expectations, they apply them not only to themselves but to each other. They reinforce each other for gender-appropriate behavior, and reject peers who violate gender roles (Matlin, 2004; Ruble et al., 2006). Here, too, the expectations are stricter for boys than for girls (Bandura & Bussey, 2004). Boys who cry easily or who like to play with girls and engage in girls' games are likely to be ostracized by other boys (David et al., 2004).

GENDER SCHEMAS AND SELF-SOCIALIZATION As a result of gender socialization, from early childhood onward children use gender schemas as a way of understanding and interpreting the world around them. Recall from Chapter 1 that *scheme* is Piaget's term for a cognitive structure for organizing and processing information. (*Scheme* and *schema* are used interchangeably in psychology.) A **gender schema** is a gender-based cognitive structure for organizing and processing information (Martin & Ruble, 2004).

According to gender-schema theory, gender is one of our most important schemas from early childhood onward. By the time we reach the end of early childhood, on the basis of our socialization we have learned to categorize a wide range of activities and objects and personality characteristics as "female" or "male." This includes not just the obvious—vaginas are female, penises are male—but many things that have no inherent "femaleness" or "maleness" and are nevertheless taught as possessing gender—the moon as "female" and the sun as "male" in traditional Chinese culture, or blue as a "boy color" and pink as a "girl color" (in Korea, pink is a "boy color," which illustrates how cultural these designations are).

Gender schemas influence how we interpret the behavior of others and what we expect from them (Frawley, 2008). This well-known story provides an example: "A little boy and his father were in a terrible automobile accident. The father died, but the boy was rushed to the hospital. As the boy was rushed into surgery, the doctor looked down at him and said, 'I cannot operate on this boy—he is my son!'"

How could the boy be the doctor's son, if the father died in the accident? The answer, of course, is that the doctor is the boy's *mother*. But people reading this story are often puzzled by it because their gender schemas have led them to assume the doctor was male. (This story is less effective than it used to be, because so many women are physicians today. Try it on someone.)

In early childhood, children tend to believe that their own preferences are true for everyone in their gender (Liben & Bigler, 2002). For example, a boy who dislikes peas may justify it by claiming

Fathers tend to promote conformity to gender roles more than mothers do.

gender schema gender-based cognitive structure for organizing and processing information, comprising expectations for males' and females' appearance and behavior

Once children learn the gender roles of their culture, they may strive to conform to them. Here, girls in Cambodia attend a dance class.

self-socialization process by which people seek to maintain consistency between their gender schemas and their behavior

parenting styles practices that parents exhibit in relation to their children and their beliefs about those practices

My Virtual Child

What kind of gender schemas will your virtual child develop? How have the schemas been influenced by the environment that you provided?

APPLYING YOUR KNOWLEDGE
. . . as a Parent

Your daughter, who had previously wanted to be a firefighter when she grows up, comes home from preschool one day and announces that she now wants to be a nurse. You ask her what made her change her mind, and she says that the boys in her class said that only men can be firefighters. What can you say to your daughter?

"boys don't like peas." Young children also tend to remember in ways that reflect their gender schemas. In one study (Liben & Signorella, 1993), children who were shown pictures that violated typical gender roles (e.g., a woman driving a truck) tended to remember them in accordance with their gender schemas (a man, not a woman, driving the truck). Throughout life, we tend to notice information that fits within our gender schemas and ignore or dismiss information that is inconsistent with them (David et al., 2004).

Once young children possess gender schemas, they seek to maintain consistency between their schemas and their behavior, a process called **self-socialization**. Boys become quite insistent about doing things they regard as boy things and avoiding things that girls do; girls become equally intent on avoiding boy things and doing things they regard as appropriate for girls (Bandura & Bussey, 2004; Tobin et al., 2010). In this way, according to a prominent gender scholar, "cultural myths become self-fulfilling prophesies" (Bem, 1981, p. 355). By the end of early childhood, gender roles are enforced not only by socialization from others but by self-socialization, as children strive to conform to the gender expectations they perceive in the culture around them.

WHAT HAVE YOU LEARNED?

1. What can parents do to help children develop effortful control?
2. Why do children become more empathic during early childhood?
3. How do children learn morality through modeling?
4. Why are fathers especially important to gender socialization?
5. How does gender-schema theory explain why Americans consider pink a "girl color"?
6. How does self-socialization lead to gender-typed behavior?

Parenting

Parents are a key part of children's lives everywhere, but how parents view their role and their approaches to discipline and punishment vary widely. First, we look at a popular model of parenting "styles" based on American parenting, then at more culturally based views of parenting.

Parenting "styles"

6.17 **LEARNING OBJECTIVE** | Describe the four types of parenting "styles" and the outcomes associated with each, and explain why those outcomes are complex.

Have you heard the joke about the man who, before he had any children, had five theories about how they should be raised? Ten years later he had five children and no theories.

Well, jokes aside, most parents do have ideas about how best to raise children, even after they have had children for awhile (Tamis-Lamonda et al., 2008). In research the investigation of this topic has involved the study of **parenting styles**, that is, the practices that parents exhibit in relation to their children and their beliefs about those practices. This research originated in the United States and has involved mainly American children and their parents, although it has now been applied in some other countries as well. ◉

◉—⌐Watch the **Video** Parenting Styles
 in **MyDevelopmentLab**

For over 50 years, American scholars have engaged in research on this topic, and the results have been quite consistent (Collins & Laursen, 2004; Maccoby & Martin, 1983; Steinberg, 2001). Virtually all of the prominent scholars who have studied parenting have described it in terms of two dimensions: demandingness and responsiveness (also known by other terms such as *control* and *warmth*). Parental **demandingness** is the degree to which parents set down rules and expectations for behavior and require their children to comply with them. Parental **responsiveness** is the degree to which parents are sensitive to their children's needs and express love, warmth, and concern for them.

Various scholars have combined these two dimensions to describe different kinds of parenting styles. For many years, the best known and most widely used conception of parenting styles was the one articulated by Diana Baumrind (1968, 1971, 1991a, 1991b). Her research on middle-class White American families, along with the research of other scholars inspired by her ideas, has identified four distinct parenting styles (Collins & Laursen, 2004; Maccoby & Martin, 1983; Steinberg, 2000) (see *Table 6.1*).

Authoritative parents are high in demandingness and high in responsiveness. They set clear rules and expectations for their children. Furthermore, they make clear what the consequences will be if their children do not comply, and they make those consequences stick if necessary. However, authoritative parents do not simply "lay down the law" and then enforce it rigidly. A distinctive feature of authoritative parents is that they *explain* the reasons for their rules and expectations to their children, and they willingly engage in discussion with their children over issues of discipline, sometimes leading to negotiation and compromise. For example, a child who wants to eat a whole bag of candy would not simply be told "No!" by an authoritative parent but something like, "No, it wouldn't be healthy and it would be bad for your teeth." Authoritative parents are also loving and warm toward their children, and they respond to what their children need and desire.

Authoritarian parents are high in demandingness but low in responsiveness. They require obedience from their children, and they punish disobedience without compromise. None of the verbal give-and-take common with authoritative parents is allowed by authoritarian parents. They expect their commands to be followed without dispute or dissent. To continue with the candy example, the authoritarian parent would respond to the child's request for a bag of candy simply by saying "No!" with no explanation. Also, authoritarian parents show little in the way of love or warmth toward their children. Their demandingness takes place without responsiveness, in a way that shows little emotional attachment and may even be hostile.

Permissive parents are low in demandingness and high in responsiveness. They have few clear expectations for their children's behavior, and they rarely discipline them. Instead, their emphasis is on responsiveness. They believe that children need love that is truly "unconditional." They may see discipline and control as having the potential to damage their children's healthy tendencies for developing creativity and expressing themselves however they wish. They provide their children with love and warmth and give them a great deal of freedom to do as they please.

Disengaged parents are low in both demandingness and responsiveness. Their goal may be to minimize the amount of time and emotion they devote to parenting.

demandingness degree to which parents set down rules and expectations for behavior and require their children to comply with them

responsiveness degree to which parents are sensitive to their children's needs and express love, warmth, and concern for them

authoritative parents in classifications of parenting styles, parents who are high in demandingness and high in responsiveness

authoritarian parents in classifications of parenting styles, parents who are high in demandingness but low in responsiveness

permissive parents in classifications of parenting styles, parents who are low in demandingness and high in responsiveness

disengaged parents in classifications of parenting styles, parents who are low in both demandingness and responsiveness

TABLE 6.1 Parenting Styles and the Two Dimensions of Parenting

Responsiveness		Demandingness	
		High	**Low**
	High	Authoritative	Permissive
	Low	Authoritarian	Disengaged

reciprocal or **bidirectional effects** in relations between two persons, the principle that each of them affects the other

TABLE 6.2 Outcomes Associated With Parenting Styles in White Middle-Class Families

Authoritative	Authoritarian	Permissive	Disengaged
Independent	Dependent	Irresponsible	Impulsive
Creative	Passive	Conforming	Behavior problems
Self-assured	Conforming	Immature	Early sex, drugs
Socially skilled			

Thus, they require little of their children and rarely bother to correct their behavior or place clear limits on what they are allowed to do. They also express little in the way of love or concern for their children. They may seem to have little emotional attachment to them.

THE EFFECTS OF PARENTING STYLES ON CHILDREN A great deal of research has been conducted on how parenting styles influence children's development. A summary of the results is shown in **Table 6.2**. In general, authoritative parenting is associated with the most favorable outcomes, at least by American standards. Children who have authoritative parents tend to be independent, self-assured, creative, and socially skilled (Baumrind, 1991a, 1991b; Collins & Laursen, 2004; Steinberg, 2000; Williams, L. R. et al., 2009). They also tend to do well in school and to get along well with their peers and with adults (Hastings et al., 2007; Spera, 2005). Authoritative parenting helps children develop characteristics such as optimism and self-regulation that in turn have positive effects on a wide range of behaviors (Jackson et al., 2005; Purdie et al., 2004).

All the other parenting styles are associated with some negative outcomes, although the type of negative outcome varies depending on the specific parenting style (Baumrind, 1991a, 1991b; Snyder et al., 2005). Children with authoritarian parents tend to be less self-assured, less creative, and less socially adept than other children. Boys with authoritarian parents are more often aggressive and unruly, whereas girls are more often anxious and unhappy (Russell et al., 2003). Children with permissive parents tend to be immature and lack self-control. Because they lack self-control, they have difficulty getting along with peers and teachers (Linver et al., 2002). Children with disengaged parents also tend to be impulsive. Partly as a consequence of their impulsiveness, and partly because disengaged parents do little to monitor their activities, children with disengaged parents tend to have higher rates of behavior problems (Pelaez et al., 2008).

A MORE COMPLEX PICTURE OF PARENTING EFFECTS Although parents undoubtedly affect their children profoundly by their parenting, the process is not nearly as simple as the cause-and-effect model just described. Sometimes discussions of parenting make it sound as though Parenting Style A automatically and inevitably produces Child Type X. However, enough research has taken place by now to indicate that the relationship between parenting styles and children's development is considerably more complex than that (Lamb & Lewis, 2005; Parke & Buriel, 2006). Not only are children affected by their parents, but parents are affected by their children. This principle is referred to by scholars as **reciprocal** or **bidirectional effects** between parents and children (Combs-Ronto et al., 2009).

Recall our discussion of evocative genotype → environment effects in Chapter 2. Children are not like billiard balls that head predictably in the direction they are propelled. They have personalities and desires of their own that they bring to the

How does the idea of reciprocal effects complicate claims of the effects of parenting styles?

parent–child relationship. Thus, children may evoke certain behaviors from their parents. An especially aggressive child may evoke authoritarian parenting; perhaps the parents find that authoritative explanations of the rules are simply ignored, and their responsiveness diminishes as a result of the child's repeated disobedience and disruptiveness. An especially mild-tempered child may evoke permissive parenting, because parents may see no point in laying down specific rules for a child who has no inclination to do anything wrong anyway.

Does this research discredit the claim that parenting styles influence children? No, but it does modify it. Parents certainly have beliefs about what is best for their children, and they try to express those beliefs through their parenting behavior (Alwin, 1988; Tamis-LeMonda et al., 2008). However, parents' actual behavior is affected not only by what they believe is best but also by how their children behave toward them and respond to their parenting. Being an authoritative parent is easier if your child responds to your demandingness and responsiveness with compliance and love, and not so easy if your love is rejected and your rules and the reasons you provide for them are ignored. Parents whose efforts to persuade their children through reasoning and discussion fall on deaf ears may be tempted either to demand compliance (and become more authoritarian) or to give up trying (and become permissive or disengaged).

Parenting in other cultures

| Describe the major cultural variations in approaches to parenting. | **LEARNING OBJECTIVE** **6.18** |

So far we have looked at the parenting styles research based mainly on American families. What does research in other cultures indicate about parenting and its effects in early childhood? 📖

One important observation is how rare the authoritative parenting style is in non-Western cultures. Remember, a distinctive feature of authoritative parents is that they do not rely on the authority of the parental role to ensure that children comply with their commands and instructions. They do not simply lay down the law and expect to be obeyed. On the contrary, authoritative parents explain the reasons for what they want children to do and engage in discussion over the guidelines for their children's behavior (Baumrind, 1971, 1991a; Steinberg & Levine, 1997).

Outside of the West, however, this is an extremely rare way of parenting. In traditional cultures, parents expect that their authority will be obeyed, without question and without requiring an explanation (LeVine et al., 2008). This is true not only in nearly all developing countries but also in developed countries outside the West, most notably Asian countries such as Japan and South Korea (Tseng, 2004; Zhang & Fuligni, 2006). Asian cultures have a tradition of **filial piety**, meaning that children are expected to respect, obey, and revere their parents throughout life (Lieber et al., 2004). The role of parent carries greater inherent authority than it does in the West. Parents are not supposed to provide reasons why they should be respected and obeyed. The simple fact that they are parents and their children are children is viewed as sufficient justification for their authority.

In Latin American cultures, too, the authority of parents is viewed as paramount. The Latino cultural belief system places a premium on the idea of *respeto*, which emphasizes respect for and obedience to parents and elders, especially the father (Cabrera & Garcia-Coll, 2004; Halgunseth et al., 2006; Harwood et al., 2002). The role of the parent is considered to be enough to command authority, without requiring that the parents explain their rules to their children. Another pillar of Latino cultural beliefs is **familismo**, which emphasizes the love, closeness, and mutual obligations of Latino family life (Halgunseth et al., 2006; Harwood et al., 2002).

Does this mean that the typical parenting style in non-Western cultures is authoritarian? No, although sometimes scholars have come to this erroneous conclusion. It

APPLYING YOUR KNOWLEDGE

Did your mother and father have the same parenting style, or not? To what extent did their parenting reflect a "style" and to what extent do you think you evoked their parenting behavior?

📖 **Read** the **Document**
An Alternative Classification of Parenting Styles in **MyDevelopmentLab**

filial piety belief that children should respect, obey, and revere their parents throughout life; common in Asian cultures

familismo cultural belief among Latinos that emphasizes the love, closeness, and mutual obligations among family members

In most cultures, parents expect to be respected and obeyed without justifying their actions. Here, a mother and daughter in Japan.

would be more accurate to state that the parenting-styles model is a cultural model, rooted in the American majority culture, and does not apply well to most other cultures. Of course, children everywhere need to have parents or other caregivers provide care for them in early childhood and beyond, and across cultures parents provide some combination of warmth and control. However, "responsiveness" is a distinctly American kind of warmth, emphasizing praise and physical affection, and "demandingness" is a distinctly American kind of control, emphasizing explanation and negotiation rather than the assertion of parental authority. Other cultures have their own culturally based forms of warmth and control, but across cultures, warmth rarely takes the American form of praise, and control rarely takes the American form of explanation and negotiation (Matsumoto & Yoo, 2006; Miller, 2004; Wang & Tamis-Lamonda, 2003).

Even within American society, the authoritative style is mainly dominant among White, middle-class families (Steinberg, 1996). Most American minority cultures, including African Americans, Latinos, and Asian Americans, have been classified by researchers as "authoritarian," but this is inaccurate and results from applying to them a model that was based on the White majority culture (Chao & Tseng, 2002). Each minority culture has its own distinctive form of warmth, but all tend to emphasize obeying parental authority rather than encouraging explanation and negotiation. Hence they have warmth as "authoritative" parents do but they view parental authority as "authoritarian" parents do; the American model of parenting styles cannot really be applied to them.

Within cultures, parenting varies depending on the personalities of the parents, their goals for their children, and the characteristics of the children that evoke particular parenting responses. Overall, however, the dominant approach to parenting in a culture reflects certain things about the underlying cultural beliefs, such as the value of independence versus independence and the status of parental authority over children (Giles-Sims & Lockhart, 2005; Hulei et al., 2006). The cultural context of parenting is so crucial that what looks like the same parental behavior in two different cultures can have two very different effects, as we will see in the next section.

Discipline and punishment

6.19 **LEARNING OBJECTIVE** Describe the main cultural variations in how parents discipline young children, and explain how cultural context influences children's responses to discipline.

In many cultures, early childhood is when issues of discipline for disapproved behavior first arise. As we have seen, it is common for cultures to be indulgent of infants and toddlers, because they are seen to be too young to exercise much judgment or self-control. However, by early childhood children become more capable of emotional and behavioral self-regulation, and when they disobey or defy the authority of others they are believed to have enough understanding to know what they were doing and to be responsible for the consequences. For this reason, early childhood is usually the age when children are first disciplined for not following expectations or not doing what is required of them.

CULTURAL VARIATIONS IN DISCIPLINE All cultures require children to learn and follow cultural rules and expectations, and all cultures have some system of discipline for misbehavior. However, cultures vary widely in the nature of the discipline, and the consequences of discipline vary depending on the cultural beliefs that underlie the approach.

In Western cultures the approach to discipline in early childhood tends to emphasize the authoritative style of explaining the consequences of misbehavior and the reasons for discipline (Huang, K.-Y., et al., 2009; Tamis-Lamonda et al., 2008). "Michael, if you don't stop banging that toy against the floor I'm going to take it away! Okay, now I'm going to take it away until you can learn to play with it nicely." Western parents also tend to use a lot of praise for compliant and obedient behavior, which is notable because the use of praise is very rare in other cultures (LeVine et al., 2008; Whiting & Edwards, 1988). Discipline for misbehavior may involve taking away privileges (as in the example just given) or a **time out** in which the child is required to sit still in a designated place for a brief period, usually only a few minutes (Morawska & Sanders, 2011). Little research has been conducted on the effectiveness of time out under normal family circumstances, but it has been shown to be effective with young children who have behavioral problems (Everett et al., 2007; Fabiano et al., 2004).

In addition to using time out, parenting researchers recommend (1) explaining the reasons for discipline; (2) being consistent so that the consequences will be predictable to the child (and hence avoidable); and (3) exercising discipline at the time of the misbehavior (not later on) so that the connection will be clear to the child (American Academy of Pediatrics, 2009). One popular approach suggests that if a parent's request to a young child is ignored or disobeyed, the parent counts a warning: "One-two-*three*," and if the request is not obeyed by "three" the child is put in time out, 1 minute for each year of their age (Phelan, 2010). I can tell you, my wife and I found that this worked like magic with our twins in early childhood; we almost never got to "three."

Other cultures have different approaches to discipline. Japan provides an interesting example of a culture where shame and withdrawal of love is the core of discipline in early childhood. Recall that *amae,* introduced in Chapter 5, is a Japanese word that describes the close attachment between mother and child (Rothbaum et al., 2000). During infancy, *amae* takes the form of an emotionally indulgent and physically close relationship between the Japanese mother and her baby. However, in toddlerhood and early childhood, a new element, shame and withdrawal of love, is added. Japanese mothers rarely respond to their children's misbehavior with loud reprimands or physical punishment. Instead, they express disappointment and withdraw their love temporarily. The child feels shame, which is a powerful inducement not to disobey again.

This system of early childhood socialization seems to work well in Japan. Japanese children have low rates of behavioral problems, and high rates of academic achievement (Stevenson & Zusho, 2002). They grow up to be Japanese adults who have low rates of crime and social problems and high levels of economic productivity, making Japan one of the most stable and economically successful societies in the world.

However, the same parental behaviors appear to have a different, more negative effect in Western countries. Among American researchers, parenting that uses shame and withdrawal of love has been described using the term **psychological control** (Barber, 2002). This kind of parenting has been found in American studies to be related to negative outcomes in early childhood and beyond, including anxious, withdrawn, and aggressive behavior, as well as problems with peers (Barber et al., 2005; Silk et al., 2003). In Finland, too, a longitudinal study that began in early childhood found psychological control to predict negative outcomes in later childhood and adolescence, especially when psychological control was combined with physical affection, as it is in *amae* (Aunola & Nurmi, 2004).

What explains this difference? Why does *amae* appear to work well in Japan but not in the West? It is difficult to say, since this question has not been researched directly. However, the answer may be some kind of interaction between the parents' behavior and the cultural belief system. In Japan, *amae* fits neatly into a larger system of cultural

"Time out" is a popular discipline strategy among middle-class American parents.

time out disciplinary strategy in which the child is required to sit still in a designated place for a brief period

psychological control parenting strategy that uses shame and withdrawal of love to influence children's behavior

APPLYING YOUR KNOWLEDGE . . . as a Nurse

Three-year-old Midori is ashamed when her Japanese mother expresses disappointment in her. How can you explain this feeling of shame from a developmental and cultural point of view?

My Virtual Child

How will you discipline your virtual child? Why did you choose that method?

beliefs about duty and obligations to others, especially to family. In the West, psychological control contrasts and perhaps collides with cultural beliefs about the value of thinking and behaving independently. It may be this friction between the parental practices and the cultural beliefs that results in negative outcomes, not the parental practices in themselves.

PHYSICAL PUNISHMENT AND ITS CONSEQUENCES Research on physical punishment (also known as **corporal punishment**) suggests a similar kind of interaction between parenting practices and cultural beliefs. Physical punishment of young children is common in most parts of the world (Curran et al., 2001). This approach to punishment has a long history, as you will see in the **Historical Focus: Beat a Child, Save a Soul** feature on page 275. Most adults in most countries around the world remember experiencing physical punishment as children. Although most countries still allow parents to spank their young children, nearly all outlaw beatings and other harsh forms of physical punishment, which the historical record shows was quite common until about 100 years ago (Straus & Donnelly, 1994).

Is physical punishment destructive to young children, or is it a form of instruction that teaches them to respect and obey adults? Here, as with *amae*, the answer appears to be very different depending on the cultural context. Many studies in the United States and Europe have been conducted on physical punishment of young children, and these studies have found a correlation between physical punishment and a wide range of antisocial behavior in children, including telling lies, fighting with peers, and disobeying parents (Alaggia & Vine, 2006; Kazdin & Benjet, 2003). Furthermore, several longitudinal studies have reported that physical punishment in early childhood increases the likelihood of bullying and delinquency in adolescence and aggressive behavior (including spousal abuse) in adulthood (Jaffee et al., 2004). On the basis of these studies, some scholars have concluded that physical punishment in early childhood increases children's compliance in the short run but damages their moral and mental health in the long run (Amato & Fowler, 2002; Gershoff, 2002).

However, studies that cast a wider cultural net report considerably more complicated findings. In one longitudinal study, White and African American families were studied when the children were in early childhood and then 12 years later, when the children were in adolescence (Lansford et al., 2004). The White children showed the familiar pattern: physical punishment in early childhood predicted aggressive and antisocial behavior in adolescence. However, for African American children, nearly the opposite pattern was found. The more physical punishment the children experienced in early childhood, the *less* likely they were to be aggressive and antisocial in adolescence. Other studies have reported similar findings of the generally beneficial results of early childhood physical punishment among African Americans (Bluestone & Tamis-Lamonda, 1999; Brody & Flor, 1998; Steele et al., 2005). Similarly, studies of traditional cultures have found that many of the parents in these cultures use physical punishment on young children, and the children nevertheless grow up to be well-behaved, productive, mentally healthy adults (LeVine et al., 2008; Whiting & Edwards, 1988).

Like the findings regarding *amae*, the findings on physical punishment show the crucial role of cultural context in how young children respond to their parents' behavior. In White American and European cultures, physical punishment is generally disapproved and not widely or frequently used (Graziano & Hamblen, 1996). In these cultures, physical punishment is likely to be combined with anger (Gunnoe & Mariner, 1997; McLoyd & Smith, 2002). In contrast, among African Americans, and in traditional cultures, the use of physical punishment in early childhood is widespread (Brody & Flor, 1998; Ispa & Halgunseth, 2004; Pinderhughes et al., 2000). Usually, it is mild in degree and is delivered not in an angry rage but calmly and sternly, as part of a "no-nonsense" parenting style (Brody & Flor, 1998). Physical punishment is often combined with parental warmth, so that children understand their parents' behavior not

corporal punishment physical punishment of children

HISTORICAL FOCUS   Beat a Child, Save a Soul

Physical punishment is a widespread parenting practice with young children, and it has a long history. It is recommended in the Bible, in the book of Proverbs written over 2,000 years ago: "Do not be afraid to beat your child. You shall beat him with the rod, and save his soul from hell." Notice that physical punishment is not meant to be harmful but helpful, a form of moral instruction that will "save [the child's] soul."

For much of the next 1,500 years, the Bible was the basis of the cultural beliefs of most of the West, including beliefs regarding family relations. Physical punishment was a standard part of parenting. It was only during the Enlightenment, beginning about 400 years ago, that Western cultural beliefs began to broaden, and as part of that process came new ideas about parenting. One influential figure in this change was John Locke (1632–1704), the British philosopher who wrote the first known parenting manual, even though he was a lifelong bachelor with no children himself (insert your own punch line here). Locke's revolutionary idea was that all children are born as a *tabula rasa,* a blank slate, rather than being filled with sin that needs to be beaten out of them. Consequently, Locke discouraged physical punishment and advocated explanation and negotiation instead, much as Western psychologists do today. He believed that if parents rewarded good behavior with esteem and made shame the consequence of bad behavior they would not have to resort to physical punishment.

John Locke was a childless bachelor who wrote the first parenting manual in the 17th century.

Another influential figure of the Enlightenment who had much to say about parenting and punishment was the French philosopher Jean Jacques Rousseau (1712–1778). Like Locke, Rousseau was no model father. He had at least five children by a variety of women but was never involved in the care of any of them. Nevertheless, for over two centuries he was tremendously influential in European views of parenting and punishment. In his book *Emile* (1763), he laid out what he believed to be an ideal program for raising children. He argued that they should be given as much freedom as possible to allow their goodness and curiosity to flourish. Locke believed children were born as blank slates, but Rousseau went further and proposed that children are born naturally good, only to be corrupted and warped by misguided parenting methods, including physical punishment. In Rousseau's view, physical punishment is unnecessary because children are born good and innocent, and it is wrong because it damages children's natural propensity for kindness.

Primarily due to Locke's and Rousseau's influence, over the course of the 18th and 19th centuries support for physical punishment gradually declined in the West (Straus & Donnelly, 1994). In recent years, physical punishment of children has even become prohibited by law in 24 countries, mainly in Europe (Curran et al., 2001). Nevertheless, physical punishment remains common in most parts of the world, as this chapter shows.

---

as a frightening and threatening loss of parental control but as a practice intended to teach them right from wrong and the importance of obeying their parents (Gunnoe & Mariner, 1997; Mosby et al., 1999). This cultural context makes the meaning and the consequences of physical punishment much different than it is in White American and European cultures.

CHILD ABUSE AND NEGLECT Although there are wide cultural variations in discipline and punishment of young children, today there is a widespread view across cultures that children should not be physically harmed and that parents have a responsibility to provide for their children's physical and emotional needs (UNICEF, 2011b). However, there are all kinds of parents in the world, and in all cultures there are some who fail to meet these basic requirements. **Child maltreatment** includes both abuse and neglect of children, specifically:

- *Physical abuse,* which entails causing physical harm to a child, including hitting, kicking, biting, burning, or shaking the child;
- *Emotional abuse,* including ridicule and humiliation as well as behavior causing emotional trauma to children such as locking them in a dark closet;

child maltreatment abuse or neglect of children, including physical, emotional, or sexual abuse

- *Sexual abuse*, meaning any kind of sexual contact with a minor; and
- *Neglect*, which is failure to meet children's basic needs of food, shelter, clothing, medical attention, and supervision.

Most research on maltreatment of young children has focused on physical abuse (Cicchetti, 2001). A variety of risk factors for physical abuse have been identified, involving characteristics of children as well as characteristics of parents. Young children are at risk for physical abuse if they are temperamentally difficult or if they are unusually aggressive or active and hence more difficult for parents to control (Li et al., 2010). Parental risk factors for physical abuse of children include poverty, unemployment, and single motherhood, all of which contribute to stress, which may in turn trigger abuse (Geeraert et al., 2004; Zielinski, 2009). Stepfathers are more likely to be abusive than biological fathers are, and child abuse is correlated with spouse abuse, suggesting that the abuser has a problem with anger management and self-control that is expressed in multiple ways (Asawa et al., 2008). Abusive parents often view their children as somehow deserving the abuse because of disobedience or because they are "no good" and will not respond to anything else (Bugental & Happaney, 2004). Parents who abuse their children were abused by their own parents in about one-third of cases (Cicchetti & Toth, 1998). ◉

Physical abuse is destructive to young children in a wide variety of ways. It impairs emotional and self-development, including self-regulation, empathy, and self-concept (Haugaard & Hazen, 2004). It is damaging to the development of friendships and social skills, because abused children find it difficult to trust others (Elliott et al., 2005). It also interferes with school performance, as abused children are often low in academic motivation and have behavior problems in the classroom (Boden et al., 2007). Furthermore, children who are abused are at risk for later emotional, social, and academic problems in adolescence and beyond (Fergusson et al., 2008; Herrenkohl et al., 2004).

What can be done to help abused children? In most cultures, there is some kind of system that removes children from their parents' care when the parents are abusive. In traditional cultures, the system tends to be informal. Children with abusive parents may go to live with relatives with whom they have a more positive, less conflictual relationship (LeVine et al., 2008). In Western countries, it is more often the formal legal system that intervenes in cases of child abuse. A state agency investigates reports of abuse, and if the report is verified the child is removed from the home. The agency may then place the child in **foster care**, in which adults approved by the agency take over the care of the child (Pew Commission on Foster Care, 2004). In the United States, about half of children in foster care are placed with relatives through the formal system (U.S. Dept. of Health & Human Services [DHHS], 2004). In addition, three times as many children are estimated to live with nonparental relatives, similar to the informal system of traditional cultures. Sometimes children in foster care return home after a period, sometimes they are adopted by their foster family, and sometimes they "age out" of foster care when they turn age 18 (Smith, 2011). Children in foster care are at high risk for academic, social, and behavioral problems, especially if they experience multiple foster-home placements (Crum, 2010; Plant & Siegel, 2008; Vig et al., 2005). ◉

Another alternative is for children to live in a *group home* staffed by the state agency that oversees child abuse and neglect cases (Dunn et al., 2010). I worked in a group home when I was an emerging adult, years ago. I still remember many of the kids vividly, especially one boy who had scars all over his back from where his parents had beaten and burned him. Group homes are usually a temporary alternative until the child can be placed in foster care or with relatives (DeSena et al., 2005).

Programs have also been developed to prevent child maltreatment. In the United States, one notable program is the *Nurse–Family Partnership* (NFP), with sites in 22 states (National Center for Children, Families and Communities, n.d.). In this program, expectant mothers who have many of the risk factors for abuse receive regular home visits by a trained nurse for two years. The nurse provides information and advice

◉—⌐**Watch** the **Video** Childhood Sexual Abuse in **MyDevelopmentLab**

◉—⌐**Watch** the **Video** Adoption and Foster Care in **MyDevelopmentLab**

foster care for maltreated children, approach in which adults approved by a state agency take over the care of the child

about how to manage crises, how to manage children's behavior without physical punishment, and how to access community agencies that provide services for families (Olds, 2010). In a 15-year follow-up comparing families who participated in the NFP to other families with similar risks, the NFP group showed a 79% reduction in child abuse and neglect (Eckenrode et al., 2001).

WHAT HAVE YOU LEARNED?

1. How do Baumrind's four parenting styles differ on the dimensions of demandingness and responsiveness?
2. What are the outcomes associated with authoritative parenting?
3. Give an example of a reciprocal or bidirectional effect between parent and child.
4. How does the Asian tradition of filial piety translate into a parenting style that differs from Western authoritative parenting?
5. What are three characteristics of effective discipline, according to American parenting researchers?
6. What are some of the negative effects of child maltreatment?

The Child's Expanding Social World

Across cultures, the social world expands considerably in early childhood. Infants and toddlers need a great deal of care, nurturance, and supervision. And, as we have seen in the previous two chapters, infants and toddlers are usually kept in close proximity to someone who will provide this for them, usually the mother, sometimes in collaboration with a father, grandmother, aunt, or older sibling.

When they reach early childhood, children still need a considerable amount of care, but they no longer need to be constantly watched by others. The anthropologist Margaret Mead (1935) proposed a general scheme many decades ago that still applies well to how most of the world's children experience the social changes of childhood (see **Table 6.3**). Recall from Chapter 5 that Mead designated children ages 0–2 with the term *lap child*, to denote their near-constant dependence on the care and monitoring of others. For early childhood, Mead proposed two terms: knee child and yard child. At ages 3–4 is the *knee child*, who is still cared for mainly by the mother but also spends time with other children, especially of the same gender. At ages 5–6 is the *yard child*, who is given more scope to venture beyond the immediate family area and into the "yard," that is, into a social world where parents are nearby but not always directly present.

Margaret Mead's scheme was the basis of a classic study of young children across cultures conducted by anthropologists Beatrice Whiting and Carolyn Edwards (1988). Whiting and Edwards studied children ages 2–10 in 12 different cultures in places around the world, including Africa, Asia, South America, and the United States. Their

TABLE 6.3	Mead's Classifications of Childhood Stages	
Age	**Term**	**Features**
0–2	Lap child	Needs constant care; doted on by others
3–4	Knee child	Still cared for mainly by mothers, but spends more time with other children
5–6	Yard child	More time spent with same-sex peers; sometimes unsupervised

Across cultures, children are given more autonomy and more responsibility in the course of early childhood. Here, a girl washes dishes outside her Guatemalan home.

goal was to see what kinds of similarities and differences exist in the social worlds of children across cultures.

They found substantial similarities worldwide in how cultures socialize young children and structure their social environments. From lap children to knee children to yard children, there is a gradual lessening of dependence on the mother and a gradual move into the social orbit of peers and older children. Like lap children, knee children receive a great deal of nurturance from mothers and from older children. However, more is required of knee children than of lap children. Knee children are expected to stop breast-feeding and to have less bodily contact with the mother. Parents and older children expect knee children to be toilet trained, to have basic manners (such as waiting their turn), and to perform minor chores. Older children exercise more dominance over knee children than over lap children, because knee children are perceived as better able to understand and follow commands.

Yard children are allowed more freedom than knee children. Yard children spend most of their time close to home, as knee children do, but 20% of the time they are outside of their immediate home area doing errands or playing. However, most cultures share a view that children cannot reason very well until about age 6 and this limits how far a yard child can be away from home or supervision.

The cultures studied by Mead and by Whiting and Edwards were mostly in developing countries, but many of the same patterns apply in developed countries. Across countries and cultures, the social world expands in early childhood to include more time and more interactions with siblings, peers, and friends. In developed countries the media world expands as well, as children not only watch TV as they have from infancy but many also begin to play electronic games as well.

Siblings and "only children"

6.20 LEARNING OBJECTIVE | Identify the most common features of sibling relationships worldwide, and describe how children with no siblings differ from other children.

A gap of 2–4 years between children is common worldwide, traditionally. In developing countries, especially in rural areas, breast-feeding often lasts at least two years, and as we have seen, breast-feeding acts as a natural contraceptive by suppressing the mother's ovulation. In economically developed countries, parents often choose to space their children by 2–4 years (maybe it takes them that long to forget how much work it is to take care of an infant!). Consequently, it is often in early childhood that children experience the birth of a younger sibling.

How do young children respond to a baby brother or sister? As we learned in Chapter 5, jealousy is the predominant emotion, initially. In their study of 12 cultures, Whiting and Edwards (1988) found a great deal of variability on most issues, but in all 12 cultures jealousy was recognized as a common response to the birth of a younger sibling. Nevertheless, there was great variability in how parents responded to the jealousy of young children, from physical punishment in Africa to trying to comfort and reassure the jealous child in the United States. From the outset, young children expressed love as well as jealousy toward their younger siblings. Like people of other ages, they enjoyed doting on the lap child.

More recent American studies show this same pattern of ambivalence toward younger siblings. Aggressive and hostile behavior is common, but so is helping, sharing, and teaching (Kramer & Kowal, 2005; Martin & Ross, 2005; Natsuaki et al., 2009). Ambivalence continues with age, when there is a younger sibling in early childhood and an older sibling in middle childhood. Middle-childhood siblings care for and teach their younger siblings, but also command and dominate them, and sometimes physically punish them (Howe & Recchia, 2009; Maynard, 2002; Pike et al., 2005; Volling, 2003). Younger siblings admire their older siblings and model their behavior after them, trying to learn to do what their older siblings can do, although sometimes resenting their authority. But even conflict between siblings can have positive effects. Studies indicate that young children with older siblings possess more advanced theory of mind understanding than children who have no older sibling (McAlister & Peterson, 2007; Randell & Peterson, 2009). One explanation of this is that, as siblings argue, compete, and cooperate, they learn better how to understand the thinking of others and accept that others have a point of view that may be different than their own.

What about children who have no siblings? This has become an increasingly common condition over the past half century, as birthrates have fallen worldwide. In the United States, about 20% of children have no siblings. In some parts of Europe and Asia, birthrates are just 1.1–1.4 children per woman, meaning that there are more children who do not have a sibling than do have one (Population Reference Bureau, 2010). What is it like to be an only child?

Having siblings is a mixed blessing, and having no siblings has mixed effects as well. In general, an "**only child**" fares at least as well as children with siblings (Brody, 2004). Their self-esteem, social maturity, and intelligence tend to be somewhat higher than children with siblings, perhaps because they have more interactions with adults (Dunn, 2004). However, in American studies they are somewhat less successful in social relations with peers, perhaps because children with siblings gain peerlike practice in social relations (Kitzmann et al., 2002).

Because of its "one-child" policy, China today has many children without siblings.

Only children have been especially common in China in recent decades. Beginning in 1978, in response to fears of overpopulation, the Chinese government instituted a "one-child policy" making it illegal for parents to have more than one child without special government approval. There were fears that this policy would create a generation of "little emperors and empresses" who were overindulged and selfish, but those fears appear to be unfounded. Like only children in the United States, only children in China demonstrate several advantages over children with siblings, including higher cognitive development, higher emotional security, and higher likeability (Jiao et al., 1996; Wang & Fong, 2009; Yang et al., 1995). Unlike their American counterparts, Chinese only children show no deficits in social skills or peer acceptance (Hart, D. et al., 2003). One unexpected benefit of the one-child policy is that girls, who in Chinese tradition have often been less favored than boys, have more opportunities in education than they did when they had to compete with brothers for family resources (Fong, 2002).

Peers and friends

> Explain how the quality of friendships changes from toddlerhood to early childhood, and describe the role of play and aggression in young children's friendships.

LEARNING OBJECTIVE 6.21

As described in Chapter 5, even toddlers are capable of forming friendships (Rubin et al., 2005). They delight in each other's company, they enjoy favorite shared activities, and they provide each other with companionship and emotional support. In early

only child child who has no siblings

peers persons who share some aspect of their status in common, such as age

childhood, friendships also have these qualities, but by this age children are more capable than toddlers of understanding and describing what a friendship entails. They regard a friend as someone you like and who likes you, and as someone who plays with you and shares toys with you (Hartup & Abecassis, 2004). By age 5 or 6, they also understand that friendship is characterized by mutual trust and support, and that a friend is someone you can rely on over time (Hay et al., 2004; Youngblade et al., 1993).

Before proceeding further, it is important to distinguish between friends and peers. Friends, as you know, are people with whom you develop a valued, mutual relationship. **Peers** are persons who share some aspect of their status in common, such as age. So, in social science research on human development, a child's peers are the same-age children who are part of the daily environment, such as the other children in the child's class at school. Some of those children may become the child's friends, others may not; a child's friends are usually peers, but not all peers become friends.

Across cultures, relations with both peers and friends tend to become more strictly segregated by gender in the course of early childhood. Boys tend to have other boys as their peers and friends, and the social world of girls is populated mostly by other females. However, cultures differ substantially in the mix of ages in peer groups. A striking difference in early childhood peer relations between traditional cultures and Western cultures is that in the West, mixed-age peer play groups are relatively rare. By age 3 or 4, most children are in some kind of preschool setting for at least part of their typical week, and preschool is the main context for their peer interactions. In contrast, children in traditional cultures often play in mixed-age groups that may include children in toddlerhood, early childhood, and middle childhood (LeVine et al., 2008).

Two of the most researched topics concerning peers and friends in early childhood are play and aggression.

PLAY IN EARLY CHILDHOOD As mentioned in Chapter 5, in toddlerhood and early childhood there are several distinct types of play, including solitary play, parallel play, simple social play, and cooperative pretend play. From toddlerhood through early childhood, solitary play and parallel play decline somewhat while simple social play and cooperative pretend play increase (Hughes & Dunn, 2007). Cooperative pretend play becomes more complex in the course of early childhood, as children's imaginations bloom and they become more creative and adept at using symbols, for example using a stick to represent a sword and a blanket over two chairs to represent a castle (Dyer & Moneta, 2006). However, even at age 5 or 6 most children display a variety of types of play, engaging in cooperative play for awhile and then making a transition to solitary play or parallel play (Robinson et al., 2003). ◉

◉—⌐Watch the Video Play Styles
in **MyDevelopmentLab**

In the course of early childhood, children become more sex-segregated in their play. In the 12-cultures studied by Whiting and Edwards (1988), across cultures children played in same-sex groups 30–40% of the time at ages 2–3, rising to over 90% of the time by age 11. American studies report similar results (Fabes et al., 2003). In one observational study, the percent of time playing in same-sex groups was 45% for 4-year-old children and 73% for 6-year-old children (Martin & Fabes, 2001). Furthermore, numerous studies have found that boys generally engage in high-activity, aggressive, competitive "rough and tumble" play in their groups, whereas girls' play tends to be quieter, more cooperative, and more likely to involve fantasy and role play (Ruble et al., 2006).

Children vary in their levels of sociability from infancy onward, and by early childhood there are distinct differences among children in how successful they are in using the social skills required for play in a group setting. Preschool social life rewards the bold, and children who are temperamentally inhibited spend a lot of their preschool time watching others play without taking part themselves (Coplan et al., 2004; Rubin et al., 2002). However, for some children it simply takes time to become accustomed to the preschool social environment. The more preschool experience children have, the

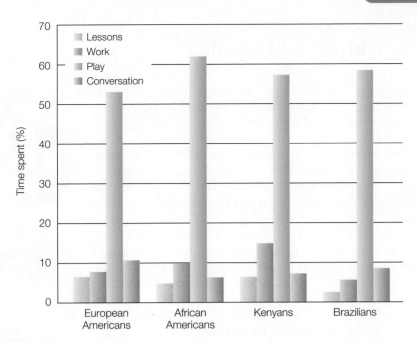

Figure 6.6 • **Play in four cultures.** Across cultures, play is the most common activity in early childhood. **Source:** Based on *A window into different cultural worlds: Young children's everyday activities in the United States, Brazil, and Kenya.* Child Development, 77, 1446–1469.

more successful they are at taking part in social play (Dyer & Moneta, 2006). Sometimes children observe other children's play as a prelude to entering the play themselves (Lindsey & Colwell, 2003). Also, some children simply enjoy playing by themselves. They may spend more time than others in solitary play, but it could be an indication of an unusually lively and creative imagination rather than a sign of being withdrawn or rejected (Coplan et al., 2004). There are also cultural differences in how shyness in early childhood is regarded by peers, as you will see in the **Cultural Focus: Shyness in China and Canada** feature on page 282.

Play in early childhood is widespread across cultures, especially in the first years of this life stage. **_Figure 6.6_** shows the results of a study comparing four cultural groups, and in all four groups the 3-year-old children spent more time in play than in any other activity (Tudge et al., 2006). However, anthropologists have observed some cultures where play is rare even in early childhood, such as the Maya of Guatemala (Gaskins, 2000). In general, the more work parents have to do, the earlier they involve children in work and the less time children have for play (Rogoff, 2003). Nevertheless, in general, children in traditional cultures have some time for play. Often their play is structured and directed by the older children in the mixed-age peer group. Outside of the West, it is rare for children to play with adults (LeVine et al., 2008).

Sometimes children's play involves imitation of adult activity, such as going to the market (Rogoff, 2003; Roopnarine et al., 1994). Other times, play is purely for fun. For example, in India, young girls play a game that involves clapping hands in time to a song. They clap against each other's hands in a complex pattern as they sing, going faster and faster as the song proceeds. The song goes through 11 verses that describe a girl's likely course through life at each age, ending with turning into a spirit. In early childhood, girls learn first by observing and listening as the older girls play, then by gradually taking part in the clapping song themselves.

AGGRESSION Early childhood is an important time for the development of aggression. As young children move more into

In most cultures, the proportion of same-gender play rises during early childhood. Here, young girls in India play a clapping game together.

CULTURAL FOCUS   Shyness in China and Canada

In studies of young children in the West, shyness has long been associated with negative characteristics such as anxiety, insecurity, and social incompetence (Rubin & Coplan, 2010). Consistently, shy children have been found to experience problems in their relations with peers and to be prone to negative self-perceptions and depression (Rubin et al.,1995). Shyness in young children has been viewed by Western researchers as a problem to be cured.

But what about in other cultural contexts? Xinyin Chen, a developmental psychologist who grew up in China and now lives in Canada, hypothesized that shyness would have a different meaning in the Chinese cultural context, and set out to compare the consequences of shyness among Chinese and Canadian children (Chen et al., 2006).

In one study conducted by Chen and his colleagues, 4-year-old children in China and Canada were invited into a laboratory setting in groups of four and observed in two 15-minute free-play interactions. Shy children were identified as those who spent the most time in onlooker behavior (watching the activities of others) or unoccupied behavior (wandering around the room alone or sitting alone doing nothing). Through this process, 50 of 200 Chinese children and 45 of 180 Canadian children were classified as shy.

Although the proportion of shy children to non-shy children was identical in the two countries, the responses shy children received from their peers was very different. When shy Canadian children made attempts to interact with their peers, the peers often reacted negatively (e.g., "No!" or "I won't do it") and rarely reacted positively with encouragement and support. In contrast, peers of shy children in China responded much more positively when shy children initiated contact, often inviting them to play or allowing them to join a game. Overall, peers in Canada tended to be antagonistic or nonresponsive toward shy children, whereas in China, peers of shy children were more often supportive and cooperative.

However, Chen and his colleagues have been conducting research in China for over 20 years now, and they have recorded striking shifts in the social implications of shyness for young Chinese children over that time. The past 20 years have been a period of dramatic social change in China, as the country has moved rapidly from a state-controlled Communist economy to free-market economy. This transition has resulted in changes in values as well, with a decline in the traditional Chinese collectivistic values of duty, respect, and obligation, and a rise in individualistic values of self-assertion and independence.

Shyness has had different social meanings in China than it does in Western countries, at least until recently.

The change in values has been reflected in Chen's research on peers' responses to shy Chinese children. In the 1990 sample Chen studied, shyness was positively associated with a variety of favorable aspects of adjustment, including peer acceptance, leadership, and academic achievement. However, by the time Chen repeated the study in 2002, the correlation had flipped. Now shyness was associated with negative adjustment, including peer rejection and depression. In just a 12-year period, the cultural meaning of shyness had reversed. As Chen observed, "the extensive change toward the capitalistic system in the economic reform and the introduction of Western ideologies may have led to the decline in the adaptive value of shyness" (Chen et al., 2006, p. 139).

▶ **Simulate** the **Experiment**
Aggression and Prosocial Behavior
in **MyDevelopmentLab**

instrumental aggression type of aggression when a child wants something and uses aggressive behavior or words to get it

hostile aggression type of aggression that entails signs of anger and intent to inflict pain or harm on others

the world of peers, they encounter more competition for resources—toys, play companions, adult attention, the last cookie—and this competition sometimes leads to conflict and aggression (Tremblay, 2002). ▶

Scholars distinguish between several different types of aggression (Underwood, 2003). **Instrumental aggression** is involved when a child wants something (toys, food, attention) and uses aggressive behavior or words to get it. A child may also exhibit signs of anger and intend to inflict pain or harm on others. This is known as **hostile aggression**. Instrumental and hostile aggression can each be expressed in several ways. *Physical aggression* includes hitting, kicking, pushing, or striking with an object. *Verbal aggression* is the use of words to hurt others, through yelling at them, calling them names, or hostile teasing. **Relational aggression** (or *social aggression*) involves damaging another person's reputation among peers through social exclusion and malicious gossip.

Physical aggression among young children has been a target of a great deal of research. There is abundant evidence that physical aggression peaks in toddlerhood and early childhood (Alink et al., 2006). One top aggression researcher, Richard Tremblay (2000), summarized a wide range of longitudinal studies extending from infancy to adulthood across many countries and found a common pattern that physical aggression peaks at 24 to 42 months—the second year of toddlerhood and the first year of early childhood—then declines. Boys are consistently more physically aggressive than girls, in early childhood and throughout the life span.

However, there is a great deal of variation around this average pattern. Not all boys are aggressive in early childhood, and not all boys and girls show a decline in aggression after age 3. One national study in the United States followed the course of physical aggression in a longitudinal study of children from age 2 to 9 (NICHD Early Childhood Research Network, 2004). The researchers identified five different "trajectory groups" with regard to aggression. The largest group declined steeply in physical aggression from age 2 to 9. However, two other groups were "low trajectory" groups that never showed much physical aggression, one was a "moderate trajectory" group that remained moderate, and one was a "high trajectory" group that remained high.

In general, individual differences in physical aggression remain stable across time, that is, children who rarely display physical aggression in early childhood are unlikely to display it in middle childhood and adolescence, and children who are especially aggressive in early childhood tend to be more aggressive than their peers in later periods as well (Brame et al., 2001; Lansford et al., 2006; Schaeffer et al., 2003; Vaillancourt et al., 2003). However, longitudinal studies show that parents who are especially patient, sensitive, and involved can reduce high aggression in early childhood to moderate aggression by middle childhood (NICHD Early Childhood Research Network, 2004; Tremblay, 2002). Early childhood is a crucial time for addressing physical aggression, because when aggression is still high at the end of early childhood it is a strong predictor of later aggressive behavior in adolescence and adulthood (Loeber et al., 2005; Tremblay & Nagin, 2005).

Across cultures, aggression is frequently a component of children's play in early and middle childhood, especially for boys (Edwards, 2005). Physical "rough-and-tumble" play such as wrestling is common among boys of the same age when they are brought together in school and playground settings (Scott & Panksepp, 2003). This aggressive play occurs in other mammals as well, and is in part a way of establishing a dominance hierarchy (Hassett et al., 2008). Aggressive play establishes who is on top and who is not, and in this way serves to avoid more serious aggression.

In contrast to physical aggression, verbal aggression rises across early childhood, at least in the Western countries where this research has been done (Dodge et al., 2006; Underwood, 2003). As children become more adept at using words, they grow capable of applying their verbal abilities to a wide range of purposes, including aggression. Also, verbal aggression becomes substituted for physical aggression across the years of early childhood as children learn that adults regard physical aggression toward peers as unacceptable and as children become more capable of restraining their physically aggressive impulses (Tremblay, 2000; Tremblay & Nagin, 2005; Tremblay et al., 2004).

Relational aggression also becomes more common in the course of early childhood (Crick et al., 2006). Like the increase in verbal aggression, the increase in relational

Physical aggression peaks in early childhood.

Watch the **Video**
Relational Aggression
in **MyDevelopmentLab**

APPLYING YOUR KNOWLEDGE
. . . as a Nurse

Do you think the 1-2-3 approach to discipline would be likely to work with a young child who has a problem with physical aggression? If not, what approach would you recommend to a parent with an aggressive child?

relational aggression type of aggression that involves damaging another person's reputation among peers through social exclusion and malicious gossip

aggression reflects children's growing cognitive and social understanding. They become more capable of understanding the complexities of social relationships, and more aware of the ways that social weapons can be used to hurt others and gain social status. They learn that a punch on the shoulder does not hurt nearly as much, or last nearly as long, as the pain of being the only one not invited to a birthday party or being the subject of a nasty rumor (Murray-Close et al., 2007; Nelson et al., 2005). Verbal and relational aggression are slightly more common among girls than among boys in early childhood, but the differences are minor, much smaller than the gap between boys and girls in physical aggression (Underwood, 2003).

Media use in early childhood

6.22	LEARNING OBJECTIVE	Identify the rates and consequences of media use in early childhood.

Early childhood is a period when children's media world expands greatly, especially in developed countries. Many types of media use increase from toddlerhood to early childhood (Lemish, 2007). The major types of media use in early childhood are television, electronic games, and recorded music.

THE NEGATIVE IMPACTS OF TELEVISION USE: VIOLENCE AND ADVERTISING Television is popular with people all over the world, including young children. In early childhood, TV-viewing time per day varies from about 1½ hours in Sweden and Germany to about 3 hours in Hungary, Turkey, and the United States (Hasebrink, 2007b). In the United States, over 30% of children ages 2–7 have a TV set in their bedroom (Scheibe, 2007). African Americans are especially high in TV consumption, with rates of over 4 hours a day in childhood compared to about 3 hours a day in other American ethnic groups (Roberts & Foehr, 2004). The most popular shows among young children are the ones made especially for them, such as cartoons and educational shows like *Sesame Street* (Lemish, 2007).

Although television is embraced everywhere for its entertainment value, many people have concerns about the effects of television, especially on children and especially with respect to violence. Content analyses have found that children's programs are even more violent than programs for adults. One study found that two-thirds of all children's programs contained violence, and about half the violence took place in cartoons (Aikat, 2007). Violence was portrayed as funny about two-thirds of the time, and in most cases the victims were not shown experiencing pain and the perpetrator of the violence was not punished. ●▶

Simulate the **Experiment** Media Violence in **MyDevelopmentLab**

What are the effects of witnessing so much TV violence on young children's development? More than five decades of research, including more than 300 studies using a variety of methods, has led to a strong consensus among scholars that watching TV violence increases children's aggression (Bushman & Chandler, 2007). The more aggressive children are, the more they like to watch TV violence, but TV violence inspires aggressive thoughts and behavior even in children who are not usually aggressive (Bushman & Huesmann, 2001). Experimental studies indicate that causation is involved, not just correlation. For example, in one early study, children in a preschool were randomly assigned to two groups (Steur et al., 1971). Over 11 days, one group watched violent cartoons, whereas the other group saw the same cartoons but with the violence removed. During playground observations following this 11-day experiment, children who had seen the violent cartoons were more likely than children in the nonviolent cartoon group to kick and hit their peers.

Young children ages 3–6 are believed to be especially vulnerable to the effects of TV violence (Bushman & Chandler, 2007). They are more likely than younger or older children to model their behavior after the behavior of others (see the discussion of social learning and modeling in Chapter 1), including TV characters. Also, they are less likely than older children to have a clear understanding of the boundary between fantasy and reality, and so more likely to believe that what they witness on TV is real.

Another important effect of TV watching in early childhood concerns advertising. In the United States, the average child sees about 40,000 TV commercials each year, mostly for toys, cereal, candy, and fast food (Scheibe, 2007). Young children are especially susceptible to advertising, as they are less aware of advertising intent than older children are. Most do not perceive a distinction between a program and an advertisement until about age 5 (Jennings, 2007). The more TV young children watch, the more they attempt to influence their parents to buy the advertised products (Valkenburg & Buijzen, 2005). Because most of the products children see advertised are unhealthy foods, concern has grown that TV advertising is one influence behind the growing international epidemic of obesity in children (Bergstrom, 2007a).

THE BENEFICIAL EFFECTS OF EDUCATIONAL TELEVISION TV has also been found to have some beneficial effects on young children. In recent decades, educational programs have been developed that are highly popular among young children. Perhaps most notable is the *Sesame Street* program, which is broadcast in 120 countries worldwide (Truglio, 2007). The content of the program is based on knowledge from developmental psychology of what will be most appealing to young children and most effective at teaching them the academic skills that will prepare them for school (Bergstrom, 2007b). Content is adapted to the culture in which the program is shown, for example addressing the stigma of AIDS in South Africa and promoting cross-cultural respect and understanding among children in the Middle East (Truglio, 2007).

Sesame Street and other programs have shown impressive positive effects on young children's development. In one study, viewing *Sesame Street* at ages 2 and 3 predicted higher scores at age 5 on tests of language development and math skills, even controlling for parents' education and income (Scantlin, 2007). In another study, children who viewed *Sesame Street* at age 5 were recontacted at ages 15 and 19 and were found to have higher grades in English, math, and science than children in the comparison group (Anderson et al., 2001). Studies of *Sesame Street* and other educational programs have shown the programs to have other positive effects as well, such as promoting imaginative play (Scantlin, 2007) and prosocial behavior such as cooperation (Bergstrom, 2007b).

ELECTRONIC GAMES AND MUSIC Although the focus of most media research concerning young children has been on television, other media are also important in their lives, notably electronic games and recorded music.

Television is now nearly universal, but playing electronic games usually depends on access to a computer, and computer access is much more variable across countries. In one international study, over 60% of households in developed countries reported having a computer, but this percentage was much lower in other regions, including eastern Europe (25%), Latin America (about 10%), and Africa (about 5%) (Hasebrink, 2007a). In U.S. studies, 70% of 4- to 6-year-olds have used a computer, and 38% of 5- to 7-year olds use a computer on a typical day, mostly for playing electronic games (Foehr, 2007). Boys play electronic games more than girls do, overall, and the kinds of games they prefer differ, with boys preferring fighting and sports games and girls preferring adventure and learning games (Kubisch, 2007). These gender differences endure through childhood and adolescence, as we will see in later chapters. Electronic games can also be played on handheld devices and mobile phones, but access to these media tends to come in middle childhood and beyond.

Listening to recorded music is also part of the daily media diet of most children in developed countries (Kinnally, 2007). Over half of parents of young children report singing to or playing music for them each day. On average, children ages 2–7 listen to music for about 45 minutes per day. Children ages 3–5 listen mostly to children's songs, but by age 6 children pay more attention to popular music and start to recognize and prefer the latest "hit songs" of the day.

Listening to recorded music is a common part of children's lives in developed countries.

Music evokes a positive response even from infants, but early childhood is an especially important time for the development of responses to music (Kinnally, 2007). It is during early childhood that children first connect musical sounds with specific emotions, for example recognizing songs in major keys as happy and songs in minor keys as sad. By age 5, children show distinct preferences for music that is harmonious rather than dissonant and has a steady rather than erratic beat. There is little research on the effects of music on young children. Research on music effects is concentrated on adolescence because of concerns about the effects of violent music on adolescent development, as we will see later in the text.

WHAT HAVE YOU LEARNED?

1. Across cultures, what is the predominant emotional response to the birth of a new sibling?
2. How do "only children" compare to children with siblings in terms of their self-esteem, intelligence, and social relations with peers?
3. How are friends different from peers?
4. How does play in traditional cultures differ from play in Western cultures during early childhood?
5. Give an example of relational aggression.
6. What gender differences exist in electronic game use during childhood?
7. Why is early childhood an especially important time for the development of responses to music?

Section 3 VIDEO GUIDE Mandatory Reporting (Length: 3:39)

This video explains the concept of mandatory reporting and includes interviews with both a doctor and a child-care worker.

1. Why is mandatory reporting so important?

2. The narrator of this video lists several occupations that are held to legal standards for mandatory reporting. Do you feel that any occupation is missing from the list? Why or why not?

3. If you were in an occupation that held you to legal mandatory reporting and you were faced with a child that you felt might be being psychologically abused, what are some ways you might try to inquire about the abuse?

Watch the **Video** Mandatory Reporting in **MyDevelopmentLab**

Summing Up

((•- **Listen** to an audio file of your chapter in **MyDevelopmentLab**

SECTION 1   PHYSICAL DEVELOPMENT

6.1 Describe the physical growth and change that takes place during early childhood.

The pace of physical development slows in early childhood. From ages 3 to 6 the typical American child grows 2–3 inches per year and adds 5–7 pounds. Average heights and weights in early childhood are considerably lower in developing countries, due to inadequate nutrition and higher likelihood of childhood diseases.

6.2 Describe the changes in brain development that take place during early childhood and the aspects of brain development that explain "infantile" amnesia.

The most notable changes in brain development during early childhood take place in the connections between neurons and in myelination. Most people experience infantile amnesia (the inability to remember anything prior to age 2) and have limited memory for personal events that happened before age 5.

6.3 Identify the main nutritional deficiencies and the primary sources of injury, illness, and mortality during early childhood in developed and developing countries.

About 80% of children in developing countries experience nutritional deficiencies, but a surprisingly high percentage of children in developed countries experience them as well. Calcium is the most common nutritional deficiency in the United States, whereas the two most common types of malnutrition in developing countries are lack of protein and lack of iron. Mortality rates in early childhood are much higher in developing countries than in developed countries but have declined substantially in recent years. In developed countries, the most common cause of injury and death by far in early childhood is motor vehicle accidents.

6.4 Describe changes in gross and fine motor abilities during early childhood, and explain how these changes may have a cultural basis.

From age 3 to 6, young children learn to make more hops in a row and hop on one foot; jump farther from a standing position and to make a running jump; climb stairs without support, alternating their feet; throw a ball farther and more accurately; become better at catching a ball; and increase their running speed and their ability to stop suddenly or change direction. In their fine motor development, children learn to pick up small objects more quickly and precisely, to draw something that is recognizable to others, to write their first letters and some short words, to put on and remove their clothes, to use scissors, and to use a knife to cut soft food. Gross and fine motor skills are culturally specific and depend on what types of activities children are exposed to.

6.5 Describe the development of handedness and identify the consequences and cultural views of left-handedness.

About 10% of children are left-handed. Being left-handed has been stigmatized in many cultures, perhaps due to its association with higher risk of developmental problems.

KEY TERMS

corpus callosum *p. 240*	reticular formation *p. 241*	infantile amnesia *p. 241*	handedness *p. 246*
cerebellum *p. 241*	hippocampus *p. 241*	anemia *p. 242*	

SECTION 2   COGNITIVE DEVELOPMENT

6.6 Explain the features of Piaget's preoperational stage of cognitive development.

Piaget viewed the preoperational stage of cognitive development (ages 2–7) as prone to a variety of errors, including centration, lack of reversibility, egocentrism, and animism. Research has shown that Piaget underestimated the cognitive abilities of early childhood.

6.7 Explain what "theory of mind" is and the evidence for how it develops during early childhood.

Theory of mind is the ability to understand thinking processes in one's self and others. By age 2, as they begin to use language more, children show increasing recognition that others have thoughts and emotions that can be contrasted with their own. By age 3, children know it is possible for them and others to imagine something that is not physically present, an understanding that becomes the basis of pretend play for many years to come. While 3-year-olds are better than 2-year-olds at understanding that others have thoughts and feelings that are different from their own, they still find it difficult to take others' perspectives. Perspective-taking ability advances considerably from age 3 to 6.

6.8 Identify the ways that cultural learning takes place in early childhood.

A great deal of cultural learning takes place in early childhood through observing and working alongside parents or siblings, and in many cultures children make important work contributions to the family during this stage.

6.9 Identify the features that are most important in preschool quality.

Children generally benefit cognitively from attending preschool, but the social effects of preschool are more mixed and in some ways, negative. Key features of high-quality preschool programs include education and training of teachers, class size and child–teacher ratio, age-appropriate materials and activities, and teacher–child interactions.

6.10 Describe the distinctive practices of Japanese preschools and how they reflect cultural values.

Preschools in Japan focus not on academic objectives but rather on group play, so that collectivist Japanese values, such as cooperation and sharing, are reinforced.

6.11 Describe early intervention programs and their outcomes.

Early intervention programs have often resulted in a rise in IQ that fades after a few years. Some early interventions via preschool have had long-term positive effects on children's development, but the effects depend greatly on the quality of the program.

6.12 Explain how advances in vocabulary and grammar occur in early childhood.

Children's vocabularies expand immensely in early childhood, from about 1,000 words at age 3 to about 2,500 words at age 6, and they readily grasp the grammatical rules of their culture with few errors by age 4.

6.13 Describe how children learn pragmatics in early childhood, and identify to what extent these social rules are culturally based.

Pragmatics guide us in knowing what to say—and what not to say—in a given social situation, and by age 4, children are sensitive to the characteristics of their conversational partner and will adjust their speech accordingly All cultures have their own rules for what kinds of speech can be used in what kinds of situations.

KEY TERMS

preoperational stage *p. 249*

conservation *p. 249*

centration *p. 250*

reversibility *p. 250*

egocentrism *p. 250*

animism *p. 250*

classification *p. 250*

symbolic function substage *p. 251*

intuitive thought substage *p. 251*

theory of mind *p. 252*

early intervention program *p. 257*

sensitive period *p. 259*

grammar *p. 259*

pragmatics *p. 260*

SECTION 3   EMOTIONAL AND SOCIAL DEVELOPMENT

6.14 Identify advances in emotional understanding and self-regulation during early childhood.

Early childhood is a key time for the development of emotional self-regulation, as children improve at effortful control.

6.15 Describe moral development in early childhood, including empathy, modeling, and morality as cultural learning.

The capacity for empathy increases in early childhood, which leads in turn to an increase in prosocial behavior. Children learn morality in part through modeling (i.e., observing the behavior of others and its consequences). Early childhood is also a time when children begin to show a capacity for moral reasoning.

6.16 Describe the roles that parents and peers play in gender socialization, and explain how gender schemas lead to self-socialization.

Children learn gender identity by age 2, but do not learn gender constancy until age 6 or 7. During early childhood they often become rigid in their views of gender roles. Parents are key agents of gender socialization, especially fathers, and conformity to gender roles is enforced by peers as well. Once young children possess gender schemas, they seek to maintain consistency between their schemas and their behavior, a process called self-socialization.

6.17 Describe the four types of parenting "styles" and the outcomes associated with each, and explain why those outcomes are complex.

American parenting research has emphasized the dimensions of demandingness and responsiveness, in combinations resulting in four categories of "parenting styles": authoritative, authoritarian, permissive, and disengaged. By American standards, authoritative parenting is associated with the most favorable outcomes. However, the relationship between parenting styles and children's development is complex due to reciprocal effects between parents and children.

6.18 Describe the major cultural variations in approaches to parenting.

The effects of parenting on young children depend substantially on cultural context. The authoritative parenting style is very rare in non-Western cultures because parents expect that their authority will be obeyed without question and without requiring an explanation.

6.19 Describe the main cultural variations in how parents discipline young children, and explain how cultural context influences children's responses to discipline.

In Western cultures the approach to discipline in early childhood tends to emphasize the authoritative approach of explaining the consequences of misbehavior and the reasons for discipline. Physical punishment and the close interdependent *amae* mother–child relationship have quite different effects on children depending on the cultural context.

6.20 Identify the most common features of sibling relationships worldwide, and describe how children with no siblings differ from other children.

Jealousy toward young siblings is very common worldwide in early childhood. "Only children" fare very well compared to children with siblings, even in China where there has been concern about the social effects of the government's "one-child" population policy.

6.21 Explain how the quality of friendships changes from toddlerhood to early childhood, and describe the role of play and aggression in young children's friendships.

Children engage in cooperative pretend play more in early childhood than in toddlerhood. Physical aggression peaks in toddlerhood and the first year of early childhood, then declines as verbal aggression rises.

6.22 Identify the rates and consequences of media use in early childhood.

In early childhood, TV-viewing time per day varies from about 1½ to 3 hours across developed countries. Abundant evidence shows that violent television promotes aggressive behavior in young children. Boys most often play electronic games involving fighting and sports, whereas girls prefer adventure and learning games. Early childhood is an especially important time for the development of responses to music, as children learn to connect musical sounds with specific emotions.

KEY TERMS

emotional self-regulation *p. 263*	gender schema *p. 267*	disengaged parents *p. 269*	child maltreatment *p. 275*
undercontrol *p. 263*	self-socialization *p. 268*	reciprocal or bidirectional effects *p. 270*	foster care *p. 276*
externalizing problems *p. 263*	parenting styles *p. 268*	filial piety *p. 271*	only child *p. 279*
overcontrol *p. 263*	demandingness *p. 269*	familismo *p. 271*	peers *p. 280*
internalizing problems *p. 263*	responsiveness *p. 269*	time out *p. 273*	instrumental aggression *p. 282*
initiative vs. guilt *p. 263*	authoritative parents *p. 269*	psychological control *p. 273*	hostile aggression *p. 282*
gender constancy *p. 266*	authoritarian parents *p. 269*	corporal punishment *p. 274*	relational aggression *p. 283*
gender roles *p. 266*	permissive parents *p. 269*		

Practice Test

✓• Study and Review in MyDevelopmentLab

1. Which of the following best describes the physical changes that take place during early childhood?
   a. Most children lose their baby fat and become more like adults in terms of their body proportions.
   b. Physical development occurs at a more rapid pace than it did in the first 3 years.
   c. Girls are slightly taller and heavier than boys.
   d. Cross-cultural comparisons have shown that only genetics plays a role in individual differences in height and weight.

2. The limited memory for personal events and experiences prior to age 5 is probably due to incomplete myelination of the
   a. reticular formation.
   b. corpus callosum.
   c. cerebellum.
   d. hippocampus.

3. Which of the following is the most common nutritional problem among young children in the United States?
   a. marasmus
   b. anemia
   c. calcium deficiency
   d. protein deficiency

4. How does motor development change between ages 3 and 6?
   a. Children's fine motor skills become refined, but their gross motor skills remain the same as they were in toddlerhood.
   b. Children's fine motor skills have been found to develop at the same rate all over the world.
   c. Children develop the same motor skills at the same pace, regardless of gender.
   d. Fine motor skill development allows children to become more independent by doing things such as dressing and feeding themselves.

5. Children who are left-handed
   a. will be more likely to learn to be right-handed in an Asian or African culture than in the United States.
   b. likely first developed this tendency during the preschool years.
   c. are often praised for their uniqueness in non-Western cultures.
   d. will always have a left-handed twin if they are monozygotic (MZ) twins.

6. A 5-year-old child draws a yellow sun in the upper corner of her paper complete with a smiley face and sunglasses. This is an example of
   a. sensorimotor thought.
   b. animism.
   c. gross motor skill refinement.
   d. centered thinking.

7. Which of the following is true regarding theory of mind?
   a. Children show a decrease in this ability from 4 to 6 years of age because they are becoming more independent.
   b. It develops the same way in all cultures with spoken language.
   c. It begins to develop, in rudimentary form, sometime in infancy.
   d. A child who demonstrates theory of mind is not yet able to think about thinking.

8. Cultural learning skills, such as learning to set the table in a developed country or to help prepare food in a traditional culture,
   a. develop as part of a social and cultural process, according to Vygotsky.
   b. must be learned in the sensorimotor stage first or they never fully develop.
   c. cannot be appropriately acquired until early adolescence.
   d. usually develop best if they take place in a formal setting.

9. As a parent of a 3-year-old you have visited several preschool programs to determine the one that will provide the highest quality experience. Which of the following should NOT be heavily weighted in your decision about which preschool to pick?
   a. whether there is a small class size
   b. whether the teachers have been formally trained and have educational credentials
   c. whether they are making good use of time by providing worksheets to practice numbers and letters
   d. whether the teachers spend a lot of time interacting with the children rather than with each other

10. In Japan
    a. learning academic skills is the number one goal of having children attend preschool.
    b. preschool is mainly a time for learning social skills.
    c. parents and preschool teachers list the same top reasons for young children to attend preschool as do their counterparts in the United States.
    d. individuality is stressed from the time children enter preschool as a way to encourage children to reach their full potential.

11. Compared to a comparison group of children with low SES who did not attend Head Start, those children who did
    a. were less likely to be placed in special education classes.
    b. improved their academic performance, but were still more likely to repeat at least two grades.
    c. showed a boost in IQ and achievement that lasted throughout their school years.
    d. showed no differences in academic performance and success.

12. Young children's use of grammar
    a. is entirely dependent on formal instruction in preschool.
    b. develops more quickly in traditional cultures.
    c. develops simply by hearing and using the language in daily interactions.
    d. is mostly incorrect until the age of 6.

13. When a 4-year-old uses infant-directed speech when talking to her neighbor's new baby, this demonstrates
    a. a sensitive period.
    b. fast mapping.
    c. classification.
    d. pragmatics.

14. A key reason why emotional outbursts decline in early childhood is that children
    a. learn strategies for regulating their emotions, in a practice known as effortful control.
    b. have a more sophisticated theory of mind at this age.
    c. at this age are no longer at risk for externalizing problems.
    d. have learned the skill of overcontrolling their emotions.

15. Which of the following statements accurately describes moral development in early childhood?
    a. Children at this age are not yet able to experience empathy.
    b. Socioemotional emotions such as shame and pride first appear.
    c. Perspective taking and being able to understand how others think and feel make children more empathic at this age.
    d. Young children inherently know the rules and expectations of their culture without needing to be taught.

16. The way we organize and process information in terms of gender-based categories is referred to as
    a. gender identity.
    b. gender constancy.
    c. self-socialization.
    d. gender schemas.

17. Research on parenting has found that
    a. the two main dimensions of parenting are demandingness and strictness.
    b. children of permissive parents tend to do better in school than children of other parenting styles because they learn to think for themselves.
    c. there are bidirectional effects between parents and their children.
    d. the outcomes for children of authoritative parents are virtually identical to outcomes for children of permissive parents.

18. Which of the following is the most accurate statement based on existing research?
    a. The typical parenting style in non-Western cultures is authoritarian.
    b. The American model of parenting does not apply well in other cultures.
    c. Providing explanations to their children is most common among non-Western parents who spend more time with their children than do American parents.
    d. Permissive parenting would be most likely in cultures that have a tradition of filial piety.

19. The use of shame as a form of discipline
    a. has resulted in positive outcomes in both the United States and Finland.
    b. is referred to as psychological control by American researchers.
    c. is associated with high rates of behavior problems in Japanese children.
    d. is universally accepted as the best method of discipline because it does not include physical punishment.

20. Which of the following is true regarding siblings?
    a. A gap of 4–8 years between children is common in many cultures across the world.
    b. "Only children" are maladjusted, meaning they are more prone to depression behavior disorders.
    c. Jealousy is a common response to the birth of a younger sibling across cultures.
    d. Research has shown that young children who have no siblings have a more advanced theory of mind than young children who have older siblings.

21. If you were a researcher observing 5-year-old children on a playground during kindergarten recess in the United States, what would you be most likely to observe?
    a. boys playing with children from other kindergarten classes rather than older boys
    b. girls playing kickball with the boys (with the girls serving as referees to be sure the boys follow the rules)
    c. boys engaging in cooperative, fantasy play
    d. the boys challenging the girls to a wrestling match

22. Watching TV during early childhood
    a. has not been associated with any positive effects on development.
    b. is a popular leisure activity all over the world.
    c. has been correlated with aggressive thoughts and behaviors, but only among males who were already extremely aggressive before viewing.
    d. has not been studied experimentally, therefore no conclusions about causation can be made.

7 Middle Childhood

Ever since my twins, Paris and Miles, were born 11 years ago, I've kept a journal of the notable events in their development.

To open this chapter on middle childhood, the life stage they have recently passed through, I present some scenes from their years ages 6 through 9.

Age 6

Actual conversation:

Miles: Daddy, I have something important to ask you.

Me: What is it?

Miles: How many people are there in the world?

Me: About 7 billion.

Miles: (long pause) I can only count to 300.

Age 7

Both twins had words of wisdom to share this month. Paris's came when we were walking home from school one day and she started talking about a scene in a book she read recently, when locusts suddenly swarm down from the sky and eat the crops the family has spent months carefully nurturing. I spoke gravely about how awful this was, all that hard work for naught, now what would they eat, etc. Then Paris observed, cheerfully, "Well, at least the locusts were happy!"

> "they went trick-or-treating separately for the first time, with friends instead of with us and each other . . ."

Miles's words of wisdom came one Sunday during brunch. We were listening to music and I went into the other room to change the CD, and during that process I banged my head hard on a shelf. Thinking no one else could hear me, I began cursing colorfully and passionately. When I walked back into the dining room the twins were staring wide-eyed, wondering about the meaning of all these new words. I apologized, explaining how I had hit my head and it REALLY hurt. "Next time," Miles advised, "just say 'Ow!'"

Age 8

Paris has become increasingly interested in doing solo baking projects. She's always helped me make bread, since she was tiny, and now she's decided that she wants to do her own baking. One day last week she made bread by herself, following a recipe in a kids' cookbook my aunt gave to her. I offered to help, fearing an inedible result that would discourage her, but she insisted on doing it on her own, and it actually turned out to be quite good. Since then she's made cookies and biscuits, with mixed results, but she's learning and clearly very keen on doing more.

Age 9

My, how they're growing up. They are now in charge of setting the table and unloading the dishwasher, and Miles makes coffee every morning.

We no longer have to take them to school or walk them home. They can handle the half-mile route on their own with no problem.

There was another milestone on Halloween, when they went trick-or-treating separately for the first time, with friends instead of with us and each other. Miles went with a group of boys who are his friends from school. Paris invited a girl from her class over, and they went with Lene. Both brought home massive amounts of candy, far more than any sane person would eat in a year.

Scenes from two children's middle childhood, in one place and time, yet many of the themes resonate more broadly. Across cultures, the transition from early childhood to middle childhood is recognized as an important shift in children's development, when they become capable of greater cognitive challenges and personal responsibility (Sameroff & Haith, 1996). In developing countries, middle childhood is often the age when children are first given important family duties, such as taking care of younger siblings, buying or selling goods, maintaining a fire, or caring for domestic animals (Weisner, 1996). According to Roy D'Andrade (1987), middle childhood is when children first show a grasp of **cultural models**, which are cognitive structures pertaining to common activities, for example buying something, herding cattle, taking care of an infant, making bread, or delivering a message to a relative's house. Children in both developed and developing countries begin formal schooling in middle childhood, which includes cultural models of "listen to the teacher," "wait your turn," and "do your homework." Children begin to grasp cultural models as early as toddlerhood, but during middle childhood their understanding of cultural models acquires greater complexity, so that they become capable of taking on a much broader range of tasks (Weisner, 1996).

Here, as elsewhere in the human life span, how we experience a given stage of life depends greatly on cultural context. Children in all cultures become more capable of useful work in middle childhood, but the nature of their work varies greatly. For many children throughout human history it has been mainly farm work—tending the fields, herding the cows, and feeding the horses. For today's children, it might be school work or household work in developed countries, and any of a wide range of work in developing countries, from household work to factory work to herding and feeding domestic animals. In this chapter we explore a wide range of cultural variations in children's experiences of middle childhood.

cultural models cognitive structures pertaining to common cultural activities

SECTION 1 PHYSICAL DEVELOPMENT

LEARNING OBJECTIVES

7.1 Identify the changes in physical and sensory development that take place during middle childhood.

7.2 Describe the negative effects of both malnutrition and obesity on development, and identify the causes of obesity.

7.3 Explain why rates of illness and injury are relatively low in middle childhood.

7.4 Explain how children's gross motor skills develop in middle childhood and how these advancements are related to participation in games and sports.

7.5 Describe the new skills that demonstrate children's advances in fine motor development in middle childhood.

Growth in Middle Childhood

body mass index (BMI) measure of the ratio of weight to height

Middle childhood is an exceptionally healthy time of life, as children become less susceptible to disease, less vulnerable to the effects of malnutrition, and less likely to have accidents that result in injury or death. However, several types of physical problems become more common in middle childhood than they were in early childhood, including nearsightedness, obesity, and asthma.

Physical growth and sensory development

7.1 | **LEARNING OBJECTIVE** | Identify the changes in physical and sensory development that take place during middle childhood.

Middle childhood is the time of life when people are most likely to be slim.

In middle childhood, physical growth continues at a slow but steady pace, about 2–3 inches (5–8 cm) per year in height and about 5–7 pounds (2½–3 kg) per year in weight. Boys continue to be slightly taller and to weigh slightly more than girls, on average. For both boys and girls, middle childhood is the time of life when they are mostly likely to be slim. Of all age groups in the life span, 6- to 10-year-olds have the lowest **body mass index (BMI)**, a measure of the ratio of weight to height (Guillaume & Lissau, 2002). Boys continue to have somewhat more muscle than girls do in middle childhood, and girls continue to have somewhat more body fat, so the average boy is stronger than the average girl. However, both boys and girls grow stronger during this stage. For example, the average 10-year-old can throw a ball twice as far as the average 6-year-old. Children run faster and longer, too, over the course of middle childhood, as lung capacity expands (Malina et al., 2004).

From age 6 to 12, children lose all 20 of their "primary teeth" and new, permanent teeth replace them. The two top front teeth are usually the first to go. The permanent teeth are adult-sized teeth that do not grow much once they come in, giving children in middle childhood a toothy smile that sometimes looks a little too big for their mouths.

Sight and hearing both change in middle childhood, hearing usually for the better, sight more likely for the worse. Hearing often improves because the tube in the inner ear that is the site of ear infections in toddlerhood and early childhood has now matured and is longer and narrower than it was before (Bluestone & Klein, 2007). This structural change makes it less likely for fluid containing bacteria to flow from the mouth to the ear, which in turn makes inner ear infections less likely.

With regard to sight, the incidence of **myopia**, also known as being *nearsighted*, rises sharply in middle childhood. This is a problem that is more likely to occur in developed countries than in developing countries. The more children read, write, and use computers, the more likely they are to develop myopia (Feldkamper & Schaeffel, 2003; Saw et al., 2002). Consequently, rates of myopia are highest in the developed countries where children are mostly likely to have access to books and computers. The eyes finish developing by age 10, so the effects of using the eyes to do a lot of close work on computers or in reading can interfere with development and lead to myopia. Myopia is also partly genetic, as MZ twins have a higher concordance rate (see Chapter 1) than DZ twins do (Pacella et al., 1999). About one-fourth of children in developed countries need glasses by the end of middle childhood (Mutti et al., 2002).

myopia visual condition of being unable to see distant objects clearly; also known as being nearsighted

Nutrition and malnutrition

> Describe the negative effects of both malnutrition and obesity on development, and identify the causes of obesity.

LEARNING OBJECTIVE 7.2

By middle childhood, children have grown large enough that they are less vulnerable to the effects of malnutrition than they were earlier. Even if they are deprived of food for a period of time, their bodies have enough resources to weather the deprivation without the effects being as severe as in earlier life stages. Nevertheless, malnutrition can have enduring negative effects in middle childhood. Obesity also becomes a problem for many children in middle childhood, especially those in developed countries.

MALNUTRITION As we have seen in previous chapters, malnutrition in early development often results in illness, disease, or death. In middle childhood, bodies are stronger and more resilient, and immune systems are better developed. Nevertheless, malnutrition has effects in middle childhood as well. Even for children who survive early malnutrition, the damage to their physical and cognitive development accumulates by middle childhood (Liu et al., 2003).

One longitudinal study in Guatemala showed how nutrition in the early years contributes to cognitive and social functioning in middle childhood (Barrett & Frank, 1987). Children who were classified in early childhood as having "high nutrient levels" were more likely than children with "low nutrient levels" to explore new environments in middle childhood and to persist in a frustrating situation. They were also more energetic, less anxious, and showed more positive emotion. A more recent study, in Ghana, reported similar results, with children who experienced mild-to-moderate malnutrition in their early years demonstrating lower levels of cognitive development in middle childhood on standardized tests and in teacher ratings, compared to children who were not malnourished (Appoh & Krekling, 2004). The malnourished children were also more likely to be rated by teachers as anxious, sad, and withdrawn (Appoh, 2004).

Other studies in other countries have found similar results, with better-nourished children scoring higher than malnourished children on a wide range of cognitive and social measures in middle childhood (Grigorenko, 2003; Wachs, 2002). However, there is a consensus that the sensitive period for long-term effects of malnutrition is from the second trimester of pregnancy through age 3 (Galler et al., 2005). Malnutrition that begins after this period does not appear to result in permanent cognitive or behavioral deficits.

APPLYING YOUR KNOWLEDGE
. . . as a Teacher
What kinds of behaviors might indicate that a child has or is developing myopia?

APPLYING YOUR KNOWLEDGE
. . . as a Policy Maker
In areas of the world where there is not enough to eat, many children in middle childhood have trouble sitting still in class because they are anxious and jumpy. How might you institute a nutrition program to help these children do better in school?

My Virtual Child

Is your virtual child at risk for malnutrition or obesity? How has your socioeconomic status impacted the risk?

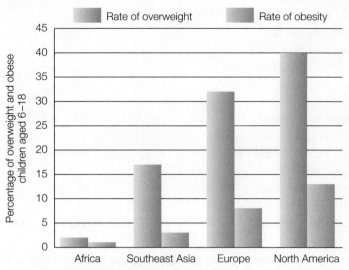

Figure 7.1 • **Rates of childhood overweight and obesity worldwide.** The highest rates occur in the most affluent regions.

Based on *Worldwide trends in childhood overweight and obesity*. International Journal of Pediatric Obesity, 1, 11–25.

Note: *The figure is based on rates for children ages 6–18.*

overweight in children, defined as having a BMI exceeding 18

obese in children, defined as having a BMI exceeding 21

OBESITY Children in developed countries have a different kind of nutritional problem, not malnutrition but overnutrition. In other words, not too few calories but too many. Although middle childhood is the stage of life when the body tends to be slimmest, for many children in developed countries being overweight is a problem. Internationally, children ages 6–10 are considered to be **overweight** if their BMI exceeds 18 and **obese** if their BMI exceeds 21 (Cole et al., 2000). Across countries, rates of overweight and obesity are highest in the most affluent regions (North America and Europe) and lowest in the poorest regions (Africa and Southeast Asia), as *Figure 7.1* shows (Wang & Lobstein, 2006). However, within the United States, rates are especially high in the least affluent ethnic minority groups, including African Americans, Latinos, and Native Americans, as shown in *Map 7.1* (Kim et al., 2002). Rates of overweight and obesity have risen sharply worldwide in recent decades (World Press Review, 2004).

A variety of changes have contributed to the rise in childhood obesity. Most important is the change in diets. Over recent decades people have become less likely to prepare meals at home and more likely to buy meals away from home, especially "fast foods" like hamburgers, french fries, and pizza that are high in fat content; then they wash it down with soft drinks high in sugar content (Nielson et al., 2002). This change reflects other social changes: Parents are less likely to prepare meals at home because they are more likely than in the past to be single parents or to be part of a dual-earner couple. Rates of overweight and obesity are rising in the populations of developing countries in part because their diets are becoming more like the diets of people in developed countries (Gu et al., 2005; Wrotniak et al., 2004).

Another contributor is television. Most children in most developed countries watch at least two hours of television a day (Roberts & Foehr, 2004). In a longitudinal study that followed a sample of American children from age 4 to 11, TV watching predicted gains in body fat (Proctor et al., 2003). Specifically, children who watched at least three hours of TV a day gained 40% more body fat over the course of the study than children who watched less than one and one-half hours a day. Other studies have shown that the more time children watch TV the less time they spend in physical exercise (Institute

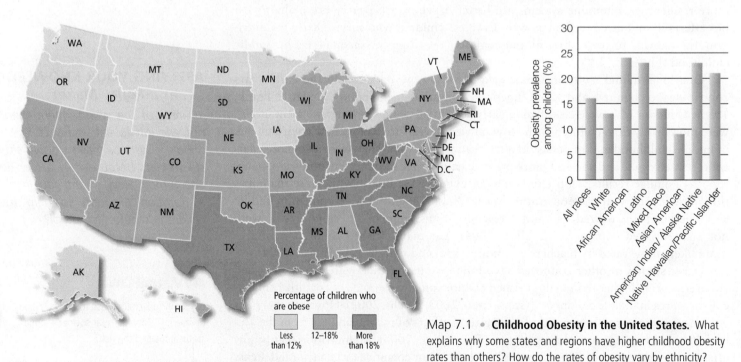

Map 7.1 • **Childhood Obesity in the United States.** What explains why some states and regions have higher childhood obesity rates than others? How do the rates of obesity vary by ethnicity?

of Medicine, 2005; Williams, 2005). Watching TV also exposes children to numerous advertisements for high-fat, high-sugar foods, which they then lobby their parents to buy (Kelly et al., 2010). Rates of overweight and obesity are especially high among African American and Latino children in part because those are also the children that tend to watch the most TV per day (Roberts & Foehr, 2004). The allure of the Internet and electronic games gives children additional reasons to stay inside rather than getting outside and playing active physical games (Anderson & Butcher, 2006).

Genetics also make a contribution to obesity. Concordance rates for obesity are higher among MZ twins than DZ twins. Adopted children tend to have BMIs that are closer to their biological parents than to their adoptive parents (Whitaker et al., 1997). Recent research has even identified a specific gene, called FTO, that sharply increases children's risk for obesity (Frayling et al., 2007). However, genetics cannot explain recent rises in obesity rates. Genetics provide only a risk for overweight and obesity, not a definite destiny.

A compelling demonstration of this comes from a naturalistic study of the Pima Indians in Arizona and Mexico (Gladwell, 1998). The Pima of Mexico live in a remote region and still maintain their traditional ways, including a traditional cultural diet that is high in vegetables and low in fats and sugars. In contrast, the Pima of Arizona have changed in recent decades and their diets have become more like the American mainstream. Consequently, they have an average BMI that is 50% higher than their counterparts in Mexico, even though the two groups are very similar genetically.

Obesity has both social and physical consequences for children. Being obese increases the likelihood that a child will be socially excluded and the object of ridicule by peers (Janssen et al., 2004; Strauss & Pollack, 2003). Other children tend to associate obesity with undesirable characteristics such as being lazy, sloppy, ugly, and stupid (Tiggemann & Anesbury, 2000). By middle childhood obesity is a risk factor for a variety of emotional and behavioral problems (Dietz, 2004; Mustillo et al., 2003; Schwimmer et al., 2003).

Physically, the consequences of obesity are equally serious. Even in middle childhood, obesity can result in diabetes, which can eventually lead to problems such as blindness, kidney failure, and stroke (Hannon et al., 2005; Ramchandani, 2004). Obesity also proves hard to shake from childhood to adulthood. About 80% of obese children remain overweight as adults (Oken & Lightdale, 2000). For adults, the range of health problems resulting from obesity is even greater—including high blood pressure, heart attack, and cancer—and more likely to be fatal (Calle et al., 2003).

What can be done to reverse the sharp increase in childhood obesity? One step is recognizing the problem. Perhaps because obese children tend to have obese parents, studies indicate that fewer than half of parents of obese children view their children as overweight (Jeffrey, 2004; Young-Hyman et al., 2003). Public policies have begun to address the problem of childhood obesity. In the United States, school lunches have been notoriously unhealthy for decades but national standards are currently being revised to provide healthier school lunches that are lower in fats and sugars (Jalonick, 2010).

Rates of obesity are rising in developing countries as diets become more like those in the developed world. This photo was taken in Mexico, which has one of the highest child obesity rates in the world.

THINKING CULTURALLY

Why do you think overweight and obesity are most common among low-income American ethnic groups even though, internationally, overweight and obesity are highest in the highest income countries?

Watch the **Video** The Problem of Childhood Obesity in **MyDevelopmentLab**

APPLYING YOUR KNOWLEDGE
. . . as a Nurse

Given that half of parents of obese children do not regard their children as obese, how would you address this issue if you were treating children who were overweight or obese?

Illness and injuries

Explain why rates of illness and injury are relatively low in middle childhood.

LEARNING OBJECTIVE **7.3**

Middle childhood is in many ways the safest, healthiest time of life. In both developed countries and developing countries, death rates are lower during middle childhood than at any other period of the life span (Hyder & Lunnen, 2009; National Center for Health Statistics [NCHS], 2009). In developed countries, by middle childhood nearly all children have been vaccinated against the diseases that may have been fatal in earlier eras, such as smallpox, typhus, and diphtheria. In developing countries, an increasing

asthma chronic illness of the lungs characterized by wheezing, coughing, and shortness of breath

proportion of children receive vaccinations in infancy, toddlerhood, and early childhood (World Health Organization [WHO], 2010c). Even children who do not receive vaccinations are less susceptible to fatal diseases in middle childhood than they were earlier in their development. Their natural immune systems have become stronger, and their bodies are bigger, stronger, and more resilient.

In developed countries, even rates of minor illnesses have declined in middle childhood in recent decades, due to public health policies. Over time, food production has become cleaner and safer, and food content more closely regulated by government agencies. The air and water have become cleaner in developed countries due to laws and restrictions by governments. For example, according to national U.S. studies, in 1978 nearly 30% of children ages 5–10 had dangerously elevated levels of lead in their blood, which can cause brain damage; by 2001, the rate had fallen to 1% (Centers for Disease Control and Prevention, 2005). This decline reflects government policies that eliminated lead from gasoline and household paint.

One exception to this trend in recent decades toward healthier development in middle childhood is **asthma**, a chronic illness of the lungs characterized by wheezing, coughing, and shortness of breath. A person with asthma has periodic "asthma attacks" in which breathing is especially difficult (Israel, 2005). An asthma attack can be triggered by cold weather, exercise, illnesses, allergies, emotional stress, or for no clear reason (Akinbami & Schoendorf, 2002). Asthma attacks can be reduced through the use of medical injections and inhalers (Glauber et al., 2001; Yoos et al., 2006).

Rates of asthma are highest in middle childhood, and are increasing worldwide (Bousquet et al., 2007; Dey & Bloom, 2005). Boys are at higher risk than girls, for reasons that are not clear (Federico & Liu, 2003). Other risk factors are low birth weight, having a parent who smokes, living in poverty, and obesity (Saha et al., 2005). Susceptibility to asthma is also transmitted genetically (Bosse & Hudson, 2007).

Why are rates of asthma higher now than in the past? The answer appears to be different for developed countries than for developing countries. In developed countries, common features of today's family households contribute to asthma, including carpets, hairy pets, and airtight windows (Tamay et al., 2007). There is also a "hygiene hypothesis" suggesting that high standards of cleanliness and sanitation expose children to fewer viruses and bacteria, and consequently they have fewer illnesses in their early years that would strengthen their immune systems and make them less susceptible to asthma (Tedeschi & Airaghi, 2006). In developing countries, air pollution has become worse as a result of increased industrialization, and air pollution can trigger asthma. One study in Mongolia compared people in rural and urban areas and found substantially higher rates of asthma in urban areas, due mainly to poorer air quality (Vinanen et al., 2007).

Middle childhood is when rates of asthma are highest. This Indian girl is using an inhaler to relieve the symptoms.

Rates of asthma are especially high among African American children, because they often live in urban neighborhoods where the air quality is poor (Pearlman et al., 2006). African Americans also have especially high rates of risk factors for asthma such as low birth weight and obesity. However, one study found that among children with asthma, the families of African American children were more likely than White families to take steps to change the environment in order to reduce risk factors that can trigger asthma attacks, with steps including use of mattress covers, use of pillow covers, cigarette smoke avoidance, pet avoidance, and carpet removal (Roy & Wisnivesky, 2010).

Like illness rates, injury rates are relatively low in middle childhood (Hyder & Lunnen, 2011; U.S. Department of Health and Human Services, 2005b). Compared to younger children, children in middle childhood are more agile and better at anticipating situations that may cause injury; compared to older children, children in middle childhood are kept closer to home and so are less likely to become involved in risky situations. The most common cause of injury in middle childhood is automobile accidents, followed by bicycle accidents (Schiller & Bernadel, 2004). The use of bicycle helmets has become common in middle childhood in recent decades, and this practice has led to a sharp decrease in the number of head injuries experienced during these years (Scheiber & Sacks, 2001).

WHAT HAVE YOU LEARNED?

1. What is myopia and why is it more likely to occur in developed countries than in developing countries?
2. Why are children in middle childhood less vulnerable to the effects of malnutrition than they were when they were younger?
3. What is the cultural basis of obesity? What are some social consequences?
4. Why are rates of asthma higher now than in the past?

Motor Development

Children advance in both gross and fine motor development during middle childhood, nearly reaching maturity in their fine motor abilities. Children become stronger and more agile, and as their gross motor skills develop, they spend more of their days in active play and organized sports. They also become capable of complex fine motor activities such as writing.

My Virtual Child

Now that your virtual child is playing organized sports, how has the typical physical development of middle childhood aided in his or her athletic ability?

Gross motor development

> Explain how children's gross motor skills develop in middle childhood and how these advancements are related to participation in games and sports.

LEARNING OBJECTIVE **7.4**

Watch a group of children on the playground of an elementary school, and you will see lots of activity. In one corner, a group of girls practices a dance routine one of them has learned from watching a TV show. In another, boys play four square, bouncing a ball into each other's square and attempting to defend their own by knocking the ball to someone else's square. In the middle, a group of boys and girls play tag, the perennial favorite.

In a variety of ways, gross motor development advances from early to middle childhood. Children's *balance* improves, allowing them to stay steady on a bike without training wheels or walk on a board across a river. They become *stronger*, so that they can jump higher and throw a ball farther. Their *coordination* advances so that they can perform movements in activities such as swimming and skating that require the synchronization of different body parts. They have greater *agility* so that they can move more quickly and precisely, for example when changing directions while playing soccer. Finally, their *reaction time* becomes faster, allowing them to respond rapidly to changing information, for example when hitting a tennis ball over the net or when catching or hitting a baseball (Kail, 2003). Increasing myelination of the *corpus callosum* connecting the two hemispheres of the brain (see Chapter 6) accelerates reaction time in middle childhood for both gross motor and fine motor tasks (Roeder et al., 2008).

As their gross motor development advances, children can enjoy a wide range of games and sports. In many countries around the world, middle childhood is a time of playing physically active games with siblings and friends, from tag and hide-and-seek to soccer, cricket, baseball, and basketball. Most of their play is informal, and takes place on the street or in a park or in the school yard when a few kids gather and decide to start a game (Kirchner, 2000). However, middle childhood is also the time when

Middle childhood is when children are most likely to be involved in organized sports.

children are most likely to be involved in organized sports. For example, Little League baseball is played in 75 countries around the world during the middle childhood years. In the United States and Canada, about half of children are involved in organized sports at least once between the ages of 5 and 14 (National Council of Youth Sports, 2008; Sport Canada, 2003). Boys are slightly more likely than girls to play on sports teams in middle childhood, but the rate of participation among girls has risen worldwide in recent decades, especially in sports such as soccer, swimming, gymnastics, and basketball (American Academy of Pediatrics, 2004; Raudsepp & Liblik, 2002; Vilhjalmsson & Krisjansdottir, 2003).

Nevertheless, in the view of public health advocates, children do not get nearly as much gross motor activity as they should, leading to high rates of obesity, as we have just seen. Middle childhood may be a time of great advancements in gross motor abilities, but physically active games and sports compete today with the electronic allurements of TV and computer games (Anderson & Butcher, 2006). In some places, schools are less likely than in the past to be a setting for physical activity. In the United States, the percentage of children involved in daily "physical education" programs during middle childhood decreased from 80% in 1969 to just 8% in 2005 (Centers for Disease Control and Prevention [CDC], 2006a; Health Management Resources, 2001). Health authorities recommend 60 minutes of physical activity a day for children ages 6–17, but few American children get that much (see http://www.cdc.gov/physicalactivity/everyone/guidelines/index.html).

Fine motor development

7.5 **LEARNING OBJECTIVE** Describe the new skills that demonstrate children's advances in fine motor development in middle childhood.

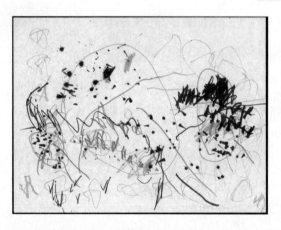

Fine motor development also makes great advances from early childhood to middle childhood. Not many 3- or 4-year-olds can tie their shoes successfully, but nearly all 8- to 9-year-olds can. In Asian cultures, only about half of 4-year-olds can use chopsticks successfully, but for children 6 years old and up it comes easily (Wong et al., 2002). In many developing countries, children become valuable as factory workers in middle childhood because of their abilities to perform intricate fine motor tasks such as weaving rugs (International Labor Organization [ILO], 2002).

Across cultures, advances in fine motor development are especially evident in two areas, drawing and writing. In early childhood, drawing skills are limited to crude depictions of two-dimensional figures. However, in the course of middle childhood children learn to indicate three-dimensional depth by overlapping objects and making near objects smaller than distant ones (Braine et al., 1993). They also learn to

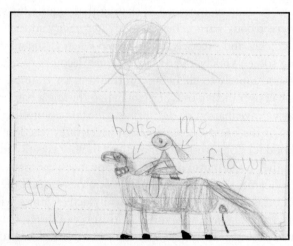

Figure 7.2 • **Change in drawing abilities from early to middle childhood.** Drawings become more realistic as fine motor development advances during middle childhood. Here are drawings that my daughter, Paris, made at ages 3 (*top*), 5 (*left*), and 7 (*right*).

draw objects in greater detail and to adjust the size and relation of objects in a drawing so that they fit together into one coherent whole (see **Figure 7.2**) (Case & Okamoto, 1996).

With regard to writing, in early childhood most children learn to write a few letters and numbers in rough form. In middle childhood, their skills greatly advance (Berninger et al., 2006). Even by age 6 most children are able to write the letters of the alphabet, their own names, and numbers from 1 to 10. In the course of the next several years, as their fine motor abilities develop, they are able to make their letters smaller and neater with more consistent height and spacing. By age 8 or 9 most children can learn to write in cursive. More generally, by the end of middle childhood their fine motor abilities have nearly reached adult maturity, whereas gross motor development will continue to advance for many years to come.

WHAT HAVE YOU LEARNED?

1. Name three ways in which gross motor skills advance during middle childhood.
2. What are some possible reasons why many children at this age are not as physically active as they should be?
3. In which two areas are advances in fine motor development most evident at this age?
4. How do writing skills improve between ages 6 and 9?

Section 1 VIDEO GUIDE Physical Fitness (Length: 3:45)

In this video, a sports and recreation director is interviewed about many aspects of physical development in the middle childhood years.

1. According to this video, what are some of the benefits of sports camps to children?

2. The person interviewed in this video discusses playing tennis versus video games. Compare and contrast these two activities. The world of gaming has changed considerably since this video was filmed; do you feel that video gaming is still a detriment to the physical health of children of this age?

3. What were some of the reasons mentioned in this video why some children are better at certain sports than others?

Watch the **Video** Physical Fitness in **MyDevelopmentLab**

LEARNING OBJECTIVES

7.6 Explain the major cognitive advances that occur during Piaget's concrete operations stage.

7.7 Describe how attention and memory change from early childhood to middle childhood, and identify the characteristics of children who have ADHD.

7.8 Describe the main features and critiques of intelligence tests, and compare and contrast Gardner's and Sternberg's approaches to conceptualizing intelligence.

7.9 Identify the advances in vocabulary, grammar, and pragmatics during middle childhood.

7.10 Explain the consequences for cognitive development of growing up bilingual.

7.11 Summarize the international variations in school enrollment during middle childhood, and compare and contrast the school socialization practices of Eastern and Western cultures.

7.12 Describe how reading and math skills develop from early childhood to middle childhood and the variations in approaches to teaching these skills.

Theories of Cognitive Development

As we have seen in previous chapters, Piaget's approach and the information processing approach offer two different but complementary ways of understanding cognitive development. First we examine Piaget's ideas about concrete operations, then we discuss information processing advances in attention and memory.

Concrete operations

7.6 **LEARNING OBJECTIVE** | Explain the major cognitive advances that occur during Piaget's concrete operations stage.

If you grew up in a Western country, perhaps you believed in Santa Claus when you were a young child. According to the story, Santa Claus rides a sleigh borne by flying reindeer around the world on Christmas Eve, and at each house he comes down the chimney and delivers toys to all the good girls and boys. Do you remember when you stopped believing it? For most children, the story starts to seem far-fetched once they get to be 7 or 8 years old (Sameroff & Haith, 1996). How could one person make it all the way around the world in one night, even with flying reindeer? How could a large man make it down a narrow chimney, dragging a sack full of toys? And what if you don't have a chimney? The loss of belief in this myth reflects gains in cognitive development, as children develop a more true-to-life understanding of the world. ◉

Middle childhood is when children develop a better grasp of what the physical world is really like and what is and is not possible, like flying reindeer. Recall from Chapter 6 that according to Piaget's theory of cognitive development, early childhood is the preoperational stage. In Piaget's view, children ages 2–6 are most notable cognitively for what they *cannot* do—they cannot perform mental operations—and for the kinds of mistakes they make.

Around age 7, children make an important cognitive advance toward becoming more systematic, planful, and logical thinkers. Piaget termed the cognitive stage from age 7 to 11 the stage of **concrete operations**. During this stage children become capable of

◉─Watch the **Video** Individual Differences in Cognitive Flexibility in **MyDevelopmentLab**

concrete operations in Piaget's theory, the cognitive stage in which children become capable of using mental operations

using mental operations, which allow them to organize and manipulate information mentally instead of relying on physical and sensory associations. According to Piaget, the advances of concrete operations are evident in new abilities for performing tasks of conservation, classification, and seriation.

ADVANCES IN CONCRETE OPERATIONS Before age 7 children usually make mistakes when performing tasks requiring an understanding of *conservation*. For example, in a task involving conservation of matter, a child may be shown two round balls of clay equal in size. The child watches as the experimenter rolls one ball into a long sausage shape and asks which shape has more clay. The preoperational child usually answers "the long one," mistaking a change in shape for a change in quantity whereas by age 7 or 8 most children will answer "the same," realizing that the quantity remains the same even if the shape changes. In the preoperational stage children are *centered* on one obvious feature of a problem, but the concrete operational child has abilities for **decentering** that the preoperational child lacks. This advance makes it possible to take more than one aspect of a problem into account, in this case width as well as length. The concrete operational child can also perform the mental operation of *reversibility* to confirm that the quantity has not changed, thus understanding that if the long shape were rolled into a ball again it would be the same size as the other ball. Conservation of matter and liquid are attained by most children by ages 7 or 8, with conservation of length, area, weight, and volume following over the next few years (refer back to Chapter 6, p. 249, Figure 6.2). Conservation is a key milestone of cognitive development because it enables the child to perceive regularities and principles in the natural world, which is the basis of being able to think logically about how the world works.

A second important cognitive achievement of concrete operations is *classification*. Although in early childhood young children can sort objects or events that share common characteristics into the same class—*red, round, sweet, dog,* for example—and can also add classes into more general categories—elephants and rabbits are both part of the larger class "animals"—they run into difficulty when a classification problem requires a mental operation. For example, in one experiment, Piaget showed a 5-year-old boy a drawing of 12 girls and 2 boys, and asked him if there were more girls or children in the drawing (Piaget, 1965). They boy answered more girls, even though he understood that girls are children.

Amusing, no doubt, at your age, but if you think about it, answering this question requires a fairly challenging mental operation, at least for a 5-year-old. He must separate the girls and boys in the drawing into two classes (girls and boys), add them to form a larger class (children), and understand that the larger class (children) can be broken down again into each of its subclasses (girls and boys). Crucially, this must be done *mentally*. The number of girls can be compared to the number of boys visually, but comparing the number of children to the number of girls cannot, because girls are part of both categories. For this reason the 5-year-old trips up on the problem, but by age 8 or 9 most children perform this mental operation easily. In another experiment, Piaget interviewed a 9-year-old boy, showing him a drawing of 12 yellow tulips, 3 red tulips, and 6 daisies:

Piaget: Which would make a bigger bunch, all the tulips or the yellow tulips?

Boy: All the tulips, of course. You'd be taking the yellow tulips as well.

Piaget: And which would be bigger, all the tulips or all the flowers?

Boy: All the flowers. If you take all the flowers, you take all the tulips, too. (adapted from Ginsburg & Opper, 1979, p. 123)

Seriation, the third achievement of concrete operations emphasized by Piaget, is the ability to arrange things in a logical order (e.g., shortest to longest, thinnest to thickest, lightest to darkest). Piaget found that preoperational children have an incomplete grasp of concepts such as *longer than* or *smaller than*. For example, when asked to arrange a set of sticks from shortest to longest, children in the preoperational age period would typically start with a short stick, then pick a long stick—but then pick another

—⌐Watch the Video Concrete Operational Thinking in **MyDevelopmentLab**

My Virtual Child

Can you think of real-life examples in which your virtual child would use classification?

decentering cognitive ability to take more than one aspect of a problem into account, such as width as well as length

seriation ability to arrange things in a logical order, such as shortest to longest, thinnest to thickest, or lightest to darkest

Seriation is one of the key cognitive abilities that develops during middle childhood, according to Piaget.

APPLYING YOUR KNOWLEDGE

What are the social implications of learning seriation? That is, how might it be related to social hierarchies in middle childhood?

short stick, then another long stick, and so on. However, by age 7 most children can accurately arrange six to eight sticks by length.

This kind of seriation task can be done visually—that is, it does not require a mental operation—but Piaget also found that during concrete operations children developed the ability to seriate mentally. Take this problem, for example. If Julia is taller than Anna and Anna is taller than Lynn, is Julia taller than Lynn? To get this right, the child has to be able to order the heights mentally from tallest to shortest: Julia, Anna, Lynn. Piaget called this **transitive inference**, the mental ability to place objects in a logical order, and he considered the achievement of this skill to be a key part of learning to think logically and systematically.

EVALUATING PIAGET'S THEORY Research testing Piaget's theory has found that, for concrete operations as for the preoperational stage, children are capable of performing some tasks at an earlier age than Piaget had claimed (Vilette, 2002). However, for Piaget it was not enough for a child to grasp *some* aspects of conservation, classification, and seriation in order to be considered a concrete operational thinker; the child had to have *complete* mastery of the tasks associated with the stage (Piaget, 1965). Thus, the difference between Piaget and his critics on this issue is more a matter of definition—"What qualifies a child as a concrete operational thinker?"—than of empirical findings. Piaget also claimed that teaching a child the principles of concrete operations would not work because their grasp of the principles of the stage has to occur naturally as part of their interaction with their environment (Piaget, 1965). Here his critics appear to be right, with many studies showing that with training and instruction, children under age 7 can learn to perform the tasks of concrete operations and also understand the underlying principles well enough to apply them to new tasks (Parameswaran, 2003).

Transporting Piaget's tasks across cultures shows that acquiring an understanding of concrete operations depends on exposure to similar tasks and materials. For example, in one study of 4- to 13-year-old children in the Maya culture of Mexico and in Los Angeles, the children in Los Angeles performed better than the Mayan children on standard tests of concrete operations, whereas the Mayan children performed better on similar concrete operations tasks that involved materials used in weaving, because these materials were familiar from their daily lives (Maynard & Greenfield, 2003).

Information processing

| 7.7 | **LEARNING OBJECTIVE** | Describe how attention and memory change from early childhood to middle childhood, and identify the characteristics of children who have ADHD. |

Ever try to play a board game with a 3-year-old? If you do, it better be short and simple. But by middle childhood, children can play a wide variety of board games that adults enjoy, too, because their powers of attention and memory have advanced. This is one reflection of how information processing improves during middle childhood. Due to increased myelination in the brain, especially of the corpus callosum connecting the two hemispheres, speed of processing information increases (Roeder et al., 2008). Consequently, the amount of time required to perform various tasks decreases in the course of middle childhood (Kail & Park, 1992). Advances are also made in the two key areas of information processing: attention and memory.

ATTENTION AND ADHD In middle childhood, children become more capable of focusing their attention on relevant information and disregarding what is irrelevant, an ability termed **selective attention** (Goldberg et al., 2001). For example, in one line of research, children of various ages were shown a series of cards, each containing one animal and one household item, and told to try and remember where the animal on each card was

transitive inference ability to place objects in a logical order mentally

selective attention ability to focus attention on relevant information and disregard what is irrelevant

located (Hagen & Hale, 1973). Nothing was mentioned about the household items. Afterward, when asked about the location of the animals on each card, older children performed better than younger children. However, when asked how many of the household items they could remember, younger children performed better than older children. The older children were capable of focusing on the information they were told would be relevant, the location of the animals, and capable of ignoring the household items as irrelevant. In contrast, the poorer performance of the younger children in identifying the locations of the animals was partly due to being distracted by the household items.

Being able to maintain attention becomes especially important once children enter school at about age 6 or 7, because the school setting requires children to pay attention to their teachers' instructions. Children with especially notable difficulties in maintaining attention may be diagnosed with **attention-deficit/hyperactivity disorder (ADHD)**, which includes problems of inattention, hyperactivity, and impulsiveness (American Academy of Pediatrics [AAP], 2005b). Children with ADHD have difficulty following instructions and waiting their turn. In the United States, it is estimated that 3–7% of children are diagnosed with ADHD. Boys are about four times more likely than girls to have ADHD (Guyer, 2000). The diagnosis is usually made by a pediatrician after evaluation of the child and consultation with parents and teachers (Sax & Kautz, 2003). Children who do not exhibit hyperactivity but who are merely inattentive may be wrongly judged "lazy" in school as their inattention gets them into trouble. 👁

ADHD is usually first diagnosed in middle childhood, once children enter school and are required to sit still for much of the day, but the majority of children with ADHD still have the disorder in adolescence (Barkley, 2002; Whalen, 2000). The causes of ADHD are unclear, but it appears to be at least partly inherited, as nearly 50% of children and adolescents with ADHD also have a sibling or parent with the disorder and MZ twins are more likely than DZ twins to be concordant for it (Guyer, 2000; Ramussen et al., 2004). Exposure to prenatal teratogens such as alcohol and tobacco is a risk factor for ADHD (Voeller, 2004). The brains of children with ADHD are slightly smaller and grow more slowly, compared to other children's brains (Durston et al., 2004). Studies using fMRI techniques have found abnormalities in the brain functioning of children with ADHD, including restricted blood flow to the frontal cortex, which controls attention and inhibits behavior (Castellanos et al., 2003). 👁

In the United States, nearly 9 of 10 children and adolescents diagnosed with ADHD receive Ritalin or other medications to suppress their hyperactivity and help them concentrate better (Kaplan et al., 2004). Medications are often effective in controlling the symptoms of ADHD, with 70% of children showing improvements in academic performance and peer relations (Harvard Mental Health Letter, 2005). However, there are concerns about side effects, including slower physical growth and higher risk of depression (Reeves & Schweitzer, 2004). Behavioral therapies are also effective, and the combination of medication and behavioral therapy is more effective than either treatment alone (American Academy of Pediatrics, 2005b). Effective behavioral therapies include parent training, classroom interventions, and summer programs (Hoza et al., 2008).

Although most research on ADHD has taken place in the United States, recently a large study of ADHD was completed in Europe, involving over 1,500 children and adolescents (ages 6–18) in 10 countries (Rothenberger et al., 2006). In this Attention-deficit/hyperactivity Disorder Observational Research in Europe (ADORE) study, pediatricians and child psychiatrists across Europe collected observational data on children and adolescents at seven time points over two years, with data including diagnosis, treatment, and outcomes. Parents also participated, and their assessments showed high agreement with the assessments of the pediatricians and child psychiatrists.

Like the American studies, ADORE found higher rates of ADHD among boys than among girls, but the ratios varied

attention-deficit/hyperactivity disorder (ADHD) diagnosis that includes problems of inattention, hyperactivity, and impulsiveness

APPLYING YOUR KNOWLEDGE
Think of any sport or game popular among children in your culture. Does speed of information processing contribute to better performance in middle childhood?

👁 **Watch** the **Video** Attention Deficit Disorder in **MyDevelopmentLab**

APPLYING YOUR KNOWLEDGE
. . . as a Teacher
What can you do to help a child who seems to have trouble paying attention to assignments?

👁 **Watch** the **Video** Speaking Out: Jimmy: ADHD in **MyDevelopmentLab**

ADHD is usually first diagnosed in middle childhood, when children are required to sit still for long periods in school.

widely among countries, from 3:1 to 16:1 (Novik et al., 2006). Symptoms of ADHD were similar among boys and girls, but girls with ADHD were more likely than boys to have additional emotional problems and to be bullied by their peers, whereas ADHD boys were more likely than girls to have conduct problems. For both boys and girls, having ADHD resulted in frequent problems in their relations with peers, teachers, and parents (Coghill et al., 2006). Parents reported frequent stresses and strains due to children's and adolescents' ADHD behavior, including frequent disruptions of family activities and worries about the future (Riley et al., 2006). In contrast to the American approach of relying heavily on Ritalin and other medications, the European approaches to treatment were diverse: medications (25%), psychotherapy (19%), combination of medications and psychotherapy (25%), other therapy (10%), and no treatment (21%) (Preuss et al., 2006).

MEMORY In early childhood, memory is often fleeting, as any parent can attest who has ever asked a 4-year-old what happened to those nice new mittens he wore out to play that morning. Mittens? What mittens?

In middle childhood the capacity of working memory enlarges. On memory tests for sequences of numbers, the length of the sequence recalled is just 4 numbers for the typical 7-year-old, but for the typical 12-year-old it has increased to 7, equal to adults (Kail, 2003). More importantly, middle childhood is the period when children first learn to use **mnemonics** (memory strategies) such as rehearsal, organization, and elaboration.

Rehearsal, which involves repeating the information over and over, is a simple but effective mnemonic. You probably use it yourself, for example when someone tells you a phone number and you are trying to remember it between the time you hear it and the time you dial it. In a classic study, John Flavell and his colleagues (1966) showed how rehearsal emerges as a memory strategy in middle childhood. They outfitted children ages 5 and 10 in a space helmet with a dark visor and displayed seven pictures of familiar objects in front of them. Each child was told that the researcher was going to point to three objects that the child was to remember (in order), pull down the space helmet visor so the child could not see for 15 seconds, then lift the visor and ask the child to point to the three objects. During the 15-second delay, nearly all of the 10-year-olds but only a few of the 5-year-olds moved their lips or recited the names of the objects aloud, showing that they were using rehearsal. At each age, rehearsers recalled the objects much more accurately than non-rehearsers.

Organization—placing things into meaningful categories—is another effective memory strategy that is used more commonly in the course of middle childhood (Schneider, 2002). Studies typically test this ability by giving people a list of items to remember, for example, shoes, zebra, baseball, cow, tennis racket, dress, raccoon, soccer goal, hat. Numerous studies have shown that if children are given a list of items to remember, they are more likely to group them into categories—clothes, animals, sports items—in middle childhood than in early childhood (Sang et al., 2002). Organization is a highly effective memory strategy, because each category serves as a *retrieval cue* for the items within the category, so that if the category can be remembered, all the items within the category are likely to be remembered as well (Schneider, 2002).

A third memory strategy that comes into greater use in middle childhood is **elaboration**, which involves transforming bits of information in a way that connects them and hence makes them easier to remember (Terry, 2003). One example of this is the standard way of teaching children the lines of the treble clef in music, EGBDF: *Every Good Boy Does Fine.* Or, if you were going to the grocery store and wanted to remember to buy butter, lettuce, apples, and milk, you could arrange the first letters of each of the items into one word, *BLAM.* The word *BLAM* serves as a retrieval cue for the items represented by each letter of the word.

Although children are more likely to use organization and elaboration in middle childhood than in early childhood, even in middle childhood and beyond, relatively few people use memory strategies on a regular basis. Instead, they rely on more concrete, practical methods. In one study, children in kindergarten and first, third, and fifth

---

APPLYING YOUR KNOWLEDGE
. . . as a Teacher

How might you encourage use of mnemonics in your class?

---

mnemonics memory strategies, such as rehearsal, organization, and elaboration

rehearsal mnemonic that involves repeating the same information over and over

organization mnemonic that involves placing things mentally into meaningful categories

elaboration mnemonic that involves transforming bits of information in a way that connects them and hence makes them easier to remember

grade were asked how they would remember to bring their ice skates to a party the next day (Kreutzer et al., 1975). At all three ages, children came up with sensible approaches such as putting the skates where they would be easy to see, writing themselves a note, and tying a string to their finger.

Another reason why memory improves from early childhood to middle childhood is that children's knowledge base expands, and the more you know, the easier it is to remember new information that is related to what you know. In a classic study illustrating this, 10-year-old chess masters and college student novice chess players were compared in their ability to remember configurations of pieces on a chess board (Chi, 1978). The 10-year-old chess masters performed far better than the college student novices, even though the college students were better at recalling a series of random numbers. In another study, 9- and 10-year-olds were separated into two groups, soccer "experts" and soccer "novices," and asked to try to remember lists of soccer items and non-soccer items (Schneider & Bjorklund, 1992). The soccer experts remembered more items on the soccer list but not the non-soccer list.

Why do young chess masters remember chess configurations better than older novices do?

Middle childhood is not only a time of advances in memory abilities but of advances in understanding how memory works, or **metamemory**. Even by age 5 or 6, most children have some grasp of metamemory (DeMarie et al., 2001; Lyon & Flavell, 1993). They recognize that it is easier to remember something that happened yesterday than something that happened long ago. They understand that short lists are easier to remember than long lists, and that familiar items are more easily remembered than unfamiliar items. However, their appraisal of their own memory abilities tends to be inflated. When children in early childhood and middle childhood were shown a series of 10 pictures and asked if they could remember all of them, more than half of the younger children but only a few older children claimed they could (none of them actually could!) (Flavell et al., 1970). In the course of middle childhood, children develop more accurate assessments of their memory abilities (Schneider & Pressley, 1997).

Intelligence and intelligence tests

> Describe the main features and critiques of intelligence tests, and compare and contrast Gardner's and Sternberg's approaches to conceptualizing intelligence.

LEARNING OBJECTIVE   **7.8**

Both the Piagetian approach and the information-processing approach describe general patterns of cognitive development and functioning, intended to apply to all children. However, at any given age there are also *individual differences* among children in their cognitive functioning. Within any group of same-age children, some will perform relatively high in their cognitive functioning and some relatively low. Even in infancy, toddlerhood, and early childhood, individual differences in cognitive development are evident, as children reach various cognitive milestones at different times, such as saying their first word. However, individual differences become more evident and more important in middle childhood, when children enter formal schooling and begin to be tested and evaluated by their teachers on a regular basis.

In the study of human development, the examination of individual differences in cognitive development has focused mainly on measurements of **intelligence**. Definitions of intelligence vary, but it is generally understood to be a person's capacity for acquiring knowledge, reasoning, and solving problems (Sternberg, 2004). Intelligence tests usually provide an overall score of general intelligence as well as several subscores that reflect different aspects of intelligence.

Let us begin by looking at the characteristics of one of the most widely used intelligence tests, and follow with an exploration of the genetic and environmental sources of

metamemory understanding of how memory works

intelligence capacity for acquiring knowledge, reasoning, and solving problems

intelligence quotient (IQ) score of mental ability as assessed by intelligence tests, calculated relative to the performance of other people the same age

individual differences. Then, we will consider two alternative ways of conceptualizing and measuring intelligence.

THE WECHSLER INTELLIGENCE TESTS The most widely used intelligence tests are the Wechsler scales, including the *Wechsler Intelligence Scale for Children (WISC-IV)* for ages 6 to 16 and the *Wechsler Adult Intelligence Scale (WAIS-IV)* for ages 16 and up.

The Wechsler scales consist of 11 subtests, of which six are Verbal subtests and five are Performance subtests. The results provide an overall **intelligence quotient**, or **IQ** score, which is calculated relative to the performance of other people of the same age, with 100 as the median score. The overall IQ can be broken down into a Verbal IQ score, a Performance IQ score, and scores for each of the 11 subtests. More detail on each of the subscales of the WISC-IV is provided in **Table 7.1**, so you can get an idea of what IQ tests really measure.

How accurate are the Wechsler IQ tests? IQ tests were originally developed to test children's abilities as they entered school, and IQ has proven to be a good predictor of children's school performance. One study of children in 46 countries found that across countries, IQ scores and school achievement scores were highly correlated (Lynn & Mikk, 2007). IQ scores are also quite good predictors of success in adulthood (Benbow & Lubinski, 2009).

IQ tests have been criticized on a variety of grounds. Critics have complained that IQ tests assess only a narrow range of abilities, and miss some of the most important aspects of intelligence, such as creativity. IQ tests have also been attacked as culturally biased, because some of the vocabulary and general knowledge items would be more familiar to someone who was part of the middle-class culture (Ogbu, 2002). However, attempts to develop "culture-fair" tests have found the same kinds of group differences as standard IQ tests have found (Johnson, te Nijenhuis, et al., 2008). It may not be possible to develop a culture-fair or culture-free IQ test, because by the time people are able to take the tests (age 6) their cognitive development has already been shaped by living in a particular cultural and social environment. Although IQ tests aspire to test raw intellectual abilities, this would not really be possible unless everyone was exposed to essentially the same environment in the years before taking the test, which is obviously

THINKING CULTURALLY

Looking at the sample IQ test items in Table 7.1, are there any that you think may reflect a cultural bias?

TABLE 7.1 The WISC-IV: Sample Items

Verbal Subtests

Information	General knowledge questions, for example, "Who wrote *Huckleberry Finn*?"
Vocabulary	Give definitions, for example, "What does *formulate* mean?"
Similarities	Describe relationship between two things, for example, "In what ways are an apple and an orange alike?" and "In what ways are a book and a movie alike?"
Arithmetic	Verbal arithmetic problems, for example, "How many hours does it take to drive 140 miles at a rate of 30 miles per hour?"
Comprehension	Practical knowledge, for example, "Why is it important to use zip codes when you mail letters?"
Digit Span	Short-term memory test. Sequences of numbers of increasing length are recited, and the person is required to repeat them.

Performance Subtests

	For all the performance tests, scores are based on speed as well as accuracy of response.
Picture arrangement	Cards depicting various activities are provided, and the person is required to place them in an order that tells a coherent story.
Picture completion	Cards are provided depicting an object or scene with something missing, and the person is required to point out what is missing (for example, a dog is shown with only three legs).
Matrix reasoning	Patterns are shown with one piece missing. The person chooses from five options the one that will fill in the missing piece accurately.
Block design	Blocks are provided having two sides all white, two sides all red, and two sides half red and half white. Card is shown with a geometrical pattern, and the person must arrange the blocks so that they match the pattern on the card.
Digit symbol	At top of sheet, numbers are shown with matching symbols. Below, sequences of symbols are given with an empty box below each symbol. The person must place matching number in the box below each symbol.

not the case. However, new approaches to studying intelligence have provided important insights into the relation between genetics and environment in performance on IQ tests, as we will discuss next. ◉➤

INFLUENCES ON INTELLIGENCE IQ scores for a population-based sample usually fall into a **normal distribution** or *bell curve*, in which most people are near the middle of the distribution and the proportions decrease at the low and high extremes, as shown in *Figure 7.3*. Persons with IQs below 70 are classified as having **mental retardation**, and those with IQs above 130 are classified as **gifted**. But what determines whether a person's score is low, high, or somewhere in the middle? Is intelligence mainly an inherited trait, or is it shaped mainly by the environment?

As noted in Chapter 2, social scientists increasingly regard the old nature–nurture debates as sterile and obsolete. Nearly all accept that both genetics and environment are involved in development, including in the development of intelligence. A variety of new findings presented in the past 20 years provide insights into how genetics and environments interact and how both contribute to intelligence. Most of these studies use the natural experiments of adoption studies or twin studies in order to avoid the problem of passive genotype → environment effects. When parents provide both genetics and environment, as they do in most families, it is very difficult to judge the relative contribution of each. Adoption and twin studies help unravel that tangle.

One important conclusion from adoption and twin studies is that the more two people in a family are alike genetically, the higher the correlation in their IQs (Brant et al., 2009). As shown in *Figure 7.4*, adopted siblings, who have none of their genotype in common, have a relatively low correlation for IQ, about 0.24. The environmental influence is apparent—ordinarily, the correlation between two genetically unrelated children would be zero—but limited. Parents and their biological children, who share half of their genotype in common, are correlated for IQ at about 0.30 to 0.40, slightly higher if they live together than if they live apart. The correlation for biological siblings is higher, about 0.50, and slightly higher still for DZ twins. Biological siblings and DZ twins share the same proportion of their genotype in common as parents and biological children do (again, about half), so the greater IQ similarity in DZ twins must be due to greater environmental similarity, from the womb onward. The highest IQ correlation of all, about 0.85, is among MZ twins, who have exactly the same genotype. Even when they are adopted by separate families and raised apart, the correlation in IQ scores of MZ twins is about 0.75 (Brant et al., 2009).

The results of these studies leave little doubt that genetics contribute strongly to IQ scores. It is especially striking that the correlation in IQ is much lower for adopted siblings, who have grown up in the same family and neighborhood and attended the same schools, than it is for MZ twins who have been raised separately and have never even known each other.

However, other adoption studies show that both environment and genetics have a strong influence on intelligence. In one study, researchers recruited a sample of adopted children whose biological mothers were at two extremes, either under 95 or above 120 (remember, 100 is the median population IQ) (Loehlin et al., 1997). All the children were

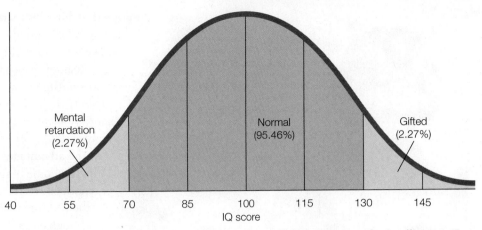

Figure 7.3 • **Bell curve for intelligence.** IQ scores for a population-based sample usually fall into this kind of pattern.

◉➤ **Simulate** the **Experiment**
Creativity in **MyDevelopmentLab**

normal distribution typical distribution of characteristics of a population, resembling a bell curve in which most cases fall near the middle and the proportions decrease at the low and high extremes

mental retardation level of cognitive abilities of persons who score 70 or below on IQ tests

gifted in IQ test performance, persons who score 130 or above

Figure 7.4 • **IQ and genetics.** The closer the genetic relationship, the higher the correlation in IQ. Based on The development etiology of high IQ. Behavior Genetics, 39, 393–405. Springer

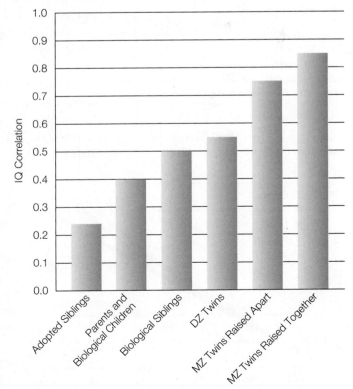

Identical twins have similar IQs, even when reared apart. Here, 6-year-old MZ twin sisters in Thailand.

adopted at birth by parents who were above average in education and income. When tested in middle childhood, children in both groups were above average in IQ. If we can assume that the high-education, high-income adoptive parents provided a healthy, stable, stimulating environment, this shows the influence of the environment for the children whose biological mothers all had IQs less than 95. On the basis of their biological mother's IQs, none of them would have been predicted to have an IQ above 95, and yet on average they were above 100, due to the advantages of an environment provided by high-education, high-income parents. However, the children whose biological mothers had IQs above 120 were significantly higher in IQ than the children whose biological mothers had IQs less than 95, even though children in both groups had an advantaged environment.

Taken together, the adoption and twin IQ studies show that both genetics and environment contribute to the development of intelligence. Specifically, every child has a genetically based *reaction range* for intelligence, meaning a range of possible developmental paths (refer back to Chapter 2). With a healthy, stimulating environment, children reach the top of their reaction range for intelligence; with a poor, unhealthy, or chaotic environment, children are likely to develop a level of intelligence toward the bottom of the reaction range. There is both an upper and a lower limit to the reaction range. Even with an optimal environment, children with relatively low intellectual abilities are unlikely to develop superior intelligence; even with a subnormal environment, children with relatively high intellectual abilities are unlikely to end up well below average in IQ.

Recent research has revealed new insights into the intricate relations between genetics and environment in the development of intelligence. Specifically, research indicates that the influence of the environment on IQ is stronger for poor children than for children of affluent families (Nesbitt, 2009; Turkheimer et al., 2009). The less stimulating the environment, the less genetics influences IQ, because all children's potentials are suppressed in an unstimulating environment. In contrast, an affluent environment generally allows children to receive the cognitive stimulation necessary to reach the top of their reaction range for IQ.

Flynn effect steep rise in the median IQ score in Western countries during the 20th century, named after James Flynn, who first identified it

Figure 7.5 • **Flynn effect.** IQ scores have risen across developed countries in recent decades.

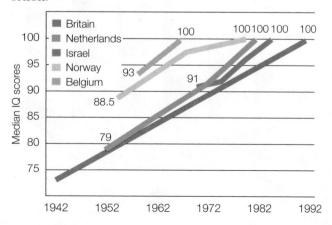

One other highly important finding that attests to the importance of environmental influences on intelligence is that the median IQ score in Western countries rose dramatically in the course of the 20th century, a phenomenon known as the **Flynn effect** after the scholar who first noted it, James Flynn (1999). From 1932 to 1997 the median IQ score among children in the United States rose by 20 points (Howard, 2001). This is a huge difference. It means that a child whose IQ was average in 1932 would be way below average by today's standard. It means that half of children today would have scored at least 120 by 1932 scoring, placing them in the "superior intelligence" range, and about one-fourth of children today would be considered by 1932 standards to have "very superior intelligence"—a classification actually held by only 3% of children in 1932 (Horton, 2001). As shown in *Figure 7.5*, similar results have been found in other countries as well (Flynn, 1999).

What explains the Flynn effect? The causes must be environmental, rather than genetic; the genes of the human population could not have changed so dramatically in such a short time. But what about the environment improved so much in the course of the 20th century as to explain such a dramatic rise in median IQ scores? Several possibilities have been identified (Rodgers & Wanstrom, 2007). Prenatal care is better now than in the early 20th century, and better prenatal care leads to better intellectual development, including higher IQs. Families are generally smaller now than in the early 20th century, and in general the fewer children in a family the higher their IQs. Far more children attend preschool now than was true in 1932, and preschool enhances young children's intellectual development. It has even been suggested that the invention of television may be one of the sources of the Flynn effect. Although television and other media are often blamed for societal ills, there is good evidence that watching educational television enhances young children's intellectual development (Scantlin, 2007).

An especially persuasive explanation has recently been proposed: the decline of infectious diseases (Eppig et al., 2010). Christopher Eppig and his colleagues note that the brain requires a great deal of the body's physical energy—87% in newborns, nearly half in 5-year-olds, and 25% in adults. Infectious diseases compete for this energy by activating the body's immune system and interfering with the body's processing of food during years when the brain is growing and developing rapidly. If this explanation is true, there should be an inverse relationship between IQ and infectious disease rates, and this pattern was evident in the researchers' analysis of data from 113 countries (as shown in *Figure 7.6*). The higher a country's infectious disease burden, the lower the country's median IQ. Thus the Flynn effect may have been primarily due to the elimination of major infectious diseases in developed countries. A Flynn effect of the future may be awaiting developing countries as they reduce and eliminate infectious diseases.

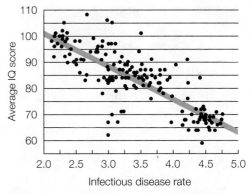

Figure 7.6 • **Inverse relation between IQ and disease.** Could this explain the Flynn effect?

OTHER CONCEPTIONS OF INTELLIGENCE: GARDNER'S AND STERNBERG'S THEORIES IQ testing has dominated research on children's intellectual development for nearly a century. However, in recent decades alternative theories of intelligence have been proposed. These theories have sought to present a conception of intelligence that is much broader than the traditional one. Two of the most influential alternative theories of intelligence have been presented by Howard Gardner and Robert Sternberg. 👁

Gardner's (1983, 2004) **theory of multiple intelligences** includes eight types of intelligence. In Gardner's view only two of them, *linguistic* and *logical–mathematical* intelligences, are evaluated by intelligence tests. The other intelligences are *spatial* (the ability to think three-dimensionally); *musical*; *bodily–kinesthetic* (the kind that athletes and dancers excel in); *naturalist* (ability for understanding natural phenomena); *interpersonal* (ability for understanding and interacting with others); and *intrapersonal* (self-understanding). As evidence for the existence of these different types of intelligence, Gardner argues that each involves distinct cognitive skills, that each can be destroyed by damage to a particular part of the brain, and that each appears in extremes in geniuses as well as in *idiots savants* (the French term for people who are low in general intelligence but possess an extraordinary ability in one specialized area). ✹

Gardner argues that schools should give more attention to the development of all eight kinds of intelligence and design programs that would be tailored to each child's individual profile of intelligences. He has proposed methods for assessing different intelligences, such as measuring musical intelligence by having people attempt to sing a song, play an instrument, or orchestrate a melody (Gardner, 1999). However, thus far neither Gardner nor others have developed reliable and valid methods (see Chapter 1) for analyzing the intelligences he proposes (Kornhaber, 2004). Gardner has also been criticized for extending the boundaries of intelligence too widely. When an adolescent displays exceptional musical ability, is this an indication of musical "intelligence" or simply of musical talent? Gardner himself has been critical of the concept of "emotional intelligence" proposed by Daniel Goleman and others (Goleman, 1997), arguing that the capacity to empathize and cooperate with others is better viewed as "emotional sensitivity" rather than intelligence (Gardner, 1999). However, Gardner is vulnerable to a similar criticism for proposing "interpersonal" and "intrapersonal" intelligences.

Sternberg's (Sternberg, R., 1983, 1988, 2002, 2003, 2005) **triarchic theory of intelligence** includes three distinct but related forms of intelligence. *Analytical intelligence* is Sternberg's term for the kind of intelligence that IQ tests measure, which involves acquiring, storing, analyzing, and retrieving information. *Creative intelligence* involves the ability to combine information in original ways to produce new insights, ideas, and

My Virtual Child

Do you see similarities between your intelligence and your virtual child's intelligence? How might your environment influence your child's intelligence test scores?

👁—**Watch** the **Video** Robert Sternberg on Cultural Influences in **MyDevelopmentLab**

✹—**Explore** the **Concept** Gardner's Multiple Intelligences in **MyDevelopmentLab**

APPLYING YOUR KNOWLEDGE

Do you agree that all the mental abilities described by Gardner are different types of intelligence? If not, which types would you remove? Are there other types you would add?

theory of multiple intelligences Gardner's theory that there are eight distinct types of intelligence

triarchic theory of intelligence Sternberg's theory that there are three distinct but related forms of intelligence

Is musical ability a type of intelligence?

problem-solving strategies. *Practical intelligence* is the ability to apply information to the kinds of problems faced in everyday life, including the capacity to evaluate social situations. Sternberg has conducted extensive research to develop tests of intelligence that measure the three types of intelligence he proposes. These tests involve solving problems, applying knowledge, and developing creative strategies. Sternberg's research on Americans has demonstrated that each person has a different profile on the three intelligences that can be assessed (Sternberg, 2005, 2007a). He proposes that the three components are universal and contribute to intelligent performance in all cultures (Sternberg, 2005), but so far the theory has been tested little outside the United States. Neither Sternberg's nor Gardner's tests are widely used among psychologists, in part because they take longer to administer and score than standard IQ tests do (Gardner, 1999).

The underlying issue in judging alternative theories of intelligence is the question of how intelligence should be defined. If intelligence is defined simply as the mental abilities required to succeed in school, the traditional approach to conceptualizing and measuring intelligence is generally successful. However, if one wishes to define intelligence more broadly, as the entire range of human mental abilities, the traditional approach may be seen as too narrow, and an approach such as Gardner's or Sternberg's may be preferred.

WHAT HAVE YOU LEARNED?

1. What advances in children's classification skills are evident during middle childhood?
2. How do American approaches to treating ADHD differ from European approaches?
3. What are some critiques of intelligence tests?
4. What are some explanations for the Flynn effect?
5. How many of Gardner's eight intelligences were emphasized in your elementary school education?

Language Development

In middle childhood, advances in language development may not be as noticeable as in the earliest years of life, but they are nevertheless dramatic. There are important advances in vocabulary, grammar, and pragmatics. Bilingual children face special challenges in language development but also benefit in some ways.

Vocabulary, grammar, and pragmatics

7.9   **LEARNING OBJECTIVE**   Identify the advances in vocabulary, grammar, and pragmatics during middle childhood.

Once they enter formal school at age 5–7 and begin reading, children's vocabulary expands as never before, as they pick up new words not just from conversations but from books. At age 6 the average child knows about 10,000 words, but by age 10 or 11 this sum has increased fourfold, to about 40,000. Part of this growth comes from children's growing abilities to understand the different forms words can take. A child who learns the meaning of *calculate* will also now understand *calculating, calculated, calculation,* and *miscalculate* (Anglin, 1993).

The grammar of children's language use becomes more complex in middle childhood. For example, they are more likely than younger children to use *conditional sentences* such as "If you let me play with that toy, I'll share my lunch with you." As in early childhood, there are SES differences in grammar development in middle childhood. Children in higher-SES families use more advanced grammatical forms than those in lower-SES families (Menon et al., 2007), and this experience may lead to higher reading scores and better performance in school.

Another important aspect of language that improves in middle childhood is *pragmatics,* the social context and conventions of language. As noted in Chapter 6, even in early childhood children have begun to understand pragmatics. For example, they realize that what people say is not always just what they mean, and that interpretation is required. They understand that "How many times do I have to tell you not to feed the dog off your plate?" is not really a question. However, in middle childhood the understanding of pragmatics grows substantially. This can be seen vividly in children's use of humor. A substantial amount of humor in middle childhood involves violating the expectations set by pragmatics. For example, here is an old joke that made my son Miles howl with laughter when he first learned it at age 8:

Man: "Waiter, what's that fly doing in my soup?"
Waiter: "I believe he's doing the backstroke, sir."

For this to be funny, you have to understand pragmatics. Specifically, you have to understand that by asking "What's that fly doing in my soup?" the man means "What are you going to do about that disgusting fly floating in my soup?" The waiter, a bit slow on his pragmatics, interprets the man to mean, "What activity is that fly engaged in?" What makes it funny is that your understanding of pragmatics leads you to expect the first response, and the second response comes as a surprise. By substituting the expected pragmatic meaning of the question with an unexpected meaning, the joke creates a humorous effect (at least if you are 8 years old).

Pragmatics are always culturally grounded, which is one reason why jokes don't travel well between cultures. To know the pragmatics of a language, you have to know well the culture of the people using the language. For example, many languages have two forms of the word "you," one form used when there is a close attachment (such as with family and close friends) and the other used with unfamiliar persons and persons with whom there is a professional but not personal relationship (such as employers or students). Knowing when and with whom to use each form of "you" requires extensive familiarity not just with the language but with the cultural norms for using the two forms in the appropriate social contexts.

Bilingualism

Explain the consequences for cognitive development of growing up bilingual.	**LEARNING OBJECTIVE** **7.10**

A rising number of children around the world grow up knowing two languages, that is, they are **bilingual**. There are two main reasons for this trend. First, with increased migration between countries, children are more likely to be exposed early to two languages, one spoken at home and one spoken with friends, teachers, and others outside the home. Second, school systems increasingly seek to teach children a second language to enhance their ability to participate in the global economy. Because the United States is the most influential country in the world economy, English is the most common second language for children around the world. For example, in China all children now begin learning English in primary school (Chang, 2008). There are many bilingual families living within the United States as well, due to the large number of immigrants that have come to the U.S. in recent decades, and they speak a variety of languages (see *Map 7.2*). 👁

As we have seen in previous chapters, children are marvelously well-suited to learning a language. But what happens when they try to learn two languages? Does learning two languages enhance their language development or impede it?

My Virtual Child

Will your virtual child be bilingual?

👁 **Watch** the **Video** Bilingual Family in **MyDevelopmentLab**

bilingual capable of using two languages

Map 7.2 • **Bilingualism in the United States.** Which states have the highest percentage of bilingual families? How might this relate to the ethnic diversity that exists within these states (refer back to Map 1.1 on page 8)?

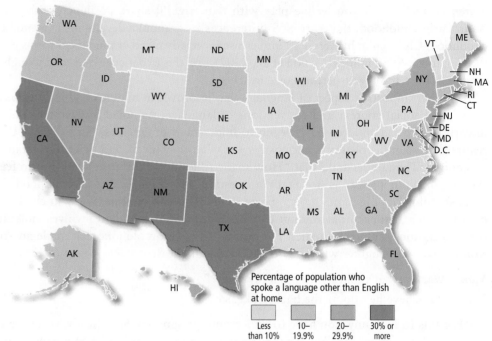

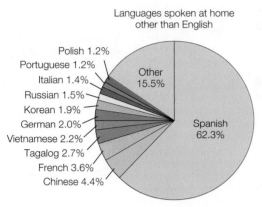

Languages spoken at home other than English

Polish 1.2%
Portuguese 1.2%
Italian 1.4%
Russian 1.5%
Korean 1.9%
German 2.0%
Vietnamese 2.2%
Tagalog 2.7%
French 3.6%
Chinese 4.4%
Other 15.5%
Spanish 62.3%

Percentage of population who spoke a language other than English at home

| Less than 10% | 10–19.9% | 20–29.9% | 30% or more |

metalinguistic skills in the understanding of language, skills that reflect awareness of the underlying structure of language

APPLYING YOUR KNOWLEDGE . . . as a Nurse

During Soroya's checkup, her American grandmother expresses concern that Soroya is being exposed to too many languages and won't be able to speak any of them well. She's learning Farsi from her mother, Turkish from her grandfather, and English from her father. What can you tell her?

Figure 7.7 • **Age and grammatical knowledge.** The challenge of learning a second language rises with age.

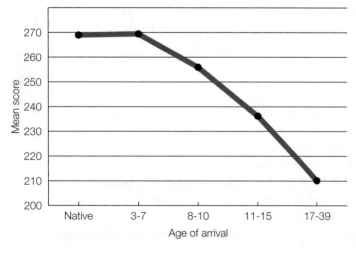

For the most part, becoming bilingual is favorable to language development. When children learn two languages, they usually become adept at using both (Genesee, 2001). Learning a secondary language does not interfere with mastering the primary language (Lessow-Hurley, 2005). One minor problem that does arise is that in early childhood there is sometimes a tendency to intermix the syntax of the two languages. For example, in Spanish dropping the subject in a sentence is grammatically correct, as in *no quiero ir.* However, if a child who is bilingual in Spanish applies this rule to English it comes out as *no want go,* which is not correct. By middle childhood, children can easily keep their two languages separate, although they may intentionally import some words from one language when speaking in the other, to create "Spanglish" (a blend of Spanish and English) or "Chinglish" (a blend of Chinese and English), for example.

When children learn their second language after already becoming fluent in a first language, it takes longer to master the second language, usually 3–5 years (Hakuta, 1999). Even so, learning a second language comes much easier in early and middle childhood than it does at later ages. For example, in one study adults who had immigrated to the United States from China or Korea at various ages were tested on their grammatical knowledge of English (Johnson & Newport, 1989). The participants who had arrived in the United States in early or middle childhood scored as well on the test as native English speakers, but beyond those periods the older the age at immigration, the less the person's grammatical knowledge (see ***Figure 7.7***). Other studies have shown that beyond the age of about 12 it is difficult for people to learn a language well enough to sound like a native speaker, that is, to speak without a noticeable accent (Birdsong, 2006). Clearly, children have a biological readiness for learning a new language that adults lack, but the decline with age is gradual and steady from childhood to adulthood (DeKeyser & Larson-Hall, 2005; Hakuta et al., 2003).

Becoming bilingual has a variety of benefits. Children who are bilingual have better **metalinguistic skills** than single-language children, meaning that they have greater awareness of the underlying structure of language (Schwartz et al., 2008). In one early study (Oren, 1981), researchers compared bilingual and single-language children ages 4–5 on metalanguage skills by instructing them to use nonsense words for familiar objects (e.g., *dimp* for dog, *wug* for car) and by asking them questions about the implications of changing object labels (if we call a dog a cow, does it give milk?). The bilingual children were consistently better than the single-language children in metalanguage understanding. Specifically, they were better at applying grammatical rules to nonsense words (one *wug,* two *wugs)* and at understanding that words are symbols for objects (calling a dog a cow won't make it give milk). Other studies have confirmed that bilingual children are better than single-language children at detecting mistakes in grammar and meaning (Bialystok, 1993, 1997). Bilingual children also score higher on more general measures of cognitive ability, such as analytical reasoning, cognitive flexibility, and cognitive complexity, indicating that becoming bilingual also has general cognitive benefits (Bialystok, 1999, 2001; Swanson et al., 2004).

In some countries, such as India, many children are not just bilingual but **multilingual**. Indian children first learn their local language, of which there are over a thousand across India (MacKenzie, 2009). Then they learn Hindi, which is the official national language, and many also learn English as well, in order to participate in the global economy. Studies indicate that by middle childhood, Indian children exposed to multiple languages use their different languages effectively in different contexts (Bhargava & Mendiratta, 2006). For example, they might use their local language at home, Hindi with friends at school, and English in their school work. However, language diversity can be an obstacle to learning for children who come to school knowing only their local language and are then faced with a school curriculum that is entirely in a new and unfamiliar language (MacKenzie, 2009). Currently, some Indian schools are changing their curriculum in the early school years to the local language before introducing Hindi or English, but others are emphasizing English from the outset of schooling in an effort to prepare children for participation in the global economy.

Many Indian children learn several languages.

WHAT HAVE YOU LEARNED?

1. What explains the huge growth in vocabulary during middle childhood?
2. What does a child's use of humor tell us about his or her language development?
3. What are some of the benefits of becoming bilingual?
4. What does it mean to be multilingual? Give an example of a culture where this is the case.

School in Middle Childhood

In the United States and other developed countries, children in middle childhood spend a great deal of their time in school and participating in school-related activities. Around the world, formal schooling is designed to ensure that children learn the knowledge and thinking skills that they will need to develop into functional and contributing members of their cultures. The rate of schooling in developing countries is increasing in recent years, especially for girls.

multilingual capable of using three or more languages

Cultural variations in school experiences

Summarize the international variations in school enrollment during middle childhood, and compare and contrast the school socialization practices of Eastern and Western cultures.	**LEARNING OBJECTIVE** 7.11

For people who have grown up in a place where going to school is a routine part of children's development in middle childhood, it is easy to assume that this has always been the case. Indeed, many developmental psychologists refer to children in middle

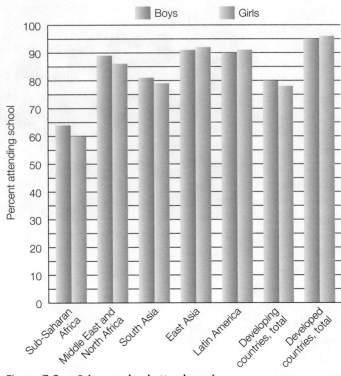

Figure 7.8 • **Primary school attendance in world regions.** Attending primary school is common but not universal, worldwide. **Source:** Based on UNICEF, State of the world's children.

My Virtual Child

How are the values of your culture likely reflected in your virtual child's schooling?

Children in many Asian countries are required to wear school uniforms, such as these children in Nepal. How is the requirement of wearing school uniforms a custom complex?

childhood as "school-age children," as if going to school is a natural, universal, and inevitable part of children's development once they reach the age of 6 or 7. However, attending school in childhood has been a typical part of children's experiences in most countries only for less than 200 years. In the United States, for example, it is estimated that prior to 1800 only about half of children attended school, and even for those who did, it lasted only a few years (Rogoff et al., 2005). Enrollment increased steadily over the 19th century, as industrialization created jobs that required literacy and people migrated from farms to urban areas, and by 1900 most children completed several years of schooling. The school year remained quite short in the late 19th century, taking place mostly during the winter months when children's labor was not needed on the farm. In 1870, the average child attending school spent only 78 days per year in school. Classrooms often mixed children of a wide range of ages. By the early 20th century, all U.S. states required children to complete elementary school. Compulsory education is associated with higher literacy rates and other skills that are useful in the job market. Furthermore, when educated is required, boys and girls attend at equal rates, unlike in many countries where school is not required of all children.

In the developed world, going to a school has become a typical part of middle childhood, but it still is not universal, as *Figure 7.8* shows (UNICEF, 2008). In Africa and South Asia, 20–40% of children ages 6–10 are not enrolled in primary school. Overall in developing countries, about one-fourth of children do not attend primary school. Until recently, boys were more likely than girls to attend primary school. School attendance requires school fees in many countries, and some poor families would use their extremely limited resources for the boys' education. Girls were often kept home because it was believed that boys' education would be of greater benefit to the family. However, in recent years this gender difference has decreased, and girls are now almost as likely as boys to obtain primary education (UNICEF, 2012).

In addition to the variations in primary-school attendance, schools around the world also have different approaches to socialization and other functions of school. Beyond cognitive skills, a primary function of school is for children to learn social skills with peers and authority figures who are unrelated to them (like teachers and the principal). Although all schooling shifts children's socialization away from family and toward a peer-intensive environment, there are differences among countries based on individualistic or collectivistic cultural beliefs. For instance, Barbara Rogoff has described the collectivistic socialization contexts of schools in Guatemala, as we'll explore in the **Cultural Focus: School Socialization in Guatemala** feature. In some countries, such as in the Middle East, school is also a place where children learn about their religion. State-sponsored education in Western countries tends not to include religious education, but religion may be emphasized in private schools. Of course, subjects covered in school may vary across cultures. This is particularly true in the subject of History, which is often taught from the point of view of the country of the school. Even in the United States, there are variations in the way American History is taught, usually with an emphasis on local experiences and point of view.

A great deal of research has focused on comparisons between schools in the United States and in Asian countries such as Japan, China, and South Korea. These Asian countries have cultural traditions going back over 2 millennia emphasizing the importance and

CULTURAL FOCUS   School Socialization in Guatemala

What do schools teach about cultural values, beliefs, and behavior? According to cultural psychologist Barbara Rogoff, an important effect of schooling on children's socialization is that it separates them from the world of adults for a substantial part of each school day and places them in a children's world with their age peers where they engage in daily social comparison and competition (Rogoff et al., 2005). In traditional cultures where children do not attend school, by middle childhood their work makes a substantial contribution to their families, in care of younger children, meal preparation, care of domestic animals, and assisting in whatever work parents do. School takes them out of that family-focused work environment and into a peer-focused book-learning environment.

Rogoff has been conducting ethnographic research in the same Guatemalan village for over 30 years, and her observations provide a vivid example of how school can change children's daily socialization experiences. Over the course of just one generation, children's experiences were transformed (see *Table 7.2*) (Rogoff et al., 2005).

For example, not a single village girl today has learned weaving, even though nearly all their mothers weaved as girls. For boys, the percentage who helped care for younger children dropped from 53% to 7% in just one generation. The percentage of boys helping with farm work also dropped from the parents' generation to the current generation.

The change in their focus from work to school was reflected in the change in their aspirations. In the parents' generation, few expected as children to continue education past grade 6; for today's children, about three-fourths expect to go beyond grade 6, and over half expect to go beyond grade 12. Both boys and girls today envision a wider range of future occupations than their parents could have imagined, including accountant, teacher, pastor, and doctor.

The introduction of schooling changes the socialization environment not only for "school-age" children but for younger children. As attending school becomes normative, parents begin to prepare their children in toddlerhood and early childhood for the verbal give-and-take of the school environment by exchanging questions and answers with them rather than issuing commands and expecting the children to participate in collaborative family work (Rogoff et al., 2005). Children's socialization environment also changes because they have fewer siblings, as attending school makes children less of an economic asset and more of an economic liability, and also because raising verbally active children is more taxing.

In sum, the spread of school attendance has made the lives—and futures—of Guatemalan children vastly different from the lives their parents knew.

TABLE 7.2 From Work to School in One Generation: Guatemalan Children and Parents

	Parents %	Children %
Girls learn weaving	87	0
Boys learn to care for younger children	53	7
Boys do farm work	57	36
Expect education beyond grade 6 (boys)	7	71
Expect education beyond grade 6 (girls)	3	76
Expect to weave as adults (girls)	43	15
Expect to do farm work as adults (boys)	77	22

Source: Based on A cultural/historical view of schooling in human development. In Developmental psychology and social change: Research, history and policy (pp. 225–263).

value of education, and the traditions remain strong today. High standards are applied to all children, as people in these countries believe that educational success is derived mainly from hard work and any child can succeed who tries hard enough (Stevenson et al., 2000). In contrast, Americans tend to believe that educational success is due mainly to innate ability, so when a child does poorly they tend to believe there is not much that can be done. Another difference is that Asian children tend to view academic striving as something they do not just for themselves but as a moral obligation to their families (Bempechat & Drago-Severson, 1999). In contrast, American children tend to view academic achievement as a mark of individual success.

Several features of Asian schools reflect collectivistic cultural beliefs emphasizing obedience and cooperation. Children are required to wear uniforms, a classic *custom complex* (see Chapter 1) underscoring diminished individuality and emphasizing conformity to the group. Children are also required to help to maintain the cleanliness and order of the school, emphasizing the collectivistic cultural value of contributing to the well-being of the community. Furthermore, children often work in groups, with students who have mastered a concept instructing those who have yet to grasp it (Shapiro & Azuma, 2004). In contrast, children in American schools typically do not wear uniforms (except in some private schools), are not required to help with school maintenance, and spend more time working alone (Stevenson & Zusho, 2002).

There are other important differences between the United States and Asian countries in the structure of the school day and year. Asian children spend more time on a typical school day learning academic subjects than American children do; Americans spend only about half as much of their school time in academic activities as children in China and Japan do, and spend more school time in art, music, and sports (Shapiro & Azuma, 2004). It is interesting to note the shift in emphasis from preschool to primary school in Japan: As mentioned in Chapter 6, Japanese preschoolers are encouraged to be very childlike and develop social skills, but by the time they are in primary school, they are expected to focus on developing academic skills. Both the school day and the school year are longer in Asian countries. The school year in Japan, Korea, and China is about 50 days longer than in the United States and about 30 days longer than in Canada (World Education Services, 2005).

How are these differences in school socialization and structure related to children's academic performance? In recent years, several excellent cross-national studies of academic performance have been conducted at regular intervals, including the Progress in International Reading Literacy Study (PIRLS) and the Trends in International Mathematics and Science Study (TIMSS). On the basis of these results, it appears that academic performance in fourth grade is related mainly to countries' economic development rather than to differences in cultural beliefs and (consequently) in educational practices (Snyder et al., 2009). The highest-performing countries have widely varying educational approaches, but they all have high levels of economic development. As a result, they are most able to afford the resources that contribute to high academic performance, from good prenatal care to high-quality preschools to well-funded primary schools. Financial resources are a factor that influences academic achievement and learning in the United States as well. Families who can afford good medical care and food and who can support children's educational development produce children who do better in school. Poverty is associated with poor grades and behavior in school (Hopson & Lee, 2011).

Learning the cognitive skills of school: Reading and mathematics

7.12   **LEARNING OBJECTIVE**   Describe how reading and math skills develop from early childhood to middle childhood and the variations in approaches to teaching these skills.

In most cultures, middle childhood is when children first learn how to read and how to do math. However, there are variations in the timing and methods of teaching these skills. ◉

Watch the **Video** The School-Age Child in **MyDevelopmentLab**

APPROACHES TO READING   Children learn language with remarkable proficiency without being explicitly taught or instructed, just from being around others who use the language and interacting with them. However, when they reach middle childhood, children must learn a whole new way of processing language, via reading, and for most children learning to read takes direct instruction. Learning to read is a relatively new development in human history. Until about 200 years ago, most people were illiterate all their lives. For example, in the United States in 1800, only about half of army recruits were even able to sign their own names on the enlistment documents (Rogoff et al., 2005). Because most human economic activity involved simple agriculture or hunting or fishing, learning to read was unnecessary for most people. They could learn what they needed to know from observing others and working alongside them, through guided participation. Today, of course, in a globalized, information-based economy, learning to read is an essential skill for most economic activity, across cultures. Consequently, children almost everywhere learn to read, usually beginning around age 6 or 7, when they enter school. 👁

Think for a moment about the cognitive skills reading requires, so that you can appreciate how complex and challenging it is. In order to read, you have to recognize that letters are symbols of sounds, and then match a speech sound to each letter or letter combination. You have to know the meanings of whole words—one or two at first, then dozens, then hundreds, eventually many thousands. As you read a sentence, you have to keep the meanings of individual words or combinations of words in working memory while you continue to read the rest of the sentence. At the end of the sentence, you must put all the word and phrase meanings together into a coherent meaning for the sentence as a whole. Then you have to combine sentences into paragraphs and derive meanings of paragraphs from the relations between the sentences; then combine paragraphs for still larger meanings; and so on. 👁

By now this process no doubt comes naturally to you, after so many years of reading. We perform the complex cognitive tasks of reading automatically after reading for some years, without thinking about the components that go into it. But what is the best way to teach children who are first learning to read? Two major approaches have emerged in educational research over the years. The **phonics approach** advocates teaching children by breaking down words into their component sounds, called phonics, then putting the phonics together into words (Gray et al., 2007). Reading in this approach involves learning gradually more complex units: phonics, then single words, then short sentences, then somewhat longer sentences, and so on. After mastering their phonics and being able to read simple words and sentences, children begin to read longer materials such as poems and stories.

The other major approach to teaching reading is the **whole-language approach** (Donat, 2006). In this view, the emphasis should be on the meaning of written language in whole passages, rather than breaking down each word into its smallest components. This approach advocates teaching children to read using complete written material, such as poems, stories, and lists of related items. Children are encouraged to guess at the meaning of words they do not know, based on the context of the word within the written material. In this view, if the material is coherent and interesting, children will be motivated to learn and remember the meanings of words they do not know.

Which approach works best? Each side has advocates, but evidence is substantial that the phonics approach is more effective at teaching children who are first learning to read (Berninger et al., 2003; Rayner et al., 2002). Children who have fallen behind in their reading progress using other methods improve substantially when taught with the phonics approach (Suggate, 2010; Vadasy & Sanders, 2011; Xue & Meisels, 2004). However, once children have begun to read they can also benefit from supplementing phonics instruction with the whole-language approach, with its emphasis on the larger meanings of written language and on using material from school subjects such as history and science to teach reading as well (Pressley et al., 2002; Silva & Martins, 2003). The International Reading Association (1999) suggests using multiple methods in teaching children to read to get the best results.

Although learning to read is cognitively challenging, most children become able readers by grade 3 (Popp, 2005). However, some children find learning to read unusually difficult. One condition that interferes with learning to read is **dyslexia**, which includes difficulty sounding out letters, difficulty learning to spell words, and a tendency

👁 **Watch** the **Video** Child Struggling with Reading in **MyDevelopmentLab**

👁 **Watch** the **Video** Literacy in **MyDevelopmentLab**

APPLYING YOUR KNOWLEDGE
. . . as a Teacher

You work in a school with many Latino children who seem to want to share stories rather than work on their own. How might you adapt literacy training to these children's inclinations?

phonics approach method of teaching reading that advocates breaking down words in their component sounds, called phonics, then putting the phonics together into words

whole-language approach method of teaching reading in which the emphasis is on the meaning of written language in whole passages, rather than breaking down words to their smallest components

dyslexia learning disability that includes difficulty sounding out letters, difficulty learning to spell words, and a tendency to misperceive the order of letters in words

learning disability cognitive disorder that impedes the development of learning a specific skill such as reading or math

numeracy understanding of the meaning of numbers

👁️—⌐**Watch** the **Video** Dyslexia Detector in **MyDevelopmentLab**

👁️—⌐**Watch** the **Video** Hands-On Learning in Elementary Math in **MyDevelopmentLab**

Street children may learn math from the transactions involving the objects they sell. Here, a boy sells candy in a park in Rio de Janeiro, Brazil.

to misperceive the order of letters in words (Snowling, 2004; Spafford & Grosser, 2005). Dyslexia is one of the most common types of **learning disabilities**, which are cognitive disorders that impede the development of learning a specific skill such as reading or math. As with other learning disabilities, children with dyslexia are not necessarily any less intelligent than other children; their cognitive problem is manifested in the skill of reading and is linked to problems in auditory and visual processing (Facoetti et al., 2003). The causes of dyslexia are not known, but boys are about three times as likely as girls to have the disability, suggesting a genetic link to the Y chromosome (Hensler et al., 2010; Vidyasagar, 2004). 👁️

LEARNING MATH SKILLS   There has been far more research on the development of reading than on the development of math skills (Berch & Mazzoccoco, 2007). Nevertheless, some interesting aspects of math development have been discovered. One is that even some nonhuman animals have a primitive awareness of **numeracy**, which means understanding the meaning of numbers, just as *literacy* means understanding the meaning of written words (Posner & Rothbart, 2007). Rats can be taught to discriminate between a two-tone and an eight-tone sequence, even when the sequences are matched in total duration. Monkeys can learn that the numbers 0 through 9 represent different quantities of rewards. In human infants the beginning of numeracy appears surprisingly early. When they are just 6 weeks old, if they are shown a toy behind a screen and see a second toy added, when the screen is then lowered they look longer and appear more surprised if one or three toys are revealed rather than the two toys they expected. 👁️

From toddlerhood through middle childhood, the development of math skills follows a path parallel to the development of language and reading skills (Doherty & Landells, 2006). Children begin to count around age 2, the same age at which their language development accelerates dramatically. They begin to be able to do simple addition and subtraction around age 5, about the same age they often learn to read their first words. In the course of middle childhood, as they become more adept readers they typically advance in their math skills, moving from addition and subtraction to multiplication and division, and increasing their speed of processing in response to math problems (Posner & Rothbart, 2007). Children who have problems learning to read frequently have problems mastering early math skills as well.

Cultures vary in their timing and approach to teaching math skills to children, with consequences for the pace of children's learning. One study compared 5-year-old children in China, Finland, and England (Aunio et al., 2008). The children in China scored highest, with children in Finland second, and the English children third. The authors related these variations to cultural differences in how math is taught and promoted. Children in China learn math beginning in preschool, and there is a strong cultural emphasis on math as an important basis of future learning and success. In contrast, English preschools usually make little attempt to teach children math skills, in the belief that they are not ready to learn math until they enter formal schooling. Across schools, there are different approaches to teaching math. Some programs emphasize basic skills and memorization and other emphasize a broader, more conceptual discovery-based understanding of math (Cavanagh, 2005).

Most children learn math skills within school, but sometimes math skills can be learned effectively in a practical setting. In a study of Brazilian street children, Geoffrey Saxe (2002) found that in selling candy they worked out complex calculations of prices and profits. Some had attended school and some had not, and the ones who had been to school were more advanced in some math skills but not in the skills necessary for them to succeed in their candy selling on the street.

WHAT HAVE YOU LEARNED?

1. What are some of the socialization functions of school across cultures?
2. What differences can be found in how children are socialized in schools in collectivistic cultures versus individualistic cultures?
3. What is currently considered the best way to teach children to read?
4. What are three main difficulties of dyslexia?
5. In what ways does the development of math skills parallel the development of language and reading skills?

Section 2 VIDEO GUIDE School and Education in Middle Childhood Across Cultures (Length: 6:49)

This video contains several interviews from various countries with children and a teacher discussing experiences with education and schooling.

1. What common educational threads do you see among the individuals in this video?

2. If you did not know that the teacher in this video was from Africa, would you think (based on her responses) that she could have been discussing teaching in the U.S.?

3. What are your thoughts on the American mother's comments that it "takes a village" to raise a child?

Watch the **Video** School and Education in Middle Childhood Across Cultures in **MyDevelopmentLab**

LEARNING OBJECTIVES

7.13 Describe the main features of emotional self-regulation and understanding in middle childhood and how other life stages compare.

7.14 Explain how different ways of thinking about the self are rooted in cultural beliefs, and summarize how self-concept and self-esteem change in middle childhood.

7.15 Describe how beliefs and behavior regarding gender change in middle childhood, including cultural variations.

7.16 Explain the distinctive features of family relations in middle childhood, and describe the consequences of parental divorce and remarriage.

7.17 Explain the main basis of friendships in middle childhood, and describe the four categories of peer social status and the dynamics between bullies and victims.

7.18 Describe the kinds of work children do in middle childhood, and explain why work patterns differ between developed and developing countries.

7.19 Summarize the rates of daily TV-watching among children worldwide, and describe the positive and negative effects of television, especially the hazards related to TV violence.

Emotional and Self-Development

Children advance in their emotional self-regulation in middle childhood and experience relatively few emotional extremes. They grow in their self-understanding, and their self-esteem is generally high, although it depends on cultural context. They grow in their understanding of gender roles, too, but in some respects they become more rigid about those roles.

Smooth sailing: Advances in emotional self-regulation

7.13 **LEARNING OBJECTIVE** | Describe the main features of emotional self-regulation and understanding in middle childhood and how other life stages compare.

Middle childhood is in some ways a golden age emotionally, a time of high well-being and relatively low volatility. In infancy, toddlerhood, and even early childhood, there are many emotional highs, but plenty of emotional lows, too. Outbursts of crying and anger are fairly frequent in the early years of life, but by middle childhood the frequency of such negative emotions has declined substantially (Shipman et al., 2003). Negative emotions will rise again in adolescence, but during middle childhood most days are free of any negative emotional extremes.

One valuable source of information about emotions in middle childhood is research using the **Experience Sampling Method (ESM)** pioneered by Reed Larson and his colleagues (Larson & Richards, 1994; Larson et al., 2002; Richards et al., 2002). The ESM involves having people wear wristwatch beepers that randomly beep during the day so that people can record their thoughts, feelings, and behavior. Each time they are "beeped," participants rate the degree to which they currently feel happy to unhappy, cheerful to irritable, and friendly to angry, as well as how hurried, tired, and competitive they are feeling. The focus of Larson's research has been on adolescence, but some of his research has

Experience Sampling Method (ESM) research method that involves having people wear beepers, usually for a period of 1 week; when they are beeped at random times during the day, they record a variety of characteristics of their experience at that moment

included middle childhood in order to chart the emotional changes that take place from middle childhood to adolescence.

The overall conclusion of ESM research with regard to middle childhood is that it is a time of remarkable contentment and emotional stability (Larson & Richards, 1994). When beeped, children in middle childhood report being "very happy" 28% of the time, a far higher percentage than for adolescents or adults. Children at this age mostly have "quite enjoyable lives" in which they "bask in a kind of naïve happiness" (Larson & Richards, 1994, p. 85). Sure, they are sad or angry occasionally, but it is almost always due to something concrete and immediate such as getting scolded by a parent or losing a game, "events that pass quickly and are forgotten" (p. 85).

Emotional self-regulation improves from early childhood to middle childhood in part because the environment requires it (Rubin, 2000). Middle childhood is often a time of moving into new contexts: primary school, civic organizations (such as the Boy Scouts and Girl Scouts), sports teams, and music groups. All of these contexts make demands for emotional self-regulation. Children are required to do what they are told (whether they feel like it or not), to wait their turn, and to cooperate with others. Expressions of emotional extremes are disruptive to the functioning of the group and are discouraged. Most children are capable of meeting these demands by middle childhood.

Emotional understanding also advances from early to middle childhood. Children become better able to understand both their own and others' emotions. They become aware that they can experience two contradictory emotions at once, an emotional state known as **ambivalence**, for example being both happy (because my team won the game) and sad (because my best friend was on the losing team) (Pons et al., 2003). They also learn how to conceal their emotions intentionally (Saarni, 1999). This allows them to show a socially acceptable emotion such as gratitude when, for example, they open a birthday present they didn't really want. In Asian cultures, children in middle childhood learn the concept of "face," which means showing to others the appropriate and expected emotion regardless of how you actually feel (Han, 2011).

In the same way that children become able to suppress or conceal their own true emotions, they come to understand that other people may display emotional expressions that do not indicate what they actually feel (Saarni, 1999). Children's understanding of others' emotions is also reflected in increased capacity for empathy (Hoffman, 2000). By middle childhood, children become better cognitively at perspective-taking, and the ability to understand how others view events fosters the ability to understand how they feel, too. Parents can help children have better peer relationships through promoting self-understanding and positive interactions. Positive interaction style with fathers is related to boys' and girls' ability to process information about social situations and to positive peer interactions, where positive interaction style with mothers is related only to girls' increased ability in these domains (Rah & Parke, 2008).

Middle childhood is an exceptionally happy time of life.

Self-understanding

Explain how different ways of thinking about the self are rooted in cultural beliefs, and summarize how self-concept and self-esteem change in middle childhood.

LEARNING OBJECTIVE 7.14

Sociologist George Herbert Mead (1934) made a distinction between what he called the *I-self* (how we believe others view us) and the *me-self* (how we view ourselves). Both the I-self and the me-self change in important ways in middle childhood. We discuss the me-self first, then the I-self, then we look at the cultural basis of conceptions of the self.

SELF-CONCEPT Our **self-concept**, that is, how we view and evaluate ourselves, changes during middle childhood from the external to the internal and from the physical to the psychological (Lerner et al., 2005; Marsh & Ayotte, 2003; Rosenberg, 1979). Up

ambivalence emotional state of experiencing two contradictory emotions at once

self-concept person's perception and evaluation of him- or herself

In middle childhood, children become more accurate in comparing themselves to others.

 **Watch** the **Video** Black Doll White Doll in **MyDevelopmentLab**

My Virtual Child

How much is self-esteem valued in your culture? How will this value influence your interactions with your virtual child?

APPLYING YOUR KNOWLEDGE ... as a Therapist

You are seeing Hiroki, a lively Japanese boy who appears to be having self-esteem problems related to his school work. How might you help him in his school work and encourage his parents to support his efforts?

social comparison how persons view themselves in relation to others with regard to status, abilities, or achievements

self-esteem person's overall sense of worth and well-being

until the age of 7 or 8, most children describe themselves mainly in terms of external, concrete, physical characteristics. ("My name is Mona. I'm 7 years old. I have brown eyes and short black hair. I have two little brothers.") They may mention specific possessions ("I have a red bicycle.") and activities they like ("I like to dance." "I like to play sports.") In the course of middle childhood, they add more internal, psychological, personality-related traits to their self-descriptions. ("I'm shy." "I'm friendly." "I try to be helpful."). They may also mention characteristics that are *not me*. ("I don't like art." "I'm not very good at math.") Toward the end of middle childhood their descriptions become more complex, as they recognize that they may be different on different occasions (Harter, 2003). ("Mostly I'm easy to get along with, but sometimes I lose my temper.")

Another important change in self-concept in middle childhood is that children engage in more accurate **social comparison**, in which they describe themselves in relation to others (Guest, 2007). A 6-year-old might describe himself by saying, "I'm really good at math," whereas a 9-year-old might say "I'm better than most kids at math, although there are a couple of kids in my class who are a little better." These social comparisons reflect advances in the cognitive ability of seriation, discussed earlier in the chapter. In the same way that children learn how to arrange sticks accurately from shortest to tallest in middle childhood, they also learn to rank themselves more accurately in abilities relative to other children. The age grading of schools promotes social comparisons, as it places children in a setting where they spend most of a typical day around other children their age. Teachers compare them to one another by giving them grades, and they notice who is relatively good and relatively not so good at reading, math, and so on.

SELF-ESTEEM **Self-esteem** is a person's overall sense of worth and well-being. A great deal has been written and discussed about self-esteem in American society in the past 50 years. Even among Western countries, Americans value high self-esteem to a greater extent than people in other countries, and the gap between Americans and non-Western countries in this respect is especially great (Triandis, 1995). For example, in traditional Japanese culture, self-criticism is a virtue and high self-esteem is a character problem (Heine et al., 1999). The belief in the value of high self-esteem is part of American individualism (Bellah et al., 1985; Rychlak, 2003).

Self-esteem declines slightly in the transition from early childhood to middle childhood, as children enter a school environment in which social comparisons are a daily experience (Lerner et al., 2005; Wigfield et al., 1997). The decline is mild, and simply reflects children's more realistic appraisal of their abilities as they compare themselves to others and are rated by teachers. For the rest of middle childhood, overall self-esteem is high for most children, reflecting the generally positive emotional states mentioned earlier. In Western countries, having low self-esteem in middle childhood is related to anxiety, depression, and antisocial behavior (Robins et al., 2005). However, inappropriately high self-esteem can also be a detriment for some children, particularly those with antisocial personality characteristics (Menon et al., 2007).

An important change in self-esteem in middle childhood is that it becomes more differentiated. In addition to overall self-esteem, children have self-concepts for several specific areas, including academic competence, social competence, athletic competence, and physical appearance (Harter, 2003; Marsh & Ayotte, 2003). Within each of these areas, self-concept is differentiated into subareas. For example, children may see themselves as good at baseball but not basketball, while also having an overall high or low evaluation of their athletic competence.

Children combine their different areas of self-concept into an overall level of self-esteem. For most children and adolescents, physical appearance is the strongest contributor to overall self-esteem (Harter, 2003; Klomsten et al., 2004). However, in other areas, children's self-concept contributes to overall self-esteem only if they value doing well in that area. For example, a child may be no good at sports, but not care about sports, in which case low athletic self-concept would have no effect on overall self-esteem.

CULTURE AND THE SELF The conception of the self that children have by middle childhood varies substantially among cultures. In discussing cultural differences in conceptions of the self scholars typically distinguish between the *independent self* promoted by individualistic cultures and the *interdependent self* promoted by collectivistic cultures (Cross & Gore, 2003; Markus & Kitayama, 1991; Shweder et al., 2006). Cultures that promote an independent, individualistic self also promote and encourage reflection about the self. In such cultures it is seen as a good thing to think about yourself, to consider who you are as an independent person, and to think highly of yourself (within certain limits, of course—no culture values selfishness or egocentrism). Americans are especially known for their individualism and their focus on self-oriented issues. It was an American who first invented the term *self-esteem* (William James, in the late 19th century), and the United States continues to be known to the rest of the world as a place where the independent self is valued and promoted (Green et al., 2005; Triandis, 1995).

However, not all cultures look at the self in this way or value the self to the same extent. In collectivistic cultures, an interdependent conception of the self prevails. In these cultures, the interests of the group—the family, the kinship group, the ethnic group, the nation, the religious institution—are supposed to come first, before the needs of the individual. This means that it is not necessarily a good thing, in these cultures, to think highly of yourself. People who think highly of themselves, who possess a high level of self-esteem, threaten the harmony of the group because they may be inclined to pursue their personal interests regardless of the interests of the groups to which they belong.

Cultural variations in views of the self influence approaches to parenting. Parents in most places and times have been more worried that their children would become too selfish than that they would have low self-esteem. As a result, parents have discouraged self-inflation as part of family socialization (LeVine & New, 2008). However, this kind of parenting works differently if it is part of a cultural norm than if it is an exception within a culture. For example, children from Asian cultures are discouraged from valuing the self highly, yet they generally have high levels of academic performance and low levels of psychological problems (Twenge & Crocker, 2002). In contrast, children within the American majority culture who are exposed to parenting that is critical and negative show negative effects such as depression and poor academic performance (Bender et al., 2007; DeHart et al., 2006). It may be that children in Asian cultures learn to expect criticism if they show signs of high self-esteem, and they see this as normal in comparison to other children, whereas American children learn to expect frequent praise, and hence they suffer more if their parents are more critical than the parents of their peers (Rudy & Grusec, 2006).

It should be added that most cultures are not purely either independent or interdependent in their conceptions of the self, but have elements of each (Killen & Wainryb, 2000). Also, with globalization, many cultures that have a tradition of interdependence are changing toward a more independent view of the self (Arnett, 2002).

Gender development

| Describe how beliefs and behavior regarding gender change in middle childhood, including cultural variations. | **LEARNING OBJECTIVE** 7.15 |

As described in Chapter 6, cultural beliefs about gender become well established by the end of early childhood. Gender roles become even more sharply divided during middle childhood. In traditional cultures, the daily activities of men and women are very

**APPLYING YOUR KNOWLEDGE
. . . as a Teacher**

What might be some of the challenges that accompany group projects in U.S. schools, given the emphasis on individualism?

THINKING CULTURALLY

Based on what you have learned so far in this book, what would you say are the economic reasons traditional cultures would promote an interdependent self?

different, and the activities of boys and girls become more differentiated in middle childhood as they begin to take part in their parents' work. In the human past, and still today in many developing countries, men have been responsible for hunting, fishing, caring for domestic animals, and fighting off animal and human attackers (Gilmore, 1990). Women have been responsible for caring for young children, tending the crops, food preparation, and running the household (Schlegel & Barry, 1991). During middle childhood, boys increasingly learn to do what men do and girls increasingly learn to do what women do.

Boys and girls not only learn gender-specific tasks in middle childhood, they are socialized to develop personality characteristics that enhance performance on those tasks: independence and toughness for boys, and nurturance and compliance for girls. In an early study of 110 traditional cultures, boys and girls were socialized to develop these gender-specific traits in virtually all cultures (Barry et al., 1957). More recent analyses of gender socialization in traditional cultures have found that these patterns persist (Banerjee, 2005; LeVine & New, 2008).

In modern developed countries, too, children's gender attitudes and behavior become more stereotyped in middle childhood. Children increasingly view personality traits as associated with one gender or the other rather than both. Traits such as "gentle" and "dependent" become increasingly viewed as feminine, and traits such as "ambitious" and "dominant" become increasingly viewed as masculine (Best, 2001; Heyman & Legare, 2004). Both boys and girls come to see occupations they associate with men (such as firefighter or astronomer) as having higher status than occupations they associate with women (such as nurse or librarian) (Liben et al., 2001). Furthermore, children increasingly perceive some school subjects as boys' areas (such as math and science) and others as girls' areas (such as reading and art) (Guay et al., 2010; Jacobs & Wiesz, 1994). Teachers may bring gender biases into the classroom, perhaps unknowingly, in ways that influence children's perceptions of which areas are gender-appropriate for them (Sadker & Sadker, 1994). Accordingly, boys come to feel more competent than girls at math and science and girls come to feel more competent than boys at verbal skills—even when they have equal abilities in these areas (Hong et al., 2003).

Socially, children become even more gender-segregated in their play groups in middle childhood than they were in early childhood. In traditional cultures, gender-segregated play is a consequence of the gender-specific work boys and girls are each doing by middle childhood. In the 12-culture analysis by Whiting and Edwards (1988) (see Chapter 6, page 277), same-gender play groups rose from a proportion of 30–40% at age 2–3 to 94% by age 8–11. However, the same pattern is true in developed countries where boys and girls are in the same schools engaged in the same daily activities (McHale et al., 2003). When boys' and girls' play groups do interact in middle childhood, it tends to be in a manner that is at once quasi-romantic and antagonistic, such as playing a game in which the girls chase the boys, or tossing mild insults at each other like the one my daughter Paris came home chanting one day at age 7:

GIRLS go to COllege to get more KNOWledge.
BOYS go to JUpiter to get more STUpider.

Thorne and Luria (1986) call this kind of gender play "border work" and sees its function as clarifying gender boundaries during middle childhood. It can also be seen as the first tentative step toward the romantic relations that will develop in adolescence.

In terms of their gender self-perceptions, boys and girls head in different directions in middle childhood (Banerjee, 2005). Boys increasingly describe themselves in terms of "masculine" traits (Serbin et al., 1993). They become more likely to avoid activities that might be considered feminine, because their peers become increasingly intolerant of anything that threatens to cross gender boundaries (Blakemore, 2003). In contrast, girls become more likely to attribute "masculine" characteristics such as "forceful" and "self-reliant" to themselves in the course of middle childhood. They do not become less likely to describe themselves as having "feminine" traits such as "warm" and

In developing countries, the kinds of work children and adults do are often divided strictly by gender. Here, a girl in Mozambique helps prepare cassava, a local food.

Why are interactions between boys and girls often quasi-romantic and antagonistic in middle childhood?

"compassionate," but they add "masculine" traits to their self-perceptions. Similarly, they become more likely during middle childhood to consider future occupations usually associated with men, whereas boys become less likely to consider future occupation associated with women (Liben & Bigler, 2002).

WHAT HAVE YOU LEARNED?

1. What kinds of emotional changes accompany the move into new contexts that often occurs in middle childhood?
2. What characterizes the interdependent conception of the self that is prevalent in collectivistic cultures?
3. Why is there such a sharp division of gender roles during middle childhood in traditional cultures?
4. How do boys and girls differ in their self-perceptions during middle childhood?

The Social and Cultural Contexts of Middle Childhood

There is both continuity and change in social contexts from early to middle childhood. Nearly all children remain within a family context, although the composition of the family may change in some cultures due to parents' divorce or remarriage. A new social context is added, as children in nearly all cultures begin formal schooling when they enter this life stage. For children in developing countries today, middle childhood may also mean entering a work setting such as a factory. In all countries, media have become an important socialization context, especially television.

Family relations

> Explain the distinctive features of family relations in middle childhood, and describe the consequences of parental divorce and remarriage.

LEARNING OBJECTIVE **7.16**

Middle childhood represents a key turning point in family relations. Up until that time, children in all cultures need, and receive, a great deal of care and supervision, from parents and older siblings and sometimes from extended family members. They lack sufficient emotional and behavioral self-regulation to be on their own for even a short period of time. However, in middle childhood they become much more capable of going about their daily activities without constant monitoring and control by others. From early childhood to middle childhood, parents and children move away from direct parental control and toward **coregulation**, in which parents provide broad guidelines for behavior but children are capable of a substantial amount of independent, self-directed behavior (Maccoby, 1984; McHale et al., 2003). Parents continue to provide assistance and instruction, and they continue to know where their children are and what they are doing nearly all the time, but there is less need for direct, moment-to-moment monitoring.

This pattern applies across cultures. In developed countries, studies have shown that children spend substantially less time with their parents in middle childhood than in early childhood (Parke, 2004). Children respond more to parents' rules and reasoning, due to advances in cognitive development and self-regulation, and parents in turn use more explanation and less physical punishment (Collins et al., 2002; Parke, 2004). Parents begin to give their children simple daily chores such as making their own beds in the morning and setting the table for dinner.

coregulation relationship between parents and children in which parents provide broad guidelines for behavior but children are capable of a substantial amount of independent, self-directed behavior

Sibling conflict remains high during middle childhood.

My Virtual Child

As your virtual child and his or her sibling engage in an increasing number of conflicts, what are some strategies you might employ to minimize the fighting?

Watch the Video A Family with Two Fathers in **MyDevelopmentLab**

In traditional cultures, parents and children also move toward coregulation in middle childhood. Children have learned family rules and routines by middle childhood and will often carry out their family duties without having to be told or urged by their parents (Weisner, 1996). Also, children are allowed to play and explore further from home once they reach middle childhood (Whiting & Edwards, 1988). Boys are allowed more of this freedom than girls are, in part because girls are assigned more daily responsibilities in middle childhood. However, girls also are allowed more scope for independent activity in middle childhood. For example, in the Mexican village described by Beverly Chinas (1992), when they reach middle childhood girls have responsibility for going to the village market each day to sell the tortillas they and their mothers have made that morning. By middle childhood they are capable of going to the market without an adult to monitor them, and they are also capable of making the monetary calculations required in selling the tortillas and providing change.

Sibling relationships also change in middle childhood. Children with an older sibling often benefit from the sibling's help with academic, peer, and parent issues (Brody, 2004). Both older and young siblings benefit from mutual companionship and assistance. However, the sibling rivalry and jealousy mentioned in Chapter 6 continue in middle childhood. In fact, sibling conflict peaks in middle childhood (Cole & Kerns, 2001). In one study that recorded episodes of conflict between siblings, the average frequency of conflict was once every 20 minutes they were together (Kramer et al., 1999). The most common source of conflict is personal possessions (McGuire et al., 2000). Sibling conflict is especially high when one sibling perceives the other as receiving more affection and material resources from the parents (Dunn, 2004). Other factors contributing to sibling conflict are family financial stress and parents' marital conflict (Jenkins et al., 2003).

DIVERSE FAMILY FORMS Children worldwide grow up in a wide variety of family environments. Some children have parents who are married while others are in single-parent, divorced, or blended families; some children are raised by heterosexual parents while others are raised by gay or lesbian parents; and still others live with extended family members or in multigenerational families. Some are adopted or live with relatives other than their parents.

Gay couples are now allowed to adopt children in some American states and some European countries, and lesbian couples often adopt children or become artificially inseminated. In the latest U.S. census, over 20% of gay couples and one-third of lesbian couples were living with children, a dramatic increase over the past 20 years (U.S. Bureau of the Census, 2010). Studies of the children of gay and lesbian couples have found that they are highly similar to other children (Goldberg, 2010; Patterson, 2002). In adolescence nearly all are heterosexual, despite the homosexual model their parents provide (Hyde & DeLamater, 2005).

Over the past 50 years, it has become increasingly common in some countries for children to be born to a single mother. The United States is one of the countries where the increase has been greatest. This is perhaps because marriage in the United States is at an all-time low: in 2010 barely half of all American adults were married (Pew Research Center, 2011). Related in part to the decline in marriage, single motherhood has increased among both Whites and African Americans, but is now highest among African Americans; over 70% of African American children are born to a single mother (U.S. Bureau of the Census, 2010). Rates of single motherhood are also high in northern Europe (Lestaeghe & Moors, 2000). However, it is more likely in northern Europe than in the United States for the father to be in the home as well, even though the mother and father may not be married. If we combine those children born to single mothers with those living with a single parent as a result of divorce, fewer than half of American children live with both biological parents throughout their entire childhood (Harvey & Fine, 2004).

What are the consequences of growing up within a single-parent household? Because there is only one parent to carry out household responsibilities such as cooking and cleaning, children in single-parent households often contribute a great deal to the functioning of the family, much like their counterparts in traditional cultures. However, the most important consequence of growing up in a single-parent family is that it greatly increases the likelihood of growing up in poverty, and growing up in poverty, in turn, has a range of negative effects on children (Harvey & Fine, 2004). Children in single-parent families generally are at higher risk for behavior problems and low school achievement when compared to their peers in two-parent families (Ricciuti, 2004).

Poverty is common in single-parent families.

Single-parent families are diverse, and many children who grow up in single-parent families function very well. When the mother makes enough money so the family is not in poverty, children in single-parent families function as well as children in two-parent families (Lipman et al., 2002). Single-father families are relatively rare, but children with a single father are no different than their peers in middle childhood on social and academic functioning (Amato, 2000). It should also be noted that having a single parent does not always mean there is only one adult in the household. In many African American families the grandmother is highly involved and provides child care, household help, and financial support to the single mother (Crowther & Rodrigues, 2003). In about one-fourth of families with an African American single mother, the grandmother also lives in the household (Lee et al., 2005).

Most children whose parents divorce spend part of their childhood in a **stepfamily**. Because mothers retain custody of the children in about 90% of divorces, most stepfamilies involve the entrance of a stepfather into the family. When a stepfather comes into the family this usually means a rise in overall family income. Stepfathers can share some of the household and child care responsibilities. Mothers' emotional well-being is typically enhanced by remarriage, at least initially (Visher et al., 2003). If mothers' lives improve in all these ways, their children's lives must improve, too, right?

Unfortunately, no. Frequently, children take a turn for the worse once a stepfather enters the family. Compared to children in nondivorced families, children in stepfamilies have lower academic achievement, lower self-esteem, and greater behavioral problems (Coleman et al., 2000; Nicholson et al., 2008). According to one estimate, about 20% of children in stepfamilies have serious problems in at least one aspect of functioning in middle childhood, compared to 10% of their peers in nondivorced families (Hetherington & Kelly, 2002). Girls respond more negatively than boys to remarriage, a reversal of their responses to divorce (Bray, 1999). If the stepfather also has children of his own that he brings into the household, making a *blended stepfamily,* the outcomes for children are even worse than in other stepfamilies (Hetherington & Kelly, 2002).

There are a number of reasons for children's negative responses to remarriage. First, remarriage represents another disruption that requires adjustment (Hetherington & Stanley-Hagan, 2002). Second, stepfathers may be perceived by children as coming in between them and their mothers, especially by girls, who may have become closer to their mothers following divorce (Bray, 1999). Third, and perhaps most importantly, children may resent and resist their stepfathers' attempts to exercise authority and discipline (Robertson, 2008). Stepfathers may be attempting to support the mother in parenting and to fulfill the family role of father, but children may refuse to regard him as a "real" father and may in fact regard him as taking their biological father's rightful place (Weaver & Coleman, 2010). When asked to draw a picture of their families, many children in stepfamilies literally leave their stepfathers out of the picture (Dunn et al., 2002).

However, it is important to add that here as elsewhere, family process counts for as much as family structure. Many stepfathers and stepchildren form harmonious, close relationships (Coleman et al., 2000). The likelihood of this outcome is enhanced if the

My Virtual Child

What are some different types of families your virtual child is likely to encounter? How will you explain the differences?

stepfamily family with children in which one of the parents is not biologically related to the children but has married a parent who is biologically related to the children

family process quality of the relationships between family members

⊙ **Watch** the **Video** Pam: Divorced Mother of Nine-Year-Old in **MyDevelopmentLab**

APPLYING YOUR KNOWLEDGE
. . . as a Nurse

A Filipino widow comes to your clinic with her twins, concerned that their father is not in their lives, but happy that they live with her parents, the twins' grandparents, who help with their care. What can you tell her?

THINKING CULTURALLY

What patterns do you see among the European countries shown in Figure 7.9? What hypothesis would you propose to explain the patterns?

Figure 7.9 • **Divorce rates, selected countries.** In many countries divorce rates have risen in recent decades. **Source:** Based on http://www.divorcemag.com/statistics/statsWorld.shtml

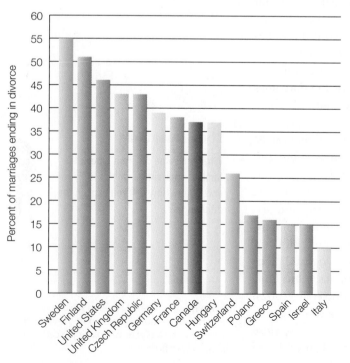

stepfather is warm and open to his stepchildren and does not immediately try to assert stern authority (Visher et al., 2003). Also, the younger the children are, the more open they tend to be to accepting the stepfather (Jeynes, 2007). The likelihood of conflict between stepfathers and stepchildren increases with the children's age from early childhood to middle childhood and again from middle childhood to adolescence (Hetherington & Kelly, 2002).

CHILDREN'S RESPONSES TO DIVORCE Rates of divorce have risen dramatically over the past half century in the United States, Canada, and northern Europe. Currently, close to half of children in many of these countries experience their parents' divorce by the time they reach middle childhood (see **Figure 7.9**). In contrast, divorce remains rare in southern Europe and in non-Western countries. ⊙

How do children respond to their parents' divorce? A wealth of American and European research has addressed this question, including several excellent longitudinal studies. Overall, most children have recovered from the impact of the divorce within two years. However, in those first two years, many children display increases in both externalizing problems (such as unruly behavior and conflict with mothers, siblings, peers, and teachers) and internalizing problems (such as depressed mood, anxieties, phobias, and sleep disturbances) (see Chapter 6) (Amato, 2000; Clarke-Stewart & Brentano, 2006). If the divorce takes place during early childhood, children often blame themselves, but by middle childhood most children are less egocentric and more capable of understanding that their parents may have reasons for divorcing that have nothing to do with them (Hetherington & Kelly, 2002).

In one renowned longitudinal study of divorces that took place when the children were in middle childhood, the researchers classified 25% of the children in divorced families as having severe emotional or behavioral problems, compared to 10% of children in two-parent nondivorced families (Hetherington & Kelly, 2002). The low point for most children came 1 year after divorce. After that point, most children gradually improved in functioning, and by two years postdivorce, girls were mostly back to normal. However, boys' problems were still evident even five years after divorce. Problems continue for some children into adolescence, and new consequences appear.

Not all children react negatively to divorce. Even if 25% have severe problems, that leaves 75% who do not. What factors influence how a divorce will affect children? Increasingly researchers have focused on **family process**, that is, the quality of the relationships between family members before, during, and after the divorce. Parents can help make the transition smoother by maintaining a positive relationship, particularly when it comes to the children. Each parent should encourage the children to have a positive relationship with the other parent. During the divorce, parents should encourage children to express their thoughts and feelings about the divorce; this can help to clear up any misunderstandings and it reminds children that their thoughts and feelings are important. When parents divorce with minimal conflict, or when parents are able to keep their conflicts private, children show far fewer problems (Amato, 2006). If divorce results in a transition from a high-conflict household to a low-conflict household, children's functioning often improves rather than deteriorates (Davies et al., 2002). It may be better for children to live in a conflict-free household headed by one parent than a high-conflict household headed by two parents who are constantly fighting.

Another aspect of family process is children's relationship to the mother after divorce. Mothers often struggle in numerous ways following divorce (Wallerstein & Johnson-Reitz, 2004). In addition to the emotional stress of the divorce and conflict with ex-husbands, they now have full responsibility for household tasks and child care.

There is increased financial stress, with the father's income no longer coming directly into the household. Most countries have laws requiring fathers to contribute to the care of their children after leaving the household, but despite these laws, mothers often receive less than full child support from their ex-husbands (Children's Defense Fund, 2005; Government of Canada, 2010). Given this pile-up of stresses, it is not surprising that the mother's parenting often takes a turn for the worse in the aftermath of divorce, becoming less warm, less consistent, and more punitive (Hetherington & Kelly, 2002).

Relationships between boys and their mothers are especially likely to go downhill after divorce. Mothers and boys sometimes become sucked into a **coercive cycle** following divorce, in which boys' less compliant behavior evokes harsh responses from mothers, which in turn makes boys even more resistant to their mothers' control, evoking even harsher responses, and so on (Patterson, 2002). However, when the mother is able to maintain a healthy balance of warmth and control despite the stresses, her children's response to divorce is likely to be less severe (Leon, 2003). ◉

Family processes involving fathers are also important in the aftermath of divorce. In about 90% of cases (across countries) mothers retain custody of the children, so the father leaves the household and the children no longer see him on a daily basis. Now fathers must get used to taking care of the children on their own, without mothers present, and children must get used to two households that may have two different sets of rules. For most children, contact with the father diminishes over time, and only 35–40% of children in mother-custody families still have at least weekly contact with their fathers within a few years of the divorce (Kelly, 2003). When the father remarries, as most do, his contact with children from the first marriage declines steeply (Dunn, 2002). However, when fathers remain involved and loving, children have fewer post-divorce problems (Dunn et al., 2004; Finley & Schwartz, 2010). Mothers can encourage an ongoing relationship between the children and their father through phone calls and visitation.

In recent decades, **divorce mediation** has developed as a way of minimizing the damage to children that may take place due to heightened parental conflict during and after divorce (Emery et al., 2005; Sbarra & Emery, 2008). In divorce mediation, a professional mediator meets with divorcing parents to help them negotiate an agreement that both will find acceptable. Research has shown that mediation can settle a large percentage of cases otherwise headed for court and lead to better functioning in children following divorce and improved relationships between divorced parents and their children, even 12 years after the settlement (Emery et al., 2005).

Relationships between mothers and sons sometimes go downhill following divorce.

◉—⌐**Watch** the **Video** Divorce and Co-parenting in **MyDevelopmentLab**

Friends and peers

Explain the main basis of friendships in middle childhood, and describe the four categories of peer social status and the dynamics between bullies and victims.

LEARNING OBJECTIVE 7.17

◉—⌐**Watch** the **Video** Parental Control of Friendships in India in **MyDevelopmentLab**

Friends rise in importance from early childhood to middle childhood, as greater freedom of movement allows children to visit and play with friends. Also, the entrance into formal schooling takes children away from the family social environment and places them in an environment where they spend a substantial amount of most days around many other children of similar age. Daily contact with other children makes it possible for them to develop friendships. ◉

In this discussion of friends and peers we will first examine the characteristics of friendships in middle childhood, then look at popularity and bullying in peer groups.

MAKING FRIENDS Why do children become friends with some peers but not others? An abundance of research over several decades has shown that the main basis of friendship is similarity, not just during middle childhood but at all ages (Rubin et al., 2008). People

coercive cycle pattern in relations between parents and children in which children's disobedient behavior evokes harsh responses from parents, which in turn makes children even more resistant to parental control, evoking even harsher responses

divorce mediation arrangement in which a professional mediator meets with divorcing parents to help them negotiate an agreement that both will find acceptable

Trust becomes more important to friendships in middle childhood.

tend to prefer being around others who are like themselves, a principle called **selective association** (Popp et al., 2008). We have already seen how gender is an especially important basis of selective association in middle childhood. Boys tend to play with boys and girls with girls, more than at either younger or older ages. Other important criteria for selective association in middle childhood are sociability, aggression, and academic orientation (Hartup, 1996). Sociable kids are attracted to each other as friends, as are shy kids; aggressive kids tend to form friendships with each other, as do kids who refrain from aggression; kids who care a lot about school tend to become friends, and so do kids who dislike school.

Although selective association is an important basis of friendship at all ages, over the course of childhood friendships change in other ways. An important change from early to middle childhood is in the relative balance of activities and trust (Rubin et al., 2008). Friendships in early childhood are based mainly on shared activities. Your friends are the kids who like to do the same things you like to do. Consequently, young children usually claim they have lots of friends, and their friends are more or less interchangeable. If you like to ride bikes, whoever is available to ride bikes with you is your friend; if you like to play with plastic action figures, your friend is whoever happens to be available to play a game with you involving those action figures. When they describe their friends, young children talk mainly about their shared activities (Damon, 1983; Rubin et al., 2008).

In middle childhood, shared activities are still an important part of friendships, but now trust, too, becomes important. Children name fewer of their peers as friends, and friendships last longer, often several years (Rose & Asher, 1999). Your friends are kids who not only like to do things you like to do, but also whom you can rely on to be nice to you almost all the time, and whom you can trust with information you would not reveal to just anyone. In one study of children in grades 3 to 6, the expectation that a friend would keep a secret increased from 25% to 72% across that age span among girls; among boys the increase came later and did not rise as high (Azmitia et al., 1998). This finding reflects a more general gender difference found in many other studies, that girls prize trust in middle childhood friendships more than boys do, and that boys' friendships focus more on shared activities, although for both genders trust is more important in middle childhood than in early childhood (Rubin et al., 2008). As trust becomes more important to friendships in middle childhood, breaches of trust (such as breaking a promise or failing to provide help when needed) also become the main reason for ending friendships (Hartup & Abecassis, 2004).

PLAYING WITH FRIENDS Even though trust becomes a more important part of friendship in early childhood, friends continue to enjoy playing together in shared activities. Recall from Chapter 6 that play in early childhood most often takes the form of simple social play or cooperative pretend play. These types of play continue in middle childhood. For example, children might play with dolls or action figures together, or they might pretend to be superheroes or animals.

What is new about play in middle childhood is that it becomes more complex and more rule-based. Children in early childhood may play with action figures, but in middle childhood there may be elaborate rules about the powers and limitations of the characters. For example, Japanese games involving Pokemon action figures are popular in middle childhood play worldwide, especially among boys (Ogletree et al., 2004). These games involve characters with an elaborate range of powers and provide children with the enjoyment of competition and mastering complex information and rules. In early childhood the information about the characters would be too abundant and the rules too complex for children to follow, but by middle childhood this cognitive challenge is exciting and pleasurable.

selective association in social relations, the principle that people tend to prefer being around others who are like themselves

In addition to games such as Pokemon, many of the games with rules that children play in middle childhood are more cognitively challenging than the games younger children play. Card games and board games become popular, and often these games require children to count, remember, and plan strategies. Middle childhood is also a time when many children develop an interest in hobbies such as collecting certain types of objects (e.g., coins, dolls) or constructing and building things (such as LEGOs, a Danish invention that is popular around the world in middle childhood). These hobbies also provide enjoyable cognitive challenges of organizing and planning (McHale et al., 2001). Recently, electronic games have become a highly popular type of game in middle childhood, and these games also present substantial cognitive challenges (Olson et al., 2008).

Although the complexity and cognitive challenges of play in middle childhood distinguish it from play in early childhood, children continue to enjoy simple games as well (Manning, 1998). According to cross-cultural studies, games such as tag and hide-and-seek are popular all over the world in middle childhood (Edwards, 2000). Children also play simple games that are drawn from their local environment, such as the herding games played by boys in Kenya in the course of caring for cattle.

Middle childhood games also reflect children's advances in gross motor development. As children develop greater physical agility and skill in middle childhood, their games with rules include various sports that require greater physical challenges than their early childhood games did. As noted earlier in the chapter, in many countries middle childhood is the time when children first join organized teams to play sports such as soccer, baseball, or basketball. Many children also play sports in games they organize themselves, often including discussions of the rules of the game (Davies, 2004).

POPULARITY AND UNPOPULARITY In addition to having friendships, children are also part of a larger social world of peers, especially once they enter primary school. Schools are usually **age graded**, which means that students at a given grade level tend to be the same age. When children are in a social environment with children of different ages, age is a key determinant of **social status**, in that older children tend to have more authority than younger children. However, when all children are about the same age, they find other ways of establishing who is high in social status and who is low. One aspect of social status in middle childhood is popularity among peers. Based on children's ratings of who they like or dislike among their peers, researchers have described four categories of social status (Cillessen & Mayeux, 2004; Rubin et al., 2008):

- *Popular children* are the ones who are most often rated as "liked" and rarely rated as "disliked."
- *Rejected children* are most often disliked and rarely liked by other children. Usually, rejected children are disliked mainly for being overly aggressive, but in about 10–20% of cases rejected children are shy and withdrawn (Hymel et al., 2004; Sandstrom & Zakriski, 2004). Boys are more likely than girls to be rejected.
- *Neglected children* are rarely mentioned as either liked or disliked; other children have trouble remembering who they are. Girls are more likely than boys to be neglected.
- *Controversial children* are liked by some children but disliked by others. They may be aggressive at times but are friendly at other times.

About two-thirds of children in American samples fall into one of these categories in middle childhood, according to most studies (Wentzel, 2003). The rest are rated in mixed ways by other children and are classified by researchers as "average."

What characteristics determine a child's social status? Abundant research indicates that the strongest influence on popularity is **social skills** such as being friendly, helpful, cooperative, and considerate (Barry & Wentzel, 2006; Cillessen & Bellmore, 2004). Children with social skills are good at perspective-taking; consequently they are good at understanding and responding to other children's needs and interests (Cassidy et al.,

age graded social organization based on grouping persons of similar ages

social status within a group, the degree of power, authority, and influence that each person has in the view of the others

social skills behaviors that include being friendly, helpful, cooperative, and considerate

What makes some children popular in middle childhood?

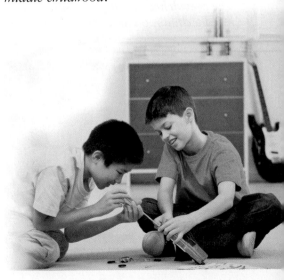

social information processing (SIP) in social encounters, evaluations of others' intentions, motivations, and behavior

2003). Other important influences on popularity are intelligence, physical appearance, and (for boys) athletic ability (McHale et al., 2003). Despite the popular idea of the "nerd" or "geek" as a kid who is unpopular for being smart, in general, intelligence enhances popularity in middle childhood (but this becomes a bit more complicated in adolescence). "Nerds" and "geeks" are unpopular because they lack social skills, not because of their intelligence.

Rejected children are usually more aggressive than other children, and their aggressiveness leads to conflicts (Coie, 2004). They tend to be impulsive and have difficulty controlling their emotional reactions, which disrupts group activities, to the annoyance of their peers. In addition to this lack of self-control, their lack of social skills and social understanding leads to conflict with others. According to Kenneth Dodge (2008), who has done decades of research on this topic, rejected children often fail in their **social information processing (SIP)**. That is, they tend to interpret their peers' behavior as hostile even when it is not, and they tend to blame others when there is conflict.

For rejected children who are withdrawn rather than aggressive, the basis of their rejection is less clear. They may be shy and even fearful of other children, but these characteristics are also found often in neglected children. What distinguishes between rejected-withdrawn and neglected children? Rejected-withdrawn children are more likely to have internalizing problems such as low self-esteem and anxiety. In contrast, neglected children are usually quite well-adjusted (Wentzel, 2003). They may not engage in social interactions with peers as frequently as other children do, but they usually have social skills equal to average children, are not unhappy, and report having friends.

Controversial children often have good social skills, as popular children do, but they are also high in aggressiveness, like rejected children (DeRosier & Thomas, 2003). Their social skills make them popular with some children, and their aggressiveness makes them unpopular with others. They may be adept at forming alliances with some children and excluding others. Sometimes they defy adult authority in ways their peers admire but do not dare to emulate (Vaillancourt & Hymel, 2006).

Social status is related to other aspects of children's development, in middle childhood and beyond, especially for rejected children. Because other children exclude them from their play and they have few or no friends, rejected children often feel lonely and they dislike going to school (Buhs & Ladd, 2001). Their aggressiveness and impulsiveness cause problems in their other social relationships, not just with peers, and they have higher rates of conflict with parents and teachers than other children do (Coie, 2004). According to longitudinal studies, being rejected in middle childhood is predictive of later conduct problems in adolescence and emerging adulthood (Miller-Johnson et al., 2003). This does not necessarily mean that being rejected causes later problems; rather, it may indicate that the aggressiveness that inspires rejection from peers in middle childhood often remains at later ages and causes problems that take other forms. Nevertheless, being rejected by peers makes it more difficult for children to develop the social skills that would allow them to overcome a tendency toward aggressiveness.

Because rejected children are at risk for a downward spiral of problems in their social relationships, psychologists have developed interventions to try to ameliorate their low social status. Some of these interventions focus on social skills, training rejected children how to initiate friendly interactions with their peers (Asher & Rose, 1997). Other programs focus on social information processing, and seek to teach rejected children to avoid jumping to the conclusion that their peers' intentions toward them are negative (Bierman, 2004). As part of the intervention, rejected children may be asked to role play hypothetical situations with peers, or watch a videotape of peer interactions with an instructor and talk about why the peers in the video acted as they did (Ladd et al., 2004). These programs have often shown success in the short term, improving rejected children's social understanding and the quality of their peer interactions, but it is unknown whether the gains from the programs are deep enough to result in enduring improvements in rejected children's peer relations.

The prevalence of bullying rises through middle childhood across countries.

BULLIES AND VICTIMS An extreme form of peer rejection in adolescence is **bullying**. Bullying is defined by researchers as having three components (Olweus, 2000; Wolak et al., 2007): *aggression* (physical or verbal); *repetition* (not just one incident but a pattern over time); and *power imbalance* (the bully has higher peer status than the victim). The prevalence of bullying rises through middle childhood and peaks in early adolescence, then declines substantially by late adolescence (Pepler et al., 2006). Bullying is an international phenomenon, observed in many countries in Europe (Dijkstra et al., 2008; Eslea et al., 2004; Gini et al., 2008), Asia (Ando et al., 2005; Hokoda et al., 2006; Kanetsuna et al., 2006), and North America (Espelage & Swearer, 2004; Pepler et al., 2008; Volk et al., 2006). Estimates vary depending on age and country, but overall about 20% of children are victims of bullies at some point during middle childhood. Boys are more often bullies as well as victims (Berger, 2007). Boys bully using both physical and verbal attacks, but girls can be bullies, too, most often using verbal methods (Pepler et al., 2004; Rigby, 2004).

There are two general types of bullies in middle childhood. Some are rejected children who are bully–victims, that is, they are bullied by children who are higher in status and they in turn look for lower-status victims to bully (Kochenderfer-Ladd, 2003). Bully–victims often come from families where the parents are harsh or even physically abusive (Schwartz et al., 2001). Other bullies are controversial children who may have high peer status for their physical appearance, athletic abilities, or social skills, but who are also resented and feared for their bullying behavior toward some children (Vaillancourt et al., 2003). Bullies of both types tend to have a problem controlling their aggressive behavior toward others, not just toward peers but in their other relationships, during middle childhood and beyond (Olweus, 2000). Bullies are also at higher risk than other children for depression (Fekkes et al., 2004; Ireland & Archer, 2004).

Victims of bullying are most often rejected, withdrawn children who are low in self-esteem and social skills (Champion et al., 2003). Because they have few friends, they often have no allies when bullies begin victimizing them (Goldbaum et al., 2003). They cry easily in response to bullying, which makes other children regard them as weak and vulnerable and deepens their rejection. Compared to other children, victims of bullying are more likely to be depressed and lonely (Baldry & Farrington, 2004; Rigby, 2004). Their low moods and loneliness may be partly a response to being bullied, but these are also characteristics that may make bullies regard them as easy targets.

How do other children respond when they witness one of their peers being bullied? One study observed American children in grades 1–6 on playgrounds and recorded bullying episodes (Hawkins et al., 2001). Other children intervened to help a victim about half the time, and when they did the bullies usually backed off. However, a study in Finland found that in 20–30% of bullying episodes, peers actually encouraged bullies and sometimes even joined in against the victim (Salmivalli & Voeten, 2004). ◉

bullying pattern of maltreatment of peers, including aggression; repetition; and power imbalance

My Virtual Child

What would you do if your virtual child began bullying other children? How would you handle the situation if your virtual child was the victim?

◉─[**Watch** the **Video** Bullying in **MyDevelopmentLab**

Work

Describe the kinds of work children do in middle childhood, and explain why work patterns differ between developed and developing countries.

LEARNING OBJECTIVE **7.18**

Increasingly in the course of middle childhood, my twins came up with ways to put themselves to work and earn money, especially my daughter Paris. For example, when she was 7 years old she invented a drink she called "Raspberry Ramble," made of apple juice, spiced tea, and crushed raspberries. She claimed we could sell large quantities of it and make a fortune. That same year, on a trip to Denmark she collected dozens of rocks on the beach and announced she was opening a "rock museum" on her bed that we could enjoy for a very reasonable price. Erik Erikson (1950), whose lifespan theory we have been discussing in each chapter (see Chapter 1), called middle childhood the stage of **industry versus inferiority**, when children become capable of doing useful work

industry versus inferiority Erikson's middle childhood stage, in which the alternatives are to learn to work effectively with cultural materials or, if adults are too critical, develop a sense of being incapable of working effectively

Children in developing countries often work long hours in poor conditions by middle childhood. Here, a young boy works in a factory in Bangladesh.

as well as their own self-directed projects, unless the adults around them are too critical of their efforts, leading them to develop a sense of inferiority instead. This part of Erikson's theory has received little research. However, it is possible to see some verification of it in the way children across cultures are regarded as more capable than they were in early childhood and in the way they are often given important work responsibilities (Rogoff, 2003; Weisner, 1996).

In developing countries, the work that children do in middle childhood is often not merely a form of play as it was for my daughter but a serious and sometimes perilous contribution to the family. In most developed countries, it is illegal to employ children in middle childhood (United Nations Development Programme, 2010). However, in a large proportion of the world middle childhood is the time when productive work begins. Children who do not attend school are usually working, often for their families on a farm or family business, but sometimes in industrial settings. With the globalization of the world economy, many large companies have moved much of their manufacturing to developing countries, where labor costs are cheaper. Cheapest of all is the labor of children. Before middle childhood, children are too immature and lacking in self-regulation to be useful in manufacturing. Their gross and fine motor skills are limited, their attention wanders too much, and they are too erratic in their behavior and their emotions. However, by age 6 or 7 children have the motor skills, the cognitive skills, and the emotional and behavioral self-regulation to be excellent workers at many jobs.

The International Labor Organization (ILO) has estimated that about 200 million children and adolescents are employed worldwide, and that 95% of them are in developing countries (ILO, 2002, 2004, 2006, 2008). As shown in **Map 7.3**, a substantial proportion of children work in Latin America, Asia, and the Middle East/North Africa, but the greatest number of child workers is found in sub-Saharan Africa. Agricultural work is the most common form of child employment, usually on commercial farms or plantations, often working alongside parents but for only one-third to one-half the pay (ILO, 2002). Children can quickly master the skills needed to plant, tend, and harvest agricultural products.

In addition, many children in these countries work in factories and shops where they perform labor such as weaving carpets, sewing clothes, gluing shoes, curing leather, and polishing gems. The working conditions are often miserable—crowded garment factories where the doors are locked and children (and adults) work 14-hour shifts, small poorly-lit huts where they sit at a loom weaving carpets for hours on end, glass factories where the temperatures are unbearably hot and children carry rods of molten glass from one station to another (ILO, 2004). Other children work in cities in a wide variety of jobs including domestic service, grocery shops, tea stalls, and delivering messages and packages. Children in developed countries are generally prohibited from work, but as you will see in the **Historical Focus: Work Among British Children in the 19th Century** feature on page 340, this is a relatively recent development.

If children's work is so often difficult and dangerous, why do parents allow their children to work, and why do governments not outlaw child labor? For parents, the simple answer is that they need the money. As we have seen, billions of people worldwide are very poor. Poor families in developing countries often depend on children's contributions to the family income for basic necessities like food and clothing. Children's work may be difficult and dangerous, but so is the work of adults; often, adults and children work in the same factories. As for governments, nearly all countries do have laws prohibiting child labor, but some developing countries do not enforce them, because of bribes from the companies employing the children or because they do not wish to incur the wrath of parents who need their children's income (Chaudhary & Sharma, 2007).

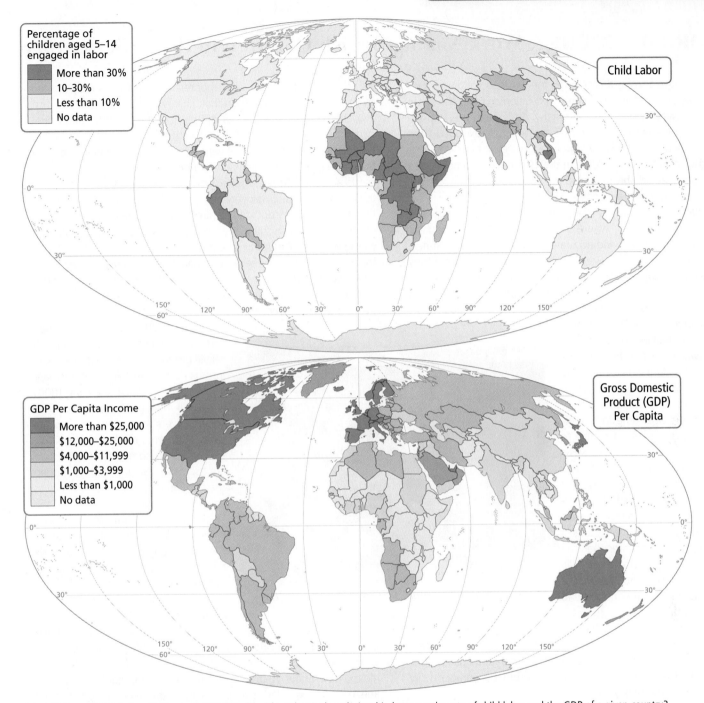

Map 7.3 • **Child Labor Rates and GDP Worldwide.** What is the relationship between the rate of child labor and the GDP of a given country? How can you explain this relationship?

Although the exploitation of children's labor in developing countries is widespread and often harsh, signs of positive changes can be seen. According to the International Labor Organization, the number of child laborers ages 5–11 is declining (ILO, 2006). This decline has taken place because the issue of child and adolescent labor has received increased attention from the world media, governments, and international organizations such as the ILO and the United Nations Children's Fund (UNICEF). Furthermore, legislative action has been taken in many countries to raise the number of years children are legally required to attend school and to enforce the often-ignored laws against employing children younger than their midteens (ILO, 2008). Amid such signs of progress, it remains true that millions of children work in unhealthy conditions all around the world (ILO, 2002, 2004, 2006, 2008).

HISTORICAL FOCUS   Work Among British Children in the 19th Century

As we have seen in this chapter, the working conditions currently experienced by children in developing countries are in many ways dangerous, unhealthy, underpaid, and exploitative. Children in developed countries are generally excluded from paid employment, but this is a relatively recent development. In fact, the working conditions of children in the 19th century in developed countries were remarkably similar to the conditions experienced today by children in developing countries.

Information on child labor in the 19th century is especially abundant in Great Britain, where government statistics were kept much more systematically and accurately than in the United States. The history of child labor in Great Britain is described in a book by Pamela Horn (1995), *Children's Work and Welfare, 1780–1890*.

Because Britain was the first country in which industrialization took place, it was also the first country in which child and adolescent labor was widely used. Textile manufacturing (the making of cloth and clothing) was the first industry to use child labor, beginning in the 1770s. For the first time textiles were being mass produced in factories rather than made one at a time in homes. Children were especially attractive to employers, partly because there was a shortage of adult workers and partly because younger workers could be paid lower wages, and with their nimble fingers they could perform much of the work even better than adults.

Many of these children had no parents and were sent to the textile mills by officials in city orphanages and institutions for the poor, who were glad to be relieved of the cost of caring for them. Children had no choice but to go and were not free to leave until they reached age 21. For those who did have parents, their parents usually did not object to them working in textile mills, but encouraged it in order to increase the family's income.

Working conditions varied in the mills, but 12- to 14-hour workdays were common, with an hour break for lunch. The work was monotonous, exhausting, and dangerous. A momentary lapse of attention could lead to serious injury, and crushed hands and fingers were common. Dust and residue from the production process damaged workers' lungs and caused stomach illnesses and eye infections.

The first attempts at government regulation of the mills were tentative, to say the least. Because the British economy depended so heavily on the young millworkers, even reformers were reluctant to advocate an end to their labor. There was also little public support

A young miner in England fixes the ropes for the coal carts.

for abolishing child labor, and labor restrictions were fiercely resisted by parents who depended on their children's income. Thus, the first law, the Health and Morals of Apprentices Act of 1802, simply limited young workers to 12 hours of labor a day! The act also mandated minimum standards of ventilation and sanitation in the mills, but these provisions were widely ignored by mill owners.

In addition, the act required employers to provide daily schooling to young workers. Employers generally complied with this, because they believed that educated children would be more compliant and productive, so the result was a significant increase in literacy among young workers. This requirement spread to other industries over the following decades and became the basis of the *half-time system,* in which young workers in factories received schooling for a half day and worked for a half day. This system survived in British society until the end of the 19th century.

In the 1830s, regulatory attention turned to mining. Just as changes in textile production had created a boom in jobs in the late 1700s, an increase in the need for coal in the early 1800s created a mining boom. Once again, children were sought as workers because they were cheap, manageable, and could do some jobs better than adults. Once again, parents urged their children to become laborers as early as possible to contribute to the family income, even though the work in the mines was especially hazardous.

A workday of 12 to 14 hours six days a week was common for young miners. Many of them descended into the mine before sunrise and came up again after sunset, so that they never saw daylight for weeks at a time except on Sundays. Accidents were common, and coal dust damaged young miners' lungs. The first reforms, in the 1842 Mines Act, prohibited boys under 10 from working in mines and required boys over age 10 to be provided with schooling by the mine owners, but did nothing about the working conditions in the mines.

Over the second half of the 19th century, legal regulations on child labor slowly and gradually reduced the exploitation of young workers in British industrial settings. Regulations increased concerning the work children could be required to do. The half-time system, once celebrated as a way of protecting young workers from exploitation, became viewed as an obstacle to their educational opportunities. Public schools were established, and attendance at school became legally required for all children in the 1880s. This essentially marked the end of child labor in Great Britain.

Media use

LEARNING OBJECTIVE **7.19**

> Summarize the rates of daily TV-watching among children worldwide, and describe the positive and negative effects of television, especially the hazards related to TV violence.

Media use is a part of daily life for most children even in early childhood, as we saw Chapter 6. But media become more prominent in children's lives from early childhood to middle childhood. Television remains the most-used media form, but time watching television rises substantially in middle childhood, to about three hours a day in the United States (Warren, 2007). As *Figure 7.10* shows, television watching varies widely across countries, but in most countries children watch television for at least two hours a day (Hasebrink, 2007b). Computer use (including Internet use and electronic games) also rises, to about an hour a day, and music (radio and recorded music) emerges as a major media source, also at about an hour a day (Warren, 2007). Magazines and books become a part of children's media diets as they learn to read in middle childhood. Unlike in early childhood, by middle childhood about one-fourth of children's media use involves **media multitasking**, the simultaneous use of more than one media form, such as playing an electronic game while watching TV (Warren, 2007). All together, media use in middle childhood occupies about four to six hours of a typical day in most developed countries.

As noted in Chapters 5 and 6, media forms and media content within each form are highly diverse, so it would be a mistake to characterize media use in childhood as solely positive or negative. There is a big difference between watching *Clifford the Big Red Dog* on TV and watching a highly violent movie or TV show; children who play on prosocial websites like *Webkinz* or *Club Penguin* can be expected to respond differently than children who play violent electronic games like *Quake* or *Mortal Kombat*.

In general, media research on middle childhood has focused on the question of negative effects, as it has at other ages, but positive effects have also been noted. With regard to television, one analysis of 34 studies found that prosocial content in children's television shows had positive effects on four areas of children's functioning: altruism, positive social interactions, self-control, and combating negative stereotypes (Kotler, 2007). Furthermore, the positive effect of prosocial content was found to be equal to or greater than the negative effects of violent content. The Internet has been shown to be a valuable resource for children to learn about a wide range of topics, for school projects or just for enjoyment (Foehr, 2007; Van Evra, 2007). Much of children's media use is simply harmless fun, such as listening to music, playing nonviolent computer games, and watching children's television shows.

The consequences of media use depend partly on whether children are light, moderate, or heavy media users (Van Evra, 2007). Light to moderate media use is generally harmless and can even be positive, especially if the media content is educational, prosocial, or at least nonviolent. In contrast, heavy media use is associated with a variety of problems in middle childhood, including obesity, anxiety, poor school performance, and social isolation. It is difficult to tell whether heavy media use is a cause or consequence of these problems; perhaps both.

Of all the problems associated with media use in middle childhood, aggression has been studied most extensively, specifically the effects of violent television on children's aggressiveness. As noted in Chapter 6, violence is common in the content of television

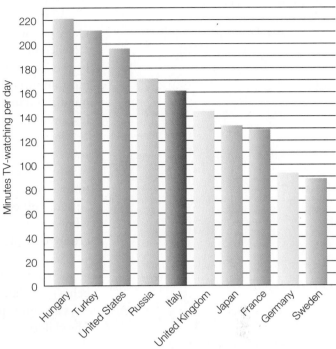

Figure 7.10 • **International television viewing rates in childhood.** In most developed countries, children watch TV for 1–3 hours a day.

Source: Based on Computer use, international. In Encyclopedia of children, adolescents, and the media (pp. 207–210).

media multitasking simultaneous use of more than one media form, such as playing an electronic game while watching TV

Watch the **Video** Violence and Video Games in **MyDevelopmentLab**

shows. It is estimated that the average child in the United States witnesses 200,000 acts of violence on television by age 18, including 16,000 murders (Aikat, 2007). The violence is not just on adults' programs that children watch along with their parents. On the contrary, an analysis of programming for children ages 5–10 on eight TV networks found that the programs depicted an average of eight acts of violence per hour, *higher* than the rate on shows for adults (Fyfe, 2006).

With such high rates of violence in the television shows that children watch most, many parents and scholars have expressed concern about the possibility that television violence may cause aggression in children. Although early childhood is considered to be the life stage of greatest vulnerability to the effects of media violence, some of the most important studies linking media violence to children's aggression have focused on middle childhood. The key studies have included field experiments, longitudinal studies, and natural experiments.

In field experiments, children's social behavior has been observed following exposure to violent television. For example, in one field experiment, there were two groups of boys at a summer camp (Bushman & Chandler, 2007). One group was shown violent films every evening for five nights; the other group watched nonviolent films during this period. Subsequently, observations of the boys' social behavior showed that the boys who watched the violent films were more likely than the boys in the nonviolent film group to display physical and verbal aggression.

Several longitudinal studies by Rowell Huesmann and colleagues have shown that watching high amounts of violent television in middle childhood predicts aggressive behavior at later life stages (Coyne, 2007; Huesmann et al., 2003). One study involved boys and girls in five countries: Australia, Finland, Israel, Poland, and the United States. The children's TV-watching patterns and aggressive behavior were assessed at age 6 and then five years later at age 11. High levels of exposure to TV violence at age 6 predicted aggressive behavior at age 11 across countries, even controlling statistically for initial aggressiveness at age 6. Studies by other researchers in South Africa and the Netherlands have reported similar results (Coyne, 2007).

Huesmann's longitudinal study in the United States extends even further into the lifespan (Huesmann et al., 1984; Huesmann et al., 2003). Television-viewing patterns and aggressive behavior were assessed in middle childhood (age 8) and again at ages 19 and 30. A correlation was found at age 8 between aggressiveness and watching violent TV, not surprisingly. But watching violent TV at age 8 also predicted aggressive behavior in boys at age 19, and by age 30 the men who had watched high amounts of violent TV at age 8 were more likely to be arrested, more likely to have traffic violations, and more likely to abuse their children. As in the other longitudinal studies by Huesmann and colleagues, the results predicting aggressive behavior at ages 19 and 30 were sustained even when aggressiveness at age 8 was controlled statistically. So, it was not simply that aggressive persons especially liked to watch violent television at all three ages, but that aggressive 8-year-olds who watched high levels of TV violence were more likely to be aggressive at later ages than similarly aggressive 8-year-olds who watched lower levels of TV violence.

Perhaps the most persuasive evidence that media violence causes aggression in children comes from a natural experiment in a Canadian town. This natural experiment is the subject of the **Research Focus: TV or Not TV** feature.

In sum, there is good reason for concern about the effects violent media content in middle childhood. However, it should be kept in mind that most of the research on the effects of media violence is correlational, and true experiments with random assignment to conditions cannot be achieved. Furthermore, it is important to remember that media can have positive effects as well. The focus of media research is generally on the negative effects, in middle childhood as in other life stages, but with nonviolent content, and if used in moderation, media use can be a positive and enjoyable part of childhood (Scantlin, 2008; Van Evra, 2007).

RESEARCH FOCUS TV or Not TV

Researchers on human development are limited in the methods they can use, because they have to take into account ethical issues concerning the rights and well-being of the people they involve in their studies. If you were a biologist studying frogs and you were interested in how frogs respond to drought, you could put some frogs into a no-water condition and other frogs into a control group with normal access to water, and no one would object (except maybe the frogs!). However, the environments of human beings cannot be changed and manipulated in the same way, especially if the change would involve a condition that is potentially unhealthy or dangerous.

One way that researchers can obtain information about human development despite this restriction it to look for opportunities for a *natural experiment*. Recall from Chapter 1 that a natural experiment is a condition that takes place without the researcher's manipulation or involvement, but that nevertheless provides important information to the perceptive observer. To go back to the frogs, if you were interested in frogs' responses to drought, you would not necessarily have to subject some frogs to a no-water condition. Instead, you could research frogs in an area where a drought was already taking place, and make use of that condition as a natural experiment.

One human development topic for which natural experiments have been available is the effect of television on children's behavior. Television use spread all over the world with remarkable speed after it was invented in the 1940s, but there are still parts of the world that do not have television or have

Many studies have shown a link between watching violent TV and aggression.

received it only recently. In the early 1980s, a perceptive group of Canadian researchers, led by Tannis MacBeth, observed that there were areas of Canada that still did not have TV, although it was spreading rapidly. They decided to take advantage of this natural experiment to observe children's behavior before and after the introduction of TV (MacBeth, 2007).

Three towns were included in the study: "Notel" (as the researchers dubbed it), which had no television at the beginning of the study, "Unitel," which had one television channel, and "Multitel," with multiple channels. The focus of the study was on middle childhood, grades 1–5. In each grade, 5 boys and 5 girls were randomly selected in each town for participation in the study. Each child's behavior was recorded by a trained observer for 21 one-minute periods over a period of two weeks across different times of day and different settings (e.g., school and home). The observers focused on aggressive behavior, using a checklist of 14 physically aggressive behaviors (such as hits, pushes, bites) and 9 verbally aggressive behaviors (such as mocking, curses, and threats). Neither children, nor parents, nor teachers were aware that the study focused on aggressive behavior or television.

In addition to the observations, the researchers obtained peer and teacher ratings of children's aggressiveness. Both of these ratings showed high agreement with the results of the observations (i.e., children rated as high in aggression by observers were also reported as highly aggressive by their peers and teachers). This demonstrated that the observations of aggression were high in external validity. That is, the high correlations between the observations and the peer and teacher ratings strengthens the likelihood that all assessments of aggression were measuring what they intended to measure.

The ratings and observations took place just before the introduction of TV to Notel and then two years later, after Notel had obtained TV reception (just one channel). Unitel and Multitel had the same number of channels at both time points. The same children were included in the study at Time 1 and Time 2.

The results of the study showed clearly and unambiguously that the introduction of television caused children in Notel to become more aggressive. Children in Notel increased their rates of both physical and verbal aggression from Time 1 to Time 2, whereas there was no change for children in Unitel or Multitel. The increase in aggression in Notel occurred for both boys and girls. Furthermore, it increased not only for Notel children who were initially high in aggressiveness but for those who were initially low in aggressiveness. In all three towns at Time 2, the more TV children watched, the more aggressive they were.

This natural experiment provides persuasive evidence that the relation between TV watching and aggressiveness in children involves not only correlation but causation. It also demonstrates that natural experiments allow researchers to obtain results that would not be possible using any other method. It would not be ethical to place children into a "TV" condition and a "Not TV" condition—especially with what we now know about TV's potential effects—but making use of the natural experiment taking place in Notel, Unitel, and Multitel allowed the researchers to obtain important results about the effects of television on children's behavior.

WHAT HAVE YOU LEARNED?

1. How does family process affect how children respond to divorce?
2. How does the principle of selective association explain friendships in middle childhood?
3. What characteristics do rejected children typically have in common?
4. What developmental changes occur by age 6 or 7 that make children more capable of work?
5. How do studies of the effects of TV violence on children distinguish correlation from causation?

Section 3 VIDEO GUIDE Friendships and Peer Relationships in Middle Childhood Across Cultures (Length: 4:09)

This video shows interviews from around the world on peer relationships and friendships in middle childhood.

1. What contributes to the increase in friendships during the middle childhood years?

2. Many of those interviewed discuss how friendships in middle childhood are often same gender. Why do you feel this self-segregation takes place?

3. The American mother presents a very chaotic and rough-and-tumble environment regarding her three boys. Do you think it is a typical situation among other U.S. homes with only boys?

👁 ⌐ **Watch** the **Video** Friendships and Peer Relationships in Middle Childhood Across Cultures in **MyDevelopmentLab**

Summing Up

((•⊣ **Listen** to an audio file of your chapter in **MyDevelopmentLab**

SECTION 1   PHYSICAL DEVELOPMENT

7.1 Identify the changes in physical and sensory development that take place during middle childhood.

In middle childhood physical growth continues at a slow but steady pace, about 2–3 inches (5–8 cm) per year in height and about 5–7 pounds (2½–3 kg) per year in weight. Children lose all 20 primary teeth and their permanent teeth begin to grow in. Ear health improves, but 25% of children become nearsighted during middle childhood.

7.2 Describe the negative effects of both malnutrition and obesity on development, and identify the causes of obesity.

Studies have shown that better-nourished children are more energetic, less anxious, show more positive emotion, and score higher than malnourished children on a wide range of cognitive measures in middle childhood. Across countries, rates of overweight and obesity are highest in the most affluent regions (North America and Europe) and lowest in the poorest regions (Africa and Southeast Asia). Obesity is a cultural phenomenon, and a variety of social and cultural changes have contributed to this problem, including diets that include more fast food and high rates of television viewing. Genetics also makes a contribution. Socially, being obese increases the likelihood that a child will be excluded and the object of ridicule by peers. Physically, obesity can result in diabetes in middle childhood, which eventually can lead to problems such as blindness, kidney failure, and stroke.

7.3 Explain why rates of illness and injury are relatively low in middle childhood.

In both developed and developing countries, middle childhood is a time of unusually high physical well-being, with low rates of illnesses and diseases due to increased immunization rates, stronger immune systems, and better public health policies. Compared to younger children, children in middle childhood are more agile and better at anticipating situations that may cause injury.

7.4 Explain how children's gross motor skills develop in middle childhood and how these advancements are related to participation in games and sports.

Children's gross motor skills improve in middle childhood due to improved balance, increased strength, better coordination, greater agility, and faster reaction time. As their gross motor development advances, children improve their performance in a wide range of games and sports and many of them participate in organized sports leagues.

7.5 Describe the new skills that demonstrate children's advances in fine motor development in middle childhood.

Fine motor development reaches nearly an adult level at this age, and across cultures, advances are especially evident in two areas: drawing and writing.

KEY TERMS

cultural models *p. 295*
body mass index (BMI) *p. 296*
myopia *p. 297*
overweight *p. 298*
obese *p. 298*
asthma *p. 300*

SECTION 2   COGNITIVE DEVELOPMENT

7.6   Explain the major cognitive advances that occur during Piaget's concrete operations stage.

According to Piaget, children progress from the preoperational stage to the stage of concrete operations during middle childhood, as they learn to think more systematically and scientifically about how the world works and avoid cognitive errors. Cognitive advances during this stage include the ability to decenter and understand conservation, improved classification skills, the understanding of seriation, and the ability to make transitive inferences.

7.7   Describe how attention and memory change from early childhood to middle childhood, and identify the characteristics of children who have ADHD.

In middle childhood, children become more capable of focusing their attention on relevant information and disregarding what is irrelevant. Children with especially notable difficulties in maintaining attention may be diagnosed with attention-deficit/hyperactivity disorder (ADHD), which includes problems of inattention, hyperactivity, and impulsiveness. Middle childhood is the period when children first learn to use memory strategies such as rehearsal, organization, and elaboration.

7.8   Describe the main features and critiques of intelligence tests, and compare and contrast Gardner's and Sternberg's approaches to conceptualizing intelligence.

Intelligence testing first becomes a reliable predictor of later development in middle childhood. Critics have complained, however, that IQ tests assess only a narrow range of abilities, and miss some of the most important aspects of intelligence, such as creativity. Average IQ scores have risen substantially over the 20th century. In recent decades, alternative theories of intelligence have sought to present a conception of intelligence that is much broader than the traditional one. These include Howard Gardner's theory of multiple intelligences and Robert Sternberg's triarchic theory of intelligence. In Gardner's theory there are eight types of intelligence, whereas Sternberg proposes three, but neither theorist has been able to develop an effective way of assessing the intelligences they proposed.

7.9   Identify the advances in vocabulary, grammar, and pragmatics during middle childhood.

Language development continues apace with massive additions to children's vocabularies once they learn to read. There is a fourfold increase in children's vocabularies between the ages of 6 and 10 or 11, and the grammar of children's language use becomes more complex. Their understanding of pragmatics also grows substantially during middle childhood, which can be seen vividly in children's use and appreciation of humor.

7.10   Explain the consequences for cognitive development of growing up bilingual.

Becoming bilingual is beneficial, most notably in the development of metalinguistic knowledge. The difficulty of learning a second language increases with age.

7.11   Summarize the international variations in school enrollment during middle childhood, and compare and contrast the school socialization practices of Eastern and Western cultures.

Attending school is a relatively recent historical development in children's lives, and even today 20–40% of children in developing countries do not attend primary school. School has important influences on children's social development because it separates children from the world of adults and places them among same-age peers. It also makes them less of an economic asset to their parents. Schools vary widely around the world depending on cultural beliefs about how children should learn, but it is economic development, not school philosophy, that mainly determines children's performance on international tests of academic performance.

7.12   Describe how reading and math skills develop from early childhood to middle childhood and the variations in approaches to teaching these skills.

In middle childhood children must learn a whole new way of processing language, via reading, and for most children learning to read takes direct instruction. This is a relatively new development in human history. Most children learn math skills within school, but sometimes math skills can be learned effectively in a practical setting.

KEY TERMS

concrete operations p. 304

decentering p. 305

seriation p. 305

transitive inference p. 306

selective attention p. 306

attention-deficit/hyperactivity
    disorder (ADHD) p. 307

mnemonics p. 308

rehearsal p. 308

organization p. 308

elaboration p. 308

metamemory p. 309

intelligence p. 309

intelligence quotient (IQ) p. 310

normal distribution p. 311

mental retardation p. 311

gifted p. 311

Flynn effect p. 312

theory of multiple intelligences p. 313

triarchic theory of intelligence p. 313

bilingual p. 315

metalinguistic skills p. 316

multilingual p. 317

phonics approach p. 321

whole-language approach p. 321

dyslexia p. 321

learning disability p. 322

numeracy p. 322

SECTION 3 EMOTIONAL AND SOCIAL DEVELOPMENT

7.13 Describe the main features of emotional self-regulation and understanding in middle childhood and how other life stages compare.

Emotionally, middle childhood is generally a time of stability and contentment as emotional self-regulation becomes firmly established and emotional understanding advances.

7.14 Explain how different ways of thinking about the self are rooted in cultural beliefs, and summarize how self-concept and self-esteem change in middle childhood.

Children's self-understanding becomes more complex in middle childhood, and they engage in more social comparison once they enter school. Their overall self-concepts are based on their self-concepts in specific areas that are important to them, which for most children includes physical appearance. In discussing cultural differences in conceptions of the self scholars typically distinguish between the *independent self* promoted by individualistic cultures and the *interdependent self* promoted by collectivistic cultures.

7.15 Describe how beliefs and behavior regarding gender change in middle childhood, including cultural variations.

Children's tasks and play become more gender-segregated in middle childhood, and their views of gender roles become more sharply defined. In traditional cultures boys and girls do separate kinds of work in middle childhood, but playing in gender-specific groups takes place across cultures.

7.16 Explain the distinctive features of family relations in middle childhood, and describe the consequences of parental divorce and remarriage.

Children become more independent during middle childhood as they and their parents move toward coregulation rather than parental dominance and control. Conflict with siblings peaks at this age. Divorce has become increasingly common in developed countries, and children (especially boys) respond negatively to divorce, particularly when it includes high conflict between parents. Parents' remarriage is also experienced negatively in middle childhood, even though it often improves the family's economic situation.

7.17 Explain the main basis of friendships in middle childhood, and describe the four categories of peer social status and the dynamics between bullies and victims.

Similarity is important as the basis of friendship in middle childhood, as it is at other ages. Trust also becomes important in middle childhood friendships. Children's play becomes more complex and rule-based in this stage. Popularity and unpopularity become prominent in peer relations once children develop the capacity for seriation and spend a considerable part of their day in age-graded schools. Rejected children have the greatest problems in peer relations and the poorest long-term prospects for social development, mainly due to their aggressiveness. Bullying is a worldwide problem in middle childhood peer relations.

7.18 Describe the kinds of work children do in middle childhood, and explain why work patterns differ between developed and developing countries.

Over 200 million children in developing countries perform paid work by the time they reach middle childhood, in a wide range of jobs ranging from agricultural work to factory work. Children in developing countries work more than children in developed countries in middle childhood because their contribution to the family income is needed.

7.19 Summarize the rates of daily TV-watching among children worldwide, and describe the positive and negative effects of television, especially the hazards related to TV violence.

Children's media use rises substantially from early childhood to middle childhood. A causal link between media violence and aggression in middle childhood has been established through field studies, longitudinal studies, and natural experiments. Prosocial TV content promotes qualities such as altruism and self-control.

KEY TERMS

Experience Sampling Method (ESM) *p. 324*
ambivalence *p. 325*
self-concept *p. 325*
social comparison *p. 326*

self-esteem *p. 326*
coregulation *p. 329*
stepfamily *p. 331*
family process *p. 332*
coercive cycle *p. 333*

divorce mediation *p. 333*
selective association *p. 334*
age graded *p. 335*
social status *p. 335*
social skills *p. 335*

social information processing (SIP) *p. 336*
bullying *p. 337*
industry versus inferiority *p. 337*
media multitasking *p. 341*

Practice Test

✔●⌐ **Study** and **Review** in **MyDevelopmentLab**

1. In middle childhood
   a. girls are usually taller and heavier than boys because they are about two years ahead in physical development.
   b. the incidence of myopia increases.
   c. ear infections are more likely than they were earlier in infancy and childhood.
   d. the average girl is stronger than the average boy.

2. Rates of overweight and obesity
   a. are rising worldwide.
   b. are lowest among African American females compared to all other ethnic groups in the United States.
   c. are lower among Latinos and Native Americans than among European Americans.
   d. are lowest in the most affluent regions of the world, such as North America and Europe.

3. In developed countries
   a. rates of lead poisoning in children have fallen over the last several decades.
   b. middle childhood is one of the least safe and healthy times of life because of children's increased need for independence.
   c. the most common cause of injury is poisoning.
   d. asthma rates are at their lowest point in decades.

4. In middle childhood,
   a. girls are more likely than their male counterparts to be involved be on a sports team because they are more collaborative.
   b. children are more likely to be involved in organized sports than they were when they were younger.
   c. children are less coordinated than they were in early childhood because they are going through an awkward phase.
   d. children have a slower reaction time than they did early in childhood because they are less impulsive.

5. By the end of middle childhood
   a. fine motor development has nearly reached adult maturity.
   b. children's drawings look about the same as they did in early childhood in terms of level of detail.
   c. improvements in fine motor skills are seen primarily among children who were educated in a formal school setting.
   d. most children are just beginning to learn to tie their shoes.

6. When capable of concrete operational thought, children
   a. still have great difficulty with seriation tasks, such as arranging items from shortest to longest.
   b. can organize and manipulate information mentally.
   c. can reason about abstractions.
   d. are likely to be misled by appearances.

7. Research on ADHD
   a. indicates that it is more prevalent among girls than boys.
   b. has shown that there is no genetic basis to this disorder.
   c. has shown that symptoms cannot be controlled by medication.
   d. has shown abnormalities in brain functioning among those with the disorder.

8. The *Wechsler Intelligence Scale for Children* (WISC-IV)
   a. is the most widely used intelligence test for children.
   b. has been criticized for focusing too much on creativity and not enough on core skills of reading and writing.
   c. has both math and performance subtests.
   d. has only been predictive of the future outcomes of gifted children.

9. Compared to younger children, those in middle childhood
   a. use less complex grammar, but longer sentences.
   b. are more serious and therefore have more difficulty understanding the punch lines in jokes.
   c. are more likely to realize that what people say is not always what they mean.
   d. are less likely to use conditional sentences (e.g., If you do this, I will do that…) because they know that it may be interpreted negatively.

10. Children who are bilingual
   a. are behind their single-language counterparts in metalinguistic skills.
   b. take longer to master the second language when they learn it after becoming fluent in the first language.
   c. learn the second language better after age 12 because they have a more sophisticated understanding of syntax by this point in development.
   d. score lower on general measures of cognitive ability than single-language children because of language confusion.

11. Compared to Asian students, American schoolchildren
   a. spend more time studying art and music.
   b. work in groups and help teach one another difficult concepts.
   c. have a longer school year.
   d. care more about the maintenance of their schools.

12. Research on reading and math skills
   a. has been conducted only in the United States and Canada.
   b. has shown that girls are more likely to be diagnosed with dyslexia than are boys.
   c. has shown that the whole-language approach is more effective than the phonics approach for children who are first learning to read.
   d. has found that even some nonhuman animals have a primitive awareness of numeracy.

13. During middle childhood,
    a. children are aware that they can experience two contradictory emotions at once.
    b. children tend to be less happy than they were in early childhood because they engage in more social comparison.
    c. children experience less emotional stability than they did at early stages in development because they are changing social contexts more often.
    d. children's emotions become more intense, so they are not yet able to conceal their true feelings.

14. A 9-year-old boy from a collectivistic culture such as China would be most likely to answer the fill-in-the-blank question, "I am _____" with which of the following?
    a. really good at math
    b. shy
    c. a son
    d. funny

15. During middle childhood
    a. both boys and girls come to see occupations they associate with men as having higher status than occupations they associate with women.
    b. play groups in traditional cultures become less gender-segregated than they were in early childhood.
    c. boys feel less competent than their female counterparts in math and science even when they have equal abilities in these areas based on their grades.
    d. gender segregation is unique to play groups in the United States.

16. Which of the following best illustrates coregulation?
    a. Siblings negotiate a conflict without resorting to physical aggression.
    b. A child takes it upon himself to set the table for dinner while his parents are in the other room.
    c. A child counts to three and tells himself to calm down after getting angry at his brother.
    d. A child describes himself in relation to others.

17. Sam is unpopular and has trouble making friends. He is aggressive and just last week started a fight by punching the boy in front of him. Which of the following is most likely the case? Sam is a(n) _____ child.
    a. neglected
    b. rejected
    c. controversial
    d. average

18. Child labor
    a. has declined worldwide in the last decade.
    b. is greatest in Mexico and Hawaii.
    c. is considered legal in most countries.
    d. statistics are not able to be monitored because no international labor organizations exist.

19. Media use in middle childhood
    a. has not been associated with any positive outcomes.
    b. has only been studied with male participants.
    c. has been associated with a number of negative outcomes later in development.
    d. has been linked with aggression only in the United States.

8

Adolescence

In the dim dawn light of a simple reed house in Tehuantepec, Mexico, 16-year-old Conchita leans over an open, barrel-shaped oven. Although it is just dawn, she has already been working for two hours making tortillas. It is difficult work, standing over the hot oven, and hazardous, too; she has several scars on her arm from the times she has inadvertently touched the hot steel. She thinks with some resentment of her younger brother, who is still sleeping and who will soon be rising and going off to school. Like most girls in her village, Conchita can neither read nor write, because it is only the boys who go to school.

But she finds consolation in looking ahead to the afternoon, when she will be allowed to go to the center of town to sell the tortillas she has made beyond those that her family will need that day. There she will see her girlfriends, who will be selling tortillas and other things for their families. And there she hopes to see the boy who spoke to her, just a few words, in the town square two Sunday evenings ago. The following Sunday evening she saw him waiting in the street across from her home, a sure sign that he is courting her. But her parents would not allow her out, so she hopes to get a glimpse of him in town.

In a suburban U.S. home in Highland Park, Illinois, 14-year-old Jodie is standing before the mirror in her bedroom with a dismayed look, trying to decide whether to change her clothes again before she goes to school. She has already changed once, from the blue sweater and white skirt to the yellow-and-white blouse and blue jeans, but now she is having second thoughts. "I look awful," she thinks to herself. "I'm getting so fat!" For the past three years her body has been changing rapidly, and now she is alarmed to find it becoming rounder and larger, seemingly with each day. Vaguely she hears her mother calling her from downstairs, probably urging her to hurry up and leave for school, but the music from her earphones is so loud it drowns out what her mother is saying.

In Amakiri, Nigeria, 18-year-old Omiebi is walking to school. He is walking quickly, because the time for school to begin is near, and he does not want to be one of the students who arrive after morning assembly has started and are required to kneel throughout the assembly. Up ahead he sees several of his fellow students, easily identifiable by their gray school uniforms, and he breaks into a trot to join them. They greet him, and together they continue walking. They joke nervously about the exam coming up for the West African School Certificate. Performance on that exam will determine to a great extent who is allowed to go on to university.

Omiebi is feeling a great deal of pressure to do well on the exam. He is the oldest child of his family, and his parents have high expectations that he will go to university and become a lawyer, then help his three younger brothers go to university or find good jobs in Lagos, the nearest big city. Omiebi is not really sure he wants to be a lawyer, and he would find it difficult to leave the girl he has recently begun seeing. However,

> *"Adolescents experience dramatic changes in physical appearance, family relations, peer relations, sexuality, and media use."*

he likes the idea of moving away from tiny Amakiri to the university in Lagos, where, he has heard, all the homes have electricity and all the latest American movies are showing in the theaters. He and his friends break into a run over the last stretch, barely making it to school in time to join their classes before the assembly starts.

Three adolescents, in three different cultures, with three very different lives. Yet all are adolescents: All have left childhood but have not yet reached adulthood; all are developing into physical and sexual maturity and learning the skills that will enable them to take part in the adult world.

As these profiles illustrate, adolescence is a time of dramatic changes. The physical changes are the most obvious, as the body goes through puberty. However, there are other dramatic changes as well, in family relations, peer relations, sexuality, and media use. Adolescents also change in how they think and talk about the world around them.

Adolescence is a cultural construction, not simply a biological phenomenon or an age range. **Puberty**—the set of biological changes involved in reaching physical and sexual maturity—is universal, and the same biological changes take place in puberty for young people everywhere, although with differences in timing and in cultural meanings, as we shall see. But adolescence is more than the events and processes of puberty. **Adolescence** is a period of the life span between the time puberty begins and the time adult status is approached, when young people are preparing to take on the roles and responsibilities of adulthood in their culture. To say that adolescence is culturally constructed means that cultures vary in how they define adult status and in the content of the adult roles and responsibilities adolescents are learning to fulfill. Almost all cultures have some kind of adolescence, but the length and content and daily experiences of adolescence vary greatly among cultures (Larson et al., 2010). There is no definite age when it begins and no definite age when it ends, but it usually begins after age 10 and ends by age 20, so it comprises most of the second decade of life.

There are two broad cultural forms that adolescence takes today. In developed countries, adolescents begin puberty early in the second decade of life, usually around age 10 or 11. They spend most of their days in school with their peers. Outside of school, too, they spend most of their leisure time with other persons their age—friends and romantic partners. A substantial proportion of their daily lives involves media use, including the Internet, television, and recorded music.

But there is another cultural form of adolescence that is prevalent in most of the developing world, including Africa, Asia, and South America. In this kind of adolescence, a typical day is spent not mostly with peers in school but with family members, working (Schlegel, 2010; Schlegel & Barry, 1991). Girls spend most of their time with their mothers and other adult women, learning the skills and knowledge necessary to fulfill the roles for women in their culture. Boys spend most of their time with adult men, learning to do what men in their culture are required to do, but they are allowed more time with friends than adolescent girls are. Some adolescent boys and girls go to school, but for others school is something they left behind by the end of childhood.

We will discuss both these forms of adolescence in the course of this chapter, and the many variations that exist within each form. We will also discuss the ways that the traditional cultural forms of adolescence are changing with exposure to industrialization and globalization.

puberty changes in physiology, anatomy, and physical functioning that develop a person into a mature adult biologically and prepare the body for sexual reproduction

adolescence period of the life span between the time puberty begins and the time adult status is approached, when young people are preparing to take on the roles and responsibilities of adulthood in their culture

LEARNING OBJECTIVES

8.1 List the physical changes that begin puberty.

8.2 Describe the normative timing of pubertal events, cultural variations, and how being early or late influences emotional and social development.

8.3 Identify the main gender differences in puberty rituals worldwide.

8.4 Describe the prevalence, symptoms, and treatment of eating disorders.

8.5 Classify adolescent substance use into four categories.

The Metamorphosis: Biological Changes of Puberty

Adolescence begins with the first notable changes of puberty, and in the course of puberty the body is transformed in many ways and reaches the capacity for sexual reproduction. Although adolescence is a culturally-constructed period of life, the biological changes of puberty are a central part of development during adolescence in all cultures. Many changes take place, and they are often dramatic. After growing at a more or less steady rate through childhood, at some time early in the second decade of life children begin a remarkable metamorphosis that includes a growth spurt, the appearance of pubic hair and underarm hair, changes in body shape, breast development and menstruation in girls, the appearance of facial hair in boys, and much more. The changes can be exciting and joyful, but adolescents experience them with other emotions as well—fear, surprise, annoyance, and anxiety. New research reveals some surprising findings in brain development, too, as we will see.

The physical changes of puberty

8.1 | LEARNING OBJECTIVE | List the physical changes that begin puberty.

My Virtual Child

Will your culture be supportive of your virtual child as he or she enters puberty? Do you see gender differences in the way puberty and the physical changes associated with it are viewed?

The word *puberty* is derived from the Latin word *pubescere*, which means "to grow hairy." This fits; during puberty hair sprouts in a lot of places where it had not been before! But adolescents do a lot more during puberty than grow hairy. Puberty entails a biological revolution that dramatically changes the adolescent's anatomy, physiology, and physical appearance. By the time adolescents reach the end of their second decade of life they look much different than before puberty, their bodies function much differently, and they are biologically prepared for sexual reproduction.

estrogens sex hormones that have especially high levels in females from puberty onward and are mostly responsible for female primary and secondary sex characteristics

androgens sex hormones that have especially high levels in males from puberty onward and are mostly responsible for male primary and secondary sex characteristics

HORMONAL CHANGES Pubertal changes begin once a threshold level of body fat is reached (Alsaker & Flammer, 2006). During middle childhood the proportion of fat in the body gradually increases, and once a threshold level is reached a series of chemical events is triggered beginning in the *hypothalamus* (refer back to Chapter 4, page 142), a bean-sized structure located in the lower part of the brain (Shalatin & Phillip, 2003). These events lead the ovaries (in girls) and testes (in boys) to increase their production of the sex hormones. There are two classes of sex hormones, the **estrogens** and the **androgens**.

With respect to pubertal development, the most important estrogen is **estradiol** and the most important androgen is **testosterone** (Shirtcliff et al., 2009).

Estradiol and testosterone are produced in both males and females, though in different ratios. By the midteens, estradiol production is about eight times as high in females as it was before puberty, but only about twice as high in males (Susman & Rogol, 2004) (see *Figure 8.1*). In contrast, testosterone production in males is about 20 times as high by the midteens as it was before puberty, but in females it is only about four times as high. These hormonal increases lead to the other bodily changes of puberty, the primary and secondary sex characteristics.

PRIMARY AND SECONDARY SEX CHARACTERISTICS Two kinds of changes take place in the body in response to increased sex hormones during puberty. **Primary sex characteristics** are directly related to reproduction: specifically, the production of ova (eggs) in females and sperm in males. **Secondary sex characteristics** are the other bodily changes resulting from the rise in sex hormones during puberty, not including the changes related directly to reproduction.

The development of ova and sperm take place quite differently (refer to Chapter 2). Females are born with all the eggs they will ever have, and they have about 40,000 eggs in their ovaries at the time they reach puberty. Once a girl reaches **menarche** (her first menstrual period) and begins having menstrual cycles, one egg develops into a mature egg, or *ovum*, every 28 days or so. Females release about 400 ova over the course of their reproductive lives.

In contrast, males have no sperm in their testes when they are born, and they do not produce any until they reach puberty. However, beginning with their first ejaculation (called **spermarche**) males produce sperm in astonishing quantities. There are between 100 and 300 million sperm in the typical male ejaculation, which means that the average male produces millions of sperm every day. If you are a man, you will probably produce over a million sperm during the time you read this chapter—even if you are a fast reader!

The secondary sex characteristics are many and varied, ranging from the growth of pubic hair to a lowering of the voice to increased production of skin oils and sweat. A summary of the major secondary sex characteristics and when they develop is shown in *Table 8.1*.

Puberty transforms physical appearance. These photos show the same boy at age 11 and age 15.

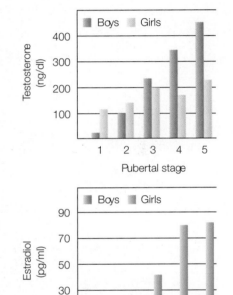

Figure 8.1 • **Hormonal changes in puberty.** Girls and boys follow very different hormonal paths at this life stage. **Source:** *Gonadal and Adrenal Hormone Correlates of Adjustment in Early Adolescence*, in Lerner & Gochs (eds.) Biological Psychological Interactions in Early Adolescence.

estradiol the estrogen most important in pubertal development among girls

testosterone the androgen most important in pubertal development among boys

primary sex characteristics production of eggs (ova) and sperm and the development of the sex organs

secondary sex characteristics bodily changes of puberty not directly related to reproduction

menarche first menstrual period

spermarche beginning of development of sperm in boys' testicles at puberty

TABLE 8.1 Timing of the Physical Changes of Puberty

Characteristic	Age Begins (boys)	Age Begins (girls)
Pubic hair	10–15	8–14
Breast development		8–13
Growth spurt	10½–16	9½–14½
Menarche		10–16½
Change in voice	11–15	
Sperm production	12–14	
Underarm hair	12–17	10–16
Skin oil and sweat	12–17	10–16

355

BRAIN DEVELOPMENT In addition to the hormonal changes and development of primary and sex characteristics, there are important neurological changes taking place in adolescents' bodies. In recent years, there has been a surge of research on neurological development in adolescence and emerging adulthood (Casey et al., 2008; Giedd, 2008; Keating, 2004). Some of the findings from this new research have been surprising and have overturned previous views of brain development in adolescence.

It has long been known that by age 6 the brain is already 95% of its adult size. However, when it comes to brain development, size is not everything. Equally if not more important are the synaptic connections between the neurons (refer back to Chapter 4). Now scientists have learned that a sharp increase in synaptic connections occurs around the time puberty begins, ages 10–12, a process called *overproduction* or *exuberance*. Earlier studies had shown that overproduction occurs during prenatal development and through the first three years of life, but now it turns out that overproduction occurs in early adolescence as well (Giedd, 2008; Giedd et al., 1999). Overproduction of synaptic connections occurs in many parts of the brain during adolescence but is especially concentrated in the frontal lobes (Keating, 2004). The frontal lobes are involved in most of the higher functions of the brain, such as planning ahead, solving problems, and making moral judgments.

The findings about overproduction in early adolescence are surprising and fascinating, but equally fascinating is what follows. Overproduction peaks at about age 11 or 12, but obviously that is not when our cognitive abilities peak. In the years that follow a massive amount of *synaptic pruning* takes place, in which the overproduction of synapses is whittled down considerably—synapses that are used remain, whereas those that are not used wither away (see Chapter 4). In fact, between the ages of 12 and 20 the average brain loses 7 to 10% of its volume through synaptic pruning (Sowell et al., 1999). Recent research using fMRI methods (refer to Chapter 5) shows that synaptic pruning is especially rapid among adolescents with high intelligence (Shaw et al., 2006). Synaptic pruning allows the brain to work more efficiently, as brain pathways become more specialized. However, as the brain specializes in this way it also becomes less flexible and less amenable to change.

Myelination is another important process of neurological growth in adolescence (refer again to Chapter 4). Myelin is a blanket of fat wrapped around the main part of the neuron, and it serves the function of keeping the brain's electrical signals on one path and increases their speed. Like overproduction, myelination was previously thought to be over prior to puberty but has now been found to continue through the teens (Giedd, 2008; Paus et al., 1999; Sowell et al., 2002). This is another indication of how brain functioning is becoming faster and more efficient during adolescence. However, like synaptic pruning, myelination also makes brain functioning less flexible and changeable.

Finally, one last recent surprise for researchers studying brain development in adolescence has been in the growth of the cerebellum (refer back to Chapter 6). This is perhaps the biggest surprise of all, because the cerebellum is part of the lower brain, well beneath the cortex, and has been long thought to be involved only in basic functions such as movement. Now, however, research shows that the cerebellum is important for many higher functions as well, such as mathematics, music, decision making, and even social skills and understanding humor. It also turns out that the cerebellum continues to grow through adolescence and well into emerging adulthood, suggesting that the potential for these functions continues to grow as well (Strauch, 2003). In fact, it is the last structure of the brain to stop growing, not completing its phase of overproduction and pruning until the mid-twenties.

The timing of puberty

My Virtual Child

How have you seen the effects of adolescent brain development in your virtual child's behavior?

8.2 **LEARNING OBJECTIVE** | Describe the normative timing of pubertal events, cultural variations, and how being early or late influences emotional and social development.

A great deal of variability exists among individuals in the timing of the development of primary and secondary sex characteristics (refer back to Table 8.1). For example, among girls underarm hair could begin to appear as early as age 10 or as late as age 16; among boys, the change in voice could begin as early as age 11 or as late as age 15. Overall, girls begin puberty two years earlier than boys, on average (Archibald et al., 2003).

The norms in Table 8.1 are for White American and British adolescents, who have been studied extensively in this area for many decades, but three studies demonstrate the variations that may exist in other groups. Among the Kikuyu, a culture in Kenya, boys show the first physical changes of puberty *before* their female peers, a reversal of the Western pattern (Worthman, 1987). In a study of Chinese girls, researchers found that pubic hair began to develop in most girls about two years after the development of breast buds, and only a few months before menarche, whereas in the Western pattern girls develop pubic hair much earlier (Lee et al., 1963). Also, in an American study (Herman-Giddens et al., 1997; Herman-Giddens et al., 2001), many African American girls were found to begin developing breast buds and pubic hair considerably earlier than White girls. At age 8, nearly 50% of the African American girls had begun to develop breasts or pubic hair or both, compared with just 15% of the White girls. This was true even though African American and White girls were similar in their ages of menarche. Similarly, pubic hair and genital development began earlier for African American boys than for White boys. Studies such as these indicate that it is important to investigate further cultural differences in the rates, timing, and order of pubertal events.

Given a similar cultural environment, variation in the order and timing of pubertal events among adolescents appears to be due to genetics. The more similar two people are genetically, the more similar they tend to be in the timing of their pubertal events, with identical twins the most similar of all (Ge et al., 2007; Marshall, 1978). However, when cultural environments vary, the timing of puberty also varies, as we shall see next.

CULTURE AND THE TIMING OF PUBERTY Culture includes a group's technologies, and technologies include food production and medical care. The age at which puberty begins is strongly influenced by the extent to which food production provides for adequate nutrition and medical care provides for good health, throughout childhood (Alsaker & Flammer, 2006; Eveleth & Tanner, 1990).

Persuasive evidence for the influence of technologies on pubertal timing comes from historical records showing a steady decrease in the average age of menarche in Western countries from the mid-19th to the late-20th century, as shown in *Figure 8.2*. This downward pattern in the age of menarche, known as a **secular trend**, has occurred in every Western country for which records exist. Menarche is not a perfect indicator of the initiation of puberty—the first outward signs of puberty appear much earlier for most girls, and of course menarche does not apply to boys. However, menarche is a reasonably good indicator of when other events have begun in girls, and it is a reasonable assumption that if the downward trend in the age of puberty has occurred for girls, it has occurred for boys as well. Menarche is also the only aspect of pubertal development for which we have records going back so many decades. Scholars believe that the downward trend in the age of menarche is due to improvements in nutrition and medical care that have taken place during the past 150 years (Archibald et al., 2003; Bullough, 1981).

Boys in Kenya reach puberty before girls do, contrary to the pattern in the West.

THINKING CULTURALLY

Among the secondary sex characteristics described here, which are viewed in your culture as enhancing sexual interest and attractiveness? Are there any that are viewed as making people less attractive?

secular trend change in the characteristics of a population over time

Figure 8.2 • **The secular trend in age of menarche.** Why did age of reaching menarche decline? **Source:** *The discovery of IQ gains over time.* American Psychologist, 54, 5–20.

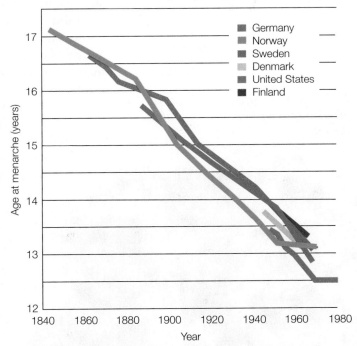

My Virtual Child

Will your virtual child likely enter puberty earlier than his or her peers? How has their environment influenced the timing?

Further evidence of the role of nutrition and medical care in pubertal timing comes from cultural comparisons in the present. The average age of menarche is lowest in developed countries (currently about 12.5 years old), where adequacy of nutrition and medical care is highest (Eveleth & Tanner, 1990; McDowell et al., 2007; Susman & Rogol, 2004). In contrast, menarche takes place at an average age as high as 15 in developing countries, where nutrition may be limited and medical care is often rare or nonexistent (Eveleth & Tanner, 1990). In countries that have undergone rapid economic development in recent decades, such as China and South Korea, a corresponding decline in the average age of menarche has been recorded (Graham et al., 1999; Park et al., 1999).

SOCIAL AND PERSONAL RESPONSES TO PUBERTAL TIMING Think back for a moment to when you were passing through puberty. What were your most memorable pubertal events? How did you respond to those events—and how did the people around you respond? I loved to sing at that age, and I distinctly remember going from soprano at age 13—the only boy in a sea of girls—to 2nd bass by age 15. I reached puberty quite a bit later than most of my peers.

Social and personal responses to puberty are intertwined, because how adolescents respond to reaching puberty depends in part on how others respond to them. In developed countries, social and personal responses may depend on whether adolescents reach puberty relatively early or relatively late compared with their peers. When adolescents spend time in school on most days, surrounded by peers, they become acutely aware of how their maturation compares to others'.

A great deal of research has been conducted on early versus late maturation among adolescents in the West, especially in the United States, extending back over a half century. The results are complex: They differ depending on gender, and the short-term effects of maturing early or late appear to differ from the long-term effects.

Research consistently shows that the effects of early maturation are usually negative for girls. Findings from a variety of Western countries concur that early-maturing girls are at risk for numerous problems, including depressed mood, negative body image, eating disorders, substance use, delinquency, aggressive behavior, school problems, and conflict with parents (Lynne et al., 2007; Mendle et al., 2007; Weichold et al., 2003; Westling et al., 2008). Early maturation is a problem for girls in part because it leads to a shorter and heavier appearance, which is a disadvantage in cultures that value slimness in females. It can also be troublesome because their early physical development draws the attention of older boys, who then introduce them to an older group of friends and to substance use, delinquency, and early sexual activity (Lynne et al., 2007; Weichold et al., 2003; Westling et al., 2008). Studies of the long-term effects of early maturation for girls are mixed, with some finding that the effects diminish by the late teens and others finding negative effects well into emerging adulthood (Graber et al., 2004; Posner, 2006; Weichold et al., 2003).

In contrast to girls, the effects of early maturation for boys are positive in some ways and negative in others. Early-maturing boys tend to have more favorable body images and higher popularity than other boys (Graber et al., 1997; Weichold et al., 2003). The earlier development of facial hair, lowered voice, and other secondary sex characteristics may make early-maturing boys more attractive to girls. Early-maturing boys may also have a long-term advantage. One study that followed early-maturing adolescent boys 40 years later found that they had achieved greater success in their careers and had higher marital satisfaction than later-maturing boys (Taga et al., 2006). However, not everything about being an early-maturing boy is favorable. Like their female counterparts, early-maturing boys tend to become involved earlier in delinquency, sex, and substance use (Westling et al., 2008; Wichstrom, 2001; Williams & Dunlop, 1999).

APPLYING YOUR KNOWLEDGE

In light of the difficulties often experienced by early-maturing girls, can you think of anything families, communities, or schools could do to assist them?

Early maturing girls are at high risk for problems, in part because they attract the interest of older boys.

Late-maturing boys also show evidence of problems. Compared to boys who mature "on time," late-maturing boys have higher rates of alcohol use and delinquency (Andersson & Magnusson, 1990; Williams & Dunlop, 1999). They also have lower grades in school (Weichold et al., 2003). There is some evidence that late-maturing boys have elevated levels of substance use and deviant behavior well into emerging adulthood (Biehl et al., 2007; Graber et al., 2004). Late-maturing girls have relatively few problems (Weichold et al., 2003).

Cultural responses: Puberty rituals

Identify the main gender differences in puberty rituals worldwide.

puberty ritual formal custom developed in many cultures to mark the departure from childhood and the entrance into adolescence

LEARNING OBJECTIVE **8.3**

My Virtual Child

What puberty rituals are part of your culture?

Does your culture have any formal way of marking the entrance from childhood to adolescence? Have you ever participated in or witnessed a bar mitzvah or bat mitzvah, the Catholic ritual of confirmation, or the *quinceañera* that takes place at age 15 for girls in Latin American cultures? These are examples of **puberty rituals** that have developed in many cultures to mark the departure from childhood and the entrance into adolescence. Puberty rituals are especially common in traditional cultures. Alice Schlegel and Herbert Barry (1991) analyzed information on adolescent development across 186 traditional cultures and reported that 68% had a puberty ritual for boys, 79% for girls (Schlegel & Barry, 1991).

For girls, menarche is the pubertal event that is most often marked by ritual (Schlegel & Barry, 1991). In fact, in many cultures menarche initiates a monthly ritual related to menstruation that lasts throughout a woman's reproductive life. It is remarkably common for cultures to have strong beliefs concerning the power of menstrual blood. Such beliefs are not universal, but they have been common in all parts of the world, in a wide variety of cultures. Menstrual blood is often believed to present a danger to the growth and life of crops, to the health of livestock, to the likelihood of success among hunters, and to the health and well-being of other people, particularly the menstruating woman's husband (Buckley & Gottlieb, 1988; Marván & Trujillo, 2010). Consequently, the behavior and movement of menstruating women are often restricted in many domains, including food preparation and consumption, social activities, religious practices, bathing, school attendance, and sexual activities (Crumbley, 2006; Mensch et al., 1998). Menarche is often believed to possess special power, perhaps because it is a girl's first menstruation, so the restrictions imposed may be even more elaborate and extensive (Yeung et al., 2005).

Traditional puberty rituals for males do not focus on a particular biological event comparable to menarche for females, but the rites for males nevertheless share some common characteristics. Typically, they require the young man to display courage, strength, and endurance (Gilmore, 1990). Daily life in traditional cultures often demands these capacities from young men in warfare, hunting, fishing, and other tasks. Thus the rituals could be interpreted as letting them know what will be required of them as adult men and testing whether they will be up to adulthood's challenges. For example, in Samoa, youth traditionally received tattoos to indicate their transition to adulthood, and the marks represented their strength in withstanding the pain of the tattoo process.

In the past, rituals for boys were often violent, requiring boys to submit to and sometimes engage in bloodletting of various kinds. Among the Amhara of Ethiopia, boys were forced to take part in whipping contests in which they faced off and lacerated each other's faces and bodies (LeVine, 1965). Among the Tewa people of New Mexico (also known as the Pueblo Indians), at some point between the ages of 12 and 15 boys were taken away from their homes, purified in ritual ceremonies, and then stripped naked and lashed on the back with a whip that drew blood and left permanent scars.

Public circumcision for boys at puberty is still practiced in some African cultures. Here, three Masai adolescents from Tanzania celebrate their successful completion of the ritual.

THINKING CULTURALLY

Are there any rituals in Western cultures that are comparable to the puberty rituals in traditional cultures? Should people in Western cultures recognize and mark the attainment of puberty more than they do now? If so, why, and how?

Although these rituals may sound cruel if you have grown up in the West, adults of these cultures believed that the rituals were necessary for boys to make the passage out of childhood toward manhood and to be ready to face life's challenges. In all these cultures, however, the rituals have declined in frequency or disappeared altogether in recent decades as a consequence of globalization (Schlegel, 2010). Because traditional cultures are changing rapidly in response to globalization, the traditional puberty rituals no longer seem relevant to the futures that young people anticipate. However, public circumcision for boys is still maintained as a puberty ritual in many African cultures (Vincent, 2008).

Female circumcision in adolescence, which involves cutting or altering the genitals, also remains common in Africa, with rates of over 70% in many countries and above 90% in Mali, Egypt, Somalia, and Djibouti (Baron & Denmark, 2006). The physical consequences of circumcision are much more severe for girls than for boys. Typically, a great deal of bleeding occurs, and the possibility of infection is high. Afterward many girls have chronic pain whenever they menstruate or urinate, and their risks of urinary infections and childbirth complications are heightened (Eldin, 2009). Critics have termed it *female genital mutilation* (FGM) and have waged an international campaign against it (Odeku et al., 2009). Nevertheless, it remains viewed in many African cultures as necessary in order for a young woman to be an acceptable marriage partner (Baron & Denmark, 2006).

WHAT HAVE YOU LEARNED?

1. How does the balance of estradiol and testosterone change for boys and girls during puberty?
2. What is the difference between primary and secondary sex characteristics?
3. How does the brain change during adolescence?
4. How do researchers explain the downward trend in the age of menarche?
5. What risks do early-maturing girls face? Do early-maturing boys face similar risks?
6. Why were puberty rituals for boys violent in some traditional cultures?

Health Issues in Adolescence

Like middle childhood, adolescence is a life stage when physical health is generally good. The immune system functions more effectively in middle childhood and adolescence than earlier in development, so susceptibility to infectious diseases is lower. Diseases that will become more common later in adulthood, such as heart disease and cancer, are very rare during adolescence. However, unlike middle childhood, adolescence is a time when problems arise not from physical functioning but from behavior. Two common problems of adolescence are eating disorders and substance use. (Automobile accidents are the number one cause of mortality in adolescence, but this topic will be discussed in Chapter 9.)

Eating disorders

8.4 **LEARNING OBJECTIVE** Describe the prevalence, symptoms, and treatment of eating disorders.

At 102 pounds I thought I would be happy. But when I lost another two pounds, I was even happier. By the time I was down to 98 pounds, I stopped getting my period. . . . Also, my hair, which was normally healthy and shiny, became very brittle and dull, and it started falling out. . . . [My skin] took on a yellowish tone that looked sick, but I didn't care. I thought I looked better than I ever had in my whole life.

Alicia, age 17 (in Alexander, 1998, p. 191)

For many adolescents, changes in the way they think about their bodies are accompanied by changes in the way they think about food. Girls, in particular, pay more attention to the food they eat once they reach adolescence, and worry more about eating too much and getting fat (Nichter, 2001). Sixty percent of American adolescent girls and 30% of boys believe they weigh too much, even though only 15% of girls and 16% of boys are actually overweight by medical standards (Centers for Disease Control and Prevention [CDC], 2008b). This dissatisfaction exists far more often among girls than among boys (Vincent & McCabe, 2000). Boys are much less likely to believe they are overweight, and much more likely to be satisfied with their bodies (Walcott et al., 2003).

These perceptions can lead adolescents to exhibit eating disordered behavior, including fasting for 24 hours or more, use of diet products, purging, and use of laxatives to control weight. According to a national U.S. study, about 20% of American adolescent girls and 10% of boys in grades 9–12 report engaging in eating disordered behavior in the past 30 days (CDC, 2008b). Similar findings have been reported in other Western countries. In a national study of German 11- to 17-year-olds, one-third of girls and 15% of boys reported symptoms of eating disorders (Herpetz-Dahlmann et al., 2008). In Finland, a large study of 14- to 15-year-olds found eating disordered behavior among 24% of girls and 16% of boys (Hautala et al., 2008).

The two most common eating disorders are **anorexia nervosa** (intentional self-starvation) and **bulimia** (binge eating combined with purging [intentional vomiting]). About 0.5% of American adolescents have anorexia nervosa and about 3% have bulimia (McKnight Investigators, 2003). Nearly all (90%) of eating disorders occur among females. Most cases of eating disorders have their onset among females in their teens and early twenties (Reijonen et al., 2003).

Anorexia is characterized by four primary symptoms:

1. inability to maintain body weight at least 85% of normal for height;
2. fear of weight gain;
3. lack of menstruation; and
4. distorted body image.

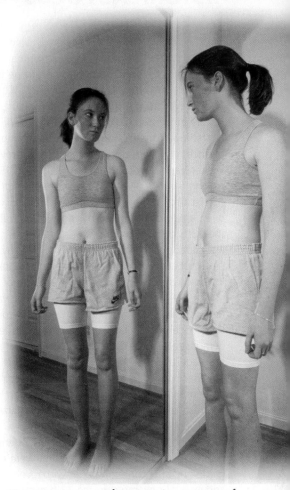

Young women with anorexia nervosa often see themselves as too fat even when they are so thin their lives are at risk.

One of the most striking symptoms of anorexia is the cognitive distortion of body image (Bowers et al., 2003; Striegel-Moore & Franko, 2006). Young women with anorexia sincerely believe themselves to be too fat, even when they have become so thin that their lives are threatened. Standing in front of a mirror with them and pointing out how emaciated they look does no good—the person with anorexia looks in the mirror and sees a fat person, no matter how thin she is. ◉

Like those with anorexia, persons with bulimia have strong fears that their bodies will become big and fat (Bowers et al., 2003). They engage in binge eating, which means eating a large amount of food in a short time. Then they purge themselves, that is, they use laxatives or induce vomiting to get rid of the food they have just eaten during a binge episode. People with bulimia often suffer damage to their teeth from repeated vomiting (because stomach acids erode tooth enamel). Unlike those with anorexia, persons with bulimia typically maintain a normal weight, because they have more or less normal eating patterns in between their episodes of bingeing and purging (Striegel-Moore & Franko, 2006). Another difference from anorexia is that persons with bulimia do not regard their eating patterns as normal. They view themselves as having a problem and often hate themselves in the aftermath of their binge episodes. ◉

Self-starvation among young women has a long history in Western countries, as described in the **Historical Focus: From Fasting Saints to Anorexic Girls** feature on page 362. Today, eating disorders are most common in cultures that emphasize slimness as part of the female physical ideal, especially Western countries (Gowen et al., 1999; Walcott et al., 2003). Presented with a cultural ideal that portrays the ideal female body

◉ ─ **Watch** the **Video** Anorexia Nervosa in **MyDevelopmentLab**

◉ ─ **Watch** the **Video** Body Image and Eating Disorders in **MyDevelopmentLab**

anorexia nervosa eating disorder characterized by intentional self-starvation

bulimia eating disorder characterized by episodes of binge eating followed by purging (self-induced vomiting)

Anorexia nervosa is generally viewed by scholars to be a modern disorder, resulting primarily from current cultural pressures for young women to be thin. However, the phenomenon of young women voluntarily, willfully reducing their food intake, even to the point of self-starvation, has a surprisingly long history in Western cultures, extending back many centuries. An examination of that history, with its illuminating similarities to and differences from present-day anorexia, is provided by Dutch scholars Walter Vandereycken and Ron Van Deth (1994) in their book *From Fasting Saints to Anorexic Girls: A History of Self-Starvation*.

Fasting, involving partial or total abstinence from food, has long been a part of both Eastern and Western religions. It was only from the 12th century onward that religious fasting in the West became associated mainly with young women. Why this happened when it did is not entirely clear, but it appears to be linked to females' being allowed greater participation in church life. For both males and females during the medieval period, religious faith was demonstrated in ways that seem extreme from the modern perspective. Men would often demonstrate their piety by such practices as self-flagellation; piercing their tongues, cheeks, or other body parts with iron pins; or sleeping on beds of thorns or iron points. For women, in contrast, extreme fasting became the characteristic path to holiness.

Young women who engaged in extreme fasting often gained great fame and were regarded by their contemporaries with reverence and awe. For example, in the 13th century an English girl became known far and wide as "Joan the Meatless" for reputedly abstaining from all food and drink except on Sundays, when she fed only on the morsel of bread distributed as part of the communion ritual. Many of these young women became anointed as saints by the Church, although official church policy discouraged extreme fasting as detrimental to physical and mental well-being. In the 16th and 17th centuries, Catholic officials sharply tightened the rules for proving fasting "miracles," in response to exposed cases of fraud as well as concern over the health of girls seeking sainthood, and extreme fasting lost its religious allure.

In place of extreme religious fasting, extreme fasting as a commercial spectacle arose. From the 16th through the 19th century, young women who had supposedly fasted for months or even years were exhibited at fairs. When these "miraculous maidens" were put to the test in conditions where they could be monitored closely, some starved to death trying to prove their legitimacy, whereas others were exposed as frauds, such as the young woman who was found to have sewn a substantial quantity of gingerbread into the hem of her dress!

During this same period, cases of self-starvation received increasing attention from physicians. The first medical description of anorexia nervosa was made by the British physician Richard Morton in 1689. All of the characteristics of Morton's clinical description of the disorder remain part of the clinical diagnosis of anorexia nervosa in the present, over three centuries later:

1. Occurs primarily in females in their teens and twenties;

2. Characterized by striking emaciation as a consequence of markedly decreased intake of food;

3. Often accompanied by constipation and amenorrhea (absence of menstruation);

4. Affected persons usually lack insight into the illness (that is, they do not believe anything is wrong with them); consequently, treatment is resisted;

5. No physical cause is responsible for the symptoms; they are psychological in origin.

Although these symptoms still define anorexia nervosa, it was only from the early 19th century onward that the disorder became

Portrait of Saint Eva Flegen of Meurs (b. 1575), who spent 14 years fasting.

motivated by a desire to conform to cultural standards of female attractiveness. In the early 19th century, the standard of beauty for young women in the West became the "hourglass figure," characterized by a substantial bosom and hips and the slimmest waist possible. In pursuit of this figure, young women had themselves laced tightly into corsets (often made of whalebone or some other unforgiving material), ignoring physicians who warned against the unhealthiness of the fashion. By the early 20th century, corsets had gone out of fashion, but in their place came an ideal of the female form as slim all over, not just the waist but the bosom and hips as well.

That this thin ideal motivated self-starvation among girls is evident from clinical reports of the time, for example, by this late-19th-century physician who, while examining an anorexic patient, "found that she wore on her skin, fashioned very tight around her waist, a rose-colored ribbon. He obtained the following confidence: the ribbon was a measure which the waist was not to exceed. 'I prefer dying of hunger to becoming as big as mamma'" (Vandereycken & Van Deth, 1994, p. 171).

Although fasting saints may seem a long way from anorexic girls, Vandereycken and Van Deth (1994) point out the striking similarities. In both cases the self-starvers were striving for an elusive perfection— the fasting girls for sainthood and the anorexic girls for the feminine ideal, a kind of secular sainthood—and typically their perfectionism extended into all aspects of their lives, not just their eating habits. In both cases, their abnormal eating patterns were often evident in childhood before developing into a fixed pattern in adolescence. Perhaps most important, in both cases their self-starvation was often a way of asserting power over not only themselves but others. By abstaining from food, they were able to establish an area over which they would have complete control, no matter what the threats or pleas from clergy, friends, or family.

as slim, at a time when their bodies are biologically tending to become less slim and more rounded, many adolescent girls feel distressed at the changes taking place in their body shape, and they attempt to resist or at least modify those changes. Young women who have an eating disorder are at higher risk for other internalizing disorders, such as depression and anxiety disorders (Johnson et al., 2002; Striegel-Moore et al., 2003; Swinbourne & Touyz, 2007). Eating disordered behavior is also related to substance use, especially cigarette smoking and binge drinking (Pisetsky et al., 2008). Within the United States, eating disorders are more common among White women than among women of other ethnic groups, probably due to a greater cultural value on female slimness. However, Latino and African American adolescent girls also experience eating disorders and body dissatisfaction (Barry & Grilo, 2002), and rates of eating disorders in minority populations are on the rise.

Although mainly a Western problem, eating disorders are increasing in parts of the world that are becoming more Westernized. For example, on the island nation of Fiji, traditionally the ideal body type for women was round and curvy. However, television was first introduced in 1995, mostly with programming from the United States and other Western countries, and subsequently the incidence of eating disorders rose substantially (Becker et al., 2007). Interviews with adolescent girls on Fiji showed that they admired the Western television characters and wanted to look like them, and that this goal in turn led to higher incidence of negative body image, preoccupation with weight, and purging behavior to control weight (Becker, 2004).

The success of treating anorexia and bulimia through hospitalization, medication, or psychotherapy is limited (Bulik et al., 2007; Grilo & Mitchell, 2010). About two-thirds of people treated for anorexia in hospital programs improve, but one-third remain chronically ill despite treatment (Steinhausen et al., 2003). Similarly, although treatments for bulimia are successful in about 50% of cases, there are repeated relapses in the other 50% of cases, and recovery is often slow (Garner & Garfinkel, 1997; Oltmanns & Emery, 2006). Adolescents and emerging adults with a history of eating disorders often continue to show significant impairments in mental and physical health, self-image, and social functioning even after their eating disorder has faded (Berkman et al., 2007; Striegel-Moore et al., 2003). About 10% of those with anorexia eventually die from starvation or from physical problems caused by their weight loss, one of the highest mortality rates of any psychiatric disorder (Polivy et al., 2003; Striegel-Moore & Franko, 2006).

Substance use

Classify adolescent substance use into four categories.	LEARNING OBJECTIVE **8.5**

Rates of substance use in adolescence vary across Western countries. A study by the World Health Organization (WHO) investigated adolescents' use of alcohol and cigarettes in 41 Western countries (WHO, 2008a). A summary of the results is shown in *Figure 8.3*. ◉

Rates of cigarette smoking are lower among adolescents in the United States and Canada than in Europe, most likely because governments in the United States and Canada have waged large-scale public health campaigns against smoking, whereas European countries have not. Cigarette smoking among young people is of particular concern, because in the long run smoking is the source of more illness and mortality than all illegal drugs combined, and because the majority of persons who smoke begin in their early teens (Cummings, 2002).

Young people use substances for a variety of purposes, which can be classified as experimental, social, medicinal, and addictive (Weiner, 1992). Young people who take part in *experimental substance use* try a substance once or perhaps a few times out of

THINKING CULTURALLY

Do advertisers who feature skinny female models and who retouch photos to make models look "perfect" bear some responsibility for anorexia rates in Western countries, or does advertising simply reflect the cultural emphasis on female slimness?

APPLYING YOUR KNOWLEDGE
. . . as a Nurse

Fifteen-year-old Ellen comes to your clinic for a yearly check-up. To your surprise, she weighs 95 pounds, down 15 pounds since her last visit. Her hair is thin and breaking, and her skin looks sallow. What would you recommend for Ellen?

◉—[**Watch** the **Video** Drugs and Alcohol in Eastern Europe in **MyDevelopmentLab**

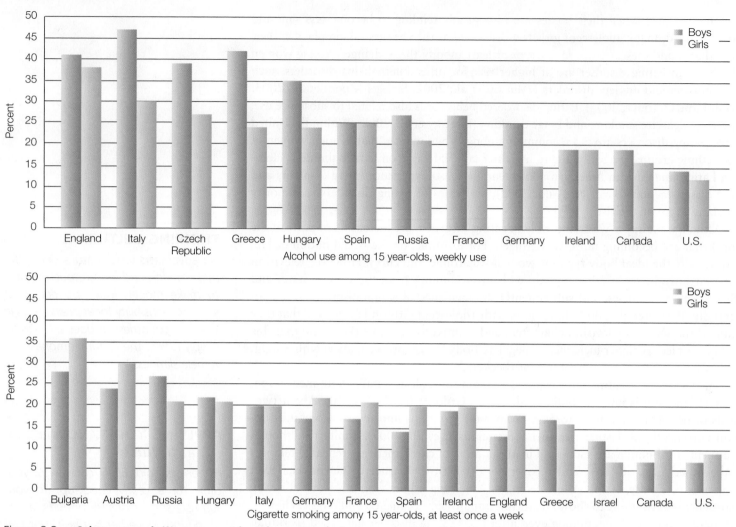

Figure 8.3 • **Substance use in Western countries.** Why are rates of substance use low in the United States and Canada? **Source:** World Health Organization (WHO). Inequalities in young people's health: Health behavior in school-aged children. Retrieved from http://www.hbsc.org/

self-medication use of substances to relieve unpleasant emotional states

Rates of smoking in adolescence are higher in Europe than in the United States and Canada. Here, young adolescents in Germany light up.

curiosity and then do not use it again. *Social substance use* involves the use of substances during social activities with one or more friends. Parties and dances are common settings for social substance use in adolescence and emerging adulthood. *Medicinal substance use* is undertaken to relieve an unpleasant emotional state such as sadness, anxiety, stress, or loneliness (Woodward & Fergusson, 2001). Using substances for these purposes has been described as a kind of **self-medication** (Reimuller et al., 2011). Young people who use substances for self-medication tend to use them more frequently than those whose purposes are mainly social or experimental. Finally, *addictive substance use* takes place when a person has come to depend on regular use of substances to feel good physically or psychologically. People who are addicted to a substance experience withdrawal symptoms such as high anxiety and tremors when they stop taking the substance (Riedel et al., 2003). Addictive substance use involves the most regular and frequent substance use of the four categories described here.

All substance use in adolescence and emerging adulthood is considered "problem behavior" in the sense that it is something that adults generally view as a problem if young people engage in it. However, the four categories described here indicate that young people may use substances in very different ways, with very different implications for their development. We'll explore substance use and abuse in further detail when we cover emerging adulthood in Chapter 9. ✴

✴ Explore the Concept Virtual Brain: Drug Addiction and Brain Reward Circuits in **MyDevelopmentLab**

WHAT HAVE YOU LEARNED?

1. In what ways is anorexia similar to and different from bulimia?
2. Why do eating disorders occur more often in Western cultures than in developing countries?
3. What are some other disorders and problems associated with having an eating disorder?
4. Why does Europe have higher rates of adolescent cigarette smoking than the United States or Canada?
5. How would you classify the substance use of an adolescent who drinks only at parties or other social gatherings?

Section 1 VIDEO GUIDE Body Image: Part 1 (Length: 4:10)

In this video two American females discuss body image, eating disorders, and the influence of the media. An American mother is also interviewed.

1. Do you feel that the two girls interviewed in this video represent the average views of U.S. female teens?

2. What impact does the media really have on adolescent females?

3. The mother interviewed in this video states that there are not many good role models for young girls today. Do you agree or disagree? Can you list at least two people who would be a good role model for a young female of today?

◉— Watch the Video Body Image: Part 1
in **MyDevelopmentLab**

LEARNING OBJECTIVES

8.6 Explain the features of hypothetical-deductive reasoning and give an example of how it is assessed.

8.7 Recall the two major critiques of Piaget's theory of formal operations.

8.8 Summarize the major changes in attention and memory that take place from middle childhood to adolescence.

8.9 Define the imaginary audience and the personal fable and explain how they reflect egocentrism in adolescence.

8.10 Produce an example of the zone of proximal development and scaffolding involving adolescents.

8.11 Compare and contrast the secondary education systems and academic performance of developed countries and developing countries.

8.12 Summarize the typical forms of adolescent work and characterize the impact it has on their development.

formal operations in Piaget's theory, cognitive stage beginning at age 11 in which people learn to think systematically about possibilities and hypotheses

hypothetical-deductive reasoning Piaget's term for the process by which the formal operational thinker systematically tests possible solutions to a problem and arrives at an answer that can be defended and explained

Piaget's Theory of Formal Operations

According to Piaget (1972), the stage of **formal operations** begins at about age 11 and reaches completion somewhere between ages 15 and 20. Children in concrete operations can perform simple tasks that require logical and systematic thinking, but formal operations allows adolescents to reason about complex tasks and problems involving multiple variables. It also includes the development of abstract thinking, which allows adolescents to think about abstract ideas such as justice and time and gives them the ability to imagine a wide range of possible solutions to a problem, even if they have had no direct experience with the problem.

Hypothetical-deductive reasoning

8.6 LEARNING OBJECTIVE | Explain the features of hypothetical-deductive reasoning and give an example of how it is assessed.

The stage of formal operations involves the development of **hypothetical-deductive reasoning**, which is the ability to think scientifically and apply the rigor of the scientific method to cognitive tasks. To demonstrate this new ability, let us look at one of the tasks Piaget used to test whether a child has progressed from concrete to formal operations, the *pendulum problem* (Inhelder & Piaget, 1958). In this task, illustrated in ***Figure 8.4***, children and adolescents are shown a pendulum (consisting of a weight hanging from a string and then set in motion) and asked to try to figure out what determines the speed at which the pendulum sways from side to side. Is it the heaviness of the weight? The length of the string? The height from which the weight is dropped? The force with which it is dropped? They are given various weights and various lengths of string to use in their deliberations.

Children in concrete operations tend to approach the problem with random attempts, often changing more than one variable at a time. They may try the heaviest

APPLYING YOUR KNOWLEDGE

Think of a real-life example of how you have used hypothetical-deductive reasoning.

weight on the longest string dropped from medium height with medium force, then a medium weight on the smallest string dropped from medium height with lesser force. When the speed of the pendulum changes, it remains difficult for them to say what caused the change, because they altered more than one variable at a time. If they happen to arrive at the right answer—it's the length of the string—they find it difficult to explain why. This is crucial, for Piaget. Cognitive advances at each stage are reflected not just in the answers children devise for problems, but in their explanations for how they arrived at the solution.

It is only with formal operations that we become able to find the right answer to a problem like this and to understand and explain why it is the right answer. The formal operational thinker approaches the pendulum problem by utilizing the kind of hypothetical thinking involved in a scientific experiment. "Let's see, it could be weight; let me try changing the weight while keeping everything else the same. No, that's not it; same speed. Maybe it's length; if I change the length while keeping everything else the same, that seems to make a difference; it goes faster with a shorter string. But let me try height, too; no change; then force; no change there, either. So it's length, and only length, that makes the difference."

Thus, the formal operational thinker changes one variable while holding the others constant and tests the different possibilities systematically. Through this process the formal operational thinker arrives at an answer that not only is correct but can be defended and explained. The capacity for this kind of thinking is at the heart of Piaget's concept of formal operations. In Piaget's research, as well as the research of many others, adolescents perform significantly better than preadolescent children at the pendulum problem and similar tasks (Elkind, 2001; Lee & Freire, 2003).

Figure 8.4 • **Pendulum problem.** How does performance on this task test formal operations?

Critiques of Piaget's theory of formal operations

Recall the two major critiques of Piaget's theory of formal operations.   **LEARNING OBJECTIVE 8.7**

Formal operations is the part of Piaget's theory that has been critiqued the most and that has been found to require the most modifications (Keating, 2004; Lee & Freire, 2003). The limitations of Piaget's theory of formal operations fall into two related categories: individual differences in the attainment of formal operations, and the cultural basis of adolescent cognitive development.

INDIVIDUAL DIFFERENCES IN FORMAL OPERATIONS As noted in Chapter 1, Piaget asserted that people develop through the same stages at about the same ages (Inhelder & Piaget, 1958). Every 8-year-old is in the stage of concrete operations; every 15-year-old should be a formal operational thinker. Furthermore, Piaget's idea of stages means that 15-year-olds should reason in formal operations in all aspects of their lives, because the same mental structure should be applied no matter what the nature of the problem (Keating, 2004).

Abundant research indicates decisively that these claims were inaccurate, especially for formal operations (Kuhn, 2008; Lee & Freire, 2003). In adolescence and even in adulthood, a great range of individual differences exists in the extent to which people use formal operations. Some adolescents and adults use formal operations over a wide range of situations; others use it selectively; still others appear to use it rarely or not at all. On any given Piagetian task of formal operations, the success rate among late adolescents and adults is only 40–60%, depending on the task and on individual factors such as educational background (Keating, 2004; Lawson & Wollman, 2003). Thus even in emerging adulthood and beyond, a large proportion of people use formal operations either inconsistently or not at all. Furthermore, even people who demonstrate the capacity for formal operations tend to use it selectively, for problems and situations in which they have the most experience and knowledge (Flavell et al., 1993). For example,

In what ways might hunting seals require formal operations?

an adolescent with experience working on cars may find it easy to apply principles of formal operations in that area but have difficulty performing classroom tasks that require formal operations. Adolescents who have had courses in math and science are more likely than other adolescents to exhibit formal operational thought (Keating, 2004; Lawson & Wollman, 2003).

CULTURAL VARIATIONS IN FORMAL OPERATIONS Questions have also been raised about the extent to which cultures differ in whether their members reach formal operations at all. By the early 1970s numerous studies indicated that cultures varied widely in the prevalence with which their members displayed an understanding of formal operations on the kinds of tasks that Piaget and others had used to measure it, and many researchers concluded that in some cultures formal operational thought does not develop, particularly in cultures that do not have formal schooling that includes training in the scientific method (Cole, 1996). More recent research suggests that people in many cultures use reasoning that could be called formal operational, provided that they are using materials and tasks familiar to them and relevant to their daily lives (Matusov & Hayes, 2000). There is widespread support among scholars for the view that the stage of formal operations constitutes a universal human potential but it takes different forms across cultures depending on the kinds of problems people encounter in their daily lives (Cole, 1996).

For example, adolescent boys in the Inuit culture of the Canadian Arctic traditionally learn how to hunt seals (Condon, 1987; Grigorenko et al., 2004). To become successful, a boy would have to think through the components involved in a hunt and test his knowledge of hunting through experience. If he were unsuccessful on a particular outing, he would have to ask himself why. Was it because of the location he chose? The equipment he took along? The tracking method he used? Or were there other causes? On the next hunt he might alter one or more of these factors to see if his success improved. This would be hypothetical-deductive reasoning, altering and testing different variables to arrive at the solution to a problem. However, in every culture there is likely to be considerable variation in the extent to which adolescents and adults display formal operational thought, from persons who display it in a wide variety of circumstances to persons who display it little or not at all.

WHAT HAVE YOU LEARNED?

1. How would a child in the concrete operations stage approach the pendulum problem differently from a formal operational thinker?
2. Do adolescents use formal operations consistently in all aspects of their lives? How does the answer to this question impact Piaget's theory of stages?
3. Can the stage of formal operations be reached in all cultures? Why or why not?
4. How might someone in a traditional culture use hypothetical-deductive reasoning in his or her daily life?

Other Changes in Adolescent Thinking

Watch the **Video** Academic Achievement and Academic Engagement Among Early Adolescents in **MyDevelopmentLab**

Piaget's theory of formal operations has inspired a great deal of research on adolescents' cognitive development. However, information processing research shows other types of gains in cognitive development from childhood to adolescence. Social cognition develops during this age as well and takes two distinctly adolescent forms. ⊙

Information processing: Selective attention and metamemory

Summarize the major changes in attention and memory that take place from middle childhood to adolescence.

As noted in previous chapters, attention and memory are the two keys to cognition in the information processing approach, and in both areas distinctive forms of cognitive development sprout in adolescence. Adolescents become more proficient at both selective and divided attention, and they become better at using memory strategies.

Are you able to read a textbook while someone else in the same room is watching television? Are you able to have a conversation at a party where music and other conversations are blaring loudly all around you? These are tasks that require *selective attention,* the ability to focus on relevant information while screening out information that is irrelevant (refer back to Chapter 7, page 310) (Hahn et al., 2009). Adolescents tend to be better than younger children at tasks that require selective attention, and emerging adults are generally better than adolescents (Manis et al., 1980; Huang-Pollock et al., 2002). Adolescents are also more adept than younger children at tasks that require **divided attention**—reading a book and listening to music at the same time, for example—but even for adolescents, divided attention may result in less efficient learning than if attention were focused entirely on one thing. One study found that watching TV interfered with adolescents' homework performance but listening to music did not (Pool et al., 2003).

Memory also improves in adolescence, especially long-term memory. Adolescents are more likely than younger children to use *mnemonic devices* (memory strategies) (refer to Chapter 7, page 312), such as organizing information into coherent patterns (Schneider, 2010). Think of what you do, for example, when you sit down to read a textbook chapter. You probably have various organizational strategies you have developed over the years (if you do not, you would be wise to develop some), such as writing a chapter outline, making notes in the margins, organizing information into categories, underlining key passages, and so on. By planning your reading in these ways, you remember (and learn) more effectively.

Another way long-term memory improves in adolescence is that adolescents have more experience and more knowledge than children do, and these advantages enhance the effectiveness of long-term memory (Keating, 1990, 2004). Having more knowledge helps you learn new information and store it in long-term memory. This is a key difference between short-term and long-term memory. The capacity of short-term memory is limited, so the more information you have in there already, the less effectively you can add new information to it. With long-term memory, however, the capacity is essentially unlimited, and the more you know, the easier it is to learn new information because you can relate it to what you already know. For example, if you have already taken an introductory psychology course and learned basic facts and terms of the field, it will be easier for you to remember the information you learn in subsequent psychology courses, because you can connect the new information to what is already in your long-term memory.

divided attention ability to focus on more than one task at a time

APPLYING YOUR KNOWLEDGE
Among the courses you have taken in your college education, for which have you found information easiest to remember, and for which has it been hardest? In what ways do the memory concepts presented here help explain why some course content is easier for you to retain?

Social cognition: The imaginary audience and the personal fable

Define the imaginary audience and the personal fable and explain how they reflect egocentrism in adolescence.

During early adolescence I believed/pretended that a movie crew was following me around and taping everything I did. They personally picked me because I was the most popular girl in school and had the most interesting life. Or so I thought!

Deena, age 21 (Arnett, unpublished data)

700 – 728

metacognition capacity to think about thinking

adolescent egocentrism type of egocentrism in which adolescents have difficulty distinguishing their thinking about their own thoughts from their thinking about the thoughts of others

imaginary audience belief that others are acutely aware of and attentive to one's appearance and behavior

personal fable belief in one's personal uniqueness, often including a sense of invulnerability to the consequences of taking risks

When I was in high school a group of us would go to the cliffs at the lake and "blind jump" at night. Usually everyone had been drinking. To add an element of danger, about 60 feet or so down the cliff there was a shelf that stuck out about 6 feet that you had to avoid. There was one guy we knew, 18 years old, who tripped when he was jumping, landed on the shelf, broke his neck and died. We all thought he must have done something stupid and that it couldn't happen to us.

Brian, age 22 (Arnett, unpublished data)

Cognitive development in adolescence includes the development of **metacognition**, which is the capacity to think about thinking. This advance includes the ability to think about not only your own thoughts but also the thoughts of others. Adolescents are generally better at metacognition than younger children are. However, when their metacognitive abilities first develop, adolescents may have difficulty distinguishing their thinking about their own thoughts from their thinking about the thoughts of others, resulting in a distinctive kind of **adolescent egocentrism**. Ideas about adolescent egocentrism were first put forward by Piaget (1967) and were developed further by David Elkind (1967, 1985; Alberts et al., 2007). According to Elkind, adolescent egocentrism has two aspects, the imaginary audience and the personal fable.

THE IMAGINARY AUDIENCE The **imaginary audience** results from adolescents' limited capacity to distinguish between their thinking about themselves and their thinking about the thoughts of others. Because they think about themselves so much and are so acutely aware of how they might appear to others, they conclude that others must also be thinking about them a great deal. Because they exaggerate the extent to which others think about them, they imagine a rapt audience for their appearance and behavior.

The imaginary audience makes adolescents much more self-conscious than they were in middle childhood. Do you remember waking up in seventh or eighth grade with a pimple on your forehead, or discovering a mustard stain on your pants and wondering how long it had been there, or saying something in class that made everybody laugh (even though you didn't intend it to be funny)? Of course, experiences like these are not much fun as an adult, either. But they tend to be worse in adolescence, because the imaginary audience makes it seem as though "everybody" knows about your humiliation and will remember it for a long, long time.

The imaginary audience is not something that simply disappears when adolescence ends. Adults are egocentric, too, to some extent. Adults, too, imagine (and sometimes exaggerate) an audience for their behavior. It is just that this tendency is stronger in adolescence, when the capacity for distinguishing between our own perspective and the perspective of others is less developed (Alberts et al., 2007).

APPLYING YOUR KNOWLEDGE
... as a Health Educator

How might you incorporate your knowledge of adolescents' risk taking and personal fables in your work?

The personal fable can lead adolescents to believe that negative consequences from taking risks "won't happen to me."

THE PERSONAL FABLE According to Elkind (1967, 1985), the belief in an imaginary audience that is highly conscious of how you look and act leads to the belief that there must be something special, something unique, about you—otherwise, why would others be so preoccupied with you? Adolescents' belief in the uniqueness of their personal experiences and their personal destiny is known as the **personal fable**.

The personal fable can be the source of adolescent anguish, when it makes them feel that "no one understands me" because no one can share their unique experience (Elkind, 1978). It can be the source of high hopes, too, as adolescents imagine their unique personal destiny leading to the fulfillment of their dreams to be a rock musician, a

professional athlete, a famous actor, or simply successful in the field of their choice. It can also contribute to risky behavior by adolescents whose sense of uniqueness leads them to believe that adverse consequences from behavior such as unprotected sex or drunk driving "won't happen to me." According to research by Elkind and his colleagues, personal fable scores increase from early to midadolescence and are correlated with participation in risk behaviors (Alberts et al., 2007).

Like the imaginary audience, the personal fable diminishes with age, but it never disappears entirely for most of us. Even most adults like to think there is something special, if not unique, about their personal experiences and their personal destiny. But the personal fable tends to be stronger in adolescence than at later ages, because with age our experiences and conversations with others lead us to an awareness that our thoughts and feelings are not as exceptional as we once might have believed (Elkind, 1978).

Culture and cognition

> Produce an example of the zone of proximal development and scaffolding involving adolescents.

LEARNING OBJECTIVE **8.10**

As noted in previous chapters, two of Vygotsky's most influential ideas are scaffolding and the zone of proximal development (see Chapter 1, page 25). The zone of proximal development is the difference between skills or tasks a person can accomplish alone and those they are capable of doing if guided by a more experienced person. Scaffolding refers to the degree of assistance provided in the zone of proximal development. In Vygotsky's view, learning always takes place via a social process, through the interactions between someone who possesses knowledge and someone who is in the process of obtaining it.

Scaffolding and the zone of proximal development continue to apply during adolescence, when the skills necessary for adult work are being learned. An example can be found in research on weaving skills among male adolescents in the Dioula culture in Ivory Coast, on the western coast of Africa (Tanon, 1994). An important part of the Dioula economy is making and selling large handmade cloths with elaborate designs. The training of weavers begins when they are age 10–12 and continues for several years. Boys grow up watching their fathers weave, but it is in early adolescence that they begin learning weaving skills themselves. Teaching takes place through scaffolding: The boy attempts a simple weaving pattern, the father corrects his mistakes, the boy tries again. When the boy gets it right, the father gives him a more complex pattern, thus raising the upper boundary of the zone of proximal development so that the boy continues to be challenged and his skills continue to improve. As the boy becomes more competent at weaving, the scaffolding provided by the father diminishes. Eventually the boy gets his own loom, but he continues to consult with his father for several years before he can weave entirely by himself.

As this example illustrates, learning in adolescence is always a cultural process, in which adolescents are acquiring the skills and knowledge that will be useful in their culture. American adolescents learn to use computers in a scaffolded way. Many teens have access to computers in school, where they learn to do assignments by word processing. Eventually, they may learn to program computers to solve problems, thus increasing their understanding of how the machines work and the potential of their use. Increasingly, the skills and knowledge of the global economy involve the ability to use information technology such as computers and the Internet. In most countries, the highest paying jobs require these kinds of skills. However, as the example of the Dioula illustrates, for the majority of the world's adolescents the most necessary skills and knowledge are those involved in making things the family can use or that other people will want to buy (Larson et al., 2010).

WHAT HAVE YOU LEARNED?

1. How do you use selective attention and divided attention in your daily life?
2. How does adolescents' experience and knowledge contribute to their long-term memory?
3. Why are adolescents often more self-conscious than they were as children?
4. How does the personal fable contribute to risky behavior in adolescence?
5. How is learning in adolescence a cultural process?

Adolescent Education and Work

Adolescence brings cognitive and social changes that help teens develop greater skills of analysis and abstract thinking that can be applied as they learn new skills in education or in work activities, or both. In turn, education and work can help adolescents develop interests that they may pursue in careers as adults. In the developed world, adolescents spend most of their day in some kind of school, and some begin to work to earn money. This is in contrast to the developing world, where youth may not have the opportunity to attend school, turning to work instead.

Schools: Secondary education around the world

8.11   **LEARNING OBJECTIVE**   Compare and contrast the secondary education systems and academic performance of developed countries and developing countries.

secondary school school attended during adolescence, after primary school

There is a great deal of diversity worldwide in the kinds of **secondary schools** (middle schools and high schools) that adolescents attend. World regions also vary in how likely adolescents are to attend secondary school at all. There is an especially sharp contrast between developed countries and developing countries. Virtually all adolescents are enrolled in secondary school in developed countries. In contrast, only about 50% of adolescents in developing countries attend secondary school (see **Map 8.1**). Furthermore, as we will see in Chapter 9, "tertiary education" (college and university) is obtained by about half of emerging adults in developed countries but is only available to the elite (and wealthy) 10% in developing countries. 📖

Read the **Document** Secondary Education Around the World in **MyDevelopmentLab**

INTERNATIONAL VARIATIONS IN SECONDARY SYSTEMS The United States is unusual in having only one institution—the "comprehensive" school—as the source of secondary education. Canada and Japan also have comprehensive secondary schools as the norm, but most other countries have several different kinds of schools that adolescents may attend. European countries usually have three types of secondary schools (Arnett, 2002b). About half of adolescents attend a *college-preparatory school* that offers a variety of academic courses. The goal is general education rather than training for any specific profession. About one-fourth of adolescents attend a *vocational school*, where they learn the skills involved in a specific occupation such as plumbing or auto mechanics. Some European countries also have a third type of secondary school, a *professional school* devoted to teacher training, the arts, or some other specific purpose (Flammer & Alsaker, 2006). About one-fourth of European adolescents usually attend this type of school.

One consequence of the European system is that adolescents must decide at a relatively early age what direction to pursue for their education and occupation. At age 15 or 16 adolescents choose which type of secondary school they will enter, and this is a

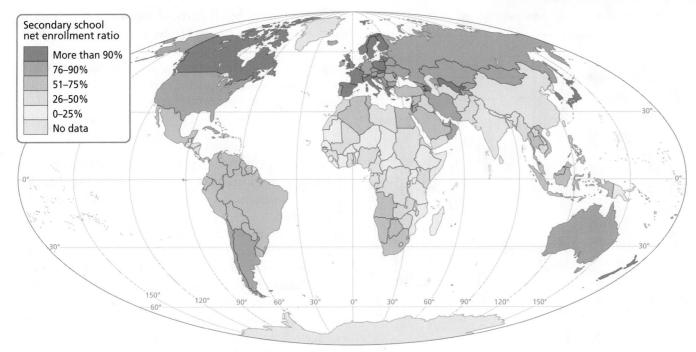

Secondary school net enrollment ratio

- More than 90%
- 76–90%
- 51–75%
- 26–50%
- 0–25%
- No data

Map 8.1 • **Secondary School Enrollment Worldwide.** Which countries have the highest enrollment rates for secondary education? Which are the lowest? What cultural and economic factors might explain these variations?

decision that is likely to have an enormous impact on the rest of their lives. Usually the decision is made by adolescents in conference with their parents and teachers, based on adolescents' interests as well as on their school performance (Motola et al., 1998). Although adolescents sometimes change schools after a year or two, and adolescents who attend a vocational school sometimes attend university, these switches are rare.

In contrast to developed countries, where attending secondary school is virtually universal for adolescents and the schools are well funded, in developing countries secondary education is often difficult to obtain and relatively few adolescents stay in school until graduation. A number of common themes recur in accounts of secondary education in developing countries (Lloyd, 2005; Lloyd et al., 2008). All developing countries have seen rising rates of enrollment in recent decades. That's about where the good news ends. Many of the schools are poorly funded and overcrowded. Many countries have too few teachers, and the teachers they have are insufficiently trained. Often families have to pay for secondary education, a cost they find difficult to afford, and families may have to pay for books and other educational supplies as well. There tends to be one education for the elite—in exclusive private schools and well-funded universities—and a much inferior education for everyone else.

What is most striking, when comparing secondary education in developed countries and developing countries, is how unequal educational opportunities are between the two. If you happen to be born in a developing country, you are likely to get an education through primary school but unlikely to have the resources to finish secondary school, and your chances of attending college are very small—especially if you are a girl. In contrast, if you happen to be born in a developed country, it is likely that you will finish secondary school and it is quite likely that you will have the opportunity to attend college if you wish—especially if you are a girl (Arnett, 2002b; Aud et al., 2011). However, it should be added that if you are a member of an ethnic minority in a developed country and your family has a low income, your chances of finishing secondary school may be only about one-half, no higher than for adolescents in many developing countries (Aud et al., 2011). In the United States, dropout rates are highest among Latinos, at more than 17%, and Native Americans, at more than 13% (Aud et al., 2011). Asian Americans and Pacific Islanders have the lowest dropout rates, at 3.4% (Aud et al., 2011).

My Virtual Child

What type of secondary education will your virtual child experience? What are the pros and cons of this when compared to the educational experiences of adolescents in other cultures?

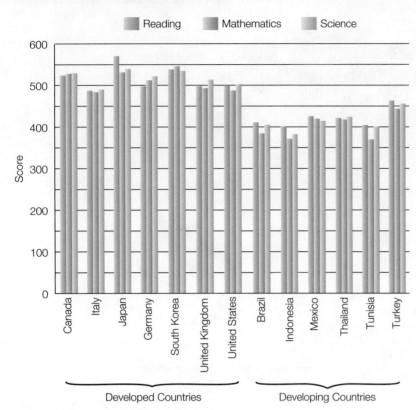

Figure 8.5 • **International performance in reading, math, and science, eighth grade.** What explains why Japan and South Korea score highest? **Source:** Based on NCES.

rote learning learning by memorization and repetition

Pressure for academic performance is high in Asian countries because the stakes are high.

Education is, in all parts of the world, the basis of many of the good things in life, from income level to physical and mental health (Lloyd, 2005; Lloyd et al., 2008; Stromquist, 2007). Yet for the majority of the world's adolescents and emerging adults, their educational fate was already largely determined at birth, simply on the basis of where they were born.

INTERNATIONAL COMPARISONS IN ACADEMIC PERFORMANCE For about 30 years, there have been international studies that compare adolescents on academic performance. *Figure 8.5* shows the most recent performance of adolescents in various countries around the world on eighth-grade achievement tests. The pattern of results is similar across reading, math, and science. In all three areas, the pattern is the same as in middle childhood, as discussed in Chapter 7: The affluent developed countries tend to perform better than the developing countries, which tend to perform below the average.

In math and science, Japan and South Korea are consistently at the top. As mentioned in Chapter 7, there are notable differences between Western and Eastern schools. In adolescence as at earlier ages, Eastern high schools focus almost exclusively on **rote learning** (memorizing information through repetition), whereas Western schools place more emphasis on promoting critical thinking and creativity (Kember & Watkins, 2010). Another crucial difference is that in the East the consequences of school performance in adolescence are much more serious and enduring. Adolescents in most Eastern countries have to take entrance exams for both high school and college. These two exams have a great influence on young people's occupational fate for the rest of their lives, because in Asian countries, obtaining a job is based primarily on the status of the schools a person has attended.

To prepare for the entrance exams, adolescents in Eastern countries are urged to apply themselves seriously at school and in their homework. In addition, from middle childhood through adolescence many of them attend "cram schools" after school or receive instruction from private tutors (Takahashi & Takeuchi, 2007). This system goes a long way toward explaining the high level of performance of children and adolescents in Eastern countries. They work intensely on their schoolwork because the stakes are so high, much higher than in Western countries, where both the higher education system and the job market are much more open and much less about people's occupational future is determined by the time they leave high school. Many adolescents (and their parents) in Western countries want to do well in secondary school so that they gain entrance into a top university, but there are many, many colleges and universities, and people who go to colleges and universities below the top tier still have a wide range of occupational options available if they perform well.

With longer school days, a longer school year, cram schools, and private tutors, Eastern adolescents have far less time for after-school leisure and informal socializing with friends than American adolescents do (Chaudhary & Sharma, 2012). In recent decades some Asian countries have reduced the length of the school day and cut the number of school days per week from six to five, but the average school day remains long and cram schools remain the norm (Takahashi & Takeuchi, 2007).

Adolescent work

Summarize the typical forms of adolescent work and characterize the impact it has on their development.

What do you remember about your jobs in adolescence, if you worked at that time? Like many adolescents, I mostly worked in low-paying restaurant jobs, mainly washing dishes and cooking hamburgers, French fries, and other greasy items. I usually didn't last long on these jobs. On one of my dishwashing jobs, the third day of work a friend and I discovered that creative use of the sprayers intended to rinse the dishes could quickly turn our boring dishwashing task into an exciting game of Spray Wars. Of course, we were fired immediately.

But what did we care? There were plenty of other jobs around, and for us not much depended on working except how much money would be available for having fun on the weekend. For adolescents in developed countries, work is usually not done as part of contributing to family survival but as a way of supporting an active leisure life. About 80% of adolescents in the United States and Canada hold at least one part-time job by the end of high school (Barling & Kelloway, 1999; Lee & Staff, 2007). Very little of the money they earn goes to their family's living expenses or saving for their future education (although adolescents in ethnic minority groups are more likely to contribute to their families) (Fuligni, 2011; Mortimer, 2003). For the most part, the money goes toward purchases for themselves, here and now: stylish clothes, music, car payments and gas, concert tickets, movies, eating out—and alcohol, cigarettes, and other drugs (Greenberger & Steinberg, 1986; Mortimer 2003).

As we have seen in previous chapters, for children in developing countries, work often begins long before adolescence. Within the family, they begin to contribute to the work required in daily life, helping with tasks such as cleaning, cooking, gathering firewood, and caring for younger siblings. By middle childhood and adolescence, many of them work in factory settings, where they do jobs such as weaving rugs and polishing gems (International Labor Organization [ILO], 2006). They also work on farms and in domestic service, and some sell goods on the street.

Unlike adolescents in developing countries, the work done by adolescents in developed countries does little to prepare them for the kind of work they are likely to be doing as adults. For example, the majority of jobs held by American and Canadian adolescents in high school involve restaurant work or retail sales (Loughlin & Barling, 1999; Staff et al., 2004). Consequently, few adolescents see their high school jobs as the basis for a future career (Mortimer et al., 2008). One exception to this is the tradition of apprenticeships in many European countries, as we'll see in the **Cultural Focus: Apprenticeships in Europe** feature on page 376.

Not only does working part-time appear not to do adolescents much good in most developed countries, it can be harmful to their development in a variety of ways. The amount of time worked per week is a crucial variable. Most studies find that up to 10 hours a week, working at a part-time job has little effect on adolescents' development. However, beyond 10 hours a week problems arise, and beyond 20 hours a week the problems become considerably worse. In the United States, employed high school sophomores work an average of 15 hours per week, and employed high school seniors work 20 hours per week (Barling & Kelloway, 1999).

Beyond 10 hours a week, the more adolescents work, the lower their grades, the less time they spend on homework, the more they cut class, the more they cheat on their schoolwork, the less committed they are to school, and the lower their educational aspirations (Marsh & Kleitman, 2005). Similarly, reports of psychological symptoms jump sharply for adolescents

My Virtual Child

Will your virtual child hold a part-time job? How will they use their earnings? How does your socioeconomic status influence this?

In the developed world, many adolescents take jobs and spend the money they earn on themselves.

CULTURAL FOCUS   Apprenticeships in Europe

Although most employment in adolescence in the United States and Canada has little relation to later jobs, many European countries have a long tradition of apprenticeships that provides excellent preparation for adult occupations. In an **apprenticeship**, an adolescent "novice" serves under contract to a "master" who has substantial experience in a profession, and through working under the master the novice learns the skills required (Hamilton & Hamilton, 2000, 2006; Vazsonyi & Snider, 2008). Although apprenticeships originally began centuries ago in craft professions such as carpentry and blacksmithing, today they are undertaken to prepare for a wide range of professions, from auto mechanics and carpenters to police officers, computer technicians, and child-care workers (Fuller et al., 2005). Apprenticeships are especially common in central and northern Europe. For example, Germany's apprenticeship program includes over 60% of all 16- to 18-year-olds (Heckhausen & Tomasik, 2002), and Switzerland's includes about one-third of the adolescents who do not attend college after secondary school (Vazsonyi & Snider, 2008).

Common features of apprenticeship programs are (Hamilton & Hamilton, 2006)

- entry at age 16, with the apprenticeship lasting two to three years;
- continued part-time schooling while in the apprenticeship, with the school curriculum closely connected to the training received in the apprenticeship;
- training that takes place in the workplace, under real working conditions; and
- preparation for a career in a respected profession that provides an adequate income.

Apprenticeships are common in Europe. These adolescents are apprenticing at a German power plant company.

This kind of program requires close coordination between schools and employers, so that what adolescents learn at school will complement and reinforce what is being learned in their apprenticeship. This means that schools consult employers with respect to the skills required in the workplace, and employers make opportunities available for adolescent apprentices. In Europe, the employers see this as worth their trouble because apprenticeships provide them with a reliable supply of well-qualified entry-level employees (Dustmann & Schoenberg, 2008).

---

apprenticeship an arrangement, common in Europe, in which an adolescent "novice" serves under contract to a "master" who has substantial experience in a profession, and through working under the master, learns the skills required to enter the profession

APPLYING YOUR KNOWLEDGE
. . . as a Teacher

As a teacher of high school students, how might you help them balance work with school?

working more than 10 hours a week and continue to rise among adolescents working 20 hours a week or more (Frone, 1999; Lee & Staff, 2007). Canadian research reports that when adolescents take on demanding jobs, they reduce their sleep by an hour per night and eliminate nearly all sports activities (Sears 2007). Adolescents who work are also more likely to use alcohol, cigarettes, and other drugs, especially if they work more than 10 hours a week (Bachman et al., 2003; Longest & Shanahan, 2007; Wu et al., 2003). A national study of adolescents in Finland also found numerous negative effects of working more than 20 hours a week (Kouvonen & Kivivuori, 2001).

Although working part-time is related to a variety of negative outcomes, a case can also be made in favor of adolescent work. Adolescents see many benefits from their work, as *Figure 8.6* shows (Aronson et al., 1996; Mortimer, 2003). They believe they gain a sense of responsibility from working, improve their abilities to manage money, develop better social skills, and learn to manage their time better. Over 40% believe that their jobs have helped them develop new occupational skills, in contrast to the portrayal of adolescent work as involving nothing but dreary tasks (although we might note that 40%, while substantial, is still a minority).

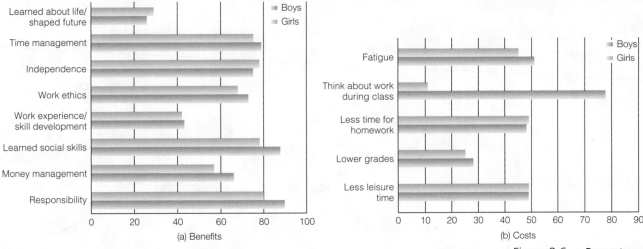

Figure 8.6 • **Percentages of Adolescents Indicating Benefits and Costs of Employment.**

WHAT HAVE YOU LEARNED?

1. How can we explain the higher academic performance of adolescents in Eastern countries compared to adolescents in Western countries?

2. What are the differences across ethnicities in the United States in high school completion rates?

3. How does access to secondary school differ across the United States, Europe, and developing countries?

4. What are some negative impacts of adolescent work in developed countries?

5. What is the recommended maximum number of hours that adolescents should work outside of school?

Section 2 VIDEO GUIDE Imaginary Audience (Length: 0:30)

In this video, an adolescent girl provides a brief personal example of the imaginary audience.

1. Explain how this adolescent's story fits with the concept of an imaginary audience.

2. How is the imaginary audience connected to the concept of a personal fable?

3. The imaginary audience doesn't entirely disappear when adolescence ends. Were their times in your own adolescence when you felt others were acutely aware of your appearance and behavior? How have these feelings changed as you have gotten older?

⊙ **Watch** the **Video** Imaginary Audience in **MyDevelopmentLab**

LEARNING OBJECTIVES

8.13 Summarize the results of the ESM studies with respect to adolescent emotionality.

8.14 Describe how self-understanding, self-concept, and self-esteem change during adolescence.

8.15 Compare and contrast the cultural patterns in gender expectations for girls and boys in adolescence.

8.16 Discriminate between Kohlberg's theory of moral development and Jensen's worldviews theory.

8.17 Describe the cultural variations in religious beliefs during adolescence as well as the sources and outcomes of religiosity within cultures.

8.18 Summarize the cultural variations in adolescents' relationships with parents, siblings, and extended family.

8.19 Describe cultural variations in adolescents' relationships with friends, and characterize their interactions with peers.

8.20 Identify cultural variations in adolescent love and sexuality, including variations in adolescent pregnancy and contraceptive use.

8.21 Explain the function of media use in adolescents' lives and apply the Media Practice Model to the playing of electronic games.

8.22 Summarize the explanations for why age and crime are so strongly correlated, and describe the multisystemic approach to combating delinquency.

8.23 Identify the different types and rates of depression and summarize the most effective treatments.

8.24 Define resilience and name the protective factors that are related to resilience in adolescence.

Emotional and Self-Development

Adolescence has long been regarded as a time of emotional volatility, and here we'll look at the history of views on this topic as well as current research. Issues of self-concept and self-esteem are also at the forefront of adolescent development, partly due to advances in cognitive development. (We will discuss identity development in more detail in Chapter 9.) Gender issues are prominent as well, because adolescence involves reaching sexual maturity.

Emotionality in adolescence: Storm and stress?

8.13 | **LEARNING OBJECTIVE** | Summarize the results of the ESM studies with respect to adolescent emotionality.

One of the most ancient and enduring observations of adolescence is that it is a time of heightened emotions (Arnett, 1999). Over 2,000 years ago, the Greek philosopher Aristotle observed that youth "are heated by Nature as drunken men by wine." About 250 years ago, the French philosopher Jean-Jacques Rousseau made a similar observation: "As the roaring of the waves precedes the tempest, so the murmur of rising passions announces the tumultuous change" of puberty and adolescence. Around the same time that Rousseau was writing, a type of German literature was developing that became known as *"sturm und drang"* literature—German for "storm and stress." In these stories, young people in their teens and early twenties experienced extreme emotions of angst, sadness, and romantic passion.

What does contemporary research tell us about the validity of these historical and popular views of adolescent emotionality? Probably the best source of data on this question is the research using the Experience Sampling Method (ESM), which involves having people wear wristwatch beepers and then beeping them randomly during the day so that they can record their thoughts, feelings, and behavior (refer back to Chapter 7, page 328) (Csikszentmihalyi & Larson, 1984; Schneider, 2006). ESM studies have also been conducted on younger children and adults, so if we compare the patterns of emotions reported by the different groups, we can get a good sense of whether adolescence is a stage of more extremes of emotions than middle childhood or adulthood.

The results indicate that adolescence in the United States is often a time of emotional volatility (Larson et al., 1980; Larson & Richards, 1994). American adolescents report feeling "self-conscious" and "embarrassed" two to three times more often than their parents and are also more likely than their parents to feel awkward, lonely, nervous, and ignored. Adolescents are also moodier when compared to younger children. Comparing preadolescent fifth graders to adolescent eighth graders, Reed Larson and Maryse Richards (1994) describe the emotional "fall from grace" that occurs during that time, as the proportion of time experienced as "very happy" declines by 50%, and similar declines take place in reports of feeling "great," "proud," and "in control." The result is an overall "deflation of childhood happiness" (p. 85) as childhood ends and adolescence begins.

Although adolescent emotionality is often attributed to "raging hormones" or some other biological source, most scholars view the emotional changes of adolescence as due to cognitive and environmental factors more than to biological changes (Buchanan et al., 1992; Susman & Rogol, 2004). According to Larson and Richards (1994), adolescents' newly developed capacities for abstract reasoning "allow them to see beneath the surface of situations and envision hidden and more long-lasting threats to their well-being" (p. 86). Larson and Richards (1994) also argue that experiencing multiple life changes and personal transitions during adolescence contributes to emotional volatility; within a short time adolescents may encounter the onset of puberty, a change of schools, and their first romantic and sexual experiences. Nevertheless, Larson and Richards (1994) emphasize that it is not just that adolescents experience potentially stressful events but *how* they experience and interpret them that underlies their emotional volatility. Even in response to the same or similar events, adolescents report more extreme and negative moods than younger children or adults.

How do emotional states change during the course of adolescence? Larson and Richards assessed their original ESM sample of fifth to eighth graders 4 years later, in ninth to twelfth grades (Larson et al., 2002). As *Figure 8.7* shows, they found that the decline in average emotional states continued through ninth and tenth grades, then leveled out. Also, the older adolescents were less volatile in their emotions, that is, the changes in their emotions from one time to the next were less extreme.

What about other cultures? Is adolescent emotionality especially an American phenomenon, or does it take place in other cultures as well? There is limited evidence to answer this question. However, in one study ESM was used with adolescents and their parents in India (Verma & Larson, 1999). The results indicated that, in India as in the United States, adolescents reported more extremes of emotion than their parents did.

Figure 8.7 • **Change in emotional states during adolescence.** Average emotional state becomes steadily more negative in the course of adolescence.

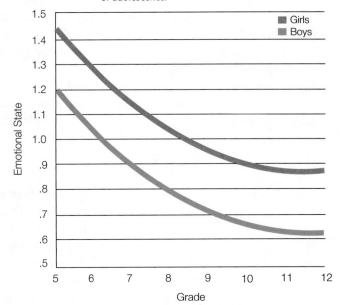

Self-development in adolescence

8.14 **LEARNING OBJECTIVE** Describe how self-understanding, self-concept, and self-esteem change during adolescence.

actual self person's perception of the self as it is, contrasted with the possible self

possible self person's conceptions of the self as it potentially may be; may include both an ideal self and a feared self

ideal self person one would like to be

feared self person one imagines it is possible to become but dreads becoming

false self self a person may present to others while realizing that it does not represent what he or she is actually thinking and feeling

Watch the **Video** Adolescence and Making Choices in **MyDevelopmentLab**

APPLYING YOUR KNOWLEDGE

Why do you think a false self is most likely to be shown to potential romantic partners? Would the false self be gradually discarded as the potential partner becomes an actual boyfriend or girlfriend, or not?

Self-conceptions become more complex in adolescence, due to advances in cognitive development. Self-esteem also becomes more complex, but overall self-esteem declines in early adolescence before rising in late adolescence and emerging adulthood.

SELF-UNDERSTANDING AND SELF-CONCEPT Self-conceptions in adolescence become more complex and more abstract. One aspect of the complexity of adolescents' self-conceptions is that they can distinguish between an **actual self** and **possible selves** (Markus & Nurius, 1986; Oyserman & Fryberg, 2006; Whitty, 2002). The actual self is your self-conception, and possible selves are the different people you imagine you could become in the future depending on your choices and experiences. Scholars distinguish two kinds of possible selves, an ideal self and a feared self (Chalk et al., 2005). The **ideal self** is the person the adolescent would like to be (for example, an adolescent may have an ideal of becoming highly popular with peers or highly successful in athletics or music). The **feared self** is the person the adolescent imagines it is possible to become but dreads becoming (for example, an adolescent might fear becoming an alcoholic, or fear becoming like a disgraced relative or friend). Both kinds of possible selves require adolescents to think abstractly. That is, possible selves exist only as abstractions, as ideas in the adolescent's mind.

The capacity for thinking about an actual, an ideal, and a feared self is a cognitive achievement, but this capacity may be troubling in some respects. If you can imagine an ideal self, you can also become aware of the discrepancy between your actual self and your ideal self, between what you are and what you wish you were. If the discrepancy is large enough, it can result in feelings of failure, inadequacy, and depression. Studies have found that the size of the discrepancy between the actual and ideal self is related to depressed mood in both adolescents and emerging adults (Moretti & Wiebe, 1999; Papadakis et al., 2006). Furthermore, the discrepancy between the actual and the ideal self is greater in mid-adolescence than in either early or late adolescence (Ferguson et al., 2010). This helps explain why rates of depressed mood rise in early adolescence and peak in mid-adolescence, as we will see in more detail later in the chapter.

A related aspect of the increasing complexity of self-conceptions is that adolescents become aware of times when they are exhibiting a **false self**, which is a self they present to others while realizing that it does not represent what they are actually thinking and feeling (Harter et al., 1997; Weir et al., 2010). With whom would you think adolescents would be most likely to exhibit their false selves—friends, parents, or potential romantic partners? Research indicates that adolescents are most likely to put on their false selves with potential romantic partners, and least likely with their close friends; parents are in between (Harter, 2006b; Sippola et al., 2007). Most adolescents indicate that they sometimes dislike putting on a false self, but many also say that some degree of false self behavior is acceptable and even desirable, to impress someone or to conceal aspects of the self they do not want others to see.

SELF-ESTEEM Several longitudinal studies show that self-esteem declines in early adolescence, then rises through late adolescence and emerging adulthood (Harter, 2006a; Robins & Trzesniewski, 2005). There are a number of reasons why self-esteem might follow this developmental pattern. The "imaginary audience" that we have discussed as part of adolescents' cognitive development can make them self-conscious in a way that decreases their self-esteem (Elkind, 1967, 1985). That is, as adolescents develop the capacity to imagine that others are especially conscious of how they look and what they say and how they act, they may suspect or fear that others are judging them harshly.

And they may be right. Adolescents in Western cultures tend to value the opinion of their peers highly, especially on day-to-day issues such as how they are dressed and what they say in social situations (Berndt, 1996). Their peers have developed new cognitive capacities for sarcasm and ridicule, which tend to be dispensed freely toward any peer who seems odd or awkward or uncool (Eder, 1995; Rosenblum & Way, 2004). So, the combination of greater peer orientation, greater self-consciousness about evaluations by peers, and peers' potentially harsh evaluations contributes to declines in self-esteem in early adolescence. Self-esteem rises in late adolescence and emerging adulthood as peers' evaluations become less important (Berndt, 1996; Robins & Trzesniewski, 2005).

As scholars have studied self-esteem, they have concluded that it has many aspects in addition to overall self-esteem. Multiple aspects of adolescent self-esteem have been investigated by Susan Harter (1990a, 1990b, 2006a). Her *Self-Perception Profile for Adolescents* distinguishes the following eight domains of adolescent self-image:

The opinions of peers become highly salient for adolescents.

- Scholastic competence
- Social acceptance
- Athletic competence
- Physical appearance
- Job competence
- Romantic appeal
- Behavioral conduct
- Close friendship

In addition to the eight subscales on specific domains of self-esteem, Harter's scale also contains a subscale for global (overall) self-esteem. Her research indicates that adolescents do not need to have a positive self-image in all domains to have high global self-esteem. Each domain of self-image influences global self-esteem only to the extent that the adolescent views that domain as important (refer back to Chapter 7, p. 330). For example, some adolescents may view themselves as having low scholastic competence, but that would influence their global self-esteem only if it was important to them to do well in school.

Nevertheless, some domains of self-esteem are more important than others to most adolescents. Research by Harter and others has found that physical appearance is most strongly related to global self-esteem, followed by social acceptance from peers (DuBois et al., 1996; Harter, 2006a; Shapka & Keating, 2005). Adolescent girls are more likely than boys to emphasize physical appearance as a basis for self-esteem. Because girls tend to evaluate their physical appearance negatively, and because physical appearance is at the heart of their global self-esteem, girls' self-esteem tends to be lower than boys' during adolescence (Robins & Trzesniewski, 2005; Shapka & Keating, 2005).

My Virtual Child

How does your virtual child rate on the different domains of self-image?

Gender intensification in adolescence

Compare and contrast the cultural patterns in gender expectations for girls and boys in adolescence.

LEARNING OBJECTIVE **8.15**

Gender is related not only to self-esteem but to many other aspects of development in adolescence. Psychologists John Hill and Mary Ellen Lynch (1983; Lynch 1991) proposed that adolescence is a particularly important time in gender socialization, especially for girls. According to their **gender-intensification hypothesis**, psychological and behavioral differences between males and females become more pronounced in the transition from childhood to adolescence because of intensified socialization pressures to conform to culturally prescribed gender roles. Hill and Lynch (1983) believe that it is this intensified socialization pressure, rather than the biological changes of puberty, that

gender-intensification hypothesis hypothesis that psychological and behavioral differences between males and females become more pronounced at adolescence because of intensified socialization pressures to conform to culturally prescribed gender roles

Watch the **Video** Adolescence: Identity and Role Development in **MyDevelopmentLab**

Watch the **Video** Gender Roles in Sports in **MyDevelopmentLab**

THINKING CULTURALLY

In your culture, what are terms for a failed man? Are there terms for a failed woman?

Watch the **Video** Sexism and Adolescent Girls in **MyDevelopmentLab**

Learning to provide for a family economically is a traditional part of the male gender role. Here, an Egyptian father and son fish together on the Nile River.

results in increased differences between males and females as adolescence progresses. Furthermore, they argue that the intensity of gender socialization in adolescence is greater for females than for males, and that this is reflected in a variety of ways in adolescent girls' development.

Since Hill and Lynch (1983) proposed this hypothesis, other studies have been presented that support it (Galambos, 2004; Shanahan et al., 2007; Wichstrom, 1999). In one study, boys and girls filled out a questionnaire on gender identity each year in sixth, seventh, and eighth grades (Galambos et al., 1990). Over this two-year period, girls' self-descriptions became more "feminine" (e.g., gentle, affectionate) and boys' self-descriptions became more "masculine" (e.g., tough, aggressive). However, in contrast to Hill and Lynch's (1983) claim that gender intensification is strongest for girls, the pattern in this study was especially strong for boys and masculinity. A more recent study found that gender stereotypes were embraced more by adolescents than by younger children, for both boys and girls (Rowley et al., 2007). Another study found that increased conformity to gender roles during early adolescence took place primarily for adolescents whose parents valued traditional gender roles (Crouter et al., 1995).

Gender intensification is often considerably stronger in traditional cultures than in the West. One striking difference in gender expectations in traditional cultures is that for boys manhood is something that has to be *achieved,* whereas girls reach womanhood inevitably, mainly through their biological changes (Lindsay & Miescher, 2003). It is true that girls are required to demonstrate various skills and character qualities before they can be said to have reached womanhood. However, in most traditional cultures womanhood is seen as something that girls attain naturally during adolescence, and their readiness for womanhood is viewed as indisputably marked when they reach menarche. Adolescent boys have no comparable biological marker of readiness for manhood. For them, the attainment of manhood is often fraught with peril and carries a definite and formidable possibility of failure. As an illustration of this, it is striking to observe how many cultures have a term for a male who is a failed man (Gilmore, 1990). In contrast, although there are certainly many derogatory terms applied to women, none of them have connotations of *failure at being a woman* the way there are terms that mean *failure at being a man.*

So, what must an adolescent boy in traditional cultures do to achieve manhood and escape the stigma of being viewed as a failed man? The anthropologist David Gilmore (1990) examined this question in traditional cultures around the world and concluded that in most cultures an adolescent boy must demonstrate three capacities before he can be considered a man: *provide, protect,* and *procreate.* He must *provide* in the sense that he must demonstrate that he has developed skills that are economically useful and that will enable him to support the wife and children he is likely to have as an adult man. For example, if what adult men mainly do is fish, the adolescent boy must demonstrate that he has learned the skills involved in fishing adequately enough to provide for a family.

Second, he must *protect,* in the sense that he must show that he can contribute to the protection of his family, kinship group, tribe, and other groups to which he belongs, from attacks by human enemies or animal predators. He learns this by acquiring the skills of warfare and the capacity to use weapons. Conflict between human groups has been a fact of life in most cultures throughout human history, so this is a pervasive requirement. Finally, he must learn to *procreate,* in the sense that he must gain some degree of sexual experience before marriage. This is not so he can demonstrate his sexual attractiveness but simply so that he can demonstrate that in marriage he will be able to perform sexually well enough to produce children.

WHAT HAVE YOU LEARNED?

1. Why is adolescence a time of emotional volatility?
2. How does your actual self differ from your possible self?
3. What are some domains of adolescent self-image as proposed by Harter?
4. Which domains of adolescent self-image are most strongly related to global self-esteem?
5. What must boys in traditional cultures do to achieve manhood?

Cultural Beliefs: Morality and Religion

As we have seen earlier in the chapter, cognitive development in adolescence entails a greater capacity for abstract and complex thinking. This capacity is applied not only to scientific and practical problems but to cultural beliefs, most notably in the areas of moral and religious development.

Moral development

Discriminate between Kohlberg's theory of moral development and Jensen's worldviews theory.

LEARNING OBJECTIVE 8.16

For most of the past half century, moral development was viewed as following a universal pattern, grounded in cognitive development. However, more recently, moral development has been argued to be fundamentally rooted in cultural beliefs. First we look at a theory of universal moral development, then at a cultural theory.

KOHLBERG'S THEORY OF MORAL DEVELOPMENT Lawrence Kohlberg (1958) presented an influential theory of moral development that dominated research on this topic for nearly a half century. Kohlberg viewed moral development as based on cognitive development, and believed that moral thinking changes in predictable ways as cognitive abilities develop, regardless of culture. He presented people with hypothetical moral dilemmas and had them indicate what behavior they believed was right or wrong in that situation, and why.

Kohlberg began his research by studying the moral judgments of 72 boys aged 10, 13, and 16 from middle-class and working-class families in the Chicago area (Kohlberg, 1958). He presented the boys with a series of fictional dilemmas, each of which was constructed to elicit their moral reasoning. For example, in one dilemma, a man must decide whether or not to steal a drug he cannot afford, to save his dying wife.

To Kohlberg, what was crucial for understanding the level of people's moral development was not whether they concluded that the actions of the persons in the dilemma were right or wrong but how they explained their conclusions; his focus was on adolescents' *moral reasoning*, not moral evaluations of right and wrong or their moral behavior. Kohlberg (1986) developed a system for classifying moral reasoning into three levels of moral development, with each level containing two stages, as follows:

Level 1: **Preconventional reasoning.** At this level, moral reasoning is based on perceptions of the likelihood of external rewards and punishments. What is right is what avoids punishment or results in rewards.
- *Stage 1: Punishment and obedience orientation.* Rules should be obeyed to avoid punishment from those in authority. In this stage, a person might avoid stealing in order to not get punished.

preconventional reasoning first level in Kohlberg's theory of moral development, in which moral reasoning is based on perceptions of the likelihood of external rewards and punishments

- *Stage 2: Individualism and purpose orientation.* What is right is what satisfies one's own needs and occasionally the needs of others, and what leads to rewards for oneself. In this stage, a person might steal to satisfy a hedonistic urge.

Level 2: **Conventional reasoning.** At this level, moral reasoning is less egocentric and the person advocates the value of conforming to the moral expectations of others. What is right is whatever agrees with the rules established by tradition and by authorities.

- *Stage 3: Interpersonal concordance orientation.* Care of and loyalty to others is emphasized in this stage, and it is seen as good to conform to what others expect in a certain role, such as being a "good husband" or a "good wife." In this stage, a person might avoid stealing in order to appear to be a "good boy" or a "good girl."
- *Stage 4: Social systems orientation.* Moral judgments are explained by reference to concepts such as social order, law, fairness, and justice. It is argued that rules and laws must be respected for social order to be maintained. In this stage, a person might avoid stealing by appealing to the importance of maintaining the laws that we have agreed to as a society.

Level 3: **Postconventional reasoning.** Moral reasoning at this level is based on the person's own independent judgments rather than on what others view as wrong or right. What is right is derived from the person's perception of objective, universal principles rather than being based on the needs of the individual (as in Level 1) or the standards of the group (as in Level 2).

- *Stage 5: Community rights and individual rights orientation.* The person reasoning at this stage views society's laws and rules as important, but also sees it as important to question them and change them if they become obstacles to the fulfillment of ideals such as freedom and equality. In this stage, a person weighs the pros and cons of stealing in terms of ideals like equality and makes efforts to change the law if necessary to further the goal of equality.
- *Stage 6: Universal ethical principles orientation.* The person has developed an independent moral code based on universal principles. When laws or social conventions conflict with these principles, it is seen as better to violate the laws or conventions than the universal principles. In this stage, a person has internalized ethical principles and weighs the act of stealing against those universal principles. The person may steal if it helps to uphold a universal principle that is seen by all as being of higher value.

Kohlberg followed his initial group of adolescent boys over the next 20 years (Colby et al., 1983), interviewing them every three or four years, and he and his colleagues also conducted numerous other studies on moral reasoning in adolescence and adulthood. The results verified Kohlberg's theory of moral development in a number of ways:

- Stage of moral reasoning tended to increase with age. However, even after 20 years, when all of the original participants were in their thirties, few of them had proceeded to Stage 5, and none had reached Stage 6 (Colby et al., 1983). Kohlberg eventually dropped Stage 6 from his coding system (Kohlberg, 1986).
- Moral development proceeded in the predicted way, in the sense that the participants did not skip stages but proceeded from one stage to the next highest over time.
- Moral development was found to be cumulative, in the sense that the participants were rarely found to slip to a lower stage over time. With few exceptions, they either remained in the same stage or proceeded to the next highest stage.

Kohlberg's goal was to propose a universal theory of moral development, a theory that would apply to people in all cultures. One reason he used hypothetical moral

conventional reasoning second level in Kohlberg's theory of moral development, in which moral reasoning is based on the expectations of others

postconventional reasoning third level in Kohlberg's theory of moral development, in which moral reasoning is based on the individual's own independent judgments rather than on what others view as wrong or right

dilemmas rather than having people talk about moral issues they had confronted in real life was that he believed that the culture-specific and person-specific *content* of moral reasoning is not important to understanding moral development. According to Kohlberg, what matters is the *structure* of moral reasoning, not the content. In other words, what matters is *how* people make their moral judgments, not whether they view certain acts as right or wrong. ✳

CULTURE AND MORAL DEVELOPMENT: THE WORLDVIEWS THEORY Does Kohlberg's theory of moral development apply universally, as he intended? Research based on Kohlberg's theory has included cross-cultural studies in countries all over the world such as Turkey, Japan, Taiwan, Kenya, Israel, and India (Gibbs et al., 2007; Snarey, 1985). Many of these studies have focused on moral development in adolescence and emerging adulthood. In general, the studies confirm Kohlberg's hypothesis that moral development as classified by his coding system progresses with age. Also, as in the American studies, participants in longitudinal studies in other cultures have rarely been found to regress to an earlier stage or to skip a stage of moral reasoning.

Nevertheless, Kohlberg's claims of a universal theory of moral development have been challenged, most notably by cultural psychologist (Richard Shweder 2003; Shweder et al., 1990; Shweder et al., 2006). As you will remember from Chapter 6 (p. 264), Shweder believes it is impossible to understand moral development unless you understand the cultural worldview that underlies it. In contrast to Kohlberg, Shweder proposed that the *content* of people's moral reasoning, including their views of right and wrong, is at the heart of moral development and cannot simply be ignored.

Shweder and his colleagues have presented an alternative to Kohlberg's theory of moral development (Shweder et al., 1997). The new theory has been developed mostly by a former student of Shweder's, Lene Jensen (1997a, 1997b, 2008, 2011). According to Jensen, the ultimate basis of morality is a person's **worldview**. A worldview is a set of cultural beliefs that explain what it means to be human, how human relations should be conducted, and how human problems should be addressed. Worldviews provide the basis for *moral reasoning* (explanations for why a behavior is right or wrong). The outcome of moral reasoning is *moral evaluations* (judgments as to whether a behavior is right or wrong), which in turn prescribe *moral behaviors*. Moral behaviors reinforce worldviews. An illustration of the worldviews theory is shown in *Figure 8.8*.

In her research, Jensen codes people's responses to moral issues according to three types of "ethics" based on different worldviews.

- The *Ethic of Autonomy* defines the individual as the primary moral authority. Individuals are viewed as having a right to do as they wish so long as their behavior does not harm others.
- The *Ethic of Community* defines individuals as members of social groups to which they have commitments and obligations. In this ethic, the responsibilities of roles in the family, community, and other groups are the basis of one's moral judgments.
- The *Ethic of Divinity* defines the individual as a spiritual entity, subject to the prescriptions of a divine authority. This ethic includes moral views based on traditional religious authorities and religious texts (e.g., the Bible, the Koran).

Studies on adolescents' moral reasoning using the worldviews approach are now in progress, but research has already been published involving emerging adults. Research conducted thus far has shown that emerging adults in the United States rely especially on the ethic of autonomy. Jensen (1995) found that American emerging adults relied on the ethic of autonomy more than midlife or older adults did when

worldview set of cultural beliefs that explain what it means to be human, how human relations should be conducted, and how human problems should be addressed

✳⌐**Explore** the **Concept** Kohlberg's Stages of Moral Reasoning in **MyDevelopmentLab**

APPLYING YOUR KNOWLEDGE
. . . as a Teacher

A middle-schooler in your class says that people should pay their fair share in taxes because we have all agreed on a system of government that relies on taxes. What stage of Kohlberg's moral development is she in?

Figure 8.8 • **Worldviews theory.** How is this theory different from Kohlberg's?

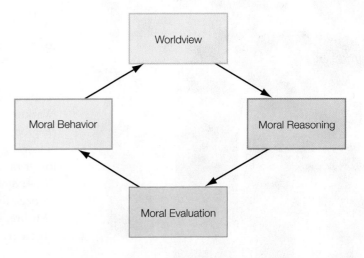

secular based on nonreligious beliefs and values

explaining their views about moral issues such as divorce and suicide. Also, Jonathan Haidt and colleagues (1993) found that college students in both the United States and Brazil used autonomy more than community on a variety of moral issues. However, one study found that emerging adults used autonomy and community in roughly equal proportions (and divinity rarely) in response to questions about the values that guide their lives and the beliefs and values they would like to pass on to the next generation (Arnett et al., 2001). Research using the three ethics has only begun, and it remains to be seen how their use changes in different cultures throughout the lifespan (Jensen, 2011).

Religious beliefs

8.17 **LEARNING OBJECTIVE** Describe the cultural variations in religious beliefs during adolescence as well as the sources and outcomes of religiosity within cultures.

TABLE 8.2 Religious Beliefs of American Adolescents

Believe in God or a universal spirit	84%
Pray at least once a week	65%
Religion important in daily life	51%
Believe in the existence of angels	63%
Attend religious services at least twice a month	52%
Involved in a church youth group	38%

Source: Based on Soul searching: The religious and spiritual lives of American teenagers. Smith, Denton.

African American adolescents are often highly religious.

Like moral development, the development of religious beliefs reaches a critical point in adolescence, because adolescence is a time when the abstract ideas involved in religious beliefs can first be fully grasped. In general, adolescents and emerging adults in developed countries are less religious than their counterparts in developing countries. Developed countries tend to be highly **secular**, which means based on nonreligious beliefs and values. In every developed country, religion has gradually faded in its influence over the past two centuries (Bellah et al., 1985). Religious beliefs and practices are especially low among adolescents in Europe. For example, in Belgium only 8% of 18-year-olds attend religious services at least once a month (Goossens & Luyckx, 2007). In Spain, traditionally a highly Catholic country, only 18% of adolescents attend church regularly (Gibbons & Stiles, 2004).

Americans are more religious than people in virtually any other developed country, and this is reflected in the lives of American adolescents (see *Table 8.2*) (Smith & Denton, 2005). However, religion has a lower priority for most of them than many her parts of their lives, including school, friendships, media, and work. Furthernore, the religious beliefs of American adolescents tend not to follow traditional doctrines. Instead, they tend to believe that religious faith is about how to be a good person and feel happy.

Many American adolescents are religious, but many others are not. What explains differences among adolescents in their religiosity? Adolescents are more likely to embrace the importance of religion when their parents talk about religious issues and participate in religious activities (King et al., 2002; Layton et al., 2011). Adolescents are less likely to be religious when their parents disagree with each other about religious beliefs, and when their parents are divorced (Smith & Denton, 2005). Ethnicity is another factor. In American society religious faith and religious practices tend to be stronger among African Americans than among Whites (Chatters et al., 2008). Latino students tend to say that religious beliefs are important to them, while this is less prevalent among Native Americans (Regnerus et al., 2004).

The relatively high rate of religiosity among African American adolescents helps explain why they have such low rates of alcohol and drug use (Stevens-Watkins & Rostosky, 2010). However, it is not only among minority groups that religiosity is associated with favorable adolescent outcomes. Across American cultural groups, adolescents who are more religious report less depression and lower rates of premarital sex, drug use, and delinquent behavior (Kerestes et al., 2004; Smith & Denton, 2005). The protective value of religious involvement is especially strong for adolescents living in the worst neighborhoods (Bridges & Moore, 2002). Religious adolescents tend to have better relationships with their parents (Smith & Denton, 2005; Wilcox, 2008). In other cultures, too, religious involvement has been found to be related to a variety of positive outcomes, for example among Indonesian Muslim adolescents (French et al., 2008).

WHAT HAVE YOU LEARNED?

1. In Kohlberg's theory, what level of moral reasoning views moral judgments as being based on the need to uphold social order?
2. Why did Kohlberg use hypothetical moral dilemmas in his research?
3. According to the worldviews theory, why is it important to know people's conceptions of right and wrong?
4. What factors influence how religious an adolescent will be?
5. What are some favorable outcomes associated with religiosity in adolescence?

My Virtual Child

Is your virtual child likely religious? What has influenced his or her religiosity?

THINKING CULTURALLY

Why do you think Americans generally are more religious than people in other developed countries?

The Social and Cultural Contexts of Adolescence

Like younger children, adolescents typically remain within the family, but social contexts of peers, romantic relations, and media often have greater prominence in adolescence than previously. Also, for some adolescents certain types of problems develop that were rare in previous life stages.

Family relationships

Summarize the cultural variations in adolescents' relationships with parents, siblings, and extended family.

LEARNING OBJECTIVE 8.18

The family is a key part of the daily social context of adolescents in all cultures, but in most cultures there are also profound changes in family relations from middle childhood to adolescence. Perhaps the most notable change in family relationships that occurs from middle childhood to adolescence in American society is the decline in the amount of time spent with family members, as described in the **Research Focus: The Daily Rhythms of Adolescents' Family Lives** feature on page 389. When adolescents do spend time with their parents, conflict is more frequent than in middle childhood, as we will see next. ◉

Watch the **Video** Parental Perspectives on Relationships with Parents in **MyDevelopmentLab**

CONFLICT WITH PARENTS

This is a dangerous world, what with all the drugs and drunk drivers and violent crime and kids disappearing and you name it. I know my kids are pretty responsible, but can I trust all their friends? Are they going to end up in some situation they can't get out of? Are they going to get in over their heads? You can never be sure, so I worry and set curfews and make rules about where they can go and who they can go with. Not because I want to be a tough dad, but because I want them to be safe.

John, father of a 16-year-old son and a 13-year-old daughter
(Alexander, 1998, p. 54)

Numerous studies have shown that adolescents and their parents agree on many of their beliefs and values, and typically they have a great deal of love and respect for one another (Moore et al., 2002; Offer & Schonert-Reichl, 1992; Smetana, 2005).

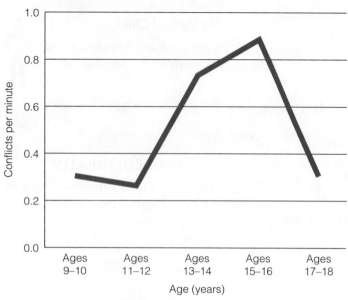

Figure 8.9 • **Parental conflict in adolescence.** Why does conflict peak in the mid-teens?

Source: The family ecology of adolescence: A dynamic systems perspective on normative development. In Blackwell handbook of adolescence (pp. 60–91).

autonomy quality of being independent and self-sufficient, capable of thinking for one's self

Nevertheless, studies in Western countries also indicate that conflict with parents increases sharply in early adolescence, compared with middle childhood, and remains high for several years before declining in late adolescence (Dworkin & Larson, 2001; Laursen et al., 1998; Shanahan et al., 2007). **Figure 8.9** shows the pattern of conflict across adolescence, from a longitudinal study that observed American mothers and sons in videotaped interactions on five occasions over eight years (Granic et al., 2003). A Canadian study found that 40% of adolescents reported arguments with their parents at least once a week (Sears, 2007). Conflict in adolescence is especially frequent and intense between mothers and daughters (Collins & Laursen, 2004). Both parents and adolescents report more frequent conflict in early adolescence than prior to adolescence; by mid-adolescence, conflict with parents tends to become somewhat less frequent but more intense before declining substantially in late adolescence (Laursen et al., 1998).

There are several reasons why conflict with parents often rises during adolescence. First, adolescence entails reaching sexual maturity, which means that sexual issues may be a source of conflict in a way they would not have been in childhood (Arnett, 1999). Early-maturing adolescents tend to have more conflict with parents than adolescents who mature "on time," perhaps because sexual issues arise earlier (Collins & Laursen, 2004). Second, advances in cognitive development make it possible for adolescents to rebut their parents' reasoning about rules and restrictions more effectively than they could have earlier. Third, and most importantly, in many cultures adolescence is a time of gaining greater independence from the family. Although parents and adolescents in these cultures usually share the same goal that the adolescent will eventually become a self-sufficient adult, they often disagree about the pace of adolescents' growing **autonomy** (Daddis & Smetana, 2006; Smetana, 2005). Parents may have concerns about adolescents' safety with respect to sexuality, automobile driving, and substance use, and so restrict adolescents' behavior in an effort to protect them from risks. Adolescents expect to be able to make their own decisions in these areas and resent their parents' restrictions, and conflict results.

However, not all cultures value and encourage increased autonomy in adolescence. In traditional cultures, it is rare for parents and adolescents to engage in the kind of frequent conflicts typical of parent–adolescent relationships in Western cultures (Larson et al., 2010). The role of parent carries greater authority in traditional cultures than in the West, and this makes it less likely that adolescents in such cultures will express disagreements and resentments toward their parents (Phinney et al., 2005). Even when they disagree with their parents, they are unlikely to express it because of their feelings of duty and respect (Phinney & Ong, 2002). Outside of the West, as we have seen in previous chapters, interdependence is a higher value than independence, not only during adolescence but throughout adulthood (Markus & Kitayama, 2003; Phinney et al., 2005). Just as a dramatic increase in autonomy during adolescence prepares Western adolescents for adult life in an individualistic culture, learning to submit to the authority of one's parents prepares adolescents in traditional cultures for an adult life in which interdependence is among the highest values and each person has a clearly designated position in a family hierarchy.

SIBLING AND EXTENDED-FAMILY RELATIONS For about 80% of American adolescents, and similar proportions in other developed countries, the family system also includes relationships with at least one sibling (U.S. Bureau of the Census, 2009). The proportion of families with siblings is even higher in developing countries, where birthrates tend to be higher and families with only one child are rare (Population Reference Bureau, 2009).

RESEARCH FOCUS   The Daily Rhythms of Adolescents' Family Lives

Adolescent researchers have found the Experience Sampling Method (ESM) to be a helpful source of information on adolescents' social lives. Reed Larson and Maryse Richards are the two scholars who have done the most to apply the ESM to adolescents and their families. In their classic book *Divergent Realities: The Emotional Lives of Mothers, Fathers, and Adolescents* (Larson & Richards, 1994), they described the results of a study that included a sample of 483 American adolescents in fifth through ninth grades, and another sample of 55 fifth through eighth graders and their parents. All were two-parent, White families. In each family, three family members (adolescent, mother, and father) were beeped at the same times, about 30 times per day between 7:30 in the morning and 9:30 at night, during the week of the study.

When beeped, adolescents and their parents paused from whatever they were doing and recorded a variety of information about where they were, whom they were with, and what they were doing. There were also items about the degree to which they felt happy to unhappy, cheerful to irritable, and friendly to angry, as well as how hurried, tired, and competitive they were feeling. The results provide "an emotional photo album . . . a set of snapshots of what [adolescents] and [their] parents go through in an average week" (Larson & Richards, 1994, p. 9).

What do the results tell us about the daily rhythms of American adolescents' family lives? One striking finding of the study was how little time adolescents and their parents actually spent together on a typical day. Mothers and fathers each averaged about an hour a day spent in shared activities with their adolescents, and their most common shared activity was watching television. The amount of time adolescents spent with their families dropped by 50% between fifth and ninth grades and declined even more sharply between ninth and twelfth grades (see *Figure 8.10*). In turn, there was an increase from fifth to ninth grade in the amount of time adolescents spent alone in their bedrooms.

The study also revealed some interesting gender differences in parent–adolescent relationships. Mothers were more deeply involved with their adolescents, both for better and for worse. The majority of mother–adolescent interactions were rated positively by both of them, especially experiences such as talking together, going out together, and sharing a meal. Adolescents, especially girls, tended to be closer to their mothers than to their fathers and had more conversations with them about relationships and other personal issues. However, adolescents' negative feelings toward their mothers increased sharply from fifth to ninth grade, and certain positive emotions decreased. For example, the proportion of interactions with the mother in which adolescents reported feeling "very close" to her fell from 68% in fifth grade to just 28% by ninth

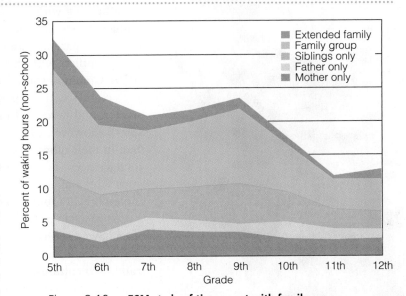

Figure 8.10 • **ESM study of time spent with family.**
Source: "Changes in Adolescent's Daily Interactions With Their Families, Ages 10–18", Developmental Psychology, 32.

grade. Also, adolescents reported more conflicts with their mothers than with their fathers, and the number of conflicts between mothers and adolescents increased from fifth to ninth grades.

As for fathers, they tended to be only tenuously involved in their adolescents' lives, a "shadowy presence," as Larson and Richards put it. For most of the time they spent with their adolescents, the mother was there as well, and the mother tended to be more directly involved with the adolescent when the three of them were together. Moms were usually on the "front lines" of parenting, whereas for fathers parenting was more of a voluntary, leisure-time activity. Fathers averaged only 12 minutes per day alone with their adolescents, and 40% of this time was spent watching TV together. Fathers and their adolescents did not talk much, and when they did, sports was the most common topic.

At the same time, however, the study showed that parents are often important sources of comfort and security for adolescents. Adolescents brought home to the family their emotions from the rest of the day. If their parents were responsive and caring, adolescents' moods improved and their negative emotions were relieved. In contrast, if adolescents felt their parents were unavailable or unresponsive, their negative feelings became even worse.

In sum, the study demonstrates the enduring importance of parents in the lives of adolescents. Also, because the study included the perspectives of fathers and mothers as well as adolescents, the results provide a vivid sense of the interconnected emotions and perspectives within the family system.

Why does conflict with parents rise from middle childhood to adolescence?

My Virtual Child

What role will extended family members play in the life of your virtual child?

APPLYING YOUR KNOWLEDGE
. . . as a Researcher

Maria, a 13-year-old girl from central Mexico, wants to accompany her younger brother when he participates in your research. As his sibling caretaker, she feels responsible for him. How might you adapt to this sibling-caretaking dynamic?

How did you get along with your siblings when you were in adolescence? My older brother Mike and I fought constantly during my adolescence, with me mostly on the losing end (until I hit my growth spurt and grew to be 6'3"; he seemed to lose interest in fighting with me after that). Relations with siblings in adolescence often involve conflict. In studies that compare adolescents' relationships with siblings to relationships with parents, grandparents, teachers, and friends, adolescents report more frequent conflicts with their siblings than with anyone else (Campione-Barr & Smetana, 2010). Common sources of conflict include teasing, possessions (e.g., borrowing a sibling's clothes without permission), responsibility for chores, name-calling, invasions of privacy, and perceived unequal treatment by parents (Noller, 2005; Updegraff et al., 2005). However, even though adolescents tend to have more conflicts with siblings than in their other relationships, conflict with siblings is lower in adolescence than at younger ages (Brody, 2004; Noller, 2005). From childhood to adolescence, relationships with siblings become more casual and less emotionally intense, mainly because adolescents gradually spend less time with their siblings (Hetherington et al., 1999).

As noted in previous chapters, by middle childhood, children in traditional cultures often have responsibility for caring for young siblings, and for many this responsibility continues into adolescence. In Schlegel and Barry's (1991) analysis of adolescence in traditional cultures, over 80% of adolescent boys and girls had frequent responsibility for caring for younger siblings. This responsibility promotes conflict between siblings, but also close attachments. Time together, and closeness, is especially high between siblings of the same gender, mainly because in traditional cultures, daily activities are often separated by gender. Caregiver relationships between siblings are also common in African American families, in part because many African American families are headed by single mothers who rely on older siblings to help with child care (Brody et al., 2003).

Adolescents in traditional cultures also tend to be close to their extended family members. In these cultures children often grow up in a household that includes not only their parents and siblings but also grandparents, and often uncles, aunts, and cousins as well. These living arrangements promote closeness between adolescents and their extended family. In Schlegel and Barry's (1991) cross-cultural analysis, daily contact was as high with grandparents as with parents for adolescents in traditional cultures, and adolescents were usually even closer to their grandparents than to their parents. Perhaps this is because parents typically exercise authority over adolescents, which may add ambivalence to adolescents' relationships with their parents, whereas grandparents are less likely to exercise authority and may focus more on nurturing and supporting adolescents.

Extended family members are also important figures in the lives of adolescents in Western majority cultures. About 80% of American adolescents list at least one member of their extended family among the people most important to them, and closeness to grandparents is positively related to adolescents' well-being (Ruiz & Silverstein, 2007). However, in the American majority culture adolescents' contact with extended family members is relatively infrequent, in part because extended family members often live many miles away. When extended family members live within the household or nearby, as is often the case in African American, Latino, and Asian American families, adolescents' closeness to them tends to resemble the pattern in traditional cultures (Fuligni et al., 1999; Suarez-Orozco & Suarez-Orozco, 1996; Oberlander et al., 2007).

Peers and friends

8.19 **LEARNING OBJECTIVE** | Describe cultural variations in adolescents' relationships with friends, and characterize their interactions with peers.

I feel close to my friends when I've had troubles and stuff. I've been able to go to them and they'll help me. Last spring I let my friend know all about me, how my family was having trouble and stuff. I felt close to her and like she would keep this and not tell anyone else about it.

13-year-old girl (Radmacher & Azmitia, 2006, p. 428)

As time spent with family decreases from middle childhood to adolescence, time spent with friends increases, in most cultures. Friends also become increasingly important in adolescents' emotional lives. In adolescence, as at other ages, friends choose one another primarily due to similarities in characteristics such as age, gender, ethnic group, personality, and leisure interests (Popp et al., 2008). 👁

FRIENDSHIPS: CULTURAL THEMES AND VARIATIONS Although family ties remain important in the lives of adolescents, friends become preferred in some ways. Adolescents indicate that they depend more on friends than on their parents or siblings for companionship and intimacy (French et al., 2001; Nickerson & Nagle, 2005; Updegraff et al., 2002). **Intimacy** is the degree to which two people share personal knowledge, thoughts, and feelings. Adolescent friends confide hopes and fears, and help each other understand what is going on with their parents, their teachers, and peers to a far greater degree than younger children do. Friends become the source of adolescents' happiest experiences, the people with whom they feel most comfortable, the persons they feel they can talk to most openly (Richards et al., 2002; Youniss & Smollar, 1985). Adolescents state that a friend is someone who understands you, someone you can share your problems with, someone who will listen when you have something important to say (Bauminger et al., 2008; Way, 2004). Younger children are less likely to mention these kinds of features and more likely to stress shared activities—we both like to play basketball, we ride bikes together, we play computer games, and so on. As noted in Chapter 7, trust also becomes important to friendships in middle childhood, and trust is one aspect of intimacy, but the importance of intimacy develops further in adolescence. 👁

There are consistent gender differences in the intimacy of adolescent friendships, with girls tending to have more intimate friendships than boys do (Bauminger et al., 2008). Girls spend more time than boys talking to their friends, and they place a higher value on talking together as a component of their friendships (Apter, 1990; Youniss & Smollar, 1985). Girls also rate their friendships as higher in affection, helpfulness, and nurturance, compared with boys' ratings of their friendships (Lempers & Clark-Lempers, 1993). And girls are more likely than boys to say they trust and feel close to their friends (Shulman et al., 1997). In contrast, even in adolescence, boys are more likely to emphasize shared activities as the basis of friendship, such as sports or hobbies (Radmacher & Azmitia, 2006).

Nevertheless, intimacy does become more important to boys' friendships in adolescence, even if not to the same extent as for girls. In one study of African American, Latino, and Asian American boys from poor and working-class families, Niobe Way (2004) reported themes of intimacy that involved sharing secrets, protecting one another physically and emotionally, and disclosing feelings about family and friends. 👁

European studies comparing relationships with parents and friends show a pattern similar to American studies (Zeijl et al., 2000). For example, a study of Dutch adolescents (ages 15 to 19) asked them who they rely on to communicate about themselves, including their personal feelings, sorrows, and secrets (Bois-Reymond & Ravesloot, 1996). Nearly half of the adolescents named their best friend or their romantic partner, whereas only 20% named one or both parents (only 3% their fathers). Another Dutch study found that 82% of adolescents named spending free time with friends as their favorite activity (Meeus, 2007). Studies

intimacy degree to which two people share personal knowledge, thoughts, and feelings

927   *936*

👁 **Watch** the **Video** Peer Pressure in **MyDevelopmentLab**

👁 **Watch** the **Video** Changes in Friendship with Age in **MyDevelopmentLab**

👁 **Watch** the **Video** Intimacy in Adolescent Friendships in **MyDevelopmentLab**

Adolescents in Western cultures tend to be happiest when with friends.

THINKING CULTURALLY

Why do you think many adolescents find it more difficult to be close to their parents than to their friends? Is this phenomenon cultural, or developmental—or both?

in other European countries confirm that adolescents tend to be happiest when with their friends and that they tend to turn to their friends for advice and information on social relationships and leisure, although they come to parents for advice about education and career plans (Hurrelmann, 1996).

As noted earlier in the chapter, adolescence in traditional cultures often entails less involvement with family and greater involvement with peers for boys but not for girls. However, for boys as well as girls the social and emotional balance between friends and family remains tilted more toward family for adolescents in developing countries than it does in the West. For example, in India, adolescents tend to spend their leisure time with family rather than friends, not because they are required to do so but because of collectivistic Indian cultural values and because they enjoy their time with family (Chaudhary & Sharma, 2012; Larson et al., 2000). Among Brazilian adolescents, emotional support is higher from parents than friends (Van Horn & Cunegatto Marques, 2000). In a study comparing adolescents in Indonesia and the United States, Indonesian adolescents rated their family members higher and their friends lower on companionship and enjoyment, compared to American adolescents (French et al., 2001). Nevertheless, friends were the primary source of intimacy in both countries. Thus, it may be that adolescents in developing countries remain close to their families even as they also develop greater closeness to their friends during adolescence, whereas in the West closeness to family diminishes as closeness to friends grows.

CLIQUES AND CROWDS So far we have focused on close friendships. Now we turn to larger groups of friends and peers. Scholars generally make a distinction between two types of adolescent social groups, cliques and crowds. **Cliques** are small groups of friends who know each other well, do things together, and form a regular social group (Brown & Klute, 2003). Cliques have no precise size—3 to 12 is a rough range—but they are small enough so that all the members of the clique feel they know each other well and they think of themselves as a cohesive group. Sometimes cliques are defined by distinctive shared activities—for example, working on cars, playing music, playing basketball, surfing the Internet—and sometimes simply by shared friendship (a group of friends who eat lunch together every day, for example).

Crowds, in contrast, are larger, reputation-based groups of adolescents who are not necessarily friends and may not spend much time together (Brown et al., 2008; Brown & Klute, 2003; Horn, 2003). A review of 44 studies on adolescent crowds concluded that five major types of crowds are found in many schools (Sussman et al., 2007):

- Elites (a.k.a. Populars, Preppies). The crowd recognized as having the highest social status in the school.
- Athletes (a.k.a. Jocks). Sports-oriented students, usually members of at least one sports team.
- Academics (a.k.a. Brains, Nerds, Geeks). Known for striving for good grades and for being socially inept.
- Deviants (a.k.a. Druggies, Burnouts). Alienated from the school social environment, suspected by other students of using illicit drugs and engaging in other risky activities.
- Others (a.k.a. Normals, Nobodies). Students who do not stand out in any particular way, neither positively nor negatively; mostly ignored by other students.

clique small group of friends who know each other well, do things together, and form a regular social group

crowd large, reputation-based group of adolescents

Cliques are often formed around shared activities. Here, South African adolescents enjoy a game of soccer.

Crowds mainly serve the function of helping adolescents to locate themselves and others within the secondary school social structure. In other words, crowds help adolescents to define their own identities and the identities of others. Knowing that others think of you as a "Brain" has implications for your identity—it means you are the kind of person who likes school, does well in school, and perhaps has more success in school than in social situations. Thinking of someone else as a "Druggie" tells you something about that person (whether it is accurate or not)—he or she uses drugs, of course, probably dresses unconventionally, and does not seem to care much about school. ⊙

BULLYING At the age of 15, Phoebe Prince immigrated to the United States from Ireland with her family. She liked her new school at first and made friends, but then a popular boy took an interest in her, and she dated him a few times. Other girls who were interested in the boy began to harass her aggressively, calling her names in school and sending vicious e-mail messages spreading false rumors about her. Friendless and persecuted in and out of school, she sank deeper and deeper into despair and finally committed suicide, to the horror of her family and her community.

This shocking true-life example shows how serious the consequences of bullying in adolescence can be. As noted in Chapter 7, bullying is common in middle childhood, but the prevalence of bullying rises through middle childhood and peaks in early adolescence, then declines substantially by late adolescence (Pepler et al., 2006). Bullying is an international phenomenon, observed in many countries in Europe (Dijkstra et al., 2008; Gini et al., 2008), Asia (Ando et al., 2005; Hokoda et al., 2006), and North America (Pepler et al., 2008; Volk et al., 2006). In a landmark study of bullying among over 100,000 adolescents ages 11–15 in 28 countries around the world, self-reported prevalence rates of being a victim of bullying ranged from 6% among girls in Sweden to 41% among boys in Lithuania, with rates in most countries in the 10–20% range (Due et al., 2005). Across countries, in this study and many others, boys are consistently more likely than girls to be bullies as well as victims. ⊙

Bullying has a variety of negative effects on adolescents' development. In the 28-country study of adolescent bullying just mentioned, victims of bullying reported higher rates of a wide range of problems, including physical symptoms such as headaches, backaches, and difficulty sleeping, as well as psychological symptoms such as loneliness, helplessness, anxiety, and unhappiness (Due et al., 2005). Many other studies have reported similar results (Olweus, 2000). Not only victims but bullies are at high risk for problems (Klomek et al., 2007). A Canadian study of bullying that surveyed adolescents for 7 years beginning at ages 10–14 found that bullies reported more psychological problems and more problems in their relationships with parents and peers than non-bullies did (Pepler et al., 2008).

A recent variation on bullying is **cyberbullying** (also called electronic bullying), which involves bullying behavior via social media (such as Facebook), e-mail, or mobile phones (Kowalski, 2008). A Swedish study of 12- to 20-year-olds found an age pattern of cyberbullying similar to what has been found in studies of "traditional" bullying, with the highest rates in early adolescence and a decline through late adolescence and emerging adulthood (Slonje & Smith, 2008). In a study of nearly 4,000 adolescents in grades 6–8 in the United States, 11% reported being victims of a cyberbullying incident at least once in the past two months; 7% indicated that they had been cyberbullies as well as victims during this time period; and 4% reported committing a cyberbullying incident (Kowalski & Limber, 2007). Notably, half of the victims did not know the bully's identity, a key difference between cyberbullying and other bullying. However, cyberbullying usually involves only a single incident, so it does not involve the repetition required in the standard definition of traditional bullying (refer to Chapter 7, page 341), and might be better termed *online harassment* (Wolak et al., 2007).

APPLYING YOUR KNOWLEDGE

Do you think you were part of any of the crowds described here, when you were in secondary school? Did you think of your peers in terms of their crowd membership?

⊙ ─ **Watch** the **Video** Adolescent Cliques in **MyDevelopmentLab**

⊙ ─ **Watch** the **Video** Peer Acceptance in **MyDevelopmentLab**

**APPLYING YOUR KNOWLEDGE
. . . as a Teacher**

Why is cyberbullying an important topic to focus on in your school?

cyberbullying bullying via electronic means, mainly through the Internet

Love and sexuality

LEARNING OBJECTIVE Identify cultural variations in adolescent love and sexuality, including variations in adolescent pregnancy and contraceptive use.

Puberty means reaching sexual maturity. Consequently, adolescence is when sexual feelings begin to stir and—in many cultures, but not all—sexual behavior is initiated. First we look at love, then at sex. ◉

●—Watch the **Video** Adolescent Sexual Behavior in **MyDevelopmentLab**

FALLING IN LOVE The prevalence of involvement in romantic relationships increases gradually over the course of adolescence. According to a study in the United States called the National Study of Adolescent Health, the percentage of adolescents reporting a current romantic relationship rises from 17% in seventh grade to 32% in ninth grade to 44% in eleventh grade (Furman & Hand, 2006). By eleventh grade, 80% of adolescents had experienced a romantic relationship at some point, even if they did not have one currently. Adolescents with an Asian cultural background tend to have their first romantic relationship later than adolescents with a European, African American, or Latino cultural background, because of Asian cultural beliefs that discourage early involvement in romantic relationships and encourage minimal or no sexual involvement before marriage (Carver et al., 2003; Connolly et al., 2004; Regan et al., 2004). ◉

●—Watch the **Video** Dating in Adolescence in **MyDevelopmentLab**

Adolescent romantic relations tend to be less formal today than in the past. Even the terms *date* and *dating* have fallen out of fashion, replaced by *going with* or *hanging out with* or *seeing* someone (Alsaker & Flammer, 1999; Furman & Hand, 2006). Adolescent boys and girls still go together to movies, sports events, and school dances, of course, but they are much more likely than before to spend time together informally. They may do things in pairs as friends, or go out in mixed-gender groups, without any specific pairing up. Before the Women's Movement of the 1960s, gender roles were much more sharply drawn in the West, and adolescent boys and girls were less likely simply to hang out together as friends. Now they often know each other as friends before they become involved romantically (Kuttler et al., 1999).

APPLYING YOUR KNOWLEDGE . . . as a Teacher

Aparajita is a 17-year-old senior in your high school class. She tells you her parents plan to help find her an appropriate husband, and though she is happy about it, she is getting harassed by her peers. What can you tell her to help her feel better?

It is not only in the West, and not only in developed countries, that adolescents experience romantic love. On the contrary, feelings of passion appear to be virtually universal among young people. One study investigated this issue systematically by analyzing the *Standard Cross-Cultural Sample,* a collection of data provided by anthropologists on 186 traditional cultures representing six distinct geographical regions around the world (Jankowiak & Fischer, 1992). The researchers concluded that there was evidence that young people fell passionately in love in *all but one* of the 186 cultures studied. In all the other cultures, even though they differed widely in geographical region, economic characteristics, and many other ways, young lovers experienced the delight and despair of passionate love, told stories about famous lovers, and sang love songs.

In the West most adolescents have a romantic partner at some point in their teens.

However, this does not mean that young people in all cultures are allowed to act on their feelings of love. On the contrary, romantic love as the basis for marriage is a fairly new cultural idea (Hatfield & Rapson, 2005). As we will see in detail in Chapter 9, in most cultures throughout most of history marriages have been arranged by parents, with little regard for the passionate desires of their children.

CULTURAL VARIATIONS IN ADOLESCENT SEXUALITY Even though adolescents in all cultures go through similar biological processes in reaching sexual maturity, cultures vary enormously in how they view adolescent sexuality. Variations among countries in sexual behavior during adolescence is due primarily to variations in cultural beliefs about the acceptability (or not) of premarital sex. The best framework for understanding this variation among countries remains a book

that is now over 50 years old, *Patterns of Sexual Behavior,* by Clellan Ford and Frank Beach (1951). These two anthropologists compiled information about sexuality from over 200 cultures. On the basis of their analysis they described three types of cultural approaches to adolescent sexuality: *permissive, semirestrictive,* and *restrictive.*

Permissive cultures tolerate and even encourage adolescent sexuality. Most of the countries of Northern Europe today would fall into this category. Adolescents in these countries usually begin an active sexual life in their late teens, and parents often allow them to have a boyfriend or girlfriend spend the night (Trost, 2012).

Semirestrictive cultures have prohibitions on premarital adolescent sex. However, in these cultures the formal prohibitions are not strongly enforced and are easily evaded. Adults in these cultures tend to ignore evidence of premarital sexual behavior as long as young people are fairly discreet. Most developed countries today would fall into this category, including the United States, Canada, and most of Europe (Regnerus & Uecker, 2011).

Restrictive cultures place strong prohibitions on adolescent sexual activity before marriage. The prohibition on premarital sex is enforced through strong social norms and by keeping boys and girls separated through adolescence. Young people in Asia and South America tend to disapprove strongly of premarital sex, reflecting the view they have been taught by their cultures (Regan et al., 2004).

In some countries, the restrictiveness of the taboo on premarital sex even includes the threat of physical punishment and public shaming. A number of Arab countries take this approach, including Algeria, Syria, and Saudi Arabia. Premarital female virginity is a matter of not only the girl's honor but the honor of her family, and if she is known to lose her virginity before marriage, the males of her family may punish her, beat her, or even kill her (Moghadam, 2004). Although many cultures also value male premarital chastity, no culture punishes male premarital sex with such severity.

Even outside the Arab world, premarital sexual standards are usually more restrictive for girls than for boys. A *double standard* in cultural views of adolescent sexuality is common worldwide, in which premarital sex is allowed for boys but forbidden for girls (Crawford & Popp, 2003; Moore & Rosenthal, 2006). In cultures where the double standard is especially strong, boys sometimes gain their first sexual experience with prostitutes or with older women who are known to be friendly to the sexual interests of adolescent boys (Davis & Davis, 2012; Howard, 1998). However, this double standard also sets up a great deal of sexual and personal tension between adolescent girls and boys, with boys pressing for girls to relax their sexual resistance and girls fearful of the shame and disgrace that will fall on them (and not on the boy) if they should give in.

ADOLESCENT PREGNANCY AND CONTRACEPTIVE USE Although cultures vary in how they view adolescent sex, nearly everywhere in the world premarital pregnancy in adolescence is viewed as undesirable. Two types of countries have low rates of premarital pregnancy: those that are permissive about adolescent sex and those that are restrictive. Northern European countries such as Denmark, Sweden, and the Netherlands have low rates of adolescent pregnancy because they are permissive about adolescent sex (Avery & Lazdane, 2008; Boyle, 2001). There are explicit safe-sex campaigns in the media. Adolescents have easy access to all types of contraception. Parents accept that their children will become sexually active by their late teens. It is not uncommon for adolescents in these countries to have a boyfriend or girlfriend stay overnight (Trost, 2012).

At the other end of the spectrum, restrictive countries such as Japan, South Korea, and Morocco strictly forbid adolescent sex (Davis & Davis, 2012;

permissive culture culture that encourages and expects sexual activity from their adolescents

semirestrictive culture culture that has prohibitions on premarital adolescent sex, but the prohibitions are not strongly enforced and are easily evaded

restrictive culture culture that places strong prohibitions on adolescent sexual activity before marriage

My Virtual Child

What are your culture's beliefs regarding adolescent sexuality? How are these beliefs communicated to your virtual child?

THINKING CULTURALLY

Is there a gender double standard for adolescent sexuality in your culture?

Why are rates of adolescent pregnancy especially high in the United States?

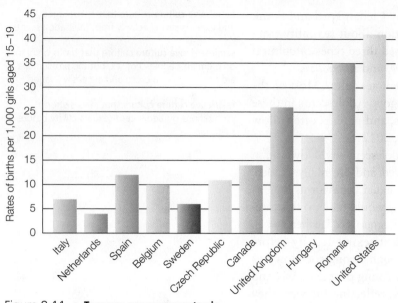

Figure 8.11 • **Teenage pregnancy rates in developed countries.** Why are rates so high in the United States? **Source:** Based on WHO, Method of delivery and pregnancy outcomes in Asia: The WHO global survey on maternal and perinatal health, 2007–2008. The Lancet, 375, 490–499.

◉⟦**Watch** the **Video** From an Objective Point of View: The Decision to Have Sex in **MyDevelopmentLab**

◉⟦**Watch** the **Video** Adolescent Sexuality in **MyDevelopmentLab**

◉⟦**Watch** the **Video** Adolescence: Identity and Role Development and Sexual Orientation in **MyDevelopmentLab**

sexual orientation a person's tendencies of sexual attraction

coming out for homosexuals, the process of acknowledging their homosexuality and then disclosing the truth to their friends, family, and others

homophobia fear and hatred of homosexuals

Hatfield & Rapson, 2005; Stevenson & Zusho, 2002). Adolescents in these countries are even strongly discouraged from dating until they are well into emerging adulthood and are seriously looking for a marriage partner. It is rare for an adolescent boy and girl even to spend time alone together, much less have sex. Some adolescents follow the call of nature anyway and violate the taboo, but violations are rare because the taboo is so strong and the shame of being exposed for breaking it is so great.

The United States has a higher rate of teenage pregnancy than any other developed country (Alan Guttmacher Institute [AGI], 2001; Teitler, 2002), as **Figure 8.11** illustrates. This is not because adolescents in the United States have more sex than those in other countries. The pregnancy rate among adolescents in Canada is less than half the rate in the United States, even though the percentages of adolescents in the two countries who are sexually active are nearly identical (AGI, 2001). Adolescents in European countries such as Sweden and Denmark are as likely as adolescents in the United States to be sexually active but much less likely to become pregnant (Avery & Lazdane, 2008; Teitler, 2002). ◉

The main reason American adolescents have high rates of teenage pregnancy may be that there is no clear cultural message regarding adolescent sexuality (Males, 2011). The semirestrictive view of adolescent sexuality prevails: Adolescent sex is not strictly forbidden, but neither is it widely accepted. As a consequence, most American adolescents have sexual intercourse at some time before they reach the end of their teens, but often those who are sexually active are not comfortable enough with their sexuality to acknowledge that they are having sex and to prepare for it responsibly by obtaining and using contraception. However, rates of teen pregnancy in the United States have declined steeply in the past two decades, especially among African Americans (Males, 2011). This may be because the threat of HIV/AIDS has made it more acceptable in the United States to talk to adolescents about sex and contraception and to provide them with sex education through the schools. ◉

SEXUAL ORIENTATION Adolescence is when most people first become fully aware of their **sexual orientation**, meaning their tendencies of sexual attraction. In American society, 2% of adolescents self-identify as lesbian, gay, or bisexual (LGB) (Michael et al., 1995; Savin-Williams, 2006). In the past in Western cultures, and still today in many of the world's cultures, most people would keep this knowledge to themselves all their lives because they would be stigmatized and persecuted if they disclosed the truth. Today in most Western cultures, however, LGBs commonly engage in a process of **coming out**, which involves a person's recognizing his or her own sexual identity and then disclosing the truth to friends, family, and others (Flowers & Buston, 2001; Savin-Williams, 2001). Awareness of an LGB sexual identity usually begins in early adolescence, with disclosure to others coming in late adolescence or emerging adulthood (Floyd & Bakeman, 2006). ◉

Given the pervasiveness of **homophobia** (fear and hatred of homosexuals) that exists in many societies (Baker, 2002), coming to the realization of an LGB identity can be traumatic for many adolescents. Lesbian, gay, or bisexual adolescents are often the targets of bullying when peers learn of their sexual identity (Mishna et al., 2009). Many parents respond with dismay or even anger when they learn that their adolescents are lesbian, gay, or bisexual. When parents reject LGB adolescents after learning of their sexual identity, the consequences are dire. One study found that LGB adolescents who experienced parental rejection were eight times more likely to report having attempted suicide, six times more likely to report high levels of depression, three times more likely to use illegal drugs, and three times more likely to have had unprotected sex than LGB adolescents whose parents were more accepting of their sexual orientation (Ryan et al., 2010).

Nevertheless, in recent years there has been a noticeable change in Western attitudes toward LGBs, constituting "a dramatic cultural shift" toward more favorable and tolerant perceptions, according to Ritch Savin-Williams (2005), a prominent researcher on LGB adolescents. Savin-Williams notes changes in popular culture, such as favorable portrayals of LGBs in television, movies, and popular songs. He also cites a national survey of 13- to 19-year-olds in the United States showing that the percentage who "don't have any problem" with homosexuality tripled over the past decade, to 54%. Of course, 54% is barely half and leaves plenty of room for continued homophobia and abuse, but it does show that public attitudes toward LGBs are becoming less hostile. Notably, the average age of coming out has declined in recent decades, from 21 in the 1970s to 16 in the present, perhaps because of growing acceptance of homosexuality (Savin-Williams, 2006). Several European countries and American states now allow same-sex marriages, another sign that people in the West are becoming more accepting of variations in sexual orientation.

Media use

Explain the function of media use in adolescents' lives and apply the Media Practice Model to the playing of electronic games.

LEARNING OBJECTIVE 8.21

No account of adolescent development would be complete without a description of the media they use. Recorded music, television, movies, magazines, electronic games, mobile phones, and the Internet are part of the daily environment for nearly all adolescents currently growing up in developed countries (and increasingly in developing countries as well). Studies across developed countries have found that adolescents use media for about six hours a day (Flammer et al., 1999; Roberts et al., 2005; Stevenson & Zusho, 2002). About one-fourth of their media use involves multiple media—listening to music while playing an electronic game, for example, or reading a magazine while watching TV (Roberts et al., 2005).

A MODEL OF ADOLESCENTS' MEDIA USES Spending six hours a day on anything means that it is a big part of your life, and many concerns have been expressed about adolescents' media use (Arnett, 2007a). Although claims are often made about the harmful effects of media on adolescents, their media use is more complex than simple cause and effect. A helpful model of the functions media play in the lives of adolescents has been presented by Jane Brown and her colleagues (Brown, 2006; Brown et al., 2002; Steele, 2006). An illustration of their model, called the *Media Practice Model,* is shown in *Figure 8.12*.

As the figure shows, the model proposes that adolescents' media use is active in a number of ways. Adolescents do not all have the same media preferences. Rather, each adolescent's identity motivates the *selection* of media products. Paying attention to certain media products leads to *interaction* with those products, meaning that the products are evaluated and interpreted. Then adolescents engage in *application* of the media content they have chosen. They may incorporate this content into their identities—for example, adolescents who respond to cigarette advertisements by taking up smoking—or they may resist the content—for example, adolescents who respond to cigarette advertisements by rejecting them as false and misleading. Their developing identity then motivates new media selections, and so on. This model reminds us that adolescents actively

Watch the **Video** Being Gay in High School in **MyDevelopmentLab**

Watch the **Video** Western Influences on the World's Societies in **MyDevelopmentLab**

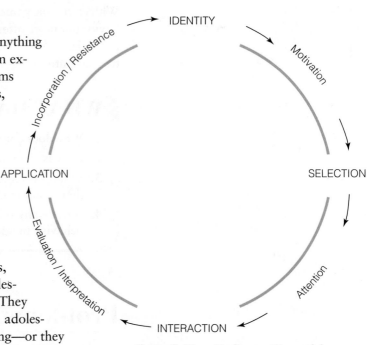

Figure 8.12 • **Media practice model.**
In this model, identity is the main motivator of media use.

select the media they use, and they respond to media content in diverse ways depending on how they interpret it and how it relates to them personally. Adolescents use media for many different purposes, but as with younger children, the focus of research on their media use has mainly been on concerns about negative effects. In the following discussion, we examine electronic games, which have been the focus of some of these concerns. (Chapter 9 will cover the use of mobile phones and social media such as Facebook.)

ELECTRONIC GAMES A relatively new type of media use among adolescents is electronic games, usually played on a computer or a handheld device. This form of media use has quickly become popular among adolescents, especially boys (Olson et al., 2008). In a study of middle school students in the United States (Olson et al., 2007), 94% reported having played electronic games during the preceding six months. Of those who played electronic games, one-third of boys and 11% of girls said they played nearly every day. A study in 10 European countries and Israel found that children ages 6 to 16 averaged more than a half hour per day playing electronic games (Beentjes et al., 2001).

The majority of adolescents' favorite electronic games involve violence. A content analysis of nearly 400 of the most popular electronic games found that 94% contained violence (Haninger & Thompson, 2004). A number of studies have examined the relation between violent electronic games and aggressiveness (Anderson et al., 2007; Brake, 2006; Funk et al., 1999; Funk et al., 2002; Funk, 2005). One study asked boys themselves about the effects of playing violent electronic games (Olson et al., 2008). The interviews showed that the boys (ages 12–14) used electronic games to experience fantasies of power and fame, and to explore what they perceived to be exciting new situations. The boys enjoyed the social aspect of electronic game playing, in playing with friends and talking about the games with friends. The boys also said they used electronic games to work through feelings of anger or stress, and that playing the games had a cathartic effect on these negative feelings. They did not believe that playing violent electronic games affected them negatively.

It seems likely that with electronic games, as with other violent media, there is a wide range of individual differences in responses, with young people who are already at risk for violent behavior being most likely to be affected by the games, as well as most likely to be attracted to them (Funk, 2003; Slater et al., 2003; Unsworth et al., 2007). With electronic games as with television, violent content may rarely provoke violent behavior but more often influence social attitudes. For example, playing violent electronic games has been found to lower empathy and raise the acceptability of violent responses to social situations (Anderson, 2004; Funk, 2005; Funk et al., 2002).

WHAT HAVE YOU LEARNED?

1. Why does conflict with parents increase during adolescence?
2. How is intimacy an important part of adolescent friendships?
3. What are some reasons that the pregnancy rate in the United States is higher than in other developed countries?
4. Is there any relation between playing violent electronic games and aggressive behavior in adolescence? Why or why not?

Problems and Resilience

After the relatively calm period of middle childhood, a variety of types of problems rise in prevalence during adolescence, including crime and delinquency and depressed mood. (Automobile accidents will be covered in Chapter 9.) However, most adolescents make it through this life stage without serious problems, and many adolescents exhibit resilience in the face of difficult conditions.

Crime and delinquency

> Summarize the explanations for why age and crime are so strongly correlated, and describe the multisystemic approach to combating delinquency.

LEARNING OBJECTIVE   **8.22**

Rates of crime begin rising in the mid-teens and peak at about age 18, then decline steadily. The great majority of crimes are committed by young people—mostly males—who are between the ages of 12 and 25 (Eisner, 2002). In the West, this finding is remarkably consistent over a period of greater than 150 years. **Figure 8.13** shows the age–crime relationship at two points, one in the 1840s and one relatively recent. At any point before, after, or in between these times, in most countries, the pattern would look very similar (Eisner, 2002; Gottfredson & Hirschi, 1990; Wilson & Herrnstein, 1985). Adolescents and emerging adults are not only more likely than children or adults to commit crimes but also more likely to be the victims of crimes (Cohen & Potter, 1999; Eisner, 2002). 👁

👁—⎡**Watch** the **Video** Risk Taking and Delinquency in **MyDevelopmentLab**

What explains the strong and consistent relationship between age and crime? One theory suggests that the key to explaining the age–crime relationship is that adolescents and emerging adults combine increased independence from parents and other adult authorities with increased time with peers and increased orientation toward peers (Wilson & Herrnstein, 1985). A consistent finding of research on crime is that crimes committed by young people in their teens and early twenties usually take place in a group, in contrast to the solitary crimes typical of adult offenders (Dishion & Dodge, 2005). Crime is an activity that in some adolescent cliques is encouraged and admired (Dishion et al., 1999). However, this theory does not explain why it is mainly boys who commit crimes, and girls, who also become more independent from parents and more peer-oriented in adolescence, rarely do.

Most surveys find that over three-fourths of adolescent boys commit at least one criminal act sometime before the age of 20 (Loeber & Burke, 2011; Moffitt, 2003).

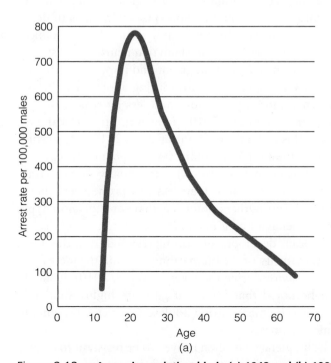

(a)

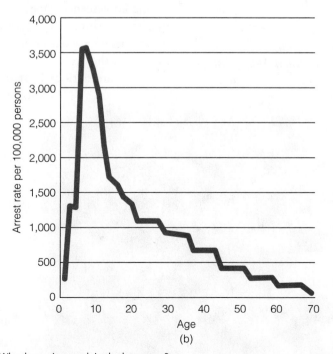

(b)

Figure 8.13 • **Age–crime relationship in (a) 1842 and (b) 1992.** Why does crime peak in the late teens?

life-course-persistent delinquent (LCPD) delinquent who shows a pattern of problems from birth onward and whose problems continue into adulthood

adolescent-limited delinquent (ALD) delinquent who shows no evidence of problems prior to adolescence and whose delinquent behavior in adolescence is temporary

However, there are obvious differences between committing one or two acts of minor crime—vandalism or underage drinking, for example—and committing crimes frequently over a long period, including more serious crimes such as rape and assault. Ten percent of young men commit over two-thirds of all offenses (Broidy et al., 2003). What are the differences between adolescents who commit an occasional minor violation of the law and adolescents who are at risk for more serious, long-term criminal behavior?

Terrie Moffitt (2003, 2007) has proposed a provocative theory in which she distinguishes between *adolescence-limited* delinquency and *life-course-persistent* delinquency. In Moffitt's view, these are two distinct types of delinquency, each with different motivations and different sources. However, the two types may be hard to distinguish from one another in adolescence, when criminal offenses are more common than in childhood or adulthood. The way to tell them apart, according to Moffitt, is to look at behavior before adolescence.

Life-course-persistent delinquents (LCPDs) show a pattern of problems from birth onward. Moffitt believes their problems originate in neuropsychological deficits that are evident in a difficult temperament in infancy and a high likelihood of attention-deficit/hyperactivity disorder (ADHD) and learning disabilities in childhood. Children with these problems are also more likely than other children to grow up in a high-risk environment (e.g., low-income family, single parent), with parents who have a variety of problems of their own. Consequently, their neurological deficits tend to be made worse rather than better by their environments. When they reach adolescence, children with the combination of neurological deficits and a high-risk environment are highly prone to engage in criminal activity. Furthermore, they tend to continue their criminal activity long after adolescence has ended, well into adulthood.

The **adolescence-limited delinquents (ALDs)** follow a much different pattern. They show no signs of problems in infancy or childhood, and few of them engage in any criminal activity after their mid-twenties. It is just during adolescence—actually, adolescence and emerging adulthood, ages 12 to 25—that they have a period of occasional criminal activity, breaking the law with behavior such as vandalism, theft, and use of illegal drugs.

As we have seen earlier in the chapter, the brain is still a long way from maturity during adolescence. Does the immaturity of the brain help explain why rates of delinquency and some other types of risk behavior are higher in adolescence than at younger ages? This theory has been proposed by researchers who claim that neurological studies show that the brain's frontal lobe areas in charge of judgment and impulse control are not mature until at least the mid-twenties; consequently, during adolescence behavior is governed more by emotions and less by reason than in later years (Steinberg, 2010). However, other researchers dispute this conclusion (Johnson et al., 2010). Some studies have found that the brain development of adolescents who engage in risky behavior is actually *more* mature in some ways than in their less risk-prone peers (Berns et al., 2009). Others point out that rates of most types of risk behavior continue to increase into the early twenties; brain development also increases during this time, so immaturity of the brain cannot explain the increase in risk behavior during these years (Males, 2010). It should also be noted that boys and girls are highly similar in brain development during adolescence, yet boys commit far more crimes.

Delinquency has often proven to be resistant to change in adolescence, but one successful approach has been to

Street children in Honduras examine watches they have stolen. What distinguishes the two types of delinquency?

intervene at several levels, including the home, the school, and the neighborhood. This is known as the *multisystemic approach* (Borduin et al., 2003; Henggler et al., 2007; Saldana & Henggler, 2006; Swenson et al., 2005). Programs based on this approach include parent training, job training and vocational counseling, and the development of neighborhood activities such as youth centers and athletic leagues. The goal is to direct the energy of delinquents into more socially constructive directions. The multisystemic approach has now been adopted by youth agencies in 32 states and 12 countries (Schoenwald et al., 2008). As *Figure 8.14* illustrates, programs using this approach have been shown to be effective in reducing arrests and out-of-home placements among delinquents (Alexander, 2001; Henggler et al., 2007; Ogden & Amlund-Hagen, 2006). Furthermore, multisystemic programs have been found to be cheaper than other programs, primarily because they reduce the amount of time that delinquent adolescents spend in foster homes and detention centers (Alexander, 2001).

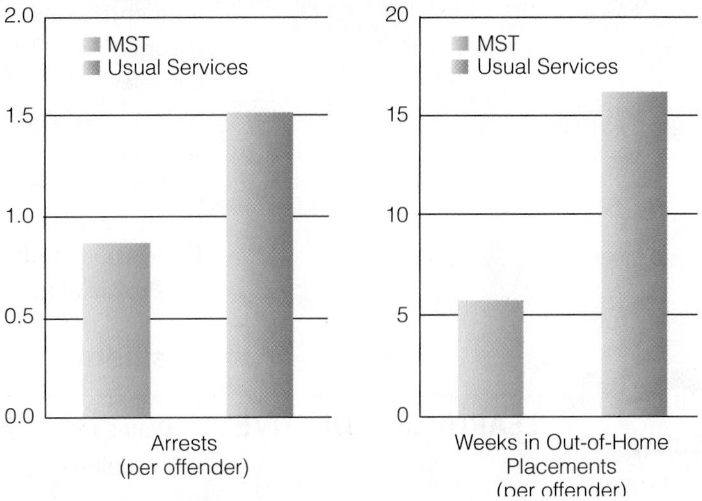

Figure 8.14 • **Multisystemic Approach to Delinquency** Why is MST more effective than other types of interventions for delinquency? **Source:** Arnett, Jeffery Jensen, Adolescence and Emerging Adulthood: A cultural approach, 3rd Ed., (c) 2007. Reprinted and electronically reproduced by permission of Pearson Education, Inc. Upper Saddle River, New Jersey.

Depression

> Identify the different types and rates of depression and summarize the most effective treatments.

LEARNING OBJECTIVE 8.23

Do you remember feeling sad at times during your teen years? As we have seen earlier in the chapter, studies of adolescents' emotional lives have found that they experience sadness and other negative emotions much more frequently than do younger children or adults.

Psychologists make distinctions between different levels of depression. **Depressed mood** is a term for a temporary period of sadness, without any related symptoms. The most serious form of depression is **major depressive disorder**, which includes a more enduring period of sadness along with other symptoms such as frequent crying, feelings of worthlessness, and feeling guilty, lonely, or worried. Major depressive disorder may also include symptoms such as difficulty sleeping and changes in appetite (American Psychiatric Association [APA], 2013).

Although a diagnosis of major depressive disorder is relatively rare in adolescence, several studies find that adolescents have higher rates of depressed mood than adults or children (Compas et al., 1998; Petersen et al., 1993; Saluja et al., 2004). Rates of depressed mood rise steeply from age 10 and reach a "mid-adolescence peak" about ages 15 to 17, then decline in the late teens and twenties (Campbell, 2006).

A variety of studies have shown that the proportion of adolescents who report experiencing depressed mood within the past six months is about 30% (Campbell, 2006). In contrast, rates of major depressive disorder among adolescents is about 6% (Campbell, 2006), which is about the same rate found in studies of adults. The most common causes of depressed mood tend to be common experiences among adolescents: conflict with friends or family members, disappointment or rejection in love, and poor performance in school (Costello et al., 2008; Larson & Richards, 1994).

One of strongest risk factors for all types of depression in adolescence and beyond is simply being female (Hammack et al., 2004). A variety of explanations have been proposed. Some scholars have suggested that body image concerns provoke depression. There is substantial evidence that adolescent girls who have a poor body image are more likely than other girls to be depressed (Graber et al., 1997; Marcotte et al., 2002; Wichstrom et al., 1999).

For adolescents as for adults, the two main types of treatment for depression are antidepressant medications and psychotherapy. Recent studies indicate that newly developed

Watch the **Video** Depression in **MyDevelopmentLab**

depressed mood enduring period of sadness, without any other related symptoms of depression

major depressive disorder clinical diagnosis that includes a range of specific symptoms such as depressed mood, appetite disturbances, sleeping disturbances, and fatigue

antidepressants such as Prozac are highly effective in treating adolescent depression (Bostic et al., 2005; Brent, 2004; Cohen et al., 2004; Emslie et al., 2002; Michael & Crowley, 2002). The combination of the newest medications and psychotherapy appear to be the most effective approach to treating adolescent depression. In one recent major study of 12- to 17-year-olds at 13 sites across the United States who had been diagnosed with major depression, 71% of the adolescents who received both Prozac and psychotherapy experienced an improvement in their symptoms (Treatment for Adolescents with Depression Study Team, 2004, 2007). Improvement rates for the other groups were 61% for Prozac alone, 43% for psychotherapy alone, and 35% for the placebo group.

Resilience in adolescence

8.24   **LEARNING OBJECTIVE**   Define resilience and name the protective factors that are related to resilience in adolescence.

resilience overcoming adverse environmental circumstances and achieving healthy development despite those circumstances

protective factors characteristics of young people that are related to lower likelihood of problems despite experiencing high-risk circumstances

APPLYING YOUR KNOWLEDGE
. . . as a Teacher

You teach in a school where many students live in poverty. How might you help students avoid high-risk behavior?

When adolescents develop problems, the source of the problems can often be traced to risk factors such as poverty, poor family relationships, abusive or neglectful parenting, and inadequate schools. However, there are also many adolescents who face dire conditions yet manage to adapt and function well. **Resilience** is the term for this phenomenon, defined as "good outcomes in spite of serious threats to adaptation and development" (Masten, 2001, p. 228). Sometimes "good outcomes" are measured as notable academic or social achievements, sometimes as psychological traits such as high well-being or self-esteem, and sometimes as the absence of notable problems. Young people who are resilient are not necessarily high achievers who have some kind of extraordinary ability. More often they display what resilience researcher Ann Masten calls the "ordinary magic" of being able to function reasonably well despite being faced with unusually difficult circumstances (Masten, 2001, p. 227).

Resilience is promoted by **protective factors** that enable adolescents to overcome the risk factors in their lives. Some of the most important protective factors identified in resilience research are:

- high intelligence: high intelligence may allow an adolescent to perform well academically despite going to a low-quality school and living in a disorderly household (Masten et al., 2006);

- physical attractiveness (Dijkstra, Lindenberg, Verhulst, Ormel, & Veenstra, 2009);

- parenting that provides an effective balance of warmth and control: effective parenting may help an adolescent have a positive self-image and avoid antisocial behavior despite growing up in poverty and living in a rough neighborhood (Brody & Flor, 1998);

- engaging in religious practices (Smith & Denton, 2005) (see section on religion above); and

- a caring adult "mentor" outside the family: a mentor may foster high academic goals and good future planning in an adolescent whose family life is characterized by abuse or neglect (Rhodes & DuBois, 2008).

A mentor can be a source of resilience for adolescents at risk for problems. Here, an adolescent girl and her mentor in the Big Sisters program.

One classic study followed a group of infants from birth through adolescence (Werner & Smith, 1982, 1992, 2001). It is known as the Kauai (pronounced *Ka-wa-ee*) study, after the Hawaiian island where the study took place. The Kauai study focused on a high-risk group of children who had four or more risk factors by age 2, such as problems in physical development, parents' marital conflict, parental drug abuse, low maternal education, and poverty. Out of this group, there was a resilient subgroup that showed good social and academic functioning and few behavior problems by ages 10–18. Compared with their less resilient peers, adolescents in the resilient group were found to benefit from several protective factors, including one well-functioning parent, higher intelligence, and higher physical attractiveness.

More recent studies have supported the Kauai findings but also broadened the range of protective factors (Masten, 2007). *Religiosity* has become recognized as an especially important protective factor. Adolescents who have a strong religious faith are less likely to have problems such as substance abuse, even when they have grown up in a high-risk environment (Howard et al., 2007; Wallace et al., 2007).

WHAT HAVE YOU LEARNED?

1. How does spending more time with peers influence adolescent crime?
2. What is the multisystemic approach to delinquency and how successful has it been?
3. Why are females more likely than males to be depressed?
4. What is a protective factor that enables adolescents to overcome risk factors in their lives?

Section 3 VIDEO GUIDE　Adolescent Conflict With Parents Across Cultures (Length: 8:19)

Adolescents from a variety of cultures are interviewed in this video. They discuss their changing relationships with their parents as well as with their friends.

1. One common thread across all of the interviewed teens was that they keep secrets from their elders. Do you feel that this is a universal trend among teens? Why or why not?

2. The narrator tells us that interdependence is valued in the Mexican village where one of the female teens is from. Do you feel that U.S. families could impact their teen's lives if they placed a higher value on interdependence rather than independence? Explain.

3. In comparing the adolescents interviewed in this clip, do you feel that gender plays an important role in parent–child conflict?

◉—[**Watch** the **Video** Adolescent Conflict with Parents Across Cultures in **MyDevelopmentLab**

Summing Up

((•—[Listen to an audio file of your chapter in **MyDevelopmentLab**

SECTION 1   PHYSICAL DEVELOPMENT

8.1   List the physical changes that begin puberty.

Increases in sex hormones lead to the development of primary and secondary sex characteristics. Recent findings in brain research show that the adolescent brain develops in some surprising ways, including a burst of overproduction (followed by synaptic pruning) and increased myelination.

8.2   Describe the normative timing of pubertal events, cultural variations, and how being early or late influences emotional and social development.

The timing of pubertal events is determined partly by genes, but puberty generally begins earlier in cultures with adequate nutrition and medical care. Early maturing girls are at risk for a wide variety of problems, in part because they draw the attention of older boys.

8.3   Identify the main gender differences in puberty rituals worldwide.

Most non-Western cultures mark puberty with a community ritual. For boys, puberty rituals often entail tests of strength and endurance, whereas for girls puberty rituals center around menarche.

8.4   Describe the prevalence, symptoms, and treatment of eating disorders.

Eating disorders are most prevalent in adolescence and emerging adulthood, and occur mainly among females. Prevalence of symptoms is higher; in some Western countries one-third of girls report eating disordered behavior such as fasting for more than 24 hours and using laxatives to control weight. Treatments for eating disorders have had mixed success.

8.5   Classify adolescent substance use into four categories.

Adolescents' substance use can be classified as experimental, social, medicinal, or addictive. Adolescents whose substance use is addictive experience withdrawal symptoms when they reduce or stop their use of the substance.

KEY TERMS

puberty *p. 353*	estradiol *p. 355*	menarche *p. 355*	anorexia nervosa *p. 361*
adolescence *p. 353*	testosterone *p. 355*	spermarche *p. 355*	bulimia *p. 361*
estrogens *p. 354*	primary sex characteristics *p. 355*	secular trend *p. 357*	self-medication *p. 364*
androgens *p. 354*	secondary sex characteristics *p. 355*	puberty ritual *p. 359*	

SECTION 2   COGNITIVE DEVELOPMENT

8.6   Explain the features of hypothetical-deductive reasoning and give an example of how it is assessed.

Hypothetical-deductive reasoning entails the ability to test solutions to a problem systematically, altering one variable while holding the others constant. The pendulum problem is one way Piaget tested the attainment of formal operations.

8.7   Recall the two major critiques of Piaget's theory of formal operations.

Piaget proposed that when adolescents reach formal operations they use it for all cognitive activities; however, research has shown that both adolescents and adults tend to use formal operations in some areas of their lives but not in others. Piaget also proposed that formal operations is a universal stage of cognitive development, but its prevalence appears to vary across cultures as measured by standard tasks, although it may be used in the course of culturally specific daily activities.

8.8   Summarize the major changes in attention and memory that take place from middle childhood to adolescence.

Information processing abilities improve in adolescence, notably selective attention, divided attention, and use of mnemonic devices.

8.9 Define the imaginary audience and the personal fable and explain how they reflect egocentrism in adolescence.

The imaginary audience is the exaggerated belief that others are paying intense attention to one's appearance and behavior. The personal fable is the belief that there is something special and unique about one's personal destiny. The imaginary audience results from adolescents' egocentric inability to distinguish their thoughts about themselves from their thoughts about others' thoughts.

8.10 Produce an example of the zone of proximal development and scaffolding involving adolescents.

Scaffolding and the zone of proximal development are evident in adolescence, when the skills necessary to adult work are being learned. For example, male adolescents in the Dioula culture in Ivory Coast are first taught simple weaving patterns but learn increasingly complex patterns as their skills improve in response to correction and instruction by their fathers, until they can weave entirely by themselves.

8.11 Compare and contrast the secondary education systems and academic performance of developed countries and developing countries.

The United States, Canada, and Japan have a comprehensive high school, but most other countries have at least three different types of secondary school. Academic performance is generally higher in developed countries than in developing countries, but highest of all in Asian developed countries, where pressure to excel is high.

8.12 Summarize the typical forms of adolescent work and characterize the impact it has on their development.

In the United States, adolescents typically perform jobs that they will not perform as adults. In developed countries, working more than 10 hours per week interferes with adolescents' school performance. In some European countries, apprenticeships are available, in which adolescents spend part of their time in school and part of their time in the workplace receiving direct occupational training.

KEY TERMS

formal operations *p. 366*

hypothetical-deductive
  reasoning *p. 366*

divided attention *p. 369*

metacognition *p. 370*

adolescent egocentrism *p. 370*

imaginary audience *p. 370*

personal fable *p. 370*

secondary school *p. 372*

rote learning *p. 374*

apprenticeship *p. 376*

SECTION 3   EMOTIONAL AND SOCIAL DEVELOPMENT

8.13 Summarize the results of the ESM studies with respect to adolescent emotionality.

Experience Sampling Method (ESM) studies show greater mood swings in adolescence than in middle childhood or adulthood. Also, there is a decline in overall emotional state from fifth grade through 10th grade.

8.14 Describe how self-understanding, self-concept, and self-esteem change during adolescence.

Self-development in adolescence is complex and may include an ideal self, a possible self, a feared self, and a false self along with an actual self. Overall self-esteem often declines in adolescence, especially for girls. Self-concept includes a variety of aspects in adolescence, but overall self-concept is strongly influenced by self-perceptions of physical attractiveness.

8.15 Compare and contrast the cultural patterns in gender expectations for girls and boys in adolescence.

Adolescence is a time of gender intensification, as young people become more aware of the gender expectations of their culture. Boys in many cultures risk becoming a failed man unless they learn to provide, protect, and procreate. Girls are generally believed to reach womanhood when they reach menarche.

8.16 Discriminate between Kohlberg's theory of moral development and Jensen's worldviews theory.

Kohlberg proposed three universal levels of moral development: preconventional reasoning, conventional reasoning, and postconventional reasoning. According to Jensen, morality develops in culturally-diverse ways based on Ethics of Autonomy, Community, and Divinity.

8.17 Describe the cultural variations in religious beliefs during adolescence as well as the sources and outcomes of religiosity within cultures.

American adolescents are more religious than adolescents in other developed countries. In general, higher religiosity is related to a variety of positive features of adolescents' development, such as better relationships with parents and lower rates of substance use.

8.18 Summarize the cultural variations in adolescents' relationships with parents, siblings, and extended family.

Adolescence is a time of increased conflict with parents in cultures that promote autonomy. Sibling conflict is not as high in adolescence as in earlier life stages, but adolescents have more conflict with siblings than in any of their other relationships. Relations with grandparents tend to be close and positive worldwide.

8.19 Describe cultural variations in adolescents' relationships with friends, and characterize their interactions with peers.

In most cultures, adolescents spend less time with family and more time with friends than they did in middle childhood. Intimacy is more important in adolescent friendships than at earlier ages. Adolescents also have groups of friends, or "cliques," and see their peers as falling into "crowds." Bullying is more common in adolescence than at other ages.

8.20 Identify cultural variations in adolescent love and sexuality, including variations in adolescent pregnancy and contraceptive use.

Cultures vary widely in their tolerance of adolescent sexuality, from permissive to semirestrictive to restrictive. Rates of adolescent pregnancy are lowest in cultures that are highly accepting of adolescent sexuality and in those that strictly forbid it. American adolescents have high rates of adolescent pregnancy, due mainly to the mixed cultural messages they receive about adolescent sexuality.

8.21 Explain the function of media use in adolescents' lives and apply the Media Practice Model to the playing of electronic games.

Adolescents are avid users of a wide range of media, from television and music to electronic games and mobile phones. Concern has been expressed about the potential negative effects of playing electronic games, mainly focusing on aggressive behavior and attitudes, but positive effects have been found in areas such as mood regulation.

8.22 Summarize the explanations for why age and crime are so strongly correlated, and describe the multisystemic approach to combating delinquency.

According to one theory, age and crime are highly correlated because adolescents are more independent from parents than at earlier ages and also more peer-oriented. The multisystemic approach entails intervening at several levels, including home, school, and neighborhood.

8.23 Identify the different types and rates of depression and summarize the most effective treatments.

Depressed mood involves a relatively brief period of sadness, whereas major depression entails a more enduring period of sadness combined with a variety of other symptoms, such as disruptions in patterns of sleeping and eating. Although major depression is rare in adolescence, depressed mood is more common in adolescence than in any other life stage, especially among adolescent girls. The most effective approach to treating adolescent depression combines the newest medications and psychotherapy.

8.24 Define resilience and name the protective factors that are related to resilience in adolescence.

Resilience means functioning well despite adverse circumstances. Some of the protective factors promoting resilience in adolescence are high intelligence, a good relationship with a parent or mentor, and physical attractiveness.

KEY TERMS

actual self *p. 380*
possible self *p. 380*
ideal self *p. 380*
feared self *p. 380*
false self *p. 380*
gender-intensification
   hypothesis *p. 381*
preconventional reasoning *p. 383*

conventional reasoning *p. 384*
postconventional
   reasoning *p. 384*
worldview *p. 385*
secular *p. 386*
autonomy *p. 388*
intimacy *p. 391*
clique *p. 392*

crowd *p. 392*
cyberbullying *p. 393*
permissive culture *p. 395*
semirestrictive culture *p. 395*
restrictive culture *p. 395*
sexual orientation *p. 396*
coming out *p. 396*
homophobia *p. 396*

life-course-persistent delinquent
   (LCPD) *p. 400*
adolescent-limited delinquent
   (ALD) *p. 400*
depressed mood *p. 401*
major depressive disorder *p. 401*
resilience *p. 402*
protective factors *p. 402*

Practice Test

✓●─ **Study** and **Review** in **MyDevelopmentLab**

1. Estradiol:
   a. is produced only in females.
   b. increases in females by the midteens.
   c. is an androgen important in pubertal development.
   d. is a sex hormone that is regulated by the amygdala.

2. Which of the following best describes pubertal timing?
   a. The average age of menarche is much later today than it was in earlier generations.
   b. Menarche takes place as late as age 15 in some developing countries, due to lack of proper nutrition and medical care.
   c. The timing of puberty has no effect on adolescent boys.
   d. The effects of early maturation are generally positive for girls.

3. Puberty rituals:
   a. developed to mark the departure from adolescence into emerging adulthood.
   b. are only carried out for females and are most often related to menstruation.
   c. are declining in many cultures as a consequence of globalization.
   d. focus on a particular biological event across all cultures.

4. In the United States, girls:
   a. who have an eating disorder are also more likely than other females to be depressed.
   b. with bulimia are usually about 20% overweight.
   c. who are Asian American are more likely to have eating disorders than are those in other ethnic groups.
   d. are more likely than boys to be satisfied with their bodies.

5. The substance use of an adolescent who drinks alcohol to relieve feelings of sadness and loneliness would be classified as:
   a. social substance use.
   b. medicinal substance use.
   c. experimental substance use.
   d. addictive substance use.

6. Compared to the concrete thinking abilities displayed in childhood, the ability to reason in adolescence:
   a. utilizes the hypothetical thinking involved in a scientific experiment.
   b. involves more random attempts at problem solving as they persist longer.
   c. differs quantitatively but not qualitatively.
   d. is not significantly different.

7. Which of the following is the most accurate statement based on research on formal operational thinking?
   a. Educational background is unlikely to impact performance on Piagetian tasks.
   b. Once people obtain formal operational thinking skills, they use them consistently across all tasks and situations.
   c. All people reach the formal operational stage of cognitive development by age 12.
   d. The way that formal operational thinking is manifested is likely different across different cultures.

8. Compared to his 7-year-old brother, a 14-year-old will have an easier time reading a book and listening to music at the same time because he's more adept at:
   a. using mnemonic devices consistently.
   b. tasks that require divided attention.
   c. tasks that require transfer of information from sensory memory to short-term memory.
   d. maximizing his metamemory.

9. Compared to his brother in college, Jonah is more likely to think that if he starts smoking marijuana, he will be able to quit when he wants to and nothing bad will happen. This way of thinking demonstrates:
   a. the personal fable.
   b. the imaginary audience.
   c. selective attention.
   d. hypothetical reasoning.

10. After learning to knit a simple scarf with her grandmother's guidance, Alexis began to knit a sweater while on break from college. She went over to her grandmother's when she had a question and was almost done when it was time to go back to school. She finished a few weeks later, needing only one Skype help session. Her grandmother recently mailed her a pattern so she can knit a handbag. This illustrates:
    a. selective attention.
    b. synaptic pruning.
    c. scaffolding.
    d. hypothetical-deductive reasoning.

11. Compared to their peers in the United States, adolescents in Eastern countries:
    a. have a shorter school day.
    b. have a shorter school year.
    c. have to take entrance exams for both high school and college.
    d. focus almost exclusively on critical thinking.

12. Adolescents in developed countries who work part-time:
    a. are less likely to use drugs and alcohol than their non-working counterparts.
    b. have higher grades in school than other students.
    c. usually contribute the majority of their earnings to support the household income.
    d. do not typically see their high school jobs as the basis for a future career.

13. A developmental psychologist would most likely use the Experience Sampling Method (ESM):
    a. to evaluate the strength of cohort differences.
    b. to examine changes in emotions at various time points.
    c. to examine how different environmental experiences affect brain development.
    d. to determine whether behavioral differences between males and females become more pronounced in the transition from childhood to adolescence.

14. Adolescents are most likely to exhibit their false selves with:
    a. close friends.
    b. dating partners.
    c. acquaintances.
    d. parents.

15. In traditional cultures, girls reach womanhood mainly through:
    a. their achievements.
    b. the same means that males reach manhood.
    c. their biological changes.
    d. protecting their young.

16. Research on Kohlberg's stages of moral development has shown that:
    a. the stage of moral reasoning achieved tends to increase with age.
    b. over time, people regress to an earlier stage of moral reasoning.
    c. people often skip stages and advance to the highest stage in adulthood.
    d. the majority of people reach Stage 5: community rights and individual rights orientation.

17. Religious faith and practices are:
    a. usually weaker among African Americans than among Whites in the United States.
    b. associated with less depression and lower rates of drug use among adolescents.
    c. highest among adolescents in Europe compared to adolescents in other countries.
    d. the main priority of most American adolescents' lives.

18. In the United States, conflict in adolescence:
    a. is especially intense and frequent between fathers and sons.
    b. steadily increases until the end of emerging adulthood.
    c. is more frequent between early maturing adolescents and their parents compared to "on-time" adolescents and their parents.
    d. is similar in frequency to that observed in traditional cultures.

19. Which of the following would you be LEAST LIKELY to hear an American female adolescent say:
    a. "If I need relationship advice I will ask my parents."
    b. "I feel most comfortable talking to my best friend about my deepest secrets."
    c. "I have the most fun when I am with my friends."
    d. "If I had the choice, I would rather hang out with my friends than go on vacation with my family."

20. On the basis of anthropological evidence, the United States would be considered a(n) _____ culture in terms of its cultural beliefs about the acceptability (or not) of premarital sex.
    a. permissive
    b. authoritarian
    c. semirestrictive
    d. restrictive

21. Research on the media use of adolescents:
    a. has found that only females report that they enjoy the social aspect of gaming.
    b. has found that adolescents in industrialized countries use media for about two hours every day.
    c. has focused primarily on the benefits, such as increasing problem-solving ability and strategizing.
    d. has shown that the content of electronic games is related to their emotional responses.

22. Which of the following best describes the relationships between age and crime?
    a. Adolescents are less likely than adults to commit crimes because they do not have enough opportunity to do so.
    b. Adolescents are less likely to be the victims of crime than are children or adults.
    c. Adolescents are likely to commit crimes alone because they worry about their reputation if they get caught.
    d. A small percentage of adolescents commit the majority of crimes.

23. Which of the following statements about depression is true?
    a. Rates of major depressive disorder are higher among adolescents than rates of depressed mood.
    b. Psychotherapy alone was as effective in treating adolescent depression as psychotherapy combined with medication.
    c. Rates of depressed mood reach a peak between the ages of 15 and 17.
    d. Boys are more likely than girls to show increases in depressed mood during adolescence.

24. Research on resilience has shown that:
    a. bouncing back from adversity requires a high level of achievement and extraordinary abilities.
    b. high intelligence characterizes many individuals who are considered resilient.
    c. as a group, girls are more resilient than boys.
    d. parenting has no influence on resilience.

9 Emerging Adulthood

Andy, age 21, lives with his girlfriend in a modest one-bedroom apartment in central Missouri. He went to college but dropped out after two years, partly because he missed home and partly because he was not sure what he wanted to study. He had been majoring in landscape architecture at college because he is "an outdoors person," but after studying it for a while he became less interested in it as a future career. He does not know what he would like to do instead, so he is working for a landscaping firm, mowing lawns and trimming shrubs, until he decides what to do next. He is also uncertain about love. Although he lives with his girlfriend, he moved in with her mainly for financial reasons and does not see her as part of his future. He is thinking of moving to San Francisco in a few months to make a new start in a new place. (Based on Arnett, 2004.)

Chunming, age 19, recently left the small Chinese village where she grew up and migrated to Guangdong, one of China's booming industrial cities. Her parents objected; in her village, it was said that girls who went to the city would be tricked into a life of prostitution. But Chunming felt there was no future for her in the village, and left anyway. In Guangdong, a cousin helped her get a job in a factory making athletic shoes. Chunming lives in a factory dormitory, where she shares a room with nine other young women who work in the factory. They work on the assembly line 10½ hours a day, 5 days a week, plus a half day on Saturday, for a salary of about 72 U.S. dollars a month. Nevertheless, she feels lucky. She dreams of finding a sweet and handsome husband, and perhaps starting a small business with him, or at least finding a job outside the factory. (Based on Chang, 2008.)

Amit, age 21, lives with his aunt and uncle in Bangalore, India, and works for an Internet company based in the United States. He spends his days answering e-mail queries from people who are having technical problems with the company's website. The Internet company provided him with training to improve his written English and to enable him to answer the technical questions he receives. He enjoys the work, but he hopes to rise in the company in the future. He misses his mother and father and three sisters, who have remained in the small village where he grew up. Nevertheless, he enjoys the freedom and diversity of city life. His parents want to arrange a marriage for him soon, with a girl from the next village whom he has not met; his parents married at age 12, and feel he is long past the age when he should have been married. But Amit would prefer to remain single for some years, and he would also prefer to choose his own wife, although he has not yet broken this news to his parents. (Based on Chaudhary & Sharma, 2012.)

Marie, age 24, is a student at a university in Denmark, studying psychology. Currently she is in Italy, collecting interviews for a research project, and living with her Brazilian boyfriend Pablo, who is studying engineering there. Her plan is to become a psychologist who works with deaf children and their families, but much of her life is up in the air right now. How much more education should she pursue, if any? She and Pablo would like to marry and have two children eventually, but when? Their lives are busy now. How could they fit children in amid their other ambitions and adventures? (Based on Arnett, 2007b.)

The lives of Andy, Chunming, Amit, and Marie are highly diverse. However, one thing they have in common is that their lives are vastly different than what their parents or grandparents experienced at a similar age. The lives of young people all over the world have changed dramatically over the past half century. This chapter is about the new life stage of *emerging adulthood* that has developed as a consequence of those changes.

> *Their lives are vastly different than what their parents or grandparents experienced at a similar age.*

SECTION 1   PHYSICAL DEVELOPMENT

LEARNING OBJECTIVES

9.1 Name the five developmental features distinctive to emerging adulthood.

9.2 Describe some of the ways emerging adulthood varies among cultures, with specific reference to European and Asian countries.

9.3 Name the indicators that emerging adulthood is a period of peak physical functioning.

9.4 Summarize college students' sleep patterns and the main elements of sleep hygiene.

9.5 Explain why young drivers have the highest rates of crashes, and name the most effective approach to reducing those rates.

9.6 Explain why rates of substance use peak in the early twenties and then decline.

The Emergence of Emerging Adulthood

Before we examine the changes in physical development that occur in emerging adulthood, let's begin with a closer look at the origins of this new life stage. Traditionally, theories of human development described a stage of adolescence followed by a stage of young adulthood (Erikson, 1950; Levinson, 1978). The transition to young adulthood was assumed to be marked by entry to adult roles, specifically marriage, parenthood, and stable work. For most people, entry into these roles took place by their early twenties.

In recent decades, however, it has increasingly been recognized that these traditional stage models no longer fit the pattern of development that most people experience, especially in developed countries. Many of the jobs available in the modern world economy are based substantially on information and technology, and require education and training that last into the early twenties or beyond. The twenties are not a time of settling into a stable occupational path but a time of exceptional instability in work, as the completion of education and training is followed by multiple job changes, for most people. Similarly, most people marry and become parents in their late twenties or early thirties rather than in their early twenties. All together, the stable structure of an adult life is constructed closer to age thirty than age twenty for most people in developed countries; "Thirty is the new twenty," as a popular American saying puts it.

As a consequence of these changes, it is increasingly recognized among scholars in human development that a new life stage has developed between adolescence and young adulthood. Rather than making the transition from adolescence to young adulthood quickly at around age twenty, most people in developed countries experience a stage of **emerging adulthood** from their late teens to at least their mid-twenties, before entering a more stable young adulthood at around age thirty (Arnett, 2004, 2007b, 2011).

Many changes have contributed to the emergence of emerging adulthood as a normative life stage in developed countries. Perhaps the most obvious indicator is the rise in the ages of entering marriage and parenthood. As recently as 1960 the median age of marriage in most developed countries was in the very early twenties, around age 21 for women and 23 for men (Douglass, 2005). However, since 1960 there has been a dramatic

emerging adulthood new life stage in developed countries, lasting from the late teens through the twenties, in which people are gradually making their way toward taking on adult responsibilities in love and work

Today in developed countries, young women exceed young men in educational attainment and have a wide range of opportunities in the workplace that they did not have before.

Map 9.1 • **Median Age at First Marriage in the United States.** Which states have the lowest and highest age of first marriages? How does the median age of marriage differ between men and women? How might you explain these differences?

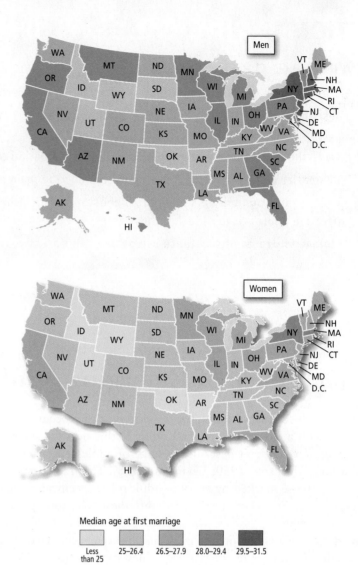

Median age at first marriage

Less than 25 | 25–26.4 | 26.5–27.9 | 28.0–29.4 | 29.5–31.5

APPLYING YOUR KNOWLEDGE

At what ages did your grandparents finish their education, marry, and have their first child? Ask them why they made those transitions at the ages they did.

APPLYING YOUR KNOWLEDGE ... as a Therapist

Kenji is a 70-year-old father of a 26-year-old unmarried daughter. He worries that his daughter will never marry. How can you help him feel better about his daughter's situation?

shift in the ages when young people in developed countries typically get married, with the median age of marriage around 30 for women, and even higher for men (by about two years, consistently across countries). **Map 9.1** shows the median age of marriage in the United States, which has a relatively low marriage age compared to other developed countries. Age at entering parenthood followed a similar rise.

But why the dramatic rise in the typical ages of entering marriage and parenthood? The invention of the birth control pill in 1964, in combination with less stringent standards of sexual morality after the sexual revolution of the 1960s and early 1970s, meant that young people no longer had to enter marriage in order to have a stable sexual relationship. Now most young people have a series of sexual relationships before entering marriage, and there is widespread tolerance for premarital sex in the context of a committed, loving relationship. Another important factor is the increase in the years devoted to pursuing education and training for an occupation. In many developed countries, over half of young people now obtain education and training beyond secondary school (Arnett, 2011). Most young people wait until they have finished school before they start thinking seriously about marriage and parenthood, and for many of them this means postponing these commitments until at least their mid-twenties.

Another key change contributing to the emergence of emerging adulthood concerns the opportunities available to women. The young women of the 1950s and early 1960s were under a great deal of social pressure to find a husband. Relatively few women attended college, and those who did were often there for the purpose of meeting their future husbands. The range of occupations open to young women was severely restricted, as it had been traditionally—secretary, waitress, teacher, nurse, perhaps a few others. Even these occupations were supposed to be temporary for young women. What they were really supposed to be focusing on was finding a husband and having children.

For the young women of the 21st century, all this has changed. In nearly every developed country, at every level of education from grade school through graduate school, girls now excel over boys. Young women's occupational possibilities are now virtually unlimited, and although men still dominate in engineering and some sciences, women are equal to men in obtaining law, business, and medical degrees. With so many options open to them, and with so little pressure on them to marry in their early twenties, the lives of young women in developed countries today have changed almost beyond recognition from what they were 50 years ago. Like young men, they typically spend the years from the late teens through at least the mid-twenties trying out various possible options before making definite choices.

My Virtual Child

Will your virtual child experience emerging adulthood? How has your culture supported this stage of development?

Five features

> Name the five developmental features distinctive to emerging adulthood.

LEARNING OBJECTIVE 9.1

What are the main features of emerging adulthood? What makes it distinct from the adolescence that precedes it and the young adulthood that follows it? There are five characteristics that distinguish emerging adulthood from other age periods (Arnett, 2004, 2006; Reifman et al., 2006). Emerging adulthood is

1. the age of identity explorations;
2. the age of instability;
3. the self-focused age;
4. the age of feeling in-between; and
5. the age of possibilities.

All of these features begin to develop before emerging adulthood and continue to develop afterward, but it is during emerging adulthood that they reach their peak (Reifman et al., 2006).

Perhaps the most distinctive characteristic of emerging adulthood is that it is the *age of identity explorations*. This means that it is an age when people explore various possibilities in love and work as they move toward making enduring choices. Through trying out these different possibilities they develop a more definite identity, that is, an understanding of who they are, what their capabilities and limitations are, what their beliefs and values are, and how they fit into the society around them. Erik Erikson (1950), who was the first to develop the idea of identity (see Chapter 1), asserted that identity is mainly an issue in adolescence, but that was over 50 years ago, and today it is mainly in emerging adulthood that identity explorations take place (Arnett, 2000, 2004, 2005b; Côté, 2005; Schwartz, 2005).

The explorations of emerging adulthood also make it the *age of instability*. As they explore different possibilities in love and work, emerging adults' lives are often unstable. A good illustration of this is in how often they move from one residence to another. As **Figure 9.1** (page 416) shows, rates of residential change in American society are much higher at ages 18–29 than at any other period of life. This is a reflection of the explorations going on in emerging adults' lives. Some move out of their parents' household for the first time in their late teens to attend a residential college, others move out simply to be independent (Goldscheider & Goldscheider, 1999). They may move again when they drop out of college or when they graduate. They may move to cohabit with a romantic partner, then move out when the relationship ends. Some move to another part of the country or the world to study or work. For nearly half of American emerging adults, their residential changes include moving back in with their parents at least once (Sassler et al., 2008). In countries where emerging adults remain home rather than moving out,

The twenties are the decade of life when people are most likely to change residence.

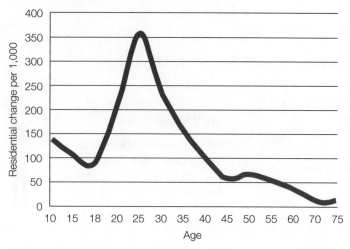

Figure 9.1 • **Rate of residential change, past year, in the United States.** Why does the rate of residential change peak in emerging adulthood?

Source: U.S. Bureau of the Census (2003).

Figure 9.2 • **Do you feel you have reached adulthood?** Emerging adults often feel adult in some ways but not others. **Source:** *Emerging adulthood: A theory of development from the late teens through the twenties.* American Psychologist, 55, 469–480.

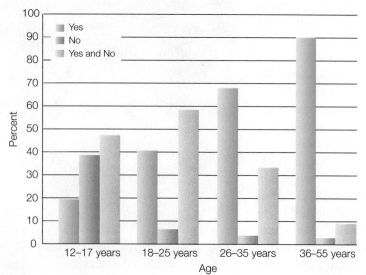

such as in most of southern Europe, they may nevertheless experience instability in education, work, and love relationships (Douglass, 2005, 2007).

Emerging adulthood is also a *self-focused age,* a time in between adolescents' reliance on parents and young adults' long-term commitments in love and work. During these years, emerging adults focus on themselves as they develop the knowledge, skills, and self-understanding they will need for adult life. In the course of emerging adulthood, they learn to make independent decisions small and large, about everything from what to have for dinner to whether or not to marry their current partner.

To say that emerging adulthood is a self-focused time is not meant critically. Being self-focused does not mean being selfish, and emerging adults are generally less egocentric than adolescents and more capable of taking the perspectives of others (Arnett, 2004). The goal of their self-focusing is learning to stand alone as a self-sufficient person, but emerging adults do not see self-sufficiency as a permanent state. Rather, they view it as a necessary step before committing themselves to lasting relationships with others, in love and work.

Another distinctive feature of emerging adulthood is that it is an *age of feeling in-between,* no longer an adolescent but not fully an adult, either. When asked, "Do you feel that you have reached adulthood?" the majority of emerging adults respond neither "yes" nor "no" but with the ambiguous "in some ways yes, in some ways no" (Arnett, 1994, 1997, 1998, 2000, 2001, 2003, 2004). As **Figure 9.2** shows, it is only when people reach their late twenties and early thirties that a clear majority feel they have reached adulthood. Most emerging adults have the subjective feeling of being in a transitional period of life, on the way to adulthood but not there yet. This "in-between" feeling in emerging adulthood has been found in a wide range of countries, including Argentina (Facio & Micocci, 2003), Israel (Mayseless & Scharf, 2003), the Czech Republic (Macek et al., 2007), China (Nelson et al., 2004), and Austria (Sirsch et al., 2009).

Finally, emerging adulthood is the *age of possibilities,* when many different futures remain possible, when little about a person's direction in life has been decided for certain. It tends to be an age of high hopes and great expectations, in part because few of their dreams have been tested in the fires of real life. In one national survey of 18- to 24-year-olds in the United States, nearly all—96%—agreed with the statement "I am very sure that someday I will get to where I want to be in life" (Hornblower, 1997). This optimism in emerging adulthood has been found in other countries as well, such as China (Nelson & Chen, 2007).

Emerging adulthood is also the age of possibilities because it is a time that holds the potential for dramatic changes. For those who have come from a troubled family, this is their chance to try to straighten the parts of themselves that have become twisted. No longer dependent on their parents, no longer subject to their parents' problems on a daily basis, they may be able to make independent decisions—perhaps to move to a different area or go to college—that turn their lives in a dramatically different direction (Arnett, 2004; Masten et al., 2006). Even for those who have come from families that are relatively happy and healthy, emerging adulthood is an opportunity to transform themselves so that they are not merely made in their parents' images but have made independent decisions about what kind of person they wish to be and how they wish to live. For this limited window of time—7, perhaps 10 years—the fulfillment of all their hopes seems possible, because for most people the range of their choices for how to live is greater than it has ever been before and greater than it will ever be again.

The cultural context of emerging adulthood

Describe some of the ways emerging adulthood varies among cultures, with specific reference to European and Asian countries.

Emerging adulthood is not a universal period of human development but a period that exists under certain conditions that have occurred only quite recently and only in some cultures. As we have seen, what is mainly required for emerging adulthood to exist is a relatively high median age of entering marriage and parenthood, in the late twenties or beyond. Postponing marriage and parenthood until the late twenties allows the late teens and most of the twenties to be devoted to other activities, such as the identity explorations just described. So, emerging adulthood exists today mainly in developed countries, including Europe, the United States, Canada, Australia, and New Zealand, along with Asian countries such as Japan and South Korea (Arnett, 2011).

Europe is the region where emerging adulthood is longest and most leisurely. The median age of entering marriage and parenthood is around 30 in most European countries (Douglass, 2007). Europe today is the location of the most affluent, generous, egalitarian societies in the world—in fact, in human history (Arnett, 2007). Governments pay for tertiary education, assist young people in finding jobs, and provide generous unemployment benefits for those who cannot find work. In northern Europe, many governments also provide housing support. Emerging adults in European societies make the most of these advantages.

The experience of emerging adulthood in Asian developed countries is markedly different than in Europe. Europe has a long history of individualism, dating back at least 500 years, and today's emerging adults represent that legacy in their focus on self-development and leisure. In contrast, Asian cultures have a shared history emphasizing collectivism and family obligations. Although Asian cultures have become more individualistic in recent decades as a consequence of globalization, the legacy of collectivism persists in the lives of emerging adults. They pursue identity explorations and self-development during emerging adulthood, like their American and European counterparts, but within narrower boundaries set by their sense of obligations to others, especially their parents (Phinney & Baldelomar, 2011). For example, in their views of the most important criteria for becoming an adult, emerging adults in the United States and Europe consistently rank *financial independence* among the most important markers of adulthood. In contrast, emerging adults with an Asian cultural background especially emphasize becoming *capable of supporting parents financially* as among the most important criteria (Arnett, 2003; Nelson et al., 2004). This sense of family obligation may curtail their identity explorations in emerging adulthood to some extent, as they pay more heed to their parents' wishes about what they should study and what job they should take and where they should live than emerging adults do in the West.

Within countries as well as between countries, emerging adulthood takes many different forms, just as we have seen for adolescence and childhood. About half of emerging adults in developed countries obtain tertiary education and training, but that leaves half who do not, and their experience of emerging adulthood is much different. Specifically, they are likely to have a much more difficult time finding a decent job in an economy that rewards educational credentials. There are other important differences across countries and cultures, such as in the degree of tolerance for premarital sex and cohabitation, as we will see later in the chapter. Thus there is not just one emerging adulthood that is experienced worldwide, but many emerging adulthoods with distinctive cultural characteristics (Arnett, 2011). Even in developed countries, there is variation across SES levels; many people

In Asian countries such as Japan, emerging adults feel an obligation to take care of their parents.

APPLYING YOUR KNOWLEDGE
. . . as a Researcher

While conducting research in India, you find that 24-year-olds in the city are mostly single, but most people of the same age in the local rural villages are already married with at least one child. What might explain this difference?

APPLYING YOUR KNOWLEDGE

Is 25 a good upper-age boundary for the end of emerging adulthood? If not, where would you put the upper-age boundary, and why?

in a lower SES do not have the luxury of an "in-between" period, and they may devote themselves to work, marriage, and children at younger ages.

Currently in developing countries, there tends to be a split between urban and rural areas in whether emerging adulthood is experienced at all. Young people in urban areas of countries such as China and India are more likely to experience emerging adulthood, because they marry later, have children later, obtain more education, and have a greater range of occupational and recreational opportunities than young people in rural areas do (Nelson & Chen, 2007). In contrast, young people in rural areas of developing countries often receive minimal schooling, marry early, and have little choice of occupation aside from agricultural work.

However, emerging adulthood is likely to become more pervasive worldwide in the decades to come, with the increasing globalization of the world economy (Arnett, 2011). Participation in tertiary education is rising in developing countries, as are median marriage ages, especially in the urban middle class. These changes open up the possibility for the spread of emerging adulthood in developing countries. It seems possible that by the end of the 21st century, emerging adulthood will be a normative period for young people worldwide, although it is likely to continue to vary in length and content both within and between countries.

WHAT HAVE YOU LEARNED?

1. What are the key reasons for the rise of emerging adulthood?
2. Why are identity issues today more prominent in emerging adulthood than in adolescence?
3. In what sense is emerging adulthood the age of possibilities?
4. What is one way the Asian pattern of emerging adulthood differs from the European pattern?
5. Does emerging adulthood exist in developing countries?

Physical Changes of Emerging Adulthood

Physical maturity is reached in many ways by the end of adolescence. By age 18, people reach their full height. The changes of puberty are over, and a degree of sexual maturity has been attained that is sufficient to allow for reproduction. However, strength and endurance continue to grow into the twenties for most people, and illness rates are especially low as the immune system is at peak effectiveness. On the other hand, health risks continue to loom in some areas, most notably automobile accidents and substance abuse.

The peak of physical functioning

9.3 **LEARNING OBJECTIVE** | Name the indicators that emerging adulthood is a period of peak physical functioning.

Do you enjoy watching the Olympics? I don't watch much TV, but the Olympics is one show I watch for many hours every two years. It's fun to marvel at the amazing physical feats performed by the athletes in events ranging from speed skating and snowboarding in the Winter Olympics to the pole vault and the 1500 meter run in the Summer Olympics. The competition exhibits human athletic performance at its highest.

Have you noticed that nearly all the athletes in the Olympics are ages 18–29? Emerging adulthood is the life stage of peak physical functioning, when the body is at its zenith of health, strength, and vigor. Physical stamina is often measured in terms of *maximum oxygen uptake,* or **VO$_2$ max,** which reflects the ability of the body to take in oxygen and transport it to various organs. VO$_2$ max peaks in the early twenties (Whaley, 2007). Similarly, **cardiac output,** the quantity of blood flow from the heart, peaks at age 25 (Lakatta, 1990; Parker et al., 2007). Reaction time is also faster in the early twenties than at any other time of life. Studies of grip strength among men show the same pattern, with a peak in the twenties followed by a steady decline (Aldwin & Spiro, 2006). The strength of the bones increases during this time as well. Even after maximum height is attained in the late teens, the bones continue to grow in density, and peak bone mass is reached in the twenties (Zumwalt, 2008).

It is not only the Olympics that demonstrate that emerging adulthood is a stage of exceptional physical functioning in terms of peak performances in athletic activity. Several studies have been conducted to determine the ages when athletes produce their best performances (Ericsson, 1990; Schulz & Curnow, 1988; Stones & Kozma, 1996; Tanaka & Seals, 2003). The peak ages have been found to vary depending on the sport, with swimmers youngest (the late teens) and golfers oldest (the early thirties). However, for most sports the peak age of performance comes during the twenties.

Emerging adulthood is also the period of the life span with the least susceptibility to physical illnesses (Gans, 1990). This is especially true in modern times, when vaccines and medical treatments have dramatically lowered the risk of diseases such as polio that used to strike mainly during these years (Hein, 1988). Emerging adults are no longer vulnerable to the illnesses and diseases of childhood, and with rare exceptions they are not yet vulnerable to diseases such as cancer and heart disease that rise in prevalence later in adulthood. Because the immune system is most effective during emerging adulthood, the late teens and early twenties are the years of fewest hospital stays and fewest days spent sick in bed at home (Gans, 1990).

In many ways, then, emerging adulthood is an exceptionally healthy time of life. However, this is not the whole story. The lifestyles of many emerging adults often include a variety of factors that undermine health, such as poor nutrition, lack of sleep, and the high stress of trying to juggle school and work or multiple jobs (Ma et al., 2002; Steptoe & Wardle, 2001). Longitudinal studies in the United States and Finland have found that physical activity, sports participation, and exercise decline from adolescence through emerging adulthood (Gordon-Larsen et al., 2004; Telama et al., 2005). These lifestyle factors often make emerging adults feel tired, weak, and depleted, despite their bodies' potential for optimal health. Furthermore, in many countries, the late teens and early twenties are the years of highest incidence of a variety of types of injury, death, and disease due to behavior. The areas of heightened risk in emerging adulthood include automobile accidents and substance abuse, as we'll see shortly. The risks associated with sexual activity, including sexually transmitted infections (STIs), will be explored later in the chapter.

VO$_2$ max ability of the body to take in oxygen and transport it to various organs; also called maximum oxygen update

cardiac output quantity of blood flow from the heart

APPLYING YOUR KNOWLEDGE . . . *as a Policy Maker*

Your state has a proposal to extend health care coverage for children of government workers from age 18 up to age 25, if the child is still in school. What have you learned in this course that would support such a proposal?

Emerging adulthood is a time of peak physical functioning. The swimmer Michael Phelps won a record seven gold medals at the 2008 Olympic games, at the age of 23, and he won four more gold medals at the 2012 Olympics.

Sleep patterns and deficits

Summarize college students' sleep patterns and the main elements of sleep hygiene.

LEARNING OBJECTIVE   **9.4**

How are you sleeping these days? If you are reading this, you are probably a college student, and if you are a college student your sleep pattern is probably not ideal—far from it. Nearly all research on sleep in emerging adulthood has focused on college students in developed countries. According to this research, college students' sleep patterns

morningness preference for going to bed early and waking up early

eveningness preference for going to bed late and waking up late

are distinctive in ways that undermine their cognitive functioning and their emotional well-being. College students are more than twice as likely as other adults to report the symptoms of *delayed sleep phase syndrome* (Brown et al., 2002). This syndrome entails a pattern of sleeping far longer on weekends and holidays than on school or work days, which leads to poor academic and job performance as well as excessive sleepiness during school and work days. College students tend to accumulate a *sleep debt* during the week as they sleep less than they need, then they try to make up their lost sleep when they have time off, with negative consequences for their cognitive and emotional functioning (Regestein et al., 2010).

College students' self-reports of their sleep patterns indicate that problems are common. Two-thirds of students report occasional sleep problems and about one-fourth report frequent severe sleep disturbances such as insomnia and insufficient sleep (Buboltz et al., 2002). Sleep disturbances are in turn related to a wide variety of problems (Millman, 2005). Poor sleep quality is related to depression and anxiety. Sleep disturbances also cause cognitive deficits in attention, memory, concentration, and critical thinking.

One reason college students and other emerging adults often have sleep problems is that the daily routines of their lives are set mostly by older adults who are likely to have different sleep preferences than they do. Sleep researchers have established that people vary in their **morningness** and **eveningness**, that is, their preference for either going to bed early and waking up early (morningness) or going to bed late and waking up late (eveningness). Furthermore, these preferences change with age, due to hormonal changes that are part of physical development, specifically, levels of *growth hormone*. One massive study of over 55,000 Europeans from childhood through late adulthood concluded that children tend toward morningness, but in the course of adolescence and the early part of emerging adulthood the balance shifts toward eveningness, with the peak of eveningness coming at about age 20–21 (slightly earlier for women than for men) (Roenneberg et al., 2007). After age 20–21, the balance shifts again toward morningness for the remainder of the life span. Other studies have found similar relations between age and sleep preferences (Brown et al., 2002). So, your 60-year-old professors may schedule their classes for 8:00 or 8:30 A.M., because that is a time of day when they feel alert and ready to go, whereas if you are in your early twenties that may well be a time of day when you feel like something scraped off the bottom of the garbage can.

However, it is not just physiological changes that contribute to college students' sleep disturbances but lifestyle factors, such as partying until late at night or waiting until the day before an exam to begin studying seriously. Have you ever stayed up all night long to study for an exam or to complete a paper due the next day? Among American college students this feat, known as an "all-nighter," is quite common. In one study of students at a four-year liberal arts college, 60% had pulled at least one all-nighter since coming to college (Thacher, 2008). Those who had pulled an all-nighter tended to have a greater preference for eveningness and had poorer overall academic achievement. Another study of all-nighters found that students who stayed up all night before exams self-rated their exam performance as better than students who slept eight hours, but their actual performance turned out to be much worse (Pilcher & Waters, 1997).

Sleep experts recommend the following practices to promote *sleep hygiene* (Brown et al., 2002):

- waking at the same time each day;
- getting regular exercise;
- taking late-afternoon naps;
- limiting caffeine intake;
- avoiding excessive alcohol intake.

APPLYING YOUR KNOWLEDGE
. . . as a Nurse

Every November, many students come to your university health clinic complaining that they can't get enough sleep. What advice do you give them?

 **Watch** the **Video** Sleep in **MyDevelopmentLab**

APPLYING YOUR KNOWLEDGE

What are some of the ways the college environment makes good sleep hygiene difficult to attain?

This may seem like common sense advice, but the actual behavior of many students contradicts these suggestions. Many drink coffee frequently during the day to stay alert, not realizing that frequent caffeine use will make it more difficult for them to sleep at night. Many believe that they can compensate for getting little sleep during the week by making it up during weekends and holidays, but this is precisely the delayed sleep phase syndrome, just discussed, that constitutes disrupted sleep. And, many drink alcohol excessively, with sleep hygiene the last thing on their minds.

Most emerging adults tend toward eveningness, not morningness.

WHAT HAVE YOU LEARNED?

1. Why do emerging adults have low rates of illnesses?
2. What are some of the lifestyle habits of emerging adults that undermine their physical health?
3. Can a "sleep debt" be paid off effectively by sleeping especially long when possible?
4. Are "all-nighters" effective as test preparation?

Risk Behavior and Health Issues

When I was 21 years old, during the summer between my junior and senior years of college, I was hungry for adventure, so I decided to take a hitchhiking trip across the United States. I stuck out my thumb down the street from my house in Michigan and proceeded to hitchhike 8,000 miles, from Michigan west to Seattle, down to Los Angeles, then all the way home again via Las Vegas. It was an adventure, all right, and in most ways a good one. I still keep in touch with an older couple I met on that trip, who were remarkably kind to me.

It strikes me today, looking back on it, that my hitchhiking trip was probably not a very good idea—to say the least—but the risks I took in emerging adulthood are not unique. Emerging adulthood is a time of life when many types of risk behavior reach their peak prevalence (Arnett, 2000). Unlike children and adolescents, emerging adults do not have their parents monitoring their behavior and setting rules for them, at least not nearly to the same extent. Unlike older adults, many emerging adults do not have the daily responsibilities of long-term commitments to a partner and children and to a long-term employer to restrain their behavior. Because emerging adulthood is the low point of **social control**—the restraints on behavior imposed by social obligations and relationships—they are more likely to take certain kinds of risks (Arnett, 2005; Hirschi, 2002). (Nobody could stop me from taking that hitchhiking trip, although my mom certainly tried.) Not all emerging adults take risks of course, but risk behavior of some kinds is more common than at other age periods. Here we examine automobile driving and substance use.

Injuries and fatalities: Automobile accidents

| Explain why young drivers have the highest rates of crashes, and name the most effective approach to reducing those rates. | **LEARNING OBJECTIVE** **9.5** |

Across developed countries, the most serious threat to the lives and health of adolescents and emerging adults comes from automobile driving (Heuveline, 2002). In the United States young people aged 16 to 24 have the highest rates of automobile accidents, injuries, and fatalities of any age group (see *Figure 9.3* on page 422) (National Highway Traffic Safety Administration [NHTSA], 2011). In other developed countries, a higher minimum driving age (usually 18) and less access to automobiles have made rates of

social control restraints on behavior imposed by social obligations and relationships

Figure 9.3 • **Rates of car injuries and fatalities by age.** Why are rates so high at ages 16–24? **Source:** Traffic Safety Facts 2009, National Highway Traffic Safety Administration, National Center for Statistics and Analysis, U.S. Department of Transportation.

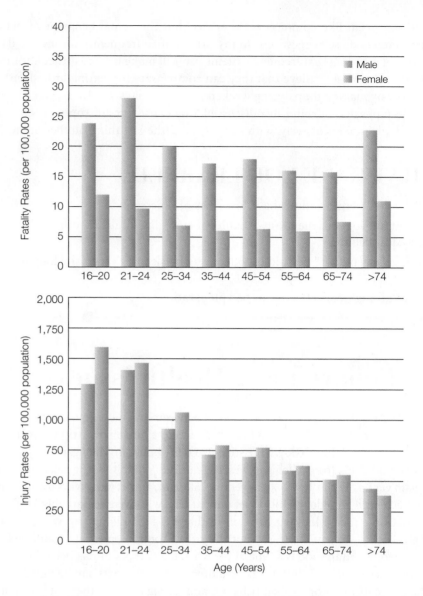

Figure 9.3 • **Rates of car injuries and fatalities by age.** Why are rates so high at ages 16–24? **Source:** Traffic Safety Facts 2009, National Highway Traffic Safety Administration, National Center for Statistics and Analysis, U.S. Department of Transportation.

||||||||||||||||||||||||||||||||||||||||||||||||||||||||||||||||||

❝I love to drive fast, but after a while driving fast just wasn't doing it any more. So I started driving without the lights on [at night], going about ninety on country roads. I even got a friend to do it. We'd go cruising down country roads, turn off the lights, and just fly. It was incredible. We'd go as fast as we could, [and] at night, with no lights it feels like you're just flying. ❞

— Nick, age 23
(in Arnett, 1996, p. 79)

||||||||||||||||||||||||||||||||||||||||||||||||||||||||||||||||||

accidents and fatalities among young people substantially lower than in the United States, but motor vehicle injuries are the leading cause of death during emerging adulthood in those countries as well (Pan et al., 2007; Twisk & Stacey, 2007).

What is responsible for these grim statistics? Is it young drivers' inexperience or their risky driving behavior? Inexperience certainly plays a large role. Rates of accidents and fatalities are extremely high in the early months of driving, but fall dramatically by one year after licensure (McKnight & Peck, 2002; Williams, 1998). Studies that have attempted to disentangle experience and age in young drivers have generally concluded that inexperience is partly responsible for young drivers' accidents and fatalities.

However, these studies and others have also concluded that inexperience is not the only factor involved. Equally important is the way young people drive and the kinds of risks they take (Ferguson, 2003). Compared to older drivers, young drivers (especially males) are more likely to drive at excessive speeds, follow other vehicles too closely, violate traffic signs and signals, take more risks in lane changing and passing other vehicles, allow too little time to merge, and fail to yield to pedestrians (Bina et al., 2006; Williams & Ferguson, 2002). They are also more likely than older drivers to report driving under the influence of alcohol. Drivers aged 21 to 24 involved in fatal accidents are more likely to have been intoxicated at the time of the accident than persons in any other age group (NHTSA, 2011). Nearly half of American college

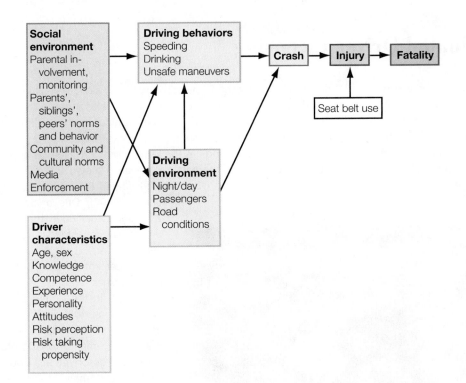

Figure 9.4 • **Shope's model of young driver crash risks.** The model shows that many factors contribute to crash risk, including social environment, driver characteristics, driving behaviors, and driving environment.

students report driving while intoxicated within the past year (Clapp et al., 2005; Glassman et al., 2010). Young people are also less likely than older drivers to wear seat belts (Williams & Ferguson, 2002), and in serious car crashes occupants not wearing seat belts are twice as likely to be killed and three times as likely to be injured, compared to those wearing seat belts (NHTSA, 2011).

What else leads to crashes among young drivers? Jean Shope (2002) of the University of Michigan has proposed a useful model (see *Figure 9.4*) that shows the importance of various factors, from parental involvement to cultural norms to media that glamorize high-speed driving. Friends' influence has been found to promote risky driving. Young drivers are more likely than older drivers to believe their friends would approve of risky driving behavior such as speeding, closely following another vehicle, and passing another car in risky circumstances (Chen et al., 2007; U.S. Department of Transportation, 1995). Driver characteristics matter, too. Personality characteristics such as sensation seeking and aggressiveness promote risky driving and subsequent crashes, and these characteristics tend to be highest in young male drivers (Shope & Bingham, 2008).

What can be done to reduce the rates of automobile accidents and fatalities among young drivers? Parental involvement and monitoring of adolescents' driving behavior has been shown to be especially important in the early months of driving, and interventions to increase parental involvement have been shown to be effective (Simons-Morton, 2007; Simons-Morton et al., 2002; Simons-Morton et al., 2006; Simons-Morton et al., 2008). However, by far the most effective approach is a program of restricted driving privileges called **graduated driver licensing (GDL)**. The GDL is a government program in which young people obtain driving privileges gradually, contingent on a safe driving record, rather than all at once. The GDL programs address a variety of the risk factors in Shope's model (refer back to Figure 9.4). The goal is to allow young people to obtain driving experience gradually, under conditions that limit the likelihood of crashes by restricting the circumstances under which novices can drive. as we'll see in the **Research Focus: Graduating Driver Licensing** feature on page 424 (Foss, 2007; Williams & Ferguson, 2002).

APPLYING YOUR KNOWLEDGE

Are you in favor of a graduated licensing program for your state or country? If so, what provisions would you include? Are such programs unfair to young people who drive safely and nevertheless have their driving privileges restricted?

graduated driver licensing (GDL) government program in which young people obtain driving privileges gradually, contingent on a safe driving record, rather than all at once

RESEARCH FOCUS   Graduated Driver Licensing

Graduated driver licensing (GDL) programs have proven to be the most effective way to reduce automobile accidents among young drivers. These programs typically include three stages (Shope, 2007). The *learning license* is the stage in which the young person obtains driving experience under the supervision of an experienced driver. For example, the GDL program in California requires young people to complete learning-license driver training of 50 hours under the supervision of a parent, of which 10 hours must take place at night.

The second stage is a period of *restricted license* driving. In this stage young drivers are allowed to drive unsupervised, but with tighter restrictions than those that apply to adults. The restrictions are based on research revealing the factors that are most likely to place young drivers at risk for crashes (Foss, 2007). For example, in some states GDL programs include *driving curfews,* which prohibit young drivers from driving late at night (e.g., in New York, between 9 P.M. and 5 A.M.) except for a specific purpose such as going to and from work. This has been found to reduce young people's crash involvement dramatically (McKnight & Peck, 2002). Also highly effective in reducing crashes is a prohibition against driving with teenage passengers when no adults are present (Williams & Ferguson, 2002).

Other restrictions include requirements for seat belt use and a "zero tolerance" rule for alcohol use, which means that young

drivers are in violation if they drive with any alcohol at all in their blood. In the restricted stage, any violations of these restrictions may result in a suspended license. It is only after the GDL period has passed—usually no more than one year—that a young person obtains a *full license* and has the same driving privileges as adults. Numerous studies in the past decade have shown the effectiveness of GDL programs (Foss, 2007; Hedlund & Compton, 2005; Shope, 2007). One analysis of 21 studies concluded that GDL programs consistently reduce young drivers' crash risk by 20 to 40 percent (Shope, 2007). Fatal crashes among 16-year-old drivers in the United States decreased by 40% in the past decade, and this improvement is attributed mainly to GDL programs (Ferguson et al., 2007). Legislators in many states have responded to this evidence by passing more of these programs. About two-thirds of American states now have some kind of GDL program, a dramatic rise over the past 10 years (Hedlund & Compton, 2005; Preusser & Tison, 2007). Graduated driver license programs have also been instituted in Canada and are becoming more common in European countries (Pan et al., 2007; Twisk & Stacey, 2007). Research indicates that these laws work in part by making it easier for parents to enforce restrictions on their adolescents' driving behavior (Hartos et al., 2005).

Substance use and abuse

9.6   **LEARNING OBJECTIVE**   Explain why rates of substance use peak in the early twenties and then decline.

binge drinking consuming five or more drinks in a row for men, four in a row for women

Many types of substance use reach their peak in emerging adulthood (Schulenberg & Maggs, 2000). The national Monitoring the Future study, which has followed up several American cohorts from high school through middle age, shows that substance use of all kinds rises through the late teens and peaks in the early twenties before declining in the late twenties (Patrick et al., 2011). **Figure 9.5** shows the pattern for marijuana use and **binge drinking** (consuming five or more drinks in a row for men, four in a row for women) (Bachman et al., 2008). Substance use, especially alcohol use, is higher among college students than among emerging adults who do not attend college (Kalb & McCormick, 1998; Okie, 2002; Schulenberg, 2000; Wechsler & Nelson, 2001). Substance use tends to be somewhat higher among men than among women, and in some cultures substance use and even abuse is considered part of becoming a man, as we'll see in the **Cultural Focus: The Young Men of Chuuk Lagoon** feature on page 426. ◉

◉ [**Watch** the **Video** Teen Drinking in **MyDevelopmentLab**

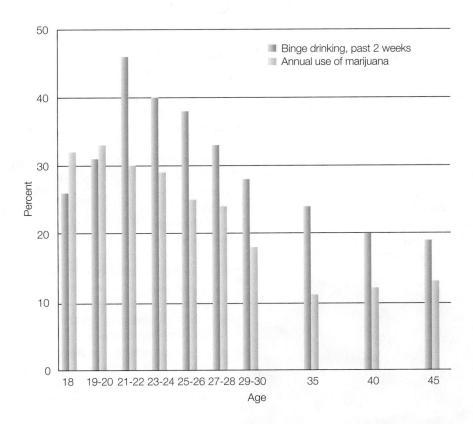

Figure 9.5 • **Marijuana use and binge drinking in emerging adulthood.** Rates of most kinds of substance use peak in the early twenties.
Source: The strong, sensitive type: Effects of gender stereotypes and leadership prototypes on the evaluation of male and female leaders. Organizational Behavior and Human Decision Processes, 106, 39–60.

Some evidence shows that substance use is also high among emerging adults in other developed countries. A study of Spanish adults reported that among 18- to 24-year-olds, rates of binge drinking in the past 30 days were 31% for men and 18% for women, far higher than in any other age group (Valencia-Martín et al., 2007). A peak in binge drinking in emerging adulthood has been found in other European countries as well (Kuntsche et al., 2004). Among female college students in Scotland, most regarded binge drinking as "harmless fun" (Guise & Gill, 2007). However, binge drinking and other types of substance use in emerging adulthood are related to a wide variety of negative consequences that range from fatal car crashes to unintended pregnancy to criminal activity to physical fights, in both Europe and the United States (Jochman & Fromme, 2010; Plant et al., 2010).

What explains the higher rates of substance use among emerging adults? Wayne Osgood has proposed a useful answer to this question. Osgood (2009; Osgood et al., 2005; Osgood et al., 1996) borrows from a sociological theory that explains all deviance on the basis of *propensity* and *opportunity*. People behave deviantly when they have a combination of sufficient propensity (that is, sufficient motivation for behaving deviantly) along with sufficient opportunity. In his explanation, Osgood especially focuses on the high degree of opportunity that emerging adults have for engaging in substance use and other deviant behavior, as a result of spending a high proportion of their time in unstructured socializing.

Osgood uses the term **unstructured socializing** to include behavior such as riding around in a car for fun, going to parties, visiting friends informally, and going out with friends. Unstructured socializing is highest in the late teens and early twenties, and emerging adults who are highest in unstructured socializing are also highest in use of alcohol and marijuana (Osgood et al., 2005; Osgood et al., 1996). Rates of most types of substance use are especially high among emerging adults who are college students because they have so many opportunities for unstructured socializing.

Osgood and others have found that the relationship between unstructured socializing and deviance holds not only for substance use but for other types of risk behavior such as crime and dangerous driving (Haynie & Osgood, 2005; Maimon & Browning, 2010).

APPLYING YOUR KNOWLEDGE

Besides unstructured socializing, what other factors might contribute to substance use in emerging adulthood?

unstructured socializing socializing with friends without any specific goal or activity; includes behavior such as riding around in a car for fun, going to parties, visiting friends informally, and going out with friends

Unstructured socializing is often the setting for risk behaviors such as substance use.

CULTURAL FOCUS The Young Men of Chuuk Lagoon

Risk behaviors such as fighting, stealing, and substance use are far more common among males than among females, everywhere in the world and in every era of the historical record (Wilson & Herrnstein, 1985). The reasons for this may be partly biological, but they are also clearly connected to gender-role socialization. In a wide range of cultures, risk behavior is in fact part of demonstrating a young man's readiness for manhood (Gilmore, 1990).

One vivid example of this can be found among the people of Chuuk Lagoon, a lagoon with a string of small islands in the South Pacific known as Micronesia. The culture of Chuuk Lagoon has been vividly described by the anthropologist Mac Marshall (1979) and summarized by David Gilmore (1990). Their accounts provide an excellent demonstration not only of the importance of gender-role socialization in the risk behavior of young males but also of the effect of globalization on young people, even in cultures in the remotest parts of the world.

The globalization of the Chuukese culture goes back more than a hundred years. Even long before that, the Chuukese were known far and wide as fierce warriors who fought frequently among themselves and made short work of any Western sailors unlucky enough to drift nearby. However, in the late 1800s, German colonists arrived and took control of the islands and of the Chuukese people. They stamped out local warfare, introduced Christianity, and also introduced alcohol, which soon became widely and excessively used by young men. After World War II, the Americans replaced the Germans in Chuuk Lagoon and introduced television, baseball, and other features of Western life. Today, Chuuk Lagoon remains an American territory.

Much has changed in Chuuk Lagoon during the century of Western influence, but there remains a strong emphasis on strictly defined gender roles. When they reach puberty, girls learn the traditional female role that includes cooking, sewing, and performing other household duties. Meanwhile, young men are expected to demonstrate their manhood in three ways: fighting, drinking large quantities of alcohol, and taking daredevil risks.

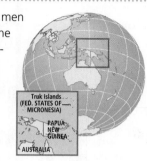

Fighting among young Chuukese men is a group activity. It takes place in the context of rivalries between clans (extended family networks). Young men fight not just for their own prestige but for the honor and prestige of their clan. On weekend evenings, they roam the streets in clan groups looking for other groups to challenge, and taking part in brawls when they find them.

How has globalization influenced the young men of Chuuk Lagoon?

Drinking alcohol is also part of the weekend group activities of young males. Beginning in adolescence and continuing through emerging adulthood, getting drunk with their clan pals is a regular part of weekend evenings. The drinking contributes to the fighting because it has the effect of diminishing any trepidation a young man might have over becoming injured. Also, on weekend days, groups of young men sometimes take risky trips in motorboats. They take long trips with limited fuel, a small motor, and nothing for sustenance except beer, risking the open sea in a small boat in order to demonstrate their bravery and thereby prove their readiness for manhood.

Although nearly all Chuukese males in their teens and twenties engage in these activities, their risk behavior escapades are limited to the weekends, and they rarely drink or fight during the week. In fact, Marshall's (1979) book about them is entitled *Weekend Warriors*. Also, when they reach about age thirty, the expectations for manhood change. At that point, they are expected to marry and settle down. They rarely fight after reaching that age, and most stop drinking alcohol entirely. The risk behavior of males in adolescence and emerging adulthood is not viewed as a social problem but, rather, as an accepted behavior during a limited period of their lives, when their culture demands it as part of fulfilling the expectations for becoming a man.

Furthermore, the relationship between unstructured socializing and deviance holds for both genders, a variety of ethnic groups, and across a wide range of developed and developing countries. Research also shows that substance use and other types of risk behavior decline in the mid- to late twenties, as role transitions such as marriage, parenthood, and full-time work cause a sharp decline in unstructured socializing (Monitoring the Future, 2003; Patrick et al., 2011).

My Virtual Child

Is excessive substance use something your virtual child will likely experience? Why or why not?

WHAT HAVE YOU LEARNED?

1. How large a role does inexperience play in crash rates among young drivers?
2. What are the main features of effective GDL programs?
3. How does substance use change between adolescence and emerging adulthood?
4. How does unstructured socializing contribute to substance use and other types of risk behavior?

Section 1 VIDEO GUIDE The Features of Emerging Adulthood (Length: 8:07)

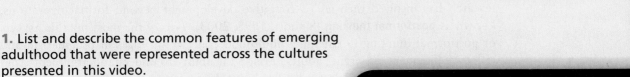

This video shows interviews with individuals from various cultures regarding the features of emerging adulthood.

1. List and describe the common features of emerging adulthood that were represented across the cultures presented in this video.

2. Emerging adulthood is described as an "unstable" time in one's life. Based on this video, why would this be an accurate description?

3. How could parents better prepare their children for this time in their life?

Watch the **Video** The Features of Emerging Adulthood in **MyDevelopmentLab**

LEARNING OBJECTIVES

9.7 Describe how growing abilities of pragmatism allow emerging adults to become better at addressing real-life problems.

9.8 Outline the development of reflective judgment in Perry's theory.

9.9 Compare and contrast the tertiary education systems and college experiences in developed countries.

9.10 Name the various long-term benefits of tertiary education.

Postformal Thinking

In Piaget's theory, formal operations is the culmination of cognitive development (see Chapter 8). Once formal operations is fully attained, by age 20 at the latest, cognitive maturation is complete. However, like many aspects of Piaget's theory of formal operations, this view has been altered by research. In fact, research indicates that cognitive development often continues in important ways during emerging adulthood. This research has inspired theories of cognitive development beyond formal operations, known as **postformal thinking** (Sinnott, 1998, 2003). Two of the most notable aspects of postformal thinking in emerging adulthood concern advances in pragmatism and reflective judgment. Emerging adults develop the ability to understand arguments, and to think reflectively and dialectically. For example, emerging adults become able to see two or more sides of a situation and reason about the merits of side. And, they can assimilate new information that contradicts their prior understanding and think in new ways about arguments, scientific findings, and situations.

Pragmatism

9.7 LEARNING OBJECTIVE | Describe how growing abilities of pragmatism allow emerging adults to become better at addressing real-life problems.

Pragmatism involves adapting logical thinking to the practical constraints of real-life situations. Theories of postformal thought emphasizing pragmatism have been developed by several scholars (Basseches, 1984, 1989; Labouvie-Vief, 1998, 2006; Labouvie-Vief & Diehl, 2002; Sinnott, 2003). The theories have in common an emphasis that the problems faced in normal adult life often contain complexities and inconsistencies that cannot be addressed with the logic of formal operations.

According to Gisela Labouvie-Vief (1982, 1990, 1998, 2006), cognitive development in emerging adulthood is distinguished from adolescent thinking by a greater recognition and incorporation of practical limitations to logical thinking. In this view, adolescents exaggerate the extent to which logical thinking will be effective in real life. In contrast, emerging adulthood brings a growing awareness of how social factors and factors specific to a given situation must be taken into account in approaching most of life's problems.

For example, in one study Labouvie-Vief (1990) presented adolescents and emerging adults with stories and asked them to predict what they thought would happen. One story described a man who was a heavy drinker, especially at parties. His wife had warned him

postformal thinking according to some theorists, the stage of cognitive development that follows formal operations and includes advances in pragmatism and reflective judgment

pragmatism theory of cognitive development proposing that postformal thinking involves adapting logical thinking to the practical constraints of real-life situations

that if he came home drunk one more time, she would leave him and take the children. Some time later he went to an office party and came home drunk. What would she do?

Labouvie-Vief found that adolescents tended to respond strictly in terms of the logic of formal operations: She said she would leave if he came home drunk once more, he came home drunk, therefore she will leave. In contrast, emerging adults considered many possible dimensions of the situation. Did he apologize and beg her not to leave? Did she really mean it when she said she would leave him? Does she have some place to go? Had she considered the possible effects on the children? Rather than relying strictly on logic and assuming an outcome of definite wrong and right answers, the emerging adults tended to be postformal thinkers in the sense that they realized that the problems of real life often involve a great deal of complexity and ambiguity. However, Labouvie-Vief (2006) emphasizes that with postformal thinking, as with formal thinking, not everyone continues to move to higher levels of cognitive complexity, and many people continue to apply earlier, more concrete thinking in emerging adulthood and beyond.

A similar theory of cognitive development in emerging adulthood has been presented by Michael Basseches (1984, 1989). Like Labouvie-Vief, Basseches (1984) views cognitive development in emerging adulthood as involving a recognition that formal logic can rarely be applied to the problems most people face in their daily lives. **Dialectical thought** is Basseches's term for the kind of thinking that develops in emerging adulthood, involving a growing awareness that problems often have no clear solution and two opposing strategies or points of view may each have some merit (Basseches, 1984). For example, people may have to decide whether to quit a job they dislike without knowing whether their next job will be more satisfying.

Some cultures may promote dialectical thinking more than others. Chinese culture traditionally promotes dialectical thought, by advocating an approach to knowledge that strives to reconcile contradictions and combine opposing perspectives by seeking a middle ground (Peng & Nisbett, 1999). In contrast, the European American approach tends to apply logic in a way that polarizes contradictory perspectives in an effort to determine which is correct.

To support this theory, one team of researchers conducted studies comparing Chinese and American college students (Peng & Nisbett, 1999). They found that the Chinese students were more likely than the Americans to prefer dialectical proverbs containing contradictions. The Chinese students were also more likely to prefer dialectical arguments, involving argument and counterargument, over arguments that used classical Western logic. In addition, when two apparently contradictory propositions were presented, the Americans tended to embrace one and reject the other, whereas the Chinese students were moderately accepting of both propositions, seeking to reconcile them.

Reflective judgment

Outline the development of reflective judgment in Perry's theory.

LEARNING OBJECTIVE 9.8

Reflective judgment, another cognitive quality that has been found to develop in emerging adulthood, is the capacity to evaluate the accuracy and logical coherence of evidence and arguments. An influential theory of the development of reflective judgment in emerging adulthood was proposed by William Perry (1970/1999), who studied college students in their late teens and early twenties. According to Perry (1970/1999), adolescents and first-year college students tend to engage in *dualistic thinking*—an act is either right or wrong, with no in-between; a statement is either true or false, regardless of the nuances or the situation to which it is being applied. In this sense, they lack reflective judgment. However, reflective judgment begins to develop for most people around age 20. First a stage of *multiple thinking* begins, in which young people come to believe that there are two or more sides to every story, two or more legitimate views of every issue, and that it can be difficult to justify one position as the only true or accurate

dialectical thought according to Basseches, a kind of thinking in emerging adulthood that involves a growing awareness that problems often have no clear solution and two opposing strategies or points of view may each have some merit

reflective judgment capacity to evaluate the accuracy and logical coherence of evidence and arguments, theorized to develop during emerging adulthood

one. In this stage people tend to value all points of view equally, even to the extent of asserting that it is impossible to make any judgments about whether one point of view is more valid than another.

By the early twenties, according to Perry, multiple thinking develops into *relativism*. Like people in the stage of multiple thinking, relativists are able to recognize the legitimacy of competing points of view. However, rather than denying that one view could be more persuasive than another, relativists attempt to evaluate the merits of competing views. Finally, by the end of their college years, many young people reach a stage of *commitment*, in which they commit themselves to certain points of view they believe to be the most valid, while being open to reevaluating their views if new evidence is presented to them.

Research on reflective judgment indicates that significant gains may take place in emerging adulthood (King & Kitchener, 2002, 2004; Kitchener et al., 2006; Kitchener et al., 1993; Pascarella & Terenzini, 1991). However, the gains that take place in emerging adulthood appear to be due more to education than to maturation (King & Kitchener, 2002, 2004; Labouvie-Vief, 2006; Pirttilae-Backman & Kajanne, 2001)— that is, people who pursue a college education during emerging adulthood show greater advances in reflective judgment than people who do not. Also, Perry and his colleagues acknowledged that the development of reflective judgment is likely to be more common in a culture that values pluralism and whose educational system promotes tolerance of diverse points of view (Perry, 1970/1999). However, thus far little cross-cultural research has taken place on reflective judgment.

WHAT HAVE YOU LEARNED?

1. In what sense are pragmatism and reflective judgment *postformal* types of cognition?
2. What is a distinctive feature of pragmatism in the Chinese context?
3. How does multiple thinking differ from relativism?
4. What cultural context is required for the development of reflective judgment?

Tertiary Education: College, University, and Training Programs

As mentioned at the outset of the chapter, one of the changes of recent decades that has led to the development of a new life stage of emerging adulthood is increasing participation in higher education. As **Map 9.2** shows, a majority of emerging adults across a wide range of developed countries now obtain **tertiary education**, which includes any kind of education or training program beyond secondary school. This has been a remarkably rapid historical change. One hundred years ago, few young people—less than 10%—obtained tertiary education in any developed country; in fact, the majority did not even attend secondary school. Those who did attend college or university were mostly men. Historically, women were deemed to be cognitively inferior to men and therefore not worthy of higher education, as we'll see in the **Historical Focus: Gender and Cognitive Development in Emerging Adulthood** feature. A hundred years later, tertiary education is now a normative experience, and in most countries women are more likely than men to obtain it. According to one worldwide survey, there were more young women than young men in tertiary education in 83 of 141 countries, including many developing countries (*"A man's world? Good news,"* 2007). 👁

APPLYING YOUR KNOWLEDGE

The Constitution of the United States specifies a minimum age of 35 before a person can be elected president. Why do you suppose this is so? What sort of cognitive qualities might be insufficiently developed before that age for a person to be capable of exercising the duties of the office?

My Virtual Child

Does your culture value dualistic thinking or reflective judgment? Which will your virtual child likely develop?

---

tertiary education education or training beyond secondary school

👁—**Watch** the **Video** Post-Secondary Education in Early Adulthood in **MyDevelopmentLab**

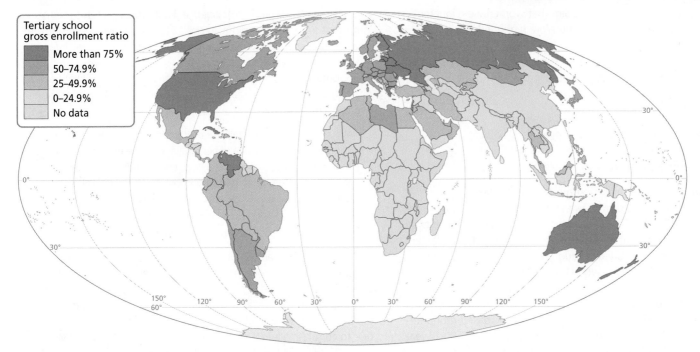

Tertiary school
gross enrollment ratio

- More than 75%
- 50–74.9%
- 25–49.9%
- 0–24.9%
- No data

Map 9.2 • **Worldwide Enrollment in Tertiary Education.** Which countries have the highest and lowest enrollment rates for higher education? How do these rates compare to the enrollment rates for secondary school (as shown in Map 8.1)? What economic and cultural factors might explain these variations?

HISTORICAL FOCUS   Gender and Cognitive Development in Emerging Adulthood

In most cultures throughout history, opportunities for obtaining education have been much more limited for females than for males. In the United States and other developed countries, this issue pertains particularly to emerging adulthood. Historically, these countries have conceded that girls should at least learn to read and write. However, there has been much more debate over, and resistance to, the idea that females should receive higher education. Many people in the 18th and 19th centuries were vehemently opposed to the idea that females should be allowed to attend colleges and universities.

Historian Linda Kerber (1997) distinguishes three periods in the history of higher education for women. The first extended from 1700 to 1775. During this time, female literacy grew (as it did for males), but no colleges or universities accepted female students. Of course, it was also rare for males to receive higher education at that time, but at least the more privileged males had this opportunity. Females were barred entirely.

In the 19th century it was widely believed that higher education was unhealthy for young women.

The second period extended from 1776 to 1833, and Kerber calls it the "Era of the Great Debate over the Capacities of Women's Minds." The question of whether women were cognitively capable of benefiting from higher education was hotly debated during this time. The final year of this period, 1833, was the year that the first women entered higher education, at Oberlin College, which was founded as a women's college. The third period, from 1833 to 1875, was marked by a steady expansion in opportunities for women to pursue higher education. By 1875, dozens of institutions accepted female students, and the debate over whether women should be allowed to pursue higher education had turned in favor of the proponents.

Arguments against allowing young women the opportunity for higher education had two main features. One was the claim that "too much" education for young women would be hazardous to them, because it would spoil their feminine qualities and because it might exhaust them and even make them ill. A second was the claim that women were inherently inferior to men intellectually, and therefore higher education would be wasted on them.

The first claim, that intellectual stimulation was hazardous to young women, was especially prevalent in the 18th century. A popular verse during that century read:

Why should girls be learn'd and wise?
Books only serve to spoil their eyes.
The studious eye but faintly twinkles
And reading paves the way to wrinkles.

In addition, many men, including medical authorities, claimed that intellectual work would disrupt women's menstrual cycles and render them infertile. Needless to say, this claim was without merit.

During the 19th century, this argument continued to be stated, but as women began to break through the barriers to higher education some men claimed that women were "scientifically" shown to be cognitively inferior. A lot of scientific activity took place in the 19th century, and a lot of pseudoscience, too. Some of the worst pseudoscience attempted to establish biologically based group differences in intelligence (Gould, 1981). Even scientists who were otherwise respectable were infected by pseudoscientific reasoning

when it came to issues of intelligence. Paul Broca, perhaps the most important figure in neurology in the 19th century, claimed that the smaller brains of women demonstrated their intellectual inferiority. He knew very well that brain size is related to body size, and that women's smaller brain size simply reflected their smaller bodies rather than inferior intelligence, but his prejudice against the cognitive capacities of women allowed him to talk himself out of it:

We might ask if the small size of the female brain depends exclusively on the small size of her body.... But we must not forget that women are, on average, a little less intelligent than men.... We are therefore permitted to suppose that the relatively small size of the female brain depends in part upon her physical inferiority and in part upon her intellectual inferiority.

(1861, quoted in Gould, 1981, p. 104)

Things have changed now. In the majority of countries worldwide, females excel over males on nearly every measure of educational achievement (United Nations Development Programme [UNDP], 2008). However, there remain parts of the world where females are not allowed the same access to education as males, due to cultural beliefs that they are less fit for mental work (Mensch et al., 1998; UNDP, 2008).

Cultural variations in tertiary education

9.9 **LEARNING OBJECTIVE** Compare and contrast the tertiary education systems and college experiences in developed countries.

APPLYING YOUR KNOWLEDGE
Should your college require certain prerequisites to graduate outside of a major? If so, how diverse should the requirements be?

Countries vary widely in how they structure tertiary education. Colleges in the United States, Canada, and Japan begin with two years of general education with no requirement of declaring a specialization or "major," which allows for the exploration of ideas that may be unrelated to any occupational future. Emerging adulthood is characterized by exploration in a variety of aspects of life, and attending college in these countries allows emerging adults to explore various possible educational directions that offer different occupational futures. You may be a business major and nevertheless enjoy courses on literature or art or philosophy that lead you to explore a variety of ideas about what it means to be human. You may be a psychology major and yet find it engaging to explore ideas in courses on astronomy or chemistry.

Tertiary education is perhaps most relaxed and undemanding in Japan. You may find this surprising, because as we have seen in Chapter 8, Japanese secondary schools are exceptionally demanding and competition to get into the best universities is fierce (Fackler, 2007). Beyond college and university, the Japanese workplace is notoriously demanding as well, requiring long hours and mandatory after-hours socializing. For the Japanese, their time of leisure and fun comes during their college years. Once they enter college, grades matter little and standards for performance are relaxed. Instead, they have "four years of university-sanctioned leisure to think and explore" (Rohlen, 1983, p. 168; Fackler, 2007). Japanese college students spend a great deal of time in unstructured socializing, walking around the city and hanging out together.

Average homework time for Japanese college students is half the homework time of junior high or high school students (Takahashi & Takeuchi, 2006). For most Japanese, this brief period in emerging adulthood is the only time in their lives, from childhood until retirement, that will be relatively free of pressure. Only during their college years are they exempt from responsibilities and allowed to enjoy extensive hours of leisure.

In Europe, the tertiary education system is structured quite differently than in the United States, Canada, and Japan. Rather than beginning with two years of general education, European students study in only one topic area from the time they enter university. Traditionally, university education in Europe often lasted six or more years because it culminated in a degree that was similar to American advanced degrees (master's or doctoral degree). However, the European system has changed recently to match the American system, with separate bachelor's, master's, and doctoral degrees (*Under threat of change*, 2008). This was done to shorten the time European emerging adults spend in university, and to promote the development of coordinated programs between European and American universities. It also reflects the growing globalization of education.

How is the European university system different from the American system? Here, Cambridge University students in England.

For most young Americans, tertiary education takes longer now than it did two or three decades ago. Currently, it takes an average of six years for students to obtain a "four-year" degree (Rooney, 2003). A number of factors explain why it takes students longer to graduate (Dey & Hurtado, 1999). Some students prefer to extend their college years to switch majors, add a minor field of study, or take advantage of internship programs or study-abroad programs. However, financial concerns are the main reason it now takes so long to graduate. Tuition rates have increased to a shocking extent and were over *four times higher* (even taking into account inflation) in 2007 than they were in 1982 in both public and private colleges and universities (Lewin, 2008). Financial aid has also shifted markedly from grants to loans, which has led many students to work long hours while attending college in order to avoid accruing excessive debt before they graduate (Dey & Hurtado, 1999; Pryor et al., 2009). African Americans and Latinos especially struggle to fund their college educations, as *Table 9.1* illustrates, and lack of money is one of the key reasons why they are less likely to obtain a college degree than Whites or Asian Americans are (McDonough & Calderone, 2006).

> **My Virtual Child**
>
> Will your virtual child attend college? What major do you think your virtual child will choose?

The benefits of tertiary education

| Name the various long-term benefits of tertiary education. | **LEARNING OBJECTIVE** 9.10 |

Is tertiary education worth the time and money it requires? It is certainly a substantial investment. Participation in tertiary education requires a great deal of money per year, paid mainly by emerging adults and their parents in the United States, and mainly by the government in other developed countries. Furthermore, the years in which emerging adults are focused on obtaining tertiary education are also years

> **THINKING CULTURALLY**
>
> *How does the way that a country structures its tertiary education system reflect on its cultural values, if at all?*

TABLE 9.1 Ethnic Differences in Financial Support for College*

"In high school, I knew that if I wanted to go to college, it would be possible for me to find financial support either from my family or from scholarships, loans, or other programs."

Whites: 86% strongly agree (0% strongly disagree)

Blacks: 9% strongly agree (42% strongly disagree)

Latinos: 9% strongly agree (33% strongly disagree)

"For as long as I wished to continue my education, it would be possible for me to find financial support either from my family or from scholarships, loans, or other programs."

Whites: 59% strongly agree

Blacks: 19% strongly agree

Latinos: 12% strongly agree

Asian Americans: 63% strongly agree

"It has been difficult for me to find the financial support to get the kind of education I really want."

Whites: 5% strongly agree

Blacks: 61% strongly agree

Latinos: 36% strongly agree

Asian Americans: 0% strongly agree

*Based on a sample of 304 emerging adults aged 20–29. The first question was not included on the Asian American questionnaire.

when most of them are not contributing to full-time economic activity. Not only are governments paying much or all of the costs of financing emerging adults' tertiary education, they are also losing the economic activity and tax revenue emerging adults would be contributing if their time and energy were not devoted mainly to tertiary education.

Nevertheless, the benefits of tertiary education are great. For societies, an educated population is a key to economic growth in a world economy that is increasingly based on information, technology, and services. This is why countries are willing to make such a large investment in the tertiary education of their emerging adults. For emerging adults themselves, the benefits are also clear. Emerging adults who obtain tertiary education tend to have considerably higher earnings, occupational status, and career attainment over the long run, compared to those who do not attend college (National Center for Education Statistics [NCES], 2011; Pascarella, 2005, 2006; Schneider & Stevenson, 1999).

Tertiary education has multiple benefits in addition to increased earnings. Ernest Pascarella and Patrick Terenzini (1991; Pascarella, 2005, 2006) have conducted research in the United States on this topic for many years. They find a variety of intellectual benefits from attending college, in areas such as general verbal and quantitative skills, oral and written communication skills, and critical thinking. These benefits hold up even after taking into account factors such as age, gender, precollege abilities, and family social class background. Pascarella and Terenzini also find that in the course of the college years students place less emphasis on college as a way to a better job and more emphasis on learning for the sake of enhancing their intellectual and personal growth.

In addition to the academic benefits, Pascarella and Terenzini describe a long list of nonacademic benefits. In the course of the college years, students develop clearer aesthetic and intellectual values. They gain a more distinct identity and become more confident socially. They become less dogmatic, less authoritarian, and less ethnocentric in their political and social views. Their self-concepts and psychological well-being improve. As with the academic benefits, these nonacademic benefits hold up even after taking into account characteristics such as age, gender, and family social class background.

WHAT HAVE YOU LEARNED?

1. What explains the cultural emphasis on unstructured socializing in Japanese colleges?

2. How has the European tertiary education system typically been structured? Why is it becoming more like the U.S. system?

3. Why does it take American students longer to graduate from college than it did a few years ago?

4. What are some of the nonacademic benefits of a college education?

Section 2 VIDEO GUIDE Post-Secondary Education Across Cultures (Length: 8:10)

In this video, emerging adults from various countries discuss their thoughts on higher education.

1. What role does family/parents play in an emerging adult's views on higher education?

2. The Mexican female states that she now regrets not gaining more education. What advice would you give to her now in dealing with this regret?

3. Compare and contrast at least two of the individuals interviewed in this video regarding their views on higher education.

●━⎨**Watch** the **Video** Post-Secondary Education
Across Cultures in **MyDevelopmentLab**

SECTION 3 EMOTIONAL AND SOCIAL DEVELOPMENT

LEARNING OBJECTIVES

9.11 Describe the course of self-esteem from adolescence through emerging adulthood and explain the reasons for this pattern.

9.12 Describe the various forms identity development can take in emerging adulthood, and consider patterns of cultural and ethnic identity.

9.13 Summarize the changes in American gender beliefs in recent decades and include findings from research on gender stereotypes among college students.

9.14 Summarize Smith and Snell's description of the religious beliefs and practices of American emerging adults.

9.15 Explain why emerging adults have often been at the forefront of political movements, and contrast this with their involvement in conventional politics.

9.16 Describe patterns of home-leaving in the United States and Europe and how this transition influences relations with parents.

9.17 Describe the role of intimacy in emerging adults' friendships and the most common activities of emerging adult friends.

9.18 Explain how romantic relationships and sexual behavior change during emerging adulthood.

9.19 Describe the transition from school to full-time work in Europe and the United States, and explain why unemployment rates among emerging adults are higher than for older adults.

9.20 Explain how emerging adults use the Internet and mobile phones to maintain social contacts.

Emotional and Self-Development

Emerging adulthood is a period when emotional and self-development turn more favorable in a variety of ways. After declining in adolescence, self-esteem now rises steadily. Identity development advances and reaches fruition in some ways, as young people move toward making enduring choices in love and work. Gender issues are confronted in new ways as emerging adults enter the workplace and encounter occupational gender expectations and sometimes gender stereotypes.

Self-esteem

9.11 | **LEARNING OBJECTIVE** | Describe the course of self-esteem from adolescence through emerging adulthood and explain the reasons for this pattern.

Think for a moment, how is your self-esteem today different from your self-esteem as an adolescent? As described in the previous chapter, self-esteem often declines during adolescence. However, for most people it rises during emerging adulthood (Galambos et al., 2006; Harter, 1999; O'Malley & Bachman, 1983; Roberts et al., 2001; Schulenberg & Zarrett, 2006). **Figure 9.6** shows this pattern.

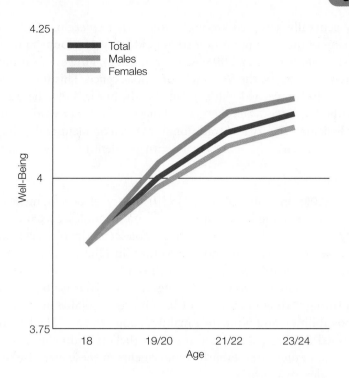

There are a number of reasons why self-esteem increases during emerging adulthood. Physical appearance is important to adolescents' self-esteem, but by emerging adulthood most people have passed through the awkward changes of puberty and may be more comfortable with how they look. Also, feeling accepted and approved by parents contributes to self-esteem, and from adolescence to emerging adulthood relationships with parents generally improve while conflict diminishes (Arnett, 2003; Galambos et al., 2006; O'Connor et al., 1996). Peers and friends are also important to self-esteem, and entering emerging adulthood means leaving the social pressure cooker of secondary school, where peer evaluations are a part of daily life and can be harsh (Gavin & Furman, 1989; Pascoe, 2007).

Also, reaching emerging adulthood usually means having more control over the social contexts of everyday life, which makes it possible for emerging adults to seek out the contexts they prefer and avoid the contexts they find disagreeable, in a way that adolescents cannot. For example, adolescents who dislike school and do poorly have little choice but to attend school, where poor grades may repeatedly undermine their self-esteem. However, emerging adults can leave school and instead engage in full-time work that they may find more gratifying and enjoyable, thus enhancing their self-esteem.

Identity development

Describe the various forms identity development can take in emerging adulthood, and consider patterns of cultural and ethnic identity.

LEARNING OBJECTIVE 9.12

As noted earlier in the chapter, a key feature of emerging adulthood is that it is the age of identity explorations. Emerging adulthood is when most people move toward making definite, long-term choices in love and work. Making these choices often involves thinking about who you are, where you want your life to go, what you believe in, and how your life fits into the world around you. During this time, explorations are made into various aspects of identity, especially love and work, culminating in commitments that set the foundation for adult life.

identity versus identity confusion in Erikson's theory, the crisis of adolescence, with two alternative paths, establishing a clear and definite identity, or experiencing identity confusion, which is a failure to form a stable and secure identity

identity status model model for researching Erikson's theory of identity development, classifying identity development into four categories: diffusion, foreclosure, moratorium, or identity achievement

It is now generally accepted among scholars that emerging adulthood is the life stage when many of the most important steps in identity development take place (Côté, 2006; Luyckx, 2006; Schachter, 2005; Schwartz, 2005). However, for most of the history of research on identity, the focus was on adolescence. This focus was due mainly to Erik Erikson's influence, as I will explain shortly, but it is also because adolescence was formerly the life stage when the main choices in love and work were made. We'll first consider Erikson's theory and traditional research on identity development in adolescence and then discuss the more recent turn to identity development in emerging adulthood.

ERIK ERIKSON'S THEORY In Erik Erikson's (1950) theory of development (refer back to Chapter 1), each stage of life has a central crisis, and in adolescence the crisis is **identity versus identity confusion**. The healthy path in adolescence involves establishing a clear and definite sense of who you are and how you fit into the world around you. The unhealthy alternative is identity confusion, which is a failure to form a stable and secure identity. Identity formation involves reflecting on what your traits, abilities, and interests are, then sifting through the range of life choices available in your culture, trying out various possibilities, and ultimately making commitments. The key areas in which identity is formed are love, work, and ideology (beliefs and values) (Erikson, 1968). In Erikson's view, a failure to establish commitments in these areas by the end of adolescence reflects identity confusion.

There are three elements essential to developing an identity according to Erikson. First, adolescents assess their own abilities and interests. By this age, most people have a pretty good idea about what their strengths and weaknesses are and what they most and least enjoy doing. Second, adolescents reflect on the *identifications* they have accumulated in childhood (Erikson, 1968). Children *identify* with their parents and other loved ones as they grow up—that is, children love and admire them and want to be like them. Thus, adolescents create an identity in part by modeling themselves after parents, friends, and others they have loved in childhood, not simply by imitating them but by integrating parts of their loved ones' behavior and attitudes into their own personality. Third, adolescents assess the opportunities available to them in their society. Many dream of a fabulous career in sports, music, or entertainment (Schneider, 2009), yet there are relatively few opportunities for people to make a living in these areas. Sometimes opportunities are restricted due to discrimination. Until fairly recently, women were discouraged or even barred from professions such as medicine and law. Today, ethnic minorities in many societies find that the doors to many professions are barred to them. In every society, adolescents need to take into account not only what they would like to do but what adults will allow them to do.

Erikson's most influential interpreter has been James Marcia (1966, 1980, 1989, 1999, 2010; Peterson et al., 2004). Marcia constructed a measure called the Identity Status Interview that classified adolescents into one of four identity statuses: *diffusion, moratorium, foreclosure,* or *achievement.* This system of four categories, known as the **identity status model**, has also been used by scholars who have constructed questionnaires to investigate identity development rather than using Marcia's interview (e.g., Adams, 1999; Benson et al., 1992; Grotevant & Adams, 1984; Kroger, 2007).

As shown in **Table 9.2**, each of these classifications involves a different combination of exploration and commitment. Erikson (1968) used the term *identity crisis* to describe the process through which young people construct their identity, but Marcia and other current scholars prefer the term *exploration* (Kroger, 2007; Peterson et al., 2004; Waterman, 2007). "Crisis" implies that the process inherently involves anguish and struggle, whereas "exploration" implies a more positive investigation of possibilities.

Diffusion is an identity status that combines no exploration with no commitment. For adolescents in a state of identity diffusion, no commitments

TABLE 9.2 The Four Identity Statuses

		Commitment	
		Yes	**No**
Exploration	**Yes**	Achievement	Moratorium
	No	Foreclosure	Diffusion

have been made among the choices available to them. Furthermore, no exploration is taking place. The person in this status is not seriously attempting to sort through potential choices and make enduring commitments.

Moratorium involves exploration but no commitment. This is a status of actively trying out different personal, occupational, and ideological possibilities. Different possibilities are being tried on and sifted through, with some being discarded and some selected, in order for adolescents to be able to determine which of the available possibilities are best suited to them.

Adolescents who are in the *foreclosure* status have not experimented with a range of possibilities but have nevertheless committed themselves to certain choices—commitment, but no exploration. This is often a result of their parents' strong influence. Marcia and most other scholars tend to see exploration as a necessary part of forming a healthy identity, and therefore see foreclosure as unhealthy. This is an issue we will discuss further shortly.

Finally, the classification that combines exploration and commitment is *identity achievement*. Identity achievement is the status of young people who have made definite personal, occupational, and ideological choices. By definition, identity achievement is preceded by a period of identity moratorium in which exploration takes place. If commitment takes place without exploration, it is considered identity foreclosure rather than identity achievement.

Although Erikson designated adolescence as the stage of the identity crisis, and research using Marcia's model has mostly focused on adolescence, studies indicate that it takes longer than scholars had expected to reach identity achievement, and in fact for most young people this status is reached—if at all—in emerging adulthood or beyond rather than in adolescence. Studies that have compared adolescents from ages 12 through 18 have found that although the proportion of adolescents in the diffusion category decreases with age and the proportion of adolescents in the identity achievement category increases with age, even by early emerging adulthood less than half are classified as having reached identity achievement (van Hoof, 1999; Kroger, 2003; Meeus et al., 1999). An example of this pattern, from an American study (Waterman, 1999) is shown in **Figure 9.7**. Similar findings were reported in a study of 12- to 27-year-olds in the Netherlands (Meeus et al., 1999).

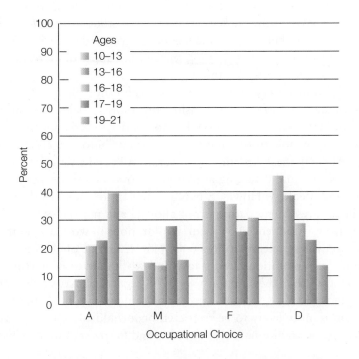

Figure 9.7 • **U.S. study on identity achievement.** With age, more young people are classified in identity achievement and fewer in diffusion. (A = achievement, M = moratorium, F = foreclosure, and D = diffusion) **Source:** Based on data from Developmental Review, Vol 19, A.S. Waterman, Issues of identity formation revisited: United States and the Netherlands, 462–479, 1999.

Studies of college students find that progress toward identity achievement also takes place during the college years, but mainly in the specific area of occupational identity rather than for identity more generally (Waterman, 1992). Some studies indicate that identity achievement may come faster for emerging adults who do not attend college, perhaps because the college environment tends to be a place where young people's ideas about themselves are challenged and they are encouraged to question previously held ideas (Lytle et al., 1997; Munro & Adams, 1997). However, for non-college emerging adults as well, the majority have not reached identity achievement by age 21 (Kroger et al., 2010; Waterman, 1999).

Even 40 years ago, Erikson observed that identity formation was taking longer and longer for young people in developed countries. He commented on the "prolonged adolescence" that was becoming increasingly common in such countries and how this was leading to a prolonged period of identity formation, "during which the young adult through free role experimentation may find a niche in some section of his society" (1968, p. 156). Considering the changes that have taken place since he made this observation in the 1960s, including much later ages of marriage and parenthood and longer education, Erikson's observation applies to far more young people today than it did then (Côté, 2000, 2006). Indeed, the conception of emerging adulthood as a distinct period of life is based to a considerable extent on the fact that, over recent decades, the late teens and early twenties have become a period of "free role experimentation" for an increasing proportion of young people (Arnett, 2000, 2004, 2007a). The achievement of an adult identity comes later, compared with earlier generations, as many emerging adults use the years of their late teens and early twenties for identity explorations in love, work, and ideology.

My Virtual Child

How have you and your culture supported your virtual child's conflict of identity versus identity confusion?

CULTURE AND IDENTITY Most of the research inspired by Erikson's theory has taken place among White middle-class adolescents in the United States, Canada, and Europe (Schwartz et al., 2011). What can we say about identity development among adolescents and emerging adults in other cultures? One observation that can be made is that although Erikson sought to ground his theory in historical and cultural context (Erikson, 1950, 1968; Kroger, 2002), his discussion of identity development nevertheless assumes an independent self that is allowed to make free choices in love, work, and ideology. The focus of Erikson's identity theory is on how young people develop an understanding of themselves as unique individuals. However, as we have discussed in earlier chapters, this conception of the self is distinctively Western and is historically recent (Markus & Kitayama, 1991; Shweder et al., 2006; Sorell & Montgomery, 2001). In most cultures until recently, the self has been understood as *interdependent*, defined in relation to others, rather than as independent. Even today, Erikson's assertions of the prominence of identity issues in adolescence may apply more to modern Western adolescents than to adolescents in other cultures.

A related cultural observation is that the exploration that Erikson viewed as a standard part of identity formation is considerably more possible in some cultures than in others (Sorell & Montgomery, 2001). In today's developed countries, there are few pressures on young people to become economic contributors in childhood or adolescence. Young people in these societies are generally allowed a long psychological moratorium in adolescence and emerging adulthood to try out various possible life choices in love, work, and ideology. However, explorations in love are clearly limited or even nonexistent in cultures where dating is not allowed and marriages are either arranged by parents or strongly influenced by them. Explorations in work are limited in cultures where the economy is simple and offers only a limited range of choices.

Limitations on exploration in both love and work tend to be narrower for girls in developing countries than they are for boys. With regard to love, some degree of sexual experimentation is encouraged for adolescent boys in most cultures, but for girls sexual experimentation is more likely to be restricted or forbidden (Schlegel, 2010). With regard to work, in most traditional cultures today and for most of human history in every culture, adolescent girls have been designated by their cultures for the roles of wife and mother, and these were essentially the only choices open to them (Mensch et al., 1998).

In terms of ideology, too, a psychosocial moratorium has been the exception in human cultures rather than the standard. In most cultures, young people have been expected to grow up to believe what adults teach them to believe, without questioning it. It is only in recent history, and mainly in Western developed countries, that these expectations have changed, and that it has come to be seen as desirable for adolescents and emerging adults to think for themselves, decide on their own beliefs, and make their life choices independently (Bellah et al., 1985; Arnett, 1998).

Another identity issue that has important cultural dimensions is how globalization influences identity, especially for adolescents and emerging adults (Arnett, 2002). Because of globalization, more young people around the world now develop a **bicultural identity** with one part of their identity rooted in their local culture while another part stems from an awareness of their relation to the global culture. For example, India has a growing, vigorous high-tech economic sector, led largely by young people. However, even the better-educated young people, who have become full-fledged members of the global economy, still mostly prefer to have an arranged marriage, in accordance with Indian tradition (Chaudhary & Sharma, 2012). They also generally expect to care for their parents in old age, again in accordance with Indian tradition. Thus they have one identity for participating in the global economy and succeeding in the fast-paced world of high technology, and another identity, rooted in Indian tradition, that they maintain with respect to their families and their personal lives.

ETHNIC IDENTITY In addition to the complex identity issues that arise as a consequence of globalization, many people experience the challenge of growing up as a member of an ethnic minority group. In fact, more people than ever experience this challenge, as worldwide immigration has climbed to unprecedented levels in recent decades (Berry et al., 2006; Phinney, 2006).

Like other identity issues, issues of ethnic identity come to the forefront in adolescence and continue to grow in importance into emerging adulthood (Pahl & Way, 2006; Portes et al., 2000; Wong, 1997). As part of their growing cognitive capacity for self-reflection, adolescents and emerging adults who are members of ethnic minorities are likely to have a sharpened awareness of what it means for them to be a member of their minority group. Group identities such as *African American, Chinese Canadian,* and *Turkish Dutch* take on a new meaning, as adolescents and emerging adults can now think about what these terms mean and how the term for their ethnic group applies to themselves. Also, as a consequence of their growing capacity to think about what others think about them, adolescents and emerging adults become more acutely aware of the prejudices and stereotypes about their ethnic group that others may hold.

For emerging adults, ethnic identity issues are likely to take on a greater prominence as they enter new social contexts such as college and the workplace, and as they meet a broader range of people from different ethnic backgrounds (Phinney, 2006). As children and adolescents they may have been mostly around people of their own ethnic group, but emerging adulthood is likely to take them into new contexts with greater ethnic diversity, sharpening their awareness of their ethnic identity (Syed & Azmitia, 2010). For example, when you entered your college environment it is likely that you came into contact with persons from a greater variety of ethnic backgrounds than you had known previously.

Because adolescents and emerging adults who are members of ethnic minorities have to confront ethnic identity issues, their identity development is likely to be more complex than for those who are part of the majority culture (Phinney, 2000, 2006; Syed & Azmitia, 2010). Consider, for example, identity development in the area of love. Love—along with dating and sex—is an area where cultural conflicts are especially likely to come up for adolescents and emerging adults who are members of ethnic minorities. Part of identity development in the American majority culture means trying

bicultural identity identity with two distinct facets, for example one for the local culture and one for the global culture, or one within one's ethnic group and one for others

APPLYING YOUR KNOWLEDGE
. . . as a Teacher

As a teacher of an increasingly diverse student population, how might you adjust your classes to address ethnic identity issues?

Biculturalism means developing a dual identity, one for the ethnic culture and one for the majority culture.

out different possibilities in love by forming emotionally intimate relationships with different people and gaining sexual experience. However, this model is in sharp conflict with the values of certain American ethnic minority groups. In most Asian American groups, for example, recreational dating is disapproved and sexual experimentation before marriage is taboo—especially for females (Qin, 2009; Talbani & Hasanali, 2000; Wong, 1997). Young people in Asian American ethnic groups face a challenge in reconciling the values of their ethnic group on such issues with the values of the majority culture, to which they are inevitably exposed through school, the media, and peers (Phinney & Rosenthal, 1992; Qin, 2009).

How, then, does identity development take place for young people who are members of minority groups within Western societies? To what extent do they develop an identity that reflects the values of the majority culture, and to what extent do they retain the values of their minority group? One scholar who has done extensive work on these questions among American minorities is Jean Phinney, (1990, 2000, 2006, 2010; Phinney & Devich-Navarro, 1997). On the basis of her research, Phinney has concluded that young people who are members of minority groups have four different ways of responding to their awareness of their ethnicity (see **Table 9.3**):

- *Assimilation* is the option that involves leaving behind the ways of one's ethnic group and adopting the values and way of life of the majority culture. This is the path that is reflected in the idea that a society is a "melting pot" that blends people of diverse origins into one national culture.
- *Marginality* involves rejecting one's culture of origin but also feeling rejected by the majority culture. Some young people may feel little identification with the culture of their parents and grandparents, nor do they feel accepted and integrated into the larger society.
- *Separation* is the approach that involves associating only with members of one's own ethnic group and rejecting the ways of the majority culture.
- *Biculturalism* involves developing a dual identity, one based in the ethnic group of origin and one based in the majority culture. Being bicultural means moving back and forth between the ethnic culture and the majority culture, and alternating identities as appropriate to the situation.

Which of these identity statuses is most common among ethnic minorities? Although ethnic identity has recently been recognized as potentially most prominent in emerging

TABLE 9.3 Four Possible Ethnic Identity Statuses

		Identification With Ethnic Group	
		High	**Low**
Identification With Majority Culture	**High**	Bicultural	Assimilated
	Low	Separated	Marginal

Examples:

Assimilation: "I don't really think of myself as Asian American, just as American."

Separation: "I am not part of two cultures. I am just Black."

Marginality: "When I'm with my Indian friends, I feel White, and when I'm with my White friends, I feel Indian. I don't really feel like I belong with either of them."

Biculturalism: "Being both Mexican and American means having the best of both worlds. You have different strengths you can draw from in different situations."

Source: Based on Variation in bicultural identification among African American and Mexican American adolescents. Journal of Research on Adolescence, 7, 3–32.

adulthood (Phinney, 2006), most research thus far has taken place on adolescents. The bicultural status is the most common status among Mexican Americans and Asian Americans, as well as among some European minority groups such as Turkish adolescents in the Netherlands (Neto, 2002; Rotheram-Borus, 1990; Phinney et al., 1994; Verkuyten, 2002). However, separation is the most common ethnic identity status among African American adolescents, and marginality is pervasive among Native American adolescents. Of course, each ethnic group is diverse and contains adolescents with a variety of different ethnic identity statuses. Adolescents tend to be more aware of their ethnic identity when they are in a context where they are in the minority. For example, in one study, Latino adolescents attending a predominately non-Latino school reported significantly higher levels of ethnic identity than adolescents in a predominately Latino or a balanced Latino/non-Latino school (Umaña-Taylor, 2005).

Is ethnic identity related to other aspects of development in adolescence and emerging adulthood? Some studies have found that adolescents who are bicultural or assimilated have higher self-esteem (e.g., Farver et al., 2002). Furthermore, several studies have found that having a strong ethnic identity is related to a variety of other favorable aspects of development, such as overall well-being, academic achievement, and lower rates of risk behavior (Giang & Wittig, 2006; St. Louis & Liem, 2005; Yasui et al., 2004; Yip & Fuligni, 2002).

Gender development: Cultural beliefs and stereotypes

Summarize the changes in American gender beliefs in recent decades and include findings from research on gender stereotypes among college students.

LEARNING OBJECTIVE 9.13

Emerging adulthood is an important time for gender development, because this is the life stage when many people become involved full-time in the workplace. Consequently, they may encounter more vividly during this stage their society's beliefs about gender in relation to occupational roles and aspirations.

What sort of cultural beliefs about gender exist for adolescents and emerging adults currently growing up in American society? The results of the General Social Survey (GSS), an annual national survey of American adults, show a clear trend toward more egalitarian gender attitudes in recent decades, as ***Figure 9.8*** shows (Cotter et al., 2011; National Opinion Research Center, 2007). Compared to 1977, American adults today are less likely to believe men are better politicians, less likely to see women as the ones who should take care of the home, more likely to believe working mothers can have warm relationships with their children, and less likely to

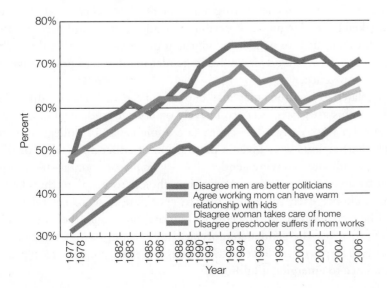

Figure 9.8 • **Change in American gender attitudes, 1977–2006.** Over recent decades, views of gender roles have become less traditional.

Would you assume a female mechanic would be less competent than a male mechanic? Gender stereotypes related to work remain strong.

believe preschoolers would suffer if mothers work. However, the results of the GSS also show that a considerable proportion of Americans—from about one-fourth to over one-third, depending on the question—continue to harbor beliefs about gender roles not unlike the ones we have seen in traditional cultures: Men should hold the power and be out in the world doing things, and women should focus on caring for children and running the household.

Given the differential gender socialization that people in American society experience in childhood and adolescence, it should not be surprising to find that by the time they reach emerging adulthood they have different expectations for males and females. Most research on gender expectations in adulthood has been conducted by social psychologists, and because social psychologists often use college undergraduates as their research participants, much of this research pertains to emerging adults' views of gender. Social psychologists have especially focused on gender stereotypes. A **stereotype** occurs when people believe others possess certain characteristics simply as a result of being a member of a particular group. Gender stereotypes, then, attribute certain characteristics to others on the basis of whether they are male or female (Kite et al., 2008).

One area of particular interest with regard to emerging adulthood is research on college students' gender stereotypes involving work. Generally, this research indicates that college students often evaluate women's work performance less favorably than men's. In one classic study, college women were asked to evaluate the quality of several articles supposedly written by professionals in a variety of fields (Goldberg, 1968). Some of the articles were in stereotypically female fields such as dietetics, some were in stereotypically male fields such as city planning, and some were in gender-neutral fields. There were two identical versions of each article, one supposedly written by, for example, "John McKay" and the other written by "Joan McKay." The results indicated that the women rated the articles more highly when they thought a man was the author. Even articles on the "female" fields were judged as better when written by a man. Other studies have found similar results with samples of both male and female college students (Cejka & Eagly, 1999; Paludi & Strayer, 1985). Recent studies have continued to find strong gender stereotypes related to work (Cabrera et al., 2009; Johnson, S. K., et al., 2008; White & White, 2006). Although not all studies have found a tendency for men's work to be evaluated more favorably, when differences are found they tend to favor men.

One recent study reported that gender stereotypes can be especially harsh for persons who have high status in gender-incongruent occupations, for example a woman who has become head of an engineering department (Brescoll et al., 2010). College students were asked to read vignettes describing a leader's successful performance or mistakes in gender-congruent or gender-incongruent professions, then evaluate the leader's competence. Leaders who made mistakes in gender-incongruent professions were rated as lowest in competence.

Gender-related evaluations may also depend on the age of the evaluator. As noted, most studies in this area have been exclusively on college students, but one study compared males who were early adolescents, late adolescents, or college students (Lobel et al., 2004). Participants were given a description of either an average or outstanding male election candidate behaving gender-stereotypically or counter-stereotypically and were asked to indicate their personal election choice, to estimate the likelihood that others would choose each candidate, and to speculate how successful the candidate would be if he were elected. Adolescents were more likely than the emerging adult college students to favor the gender-stereotypical candidate. No differences were found between the two stages of adolescence. This suggests that gender stereotypes may wane from adolescence to emerging adulthood.

APPLYING YOUR KNOWLEDGE

Do you think your professors evaluate your work without regard to your gender? Does it depend on the subject area?

stereotype belief that others possess certain characteristics simply as a result of being a member of a particular group

WHAT HAVE YOU LEARNED?

1. How is having control over social contexts related to the rise in self-esteem during emerging adulthood?

2. Why did Erikson emphasize adolescence as the crucial time for identity development and why has the focus now shifted to emerging adulthood?

3. What are the consequences of globalization for identity development and why are those consequences more evident in emerging adulthood than in other life stages?

4. What are the four categories of ethnic identity development and to what other aspects of development are they related?

5. What can be concluded from studies of gender stereotypes among college students?

Cultural Beliefs

Children and adolescents learn the cultural beliefs distinctive to their culture, and by emerging adulthood they have developed a worldview composed of these beliefs. However, beliefs continue to develop during emerging adulthood and beyond. In emerging adulthood there are notable developments in religious and political beliefs and behavior.

Religious development

Summarize Smith and Snell's description of the religious beliefs and practices of American emerging adults.

LEARNING OBJECTIVE 9.14

In American studies, religiosity generally declines from adolescence through emerging adulthood. Both religious participation and religious beliefs decline throughout the teens and are lower in the late teens and early twenties than at any other period of the life span (Hoge et al., 1993; Smith & Snell, 2009; Wallace & Williams, 1997). This pattern may reflect the individualism of American society. Emerging adults often feel they need to make a break with their parents' religious beliefs and practices to establish that they are making their own decisions about their beliefs and values (Arnett & Jensen, 2002).

A recent study by Christian Smith and Patricia Snell goes into greater depth and detail than previous studies on religious development among American emerging adults (Smith & Snell, 2010). The study included survey data on over 2,500 emerging adults (ages 18–23) in 37 states; 250 subjects were interviewed. Most of the emerging adults in the study had been included in Smith's earlier study of adolescents' religious development five years earlier (described in Chapter 8).

Overall, there was a decline in religiosity from adolescence to emerging adulthood, both in behavior and in beliefs. Only about 30% of emerging adults attended religious services at least once a month; over half attended only a few times a year or less. Beliefs were stronger than behavior; 44% reported that religious faith is "very" or "extremely" important in their lives, and 75% reported believing in God. Nevertheless, these percentages were lower than they had been in adolescence.

Just as in adolescence, in emerging adulthood religious beliefs were highly individualized. Few emerging adults accepted a standard religious doctrine; instead, they adopted a make-your-own approach to their religious beliefs, constructed partly from what they had learned from their parents but also from many other sources. Consequently, religious denomination did not hold much meaning for most of them. They could state they were "Catholic" or "Presbyterian" or "Jewish" without actually believing much of what is stated in the traditional doctrine of that faith and without participating in it. In fact, 38% of "Protestants" and 35% of "Catholics" reported that they

TABLE 9.4 Smith and Snell's Five Religious Categories	
Category	**Description**
Selective adherents (30%)	Many in this group identify with a particular denomination, but they believe only part of the doctrine while rejecting other parts and adding other beliefs outside the doctrine.
Religiously indifferent/disconnected (30%)	This group includes emerging adults who have little knowledge of or opinion on religion.
Spiritually open (15%)	People in this group believe there is "something out there," some kind of god or higher power, but are not sure what form it takes and they do not locate themselves in any religious tradition.
Committed traditionalists (15%)	Includes people of strong conservative faith. They are the only ones who accept a religious doctrine and a religious tradition. They are the group most likely to attend religious services.
Irreligious (10%)	Actively hostile to religion.

Source: Based on Smith, Snell. Souls in transition: The religious lives of emerging adults in America. 2010.

In most cultures through history, young people have been expected to believe what their parents believe, not to decide on their own beliefs. Here, a young Israeli man prays.

never attend religious services. This individualized approach to religion led to great religious diversity in emerging adulthood, which Smith and Snell (2010) grouped into five categories (see **Table 9.4**).

Although emerging adults' religious beliefs and practices are diverse, there are common themes that apply to most of them, according to Smith and Snell (2010). Emerging adults tend to believe that what is most important about religion is the belief in God and the encouragement to try to be a good person. Consequently, few of them view the differences between different religions as important. They are tolerant of religious differences and do not believe there is any way to determine if one religion is more true than another.

Just as in adolescence, religious faith in emerging adulthood tends to be associated with a variety of other positive characteristics. Smith and Snell (2010) found religious belief and participation among emerging adults to be related to higher well-being and lower rates of participation in a variety of types of risk behavior. Another study, comparing African American and European American emerging adults, reported that African Americans were more likely to cope with stress by relying on their religious beliefs, and in turn they experienced fewer anxiety symptoms than European American emerging adults did (Chapman & Steger, 2010). This is consistent with studies in other age periods showing that African Americans tend to be more religious than Whites are (Dilworth-Anderson et al., 2007).

Political development

9.15   **LEARNING OBJECTIVE**   Explain why emerging adults have often been at the forefront of political movements, and contrast this with their involvement in conventional politics.

In most countries, 18 is the age when people first receive the right to vote, so political development might be expected to be an important issue in emerging adulthood. However, political involvement tends to be very low among emerging adults. In Europe as well as in Canada and the United States, emerging adults' political participation is strikingly low by conventional measures such as voting rates and involvement in political parties (Barrio et al., 2007; Botcheva et al., 2007; Meeus, 2007; Sears et al., 2007). Emerging adults tend to have lower political participation not only in comparison to adults but in comparison to previous generations of young people. They tend to be skeptical of the motivations of politicians, and to see the activities of political parties as irrelevant to their lives. One recent study of young people in eight European countries found that low levels of trust in political authorities and political systems were consistent from adolescence through emerging adulthood (Hooghe & Wilkenfeld, 2008).

However, the rejection of conventional politics should not be construed as a lack of interest in improving the state of their communities, their societies, and the world. On the contrary, emerging adults in many countries are more likely than older adults to be involved in organizations devoted to particular issues, such as environmental protection and efforts against war and racism (Goossens & Luyckx, 2007; Meeus, 2007). In one nationwide survey of college freshmen in the United States, only 28% said they were interested in politics, but 81% had done volunteer work and 45% had participated in a political demonstration (Kellogg, 2001). Often frustrated by and alienated from conventional political processes, emerging adults choose instead to direct their energies toward specific areas of importance to them, where they believe they are more likely to see genuine progress.

Furthermore, emerging adults have often been involved in movements at the political extremes, including peaceful protests, uprisings, revolutionary movements, and terrorism. The leaders of politically extreme groups are usually in midlife or later, but many of their most zealous followers are often emerging adults. There are many recent historical examples of this, including the terrorist attacks by Muslim extremists against Western (especially American) targets—most notably the attacks of September 11, 2001 (Sen & Samad, 2007). The collapse of Communism in Eastern Europe in 1989 was initiated by emerging adults through strikes, demonstrations, and the formation of new youth-oriented political parties (Botcheva et al., 2007; Flanagan & Botcheva, 1999; Macek, 2006). Recent protests against governments in the Middle East have also involved emerging adults more than any other age group (Hvistendahl, 2011).

Why are emerging adults especially likely to be involved in extreme political movements? One reason is that they have fewer social ties and obligations than people in other age periods (Arnett, 2005b). Children and adolescents can be restrained from involvement by their parents. Young, middle, and older adults can be deterred from involvement by their commitments to others who depend on them, especially a spouse and children. However, emerging adulthood is a time when social commitments and social control are at their low point. Emerging adults have more freedom than people at other age periods, and this freedom allows some of them to become involved in extreme political movements.

Another possibility is that their involvement is identity-related. Recall that one of the key developmental features of emerging adulthood is that it is a time of identity explorations. One aspect of identity explorations is ideology or worldview (Arnett, 2004; Erikson, 1968). Emerging adulthood is a time when people are looking for an ideological framework for explaining the world, and some emerging adults may be attracted to the definite answers provided by extreme political movements. Embracing an extreme political ideology may relieve the discomfort that can accompany the uncertainty and doubt of ideological explorations. Still, these explanations beg the question, since only a small minority of emerging adults are involved in these extreme movements, why them and not the others?

Emerging adults have often been at the forefront of political movements. Here, emerging adults participate in antigovernment protests in Tahrir Square in Cairo, Egypt. Demonstrations such as this led to the peaceful overthrow of the government in 2011.

WHAT HAVE YOU LEARNED?

1. How do religious beliefs and practices in emerging adulthood compare to adolescence, and what are some reasons for the differences?

2. What are some of the positive characteristics associated with religious faith in emerging adulthood?

3. How does emerging adults' participation in conventional politics compare to other adult age groups?

4. What are some examples of how emerging adults have been in the front lines of political movements?

The Social and Cultural Contexts of Emerging Adulthood

Emerging adulthood is a life stage in which sociocultural contexts change in some profound and dramatic ways. After living within a family context from infancy through adolescence, emerging adults in many countries move out of their parents' household, diminishing their parents' influence and giving them more control over their daily lives. Friends are highly important, especially for emerging adults who are currently without a romantic relationship. Romantic relationships take on new importance, as intimacy deepens and emerging adults move toward making an enduring commitment to a love partner. The school context changes, as many emerging adults leave school and those who remain engage in more specific education and training for an occupation. Work becomes a much more important context, as most emerging adults engage in full-time work by their mid-twenties. Media remain a source of entertainment and enjoyment, especially the Internet and mobile phones.

Family relationships

9.16 | **LEARNING OBJECTIVE** | Describe patterns of home-leaving in the United States and Europe and how this transition influences relations with parents.

In most Western majority cultures, most young people move out of their parents' home sometime during emerging adulthood. In the United States, leaving home typically takes place around ages 18 to 19 (De Marco & Berzin, 2008). The most common reasons for leaving home stated by emerging adults are going to college, cohabiting with a partner, or simply the desire for independence (Goldscheider & Goldscheider, 1999; Seiffge-Krenke, 2009).

Typically, relationships between parents and emerging adults improve once the young person leaves home. In this case, at least, absence makes the heart grow fonder. Numerous studies have confirmed that emerging adults report greater closeness and fewer negative feelings toward their parents after moving out (Aquilino, 2006; O'Connor et al., 1996; Smetana et al., 2004). Furthermore, emerging adults who move out tend to get along better with their parents than those who remain at home. For example, in one study of 21-year-olds, the emerging adults who had moved at least an hour away (by car) from their parents reported the highest levels of closeness to their parents and valued their parents' opinions most highly (Dubas & Petersen, 1991). Emerging adults who remained at home had the poorest relations with their parents, and those who had moved out but remained within an hour's drive were in between the other two groups.

What explains these patterns? Some scholars have suggested that leaving home leads young people to appreciate their parents more (Arnett, 2004; Katchadourian & Boli, 1985). Another factor may be that it is easier to be fond of someone you no longer live with. Once emerging adults move out, they no longer experience the day-to-day friction with their parents that inevitably results from living with others. They can now control the frequency and timing of their interactions with their parents in a way they could not when they were living with them. They can visit their parents for the weekend, for a holiday, or for dinner, enjoy the time together, and still maintain full control over their daily lives. As a 24-year-old woman in my research put it, "I don't have to talk to them when I don't want to, and when I want to, I can" (Arnett, 2004, p. 49).

In the United States, although most emerging adults move out of their parents' home in their late teens, a substantial proportion (about one-fourth) stay home through their early twenties (Goldscheider & Goldscheider, 1999). Staying at home is more common among Latinos, Blacks, and Asian Americans than among White Americans (Fuligni & Witkow, 2004). The reason for this is sometimes economic, especially for Latinos and African Americans, who have high rates of unemployment in emerging adulthood (U.S. Bureau of the Census, 2011). However, another important reason appears to be the greater emphasis on family closeness and interdependence in minority cultures, and less emphasis on being independent as a value in itself. For example, one emerging adult in my research (Arnett, 2004) lived with her Chinese American mother and Mexican American father throughout her college years at the University of California-Berkeley. She enjoyed the way staying home allowed her to remain in close contact with them. "I loved living at home. I respect my parents a lot, so being home with them was actually one of the things I liked to do most," she said. "Plus, it was free!" (Arnett, 2004, p. 54). For Latinos and Asian Americans, an additional reason for staying home is specific to young women, and concerns the high value placed on virginity before marriage.

About 40% of American emerging adults "return to the nest" to live at least once after they leave (Aquilino, 2006; Goldscheider & Goldscheider, 1999). There are many reasons why emerging adults sometimes move home again (Goldscheider & Goldscheider, 1999). For those who left home for college, moving back home may be a way of bridging their transition to postcollege life after they graduate or drop out. It gives them a chance to decide what to do next, be it graduate school, a job near home, or a job farther away. For those who left home for independence, some may feel that the glow of independence dims after a while as the freedom of doing what they want when they want becomes outweighed by the burden of taking care of a household and paying all their own bills. An early divorce or a period of military service are other reasons emerging adults give for returning home (Goldscheider & Goldscheider, 1999). Under these circumstances, too, coming home may be attractive to young people as a transition period, a chance to get back on their feet before they venture again into the world.

There are a number of possible outcomes when emerging adults move back home (Arnett, 2004). For some, the return home is welcome and the transition is managed easily. A successful transition home is more likely if parents recognize the change in their children's maturity and treat them as adults rather than adolescents. For others, however, the return home is a bumpy transition. Parents may have come to enjoy having the nest all to themselves, without children to provide for and feel responsible for. Emerging adults may find it difficult to have parents monitoring them daily again, after a period when they had grown used to managing their own lives. In my research (Arnett, 2004), after Mary moved home she was dismayed to find that her mother would wait up for her when she went out with her boyfriend, just like it was high school all over again. They did not argue openly about it, but it made Mary feel "like she was sort of 'in my territory' or something" (p. 53). For many emerging adults, moving back home results in ambivalence. They are grateful for the support their parents provide, even as they resent returning to the subordinate role of a dependent child (White, 2002). Perhaps because of this ambivalence, the return home tends to be brief, with two-thirds of emerging adults moving out again within one year (Aquilino, 2006).

In European countries, emerging adults tend to live with their parents longer than in the United States, especially in southern and eastern Europe (Douglass, 2005, 2007; Kins et al., 2009). For example, in Greece, Italy, and Spain, more than 50% of men and women in their twenties live with their parents, with the numbers over 80% for men. In the United States, more than 50% of White men in their twenties live with their parents, while the figure is close to 70% for Black and Latino males. In Europe and in the United States, the figures are lower for females than for males. This is probably because females tend to marry at a slightly younger age than do males (Iacovou, 2002).

APPLYING YOUR KNOWLEDGE
. . . as a Parent

Your 25-year-old son wants to move back in with you after college to work on a film, and your spouse is embarrassed that he can't make it on his own. How can you help your spouse get over these concerns and adjust to having your son back at home?

My Virtual Child

How will your relationship with your virtual child change during emerging adulthood? What do you think would happen if your child had been raised in a different culture?

Emerging adults in southern Europe often live with parents through their twenties. Here, an Italian family enjoys an outdoor dinner together.

|||||||||||||||||||||||||||||||||||||||||||||||||

❝*In high school I was rude, inconsiderate, and got into many fights with my mom. Since coming to college I realize how much she means to me and how much she goes out of her way for me. I've grown to have a true appreciation for her.*❞

— Matt, age 21
(in Arnett, 2004, p. 57)

|||||||||||||||||||||||||||||||||||||||||||||||||

There are a number of practical reasons why European emerging adults stay home longer. European university students are more likely than American students to continue to live at home while they attend university. European emerging adults who do not attend university may have difficulty finding or affording an apartment of their own. However, also important are European cultural values that emphasize mutual support within the family while also allowing young people substantial autonomy. Young Europeans find that they can enjoy a higher standard of living by staying at home rather than living independently, and at the same time enjoy substantial autonomy. Italy provides a good case in point (Chisholm & Hurrelmann, 1995; Kraus, 2005). Ninety-four percent of Italians aged 15 to 24 live with their parents, the highest percentage in the European Union (EU), and many of them continue to live with their parents even into their late twenties and early thirties (Bonino et al., 2012). However, only 8% of them view their living arrangements as a problem—the lowest percentage among EU countries. Many European emerging adults remain at home contentedly through their early twenties, by choice rather than necessity.

There is more to the changes in relationships with parents from adolescence to emerging adulthood than simply the effects of moving out, staying home, or moving back in. Emerging adults also grow in their ability to understand their parents (Arnett, 2004). Adolescence is in some ways an egocentric period (refer back to Chapter 8) and adolescents often have difficulty taking their parents' perspectives. They sometimes evaluate their parents harshly, magnifying their deficiencies and becoming easily irritated by their imperfections. As emerging adults mature and begin to feel more adult themselves, they become more capable of understanding how their parents look at things. They come to see their parents as persons and begin to realize that their parents, like themselves, have a mix of qualities, merits as well as faults.

There has been little research on sibling relationships in emerging adulthood (Aquilino, 2006). However, one study of adolescents and emerging adults in Israel found that emerging adults spent less time with their siblings than adolescents did but also felt more emotional closeness and warmth toward their siblings (Scharf et al., 2005). Conflict and rivalry were also reported to be less intense by emerging adults than by adolescents. Qualitative analyses showed that emerging adults had a more mature perception of their relationship with their siblings than adolescents did, in the sense that they were better able to understand their siblings' needs and perspectives.

Friendships

9.17 **LEARNING OBJECTIVE** Describe the role of intimacy in emerging adults' friendships and the most common activities of emerging adult friends.

In a number of ways, friendships may be especially important in emerging adulthood. The majority of emerging adults move away from home and so lose the daily social support they may have received from their parents and siblings. Even for the ones who return home or remain home, they may rely less on their parents for social support as they strive toward becoming self-sufficient and making their own decisions (Arnett, 2004). Consequently, they may turn more to friends than to parents for companionship and support.

As we have seen, intimacy becomes more important to friendships in adolescence than it had been in middle childhood, and that trend may continue into emerging adulthood. In one study (Radmacher & Azmitia, 2006), early adolescents (ages 12–13) and emerging adults (ages 18–20) described a time when they felt especially close to a friend. Emerging adults' accounts contained more self-disclosure and fewer shared activities, compared to early adolescents. Among the emerging adults (but not the early adolescents) there was a gender difference. Self-disclosure promoted emotional closeness for young women, whereas for young men shared activities were usually the basis of feeling emotional closeness.

What kinds of things do emerging adults do with their friends? Much of their time together is unstructured socializing (described earlier in the chapter), in activities such as visiting each other informally and going out together. Some drink alcohol or use drugs together, and as we have seen earlier, unstructured socializing and substance use often take place together (Osgood, 2009). Emerging adults also participate in media-related activities together, such as watching TV or playing electronic games (Brown, 2006) (see Social Uses of Media, later in the chapter). And emerging adults seem to be always connected through social media and cell phones. Many enjoy playing sports or exercising together (Malebo et al., 2007). Overall, leisure activities with friends decline steadily in the course of the twenties as emerging adults form close romantic relationships and begin to enter adult responsibilities such as stable work, marriage, and parenthood (Osgood, 2009).

APPLYING YOUR KNOWLEDGE
What are some other reasons why leisure activities with friends might decline in the course of emerging adulthood, other than those mentioned here?

Love and sexuality

> Explain how romantic relationships and sexual behavior change during emerging adulthood.

LEARNING OBJECTIVE 9.18

Emerging adulthood is a time of gradually building the structure of an adult life in love and work. In many cultures, explorations in love are part of this process, as emerging adults experience a series of romantic and sexual relationships in the course of deciding on a long-term partner.

IN SEARCH OF A SOUL MATE: FINDING A ROMANTIC PARTNER A key part of emerging adulthood involves moving away from one's family, not just geographically but socially and emotionally, and toward a new love partner, in marriage or another long-term romantic partnership. Jennifer Tanner (2006) calls this process "recentering." For children and adolescents, the center of their emotional lives is within their family, with their parents and siblings. For adults, the center of their emotional lives is usually with a new family constellation, mainly a romantic partner, and usually children as well. Emerging adulthood is when the change takes place, as the center of emotional life is transferred from the original family to a long-term romantic partner. Parents and siblings remain important, of course. As we have seen, relations with them even improve in many ways. But the center of emotional life usually moves to a romantic partner. 👁

When they talk about what they are looking for in a romantic partner, emerging adults around the world mention a wide variety of ideal qualities (Gibbons & Stiles, 2004; Hatfield & Rapson, 2005). Sometimes these are qualities of the person, the individual: intelligent, attractive, or funny. But most often they mention interpersonal qualities, qualities a person brings to a relationship, such as kind, caring, loving, and trustworthy. Emerging adults hope to find someone who will treat them well and who will be capable of an intimate, mutually loving, durable relationship.

In romantic relationships as in friendships, intimacy becomes more important in emerging adulthood than it had been in adolescence. One study investigated views of the functions of love relationships among early adolescents (sixth grade), late adolescents (eleventh grade), and college students (Roscoe et al., 1987). The early and late adolescents both considered recreation to be the most important function, followed by intimacy, and then status. In contrast, for the college students intimacy ranked highest, followed by companionship, with recreation a bit lower, and status much lower. A more recent study reported similar results (Montgomery, 2005). 👁

In addition to looking for intimacy, emerging adults also seek a romantic partner who will be like themselves in many ways. Opposites rarely attract; on the contrary, birds of a feather flock together. A long line of studies has established that emerging adults, like people of other ages, tend to have romantic relationships with people who are similar to themselves in characteristics such as personality, intelligence, social class,

👁 **Watch** the **Video** Rules for Dating in **MyDevelopmentLab**

👁 **Watch** the **Video** Love in the 21st Century in **MyDevelopmentLab**

cohabitation unmarried romantic partners living together

◉⊣ **Watch** the **Video** Relationships and Love in **MyDevelopmentLab**

THINKING CULTURALLY

What are some cultural explanations for why cohabiting couples in Europe stay together as long as married couples, but those in the United States often break up within five years?

❝*I don't see how people can get married without living together. I wanted to make sure that she doesn't throw her socks on top of the sink and if she puts the top back on the toothpaste and stuff. All those little things.*❞
—*Pete, age 25*
(in Arnett, 2004, p. 108)

ethnic background, religious beliefs, and physical attractiveness (Furman & Simon, 2008; Markey & Markey, 2007). Scholars attribute this to what they call *consensual validation,* which means that people like to find in others a match, or *consensus,* with their own characteristics. Finding this consensus reaffirms, or *validates,* their own way of looking at the world. The more similar your love partner is to you, the more likely you are to reaffirm each other, and the less likely you are to have conflicts that spring from having different views and preferences. ◉

COHABITATION   For many emerging adults in the West, the next step after forming an exclusive, enduring relationship with a romantic partner is not marriage but moving in together. In the United States and Canada as well as in northern European countries, **cohabitation** before marriage is now experienced by at least two-thirds of emerging adults (Kiernan, 2002; Lichter et al., 2010). The percentage is highest in the Scandinavian countries, where nearly all young people cohabit before marriage (Syltevik, 2010). Cohabitation tends to be brief and unstable for young Americans. One study found that half of cohabiting relationships lasted less than a year, and only one in 10 couples were together five years later (Bumpass & Liu, 2000). In contrast, cohabiting couples in European countries tend to stay together as long as married couples (Hacker, 2002).

However, in Europe there are distinct differences in cohabitation between north and south (Kiernan, 2002, 2004). Emerging adults in southern Europe are considerably less likely than their counterparts in the north to cohabit; most emerging adults in southern Europe live at home until marriage (Douglass, 2005), especially females. Perhaps due to the Catholic religious tradition in the south, cohabitation carries a moral stigma there that it does not have in the north. Cohabitation is also rare in Asian cultures, most of which have a long tradition of sexual conservatism and virginity at marriage.

Young people choose to cohabit sometimes for practical reasons—two together can live more cheaply than two separately—and sometimes because they wish to enhance the likelihood that when they marry, it will last. Indeed, in a national (American) survey of 20- to 29-year-olds, 62% agreed that "Living together with someone before marriage is a good way to avoid eventual divorce" (Popenoe & Whitehead, 2001). Emerging adults from divorced families are especially likely to cohabit, because they are especially determined to avoid their parents' fate (Cunningham & Thornton, 2007). However, cohabitation before marriage is related to higher rather than lower likelihood of later divorce (Cohan & Kleinbaum, 2002; Kiernan, 2002, 2004).

This may be because cohabiting couples become used to living together while maintaining separate lives in many ways, especially financially, so that they are unprepared for the compromises required by marriage. Also, even before entering cohabitation, emerging adults who cohabit tend to be different from emerging adults who do not, in ways that are related to higher risk of divorce—less religious, more skeptical of the institution of marriage, and more accepting of divorce (Cohan & Kleinbaum, 2002; Stanley et al., 2004; Wu, 1999). However, one analysis concluded that cohabitation itself increases the risk of divorce, because it leads some couples who are not compatible to marry anyway, out of "the inertia of cohabitation" (Stanley et al., 2006).

SEXUALITY   In their sexual behavior as in other aspects of their lives, there is a great deal of diversity among emerging adults. The most common pattern among American 18- to 24-year-olds is to have had one partner in the past year (Lefkowitz & Gillen, 2006; Regnerus & Uecker, 2011). However, emerging adults are more likely than adults in older age groups to have had either more or fewer sexual partners. About one-third of 18- to 23-year-olds report having had two or more partners in the past year, but about one-fourth report having had sex not at all in the past year (Regnerus & Uecker, 2011). At the beginning of emerging adulthood, age 18, about half of Americans have had intercourse at least once, and by age 25 nearly all emerging adults have had intercourse at least once, but those who have their first episode of intercourse relatively late tend to be "active abstainers" rather than "accidental abstainers" (Lefkowitz, 2006). That is, they remain virgins longer because they have chosen to wait rather than because they had no opportunity for sex. Common reasons for abstaining are fear of pregnancy, fear of sexually-transmitted infections (STIs), religious or moral beliefs, and the feeling one has not yet met the right person (Lefkowitz et al., 2004; Sprecher & Regan, 1996).

Sexual behavior in emerging adulthood most commonly takes place in the context of a close romantic relationship (Lefkowitz, 2006). However, emerging adults are more likely than adults in older age groups to engage in recreational sex or "hooking up." In one study, 30% of American emerging adult college students reported having at least one episode of hooking up that included intercourse, and an additional 48% reported at least one episode of hooking up that did not involve intercourse (Paul et al., 2000). Male emerging adults are more likely than females to have sexual attitudes that favor recreational sex. They tend to be more likely than females to be willing to have intercourse with someone they have known for only a few hours, to have sex with two different partners in the same day, and to have sex with someone they do not love (Knox et al., 2001).

Frequently, episodes of hooking up are fueled by alcohol. In various studies, from one-fourth to one-half of emerging adults report having consumed alcohol before their most recent sexual encounter (Lefkowitz, 2006), and emerging adults who drink often are more likely than others to have had multiple sexual partners (Regnerus & Uecker, 2011). The college environment is especially conducive to hooking up since it brings together so many emerging adults in a common setting that includes frequent social events that involve alcohol use (Sperber, 2001).

Most American emerging adults are quite responsible about contraceptive use, although certainly not all of them. Only about 10% of sexually active emerging adults report never using contraception, but an additional 35% of them report inconsistent or ineffective contraceptive use (Hogben & Williams, 2001; Regnerus & Uecker, 2011). Over 80% of emerging adults report using condoms during a hookup (Corbin & Fromme, 2002; Paul et al., 2000). As a romantic relationship develops between emerging adults, they often move from condom use to oral contraceptives, because they believe sex feels better without a condom or because switching to oral contraceptives signifies a deeper level of trust and commitment (Hammer et al., 1996; Lefkowitz, 2006).

Surveys have been conducted in numerous countries that demonstrate the wide variability in cultural approaches to premarital sexuality around the world (Hatfield & Rapson, 2005). *Table 9.5* shows some examples. Premarital sex is common in Western European countries. Rates of premarital sex are somewhat lower in the countries of South America, although the large differences in reported premarital sex by male and female adolescents in countries such as Brazil and Chile suggest that males exaggerate their sexual activity or females underreport theirs (or both). Finally, premarital sex is least common in Asian countries such as Japan and South Korea, where the emphasis on female virginity before marriage is still very strong. Missing from the table are figures from the Arab countries—no Arab country allows social scientists to ask adolescents about their sexual behavior—but ethnographic studies indicate that rates of premarital sex in those countries are even lower than in Asia because of the severe penalties for girls who violate the prohibition (Davis & Davis, 2012).

In the United States, use of the Internet for pornography is widespread among emerging adults. In a study of college students at six sites around the country, 87% of the young men and 31% of young women reported viewing Internet pornography (Carroll et al., 2008). Notably, 67% of the young men and 49% of the young women agreed that viewing pornography is acceptable, which means that many of the young men

Premarital sex in emerging adulthood is accepted in some cultures and forbidden in others.

TABLE 9.5 Percentage of Young Men and Women Who Have Engaged in Premarital Sex

Country	Age	Men (percent)	Women (percent)
United States	20	80	78
Norway	20	78	86
United Kingdom	19–20	84	85
Germany	20	78	83
Mexico	15–19	44	13
Brazil	15–19	73	28
Chile	15–19	48	19
Colombia	20	89	65
Liberia	18–21	93	82
Nigeria	19	86	63
Hong Kong	27	38	24
Japan	16–21	15	7
Republic of Korea	12–21	17	4

Source: Based on data from Love and sex: Cross-cultural perspectives (2nd edition).

who reported viewing pornography did not view this behavior as acceptable, whereas many young women who did not view pornography believed it was acceptable to do so. Viewing pornography was related to risk behaviors, specifically sexual risk behaviors and substance use, but of course this is a correlation rather than causation; it does not show that viewing pornography causes emerging adults to take sexual risks. A study of Swedish emerging adults found even higher rates of viewing Internet pornography among young men and women (Häggström-Nordin et al., 2005). Ninety-eight percent of young men and 72% percent of young women in this study had ever viewed pornography. In a qualitative study by this research team (Häggström-Nordin et al., 2005), Swedish emerging adults expressed mixed feelings about pornography viewing. They described it as interesting and pleasurable to view, but also expressed the concerns about the submissive and degrading ways women are depicted in pornography and the separation of sex from intimacy.

SEXUALLY TRANSMITTED INFECTIONS (STIS) Emerging adults in Western countries may view sex as a normal and enjoyable part of life, but that does not mean it is unproblematic. The long period between the initiation of sexual activity in adolescence and the entry into marriage in young adulthood typically includes sex with a series of romantic partners as well as occasional episodes of hooking up, and in the course of these years unintended pregnancies are not unusual. Although responsible contraceptive use is the norm among emerging adults, inconsistent and ineffective use of contraception is common enough to make emerging adulthood the age period when both abortion and nonmarital childbirth are most common, across many countries (Jones et al., 2002; Singh et al., 2001). ◉

Emerging adulthood is also the peak period for **sexually transmitted infections (STIs)**, which are infections transmitted through sexual contact, including chlamydia, gonorrhea, syphilis, human papilloma virus (HPV), herpes simplex virus 2 (HSV-2), and HIV/AIDS (Weinstock et al., 2004). One-half of STIs in the United States occur in people who are aged 15–24 (Weinstock et al., 2004). Rates of STIs are higher in emerging adulthood than in any other life stage, in both the United States and Europe (Lehtinen et al., 2006).

Why are emerging adults particularly at risk for STIs? Although few emerging adults have sex with numerous partners, hooking up occasionally with a temporary partner is

◉—[**Watch** the **Video** Choices: Good, Bad, Ugly in **MyDevelopmentLab**

sexually transmitted infection (STI) infection transmitted through sexual contact

quite common. Even if sex takes place in a committed relationship, most youthful love relationships do not endure for long and partners eventually break up and move on. In this way, young people gain experience with love and sex and see what it is like to be involved with different people. Unfortunately, having sex with a variety of people, even within a series of relationships, carries with it a substantial risk for STIs. 👁

The symptoms and consequences of STIs vary widely, from the merely annoying (pubic lice or "crabs") to the deadly (HIV/AIDS). Some STIs, such as chlamydia, gonorrhea, syphilis, and HPV, may increase the risk of infertility for women (Mills et al., 2006). Fortunately, chlamydia, gonorrhea, and syphilis can be treated effectively with antibiotics. Also, a vaccine for HPV is now available, and public health advocates in many Western countries are vigorously promoting that adolescents be vaccinated before they become sexually active (Kahn, 2007; Woodhall et al., 2007). Herpes simplex 2 cannot be cured, but medications can relieve the symptoms and speed up the healing process when an episode occurs (King, 2005).

The most deadly STI, HIV/AIDS (see Chapter 2), has proven to be extremely difficult to treat, because the virus has the ability to change itself and thus render previously developed medications ineffective. AIDS has been most devastating in southern Africa, where 10 of every 11 new HIV infections worldwide take place (see **Map 9.3**) (Bankole et al., 2004). Worldwide, incidence of new HIV infections has decreased in recent years among young people, due to a decline in risky sexual practices such as having multiple sexual partners (UNAIDS, 2010). 👁

In recent years effective drug treatments for slowing the progress of AIDS have been developed so that those with HIV might live longer. The cost of these drug treatments was initially extremely high, but now the cost has declined and the drugs are widely available even in developing countries, mainly through international aid organizations (UNAIDS, 2010). Prevention programs to reduce HIV risk among emerging adults have been conducted in many developing countries, and have been successful in changing young people's behavior to reduce their HIV risk, particularly through the use and distribution of condoms (Bankole et al., 2004; Magnussen et al., 2004). 👁➤

👁─⎡**Watch** the **Video** Intimate Danger in **MyDevelopmentLab**

👁─⎡**Watch** the **Video** Nightmare on AIDS Street in **MyDevelopmentLab**

👁➤─⎡**Simulate** the **Experiment** AIDS Timeline in **MyDevelopmentLab**

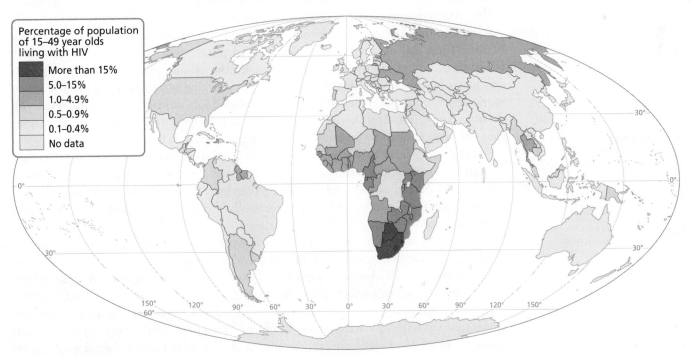

Map 9.3 • **HIV Population Worldwide.** Which countries have the highest population of adults living with HIV? How might you explain these variations?

Finding adult work

9.19   **LEARNING OBJECTIVE**   Describe the transition from school to full-time work in Europe and the United States, and explain why unemployment rates among emerging adults are higher than for older adults.

Watch the **Video** Career and Personality in **MyDevelopmentLab**

> **❝** *I didn't really choose my job [as a bank teller]. It chose me. I needed the money. I was so broke! And they pay well. But I hate my job! There's no opportunity for growth there. I want to do something in maybe the health care field or fashion industry.* **❞**
>
> —Wendy, age 25
> (in Arnett, 2004, p. 151)

Watch the **Video** Discover Me: Match Personalities to Careers in **MyDevelopmentLab**

As we have seen in Chapter 8, some adolescents in developed countries work part-time, but few of them see their part-time jobs as the beginning of the kind of work they expect to be doing as adults. Most emerging adults, in contrast, are looking for a job that will turn into a career, a long-term occupation, something that will not only bring in a paycheck but provide personal fulfillment (Taylor, 2005).

Work in emerging adulthood focuses on identity questions: What do I really want to do? What am I best at? What do I enjoy the most? How do my abilities and desires fit in with the kinds of opportunities that are available to me? In asking themselves what kind of work they want to do, emerging adults are also asking themselves what kind of person they are. In the course of emerging adulthood, as they try out various jobs they begin to answer their identity questions, and they develop a better sense of what work suits them best.

THE TRANSITION TO WORK   For most American emerging adults, the road to a stable, long-term job is a long and winding one, with many brief, low-paying, dreary jobs along the way. The average American holds seven to eight different jobs between the ages of 18 and 30, and 1 in 4 young workers has over 10 different jobs during this period (U.S. Department of Labor, 2010).

Some emerging adults engage in systematic exploration as they look for a career path that they wish to settle into for the long term. They think about what they want to do, they try a job or a college major in that area to see if the fit is right, and if it is not they try another path until they find something they like better. But for many others, *exploration* is a bit too lofty a word to describe their work history during their late teens and early twenties (Arnett, 2004; Mortimer et al., 2002). Often it is not nearly as systematic, organized, and focused as "exploration" implies. *Meandering* might be a more accurate word, or maybe *drifting* or even *floundering* (Hamilton & Hamilton, 2006). Many emerging adults express a sense that they did not really choose their current job, they just one day found themselves in it. In my interviews with emerging adults, "I just fell into it" is a frequently used phrase when they describe how they found their current job (Arnett, 2004). Yet even the meandering process of trying various jobs often serves the function of helping emerging adults sort out what kind of work they want to do. When you are in a dead-end job, at least you find out what you do *not* want to do. And there is also the possibility that as you drift through various jobs you may happen to drift into one you enjoy, one that unexpectedly clicks.

Although at least half of young people in developed countries now obtain tertiary education in some form, a substantial proportion of emerging adults finish their education after secondary school and enter the workplace. What are the work prospects like for these emerging adults, and how successfully are they able to make the transition from school to the workplace?

For the most part, they struggle to find work that pays them enough to live on, much less the identity-based work that is the ideal for many emerging adults. Because the economy in developed countries has shifted from manufacturing to information, technology, and services over the past half century, tertiary education is more important than ever in obtaining jobs that pay well. Those who lack the training, knowledge, and credentials conferred by tertiary education are at a great disadvantage in the modern economy. In the last half of the 20th century, emerging adults with no tertiary education were "in a free-fall of declining earnings and diminished expectations" (Halpern, 1998, p. xii), and their prospects have not improved in the early years of the 21st century.

Is there anything that can be done about the dismal job prospects of emerging adults who have no tertiary education or training? Richard Murnane (an economist) and Frank Levy (a scholar on education) have researched the job skills needed by these emerging adults in order to succeed in the workplace (Murnane & Levy, 1997). Murnane and Levy conducted observations in a variety of factories and offices to gain information about the kinds of jobs now available to high school graduates and the kinds of skills required by those jobs. They focused not on routine jobs that require little skill and pay low wages but on the most promising new jobs available to high school graduates in the changing economy, jobs that offer the promise of career development and middle-class wages. They concluded that six basic skills are necessary for success at these new jobs:

1. reading at a ninth-grade level or higher;
2. doing math at a ninth-grade level or higher;
3. solving semistructured problems;
4. communicating orally and in writing;
5. using a computer for word processing and other tasks;
6. collaborating in diverse groups.

Today, high-paying manufacturing jobs are scarce in developed countries.

The good news is that all six of what Murnane and Levy (1997) call the *new basic skills* could be taught to adolescents by the time they leave high school. The bad news is that many American adolescents currently graduate from high school without learning them adequately. Murnane and Levy focused on reading and math skills because those are the skills on which the most data are available. They concluded that the data reveal a distressing picture: close to half of all 17-year-olds cannot read or do math at the level needed to succeed at the new jobs. The half who do have these skills are also the half who are most likely to go to college rather than seeking full-time work after high school. More recently, Murnane and Levy (2004) focused on the growing importance of computer skills, again concluding that high schools are failing to provide adolescents with the knowledge they need to succeed in the new economy.

Of course, this does not mean that the current situation cannot be changed. There is certainly no reason that high schools could not be expected to require that students master the new basic skills by the time they graduate. The results of Murnane and Levy's research suggest that it may be wise for administrators of high schools and job-training programs to revise their curricula to fit the requirements of the new information- and technology-based economy.

UNEMPLOYMENT Although most young people in developed countries are able to find a job once they leave high school or college, this is not true for all of them. In both Europe and the United States, the unemployment rate for emerging adults is consistently *twice as high* as for adults beyond age 25 (Wolbers, 2007). In both Europe and the United States unemployment has been found to be associated with higher risk for depression, especially for emerging adults who lack strong parental support (Axelsson & Ejlertsson, 2002; Bjarnason & Sigurdardottir, 2003; Hämäläinen et al., 2005). The relation between unemployment and depression has also been found in longitudinal studies (Dooley et al., 2000), which indicates that unemployment leads to depression more often than being depressed makes it hard to find a job.

To say that someone is unemployed does not just mean that the person does not have a job. A large proportion of young people in their late teens and early twenties are attending high school or college, but they are not classified as unemployed because school is considered to be the focus of their efforts, not work. People whose time is mainly devoted to caring for their own children also would not be classified as unemployed. **Unemployment** refers only to people who are not in school, are not working, and are looking for a job.

66*At first I majored in journalism. Then I got a part-time job at a pre-school. They asked me to teach a three-year-old classroom and I did it and I loved it and I thought 'You know, this is what I need to do.' So I changed my major to education. I love teaching. I can't imagine doing anything else.*99

—Kim, age 23
(in Arnett, 2004, p. 147)

unemployment work status of adults who are not in school, are not working, and are looking for a job

Figure 9.9 • **U.S. unemployment rates for emerging adults (ages 16–24).** What explains the differences among ethnic groups?
Source: Based on U.S. Bureau of the Census, 2010.

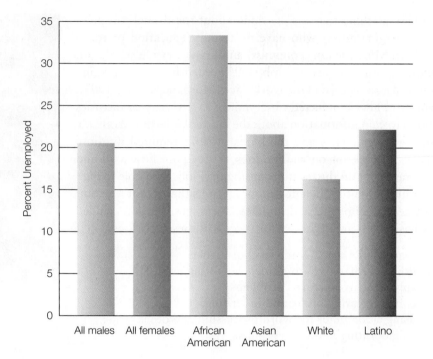

Unemployment rates in emerging adulthood are especially high among African Americans and Latinos. Here, young African Americans seek opportunities at a job fair.

This status applies to a substantial proportion of young people in the United States. **Figure 9.9** shows the unemployment rates for young people in their late teens and early twenties. As you can see from the figure, unemployment is extremely high among young people who drop out of high school. *Over half of* high school dropouts aged 18 to 21 are unemployed (NCES, 2009). Also, unemployment is especially concentrated among Black and Latino emerging adults.

What explains the high rates of unemployment among minority groups? Today, most of the new jobs, and certainly the best jobs, require people to have at least a minimal level of information skills such as basic math knowledge and ability to use a computer. Those skills come from education, and young African Americans and Latinos tend to obtain less education than young Whites or Asian Americans. This is especially true for Latinos, as educational attainment is lower among Latinos than among Whites, African Americans, or Asian Americans (Hamilton & Hamilton, 2006). Among African American adolescents, the dropout rate from high school is only slightly higher than for Whites, but the proportion of Blacks obtaining a college degree is only half as high as for Whites (Aud et al., 2011). Without educational credentials, gaining access to jobs in the new economy is difficult.

Social uses of media

9.20 **LEARNING OBJECTIVE** Explain how emerging adults use the Internet and mobile phones to maintain social contacts.

Emerging adults' media use is diverse, from television and recorded music to electronic games, the Internet, and mobile phones. There is surprisingly little research on emerging adults' uses of television and music, perhaps because of an assumption that the effects of these media are more profound for children and adolescents. Instead, research has focused mainly on Internet use and mobile phones.

INTERNET USE Internet use is high worldwide among emerging adults. In a survey of Internet use among persons ages 18 and over in 13 countries in Europe, Asia, and the Americas, Internet use was over 80% among 18- to 24-year-olds in all countries but one (World Internet Project, 2008). Furthermore, in all countries Internet use was higher among emerging adults than in any other age group. The Internet can be an extremely valuable tool, but like other media forms its effects can be negative at the extremes of use. One study of college students in the UK found a negative correlation between grade performance and hours per week spent online (Englander et al., 2010). Another study, of Chinese college students in eight universities, found that heavy Internet use (more than 15 hours a week) was related to poorer academic performance as well as to symptoms of depression (Huang, R. L., et al., 2009).

The use of the Internet for **social-networking websites** such as Facebook is highly popular among emerging adults. Facebook was originally developed by and for college students, and college students and other emerging adults are still the main users, although it has rapidly become widely used by adolescents and adults as well (Baker & Moore, 2008; Raacke & Bonds-Raacke, 2008). Facebook is by far the most popular social-networking website, surpassing 800 million members worldwide in 2011. Among 18- to 29-year-olds in the United States, 72% use social-networking websites, the same rate as for teens and nearly twice the rate of persons age 30 and older (Lenhart et al., 2010).

Social-networking profiles are an arena for identity presentation and reflect the prominence of identity issues in emerging adulthood (Davis, 2010; Mazur & Kozarian, 2010). Users of social-networking websites construct a profile describing themselves, containing information about topics such as their family, their romantic partner (if they have one), and their interests (Magnuson & Dundes, 2008). Most profiles also include a photo (Hinduja & Patchin, 2008). Many users have a blog linked to their profile, where they record their thoughts and feelings and experiences. Page design, images, and links are expressions of self that enable users to communicate a style and personality (Stern, 2002; Zhao et al., 2008).

Having a profile also allows users to maintain and expand their social networks. Emerging adults use the sites mainly to keep in touch with old friends and current friends and to make new ones (Ellison et al., 2007; Raacke & Bonds-Raacke, 2008). This function is especially important in emerging adulthood, because emerging adults often leave home and the network of friends they formed in secondary school. Furthermore, emerging adults frequently change educational settings, jobs, and residences. Social-networking websites allow them to keep in contact with the friends they leave behind as they move through emerging adulthood, and to make new friends in each new place (Subrahmanyam et al., 2008).

MOBILE PHONES Like the Internet, the pervasiveness and popularity of mobile phones have skyrocketed in the past decade, and like the Internet, mobile phones are especially popular among adolescents and emerging adults (Madell & Muncer, 2004). For example, mobile phones are used by over 90% of 18- to 24-year-olds in Sweden (Axelsson, 2010). In the United States, 93% of 18- to 19-year-olds own a mobile phone, a higher rate than in any other age group (Lenhart, 2010). Mobile phones are used by young people not only for calling someone but also for text messaging. A study of Japanese adolescents found that they used their mobile phones much more often for text messaging than for talking (Kamibeppu & Sugiura, 2005). More than half of those who owned a mobile phone sent at least 10 text messages a day to their friends. Similar results have been found in Western developed countries (Axelsson, 2010).

Mobile phones resemble e-mail and social-networking websites as a way for adolescents and emerging adults to remain in contact with each other when they are apart, virtually all day long. The social worlds of young people are no longer neatly divided into time with family and time with friends or at school. Rather, the new media allow the world of friends to be a nearly constant presence in their lives. The limited evidence so far indicates that young people enjoy the way the new media allow them to keep in touch with their friends. In one study in Italy, adolescents reported many of their happiest moments took

social-networking website website that allows people to establish and maintain electronic contact with a wide social group

APPLYING YOUR KNOWLEDGE

If you have a Facebook profile, how does your profile reflect your identity? What kind of image are you seeking to project to others who might view your profile, and why?

My Virtual Child

Based on what you have observed, what career do you think might best fit your virtual child's interests and abilities?

APPLYING YOUR KNOWLEDGE

In the days before mobile phones, college students may have been in contact with their parents a few times a month by letters or telephone; now the rate is 13 text messages a week plus phone calls and e-mail messages. What are some possible consequences, positive or negative, of today's pattern of more frequent contact?

place while communicating with friends on the Internet or using their mobile phones (Bassi & Antonella, 2004). A study of emerging adults in Sweden reported that they were in contact with friends and family throughout the day via texting (Axelsson, 2010).

Emerging adults who have moved out of their parents' household often use their mobile phones to keep in contact with their parents. In one study of American college students, the students sent an average of 13 text messages a week to their parents (Hofer & Moore, 2010). Students valued texting as a way to keep in touch with their parents as they went about their busy days at school, allowing for parental support while also giving them room to run their own lives.

Many mobile phones are not just "phones" but digital devices that allow access to the Internet, videos, television, and direct video conversations (Hundley & Shyles, 2010). The new technologies are adopted quickly by emerging adults, who use them regularly.

Texting allows emerging adults to keep in contact with family and friends all day long.

WHAT HAVE YOU LEARNED?

1. In what ways do emerging adults tend to view their parents differently than adolescents do, and how does this change influence relations with parents?

2. What are some ways that friendships in emerging adulthood differ from friendships in adolescence?

3. Why are rates of abortion and nonmarital childbirth highest in emerging adulthood?

4. What are the main differences between adolescents' and emerging adults' expectations for work?

5. How can the popularity of social networking in emerging adulthood be explained by emerging adults' developmental needs?

Section 3 VIDEO GUIDE Media Use in Emerging Adulthood Across Cultures (Length: 5:42)

Emerging adults from various countries are interviewed in this video about their media and technology use.

1. What are the common themes mentioned by the individuals interviewed in this video regarding their use of media and technology?

2. The U.S. emerging adult interviewed in this video mentions a heavy reliance on Facebook as a "tool" to stay connected. Do you feel his use of social media is typical among most Americans his age?

3. The narrator and emerging adults mention several forms of technology and media use. Which of these forms do you rely on the most? How has this changed over the past year; five years; ten years?

◉—[**Watch** the **Video** Media Use in Emerging Adulthood Across Cultures in **MyDevelopmentLab**

Summing Up

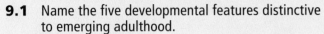

((•—[**Listen** to an audio file of your chapter in **MyDevelopmentLab**

SECTION 1 PHYSICAL DEVELOPMENT

9.1 Name the five developmental features distinctive to emerging adulthood.

Emerging adulthood is the age of identity explorations, the age of instability, the self-focused age, the age of feeling in-between, and the age of possibilities.

9.2 Describe some of the ways emerging adulthood varies among cultures, with specific reference to European and Asian countries.

Emerging adulthood is longest and most leisurely in Europe, where education often lasts well into the twenties and the median age of entering marriage and parenthood is around 30. Cohabitation is especially high in northern Europe, and living with parents through most of the twenties is common in southern Europe. In Asian countries, emerging adults balance their identity explorations with a sense of obligation to family. They seek to become capable of supporting their parents, which is seen as a key marker of becoming an adult. Emerging adulthood is rare but growing in developing countries.

9.3 Name the indicators that emerging adulthood is a period of peak physical functioning.

Emerging adulthood is a time of peak physical functioning as indicated in measures such as VO_2 max and grip strength. However, many emerging adults feel less than optimally healthy and energetic due to lifestyle factors such as poor nutrition, lack of sleep, and the strain of balancing school and work obligations.

9.4 Summarize college students' sleep patterns and the main elements of sleep hygiene.

College students' sleep patterns are often irregular and disrupted, so that they accumulate a large sleep debt during the week and then try to compensate on weekends. Part of the problem is that they tend toward eveningness in their twenties, whereas the older adults who set emerging adults' work and class schedules tend toward morningness. Good sleep hygiene includes waking up at the same time each day, getting regular exercise, and limiting caffeine and alcohol consumption.

9.5 Explain why young drivers have the highest rates of crashes, and name the most effective approach to reducing those rates.

Rates of automobile fatalities are high in adolescence and emerging adulthood due to a combination of inexperience and risky driving behaviors, but have been reduced substantially by GDL programs.

9.6 Explain why rates of substance use peak in the early twenties and then decline.

Substance use rates peak in the early twenties primarily because this is when social control is lowest. The decline in substance use in the late twenties and beyond is primarily due to taking on new social roles such as spouse and parent, which provide new sources of social control.

KEY TERMS

emerging adulthood *p. 413*
VO_2 max *p. 419*
cardiac output *p. 419*

morningness *p. 420*
eveningness *p. 420*
social control *p. 421*

graduated driver
  licensing (GDL) *p. 423*

binge drinking *p. 424*
unstructured socializing *p. 425*

SECTION 2 COGNITIVE DEVELOPMENT

9.7 Describe how growing abilities of pragmatism allow emerging adults to become better at addressing real-life problems.

In contrast to the thinking of formal operations, which emphasizes scientific approaches to problems, pragmatism recognizes that the problems people confront in their daily lives are often complex and ambiguous and do not submit to definite answers.

9.8 Outline the development of reflective judgment in Perry's theory.

William Perry found that college students' reflective judgment develops through stages of dualistic thinking, multiple thinking, relativism, and commitment, but other research indicates this pattern is due more to education than to maturation.

461

9.9 Compare and contrast the tertiary education systems and college experiences in developed countries.

Participation in tertiary education has risen dramatically in recent decades. A majority of emerging adults now obtain tertiary education in most developed countries, with women consistently attaining higher educational achievement than men. Countries vary greatly in their tertiary education systems, with Europe the most structured and Japan the least.

9.10 Name the various long-term benefits of tertiary education.

Tertiary education has been shown to have many benefits, occupationally and financially as well as personally. Benefits include greater earnings and better verbal and quantitative skills as well as nonacademic benefits such as developing a clearer identity and more definite values.

KEY TERMS

postformal thinking *p. 428*   dialectical thought *p. 429*   reflective judgment *p. 429*   tertiary education *p. 430*
pragmatism *p. 428*

SECTION 3 EMOTIONAL AND SOCIAL DEVELOPMENT

9.11 Describe the course of self-esteem from adolescence through emerging adulthood and explain the reasons for this pattern.

Self-esteem often rises for emerging adults because they have moved beyond some of the difficult issues of adolescence and they have more control over their lives.

9.12 Describe the various forms identity development can take in emerging adulthood, and consider patterns of cultural and ethnic identity.

In the identity status model, James Marcia proposed four categories of identity development: diffusion, moratorium, foreclosure, and achievement. Research indicates that for most people identity achievement is not reached until emerging adulthood or beyond. Cultures influence identity development by the extent to which they allow or restrict their young people's opportunities to make choices in love and work. Today, globalization often influences the cultural context of identity development, resulting in bicultural identities. For members of ethnic minorities, there are a variety of possible forms their ethnic identity may take, including assimilation, marginality, separation, and biculturalism.

9.13 Summarize the changes in American gender beliefs in recent decades and include findings from research on gender stereotypes among college students.

Beliefs about gender roles have become less restrictive in American society over the last half century. However, gender stereotypes persist in occupational roles, in the expectations for men and women to perform different kinds of jobs, and in less favorable evaluations of women's work performance.

9.14 Summarize Smith and Snell's description of the religious beliefs and practices of American emerging adults.

Religious beliefs and practices decline in emerging adulthood, reaching their lowest point in the life span. Emerging adults tend to hold highly individualized religious beliefs rather than adhering to a traditional doctrine.

9.15 Explain why emerging adults have often been at the forefront of political movements, and contrast this with their involvement in conventional politics.

Political participation is low in emerging adulthood with respect to conventional measures such as voting. However, emerging adults are more likely than older adults to engage in volunteer work and to join extreme political movements, due to their ideological identity search and their lack of binding social commitments.

9.16 Describe patterns of home-leaving in the United States and Europe and how this transition influences relations with parents.

Emerging adults in the United States and northern Europe usually move out of their parents' household at age 18 or 19 to live on their own or with a friend or romantic partner. In southern Europe, emerging adults usually remain at home but enjoy doing so. Relations with parents often improve as emerging adults become better at taking their parents' perspectives.

9.17 Describe the role of intimacy in emerging adults' friendships and the most common activities of emerging adult friends.

Friends are important to emerging adults, especially to those without a current romantic partner, and intimacy is more important to their friendships than it is in childhood or adolescence. Common activities among friends include unstructured socializing, which may involve alcohol use and media use. Activities with friends decline steadily during the twenties as emerging adults form stable romantic partnerships.

9.18 Explain how romantic relationships and sexual behavior change during emerging adulthood.

Today's emerging adults often seek a "soul mate" who provides an ideal fit with their own identity. However, in Asian countries dating relationships are discouraged in adolescence and emerging adulthood and parents are often deeply involved in the choice of a marriage partner. Cohabitation is now normative in most Western countries. In northern Europe cohabitation relationships are as enduring as marriages, but in the United States they typically dissolve within a year or two. Worldwide, emerging adults' premarital sexual behavior varies greatly across countries and cultures. STIs are more common in emerging adulthood than in any other age group, including chlamydia, HPV, herpes, and HIV/AIDS. Of particular concern is HIV/AIDS because it is fatal and because it is alarmingly prevalent in some African countries.

9.19 Describe the transition from school to full-time work in Europe and the United States, and explain why unemployment rates among emerging adults are higher than for older adults.

Emerging adults tend to seek identity-based work that fits their abilities and interests. In developed countries the best jobs require tertiary education, and emerging adults often struggle in the job market because they lack basic skills as well as educational credentials. Across developed countries unemployment peaks in emerging adulthood. In the United States, unemployment is especially high among African Americans and Latinos because they are more likely to lack educational credentials.

9.20 Explain how emerging adults use the Internet and mobile phones to maintain social contacts.

Today's emerging adults are the "new media generation," having grown up with the Internet, and they eagerly adopt new technologies such as mobile phones. Many emerging adults use the Internet for social networking and to access pornography. Mobile phones are used for phone calls but they are more often used for text messaging.

KEY TERMS

identity versus identity
   confusion *p. 438*

identity status model *p. 438*

bicultural identity *p. 441*

stereotype *p. 444*

cohabitation *p. 452*

sexually transmitted
   infection (STI) *p. 454*

unemployment *p. 457*

Practice Test

✔●⌐ **Study** and **Review** in **MyDevelopmentLab**

1. In emerging adulthood
   a. rates of residential change in American society are much higher at ages 18–29 than at any other period of life.
   b. there is a sense of optimism about being able to "get where I want to be in life" among those from individualistic cultures, but not for those from collectivistic cultures.
   c. the focus on self-exploration means that individuals are more egocentric than their adolescent counterparts.
   d. the feeling "in-between" is unique to those in the United States and Canada because emerging adults in other cultures tend to remain at home rather than moving out.

2. Emerging adults who live in _____ would emphasize becoming capable of supporting parents financially as among the most important criteria for becoming an adult.
   a. Canada
   b. Japan
   c. the United States
   d. Europe

3. Which of the following is true of emerging adults' health?
   a. Most emerging adults experience an increased susceptibility to physical illness due to the increased stressors associated with this developmental period.
   b. For most sports, the peak age of performance comes during adolescence and athletic abilities begin to decline in the early twenties.
   c. During emerging adulthood the immune system is weak.
   d. The heart is strong during emerging adulthood and reaction time is faster than at any other time of life.

4. Which of the following statements best summarizes the current research on sleep patterns of emerging adults?
   a. The research showing delayed sleep phase syndrome and sleep debt is based almost exclusively on low-income emerging adults who work full-time rather than attending college.
   b. The preference of being a morning person versus a night person changes with age due to increased levels of cortisol.
   c. Sleep debt has negative consequences for both cognitive and emotional functioning.
   d. Students who stayed up all night before exams thought they did worse than their peers who got a full-night's sleep.

5. Researchers who study young drivers have found that
   a. increased parental monitoring does not reduce automobile accidents because adolescents spend so much time with their friends.
   b. driving curfews have been found to reduce their crash involvement dramatically.
   c. inexperience is the only factor found to be significantly correlated with accidents and fatalities.
   d. the best way to reduce automobile accidents and fatalities is for parents to encourage their children to gain more experience driving with their friends who have taken driver's education and who will serve as role models for safe driving.

6. Binge drinking
   a. peaks in emerging adulthood in the United States, but not in Europe where adolescents are often allowed to drink alcohol with their meals.
   b. has not been studied longitudinally because of the difficulty getting IRB approval to ask about alcohol use among high school students.
   c. is highest among single mothers in their early twenties who do not go to college.
   d. is more likely among emerging adults than those in other age groups because they spend more time in unstructured socializing.

7. Dialectical thought
   a. relies strictly on emotion in solving real-life problems.
   b. has been found to characterize emerging adults in individualistic cultures more than those in collectivistic cultures.
   c. refers to the need for explaining human actions in terms of logical principles.
   d. involves the growing awareness that problems often have no clear-cut solution.

8. Reflective judgment
   a. is a synonym for dualism.
   b. increases over time for all emerging adults as a result of maturation, regardless of their educational background or the skills required in their job.
   c. is more likely to characterize students in their first year of college than those in their senior year because first-year college students are more open to new ideas.
   d. is more likely to develop in cultures that value pluralism.

9. An emerging adult from _____ would be most likely to express the following sentiment upon first entering college: "In many ways, college is easier than high school; it's a relief to spend less time on homework and to have more time to explore my options."
   a. Canada
   b. Japan
   c. the United States
   d. Germany

10. Research has shown that over the course of the college years,
    a. students become more authoritarian in their political and social views.
    b. students become less ethnocentric in their political and social views.
    c. females obtain mostly academic benefits, whereas males obtain nonacademic benefits.
    d. males become more confident socially, whereas females report a slight decrease in social confidence.

11. For most people, self-esteem
    a. rises during emerging adulthood.
    b. declines during emerging adulthood.
    c. stays about the same as it was in adolescence.
    d. declines during the first half of emerging adulthood and increases in later emerging adulthood.

12. Which of the following ethnic identity statuses is reflected in the idea of the American "melting pot"?
    a. assimilation   c. separation
    b. marginality   d. biculturalism

13. Which of the following is true of gender-related evaluations of work?
    a. Generally, research indicates that college students often evaluate women's work performance more favorably than men's.
    b. College students evaluate work done by someone of their own gender higher than work done by someone of the opposite gender.
    c. Some studies have found that evaluations can be especially harsh when a person's behavior violates stereotypical gender expectations.
    d. Gender-related evaluations do not depend on characteristics of the evaluators, such as their age.

14. Which of the following best describes religious beliefs in emerging adulthood?
    a. There is an overall decline in religious behavior, but not religious beliefs from adolescence to emerging adulthood.
    b. Emerging adults are not tolerant of religious differences.
    c. In emerging adulthood, religious beliefs are highly individualized.
    d. Emerging adults place great emphasis on the religious doctrine of their faith.

15. Which of the following is true of emerging adults' political beliefs?
    a. Unlike their counterparts in Canada or Western Europe, emerging adults' political participation is very low in the United States.
    b. Emerging adults tend to see the activities of political parties as highly relevant to their lives.
    c. Emerging adults tend to be skeptical of the motivations of politicians.
    d. Emerging adults tend to have higher conventional political participation compared to previous generations of young people.

16. _____ are most likely to be living on their own rather than with their parents in their early twenties.
    a. Latinos
    b. African Americans
    c. White Americans
    d. Asian Americans

17. Leisure activities with friends
    a. decline steadily in the course of the twenties.
    b. decline for women, but not for men in the course of the twenties.
    c. increase slightly in the course of the twenties.
    d. stay at about the same level in the course of the twenties as they were during adolescence.

18. Male emerging adults are more likely than females to
    a. have negative attitudes toward recreational sex.
    b. suffer severe punishments if they have premarital sex.
    c. be willing to have intercourse with someone they have known for only a few hours.
    d. have sex in the context of a close romantic relationship.

19. Based on Murnane and Levy's (1997) research, which of the following is NOT considered one of the six basic skills necessary for success at the most promising new jobs available to high school graduates in the changing economy?
    a. being able to communicate in writing
    b. being able to collaborate in diverse groups
    c. being able to read at the ninth-grade level or higher
    d. being able to conduct statistical analyses

20. Based on the current research, which is a true statement about media use in emerging adulthood?
    a. In all countries, Internet use is higher among adolescents than among emerging adults because increased responsibilities among emerging adults reduce time they can spend online.
    b. Social networking profiles are a way for individuals to express their identity.
    c. Most emerging adults prefer face-to-face interactions to social contact via the Internet; therefore, use of social networking sites has decreased in the past few years as the novelty has worn off.
    d. Cross-cultural research has shown that more women than men view pornography on the Internet.

Practice Test Answer Key

Chapter 1

1. B (L.O. 1.1) *p. 7*
2. B (L.O. 1.2) *p. 11*
3. C (L.O. 1.3) *p. 13*
4. C (L.O. 1.4) *p. 15*
5. B (L.O. 1.5) *p. 17*
6. C (L.O. 1.6) *p. 21*
7. A (L.O. 1.7) *p. 23*
8. D (L.O. 1.8) *p. 26*
9. B (L.O. 1.9) *p. 29*
10. A (L.O. 1.10) *p. 31*
11. C (L.O. 1.11) *p. 33*
12. D (L.O. 1.12) *p. 38*

Chapter 2

1. B (L.O. 2.1) *p. 47*
2. B (L.O. 2.2) *p. 50*
3. A (L.O. 2.3) *p. 52*
4. C (L.O. 2.4) *p. 53*
5. A (L.O. 2.5) *p. 54*
6. D (L.O. 2.6) *p. 57*
7. D (L.O. 2.7) *p. 58*
8. B (L.O. 2.8) *p. 61*
9. D (L.O. 2.9) *p. 62*
10. C (L.O. 2.10) *p. 63*
11. C (L.O. 2.11) *p. 64*
12. B (L.O. 2.12) *p. 66*
13. B (L.O. 2.13) *p. 68*
14. B (L.O. 2.14) *p. 74*
15. D (L.O. 2.15) *p. 76*
16. B (L.O. 2.16) *p. 77*
17. D (L.O. 2.17) *p. 78*
18. D (L.O. 2.18) *p. 80*

Chapter 3

1. C (L.O. 3.1) *p. 91*
2. A (L.O. 3.2) *p. 92*
3. C (L.O. 3.3) *p. 95*
4. A (L.O. 3.4) *p. 96*
5. D (L.O. 3.5) *p. 100*
6. C (L.O. 3.6) *p. 103*
7. B (L.O. 3.7) *p. 107*
8. A (L.O. 3.8) *p. 108*
9. B (L.O. 3.9) *p. 111*
10. C (L.O. 3.10) *p. 112*
11. B (L.O. 3.11) *p. 113*
12. C (L.O. 3.12) *p. 117*
13. A (L.O. 3.13) *p. 118*
14. D (L.O. 3.14) *p. 122*
15. D (L.O. 3.15) *p. 125*
16. B (L.O. 3.16) *p. 125*

Chapter 4

1. B (L.O. 4.1) *p. 135*
2. B (L.O. 4.2) *p. 137*
3. A (L.O. 4.3) *p. 140*
4. C (L.O. 4.4) *p. 143*
5. B (L.O. 4.5) *p. 144*
6. B (L.O. 4.6) *p. 147*
7. D (L.O. 4.7) *p. 151*
8. A (L.O. 4.8) *p. 154*
9. C (L.O. 4.9) *p. 155*
10. C (L.O. 4.10) *p. 156*
11. A (L.O. 4.11) *p. 158*
12. C (L.O. 4.12) *p. 159*
13. A (L.O. 4.13) *p. 160*
14. C (L.O. 4.14) *p. 161*
15. D (L.O. 4.15) *p. 162*
16. A (L.O. 4.16) *p. 164*
17. C (L.O. 4.17) *p. 166*
18. C (L.O. 4.18) *p. 169*
19. B (L.O. 4.19) *p. 170*
20. B (L.O. 4.20) *p. 171*
21. D (L.O. 4.21) *p. 173*
22. B (L.O. 4.22) *p. 174*

Chapter 5

1. A (L.O. 5.1) *p. 183*
2. B (L.O. 5.2) *p. 185*
3. A (L.O. 5.3) *p. 186*
4. B (L.O. 5.4) *p. 187*
5. D (L.O. 5.5) *p. 189*
6. A (L.O. 5.6) *p. 191*
7. B (L.O. 5.7) *p. 194*
8. A (L.O. 5.8) *p. 197*
9. C (L.O. 5.9) *p. 199*
10. C (L.O. 5.10) *p. 201*
11. A (L.O. 5.11) *p. 204*
12. B (L.O. 5.12) *p. 208*
13. D (L.O. 5.13) *p. 211*
14. B (L.O. 5.14) *p. 212*
15. A (L.O. 5.15) *p. 214*
16. C (L.O. 5.16) *p. 217*
17. B (L.O. 5.17) *p. 220*
18. D (L.O. 5.18) *p. 223*
19. B (L.O. 5.19) *p. 226*
20. B (L.O. 5.20) *p. 228*
21. C (L.O. 5.21) *p. 229*

Chapter 6

1. A (L.O. 6.1) *p. 239*
2. D (L.O. 6.2) *p. 240*
3. C (L.O. 6.3) *p. 241*
4. D (L.O. 6.4) *p. 245*
5. A (L.O. 6.5) *p. 246*
6. B (L.O. 6.6) *p. 248*
7. C (L.O. 6.7) *p. 252*
8. A (L.O. 6.8) *p. 253*
9. C (L.O. 6.9) *p. 254*
10. B (L.O. 6.10) *p. 256*
11. A (L.O. 6.11) *p. 257*
12. C (L.O. 6.12) *p. 259*
13. D (L.O. 6.13) *p. 260*
14. A (L.O. 6.14) *p. 262*
15. C (L.O. 6.15) *p. 264*
16. D (L.O. 6.16) *p. 266*
17. C (L.O. 6.17) *p. 268*
18. B (L.O. 6.18) *p. 271*
19. B (L.O. 6.19) *p. 272*
20. C (L.O. 6.20) *p. 278*
21. A (L.O. 6.21) *p. 279*
22. B (L.O. 6.22) *p. 284*

Chapter 7

1. B (L.O. 7.1) *p. 296*
2. A (L.O. 7.2) *p. 297*
3. A (L.O. 7.3) *p. 299*
4. B (L.O. 7.4) *p. 301*
5. A (L.O. 7.5) *p. 302*
6. B (L.O. 7.6) *p. 304*
7. D (L.O. 7.7) *p. 306*
8. A (L.O. 7.8) *p. 309*
9. C (L.O. 7.9) *p. 314*
10. B (L.O. 7.10) *p. 315*
11. A (L.O. 7.11) *p. 317*
12. D (L.O. 7.12) *p. 320*
13. A (L.O. 7.13) *p. 324*
14. C (L.O. 7.14) *p. 325*
15. A (L.O. 7.15) *p. 327*
16. B (L.O. 7.16) *p. 329*
17. B (L.O. 7.17) *p. 333*
18. A (L.O. 7.18) *p. 337*
19. C (L.O. 7.19) *p. 341*

Chapter 8

1. B (L.O. 8.1) *p. 354*
2. B (L.O. 8.2) *p. 356*
3. C (L.O. 8.3) *p. 359*
4. A (L.O. 8.4) *p. 360*
5. B (L.O. 8.5) *p. 363*
6. A (L.O. 8.6) *p. 366*
7. D (L.O. 8.7) *p. 367*
8. B (L.O. 8.8) *p. 369*
9. A (L.O. 8.9) *p. 369*
10. C (L.O. 8.10) *p. 371*
11. C (L.O. 8.11) *p. 372*
12. D (L.O. 8.12) *p. 375*
13. B (L.O. 8.13) *p. 378*
14. B (L.O. 8.14) *p. 380*
15. C (L.O. 8.15) *p. 381*
16. A (L.O. 8.16) *p. 383*
17. B (L.O. 8.17) *p. 386*
18. C (L.O. 8.18) *p. 387*
19. A (L.O. 8.19) *p. 390*
20. C (L.O. 8.20) *p. 394*
21. D (L.O. 8.21) *p. 397*
22. D (L.O. 8.22) *p. 399*
23. C (L.O. 8.23) *p. 401*
24. B (L.O. 8.24) *p. 402*

Chapter 9

1. A (L.O. 9.1) *p. 415*
2. B (L.O. 9.2) *p. 417*
3. D (L.O. 9.3) *p. 418*
4. C (L.O. 9.4) *p. 419*
5. B (L.O. 9.5) *p. 421*
6. D (L.O. 9.6) *p. 424*
7. D (L.O. 9.7) *p. 428*
8. D (L.O. 9.8) *p. 429*
9. B (L.O. 9.9) *p. 432*
10. B (L.O. 9.10) *p. 434*
11. A (L.O. 9.11) *p. 436*
12. A (L.O. 9.12) *p. 437*
13. C (L.O. 9.13) *p. 443*
14. C (L.O. 9.14) *p. 445*
15. C (L.O. 9.15) *p. 446*
16. C (L.O. 9.16) *p. 448*
17. A (L.O. 9.17) *p. 450*
18. C (L.O. 9.18) *p. 451*
19. D (L.O. 9.19) *p. 456*
20. B (L.O. 9.20) *p. 458*

accommodation cognitive process of changing a scheme to adapt to new information

active genotype→environment effects in the theory of genotype→environment effects, the type that results when people seek out environments that correspond to their genotypic characteristics

actual self person's perception of the self as it is, contrasted with the possible self

adolescence period of the life span between the time puberty begins and the time adult status is approached, when young people are preparing to take on the roles and responsibilities of adulthood in their culture

adolescent egocentrism type of egocentrism in which adolescents have difficulty distinguishing their thinking about their own thoughts from their thinking about the thoughts of others

adolescent-limited delinquent (ALD) delinquent who shows no evidence of problems prior to adolescence and whose delinquent behavior in adolescence is temporary

age graded social organization based on grouping persons of similar ages

AIDS (acquired immune deficiency syndrome) sexually transmitted infection caused by HIV, resulting in damage to the immune system

allele on a pair of chromosomes, each of two forms of a gene

amae Japanese word for very close, physical, indulgent relationship between the mother and her young child

ambivalence emotional state of experiencing two contradictory emotions at once

amniocentesis prenatal procedure in which a needle is used to withdraw amniotic fluid containing fetal cells from the placenta, allowing possible prenatal problems to be detected

amnion fluid-filled membrane that surrounds and protects the developing organism in the womb

androgens sex hormones that have especially high levels in males from puberty onward and are mostly responsible for male primary and secondary sex characteristics.

anemia dietary deficiency of iron that causes problems such as fatigue, irritability, and attention difficulties

animalcule microscopic human being

animism tendency to attribute human thoughts and feelings to inanimate objects and forces

anorexia nervosa eating disorder characterized by intentional self-starvation

anoxia deprivation of oxygen during birth process and soon after that can result in serious neurological damage within minutes

Apgar scale neonatal assessment scale with five subtests: Appearance (color), Pulse (heart rate), Grimace (reflex irritability), Activity (muscle tone), and Respiration (breathing)

apprenticeship an arrangement, common in Europe, in which an adolescent "novice" serves under contract to a "master" who has substantial experience in a profession, and through working under the master, learns the skills required to enter the profession

artificial insemination procedure of injecting sperm directly into the uterus

assimilation cognitive process of altering new information to fit an existing scheme

assisted reproductive technologies (ART) methods for overcoming infertility that include artificial insemination, fertility drugs, and IVF

asthma chronic illness of the lungs characterized by wheezing, coughing, and shortness of breath

attachment theory Bowlby's theory of emotional and social development, focusing on the crucial importance of the infant's relationship with the primary caregiver

attention-deficit/hyperactivity disorder (ADHD) diagnosis that includes problems of inattention, hyperactivity, and impulsiveness

authoritarian parents in classifications of parenting styles, parents who are high in demandingness but low in responsiveness

authoritative parents in classifications of parenting styles, parents who are high in demandingness and high in responsiveness

autism developmental disorder marked by a lack of interest in social relations, abnormal language development, and repetitive behavior

autism spectrum disorder a category of developmental disorders that includes autism, Asperger syndrome, and Pervasive Developmental Disorder Not Otherwise Specified

autonomy quality of being independent and self-sufficient, capable of thinking for one's self

autonomy vs. shame and doubt in Erikson's lifespan theory, the main crisis of the toddlerhood stage, when toddlers gain a healthy confidence in their ability to make choices and express them to others *or* parents are harsh and impatient and toddlers experience shame and doubt that undermines their trust in themselves

axon part of the neuron that transmits electric impulses and releases neurotransmitters

babbling repetitive prelanguage consonant–vowel combinations such as "ba-ba-ba" or "do-do-do-do," made by infants universally beginnning at about 6 months old

Bayley Scales of Infant Development widely used assessment of infant development from age 3 months to 3½ years

behavior genetics field in the study of human development that aims to identify the extent to which genes influence behavior, primarily by comparing persons who share different amounts of their genes

behaviorism theory that all thought and behavior can be explained in terms of learning mechanisms

bicultural identity identity with two distinct facets, for example one for the local culture and one for the global culture, or one within one's ethnic group and one for others

bilingual capable of using two languages

binge drinking consuming five or more drinks in a row for men, four in a row for women

binocular vision   ability to combine the images of the two eyes into one image

blastocyst   ball of about 100 cells formed by about one week following conception

body mass index (BMI)   measure of the ratio of weight to height

bonding   concept that in humans the first few minutes and hours after birth are critical to mother–infant relationships

Brazelton Neonatal Behavioral Assessment Scale (NBAS)   27-item scale of neonatal functioning with overall ratings "worrisome," "normal," and "superior"

breech presentation   positioning of the fetus so that feet or buttocks, rather than the head, are positioned to come first out of the birth canal

Broca's area   portion of the left frontal lobe of the human brain that is specialized for language production

bulimia   eating disorder characterized by episodes of binge eating followed by purging (self-induced vomiting)

bullying   pattern of maltreatment of peers, including aggression; repetition; and power imbalance

cardiac output   quantity of blood flow from the heart

caste system   in Hindu culture of India, an inherited social hierarchy, determined by birth

centration   Piaget's term for young children's thinking as being centered or focused on one noticeable aspect of a cognitive problem to the exclusion of other important aspects

cephalocaudal principle   principle of biological development that growth tends to begin at the top, with the head, and then proceeds downward to the rest of the body

cerebellum   structure at the base of the brain involved in balance and motor movements

cerebral cortex   outer portion of the brain, containing four regions with distinct functions

cesarean delivery, or C-section   type of birth in which mother's abdomen is cut open and fetus is retrieved directly from the uterus

child maltreatment   abuse or neglect of children, including physical, emotional, or sexual abuse

chorionic villus sampling (CVS)   prenatal technique for diagnosing genetic problems, involving taking a sample of cells at 5–10 weeks gestation by inserting a tube into the uterus

chromosome   sausage-shaped structure in the nucleus of cells, containing genes, which are paired, except in reproductive cells

civilization   form of human social life, beginning about 5,000 years ago, that includes cities, writing, occupational specialization, and states

classification   ability to understand that objects can be part of more than one cognitive group, for example an object can be classified with red objects as well as with round objects

clique   small group of friends who know each other well, do things together, and form a regular social group

coercive cycle   pattern in relations between parents and children in which children's disobedient behavior evokes harsh responses from parents, which in turn makes children even more resistant to parental control, evoking even harsher responses

cognitive constructivist theory   Piaget's theory that the development of knowledge is driven by the child's interaction with objects in the world

cohabitation   unmarried romantic partners living together

cohort effect   in scientific research, an explanation of group differences among people of different ages based on the fact that they grew up in different *cohorts* or historical periods

colic   infant crying pattern in which the crying goes on for more than 3 hours a day over more than 3 days at a time for more than 3 weeks

collectivistic   cultural values such as obedience and group harmony

colostrum   thick, yellowish, milky liquid produced by mammalian mothers during the first days following birth, extremely rich in protein and antibodies that strengthen the baby's immune system

coming out   for homosexuals, the process of acknowledging their homosexuality and then disclosing the truth to their friends, family, and others

concordance rate   degree of similarity in phenotype among pairs of family members, expressed as a percentage

concrete operations   in Piaget's theory, the cognitive stage in which children become capable of using mental operations

conditioning   the process by which a particular stimulus becomes linked to a particular response

confounded   problem in statistical analyses when variables are entwined in people's lives in a way that is not easy to disentangle

conservation   mental ability to understand that the quantity of a substance or material remains the same even if its appearance changes

contexts   settings and circumstances that contribute to variations in pathways of human development, including SES, gender, and ethnicity, as well as family, school, community, media, and culture

conventional reasoning   second level in Kohlberg's theory of moral development, in which moral reasoning is based on the expectations of others

cooing   prelanguage "oo-ing" and "ah-ing," and gurgling sounds babies make beginning at about 2 months old

coregulation   relationship between parents and children in which parents provide broad guidelines for behavior but children are capable of a substantial amount of independent, self-directed behavior

corporal punishment   physical punishment of children

corpus callosum   band of neural fibers connecting the two hemispheres of the brain

correlation   statistical relationship between two variables such that knowing one of the variables makes it possible to predict the other

cosleeping   cultural practice in which infants and sometimes older children sleep with one or both parents

crossing over   at the outset of meiosis, the exchange of genetic material between paired chromosomes

cross-sectional research   research design that involves collecting data from people of a variety of ages on a single occasion

crowd   large, reputation-based group of adolescents

cultural models   cognitive structures pertaining to common cultural activities

culture   total pattern of a group's customs, beliefs, art, and technology

custom complex   distinctive cultural pattern of behavior that reflects underlying cultural beliefs

cyberbullying   bullying via electronic means, mainly through the Internet

decentering   cognitive ability to take more than one aspect of a problem into account, such as width as well as length

deferred imitation   ability to repeat actions observed at an earlier time

delivery   second stage of the birth process, during which the fetus is pushed out of the cervix and through the birth canal

demandingness   degree to which parents set down rules and expectations for behavior and require their children to comply with them

dendrite   part of the neuron that receives neurotransmitters

dependent variable in an experiment, the outcome that is measured to calculate the results of the experiment by comparing the experimental group to the control group

depressed mood enduring period of sadness, without any other related symptoms of depression

depth perception ability to discern the relative distance of objects in the environment

developed countries world's most economically developed and affluent countries, with the highest median levels of income and education

developing countries countries that have lower levels of income and education than developed countries but are experiencing rapid economic growth

developmental quotient (DQ) in assessments of infant development, the overall score indicating developmental progress

dialectical thought according to Basseches, a kind of thinking in emerging adulthood that involves a growing awareness that problems often have no clear solution and two opposing strategies or points of view may each have some merit

disengaged parents in classifications of parenting styles, parents who are low in both demandingness and responsiveness

dishabituation following habituation, the revival of attention when a new stimulus is presented

disorganized–disoriented attachment classification of parent–child attachment in which the child seems dazed and detached, with possible outbursts of anger, when the parent leaves the room, and exhibits its fear upon parent's return

displacement effect in media research, term for how media use occupies time that may have been spent on other activities

divided attention ability to focus on more than one task at a time

divorce mediation arrangement in which a professional mediator meets with divorcing parents to help them negotiate an agreement that both will find acceptable

dizygotic (DZ) twins twins that result when two ova are released by a female instead of one, and both are fertilized by sperm; also called fraternal twins

DNA (deoxyriboynucleic acid) long strand of cell material that stores and transfers genetic information in all life forms

dominant–recessive inheritance pattern of inheritance in which a pair of chromosomes contains one dominant and one recessive gene, but only the dominant gene is expressed in the phenotype

Down syndrome genetic disorder due to carrying an extra chromosome on the 21st pair

dyslexia learning disability that includes difficulty sounding out letters, difficulty learning to spell words, and a tendency to misperceive the order of letters in words

early intervention program program directed at young children who are at risk for later problems, intended to prevent problems from developing

ecological theory Bronfenbrenner's theory that human development is shaped by five interrelated systems in the social environment

ectoderm in the embryonic period, the outer layer of cells, which will eventually become the skin, hair, nails, sensory organs, and nervous system (brain and spinal cord)

EEG (electroencephalogram) device that measures the electrical activity of the cerebral cortex, allowing researchers to measure overall activity of the cerebral cortex as well as activation of specific parts of it

egocentrism cognitive inability to distinguish between one's own perspective and another person's perspective

elaboration mnemonic that involves transforming bits of information in a way that connects them and hence makes them easier to remember

electronic fetal monitoring (EFM) method that tracks the fetus's heartbeat, either externally through the mother's abdomen or directly by running a wire through the cervix and placing a sensor on the fetus's scalp

embryonic disk in the blastocyst, the inner layer of cells, which will go on to form the embryo

embryonic period weeks 3–8 of prenatal development

emerging adulthood new life stage in developed countries, lasting from the late teens through the twenties, in which people are gradually making their way toward taking on adult responsibilities in love and work

emotional contagion in infants, crying in response to hearing another infant cry, evident beginning at just a few days old

emotional self-regulation ability to exercise control over one's emotions

empathy ability to understand and respond helpfully to another person's distress

endoderm in the embryonic period, the inner layer of cells, which will become the digestive system and the respiratory system

epidural during birth process, injection of an anesthetic drug into the spinal fluid to help the mother manage the pain while also remaining alert

epigenesis in development, the continuous bidirectional interactions between genes and environment

estradiol the estrogen most important in pubertal development among girls

estrogens sex hormones that have especially high levels in females from puberty onward and are mostly responsible for female primary and secondary sex characteristics

ethnicity group identity that may include components such as cultural origin, cultural traditions, race, religion, and language

ethnographic research research method that involves spending extensive time among the people being studied

ethology study of animal behavior

eveningness preference for going to bed late and waking up late

evocative genotype→environment effects in the theory of genotype →environment effects, the type that results occur when a person's inherited characteristics evoke responses from others in the environment

evolutionary psychology branch of psychology that examines how patterns of human functioning and behavior have resulted from adaptations to evolutionary conditions

Experience Sampling Method (ESM) research method that involves having people wear beepers, usually for a period of 1 week; when they are beeped at random times during the day, they record a variety of characteristics of their experience at that moment

experimental research method research method that entails comparing an *experimental group* that receives a treatment of some kind to a *control group* that receives no treatment

externalizing problems problems that involve others, such as aggression

extremely low birth weight term for neonates who weigh less than 1,000 grams (about 2.2 lb) at birth

false self self a person may present to others while realizing that it does not represent what he or she is actually thinking and feeling

familismo cultural belief among Latinos that emphasizes the love, closeness, and mutual obligations among family members

family process quality of the relationships between family members

fast mapping learning and remembering a word for an object after just one time of being told what the object is called

feared self   person one imagines it is possible to become but dreads becoming

fetal alcohol spectrum disorder (FASD)   set of problems that occur as a consequence of high maternal alcohol use during pregnancy, including facial deformities, heart problems, misshapen limbs, and a variety of cognitive problems

fetal period   in prenatal development, the period from week 9 until birth

filial piety   belief that children should respect, obey, and revere their parents throughout life; common in Asian cultures

fine motor development   development of motor abilities involving finely tuned movements of the hands such as grasping and manipulating objects

Flynn effect   steep rise in the median IQ score in Western countries during the 20th century, named after James Flynn, who first identified it

fMRI (functional magnetic resonance imaging)   method of monitoring brain activity in which a person lies inside a machine that uses a magnetic field to record changes in blood flow and oxygen use in the brain in response to different kinds of stimulation

follicle   during the female reproductive cycle, the ovum plus other cells that surround the ovum and provide nutrients

fontanels   soft spots on the skull between loosely joined pieces of the skull that shift during birth process to assist passage through the birth canal

formal operations   in Piaget's theory, cognitive stage beginning at age 11 in which people learn to think systematically about possibilities and hypotheses

foster care   for maltreated children, approach in which adults approved by a state agency take over the care of the child

gametes   cells, distinctive to each sex, that are involved in reproduction (egg cells in the ovaries of the female and sperm in the testes of the male)

gender   cultural categories of "male" and "female"

gender constancy   understanding that maleness and femaleness are biological and cannot change

gender identity   awareness of one's self as male or female

gender roles   cultural expectations for appearance and behavior specific to males or females

gender schema   gender-based cognitive structure for organizing and processing information, comprising expectations for males' and females' appearance and behavior

gender-intensification hypothesis   hypothesis that psychological and behavioral differences between males and females become more pronounced at adolescence because of intensified socialization pressures to conform to culturally prescribed gender roles

gene   segment of DNA containing coded instructions for the growth and functioning of the organism

gene therapy   method of treating genetic disorders that involves replacing the affected genes with genes that do not have the disorder

genome   entire store of an organism's hereditary information

genotype   organism's unique genetic inheritance

germinal period   first 2 weeks after conception

gestation   in prenatal development, elapsed time since conception

gifted   in IQ test performance, persons who score 130 or above

globalization   increasing connections between different parts of the world in trade, travel, migration, and communication

goodness-of-fit   theoretical principle that children develop best if there is a good fit between the temperament of the child and environmental demands

graduated driver licensing (GDL)   government program in which young people obtain driving privileges gradually, contingent on a safe driving record, rather than all at once

grammar   a language's distinctive system of rules

gross motor development   development of motor abilities including balance and posture as well as whole-body movements such as crawling

guided participation   teaching interaction between two people (often an adult and a child) as they participate in a culturaslly valued activity

habituation   gradual decrease in attention to a stimulus aftere repeated presentations

handedness   preference for using either the right or left hand in gross and fine motor activities

heritability   statistical estimate of the extent to which genes are responsible for the differences among persons within a specific population, with values ranging from 0 to 1.00

hippocampus   stucture involved in transfer of information from short-term to long-term memory

holophrase   single word that is used to represent a whole sentence

hominid   evolutionary line that led to modern humans

Homo sapiens   species of modern humans

homophobia   fear and hatred of homosexuals

hostile aggression   type of aggression that entails signs of anger and intent to inflict pain or harm on others

human development   way people grow and change across the life span; includes people's biological, cognitive, psychological, and social functioning

hunter–gatherer   social and economic system in which economic life is based on hunting (mostly by males) and gathering edible plants (mostly by females)

hypothesis   in the scientific process, a researcher's idea about one possible answer to the question proposed for investigation

hypothetical-deductive reasoning   Piaget's term for the process by which the formal operational thinker systematically tests possible solutions to a problem and arrives at an answer that can be defended and explained

ideal self   person one would like to be

identity status model   model for researching Erikson's theory of identity development, classifying identity development into four categories: diffusion, foreclosure, moratorium, or identity achievement

identity versus identity confusion   in Erikson's theory, the crisis of adolescence, with two alternative paths, establishing a clear and definite identity, or experiencing identity confusion, which is a failure to form a stable and secure identity

imaginary audience   belief that others are acutely aware of and attentive to one's appearance and behavior

imprinting   instant and enduring bond to the first moving object seen after birth; common in birds

in vitro fertilization (IVF)   form of infertility treatment that involves using drugs to stimulate the growth of multiple follicles in the ovaries, removing the follicles and combining them with sperm, then transferring the most promising zygotes to the uterus

incomplete dominance   form of dominant–recessive inheritance in which the phenotype is influenced primarily by the dominant gene but also to some extent by the recessive gene

independent variable   in an experiment, the variable that is different for the experimental group than for the control group

individualistic   cultural values such as independence and self-expression

industry versus inferiority Erikson's middle childhood stage, in which the alternatives are to learn to work effectively with cultural materials or, if adults are too critical, develop a sense of being incapable of working effectively

infant-directed (ID) speech special form of speech that adults in many cultures direct toward infants, in which the pitch of the voice becomes higher than in normal speech, the intonation is exaggerated, and words and phrases are repeated

infantile amnesia inability to remember anything that happened prior to age 2

infertility inability to attain pregnancy after at least a year of regular sexual intercourse

infertility belt geographical area in central Africa with infertility rates as high as 30%, apparently due to high rates of malnutrition and STIs

infinite generativity ability to take the word symbols of a language and combine them in a virtually infinite number of new ways

information processing approach approach to understanding cognitive functioning that focuses on cognitive processes that exist at all ages, rather than on viewing cognitive developing in terms of discontinuous stages

informed consent standard procedure in social scientific studies that entails informing potential participants of what their participation would involve, including any possible risks, and giving them the opportunity to agree to participate or not

initiative vs. guilt in Erikson's lifespan theory, the early childhood stage, in which the alternatives are learning to plan activities in a purposeful way, or being afflicted with excess guilt that undermines initiative

insecure–avoidant attachment classification of parent–child attachment in which there is relatively little interaction between them and the child shows little response to the parent's absence and may resist being picked up when the parent returns

insecure–resistant attachment classification of parent–child attachment in which the child shows little exploratory behavior when the parent is present, great distress when the parent leaves the room, and ambivalence upon the parent's return

instrumental aggression type of aggression when a child wants something and uses aggressive behavior or words to get it

intelligence capacity for acquiring knowledge, reasoning, and solving problems

intelligence quotient (IQ) score of mental ability as assessed by intelligence tests, calculated relative to the performance of other people the same age

intermodal perception integration and coordination of information from the various senses

internalizing problems problems that entail turning distress inward, toward the self, such as depression and anxiety

intervention program intended to change the attitudes or behavior of the participants

intimacy degree to which two people share personal knowledge, thoughts, and feelings

intuitive thought substage second substage of the preoperational stage, lasting from age 4 to 7, during which children begin to understand how one event leads to another event but cannot say why they know what they know

kangaroo care recommended care for preterm and low-birth-weight neonates, in which mothers or fathers are advised to place the baby skin-to-skin on their chests for 2–3 hours a day for the early weeks of life

kwashiorkor protein deficiency in childhood, leading to symptoms such as lethargy, irritability, thinning hair, and swollen body, which may be fatal if not treated

labor first stage of the birth process, in which the cervix dilates and the muscles of the uterus contract to push the fetus into the vagina toward the cervix

language acquisition device (LAD) according to Chomsky, innate feature of the brain that that enables children to perceive and grasp quickly the grammatical rules in the language around them

lateralization specialization of functions in the two hemispheres of the brain

learning disability cognitive disorder that impedes the development of learning a specific skill such as reading or math

let-down reflex in females, a reflex that causes milk to be released to the tip of the nipples in response to the sound of her infant's cry, seeing its open mouth, or even thinking about breast-feeding

life-course-persistent delinquent (LCPD) delinquent who shows a pattern of problems from birth onward and whose problems continue into adulthood

longitudinal research research design in which the same persons are followed over time and data are collected on two or more occasions

low birth weight term for neonates weighing less than 2,500 grams (5.5 lb)

major depressive disorder clinical diagnosis that includes a range of specific symptoms such as depressed mood, appetite disturbances, sleeping disturbances, and fatigue

majority culture within a country, the cultural group that sets most of the norms and standards and holds most of the positions of political, economic, intellectual, and media power

mammary glands in females, the glands that produce milk to nourish babies

marasmus disease in which the body wastes away from lack of nutrients

maturation concept that an innate, biologically based program is the driving force behind development

media multitasking simultaneous use of more than one media form, such as playing an electronic game while watching TV

median in a distribution of data, the score that is precisely in the middle, with half the distribution lying above and half below

meiosis process by which gametes are generated, through separation and duplication of chromosome pairs, ending in four new gametes from the original cell, each with half the number of chromosomes of the original cell

menarche first menstrual period

mental representations Piaget's final stage of sensorimotor development in which toddlers first think about the range of possibilities and then select the action most likely to achieve the desired outcome

mental retardation level of cognitive abilities of persons who score 70 or below on IQ tests

mental structures in Piaget's theory of cognitive development, the cognitive systems that organize thinking into coherent patterns so that all thinking takes place on the same level of cognitive functioning

mesoderm in the embryonic period, the middle of the three cell layers, which will become the muscles, bones, reproductive system, and circulatory system

meta-analysis statistical technique that combines the results from many studies into one summary statistic to evaluate the overall outcome of research in an area

metacognition   capacity to think about thinking

metalinguistic skills   in the understanding of language, skills that reflect awareness of the underlying structure of language

metamemory   understanding of how memory works

micronutrients   dietary ingredients essential to optimal physical growth, including iodine, iron, zinc, and vitamins A, B_{12}, C, and D

midwife   person who assists in pregnant women's prenatal care and the birth process

mitosis   process of cell replication in which the chromosomes duplicate themselves and the cell divides into two cells, each with the same number of chromosomes as the original cell

mnemonics   memory strategies, such as rehearsal, organization, and elaboration

monozygotic (MZ) twins   twins who have exactly the same genotype; also called identical twins

morningness   preference for going to bed early and waking up early

Moro reflex   reflex in response to a sensation of falling backward or to a loud sound, in which the neonate arches its back, flings out its arms, and then brings its arms quickly together in an embrace

multilingual   capable of using three or more languages

myelination   process of the growth of the myelin sheath around the axon of a neuron

myopia   visual condition of being unable to see distant objects clearly; also known as being nearsighted

natural childbirth   approach to childbirth that avoids medical technologies and interventions

natural experiment   situation that exists naturally but provides interesting scientific information

natural selection   evolutionary process in which the offspring best adapted to their environment survive to produce offspring of their own

nature–nurture debate   debate among scholars as to whether human development is influenced mainly by genes (nature) or environment (nurture)

neonatal jaundice   yellowish pallor common in the first few days of life due to immaturity of the liver

neonate   newborn baby, up to 4 weeks old

neural tube   in the embryonic period, the part of the ectoderm that will become the spinal cord and brain

neuron   cell of the nervous system

neurotransmitter   chemical that enables neurons to communicate across synapses

normal distribution   typical distribution of characteristics of a population, resembling a bell curve in which most cases fall near the middle and the proportions decrease at the low and high extremes

numeracy   understanding of the meaning of numbers

obese   in children, defined as having a BMI exceeding 21

object permanence   awareness that objects (including people) continue to exist even when we are not in direct sensory or motor contact with them

obstetrics   field of medicine that focuses on prenatal care and birth

only child   child who has no siblings

opposable thumb   position of the thumb apart from the fingers, unique to humans, that makes possible fine motor movements

oral rehydration therapy (ORT)   treatment for infant diarrhea that involves drinking a solution of salt and glucose mixed with clean water

organization   mnemonic that involves placing things mentally into meaningful categories

overcontrol   trait of having excessive emotional self-regulation

overextension   use of a single word to represent a variety of related objects

overproduction/exuberance   burst in the production of dendritic connections between neurons

overregularization   applying grammatical rules even to words that are the exception to the rule

overweight   in children, defined as having a BMI exceeding 18

ovum   mature egg that develops in ovaries, about every 28 days in human females

oxytocin   hormone released by pituitary gland that causes labor to begin

parenting styles   practices that parents exhibit in relation to their children and their beliefs about those practices

passive genotype→environment effects   in the theory of genotype→environment effects, the type that results from the fact that in a biological family, parents provide both genes and environment to their children

peer-review   in scientific research, the system of having other scientists review a manuscript to judge its merits and worthiness for publication

peers   persons who share some aspect of their status in common, such as age

permissive culture   culture that encourages and expects sexual activity from their adolescents

permissive parents   in classifications of parenting styles, parents who are low in demandingness and high in responsiveness

personal fable   belief in one's personal uniqueness, often including a sense of invulnerability to the consequences of taking risks

phenotype   organism's actual characteristics, derived from its genotype

phonics approach   method of teaching reading that advocates breaking down words in their component sounds, called phonics, then putting the phonics together into words

placebo effect   psychological phenomenon in which people believe something affects them and it does, just by virtue of the power of their belief

placenta   in the womb, gatekeeper between mother and fetus, protecting the fetus from bacteria and wastes in the mother's blood, and producing hormones that maintain the blood in the uterine lining and cause the mother's breasts to produce milk

plasticicty   degree to which development can be influenced by environmental circumstances

polygenic inheritance   expression of phenotypic characteristics due to the interaction of multiple genes

polygyny   cultural tradition in which men have more than one wife

population   in research, the entire category of people represented by a sample

possible self   person's conceptions of the self as it potentially may be; may include both an ideal self and a feared self

postconventional reasoning   third level in Kohlberg's theory of moral development, in which moral reasoning is based on the individual's own independent judgments rather than on what others view as wrong or right

postformal thinking   according to some theorists, the stage of cognitive development that follows formal operations and includes advances in pragmatism and reflective judgment

postpartum depression   in parents with a new baby, feelings of sadness and anxiety so intense as to interfere with the ability to carry out simple daily tasks

pragmatics   social and cultural context of language that guides people as to what is appropriate to say and not to say in a given social situation

pragmatism   theory of cognitive development proposing that postformal thinking involves adapting logical thinking to the practical constraints of real-life situations

preconventional reasoning   first level in Kohlberg's theory of moral development, in which moral reasoning is based on perceptions of the likelihood of external rewards and punishments

preoperational stage   cognitive stage from age 2 to 7 during which the child becomes capable of representing the world symbolically—for example, through the use of language—but is still very limited in ability to use mental operations

preterm   babies born at 37 weeks gestation or less

primary attachment figure   person who is sought out when a child experiences some kind of distress or threat in the environment

primary emotions   most basic emotions, such as anger, fear, disgust, surprise, and happiness

primary sex characteristics   production of eggs (ova) and sperm and the development of the sex organs

private speech   in Vygotsky's theory, self-guiding and self-directing comments children make to themselves as they learn in the zone of proximal development and have conversations with those guiding them; first spoken aloud, then internally

procedure   the way a study is conducted and the data are collected

prosocial behavior   positive behavior toward others, including kindness, friendliness, and sharing

protective factors   characteristics of young people that are related to lower likelihood of problems despite experiencing high-risk circumstances

proximodistal principle   principle of biological development that growth proceeds from the middle of the body outward

psychological control   parenting strategy that uses shame and withdrawal of love to influence children's behavior

psychosexual theory   Freud's theory proposing that sexual desire is the driving force behind human development

psychosocial theory   Erikson's theory that human development is driven by the need to become integrated into the social and cultural environment

puberty   changes in physiology, anatomy, and physical functioning that develop a person into a mature adult biologically and prepare the body for sexual reproduction

puberty ritual   formal custom developed in many cultures to mark the departure from childhood and the entrance into adolescence

qualitative   data that is collected in nonnumerical form

quantitative   data that is collected in numerical form

rapid eye movement (REM) sleep   phase of the sleep cycle in which a person's eyes move back and forth rapidly under the eyelids; persons in REM sleep experience other physiological changes as well

reaction range   range of possible developmental paths established by genes; environment determines where development takes place within that range

reciprocal or **bidirectional effects**   in relations between two persons, the principle that each of them affects the other

reflective judgment   capacity to evaluate the accuracy and logical coherence of evidence and arguments, theorized to develop during emerging adulthood

reflex   automatic response to certain kinds of stimulation

regulator gene   gene that directs the activities of other genes

rehearsal   mnemonic that involves repeating the same information over and over

relational aggression   type of aggression that involves damaging another person's reputation among peers through social exclusion and malicious gossip

reliability   in scientific research, the consistency of measurements across different occasions

research design   plan for when and how to collect the data for a study

research method   in the scientific process, the approach to investigating the hypothesis

resilience   overcoming adverse environmental circumstances and achieving healthy development despite those circumstances

responsiveness   degree to which parents are sensitive to their children's needs and express love, warmth, and concern for them

restrictive culture   culture that places strong prohibitions on adolescent sexual activity before marriage

reticular formation   part of the lower brain, involved in attention

reversibility   ability to reverse an action mentally

rooting reflex   reflex that causes the neonate to turn its head and open its mouth when it is touched on the cheek or the side of the mouth; helps the neonate find the breast

rote learning   learning by memorization and repetition

sample   subset of a population for which data are collected in a scientific study

scaffolding   degree of assistance provided to the learner in the zone of proximal development, gradually decreasing as the learner's skills develop

schemes   cognitive structures for processing, organizing, and interpreting information

scientific method   process of scientific investigation, involving a series of steps from identifying a research question through forming a hypothesis, selecting research methods and designs, collecting and analyzing data, and drawing conclusions

secondary emotions   emotions that require social learning and sense of self, such as embarrassment, shame, and guilt; also called sociomoral emotions

secondary school   school attended during adolescence, after primary school

secondary sex characteristics   bodily changes of puberty not directly related to reproduction

secondhand smoke   smoke from a cigarette inhaled by those near the smoker

secular   based on nonreligious beliefs and values

secular trend   change in the characteristics of a population over time

secure attachment   healthiest classification of parent–child attachment, in which the child uses the parent as a secure base from which to explore, protests when separated from parent, and is happy when the parent returns

secure base   role of primary attachment figure, allows child to explore world while seeking comfort when threats arise

selective association   in social relations, the principle that people tend to prefer being around others who are like themselves

selective attention   ability to focus attention on relevant information and disregard what is irrelevant

self-concept   person's perception and evaluation of him- or herself

self-esteem   person's overall sense of worth and well-being

self-medication   use of substances to relieve unpleasant emotional states

self-recognition ability to recognize one's image in the mirror as one's self

self-reflection capacity to think about one's self as one would think about other persons and objects

self-socialization process by which people seek to maintain consistency between their gender schemas and their behavior

semirestrictive culture culture that has prohibitions on premarital adolescent sex, but the prohibitions are not strongly enforced and are easily evaded

sensitive period in the course of development, a period when the capacity for learning in a specific area is especially pronounced

sensorimotor stage in Piaget's theory, the first two years of cognitive development, which involves learning how to coordinate the activities of the senses with motor activities

separation anxiety discomfort experienced by infants and young children when apart from attachment figures, especially when a stranger is present

seriation ability to arrange things in a logical order, such as shortest to longest, thinnest to thickest, or lightest to darkest

sex biological status of being male or female

sex chromosomes chromosomes that determine whether an organism is male (XY) or female (XX)

sexual orientation a person's tendencies of sexual attraction

sexually transmitted infection (STI) infection transmitted through sexual contact

small for date term applied to neonates who weigh less than 90% of other neonates who were born at the same gestational age

social comparison how persons view themselves in relation to others with regard to status, abilities, or achievements

social constructivist theory Vygotsky's theory that child development is driven by the child's interaction with more experienced others in social contexts

social control restraints on behavior imposed by social obligations and relationships

social information processing (SIP) in social encounters, evaluations of others' intentions, motivations, and behavior

social learning theory focus on learning by observing social models without any direct reinforcement

social referencing term for process of becoming more adept at observing others' emotional responses to ambiguous and uncertain situations, and using that information to shape one's own emotional responses

social skills behaviors that include being friendly, helpful, cooperative, and considerate

social smile expression of happiness in response to interacting with others, first appearing at age 2–3 months

social status within a group, the degree of power, authority, and influence that each person has in the view of the others

social-networking website website that allows people to establish and maintain electronic contact with a wide social group

socioeconomic status (SES) person's social class, including educational level, income level, and occupational status

sociomoral emotions emotions evoked based on learned culturally based standards of right and wrong; also called *secondary emotions*

sound localization perceptual ability for telling where a sound is coming from

spermarche beginning of development of sperm in boys' testicles at puberty

state centralized political system that is an essential feature of a civilization

stepfamily family with children in which one of the parents is not biologically related to the children but has married a parent who is biologically related to the children

stereotype belief that others possess certain characteristics simply as a result of being a member of a particular group

Strange Situation laboratory assessment of attachment entailing a series of introductions, separations, and reunions involving the child, the mother, and an unfamiliar person

stranger anxiety fear in response to unfamiliar persons, usually evident in infants by age 6 months

sudden infant death syndrome (SIDS) death within the first year of life due to unknown reasons, with no apparent illness or disorder

surfactant substance in lungs that promotes breathing and keeps the air sacs in the lungs from collapsing

swaddling practice of infant care that involves wrapping an infant tightly in cloths or blankets

symbolic function substage first substage of the preoperational stage, lasting from about age 2 to age 4, when the child first becomes capable of representational thought and of using symbols to represent the world

synaptic density density of synapses among neurons in the brain; peaks around age 3

synaptic pruning process in brain development in which dendritic connections that are used become stronger and faster and those that are unused whither away

teething period of discomfort and pain experienced by infants as their new teeth break through their gums

telegraphic speech two-word phrases that strip away connecting words, such as *the* and *and.*

temperament innate responses to the physical and social environment, including qualities of activity level, irritability, soothability, emotional reactivity, and sociability

teratogen behavior, environment, or bodily condition that can have damaging influence on prenatal development

tertiary education education or training beyond secondary school

testosterone the androgen most important in pubertal development among boys

theory framework that presents a set of interconnected ideas in an original way and inspires further research

theory of genotype→environment effects theory proposing that genes influence the kind of environment we experience

theory of mind ability to understand thinking processes in one's self and others

theory of multiple intelligences Gardner's theory that there are eight distinct types of intelligence

time out disciplinary strategy in which the child is required to sit still in a designated place for a brief period

total fertility rate (TFR) in a population, the number of births per woman

traditional culture in developing countries, a rural culture that adheres more closely to cultural traditions than people in urban areas do

transitive inference ability to place objects in a logical order mentally

triarchic theory of intelligence Sternberg's theory that there are three distinct but related forms of intelligence

trimester one of the three 3-month periods of prenatal development

trophoblast in the blastocyst, the outer layer of cells, which will go on to form structures that provide protection and nourishment to the embryo

trust-versus-mistrust in Erikson's psychosocial theory, the first stage of development, during infancy, in which the central crisis is the need to establish a stable attachment to a loving and nurturing caregiver

ultrasound machine that uses sound waves to produce images of the fetus during pregnancy

umbilical cord structure connecting the fetus to the placenta

undercontrol trait of having inadequate emotional self-regulation

underextension applying a general word to a specific object

unemployment work status of adults who are not in school, are not working, and are looking for a job

unstructured socializing socializing with friends without any specific goal or activity; includes behavior such as riding around in a car for fun, going to parties, visiting friends informally, and going out with friends

validity in scientific research, the extent to which a research method measures what it claims to measure

very low birth weight term for neonates who weigh less than 1,500 grams (3.3 lb) at birth

VO₂ max ability of the body to take in oxygen and transport it to various organs; also called maximum oxygen update

weaning cessation of breast-feeding

Wernicke's area portion of the left temporal lobe of the human brain that is specialized for language comprehension

wet nursing cultural practice, common in human history, of hiring a lactating woman other than the mother to feed the infant

whole-language approach method of teaching reading in which the emphasis is on the meaning of written language in whole passages, rather than breaking down words to their smallest components

worldview set of cultural beliefs that explain what it means to be human, how human relations should be conducted, and how human problems should be addressed

X-linked inheritance pattern of inheritance in which a recessive characteristic is expressed because it is carried on the male's X chromosome

zone of proximal development difference between skills or tasks that children can accomplish alone and those they are capable of performing if guided by an adult or a more competent peer

zygote following fertilization, the new cell formed from the union of sperm and ovum

References

A man's world? Good news. The education gap between men and women is narrowing. (2007, November 3). *The Economist, 75.*

A special report on the human genome. (2010). *The Economist.* Retrieved from http://www.economist.com/node/16349358

Abbott, S. (1992). Holding on and pushing away: Comparative perspectives on an eastern Kentucky child-rearing practice. *Ethos, 20,* 33–65.

Abrejo, F. G., Shaikh, B. T., & Rizvi, N. (2009). And they kill me, only because I am a girl . . . a review of sex-selective abortions in South Asia. *European Journal of Contraception and Reproductive Health Care, 14,* 10–16.

Adams, G. R. (1999). *The objective measure of ego identity status: A manual on test theory and construction.* Guelph, Ontario, Canada: Author.

Adamson, L., & Frick, J. (2003). The still face: A history of a shared experimental paradigm. *Infancy, 4,* 451–473.

Adolph, K. E., & Berger, S. E. (2005). Physical and motor development. In M. H. Bornstein & M. E. Lamb (Eds.), *Developmental science: An advanced textbook* (5th ed., pp. 223–281). Mahwah, NJ: Erlbaum.

Adolph, K. E., & Berger, S. E. (2006). Motor development. In W. Damon & R. Lerner (Series Eds.), & D. Kuhn & R. Sieglery (Vol. Eds.), *Handbook of child psychology: Vol. 2. Cognition, perception and language* (6th ed., pp. 161–213). New York, NY: Wiley.

Adolph, K. E., Karasik, L. B., & Tamis-Lemonda, C. S. (2010). Motor skill. In M. H. Bornstein (Ed.), *Handbook of cultural developmental science* (pp. 61–88). New York, NY: Psychology Press.

Aikat, D. (2007). Violence, extent and responses to. In J. J. Arnett (Ed.), *Encyclopedia of children, adolescents, and the media* (Vol. 2, pp. 852–854). Thousand Oaks, CA: Sage.

Ainsworth, M. D. S., & Bell, S. M. (1969). Some contemporary patterns of mother–infant interaction in the feeding situation. In A. Ambrose (Ed.), *Stimulation in early infancy* (pp. 133–170). London, UK: Academic Press.

Ainsworth, M. D. S., Behar, M. C., Waters, E., & Wall, S. (1978). *Patterns of attachment: A psychological study of the strange situation.* Oxford, UK: Erlbaum.

Ainsworth, M. S. (1977). Infant development and mother–infant interaction among Ganda and American families. In P. H. Leiderman, S. R. Tulkin, & A. Rosenfeld (Eds.), *Culture and infancy: Variations in the human experience* (pp. 119–149). New York, NY: Academic Press.

Akhtar, N. (2005). Is joint attention necessary for early language learning? In B. D. Homer & C. S. Tamis-LeMonda (Eds.), *The development of social cognition and communication* (pp. 165–179). Mahwah, NJ: Erlbaum.

Akhtar, N., & Tomasello, M. (2000). The social nature of words and word learning. In R. M. Golinkoff, K. Hirsh-Pasek, L. Bloom, L. B. Smith, A. L. Woodward, & N. Akhtar (Eds.), *Becoming a word learner: A debate on lexical acquisition* (pp. 115–135). New York, NY: Oxford University Press.

Akimoto, S. A., & Sanbonmatsu, D. M. (1999). Differences in self-effacing behavior between European and Japanese Americans: Effect on competence evaluations. *Journal of Cross-Cultural Psychology, 30,* 159–177.

Akinbami, L. J., & Schoendorf, K. C. (2002). Trends in childhood asthma: Prevalence, health care utilization, and mortality. *Pediatrics, 110,* 315–322.

Aksu-Koç, A. A., & Slobin, D. I. (1985). The acquisition of Turkish. *The cross-linguistic study of language acquisition, Vol. 1: The data; Vol. 2: Theoretical issues* (pp. 839–878). Hillsdale, NJ, England: Erlbaum.

Akshoomoff, N. A., Feroleto, C. C., Doyle, R. E., & Stiles, J. (2002). The impact of early unilateral brain injury on perceptual organization and visual memory. *Neuropsychologia, 40,* 539–561.

Alaggia, R., & Vine, C. (Eds.). (2006). *Cruel but not unusual: Violence in Canadian families.* Waterloo, Ontario, Canada: Wilfrid Laurier University Press.

Alan Guttmacher Institute (AGI) (2001). *Teenage sexual and reproductive behavior in developed countries: Can more progress be made?* New York: Author. Retrieved from www.agi-usa.org

Alberts, A., Elkind, D., & Ginsberg, S. (2007). The personal fable and risk-taking in early adolescence. *Journal of Youth and Adolescence, 36,* 71–76.

Aldridge, M. A., Stillman, R. D., & Bower, T. G. R. (2001). Newborn categorization of vowel-like sounds. *Developmental Science, 4,* 220–232.

Aldwin, C. M., & Spiro, A. III (2006). *Health, behavior, and optimal aging: A life span developmental perspective.* San Diego, CA: Academic Press.

Alexander, B. (2001, June). Radical idea serves youth, saves money. *Youth Today,* pp. 1, 42–44.

Alexander, R. B. (1998). *Changing bodies, changing lives: A book for teens on sex and relationships* (Expanded 3rd ed.). New York, NY: Three Rivers Press.

Alexander, G. M., & Hines, M. (2002). Sex differences in response to children's toys in nonhuman primates. *Evolution and Human Behavior, 23,* 467–479.

Alink, L. R. A., Mesman, J., van Zeijl, J., Stolk, M. N., Juffer, F., Koot, H. M., . . . van IJzendoorn, M. H. (2006). The early childhood aggression curve: Development of physical aggression in 10- to 50-month-old children. *Child Development, 77,* 954–966.

Alsaker, F. D., & Flammer, A. (1999). *The adolescent experience: European and American adolescents in the 1990s.* Mahwah, NJ: Erlbaum.

Alsaker, F. D., & Flammer, A. (2006). Pubertal maturation. In S. Jackson & L. Goossens (Eds.), *Handbook of adolescent development* (pp. 30–50). New York, NY: Psychology Press.

Althabe, F., Buekens, P., Bergell, E., Belizán, J. M., Kropp, N., Wright, L., Cogo, N., and Moss, N. (2005). A cluster randomized controlled trial of a behavioral intervention to facilitate the development and implementation of clinical practice guidelines in Latin American maternity hospitals: the Guidelines Trial. *BMC Women's Health, 5:*4.

Alvarez, M. (2004). Caregiving and early infant crying in a Danish community. *Journal of Developmental and Behavioral Pediatrics, 25,* 91–98.

Alwin, D. F. (1988). From obedience to autonomy: Changes in traits desired in children, 1928–1978. *Public Opinion Quarterly, 52,* 33–52.

Al-Mateen, C. S., & Afzal, A. (2004). The Muslim child, adolescent, and family. *Child and Adolescent Psychiatry Clinics of North America, 13,* 183–200.

Amato, P. R. (2000). Diversity within single-parent families. In D. H. Demo, K. R. Allen, & M. A. Fine (Eds.), *Handbook of family diversity* (pp. 149–172). New York, NY: Oxford University Press.

Amato, P. R. (2006). Marital discord, divorce, and children's well-being: Results from a 20-year longitudinal study of two generations. In A. Clarke-Steward & J. Dunn (Eds.), *Families count: Effects on child and adolescent development* (pp. 179–202). New York, NY: Cambridge University Press.

Amato, P. R., & Fowler, F. (2002). Parenting practices, child adjustment, and family diversity. *Journal of Marriage and the Family, 64,* 703–716.

American Academy of Pediatrics Committee on Public Education. (2001). Children, adolescents, and television. *Pediatrics, 107,* 423–426.

American Academy of Pediatrics. (2004). *Sports programs.* Retrieved from http://www.medem.com/medlb/article_detaillb_for_printer.cfm?article_ID=ZZZD2QD5M7C&sub_cat=405/

American Academy of Pediatrics. (2005a). Breastfeeding and the use of human milk: Policy statement. *Pediatrics, 115,* 496–506.

American Academy of Pediatrics, Subcommittee on Attention-Deficit Hyperactivity Disorder. (2005b). Treatment of attention-deficit hyperactivity disorder. *Pediatrics, 115,* e749–e757.

American Academy of Pediatrics. (2009). *Toilet training.* Retrieved from http://www2.aap.org/publiced/BR_ToiletTrain.htm

American Academy of Pediatrics (2009). Disciplining your child. HealthyChildren.org. Retrieved September 1, 2012, from http://www.healthychildren.org/English/family-life/family-dynamics/communication-discipline/pages/Disciplining-Your-Child.aspx?nfstatus=401&nftoken=00000000-0000-0000-0000-000000000000&nfstatusdescription=ERROR%3a+No+local+token

American Academy of Pediatrics. (2011). *AAP issues new guidelines for identifying and managing newborn jaundice.* Retrieved from http://www.aap.org/family/jaundicefeature.htm

American Academy of Pediatrics Task Force on Infant Positioning and SIDS (AAPTFIPS). (2005). Changing concepts of sudden infant death syndrome. *Pediatrics, 105,* 650–656.

American Pregnancy Association. (2011). *In-vitro fertilization (IVF).* Retrieved from http://www.americanpregnancy.org/infertility/ivf.html/

American Psychiatric Association. (2013). *Diagnostic and statistical manual of mental disorders (DSM-5).* Arlington, VA: American Psychiatric Association.

Ammaniti, M., Speranza, A. M., & Fedele, S. (2005). Attachment in Infancy and in Early and Late Childhood: A Longitudinal Study. In K. A. Kerns R. A. Richardson (Ed.), *Attachment in middle childhood* (pp. 115–136). New York, NY: Guilford Press.

Amsterlaw, J., & Wellman, H. (2006). Theories of mind in transition: A microgenetic study of the development of false belief understanding. *Journal of Cognition and Development, 7,* 139–172.

Anand, S., & Krosnick, J. A. (2005). Demographic predictors of media use among infants, toddlers, and preschoolers. *American Behavioral Scientist, 48*(5), 539–561.

Anders, T. F., & Taylor, T. (1994). Babies and their sleep environment. *Children's Environments, 11,* 123–134.

Anderson, C. A. (2004). An update on the effects of playing violent video games. *Journal of Adolescence, 27,* 113–122.

Anderson, C. A., Gentile, D. A., & Buckley, K. E. (2007). *Violent video game effects on children and adolescents: Theory, research, and public policy.* New York, NY: Oxford University Press.

Anderson, D. R., Huston, A. C., Schmitt, K., Linebarger, D. L., & Wright, J. C. (2001). Early childhood viewing and adolescent behavior: The recontact study. *Monographs of the Society for Research in Child Development, 66*(1, Serial No. 264).

Anderson, E. (2000). Exploring register knowledge: The value of "controlled improvisation." In L. Menn & N. B. Ratner (Eds.), *Methods for studying language production* (pp. 225–248). Mahwah, NJ: Erlbaum.

Anderson, P., & Butcher, K. (2006). Childhood obesity: Trends and potential causes. *The Future of Children, 16,* 19–45.

Anderson, V., & Jacobs, R. (Eds.). (2008). *Executive functions and the frontal lobes: A lifespan perspective.* Philadelphia, PA: Taylor & Francis.

Andersson, T., & Magnusson, D. (1990). Biological maturation in adolescence and the development of drinking habits and alcohol abuse in young males: A prospective longitudinal study. *Journal of Youth and Adolescence, 19,* 33–42.

Ando, M., Asakura, T., & Simons-Morton, B. (2005). Psychosocial influences in physical, verbal and indirect bullying among Japanese early adolescents. *Journal of Early Adolescence, 25,* 268–297.

Andrews, G., Halford, G., & Bunch, K. (2003). Theory of mind and relational complexity. *Child Development, 74,* 1476–1499.

Anglin, J. M. (1993). Vocabulary development: A morphological analysis. *Monographs of the Society for Research in Child Development, 58*(10, Serial No. 238).

Apgar, V. (1953). Proposal for a new method of evaluation of newborn infant. *Anesthesia and Analgesia, 32,* 260–267.

Appoh, L. Y. (2004). Consequences of early malnutrition for subsequent social and emotional behaviour of children in Ghana. *Journal of Psychology in Africa; South of the Sahara, the Caribbean, and Afro-Latin America, 14,* 87–94.

Appoh, L. Y., & Krekling, S. (2004). Effects of early childhood malnutrition on cognitive performance of Ghanaian children. *Journal of Psychology in Africa; South of the Sahara, the Caribbean, and Afro-Latin America, 14,* 1–7.

Apter, T. (1990). *Altered loves: Mothers and daughters during adolescence.* New York, NY: St. Martin's.

Aquilino, W. S. (2006). Family relationships and support systems in emerging adulthood. In J. J. Arnett & J. Tanner (Eds.), *Coming of age in the 21st century: The lives and contexts of emerging adults* (pp. 193–218). Washington, DC: American Psychological Association.

Archibald, A. B., Graber, J. A., & Brooks-Gunn, J. (2003). Pubertal processes and physiological growth in adolescence. In G. Adams & M. Berzonsky (Eds.), *Blackwell handbook of adolescence.* Malden, MA: Blackwell.

Arditi-Babchuk, H., Eidelman, A. I., & Feldman, R. (2009). Rapid eye movement (REM) in premature neonates and developmental outcome at 6 months. *Infant Behavior & Development, 32,* 27–32.

Arnett, J. (1994). Are college students adults? Their conceptions of the transition to adulthood. *Journal of Adult Development, 1,* 154–168.

Arnett, J. J. (1996). *Metalheads: Heavy metal music and adolescent alienation.* Boulder, CO: Westview Press.

Arnett, J. J. (1997). Young people's conceptions of the transition to adulthood. *Youth & Society, 29,* 1–23.

Arnett, J. J. (1998). Learning to stand alone: The contemporary American transition to adulthood in cultural and historical context. *Human Development, 41,* 295–315.

Arnett, J. J. (1999). Adolescent storm and stress, reconsidered. *American Psychologist, 54,* 317–326.

Arnett, J. J. (2000). Emerging adulthood: A theory of development from the late teens through the twenties. *American Psychologist, 55,* 469–480.

Arnett, J. J. (2001). Conceptions of the transition to adulthood: Perspectives from adolescence to midlife. *Journal of Adult Development, 8,* 133–143.

Arnett, J. J. (2002a). Adolescents in Western countries in the 21st century: Vast opportunities—for all? In B. B. Brown, R. W. Larson, & T. S. Saraswathi (Eds.), *The world's youth: Adolescence in eight regions of the globe* (pp. 307–343). New York, NY: Cambridge University Press.

Arnett, J. J. (2002b). The psychology of globalization. *American Psychologist, 57,* 774–483.

Arnett, J. J. (2003). Conceptions of the transition to adulthood among emerging adults in American ethnic groups. *New Directions in Child and Adolescent Development, 100,* 63–75.

Arnett, J. J. (2004). *Emerging adulthood: The winding road from the late teens through the twenties.* New York, NY: Oxford University Press.

Arnett, J. J. (2005a). The Vitality Criterion: A new standard of publication for *Journal of Adolescent Research. Journal of Adolescent Research, 20,* 3–7.

Arnett, J. J. (2005b). The developmental context of substance use in emerging adulthood. *Journal of Drug Issues, 35,* 235–253.

Arnett, J. J. (2006). G. Stanley Hall's adolescence: Brilliance and nonsense. *History of Psychology, 9,* 186–197.

Arnett, J. J. (2007a). Introduction. In J. J. Arnett (Ed.), *Encyclopedia of children, adolescents, and the media, Volume 1: A-K* (pp. xxxv–xxxvi). Thousand Oaks, CA: Sage.

Arnett, J.J. (2007b). The long and leisurely route: Coming of age in Europe today. *Current History, 106,* 130–136.

Arnett, J. J. (2008). The neglected 95%: Why American psychology needs to become less American. *American Psychologist, 63,* 602–614.

Arnett, J. J. (2011). Emerging adulthood(s): The cultural psychology of a new life stage. In L. A. Jensen (Ed.), *Bridging cultural and developmental psychology: New syntheses in theory, research, and policy.* New York, NY: Oxford University Press.

Arnett, J. J., & Jensen, L. A. (2002). A congregation of one: Individualized religious beliefs among emerging adults. *Journal of Adolescent Research, 17,* 451–467.

Arnett, J. J., & Tanner, J. L. (2009). Toward a cultural-developmental stage theory of the life course. In K. McCartney & R. Weisberg (Eds.), *Development and experience: A festschrift in honor of Sandra Wood Scarr* (pp. 17–38). New York, NY: Taylor & Francis.

Aronson, P. J., Mortimer, J. T., Zierman, C., & Hacker, M. (1996). Generational differences in early work experiences and evaluations. In J. T. Mortimer M. D. Finch (Ed.), *Adolescents, work, and family: An intergenerational developmental analysis,* Understanding families. (pp. 25–62). Thousand Oaks, CA: Sage.

Asawa, L. E., Hansen, D. J., & Flood, M. F. (2008). Early childhood intervention programs: Opportunities and challenges for preventing child maltreatment. *Education and Treatment of Children, 31,* 73–110.

Ashcraft, M. H. (2009). *Cognition.* Upper Saddle River, NJ: Prentice Hall.

Asher, S. R., & Rose, A. J. (1997). Promoting children's social–emotional adjustment with peers. In P. Salovey & D. J. Sluyter (Eds.), *Emotional development and emotional intelligence* (pp. 193–195). New York, NY: Basic Books.

Aslin, R. N., Jusczyk, P. W., & Pisoni, D. B. (1998). Speech and auditory processing during infancy: Constraints on and precursors to language. In W. Damon (Ed.), *Handbook of child psychology* (5th ed., Vol. 2). New York, NY: Wiley.

Atella, L. D., DiPietro, J., Smith, B. A., & St. James-Roberts, I. (2003). More than meets the eye: Parental and infant contributors to maternal and paternal reports of early infant difficultness. *Parenting: Science and Practice, 3,* 265–284.

Atkinson, J. (2000). *The developing visual brain.* Oxford, UK: Oxford University Press.

Atkinson, L., & Goldberg, S. (Eds.). (2004). *Attachment issues in psychopathology and intervention.* Mahwah, NJ: Erlbaum.

Atkinson, L., Chisholm, V. C., Scott, B., Goldberg, S., Vaughn, B. E., Blackwell, J., Dickens, S., Tam, F. (1999). Maternal sensitivity, child functional level, and attachment in Down syndrome. *Monographs of the Society for Research in Child Development, 64,* 45–66.

Aud, S., Hussar, W., Kena, G., Bianco, K., Frohlich, L., Kemp, J., & Tahan, K. (2011). *The Condition of Education 2011* (NCES 2011-033). U.S. Department of Education, National Center for Education Statistics. Washington, DC: U.S. Government Printing Office.

Aunio, P., Aubrey, C., Godfrey, R., Pan, Y., & Liu, Y. (2008). Children's early numeracy in England, Finland and People's Republic of China. *International Journal of Early Years Education, 16,* 203–221.

Aunola, K., & Nurmi, J. E. (2004). Maternal affection moderates the impact of psychological control on a child's mathematical performance. *Developmental Psychology, 40,* 965–978.

Avery, L., & Lazdane, G. (2008). What do we know about sexual and reproductive health among adolescents in Europe? *European Journal of Contraception and Reproductive Health, 13,* 58–70.

Axelsson, A. S. (2010). Perpetual and personal: Swedish youth adults and their use of mobile phones. *New Media & Society, 12,* 35–54.

Axelsson, L., & Ejlertsson, G. (2002). Self-reported health, self-esteem and social support among young unemployed people: A population-based study. *International Journal of Social Welfare, 11,* 111–119.

Azmitia, M., Kamprath, N., & Linnet, J. (1998). Intimacy and conflict: The dynamics of boys' and girls' friendships during middle childhood and early adolescence. In L. Meyer, H. Park, M. Gront-Scheyer, I. Schwartz, & B. Harry (Eds.), *Making friends: The influences of culture and development* (pp. 171–189). Baltimore, MD: Brookes.

Axia, G., Bonichini, S., & Benini, F. (1999). Attention and reaction to distress in infancy: A longitudinal study. *Developmental Psychology, 35,* 500–504.

Bachman, J. G., O'Malley, P. M., Schulenberg, J. E., Johnston, L. D., Freedman-Doan, P., & Messersmith, E. E. (2008). *The education-drug use connection: How successes and failures in school relate to adolescent smoking, drinking, drug use, and delinquency.* New York, NY: Erlbaum.

Bachman, J. G., Safron, D. J., Sy, S. R., & Schulenberg, J. E. (2003). Wishing to work: New perspectives on how adolescents' part-time work intensity is linked to educational engagement, substance use, and other problem behaviors. *International Journal of Behavioral Development, 27,* 301–315.

Baer, J. S., Sampson, P. D., Barr, H. M., Connor, P. D., & Streissguth, A. P. (2003). A 21-year longitudinal analysis of the effects of prenatal alcohol exposure on young adult drinking. *Archives of General Psychiatry, 60,* 377–385.

Bahl, R., Frost, C., Kirkwood, B. R., Edmond, K., Martines, J., Bhandari, N., & Arthur, P. (2005). Infant feeding patterns and risks of death and hospitalization in the first half of infancy: multicentre cohort study. *Bulletin of the World Health Organization, 83*(6), 418–426.

Baildum, E. M., Hillier, V. F., Menon, S., Bamford, F. N., Moore, W. M. O., & Ward, B. S. (2000). Attention to infants in the first year. *Child: Care, Health and Development, 26,* 199–216.

Baillargeon, R. (2008). Innate ideas revisited: For a principle of persistence in infants' physical reasoning. *Perspectives on Psychological Science, 3*(Special issue: From philosophical thinking to psychological empiricism), 2–13.

Baker, J. M. (2002). *How homophobia hurts children: Nurturing diversity at home, at school, and in the community.* New York, NY: Haworth Press.

Baker, J. R., & Moore, S. M. (2008). Distress, coping and blogging: Comparing new MySpace users by their intention to blog. *CyberPsychology & Behavior, 11,* 81–85.

Bakermans-Kranenburg, M. J., van Uzendoorn, M. H., Bokhorst, C. L., & Schuengel, C. (2004). The importance of shared environment in infant–father attachment: A behavioral genetic study of the attachment q-sort. *Journal of Family Psychology, 18,* 545–549.

Baldry, A. C., & Farrington, D. P. (2004). Evaluation of an intervention program for the reduction of bullying and victimization in schools. *Aggressive Behavior, 30,* 1–15.

Balodis, I. M., Wynne-Edwards, K. E., & Olmstead, M. C. (2011). The stress-response-dampening effects of placebo. *Hormones and behavior, 59,* 465–472.

Baltes, P. B., Lindenberger, U., & Staudinger, U. M. (2006). Life span theory in developmental psychology. In W. Damon & R. M. Lerner (Eds.), *Handbook of child psychology* (Vol. 1., pp. 569–664). New York, NY: Wiley.

Bandura, A. (1977). *Social learning theory.* New York, NY: General Learning Press.

Bandura, A. (2002). Social cognitive theory in cultural context. *Applied Psychology: An International Review, 51*(Special Issue), 269–290.

Bandura, A., & Bussey, K. (2004). On broadening the cognitive, motivational, and sociostructural scope of theorizing about gender development and functioning: Comments on Martin, Buble and Szkrybalo (2002). *Psychological Bulletin, 130,* 691–701.

Bandura, A., Ross, D., & Ross, S. A. (1961). The transmission of aggression through imitation of aggressive models. *Journal of Abnormal and Social Psychology, 63,* 575–582.

Banerjee, R. (2005). Gender identity and the development of gender roles. In S. Ding & K. Littleton (Eds.), *Children's personal and social development* (pp. 142–179). Malden, MA: Blackwell.

Bankole, A., Singh, S., Woong, V., & Wulf, D. (2004). *Risk and protection: Youth and HIV/AIDS in sub-Saharan Africa.* Washington, DC: Alan Guttmacher Institute.

Banks, M. S. (2005). The benefits and costs of combining information between and within the senses. In J. J. Reiser, J. J. Lockman, & C. A. Nelson (Eds.), *Action as an organizer of learning and development* (pp. 161–198). Mahwah, NJ: Erlbaum.

Barber, B. K. (Ed.). (2002). *Intrusive parenting: How psychological control affects children and adolescents.* Washington, DC: American Psychological Association.

Barber, B. K., Stolz, H. E., & Olsen, J. A. (2005). Parental support, psychological control, and behavioral control: Assessing relevance across time, culture, and method: IV. Assessing relevance across time: U.S. analyses and results. *Monographs of the Society for Research in Child Development, 70*(4).

Barkley, R. A. (2002). Major life activity and health outcomes associated with attention-deficit/hyperactivity disorder. *Journal of Clinical Psychiatry, 63,* 10–15.

Barling, J., & Kelloway, E. K. (1999). *Young workers: Varieties of experience.* Washington, DC: American Psychological Association.

Barnett, D., Ganiban, J., & Cicchetti, D. (1999). Maltreatment, negative expressivity, and the development of type D attachments from 12 to 24 months of age. *Monographs of the Society for Research in Child Development, 64,* 97–118.

Barnett, W. S., & Hustedt, J. T. (2005). Head Start's lasting benefits. *Infants and Young Children, 18,* 16–24.

Baron, E. M., & Denmark, F. L. (2006). An exploration of female genital mutilation. In F. L. Denmark, H. H. Krauss, E. Halpern, & J. A. Sechzer (Eds.), *Violence and exploitation against women and girls* (pp. 339–355). Malden, MA: Blackwell.

Barone, J. G., Jasutkar, N., & Schneider, D. (2009). Later toilet training is associated with urge incontinence in children. *Journal of Pediatric Urology, 5,* 458–461.

Barr, H. M., & Streissguth, A. P. (2001). Identifying maternal self-reported alcohol use associated with Fetal Alcohol Spectrum Disorders. *Alcoholism: Clinical and Experimental Research, 25,* 283–287.

Barr, R. G. (2009). The phenomena of early infant crying and colic. Paper presented at the Centre for Community and Child Health, Melbourne, Australia, March 2.

Barr, R. G., & Gunnar, M. (2000). Colic: The 'transient responsivity' hypothesis. In R. G. Barr, B. Hopkins, & J. A. Green (Eds.), *Crying as a sign, a symptom, and a signal* (pp. 41–66). Cambridge, UK: Cambridge University Press.

Barr, R., & Hayne, H. (2003). It's not what you know, it's who you know: Older siblings facilitate imitation during infancy. *Child Development, 70,* 1067–1081.

Barrett, D. E., & Frank, D. A. (1987). *The effects of undernutrition on children's behavior.* New York, NY: Gordon & Breach.

Barrett, K. C., & Nelson-Goens, G. C. (1997). Emotion communication and the development of the social emotions. *New Directions for Child Development, 77,* 69–88.

Barrio, C., Morena, A., & Linaza, J. L. (2007). Spain. In J. J. Arnett, R. Ahmed, B. Nsamenang, T. S. Saraswathi, & R. Silbereisen (Eds.), *International encyclopedia of adolescence.* New York, NY: Routledge.

Barry, D. T., & Grilo, C. M. (2002). Eating and body image disturbances in adolescent psychiatric inpatients: Gender and ethnicity patterns. *International Journal of Eating Disorders, 32*(3), 335–343.

Barry, H. III, Bacon, M. K., & Child I. L. (1957). A cross-cultural survey of some sex differences in socialization. *Journal of Abnormal Social Psychology, 55,* 327–332.

Bartoshuk, L. M., & Beauchamp, G. K. (1994). Chemical senses. *Annual Review of Psychology, 45,* 419–449.

Basseches, M. (1984). *Dialectical thinking and adult development.* Norwood, NJ: Ablex.

Basseches, M. (1989). Dialectical thinking as an organized whole: Comments on Irwin and Kramer. In M. L. Commons, J. D. Sinnott, F. A. Richards, & C. Armon (Eds.), *Adult development, Vol. 1: Comparisons and applications of developmental models* (pp. 161–178). New York, NY: Praeger.

Bassi, M., & Antonella, D. F. (2004). Adolescence and the changing context of optimal experience in time: Italy 1986–2000. *Journal of Happiness Studies, 5,* 155–179.

Bates, B., & Turner, A. N. (2003). Imagery and symbolism in the birth practices of traditional cultures. In L. Dundes (Ed.), *The manner born: Birth rites in cross-cultural perspective* (pp. 85–97). Walnut Creek, CA: Altamira Press.

Batzer, F. R., & Ravitsky, V. (2009). Preimplantation genetic diagnosis: Ethical considerations. In V. Ravitsky, A. Fiester, & A. L. Caplan (Eds.), *The Penn Center guide to bioethics* (pp. 339–354). New York, NY: Springer.

Bauer, P. J. (2006). Event memory. In W. Damon & R. Lerner (Eds.), *Handbook of child psychology: Vol. 2. Cognition, perception and language* (6th ed., pp. 373–425). New York, NY: Wiley.

Bauer, P. J., Wenner, J. A., Dropik, P. I., & Wewerka, S. S. (2000). Parameters of remembering and forgetting in the transition from infancy to early childhood. *Monographs of the Society for Research in Child Development, 65,* 1–204.

Bauer, P. J., Wiebe, S. A., Carver, L. J., Waters, J. M., & Nelson, C. A. (2003). Developments in long-term explicit memory late in the first year of life: Behavioral and electrophysiological indices. *Psychological Science, 14,* 629–635.

Bauer, P. J., Wiebe, S. A., Waters, J. M., & Banston, S. K. (2001). Reexposure breeds recall: Effects of experience on 9-month olds' ordered recall. *Journal of Experimental Child Psychology, 80,* 174–200.

Bauer, P. M., Hanson, J. L., Pierson, R. K., Davidson, R. J., & Pollak, S. D. (2009). Cerebellar volume and cognitive functioning in children who experienced early deprivation. *Biological Psychiatry, 66,* 1100–1106.

Bauminger, N., Finzi-Dottan, R., Chason, S., & Har-Even, D. (2008). Intimacy in adolescent friendship: The roles of attachment, coherence, and self-disclosure. *Journal of Social and Personal Relationships, 25,* 409–428.

Baumrind, D. (1968). Authoritative vs. authoritarian parental control. *Adolescence, 3,* 255–272.

Baumrind, D. (1971). Current patterns of parental authority. *Developmental Psychology Monograph, 4*(No. 1, Pt. 2).

Baumrind, D. (1991a). Effective parenting during the early adolescent transition. In P. A. Cowan & E. M. Hetherington (Ed.), *Advances in family research* (Vol. 2, pp. 111–163). Hillsdale, NJ: Erlbaum.

Baumrind, D. (1991b). The influence of parenting style on adolescent competence and drug use. *Journal of Early Adolescence, 11,* 56–95.

Baumrind, D. (1993). The average expectable environment is not enough: A response to Scarr. *Child Development, 64,* 1299–1317.

Bayley, N. (2005). *Bayley Scales of Infant and Toddler Development, Third Edition* (Bayley-III). San Antonio, TX: Harcourt Assessment.

Beck, C.T. (2002). Theoretical perspectives on postpartum depression and their treatment implications. *American Journal of Maternal/Child Nursing, 27,* 282–287.

Becker, A. E. (2004). Television, disordered eating, and young women in Fiji: Negotiating body image and identity during rapid social change. *Culture, Medicine, and Psychiatry, 28,* 533–559.

Becker, A. E., Fay, K., Gilman, S. E., & Striegel-Moore, R. (2007). Facets of acculturation and their diverse relations to body shape concern in Fiji. *International Journal of Eating Disorders, 40,* 42–50.

Beckett, C., Maughan, B., Rutter, M., Castle, J., Colvert, E., Groothues, C., . . . Sonuga-Barke, E. J. S. (2006). Do the effects of early severe deprivation on cognition persist into early adolescence? Findings from the English and Romanian adoptees study. *Child Development, 77,* 696–711.

Beentjes, J. W. L., Koolstra, C. M., Marseille, N., & van der Voort, T. H. A. (2001). Children's use of different media: For how long and why? In S. M. Livingstone & M. Bovill (Eds.), *Children and their changing media environment: A European comparative study* (pp. 85–112). Hillsdale, NJ: Erlbaum.

Bel, A., & Bel, B. (2007). Birth attendants: Between the devil and the deep blue sea. In B. Bel, J. Brouwer, B. T. Das, V. Parthasarathi, & G. Poitevin (Eds.), *Communication processes 2: The social and the symbolic* (pp. 353–385). Thousand Oaks, CA: Sage.

Bell, M. A. (1998). Frontal lobe function during infancy: Implications for the development of cognition and attention. In J. E. Richards (Ed.), *Cognitive neuroscience of attention: A developmental perspective* (pp. 327–362). Mahwah, NJ: Erlbaum.

Bell, M. A., & Wolfe, C. D. (2007). The cognitive neuroscience of early socioemotional development. In C. A. Brownell & C. B. Kopp (Eds.), *Socioemotional development in the toddler years: Transitions and transformations* (pp. 345–369). New York, NY: Guilford Press.

Bell, S. M., & Ainsworth, M. D. S. (1972). Infant crying and maternal responsiveness. *Child Development, 43,* 1171–1190.

Bellah, R. N., Madsen, R., Sullivan, W. M., Swidler, A., & Tipton, S. M. (1985). *Habits of the heart: Individualism and commitment in American life.* New York, NY: Harper & Row.

Bellamy, C. (2005). *The state of the world's children: 2005.* New York, NY: UNICEF.

Belsky, J. (2006). Early child care and early child development: Major findings from the NICHD Study of Early Child Care. *European Journal of Developmental Psychology, 3,* 95–110.

Bem, S. L. (1981). Gender schema theory: A cognitive account of sex-typing. *Psychological Review, 88,* 354–364.

Bempechat, J., & Drago-Severson, E. (1999). Cross-national differences in academic achievement: Beyond etic conceptions of children's understandings. *Review of Educational Research, 69,* 801–813.

Benbow, C. P., & Lubinski, D. (2009). Extending Sandra Scarr's ideas about development to the longitudinal study of intellectually precocious youth. In K. McCartney & R. A. Weinberg (Eds.), *Experience and development: A festschrift in honor of Sandra Wood Scarr* (pp. 231–252). New York, NY: Psychology Press.

Bender, H. L., Allen, J. P., McElhaney, K. B., Antonishak, J., Moore, C. M., Kelly, H. O., & Davis, S. M. (2007). Use of harsh physical discipline and developmental outcomes in adolescence. *Development and Psychopathology, 19,* 227–242.

Benson, M., Harris, P., & Rogers, C. (1992). Identity consequences of attachment to mothers and fathers among late adolescents. *Journal of Research on Adolescents, 2,* 187–204.

Berch, D., & Mazzocco, M. (2007). Why is math so hard for some children? *The nature and origins of mathematical learning difficulties and disabilities.* Baltimore, MD: Brookes.

Berger, K. S. (2007). Update on bullying at school: Science forgotten? *Developmental Review, 27,* 90–126.

Berger, S. E., Adolph, K. E., & Lobo, S. A. (2005). Out of the toolbox: Toddlers differentiate wobbly and wooden handrails. *Child Development, 76,* 1294–1307.

Bergstrom, A. (2007a). Food advertising, international. In J. J. Arnett (Ed.), *Encyclopedia of children, adolescents, and the media* (pp. 347–348). Thousand Oaks, CA: Sage.

Bergstrom, A. (2007b). Cartoons, educational. In J. J. Arnett (Ed.), *Encyclopedia of children, adolescents, and the media* (pp. 137–140). Thousand Oaks, CA: Sage.

Bergström, L., Richards, L., Morse, J. M., & Roberts, J. (2010). How caregivers manage pain and distress in second-stage labor. *Journal of Midwifery & Women's Health, 55,* 38–45.

Bergström, M., Kieler, H., & Waldenström, U. (2009). Effects of natural childbirth preparation versus standard antenatal education on epidural rates, experience of childbirth and parental stress in mothers and fathers: A randomised controlled multicentre trial. *BJOG: An International Journal of Obstetrics & Gynaecology 116,* 1167–1176.

Berkman, N. D., Lohr, K. N., & Bulik, C. M. (2007). Outcomes of eating disorders: A systematic review of the literature. *International Journal of Eating Disorders, 40,* 293–309.

Berko, J. (1958). The child's learning of English morphology. *Word, 14,* 150–177.

Berndt, T. J. (1996). Transitions in friendship and friends' influence. In J. A. Graber, J. Brooks-Gunn, & A. C. Petersen (Eds.), *Transitions through adolescence: Interpersonal domains and context* (pp. 57–84). Mahwah, NJ: Erlbaum.

Berney, T. (2009). Ageing in Down Syndrome. In G. O'Brien, & L. Rosenbloom (Eds.), *Developmental disability and ageing* (pp. 31–38). London, UK: Mac Keith Press.

Berninger, V. W., Abbott, R. D., Jones, J., Wolf, B. J., Gould, L., Anderson-Youngstrom, M., . . . Apel, K. (2006). Early development of language by hand: Composing, reading, listening, and speaking connections; three letter-writing modes; and fast mapping in spelling. *Developmental Neuropsychology, 29*(Special issue on writing), 61–92.

Berninger, V. W., Vermeulen, K., Abbott, R. D., McCutchen, D., Cotton, S., & Cude, J. (2003). Naming speed and phonological awareness as predictors of reading development. *Journal of Educational Psychology, 95,* 452–464.

Berns, G. S., Moore, S., & Capra, C. M. (2009). Adolescent engagement in dangerous behaviors is associated with increased white matter maturity of frontal cortex. *PLoS ONE, 4*(8), e6773.

Berry, J. W., Phinney, J. S., Sam, D. L., & Vedder, P. (Eds.). (2006). *Immigrant youth in cultural transition: Acculturation, identity, and adaptation across national contexts.* Mahwah, NJ: Erlbaum.

Berry, R. J., Li, Z., Erickson, J. D., Li, S., Moore, C. A., Wang, H., . . . Correa, A. (1999). Prevention of neural-tube defects with folic acid in China. *New England Journal of Medicine, 341,* 1485–1490.

Berthier, N. E., & Carrico, R. L. (2010). Visual information and object size in infant reaching. *Infant Behavior and Development, 33,* 555–566.

Best, D. L. (2001). Gender concepts: Convergence in cross-cultural research and methodologies. *Cross-cultural Research: The Journal of Comparative Social Science, 35,* 23–43.

Bhargava, S., & Mendiratta, A. (2006). Understanding language patterns of multilingual children (8–10 years) belonging to high socio-economic class. *Social Science International, 22,* 148–158.

Bialystok, E. (1993). Metalinguistic awareness: The development of children's representations in language. In C. Pratt & A. Garton (Eds.), *Systems of representation in children* (pp. 211–233). London, UK: Wiley.

Bialystok, E. (1997). Effects of bilingualism and biliteracy on children's emerging concepts of print. *Developmental Psychology, 33,* 429–440.

Bialystok, E. (1999). Cognitive complexity and attentional control in the bilingual mind. *Child Development, 70,* 636–644.

Bialystok, E. (2001). *Bilingualism in development: Language, literacy, and cognition.* New York, NY: Cambridge University Press.

Bibok, M. B., Müller, U., & Carpendale, J. I. M. (2009). Childhood. In U. Müller, J. I. M. Carpendale, & L. Smith (Eds.), *The Cambridge companion to Piaget* (pp. 229–254). New York, NY: Cambridge University Press.

Biehl, M. C., Natsuaki, M. N., & Ge, X. (2007). The influence of pubertal timing on alcohol use and heavy drinking trajectories. *Journal of Youth and Adolescence, 36,* 153–167.

Bierman, K. L. (2004). *Peer rejection.* New York, NY: Guilford Press.

Bigelow, A. E., & Dugas, K. (2008). Relations among preschool children's understanding of visual perspective taking, false belief, and lying. *Journal of Cognition and Development, 9*(4), 411–433.

Bina, M., Graziano, F., & Bonino, S. (2006). Risky driving and lifestyles in adolescence. *Accident Analysis & Prevention, 38,* 472–481.

Birch, L. L., Fisher, J. O., & Davison, K. K. (2003). Learning to overeat: Maternal use of restrictive feeding practices promotes girls' eating in the absence of hunger. *American Journal of Clinical Nutrition, 78,* 215–220.

Birdsong, D. (2006). Age and second language acquisition and processing: A selective overview. *Language Learning, 56*(Suppl. s1), 9–49.

Bjarnason, T., & Sigurdardottir, T. J. (2003). Psychological distress during unemployment and beyond: Social support and material deprivation among youth in six Northern European counties. *Social Science & Medicine, 56,* 973–985.

Black, R. E., Williams, S. M., Jones, I. E., & Goulding, A. (2002). Children who avoid drinking cow milk have lower dietary calcium intakes and poor bone health. *American Journal of Clinical Nutrition, 76,* 675–680.

Blair, J. M., Hanson, D. L., Jones, H., & Dwokin, M. S. (2004). Trends in pregnancy rates among women with human immunodeficiency virus. *Obstetrics and Gynecology, 103,* 663–668.

Blakemore, J. E. O. (2003). Children's beliefs about violating gender norms: Boys shouldn't look like girls, and girls shouldn't act like boys. *Sex Roles, 48,* 411–419.

Bloch, M., Klein, E., Koren, D., & Rotenberg, N. (2006). Risk factors for early postpartum depressive symptoms. *General Hospital Psychiatry, 28,* 3–8.

Bloom, L. (1998). Language acquisition in its developmental context. In W. Damon (Ed.), & D. Kuhn & R. S. Siegler (Vol. Eds.), *Handbook of Child Psychology* (5th ed.): *Vol. 2. Cognition, perception and language* (pp. 309–370). New York, NY: Wiley.

Bloom, L., Lifter, K., & Broughton, J. (1985). The convergence of early cognition and language in the second year of life: Problems in conceptualization and measurement. In M. Barrett (Ed.), *Single word speech* (pp. 149–181). New York, NY: Wiley.

Bloom, P. (2000). *How children learn the meanings of words.* Cambridge, MA: MIT Press.

Bluestone, C. D., & Klein, J. O. (2007). *Otitis media in infants and children.* New York, NY: Decker.

Bluestone, C., & Tamis-LeMonda, C. S. (1999). Correlates of parenting styles in predominately working- and middle-class African American mothers. *Journal of Marriage and the Family, 61,* 881–893.

Blum, N. J., Taubman, B., & Nemeth, N. (2004). Why is toilet training occurring at older ages? A study of factors associated with later training. *Journal of Pediatrics, 145,* 107–111.

Blumenthal, J., Jeffries, N. O., Castellanos, F. X., Liu, H., Zidjdenbos, A., Paus, T., . . . Giedd, J. N. (1999). Brain development during childhood and adolescence: A longitudinal MRI study. *Nature Neuroscience, 10,* 861–863.

Bochner, S., & Jones, J. (2008). Frontmatter. *Child Language Development* (pp. i–xiv). Whurr Publishers Ltd. Retrieved from http://onlinelibrary.wiley.com/doi/10.1002/9780470699126.fmatter/summary

Boden, J. M., Horwood, L. J., & Fergusson, D. M. (2007). Exposure to childhood sexual and physical abuse and subsequent educational achievement outcomes. *Child Abuse and Neglect, 31,* 1101–1114.

Bois-Reymond, M., & Ravesloot, J. (1996). The roles of parents and peers in the sexual and relational socialization of adolescents. In K. Hurrelmann & S. Hamilton (Eds.), *Social problems and social contexts in adolescence: Perspectives across boundaries* (pp. 175–197). Hawthorne, NY: Aldine de Gruyter.

Bolzani, L. H., Messinger, D. S., Yale, M., & Dondi, M. (2002). Smiling in infancy. In M. H. Abel (Ed.), *An empirical reflection on the smile* (pp. 111–136). Lewiston, NY: Edwin Mellen Press.

Bonino, S., & Cattelino, E. (2012). Italy. In J. J. Arnett (Ed.), *Adolescent psychology around the world.* New York, NY: Taylor & Francis.

Bong, C. L., Hilliard, J., & Seefelder, C. (2008). Severe methemoglobinemia from topical benzocaine 7.5% (Baby Orajel) use for teething pain in a toddler. *Clinical Pediatrics, 48*(2), 209–211.

Booth, D. A., Higgs, S., Schneider, J., & Klinkenberg, I. (2010). Learned liking versus inborn delight: Can sweetness give sensual pleasure or is it just motivating? *Psychological Science, 21,* 1656–1663.

Borduin, C. M., Schaeffer, C. M., & Ronis, S. T. (2003). Multisystemic treatment of serious antisocial behavior in adolescents. In C. A. Essau (Ed.), *Conduct and oppositional defiant disorders: Epidemiology, risk factors, and treatment* (pp. 299–318). Mahwah, NJ: Erlbaum.

Borgaonkar, D. S. (1997). Chromosomal variation in man: A catalog of chromosomal variants and anomalies (8th ed.). New York, NY: Wiley.

Bornstein, M. H. (2006). Parenting science and practice. In W. Damon & R. Lerner (Eds.), & K. A. Renninger & L. E. Sigel (Vol. Eds.), *Handbook of child psychology: Vol. 4. Child psychology in practice* (6th ed., pp. 893–949). New York, NY: Wiley.

Bornstein, M. H., Slater, A., Brown, E., Robers, E., & Barrett, J. (1997). Stability of mental development from infancy to later childhood: Three "waves" of research. In G. Bremner, A. Slater, & G. Butterworth (Eds.), *Infant development: Recent advances* (pp. 191–215). East Sussex, UK: Psychology Press.

Bortolus, R., Parazzini, F., Chatenoud, L., Benzi, G., Bianchi, M. M., & Marini, A. (1999). The epidemiology of multiple births. *Human Reproduction Update, 5,* 179–187.

Boschi-Pinto, C., Lanata, C. F., & Black, R. E. (2009). The global burden of childhood diarrhea. *Maternal and Child Health, 3,* 225–243.

Bosse, Y., & Hudson, T. J. (2007). Toward a comprehensive set of asthma susceptibility genes. *Annual Review of Medicine, 58,* 171–184.

Bostic, J. Q., Rubin, D. H., Prince, J., & Schlozman, S. (2005). Treatment of depression in children and adolescents. *Journal of Psychiatric Practice, 11,* 141–154.

Botcheva, L., Kalchev, P., & Lederman, P. H. (2007). Bulgaria. In J. J. Arnett, R. Ahmed, B. Nsamenang, T. S. Saraswathi, & R. Silbereisen (Eds.), *International encyclopedia of adolescence.* New York, NY: Routledge.

Bottenberg, P., Van Melkebeke, L., Louckx, F., & Vandenplas, Y. (2008). Knowledge of Flemish paediatricians about children's oral health—Results of a survey. *Acta Paediatrica, 97,* 959–963.

Bouchard, T. J., & McGue, M. (2003). Genetic and environmental influences on human psychological differences. *Journal of Neurobiology, 54,* 4–45.

Bousquet, J., Dahl, R., & Khaltaev, N. (2007). Global alliance against chronic respiratory diseases. *Allergy, 62,* 216–223.

Bower, B. (1985). The left hand of math and verbal talent. *Science News, 127,* 263.

Bowers, W. A., Evans, K., LeGrange, D., & Andersen, A. E. (2003). Treatment of adolescent eating disorders. In M. A. Reinecke & F. M. Dattilio (Eds.), *Cognitive therapy with children and adolescents: A casebook for clinical practice* (2nd ed., pp. 247–280). New York, NY: Guilford Press.

Bowlby, J. (1967). *Childhood mourning and psychiatric illness*. New York, NY: International Universities Press.

Bowlby, J. (1969/1982). *Attachment and loss: Vol. 1. Attachment.* (2nd ed.). New York, NY: Basic Books.

Bowlby, J. (1980). *Attachment and loss: Vol. 3. Loss: Sadness and depression.* New York, NY: Basic Books.

Boyle, P. (2001). Why are Dutch teens so sexually safe? *Youth Today, 10*, 1, 34.

Braine, L. G., Schauble, L., Kugelmass, S., & Winter, A. (1993). Representation of depth by children: Spatial strategies and lateral biases. *Developmental Psychology, 29*, 466–479.

Brake, D. (2006). Electronic games, effects. In J. J. Arnett (Ed.), *Encyclopedia of children, adolescents, and the media*. Thousand Oaks, CA: Sage.

Brambati, B., & Tului, L. (2005). Chronic villus sampling and amniocentesis. *Current Opinion in Obstetrics and Gynecology, 17*, 197–201.

Brame, B., Nagin, D. S., & Tremblay, R. E. (2001). Developmental trajectories of physical aggression from school entry to late adolescence. *Journal of Child Psychology and Psychiatry, 42*, 503–512.

Brant, A. M., Haberstick, B. C., Corley, R. P., Wadsworth, S. J., DeFries, J. C., & Hewitt, J. K. (2009). The development etiology of high IQ. *Behavior Genetics, 39*, 393–405.

Bray, J. H. (1999). From marriage to remarriage and beyond: Findings from the Developmental Issues in Stepfamilies Research Project. In E. M. Hetherington (Ed.), *Coping with divorce, single parenting, and remarriage: A risk and resiliency perspective* (pp. 295–319). Mahwah, NJ: Erlbaum.

Brazelton, T. B., & Sparrow, J. D. (2004). *Toilet training the Brazelton way.* Cambridge, MA: deCapo Press.

Brazelton, T. B., Koslowski, B., & Tronick, E. (1976). Neonatal behavior among urban Zambians and Americans. *Journal of the American Academy of Child Psychiatry, 15*, 97–107.

Breger, L. (2000). *Freud: Darkness in the midst of vision.* New York, NY: Wiley.

Brent, D. A. (2004). Antidepressants and pediatric depression: The risk of doing nothing. *New England Journal of Medicine, 35*, 1598–1601.

Brescoll, V. L., Dawson, E., & Uhlmann, E. L. (2010). Hard won and easily lost: The fragile status of leaders in gender-stereotype-incongruent occupations. *Psychological Science, 21*, 1640–1642.

Bretherton, I., & Munholland, K. (1999). Internal working models in attachment relationships: A construct revisited. In J. Cassidy & P. R. Shaver (Eds.), *Handbook of attachment: Theory, research, and clinical applications* (pp. 89–111). New York, NY: Guilford Press.

Bridges, L., & Moore, K. (2002). Religious involvement and children's well-being: What research tells us (and what it doesn't). *Child Trends Research Brief.* Washington, DC: Author. Retrieved from www.childtrends.org

Brody, G. (2004). Siblings' direct and indirect contributions to child development. *Current Directions in Psychological Science, 13*, 124–126.

Brody, G. H., & Flor, D. L. (1998). Maternal resources, parenting practices, and child competence in rural, single-parent African American families. *Child Development, 69*, 803–816.

Brody, G. H., Kim, S., Murry, V. M., & Brown, A. C. (2003). Longitudinal direct and indirect pathways linking older sibling competence to the development of young sibling competence. *Developmental Psychology, 39*, 618–628.

Broidy, L. M., Nagin, D. S., Tremblay, R. E., Bates, J. E., Brame, B., Dodge, K. A., et al. (2003). Developmental trajectories of childhood disruptive behaviors and adolescent delinquency: A six-site, cross-national study. *Developmental Psychology, 39*, 222–245.

Bronfenbrenner, U. (1980). *The ecology of human development.* Cambridge, MA: Harvard University Press.

Bronfenbrenner, U. (2000). Ecological theory: In A. Kazdin (Ed.), *Encyclopedia of psychology*. Washington, DC: America Psychological Association.

Bronfenbrenner, U. (Ed.). (2005). *Making human beings human: Bioecological perspectives on human development.* Thousand Oaks, CA: Sage.

Bronfenbrenner, U., & Morris, P. A. (1998). The ecology of developmental processes. In W. Damon (Series Ed.) and R. Lerner (Vol. Ed.), *Handbook of child psychology, Vol 1: Theoretical models of human development* (pp. 993–1028). New York, NY: Wiley.

Brooks, R., & Meltzoff, A. N. (2005). The development of gaze following and its relation to language. *Developmental Science, 8*, 535–543.

Brooks-Gunn, J. (2003). Do you believe in magic? What we can expect from early childhood intervention programs. *Social Policy Report of the Society for Research in Child Development, 17*, 3–14.

Brotanek, J. M., Gosz, J., & Weitzman, M. (2007). Iron deficiency in early childhood in the United States: Risk factors and racial/ethnic disparities. *Pediatrics, 120*, 568–575.

Brown, A. M., & Miracle, J. A. (2003). Early binocular vision in human infants: Limitations on the generality of the Superposition Hypothesis. *Vision Research, 43*, 1563–1574.

Brown, A. S., & Susser, E. S. (2002). In utero infection and adult schizophrenia. *Mental Retardation and Developmental Disabilities Research Reviews, 8*, 51–57.

Brown, B. B., & Klute, C. (2003). Friendships, cliques, and crowds. In R. G. Adams & D. M. Berzonsky (Eds.), *Blackwell handbook of adolescence* (pp. 330–348). Malden, MA: Blackwell.

Brown, B. B., Herman, M., Hamm, J. V., & Heck, D. K. (2008). Ethnicity and image: Correlates of crowd affiliation among ethnic minority youth. *Child Development, 79*, 529–546.

Brown, J. D. (2006). Emerging adults in a media-saturated world. In J. J. Arnett & J. Tanner (Eds.), *Coming of age in the 21st century: The lives and contexts of emerging adults* (pp. 279–299). Washington, DC: American Psychological Association.

Brown, J. D., Steele, J., & Walsh-Childers, K. (Eds.). (2002). *Sexual teens, sexual media.* Mahwah, NJ: Erlbaum.

Brown, J. D., Steele, J. R., & Walsh-Childers, K. (2002). Introduction. In J. D. Brown, J. R. Steele, & K. Walsh-Childers (Eds.) Sexual teens, sexual media: Investigating media's influence on adolescent sexuality (pp. 1-25). Mahwah, NJ: Taylor & Francis.

Brown, R. (1973). *A first language: The early stages.* Cambridge, MA: Harvard University Press.

Brownell, C. A., & Kopp, C. B. (2007). *Socioemotional development in the toddler years.* New York, NY: Guilford Press.

Brumberg, J. J. (1997). *The body project: An intimate history of American girls.* New York, NY: Random House.

Bryant, G. A., & Barrett, H. C. (2007). Recognizing intentions in infant–directed speech: Evidence for universals. *Psychological Science, 18*, 746–751.

Bryder, L. (2009). From breast to bottle: a history of modern infant feeding. *Endeavour 33*, 54–59.

Buboltz, W. C., Soper, B., Brown, F., & Jenkins, S. (2002). Treatment approaches for sleep difficulties in college students. *Counseling Psychology Quarterly, 15*, 229–237.

Buchanan, C. M., Eccles, J. S., & Becker, J. B. (1992). Are adolescents the victims of raging hormones? Evidence for activational effects of hormones on moods and behavior at adolescence. *Psychological Bulletin, 111*, 62–107.

Buckley, T., & Gottlieb, A. (1988). *Blood magic: The anthropology of menstruation.* Berkeley: University of California Press.

Bugental, D. B., & Grusec, J. E. (2006). Socialization processes. In N. Eisenberg, W. Damon, & R. M. Lerner (Eds.), *Handbook of child psychology: Vol. 3. Social, emotional, and personality development* (6th ed., pp. 366–428, xxiv, 1128). Hoboken, NJ: Wiley.

Bugental, D. B., & Happaney, K. (2004). Predicting infant maltreatment in low-income families: The interactive effects of maternal attributions and child status at birth. *Developmental Psychology, 40*, 234–243.

Buhs, E. S., & Ladd, G. W. (2001). Peer rejection as antecedent of young children's school adjustment: An examination of mediating processes. *Developmental Psychology, 37*, 550–560.

Bulik, C. M., Berkman, N. D., Brownley, K. A., Sedway, L. A., & Lohr, K. N. (2007). Anorexia nervosa treatment: A systematic review of randomized controlled trials. *International Journal of Eating Disorders, 40*, 310–320.

Bullough, V. L. (1981). Comments on Mosher's "Three dimensions of depth involvement in human sexual response." *Journal of Sex Research, 17*, 177–178.

Bumpass, L., & Liu, H. H. (2000, March). Trends in cohabitation and implications for children's family contexts in the United States. *Population Studies, 54*, 29–41.

Burnham, M., Goodlin-Jones, B., & Galyor, E. (2002). Nighttime sleep–wake patterns and self-soothing from birth to one year of age: A longitudinal intervention study. *Journal of Child Psychology & Psychiatry & Allied Disciplines, 43*, 713–725.

Bushman, B. J., & Chandler, J. J. (2007). Violence, effects of. In J. J. Arnett (Ed.), *Encyclopedia of children, adolescents, and the media* (Vol. 2, pp. 847–850). Thousand Oaks, CA: Sage.

Bushman, B. J., & Huesmann, L. R. (2001). Effects of televised violence on aggression. In D. G. Singer & J. L. Singer (Eds.), *Handbook of children and the media* (pp. 223–254). Thousand Oaks, CA: Sage.

Buss, A. H. (1995). *Personality, temperament, social behavior, and the self.* Boston, MA: Allyn & Bacon.

Buss, D. (2000). Evolutionary psychology. In A. Kazdin (Ed.), Encyclopedia of psychology (pp. 277–280). Washington, DC, and New York: American Psychological Association and Oxford University Press.

Buss, D. M. (2004). *Evolutionary psychology: The new science of the mind* (2nd ed.). Boston; London: Pearson/Allyn and Bacon.

Buss, K. A., & Goldsmith, H. H. (1998). Fear and anger regulation in infancy: Effects on the temporal dynamics of affective expression. *Child Development, 69,* 359–374.

Buss, K. A., & Plomin, R. (1984). *Temperament: Early developing personality traits.* Hillsdale, NJ: Erlbaum.

Bussey, K. (1992). Lying and truthfulness: Children's definitions, standards, and evaluative reactions. *Child Development, 63,* 129–137.

Bussey, K., & Bandura, A. (2004). Social cognitive theory of gender development and functioning. In A. H. Eagly, A. Beall, & R. Sternberg (Eds.), *The psychology of gender* (2nd ed., pp. 92–119). New York, NY: Guilford Press.

Cabrera, N. J., & Garcia-Coll, C. (2004). Latino fathers: Uncharted territory in need of much exploration. In M. E. Lamb (Ed.), *The role of the father in child development* (4th ed., pp. 98–120). Hoboken, NJ: Wiley.

Cabrera, S. F., Sauer, S. J., & Thomas-Hunt, M. C. (2009). The evolving manager stereotype: The effects of industry gender typing on performance expectations for leaders and their teams. *Psychology of Women Quarterly, 33,* 419–428.

Caetano, R., Ramisetty-Mikler, S., Floyd, L. R., & McGrath, C. (2006). The epidemiology of drinking among women of child-bearing age. *Alcoholism: Clinical and Experimental Research, 30,* 1023–1030.

Calkins, S. D. (2002). Does aversive behavior during toddlerhood matter? The effects of difficult temperament on maternal perceptions and behavior. *Child Development, 67,* 523–540.

Call, J. (2001). Object permanence in orangutans, chimpanzees, and children. *Journal of Comparative Psychology, 115,* 159–171.

Callahan, C. M., Boustani, M. A., Unverzagt, F. W., Austrom, M. G., Damush, T. M., Perkins, et al. (2005). Effectiveness of collaborative care for older adults with Alzheimer disease in primary care: A randomized controlled trial. *JAMA: Journal of the American Medical Association, 295,* 2148–2157.

Calle, E. E., Rodriguez, C., Walker-Thurmond, K., & Thun, M. J. (2003). Overweight, obesity, and mortality from cancer in a prospectively studied cohort of U.S. adults. *New England Journal of Medicine, 348,* 1625–1638.

Cameron, J. L. (2001). Effects of sex hormones on brain development. In C. A. Nelson & M. Luciana (Eds.), *Handbook of developmental cognitive neuroscience* (pp. 59–78).

Campbell, A., Shirley, L., & Candy, J. (2004)t. A longitudinal study of gender-related cognition and behavior. *Developmental Science, 7,* 1–9.

Campbell, E., Ramey, C., & Pungello, E. (2002). Early childhood education: Young adult outcomes from the Abecedarian Project. *Applied Developmental Science, 6,* 42–57.

Campbell, J. M. (2006). Depressive disorders. *Psychodiagnostic assessment of children: Dimensional and categorical approaches.* (pp. 169–209). Hoboken, NJ: Wiley.

Campione-Barr, N., & Smetana, J. G. (2010). 'Who said you could wear my sweater?' Adolescent siblings' conflicts and associations with relationship quality. *Child Development, 81,* 464–471.

Campos, J. J., Langer, A., & Krowitz, A. (1970). Cardiac responses on the visual cliff in prelocomotor human infants. *Science, 170,* 196–197.

Camras, L. A., Lambrecht, L., & Michel, G. F. (1996). Infant "surprise" expressions as coordinative motor structures. *Journal of Nonverbal Behavior, 20,* 183–195.

Capone, G. T., & Kaufmann, W. E. (2008). Human brain development. Capute and Accardo's neurodevelopmental disabilities in infancy and childhood: Vol 1: *Neurodevelopmental diagnosis and treatment* (3rd ed.) (pp. 27–59). Baltimore, MD: Paul H. Brookes Publishing.

Capone, N. C., & McGregor, K. K. (2005). The Effect of Semantic Representation on Toddlers' Word Retrieval. *Journal of Speech Language and Hearing Research, 48*(6), 1468–1480.

Carlson, S. M. (2003). Executive function in context: Development, measurement, theory and experience. *Monographs of the Society for Research in Child Development, 68*(3, Serial No. 274*),* 138–151.

Carr, J. (2002). Down syndrome. In P. Howlin & O. Udwin (Eds.), *Outcomes in neurodevelopmental and genetic disorders* (pp. 169–197). New York, NY: Cambridge University Press.

Carroll, J. L., & Wolpe, P. R. (2005). *Sexuality now: Embracing diversity:* Wadsworth.

Carroll, J. S., Padilla-Walker, L. M., Nelson, L. J., Olson, C. D., Barry, C. M., & Madsen, S. D. (2008). Generation XXX: Pornography acceptance and use among emerging adults. *Journal of Adolescent Research, 23,* 6–30.

Carter, K. C., & Carter, B. R. (2005). *Childbed fever. A scientific biography of Ignaz Semmelweis.* Edison, NJ: Transaction.

Carter-Saltzman, L. (1980). Biological and sociocultural effects on handedness: Comparison between biological and adoptive families. *Science, 209,* 1263–1265.

Carver, K., Joyner, K., & Udry, J. R. (2003). National estimates of adolescent romantic relationships. In P. Florsheim (Ed.), *Adolescent romantic relations and sexual behavior: Theory, research, and practical implications* (pp. 23–56). Mahwah, NJ: Erlbaum.

Case, R. (1999). Conceptual development in the child and the field: A personal view of the Piagetian legacy. In E. K. Skolnick, K. Nelson, S. A. Gelman, & P. H. Miller (Eds.), *Conceptual Development.* Mahwah, NJ: Erlbaum.

Case, R., & Okamato, Y. (Eds.). (1996). The role of central conceptual structures in the development of children's thought. *Monographs of the Society for Research in Child Development, 61*(1–2, Serial No. 246).

Casey, B. J., Getz, S., & Galvan, A. (2008). The adolescent brain. *Developmental Review, 28,* 62–77.

Casey, B. M., McIntire, D. D., & Leveno, K. J. (2001). The continuing value of Apgar score for the assessment of the newborn infants. *New England Journal of Medicine, 344,* 467–471.

Casey Foundation (2010). *2010 Kids Count data book.* Baltimore, MD: Annie E. Casey Foundation.

Caspi, A., & Moffitt, T. E. (2006). Gene-environment interactions in psychiatry: Joining forces with neuroscience. *Nature Reviews Neuroscience, 7*(7), 583–590.

Cassidy, J., & Shaver, P. R. (2008). *Handbook of attachment: Theory, research, and clinical applications.* New York, NY: Guilford Press.

Cassidy, K. W., Werner, R. S., Rourke, M., Zubernis, L. S., & Balaraman, G. (2003). The relationship between psychological understanding and positive social behaviors. *Social Development, 12,* 198–221.

Cassidy, T. (2006). *Birth: The surprising history of how we are born.* New York, NY: Atlantic Monthly Press.

Cassidy, T. (2008). *Taking Great Pains: An Abridged History of Pain Relief in Childbirth.* Retrieved from http://wondertime.go.com/learning/article/childbirth-pain-relief.html

Castellanos, F. X., Sharp, W. S., Gottesman, R. F., Greenstein, D. K., Giedd, J. N., & Rapoport, J. L. (2003). Anatomic brain abnormalities in monozygotic twins discordant for attention-deficit hyperactivity disorder. *American Journal of Psychiatry, 160,* 1693–1695.

Cavallini, A., Fazzi, E., & Viviani, V. (2002). Visual acuity in the first two years of life in healthy term newborns: An experience with the Teller Acuity Cards. *Functional Neurology: New Trends in Adaptive & Behavioral Disorders, 17,* 87–92.

Cavanagh, S. (2005). Poor math scores on world stage trouble U.S. *Education Week, 25*(1), 18.

Cejka, M. A., & Eagly, A. H. (1999). Gender-stereotypic images of occupations correspond to the sex segregation of employment. *Personality and Social Psychology Bulletin, 25,* 413–423.

Centers for Disease Control and Prevention (CDC). (2002). Infant mortality and low birth weight among Black and White infants: United States, 1980–2000. *Morbidity & Mortality Weekly Report, 51,* 589–592.

Centers for Disease Control and Prevention (CDC). (2005). Blood Lead Levels—United States, 1999–2002. *Morbidity and Mortality Weekly Report, 54*(20): 513–516.

Centers for Disease Control and Prevention (CDC). (2006a). School health policies and programs study (SHPPS). *Journal of School Health.* 2007, 27(8).

Centers for Disease Control and Prevention (CDC). (2006b). Vaccine preventable deaths and the global immunization vision and strategy, 2006–15. *Mortality and Morbidity Weekly Report, 55,* 511–515.

Centers for Disease Control and Prevention (CDC). (2008a). Breastfeeding in the United States: Findings from the National Health and Nutrition Examination Surveys, 1999–2006. *NCHS Data Brief, No. 5.*

Centers for Disease Control and Prevention (CDC). (2008b). Youth risk behavior surveillance: United States 2007. *Morbidity and Mortality Weekly Report, 57:* SS-4.

Centers for Disease Control and Prevention. (2009). Defining overweight and obesity. Retrieved from http://www.cdc.gov/obesity/defining.html

Centers for Disease Control and Prevention (CDC). (2010a). *Neonatal mortality rates, by race and Hispanic origin of mother, and state: United States, average annual 1989–1991, 2001–2003, and 2004–2006.* Retrieved from http://www.cdc.gov/nchs/data/hus/2010/019.pdf

Centers for Disease Control and Prevention (CDC). (2010b). Pediatric nutrition surveillance system, 2010. Atlanta, GA: CDC.

Centers for Disease Control and Prevention (CDC). (2010c). *U.S. Obesity Trends: Trends by State 1985–2009.* Atlanta, GA: Author.

Centers for Disease Control and Prevention (CDC). (2011a). *Autism spectrum disorders (ASDs).* Retrieved from http://www.cdc.gov/ncbddd/autism/data.html

Centers for Disease Control and Prevention (CDC). (2011b). *Spina bifida fact sheet.* Retrieved from http://www.cdc.gov/ncbddd/spinabifida/documents/spina–bifida-fact-sheet1209.pdf

Chalk, L. M., Meara, N. M., Day, J. D., & Davis, K. L. (2005). Occupational possible selves: Fears and aspirations of college women. *Journal of Career Assessment, 13,* 188–203.

Chambers, M. L., Hewitt, J. K., Schmitz, S., Corley, R. P., & Fulker, D. W. (2001). Height, weight, and body mass index. In R. N. Emde & J. K. Hewitt (Eds.), *Infancy to early childhood: Genetic and environmental influences on developmental change* (pp. 292–306). New York, NY: Oxford University Press.

Champion, K. M., Vernberg, E. M., & Shipman, K. (2003). Non-bullying victims of bullies: Aggression, social skills, and friendship characteristics. *Journal of Applied Developmental Psychology, 24,* 535–551.

Chang, L. (2008). *Factory girls: From village to city in a changing China.* New York, NY: Spiegel & Grau.

Chao, R., & Tseng, V. (2002). Parenting of Asians. In M. H. Bornstein (Ed.), *Handbook of parenting, Vol. 4: Social conditions and applied parenting* (pp. 59–93). Mahwah, NJ: Erlbaum.

Chapman, L. K., & Steger, M. F. (2010). Race and religion: differential prediction of anxiety symptoms by religious coping in African American and European American young adults. *Depression and Anxiety, 27*(3), 316–322

Charpak, N., Ruiz-Pelaez, J. G., & Figueroa, Z. (2005). Influence of feeding patterns and other factors on early somatic growth of healthy, preterm infants in home-based kangaroo mother care: A cohort study. *Journal of Pediatric Gastroenterology and Nutrition, 41,* 430–437.

Chatters, L. M., Taylor, R. J., Lincoln, K. D., & Jackson, J. S. (2008). Religious coping among African Americans, Caribbean Blacks, and non-Hispanic Whites. *Journal of Community Psychology, 36*(3), 371–386.

Chaudhary, N., & Sharma, N. (2007). India. In J. J. Arnett (Ed.), *International encyclopedia of adolescence* (pp. 442–459). New York, NY: Routledge.

Chaudhary, N., & Sharma, P. (2012). India. In J. J. Arnett (Ed.), *Adolescent psychology around the world.* New York, NY: Taylor & Francis.

Chen, X. (2011). Culture, peer relationships, and human development. In L. A. Jensen (Ed.), *Bridging cultural and developmental approaches to psychology* (pp. 92–111). New York, NY: Oxford University Press.

Chen, X., Cen, G., Li, D., & He, Y. (2005). Social functioning and adjustment in Chinese children: The imprint of historical time. *Child Development, 76,* 182–195.

Chen, X., French, D. C., & Schneider, B. H. (2006). *Peer relationships in cultural context.* Cambridge University Press.

Chen, K., Shen, H., Chen, S., & Li, J. (2010). A research on Chinese children's Animal Drawing Test. *Chinese Journal of Clinical Psychology, 18*(6), 723–724.

Chen, X., Wang, L., & DeSouza, A. (2007). Temperament, socioemotional functioning, and peer relationships in Chinese and North American children. In X. Chen, D. C. French, & B. H. Schneider (Eds.), *Peer relationships in cultural context* (pp. 123–146). New York, NY: Cambridge University Press.

Chess, S., & Thomas, A. (1984). *Origins and evolution of behavior disorders.* New York, NY: Brunner/Mazel.

Chi, D. L., Momany, E. T., Neff, J., Jones, M. P., Warren, J. J., Slayton, R. L., . . . Damiano, P. C. (2011). Impact of chronic condition status and the severity on the time of first dental visit for newly Medicaid-enrolled children in Iowa. *Health Services Research, 46,* 572–595.

Chi, M. T. (1978). Knowledge structures and memory development. In R. S. Siegler (Ed.), *Children's thinking: What develops?* (pp. 73–96). Hillsdale, NJ: Erlbaum.

Children's Defense Fund (2005). *State of America's children.* Washington, DC: Author.

Chinas, L. (1992). *The Isthmus Zapotecs: A matrifocal culture of Mexico.* New York, NY: Harcourt Brace Jovanovich College Publishers.

Chisholm, L., & Hurrelmann, K. (1995). Adolescence in modern Europe: Pluralized transition patterns and their implications for personal and social risks. *Journal of Adolescence, 18,* 129–158.

Chomsky, N. (1957). *Deep structure, surface structure, and semantic interpretation.* The Hague, The Netherlands: Mouton.

Chomsky, N. (1965). *Aspects of a theory of syntax.* Cambridge, MA: MIT Press.

Chomsky, N. (1969). *Deep structure, surface structure, and semantic interpretation.* Indiana University Linguistics Club.

Chuang, M. E., Lamb, C. P., & Hwang, C. P. (2004). Internal reliability, temporal stability, and correlates of individual differences in parental involvement: A 15-year longitudinal study in Sweden. In R. D. Day & M. E. Lamb (Eds.), *Conceptualizing and measuring father involvement* (pp. 129–148). Mahwah, NJ: Erlbaum.

Chumlea, W. C., Schubert, C. M., Roche, A. F., Kulin, H. E., Lee, P. A., Himes, J. H., & Sun, S. S. (2003). Age at menarche and racial comparisons in US girls. *Pediatrics, 111*(1), 110–113.

Cicchetti, D. (2001). How a child builds a brain. In W. W. Hartup & R. A. Weinberg (Eds.), *Child psychology in retrospect and prospect* (pp. 23–71). Mahwah, NJ: Erlbaum.

Cicchetti, D., & Toth, S. L. (1998). Perspectives on research and practice in developmental psychology. In W. Damon (Series Ed.) & I. E. Sigel & K. A. Renninger (Vol. Eds.), *Handbook of child psychology* (Vol. 4, pp. 479–583). New York, NY: Wiley.

Cillessen, A. H. N., & Bellmore, A. D. (2004). Social skills and interpersonal perception in early and middle childhood. In P. K. Smith & C. H. Hart (Eds.), *Blackwell handbook of childhood social development* (pp. 355–374). Malden, MA: Blackwell.

Cillessen, A. H. N., & Mayeux, L. (2004). From censure to reinforcement: Developmental changes in the association between aggression and social status. *Child Development, 75,* 147–163.

Cipriano, E. A., & Stifter, C. A. (2010). Predicting preschool effortful control from toddler temperament and parenting behaviour. *Journal of Applied Developmental Psychology, 31,* 221–230.

Clapp, J. D., Johnson, M., Voas, R. B., Lange, J. E., Shillington, A., & Russell, C. (2005). Reducing DUI among U.S. college students: Results of an environmental prevention trial. *Addiction, 100,* 327–334.

Clark, E. V. (1995). The lexicon and syntax. In J. L. Miller & P. D. Eimas (Eds.), *Speech, language, and communication* (pp. 303–337). San Diego, CA: Academic Press.

Clark, J. J. (2010). Life as a source of theory: Erik Erikson's contributions, boundaries, and marginalities. In T. W. Miller (Ed.), *Handbook of stressful transitions across the lifespan* (pp. 59–83). New York, NY: Springer.

Clarke-Stewart, A., & Brentano, C. (2006). *Divorce: Causes and consequences.* New Haven, CT: Yale University Press.

Clarke-Stewart, K., & Allhusen, V. (2002). Nonparental caregiving. In M. Bornstein (Ed.), *Handbook of parenting: Vol. 3: Being and becoming a parent* (2nd ed., pp. 215–252). Mahwah, NJ: Erlbaum.

Clarke-Stewart, K., Fitzpatrick, M., Allhusen, V., & Goldberg, W. (2000). Measuring difficult temperament the easy way. *Developmental and Behavioral Pediatrics, 21,* 207–223.

Clay, E. C., & Seehusen, D. A. (2004). A review of postpartum depression for the primary care physician. *Southern Medical Journal, 97,* 157–162.

Coghill, D., Spiel, G., Baldursson, G., Döpfner, M., Lorenzo, M. J., Ralston, S.J., & Rothenberger, A., & ADORE Study Group (2006). Which factors impact on clinician-rated impairment in children with ADHD? *European Child & Adolescent Psychiatry, 15*(Suppl. 1), I30–I37.

Cohan, C. L., & Kleinbaum, S. (2002). Toward a greater understanding of the cohabitation effect: Premarital cohabitation and marital communication. *Journal of Marriage & the Family, 64,* 180–192.

Cohen, D., Gerardin, P., Mazet, P., Purper-Ouakil, D., & Flament, M. F. (2004). Pharmacological treatment of adolescent major depression. *Journal of Child and Adolescent Psychopharmacology, 14,* 19–31.

Cohen, L. R., & Potter, L. B. (1999). Injuries and violence: Risk factors and opportunities. *Adolescent Medicine: State of the Art Reviews, 10,* 125–135.

Cohn, J. F., & Tronick, E. Z. (1983). Three-month-old infants' reaction to stimulated maternal depression. *Child Development, 23,* 185–193.

Coie, J. (2004). The impact of negative social experiences on the development of antisocial behavior. In J. B. Kupersmidt & K. A. Dodge (Eds.), *Children's peer relations: From the development to intervention.* Washington, DC: American Psychological Association.

Colby, A., Kohlberg, L., Gibbs, J., & Lieberman, M. (1983). A longitudinal study of moral judgment. *Monographs of the Society for Research in Child Development, 48*(1–2).

Cole, A., & Kerns, K. A. (2001). Perceptions of sibling qualities and activities in early adolescents. *Journal of Early Adolescence, 21,* 204–226.

Cole, M. (1996). *Cultural psychology: A once and future discipline.* Cambridge, MA: Harvard University Press.

Cole, P. M., Teti, L. O., & Zahn-Waxler, C. (2003). Mutual emotion regulation and the stability of conduct problems between preschool and early school age. *Development and Psychopathology, 15,* 1–18.

Cole, T. J., Bellizzi, M. C., Flegal, K. M., & Dietz, W. H. (2000). Establishing a standard definition for child overweight and obesity worldwide: International survey. *British Medical Journal, 320,* 1240–1243.

Coleman, M., Ganong, L., & Fine, M. (2000). Reinvestigating remarriage: Another decade of progress. *Journal of Marriage and the Family, 62,* 1288–1307.

Collier-Baker, E., & Suddendorf, T. (2006). Do chimpanzees and 2-year-old children understand double invisible displacement? *Journal of Comparative Psychology, 120,* 89–97.

Collins, W. A., & Laursen, B. (2004). Parent–adolescent relationships and influences. In R. M. Lerner & L. Steinberg (Eds.), *Handbook of adolescent psychology* (2nd ed., pp. 331–361). New York, NY: Wiley.

Collins, W. A., Maccoby, E. E., Steinberg, L., Hetherington, E. M., & Bornstein, M. H. (2000). Contemporary research on parenting: The case for nature and nurture. *American Psychologist, 55,* 218–232.

Collins, W. A., Madsen, S. D., & Susman-Stillman, A. (2002). Parenting during middle childhood. In M. H. Bornstein (Ed.), *Handbook of parenting: Vol. 1* (2nd ed., pp. 73–101). Mahwah, NJ: Erlbaum.

Colombo, J. (2002). Infant attention grows up: The emergence of a developmental cognitive neuroscience perspective. *Current Directions in Psychological Science, 11,* 196–200.

Colombo, J., & Mitchell, D. W. (2009). Infant visual habituation. *Neurobiology of Learning and Memory, 92,* 225–234.

Combs-Ronto, L. A., Olson, S. L., Lunkenheimer, E. S., & Sameroff, A. J. (2009). Interactions between maternal parenting and children's early disruptive behaviour: Bidirectional associations across the transition from preschool to school entry. *Journal of Abnormal Child Psychology, 37,* 1151–1163.

Compas, B. E., Connor, J. K., & Hinden, B. R. (1998). New perspectives on depression during adolescence. In R. Jessor (Ed.), *New perspectives on adolescent risk behavior* (pp. 319–362). New York, NY: Cambridge University Press.

Condon, R. G. (1987). *Inuit youth: Growth and change in the Canadian Arctic.* New Brunswick, NJ: Rutgers University Press.

Connolly, J., Craig, W., Goldberg, A., & Pepler, D. (2004). Mixed-gender groups, dating, and romantic relationships in early adolescence. *Journal of Research on Adolescence, 14,* 185–207.

Connolly, M., & Sullivan, D. (2004). *The essential c-section guide: Pain control, healing at home, getting your body back, and everything else you need to know about a cesarean birth.* New York, NY: Broadway Books.

Coovadia, H. M., & Wittenberg, D. F. (Eds.) (2004). *Pediatrics and child health: A manual for health professionals in developing countries.* (5th ed.). New York, NY: Oxford University Press.

Coplan, R. J., Prakash, K., O'Neil, K., & Arner, M. (2004). Do you "want" to play? Distinguishing between conflicted shyness and social disinterest in early childhood. *Developmental Psychology, 40,* 244–258.

Corbin, W. R., & Fromme, K. (2002). Alcohol use and serial monogamy as risks for sexually transmitted diseases in young adults. *Health Psychology, 21,* 229–236.

Corby, B. C., Menon, M., Hodges, E. V. E., & Perry, D. G. (2007). The developmental costs of high self-esteem for antisocial children. *Child Development, 78*(6), 1627–1639.

Cornelius, M. D., Day, N. L., De Genna, N. M., Goldschmidt, L., Leech, S. L., & Willford, J. A. (2011). Effects of prenatal cigarette smoke exposure on neurobehavioral outcomes in 10-year-old children of adolescent mothers. *Neurotoxicology and Teratology, 33,* 137–144.

Cosminsky, S. (2003). Cross-cultural perspectives on midwifery. In L. Dundes (Ed.), *The manner born: Birth rites in cross-cultural perspective* (pp. 69–84). Walnut Creek, CA: Altamira Press.

Costello, D. M., Swendsen, J., Rose, J. S., & Dierker, L. C. (2008). Risk and protective factors associated with trajectories of depressed mood from adolescence to early adulthood. *Journal of Consulting and Clinical Psychology, 76,* 173–183.

Côté, J. (2000). *Arrested adulthood: The changing nature of maturity and identity in the late modern world.* New York: New York University Press.

Côté, J. (2005). Editor's introduction. *Identity, 5,* 95–96.

Côté, J. (2006). Emerging adulthood as an institutionalized moratorium: Risks and benefits to identity formation. In J. J. Arnett & J. L. Tanner (Eds.), *Emerging adults in America: Coming of age in the 21st century* (pp. 85–116). Washington, DC: American Psychological Association Press.

Cotter, D., Hermsen, J. M., & Vanneman, R. (2011). The end of the gender revolution? Gender role attitudes from 1977 to 2008. *American Journal of Sociology, 117*(1), 259–289.

Coughlin, C. R. (2009). Prenatal choices: Genetic counseling for variable genetic diseases. In V. Ravitsky, A. Fiester, A. L. Caplan (Eds.), *The Penn Center guide to bioethics* (pp. 415–424). New York, NY: Springer.

Courage, M. L., Howe, M. L., & Squires, S. E. (2004). Individual differences in 3.5 month olds' visual attention: What do they predict at 1 year? *Infant Behavior and Development, 127,* 19–30.

Courage, M., & Cowan, N. (Eds.). (2009). *The development of memory in infancy and childhood* (2nd ed.). New York, NY: Psychology Press.

Courage, M. L., & Setliff, A. E. (2009). Debating the impact of television and video material on very young children: Attention, learning, and the developing brain. *Child Development Perspectives, 3*(1), 72–78.

Coyne, S. (2007). Violence, longitudinal studies of. In J. J. Arnett (Ed.), *Encyclopedia of children, adolescents, and the media* (Vol. 2, pp. 859–860). Thousand Oaks, CA: Sage.

Craig, H. K., Zhang, L., Hensel, S. L., & Quinn, E. J. (2009). African American English-speaking students: An examination of the relationship between dialect shifting and reading outcomes. *Journal of Speech, Language, and Hearing Research;Journal of Speech, Language, and Hearing Research, 52*(4), 839–855.

Crain, W. (2000). *Theories of development: Concepts and applications.* Upper Saddle River, NJ: Prentice Hall.

Cratty, B. J. (1986). *Perceptual and motor development in infants and children* (3rd ed.). Englewood Cliffs, NJ: Prentice-Hall.

Crawford, C., & Krebs, D. (2008). *Foundations of evolutionary psychology.* New York: Erlbaum.

Crawford, M., & Popp, D. (2003). Sexual double standards: A review and methodological critique of two decades of research. *Journal of Sex Research, 40,* 13–26.

Crick, N. R., Ostrov, J. M., Burr, J. E., Cullerton-Sen, C., Jansen-Yeh, E., & Ralston, P. (2006). A longitudinal study of relational and physical aggression in preschool. *Journal of Applied Developmental Psychology, 27,* 254–268.

Crncec, R., Matthey, S., & Nemeth, D. (2010). Infant sleep problems and emotional health: A review of two behavioural approaches. *Journal of Reproductive and Infant Psychology, 28,* 44–54.

Cross, S. E., & Gore, J. S. (2003). Cultural models of the self. In E. S. Cross, S. J. Gore, & R. M. Leary (Eds.), *Handbook of self and identity* (pp. 536–564). New York, NY: Guilford Press.

Crouter, A. C., Manke, B. A., & McHale, S. M. (1995). The family context of gender intensification in early adolescence. *Child Development, 66,* 317–329.

Crow, J. F. (2003). There's something curious about parental–age effects. *Science, 301,* 606–607.

Crowther, M., & Rodriguez, R. (2003). A stress and coping model of custodial grandparenting among African Americans. In B. Hayslip & I. Patrick (Eds.), *Working with custodial grandparents* (pp. 145–162). New York, NY: Springer.

Crum, W. (2010). Foster parent parenting characteristics that lead to increased placement stability or disruption. *Children and Youth Services Review, 32,* 185–190.

Crumbley, D. H. (2006). "Power in the blood": Menstrual taboos and women's power in an African Instituted Church. In R. M. Griffith & B. D. Savage, *Women and religion in the African diaspora: Knowledge, power, and performance* (pp. 81–97). Baltimore, MD: Johns Hopkins University Press.

Csibra, G., Davis, g., Spratling, M. W., & Johnson, M. H. (2000). Gamma oscillations and object processing in the infant brain. *Science, 290,* 1582–1585.

Csikszentmihalyi, M., & Larson, R. W. (1984). *Being adolescent: Conflict and growth in the teenage years.* New York, NY: Basic Books.

Cummings, K. M. (2002). Marketing to America's youth: Evidence from corporate documents. *Tobacco Control, 11*(Suppl. 1), i5–i17.

Cunningham, M., & Thorton, A. (2007). Direct and indirect influences of parents' marital instability on children's attitudes toward cohabitation in young adulthood. *Journal of Divorce & Remarriage, 46,* 125–143.

Curran, K., DuCette, J., Eisenstein, J., & Hyman, I. A. (2001, August). *Statistical analysis of the cross-cultural data: The third year.* Paper presented at the meeting of the American Psychological Association, San Francisco, CA.

D'Andrade, R. (1987). A folk model of the mind. In D. Holland & N. Quinn (Eds.), *Cultural models in language and thought* (pp. 112–148). New York, NY: Cambridge Universtiy Press.

da Motta, C. C. L., Naziri, D., & Rinne, C. (2006). The Influence of emotional support during childbirth: A clinical study. *Journal of Prenatal & Perinatal Psychology & Health, 20,* 325–341.

Daddis, C., & Smetana, J. (2005). Middle-class African American families' expectations for adolescents' behavioural autonomy. *International Journal of Behavioral Development, 29,* 371–381.

Dale, P. S., & Goodman, J. C. (2005). Commonality and individual differences in vocabulary growth. In M. Tomasello & D. I. Slobin (Eds.), *Beyond nature–nurture: Essays in honor of Elizabeth Bates* (pp. 41–78). Mahwah, NJ: Erlbaum.

Damon, W. (1983). *Social and personality development.* New York, NY: Norton.

Daniels, P., Godfrey, F. N., & Mayberry, R. (2006). Barriers to prenatal care among Black women of low socioeconomic status. *American Journal of Health Behavior, 30,* 188–198.

Darwin, C. (1859). *On the origin of species.* London, UK: John Murray.

Darwin, C. (1872). *The expression of the emotions in man and animals.* New York, NY: Appleton.

Dasen, P., Inhelder, B., Lavalle, M., & Retschitzki, J. (1978). *Naissance de l'intelligence chez l'enfant Baoule de Cote d'Ivoire.* Berne: Hans Huber.

Daum, M. M., Prinz, W., & Aschersleben, G. (2011). Perception and production of object-related grasping in 6-month-olds. *Journal of Experimental Child Psychology, 108*(4), 810–818.

David, B., Grace, D., & Ryan, M. K. (2004). The gender wars: A self-categorization perspective on the development of gender identity. In M. Bennett & S. Fabio (Eds.), *The development of the social self* (pp. 135–157). East Sussex, England: Psychology Press.

Davies, P. T., Harold, G. T., Goeke-Morey, M. C., & Cummings, E. M. (2002). Child emotional security and interparental conflict. *Monography of the Society for Research in Child Development, 67*(3, Serial No. 270).

Davies, R. (2004). New understandings of parental grief. *Journal of Advanced Nursing, 46,* 506–513.

Davis, D. W. (2003). Cognitive outcomes in school-age children born prematurely. *Neonatal Network, 22,* 27–38.

Davis, K. (2010). Coming of age online: The developmental underpinnings of girls' blogs. *Journal of Adolescent Research, 25,* 145–171.

Davis, K. F., Parker, K. P., & Montgomery, G. L. (2004). Sleep in infants and young children. Part I: Normal sleep. *Journal of Pediatric Health Care, 18,* 65–71.

Davis, S. S., & Davis, D. A. (2007). Morocco. In J. J. Arnett, R. Ahmed, B. Nsamenang, T. S. Saraswathi, & R. Silbereisen (Eds.), *International encyclopedia of adolescence* (pp. 645–655). New York, NY: Routledge.

Davis, S., & Davis, D. (2012). Morocco. In J. J. Arnett (Ed.), *Adolescent Psychology Around the World.* New York, NY: Taylor & Francis.

Dawson, G., Meltzoff, A. N., Osterling, J., Rinaldi, J., & Brown, E. (1998). Children with autism fail to orient to naturally occurring social stimuli. *Journal of Autism & Developmental Disorders, 28,* 479–485.

Day, R. D., & Lamb, M. E. (Eds.). (2004). *Conceptualizing and measuring father involvement.* Mahwah, NJ: Erlbaum.

de Haan, M., & Johnson, M. H. (2003). Mechanisms and theories of brain development. In M. de Haan & M. H. Johnson (Eds.), *The cognitive neuroscience of development* (pp. 1–18). Hove, UK: Psychology Press.

De Marco, A. C., & Berzin, S. C. (2008). The influence of family economic status on home-leaving patterns during emerging adulthood. *Families in Society, 89,* 208–218.

de Villarreal, L. E. M., Arredondo, P. Hernández, R., & Villarreal, J. Z. (2006). Weekly administration of folic acid and epidemiology of neural tube defects. *Maternal and Child Health Journal, 10,* 397–401.

de Villiers, P. A., & de Villiers, J.G. (1978). *Language acquisition.* Cambridge, MA: Harvard University Press.

de Vonderweid, U., & Leonessa, M. (2009). Family centered neonatal care. *Early Human Development, 85,* S37–S38.

de Weerd, A. W., & van den Bossche, A. S. (2003). The development of sleep during the first months of life. *Sleep Medicine Reviews, 7,* 179–191.

DeCasper, A. J., & Spence, M. J. (1986). Prenatal maternal speech influences newborns' perception of speech sounds. *Infant Behavior and Development, 9,* 133–150.

DeHart, T., Pelham, B., & Tennen, H. (2006). What lies beneath: Parenting style and implicit self-esteem. *Journal of Experimental Social Psychology, 42,* 1–17.

DeKeyser, R., & Larson-Hall, J. (2005). What does the critical period really mean? In J. F. Kroll & A. M. B. de Groot (Eds.), *Handbook of bilingualism: Psycholinguistic approaches* (pp. 88–108). Oxford, UK: Oxford University Press.

Delaney, C. (2000). Making babies in a Turkish village. In J. DeLoache & A. Gottlieb (Eds.), *A world of babies: Imagined childcare guides for seven societies* (pp. 117–144). New York, NY: Cambridge University Press.

DeLoache, J. S., Chiong, C., Sherman, K., Islam, N., Vanderborght, M., Troseth, G. L., . . . O'Doherty, K. (2010). Do babies learn from baby media? *Psychological Science, 21,* 1570–1574.

DeLoache, J., & Gottlieb, A. (2000). *A world of babies: Imagined childcare guides for seven societies.* New York, NY: Cambridge University Press.

DeMarie, D., Abshier, D. W., & Ferron, J. (2001, April). *Longitudinal study of predictors of memory improvement over the elementary school years: Capacity, strategies, and metamemory revisited.* Paper presented at the meeting of the Society for Research in Child Development, Minneapolis, MN.

DeMeo, J. (2006). *Saharasia: The 4000 bce origins of child abuse, sex-repression, warfare and social violence, in the deserts of the old world* (Revised 2nd ed.). El Cerrito, CA: Natural Energy Works.

Demetriou, A., & Raftopoulos, A. (Eds.). (2004). *Cognitive developmental change: Theories, models and measurement.* New York, NY: Cambridge University Press.

Dennis, C. L. (2004). Can we identify mothers at risk for postpartum depression in the immediate postpartum period using the Edinburgh Postnatal Depression Scale? *Journal of Affective Disorders, 78,* 163–169.

DeParle, J. (2010, June 27). A world on the move. *The New York Times,* pp. WK1, 4.

Derom, C., Thiery, E., Vlientinck, R., Loos, R., & Derom, R. (1996). Handedness in twins according to zygosity and chorion type: A preliminary report. *Behavior Genetics, 26,* 407–408.

DeRosier, M. E., & Thomas, J. M. (2003). Strengthening sociometric prediction: Scientific advances in the assessment of children's peer relations. *Child Development, 75,* 1379–1392.

DeSena, A. D., Murphy, R. A., Douglas-Palumberi, H., Blau, G., Kelly, B., Horwitz, S. M., & Kaufman, J. (2005). SAFE homes: Is it worth the cost? An evaluation of a group home permanency planning program for children who first enter out-of-home care. *Child Abuse and Neglect, 29,* 627–643.

Dewar, G. (2010). What the scientific evidence reveals about the timing of toilet training. Retrieved from http://www.parentingscience.com/science-of-toilet-training.html

De Wals, P., Tairou, F., Van Allen, M. I., Uh, S. H., Lowry, R. B., Sibbald, B., Evans, J. A., et al. (2007). Reduction in neural-tube defects after folic acid fortification in Canada. *New England Journal of Medicine, 357*(2), 135–142.

Dey, A. N., & Bloom, B. (2005). Summary health statistics for U.S. children: National Health Interview Survey, 2003. *Vital Health Statistics, 21,* 217–227.

Dey, E. L., & Hurtado, S. (1999). Students, colleges, and society: Considering the interconnections. In P. G. Altbach, R. O. Berndahl, & P. J. Gumport (Eds.), *American higher education in the twenty-first century: Social, political, and economic challenges* (pp. 298–322). Baltimore, MD: Johns Hopkins University Press.

Diamond, A. (2004). Normal development of prefrontal cortex from birth to young adulthood: Cognitive functions, anatomy, and biochemistry. In D. T. Stuff & R. T. Knight (Eds.), *Principles of frontal lobe function* (pp. 466–503). New York, NY: Oxford University Press.

Diamond, A. D. (1985). Development of the ability to use recall to guide action, as indicated by infants' performance on AB. *Child Development, 56,* 868–883.

Diamond, J. (1992). *The third chimpanzee: The evolution and future of the human animal.* New York, NY: Harper Perennial.

Dick, F., Dronkers, N. F., Pizzamiglio, L., Saygin, A. P., Small, S. L., & Wilson, S. (2004). Language and the brain. In M. Tomasello & D. I. Slobin (Eds.), *Beyond nature–nurture: Essays in honor of Elizabeth Bates* (pp. 237–260). Mahwah, NJ: Erlbaum.

Diener, M. (2000). Gifts from gods: A Balinese guide to early child rearing. In J. DeLoache & A. Gottlieb (Eds.), *A world of babies: Imagined childcare guides for seven societies* (pp. 91–116). New York, NY: Cambridge University Press.

Dieter, J. N. I., Field, T., Hernandez-Reif, M., Emory, E. K., & Redzepi, M. (2003). Stable preterm infants gain more weight and sleep less after five days of massage therapy. *Journal of Pediatric Psychology, 28*(6), 403–411.

Dietz, W. H. (2004). Overweight in childhood and adolescence. *New England Journal of Medicine, 350,* 855–857.

Dijkstra, J. K., Lidenberg, S., & Veenstra, R. (2008). Beyond the class norm: Bullying behavior of popular adolescents and its relation to peer acceptance and rejection. *Journal of Abnormal Child Psychology, 36,* 1289–1299.

Dijkstra, J. K., Lindenberg, S., Verhulst, F. C., Ormel, J., & Veenstra, R. (2009). The relation between popularity and aggressive, destructive, and norm-breaking behaviors: Moderating effects of athletic abilities, physical attractiveness, and prosociality. *Journal of Research on Adolescence, 19*(3), 401–413.

Dilworth-Anderson, Boswell, G., & Cohen, M. D. (2007). Spiritual and religious coping values and beliefs among African American caregivers: A qualitative study. *Journal of Applied Gerontology, 26,* 355–369.

DiPietro, J., Hilton, S., Hawkins, M., Costigan, K., & Pressman, E. (2002). Maternal stress and affect influence fetal neurobehavioral development. *Developmental Psychology, 38,* 659–668.

Dishion, T. J., & Dodge, K. A. (2005). Peer contagion in interventions for children and adolescents: Moving towards an understanding of the ecology and dynamics of change. *Journal of Abnormal Child Psychology, 33,* 395–400.

Dishion, T. J., McCord, J., & Poulin, F. (1999). When interventions harm: Groups and problem behavior. *American Psychologist, 54,* 755–764.

Dixon Jr., W. E., & Salley, B. J. (2006). "Shhh! We're tryin' to concentrate": Attention and environmental distracters in novel word learning. *The Journal of Genetic Psychology: Research and Theory on Human Development, 167*(4), 393–414.

Dobson, V. (2000). Review of The developing visual brain. *Perception, 29*(12), 1501–1503.

Dodge, K. A. (2007). The nature–nurture debate and public policy. In G. W. Ladd (Ed.), *Appraising the human developmental sciences: Essays in honor of Merrill-Palmer Quarterly* (pp. 262–271). Detroit, MI: Wayne State University Press.

Dodge, K. A. (2008). Framing public policy and prevention of chronic violence in American youths. *American Psychologist, 63,* 573–590.

Dodge, K. A., Coie, J.D., & Lynam, D. (2006). Aggression and antisocial behavior in youth. In W. Damon & R. Lerner (Eds.), & N. Eisenberg (Vol. Ed.), *Handbook of child psychology: Vol. 3. Social, emotional and personality development* (6th ed., pp. 719–788). New York, NY: Wiley.

Doheny, K. (2009). Obese women more likely to have babies with birth defects, study shows. *WebMD Health News.* Retrieved from http://www.webmd.com/baby/news/20090210/obesity-carries-pregnancy-risks

Doherty, I., & Landells, J. (2006). Literacy and numeracy. In J. Clegg & J. Ginsborg (Eds.), *Language and social disadvantage: Theory into practice* (pp. 44–58). Hoboken, NJ: Wiley.

Domsch, H., Lohaus, A., & Thomas, H. (2010). Infant attention, heart rate, and looking time during habituation/dishabituation. *Infant Behavior & Development, 33,* 321–329.

Donat, D. (2006). Reading their way: A balanced approach that increases achievement. *Reading & Writing Quarterly: Overcoming Learning Difficulties, 22,* 305–323.

Donovan, J., & Zucker, C. (2010, October). Autism's first child. *The Atlantic,* pp. 78–90.

Douglass, C. B. (2005). *Barren states: The population "implosion" in Europe.* New York, NY: Berg.

Douglass, C. B. (2007). From duty to desire: Emerging adulthood in Europe and its consequences. *Child Development Perspectives, 1,* 101–108.

Doyle, L. W., Faber, B., Callanan, C., Ford, G. W., & Davis, N. M. (2004). Extremely low birth weight and body size in early adulthood. *Archives of Disorders in Childhood, 89,* 347–350.

Dubas, J. S., & Petersen, A. (1991). A longitudinal investigation of adolescents' changing perceptions of pubertal timing. *Developmental Psychology, 27,* 580–586.

DuBois, D., Felner, R., Brand, S., Phillip, R., & Lease, A. (1996). Early adolescent self-esteem: A developmental–ecological framework and assessment strategy. *Journal of Research on Adolescence, 6,* 543–579.

Due, P., Holstein, B. E., Lunch, J., Diderichsen, F., Gabhain, S. N., Scheidt, P., & Currie, C. (2005). The health behavior in school-aged children bullying working group. *European Journal of Public Health, 15,* 128–132.

Dunn, D. M., Culhane, S. E., & Taussig, H. N. (2010). Children's appraisals of their experiences in out-of-home care. *Children and Youth Services Reviews, 32,* 1324–1330.

Dunn, J. (1988). *The beginnings of social understanding.* Cambridge, MA: Harvard University Press.

Dunn, J. (2002). The adjustment of children in stepfamilies: Lessons from community studies. *Child and Adolescent Mental Health, 7,* 154–161.

Dunn, J. (2004). Sibling relationships. In P. K. Smith & C. H. Hart (Eds.), *Handbook of childhood social development* (pp. 223–237). Malden, MA: Blackwell.

Dunn, J., Cheng, H., O'Connor, T. G., & Bridges, L. (2004). Children's perspectives on their relationships with their nonresident fathers: Influences, outcomes and implications. *Journal of Child Psychology and Psychiatry, 45,* 553–566.

Dunn, J., & Kendrick, C. (1982). *Siblings: Love, envy, and understanding.* London, UK: Grant McIntyre.

Dunn, J., & Munn, P. (1985). Becoming a family member: Family conflict and the development of social understanding in the second year. *Child Development, 56,* 480–492.

Dunn, J., O'Connor, T. G., & Levy, I. (2002). Out of the picture: A study of family drawings by children from step-, single-parent and non-step families. *Journal of Clinical Child and Adolescent Psychology, 31*(4), 505–512.

Durston, S., Pol, H. E. H., Schnack, H. G., Buitelaar, J. K., Steenhuis, M. P., & Minderaa, R. B. (2004). Magnetic resonance imaging of boys with attention-deficit/hyperactivity disorder and their unaffected siblings. *Journal of the American Academy of Child and Adolescent Psychiatry, 43,* 332–340.

Dustmann, C., & Schoenberg, U. (2008). Why does the German apprenticeship system work? In K. U. Mayer & H. Solga (Eds.), *Skill information: Interdisciplinary and cross-national perspective* (p. 85–108). New York, NY: Cambridge University Press.

Dworkin, J. B., & Larson, R. (2001). Age trends in the experience of family discord in single-mother families across adolescence. *Journal of Adolescence, 24,* 529–534.

Dyer, S., & Moneta, G. (2006). Frequency of parallel, associative and co-operative play in British children of different socio-economic status. *Social Behavior and Personality, 34,* 587–592.

Eberhart-Phillips, J. E., Frederick, P. D., & Baron, R. C. (1993). Measles in pregnancy: A descriptive study of 58 cases. *Obstetrics and Gynecology, 82,* 797–801.

Eckenrode, J., Zielinski, D., Smith, E., Marcynyszyn, L. A., Henderson, C. R., Jr., & Kitzman, H. (2001). Child maltreatment and the early onset of problem behaviors: Can a program of nurse home visitation break the link? *Development and Psychopathology, 13,* 873–890.

Eder, D. (1995). *School talk: Gender and adolescent culture.* New Brunswick, NJ: Rutgers University Press.

Edwards, C. P. (2000). Children's play in cross-cultural perspective: A new look at the Six Cultures study. *Cross-Cultural Research: The Journal of Comparative Social Science, 34,* 318–338.

Edwards, C. P. (2005). Children's play in cross-cultural perspective: A new look at the "six cultures" study. In F. F. McMahon, D. E. Lytle, B. Sutton-Smith (Eds.), *Play: An interdisciplinary synthesis* (pp. 81–96). Lanham, MD: University Press of America.

Egeland, B., & Carlson, B. (2004). Attachment and psychopathology. In L. Atkinson & S. Goldberg (Eds.), *Attachment issues in psychopathology and intervention* (pp. 27–48). Mahwah, NJ: Erlbaum.

Ehrenberg, H. M., Dierker, L., Milluzzi, C., & Mercer, B. M. (2003). Low maternal weight, failure to thrive in pregnancy, and adverse pregnancy outcomes. *American Journal of Obstetrics and Gynecology, 189,* 1726–1730.

Ehrenreich, B. (2010). *Witches, midwives, and nurses: A history of women healers.* New York, NY: Feminist Press.

Eiden, R. D., & Reifman, A. (1996). Effects of Brazelton demonstrations on later parenting: A meta-analysis. *Journal of Pediatric Psychology, 21,* 857–868.

Eisenberg, A., Murkoff, H., & Hathaway, S. (2008). *What to expect the first year.* New York, NY: Workman.

Eisenberg, A., Murkoff, H., & Hathaway, S. (1994). *What to expect the toddler years* (1st ed.). New York, NY: Workman Publishing Company.

Eisenberg, N., & Eggum, N. D. (2008). Empathy-related and prosocial responding: Conceptions and correlates during development. In B. A. Sullivan, M. Snyder, & J. L. Sullivan (Eds.), *Cooperation: The political psychology of effective human interaction* (pp. 53–74). Malden, MA: Blackwell.

Eisenberg, N., & Fabes, R. A. (2006). Emotion regulation and children's socioemotional competence. In L. Balter & C. S. Tamis-LeMonda (Eds.), *Child psychology: A handbook of contemporary issues* (2nd ed., pp. 357–381). New York, NY: Psychology Press.

Eisenberg, N., & Valiente, C. (2004). Empathy-related responding: Moral, social and socialization correlates. In A. G. Miller (Ed.), *Social psychology of good and evil*. New York, NY: Guilford Press.

Eisenberg, N., Zhou, Q, Liew, J., Champion, C., & Pidada, S. U. (2006). Emotion, emotion-regulated regulation, and social functioning. In X. Chen, D. C. French, & B. H. Schneider (Eds.), *Peer relationships in cultural context* (pp. 170–199). New York, NY: Cambridge University Press.

Eisner, M. (2002). Crime, problem drinking, and drug use: Patterns of problem behavior in cross-national perspective. *Annals of the American Academy of Political and Social Science, 580,* 201–225.

Ekman, P. (2003). *Emotions revealed.* New York, NY: Times Books.

Eldin, A. S. (2009). Female mutilation. In P. S. Chandra, H. Herrman, J. Fisher, M. Kastrup, U. Niaz, M. B. Rondón, & A. Okasha (Eds.), *Contemporary topics in women's mental health: Global perspectives in a changing society* (pp. 485–498). Hoboken, NJ: Wiley.

Elkind, D. (1967). Egocentrism in adolescence. *Child Development, 38,* 1025–1034.

Elkind, D. (1978). Understanding the young adolescent. *Adolescence, 13,* 127–134.

Elkind, D. (1985). Egocentrism redux. *Developmental Review, 5,* 218–226.

Elkind, D. (2001). *The hurried child: Growing up too fast too soon (25th anniversary ed.)* (Vol. xxxiv). Cambridge, MA: Da Capo Press.

Elliott, G. C., Cunningham, S. M., Linder, M., Colangelo, M., & Gross, M. (2005). Child physical abuse and self-perceived social isolation among adolescents. *Journal of Interpersonal Violence, 20,* 1663–1684.

Ellison, N. C., Steinfield, C., & Lampe, C. (2007). The benefits of Facebook "friends": Social capital and college students' use of online social network sites. *Journal of Computer-Mediated Communication, 12,* 1143–1168.

Ember, C. R., Ember, M., & Peregrine, P. N. (2011). *Anthropology* (13th edition). New York, NY: Pearson.

Emery, R. E., Sbarra, D., & Grover, T. (2005). Divorce mediation: Research and reflections. *Family Court Review, 43,* 22–37.

Emslie, G. J., Heiligenstein, J. H., & Wagner, K. D. (2002). Fluoxetine for acute treatment of depression in children and adolescents: A placebo-controlled randomized clinical trial. *Journal of the American Academy of Child & Adolescent Psychiatry,* 1205–1214.

Englander, F., Terregrossa, R. A., & Wang, Z. (2010). Internet use among college students: Tool or toy? *Educational Review, 62,* 85–96.

Engle, P. I., & Breaux, C. (1998). Fathers' involvement with children: Perspectives from developing countries. *Social Policy Report, XII(1),* 1–21.

Engler, A. J., Ludington-Hoe, S. M., Cusson, R. M., Adams, R., Bahnsen, M., Brumbaugh, E., . . . Williams, D. (2002). Kangaroo care: National survey of practice, knowledge, barriers, and perceptions. *American Journal of Maternal/Child Nursing, 27,* 146–153.

Eppig, C., Fincher, C. L., & Thornhill, R. (2010). Parasite prevalence and the worldwide distribution of cognitive ability. *Proceedings of the Royal Society B, 277,* 3801–3808.

Erickson, K. I., & Korol, D. L. (2009). The effects of hormone replacement therapy on the brains of postmenopausal women: A review of human neuroimaging studies. In W. J. Chodzko-Zajko, A. F. Kramer, & L. Poon (Eds.), *Enhancing cognitive functioning and brain plasticity (aging, exercise, and cognition)* (pp. 133–158). Champaign, IL: Human Kinetics.

Ericsson, K. A. (1990). Peak performance and age: An examination of peak performance in sports. In P. Baltes & M. M. Baltes (Eds.), *Successful aging* (pp. 164–196). Cambridge, MA: Cambridge University Press.

Erikson, E. H. (1950). *Childhood and society.* New York, NY: Norton.

Erikson, E. H. (1968). *Identity: Youth and crisis.* New York, NY: Norton.

Eriksson, C., Hamberg, K., & Salander, P. (2007). Men's experiences of intense fear related to childbirth investigated in a Swedish qualitative study. *Journal of Men's Health & Gender, 4,* 409–418.

Erlandsson, K., & Lindgren, H. (2009). From belonging to belonging through a blessed moment of love for a child—The birth of a child from the fathers' perspective. *Journal of Men's Health,* 338–344.

Eslea, M., Menesini, E., Morita, Y., O'Moore, M., Mora-Nerchan, J. A., Pereira, B., & Smith, P. K. (2004). Friendship and loneliness among bullies and victims: Data from seven countries. *Aggressive Behavior, 30,* 71–83.

Espelage, D. L., & Swearer, S. M. (2004). *Bullying in American schools.* Mahwah, NJ: Erlbaum.

Espy, K. A., Fang, H., Johnson, C., Stopp, C., Wiebe, S. A., & Respass, J. (2011). Prenatal tobacco exposure: Developmental outcomes in the neonatal period. *Developmental Psychology, 47,* 153–169.

Eveleth, P. B., & Tanner, J. M. (1990). *Worldwide variation in human growth.* Cambridge, MA: Cambridge University Press.

Everett, G. E., Olmi, D. J., Edwards, R. P., Tingstrom, D. H., Sterling-Turner, H. E., & Christ, T. J. (2007). An empirical investigation of time-out with and without escape extinction to treat escape-maintained noncompliance. *Behavior Modification, 31,* 412–434.

Fabes, R. A., Martin, C. L., & Hanish, L. D. (2003). Young children's play qualities in same-, other-, and mixed-sex peer groups. *Child Development, 74,* 921–932.

Fabiano, G. A., Pelham, Jr., W. E., Manos, M. J., Gnagy, E. M., Chronis, A. M., Onvango, A. N., . . . Swain, S. (2004). An evaluation of three time-out procedures for children with attention deficit/hyperactivity disorder. *Behavior Therapy, 35,* 449–469.

Facio, A., & Micocci, F. (2003). Emerging adulthood in Argentina. In J. J. Arnett & N. Galabmos (Eds.), *New Directions in Child and Adolescent Development, 100,* 21–31.

Facoetti, A., Lorusso, M. L., Paganoni, P., Cattaneo, C., Galli, R., Umiltà, C., & Mascetti, G. G. (2003). Auditory and visual automatic attention deficits in developmental dyslexia. *Cognitive Brain Research, 16(2),* 185–191.

Fackler, M. (2007, June 22). As Japan ages, universities struggle to fill classrooms. *The New York Times,* p. A3.

Facoetti, A., Lorusso, M. L., Paganoni, P., Cattaneo, C., Galli, R., Umiltà, C., & Mascetti, G. G. (2003). Auditory and visual automatic attention deficits in developmental dyslexia. *Cognitive Brain Research, 16(2),* 185–191.

Fagan, J. F., Holland, C. R., & Wheeler, K. (2007). The prediction, from infancy, of adult IQ and achievement. *Intelligence, 35,* 225–231.

Farver, J. A., Bhadha, B. R., & Narang, S. K. (2002). Acculturation and psychological functioning in Asian Indian adolescents. *Social Development, 11,* 11–29.

Fearon, P., O'Connell, P., Frangou, S., Aquino, P., Nosarti, C., Allin, M., . . . Murray, R. (2004). Brain volumes in adult survivors of very low birth weight: A sibling–controlled study. Q *Pediatrics, 114,* 367–371.

Federico, M. J., & Liu, A. H. (2003). Overcoming childhood asthma disparities of the inner-city poor. *Pediatric Clinics of North America, 50,* 655–675.

Feigenbaum, P. (2002). Private speech: Cornerstone of Vygotsky's theory of the development of higher psychological processes. In D. Robbins & A. Stetsenko (Eds.), *Voices within Vygotsky's non-classical psychology: Past, present, future* (pp. 161–174). Hauppauge, NY: Nova Science.

Fekkes, M., Pijpers, F. I., & Verloove-Vanhorick, S. P. (2004). Bullying behavior and associations with psychosomatic complaints and depression in victims. *Journal of Pediatrics, 144,* 17–22.

Feldkamper, M., & Schaeffel, F. (2003). Interactions of genes and environment in myopia. *Developmental Opthamology, 37,* 34–49.

Feldman, R., & Eidelman, A. I. (2003). Skin-to-skin contact (kangaroo care) accelerates autonomic and neurobehavioral maturation in preterm infants. *Developmental Medicine and Child Neurology, 45,* 274–281.

Feldman, R., Weller, A., Sirota, L., & Eidelman, A. I. (2003). Testing a family intervention hypothesis: The contribution of mother–infant skin-to-skin (kangaroo care) to family interaction, proximity, and touch. *Journal of Family Psychology, 17,* 94–107.

Feldman-Salverlsberg, P. (2002). Is infertility an unrecognized public health and population problem? The view from the Cameroon grassfields. In M. C. Inhorn & F. van Balen (Eds.), *Infertility around the globe: New thinking on childlessness, gender, and reproductive technologies* (pp. 215–231). Berkeley: University of California Press.

Ferber, S. G., & Makhoul, I. R. (2004). The effect of skin-to-skin contact (kangaroo care) shortly after birth on the neurobehavioral responses of the term newborn: A randomized, controlled trial. *Pediatrics, 113,* 858–865.

Ferber, S. G., Kuint, J., Weller, A., Feldman, S. D., Arbel, E., & Kohelet, D. (2002). Massage therapy by mothers and trained professionals enhances weight gain in preterm infants. *Early Human Development, 67,* 37–45.

Ferguson, G. M., Hafen, C. A., & Laursen, B. (2010). Adolescent psychological and academic adjustment as a function of discrepancies between actual and ideal self-perceptions. *Journal of Youth and Adolescence, 39,* 1485–1497.

Ferguson, S. A. (2003). Other high-risk factors for young drivers—how graduated licensing does, doesn't, or could address them. *Journal of Safety Research, 34,* 71–77.

Ferguson, S. A., Teoh, E. R., & McCartt, A. T. (2007). Progress in teenage crash risk during the last decade. *Journal of Safety Research, 38,* 137–145.

Fergusson, D. M., Boden, J. M., & Horwood, L. J. (2008). Exposure to childhood sexual and physical abuse and adjustment in early adulthood. *Child Abuse and Neglect, 32,* 607–619.

Fernald, A., & O'Neill, D. K. (1993). Peekaboo across cultures: How mothers and infants play with voices, faces, and expectations. In K. MacDonald (Ed.), *Parent–child play* (pp. 259–285). Albany: State University of New York Press.

Fernald, A., Perfors, A., & Marchman, V. A. (2006). Picking up speed in understanding: Speech processing efficiency and vocabulary growth across the 2nd year. *Developmental Psychology, 42,* 98–116.

Field, M. J., & Behrman, R. E. (Eds.). (2002). *When children die.* Washington, DC: National Academies Press.

Field, T. M. (1998). Massage therapy effects. *American Psychologist, 53,* 1270–1281.

Field, T. M. (2001). Massage therapy facilitates weight gain in preterm infants. *Current Directions in Psychological Science, 10,* 51–55.

Field, T. M. (2004). Massage therapy effects on depressed pregnant women. *Journal of Psychosomatic Obstetrics and Gynaecology, 25,*115–122.

Field, T., Diego, M., & Hernandez-Reif, M. (2010). Preterm infant massage therapy: A review. *Infant Behavior and Development, 33,* 115–124.

Field, T., Hernandez-Reif, M., & Diego, M. (2006). Newborns of depressed mothers who received moderate versus light pressure massage during therapy. *Infant Behavior and Development, 29,* 54–58.

Fildes, V. (1995). The culture and biology of breastfeeding: An historical review of Western Europe. In P. Stuart-Macadam & K. A. Dettwyler (Eds.), *Breastfeeding: Biocultural perspectives* (pp. 101–131). Hawthorne, NY: Aldein de Gruyter.

Filipek, P. A., Accardo, P. J., Ashwal, S., Baranek, G. T., Cook, E. H., Dawson, G., . . . Volkmar, F. R. (2000). Practice parameter: Screening and diagnosis of autism: Report of the Quality Standards Subcommittee of the American Academy of Neurology and the Child Neurology Society. *Neurology, 55,* 468–479.

Finkel, M. (2007a). Bedlam in the blood: Malaria. *National Geographic*, July, 32–67.

Finkel, M. (2007b). Stopping a global killer. *National Geographic Magazine*. Retrieved from http://ngm.nationalgeographic.com/2007/07/malaria/finkel-text

Finley, G. E., & Schwartz, S. J. (2010). The divided world of the child: Divorce and long-term psychosocial adjustment. *Family Court Review, 48,* 516–527.

Finn, C. A. (2001). Reproductive ageing and the menopause. *International Journal of Developmental Biology, 45,* 613–617.

Fisch, H., Hyun, G., Golden, R., Hensle, T. W., Olsson, C. A., & Liberson, G. L. (2003). The influence of paternal age on Down syndrome. *Journal of Urology, 169,* 2275–2278.

Fisher, C. B. (2003). A goodness–of–fit ethic for child assent to nonbeneficial research. *The American Journal of Bioethics, 3,* 27–28.

Flammer, A., & Alsaker, F. D. (2006). Adolescents in school. In S. Jackson & L. Goossens (Eds.), *Handbook of adolescent development: European perspectives* (pp. 223–245). Hove, UK: Psychology Press.

Flammer, A., Alsaker, F. D., & Noack, P. (1999). Time use by adolescents in international perspective: The case of leisure activities. In F. D. Alsaker & A. Flammer (Eds.), *The adolescent experience: European and American adolescents in the 1990s* (pp. 33–60). Mahwah, NJ: Erlbaum.

Flanagan, C., & Botcheva, L. (1999). Adolescents' preference for their homeland and other countries. In F. D. Alsaker & A. Flammer (Eds.), *The adolescent experience: European and American adolescents in the 1990s* (pp. 131–144). Mahwah, NJ: Erlbaum.

Flannery, K. A., & Liederman, J. (1995). Is there really a syndrome involving the co-occurrence of neurodevelopmental disorder, talent, non–right handedness and immune disorder among children? *Cortex, 31,* 503–515.

Flavell, J. H., Beach, D. R., & Chinsky, J. M. (1966). Spontaneous verbal rehearsal in a memory task as a function of age. *Child Development, 37,* 283–299.

Flavell, J. H., Friedrichs, A., & Hoyt, J. (1970). Developmental changes in memorization process. *Cognitive Psychology, 1,* 324–340.

Flavell, J. H., Miller, P. H., & Miller, S. A. (1993). *Cognitive development (3rd ed.)* (Vol. vii). Englewood Cliffs, NJ: Prentice-Hall.

Flavell, J. H., Miller, P. H., & Miller, S. A. (2002). *Cognitive development* (4th ed.). Upper Saddle River, NJ: Prentice Hall.

Fleming, T. P. (2006). The periconceptional and embryonic period. In P. Gluckman, & M. Hanson (Eds.), *Developmental origins of health and disease* (pp. 51–61). New York, NY: Cambridge University Press.

Flowers, P., & Buston, K. (2001). "I was terrified of being different": Exploring gay men's accounts of growing up in a heterosexist society. *Journal of Adolescence, 24,* 51–66.

Floyd, F., & Bakeman, R. (2006). Coming-out across the life course: Implications of age and historical context. *Archives of Sexual Behavior, 35,* 287–297.

Flynn, J. R. (1999). The discovery of IQ gains over time. *American Psychologist, 54,* 5–20.

Foehr, U. (2007). Computer use, age differences in. In J. J. Arnett (Ed.), *Encyclopedia of children, adolescents, and the media, Vol. 1* (pp. 202–204). Thousand Oaks, CA: Sage.

Fogel, A., Hsu, H., Nelson-Goens, G. C., Shapiro, A. F., & Secrist, C. (2006). Effects of normal and perturbed social play on the duration and amplitude of different types of infant smiles. *Developmental Psychology, 42,* 459–473.

Fomon, S. J., & Nelson, S. E. (2002). Body composition of the male and female reference infants. *Annual Review of Nutrition, 22,* 1–17.

Fong, V. L. (2002). China's one-child policy and the empowerment of urban daughters. *American Anthropologist, 104,* 1098–1109.

Fontanel, B., & d'Harcourt, C. (1997). *Babies: History, art and folklore.* New York, NY: Abrams.

Fontes, L. A., & O'Neill-Arana, M. R. (2008). Assessing for child maltreatment in culturally diverse families. In L. A. Suzuki & J. G. Ponterotto (Eds.), *Handbook of multicultural assessment: Clinical, psychological, and educational applications* (pp. 627–650). San Francisco, CA: Jossey-Bass.

Ford, C. S. (1945). *A comparative study of human reproduction.* New Haven, CT: Yale University Press.

Foss, R. D. (2007). Improving graduated driver licensing systems: A conceptual approach and its implications. *Journal of Safety Research, 38,* 185–192.

Fox, M. K., Pac, S., Devaney, B., & Jankowski, L. (2004). Feeding infants and toddlers study: What foods are infants and toddlers eating? *American Dietetic Association Journal, 104*(Suppl.), S22–S30.

Frankenburg, W. K., Dodds, J., Archer, P., Shapiro, H., & Bresnick, B. (1992). The Denver II: A major revision and restandardization of the Denver Developmental Screening Test. *Pediatrics, 89,* 91–97.

Fransen, M., Meertens, R., & Schrander-Stumpel, C. (2006). Communication and risk presentation in genetic counseling: Development of a checklist. *Patient Education and Counseling, 61,* 126–133.

Frawley, T. J. (2008). Gender schema and prejudicial recall: How children misremember, fabricate, and distort gendered picture book information. *Journal of Research in Childhood Education, 22,* 291–303.

Frayling, T. M., Timpson, N. J., Weedon, M. N., Zeggini, E., Freathy, R. M., Lindgren, C. M., . . . McCarthy, M. I. (2007). A common variant in the *FTO* gene is associated with body mass index and predisposes children and adult obesity. *Science, 316,* 889–894.

Freedman, D. S., Khan, L. K., Serdula, M. K., Ogden, C. L., & Dietz, W. H. (2006). Racial and ethnic differences in secular trends for childhood BMI, weight, and height. *Obesity,* 301–308.

French, D. C., Eisenberg, N., Vaughan, J., Purwono, U., & Suryanti, T. A. (2008). Religious involvement and the social competence and adjustment of Indonesian Muslim adolescents. *Developmental Psychology, 44,* 597–611.

French, D. C., Rianasari, J. M., Piadada, S., Nelwan, P., & Buhrmester, D. (2001). Social support of Indonesian and U.S. children and adolescents by family members and friends. *Merrill-Palmer Quarterly, 47,* 377–394.

Frick, P. J., & Kimonis, E. R. (2005). Externalizing disorders of childhood and adolescence. In E. J. Maddux & A. B. Winstead (Eds.), *Psychopathology: Foundations for a contemporary understanding* (pp. 325–351). Mahwah, NJ: Lawrence.

Friedman, H. S., & Martin, L. R. (2011). *The longevity project.* New York, NY: Penguin.

Fritz, G., & Rockney, R. (2004). Summary of the practice parameter for the assessment and treatment of children and adolescents with enuresis. *Work Group on Quality Issues: Journal of the American Academy of Child & Adolescent Psychiatry, 43,* 123–125.

Frone, M. R. (1999). Developmental consequences of youth employment. In J. Barling & E. K. Kelloway (Eds.), *Youth workers: Varieties of experience* (pp. 89–128). Washington, DC: American Psychological Association.

Frydenberg, E., & Lodge, J. (2007). Australia. In J.J. Arnett (Ed.), *International encyclopedia of adolescence.* New York, NY: Routledge.

Fuligni, A. J. (2011). Social identity, motivation, and well being among adolescents from Asian and Latin American backgrounds. In G. Carlo, L. J. Crockett, & M. A. Carranza (Eds.), *Health disparities in youth and families: Research and applications* (pp. 97–120). New York, NY: Springer.

Fuligni, A. J., Witkow, M. (2004). The postsecondary educational progress of youth from immigrant families. *Journal of Research on Adolescence, 14,* 159–183.

Fuligni, A., Tseng, V., & Lam, M. (1999). Attitudes toward family obligation among American adolescents with Asian, Latin American, and European backgrounds. *Child Development, 70,* 1030–1044.

Fuller, A., Beck, V., & Unwin, L. (2005). The gendered nature of apprenticeship: Employers' and young peoples' perspectives. *Education & Training, 47,* 298–311.

Funk, J. B. (2003). Violent video games: Who's at risk? In D. Ravitch & J. P. Viteritti (Eds.), *Kid stuff: Marketing sex and violence to America's children* (pp. 168–192). Baltimore, MD: Johns Hopkins University Press.

Funk, J. B. (2005). Children's exposure to violent video games and desensitization to violence. *Child & Adolescent Psychiatric Clinics of North America, 14,* 387–404.

Funk, J. B., Flores, B., Buchman, D. D., & Germann, J. N. (1999). Rating electronic video games: Violence is in the eye of the beholder. *Youth & Society, 30,* 283–312.

Funk, J. B., Hagan, J., Schimming, J., Bullock, W. A., Buchman, D. D., & Myers, M. (2002). Aggression and psychopathology in adolescents with a preference for violent electronic games. *Aggressive Behavior, 28,* 134–144.

Furman, W., & Hand, L. S. (2006). The slippery nature of romantic relationships: Issues in definition and differentiation. In A. C. Crouter & A. Booth (Eds.), *Romance and sex in adolescence and emerging adulthood: Risks and opportunities* (pp. 171–178). The Penn State University family issues symposia series. Mahwah, NJ: Erlbaum.

Furman, W., & Simon, V. A. (2008). Homophily in adolescent romantic relationships. In M. J. Prinstein & K. A. Dodge (Eds.), *Understanding peer influence in children and adolescents* (pp. 203–224). New York, NY: Guilford Press.

Futagi, Y., Toribe, Y., & Suzuki, Y. (2009). Neurological assessment of early infants. *Current Pediatric Reviews, 5,* 65–70.

Fyfe, K. (2006). Wolves in sheep's clothing: A content analysis of children's television. Retrieved from http://www.parentstelevision.org/

Galambos, N., Almeida, D., & Petersen, A. (1990). Masculinity, femininity, and sex role attitudes in early adolescence: Exploring gender intensification. *Child Development, 61,* 1905–1914.

Galambos, N. L. (2004). Gender and gender role development in adolescence. In R. Lerner & L. Steinberg (Eds.), *Handbook of adolescent psychology.* New York, NY: Wiley.

Galambos, N. L., Barker, E. T., & Krahn, H. J. (2006). Depression, anger, and self-esteem in emerging adulthood: Seven-year trajectories. *Developmental Psychology, 42,* 350–365.

Gale, C. R., Godfrey, K. M., Law, C. M., Martyn, C. N., & O'Callaghan, F. J. (2004). Critical periods of brain growth and cognitive function in children. *Brain: A Journal of Neurology, 127,* 321–329.

Gall, S. (Ed.). (1996). *Multiple pregnancy and delivery.* St. Louis, MO: Mosby.

Galler, J. R., Bryce, C. P., Waber, D., Hock, R. S., Exner, N., Eaglesfield, D., . . . Harrison, R. (2010). Early childhood malnutrition predicts depressive symptoms at ages 11–17. *Journal of Child Psychology and Psychiatry, 51,* 789–798.

Galler, J. R., Waber, D., Harrison, R., & Ramsey, F. (2005). Behavioral effects of childhood malnutrition. *The American Journal of Psychiatry, 162,* 1760–1761.

Ganger, J., & Brent, M. R. (2004). Reexamining the vocabulary spurt. *Developmental Psychology, 40,* 621–632.

Ganiban, J. M., Ulbricht, J., Saudino, K. J., Reiss, D., & Neiderhiser, J. M. (2011). Understanding child-based effects on parenting: Temperament as a moderator of genetic and environmental contributions to parenting. *Developmental Psychology, 47(3),* 676–692.

Gans, J. (1990). *America's adolescents: How healthy are they?* Chicago, IL: American Medical Association.

Gardiner, H. W. (2001). Child and adolescent development: Cross-cultural perspectives. In L. L. Adler & U. P. Gielen (Eds.), *Cross-cultural topics in psychology* (pp. 63–79). Westport, CT: Praeger.

Gardner, H. (1983). *Frames of mind.* New York, NY: Basic Books.

Gardner, H. (1999). Who owns intelligence? *Atlantic Monthly, 283,* 67–76.

Gardner, H. (2004). *Frames of mind: The theory of multiple intelligences.* New York, NY: Basic Books.

Garner, D. M., & Garfinkel, P. E. (Eds.). (1997). *Handbook of treatment for eating disorders* (2nd ed.). New York, NY: Guilford Press.

Garrison, M. M., & Christakis, D. A. (2005). *A teacher in the living room? Educational media for babies, toddlers and preschoolers.* Menlo Park, CA: The Henry J. Kaiser Family Foundation.

Gartstein, M. A., Gonzalez, C., Carranza, J. A., Ahadi, S. A., Ye, R., Rothbart, M. K., & Yang, S. W. (2006). Studying cross-cultural differences in the development of infant temperament: People's Republic of China, the United States of America, and Spain. *Child Psychiatry and Human Development, 37,* 145–161.

Gaskins, S. (2000). Children's daily activities in a Mayan village: A culturally grounded description. *Cross-Cultural Research, 34,* 375–389.

Gavin, A. R., Hill, K. G., Hawkins, J. D., & Maas, C. (2011). The role of maternal early-life and later-life risk factors on offspring low birth weight: Findings from a three-generational study. *Journal of Adolescent Health, 49,* 166–171.

Gavin, L., & Furman, W. (1989). Age differences in adolescents' perceptions of their peer groups. *Developmental Psychology, 25,* 827–834.

Gazzaniga, M. (2008). *Human: The science behind what makes us unique.* New York, NY: Ecco.

Ge, X., Natsuaki, M. N., Neiderhiser, J. M., & Reiss, D. (2007). Genetic and environmental influences on pubertal timing: Results from two national sibling studies. *Journal of Research on Adolescence, 17,* 767–788.

Geangu, E., Benga, O., Stahl, D., & Striano, T. (2010). Contagious crying beyond the first days of life. *Infant Behavior & Development, 33,* 279–288.

Geary, D. C. (2010). *Male, female: The evolution of human sex differences* (2nd ed.). Washington, DC: American Psychological Association.

Geeraert, L., Van den Noortgate, W., Grietens, H., & Onghena, P. (2004). The effects of early prevention programs for families with young children at risk for physical child abuse and neglect: A meta-analysis. *Child Maltreatment, 9,* 277–291.

Gelman, R. (1969). Conservation acquisition: A problem of learning to attend to relevant attributes. *Journal of Experimental Child Psychology, 7,* 67–87.

Gelman, S. A., Taylor, M. G., & Nguyen, S. P. (2004). Mother–child conversations about gender. *Monographs of the Society for Research in Child Development, 69(Serial No. 275),* pp. 1–127.

Genesoni, L., & Tallandini, M. A. (2009). Men's psychological transition to fatherhood: An analysis of the literature, 1989–2008. *Birth: Issues in Perinatal Care, 36,* 305–318.

Genesee, F. (2001). Portrait of the bilingual child. In V. Cook (Ed.), *Portraits of the second language user* (pp. 170–196). Clevedon, UK: Multilingual Matters.

George, C., & Solomon, J. (1999). Attachment and caregiving: The caregiving behavioural system. In J. Cassidy & P. R. Shaver (Eds.), *Handbook of attachment: Theory, research, and clinical applications* (pp. 649–670). New York, NY: Guilford Press.

Gergen, K. (2011). The acculturated brain. *Theory and Psychology, 20,* 1–20.

Germo, G. R., Chang, E. S., Keller, M. A., & Goldberg, W. A. (2007). Child sleep arrangements and family life: perspectives from mothers and fathers. *Infant and Child Development, 16(4),* 433–456.

Gershoff, E. T. (2002). Corporal punishment by parents and associated child behaviors and experiences: A meta-analytic and theoretical review. *Psychological Bulletin, 128,* 539–579.

Gesell, A. (1946). The ontogenesis of infant behaviour. In L. Carmichael (Ed.), *Manual of child psychology* (pp. 295–331). Hoboken, NJ: Wiley.

Gesell, A. L. (1934). *Infancy and human growth.* New York, NY: Macmillan.

Gewirtz, J. (1977). Maternal responding and the conditioning of infant crying: Directions of influence within the attachment–acquisition process. In B. C. Etzel, J. M. LeBlanc, & D. M. Baer (Eds.), *New developments in behavioral research* (pp. 31–57). Hillsdale, NJ: Erlbaum.

Giang, M. T., & Wittig, M. A. (2006). Implications of adolescents' acculturation strategies for personal and collective self-esteem. *Cultural Diversity and Ethnic Minority Psychology, 12,* 725–739.

Gibbons, J. L., & Stiles, D. A. (2004). *The thoughts of youth: An international perspective on adolescents' ideal persons.* Greenwich, CT: IAP Information Age.

Gibbs, J. C. (2003). *Moral development and reality: Beyond the theories of Kohlberg and Hoffman.* Thousand Oaks, CA: Sage.

Gibbs, J. C., Basinger, K. S., Grime, R. L., & Snarey, J. R. (2007). Moral judgment development across cultures: Revisiting Kohlberg's universality claims. *Developmental Review, 27,* 443–500.

Gibson, E. J., & Walk, R. D. (1960). The "visual cliff." *Scientific American, 202,* 64–71.

Gibson, J. H., Harries, M., Mitchell, A., Godfrey, R., Lunt, M., & Reeve, J. (2000). Determinants of bone density and prevalence of osteopenia among female runners in their second to seventh decades of age. *Bone, 26,* 591–598.

Giddens, A. (2000). *Runaway world: How globalization is reshaping our lives.* New York, NY: Routledge.

Giedd, J. N. (2008). The teen brain: Insights from neuroimaging. *Journal of Adolescent Health, 42,* 335–343.

Giedd, J. N., Blumenthal, J., & Jeffries, N. O. (1999). Brain development during childhood and adolescence: A longitudinal MRI study. *Nature Neuroscience, 2,* 861–863.

Giles-Sims, J., & Lockhart, C. (2005). Culturally shaped patterns of disciplining children. *Journal of Family Issues, 26,* 196–218.

Gilmore, D. (1990). *Manhood in the making: Cultural concepts of masculinity.* New Haven, CT: Yale University Press.

Gini, G., Albierto, P., Benelli, B., & Altoe, G. (2008). Determinants of adolescents' active defending and passive bystander behavior in bullying. *Journal of Adolescence, 31,* 93–105.

Ginsburg, H. P., & Opper, S. (1979). *Piaget's theory of intellectual development.* Englewood Cliffs, NJ: Prentice Hall.

Giscombé, C. L., & Lobel, M. (2005). Explaining disproportionately high rates of adverse birth outcomes among African Americans: The impact of stress, racism, and related factors in pregnancy. *Psychological Bulletin, 131,* 662–683.

Gladwell, M. (1998, February 2). The Pima paradox. *The New Yorker,* pp. 44–57.

Glassman, T. J., Dodd, V., Miller, E. M., & Braun, R. E. (2010). Preventing high-risk drinking among college students: A social marketing case study. *Social Marketing Quarterly, 16,* 92–110.

Glauber, J. H., Farber, H. J., & Homer, C. J. (2001). Asthma clinical pathways: Toward what end? *Pediatrics, 107,* 590–592.

Godfrey, J. R., & Meyers, D. (2009). Toward optimal health: Maternal benefits on breastfeeding. *Journal of Women's Health, 18,* 1307–1310.

Goldbaum, S., Craig, W. M., Pepler, D., & Connolly, J. (2003). Developmental trajectories of victimization: Identifying risk and protective factors. *Journal of Applied School Psychology, 19,* 139–156.

Goldberg, A. E. (2010). *Lesbian and gay parents and their children.* Washington, DC: American Psychological Association.

Goldberg, M. C., Maurer, D., & Lewis, T. L. (2001). Developmental changes in attention: The effects of endogenous cueing and of distracters. *Developmental Science, 4,* 209–219.

Goldberg, P. H. (1968). Are women prejudiced against women? *Transaction, 5,* 28–30.

Goldfield, B. A., & Reznick, J. S. (1990). Early lexical acquisition: Rate, content and the vocabulary spurt. *Journal of Child Language, 17,* 171–183.

Goldin-Meadow, S. (2009). Using the hands to study how children learn language. In J. Colombo, L. Freund, & P. McCardle (Eds.), *Infant pathways to language: Methods, models, and research disorders* (pp. 195–210). New York, NY: Psychology Press.

Goldman, B. D., & Buysse, V. (2007). Friendships in very young children. In O. N. Saracho B. Spodek (Ed.), Contemporary perspectives on socialization and social development in early childhood education, Contemporary perspectives on early childhood education. (pp. 165–192). Charlotte, NC, US: IAP Information Age Publishing.

Goldscheider, F., & Goldscheider, C. (1999). *The changing transition to adulthood: Leaving and returning home.* Thousand Oaks, CA: Sage.

Goldsmith, H. H. (2009). Genetics of emotional development. In R. J. Davidson, K. R. Scherer, & H. H. Goldsmith (Eds.), *Handbook of affective sciences* (pp. 300–319). New York, NY: Oxford University Press.

Goldstein, B. (1976). *Introduction to human sexuality.* New York, NY: McGraw-Hill.

Goleman, D. (1997). *Emotional intelligence.* New York, NY: Bantam.

Goode, E. (1999, May 20). Study finds TV trims Fiji girls' body image and eating habits. *The New York Times,* p. A1.

Goode, E. (1999). Pediatricians renew battle over toilet training. *New York Times on the Web.* Retrieved from http://www.nytimes.com/library/nationalscience/011299sci-toilettraining.html

Goodwin, C. J. (2009). *Research in psychology: Methods and design.* New York, NY: Wiley.

Goossens, L., & Luyckx, K. (2007). Belgium. In J. J. Arnett, U. Gielen, R. Ahmed, B. Nsamenang, T. S. Saraswathi, & R. Silbereisen (Eds.), *International encyclopedia of adolescence* (pp. 64–76). New York, NY: Routledge.

Gopnik, A., & Astington, J. W. (1998). Children's understanding of representational change and its relation to the understanding of false belief and the appearance–reality distinction. *Child Development, 59,* 26–37.

Gopnik, A., Meltzoff, A. N., & Kuhl, P. K. (1999). *The scientist in the crib: Minds, brains, and how children learn.* New York, NY: William Morrow.

Gordon-Larsen, P., Nelson, M. C., & Popkin, B. M. (2004). Longitudinal physical activity and sedentary behavior trends: Adolescence to adulthood. *American Journal of Preventitive Medicine, 27,* 277–283.

Gottesman, I. I. (1994). *Schizophrenia genetics: The origins of madness.* New York, NY: Freeman.

Gottesman, I. I. (2004). Postscript: Eyewitness to maturation. In L. E. DiLalla (Ed.), *Behavior genetics principles.* Washington, DC: American Psychological Association.

Gottfredson, M., & Hirschi, T. (1990). *A general theory of crime.* Stanford, CA: Stanford University Press.

Gottlieb, A. (2000). Luring your child into this life: A Beng path for infant care. In J. DeLoache & A. Gottlieb (Eds.), *A world of babies: Imagined childcare guides for seven societies* (pp. 55–89). New York, NY: Cambridge University Press.

Gottlieb, G. (2004). Normally occurring environmental and behavioral influences on gene activity. In C. G. Coll, E. L. Bearer, & R. M. Lerner (Eds.), *Nature and nature: The complex interplay of genetic and environmental influences on human behavior and development* (pp. 85–106). Mahwah, NJ: Erlbaum.

Gottlieb, G., & Lickliter, R. (2007). Probabilistic epigenesis. *Developmental Science, 10,* 1–11.

Gould, S. J. (1981). *The mismeasure of man.* New York, NY: Norton.

Gowen, L. K., Hayward, C., Killen, J. D., Robinson, T. N., & Taylor, C. B. (1999). Acculturation and eating disorder symptoms in adolescent girls. *Journal of Research on Adolescence, 9,* 67–83.

Government of Canada. (2010). Child and spousal support in metropolitan and non-metropolitan areas 2009/2010. Component of Statistics Canada catalogue no. 85-002-X.

Graber, J. A., Lewinsohn, P. M., Seeley, J. R., & Brooks-Gunn, J. (1997). Is psychopathology associated with the timing of pubertal development? *Journal of the American Academy of Child and Adolescent Psychiatry, 36,* 1768–1776.

Graber, J. A., Seeley, J. R., Brooks-Gunn, J., & Lewinsohn, P. M. (2004). Is pubertal timing associated with psychopathology in young adulthood? *Journal of the American Academy of Child & Adolescent Psychiatry, 43,* 718–726.

Graham, M. J., Larsen, U., & Xu, X. (1999). Secular trend in age of menarche in China: A case study of two rural counties in Anhui province. *Journal of Biosocial Science, 31,* 257–267.

Granic, I., Dishion, T. J., & Hollenstein, T. (2003). The family ecology of adolescence: A dynamic systems perspective on normative development. In G. R. Adams & M. D. Berzonsky (Eds.), *Blackwell handbook of adolescence* (pp. 60–91). Malden, MA: Blackwell.

Gray, C., Ferguson, J., Behan, S., Dunbar, C., Dunn, J., & Mitchell, D. (2007). Developing young readers through the linguistic phonics approach. *International Journal of Early Years Education, 15,* 15–33.

Graziano, A. M., & Hamblen, J. L. (1996). Subabusive violence in child rearing in middle-class American families. *Pediatrics, 98,* 845–848.

Green, E. G. T., Deschamps, J. C., & Paez, D. (2005)l. Variation of individualism and collectivism within and between 20 countries: A typological analysis. *Journal of Cross-Cultural Psychology, 36,* 321–339.

Greenberger, E., & Steinberg, L. (1986). *When teenagers work: The psychological social costs of adolescent employment.* New York, NY: Basic Books.

Greenfield, P. M. (2005). Paradigms of cultural thought. In K. J. Holyoak, & R. G. Morrison (Eds.), *The Cambridge Handbook of Thinking and Reasoning* (pp. 663–682). New York, NY: Cambridge University Press.

Greenfield, P. M., Keller, H., Fuligni, A., & Maynard, A. (2003). Cultural pathways through universal development. *Annual Review of Psychology, 54*(1), 461–490.

Greve, T. (2003). Norway: The breastfeeding top of the world. *Midwifery Today International, 67,* 57–59.

Grigorenko, E. (2003). Intraindividual fluctuations in intellectual functioning: Selected links between nutrition and the mind. In R. Sternberg & J. Lautrey (Eds.), *Models of intelligence: International perspectives.* Washington, DC: American Psychological Association.

Grigorenko, E. L., Lipka, J., Meier, E., Mohatt, G., Sternberg, R. J., & Yanez, E. (2004). Academic and practical intelligence: A case study of the Yup'ik in Alaska. *Learning and Individual Differences, 14,* 183–207.

Grilo, C. M., & Mitchell, J. E. (Eds.). (2010). *The treatment of eating disorders: A clinical handbook.* New York, NY: Guilford Press.

Grolnick, W. S., McMenamy, J. M., & Kurowski, C. O. (2006). Emotional self-regulation in infancy and toddlerhood. In L. Balter & C. S. Tamis-Lamonda (Eds.), *Child psychology: A book of contemporary issues* (pp. 3–25). New York, NY: Psychology Press.

Grossman, K. E., Grossman, K., & Waters, E. (Eds.). (2005). *Attachment from infancy to adulthood: The major longitudinal studies.* New York, NY: Guilford Press.

Grotevant, H. D., & Adams, G. R. (1984). Development of an objective measure to assess ego identity in adolescence: Validation and replication. *Journal of Youth and Adolescence, 13,* 419–438.

Grunbaum, A. (2006). Is Sigmund Freud's psychoanalytic edifice relevant to the 21st century? *Psychoanalytic Psychology, 23,* 257–284.

Gu, D., Reynolds, K., Wu, N., Chen, J., Duan, X., Reynolds, R. F., et al. (InterASIA Collaborative Group) (2005). Prevalence of the metabolic syndrome and overweight among adults in China. *Lancet, 365,* 1398–1405.

Guasti, M. T. (2000). An excursion into interrogatives in early English and Italian. In M. A. Friedemann & L. Rizzi (Eds.), *The acquisition of syntax* (pp. 105–128). Harlow, England: Longman.

Guay, F., Chanal, J., Ratelle, C. F., Marsh, H. W., Larose, S., & Boivin, M. (2010). Intrinsic, identified, and controlled types of motivation for school subjects in young elementary school children. *British Journal of Educational Psychology, 80,* 711–735.

Guernsey, L. (2007). *Into the minds of babes: How screen time affects children from birth to age 5.* New York, NY: Perseus.

Guest, A. M. (2007). Cultures of childhood and psychosocial characteristics: Self-esteem and social comparison in two distinct communities. *Ethos, 35,* 1–32.

Guillaume, M., & Lissau, I. (2002). Epidemiology. In W. Burniat, T. Cole, I. Lissau, & E. M. E. Poskitt (Eds.), *Child and adolescent obesity: Causes and consequences, prevention and management* (pp. 28–49). Cambridge, MA: Cambridge University Press.

Guise, J. M. F., & Gill, J. S. (2007). "Binge drinking? It's good, it's harmless fun": A discourse analysis of female undergraduate drinking in Scotland. *Health Education Research, 22,* 895–906.

Gunnoe, M. L., & Mariner, C. L. (1997). Toward a developmental–contextual model of the effects of parental spanking on children's aggression. *Archives of Pediatrics and Adolescent Medicine, 151,* 768–775.

Guyer, B. (2000). *ADHD.* Boston, MA: Allyn & Bacon.

Haan, M. D., & Matheson, A. (2009). The development and neural bases of processing emotion in faces and voices. In M. D. H. & M. R. Gunnar, *Handbook of developmental social neuroscience* (pp. 107–121). New York, NY: Guilford Press.

Hack, M., Taylor, G., Drotar, D., Schluchter, M., Cartar, L., Wilson-Costello, D., . . . Morrow, M. (2005). Poor predictive validity of the Bayley Scales of Infant Development for cognitive function of extremely low birth weight children at school age. *Pediatrics, 116,* 333–341.

Hacker, J. (2002). *The divided welfare state: The battle over public and private social benefits in the United States.* New York, NY: Cambridge University Press.

Hadjikhani, N., Chabris, C. F., Joseph, R. M., Clark, J., McGrath, L., Aharon, L., . . . Harris, G. J. (2004). Early visual cortex organization in autism: An fMRI study. *Neuroreport: For Rapid Communication of Neuroscience Research, 15,* 267–270.

Haffner, W. H. J. (2007). Development before birth. In M. L. Batshaw, L. Pellegrino, & N. J. Roizen (Eds.), *Children with disabilities* (pp. 23–33). Baltimore, MD: Brookes.

Hagen, J., & Hale, G. (1973). The development of attention in children. In A. Pick (Ed.), *Minnesota symposium on child psychology* (Vol. 7, pp. 117–140). Minneapolis: University of Minnesota Press.

Häggström-Nordin, E., Hanson, U., & Tydén, T. (2005). Associations between pornography consumption and sexual practices among adolescents in Sweden. *International Journal of STD & AIDS, 16*(2), 102–107.

Hahn, B., Ross, T. J., Wolkenberg, F. A., Shakleya, D. M., Huestis, M. A., & Stein, E. A. (2009). Performance effects of nicotine during selective attention, divided attention, and simple stimulus detection: An fMRI study. *Cerebral Cortex, 19,* 1990–2000.

Haidt, J., Koller, S. H., & Dias, M. G. (1993). Affect, culture, and morality, or is it wrong to eat your dog? *Journal of Personality and Social Psychology, 65,* 613–628.

Hakuta, K. (1999). The debate on bilingual education. *Developmental and Behavioral Pediatrics, 20,* 36–37.

Hakuta, K., Bialystok, E., & Wiley, E. (2003). Critical evidence: A test of the critical-period hypothesis for second-language acquisitions. *Psychological Science, 14,* 31–38.

Hale, C. M., & Tager-Flusberg, H. (2005). Social communication with children with autism: The relationship between theory of mind and discourse development. *Autism, 9,* 157–178.

Halford, G. S. (2005). Development of thinking. In K. J. Holyoak & Robert G. Morrison (Eds.), *The Cambridge handbook of thinking and reasoning* (pp. 529–558). New York, NY: Cambridge University Press.

Halgunseth, L. C., Ispa, J. M., & Rudy, D. (2006). Parental control in Latino families: An integrated review of the literature. *Child Development, 77,* 1282–1297.

Halpern, S. (1998). *The forgotten half revisited: American youth and young families, 1988–2008.* Washington, DC: American Youth Policy Forum.

Hämäläinen, J., Poikolainen, K., Isometsa, E., Kaprio, J., Heikkinen, M., Lindermman, S., & Aro, H. (2005). Major depressive episode related to long unemployment and frequent alcohol intoxication. *Nordic Journal of Psychiatry, 59,* 486–491.

Hamilton, S. F., & Hamilton, M. A. (2000). Research, intervention, and social change: Improving adolescents' career opportunities. In L. J. Crockett & R. K. Silbereisen (Eds.), *Negotiating adolescence in times of social change* (pp. 267–283). New York, NY: Cambridge University Press.

Hamilton, S., & Hamilton, M. A. (2006). School, work, and emerging adulthood. In J. J. Arnett & J. L. Tanner (Eds.), *Coming of age in the 21st century: The lives and contexts of emerging adults* (pp. 257–277). Washington, DC: American Psychological Association.

Hammack, P. L., Robinson, W., L., Crawford, I., & Li, S. (2004). Poverty and depressed mood among urban African-American adolescents: A family stress perspective. *Journal of Child & Family Studies, 13,* 309–323.

Hammer, J. C., Fisher, J. D., Fitzgerald, P., & Fisher, W. A. (1996). When two heads aren't better than one: AIDS risk behavior in college-age couples. *Journal of Applied Social Psychology, 26,* 375–397.

Han, C. (2011). Embitterment in Asia: Losing face, inequality, and alienation under historical and modern perspectives. In M. Linden & A. Maercker (Eds.), *Embitterment: Societal, psychological, and clinical perspectives* (pp. 168–176). New York, NY: Springer.

Haninger, K., & Thompson, K. M. (2004). Content and ratings of teen rated video games. *JAMA: Journal of the American Medical Association, 291,* 856–865.

Hannon, T. S., Rao, G., & Arslanian, S. A. (2005). Childhood obesity and Type 2 diabetes mellitus. *Pediatrics, 116,* 473–480.

Hansen, M., Bower, C., Milne, E., Klerk, N. D., & J. Kurinczuk, J. (2005). Assisted reproductive technologies and the risk of birth defects—a systematic review. *Human Reproduction, 20*(2), 328–338.

Harlow, H. F. (1958). The nature of love. *American Psychologist, 13,* 673–685.

Hart, B., & Risley, T. R. (1995). *Meaningful differences in the everyday experience of young American children.* Baltimore, MD: Brookes.

Hart, B., & Risley, T. R. (1999). *The social world of children learning to talk.* Baltimore, MD: Brookes.

Hart, C. H., Burts, D. C., Durland, M. A., Charlesworth, R., DeWolf, M., & Fleege, P.O. (1998). Stress behaviors and activity type participation of preschoolers in more and less developmentally appropriate classrooms: SES and sex differences. *Journal of Research in Childhood Education, 12,* 176–196.

Hart, C. H., Newell, L. D., & Olsen, S. F. (2003). Parenting skills and social-communicative competence in childhood. In J. O. Greene & B. R. Burleson (Eds.), *Handbook of communication and social interaction skills* (pp. 753–797). Mahwah, NJ: Erlbaum.

Harter, S. (1990a). Processes underlying adolescent self-concept formation. In R. Montemayor, G. R. Adams, & T. P. Gullotta (Eds.), *From childhood to adolescence: A transitional period?* Newbury Park, CA: Sage.

Harter, S. (1990b). Self and identity development. In S. S. Feldman & G. R. Elliott (Eds.), *At the threshold: The developing adolescent* (pp. 352–387). Cambridge, MA: Harvard University Press.

Harter, S. (1999). *The construction of the self: A developmental perspective.* New York, NY: Guilford.

Harter, S. (2003). The development of self-representations during childhood and adolescence. In M. R. Leary & J. P. Tangney (Eds.), *Handbook of self and identity* (pp. 610–642). New York, NY: Guilford.

Harter, S. (2006a). The development of self-esteem. In M. H. Kernis (Ed.), *Self-esteem issues and answers: A sourcebook of current perspectives* (pp. 144–150). New York, NY: Psychology Press.

Harter, S. (2006b). The self. In W. Damon & R. Lerner (Eds.), & N. Eisenberg (Vol. Ed.), *Handbook of child psychology: Vol. 3. Social, emotional and personality development* (6th ed., pp. 505–570). New York, NY: Wiley.

Harter, S., Waters, P. L., & Whitesell, N. R. (1997). Lack of voice as a manifestation of false-self behavior among adolescents: The school setting as a stage upon which the drama of authenticity is enacted. *Educational Psychologist, 32,* 153–173.

Hartos, J. L., Simons-Morton, B. G., Beck, K. H., & Leaf, W. A. (2005). Parent-imposed limits on high-risk adolescent driving: Are they stricter with graduated driver licensing? *Accident Analysis & Prevention, 37,* 557–562.

Hartup, W. W. (1996). The company they keep: Friendships and their developmental significance. *Child Development, 67,* 1–13.

Hartup, W. W., & Abecassis, M. (2004). Friends and enemies. In P. K. Smith & C. H. Hart (Eds.), *Blackwell handbook of childhood social development* (pp. 285–306). Malden, MA: Blackwell.

Harvard Mental Health Letter (HMHL) (2005). The treatment of attention deficit disorder: New evidence. *Harvard Mental Health Letter, 21,* 6.

Harvey, J. H., & Fine, M. A. (2004). *Children of divorce: Stories of loss and growth.* Mahwah, NJ: Erlbaum.

Harwood, R., Leyendecker, B., Carlson, V., Asencio, M., & Miller, A. (2002). Parenting among Latino families in the U.S. In M. H. Bornstein (Ed.), *Handbook of parenting, Vol. 4. Social conditions and applied parenting* (2nd ed., pp. 21–46). Mahwah, NJ: Erlbaum.

Hasebrink, U. (2007a). Computer use, international. In J. J. Arnett (Ed.), *Encyclopedia of children, adolescents, and the media* (pp. 207–210). Thousand Oaks, CA: Sage.

Hasebrink, U. (2007b). Television, international viewing patterns and. In J. J. Arnett (Ed.), *Encyclopedia of children, adolescents, and the media* (pp. 808–810). Thousand Oaks, CA: Sage.

Hassett, J. M., Siebert, E. R., & Wallen, K. (2008). Sex differences in rhesus monkey toy preference parallel those of children. *Hormones and Behavior, 54,* 359–364.

Hassold, T. J., & Patterson, D. (Eds.) (1999). *Down syndrome: A promising future, together.* New York, NY: Wiley-Liss.

Hastings, P. D., McShane, K. E., Parker, R., & Ladha, F. (2007). Ready to make nice: Parental socialization of young sons' and daughters' prosocial behaviors with peers. *The Journal of Genetic Psychology: Research and Theory on Human Development, 168,* 177–200.

Hatfield, E., & Rapson, R. L. (1996). *Love and sex: Cross-cultural perspectives.* Boston, MA: Allyn & Bacon.

Hatfield, E., & Rapson, R. L. (2005). *Love and sex: Cross-cultural perspectives* (2nd edition). Boston, MA: Allyn & Bacon.

Haugaard, J. L., & Hazan, C. (2004). Recognizing and treating uncommon behavioral and emotional disorders in children and adolescents who have been severely maltreated: Reactive attachment disorder. *Child Maltreatment, 9,* 154–160.

Hautala, L. A., Junnila, J., Helenius, H., Vaananen, A. M., Liuksila, P. R., Raiha, H., et al. (2008). Towards understanding gender differences in disordered eating among adolescents. *Journal of Clinical Nursing, 17,* 1803–1813.

Hawkins, A. J., Lovejoy, K. R., Holmes, E. K., Blanchard, V. L., & Fawcett, E. (2008). Increasing fathers' involvement in child care with a couple–focused intervention during the transition to parenthood. *Family Relations, 57,* 49–59.

Hawkins, D. L., Pepler, D. J., & Craig, W. M. (2001). Naturalistic observations of peer intervention in bullying. *Social Development, 10,* 512–527.

Hay, D., Payne, A., & Chadwick, A. (2004). Peer relations in childhood. *Journal of Child Psychology & Psychiatry & Allied Disciplines, 45,* 84–108.

Hayashi, A., Karasawa, M., & Tobin, J. (2009). The Japanese preschool's pedagogy of feeling: Cultural strategies for supporting young children's emotional development. *Ethos, 37,* 32–49.

Haynie, D. L., & Osgood, D. W. (2005). Reconsidering peers and delinquency: How do peers matter? *Social Forces, 84,* 1109–1130.

Health Management Resources. (2001). *Child health and fitness.* Boston, MA: Author.

Heckhausen, J., & Tomasik, M. J. (2002). Get an apprenticeship before school is out: How German adolescents adjust vocational aspirations when getting close to a developmental deadline. *Journal of Vocational Behavior, 60,* 199–219.

Hedlund, J., & Compton, R. (2005). Graduated driver licensing research in 2004 and 2005. *Journal of Safety Research, 36,* 109–119.

Heffner, L. J. (2004). Advanced maternal age—How old is too old? *New England Journal of Medicine, 351*(19), 1927–1929.

Hein, K. (1988). *Issues in adolescent health: An overview.* Washington, DC: Carnegie Council on Adolescent Development.

Heine, S. H., Lehman, D. R., Markus, H. R., & Kitayama, S. (1999). Is there a universal need for positive self-regard? *Psychological Review, 106,* 766–794.

Helwig, C. C. (2008). The moral judgment of the child reevaluated: Heteronomy, early morality, and reasoning about social justice and inequalities. In C. Wainryb, J. G. Smetana, & E. Turiel (Eds.), *Social development, social inequalities, and social justice* (pp. 27–51). New York, NY: Taylor & Francis.

Henggeler, S. W., Sheidow, A. J., & Lee, T. (2007). Multisystemic treatment of serious clinical problems in youths and their families. In D. W. Springer & A. R. Roberts (Eds.), *Handbook of forensic mental health with victims and offenders: Assessment, treatments, and research* (pp. 315–345). New York, NY: Springer.

Henrichs, J., Schenk, J. J., Barendregt, C. S., Schmidt, H. G., Steegers, E. A. P., Hofman, A., . . . Tiemeier, H. (2010). Fetal growth from mid– to late pregnancy is associated with infant development: The Generation R study. *Developmental Medicine & Child Neurology, 52,* 644–651.

Hensler, B. A., Schatschneider, C., Taylor, J., & Wagner, R. K. (2010). Behavioral genetic approach to the study of dyslexia. *Journal of Developmental and Behavioral Pediatrics, 31*(Special Issue: The genetics and genomics of childhood neurodevelopmental disorders: An update), 525–532.

Hepper, P. G., Wells, D. L., & Lynch, C. (2005). Prenatal thumb sucking is related to postnatal handedness. *Neuropsychologia, 43,* 313–315.

Herman-Giddens, M., Slora, E., Wasserman, R., Bourdony, C., Bhapkar, M., Koch, G., & Hasemeier, C. (1997). Secondary sexual characteristics and menses in young girls seen in office practice: A study from the Pediatric Research in Office Settings Network. *Pediatrics, 88,* 505–512.

Herman-Giddens, M., Wang, L., & Koch, G. (2001). Secondary sexual characteristics in boys. *Archives of Pediatrics and Adolescent Medicine, 155,* 1022–1028.

Herpetz-Dahlmann, B., Wille, N., Holling, J., Vloet, T. D., Ravens-Sieberer, U. [BELLA study group (Germany)]. (2008). Disordered eating behavior and attitudes, associated psychopathology and health-related quality of life: Results of the BELLA study. *European Child & Adolescent Psychiatry, 17*(Suppl. 1), 82–91.

Herrenkohl, T. I., Mason, W. A., Kosterman, R., Lengua, L. J., Hawkins, J. D., & Abbott, R. D. (2004). Pathways from physical childhood abuse to partner violence in young adulthood. *Violence and Victims, 19,* 123–136.

Herrera, E., Reissland, N., & Shepherd, J. (2004). Maternal touch and maternal child-directed speech: Effects of depressed mood in the postnatal period. *Journal of Affective Disorders, 81,* 29–39.

Hetherington, E. M., & Kelly, J. (2002). *For better or worse: Divorce reconsidered.* New York, NY: Norton.

Hetherington, E. M., & Stanley-Hagan, M. (2002). Parenting in divorced and remarried families. In M. H. Bornstein (Ed.), *Handbook of parenting* (pp. 287–299). Mahwah, NJ: Erlbaum.

Hetherington, E. M., Henderson, S., & Reiss, D. (1999). Adolescent siblings in stepfamilies: Family functioning and adolescent adjustment. *Monographs of the Society for Research in Child Development, 64*(4).

Heuveline, P. (2002). An international comparison of adolescent and young adult morality. *Annals of the American Academy of Political Social Science, 580,* 172–200.

Hewlett, B. S. (2004). Fathers in forager, farmer and pastoral cultures. In M. E. Lamb (Ed.), *The role of the father in child development* (94th ed., pp. 182–195). New York, NY: Wiley.

Heyman, G. D., & Legare, C. H. (2004). Children's beliefs about gender differences in the academic and social domains. *Sex Roles, 50,* 227–239.

Hildreth, K., Sweeney, B., & Rovee-Collier, C. (2003). Differential memory-preserving effects of reminders at 6 months. *Journal of Experimental Child Psychology, 84,* 41–62.

Hill, J., & Lynch, M. (1983). The intensification of gender-related role expectations during early adolescence. In J. Brooks-Gunn & A. Petersen (Eds.), *Girls at puberty: Biological and psychosocial perspectives* (pp. 201–228). New York, NY: Plenum.

Hinduja, S., & Patchin, J. W. (2008). Personal information of adolescents on the Internet: A quantitative content analysis of MySpace. *Journal of Adolescence, 31,* 125–146.

Hines, M. (2004). Neuroscience and intersex. *The Psychologist, 17*(8), 455–458.

Hinojosa, T., Sheu, C. F., & Michael, G. F. (2003). Infant hand-use preference for grasping objects contributes to the development of a hand-use preference for manipulating objects. *Developmental Psychobiology, 43,* 328–334.

Hirschi, T. (2002). *Causes of delinquency.* Piscataway, NJ: Transaction.

Hiscock, H., & Jordan, B. (2004). Problem crying in infancy. *Medical Journal of Australia, 181,* 507–512.

Hjelmsedt, A., Andersson, L., Skoog-Svanberg, A., Bergh, T., Boivin, J., & Collins, A. (1999). Gender differences in psychological reactions to infertility among couples seeking IVF- and ICSI-treatment. *Acta Obstet Gynecol Scand, 78,* 42–48.

Hla, M. M., Novotny, R., Kieffer, E. C., Mor, J., & Thiele, M. (2003). Early weaning among Japanese women in Hawaii. *Journal of Biosocial Science, 35*(2), 227–241.

Ho, D. Y. F. (1987). Fatherhood in Chinese culture. In M. E. Lamb (Ed.), *The father's role: Cross-cultural perspectives* (pp. 227–245). Hillsdale, NJ: Erlbaum.

Hodnett, E. D., Gates, S., Hofmeyr, G. J., & Sakala, C. (2007). Continuous support for women during childbirth. *Cochrane Database of Systematic Reviews, 3.*

Hofer, K., & Moore, A. S. (2010). *The iConnected parent: Staying close to your kids in college (and beyond) while letting them grow up.* New York, NY: Free Press.

Hoff, E. (2009). *Language development.* Belmont, CA: Wadsworth.

Hoffman, M. (2007). The origins of empathic morality in toddlerhood. In C. A. Brownell & C. B. Kopp (Eds.), *Socioemotional development in the toddler years* (pp. 132–145). New York, NY: Guilford Press.

Hoffman, M. L. (2000). *Empathy and moral development.* New York, NY: Cambridge University Press.

Hofman, P. L., Regan, F., Jackson, W. E., Jefferies, C., Knight, D. B., Robinson, E. M., & Cutfield, W. S. (2004). Premature birth and later insulin resistance. *New England Journal of Medicine, 351,* 2179–2186.

Hofmeyr, G. J. (2002). Interventions to help external cephalic version for breech presentation at term. *Cochrane Database of Systematic Reviews, 2,* CD000184.

Hogan, M. C., Foreman, K. J., Naghavi, M., Ahn, S. Y., Wang, M., Makela, S. M., . . . Murray, C. J. L. (2010). Maternal mortality for 181 countries, 1980–2008: A systematic analysis of progress toward Millennium Development Goal 5. *The Lancet, 375,* 1–15.

Hogben M., & Williams S. P. (2001). Exploring the context of women's relationship perceptions, sexual behavior, and contraceptive strategies. *Journal of Psychology and Human Sexuality, 13,* 1–20.

Hoge, D. R., Johnson, B., & Luidens, D. A. (1993). Determinants of church involvement of young adults who grew up in the Presbyterian churches. *Journal for the Scientific Study of Religion, 32,* 242–255.

Hoh, J., & Ott, J. (2003). Mathematical multi-locus approaches to localizing complex human trait genes. *Nature Reviews Genetics, 4,* 701–709.

Hokoda, A., Lu, H. H., A., & Angeles, M. (2006). School bullying in Taiwanese adolescents. *Journal of Emotional Abuse, 64,* 69–90.

Holodynski, M. (2009). Milestones and mechanisms of emotional development. In B. Röttger-Rössler & H. J. Markowitsch (Eds.), *Emotions as bio-cultural processes* (pp. 139–163). New York, NY: Springer Science + Business Media.

Holsti, L., & Grunau, R. E. (2010). Considerations for using sucrose to reduce procedural pain in preterm infants. *Pediatrics, 125,* 1042–1049.

Holtzen, D. W. (2000). Handedness and professional tennis. *International Journal of Neuroscience, 105,* 101–119.

Honein, M. A., Paulozzi, L. J., Mathews, T. J., Erickson, J. D., & Wong, L. C. (2001). Impact of folic acid fortification of the U.S. food supply on the occurrence of neural tube defects. *The Journal of the American Medical Association, 285,* 2981–2986.

Hong, Z. R., Veach, P. M., & Lawrenz, F. (2003). An investigation of the gender stereotyped thinking of Taiwanese secondary school boys and girls. *Sex Roles, 48,* 495–504.

Hood, B., Cole-Davies, V., & Dias, M. (2003). Looking and search measures of object knowledge in preschool children. *Developmental Psychology, 39,* 61–70.

Hooghe, M., & Wilkenfeld, B. (2008). The stability of political attitudes and behaviors across adolescence and early adulthood: A comparison of survey data on adolescents and young adults in eight countries. *Journal of Youth and Adolescence, 37,* 155–167.

Hopkins, B., & Westra, T. (1990). Motor development, maternal expectations and the role of handling. *Infant Behavior and Development, 13,* 117–122.

Hopkins-Golightly, T., Raz, S., & Sander, C. (2003). Influence of slight to moderate risk for hypoxia on acquisition of cognitive and language function in the preterm infant: A cross-sectional comparison with preterm-birth controls. *Neuropsychology, 17,* 3–13.

Hopson, L. M., & Lee, E. (2011). Mitigating the effect of family poverty on academic and behavioral outcomes: The role of school climate in middle and high school. *Children and Youth Services Review, 33*(11), 2221–2229.

Horn, K., Dino, G., Kalsekar, I., & Mody, R. (2005). The impact of *Not on Tobacco* on teen smoking cessation: End-program evaluation results, 1998–2003. *Journal of Adolescent Research, 20,* 640–661.

Horn, P. (1995). *Children's work and welfare,* 1780–1890. Cambridge University Press.

Horn, S. (2003). Adolescents' reasoning about exclusion from social groups. *Developmental Psychology, 39,* 71–84.

Hornblower, M. (1997, June 9). Great Xpectations. *Time,* 58–68.

Horton, D. M. (2001). The disappearing bell curve. *Journal of Secondary Gifted Education, 12,* 185–188.

Howard, A. (1998). Youth in Rotuma, then and now. In G. Herdt & S. C. Leavitt (Eds.), *Adolescence in Pacific island societies* (pp. 148–172). Pittsburgh, PA: University of Pittsburgh Press.

Howard, K. S., Carothers, S. S., Smith, L. E., & Akai, C. E. (2007). Overcoming the odds: Protective factors in the lives of children. In J. G. Borkowski, J. R. Farris, T. L. Whitman, S. S. Carothers, K. Weed, & D. A. Keogh (Eds.), *Risk and resilience: Adolescent mothers and their children grow up* (pp. 205–232). Mahwah, NJ: Erlbaum.

Howard, R. W. (2001). Searching the real world for signs of rising population intelligence. *Personality & Individual Differences, 30,* 1039–1058.

Howe, M. L., Courage, M. L., Rooksby, M. (2009). The genesis and development of autobiographical memory. In M. L. Courage & N. Cowan (Eds.), *The development of memory in infancy and childhood* (2nd ed., pp. 177–196). New York, NY: Psychology Press.

Howe, N., & Recchia, H. (2009). Individual differences in sibling teaching in early and middle childhood. *Early Education and Development, 20,* 174–197.

Howe, N., Aquan-Assee, J., & Bukowski, W. M. (2001). Predicting sibling relations over time: Synchrony between maternal management styles and sibling relationship quality. *Merrill-Palmer Quarterly, 47,* 121–141.

Howes, C. (1985). Sharing fantasy: Social pretend play in toddlers. *Child Development, 56,* 1253–1258.

Howes, C. (1996). The earliest friendships. In W. M. Bukowski, A. F. Newcomb, & W. W. Hartup (Eds.), *The company they keep: Friendship in childhood and adolescence* (pp. 66–86). Boston, MA: Cambridge University Press.

Hoza, B., Kaiser, N., & Hurt, E. S. (2008). Evidence-based treatments for attention-deficit/hyperactivity disorder (ADHD). In G. Ric, T. D. Elkin, & M. C. Robers (Eds.), *Handbook of evidence-based therapies for children and adolescents: Bridging science and practice. Issues in clinical child psychology* (pp. 197–219). New York, NY: Springer.

Huang, K. Y., Caughy, M. O., Lee, L. C., Miller, T., & Genevro, J. (2009). Stability of maternal discipline practices and the quality of mother–child interaction during toddlerhood. *Journal of Applied Developmental Psychology, 30,* 431–441.

Huang, R. L., Lu, Z., Liu, J. J., You, Y. M., Pan, Z. Q., Wei, Z., . . . Wang, Z. Z. (2009). Features and predictors of problematic Internet use in Chinese college students. *Behaviour & Information Technology, 28,* 485–490.

Huang-Pollock, C. L., Carr, T. H., & Nigg, J. T. (2002). Development of selective attention: Perceptual load influences early versus late attentional selection in children and adults. *Developmental Psychology, 38,* 363–375.

Huesmann, L. R., Eron, L. D., Lefkowitz, M. M., & Walder, L. O. (1984). Stability of aggression over time and generations. *Developmental Psychology, 20,* 1120–1134.

Huesmann, L. R., Moise-Titus, J., Podolski, C., & Eron, L. D. (2003). Longitudinal relations between children's exposure to TV violence and their aggressiveness in young adulthood, 1977–1992. *Developmental Psychology, 39,* 201–221.

Huffman, L. R., & Speer, P. W. (2000). Academic performance among at-risk children: The role of developmentally appropriate practices. *Early Childhood Research Quarterly, 15,* 167–184.

Hughes, C., & Dunn, J. (2007). Children's relationships with other children. In C. A. Brownell & C. B. Kopp (Eds.), *Socioemotional development in the toddler years* (pp. 177–200). New York, NY: Guilford Press.

Hulei, E., Zevenbergen, A., & Jacobs, S. (2006). Discipline behaviors of Chinese American and European American mothers. *Journal of Psychology: Interdisciplinary and Appeal, 140,* 459–475.

Hundley, H. L., & Shyles, L. (2010). U.S. teenagers' perceptions and awareness of digital technology: A focus group approach. *New Media & Society, 12,* 417–433.

Hunnius, S., de Wit, T. C. J., Vrins, S., & von Hofsten, C. (2011). Facing threat: Infants' and adults' visual scanning of faces with neutral, happy, sad, angry, and fearful emotional expressions. *Cognition and Emotion, 25,* 193–205.

Hunt, E. (1989). Cognitive science: Definition, status, and questions. *Annual Review of Psychology, 40,* 603–629.

Hunziker, U. A., & Barr, R. G. (1986). Increased carrying reduces infant crying: A randomized controlled trial. *Pediatrics, 77,* 641–648.

Hurrelmann, K. (1996). The social world of adolescents: A sociological perspective. In K. Hurrelmann & S. Hamilton (Eds.), *Social problems and social contexts in adolescence: Perspectives across boundaries* (pp. 39–62). Hawthorne, NY: Aldine de Gruyter.

Hursti, U. K. (1999). Factors influencing children's food choice. *Annals of Medicine, 31,* 26–32.

Huttenlocher, P. R. (2002). *Neural plasticity: The effects of environment on the development of the cerebral cortex.* Cambridge, MA: Harvard University Press.

Hvistendahl, M. (2011). Young and restless can be a volatile mix. *Science, 333*(6042), 552–554.

Hyde, J. S., & DeLamater, J. D. (2005). *Understanding human sexuality* (9th ed.). Boston, MA: McGraw Hill.

Hyder, A. A., & Lunnen, J. (2009). Reduction of childhood mortality through millennium, development goal 4. *BMJ, 342.*

Hyder, A. A., & Lunnen, J. (2011). Reduction of childhood mortality through millennium development goal 4. *BMJ, 342*–357.

Hymel, S., McDougall, P., & Renshaw, P. (2004). Peer acceptance/rejection. In P. K. Smith & C. H. Hart (Eds.), *Blackwell handbook of childhood social development* (pp. 265–284). Malden, MA: Blackwell.

Iacovou, M. (2002). Regional differences in the transition to adulthood. *Annals of the American Academy of Political Science Studies, 580,* 40–69.

Iannelli, V. I. (2007). *Tummy time: Infants.* About.com Guide. Retrieved from http://pediatrics. about.com/od/infants/a/0607_tummy_time.htm

Iglowstein, I., Jenni, O. G., Molinari, L., & Largo, R. H. (2003). Sleep duration from infancy to adolescence: Reference values and generational trends. *Pediatrics, 111,* 302–307.

Iles, J., Slade, P., & Spiby, H. (2011). Posttraumatic stress symptoms and postpartum depression in couples after childbirth: The role of partner support and attachment. *Journal of Anxiety Disorders, 25,* 520–530.

Ilich, J. Z., & Brownbill, R. A. (2010). Nutrition through the life span: Needs and health concerns in critical periods. In T. W. Miller (Ed.), *Handbook of stressful transitions across the lifespan* (pp. 625–641). New York, NY: Springer.

Inhelder, B., & Piaget, J. (1958). *The growth of logical thinking from childhood to adolescence.* New York, NY: Basic Books.

Inhorn, M. C., & van Balen, F. (2002). *Infertility around the globe: New thinking on childlessness, gender, and reproductive technologies.* Berkeley: University of California Press.

Institute of Medicine of the National Academies. (2005). *Preventing childhood obesity: Health in the balance.* Washington, DC.

International Genome Sequencing Consortium. (2004). Finishing euchromatic sequence of the human genome. *Nature, 431,* 931–945.

International Labor Organization (ILO). (2002). *A future without child labour.* New York, NY: Author.

International Labor Organization (ILO). (2004). *Investing in every child. An economic study of the costs and benefits of eliminating child labour.* New York, NY: Author.

International Labor Organization (ILO). (2006). *The end of child labour: Within reach.* Geneva, Switzerland: International Labour Office.

International Labor Organization (ILO). (2011). *Global employment trends 2011.* Geneva, Switzerland: Author.

International Labor Organization (ILO). (2008, June 12). *World day against child labour 2008—Education: The right response to child labour.* Retrieved from http://www.ilo.org/ipec/Campaignandadvocacy/WDACL/2008/lang–en/index.htm

International Obesity Taskforce. (2008). *Global prevalence of adult obesity.* Retrieved from http://www.iotf.org/database/documents/GlobalPrevalenceofAdultObesity16December08.pdf

International Reading Association. (1999). Using multiple methods of beginning reading instruction. Newark, DE: International Reading Association.

Ip, S., Chung, M., Raman, G., Chew, P., Magula, N., DeVine, D., . . . Lau, J. (2007). *Breastfeeding and maternal and infant health outcomes in developed countries. Evidence Report/Technology Assessment No. 153.* Rockville, MD. Agency for Healthcare Research and Quality.

Ireland, J. L., & Archer, N. (2004). Association between measures of aggression and bullying among juvenile young offenders. *Aggressive Behavior, 30,* 29–42.

Ispa, J. M., & Halgunseth, L. C. (2004). Talking about corporal punishment: Nine low-income African American mothers' perspectives. *Early Childhood Research Quarterly, 19,* 463–484.

Israel, E. (2005). Introduction: The rise of the age of individualism—variability in the pathobiology, response to treatment, and treatment outcomes in asthma. *Journal of Allergy and Clinical Immunology, 115,* S525.

Iverson, R., Kuhl, P. K., Akahane-Yamada, R., Diesch, E., Tohkura, Y., & Kettermann, A. (2003). A perceptual interference account of acquisition difficulties for non-native phonemes. *Cognition, 87,* B47–B57.

Izard, C. E., & Ackerman, B. P. (2000). Motivational, organizational, and regulatory functions of discrete emotions. In M. Lewis & J. M. Haviland-Jones (Eds.), *Handbook of emotions,* (2nd ed., pp. 253–264). New York, NY: Guilford Press.

Jaakkola, J. J., & Gissler, M. (2004). Maternal smoking in pregnancy, fetal development, and childhood asthma. *American Journal of Public Health, 94,* 136–140.

Jackson, L. M., Pratt, M. W., Hunsberger, B., & Pancer, S. M. (2005). Optimism as a mediator of the relation between perceived parental authoritativeness and adjustment among adolescents: Finding the sunny side of the street. *Social Development, 14,* 273–304.

Jacobs, J. E., & Weisz, V. (1994). Gender stereotypes: Implications for gifted education. *Roeper Review, 16,* 152–155.

Jaeger, S. (1985). The origin of the diary method in developmental psychology. In G. Eckardt, W. G. Bringmann, & L. Sprung (Eds.), *Contributions to a history of developmental psychology* (pp. 63–74). New York, NY: Mouton.

Jaffee, S. R., Caspi, A., Moffitt, T. E., Polo-Tomas, M., Price, T. S., & Taylor, A. (2004). The limits of child effects: Evidence for genetically mediated child effects on corporal punishment but not on physical maltreatment. *Developmental Psychology, 40,* 1047–1058.

Jahromi, L. B., Putnam, S. P., & Stifter, C. A. (2004). Maternal regulation of infant reactivity from 2 to 6 months. *Developmental Psychology, 40,* 477–487.

Jalonick, M. C. (2010, December 13). Obama signs historic school lunch nutrition bill. Retrieved from http://www.salon.com/food/feature/2010/12/13/us_obama_child_nutrition

James, C., Hadley, D. W., Holtzman, N. A., & Winkelstein, J. A. (2006). How does the mode of inheritance of a genetic condition influence families? A study of guilt, blame, stigma, and understanding of inheritance and reproductive risks in families with X-linked and autosomal recessive diseases. *Genetics in Medicine, 8,* 234–242.

James, D. K. (2010). Fetal learning: A critical review. *Infant and Child Development, 19,* 45–54.

Jankowiak, W. R., & Fischer, E. F. (1992). A cross-cultural perspective on romantic love. *Ethology, 31,* 149–155.

Janssen, I., Katzmarzyk, P. T., Ross, R., Leon, A. S., Skinner, J. S., Rao, D. C., Wilmore, J. H., . . . Bouchard, C. (2004). Fitness alters the associations of BMI and waist circumference with total and abdominal fat. *Obesity Research, 12,* 525–537.

Jeffrey, J. (2004, November). Parents often blind to their kids' weight. *British Medical Journal Online.* Retrieved from content.health.msn.com/content/article/97/104292.htm

Jenkins, J. M., Rabash, J., & O'Connor, T. G. (2003). The role of the shared family context in differential parenting. *Developmental Psychology, 39,* 99–113.

Jennings, N. (2007). Advertising, viewer age and. In J. J. Arnett (Ed.), *Encyclopedia of children, adolescents, and the media* (pp. 55–57). Thousand Oaks, CA: Sage,

Jensen, L. A. (1995). Habits of the heart revisited: Autonomy, community, and divinity in adults' moral language. *Qualitative Sociology, 18,* 71–86.

Jensen, L. A. (1997a). Culture wars: American moral divisions across the adult life span. *Journal of Adult Development, 4,* 107–121.

Jensen, L. A. (1997b). Different worldviews, different morals: America's culture war divide. *Human Development, 40,* 325–344.

Jensen, L. A. (2008). Coming of age in a multicultural world: Globalization and adolescent cultural identity formation. In D. L. Browning (Ed.), *Adolescent identities: A collection of readings* (pp. 3–17). Relational perspectives book series. New York, NY: Analytic Press.

Jensen, L. A. (Ed.). (2011). *Bridging cultural and developmental psychology.* New York, NY: Oxford University Press.

Jensen, L. A., Arnett, J. J., & McKenzie, J. (2011). Globalization and cultural identity developments in adolescence and emerging adulthood. In Schwartz, S. J., Luyckx, K., & Vignoles, V. L. (Eds.), *Handbook of identity theory and research.* New York, NY: Springer.

Jequier, A. (2011). *Male infertility: A clinical guide.* New York, NY: Cambridge University Press.

Jessor, R., Colby, A., & Shweder, R. A. (1996). *Ethnography and human development: Context and meaning in social inquiry.* Chicago, IL: University of Chicago Press.

Jeynes, W. (2007). The impact of parental remarriage on children: A meta-analysis. *Marriage & Family Review, 40,* 75–102.

Jiao, S., Ji, G., & Jing, Q. (1996). Cognitive development of Chinese urban only children and children with siblings. *Child Development, 67,* 387–395.

Jochman, K. A., & Fromme, K. (2010). Maturing out of substance use: The other side of etiology. In L. Scheier (Ed.), *Handbook of drug use etiology: Theory, methods, and empirical findings* (pp. 565–578). Washington, DC: American Psychological Association.

Johnson, B., Redding, C., DiClemente, R., Mustanski, B., Dodge, B., Sheeran, P., Warren, M., et al. (2010). A network-individual-resource model for HIV prevention. *AIDS and Behavior, 14*(0), 204–221.

Johnson, D. J., Jaeger, E., Randolph, S. M., Cauce, A. M., Ward, J., & National Institute of Child Health and Human Development: Early Child Care Research Network. (2003). Studying the effects of early child care experiences on the development of children of color in the United States: Toward a more inclusive research agenda. *Child Development, 74,* 1227–1244.

Johnson, D. M. (2005). Mind, brain, and the upper Paleolithic. In C. E. Erneling & D. M. Johnson (Eds.), *The mind as a scientific object: Between brain and culture* (pp. 499–510). New York, NY: Oxford University Press.

Johnson, J. G., Cohen, P., Kasen, S., & Brook, J. S. (2002). Eating disorders during adolescence and the risk for physical and mental disorders during early adulthood. *Archives of General Psychiatry, 59,* 545–552.

Johnson, J. S., & Newport, E. L. (1989). Critical period effects in second language learning: The influence of maturational state on the acquisition of English as a second language. *Cognitive Psychology, 21*(1), 60–99.

Johnson, M. C. (2000). The view from the Wuro: A guide to child rearing for Fulani parents. In J. DeLoache & A. Gottlieb (Eds.), *A world of babies: Imagined childcare guides for seven societies* (pp. 171–198). New York, NY: Cambridge University Press.

Johnson, M. D. (2008). *Human biology: Concepts and current issues.* Upper Saddle River, NJ: Prentice Hall.

Johnson, M. H. (2001). Functional brain development in humans. *Nature Reviews Neuroscience, 2,* 475–483.

Johnson, S. K., Murphy, S. R., Zewdie, S., & Reichard, R. J. (2008). The strong, sensitive type: Effects of gender stereotypes and leadership prototypes on the evaluation of male and female leaders. *Organizational Behavior and Human Decision Processes, 106,* 39–60.

Johnson, W., te Nijenhuis, J., & Bouchard, T. J., Jr. (2008). Still just 1 g: Consistent results from five tests batteries. *Intelligence, 36,* 81–95.

John-Steiner, V., & Mahn, H. (2003). Sociocultural contexts for teaching and learning. *Handbook of psychology.* John Wiley & Sons, Inc. Retrieved from http://onlinelibrary.wiley.com/doi/10.1002/0471264385.wei0707/abstract

John-Steiner, V., & Mahn, H. (2003). Sociocultural contexts for teaching and learning. In A. Reynolds, M. William & G. E. Miller (Eds.), *Handbook of psychology: Educational psychology* (Vol. 7, pp. 125–151). New York: John Wiley and Sons.

Johnston, L. D., O'Malley, P. M., Bachman, J. G., & Schulenberg, J. E. (2008). *Monitoring the future: National survey results on drug use, 1975–2007: Volume II, College students and adults ages 19–45* (NIH Publication No. 08-6418B). Bethesda, MD: National Institute on Drug Abuse.

Jones, E., & Kay, M. A. (2003). The cultural anthropology of the placenta. In L. Dundes (Ed.), *The manner born: Birth rites in cross-cultural perspective* (pp. 101–116). Walnut Creek, CA: Altamira Press.

Jones, R. E. (2006). *Human reproductive biology.* New York, NY: Academic Press.

Jones, R. K., Darroch, J. E., & Henshaw, S. K. (2002). Contraceptive use among U.S. women having abortions in 2000–2001. *Perspectives on Sexual and Reproductive Health, 34,* 294–303.

Jordan, B. (1993). *Birth in four cultures: A cross-cultural investigation of childbirth in Yucatan, Holland, Sweden, and the United States.* Long Grove, IL: Waveland Press.

Jordan, B. (1994). *Birth in four cultures.* Long Grove, IL: Waveland Press.

Joyce, D. (2010). *Essentials of temperament assessment.* Hoboken, NJ: Wiley.

Kagan, J. (1994). *Galen's prophecy: Temperament in human nature.* New York, NY: Basic Books.

Kagan, J. (1998). Biology and the child. In N. Eisenberg (Ed.), *Handbook of child psychology: Vol. 3. Social, emotional, and personality development* (5th ed., pp. 177–236). New York, NY: Wiley.

Kagan, J. (2000). Temperament. In A. Kazdin (Ed.), *Encyclopedia of psychology* (Vol. 8, pp. 34–37). Washington, DC: American Psychological Association.

Kagan, J. (2003). Behavioral inhibition as a temperamental category. In R. J. Davidson, K. R. Scherer, & H. H. Goldsmith (Eds.), *Handbook of affective science* (pp. 320–331). New York, NY: Oxford University Press.

Kagan, J., & Fox, N. A. (2006). Biology, culture, and temperamental biases. In W. Damon & R. Lerner (Eds.), & N. Eisenberg (Vol. Ed.), *Handbook of child psychology: Vol. 3. Social, emotional, and personality development* (6th ed., pp. 167–225). New York, NY: Wiley.

Kagan, J., & Herschkowitz, E. C. (2005). *Young mind in a growing brain.* Mahwah, NJ: Erlbaum.

Kagan, J., Kearsley, R. B., & Zelazo, P. R. (1978). *Infancy: Its place in human development.* Cambridge, MA: Harvard University Press.

Kahana-Kalman, R., & Walker-Andrews, A. S. (2001). The role of person familiarity in young infants' perception of emotional expressions. *Child Development, 72,* 352–369.

Kahn, J. A. (2007). Maximizing the potential public health impact of HPV vaccines: A focus on parents. *Journal of Adolescent Health, 20,* 101–103.

Kail, R. V. (2003). Information processing and memory. In M. H. Bornstein, L. Davidson, C. L. M. Keyes, K. A. Moore, and the Center for Child Well-Being (Eds.), *Well-being: Positive development across the life course* (pp. 269–280). Mahwah, NJ: Erlbaum.

Kail, R., & Park, Y. (1992). Global developmental change in processing time. *Merrill-Palmer Quarterly, 38,* 525–541.

Kainz, G., Eliasson, M., & von Post, I. (2010). The child's father, an important person for the mother's well-being during the childbirth: A hermeneutic study. *Health Care for Women International, 31,* 621–635.

Kakar, S. (1998). The search for the middle age in India. In R. A. Shweder (Ed.), *Welcome to middle age! (and other cultural fictions)* (pp. 75–98). Chicago, IL: University of Chicago Press.

Kakar, S., & Kakar, K. (2007). *The Indians: Portrait of a people.* New York, NY: Penguin.

Kalb, C., & McCormick, J. (1998, September 21). Bellying up to the bar. *Newsweek,* 89.

Kalter, H. (2010). *Teratology in the twentieth century plus ten.* New York, NY: Springer.

Kamibeppu, K., & Sugiura, H. (2005). Impact of the mobile phone on junior high-school students' friendships in the Tokyo metropolitan area. *Cyber Psychology & Behavior, 8,* 121–130.

Kane, P., & Garber, J. (2004). The relations among depression in fathers, children's psychopathology, and father–child conflict: A meta-analysis. *Child Psychology Review, 24,* 339–360.

Kanetsuna, T., Smith, P., & Morita, Y. (2006). Coping with bullying at school: Children's recommended strategies and attitudes to school-based intervention in England and Japan. *Aggressive Behavior, 32,* 570–580.

Kaplan, B. J., Fisher, J. E., Crawford, S. G., Field, C. J., & Kolb, B. (2004). Improved mood and behavior during treatment with a mineral-vitamin supplement: An open-label case series of children. *Journal of Child and Adolescent Psychopharmacology, 14*(1), 115–122.

Kaplan, B. J., Crawford, S. G., Field, C. J., Simpson, J., & Steven, A. (2007). Vitamins, minerals, and mood. *Psychological Bulletin, 133,* 747–760.

Kaplan, H., & Dove, H. (1987). Infant development among the Ache of Eastern Paraguay. *Developmental Psychology, 23,* 190–198.

Karlsson, J. L. (2006). Specific genes for intelligence. In L. V. Wesley (Ed.), *Intelligence: New research* (pp. 23–46). Hauppauge, NY: Nova Science.

Katchadourian, H., & Boli, J. (1985). *Careerism and intellectualism among college students.* San Francisco, CA: Jossey-Bass.

Katz, L. F., & Windecker-Nelson, B. (2004). Parental meta-emotion philosophy in families with conduct-problem children: Links with peer relations. *Journal of Abnormal Child Psychology, 32,* 385–398.

Kavšek, M. (2003). Development of depth and object perception in infancy. In G. Schwarzer & H. Leder (Eds.), *The development of face processing* (pp. 35–52). Ashland, OH: Hogrefe & Huber.

Kavšek, M. (2004). Predicting later IQ from infant visual habituation and dishabituation: A meta-analysis. *Journal of Applied Developmental Psychology, 25,* 369–393.

Kavšek, M., & Bornstein, M. H. (2010). Visual habituation and dishabituation in preterm infants: A review and meta-analysis. *Research in Developmental Disabilities, 31,* 951–975.

Kazdin, A. E., & Benjet, C. (2003). Spanking children: Evidence and issues. *Current Directions in Psychological Science, 12,* 99–103.

Keating, D. (1990). Adolescent thinking. In S. Feldman & G. Elliott (Eds.), *At the threshold: The developing adolescent* (pp. 54–89). Cambridge, MA: Harvard University Press.

Keating, D. (2004). Cognitive and brain development. In L. Steinberg & R. M. Lerner (Eds.), *Handbook of adolescent psychology* (2nd ed., pp. 45–84). New York, NY: Wiley.

Keegan, R. T., & Gruber, H. E. (1985). Charles Darwin's unpublished "Diary of an infant": An early phase in his psychological work. In G. Eckardt, W. G. Bringmann, & L. Sprung (Eds.), *Contributions to a history of developmental psychology* (pp. 127–145). New York, NY: Mouton.

Keen, R. (2005). Using perceptual representations to guide reaching and looking. In J. J. Reiser, J. J. Lockman, & C. A. Nelson (Eds.), *Action as an organizer or learning and development: Minnesota Symposia on Child Psychology* (Vol. 33, pp. 301–322). Mahwah, NJ: Erlbaum.

Keller, M. A., & Goldberg, W. A. (2004). Co-sleeping: Help or hindrance for young children's independence? *Infant and Child Development, 13,* 369–388.

Kellman, P. J., & Arterberry, M. E. (2006). Infant visual perception. In W. Damon & R. Lerner (Eds.), & D. Kuhn & R. Siegler (Vol. Eds.), *Handbook of child psychology: Vol. 2. Cognition, perception, and language* (6th ed., pp. 109–160). New York, NY: Wiley.

Kellogg, A. (2001, January). Looking inward, freshman care less about politics and more about money. *Chronicle of Higher Education,* A47–A49.

Kelly, B., Halford, J. C. G., Boyland, E. J., Chapman, K., Bautista-Castaño, I., Berg, C., et al. (2010). Television food advertising to children: A global perspective. *American Journal of Public Health, 100,* 1730–1736.

Kelly, J. B. (2003). Changing perspectives on children's adjustment following divorce: A view from the United States. *Childhood: A Global Journal of Child Research, 10,* 237–254.

Kelly, Y., Sacker, A., Schoon, I., & Nazroo, J. (2006). Ethnic differences in achievement of developmental milestones by 9 months of age: the Millennium Cohort Study. *Developmental Medicine & Child Neurology, 48*(10), 825–830.

Kelly, Y., Nazroo, J., Sacker, A., & Schoon, I. (2006). Ethnic differences in achievement of developmental milestones by 9 months of age: The Millenium Cohort Study. *Developmental Medicine & Child Neurology, 48,* 825–830.

Kember, D., & Watkins, D. (2010). Approaches to learning and teaching by the Chinese. In M. Harris (Ed.), *The Oxford handbook of Chinese psychology* (pp. 169–185). New York, NY: Oxford University Press.

Kenneally, C. (2007). *The first word: The search for the origins of language.* New York, NY: Penguin.

Kent, M. M., & Haub, C. (2005). Global demographic divide. *Population Bulletin, 60,* 1–24.

Kerber, L. K. (1997). *Toward an intellectual history of women.* Chapel Hill: University of North Carolina Press.

Kerestes, M., Youniss, J., & Metz, E. (2004). Longitudinal patterns of religious perspective and civic integration. *Applied Developmental Science, 8,* 39–46.

Kesson, A. M. (2007). Respiratory virus infections. *Paediatric Respiratory Reviews, 8,* 240–248.

Kiang, L., Moreno, A. J., & Robinson, J. L. (2004). Maternal preconceptions about parenting predict child temperament, maternal sensitivity, and children's empathy. *Developmental Psychology, 40,* 1081–1092.

Kidd, S. A., Eskenazi, B., & Wyrobek, A. J. (2001). Effects of male age on semen quality and fertility: a review of the literature. *Fertility and Sterility, 75*(2), 237–248.

Kidd, E., & Lum, J. A. G. (2008). Sex differences in past tense overregularization. *Developmental Science, 11*(6), 882–889.

Kiernan, K. (2002). Cohabitation in Western Europe: Trends, issues, and implications. In A. Booth & A. C. Crouter (Eds.), *Just living together: Implications of cohabitation on families, children, and social policy* (pp. 3–31). Mahwah, NJ: Erlbaum.

Kiernan, K. (2004). Cohabitation and divorce across nations and generations. In P. L. Chase-Lansdale, K. Kiernan, & R. J. Friedman (Eds.), *Human development across lives and generations: The potential for change* (pp. 139–170). New York, NY: Cambridge University Press.

Killen, M., & Wainryb, C. (2000). Independence and interdependence in diverse cultural contexts. In S. Harkness, C. Raeff, & C. M. Super (Eds.), *Variability in the social construction of the child* (pp. 5–21). San Francisco, CA: Jossey-Bass.

Kim, M., McGregor, K. K., & Thompson, C. K. (2000). Early lexical development in English- and Korean-speaking children: Language-general and language-specific patterns. *Journal of Child Language, 27,* 225–254.

Kim, S. Y. S., Barton, D. A., Obarzanek, E., McMahon, R. P., Kronsberg, S., & Waclawiw, M. A. (2002). Obesity development during adolescence in a biracial cohort: The NHLBI Growth and Health Study. *Pediatrics, 110,* 354–358.

King, B. M. (2005). *Human sexuality today* (5th ed.). Upper Saddle River, NJ: Prentice Hall.

King, P. E., Furrow, J. L., & Roth, N. (2002). The influence of families and peers on adolescent religiousness. *Journal of Psychology and Christianity, 21,* 109–120.

King, P. M., & Kitchener, K. S. (2002). The reflective judgment model: Twenty years of research on epistemic cognition. In B. K. Hofner & P. R. Pintrich (Eds.), *Personal epistemology: The psychology of beliefs about knowledge and knowing* (pp. 37–61). Mahwah, NJ: Erlbaum.

King, P. M., & Kitchener, K. S. (2004). Reflective judgment: Theory and research on the development of epistemic judgment through adulthood. *Educational Psychologist, 39,* 5–18.

Kinnally, W. (2007). Music listening, age effects on. In J. J. Arnett (Ed.), *Encyclopedia of children, adolescents, and the media* (pp. 585–586). Thousand Oaks, CA: Sage.

Kinney, H. C., & Thach, B. T. (2009). Medical progress: The sudden infant death syndrome. *The New England Journal of Medicine, 361,* 795–805.

Kins, E., Beyers, W., Soenens, B., & Vansteenkiste, M. (2009). Patterns of home leaving and subjective well-being in emerging adulthood: The role of motivational processes and parental autonomy support. *Developmental Psychology, 45,* 1416–1429.

Kirchner, G. (2000). *Children's games from around the world.* Boston, MA: Allyn & Bacon.

Kirkorian, H. L., Wartella, E. A., & Anderson, D. R. (2008). Media and young children's learning. *The Future of Children, 18*(1), 39–61.

Kisilevsky, B. S., Hains, S. M., Lee, K., Xic, X., Huang, H., Ye, H. H., Zhang, K. & Wang, Z. (2003). Effects of experience on fetal voice recognition. *Psychological Science, 14,* 220–224.

Kitchener, K. S., King, P. M., & DeLuca, S. (2006). Development of reflective judgment in adulthood. In C. Hoare (Ed.), *Handbook of adult development and learning* (pp. 73–98). New York, NY: Oxford University Press.

Kitchener, K. S., Lynch, C. L., Fischer, K. W., & Wood, P. K. (1993). Developmental range of reflective judgment: The effect of contextual support and practice on developmental stage. *Developmental Psychology, 29,* 893–906.

Kite, M. E., Deaux, K., & Hines, E. (2008). Gender stereotypes. In F. L. Denmark & M. A. Paludi (Eds.), *Psychology of women: A handbook of issues and theories* (2nd ed., pp. 205–236). Westport, CT: Praeger.

Kitzmann, K. M., Cohen, R., & Lockwood, R. L. (2002). Are only children missing out? Comparison of the peer-related social competence of only children and siblings. *Journal of Social and Personal Relationships, 19,* 299–316.

Klahr, D., & MacWhinney, B. (1998). Information processing. In D. Kuhn & R. S. Siegler (Eds.), *Handbook of child psychology: Vol. 2. Cognition, perception, and language* (5th ed., pp. 631–678). New York, NY: Wiley.

Klass, C. S. (2008). *The home visitor's guidebook: Promoting optimal parent and child development* (3rd ed.). Baltimore, MD: Brookes.

Klaus, M. H., & Kennell, J. H. (1976). *Maternal–infant bonding: The impact of early separation or loss on family development.* St. Louis, MO: Mosby.

Klomek, A. B., Marrocco, F., Kleinman, M., Schonfeld, I. S., & Gould, M. S. (2007). Bullying, depression, and suicidality in adolescents. *Journal of the American Academy of Child & Adolescent Psychiatry, 46,* 40–49.

Klomsten, A. T., Skaalvik, E. M., & Espnes, G. A. (2004). Physical self-concept and sports: Do gender differences exist? *Sex Roles, 50,* 119–127.

Knecht, S., Drager, B., Deppe, M., Bobe, L., Lohmann, H., Floel, A., . . . Henningsen, H. (2000). Handedness and hemispheric language dominance in healthy humans. *Brain, 135,* 2512–2518.

Knect, S., Jansen, A., Frank, A., van Randenborgh, J., Sommer, J., Kanowski, M., & Heinze, H. J. (2003). How atypical is atypical language dominance? *Neuroimage, 18,* 917–927.

Knickmeyer, R. C., & Baron-Cohen, S. (2006). Fetal testosterone and sex differences. *Early Human Development, 82*(12), 755–760.

Knox, D., Sturdivant, L., & Zusman, M. E. (2001). College student attitudes toward sexual intimacy. *College Student Journal, 35,* 241–243.

Kochanek, K. D., Murphy, S. I., Anderson, R. B., & Scott, C. (2004). Deaths: Final data for 2002. *National Vital Statistics Report, 53,* 1–116.

Kochanska, G. (2002). Mutually responsive orientation between mothers and their young children: A context for the early development of conscience. *Current Directions in Psychological Science, 11,* 191–195.

Kochenderfer-Ladd, B. (2003). Identification of aggressive and asocial victims and the stability of their peer victimization. *Merrill-Palmer Quarterly, 49,* 401–425.

Kohlberg, L. (1958). *The development of modes of moral thinking and choice in the years 10 to 16.* Unpublished doctoral dissertation. University of Chicago.

Kohlberg, L. (1986). A current statement on some theoretical issues. In S. Modgil & C. Modgil (Eds.), *Lawrence Kohlberg.* Philadelphia, PA: Falmer.

Kopp, C. B. (1989). Regulation of distress and negative emotions: A developmental view. *Developmental Psychology, 25,* 343–354.

Kopp, C. B. (2003). *Baby steps: A guide to your child's social, physical, mental, and emotional development in the first two years.* New York, NY: Owl.

Korkman, M., Kettunen, S., & Autti-Rämö, I. (2003). Neurocognitive impairment in early adolescence following prenatal alcohol exposure of varying duration. *Child Neuropsychology, 9*(2), 117–128.

Kornhaber, M. L. (2004). Using multiple intelligences to overcome cultural barriers to identifications for gifted education. In D. Boothe & J. C. Stanley. (Eds.), *In the eyes of the beholder: Critical issues for diversity in gifted education* (pp. 215–225). Waco, TX: Prufrock Press.

Kostandy, R. R., Ludington-Hoe, S. M., Cong, X., Abouelfettoh, A., Bronson, C., Stankus, A., & Jarrell, J. R. (2008). Kangaroo care (skin contact) reduces crying response to pain in preterm neonates: Pilot results. *Pain Management Nursing, 9,* 55–65.

Kotkin, J. (2010). *The next hundred million: America in 2050.* New York, NY: Penguin.

Kotler, J. (2007). Television, prosocial content and. In J. J. Arnett (Ed.), *Encyclopedia of children, adolescents, and the media, Vol. 2* (pp. 817–819). Thousand Oaks, CA: Sage.

Kostovic, I., & Vasung, L. (2009). Insights from in vitro magnetic resonance imaging of cerebral development. *Seminars in Perinatology, 33,* 220–233.

Kouvonen, A., & Kivivuori, J. (2001). Part-time jobs, delinquency and victimization among Finnish adolescents. *Journal of Scandinavian Studies in Criminology and Crime Prevention, 2*(2), 191–212.

Kowalski, R. (2008). *Cyberbullying: Bullying in the digital age.* Malden, MA: Blackwell.

Kowalski, R. M., & Limber, S. P. (2007). Electronic bullying among middle school students. *Journal of Adolescent Health, 41,* S22–S30.

Kramer, L., & Kowal, A. K. (2005). Sibling relationship quality from birth to adolescence: The enduring contributions of friends. *Journal of Family Psychology, 19*(Special issue: Sibling Relationship Contributions to Individual and Family Well-Being), 503–511.

Kramer, L., Perozynski, L., & Chung, T. (1999). Parental responses to sibling conflict: The effects of development and parent gender. *Child Development, 70,* 1401–1414.

Kramer, M. S., Aboud, F., Mironova, E., Vanilovich, I., Platt, R. W., Matush, L., . . . Promotion of Breastfeeding Intervention Trial (PROBIT) Study Group (2008). Breastfeeding and child cognitive development: New evidence from a large randomized trial. *Archives of General Psychiatry, 65,* 578–584.

Kramer, M. S., Lidia, M., Vanilovich, I., Platt, R. W., & Bogdanovich, N. (2009). A randomized breast-feeding promotion intervention did not reduce child obesity in Belarus. *Journal of Nutrition, 139,* 417S–421S.

Kraus, E. L. (2005). "Toys and perfumes:" Imploding Italy's population paradox and motherly myths. In C. B. Douglass (Ed.), *Barren states: The population "implosion" in Europe* (pp. 159–182). New York, NY: Berg.

Kreutzer, M., Leonard, C., & Flavell, J. H. (1975). An interview study of children's knowledge about memory. *Monographs of the Society for Research in Child Development, 40*(1, Serial No. 159).

Kroger, J. (2002). Commentary on "Feminist perspectives on Erikson's theory: Their relevance for contemporary identity development research." *Identity, 2,* 257–266.

Kroger, J. (2003). Identity development during adolescence. In G. Adams & M. Berzonsky (Eds.), *Blackwell handbook of adolescence* (pp. 205–225). Malden, MA: Blackwell.

Kroger, J. (2007). *Identity development: Adolescence through adulthood* (2nd ed.). Thousand Oaks, CA: Sage.

Kroger, J., Martinussen, M., & Marcia, J. E. (2010). Identity status change during adolescence and young adulthood: A meta-analysis. *Journal of Adolescence, 33,* 683–698.

Kubisch, S. (2007). Electronic games, age and. In J. J. Arnett (Ed.), *Encyclopedia of children, adolescents, and the media* (pp. 264–265). Thousand Oaks, CA: Sage.

Kuhl, P. K. (2004). Early language acquisition: Cracking the speech code. *Nature Reviews Neuroscience, 5,* 831–843.

Kuhn, D. (2008). Formal operations from a twenty-first century perspective. *Human Development, 51*(Special issue: Celebrating a Legacy of Theory with New Directions for Research on Human Development), 48–55.

Kuntsche, E., Rehm, J., & Gmel, G. (2004). Characteristics of binge drinkers in Europe. *Social Science & Medicine, 59,* 113–127.

Kuttler, A. F., La Greca, A. M., & Prinstein, M. J. (1999). Friendship qualities and social-emotional functioning of adolescents with close, cross-sex friendships. *Journal of Research on Adolescence, 9,* 339–366.

Labouvie-Vief, G. (1982). Dynamic development and mature autonomy: A theoretical prologue. *Human Development, 25,* 161–191.

Labouvie-Vief, G. (1990). Modes of knowledge and the organization of development. In M. L. Commons, J. D. Sinnott, F. A. Richards, & C. Armon (Eds.), *Models and methods in the study of adolescent and adult thought* (pp. 43–62). New York, NY: Praeger.

Labouvie-Vief, G. (1998). Cognitive-emotional integration in adulthood. In K. W. Schaie & M. P. Lawton (Eds.), *Annual review of gerontology and geriatrics, Vol. 17: Focus on emotion and adult development* (pp. 206–237). New York, NY: Springer.

Labouvie-Vief, G. (2006). Emerging structures of adult thought. In J. J. Arnett & J. Tanner (Eds.), *Emerging adults in America: Coming of age in the 21st century* (pp. 59–84). Washington, DC: American Psychological Association.

Labouvie-Vief, G., & Diehl, M. (2002). Cognitive complexity and cognitive-affective integration: Related or separate domains of adult development? *Psychology and Aging, 15,* 490–594.

Ladd, G. W., Buhs, E., & Troop, W. (2004). School adjustment and social skills training. In P. K. Smith & C. H. Hart (Eds.), *Blackwell handbook of childhood social development* (pp. 394–416). Malden, MA: Blackwell.

Laible, D. (2004). Mother–child discourse in two contexts: Links with child temperament, attachment security and socioemotional competence. *Developmental Psychology, 40,* 979–992.

Lakatta, E. G. (1990). Heart and circulation. In E. L. Schneider & J. W. Rowe (Eds.), *Handbook of the biology of aging* (3rd ed., pp. 181–217). San Diego, CA: Academic Press.

Lamb, M. E. (1994). Infant care practices and the application of knowledge. In C. B. Fisher & R. M. Lerner (Eds.), *Applied developmental psychology* (pp. 23–45). New York, NY: McGraw-Hill.

Lamb, M. E. (2000). The history of research on father involvement: An overview. In H. E. Peters, G. W. Peterson, S. K. Steinmetz, & R. D. Day (Eds.), *Fatherhood: Research, interventions, and policies* (pp. 23–42). New York, NY: Haworth Press.

Lamb, M. E., & Lewis, C. (2005). The role of parent–child relationships in child development. In M. H. Bornstein & M. E. Lamb (Eds.), *Developmental psychology* (5th ed., pp. 429–468). Mahwah, NJ: Erlbaum.

Lampl, M., Johnson, M. L., & Frongillo, E. A., Jr. (2001). Mixed distribution analysis identifies saltation and stasis growth. *Annals of Human Biology, 28,* 403–411.

Lander, E. S., Linton, L. M., & Birren, B. (2001). Initial sequencing and analysis of the human genome. *Nature, 409,* 860–921.

Lane, B. (2009). *Epidural rates in the U.S. and around the world: How many mothers choose to use an epidural to provide pain relief?* Retrieved from http://www.suite101.com/content/epidural-for-labor-a168170

Lansford, J. E., Deater-Deckard, K., Dodge, K. A., Bates, J. E., & Pettit, G. S. (2004). Ethnic differences in the link between physical discipline and later adolescent externalizing behaviors. *Journal of Child Psychology and Psychiatry, 45,* 801–812.

Lansford, J. E., Malone, P. S., Dodge, K. A., Crozier, J. C., Pettit, G. S., & Bates, J. E. (2006). A 12-year prospective study of patterns of social information processing problems and externalizing behaviors. *Journal of Abnormal Child Psychology, 34,* 715–724.

Larson, R. W., Csikszentmihalyi, M., & Graef, R. (1980). Mood variability and the psycho-social adjustment of adolescents. *Journal of Youth & Adolescence, 9,* 469–490.

Larson, R. W., Moneta, G., Richards, M. H., & Wilson, S. (2002). Continuity, stability, and change in daily emotional experience across adolescence. *Child Development, 73,* 1151–1165.

Larson, R. W., Richards, M. H., Moneta, G., Holmbeck, G., & Duckett, E. (1996). Changes in adolescents' daily interactions with their families from ages 10 to 18: Disengagement and transformation. *Developmental Psychology, 32*(4), 744–754.

Larson, R. W., Wilson, S., & Rickman, A. (2010). Globalization, societal change, and adolescence across the world. In R. Lerner & L. Steinberg (Eds.), *Handbook of adolescent psychology* (3rd ed., pp. 590–622). Hoboken, NJ: Wiley.

Larson, R., & Richards, M. H. (1994). *Divergent realities: The emotional lives of mothers, fathers, and adolescents.* New York, NY: Basic Books.

Larson, R., Verman, S., & Dwokin, J. (2000, March). Adolescence without family disengagement: The daily family lives of Indian middle-class teenagers. Paper presented at the biennial meeting of the Society for Research on Adolescence, Chicago, IL.

Lauersen, N. H., & Bouchez, C. (2000). *Getting pregnant: What you need to know right now.* New York, NY: Fireside.

Laursen, B., Coy, K. C., & Collins, W. A. (1998). Reconsidering changes in parent–child conflict across adolescence: A meta-analysis. *Child Development, 69,* 817–832.

Lavzer, J. L., & Goodson, B. D. (2006). The "quality" of early care and education settings: Definitional and measurement issues. *Evaluation Review, 30,* 556–576.

Lawson, A. E., & Wollman, W. T. (2003). Encouraging the transition from concrete to formal operations: An experiment. *Journal of Research in Science Teaching, 40*(Suppl.), S33–S50.

Layton, E., Dollahite, D. C., & Hardy, S. A. (2011). Anchors of religious commitment in adolescents. *Journal of Adolescent Research, 26,* 381–413.

Le, H. N. (2000). Never leave your little one alone: Raising an Ifaluk child. In J. DeLoache & A. Gottlieb (Eds.), *A world of babies: Imagined childcare guides for seven societies* (pp. 199–222). New York, NY: Cambridge University Press.

Leakey, R. (1994). *The origins of humankind.* New York, NY: Basic Books.

Leaper, C., & Smith, T. E. (2004). A meta-analytic review of gender variations in children's language use: Talkativeness, affiliative speech, and assertive speech. *Developmental Psychology, 40,* 993–1027.

Leathers, H. D., & Foster, P. (2004). *The world food problem: Tackling causes of undernutrition in the third world.* Boulder, CO: Rienner.

Lee, H. M., Bhat, A., Scholz, J. P., & Galloway, J. C. (2008). Toy-oriented changes during early arm movements: IV: Shoulder–elbow coordination. *Infant Behavior and Development, 31,* 447–469.

Lee, J. C., & Staff, J. (2007). When work matters: The varying impact of work intensity on high school dropouts. *Sociology of Education, 80,* 158–178.

Lee, K., & Freire, A. (2003). Cognitive development. In A. Slater & G. Bremner (Eds.), *An introduction to developmental psychology* (pp. 359–387). Malden, MA: Blackwell.

Lee, M. M. C., Chang, K. S. F., & Chan, M. M. C. (1963). Sexual maturation of Chinese girls in Hong Kong. *Pediatrics, 32,* 389–398.

Lee, R. D., Ensminger, M. E., & Laveist, T. A. (2005). The responsibility continuum: Never primary, coresident and caregiver-heterogeneity in the African-American grandmother experience. *The International Journal of Aging and Human Development, 60*(Special Issue: Diversity among grandparent caregivers), 295–304.

Lee, S. A. S., Davis, B., & MacNeilage, P. (2010). Universal production patterns and ambient language influences in babbling: A cross-linguistic study of Korean- and English-learning infants. *Journal of Child Language, 37,* 293–318.

Lee, V. E., & Burkam, D. T. (2002). *Inequality at the starting gate.* Washington, DC: Economic Policy Institute.

Lefkowitz, E. S., & Gillen, M. M. (2006). 'Sex is just a normal part of life': Sexuality in emerging adulthood. In J. J. Arnett & J. L. Tanner (Eds.), *Emerging adults in America: Coming of age in the 21st century* (pp. 235–255). Washington, DC: American Psychological Association.

Lefkowitz, E. S., Gillen, M. M., Shearer, C. L., & Boone, T. L. (2004). Religiosity, sexual behaviors, and sexual attitudes during emerging adulthood. *Journal of Sex Research, 41,* 150–159.

Lehtinen, M., Paavonen, J., & Apter, D. (2006). Preventing common sexually transmitted infections in adolescents: Time for rethinking. *The European Journal of Contraception and Reproductive Health Care, 11,* 247–249.

Lemish, D. (2007). *Children and television: A global perspective.* Oxford, UK: Blackwell.

Lempers, J. D., & Clark-Lempers, D. S. (1993). A functional comparison of same-sex and opposite-sex friendship during adolescence. *Journal of Adolescent Research, 8,* 89–108.

Lenhart, A., Purcell, K., Smith, A., & Zickuhr, K. (2010). *Social media and mobile Internet use among teens and young adults.* Washington, DC: Pew Research Center.

Leon, K. (2003). Risk and protective factors in young children's adjustment to parental divorce: A review of the research. *Family Relations, 52,* 258–270.

Leonard, L. (2002). Problematizing fertility: "Scientific" accounts and Chadian women's narratives. In M. C. Inhorn & F. van Balen (Eds.), *Infertility around the globe: New thinking on childlessness, gender, and reproductive technologies* (pp. 193–213). Berkeley, CA: University of California Press.

Lerner, R. M. (2006). Developmental science, developmental systems, and contemporary theories of human development. In W. Damon & R. M. Lerner (Eds.), *Handbook of child psychology, Vol. 1: Theoretical models of human development* (5th ed., pp. 1–17). New York, NY: Wiley.

Lerner, R. M., Theokas, C., & Jelicic, H. (2005). Youth as active agents in their own positive development: A developmental systems perspective. In W. Greve, L. Rothermund, & D. Wentura, *The adaptive self: Personal continuity and intentional self-development* (pp. 31–47). Göttingen, Germany: Hogrefe & Huber.

Lessow-Hurley, J. (2005). *The foundations of dual language instruction* (4th ed.). Boston, MA: Allyn & Bacon.

Lestaeghe, R., & Moors, G. (2000). Recent trends in fertility and household formation in the industrialized world. *Review of Population and Social Policy, 9,* 121–170.

Levinson, D. J. (1978). *The seasons of a man's life.* New York, NY: Knopf.

Levine, D. N. (1965). *Wax & gold: tradition and innovation in Ethiopian culture.* University of Chicago Press.

LeVine, R. A. (1977). Child rearing as cultural adaptation. In P. H. Leiderman, S. R. Tulkin, & A. Rosenfeld (Eds.), *Culture and infancy: Variations in the human experience* (pp. 15–27). New York, NY: Academic Press.

LeVine, R. A. (1994). *Child care and culture.* Cambridge, UK: Cambridge University Press.

LeVine, R. A., Dixon, S., LeVine, S. E., Richman, A., Keefer, C., Liederman, P. H., & Brazelton, T. B. (2008). The comparative study of parenting. In R. A. LeVine & R. S. New, *Anthropology and child development: A cross-cultural reader* (pp. 55–65). Malden, MA: Blackwell.

LeVine, R. A., Dixon, S., LeVine, S., Richman, A., Leiderman, P. H., Keefer, C. H., & Brazelton, T. B. (1994). *Childcare and culture: Lessons from Africa.* New York, NY: Cambridge University Press.

LeVine, R. A., & New, R. S. (Eds.) (2008). *Anthropology and child development: A cross-cultural reader.* Malden, MA: Blackwell.

Levi-Strauss, C. (1963). The effectiveness of symbols. In C. Levi-Strauss (Ed.) *Structural anthropology* (pp. 181–200). New York, NY: Basic Books.

Levitin, D. (2007). *This is your brain on music.* New York, NY: Plume.

Lewin, T. (2008, December 3). Higher education may soon be unaffordable for most Americans, report says. *The New York Times,* p. A17.

Lewis, C., Freeman, N. H., Kyriakidou, C., Maridaki-Kassotaki, K., & et al. (1996). Social influences on false belief access: Specific sibling influences or general apprenticeship? *Child Development;Child Development, 67*(6), 2930–2947.

Lewis, M. (2000). The emergence of human emotions. In M. Lewis & J. M. Haviland-Jones (Eds.), *Handbook of emotions* (2nd ed., pp. 265–280). New York, NY: Guilford Press.

Lewis, M. (2002). Early emotional development. In A. Slater & M. Lewis (Eds.), *Introduction to infant development* (pp. 216–232). New York, NY: Oxford University Press.

Lewis, M. (2008). The emergence of human emotions. In L. F. Barrett, J. M. Haviland-Jones, & M. Lewis, M. (Eds.), *Handbook of emotions* (3rd ed., pp. 304–319). New York, NY: Guilford Press.

Lewis, M. (2010). The development of anger. In M. Potegal, G. Stemmler, & C. Spielberger (Eds.), *International handbook of anger: Constituent and concomitant biological, psychological, and social processes* (pp. 177–191). New York, NY: Springer.

Lewis, M., & Brooks-Gunn, J. (1979). *Social cognition and the acquisition of self.* New York, NY: Plenum.

Lewis, M., & Ramsay, D. S. (1999). Effect of maternal soothing on infant stress response. *Child Development, 70*(1), 11–20.

Lewis, M., & Ramsay, D. S. (2004). Development of self-recognition, personal pronoun use, and pretend play during the 2nd year. *Child Development, 75,* 1821–1831.

Lewis, R. (2005). *Human genetics* (6th ed.). New York, NY: McGraw-Hill.

Lewis, S. N., West, A. F., Stein, A., Malmberg, L. E., Bethell, K., Barnes, J., . . . Leach, P. (2009). A comparison of father–infant interaction between primary and non–primary care giving fathers. *Child Care, Health, and Development, 35,* 199–207.

Li, F., Godinet, M. T., & Arnsberger, P. (2010). Protective factors among families with children at risk of maltreatment: Follow up to early school years. *Children and Youth Services Review, 33,* 139–148.

Liben, L. S., & Bigler, R. S. (2002). The developmental course of gender differentiation: Conceptualizing, measuring, and evaluating constructs and pathways. *Monographs of the Society for Research in Child Development, 6*(4, Series. No. 271).

Liben, L. S., & Signorella, M. L. (1993). Gender-schematic processing in children: The role of initial interpretation of stimuli. *Developmental Psychology, 29,* 141–149.

Liben, L. S., Bigler, R. S., & Krogh, H. R. (2001). Pink and blue collar jobs: Children's adjustments of job status and job aspirations in relation to sex of worker. *Journal of Experimental Child Psychology, 79,* 346–363.

Lichter, D. T., Turner, R. N., & Sassler, S. (2010). National estimates of the rise of serial cohabitation. *Social Science Research, 39,* 754–765.

Lieber, E., Nihira, K., & Mink, I. T. (2004). Filial piety, modernization, and the challenges of raising children for Chinese immigrants: Quantitative and qualitative evidence. *Ethos, 32,* 324–347.

Lillard, A. S. (2007). Pretend play in toddlers. In C. A. Brownell & C. B. Kopp (Eds.), *Socioemotional development in the toddler years* (pp. 149–176). New York, NY: Guilford Press.

Lillard, A. S. (2008). *Montessori: The science behind the genius.* New York, NY: Oxford University Press.

Lillard, A. S., & Else-Quest, N. (2006). Evaluating Montessori education. *Science, 313,* 1893–1894.

Lindsay, L. A., & Miescher, S. F. (Eds.). (2003). *Men and masculinities in modern Africa.* Portsmouth, NH: Heinemann.

Lindsey, E., & Colwell, M. (2003). Preschooler's emotional competence: Links to pretend and physical play. *Child Study Journal, 33,* 39–52.

Linebarger, D. L., & Walker, D. (2005). Infants' and Toddlers' Television Viewing and Language Outcomes. *American Behavioral Scientist, 48*(5), 624–645.

Linver, M. R., Brooks-Gunn, J., & Kohen, D. E. (2002). Family processes as pathways from income to young children's development. *Developmental Psychology, 38,* 719–734.

Lipman, E. L., Boyle, M. H., Dooley, M. D., & Offord, D. R. (2002). Child well-being in single-mother families. *Journal of the American Academy of Child and Adolescent Psychiatry, 41,* 75–82.

Lipsitt, L. P. (2003). Crib death: A biobehavioral phenomenon? *Psychological Science, 12,* 164–170.

Liston, C., & Kagan, J. (2002). Brain development: Memory enhancement in early childhood. *Nature, 419*(6910), 896–896.

Litovsky, R. Y., & Ashmead, D. H. (1997). Development of binatural and spatial hearing in infants and children. In R. H. Gilkey & T. R. Anderson (Eds.), *Binaural and spatial hearing in real and virtual environments* (pp. 571–592). Mahwah, NJ: Erlbaum.

Liu, J., Raine, A., Venables, P. H., Dalais, C., & Mednick, S. A. (2003). Malnutrition at age 3 years and lower cognitive ability at age 11 years. *Archives of Paediatric and Adolescent Medicine, 157,* 593–600.

Lloyd, C. B., Grant, M., & Ritchie, A. (2008). Gender differences in time use among adolescents in developing countries: Implications of rising school enrollment rates. *Journal of Research on Adolescence, 18,* 99–120.

Lloyd, C. (Ed.). (2005). *Growing up global: The changing transitions to adulthood in developing countries.* Washington, DC: National Research Council and Institute of Medicine.

Lobel, T. E., Nov-Krispin, N., Schiller, D., Lobel, O., & Feldman, A. (2004). Gender discriminatory behavior during adolescence and young adulthood: A developmental analysis. *Journal of Youth and Adolescence, 33*(6), 535–546.

Loeb, S., Fuller, B., Kagan, S. L., & Carrol, B. (2004). Child care in poor communities: Early learning effects on type, quality, and stability. *Child Development, 75,* 47–65.

Loeber, R., & Burke, J. D. (2011). Developmental pathways in juvenile externalizing and internalizing problems. *Journal of Research on Adolescence, 21,* 34–46.

Loeber, R., Lacourse, E., & Homish, D. L. (2005). Homicide, violence, and developmental trajectories. In R. E. Tremblay, W. W. Hartup, & J. Archer (Eds.), *Developmental origins of aggression* (pp. 202–222). New York, NY: Guilford Press.

Loehlin, J. C., Horn, J. M., & Willerman, L. (1997). Heredity, environment, and IQ in the Texas Adoption Project. In R. J. Sternberg & E. L. Grigrenko (Eds.), *Intelligence, heredity, and environment* (pp. 105–125). New York, NY: Cambridge University Press.

Lohaus, A., Keller, H., Ball, J., Voelker, S., & Elben, C. (2004). Maternal sensitivity in interactions with three- and 12-month-old infants: Stability, structural composition, and developmental consequences. *Infant and Child Development, 13,* 235–252.

Longest, K. C., & Shanahan, M. J. (2007). Adolescent work intensity and substance use: The meditational and moderational roles of parenting. *Journal of Marriage & Family, 69,* 703–720.

Lord, C. E. (2010). Autism: From research to practice. *American Psychologist, 65*(8), 815–826.

Lorenz, J. M., Wooliever, D. E., Jetton, J. R., & Paneth, N. (1998). A quantitative review of mortality and developmental disability in extremely premature newborns. *Archives of Pediatric Medicine, 152,* 425–435.

Lorenz, K. (1957). Companionship in bird life. In C. Scholler (Ed.), *Instinctive behavior: The development of a modern concept* (pp. 83–128). New York, NY: International Universities Press.

Lorenz, K. Z. (1965). *Evolution and the modification of behavior.* Chicago, IL: University of Chicago Press.

Loughlin, C., & Barling, J. (1999). The nature of youth employment. In J. Barling & E. K. Kelloway (Eds.), *Youth workers: Varieties of experience* (pp. 17–36). Washington, DC: American Psychological Association.

Lourenco, O. (2003). Making sense of Turiel's dispute with Kohlberg: The case of the child's moral competence. *New Ideas in Psychology, 21,* 43–68.

Lovas, G. S. (2011). Gender and patterns of language development in mother-toddler and father-toddler dyads. *First Language, 31*(1), 83–108.

Lung, F. W., Chiang, T. L., Lin, S. J., Feng, J. Y., Chen, P. F., & Shu, B. C. (2011). Gender differences of children's developmental trajectory from 6 to 60 months in the Taiwan Birth Cohort Pilot Study. *Research in Developmental Disabilities, 32*(1), 100–106.

Luyckx, K. (2006). *Identity formation in emerging adulthood: Developmental trajectories, antecedents, and consequences.* Dissertation, Catholic University, Leuven, Belgium.

Lynch, M. E. (1991). Gender intensification. In R. M. Lerner, A. C. Petersen, & J. Brooks-Gunn (Eds.), *Encyclopedia of adolescence* (Vol. 1). New York, NY: Garland.

Lynn, R., & Mikk, J. (2007). National differences in intelligence and educational attainment. *Intelligence, 35,* 115–121.

Lynne, S. D., Graber, J. A., Nichols, T. R., Brooks-Gunn, J., & Botvin, G. J. (2007). Links between pubertal timing, peer influences, and externalizing behaviors among urban students followed through middle school. *Journal of Adolescent Health, 40,* e7–e13.

Lyon, E. (2007). *The big book of birth.* New York, NY: Plume.

Lyon, T. D., & Flavell, J. H. (1993). Young children's understanding of forgetting over time. *Child Development, 64,* 789–800.

Lyons-Ruth, K., Bronfman, E., Parsons, E. (1999). Maternal frightened, frightening, or atypical behavior and disorganized infant attachment patterns. *Monographs of the Society for Research in Child Development, 64*(3, Serial No. 258), 67–96.

Lytle, L. J., Bakken, L., & Romig, C. (1997). Adolescent female identity development. *Sex Roles, 37*, 175–185.

Ma, J., Betts, N. M., Horacek, T., Georgiou, C., White, A., & Nitzke, S. (2002). The importance of decisional balance and self-efficacy in relation to stages of change for fruit and vegetable intakes by young adults. *American Journal of Health Promotion, 16*, 157–166.

MacBeth, T. M. (2007). Violence, natural experiments and. In J. J. Arnett (Ed.), *Encyclopedia of children, adolescents, and the media* (Vol. 2, pp. 864–867). Thousand Oaks, CA: Sage.

Maccoby, E. E. (1984). Socialization and developmental change. *Child Development, 55*, 317–328.

Maccoby, E. E. (2002). Gender and group process: A developmental perspective. *Current Directions in Psychological Science, 11*, 54–57.

Maccoby, E. E., & Lewis, C. C. (2003). Less day care or different day care? *Child Development, 76*, 1069–1075.

Maccoby, E., & Martin, J. (1983). Socialization in the context of the family: Parent–child interaction. In P. H. Mussen (Ed.) & E. M. Hetherington (Vol. Ed.), *Handbook of child psychology. Vol. 4: Socialization, personality, and social development* (4th ed., pp. 1–101). New York, NY: Wiley.

MacDorman, M. F., Menacker, F., & Declercq, E. (2010). Trends and characteristics of home and other out-of-hospital births in the United States, 1990–2006. *National Vital Statistics Reports, 58*, 1–14, 16.

Macek, P. (2006). Czech Republic. In J. J. Arnett (Ed.), *International encyclopedia of adolescence* (pp. 206–219). New York, NY: Routledge.

Macek, P., Bejcek, J., & Vanickova, J. (2007). Contemporary Czech emerging adults: Generation growing up in the period of social changes. *Journal of Adolescent Research, 22*, 444–475.

Macfie, J., Cicchetti, D., & Toth, S. L. (2001). The development of dissociation in maltreated preschool-aged children, *Development and Psychopathology, 13*, 233–254.

Machado, A., & Silva, F. J. (2007). Toward a richer view of the scientific method: The role of conceptual analysis. *American Psychologist, 62*, 671–681.

MacKenzie, P. J. (2009). Mother tongue first multilingual education among the tribal communities in India. *International Journal of Bilingual Education and Bilingualism, 12*, 369–385.

Madell, D., & Muncer, S. (2004). Back from the beach but hanging on the telephone? English adolescents' attitudes and experiences of mobile phones and the Internet. *CyberPsychology & Behavior, 73*, 359–367.

Madlon-Kay, D. J. (2002). Maternal assessment of neonatal jaundice after hospital discharge. *The Journal of Family Practice, 51*, 445–448.

Magnuson, M. J., & Dundes, L. (2008). Gender differences in "social portraits" reflected in MySpace profiles. *CyberPsychology & Behavior, 11*, 239–241.

Magnussen, L., Ehiri, J. E., Ejere, H. O. D., & Jolly, P. E. (2004). Interventions to prevent HIV/AIDS among adolescents in less developed countries: Are they effective? *International Journal of Adolescent Medicine & Health, 16*, 303–323.

Maheshwari, A., Hamilton, M., & Bhattacharya, S. (2008). Effect of female age on the diagnostic categories of infertility. *Human Reproduction, 23*, 538–542.

Maimon, D., & Browning, C. R. (2010). Unstructured socializing, collective efficacy, and violent behavior among urban youth. *Criminology: An Interdisciplinary Journal, 48*, 443–474.

Malebo, A., van Eeden, C., & Wissing, M. P. (2007). Sport participation, psychological well-being, and psychosocial development in a group of young black adults. *South African Journal of Psychology, 37*, 188–206.

Males, M. (2010). Is jumping off the roof always a bad idea? A rejoinder on risk taking and the adolescent brain. *Journal of Adolescent Research, 25*, 48–63.

Males, M. (2011). Adolescent apartheid. *Journal of Applied Developmental Psychology, 32*(3), 160–161.

Malina, R. M., Bouchard, C., & Bar-Or, O. (2004). *Growth, maturation and physical activity* (2nd ed.). Champaign, IL: Human Kinetics.

Mandel, D. R., Lusczyk, P. W., & Pisoni, D. B. (1995). Infants' recognition of the sound patterns of their own names. *Psychological Science, 6*, 314–317.

Mange, E. J., & Mange, A. P. (1998). *Basic human genetics* (2nd ed.). Sunderland, MA: Sinauer Associates.

Manis, F. R., Keating, D. P., & Morrison, F. J. (1980). Developmental differences in the allocation of processing capacity. *Journal of Experimental Child Psychology, 29*, 156–169.

Manning, M. L. (1998). Play development from ages eight to twelve. In D. P. Fromberg & D. Bergen, *Play from birth to twelve and beyond* (pp. 154–161). London, UK: Garland.

Maratsos, M. (1998). The acquisition of grammar. In W. Damon (Ed.), & D. Kuhn & R. S. Siegler (Vol. Eds.), *Handbook of child psychology* (5th ed.): *Vol. 2. Cognition, perception and language* (pp. 421–466). New York, NY: Wiley.

Marcia, J. (1966). Development and validation of ego identity status. *Journal of Personality and Social Psychology, 3*, 551–558.

Marcia, J. (1980). Identity in adolescence. In J. Adelson (Ed.), *Handbook of adolescent Psychology* (pp. 159–187). New York, NY: Wiley.

Marcia, J. (1989). Identity and intervention. *Journal of Adolescence, 12*, 401–410.

Marcia, J. E. (1999). Representational thought in ego identity, psychotherapy, and psychosocial developmental theory. In I. E. Siegel (Ed.), *Development of mental representation: Theories and applications* (pp. 391–414). Mahwah, NJ: Erlbaum.

Marcia, J. E. (2010). Life transitions and stress in the context of psychosocial development. In T. W. Miller (Ed.), *Handbook of stressful transitions across the lifespan* (pp. 19–34). New York, NY: Springer.

Marcon, R. A. (1999). Positive relationships between parent–school involvement and public school inner-city preschoolers' development and academic performance. *School Psychology Review, 28*, 395–412.

Marcotte, D., Fortin, L., Potvin, P., & Papillon, M. (2002). Gender differences in depressive symptoms during adolescence: Role of gender-typed characteristics, self-esteem, body image, stressful life events, and pubertal status. *Journal of Emotional and Behavioral Disorders, 10*, 29–42.

Marcovitch, S., Zelazo, P., & Schmuckler, M. (2003). The effect of the number of A trials on performance on the A-not-B task. *Infancy, 3*, 519–529.

Markey, P. M., & Markey, C. N. (2007). Romantic ideals, romantic obtainment, and relationship experiences: The complementarity of interpersonal traits among romantic partners. *Journal of Social and Personal Relationships, 24*, 517–533.

Markman, E. M., & Jaswal, V. K. (2004). Acquiring and using a grammatical form class: Lessons from the proper-count distinction. In D. G. Hall & S. R. Waxman (Eds.), *Weaving a lexicon* (pp. 371–409). Cambridge, MA: MIT Press.

Markus, H. R., & Kitayama, S. (2003). Culture, self, and the reality of the social. *Psychological Inquiry, 14*, 277–283.

Markus, H., & Kitayama, S. (1991). Culture and the self: Implications for cognition, emotion, and motivation. *Psychological Review, 98*, 224–253.

Markus, H., & Nurius, R. (1986). Possible selves. *American Psychologist, 41*, 954–969.

Marlier, L, Schaal, B., & Soussignan, R. (1998). Neonatal responsiveness to the odor of amniotic and lacteal fluids: A test of perinatal chemosensory continuity. *Child Development, 69*, 611–623.

Marlow, N., Wolke, D., Bracewell, M. A., & Samara, M. (2005). Neurologic and developmental disability at six years of age after extremely preterm births. *New England Journal of Medicine, 352*, 9–19.

Marsh, H. W., & Ayotte, V. (2003). Do multiple dimensions of self-concept become more differentiated with age? The differential distinctiveness hypothesis. *Journal of Educational Psychology, 95*, 687–706.

Marsh, H., & Kleitman, S. (2005). Consequences of employment during high school: Character building, subversion of academic goals, or a threshold? *American Educational Research Journal, 42*, 331–369.

Marsh, M., & Ronner, W. (1996). *The empty cradle: Infertility in America from colonial times to the present*. Baltimore, MD: Johns Hopkins University Press.

Marshall, M. (1979). *Weekend warriors: alcohol in a Micronesian culture*. Explorations in world ethnology (1st ed.). Palo Alto, CA: Mayfield.

Marshall, W. (1978). Puberty. In F. Falkner & J. Tanner (Eds.), *Human growth* (Vol. 2). New York, NY: Plenum.

Martin, A., Brooks-Gunn, J., Klebanov, P., Buka, S., & McCormick, M. (2008). Long-term maternal effects of early childhood intervention: Findings from the Infant Health and Development Program (IHDP). *Journal of Applied Developmental Psychology, 29*, 101–117.

Martin, C. K., & Fabes, R. A. (2001). The stability and consequences of young children's same-sex peer interactions. *Developmental Psychology, 37*, 431–446.

Martin, C. L., & Rubie, D. (2004). Children's search for gender cues: Cognitive perspectives on gender development. *Current Directions in Psychological Science, 13*, 67–70.

Martin, J. A., Hamilton, B. E., Sutton, P. D., Ventura, S. J., Menacker, F., & Munson, M. L (2005). Births: Final data for 2003. *National vital statistics Reports, 54*, 1–116.

Martin, J. A., Park, M. M., & Sutton, P. D. (2002). Births: Preliminary data for 2001. *National Vital Statistics Reports, 50*(10). Hyattsville, MD: National Center for Health Statistics.

Martin, J. L, & Ross, H. S. (2005). Sibling aggression: Sex differences and parents' reactions. *International Journal of Behavioral Development, 29,* 129–138.

Martin, P., & Midgley, E. (2010). *Immigration in America, 2010.* Washington, DC: Population Reference Bureau.

Martin, W., & Freitas, M. (2002). Mean mortality among Brazilian left- and right-handers: Modification or selective elimination. *Laterality, 7,* 31–44.

Martini, M. (1996). "What's new?" at the dinner table: Family dynamics during mealtimes in two cultural groups in Hawaii. *Early Development and Parenting, 5*(1), 23–34.

Martins, C., & Gaffan, E. A. (2000). Effects of maternal depression on patterns of infant–mother attachment: A meta-analytic investigation. *Journal of Child Psychology and Psychiatry, 41,* 737–746.

Martlew, M., & Connolly, K. J. (1996). Human figure drawings by schooled and unschooled children in Papua New Guinea. *Child Development, 67,* 2743–2762.

Marván, M. L., & Trujillo, P. (2010). Menstrual socialization, beliefs, and attitudes concerning menstruation in rural and urban Mexican women. *Health Care for Women International, 31,* 53–67.

Mascolo, M. F., & Fischer, K. W. (2007). The codevelopment of self and socio-moral emotions during the toddler years. In C. A. Brownell & C. B. Kopp (Eds.), *Socioemotional development in the toddler years* (pp. 66–99). New York, NY: Guilford Press.

Masten, A. S. (2001). Ordinary magic: Resilience processes in development. *American Psychologist, 56*(3), 227–238.

Masten, A. S. (2007). Competence, resilience, and development in adolescence: Clues for prevention science. In D. Romer & E. F. Walker (Eds.), *Adolescent psychopathology and the developing brain: Integrating brain and prevention science* (pp. 31–52). New York, NY: Oxford University Press.

Masten, A. S., Obradovic, J., & Burt, K. B. (2006). Resilience in embracing emerging adulthood: Developmental perspectives on continuity and transformation. In J. J. Arnett & J. L. Tanner (Eds.), *Emerging adults in America: Coming of age in the 21st century* (pp. 173–190). Washington, DC: American Psychological Association.

Matlin, M. W. (2004). *The psychology of women* (5th ed.). Belmont, CA: Wadsworth.

Matsumoto, D., & Yoo, S. H. (2006). Toward a new generation of cross-cultural research. *Perspectives on Psychological Science, 1,* 234–250.

Mattson, S. N., Roesch, S. C., Fagerlund, Å., Autti-Rämö, I., Jones, K. L., May, P. A., . . . CIFASD. (2010). Toward a neurobehavioral profile of fetal alcohol spectrum disorders. *Alcoholism: Clinical and Experimental Research, 34,* 1640–1650.

Matusov, E., & Hayes, R. (2000). Sociocultural critique of Piaget and Vygotsky. *New Ideas in Psychology, 18,* 215–239.

Maynard, A. E. (2002). Cultural teaching: The development of teaching skills in Zinacantec Maya sibling interactions. *Child Development, 73*(3), 969–982.

Maynard, A. E. (2008). What we thought we knew and how we came to know it: Four decades of cross-cultural research from a Piagetian point of view. *Human Development, 51*(Special issue: Celebrating a legacy of theory with new directions for research on human development), 56–65.

Maynard, A. E., & Greenfield, P. M. (2003). Implicit cognitive development in cultural tools and children: Lessons from Maya Mexico. *Cognitive Development, 18*(Special Issue: The sociocultural construction of implicit knowledge), 485–510.

Maynard, A. E., & Martini, M. I. (Eds.). (2005). *Learning in cultural context: Family, peers, and school.* New York, NY: Kluwer.

Mayo Clinic Staff. (2011). *Stages of Labor: Baby, it's time!* Retrieved from http://www.mayoclinic.com/health/stages-of-labor/PR00106/NSECTION GROUP=2

Mayseless, O., & Scharf, M. (2003). What does it mean to be an adult? The Israeli experience. In J. J. Arnett & N. Galambos (Eds.), *New directions in child and adolescent development* (Vol. 100, pp. 5–20). San Francisco, CA: Jossey-Boss.

Mazuka, R., Kondo, T., & Hayashi, A. (2008). Japanese mothers' use of specialized vocabulary in infant-directed speech: Infant–directed vocabulary in Japanese. In N. Masataka (Ed.), *The origins of language: Unraveling evolutionary forces* (pp. 39–58). New York, NY: Springer.

Mazur, E., & Kozarian, L. (2010). Self-presentation and interaction in blogs of adolescents and young emerging adults. *Journal of Adolescent Research, 25,* 124–144.

McAlister, A., & Peterson, C. (2007). A longitudinal study of child siblings and theory of mind development. *Cognitive Development, 22,* 258–270.

McArdle, W. D., Katch, F. I., & Katch, V. L. (2009). *Exercise physiology: Nutrition, energy, and human performance.* Lippincott Williams & Wilkins.

McCarthy, G., & Maughan, B. (2010). Negative childhood experiences and adult love relationships: The role of internal working models of attachment. *Attachment & Human Development, 12*(5), 445–461.

McCartney, K., & Berry, D. (2009). Whether the environment matters more for children in poverty. In K. McCartney and R. A. Weinberg (Eds.), *Experience and development: A festschrift in honor of Sandra Wood Scarr* (pp. 99–124). New York, NY: Psychology Press.

McCarty, M. E., Clifton, R. K., & Collard, R. R. (2001). The beginnings of tool use by infants and toddlers. *Infancy, 2*(2), 233–256.

McClure, V. S. (2000). *Infant massage—Revised Edition: A handbook for loving parents.* New York, NY: Bantam.

McDonough, P. M., & Calderone, S. (2006). The meaning of money: Perceptual differences between college counselors and low-income families about college costs and financial aid. *American Behavioral Scientist, 49,* 1703–1718.

McDowell, M. A., Brody, D. J., & Hughes, J. P. (2007). Has age at menarche changed? Results from the National Health and Nutrition Examination Survey (NHANES) 1999–2004. *Journal of Adolescent Health, 40,* 227–231.

McFalls, J. A. (2007). Population: A lively introduction. *Population Bulletin, 62,* 1–31.

McGregor, I. A., Thomson, A. M., & Billewicz, W. Z. (1968). The development of primary teeth in children from a group of Gambian villages, and critical examination of its use for estimating age. *British Journal of Nutrition, 22*(02), 307–314.

McGue, M., & Christensen, K. (2002). The heritability of level and rate-of-change in cognitive functioning in Danish twins aged 70 years and older. *Experimental Aging Research, 28,* 435–451.

McGuire, S., Manke, B., Eftekhari, A., & Dunn, J. (2000). Children's perceptions of sibling conflict during middle childhood: Issues and sibling (Dis)similarity. *Social Development, 9,* 173–190.

McHale, S. M., Crouter, A. C., Tucker, C. J. (2001). Free-time activities in middle childhood: Links with adjustment in early adolescence. *Child Development, 72,* 1764–1778.

McHale, S., Dariotis, J., & Kauh, T. (2003). Social development and social relationships in middle childhood. In R. Lerner & M. Easterbrooks (Eds.), *Handbook of psychology: Developmental psychology* (Vol. 6., pp. 241–265). New York, NY: Wiley.

McKenna, J. J., & McDade, T. (2005). Why babies should never sleep alone: A review of the co-sleeping controversy in relation to SIDS, bedsharing, and breastfeeding. *Paediatric Respiratory Reviews, 6,* 134–152.

McKenzie, A. (2004). *The safe baby book: The complete safety guide for parents and carers of babies and toddlers.* Victoria, Canada: Trafford.

McKinsey Global Institute. (2010). *Lions on the move: The progress and potential of Africa's economies.* Washington, DC: Author.

McKnight Investigators. (2003). Risk factors for the onset of eating disorders in adolescent girls: Results on the McKnight longitudinal risk factor study. *American Journal of Psychiatry, 160,* 248–254.

McKnight, A. J., & Peck, R. C. (2002). Graduated licensing: What works? *Injury Prevention, 8*(Suppl. 2), ii32–ii38.

McLoyd, V. C., & Smith, J. (2002). Physical discipline and behavior problems in African-American, European-American, and Hispanic children: Emotional support as a moderator. *Journal of Marriage and the Family, 64,* 40–53.

McLuhan, M. (1960). *The Gutenberg galaxy.* Toronto, Canada: University of Toronto Press.

McNamara, F., & Sullivan, C. E. (2000). Obstructive sleep apnea in infants. *Journal of Pediatrics, 136,* 318–323.

Mead, G. H. (1934). *Mind, self, and society.* Chicago, IL: University of Chicago Press.

Mead, M. (1930/2001). *Growing up in New Guinea.* New York, NY: Anchor.

Mead, Margaret. [1935/1968]. *Sex and temperament: In three primitive societies.* New York, NY: Dell.

Mechling, J. (2008). Toilet training. In *Encyclopedia of children and childhood in history and society.* Retrieved from http://www.faqs.org/childhood/Th-W/Toilet-Training.html

Medina, J. A. S., Rubio, D. A., & Benítez, M. L. D. la M. (2009). Private speech beyond childhood: Testing the developmental hypothesis. In A. Winsler, C. Fernyhough, & I. Montero (Eds.), *Private speech, executive functioning, and the development of verbal self-regulation* (pp. 188–197). New York, NY: Cambridge University Press.

Medline. (2008). Kwashiorkor. *Medline Plus medical encyclopedia*. Retrieved from http://www.nlm.nih.gov/MEDLINEPLUS/ency/article/001604.htm

Meeus, W. (2007). Netherlands. In J. J. Arnett, R. Ahmed, B. Nsamenang, T. S. Saraswathi, & R. Silbereisen (Eds.), *International encyclopedia of adolescence* (pp. 666–680). New York, NY: Routledge.

Meeus, W., Iedema, J., Helsen, M., & Vollebergh, W. (1999). Patterns of adolescent identity development: Review of literature and longitudinal analysis. *Developmental Review, 19,* 419–461.

Meltzoff, A. N., & Moore, M. K. (1994). Imitation, memory, and the representation of persons. *Infant Behavior and Development, 17,* 83–99.

Mendle, J., Turkheimer, E., & Emery, R. E. (2007). Detrimental psychological outcomes associated with early pubertal timing in adolescent girls. *Developmental Review, 27,* 151–171.

Menella, J. (2000, June). The psychology of eating. Paper presented at the annual meeting of the American Psychological Society, Miami, FL.

Menon, M., Tobin, D. D., Corby, B. C., Menon, M., Hodges, E. V. E., & Perry, D. G. (2007). The developmental costs of high self-esteem for antisocial children. *Child Development 78(6),* 1627–1639.

Menon, M., Tobin, D. D. Facoetti, A., Lorusso, M. L., Paganoni, P., Cattaneo, C., . . . Mascetti, G. G. (2003). Auditory and visual automatic attention deficits in developmental dyslexia. *Cognitive Brain Research*, 16(2), 185–191.

Mensch, B. S., Bruce, J., & Greene, M. E. (1998). *The uncharted passage: Girls' adolescence in the developing world*. New York, NY: Population Council.

Menyuk, P., Liebergott, J., & Schultz, M. (1995). *Early language development in full-term and premature infants*. Hillsdale, NJ: Erlbaum.

Merewood, A., Mehta, S. D., Chamberlain, L. B., Phillipp, B. L., & Bauchner, H. (2005). Breastfeeding rates in U.S. baby-friendly hospitals: Results of a national survey. *Pediatrics, 116,* 628–634.

Merten, S., Dratva, J., & Achermann-Liebrich, U. (2005). Do baby-friendly hospitals influence breastfeeding duration on a national level? *Pediatrics, 116,* c702–c708.

Merz, E. (2006). *Ultrasound in obstetrics and gynecology*. Stuttgart, Germany: Verlag.

Mesman, J., van IJzendoorn, M. H., Bakermans-Kranenburg, M. J. (2009). The many faces of the Still-Face Paradigm: A review and meta–analysis. *Developmental Review, 29,* 120–162.

Messinger, D. S., & Lester, B. M. (2008). Prenatal substance exposure and human development. In A. Fogel, B. J. King, & S. G. Shanker (Eds.), *Human development in the 21st century: Visionary policy ideas from systems scientists* (pp. 225–232). Bethesda, MD: Council on Human Development.

Meyers, C., Adam, R., Dungan, J., & Prenger, V. (1997). Aneuploidy in twin gestations: When is maternal age advanced? *Obstetrics and Gynecology, 89,* 248–251.

Michael, K. D., & Crowley, S. L. (2002). How effective are treatments for child and adolescent depression? A meta-analytic review. *Clinical Psychology Review, 22,* 247–269.

Michael, R. T., Gagnon, J. H., Laumann, E. O., & Kolata, G. (1995). *Sex in America: A definitive study*. New York, NY: Warner Books.

Milan, S., Snow, S., & Belay, S. (2007). The context of preschool children's sleep: Racial/ethnic differences in sleep locations, routines, and concerns. *Journal of Family Psychology, 21*(Special issue: *Carpe noctem*: Sleep and family processes), 20–28.

Miller, J. G. (2004). The cultural deep structure of psychological theories of social development. In R. J. Sternberg & E. L. Grigorenko (Eds.), *Culture and competence: Contexts of life success* (pp. 111–138). Washington, DC: American Psychological Association.

Miller, P. J., Fung, H., & Mintz, J. (2010). Self-construction through narrative practices: A Chinese and American comparison of early socialization. In R. A. LeVine (Ed.), *Psychological anthropology: A reader on self in culture*, Blackwell anthologies in social and cultural anthropology (pp. 193–219). Wiley-Blackwell: Wiley-Blackwell.

Miller, P. J., Wiley, A. R., Fung, H., & Liang, C. H. (1997). Personal storytelling as a medium of socialization in Chinese and American families. *Child Development, 68,* 557–568.

Miller-Johnson, S., Costanzo, P. R., Cole, J. D., Rose, M. R., & Browne, D. C. (2003). Peer social structure and risk-taking behaviour among African American early adolescents. *Journal of Youth & Adolescence, 32,* 375–384.

Millman, R. P. (2005). Excessive sleepiness in adolescents and young adults: Causes, consequences, and treatment strategies. *Pediatrics, 115,* 1774–1786.

Mills, N., Daker-White, G., Graham, A., Campbell, R., & The Chlamydia Screening Studies (ClaSS) Group. (2006). Population screening for *Chlamydia trachomatis* infection in the UK: A qualitative study of the experiences of those screened. *Family Practice, 23,* 550–557.

Minami, M., & McCabe, A. (1995). Rice balls and bear hunts: Japanese and North American family narrative patterns. *Journal of Child Language, 22,* 423–445.

Mindell, J. A., Sadeh, A., Kohyama, J., & How, T. H. (2010). Parental behaviors and sleep outcomes in infants and toddlers: A cross-cultural comparison. *Sleep Medicine, 11,* 393–399.

Mintz, T. H. (2005). Linguistic and conceptual influences on adjective acquisition in 24- and 36-month-olds. *Developmental Psychology, 41,* 17–29.

Mishna, F., Newman, P. A., Daley, A., & Solomon, S. (2009). Bullying of lesbian and gay youth: A qualitative investigation. *British Journal of Social Work, 39,* 1598–1614.

Mistry, J., & Saraswathi, T. (2003). The cultural context of child development. In R. Lerner & M. Easterbrooks (Eds.), *Handbook of psychology: Developmental psychology* (Vol. 6, pp. 267–291). New York, NY: Wiley.

Mitchell, A., & Boss, B. J. (2002). Adverse effects of pain on the nervous systems of newborns and young children: A review of the literature. *Journal of Neuroscience and Nursing, 34,* 228–235.

Moffitt, T. E. (2003). Life-course-persistent and adolescence-limited antisocial behavior: A 10-year research review and a research agenda. In B. B. Lahey & T. E. Moffitt (Eds.), *Causes of conduct disorder and juvenile delinquency* (pp. 49–75). New York, NY: Guilford Press.

Moffitt, T. E. (2007). A review of research on the taxonomy of life-course persistent versus adolescence-limited antisocial behavior. In D. J. Flannery, A. T. Vazsonyi, & I. D. Waldman (Eds.), *The Cambridge handbook of violent behavior and aggression* (pp. 49–74). New York, NY: Cambridge University Press.

Moghadam, V. M. (2004). Patriarchy in transition: Women and the changing family in the Middle East. *Journal of Comparative Family Studies, 35,* 137–162.

Monitoring the Future. (2003). *ISR study finds drinking and drug use decline after college*. Ann Arbor, MI: Author. Retrieved from www.umich.edu/newsinfo/releases/2002/Jan02/r013002a.html

Montessori, M. (1964). *The Montessori method*. New York, NY: Schocken.

Montgomery, M. J. (2005). Psychosocial intimacy and identity: From early adolescence to emerging adulthood. *Journal of Adolescent Research, 20,* 346–374.

Moon, R. Y., Kington, M., Oden, R., Iglesias, J., & Hauck, F. R. (2007). Physician recommendations regarding SIDS risk reduction: A national survey of pediatricians and family physicians. *Clinical Pediatrics, 46,* 791–800.

Moore, D. (2001). *The dependent gene*. New York, NY: Freeman.

Moore, G. A., Cohn, J. F., & Campbell, S. B. (1997). Mothers' affective behavior with infant siblings: Stability and change. *Developmental Psychology, 33,* 856–860.

Moore, J. L. (2010). The neuropsychological functioning of prisoners of war following repatriation. In C. H. Kennedy & J. L. Moore (Eds.), *Military neuropsychology* (pp. 267–295). New York, NY: Springer.

Moore, K. A., Chalk, R., Scarpa, J., & Vandivere, S. (2002, August). Family strengths: Often overlooked, but real. *Child Trends Research Brief,* 1–8.

Moore, K. L., & Persaud, T. V. N. (2003). *Before we are born* (6th ed.). Philadelphia, PA: Saunders.

Moore, S., & Rosenthal, D. (2006). *Sexuality in adolescence: Current trends*. New York, NY: Routledge.

Morawska, A., & Sanders, M. (2011). Parental use of time out revisited: A useful or harmful parenting strategy? *Journal of Child and Family Studies, 20,* 1–8.

Morelli, G., Rogoff, B., Oppenheim, D., & Goldsmith, D. (1992). Cultural variation in infants' sleeping arrangements: Question of independence. *Developmental Psychology, 39,* 604–613.

Morelli, G., & Rothbaum, F. (2007). Situating the child in context: Attachment relationships and self-regulation in different cultures. In S. Kitayama & D. Cohen (Eds.), *Handbook of cultural psychology* (pp. 500–527). New York, NY: Guilford Press.

Moretti, M. M., & Wiebe, V. J. (1999). Self-discrepancy in adolescence: Own and parental standpoints on the self. *Merrill-Palmer Quarterly, 45,* 624–649.

Morgan, M. A., Cragan, J. D., Goldenberg, R. L., Rasmussen, S. A., & Schulkin, J. (2010)b. Management of prescription and nonprescription drug use during pregnancy. *Journal of Maternal–Fetal and Neonatal Medicine, 23,* 813–819.

Morra, S., Gobbo, C., Marini, Z., & Sheese, R. (2008). *Cognitive development: Neo-Piagetian perspectives*. New York, NY: Taylor & Francis.

Morrongiello, B. A., Fenwick, K. D., Hillier, L., & Chance, G. (1994). Sound localization in newborn human infants. *Developmental Psychobiology, 27,* 519–538.

Mortimer, J. T. (2003). *Working and growing up in America.* Cambridge, MA: Harvard University Press.

Mortimer, J. T., Vuolo, M., Staff, J., Wakefield, S., & Xie, W. (2008). Tracing the timing of "career" acquisition in a contemporary youth cohort. *Work and Occupations, 35,* 44–84.

Mortimer, J. T., Zimmer-Gembeck, M. J., Holmes, M., & Shanahan, M. J. (2002). The process of occupational decision making: Patterns during the transition to adulthood. *Journal of Vocational Behavior, 61,* 439–465.

Mosby, L., Rawls, A. W., Meehan, A. J., Mays, E., & Pettinari, C. J. (1999). Troubles in interracial talk about discipline: An examination of African American child rearing narratives. *Journal of Comparative Family Studies, 30,* 489–521.

Motola, M., Sinisalo, P., & Guichard, J. (1998). Social habitus and future plans. In J. Nurmi (Ed.), *Adolescents, cultures, and conflicts* (pp. 43–73). New York, NY: Garland.

Mugford, M. (2006). Cost effectiveness of prevention and treatment of neonatal respiratory distress (RDS) with exogenous surfactant: What has changed in the last three decades? *Early Human Development, 82,* 105–115.

Muller, F., Rebiff, M., Taillandier, A., Qury, J. F., & Mornet, E. (2000). Parental origin of the extra chromosome in prenatally diagnosed fetal trisomy. *Human Genetics, 106,* 340–344.

Mumme, D. L., & Fernald, A. (2003). The infant as onlooker: Learning from emotional reactions observed in a television scenario. *Child Development, 74,* 221–237.

Munro, G., & Adams, G. R. (1977). Ego-identity formation in college students and working youth. *Developmental Psychology, 13,* 523–524.

Muret-Wagstaff, S., & Moore, S. G. (1989). The Hmong in America: Infant behavior and rearing practices. In J. K. Nugent, B. M. Lester, & T. B. Brazelton (Eds.), *Biology, culture, and development* (Vol. 1, pp. 319–339). Norwood, NJ: Ablex.

Murkoff, H. E., Eisenberg, A., Mazel, S., & Hathaway, S. E. (2003). *What to expect the first year* (2nd ed.). New York, NY: Workman.

Murkoff, H., & Mazel, S. (2008). *What to expect when you're expecting.* New York, NY: Workman.

Murnane, R. J., & Levy, F. (1997). *Teaching the new basic skills: Principles for educating children to thrive in a changing economy.* New York, NY: Free Press.

Murray-Close, D., Ostrov, J., & Crick, N. (2007). A short-term longitudinal study of growth and relational aggression during middle childhood: Associations with gender, friendship, intimacy, and internalizing problems. *Development and Psychopathology, 19,* 187–203.

Mustillo, S., Worthman, C., Erkanli, A., Keeler, G., Angold, A., Costello, E. J. (2003). Obesity and psychiatric disorder: Developmental trajectories. *Pediatrics, 111,* 851–859.

Mutti, D. O., Mitchell, G. L., Moeschberger, M. L., Jones, L. A., & Zadnik, K. (2002). Parental myopia, near work, school achievement, and children's refractive error. *Investigative Opthamology and Visual Science, 43,* 3633–3640.

Nakano, H., & Blumstein, S. E. (2004). Deficits in thematic processes in Broca's and Wernicke's aphasia. *Brain and Language, 88,* 96–107.

Napier, K., & Meister, K. (2000). *Growing healthy kids: A parents' guide to infant and child nutrition.* New York, NY: American Council on Science and Health.

Narayanan, U., & Warren, S. T. (2006). Neurobiology of related disorders: Fragile X syndrome. In S. O. Moldin & J. L. R. Rubenstein, *Understanding autism: From basic neuroscience to treatment* (pp. 113–131). Washington, DC: Taylor & Francis.

National Association for the Education of Young Children. (2010). 2010 NAEYC standards for initial & advanced early childhood professional preparation programs. Washington, DC: Author.

National Center for Children, Families and Communities. (n.d.). *Nurse-family partnership.* Retrieved from http://www.nccfc.org/pdfs/descriptionNFP.pdf

National Center for Education in Maternal and Child Health. (2002). *Bright futures in practice: Nutrition pocket guide.* Washington, DC: Georgetown University.

National Center for Education Statistics. (2011). The condition of education: 2011. Washington, DC: USDOE.

National Center for Health Statistics. (2000a). *Health United States, 1999.* Atlanta, GA: Centers for Disease Control and Prevention.

National Center for Health Statistics. (2000b). *Growth charts.* Atlanta, GA: Centers for Disease Control and Prevention.

National Center for Health Statistics. (2004). *Health United States, 2003.* Atlanta, GA: Centers for Disease Control and Prevention.

National Center for Health Statistics. (2005). *Health, United States, 2005. With chartbook on trends in the health of Americans.* Hyattsville, MD: Author.

National Center for Health Statistics. (2009). *Health, United States, 2009.* Hyattsville, MD: Centers for Disease Control and Prevention.

National Council of Youth Sports. (2002). *Report on trends and participation in youth sports.* Stuart, FL: Author.

National Highway Traffic Safety Administration. (2011). *Traffic safety facts, 2009 data:* Older population. Washington, DC: U.S. Department of Transportation.

National Institute of Child Health and Development (NICHD). (2004). Follow-up care of high-risk infants. *Pediatrics, 114,* 1377–1397.

National Institute of Drug Abuse. (2001). *Marijuana.* Washington, DC: National Institutes of Health.

National Opinion Research Center. (2007). General Social Survey 1972–2006. Chicago, IL: National Opinion Research Center.

National Sudden and Unexpected Infant/Child Death & Pregnancy Loss Resource Center. (2010). *Statistics overview.* Retrieved from http://sidcenter.org/Statistics.html

National Women's Health Information Center. (2011). *Infertility.* Retrieved from http://www.womenshealth.gov/faq/infertility.cfm#f

Natsopoulos, D., Kiosseoglou, G., Xeroxmeritou, A., & Alevriadou, A. (1998). Do the hands talk on the mind's behalf? Differences in language between left- and right-handed children. *Brain and Language, 64,* 182–214.

Natsuaki, M. N., Ge, X., Reiss, D., & Neiderhiser, J. M. (2009). Aggressive behavior between siblings and the development of externalizing problems: Evidence from a genetically sensitive study. *Developmental Psychology, 45,* 1009–1018.

Neberich, W., Penke, L., Lenhart, J., & Asendorph, J. B. (2010). Family of origin, age at menarche, and reproductive strategies: A test of four evolutionary–developmental models. *European Journal of Developmental Psychology, 7,* 153–177.

Nelson, D. A., Robinson, C. C., & Hart, C. H. (2005). Relational and physical aggression of preschool-age children: Peer status linkages across informants. *Early Education and Development, 16,* 115–139.

Nelson, L. J., & Chen, X. (2007). Emerging adulthood in China: The role of social and cultural factors. *Child Development Perspectives, 1,* 86–91.

Nelson, L. J., Badger, S., & Wu, B. (2004). The influence of culture in emerging adulthood: Perspectives of Chinese college students. *International Journal of Behavioral Development, 28,* 26–36.

Nesbitt, R. E. (2009). *Intelligence and how to get it: Why schools and cultures matter.* New York, NY: Norton.

Neto, F. (2002). Acculturation strategies among adolescents from immigrant families in Portugal. *International Journal of Intercultural Relations, 26,* 17–38.

Newcombe, N. S., Lloyd, M. E., & Ratliff, K. R. (2007). Development of episodic and autobiographical memory: A cognitive neuroscience perspective. In R. V. Kail (Ed.), *Advances in child development and behavior* (Vol. 35, pp. 37–85). San Diego, CA: Elsevier Academic Press.

Newcombe, N., & Huttenlocher, J. (1992). Children's early ability to solve perspective-taking problems. *Developmental Psychology, 28*(4), 635–643.

Newman, R. S. (2008). The level of detail in infants' word learning. *Current Directions in Psychological Science, 17*(3), 229–232.

Newton, N., & Newton, M. (2003). Childbirth in cross–cultural perspective. In L. Dundes (Ed.), *The manner born: Birth rites in cross–cultural perspective* (pp. 9–32). Walnut Creek, CA: AltaMira.

NICHD (National Institute of Child Health and Human Development) Early Child Care Research Network. (1997). The effects of infant child care on infant–mother attachment security: Results of the NICHD Study of Early Child Care. *Child Development, 68,* 860–879.

NICHD Early Child Care Research Network. (2000). Factors associated with fathers' caregiving activities and sensitivity with young children. *Developmental Psychology, 14,* 200–219.

NICHD Early Child Care Research Network (2004). Trajectories of physical aggression from toddlerhood to middle childhood. *Monographs of the Society for Research in Child Development, 69* (Serial No. 278), vii–129.

NICHD Early Child Care Research Network (2006a). Infant-mother attachment classification: Risk and protection in relation to changing maternal caregiving quality. *Developmental Psychology, 42,* 38–58.

NICHD Early Child Care Research Network (2006b). *Child care and child development: Results from the NICHD study of early child care and youth development.* New York, NY: Guilford.

Nichols, S. R., Svetlova, M., & Brownell, C. A. (2009). The role of social understanding and empathic disposition in young children's responsiveness to distress in parents and peers. *Cognition, Brain, Behavior: An Interdisciplinary Journal, 13*(4), 449–478.

Nicholson, J. M., Sanders, M. R., Halford, W. K., Phillips, M., & Whitton, S. W. (2008). The prevention and treatment of children's adjustment problems in stepfamilies. In J. Pryor (Ed.), *The international handbook of stepfamilies: Policy and practice in legal, research, and clinical environments* (pp. 485–521). Hoboken, NJ: Wiley.

Nichter, M. (2001). *Fat talk: What girls and their parents say about dieting.* Cambridge, MA: Harvard University Press.

Nickerson, A. B., & Nagle, R. J. (2005). Parent and peer attachment in late childhood and early adolescence. *Journal of Early Adolescence, 25,* 223–249.

Nielsen, S. J., Siega-Riz, A. M., & Popkin, B. M. (2002). Trends in energy intake between 1977 and 1986: Similar shifts seen across age groups. *Obesity Research, 10,* 370–378.

Nihart, M. A. (1993). Growth and development of the brain. *Journal of Child and Adolescent Psychiatric and Mental Health Nursing, 6,* 39–40.

Noia, G., Cesari, E., Ligato, M. S., Visconti, D., Tintoni, M., Mappa, I., . . . Caruso, A. (2008). Pain in the fetus. *Neonatal Pain, 2,* 45–55.

Nolan, K., Schell, L. M., Stark, A. D., & Gomez, M. I. (2002). Longitudinal study of energy and nutrient intakes for infants from low-income, urban families. *Public Health Nutrition, 5,* 405–412.

Noller, P. (2005). Sibling relationships in adolescence: Learning and growing together. *Personal Relationships, 12,* 1–22.

Nottelmann, E. D., Susman, E. J., Blue, J. H., Inoff-Germain, G., Dorn, L. D., Loriaux, D. L., Cutler Jr., G. B., et al. (1987). Gonadal and adrenal hormone correlates of adjustment in early adolescence. In R. M. Lerner T. T. Foch (Ed.), Biological-psychosocial interactions in early adolescence, Child psychology. (pp. 303–323). Hillsdale, NJ, England: Erlbaum.

Novik, T. S., Hervas, A., Ralston, S. J., Dalsgaard, S., Rodrigues Pereira, R., Lorenzo, M. J., & ADORE Study Group. (2006). Influence of gender on attention deficit/hyperactivity disorder in Europe—ADORE. *European Child & Adolescent Psychiatry, 15*(Suppl. 1), 5–24.

Nsamengnang, B. A. (1992). Perceptions of parenting among the Nso of Cameroon. *Father–child relations: Cultural and biosocial contexts* (pp. 321–344). New York, NY: De Gruyter.

Nugent, K. J., Petrauskas, B. J., & Brazelton, T. B. (Eds.). (2009). *The newborn as a person: Enabling healthy infant development worldwide.* Hoboken, NJ: Wiley.

Nugent, K., & Brazelton, T. B. (2000). Preventive infant mental health: Uses of the Brazelton scale. In J. D. Osofsky & H. E. Fitzgerald (Eds.), *WAIMH Handbook of infant mental health* (Vol. 2). New York, NY: Wiley.

Nuland, S. B. (2003). *The doctor's plague: Germs, childbed fever, and the strange story of Ignac Semmelweis.* New York, NY: Norton.

Nwokah, E. E., Hsu, H., Davies, P., & Fogel, A. (1999). The integration of laughter and speech in vocal communication: A dynamic systems perspective. *Journal of Speech and Hearing Research, 42,* 880–894.

Nylen, K., Moran, T., Franklin, C., & O'Hara, M. (2006). Maternal depression: A review of relevant treatment approaches for mothers and infants. *Infant Mental Health Journal, 27,* 327–343.

O'Connor, T. G., & Croft, C. M. (2001). A twin study of attachment in preschool children. *Child Development, 72,* 1501–1511.

O'Connor, T. G., Allen, J. P., Bell, K. L., & Hauser, S. T. (1996). Adolescent–parent relationships and leaving home in young adulthood. *New Directions in Child Development, 71,* 39–52.

O'Connor, T. G., Rutter, M., Beckett, C., Keaveney, L., Dreppner, J. M., & the English and Romanian Adoptees Study Team. (2000). The effects of global severe privation on cognitive competence: Extension and longitudinal follow-up. *Child Development, 71,* 376–390.

O'Malley, P., & Bachman, J. (1983). Self-esteem: Change and stability between ages 13 and 23. *Developmental Psychology, 19,* 257–268.

Oates, M. R., Cox, J. L., Neema, S., Asten, P., Glangeaud-Freudenthal, N., Figueiredo, B., . . . TCS–PND Group. (2004). Postnatal depression across countries and cultures: A qualitative study. *British Journal of Psychiatry, 184,* s10–s16.

Oberlander, S. E., Black, M. M., & Starr, R. H., Jr. (2007). African American adolescent mothers and grandmothers: A multigenerational approach to parenting. *American Journal of Community Psychology, 39,* 37–46.

Odeku, K., Rembe, S., & Anwo, J. (2009). Female genital mutilation: A human rights perspective. *Journal of Psychology in Africa, 19*(Special issue: Violence against children in Africa), 55–62.

Offer, D., & Schonert-Reichl, K. A. (1992). Debunking the myths of adolescence: Findings from recent research. *Journal of the American Academy of Child & Adolescent Psychiatry, 31,* 1003–1014.

Office of Head Start (2010). Head Start program fact sheet. Washington, DC: U.S. Department of Health and Human Services.

Ogbu, J. U. (2002). Cultural amplifiers of intelligence: IQ and minority status in cross-cultural perspective. In J. M. Fish (Ed.), *Race and intelligence: Separating science from myth* (pp. 241–278). Mahwah, NJ: Erlbaum.

Ogden, C. L., Kuczmarski, R. J., Flegal, K. M., Mei, Z., Guo, S., Wei, R., . . . Johnson, C. L. (2002). Centers for Disease Control and Prevention 2000 growth charts for the United States: Improvements to the 1977 National Center for Health Statistics version. *Pediatrics, 109,* 45–60.

Ogden, T., & Amlund-Hagen, K. (2006). Multisystemic treatment of serious behavior problems in youth: Sustainability of therapy effectiveness two years after intake. *Child and Adolescent Mental Health, 11,* 142–149.

Ogletree, S. M., Martinez, C. N., Turner, T. R., & Mason, M. (2004). Pokémon: Exploring the role of gender. *Sex Roles, 50*(11–12), 851–859.

Ohgi, S., Arisawa, K., Takahashi, T., Kusomoto, T., Goto, Y., & Saito, A .T. (2003). Neonatal behavioral assessment scale as a predictor of later developmental disabilities of low birth-weight and/or premature infants. *Brain Development, 25,* 313–321.

Oken, E., & Lightdale, J. R. (2000). Updates in pediatric nutrition. *Current Opinion in Pediatrics, 12,* 282–290.

Okie, S. (2002, April 10). Study cites alcohol link in campus deaths. *The Washington Post,* p. A2.

Olds, D. L. (2010). The nurse–family partnership: From trials to practice. In A. J. Reynolds, A. J. Rolnick, M. M. Englund, & J. A. Temple (Eds.), *Childhood programs and practices in the first decade of life: A human capital integration* (pp. 49–75). New York, NY: Cambridge University Press.

Ollendick, T. H., Shortt, A. L., & Sander, J. B. (2008). Internalizing disorders in children and adolescents. In J. E. Maddux & B. A. Winstead (Eds.), *Psychopathology: Foundations for a contemporary understanding* (2nd ed., pp. 375–399). New York, NY: Routledge.

Oller, D. K., Eilers, R. E., Urbano, R., & Cobo-Lewis, A. B. (1997). Development of precursors to speech in infants exposed to two languages. *Journal of Child Language, 24,* 407–425.

Olson, C. K., Kutner, L. A., & Warner, D. E. (2008). The role of violent video game content in adolescent development: Boys' perspectives. *Journal of Adolescent Research, 23,* 55–75.

Olson, C. K., Kutner, L. A., Warner, D. E., Almerigi, J., Baer, L., Nicholi, A. M., & Beresin, E. V. (2007). Factors correlated with violent video game use by adolescent boys and girls. *Journal of Adolescent Health, 41,* 77–83.

Olson, C. M. (2008). Achieving a healthy weight gain during pregnancy. *Annual Review of Nutrition, 28*(1), 411–423.

Oltmanns, T. F., & Emery, R. E. (2006). *Abnormal psychology* (6th ed.). Upper Saddle River, NJ: Prentice Hall.

Olweus, D. (2000). Bullying. In A. E. Kazdin (Ed.), *Encyclopedia of psychology* (Vol. 1, pp. 487–489). Washington, DC: American Psychological Association.

Oren, D. L. (1981). Cognitive advantages of bilingual children related to labeling ability. *The Journal of Educational Research, 74*(3), 163–169.

Organisation for Economic Co-operation and Development. (2009). *Health at a glance 2009: OECD indicators.*

Organisation for Economic Co-operation and Development. (2010). Incidence of employment by usual weekly hours worked. *StatExtracts.* Retrieved from http://stats.oecd.org/Index.aspx?DataSetCode%20%09=USLHRS_I

Osgood, D. W. (2009). Illegal behavior: A presentation to the Committee on the Science of Adolescence of the National Academies. Washington, DC.

Osgood, D. W., Anderson, A. L., & Shaffer, J. N. (2005). Unstructured leisure in the afterschool hours. In L. J. Mahoney, R. W. Larson, & J. S. Eccles (Eds.), *Organized activities as contexts of development: Extracurricular activities, after-school and community programs* (pp. 45–64). Mahwah, NJ: Erlbaum.

Osgood, D. W., Wilson, J. K., Bachman, J. G., O'Malley, P. M., & Johnston, L. D. (1996). Routine activities and individual deviant behavior. *American Sociological Review, 61,* 635–655.

Oster, H., Hegley, D., & Nagel, L. (1992). Adult judgments and fine-grained analysis of infant facial expressions: Testing the validity of a priori coding formulas. *Developmental Psychology, 28,* 1115–1131.

Out, D., Pieper, S., Bakermans-Kranenburg, M. J., Zeskind, P. S., & van IJzendoorn, M. H. (2010). Intended sensitive and harsh caregiving responses to infant crying: The role of cry pitch and perceived urgency in an adult twin sample. *Child Abuse & Neglect, 34,* 863–873.

Overpeck, M. D., Brenner, R. A., Trumble, A. C., Smith, G. S., MacDorman, M. F., & Berendes, H. W. (1999). Infant injury deaths with unknown intent: What else do we know? *Injury Prevention, 5,* 272–275.

Owen, C. G., Whincup, P. H., Odoki, K., Gilg, J. A., & Cook, D. G. (2002). Infant feeding and blood cholesterol: A study in adolescents and a systematic review. *Pediatrics, 110,* 597–608.

Owens, J. A. (2004). Sleep in children: Cross-cultural perspectives. *Sleep and Biological Rhythms, 2*(3), 165–173.

Oyserman, D., & Fryberg, S. (2006). The possible selves of diverse adolescents: Content and function across gender, race and national origin. In C. Dunkel & J. Kerpelman (Eds.), *Possible selves: Theory, research and applications* (pp. 17–39). Hauppauge, NY: Nova Science.

Pacella, R., McLellan, M., Grice, K., Del Bono, E. A., Wiggs, J. L., & Gwiazda, J. E. (1999). Role of genetic factors in the etiology of juvenile-onset myopia based on the longitudinal study of refractive error. *Optometry and Vision Science, 76,* 381–386.

Pahl, K., & Way, N. (2006). Longitudinal trajectories of ethnic identity among urban Black and Latino adolescents. *Child Development, 77,* 1403–1415.

Paludi, M. A., & Strayer, L. A. (1985). What's in an author's name? Differential evaluations of performance as a function of author's name. *Sex Roles, 12,* 353–362.

Pan, B. A., & Snow, C. E. (1999). The development of conversation and discourse skills. In M. Barrett (Ed.), *The development of language* (pp. 229–249). Hove, UK: Psychology Press.

Pan, S. Y., Desmeules, M., Morrison, H., Semenciw, R., Ugnat, A. M., Thompson, W., & Mao, Y. (2007). Adolescent injury deaths and hospitalization in Canada: Magnitude and temporal trends (1979–2003). *Journal of Adolescent Health, 41,* 84–92.

Pankow, L. J. (2008). Genetic theory. In B. A. Thyer, K. M. Sowers, & C. N. Dulmus (Eds.), *Comprehensive handbook of social work and social welfare: Vol. 2. Human behavior in the social environment* (pp. 327–353). Hoboken, NJ: John Wiley & Sons.

Papadakis, A. A., Prince, R. P., Jones, N. P., & Strauman, T. J. (2006). Self-regulation, rumination, and vulnerability to depression in adolescent girls. *Development and Psychopathology, 18,* 815–829.

Paquette, D. (2004). Theorizing the father–child relationship: Mechanisms and developmental outcomes. *Human Development, 47,* 193–219.

Parameswaran, G. (2003). Age, gender, and training in children's performance of Piaget's horizontality task. *Educational Studies, 29,* 307–319.

Park, S. H., Shim, Y. K., Kim, H. S., & Eun, B. L. (1999). Age and seasonal distribution of menarche in Korean girls. *Journal of Adolescent Health, 25,* 97.

Parke, R. D. (2004). Development in the family. *Annual Review of Psychology, 55,* 363–399.

Parke, R. D., & Buriel, R. (2006). Socialization in the family: Ethnic and ecological perspectives. In W. Damon & R. Lerner (Eds.), & N. Eisenberg (Vol. Ed.), *Handbook of child psychology: Vol. 3. Social, emotional and personality development* (6th ed., pp. 429–504). New York, NY: Wiley.

Parker, E. D., Schmitz, K. H., Jacobs, D. R., Jr., Dengel, D. R., & Schreiner, P. J. (2007). Physical activity in young adults and incident hypertension over 15 years of follow-up: The CARDIA study. *American Journal of Public Health, 97,* 703–709.

Parker, J. D. (1994). Ethnic differences in midwife-attended US births. *American Journal of Public Health, 84*(7), 1139–1141.

Parten, M. (1932). Social play among preschool children. *Journal of Abnormal Social Psychology, 27,* 243–269.

Pascalis, O., & Kelly, D. J. (2009). The origins of face processing in humans: Phylogeny and ontogeny. *Perspectives on Psychological Science, 4,* 200–209.

Pascarella, E. T. (2005). Cognitive impacts of the first year of college. In R. S. Feldman (Ed.), *Improving the first year of college: Research and practice* (pp. 111–140). Mahwah, NJ: Erlbaum.

Pascarella, E. T. (2006). How college affects students: Ten directions for future research. *Journal of College Student Development, 47,* 508–520.

Pascarella, E., & Terenzini, P. (1991). *How college affects students: Findings and insights from twenty years of research.* San Francisco, CA: Jossey-Bass.

Pascoe, C. J. (2007). *Dude, you're a fag: Masculinity and sexuality in high school.* Berkeley: University of California Press.

Pashigian, M. J. (2002). Conceiving the happy family: Infertility and marital politics in northern Vietnam. In M.C. Inhorn & F. van Balen (Eds.), *Infertility around the globe: New thinking on childlessness, gender, and reproductive technologies* (pp. 134–150). Berkeley: University of California Press.

Pathman, T., Samson, Z., Dugas, K., Cabeza, R., & Bauer, P. J. (2011). A "snapshot" of declarative memory: Differing developmental trajectories in episodic and autobiographical memory. *Memory, 19*(8), 825–835.

Patrick, M. E., Schulenberg, J. E., O'Malley, P. M., Maggs, J. L., Kloska, D. D., Johnston, L. D., & Bachman, J. G. (2011). Age-related changes in reasons for using alcohol and marijuana from ages 18 to 30 in a national sample. *Psychology of Addictive Behaviors, 25,* 330–339.

Patterson, G. R. (2002). The early development of coercive family process. In J. B. Reid, G. R. Patterson, & J. Snyder (Eds.), *Antisocial behavior in children and adolescents: A developmental analysis and model for intervention* (pp. 25–44). Washington, DC: American Psychological Association.

Patterson, M. L., & Werker, J. F. (2002). Infants' ability to match dynamic phonetic and gender information in the face and voice. *Journal of Experimental Child Psychology, 81,* 93–115.

Paul, E. L., McManus, B., & Hayes, A. (2000). "Hookups": Characteristics and correlates of college students' spontaneous and anonymous sexual experiences. *The Journal of Sex Research, 37,* 76–88.

Paus, T., Zijdenbos, A., Worsley, K., Collins, D. L., Blumenthal, J., Giedd, J. N., . . . Evans, A. C. (1999). Structural maturation of neural pathways in children and adolescents: In vivo study. *Science, 19,* 1908–1911.

Pearlman, D., Zierler, S., Meersman, S., Kim, H., Viner-Brown, S., & Caron, C. (2006). Race dispartites in childhood asthma: Does where you live matter? *Journal of the National Medical Association, 98,* 239–247.

Peirano, P., Algarin, C., & Uauy, R. (2003). Sleep–wake states and their regulatory mechanism throughout early human development. *Journal of Pediatrics, 143*(Suppl.), S70–S79.

Pelaez, M., Field, T., Pickens, J. N., & Hart, S. (2008). Disengaged and authoritarian parenting behavior of depressed mothers with their toddlers. *Infant Behavior and Development, 31,* 145–148.

Peng, K., & Nisbett, R. E. (1999). Culture, dialectics, and reasoning about contradiction. *American Psychologist, 54,* 741–754.

Pennington, B. F., Moon, J., Edgin, J., Stedron, J., & Nadel, L. (2003). The neuropsychology of Down syndrome: Evidence for hippocampal dysfunction. *Child Development, 74,* 75–93.

Pepler, D. J., Craig, W. M., Connolly, J. A., Yuile, A., McMaster, L., & Jiang, D. (2006). A developmental perspective on bullying. *Aggressive Behavior, 32,* 376–384.

Pepler, D. J., Jiang, D., Craig, W. M., & Connolly, J. A. (2008). Developmental trajectories of bullying and associated factors. *Child Development, 79,* 325–338.

Pepler, D., Craig, W., Yuile, A., & Connolly, J. (2004). Girls who bully: A developmental and relational perspective. In M. Putallaz & K. L. Bierman (Eds.), *Aggression, antisocial behavior, and violence among girls: A developmental perspective* (pp. 90–109). New York, NY: Guilford Press.

Perner, J., Ruffman, T., & Leekam, S. R. (1994). Theory of mind is contagious: You catch it from your sibs. *Child Development; Child Development, 65*(4), 1228–1238.

Perry, W. G. (1970/1999). *Forms of ethical and intellectual development in the college years: A scheme.* San Francisco, CA: Jossey-Bass.

Petersen, A. C., Compas, B. E., Brooks-Gunn, J., Stemmler, M., Ey, S., & Grant, K. E. (1993). Depression in adolescence. *American Psychologist, 48,* 155–168.

Peterson, C. C. (2000). Influence of siblings' perspectives on theory of mind. *Cognitive Development, 15*(4), 435–455.

Peterson, C., & Whalen, N. (2001). Five years later: Children's memory for medical emergencies. *Applied Cognitive Psychology, 15*(Special issue: Trauma, stress, and autobiographical memory), S7–S24.

Peterson, D. M., Marcia, J. E., & Carpendale, J. I. M. (2004). Identity: Does thinking make it so? In C. Lightfoot & M. Chandler (Eds.), *Changing conceptions of psychological life* (pp. 113–126). Mahwah, NJ: Erlbaum.

Pew Commission on Children on Foster Care (2004). *Safety, permanence and well-being for children in foster care.* Retrieved from: http://pewfostercare .org/research/docs/FinalReport.pdf

Pew Research Center. (2001). Barely half of U.S. adults are married—A record low, December 14, 2011.

Phelan, T. W. (2010). *1-2-3 magic: Effective discipline for children 2–12.* New York, NY: Child Management.

Phinney, J. S. (1990). Ethnic identity in adolescents and adults: A review of research. *Psychological Bulletin, 108,* 499–514.

Phinney, J. S. (2000, March). *Identity formation among U.S. ethnic adolescents from collectivist cultures.* Paper presented at the biennial meeting of the Society of Research on Adolescence, Chicago, IL.

Phinney, J. S. (2006). Ethnic identity in emerging adulthood. In J. J. Arnett & J. L. Tanner (Eds.), *Emerging adults in America: Coming of age in the 21st century* (pp. 117–134). Washington, DC: American Psychological Association.

Phinney, J. S. (2010). Understanding development in cultural contexts: How do we deal with the complexity? *Human Development, 53*(1), 33–38.

Phinney, J. S., & Baldelomar, O. A. (2011). Identity development in multiple cultural contexts. In L. A. Jensen (Ed.), *Bridging cultural and developmental psychology: New syntheses in theory, research and policy* (pp. 161–186). New York, NY: Oxford University Press.

Phinney, J. S., & Devich-Navarro, M. (1997). Variation in bicultural identification among African American and Mexican American adolescents. *Journal of Research on Adolescence, 7,* 3–32.

Phinney, J. S., & Ong, A. D. (2002). Adolescent–parent disagreement and life satisfaction in families from Vietnamese and European American backgrounds. *International Journal of Behavioral Development, 26,* 556–561.

Phinney, J. S., & Rosenthal, D. A. (1992). Ethnic identity in adolescence: Process, context, and outcome. In G. R. Adams, T. P. Gullotta, & R. Montemayor (Eds.), *Adolescent identity formation* (pp. 145–172). Newbury Park, CA: Sage.

Phinney, J. S., DuPont, S., Espinosa, A., Revill, J., & Sanders, K. (1994). Ethnic identity and American identification among ethnic minority adolescents. In A. M. Bouvy, F. J. R. van de Vijver, P. Boski, & P. Schmitz (Eds.), *Journeys into cross-ultural psychology* (pp. 167–183). Amsterdam, The Netherlands: Swets & Zeitlinger.

Phinney, J. S., Kim-Jo, T., Osorio, S., & Vilhjalmsdottir, P. (2005). Autonomy and relatedness in adolescent-parent disagreements: Ethnic and developmental factors. *Journal of Adolescent Research, 20,* 8–39.

Piaget, J. (1936/1952). *The origins of intelligence in children.* New York, NY: Norton.

Piaget, J. (1954). *The construction of reality in the child.* New York, NY: Basic Books.

Piaget, J. (1965). *The moral judgment of the child.* New York, NY: Free Press. (Original work published 1932).

Piaget, J. (1967). *Six psychological studies.* New York, NY: Random House.

Piaget, J. (1972). Intellectual evolution from adolescence to adulthood. *Human Development, 15,*1–12.

Piaget, J. (2002). The epigenetic system and the development of cognitive functions. In R. O. Gilmore, M. H. Johnson, & Y. Munakata (Eds.), *Brain development and cognition: A reader* (2nd ed., pp. 29–35). Malden, MA: Blackwell.

Piaget, J., & Inhelder, B. (1969). *The child's conception of space* (F. J. Langdon & J. L. Lunger, Trans.). New York, NY: Norton.

Piek, J. P., Dawson, L., Smith, L., & Gasson, N. (2008). The role of early fine and gross motor development on later motor and cognitive ability. *Human Movement Science, 27,* 668–681.

Pickett, K. E., Luo, Y., & Lauderdale, D. S. (2005). Widening social inequalities in risk for sudden infant death syndrome. *American Journal of Public Health, 95*(11), 1976–1981.

Pierroutsakos, S. L. (2000). Infants of the dreaming. In J. DeLoache & A. Gottlieb (Eds.), *A world of babies: Imagined childcare guides for seven societies* (pp. 145–170). New York, NY: Cambridge University Press.

Pierroutsakos, S. L., & Troseth, G. L. (2003). Video verite: Infants' manual investigation of objects on video. *Infant Behavior & Development, 26,* 183–199.

Pike, A., Coldwell, J., & Dunn, J. F. (2005). Sibling relationships in early/middle childhood: Links with individual adjustment. *Journal of Family Psychology, 19,* 523–532.

Pilcher, J. J., & Walters, A. S. (1997). How sleep deprivation affects psychological variables related to college students' cognitive performance. *Journal of American College Health, 46,* 121–126.

Pinderhughes, E. E., Dodge, K. A., Bates, J. E., Pettit, G. S., & Zelli, A. (2000). Discipline responses: Influences of parents' socioeconomic status, ethnicity, beliefs about parenting, stress, and cognitive-emotional processes. *Journal of Family Psychology, 14* (3), 380–400.

Pinker, S. (1994). *The language instinct.* New York, NY: Williams Morrow.

Pinker, S. (2002). *The blank slate: The modern denial of human nature.* New York, NY: Penguin.

Pipp, S., Fischer, K. W., & Jennings, S. (1987). Acquisition of self- and mother knowledge in infancy. *Developmental Psychology, 23,* 86–96.

Pirttilae-Backman, A. M., & Kajanne, A. (2001). The development of implicit epistemologies during early adulthood. *Journal of Adult Development, 8,* 81–97.

Pisetsky, E. M., Chao, Y. M., Dierker, L. C., May, A. M., & Striegel-Moore, R. H. (2008). Disordered eating and substance use in high school students: Results from the Youth Risk Behavior Surveillance System. *International Journal of Eating Disorders, 41,* 464–470.

Pizzamiglio, A. P., Saygin, S. L., Small, S., & Wilson, S. (2005). Language and the brain. In M. Tomasello & D. A. Slobin (Eds.), *Beyond nature-nurture* (pp. 237–260). Mahwah, NJ: Erlbaum.

Plant, M., Miller, P., Plant, M., Gmel, G., Kuntsche, S., Bergmark, K., . . . Vidal, A. (2010). The social consequences of binge drinking among 24- to 32-year-olds in six European countries. *Substance Use & Misuse, 45,* 528–542.

Plant, R. W., & Siegel, L. (2008). Children in foster care: Prevention and treatment of mental health problems. In T. P. Gullotta & G. M. Blau (Eds.), *Family influences on childhood behavior and development: Evidence-based prevention and treatment approaches* (pp. 209–230).

Pleck, J. H., & Masciadrelli, B. P. (2004). Paternal involvement by U.S. residential fathers: Levels, sources and conequences. In M. E. Lamb (Ed.), *The role of the father in child development* (4th ed., pp. 272–306). New York, NY: Wiley.

Plomin, R. (2009). The nature of nurture. In K. McCartney & R. A. Weinberg (Eds.), *Experience and development: A festschrift in honor of Sandra Wood Scarr* (pp. 61–80). New York, NY: Psychology Press.

Plotkin, S. A., Katz, M., & Cordero, J. F. (1999). The eradication of rubella. *JAMA: Journal of the American Medical Association, 306,* 343–450.

Polivy, J., Herman, C. P., Mills, J. S., & Wheeler, H. B. (2003). Eating disorders in adolescence. In R. G. Adams & D. M. Berzonsky (Eds.), *Blackwell handbook of adolescence* (pp. 523–549). Malden, MA: Blackwell.

Pollitt, E., Golub, M., Gorman, K., Gratham-McGregor, S., Levitsky, D., Schurch, B., . . . Wachs, T. (1996). A reconceptualization of the effects of undernutrition on children's biological, psychosocial, and behavioral development. *Social Policy Report, 10,* 1–28.

Pons, F., Lawson, J., Harris, P. L., & de Rosnay, M. (2003). Individual differences in children's emotion understanding: Effects of age and language. *Scandinavian Journal of Psychology, 44,* 347–353.

Pool, M. M., Koolstra, C. M., & van der Voort, T. H. A. (2003). The impact of background radio and television on high school students' homework performance. *Journal of Communication, 53,* 74–87.

Popenoe, D., & Whitehead, B. D. (2001). *The state of our unions, 2001: The social health of marriage in America.* Report of the National Marriage Project, Rutgers, New Brunswick, NJ. Retrieved from http://marriage.rutgers.edu

Popp, D., Lauren, B., Kerr, M., Stattin, H., & Burk, W. K. (2008). Modeling homophily over time with an actor–partner independence model. *Developmental Psychology, 44,* 1028–1039.

Popp, M. S. (2005). *Teaching language and literacy in elementary classrooms.* Mahwah, NJ: Erlbaum.

Population Reference Bureau (PRB). (2009). *2009 World Population Data Sheet.* Washington, DC: Author.

Population Reference Bureau (PRB). (2010). *World population data sheet.* Washington, DC.

Porath, M., Korp, L., Wendrich, D., Dlugay, V., Roth, B., & Kribs, A. (2011). Surfactant in spontaneous breathing with nCPAP: Neurodevelopmental outcome at early school age of infants = 27 weeks. *Acta Paediatrica, 100,* 352–359.

Porges, S. W., & Lispitt, L. P. (1993). Neonatal responsivity to gustatory stimulation: The gustatory-vagal hypothesis. *Infant Behavior & Development, 16,* 487–494.

Porter, R. H., & Rieser, J. J. (2005). Retention of olfactory memories by newborn infants. In R. T. Mason, P. M. LeMaster, & D. Müller-Schwarze (Eds.), *Chemical Signals in Vertebrates* (pp. 300–307). New York, NY: Springer.

Portes, P. R., Dunham, R., & Castillo, K. D. (2000). Identity formation and status across cultures: Exploring the cultural validity of Eriksonian theory. In A. Comunian & U. P. Gielen (Eds.), *International perspectives on human development* (pp. 449–459). Lengerich, Germany: Pabst Science.

Posada, G., Gao, Y., Wu, F., Posada, R., Tascon, M., Schoelmerich, A., . . . Synnevaag, B. (1995). The secure-base phenomenon across cultures: Children's behavior, mothers' preferences, and experts' concepts. *Monographs of the Society for Research in Child Development, 60, 27–48*.

Posner, M. I., & Rothbart, M. K. (2007). Numeracy. In M. I. Posner & M. K. Rothbart, *Educating the human brain* (pp. 173–187). Washington, DC: American Psychological Association.

Posner, R. B. (2006). Early menarche: A review of research on trends in timing, racial differences, etiology and psychosocial consequences. *Sex Roles, 54,* 315–322.

Potegal, M., & Davison, R. J. (2003). Temper tantrums in young children, 1: Behavioral composition. *Journal of Developmental & Behavioral Pediatrics, 24,* 140–147.

Powls, A., Botting, N., Cooke, R. W. I., & Marlow, N. (1996). Handedness in very-low birth-weight (VLBW) children at 12 years of age: Relation to perinatal and outcome variables. *Developmental Medicine and Child Neurology, 38,* 594–602.

Pressley, M., Wharton-McDonald, R., Raphael, L. M., Bogner, K., & Roehrig, A. (2002). Exemplary first-grade teaching. In B. M. Taylor & P. D. Pearson (Eds.), *Teaching reading: Effective schools, accomplished teachers* (pp. 73–88). Mahwah, NJ: Erlbaum.

Pretorius, E., Naude, H., & Van Vuuren, C. J. (2002). Can cultural behavior have a negative impact on the development of visual integration pathways? *Early Child Development and Care, 123,* 173–181.

Preuss, U., Ralston, S. J., Baldursson, G., Falissard, B., Lorenzo, M. J., Rodrigues Pereira, R., . . . ADORE Study Group. (2006). Study design, baseline patient characteristics and intervention in a cross-cultural framework: Results from the ADORE study. *European Child & Adolescent Psychiatry, 15*(Suppl. 1), 4–19.

Preusser, D. F., & Tison, J. (2007). GDL then and now. *Journal of Safety Research, 38,* 159–163.

Price Waterhouse Coopers. (2011). The accelerating shift of global economic power: Challenges and opportunities. Retrieved from http://www.pwc.com/en_GX/gx/world-2050/pdf/world-in-2050-jan-2011.pdf

Proctor, M. H., Moore, L. L., Gao, D., Cupples, L. A., Bradlee, M. L., Hood, M. Y., & Ellison, R. C. (2003). Television viewing and change in body fat from preschool to early adolescence: The Framingham Children's Study. *International Journal of Obesity, 27,* 827–833.

Provins, K. A. (1997). Handedness and speech: A critical reappraisal of the role of genetic and environmental factors in the cerebral lateralization of function. *Psychological Review, 104,* 554–571.

Pryor, J. H., Hurtado, S., DeAngelo, L., Palucki Blake, L., & Tran, S. (2009). *The American freshman: National norms fall 2009.* Los Angeles, CA: Higher Education Research Institute, UCLA.

Purdie, N., Carroll, A., & Roche, L. (2004). Parenting and adolescent self-regulation. *Journal of Adolescence, 27,* 663–676.

Qin, D. B. (2009). Being "good" or being "popular": Gender and ethnic identity negotiations of Chinese immigrant adolescents. *Journal of Adolescent Research, 24,* 37–66.

Quinn, C. T., Rogers, Z. R., & Buchanan, G. R. (2004). Survival of children with sickle cell disease. *Blood, 103,* 4023–4027.

Quinn, P. C., Eimas, P. D., & Rosenkranz, S. L. (1993). Evidence for representations of perceptually similar natural categories by 3-month-old and 4-month-old infants. *Perception, 22,* 463–475.

Raacke, J., & Bonds-Raacke, J. (2008). MySpace and Facebook: Applying the uses and gratifications theory to exploring friend-networking sites. *Cyber-Psychology & Behavior, 11,* 169–174.

Raag, T. (2003). Racism, gender identities and young children: Social relations in a multi-ethnic, inner-city primary school. *Archives of Sexual Behavior, 32,* 392–393.

Radmacher, K., & Azmitia, M. (2006). Are there gendered pathways to intimacy in early adolescents' and emerging adults' friendships? *Journal of Adolescent Research, 21,* 415–448.

Rah, Y., & Parke, R. D. (2008). Pathways between parent-child interactions and peer acceptance: The role of children's social information processing. *Social Development, 17*(2): 341–357.

Raikes, H. H., Chazan-Cohen, R., Love, J. M., & Brooks-Gunn, J. (2010). Early Head Start impacts at age 3 and a description of the age 5 follow-up study. In A. J. Reynolds, A. J. Rolnick, & M. M. Englund (Eds.), *Childhood programs and practices in the first decade of life: A human capital integration* (pp. 99–118). New York, NY: Cambridge University Press.

Rajaratnam, J. K., Marcus, J. R., Flaxman, A. D., Wang, H., Levin-Rector, A., Dwyer, L., . . . Murray, C. J. L. (2003). Neonatal, postneonatal, childhood, and under–5 mortality for 187 countries, 1970–2010: A systematic analysis of progress towards Millennium Development Goal 4. *Pediatrics, 111,* e61–e66.

Ralph, K., Harrington, K., & Pandha, H. (2004). Recent developments and current status of gene therapy using viral vectors in the United Kingdom. *British Medical Journal, 329,* 839–842.

Ramchandani, N. (2004). Diabetes in children: A burgeoning health problem among overweight young Americans. *American Journal of Nursing, 104,* 65–68.

Ramchandani, P., Stein, A., Evans, J., O'Connor, T. G., & the ALSPAC Study Team. (2005). Paternal depression in the postnatal period and child development: A prospective population study. *Lancet, 365,* 2201–2205.

Ramos, M. C., Guerin, D. W., Gottfried, A. W., Bathurst, K., & Oliver, P. H. (2005). Family conflict and children's behavior problems: The moderating role of child temperament. *Structural Equation Modeling, 12,* 278–298.

Ramsay, D., & Lewis, M. (2001). Temperament, stress, and soothing. In T. D. Wachs & G. A. Kohnstamm (Eds.), *Temperament in context* (pp. 23–41). Mahwah, NJ: Erlbaum.

Randell, A. C., & Peterson, C. C. (2009). Affective qualities of sibling disputes, mothers' conflict attitudes, and children's theory of mind development. *Social Development, 18,* 857–874.

Rao, R., & Georgieff, M. K. (2001). Neonatal iron nutrition. *Seminars in Neonatology, 6,* 425–435.

Rasmussen, E. R., Neuman, R. J., Heath, A. C., Levy, F., Hay, D. A., & Todd, R. D. (2004). Familial clustering of latent class and DSM-IV defined attention-deficit hyperactivity disorder (ADHD) subtypes. *Journal of Child Psychology and Psychiatry, 45,* 589–598.

Raudsepp, L., & Liblik, R. (2002). Relationship of perceived and actual motor competence in children. *Perception and Motor Skills, 94,* 1059–1070.

Rauscher, F. H. (2003). Can music instruction affect children's cognitive development? *ERIC Digest, EDO-PS-03-12.*

Rauscher, F. H., Shaw, G. L., & Ky, K. N. (1993). Listening to Mozart enhances spatial-temporal reasoning: Towards a neurophysiological basis. *Neuroscience Letters, 185,* 44–47.

Ravn, M. N. (2005). A matter of free choice? Some structural and cultural influences on the decision to have or not to have children in Norway. In C. B. Douglas (Ed.), *Barren states: The population "implosion" in Europe* (pp. 29–47). New York, NY: Berg.

Rayner, K., Foorman, B. R., Perfetti, C. A., Pesetsky, D., & Seidenberg, M. S. (2002). How should reading be taught? *Scientific American, 286,* 84–91.

Redcay, E., Haist, F., & Courchesne, E. (2008). Functional neuroimaging of speech perception during a pivotal period in language acquisition. *Developmental Science, 11*(2), 237–252.

Reddy, U. M., & Mennuti, M. T. (2006). Incorporating first-trimester Down syndrome studies into prenatal screening. *Obstetrics and Gynecology, 107,* 167–173.

Redshaw, M. E. (1997). Mothers of babies requiring special care: Attitudes and experiences. *Journal of Reproductive & Infant Psychology, 15,* 109–120.

Reese, D. (2000). A parenting manual, with words of advice for Puritan mothers. In J. DeLoache & A. Gottlieb (Eds.), *A world of babies: Imagined childcare guides for seven societies* (pp. 29–54). New York, NY: Cambridge University Press.

Reeves, G., & Schweitzer, J. (2004). Pharmacological management of attention deficit hyperactivity disorder. *Expert Opinions in Pharmacotherapy, 5,* 1313–1320.

Regan, P. C., Durvasula, R., Howell, L., Ureno, O., & Rea, M. (2004). Gender, ethnicity, and the developmental timing of the first sexual and romantic experiences. *Social Behavior & Personality, 32,* 667–676.

Regestein, Q., Natarajan, V., Pavlova, M., Kawasaki, S., Gleason, R., & Koff, E. (2010). Sleep debt and depression in female college students. *Psychiatry Research, 176*(1), 34–39.

Regev, R. H., Lusky, A., Dolfin, T., Litmanovitz, I., Arnon, S., & Reichman, B. (2003). Excess mortality and morbidity among small-for-gestational-age premature infants: a population-based study. *The Journal of Pediatrics,* 143(2), 186–191.

Regnerus, M., & Uecker, J. (2011). *Premarital sex in America: How young Americans meet, mate, and think about marrying.* New York, NY: Oxford University Press.

Regnerus, M. D., Smith, C., & Smith, B. (2004). Social Context in the Development of Adolescent Religiosity. *Applied Developmental Science, 8*(1), 27–38.

Reid, C. (2004). Kangaroo care. *Neonatal Network, 23,* 53.

Reifman, A., Arnett, J. J., & Colwell, M. J. (2006). Emerging adulthood: Theory, assessment, and application. *Journal of Youth Development, 1,* 1–12.

Reijonen, J. H., Pratt, H. D., Patel, D. R., & Greydanus, D. E. (2003). Eating disorders in the adolescent population: An overview. *Journal of Adolescent Research, 18,* 209–222.

Reimuller, A., Shadur, J., & Hussong, A. M. (2011). Parental social support as a moderator of self-medication in adolescents. *Addictive Behaviors, 36,* 203–208.

Resnick, G. (2010). Project Head Start: Quality and links to child outcomes. In A. J. Reynolds, A. J. Rolnick, M. M. Englund, & J. A. Temple (Eds.), *Childhood programs and practices in the first decade of life: A human capital integration* (pp. 121–156). New York, NY: Cambridge University Press.

Reynolds, K., Lewis, L. B., Nolen, J. D. L., Kinney, G. L., Sathya, B., & He, J. (2003). Alcohol consumption and risk of stroke: A meta-analysis. *Journal of the American Medical Association, 289,* 579–588.

Reznick, J. S., Corley, R., & Robinson, J. (1997). A longitudinal study of intelligence in the second year. *Monographs of the Society for Research in Child Development, 62,* 1–154.

Rhodes, J. R., & DuBois, D. L. (2008). Mentoring relationships and programs for youth. *Current Directions in Psychological Science, 17,* 254–258.

Ricciuti, H. N. (2004). Single parenthood, achievement, and problem behavior in White, Black, and Hispanic children. *Journal of Educational Research, 97,* 196–206.

Richards, M. H., Crowe, P. A., Larson, R., & Swarr, A. (2002). Developmental patterns and gender differences in the experience of peer companionship in adolescence. *Child Development, 69,* 154–163.

Richman, A. L., Miller, P. M., & LeVine, R. A. (2010). Cultural and educational variations in maternal responsiveness. In R. A. LeVine (Ed.), *Psychological anthropology: A reader on self in culture* (pp. 181–192). Malden, MA: Wiley-Blackwell.

Rideout, V. J., & Hamel, E. (2006). *The media family: Electronic media in the lives of infants, toddlers, preschoolers, and their parents.* Menlo Park, CA: The Henry J. Kaiser Family Foundation.

Rideout, V. J., Vandewater, E. A., & Wartella, E. A. (2003). *Zero to six: Electronic media in the lives of infants, toddlers and preschoolers.* Menlo Park, CA: The Henry J. Kaiser Family Foundation.

Ridley, M. (2010). *The rational optimist: How prosperity evolves.* New York, NY: Harper.

Riedel, B. W., Robinson, L. A., Klesges, R. C., & McLain-Allen, B. (2003). Ethnic differences in smoking withdrawal effects among adolescents. *Addictive Behaviors, 28,* 129–140.

Rigby, K. (2004). Bullying in childhood. In P. K. Smith & C. H. Hart (Eds.), *Blackwell handbook of childhood social development.* Malden, MA: Blackwell.

Righetti, P. L., Dell'Avanzo, M., Grigio, M., & Nicolini, U. (2005). Maternal/paternal antenatal attachment and fourth-dimensional ultrasound technique: A preliminary report. *British Journal of Psychology, 96,* 129–137.

Righetti-Veltema, M., Conne-Perreard, E., Bousquest, A., & Manzano, J. (2002). Postpartum depression and mother-infant relationship at 3 months old. *Journal of Affective Disorders, 70,* 291–306.

Riley, A. W., Lyman, L. M., Spiel, G., Döpfner, M., Lorenzo, M. J., Ralston, S. J., & ADORE Study Group. (2006). The Family Strain Index (FSI). Reliability, validity, and factor structure of a brief questionnaire for families of children with ADHD. *European Child & Adolescent Psychiatry, 15*(Suppl. 1), 72–78.

Roberto, C. A., Steinglass, J., Mayer, L. E. S., Attia, E., & Walsh, B. T. (2008). The clinical significance of amenorrhea as a diagnostic criterion for anorexia nervosa. *International Journal of Eating Disorders, 41,* 559–563.

Roberts, B. W., Caspi, A., & Moffitt, T. E. (2001). The kids are alright: Growth and stability in personality development from adolescence to adulthood. *Journal of Personality and Social Psychology, 81,* 670–683.

Roberts, D. F., & Foehr, U. G. (2004). *Kids and media in America.* Cambridge, MA: Cambridge University Press.

Roberts, D. F., Foehr, U. G., & Rideout, V. (2005). *Generation M: Media in the lives of 8–18 year-olds.* Washington, DC: The Henry J. Kaiser Family Foundation.

Roberts, R. G., Deutchman, M., King, V. J., Fryer, G. E., & Miyoshi, T. J. (2007). Changing policies on vaginal birth after cesarean: Impact on access. *Birth: Issues in Perinatal Care, 34,* 316–322.

Robertson, J. (2008). Stepfathers in families. In J. Pryor (Ed.), *The international handbook of stepfamilies: Policy and practice in legal, research, and clinical environments* (pp. 125–150). Hoboken, NJ: Wiley.

Robins, R. W., Gosling, S. D., & Craik, K. H. (1999). An empirical analysis of trends in psychology. *American Psychologist, 54,* 117–128.

Robins, R. W., & Trzesniewski, K. H. (2005). Self-esteem development across the lifespan. *Current Directions in Psychological Science, 14,* 158–162.

Robinson, C. C., Anderson, G. T., Porter, C. L., Hart, C. H., & Wouden-Miller, M. (2003). Sequential transition patterns of preschoolers' social interactions during child-initiated play: Is parallel-aware play a bi-directional bridge to other play states? *Early Childhood Research Quarterly, 18,* 3–21.

Robinson, J. L., Klute, M. M., Faldowski, R., Pan, B., Staerkel, F., Summers, J. A., & Wall, S. (2009). Mixed approach programs in the Early Head Start Research and Evaluation Project: An in-depth view. *Early Education and Development, 20,* 893–919.

Rochat, P., & Hespos, S. J. (1997). Differential rooting responses by neonates: Evidence for an early sense of self. *Early Development and Parenting, 6,* 105–112.

Rodgers, J. L., & Wanstrom, L. (2007). Identification of a Flynn Effect in the NLSY: Moving from the center to the boundaries. *Intelligence, 35,* 187–196.

Rodier, P. M. (2009). *Science under attack: Vaccines and autism.* Berkeley: University of California Press.

Roeder, M. B., Mahone, E. M., Larson, J. G., Mostofsky, S., Cutting, L. E., Goldberg, M. C., & Denckla, M. B. (2008). Left–right differences on timed motor examination in children. *Child Neuropsychology, 14,* 249–262.

Roenneberg, T., Kuehnle, T., Juda, M., Kantermann, T., Allebrandt, K., Gordijn, M., & Merrow, M. (2007). Epidemiology of the human circadian clock. *Sleep Medicine Reviews, 11,* 429–438.

Rogoff, B. (1990). Apprenticeship in thinking: *Cognitive development in social context.* New York, NY: Oxford University Press.

Rogoff, B. (1995). Observing sociocultural activities on three planes: Participatory appropriation, guided participation, and apprenticeship. In J. V. Wertsch, P. del Rio, & A. Alvarez (Eds.), *Sociocultural studies of the mind* (pp. 273–294). New York, NY: Cambridge University Press.

Rogoff, B. (1998). Cognition as a collaborative process. In D. Kuhn & R. S. Siegler (Eds.), *Handbook of child psychology: Vol. 2. Cognition, perception, and language* (5th ed., pp. 679–744). New York, NY: Wiley.

Rogoff, B. (2003). *The cultural nature of human development.* New York, NY: Oxford University Press.

Rogoff, B., Correa-Chávez, M., & Cotuc, M. N. (2005). A cultural/historical view of schooling in human development. In D. B. Pillemer & S. H. White (Eds.), *Developmental psychology and social change: Research, history and policy* (pp. 225–263). New York, NY: Cambridge University Press.

Rogoff, B., Paradise, R., Arauz, R. M., Correa-Chavez, M., & Angelillo, C. (2003). Firsthand learning through intent participation. *Annual Review of Psychology, 54,* 175–203.

Rohlen, T. P. (1983). *Japan's high schools.* Berkeley: University of California Press.

Roizen, N. J., & Patterson, D. (2003). Down's syndrome. *Lancet, 361,* 1281–1289.

Rooney, M. (2003, March 19). Fewer college students graduate in 4 years, survey finds. *Chronicle of Higher Education: Today's news* (pp. 1–2). Retrieved from http://chronicle.com/daily/2003/03/2003031901n.htm

Roopnarine, J. L., Hossain, Z., Gill, P., & Brophy, H. (1994). Play in the East Indian context. In J. L. Roopnarine, J. E. Johnson, & F. H. Hooper (Eds.), *Children's play in diverse cultures* (pp. 9–30). Albany: State University of New York Press.

Rothstein-Fisch, C., Greenfield, P. M., Trumbull, E., Keller, H., & Quiroz, B. (2010). Uncovering the role of culture in learning, development, and education. In D. D. Preiss & R. J. Sternberg (Eds.), *Innovations in educational psychology: Perspectives on learning, teaching, and human development.* (pp. 269–294). New York, NY: Springer.

Roscoe, B., Dian, M. S., & Brooks, R. H. (1987). Early, middle, and late adolescents' views on dating and factors influencing partner selection. *Adolescence, 22,* 59–68.

Rose, A. J., & Asher, S. R. (1999). Children's goals and strategies in response to conflicts to conflicts within a friendship. *Developmental Psychology, 35,* 69–79.

Rose, P. (2004). The forest dweller and the beggar. *American Scholar, 73,* 5–11.

Rose, S. A., Feldman, J. F., Jankowski, J. J., & Van Rossem, R. (2005). Pathways from prematurity and infant abilities to later cognition. *Child Development, 76,* 1172–1184.

Rosenberg, M. (1979). *Conceiving the self.* New York, NY: Basic Books.

Rosenbloom, S. R., & Way, N. (2004). Experiences of discrimination among African American, Asian American, and Latino adolescents in an urban high school. *Youth & Society, 35,* 420–451.

Rosnow, R. L., & Rosenthal, R. L. (2005). *Beginning behavioral research* (5th ed.). Upper Saddle River, NJ: Prentice Hall.

Ross, H. S., & Lollis, S. P. (1989). A social relations analysis of toddler peer relationships. *Child Development, 60,* 1082–1091.

Rothbart, M. K. (2004). Emotion-related regulation: Sharpening the definition. *Child Development, 75,* 334–339.

Rothbart, M. K., & Bates, J. E. (2006). Temperament. In W. Damon & R. Lerner (Series Eds.), & N. Eisenberg (Vol. Ed.), *Handbook of child psychology: Vol. 3. Social, emotional, and personality development* (6th ed., pp. 99–166). New York, NY: Wiley.

Rothbart, M. K., Ahadi, S. A., & Evans, D. E. (2000). Temperament and personality: Origins and outcome. *Journal of Personality and Social Psychology, 78,* 122–135.

Rothbart, M. K., Sheese, B. E., Rueda, M. R., & Posner, M. I. (2011). Developing Mechanisms of Self-Regulation in Early Life. *Emotion Review, 3*(2), 207–213.

Rothbaum, F., Kakinuma, M., Nagaoka, R., & Azuma, H. (2007). Attachment and *amae*: Parent–child closeness in the United States & Japan. *Journal of Cross-Cultural Psychology, 38,* 465–486.

Rothbaum, F., & Morelli, G. (2005). Attachment and culture: Bridging relativism and universalism. In W. Friedlmeier, P. Chakkarath, & B. Schwarz (Eds.), *Culture and human development: The importance of cross-cultural research to the social sciences* (pp. 99–124). Lisse, The Netherlands: Swets & Zeitlinger.

Rothbaum, F., Weisz, J., Pott, M., Miyake, K., & Morelli, G. (2000). Attachment and culture: Security in the United States and Japan. *American Psychologist, 55,* 1093–1104.

Rothbaum, F., Weisz, J., Pott, M., Miyake, K., & Morelli, G. (2001). Deeper into attachment and culture. *American Psychologist, 56,* 827–829.

Rothenberger, A., Coghill, D., Dopfner, M., Falissard, B., & Stenhausen, H. C. (2006). Naturalistic observational studies in the framework of ADHD health care. *European Child and Adolescent Psychiatry, 15*(Suppl. 1), 1–3.

Rotheram-Borus, M. J. (1990). Adolescents' reference group choices, self-esteem, and adjustment. *Journal of Personality and Social Psychology, 59,* 1075–1081.

Rothstein-Fisch, C., Greenfield, P. M., Trumbull, E., Keller, H., & Quiroz, B. (2010). Uncovering the role of culture in learning, development, and education. Innovations in educational psychology: Perspectives on learning, teaching, and human development. (pp. 269–294). New York, NY: Springer.

Rovee-Collier, C. K. (1999). The development of infant memory. *Current Directions in Psychological Science, 8,* 80–85.

Rowley, S. J., Kurtz-Costes, B., Mistry, R., & Feagans, L. (2007). Social status as a predictor of race and gender stereotypes in late childhood and early adolescence. *Social Development, 16,* 150–168.

Roy, A., & Wisnivesky, J. P. (2010). Comprehensive use of environmental control practices among adults with asthma. *Allergy and Asthma Proceedings, 31,* 72–77.

Rozin, P. (2006). Domain denigration and process preference in academic psychology. *Perspectives on Psychological Science, 1,* 365–376.

Rubin, K. H. (2000). Peer interactions, relationships, and groups. Paper presented at the *ISSBD Preconference Workshop on Human Development and Psychological Adaptation,* Peking University, Beijing, China.

Rubin, K. H., Coplan, R. J., Fox, N. A., & Calkins, S. D. (1995). Emotionality, emotion regulation, and preschoolers' social adaptation. *Development and Psychopathology, 7,* 49–62.

Rubin, K. H., & Coplan, R. J. (Eds.). (2010). *The development of shyness and social withdrawal.* New York, NY: Guilford Press.

Rubin, K. H., Bukowski, W., & Parker, J. G. (2006). Peer interactions, relationships, and groups. In W. Damon & R. Lerner (Eds.), & N. Eisenberg (Vol. Ed.), *Handbook of child psychology: Vol. 3. Social, emotional and personality development* (6th ed., pp. 571–645). New York, NY: Wiley.

Rubin, K. H., Burgess, K. B., & Hastings, P. D. (2002). Stability and social-behavioral consequences of toddlers' inhibited temperament and parenting behaviors. *Child Development, 73,* 483–495.

Rubin, K. H., Coplan, J., Chen, X., Buskirk, A. A., & Wojslawowicz, J. C. (2005). Peer relationships in childhood. In M. H. Bornstein & M. E. Lamb (Eds.), *Developmental science: An advanced textbook* (pp. 469–512). Mahwah, NJ: Erlbaum.

Rubin, K., Fredstrom, B., & Bowker, J. (2008). Future directions in friendship in childhood and early adolescence. *Social Development, 17,* 1085–1096.

Ruble, D. N., Martin, C. L., & Berenbaum, S. (2006). Gender development. In W. Damon & R. M. Lerner (Series Eds.), & N. Eisenberg (Vol. Ed.), *Handbook of child psychology: Vol. 3. Social, emotional and personality development* (6th ed., pp. 858–932). Hoboken, NJ: Wiley.

Rucker, J. H., & McGuffin, P. (2010). Polygenic heterogeneity: A complex model of genetic inheritance in psychiatric disorders. *Biological Psychiatry, 68,* 312–313.

Rückinger, S., Beyerlein, A., Jacobsen, G., von Kries, R., & Vik, T. (2010). Growth in utero and body mass index at age 5 years in children of smoking and non-smoking mothers. *Early Human Development, 86,* 773–777.

Rudy, D., & Grusec, J. (2006). Authoritarian parenting in individualist and collectivist groups: Associations with maternal emotion and cognition and children's self esteem. *Journal of Family Psychology, 43,* 302–319.

Ruiz, S. A., & Silverstein, M. (2007). Relationships with grandparents and the emotional well-being of late adolescent and young adult grandchildren. *Journal of Social Issues, 63,* 793–808.

Russell, A., Hart, C. H., Robinson, C. C., & Olsen, S. F. (2003). Children's sociable and aggressive behavior with peers: A comparison of the U.S. and Australian, and contributions of temperament and parenting styles. *International Journal of Behavioral Development, 27,* 74–86.

Rutter, M. (1996). Clinical implications of attachment concepts: Retrospect and prospect. *Annual Progress in Child Psychiatry & Child Development,* 127–156.

Rutter, M. (2012). Gene–environment interdependence. *European Journal of Developmental Psychology, 9*(4), 391–412.

Rutter, M., O'Connor, T. G., and the English and Romanian Adoptees Study Team. (2004). Are there biological programming effects for psychological development? Findings from a study of Romanian adoptees. *Developmental Psychology, 40,* 81–94.

Ryan, A.S., Zhou, W., & Arensberg, M.B. (2006). The effects of employment status on breastfeeding in the United States. *Women's Health Issues, 16,* 243–251.

Ryan, C., Huebner, D., Diaz, R. M., & Sanchez, J. (2009). Family rejection as a predictor of negative health outcomes in white and Latino lesbian, gay and bisexual young adults. *Pediatrics, 123,* 346–352.

Rychlak, J. F. (2003). The self takes over. In J. F. Rychlak, *The human image in postmodern America* (pp. 69–82). Washington, DC: American Psychological Association.

Saarni, C. (1999). *The development of emotional competence.* New York, NY: Guilford Press.

Sachs, B. P., Kobelin, C., Castro, M. A., & Frigoletto, F. (1999). The risks of lowering the cesarean-delivery rate. *New England Journal of Medicine, 340,* 54–57.

Sadker, M., & Sadker, D. (1994). *Failing at fairness: How America's schools cheat girls.* New York, NY: Scribner.

Safe Kids Worldwide. (2002). Childhood injury worldwide: Meeting the challenge. Retrieved from http://www.safekidsworldwide.org

Safe Kids Worldwide. (2009). *News and facts.* Retrieved from www.safekids.org

Saffran, J. R., Werker, J. F., & Werner, L. A. (2006). The infant's auditory world: Hearing, speech and the beginnings of language. In W. Damon & R. Lerner (Eds.), & D. Kuhn & R. Siegler (Vol. Eds.), *Handbook of child psychology: Vol. 2. Cognition, perception, and language* (6th ed., pp.58–108). New York, NY: Wiley.

Saha, C., Riner, M. E., & Liu, G. (2005). Individual and neighborhood-level factors in predicting asthma. *Archives of Pediatrics and Adolescent Medicine, 159,* 759–763.

Saigal, S., den Ouden, L., Wolke, D., Hoult, L., Paneth, N., Streiner, D. L., Whitaker, A., & Pinto-Martin, J. (2003). School-age outcomes in children who were extremely low birth weight from four international population-based cohorts. *Pediatrics, 112,* 943–950.

Saldana, L., & Henggeler, S. W. (2006). Multisystemic therapy in the treatment of adolescent conduct disorder. In W. M. Nelson, III, A. J. Finch, Jr., & K. L. Hart (Eds.), *Conduct disorders: A practitioner's guide to comparative treatments* (pp. 217–258). New York, NY: Springer.

Salkind, N. J. (2009). *Exploring research.* Upper Saddle River, NJ: Prentice Hall.

Salmivalli, C., & Voeten, M. (2004). Connections between attitudes, group norms, and behaviour in bullying situations. *International Journal of Behavioral Development, 28,* 246–258.

Saluja, G., Iachan, R., & Scheidt, P. (2004). Prevalence and risk factors for depressive symptoms among young adolescents. *Archives of Pediatrics and Adolescent Medicine, 158,* 760–765.

Sameroff, A. J., & Haith, M. M. (1996). *The five to seven year shift: The age of reason and responsibility.* Chicago, IL: University of Chicago Press.

Samuels, H. R. (1980). The effect of an older sibling on infant locomotor exploration of a new environment, *Child Development, 51,* 607–609.

Sandberg, J. F., & Hofferth, S. L. (2001). Changes in children's time with parents: United States, 1981–1997. *Demography, 38,* 423–436.

Sandstrom, M. J., & Zakriski, A. L. (2004). Understanding the experience of peer rejection. In J. B. Kupersmidt & K. A. Dodge (Eds.), *Children's peer relations: From development to intervention.* Washington, DC: American Psychological Association.

Sang, B., Miao, X., & Deng, C. (2002). The development of gifted and nongifted young children in metamemory knowledge. *Psychological Science (China), 25,* 406–424.

Sansavini, A., Bertoncini, J., & Giovanelli, G. (1997). Newborns discriminate the rhythm of multisyllabic stressed words. *Developmental Psychology, 33,* 3–11.

Sarrell, E. M., Horev, Z., Cohen, Z., & Cohen, H. A. (2005). Parents' and medical personnel's beliefs about infant teething. *Patient Education and Counseling, 57,* 122–125.

Sassler, S., Ciambrone, D., & Benway, G. (2008). Are they really mama's boys/daddy's girls? The negotiation of adulthood upon returning to the parental home. *Sociological Forum, 23,* 670–698.

Saudino, K. J. (2003). Parent ratings of infant temperament: Lessons from twin studies. *Infant Behavior and Development, 26,* 100–107.

Savin-Williams, R. (2001). *Mom, Dad, I'm gay.* Washington, DC: American Psychological Association.

Savin-Williams, R. C. (2005). *The new gay teenager.* New York, NY: Trilateral.

Savin-Williams, R. C. (2006). Who's Gay? Does It Matter? *Current Directions in Psychological Science, 15*(1), 40–44.

Saw, S. M., Carkeet, A., Chia, K. S., Stone, R. A., & Tan, D. T. (2002). Component dependent risk factors for ocular parameters in Singapore Chinese children. *Opthamology, 109,* 2065–2071.

Sawnani, H., Jackson, T., Murphy, T., Beckerman, R., & Simakajornboon, N. (2004). The effect of maternal smoking on respiratory and arousal patterns in preterm infants during sleep. *American Journal of Respiratory and Critical Care Medicine, 169,* 733–738.

Sax, L., & Kautz, K. J. (2003). Who first suggests the diagnosis of attention deficit/hyperactivity disorder? *Annals of Family Medicine, 1,* 171–174.

Saxe, G. B. (2002). Candy selling and math learning. In C. Desforges & R. Fox (Eds.), *Teaching and learning: The essential readings* (pp. 86–106). Malden, MA: Blackwell.

Sbarra, D. A., & Emery, R. E. (2008). Deeper into divorce: Using actor–partner analyses to explore systemic differences in coparenting conflict following custody dispute resolution. *Journal of Family Psychology, 22,* 144–152.

Scantlin, R. (2007). Educational television, effects of. In J. J. Arnett (Ed.), *Encyclopedia of children, adolescents, and the media* (pp. 255–258). Thousand Oaks, CA: Sage.

Scantlin, R. (2008). Media use across childhood: Access, time, and content. The handbook of children, media, and development., Handbooks in communication and media. (pp. 51–73). Malden, MA: Blackwell.

Scarr, S. (1993). Biological and cultural diversity: The legacy of Darwin for development. *Child Development, 54,* 424–435.

Scarr, S., & McCartney, K. (1983). How people make their own environments: A theory of genotype environment effects. *Child Development, 54,* 424–435.

Schaal, B., Marlier, L., & Soussignan, R. (2000). Human fetuses learn odours from their pregnant mother's diet. *Chemical Senses, 25,* 729–737.

Schachter, E. P. (2005). Erikson meets the postmodern: Can classic identity theory rise to the challenge? *Identity, 5,* 137–160.

Schachter, S. C., & Ransil, B. J. (1996). Handedness distributions in nine professional groups. *Pereptual and Motor Skills, 82,* 51–63.

Schaeffer, C., Petras, H., & Ialongo, B. (2003). Modeling growth in boys' aggressive behavior across elementary school: Links to later criminal involvement, conduct disorder, and antisocial personality disorder. *Developmental Psychology, 39,* 1020–1035.

Scharf, M., Shulman, S., & Avigad-Spitz, L. (2005). Sibling relationships in emerging adulthood and in adolescence. *Journal of Adolescent Research, 20,* 64–90.

Scheibe, C. (2007). Advertising on children's programs. In J. J. Arnett (Ed.), *Encyclopedia of children, adolescents, and the media* (pp. 59–60). Thousand Oaks, CA: Sage.

Scheiber, R. A., & Sacks, J. J. (2001). Measuring community bicycle helmet use among children. *Public Health Reports, 116,* 113–121.

Scheiwe, K., & Willekins, H. (2009). *Childcare and preschool development in Europe.* New York, NY: Palgrave MacMillan.

Scher, A., Epstein, R., & Tirosh, E. (2004). Stability and changes in sleep regulation: A longitudinal study from 3 months to 3 years. *International Journal of Behavioral Development, 28,* 268–274.

Scherzer, A. L. (2009). Experience in Cambodia with the use of a culturally relevant developmental milestone chart for children in low- and middle-income countries. *Journal of Policy and Practice in Intellectual Disabilities, 6,* 287–292.

Schieffelin, B. B. (1986). The acquisition of Kaluli. In D. Slobin (Ed.), *The cross-linguistic study of language acquisition* (pp. 525–593). Hillsdale, NJ: Erlbaum.

Schieffelin, B. B. (1990). *The give and take of everyday life: Language socialization of Kaluli children.* New York, NY: Cambridge University Press.

Schiller, J. S., & Bernadel, L. (2004). Summary health statistics for the U.S. population: National Health Interview Survey, 2002. *Vital and health statistics. Series 10, Data from the National Health Survey,* (220), 1–101.

Schlegel, A. (2010). Adolescent ties to adult communities: The intersection of culture and development. In L. Jensen (Ed.), *Bridging cultural and developmental approaches to psychology* (pp. 138–159). New York, NY: Oxford University Press.

Schlegel, A., & Barry, H. (1991). *Adolescence: An anthropological inquiry.* New York, NY: Free Press.

Schmidt, L., Holstein, B., Christensen, U., & Boivin, J. (2005). Does infertility cause marital benefit? An epidemiological study of 2250 men and women in fertility treatment. *Patient Education and Counseling, 59,* 244–251.

Schneider, B. (2006). In the moment: The benefits of the Experience Sampling Method. In M. Pitt-Catsouphes, E. E. Kossek, & S. Sweet (Eds.), *The work and family handbook: Multi-disciplinary perspectives, methods, and approaches* (pp. 469–488). Mahwah, NJ: Erlbaum.

Schneider, B. (2009). Challenges of transitioning into adulthood. In I. Schoon & R. K. Silbereisen (Eds.), *Transitions from school to work: Globalization, individualization, and patterns of diversity* (pp. 265–290). New York, NY: Cambridge University Press.

Schneider, B., & Stevenson, D. (1999). *The ambitious generation: America's teenagers, motivated but directionless.* New Haven, CT: Yale University Press.

Schneider, W. (2002). Memory development in childhood. In U. Goswami (Ed.), *Blackwell handbook of childhood cognitive development* (pp. 236–256). Malden, MA: Blackwell.

Schneider, W. (2010). Metacognition and memory development in childhood and adolescence. In H. S. Waters & W. Schneider (Eds.), *Metacognition, strategy use, and instruction* (pp. 54–81). New York, NY: Guilford Press.

Schneider, W., & Bjorklund, D. F. (1992). Expertise, aptitude, and strategic remembering. *Child Development, 63,* 461–473.

Schneider, W., & Pressley, M. (1997). *Memory development between two and twenty* (2nd ed.). Mahwah, NJ: Erlbaum.

Schoenwald, S. K., Heiblum, N., Saldana, L., & Henggeler, S. W. (2008)a. The international implementation of multisystemic therapy. *Evaluation & the Health Professions, 31,* 211–225.

Schoolcraft, W. (2010). *If at first you don't conceive: A complete guide to infertility from one of the nation's leading clinics.* New York, NY: Rodale Books.

Schott, J. M., & Rossor, M. N. (2003). The grasp and other primitive reflexes. *Journal of Neurological and Neurosurgical Psychiatry, 74,* 558–560.

Schulenberg, J. (2000, April). *College students get drunk, so what? National panel data on binge drinking trajectories before, during and after college.* Paper presented at the biennial meeting of the Society for Research on Adolescence, Chicago, IL.

Schulenberg, J. E., & Zarrett, N. R. (2006). Mental health during emerging adulthood: Continuity and discontinuity in courses, causes, and functions. In J. J. Arnett & J. L. Tanner (Eds.), *Emerging adults in America: Coming of age in the 21st century* (pp. 135–172). Washington, DC: American Psychological Association.

Schulenberg, J., & Maggs, J. L. (2000). *A developmental perspective on alcohol use and heavy drinking behavior during adolescence and the transition to adulthood.* Washington, DC: National Institute on Alcohol Abuse and Alcoholism.

Schulz, R., & Curnow, C. (1988). Peak performance and age among superathletes: Track and field, swimming, baseball, tennis, and golf. *Journal of Gerontology, 43*(5), P113–P120.

Schulze, P. A., & Carlisle, S. A. (2010). What research does and doesn't say about breastfeeding: A critical review. *Early Child Development and Care, 180,* 703–718.

Schum, T. R., McAuliffe, T. L., Simms, M. D., Walter, J. A., Lewis, M., & Pupp, R. (2001). Factors associated with toilet training in the 1990s. *Ambulatory Pediatrics, 1,* 79–86.

Schwalb, D. W., Nakawaza, J., Yamamoto, T., & Hyun, J. H. (2004). Fathering in Japanese, Chinese, and Korean cultures: A review of the research literature. In M. E. Lamb (Ed.), *The role of the father in child development* (4th ed., pp. 146–181). Hoboken, NJ: Wiley.

Schwartz, S. J., Beyers, W., Luyckx, K., Soenens, B., Zamboanga, B. L., Forthun, L. F., Hardy, S. A., et al. (2011). Examining the light and dark sides of emerging adults' identity: A study of identity status differences in positive and negative psychosocial functioning. *Journal of Youth and Adolescence, 40*(7), 839–859.

Schwartz, D., Proctor, L. J., & Chien, D. H. (2001). The aggressive victim of bullying: Emotional and behavioral dysregulation as a pathway to victimization by peers. In J. Juonen & S. Graham (Eds.), *Peer harassment in school: The plight of the vulnerable and victimized* (pp. 147–174). New York, NY: Guilford Press.

Schwartz, M., Share, D. L., Leikin, M., & Kozminsky, E. (2008). On the benefits of bi-literacy: Just a head start in reading or specific orthographic insights? *Reading and Writing, 21,* 905–927.

Schwartz, S. J. (2005). A new identity for identity research: Recommendations for expanding and refocusing the identity literature. *Journal of Adolescent Research, 20,* 293–308.

Schweinle, A., & Wilcox, T. (2004). Intermodal perception and physical reasoning in young infants. *Infant Behavior & Development, 27,* 246–265.

Schweinhart, L. J., Montie, J., Xiang, Z., Barnett, W. S., & Belfield, C. R. (2004). *Lifetime effects: The High/Scope Perry Preschool Study through age 40.* Boston, MA: Strategies for Children. Retrieved from www.highscope.org/Research/PerryProject/perrymain.htm

Schwimmer, J. B., Burwinkle, T. M., & Varni, J. W. (2003). Health-related quality of life of severely obese children and adolescents. *JAMA: Journal of the American Medical Association, 289,* 1813–1819.

Scott, E., & Panksepp, J. (2003). Rough-and-tumble play in human children. *Aggressive Behavior, 29,* 539–551.

Seach, K. A., Dharmage, S. C., Lowe, A. J., & Dixon, J. B. (2010). Delayed introduction of solid feeding reduces child overweight and obesity at 10 years. *International Journal of Obesity, 34,* 1475–1479.

Sears, H. (2007). Canada. In J. J. Arnett (Ed.), *International encyclopedia of adolescence.* New York, NY: Routledge.

Sears, H. (2012). Canada. In J. J. Arnett (Ed.), *Adolescent psychology around the world.* New York, NY: Taylor & Francis.

Segal, A. F. (2004). *Life after death: A history of the afterlife in Western religion.* New York, NY: Doubleday.

Segall, M. H., Dasen, P. R., Berry, J. W., & Poortinga, Y. H. (1999). *Human behavior in global perspective: An introduction to cross-cultural psychology.* Boston, MA: Allyn & Bacon.

Seiffge-Krenke, I. (2009). Leaving-home patterns in emerging adults: The impact of earlier parental support and developmental task progression. *European Psychologist, 14*(3), 238–248.

Selander, J. (2011). *Cultural beliefs honor placenta.* Retrieved from http://placentabenefits.info/culture.asp

Sellen, D. W. (2001). Comparison of infant feeding patterns reported for nonindustrial populations with current recommendations. *Journal of Nutrition, 131,* 2707–2715.

Sembuya, R. (2010). Mother or nothing: The agony of infertility. *Bulletin of the World Health Organization, 88,* 881–882.

Sen, K., & Samad, A. Y. (Eds.). (2007). *Islam in the European Union: Transnationalism, youth, and the war on terror.* New York, NY: Oxford University Press.

Serbin, L. A., Powlishta, K. K., & Gulko, J. (1993). The development of sex typing in middle childhood. *Monographs of the Society for Research in Child Development, 58*(2, Serial No. 232).

Shalatin, S., & Phillip, M. (2003). The role of obesity and leptin in the pubertal process and pubertal growth: A review. *International Journal of Obesity and Related Metabolic Disorders, 27,* 869–874.

Shanahan, L., McHale, S. M., Osgood, D. W., & Crouter, A. C. (2007). Conflict frequency with mothers and fathers from middle childhood to late adolescence: Within- and between-families comparisons. *Developmental Psychology, 43,* 539–550.

Shapiro, L. J., & Azuma, H. (2004). Intellectual, attitudinal, and interpersonal aspects of competence in the United States and Japan. In R. J. Sternberg & E. L. Grigorenko (Eds.), *Culture and competence: Contexts of life success* (pp. 187–206). Washington, DC: American Psychological Association.

Shapka, J. D., & Keating, D. P. (2005). Structure and change in self-concept during adolescence. *Canadian Journal of Behavioural Science, 37,* 83–96.

Shaughnessy, J., Zechmeister, E., & Zechmeister, J. (2011). *Research methods in psychology* (11th ed.). New York, NY: McGraw-Hill.

Shaw, P., Greenstein, D., Lerch, J., Clasen, L., Lenroot, R., Gogtay, N., & Evans, A. (2006). Intellectual ability and cortical development in children and adolescents. *Nature, 440,* 676–679.

Shields, L., Mamun, A. A., O'Callaghan, M., Williams, G. M., & Najman, J. M. (2010). Breastfeeding and obesity at 21 years: A cohort study. *Journal of Clinical Nursing, 19,* 1612–1617.

Shipman, K. L., Zeman, J., Nesin, A. E., & Fitzgerald, M. (2003). Children's strategies for displaying anger and sadness: What works with whom? *Merrill-Palmer Quarterly, 49,* 100–122.

Shirtcliff, E. A., Dahl, R E., & Pollak, S. D. (2009). Pubertal development: Correspondence between hormonal and physical development. *Child Development, 80,* 327–337.

Shonkoff, J. P., & Phillips, D. A. (Eds.). (2000). *From neurons to neighborhoods: The science of early childhood development.* Washington, DC: National Academy Press.

Shope, J. T. (2002). Discussion paper. *Injury Prevention, 8*(Suppl. 2), ii14–ii16.

Shope, J. T. (2007). Graduated driver licensing: Review of evaluation results since 2002. *Journal of Safety Research, 38,* 165–175.

Shope, J. T., & Bingham, C. R. (2008). Teen driving: Motor-vehicle crashes and factors that contribute. *American Journal of Preventative Medicine, 35*(3, Suppl. 1), S261–S271.

Shorten, A. (2010). Bridging the gap between mothers and medicine: "New insights" from the NIH Consensus Conference on VBAC. *Birth: Issues in Perinatal Care, Vol 3,* 181–183.

Shreeve, J. (2010, July). The evolutionary road. *National Geographic,* 34–50.

Shulman, S., Laursen, B., Kalman, Z., & Karpovsky, S. (1997). Adolescent intimacy revisited. *Journal of Youth & Adolescence, 26,* 597–617.

Shumaker, D. M., Miller, C., Ortiz, C., & Deutsch, R. (2011). The forgotten bonds: The assessment and contemplation of sibling attachment in divorce and parental separation. *Family Court Review, 49*(1), 46–58.

Shweder, R. A. (2003). *Why do men barbecue? Recipes for cultural psychology.* Cambridge, MA: Harvard University Press.

Shweder, R. A. (Ed.) (2009). *The child: An encyclopedic companion.* Chicago, IL: The University of Chicago Press.

Shweder, R. A., Goodnow, J. J., Hatano, G., LeVine, R. A., Markus, H. R., & Miller, P. J. (2006). The cultural psychology of development: One mind, many mentalities. In W. Damon & R. Lerner (Eds.), & R. M. Lerner (Vol. Eds.), *Handbook of child psychology: Vol. 1. Theoretical models of human development* (6th ed., pp. 716–792). New York, NY: Wiley.

Shweder, R. A., Mahapatra, M., & Miller, J. G. (1990). Culture and moral development. In J. W. Stigler, R. A. Shweder, & G. Herdt (Eds.), *Cultural psychology* (pp. 130–204). New York, NY: Cambridge University Press.

Shweder, R. A., Much, N. C., Mahapatra, M., & Park, L. (1997). The "big three" of morality (autonomy, community, divinity) and the "big three" explanations of suffering. In A. Brandt & D. Rozin (Eds.), *Morality and health* (pp. 119–169). New York, NY: Routledge.

Sidorowicz, L. S., & Lunney, G. S. (1980). Baby X revisited. *Sex Roles, 6,* 67–73.

Sigman, M. (1999). Developmental deficits in children with Down syndrome. In H. Tager-Flusberg (Ed.), *Neurodevelopmental disorders: Developmental cognitive neuroscience* (pp. 179–195). Cambridge, MA: MIT Press.

Sigman, M., Cohen, S., & Beckwith, L. (2000). Why does infant attention predict adolescent intelligence? In D. Muir & A. Slater (Eds.), *Infant development: The essential readings* (pp. 239–253). Malden, MA: Blackwell.

Silk, J. S., Morris, A. S., Kanaya, T., & Steinberg, L. (2003). Psychological control and autonomy granting: Opposite ends of a continuum or distinct constructs? *Journal of Research on Adolescence, 13,* 113–128.

Silva, C., & Martins, M. (2003). Relations between children's invented spelling and the development of phonological awareness. *Educational Psychology, 23,* 3–16.

Simkin, P. (2007). *The birth partner, Third edition: A complete guide to childbirth for dads, doulas, and all other labor companions.* Boston, MA: Harvard Common Press.

Simons, S. H. P., van Dijk, M., Anand, K. S., Roofhooft, D., van Lingen, R., & Tibboel, D. (2003). Do we still hurt newborn babies: A prospective study of procedural pain and analgesia in neonates. *Archives of Pediatrics & Adolescent Medicine, 157,* 1058–1064.

Simons-Morton, B. (2007). Parent involvement in novice teen driving: Rationale, evidence of effects, and potential for enhancing graduated driver licensing effectiveness. *Journal of Safety Research, 38,* 192–202.

Simons-Morton, B. G., Hartos, J. L., & Leaf, W. A. (2002). Promoting parental management of teen driving. *Injury Prevention, 8*(Suppl. 2), ii24–ii31.

Simons-Morton, B. G., Hartos, J. L., Leaf, W. A., & Preusser, D. F. (2006). Increasing parent limits on novice young drivers: Cognitive mediation of the effect of persuasive messages. *Journal of Adolescent Research, 21,* 83–105.

Simons-Morton, B. G., Ouimet, M. C., & Catalano, R. F. (2008). Parenting and the young driver problem. *American Journal of Preventative Medicine, 35*(3, Suppl. 1), S294–S303.

Singer, J. L., & Singer, D. G. (1998). *Barney & Friends* as entertainment and education: Evaluating the quality and effectiveness of a television series for preschool children. In J. K. Asamen & G. L. Berry (Eds.), *Research paradigms, television and social behavior* (pp. 305–367). Thousand Oaks, CA: Sage.

Singerman, J., & Lee, L. (2008). Consistency of the Babinski reflex and its variants. *European Journal of Neurology, 15,* 960–964.

Singh, L., Nestor, S., Parikh, C., & Yull, A. (2009). Influences of infant-directed speech on early word recognition. *Infancy, 14,* 654–666.

Singh, S., Darroch, J. E., & Frost, J. J. (2001). Socioeconomic disadvantage and adolescent women's sexual and reproductive behavior: The case of five developed countries. *Perspectives on Sexual and Reproductive Health, 33,* 251–258 & 289.

Sinnott, J. D. (1998). *The development of logic in adulthood: Postformal thoughts and its applications.* New York, NY: Plenum.

Sinnott, J. D. (2003). Postformal thought and adult development: Living in balance. In J. Demick & C. Andreotti (Eds.), *Handbook of adult development* (pp. 221–238). New York, NY: Kluwer.

Sippola, L. K., Buchanan, C. M., & Kehoe, S. (2007). Correlates of false self in adolescent romantic relationships. *Journal of Clinical Child and Adolescent Psychology, 36,* 515–521.

Sirsch, U., Dreher, E., Mayr, E., & Willinger, U. (2009). What does it take to be an adult in Austria? Views on adulthood in Austrian adolescents, emerging adults, and adults. *Journal of Adolescent Research, 24,* 275–292.

Slater, A., Field, T., & Hernandez-Reif, M. (2002). The development of the senses. In A. Slater & M. Lewis (Eds.), *Introduction to infant development.* New York, NY: Oxford University Press.

Slater, M. D., Henry, K. L., Swaim, R. C., & Anderson, L. L. (2003). Violent media content and aggressiveness in adolescents: A downward spiral model. *Communication Research, 30,* 713–736.

Slobin, D. (1972, July). Children and language: They learn the same way around the world. *Psychology Today,* 71–76.

Slonje, R., & Smith, P. K. (2008). Cyberbullying: Another main type of bullying? *Scandinavian Journal of Psychology, 49,* 147–154.

Small, M. (2001). *Kids: How biology and culture shape the way we raise young children.* New York, NY: Anchor.

Small, M. F. (1998). *Our babies, ourselves: How biology and culture shape the way we parent.* New York, NY: Anchor.

Small, M. F. (2005). The natural history of children. In Sharna Olfman (Ed.), *Childhood lost: How American culture is failing our kids* (pp. 3–17). Westport, CT: Praeger.

Smetana, J. G. (2005). Adolescent–parent conflict: Resistance and subversion as developmental processes. In L. Nucci (Ed.), *Conflict, contradiction, and contrarian elements in moral development and education* (pp. 69–91). Mahwah, NJ: Erlbaum.

Smetana, J. G., Metzger, A., & Campione-Barr, N. (2004). African American late adolescents' relationships with parents: Developmental transitions and longitudinal patterns. *Child Development, 75,* 932–947.

Smith, C., & Denton, M. L. (2005). *Soul searching: The religious and spiritual lives of American teenagers.* New York, NY: Oxford University Press.

Smith, C., & Snell, P. (2009). *Souls in transition: The religious lives of emerging adults in America.* New York, NY: Oxford University Press.

Smith, K., Downs, B., & O'Connell, M. (2001). Maternity leave and employment patterns: 1961–1995. *Current Population Reports P70(79)* (pp. 1–21). Washington, DC: U.S. Bureau of the Census.

Smith, W. B. (2011). *Youth leaving foster care: A developmental, relationship-based approach to practice.* New York, NY: Oxford University Press.

Snarey, J. R. (1985). Cross-cultural universality of social moral development: A review of Kohlbergian research. *Psychological Bulletin, 97,* 202–232.

Snow, R. (2010). The social body: Gender and the burden of disease. In G. Sen and P. Ostlin (Eds.), *Gender equity in health: The shifting frontiers of evidence and action* (pp. 47–69). New York, NY: Taylor & Francis.

Snowling, M. J. (2004). Reading development and dyslexia. In U. Goswami (Ed.), *Blackwell handbook of childhood cognitive development.* Malden, MA: Blackwell.

Snyder, J., Cramer, A., & Afrank, J. (2005). The contributions of ineffective discipline and parental hostile attributions of child misbehavior to the development of conduct problems at home and school. *Developmental Psychology, 41,* 30–41.

Snyder, T. D., Dillow, S. A., & Hoffman, C. M. (2009, March). Digest of Education Statistics, 2008. NCES 2009-020. National Center for Education Statistics. Available from: ED Pubs. P.O. Box 1398, Jessup, MD 20794-1398. Tel: 877-433-7827; Web site: http://nces.ed.gov/help/orderinfo.asp. Retrieved from http://www.eric.ed.gov/ERICWebPortal/contentdelivery/servlet/ERICServlet?accno=ED504502

Soderstrom, M. (2007). Beyond babytalk: Re-evaluating the nature and content of speech input to preverbal infants. *Developmental Review, 27,* 501–532.

Soken, N. H., & Pick, A. D. (1992). Intermodal perception of happy and angry expressive behaviors by seven-month-old infants. *Child Development, 63,* 787–795.

Sokol, R. J., Delaney-Black, V., & Nordstrom, B. (2003). Fetal alcohol spectrum disorder. *JAMA: Journal of the American Medical Association, 290,* 2996–2999.

Sorell, G. T., & Montgomery, M. J. (2001). Feminist perspectives on Erikson's theory: Their relevance for contemporary identity development research. *Identity, 1,* 97–128.

Sowell, E. R., Thompson, P. M., Holmes, C. J., Jernigan, T. I., & Toga, A. W. (1999). In vivo evidence for post-adolescence brain maturation in frontal and striatal regions. *Nature Neuroscience, 2,* 859–861.

Sowell, E., Trauner, D., Ganst, A., & Jernigan, T. (2002). Development of cortical and subcortical brain structures in childhood and adolescence: A structural MRI study. *Developmental Medicine and Child Neurology, 44,* 4–16.

Spafford, C. S., & Grosser, G. S. (2005). *Dyslexia and reading difficulties* (2nd ed.). Boston, MA: Allyn & Bacon.

Spelke, E. S. (1979). Perceiving bimodally specified events in infancy. *Developmental Psychology, 5,* 626–636.

Spence, M. J., & DeCasper, A. J. (1987). Prenatal experience with low-frequency maternal voice sounds influences neonatal perception of maternal voice samples. *Infant Behavior and Development, 10,* 133–142.

Spencer, J. P., Verejiken, B., Diedrich, F. J., & Thelen, E. (2000). Posture and the emergence of manual skills. *Developmental Science, 3,* 216–233.

Spera, C. (2005). A review of the relationship among parenting practices, parenting styles, and adolescent school achievement. *Educational Psychology Review, 17,* 125–146.

Sperber, M. (2000). Beer and circus: How big-time college sports is crippling undergraduate education. New York, NY: Holt.

Spitz, R. (1945). Hospitalism: An inquiry into the genesis of psychiatric conditions in early childhood. In A. Freud, H. Hartmann, & E. Kris (Eds.), *The psychoanalytic study of the child* (pp. 53–74). New York, NY: International Universities Press.

Spock, B. (1966). *Baby and child care.* New York, NY: Pocket Books.

Spock, B., & Needleman, R. (2004). *Dr. Spock's baby and child care* (8th ed.). New York, NY: Pocket Books.

Sprecher, S., & Regan, P. C. (1996). College virgins: How men and women perceive their sexual status. *Journal of Sex Research, 33,* 3–15.

Sroufe, L. A., Carlson, E., & Schulman, S. (1993). Individuals in relationships: Development from infancy through adolescence. In D. C. Funder, R. D. Parke, C. Tomlinson-Keasey, & K. Widaman (Eds.), *Studying lives through time: Personality and development* (pp. 51–60). Norwood, NJ: Ablex.

Sroufe, L. A., Egeland, B., Carlson, E. A., & Collins, W. A. (2005). *The development of the person: The Minnesota study of risk and adaptation from birth to adulthood.* New York, NY: Guilford Press.

St. James-Roberts, I., & Plewis, I. (1996). Individual differences, daily fluctuations, and developmental changes in amounts of infant waking, fussing, crying, feeding, and sleeping. *Child Development, 67,* 2527–2540.

St. James-Roberts, I., Bargn, J. G., Peter, B., Adams, D., & Hunt, S. (2003). Individual differences in responsivity to a neurobehavioural examination predict crying patterns of 1–week–old infants at home. *Developmental Medicine & Child Neurology, 45,* 400–407.

St. Louis, G. R., & Liem, J. H. (2005). Ego identity, ethnic identity, and psychosocial well-being of ethnic minority and majority college students. *Identity, 5,* 227–246.

Staff, J., Mortimer, J. T., & Uggen, C. (2004). Work and leisure in adolescence. In R. M. Lerner & L. Steinberg (Eds.), *Handbook of adolescent psychology* (2nd ed., pp. 429–450). Hoboken, NJ: Wiley.

Stanley, S. M., Rhoades, G. K., & Markman, H. J. (2006). Sliding versus deciding: Inertia and the premarital cohabitation effect. *Family Relations, 55,* 499–509.

Stanley, S. M., Whitton, S. W., & Markman, H. J. (2004). Maybe I do: Interpersonal commitment levels and premarital or non-marital cohabitation. *Journal of Family Issues, 25,* 496–519.

Steele, J. (2006). Media practice model. In J. J. Arnett (Ed.), *Encyclopedia of children, adolescents, and the media.* Thousand Oaks, CA: Sage.

Steele, R. G., Nesbitt-Daly, J. S., Daniel, R. C., & Forehand, R. (2005). Factor structure of the Parenting Scale in a low-income African American sample. *Journal of Child and Family Studies, 14,* 535–549.

Steinberg, L. (1996). *Beyond the classroom: Why school reform has failed and what parents need to do.* New York, NY: Simon & Schuster.

Steinberg, L. (2000, April). *We know some things: Parent–adolescent relations in retrospect and prospect.* [Presidential Address]. Presented at the biennial meeting of the Society for Research on Adolescence, Chicago, IL.

Steinberg, L. D. (2001). We know some things: Parent–adolescent relationships in retrospect and prospect. *Journal of Research on Adolescence, 11,* 1–19.

Steinberg, L. (2010). A dual systems model of adolescent risk-taking. *Developmental Psychobiology, 52*(3), 216–224.

Steinberg, L., & Levine, A. (1997). *You and your adolescent: A parents' guide for ages 10 to 20* (rev. ed.). New York, NY: HarperCollins.

Steinhausen, H. C., Boyadjieva, S., Griogoroiu-Serbanescue, M., & Neumarker, K. J. (2003). The outcome of adolescent eating disorders: Findings from an international collaborative study. *European Child & Adolescent Psychiatry, 12,* i91–i98.

Steptoe, A., & Wardle, J. (2001). Locus of control and health behaviour revisited: A multivariate analysis of young adults from 18 countries. *British Journal of Psychology, 92*(4), 659–672.

Stern, S. (2002). Sexual selves on the World Wide Web: Adolescent girls' home pages as sites for sexual self-expression. In J. D. Brown, J. R. Steele, & K. Walsh-Childers (Eds.), *Sexual teens, sexual media: Investigating media's influence on adolescent sexuality* (pp. 265–285). Mahwah, NJ: Erlbaum.

Sternberg, R. (1983). Components of human intelligence. *Cognition, 15,* 1–48.

Sternberg, R. (1988). *The triarchic mind: A new theory of human intelligence.* New York, NY: Viking Penguin.

Sternberg, R. J. (2002). Intelligence is not just inside the head: The theory of successful intelligence. In J. Aronson (Ed.), *Improving academic achievement* (pp. 227–244). San Diego, CA: Academic Press.

Sternberg, R. J. (2003). Our research program validating the triarchic theory of successful intelligence: Reply to Gottfredson. *Intelligence, 31,* 399–413.

Sternberg, R. J. (2004). Cultural and intelligence. *American Psychologist, 59,* 325–338.

Sternberg, R. J. (2005). The triarchic theory of successful intelligence. In D. P. Flanagan & P. L. Harrison (Eds.), *Contemporary Intellectual Assessment: Theories, Tests and Issues* (pp. 103–119). New York, NY: Guilford Press.

Sternberg, R. J. (2007a). Intelligence and culture. In S. Kitayama & D. Cohen (Eds.), *Handbook of cultural psychology* (pp. 547–568). New York, NY: Guilford Press.

Sternberg, R. J. (2007b). *Wisdom, intelligence, and creativity synthesized.* New York, NY: Cambridge University Press.

Sternberg, C. R., Campos, J. J., & Emde, R. N. (1983). The facial expression of anger in seven month infants. *Child Development, 54,* 178–184.

Steur, F. B., Applefield, J. M., & Smith, R. (1971). Televised aggression and interpersonal aggression of preschool children. *Journal of Experimental Child Psychology, 11,* 442–447.

Stevenson, H. W., & Zusho, A. (2002). Adolescence in China and Japan: Adapting to a changing environment. In B. B. Brown, R. Larson, & T. S. Sarasawthi (Eds.), *The World's Youth: Adolescence in Eight Regions of the Globe* (pp. 141–170). New York, NY: Cambridge University Press.

Stevenson, H. W., Lee, S., & Mu, X. (2000). Successful achievement in mathematics: China and the United States. In C. F. M. van Lieshout & P. G. Heymans (Eds.), *Developing talent across the lifespan* (pp. 167–183). Philadelphia, PA: Psychology Press.

Stevens-Watkins, D., & Rostosky, S. (2010). Binge drinking in African American males from adolescence to young adulthood: The protective influence of religiosity, family connectedness, and close friends' substance use. *Substance Use & Misuse, 45,* 1435–1451.

Stipek, D. J., Gralinski, J. H., & Kopp, C. B. (1990). Self-concept development in toddler years. *Developmental Psychology, 26,* 972–977.

Stoll, B., Hansen, N. I., Adams-Chapman, I., Fanaroff, A. A., Hintz, S. R., Vohr, B., . . . Human Development Neonatal Research Network (2004). Neurodevelopmental and growth impairment among extremely low–birth–weight infants with neonatal infection. *JAMA: Journal of the American Medical Association, 292,* 2357–2365.

Stone, V. E., Baron-Cohen, S., & Knight, R. T. (1998). Frontal lobe contributions to theory of mind. *Journal of Cognitive Neuroscience, 10*(5), 640–656.

Stones, M. J., & Kozma, A. (1996). Activity, exercise, and behavior. In J. E. Birren & K. W. Schaie (Eds.), *Handbook of psychology and aging* (4th ed., pp. 338–352). San Diego, CA: Academic Press.

Stotland, N. E., Gilbert, P., Bogetz, A., Harper, C. C., Abrams, B., & Gerbert, B. (2010). Excessive weight gain in pregnancy: How do prenatal care providers approach counseling? *Journal of Women's Health, 19,* 807–814.

Strang-Karlsson, S., Räikkönen, K., Pesonen, A-K., Kajantie, E., Paavonen, J., Lahti, J., . . . Andersson, S. (2008). Very low birth weight and behavioral symptoms of Attention Deficit Hyperactivity Disorder in young adulthood: The Helsinki Study of very-low-birth-weight adults. *American Journal of Psychiatry, 165,* 1345–1353.

Strauch, B. (2003). *The primal teen: What the new discoveries about the teenage brain tell us about our kids.* New York, NY: Anchor.

Straus, M. A., & Donnelly, D. A. (1994). *Beating the devil out of them: Corporal punishment in American families.* New York, NY: Lexington Books.

Strauss, R. S., & Pollack, H. A. (2003). Social marginalization of overweight children. *Archives of Pediatric and Adolescent Medicine, 157,* 746–752.

Striegel-Moore, R. H., & Franko, D. L. (2006). Adolescent eating disorders. In C. A. Essau (Ed.), *Child and adolescent psychopathology: Theoretical and clinical implications* (pp. 160–183). New York, NY: Routledge.

Striegel-Moore, R. H., Seeley, J. R., & Lewinsohn, P. M. (2003). Psychosocial adjustment in young adulthood of women who experienced an eating disorder in adolescence. *Journal of the American Academy of Child & Adolescent Psychiatry, 42,* 587–593.

Stromquist, N. P. (2007). Gender equity education globally. In S. S. Klein, B. Richardson, D. A. Grayson, L. H. Fox, C. Kramarae, D. S. Pollard, & C. A. Dwyer (Eds.), *Handbook for achieving gender equity through education* (2nd ed., pp. 33–42). Mahwah, NJ: Erlbaum.

Suarez-Orozco, C., & Suarez-Orozco, M. (1996). *Transformations: Migration, family life and achievement motivation among Latino adolescents.* Palo Alto, CA: Stanford University Press.

Subrahmanyam, K., Reich, S. M., Waechter, N., & Espinoza, G. (2008). Online and offline social networks: Use of social networking sites by emerging adults. *Journal of Applied Developmental Psychology, 29*(6), 420–433.

Suggate, S. P. (2010). Why what we teach depends on when: Grade and reading intervention modality moderate effect size. *Developmental Psychology, 46*(6), 1556–1579.

Sullivan, C., & Cottone, R. R. (2010). Emergent characteristics of effective cross-cultural research: A review of the literature. *Journal of Counseling and Development, 88,* 357–362.

Sullivan, J. L. (2003). Prevention to mother-to-child transmission of HIV—what next? *Journal of Acquired Immune Deficiency Syndrome* (Suppl. 1), *34,* S67–S72.

Super, C. M., & Harkness, S. (1986). The developmental niche: A conceptualization at the interface of child and culture. *International Journal of Behavior Development, 9,* 545–569.

Super, C. M., & Harkness, S. (2009). The developmental niche of the newborn in rural Kenya. In K. J. Nugent, B. J. Petrauskas, & T. B. Brazelton (Eds.), *The newborn as a person: Enabling healthy infant development worldwide* (pp. 85–97). Hoboken, NJ: Wiley.

Super, C. M., Harkness, S., van Tijen, N., van der Vlugt, E., Fintelman, M., & Dijkstra, J. (1996). The three R's of Dutch childrearing and the socialization of infant arousal. In S. Harkness & C. M. Super (Eds.), *Parents' cultural belief systems: Their origins, expressions and consequences* (pp. 447–466). New York, NY: Guilford Press.

Susser, I. (2011). *AIDS, sex, and sulture: Global politics and survival in Southern Africa.* Wiley.

Susman, E. J., & Rogol, A. (2004). Puberty and psychological development. In R. M. Lerner & L. Steinberg (Eds.), *Handbook of adolescent psychology* (2nd ed., pp. 15–44). Hoboken, NJ: Wiley.

Sussman, S., Pokhrel, P., Ashmore, R. D., & Brown, B. B. (2007). Adolescent peer group identification and characteristics: A review of the literature. *Addictive Behaviors, 32,* 1602–1627.

Svetlova, M., Nichols, S. R., & Brownell, C. A. (2010). Toddlers prosocial behavior: From instrumental to empathic to altruistic helping. *Child Development, 81*(6), 1814–1827.

Swanson, H., Saez, L., & Gerber, M. (2004). Literacy and cognitive functioning inbilingual and nonbilingual children at or not at risk for reading disabilities. *Journal of Educational Psychology, 96,* 3–18.

Swenson, C. C., Henggeler, S. W., Taylor, I. S., & Addison, O. W. (2005). *Multisystemic therapy and neighborhood partnerships: Reducing adolescent violence and substance abuse.* New York, NY: Guilford Press.

Swinbourne, J. M., & Touyz, S. W. (2007). The comorbidity of eating disorders and anxiety disorders: A review. *European Eating Disorders Review, 15,* 253–274.

Swingley, D. (2010). Fast mapping and slow mapping in children's word learning. *Language Learning and Development, 6,* 179–183.

Syed, M., & Azmitia, M. (2010). Narrative and ethnic identity exploration: A longitudinal account of emerging adults' ethnicity-related experiences. *Developmental Psychology, 46,* 208–219.

Syltevik, L. J. (2010). Sense and sensibility: Cohabitation in "cohabitation land." *The Sociological Review, 58,* 444–462.

Symons, D. K. (2001). A dyad-oriented approach to distress and mother–child relationship outcomes in the first 24 months. *Parenting: Science and Practice, 1,* 101–122.

Taga, K. A., Markey, C. N., & Friedman, H. S. (2006). A longitudinal investigation of associations between boys' pubertal timing and adult behavioral health and well-being. *Journal of Youth and Adolescence, 35,* 401–411.

Takahashi, K., & Takeuchi, K. (2007). Japan. In J. J. Arnett (Ed.), *International encyclopedia of adolescence* (pg #s?). New York, NY: Routledge.

Talbani, A., & Hasanali, P. (2000). Adolescent females between tradition and modernity: Gender role socialization in south Asian immigrant families. *Journal of Adolescence, 23,* 615–627.

Tamaru, S., Kikuchi, A., Takagi, K., Wakamatsu, M., Ono, K., Horikoshi, T., Kihara, H., & Nakamura, T. (2011). Neurodevelopmental outcomes of very low birth weight and extremely low birth weight infants at 18 months of corrected age associated with prenatal risk factors. *Early Human Development, 87,* 55–59.

Tamay, Z., Akcay, A., Ones, U., Guler, N., Kilie, G., & Zencir, M. (2007). Prevalence and risk factors for allergic rhinitis in primary school children. *International Journal of Pediatric Otorhinolaryngology, 71,* 463–471.

Tamis-LeMonda, C. S., Bornstein, M. H., & Baumwell, L. (2001). Maternal responsiveness and children's achievement of language milestones. *Child Development, 72,* 749–767.

Tamis-LeMonda, C. S., Way, N., Hughes, D., Yoshikawa, H., Kalman, R. K., & Niwa, E. Y. (2008). Parents' goals for children: The dynamic coexistence of individualism and collectivism in cultures and individuals. *Social Development, 17,* 183–209.

Tanaka, H., & Seals, D. R. (2003). Dynamic exercise performance in master athletes: Insight into the effects of primary human aging on physiological functional capacity. *Journal of Applied Physiology, 95,* 2152–2162.

Tanner, J. L. (2006). Recentering during emerging adulthood: A critical turning point in life span human development. In J. J. Arnett & J. L. Tanner (Eds.),

Emerging adults in America: Coming of age in the 21st century (pp. 21–55). Washington, DC: American Psychological Association.

Tanon, F. (1994). *A cultural view on planning: The case of weaving in Ivory Coast.* Tilburg, The Netherlands: Tilburg University Press.

Tardif, T., Wellman, H. M., & Cheung, K. M. (2004). False belief understanding in Canontese-speaking children. *Journal of Child Language, 31,* 779–800.

Taylor, A. (2005). It's for the rest of your life: The pragmatics of youth career decision making. *Youth & Society, 36,* 471–503.

Taylor, H. G., Klein, N., & Hack, M. (2000). School-age consequences of <750 g birth weight: A review and update. *Developmental Neuropsychology, 17,* 289–321.

Taylor, M. J. (2006). Neural Bases of Cognitive Development. In E. Bialystok & F. I. M. Craik (Eds.), *Lifespan cognition: Mechanisms of change* (pp. 15–26.) New York, NY: Oxford University Press.

Tedeschi, A., & Airaghi, L. (2006). Is affluence a risk factor for bronchial asthma and type 1 diabetes? *Pediatric Allergy and Immunology, 17,* 533–537.

Teitler, J. O. (2002). Trends in youth sexual initiation and fertility in developed counties: 1960–1995. *Annals of the American Academy of Political Science Studies, 580,* 134–152.

Telama, R., Yang, X., Viikari, J., Välimäki, I., Wanne, O., & Raitakari, O. (2005). Physical activity from childhood to adulthood: A 21-year tracking study. *American Journal of Preventative Medicine, 28,* 267–273.

Terry, W. S. (2003). *Learning and memory* (2nd ed.). Boston, MA: Allyn & Bacon.

Teti, D. M., Sakin, K., Kucera, E., Corns, K. M., & Eiden, R.D. (1996). And baby makes four: Predictors of attachment security among preschool-aged first-borns during the transition to sibling-hood. *Child Development, 68,* 579–596.

Thach, B. T. (2009). Does swaddling decrease or increase the risk for Sudden Infant Death syndrome? *Journal of Pediatrics, 155,* 461–462.

Thacher, P. V. (2008). University students and the "all nighter": Correlates and patterns of students' engagement in a single night of total sleep deprivation. *Behavioral Sleep Medicine, 6,* 16–31.

Thacker, S. B., & Stroup, D. E. (2003). Revisiting the use of the electronic fetal monitor. *Lancet, 361,* 445–446.

Tharpe, A. M., & Ashmead, D. H. (2001). A longitudinal investigation of infant auditory sensitivity. *AJA: American Journal of Audiology, 10,* 104–112.

Thelen, E. (2001). Dynamic mechanisms of change in early percetual-motor development. In J. L. McClelland & R. S. Siegler (Eds.), *Mechanisms of cognitive development: Behavioral and neural perspectives* (pp. 161–184). Mahwah, NJ: Erlbaum.

Thiessen, E. D., Hill, E. A., & Saffran, J. R. (2005). Infant-directed speech facilitates word segmentation. *Infancy, 7,* 53–71.

Thomas, A., & Chess, S. (1977). *Temperament and development.* New York, NY: Brunner/Mazel.

Thomas, A., Chess, S., & Birch, H. G. (1968). *Temperament and behavior disorders in children.* New York: NY University Press.

Thompson, C. J. (2005). Consumer risk perceptions in a community of reflexive doubt. *The Journal of Consumer Research, 32,* 235–248.

Thompson, P. M., Giedd, J. N., Woods, R. P., MacDonald, D., Evans, A. C. & Toga, A. W. (2000). Growth patterns in the developing brain detected by using continuum mechanical tensor maps. *Nature, 404,* 190–193.

Thompson, R. A. (1998). Early sociopersonality development. In W. Damon (Editor-in-Chief), & N. Eisenberg (Vol. Ed.), *Handbook of child psychology: Vol. 3. Social, emotional and personality development* (5th ed., pp. 25–104). New York, NY: Wiley.

Thompson, R. A. (2006). The development of the person: Social understanding, relationships, conscience, self. In W. Damon & R. Lerner (Eds.), & N. Eisenberg (Vol. Ed.), *Handbook of child psychology: Vol. 3. Social, emotional and personality development* (6th ed., pp. 24–98). New York, NY: Wiley.

Thompson, R. A. (2008). Attachment-related mental representations: Introduction to the special issue. *Attachment & Human Development, 10*(4), 347–358.

Thompson, P. M., Giedd, J. N., Woods, R. P., MacDonald, D., Evans, A. C., Toga, A. W., & others. (2000). Growth patterns in the developing brain detected by using continuum mechanical tensor maps. *Nature, 404*(6774), 190–192.

Thompson, R. A., & Goodvin, R. (2007). Taming the tempest in the teapot: Emotional regulation in toddlers. In C. A. Brownell & C. B. Kopp (Eds.), *Socioemotional development in the toddler years* (pp. 320–341). New York, NY: Guilford Press.

Thompson, R. A., & Nelson, C. A. (2001). Developmental science and the media. *American Psychologist, 56,* 5–15.

Thompson, R. A., & Raikes, H. A. (2003). Toward the next quarter-century: Conceptual and methodological challenges for attachment theory. *Development and Psychopathology, 15,* 691–718.

Thorne, B., & Luria, Z. (1986). Sexuality and gender in children's daily worlds. *Social Problems, 33*(3), 176–190.

Tierra, L., & Tierra, M. (1998). *Chinese traditional herbal medicine.* Twin Lakes, WI: Lotus Light.

Tiggemann, M., & Anesbury, T. (2000). Negative stereotyping of obesity in children: The role of controllability beliefs. *Journal of Applied Social Psychology, 30,* 1977–1993.

Tobach, E. (2004). Development of sex and gender: Biochemistry, physiology, and experience. In A. M. Paludi (Ed.), *Praeger guide to the psychology of gender* (pp. 240–270). Westport, CT: Praeger.

Tobin, D. D., Menon, M., Menon, M., Spatta, B. C., Hodges, E. V. E., & Perry, D. G. (2010). The intrapsychics of gender: A model of self-socialization. *Psychologival Review, 117,* 601–622.

Tobin, J., Hsueh, Y., & Karasawa, M. (2009). *Preschool in three cultures revisited: China, Japan, and the United States.* Chicago, IL: University of Chicago Press.

Tomasello, M., & Rakoczy, H. (2003). What makes human cognition unique? From individual to shared to collective intentionality. *Mind and Language, 18,* 121–147.

Tough, S., Clarke, M., & Cook, J. (2007). Fetal alcohol spectrum disorder prevention approaches among Canadian physicians by proportion of native/aboriginal patients: Practices during the preconception and prenatal periods. *Maternal and Child Health Journal, 11,* 385–393.

Trainor, L. J., Austin, C. M., & Desjardins, R. N. (2000). Is infant-directed speech prosody a result of the vocal expression of emotion? *Psychological Science, 11,* 188–195.

Trajanovska, M., Manias, E., Cranswick, N., & Johnston, L. (2010). Parental management of childhood complaints: Over-the-counter medicine use and advice-seeking behaviours. *Journal of Clinical Nursing, 19,* 2065–2075.

Treatment for Adolescents with Depression Study Team (2007). Long-term effectiveness and safety outcomes. *Archives of General Psychiatry, 64,* 1132–1143.

Trehub, S. E. (2001). Musical predispositions in infancy. *Annals of the New York Academy of Sciences, 930,* 1–16.

Trehub, S. E., Thorpe, L. A., & Morrongiello, B. A. (1985). Infants' perception of melodies: Changes in a single tone. *Infant Behavior and Development, 8,* 213–223.

Tremblay, R. E. (2000). The development of aggressive behaviour during childhood: What have we learned in the past century? *International Journal of Behavioral Development, 24,* 129–141.

Tremblay, R. E. (2002). Prevention of injury by early socialization of aggressive behavior. *Injury Prevention, 8*(Suppl. IV), 17–21.

Tremblay, R. E., & Nagin, D. S. (2005). Developmental origins of physical aggression in humans. In R. E. Tremblay, W. W. Hartup, & J. Archer (Eds.), *Developmental origins of aggression* (pp. 83–106). New York, NY: Guilford Press.

Tremblay, T., Monetta, L., & Joanette, Y. (2004). Phonological processing of words in right- and left-handers. *Brain and Cognition, 55,* 427–432.

Triandis, H. C. (1995). *Individualism and collectivism.* Boulder, CO: Westview Press.

Tronick, E. (2007). *The neurobehavioral and social-emotional development of infants and children.* New York, NY: W. W. Norton.

Trost, K. (2012). Norway. In J. J. Arnett (Ed.), *Adolescent psychology around the world.* New York, NY: Taylor & Francis.

Truglio, R. T. (2007). Sesame Workshop. In J. J. Arnett (Ed.), *Encyclopedia of children, adolescents, and the media* (pp. 749–750). Thousand Oaks, CA: Sage.

Tseng, V. (2004). Family interdependence and academic adjustments in college: Youth from immigrant and U.S. born families. *Child Development, 75,* 966–983.

Tudge, J. R. H., Doucet, F., Odero, D., Sperb, T. M., Piccinini, C. A., & Lopes, R. S. (2006). A window into different cultural worlds: Young children's everyday activities in the United States, Brazil, and Kenya. *Child Development, 77,* 1446–1469.

Turkheimer, E., Harden, K. P., D'Onofrio, B., & Gottesman, I. I. (2009). The Scarr-Rowe interaction between measured socioeconomic status and the heritability of cognitive ability. In K. McCartney & R. A. Weinberg (Eds.), *Experience and development: A festschrift in honor of Sandra Wood Scarr* (pp. 81–98). New York, NY: Psychology Press.

Twenge, J. M., & Crocker, J. (2002). Race and self-esteem: Meta-analyses comparing Whites, Blacks, Hispanics, Asians, and America Indians and comment on Gray-Little and Hafdahl (2000). *Psychological Bulletin, 128,* 371–408.

Twenge, J. M. (2006). *Generation me: Why today's young Americans are more confident, assertive, entitled—and more miserable than ever before.* New York, NY: Free Press.

Twisk, D. A. M., & Stacey, C. (2007). Trends in young driver risk and countermeasures in European countries. *Journal of Safety Research, 38,* 245–257.

Tyano, S., Keren, M., Herrman, H., & Cox, J. (2010). *The competent fetus.* New York, NY: Wiley.

U.S. Bureau of the Census. (2003). *Statistical abstracts of the United States.* Washington, DC: U.S. Government Printing Office.

U.S. Bureau of the Census. (2006). *Statistical abstracts of the United States.* Washington, DC: U.S. Government Printing Office.

U.S. Bureau of the Census. (2009). *Statistical abstracts of the United States.* Washington, DC: U.S. Government Printing Office.

U.S. Bureau of the Census. (2010). *Statistical abstracts of the United States.* Washington, DC: U.S. Government Printing Office.

U.S. Bureau of the Census. (2011). *Statistical abstract of the United States.* Washington, DC: Author.

U.S. Department of Health and Human Services. (2004). *Trends in the well-being of America's children and youth, 2003* (No. 017–022–01571–4). Washington, DC: U.S. Government Printing Office.

U.S. Department of Labor. (1932). *Infant care.* Children's Bureau, Publication 8.

U.S. Department of Transportation. (1995). *The economic costs of motor vehicle crashes, Technical report 1994.* Washington, DC: National Highway Traffic Safety Administration.

Umaña-Taylor, A. J. (2005). Self-esteem and ethnic identity among Latino adolescents. *Directions in Rehabilitation Counseling, 16,* 9–18.

UNAIDS. (2010). UNAIDS report on the global AIDS epidemic. Retrieved from http://www.unaids.org/globalreport/documents/20101123_GlobalReport_full_en.pdf

Under threat of change, slowly but surely, universities in France—and all across Europe—are reforming. (2008, June 7). *The Economist,* 62.

Underwood, M. (2003). *Social-aggression among girls.* New York, NY: Guilford Press.

UNESCO. (2006). EFA global monitoring report: Strong foundations: Early childhood care and education. Paris, France: Author.

UNICEF. (2004a). *Low birth weight: Country, regional, and global estimates.* New York, NY:Author.

UNICEF. (2004b). *The state of the world's children 2002.* Geneva, Switzerland: Author.

UNICEF. (2008). *State of the world's children.* New York, NY: Author.

UNICEF. (2009). *State of the world's children, 2009.* New York, NY: Author.

UNICEF. (2011a). *Breastfeeding Initiatives Exchange.* Retrieved from http://www.unicef.org/programme/breastfeeding/

UNICEF. (2011b). *The state of the world's children.* New York, NY: UNICEF.

UNICEF. (2012). *The State of the World's Children.* New York, NY: United Nations.

United Nations Development Programme (UNDP). (2006). *Human development report.* New York, NY: Author.

United Nations Development Programme. (2008). *Human development report.* New York, NY: Author.

United Nations Development Programme. (2010). *Human development report.* New York, NY: Author.

United Nations Development Programme (UNDP). (2011). *Human development report.* New York, NY: Author.

United States Department of Labor. (2010). *Number of jobs held, labor market activity, and earnings growth among younger baby boomers: Results from more than two decades of a longitudinal study.* Washington, DC: Bureau of Labor Statistics.

Unsworth, G., Devilly, G. J., & Ward, T. (2007). The effect of playing violent video games on adolescents: Should parents be quaking in their boots? *Psychology, Crime, & Law, 13,* 383–394.

Updegraff, K. A., McHale, S. M., & Crouter, A. (2002). Adolescents' sibling relationship and friendship experiences: Developmental patterns and relationship linkages. *Social Development, 11,* 182–204.

Updegraff, K. A., Thayer, S. M., Whiteman, S. D., Denning, D. J., & McHale, S. M. (2005). Relational aggression in adolescents' sibling relationships: Links to sibling and parent–adolescent relationship quality. *Family Relations, 54,* 373–385.

Vadasy, P. F., & Sanders, E. A. (2011). Efficacy of supplemental phonics-based instruction for low-skilled first graders: How language minority status and pretest characteristics moderate treatment response. *Scientific Studies of Reading, 15*(6), 471–497.

Vaillancourt, T., & Hymel, S. (2006). Aggression and social status: The moderating roles of sex and peer-values characteristics. *Aggressive Behavior, 32*, 396–408.

Vaillancourt, T., Brendgen, M., Boivin, M., & Tremblay, R. E. (2003). A longitudinal confirmatory factor analysis of indirect and physical aggression: Evidence of two factors over time? *Child Development, 74*, 1628–1638.

Valencia-Martín, J. L., Galan, I., & Rodríguez-Artalejo, F. (2007). Binge drinking in Madrid, Spain. *Alcoholism: Clinical and Experimental Research, 31*, 1723–1730.

Vallejo, M. C., Ramesh, V., Phelps, A. L., & Sah, N. (2007). Epidural labor analgesia: Continuous infusion versus patient-controlled epidural analgesia with background infusion versus without a background infusion. *The Journal of Pain, 8*, 970–975.

Valkenburg, P. M., & Buijzen, M. (2005). Identifying determinants of young children's brand awareness: Television, parents, and peers. *Journal of Applied Developmental Psychology, 26*(4), 456–468.

van Balen, F. v., & Inhorn, M. C. (2002). Interpreting infertility: A view from the social sciences. In M. C. Inhorn & F. v. Balen, *Infertility around the globe: New thinking on childlessness, gender, and reproductive technologies* (pp. 3–32). Berkeley, CA: University of California Press.

van Beinum, F. J. (2008). Frames and babbling in hearing and deaf infants. In B. L. Davis & K. Zajdó (Eds.), *The syllable in speech production* (pp. 225–241). New York, NY: Erlbaum.

Van de Poel, E. V., Hosseinpoor, A. R., Speybroek, N., Van Ourti, T., & Vega, J. (2008). Socioeconomic inequality in malnutrition in developing countries. *Bulletin of the World Health Organization, 86*, 282–291.

Van Evra, J. (2007). School-age children, impact of media on. In J. J. Arnett (Ed.), *Encyclopedia of children, adolescents, and the media* (pp. 739–742). Thousand Oaks, CA: Sage.

Van Hecke, A. V., Mundy, P. C., Acra, C. F., Block, J. J., Delgado, C. E. F., Parlade, M. V., . . . Pomares, Y. B. (2007). Infant joint attention, temperament, and social competence in preschool children. *Child Development, 78*, 53–69.

Van Hoof, A. (1999). The identity status approach: In need of fundamental revision and qualitative change. *Developmental Review, 19*, 622–647.

Van Horn, K. R., & Cunegatto, M. J. (2000). Interpersonal relationships in Brazilian adolescents. *International Journal of Behavioral Development, 24*, 199–203.

van IJzendoorn, M. H., & Hubbard, F. O. A. (2000). Are infant crying and maternal responsiveness during the first year related to infant–mother attachment at 15 months? *Attachment and Human Development, 2*, 371–391.

van IJzendoorn, M. H., & Kroonenberg, P. M. (1988). Cross-cultural patterns of attachment: A meta-analysis of the Strange Situation. *Child Development, 59*, 147–156.

van IJzendoorn, M. H., & Sagi-Schwartz, A. (2008). Cross-cultural patterns of attachment: Universal and contextual dimensions. In J. Cassidy & P. R. Shaver (Eds.), *Handbook of attachment: Theory, research, and clinical applications* (2nd ed., pp. 880–905). New York, NY: Guilford Press.

van IJzendoorn, M. H., Schuengel, C., & Bakermans-Kranenburg, M. J. (1999). Disorganized attachment in early childhood: Meta-analysis of precursors, concomitants and sequelae. *Development and Pscyhopathology, 11*, 225–249.

van IJzendoorn, M. H., Vereijken, C. M. J. L., Bakermans-Kraneburg, M. J., & Riksen-Walraven, J. M. (2004). Assessing attachment security with the Attachment Q Sort: Meta-analytic evidence for the validity of the Observer AQS. *Child Development, 75*, 1188–1213.

van Sleuwen, B. E., Engelberts, A. C., Boere-Boonekamp, M. M., Kuis, W., Schulpen, T. W. J., & L'Hoir, M. P. (2007). Swaddling: A systematic review. *Pediatrics, 120*, e1097–e1106.

Vandell, D. L. (2004). Early child-care: The known and the unknown. *Merrill-Palmer Quarterly, 50* (Special Issue: The maturing of human developmental sciences: Appraising past, present and prospective agendas), 387–414.

Vandell, D. L., Burchinal, M. R., Belsky, J., Owen, M. T., Friedman, S. L., Clarke-Stewart, A., . . . Weinraub, M. (2005). Early child care and children's development in the primary grades: Follow-up results from the NICHD Study of Early Child Care. Paper presented at the biennial meeting of the Society for Research in Child Development, Atlanta, GA.

Vandereycken, W., & Van Derth, R. (1994). *From fasting saints to anorexic girls: The history of self-starvation.* New York, NY: New York University Press.

Varendi, H., Christensson, K., Porter, R. H., & Wineberg, J. (1998). Soothing effect of amniotic fluid smell in newborn infants. *Early Human Development, 51*, 47–55.

Vazsonyi, A. T., & Snider, J. B. (2008). Mentoring, competencies, and adjustment in adolescents: American part-time employment and European apprenticeships. *International Journal of Behavioral Development, 32*, 46–55.

Verkuyten, M. (2002). Multiculturalism among minority and majority adolescents in the Netherlands. *International Journal of Intercultural Relations, 26*, 91–108.

Verma, R. P., Shibli, S., Fang, H., & Komaroff, E. (2009). Clinical determinants and the utility of early postnatal maximum weight loss in fluid management of extremely low birth weight infants. *Early Human Development, 85*, 59–64.

Verma, S., & Larson, R. (1999). Are adolescents more emotional? A study of daily emotions of middle class Indian adolescents. *Psychology and Developing Societies, 11*, 179–194.

Vidyasagar, T. R. (2004). Neural underpinnings of dyslexia as a disorder of visuospatial attention. *Clinical and Experimental Optometry, 87*, 4–10.

Vig, S., Chinitz, S., & Shulman, L. (2005). Young children in foster care: Multiple vulnerabilities and complex service needs. *Infants and Young Children, 18*, 147–160.

Vilette, B. (2002). Do young children grasp the inverse relationship between addition and subtraction? Evidence against early arithmetic. *Cognitive Development, 17*, 1365–1383.

Vilhjalmsson, R., & Kristjansdottir, G. (2003). Gender differences in physical activity in older children and adolescents: The central role of organized sport. *Social Science Medicine, 56*, 363–374.

Vinanen, A., Munhbayarlah, S., Zevgee, T., Narantsetseg, L., Naidansuren, T. S., Koskenvuo, M., . . . Terho, E. O. (2007). The protective effect of rural living against atopy in Mongolia. *Allergy, 62*, 272–280.

Vincent, L. (2008). "Boys will be boys": Traditional Xhosa male circumcision, HIV and sexual socialization in contemporary South Africa. *Culture, Health, and Sexuality, 10*, 431–446.

Vincent, M. A., & McCabe, M. P. (2000). Gender differences among adolescents in family and peer influences on body dissatisfaction, weight loss, and binge eating disorders. *Journal of Youth & Adolescence, 29*, 205–221.

Vinden, P. G. (1996). Junin Quechua children's understanding of mind. *Child Development, 67*, 1707–1716.

Visher, E. B., Visher, J. S., & Pasley, K. (2003). Remarriage families and stepparenting. In F. Walsh (Ed.), *Normal family processes* (pp. 153–175). New York, NY: Guilford.

Vlaardingerbroek, J., van Goudoever, J. B., & van den Akker, C. H. P. (2009). Initial nutritional management of the preterm infant. *Early Human Development, 85*, 691–695.

Voeller, K. K. (2004). Attention-deficit hyperactivity disorder. *Journal of Child Neurology, 19*, 798–814.

Volk, A., Craif, W., Bryce, W., & King, M. (2006). Adolescent risk correlates of bullying and different types of victimization. *International Journal of Adolescent Medicine and Health, 18*, 575–586.

Volling, B. L. (2003). Sibling relationships. In M. H. Bornstein, L. Davidson, C. L.M. Keyes, & K. A. Moore (Eds.), *Well-being: Positive development across the life course* (pp. 205–220). Mahwah, NJ: Erlbaum.

Vondra, J. L., & Barnett, D. (Eds.). (1999). Atypical attachment in infancy and early childhood among children at developmental risk. *Monographs of the Society for Research in Child Development, 64*(3,Serial No. 258).

Vouloumanos, A., & Werker, J. F. (2004). Tuned to the signal: The privileged status of speech for young infants. *Developmental Science, 7*, 270–276.

Vouloumanos, A., Hauser, M. D., Werker, J. F., & Martin, A. (2010). The tuning of human neonates' preference for speech. *Child Development, 81*, 517–527.

Wachs, T. (2002). Nutritional deficiencies as a biological context for development. In W. Hartup, W. Silbereisen, & K. Rainer (Eds.), *Growing points in developmental science: An introduction* (pp. 64–84). Philadelphia, PA: Psychology Press.

Wagner, C. L., & Greer, F. R. (2008). Prevention of rickets and Vitamin D deficiency in infants, children, and adolescents. *Pediatrics, 122*(5), 1142–1152.

Wahlbeck, K., Forsén, T., Osmond, C., Barker, D. J. P., & Eriksson, J. G. (2001). Association of schizophrenia with low maternal body mass index, small size at birth, and thinness during childhood. *Archives of General Psychiatry, 58*, 48–52.

Walcott, D. D., Pratt, H. D., & Patel, D. R. (2003). Adolescents and eating disorders: Gender, racial, ethnic, sociocultural and socioeconomic issues. *Journal of Adolescent Research, 18,* 223–243.

Wallace, J. M., & Williams, D. R. (1997). Religion and adolescent health-compromising behavior. In J. Schulenberg, J. L. Maggs, & K. Hurrelmann (Eds.), *Health risks and developmental transitions during adolescence* (pp. 444–468). New York, NY: Cambridge University Press.

Wallace, J. M., Yamaguchi, R., Bachman, J. G., O'Malley, P. M., Schulenberg, J. E., & Johnston, L. D. (2007). Religiosity and adolescent substance use: The role of individual and contextual influences. *Social Problems, 54,* 308–327.

Wallerstein, J. S., & Johnson-Reitz, K. (2004). Communication in divorced and single parent families. In A. L. Vangelisti (Ed.), *Handbook of family communication* (pp. 197–214). Mahwah, NJ: Erlbaum.

Walshaw, C. A. (2010). Are we getting the best from breastfeeding? *Acta Pædiatrica, 99*(9), 1292–1297.

Wang, Q. (2006). Relations of maternal style and child self-concept to autobiographical memories in Chinese, Chinese immigrant, and European American 3-year-olds. *Child Development, 77*(6), 1794–1809.

Wang, S., Baillargeon, R., & Paterson, S. (2005). Detecting continuity violations in infancy: A new account and new evidence from covering and tube events. *Cognition, 95,* 129–173.

Wang, S., & Tamis-LeMonda, C. (2003). Do childrearing values in Taiwan and the United States reflect cultural values of collectivism and individualism? *Journal of Cross-Cultural Psychology, 34,* 629–642.

Wang, Y., & Fong, V. L. (2009). Little emperors and the 4:2:1 generation: China's singletons. *Journal of the American Academy of Child & Adolescent Psychiatry, 48,* 1137–1139.

Wang, Y., & Lobstein, T. (2006). Worldwide trends in childhood overweight and obesity. *International Journal of Pediatric Obesity, 1,* 11–25.

Wang, Y., Wang, X., Kong, Y., Zhang, J. H., & Zeng, Q. (2010). The Great Chinese Famine leads to shorter and overweight females in Chongqing Chinese population after 50 years. *Obesity, 18,* 588–592.

Warnock, F. F., Castral, T. C., Brant, R., Sekilian, M., Leite, A. M., De La Presa Owens, S., & Schochi, C. G. S. (2010). Brief report: Maternal Kangaroo Care for neonatal pain relief: A systematic narrative review. *Journal of Pediatric Psychology, 35,* 975–984.

Warnock, F., & Sandrin, D. (2004). Comprehensive description of newborn distress behavior in response to acute pain (newborn male circumcision). *Pain, 107,* 242–255.

Warren, R. (2007). Electronic media, children's use of. In J. J. Arnett (Ed.), *Encyclopedia of children, adolescents, and the media* (Vol. 1, pp. 286–288). Thousand Oaks, CA: Sage.

Warren, S. L., & Simmens, S. J. (2005). Predicting toddler anxiety/depressive symptoms: Effects of caregiver sensitivity of temperamentally vulnerable children. *Infant of Medical Health Journal, 26,* 40–55.

Waterman, A. S. (1992). Identity as an aspect of optimal functioning. In G. R. Adams, T. P. Gullotta, & R. Montemayor (Eds.), *Adolescent identity formation* (Vol. 4, pp. 50–72). Newbury Park, CA: Sage.

Waterman, A. S. (1999). Issues of identity formation revisited: United States and the Netherlands. *Developmental Review, 19,* 462–479.

Waterman, A. S. (2007). Doing well: The relationship of identity status to three conceptions of well-being. *Identity, 7,* 289–307.

Watkin, P. M. (2011). The value of the neonatal hearing screen. *Paediatrics and Child Health, 21,* 37–41.

Watson, J. B. (1928). *Psychological Care of Infant and Child.* New York, NY: Norton.

Watson, John B. *Behaviorism* (revised edition). (1930). Chicago, IL: University of Chicago Press.

Waxman, S. R. (2003). Links between object categorization and naming: Origins and emergence in human infants. In D. H. Rakison & L. M. Oakes (Eds.), *Early category and concept development: Making sense of the blooming, buzzing confusion* (pp. 193–209). New York, NY: Oxford University Press.

Waxman, S. R., & Lidz, J. L. (2006). Early word learning. In W. Damon & R. Lerner (Eds.), & D. Kuhn & R. Siegler (Vol. Eds.), *Handbook of child psychology: Vol. 2. Cognition, perception and language* (6th ed., pp. 299–335). New York, NY: Wiley.

Way, N. (2004). Intimacy, desire, and distrust in the friendships of adolescent boys. In N. Way & J. Y. Chu (Eds.), *Adolescent boys: Exploring diverse cultures of boyhood* (pp. 167–196). New York: New York University Press.

Weaver, R. F. (2005). *Molecular Biology* (3rd ed.). New York, NY: McGraw-Hill.

Weaver, S. E., & Coleman, M. (2010). Caught in the middle mothers in stepfamilies. *Journal of Social and Personal Relationships, 27,* 305–326.

Weber, D. S. (2006). Media Use by Infants and Toddlers: A Potential for Play. In D. G. Singer, R. M. Golinkoff, & K. Hirsh-Pasek (Eds.), *Play = learning: How play motivates and enhances children's cognitive and social-emotional growth* (pp. 169–191). New York, NY: Oxford University Press.

Wechsler, H., & Nelson, T. F. (2001). Binge drinking and the American college student: What's the five drinks? *Psychology of Addictive Behaviors, 15,* 287–291.

Weekley, A. (2007). *Placentophagia: Benefits of eating the placenta.* Retrieved from http://www.associatedcontent.com/article/289824/placentophagia_benefits_of_eating_the.html?cat=51

Weichold, K., Silbereisen, R. K., & Schmitt-Rodermund, E. (2003). Short-term and long-term consequences of early vs. late physical maturation in adolescents. In C. Haywood (Ed.), *Puberty and psychopathology* (pp. 241–276). Cambridge, MA: Cambridge University Press.

Weinberg, R. A. (2004). The infant and the family in the twenty-first century. *Jouranl of the American Academy of Child & Adolescent Psychiatry, 43,* 115–116.

Weiner, I. B. (1992). *Psychological disturbance in adolescence* (2nd ed.). New York, NY: Wiley.

Weinfeld, N. S., Whaley, G. J. L., & Egeland, B. (2004). Continuity, discontinuity, and coherence in attachment from infancy to late adolescence: Sequelae of organization and disorganization. *Attachment and Human Development, 6,* 73–97.

Weinstock, H., Berman, S., & Cates, W. (2004). Sexually transmitted diseases among American youth: Incidence and prevalence estimates, 2000. *Perspectives on Sexual and Reproductive Health, 36,* 6–10.

Weir, K. F., & Jose, P. E. (2010). The perception of false self scale for adolescents: Reliability, validity, and longitudinal relationships with depressive and anxious symptoms. *British Journal of Developmental Psychology, 28,* 393–411.

Weisner, T. S. (1996). The 5 to 7 transition as an ecocultural project. In A. J. Sameroff & M. M. Haith, *The five to seven year shift: The age of reason and responsibility* (pp. 295–326). Chicago, IL: University of Chicago Press.

Weissman, M. M., Warner, V., Wickramaratne, P. J., & Kandel, D. B. (1999). Maternal smoking during pregnancy and psychopathology in offspring followed to adulthood. *Journal of the American Academy of Child & Adolescent Psychiatry, 38,* 892–899.

Wendland-Carro, J., Piccinini, C. A., & Millar, W. S. (1999). The role of an early intervention on enhancing the quality of mother–infant interaction. *Child Development, 70,* 713–731.

Wentzel, K. R. (2003). Sociometric status and adjustment in middle school: A longitudinal study. *The Journal of Early Adolescence, 23,* 5–38.

Werker, J. F., & Fennell, C. T. (2009). Infant speech perception and later language acquisition: Methodological underpinnings. In J. Colombo, P. McCardle, & L. Freund (Eds.), *Infant pathways to language: Methods, models, and research disorders* (pp. 85–98). New York, NY: Psychology Press.

Werner, E. E., & Smith, R. S. (1982). *Vulnerable but invincible: A study of resilient children.* New York, NY: McGraw-Hill.

Werner, E. E., & Smith, R. S. (1992). *Overcoming the odds: High-risk children from birth to adulthood.* Ithaca, NY: Cornell University Press.

Werner, E. E., & Smith, R. S. (2001). *Journeys from childhood to midlife: Risk, resilience, and recovery.* Ithaca, NY: Cornell University Press.

Werner, E., Dawson, G., Osterling, J., & Dinno, N. (2000). Recognition of autism spectrum disorder before one year of age. A retrospective study based on home videotapes. *Journal of Autism & Developmental Disorders, 30,* 157–162.

Werner, L. A., & Marean, G. C. (1996). *Human auditory development.* Boulder, CO: Westview Press.

Westfall, R. E., & Benoit, C. (2004). The rhetoric of "natural" in natural childbirth: Childbearing women's perspectives on prolonged pregnancy and induction of labour. *Social Science & Medicine, 59,* 1397–1408.

Westling, E., Andrews, J. A., Hampson, S. E., & Peterson, M. (2008). Pubertal timing and substance use: The effects of gender, parental monitoring and deviant peers. *Journal of Adolescent Health, 42,* 555–563.

Westoff, C. F. (2003). *Trends in marriage and early childbearing in developing countries.* DHS Comparative Reports No. 5. Calverton, MD: ORC Macro.

Whalen, C. K. (2000). Attention deficit hyperactivity disorder. In A. Kazdin (Ed.), *Encyclopedia of psychology.* Washington, DC: American Psychological Association.

Whaley, D. E. (2007). A life span developmental approach to studying sport and exercise behavior. In G. Tenenbaum & R. C. Eklund (Eds.), *Handbook of sport psychology* (3rd ed., pp. 645–661).

Whitaker, R. C., Wright, J. A., Pepe, M. S., Seidel, K. D., & Dietz, W. H. (1997). Predicting obesity in young adulthood from childhood and parental obesity. *The New England Journal of Medicine, 337,* 869–873.

White, M. J., & White, G. B. (2006). Implicit and explicit occupational gender stereotypes. *Sex Roles, 55,* 259–266.

White, N. R. (2002). "Not under my roof!" Young people's experience of home. *Youth and Society, 34,* 214–231.

Whiting, B. B., & Edwards, C. P. (1988). *Children of different worlds: The formation of social behavior.* Cambridge, MA: Harvard University Press.

Whitty, M. (2002). Possible selves: An exploration of utility of a narrative approach. *Identity, 2,* 211–228.

Wichstrom, L. (1999). The emergence of gender difference in depressed mood during adolescence: The role of intensified gender socialization. *Developmental Psychology, 35,* 232–245.

Wichstrom, L. (2001). The impact of pubertal timing on adolescents' alcohol use. *Journal of Research on Adolescence, 11,* 131–150.

Wigfield, A., Eccles, J. S., Yoon, K. S., Harold, R. D., Arbreton, A. J., Freedman-Doan, C., & Blumenfeld, P. C. (1997). Changes in children's competence beliefs and subjective task values across the elementary school years: A three-year study. *Journal of Educational Psychology, 89,* 451–469.

Wilcox, A. J., Weinberg, C. R., & Baird, D. D. (1995). Timing of sexual intercourse in relation to ovulation: Effects on the probability of contraception, survival of the pregnancy, and sex of the baby. *New England Journal of Medicine, 333,* 1517–1519.

Wilcox, W. B. (2008). Focused on their families: Religion, parenting, and child well-being. In K. K. Kline (Ed.), *Authoritative communities: The scientific case for nurturing the whole child* (pp. 227–244). The Search Institute series on developmentally attentive community and society. New York, NY: Springer.

Willford, J. A., Leech, S. L., & Day, N. L. (2006). Moderate prenatal alcohol exposure and cognitive status of children at age 10. *Alcoholism: Clinical and Experimental Research, 30*(6), 1051–1059.

Williams A. F. (1998). Risky driving behavior among adolescents. In R. Jessor (Ed.), *New perspectives on adolescent risk behavior* (pp. 221–237). New York, NY: Cambridge University Press.

Williams, A. F., & Ferguson, S. A. (2002). Rationale for graduated licensing and the risks it should address. *Injury Prevention, 8* (Suppl II), ii9–ii16.

Williams, D. R. (2005). The health of U.S. racial and ethnic populations. *Journals of Gerontology, 60B*(Special Issue II), 53–62.

Williams, J. M., & Dunlop, L. C. (1999). Pubertal timing and self-reported delinquency among male adolescents. *Journal of Adolescence, 22,* 157–171.

Williams, L. R., Degnan, K. A., Perez-Edgar, K. E., Henderson, H. A., Rubin, K. H., Pine, D. S., et al. (2009). Impact of behavioral inhibition and parenting style on internalizing and externalizing problems from early childhood through adolescence. *Journal of Abnormal Child Psychology, 37,* 1063–1075.

Willinger, M., Ko, C. W., Hoffman, J. J., Kessler, R. C., & Corwin, M. J. (2003). Trends in infant bed sharing in the United States. *Archives of Pediatrics and Adolescent Medicine, 157,* 43–49.

Wilson, J. Q., & Herrnstein, R. J. (1985). *Crime and human nature.* New York, NY: Simon and Schuster.

Winsler, A. (2009). Still talking to ourselves after all these years: A review of current research on private speech. In A. Winsler, C. Fernyhough, & I. Montero (Eds.), *Private speech, executive functioning, and the development of verbal self-regulation* (pp. 3–41). New York, NY, US: Cambridge University Press.

Wolak, J., Mitchell, K. J., & Finkelhor, D. (2007). Does online harassment constitute bullying? An exploration of online harassment by known peers and online-only contacts. *Journal of Adolescent Health, 41*(Suppl. 6), S51–S58.

Wolf, J. B. (2007). Is breast really best? Risk and total motherhood in the national breastfeeding awareness campaign. *Journal of Health Politics, Policy and Law, 32,* 595–63.

Wong, C. A. (1997, April). *What does it mean to be African-American or European-American growing up in a multi-ethnic community?* Paper presented at the biennial meeting of the Society for Research in Child Development, Washington, DC.

Wong, S., Chan, K., Wong, V., & Wong, W. (2002). Use of chopsticks in Chinese children. *Child: Care, Health, & Development, 28,* 157–161.

Wood, A. G., Harvey, A. S., Wellard, R. M., Abbott, D. F., Anderson, V., Kean, M., . . . Jackson, G. D. (2004). Language cortex activation in normal children. *Neurology, 63,* 1035–1044.

Wood, E., Desmarais, S., & Gugula, S. (2002). The impact of parenting experience on gender stereotyped toy play of children. *Sex Roles, 47,* 39–49.

Wood, R. M., & Gustafson, G. E. (2001). Infant crying and adults' anticipated caregiving responses: Acoustic and contextual influences. *Child Development, 72,* 1287–1300.

Woodhall, S. C., Lehtinen, M., Verho, T., Huhtala, H., Hokkanen, M., & Kosunen, E. (2007). Anticipated acceptance of HPV vaccination at the baseline of implementation: A survey of parental and adolescent knowledge and attitudes in Finland. *Journal of Adolescent Health, 40,* 466–469.

Woodward, A. L., & Markman, E. M. (1998). Early word learning. In W. Damon (Ed.), & D. Kuhn & R. S. Siegler (Vol. Eds.), *Handbook of child psychology: Vol. 2. Cognition, perception and language* (5th ed., pp. 371–420). New York, NY: Wiley.

Woodward, E. H., & Gridina, N. (2000). *Media in the home, 2000: The fifth annual survey of parents and children.* Philadelphia: The Annenberg Public Policy Center of the University of Pennsylvania. Retrieved from http://www.appcpenn.org/mediainhome/survey/survey7.pdf

Woodward, L., & Fergusson, D. (1999). Early conduct problems and later risk of teenage pregnancy in girls. *Development and Psychopathology, 11,* 127–142.

Woodward, L. J., & Fergusson, D. M. (2001). Life course outcomes of young people with anxiety disorders in adolescence. *Journal of the American Academy of Child & Adolescent Psychiatry, 40*(9), 1086–1093.

World Bank. (2011). India's undernourished children: A call for action. Retrieved from http://web.worldbank.org/WBSITE/EXTERNAL/COUNTRIES/SOUTHASIAEXT/0,,contentMDK:20916955~pagePK:146736~piPK:146830~theSitePK:223547,00.html

World Education Services. (2005). World education database. Retrieved from www.wes.org

World Health Organization (WHO). (2000a). *Healthy life expectancy rankings.* Geneva: Author.

World Health Organization (WHO). (2000b). WHO Global Data Bank on Breast-feeding. Retrieved from http://www.who.int/nut/db_bfd.htm

World Health Organization (WHO). (2002). Micronutirent deficiencies. Retrieved from http://www.who.int/nut/#mic

World Health Organization (WHO). (2004). *Infecundity, infertility, and childlessness in developing countries. Demographic and Health Surveys (DHS) Comparative reports No. 9.* Geneva, Switzerland: Author.

World Health Organization (WHO). (2008a). *Inequalities in young people's health: Health behavior in school-aged children.* Retrieved from http://www.hbsc.org/

World Health Organization (WHO). (2008b). Significant caries index: Data for some selected countries. Retrieved from www.whocollab.od.mah.se/sicdata.html

World Health Organization (WHO). (2009). *Department of making pregnancy safer: Annual report.* Geneva, Switzerland: Author.

World Health Organization (WHO). (2010a). Method of delivery and pregnancy outcomes in Asia: The WHO global survey on maternal and perinatal health, 2007–2008. *The Lancet, 375,* 490–499.

World Health Organization (WHO). (2010b). *Towards universal access: Scaling up priority HIV/AIDS interventions in the health sector.* Geneva, Switzerland.

World Health Organization (WHO). (2010c). *World Health Statistics 2010.* Geneva, Switzerland.

World Health Organization (WHO). (2011a). Cigarette consumption. Retrieved February 21, 2011, from http://www.who.int/tobacco/en/atlas8.pdf

World Health Organization (WHO). (2011b). *Vacuum extraction versus forceps for assisted vaginal delivery.* Retrieved from http://apps.who.int/rhl/pregnancy_childbirth/childbirth/2nd_stage/facom/en/

World Health Organization. (2012). Tobacco. Fact sheet number 339. New York, NY: World Health Organization.

World Internet Project. (2008). Center for the digital future at USC Annenberg with 13 partner countries release the first World Internet Project report. Retrieved from http://www.worldinternetproject.net

World Press Review. (2004). Obesity: A worldwide issue. Retrieved from www.worldpress.org/Africa/1961.cfm

Worthman, C. M. (1987). Interactions of physical maturation and cultural practice in ontogeny: Kikuyu adolescents. *Cultural Anthropology, 2,* 29–38.

Wrangham, R. (2009). *Catching fire: How cooking made us human*. New York, NY: Basic Books.

Wright, V. C., Schieve, L. A., Reynolds, M. A., Jeng, G., & Kissin, D. (2004). Assisted reproductive technology surveillance—United States 2001. *Morbidity and Mortality Weekly Report, 53,* 1–20.

Wrotniak, B. H., Epstein, L. H., Raluch, R. A., & Roemmich, J. N. (2004). Parent weight change as a predictor of child weight change in family-based behavioral obesity treatment. *Archives of Pediatric and Adolescent Medicine, 158,* 342–347.

Wu, L., Schlenger, W., & Galvin, D. (2003). The relationship between employment and substance abuse among students aged 12 to 17. *Journal of Adolescent Health, 32,* 5–15.

Wu, Z. (1999). Premarital cohabitation and the timing of first marriage. *Canadian Review of Sociology and Anthropology, 36,* 109–127.

Xue, Y., & Meisels, S. J. (2004). Early literacy instruction and learning in kindergarten: Evidence from the early childhood longitudinal study—kindergarten classes of 1998–1999. *American Educational Research Journal, 41,* 191–229.

Yang, B., Ollendick, T. H., Dong, Q., Xia, Y., & Lin, L. (1995). Only children and children with siblings in the People's Republic of China: Levels of fear, anxiety, and depression. *Child Development, 66,* 1301–1311.

Yasui, M., Dorham, C. L., & Dishion, T. J. (2004). Ethnic identity and psychological adjustment: A validity analysis for European American and African American adolescents. *Journal of Adolescent Research, 19,* 807–825.

Yeung, D. Y. L., & Tang, C. S. K., & Lee, A. (2005). Psychosocial and cultural factors influencing expectations of menarche: A study on Chinese premenarcheal teenage girls. *Journal of Adolescent Research, 20,* 118–135.

Yip, T., & Fulgni, A. J. (2002). Daily variation in ethnic identity, ethnic behaviors, and psychological well-being among American adolescents of Chinese descent. *Child Development, 73,* 1557–1572.

Yoos, H. L., Kitzman, H., Halterman, J. S., Henderson, C., Sidora-Arcoleo, K., & McMullen, A. (2006). Treatment regimens and health care utilization in children with persistent asthma symptoms. *Journal of Asthma, 43,* 385–391.

Youngblade, L. M., Park, K. A., & Belsky, J. (1993). Measurement of young children's close friendship: A comparison of two independent assessment systems and their associations with attachment security. *International Journal of Behavioral Development, 16*(4), 563–587.

Young-Hyman, D., Schlundt, D. G., Herman-Wenderoth, L., & Bozylinski, K. (2003). Obesity, appearance, and psychosocial adaptation in young African American children. *Journal of Pediatric Psychology, 28,* 463–472.

Youniss, J., & Smollar, J. (1985). *Adolescent relations with mothers, fathers, and friends*. Chicago, IL: University of Chicago Press.

Zach, T., Pramanik, A., & Ford, S. P. (2001). Multiple births. *eMedicine*. Retrieved from www.mypage.direct.ca/csamson/multiples/2twinningrates.html

Zald, D. H. (2003). The human amygdala and the emotional evaluation of sensory stimuli. *Brain Research Review, 41,* 88–123.

Zehle, K., Wen, L. M., Orr, N., & Rissel, C. (2007). "It's not an issue at the moment": A qualitative study of mothers about childhood obesity. *MCN: The American Journal of Maternal/Child Nursing, 32,* 36–41.

Zeijl, E., te Poel, Y., de Bois-Reymond, M., Ravesloot, J., & Meulmann, J. J. (2000). The role of parents and peers in the leisure activities of young adolescents. *Journal of Leisure Research, 32,* 281–302.

Zeskind, P. S., & Lester, B. M. (2001). Analysis of infant crying. In L. T. Singer & P. S. Zeskind (Eds.), *Biobehavioral assessment of the infant* (pp. 149–166). New York, NY: Guilford Press.

Zeskind, P. S., Klein, L., & Marshall, T. R. (1992). Adults' perceptions of experimental modifications of durations and expiratory sounds in infant crying. *Developmental Psychology, 28,* 1153–1162.

Zhang, W., & Fuligni, A. J. (2006). Authority, autonomy, and family relationships among adolescents in urban and rural China. *Journal of Research on Adolescence, 16,* 527–537.

Zhao, S., Grasmuck, S., & Martin, J. (2008). Identity construction on Facebook: Digital empowerment in anchored relationships. *Computers in Human Behavior, 24,* 1816–1836.

Zielinski, D. S. (2009). Child maltreatment and adult socioeconomic well-being. *Child Abuse and Neglect, 33,* 666–678.

Zigler, E., & Styfco, S. J. (Eds.). (2004). *The Head Start debates*. Baltimore: Brookes.

Zimmermann, M. B., Pieter, L. J., & Chandrakant, S. P. (2008). Iodine-deficiency disorders. *The Lancet, 372,* 1251 – 1262.

Zumwalt, M. (2008). Effects of the menstrual cycle on the acquisition of peak bone mass. In J. J. Robert-McComb, R. Norman, & M. Zumwalt (Eds.), *The active female: Health issues throughout the lifespan* (pp. 141–151). Totowa, NJ: Humana Press.

Zuzanek, J. (2000). *The effects of time use and time pressure on child–parent relationships*. Waterloo, Ontario, Canada: Otium.

Credits

Text and Art

Chapter 2

Figure 2.8, p. 75: Feldman, Robert S, Development Across the Life Span, 6th Ed., © 2011. Reprinted Electronically reproduced by permission of Pearson Education, Inc. Upper Saddle River, New Jersey.

Figure 2.9, p. 78: Feldman, Robert S, Development Across the Life Span, 6th Ed., © 2011. Reprinted Electronically reproduced by permission of Pearson Education, Inc. Upper Saddle River, New Jersey.

Chapter 3

Table 3.3, p. 123: Used by permission of Ronald Barr.

Chapter 4

Figure 4.5, p. 149: Based on Childcare and culture: Lessons from Africa, Levine (1994)

Chapter 6

Figure 6.4, p. 258: From L.J. Schweinhart, J. Montie, Z. Xiang, W.S. Barnett, C.R. Belfield, Lifetime Effects: The HighScope Perry Preschool Study Through Age 40. Ypsilanti, MI: HighScope Press, © 2005. Reprinted with Permission.

Figure 6.5, p. 260: By permission of Jean Berko Gleason

Chapter 7

Extract: *Piaget:* Which would make a bigger bunch, ..., **p. 305:** Ginsberg & Opper, Piagets Theory of Intellectual Development, 2nd Ed. © 1979. Reprinted and electronically reproduced by permission of Pearson Education, Inc.

Figure 7.6, p. 313: Christopher Eppig, Corey L. Fincher, Randy Thornhill. Parasite prevalence and the worldwide distribution of cognitive ability. Proceedings of the Royal Society B, 277, 3801–3808.

Figure 7.7, p. 316: Based on data from Cognitive Psychology, Jacqueline S. Johnson, Elissa L. Newport, Critical period effects in second language learning: The influence of maturational state on the acquisition of English as a second language, 1989.

Chapter 8

Figure 8.7, p. 379: Child Development. Art: "Change in Emotional States During Adolescence" by R.W. Larson et al. In. "Continuity, stability, and change in daily emotional experience across adolescence". Volume 73 (2002) **pp. 1151–1165.** Reproduced with permission of John Wiley & Sons Ltd.

Figure 8.8, p. 385: Arnett, Jeffery Jensen, Adolescence and Emerging Adulthood: A cultural approach, 3rd Ed., © 2007. Reprinted and electronically reproduced by permission of Pearson Education, Inc. Upper Saddle River, New Jersey.

Figure 8.12, p. 397: Arnett, Jeffery Jensen, Adolescence and Emerging Adulthood: A cultural approach, 3rd Ed., © 2007. Reprinted and electronically reproduced by permission of Pearson Education, Inc. Upper Saddle River, New Jersey.

Figure 8.14, p. 401: Arnett, Jeffery Jensen, Adolescence and Emerging Adulthood: A cultural approach, 3rd Ed., © 2007. Reprinted and electronically reproduced by permission of Pearson Education, Inc. Upper Saddle River, New Jersey.

Chapter 9

Figure 9.4, p. 423: Arnett, Jeffery Jensen, Adolescence and Emerging Adulthood: A cultural approach, 3rd Ed., © 2007. Reprinted and electronically reproduced by permission of Pearson Education, Inc. Upper Saddle River, New Jersey.

Table 9.1, p. 434: By permission of Oxford University Press, Inc.

Figure 9.6, p. 437: Monitoring the Future: www.umich.edu/newsinfo/releases/2002/Jan02/r013002a.html.

Figure 9.7, p. 439: Based on data from Developmental Review, Vol 19, A.S. Waterman, Issues of identity formation revisited: United States and the Netherlands, 462–479, 1999.

Figure 9.8, p. 443: Reprinted by permission from NORC. General Social Survey (GSS), 1977–2006.

Photographs

Front Matter

p. iii, Jeffrey Jensen Arnett; **p. v,** Gregory Holmgren/Alamy; **p. v,** Jenny Matthews/Alamy; **p. vi,** Pakistan Images/Alamy; **p. vi,** James Pauls/iStockphoto; **p. vii,** Somos Group 25/Somos Images/Alamy; **p. vii,** David Grossman/Alamy; **p. viii,** Friedrich Stark/Alamy; **p. viii,** Ashley Maynard; **p. ix,** Westend61 GmbH/Alamy; **p. xxiv,** Jeffrey Jensen Arnett; **p. xxv,** Ashley Maynard; **p. xxvbl,** David Foss

Chapter 1

pp. 2–3, Gregory Holmgren/Alamy; **p. 4,** Sylvaine Poitau/Alamy; **p. 6,** ADB Travel/dbimages/Alamy Limited; **p. 7,** ADB Travel/dbimages/Alamy Limited; **p. 10t,** © Picture Contact BV/Alamy' **p. 10b,** © S. Forster/Alamy; **p. 12,** Imagestate Media Partners Limited–Impact Photos/Alamy; **p. 13,** AP Photo/Daniel Maurer; **p. 16,** Pearson Education; **p. 17,** iofoto/Shutterstock; **p. 18,** Ethno Images, Inc./Alamy; **p. 20,** PHOTOEDIT/PhotoEdit; **p. 23,** iofoto/Shutterstock; **p. 26,** Imagestate Media Partners Limited–Impact Photos/Alamy; **p. 28t,** Vladimir Melnik/Shutterstock.com; **p. 28b,** Pearson Education; **p. 29,** Bettmann/Corbis; **p. 30,** Paul Burns/Blend Images/Alamy limited; **p. 34,** Pearson Education; **p. 35,** Bettmann/Corbis; **p. 36,** © English Heritage Photo Library; **p. 37,** © Jeff Greenberg/Alamy; **p. 39l,** CK Archive; **p. 39cl,** CK Archive; **p. 39cr,** CK Archive; **p. 39r,** CK Archive; **p. 40,** Pearson Education; **p. 41t,** ADB Travel/dbimages/Alamy Limited; **p. 41b,** iofoto/Shutterstock; **p. 42,** Bettmann/Corbis

Chapter 2

pp. 44–45, Jenny Matthews/Alamy; **p. 46,** © Janine Wiedel Photolibrary/Alamy; **p. 47,** Getty Images/Comstock/Thinkstock; **p. 48,** SPL/Photo Researchers, Inc; **p. 50,** Martin Shields/Alamy; **p. 53,** Getty Images/Comstock/Thinkstock; **p. 54,** dbtravel/dbimages/Alamy; **p. 55,** Jeff Randall/Digital Vision/Getty Images; **p. 56,** Oskar and Jack/Lichtfilm; **p. 59,** David M. Phillips/Photo Researchers; **p. 60,** Pearson Education; **p. 61t,** Keith Brofsky/Photodisc/Thinkstock; **p. 61b,** R. Rawlins PhD/Custom Medical Stock Photo/Newscom; **p. 62,** kage–mikrofotografie/doc–stock/Alamy; **p. 63t,** Dr. M.A. Ansary/Photo Researchers, Inc.; **p. 63b,** Neil Bromhall/Photo Researchers, Inc.; **p. 65,** The Highland Support Project, a nonprofit local to Richmond, Virginia, is always accepting donations in support of midwifery training in Guatemala. For more information, please contact service project coordinator Rachel Triplett, at Rachel@highlandsupportproject.org; **p. 68,** Leland Bobbe/Stone/Getty Images; **p. 70,** Sue Cunningham Photographic/Alamy; **p. 71t,** Gideon Mendel/Corbis News/Corbis; **p. 71b,** FotoSearch/glow Images; **p. 73,** Pearson Education; **p. 74,** Машков Юрпñ/ITAR–TASS/Newscom; **p. 75,** Alex Segre/Alamy; **p. 76,** Keith Brofsky/Photodisc/Thinkstock; **p. 79,** Машков Юрпñ/ITAR–TASS/Newscom; **p. 80,** Wellcome Library, London; **p. 82,** Pearson Education; **p. 83,** Getty Images/Comstock/Thinkstock; **p. 84,** Keith Brofsky/Photodisc/Thinkstock; **p. 85,** Машков Юрпñ/ITAR–TASS/Newscom

Chapter 3

pp. 88–89, Pakistan Images/Alamy; **p. 90,** Pearson Education–Addison-Wesley; **p. 91,** Angela Hampton Picture Library/Alamy; **p. 97,** Borderlands/Alamy; **p. 99,** Paul Gapper/Alamy; **p. 101,** Emilio Ereza/Alamy; **p. 102t,** Bush/Stringer/Hulton Archive/Getty Images; **p. 102b,** Angela Hampton Picture Library/Alamy; **p. 103,** Angela Hampton/Bubbles Photolibrary/Alamy Limited; **p. 105,** Pearson Education; **p. 106t,** Jake Lyell/Alamy; **p. 106b,** Buddy Mays/Alamy; **p. 109,** Jake Lyell/Alamy; **p. 110,** Hypermania/Alamy; **p. 112,** Rohit Seth/Shutterstock.com; **p. 113,** Picture Partners/Alamy; **p. 114,** Kathleen Nelson/Alamy; **p. 116,** Pearson Education; **p. 117,** Michel Renaudeau/Age Fotostock; **p. 118,** Henri Roger/Roger-Viollet/The Image Works; **p. 119,** Michel Renaudeau/Age Fotostock; **p. 120,** Pavel Filatov/Alamy; **p. 123,** BananaStock/Thinkstock; **p. 124,** Gale Zucker/Aurora Photos/Alamy; **p. 125,** Nina Leen/Time Life Pictures/Getty Images; **p. 126,** VOISIN/PHANIE/Photo Researchers, Inc.; **p. 127t,** Pearson Education; **p. 127b,** Angela Hampton Picture Library/Alamy; **p. 128,** Jake Lyell/Alamy; **p. 129,** Michel Renaudeau/Age Fotostock

Name Index

Subject Index